DIGEST OF
UNITED STATES PRACTICE
IN INTERNATIONAL LAW

2007

Digest of
United States Practice
in International Law

2007

Sally J. Cummins
Editor

Office of the Legal Adviser
United States Department of State

UNIVERSITY PRESS

INTERNATIONAL LAW INSTITUTE

The *Digest of United States Practice in International Law* is co-published by Oxford University Press and the International Law Institute under agreement with the United States Department of State, Office of the Legal Adviser. The contents of the *Digest*, including selection of documents and preparation of editorial commentary, are entirely under the auspices of the Office of the Legal Adviser.

INTERNATIONAL LAW INSTITUTE

For fifty years the International Law Institute has addressed issues of interest to the international legal community through research, publishing, training, and technical assistance. For information on the activities of the Institute:

Publishing Office
International Law Institute
The Foundry Building
1055 Thomas Jefferson St., NW
Washington, DC 20007

202-247-6006
202-247-6010 (fax)
e-mail: pub@ili.org
Internet: www.ili.org

If you would like to be placed on Standing Order status for the *Digest of United States Practice in International Law*, whereby you will automatically receive and be billed for new annual volumes as they publish, please contact a Customer Service Representative.

In the United States, Canada, Mexico, Central and South America, contact:

Customer Service
Oxford University Press USA
2001 Evans Road
Cary, NC 27513
Email: custserv.us@oup.com
Phone (toll free in US): 1-866-445-8685
Phone (international customers): 1-919-677-0977
Fax: 1-919-677-1303

In the United Kingdom, Europe, and Rest of World, contact:

Customer Service
Oxford University Press
Saxon Way West, Corby
Northants, NN18 9ES
United Kingdom
Email: bookorders.uk@oup.com
Phone: +44 1536 741017
Fax: +44 1536 454518

ISBN: 978-0-19-537997-6 (2007, Hardback)

Table of Contents

Preface

I welcome this latest edition of the *Digest of United States Practice in International Law* for the calendar year 2007. This is the 10th edition of the *Digest* published by the International Law Institute, and the fourth edition co-published with Oxford University Press. We have been very pleased with our co-publishing relationship with them, and are looking forward to their making the *Digest* even more widely available online, preparations for which are now underway.

It is my hope that practitioners and scholars will find this new edition, tracking highly important developments in the state practice of the United States during last year, to be useful.

As always, the Institute is also very pleased to work with the Office of the Legal Adviser to make the *Digest* available for the use of the international legal community.

Don Wallace, Jr.
Chairman
International Law Institute

Introduction

I am pleased to introduce the *Digest of United States Practice in International Law* for 2007. This year's *Digest* reflects the broad range of legal issues that engaged the Department of State and other parts of the U.S. government during the year.

In 2007, the conflicts in Iraq, Afghanistan, and elsewhere continued to raise novel and important legal issues. The conflict with al Qaeda and other terrorist groups, in particular, presents the question of how to deal with transnational terrorists that do not fit neatly within existing legal frameworks. My colleagues and I continued to pursue an extensive bilateral and multilateral dialogue with our international counterparts with a view to developing a common legal approach to these issues. In addition, litigation in U.S. courts during the year addressed questions regarding the appropriate legal framework applicable to detainees held by the United States.

In the area of human rights law, the United States provided extensive submissions to UN bodies, including reports on U.S. implementation of the two protocols to the Convention on the Rights of the Child and of the Convention on the Elimination of All Racial Discrimination, as well as follow-up responses on implementation of the International Covenant on Civil and Political Rights (ICCPR) and the Convention Against Torture. The United States also submitted observations on UN Human Rights Committee General Comment 31 on the ICCPR, a report on the non-refoulement obligation under the Refugee Convention and Protocol, and views on responding to religious defamation.

In U.S. courts, the Executive Branch worked to implement the decision of the International Court of Justice requiring that certain Mexicans on death row in the United States obtain review and reconsideration of their convictions and sentences in light of Vienna Convention violations. We also continued our efforts, not yet finished, to obtain Senate approval of the UN Convention on the

Law of the Sea and the accompanying 1994 Agreement. At the same time, the United States issued a new policy for the repression of piracy and acted to preserve its freedom of navigation rights by protesting infringements by other countries.

It was an active year for U.S. treaty practice generally. In 2007, the President transmitted to the Senate for advice and consent a number of important multilateral treaties. These include treaties addressing nuclear terrorism, safety of maritime navigation, protection of nuclear material, pollution from land-based sources and activities, and bilateral defense trade cooperation. In addition, important treaties on child adoption, extradition, maritime conservation, and the law of war entered into force during the year. The United States also signed many new agreements, including those on air transport, classified information sharing, and access to airline passenger-name records with the European Union, and a multilateral convention on recovery of family support maintenance.

The United States remained engaged in efforts to restore and preserve peace in trouble spots around the world, and continued efforts in support of the nonproliferation of weapons of mass destruction. We maintained our active role in resolving outstanding nonproliferation issues with North Korea and Iran, and reached agreement on nuclear cooperation with Russia.

The United States continued to be a major participant in international arbitrations in the WTO and NAFTA systems and supported the establishment of the Special Tribunal for Lebanon. Immunity of foreign governments and their officials continued to be an active issue in U.S. courts. In one of two cases raising questions of immunity in 2007, the Supreme Court ruled that U.S. courts have jurisdiction over suits to establish the validity of a tax lien on real property owned by a foreign sovereign.

The *Digest* reflects the commitment of the Office of the Legal Adviser to providing current information and documentation on a timely basis that reflects U.S. views in various areas of international law. It remains, in the truest sense, a collaborative undertaking, requiring the sustained effort of the attorneys and paralegals who work in the office. I am grateful to all those who contribute to this effort. I thank in particular Anna Conley, a former student intern, for assistance with the international civil litigation section of Chapter 15. Very special thanks also go to Joan Sherer, the Department's Senior Reference Librarian for legal matters. Finally, I thank *Digest* editor Sally Cummins who, with this, has edited her final volume of the *Digest*. Her extraordinary efforts over the years have brought the *Digest* up to date and have made it the great work of reference that it is.

We continue to value our rewarding collaboration with the International Law Institute and Oxford University Press as co-publishers. The Institute's Director, Professor Don Wallace, and editor William Mays again have our sincere thanks for their superb support and guidance.

Comments and suggestions from readers are always welcome.

John B. Bellinger, III
The Legal Adviser
Department of State

Note from the Editor

Publication of the *Digest of United States Practice in International Law* for calendar year 2007 brings the new *Digest* series current for the period 1989–2007. I thank first of all my colleagues in the Office of the Legal Adviser and those in other offices and departments in the U.S. Government who make this cooperative venture possible. As always, I am also grateful to the International Law Institute and Oxford University Press for their valuable contributions in publishing the *Digest*.

The 2007 volume continues the general organization and approach adopted in 2000. In order to provide broad coverage of significant developments as soon as possible after the end of the covered year, we rely on the text of relevant original source documents introduced by relatively brief explanatory commentary to provide context. Entries in each annual *Digest* pertain to material from the relevant year, leaving it to the reader to check for updates. As in other volumes, however, we note the release of several U.S. Supreme Court decisions before the Court recessed at the end of June 2008; relevant aspects of the decisions will be discussed in *Digest 2008*. This volume continues the practice of providing cross-references to related entries within the volume and to prior volumes of the *Digest*.

In one organizational change, this year we have relocated the discussion of litigation under the Alien Tort Statute from the human rights chapter (Chapter 6) to the foreign relations chapter (Chapter 5). This placement reflects the fact that claims under the ATS are not limited to human rights violations and that recent litigation has frequently focused on the scope of the application of the statute.

As in previous volumes, our goal is to assure that the full texts of documents excerpted in this volume are available to the reader to the extent possible. For many documents we have provided a specific internet cite in the text. We realize that internet citations are subject to change, but we have provided the best address available at the time of publication. Where documents are not readily available elsewhere, we have placed them on the State Department website, at *www.state.gov/s/l/c8183.htm*.

Other documents are available from multiple public sources, both in hard copy and from various online services. The United Nations Official Document System is available to the public without charge for UN-related documents of all types at *http://documents. un.org/*. The UN's home page at *www.un.org* also remains a valuable source.

The U.S. Government Printing Office provides access to government publications at *www.gpoaccess.gov*, including the Federal Register and Code of Federal Regulations; the Congressional Record and other congressional documents and reports; the U.S. Code, Public and Private Laws, and Statutes at Large; and Public Papers of the President and the Weekly Compilation of Presidential Documents. On treaty issues, this site offers Senate Treaty Documents (for the President's transmittal of treaties to the Senate for advice and consent, with related materials) available at *www.gpoaccess.gov/serialset/ cdocuments/index.html*, and Senate Executive Reports (for the Senate Committee on Foreign Relations reports of treaties to the Senate for vote on advice and consent), available at *www.gpoaccess. gov/serialset/creports/index.html*. In addition, the Office of the Legal Adviser now provides a wide range of current treaty information at *www.state.gov/s/l/treaty/* and the Library of Congress provides extensive treaty and other legislative resources at *http:// thomas.loc.gov*.

The U.S. government's official web portal is *www.firstgov.gov*, with links to government agencies and other sites; the State Department's home page is *www.state.gov*.

While court opinions are most readily available through commercial online services and bound volumes, some materials are available through links to individual federal court websites provided at *www.uscourts.gov/links.html*. The official Supreme Court website is maintained at *www.supremecourtus.gov*. The Office of the Solicitor General in the Department of Justice makes its briefs filed in the Supreme Court available at *www.usdoj.gov/osg*.

Selections of material in this volume were made based on judgments as to the significance of the issues, their possible relevance for future situations, and their likely interest to scholars and other academics, government lawyers, and private practitioners.

As always, we welcome suggestions from those who use these volumes.

Sally J. Cummins

CHAPTER 1

Nationality, Citizenship, and Immigration

A. NATIONALITY AND CITIZENSHIP

1. Non-Citizen Nationals: Taiwan Claimants

On April 5, 2007, the United States filed a motion to dismiss a case brought by individuals residing in Taiwan who claimed that the American Institute on Taiwan or its officials "denied individual [p]laintiffs' rights and privileges as United States nationals" and sought a declaratory judgment that they were United States nationals. *Lin v. United States,* Civil Action No. 06-1825 (RMC) (D.D.C.). The United States argued that the Immigration and Nationality Act ("INA") did not provide a basis for the claims:

> . . . [INA]§ 360, 8 U.S.C. § 1503 . . . allows an individual to bring a declaratory judgment action if a person claims to be a United States national and is denied "such right or privilege . . . upon the ground that he is not a national of the United States." . . . But plaintiffs are not nationals of the United States. . . . In charting the United States relations with Taiwan, the political branches have repudiated plaintiffs' claim that the United States is sovereign over Taiwan. Therefore, plaintiffs do not state a claim upon which relief may be granted because they could not have been denied rights and privileges as United States nationals if they are not United States nationals.

1

Sections of the U.S. motion demonstrating that the United States does not exercise sovereignty over Taiwan, and that determinations of sovereignty are reserved to the executive branch and are nonjusticiable political questions, are addressed in Chapter 9.A.2. Excerpts below address plaintiffs' claim to be non-citizen nationals. The case was pending at the end of 2007. (Citations to other submissions in the case are omitted.)

The full text of the U.S. motion to dismiss and supporting memorandum is available at *www.state.gov/s/l/c8183.htm.*

* * * *

Merely being from Taiwan does not meet the statutory definition of who is considered a national of the United States. The statute explicitly states that "[t]he term 'national of the United States' means (A) a citizen of the United States, or (B) a person who, though not a citizen of the United States, owes permanent allegiance to the United States." *See* 8 U.S.C. § 1101(a)(22). Plaintiffs are not alleging that they are citizens, so their entire basis for claiming nationality status is 8 U.S.C. § 1101(a)(22)(B). Plaintiffs' manifestation that the "Taiwanese people owe permanent allegiance to the United States," is not sufficient for them to fall under that statutory provision. . . . Rather, that provision must be "read in the context of the general statutory scheme" and "the only 'non-citizen nationals' currently recognized by our law are persons deemed to be so under 8 U.S.C. § 1408." *Marquez-Almanzar* [*v. INS*, 418 F.3d 210 (2nd Cir. 2005)] at 217, 219.

The individual plaintiffs have failed to state a claim that they meet the criteria under 8 U.S.C. § 1408 for being considered United States non-citizen nationals. Section 1408 defines a non-citizen national as a "person born in an outlying possession of the United States on or after the date of the formal acquisition of such possession." *See* 8 U.S.C. § 1408(1).[3] But, Taiwan is not an outlying

---

3   Section 1408 defines three other situations for a person to be considered a non-citizen national, but plaintiffs are not making any allegations related to those situations. Plaintiffs have not alleged that their parents are

possession of the United States. The statute defines "outlying possessions of the United States" as being "American Samoa and Swains Island." *See* 8 U.S.C. § 1101(a)(29); *see also Miller v. Albright,* 523 U.S. 420, 467 n.2 (1998) (Ginsburg, J., dissenting) ("[n]ationality and citizenship are not entirely synonymous; one can be a national of the United States and yet not a citizen. 8 U.S.C. § 1101(a)(22). The distinction has little practical impact today, however, for the only remaining noncitizen nationals are residents of American Samoa and Swains Island.") (emphasis added); *Abur v. Republic of Sudan,* 437 F. Supp. 2d at 176–77. Considering that plaintiffs are not nationals by virtue of being from Taiwan, plaintiffs have failed to state a claim upon which relief may be granted because they are not entitled to rights or privileges as United States nationals.

Besides it being clear from the statute that Taiwan is not considered an outlying possession of the United States, the political branches have also made it clear that the United States does not exercise sovereignty over Taiwan. This alleged sovereignty by the United States over Taiwan is the foundation for plaintiffs' claim that they are United States nationals. . . . Because plaintiffs cannot claim they are nationals of the United States merely because they are from Taiwan, plaintiffs have failed to state a claim under the INA § 360, 5 U.S.C. §§ 1503.

*   *   *   *

2. Renunciation of Citizenship Within the United States

On May 17, 2007, the U.S. District Court for the District of Columbia dismissed a claim for a writ of mandamus seeking to compel the Secretary of State to issue a Certificate of Loss

---

nationals and have residences in the United States, *see* 8 U.S.C. § 1408(2), that they are of an unknown parentage found in an outlying possession of the United States while under the age of five, 8 U.S.C. § 1408(3), or that one of each of their parents are nationals of the United States and who were present in the United States for at least seven years during a "continuous period of ten years," *see* 8 U.S.C. § 1408(4). Rather, they have alleged that they are entitled to nationality status because of their claim that the "United States is holding sovereignty over Taiwan."

of Citizenship. *Kemp v. Rice,* 2007 U.S. Dist. LEXIS 35903 (D.D.C. 2007). In its motion to dismiss, filed February 26, 2007, the United States demonstrated that the case "should be treated as a renunciation of U.S. nationality under INA section 349 and should be dismissed because Petitioner has not alleged or demonstrated that he has complied with the statutory scheme through which renunciation of U.S. nationality in the United States can be accomplished." The United States also addressed the distinction between citizenship and nationality (*see* A.1. *supra*), in this case concluding that it was irrelevant:

> INA section 349, 8 U.S.C. 1481, provides the exclusive means under United States law for renunciation of allegiance to the United States. Drawing no distinction between citizenship and nationality—indeed, the provision is entitled "Loss of Nationality by Native-Born or Naturalized Citizen"—section 349 provides for renunciation of nationality when the statutory requisites are satisfied.

Citations to other submissions in the case have been omitted from the excerpts below.

The full texts of the U.S. motion and supporting memorandum are available at *www.state.gov/s/l/c8183.htm.*

*   *   *   *

1. Petitioner Has Failed To Take Appropriate Steps to Renounce His Citizenship

Preliminarily, it should be noted that Petitioner names the Secretary of State as the Respondent. In this case, the Secretary is an improper party because the Petitioner is physically located within the United States. The INA authorizes the United States Attorney General, or any officer designated by him, to approve renunciation of an individual's United States citizenship, who may be physically present in the United States, if certain conditions are met. *See* . . . INA section 349(a)(6), (codified at 8 U.S.C. §1481(a)(6)). If not physically present in the United States, renunciation may be [e]ffected through 8 U.S.C. § 1481 (a)(5). One may invoke the statutory provision of expatriation, found at § 1481(a)(5), which requires a "formal renunciation of nationality before a diplomatic or consular officer of the United States in *a foreign state*, in such form as may be prescribed by the Secretary of State. . . ." 8 U.S.C. § 1481 (a)(5) (emphasis added). The Secretary of State has implemented this provision by setting forth the manner and form of the renunciation in a regulation. *See* 22 C.F.R. § 50.50. Accordingly, this method would be an option for Petitioner once he is released from incarceration in Michigan. *See Koos v. Hom*, 204 F. Supp. 2d 1099, 1108 (W.D.Tenn. 2002).

Here, Petitioner is physically present in the United States. He has filed his Complaint against the Secretary, rather than the United States Attorney General. He does not allege that he has attempted to file the appropriate forms with the United States Attorney General to effectuate his renunciation. Accordingly, the Court lacks jurisdiction and Petitioner's Amended Complaint should be dismissed.

2. Mandamus Does Not Lie For Discretionary Acts

* * * *

. . . [A]ccording to traditional doctrine, a writ of mandamus will issue "only where the duty to be performed is ministerial[3] and the obligation to act peremptory, and clearly defined. The law must not only authorize the demanded action, but require it; the duty must be clear and undisputable." *13th Regional*, 654 F.2d at 760 (citations omitted); *See Wilbur v. United States*, 281 U.S. 206, 218–19 (1929). . . .

. . . The party seeking mandamus has the burden of showing that its right to issuance of the writ is clear and indisputable. . . .

---

[3] A ministerial act is one in which the law prescribes and defines a duty to be performed with such precision as to leave nothing to the exercise of discretion or judgment. . . .

Petitioner has failed to satisfy that burden here. The statute governing voluntary renunciation of citizenship, upon which Petitioner relies, provides in pertinent part[4]:

(a) A person who is a national of the United States whether by birth or naturalization, shall lose his nationality by voluntarily performing any of the following acts with the intention of relinquishing United States nationality:

*   *   *   *

(6) making in the United States a formal written renunciation of nationality in such form as may be prescribed by, and before such officer as may be designated by, the Attorney General, whenever the United States shall be in a state of war and the Attorney General shall approve such renunciation as not contrary to the interests of national defense.

8 U.S.C. § 1481(a)(6). This provision was enacted in 1944 to allow the government to continue to lawfully detain U.S. citizens of Japanese origin during the second World War ("WWII") by having them renounce their citizenship. *Tadayasu v. Clark*, 77 F. Supp. 806, 809–810 (N.D. Cal. 1948), *reversed in part on other grounds*, 186 F.2d 766 (9th Cir.), *cert. denied*, 342 U.S. 832 (1951).

Regulations promulgated to implement the 1944 amendment, 9 Fed. Reg. 12241 (Oct. 10, 1944) (codified at then-8 C.F.R. § 316.1, et seq. (1944)), provided an administrative process for renouncing citizenship within the United States by requesting from the Department of Justice an "Application for Renunciation of United States Nationality." However, the regulations specifically provided that they were effective only until the "cessation of the *present* state of war unless sooner terminated by the Attorney General." *Id.* Thus, the regulations ceased to have effect at the end

---

4   The only other potential way for Petitioner to effectuate a loss of nationality, while physically remaining in the United States, is to show that he has committed treason. *See* 8 U.S.C. § 1483(a) citing 8 U.S.C. § 1481(a)(7); 8 U.S.C. § 1488. Petitioner makes no such claim here, rendering this provision of the law inapplicable to the instant matter.

of WWII, and no longer exist. Therefore, Petitioner cannot avail himself of the procedure contained therein.[5]

Moreover, Section 1481(a)(6) imposes no duty on the Attorney General or the Secretary to act.[6] The statute merely provides that the applicant must make a formal renunciation "in such form as *may* be prescribed by . . . the Attorney General," thereby vesting discretion in the Attorney General, as to whether and when to set forth a procedure for renunciations of citizenship in the United States. The Attorney General has not exercised his discretion under this statutory section to establish a renunciation procedure and has never promulgated regulations to implement the provision. *See Koos v. Hom*, 204 F. Supp. at 1108 (renunciation request denied under Section 1481(a)(6) as § 1481(a)(6) is presently inoperative and the Attorney General has not prescribed procedures for such renunciations).

The statute also contemplates that the Attorney General has the discretion to determine whether, even when all other elements have been met, a renunciation is or is not contrary to the interests of national defense. 8 U.S.C. § 1481(a)(6). The phrase in "the interests of national defense" is extremely broad. Moreover, it is inherently enmeshed with policy judgments specific to the particular programs run by that agency. The phrase goes to the heart of the presumption against the courts becoming overly involved in foreign policy matters such as immigration. *See, e.g., INS v. Aguirre-Aguirre*, 526 U.S. 415, 424–25 (1999).

---

[5] A statutory provision virtually identical to the 1944 version was adopted in 1952, which is currently codified at 8 U.S.C. § 1481(a)(6). However, the Attorney General has never promulgated regulations to implement this provision.

[6] The more commonly invoked statutory provision of expatriation is found at § 1481(a)(5), which requires a "formal renunciation of nationality before a diplomatic or consular officer of the United States in *a foreign state*, in such form as may be prescribed by the Secretary of State. . . ." 8 U.S.C. § 1481 (a)(5) (emphasis added). The Secretary of State has implemented this provision by setting forth the manner and form of the renunciation in a regulation. *See* 8 C.F.R. § 50.50. This method may be an option for Petitioner once he is released from incarceration in Michigan. *See Koos*, 204 F. Supp. 2d at 1108.

In sum, in the instant matter, assuming that Petitioner is a U.S. citizen, (fn. omitted) he has not alleged that (1) he made a formal written statement of renunciation in the form prescribed by the Attorney General and before a duly authorized officer designated by the Attorney General; (2) that the United States is (or was at the time of the purported renunciation) in a state of war; (3) and that the purported renunciation would not be contrary to interests of national defense. Indeed, the Petitioner has not attached to his Amended Complaint any written documentation to substantiate his claim. Consequently, he is not entitled to the relief sought and his complaint must be dismissed. *See Toler v. Gonzales*, 2006 WL 3208664 (D.D.C. Nov. 7, 2006).

*   *   *   *

B. PASSPORTS

1. Passport Regulations

a. *Western Hemisphere Travel Initiative: Documents required for travelers departing or arriving by sea and land*

On June 26, 2007, the Department of Homeland Security and the Department of State issued a joint notice of proposed rulemaking to implement a statutory requirement that U.S. citizens and nonimmigrant aliens from Canada, Bermuda, and Mexico entering the United States at sea and land ports-of-entry from Western Hemisphere countries must present passports or such alternative documents as the Secretary of Homeland Security designates as satisfactorily establishing identity and citizenship for entry into the United States. 72 Fed. Reg. 35,088 (June 26, 2007). As explained in the Background section of the notice, "[t]he current document requirements . . . generally depend on the nationality of the traveler and whether or not the traveler is entering the United States from a country within the Western Hemisphere." Further excerpts below from the Background section explain the statutory requirements and the proposed regulations (most footnotes omitted). The

Western Hemisphere Travel Initiative is discussed in *Digest 2005* at 1–5 and *Digest 2006* at 4–11.

The final rule on air ports-of-entry was published on November 24, 2006, 71 Fed. Reg. 68,412 (Nov. 24, 2006).

---

*   *   *   *

C. Statutory and Regulatory History

This NPRM is the second phase of a joint DHS and DOS plan, known as the Western Hemisphere Travel Initiative (WHTI), to implement section 7209 of the Intelligence Reform and Terrorism Prevention Act of 2004, as amended (hereinafter IRTPA), [Pub. L. No. 108-458, as amended, 118 Stat. 3638 (Dec. 17, 2004)]. A brief discussion of IRTPA and related regulatory efforts follows.

1. Intelligence Reform and Terrorism Prevention Act of 2004

Section 7209 of IRTPA requires that the Secretary of Homeland Security, in consultation with the Secretary of State, develop and implement a plan to require travelers entering the United States to present a passport, other document, or combination of documents, that are "deemed by the Secretary of Homeland Security to be sufficient to denote identity and citizenship." Section 7209 expressly provides that U.S. citizens and nationals for whom documentation requirements have previously been waived on the basis of reciprocity under section 212(d)(4)(B) of the INA (8 U.S.C 1182(d)(4)(B)) (*i.e.*, citizens of Canada, Mexico, and Bermuda) will be required to comply.[10]

---

[10]   Section 7209 does not apply to Lawful Permanent Residents, who will continue to be able to enter the United States upon presentation of a valid Form I-551, Permanent Resident Card, or other valid evidence of permanent resident status. See section 211(b) of the INA, 8 U.S.C. 1181(b). It also does not apply to alien members of the United States Armed Forces traveling under official orders who present military identification. See section 284 of the INA, 8 U.S.C. 1354. Additionally, section 7209 does not apply to nonimmigrant aliens from anywhere other than Canada, Mexico, or Bermuda. See section 212(d)(4)(B) of the INA, 8 U.S.C 1182(d)(4)(B). Such nonimmigrant aliens are currently required to show a passport for admission into the United States.

Section 7209 limits the President's authority to waive generally applicable documentation requirements after the complete implementation of the plan required by IRTPA. With respect to nonimmigrant aliens currently granted a passport waiver under section 212(d)(4)(B) of the INA (*i.e.*, nationals of contiguous territory or adjacent islands), the President may not waive the document requirement imposed by IRTPA. With respect to U.S. citizens, once WHTI is completely implemented, the President may waive the new documentation requirements for departing or entering the United States only in three specific circumstances: (1) When the Secretary of Homeland Security determines that "alternative documentation" that is the basis of the waiver is sufficient to denote identity and citizenship; (2) in an individual case of an unforeseen emergency; or (3) in an individual case based on "humanitarian or national interest reasons."

Accordingly, U.S. citizens and those nonimmigrant aliens who currently are not required to present passports, pursuant to sections 215(b) and 212(d)(4)(B) of the INA respectively, will be required to present a passport or other acceptable document that establishes identity and citizenship deemed sufficient by the Secretary of Homeland Security when entering the United States from any location, including from countries within the Western Hemisphere. The principal groups affected by this provision of IRPTA are citizens of the United States, Canada, and Bermuda entering the United States from within the Western Hemisphere and Mexican nationals in possession of a [Border Crossing Card ("BCC")] entering the United States from contiguous territory.

*   *   *   *

IV. Proposed WHTI Document Requirements for U.S. Citizens and Nonimmigrant Aliens

*   *   *   *

A. *U.S. Citizens Arriving by Sea or Land*

Under this proposed rule, most U.S. citizens entering the United States at all sea or land ports-of-entry would be required to have either (1) A U.S. passport; (2) a U.S. passport card; (3) a trusted traveler card (NEXUS, FAST, or SENTRI [in certain circumstances]);

(4) a valid [Merchant Mariner Document] when traveling in conjunction with official maritime business; or (5) a valid U.S. Military identification card when traveling on official orders or permit.

1. Passport Book

U.S. passports are internationally recognized, secure documents that demonstrate the individual's identity and citizenship and continue to be specifically authorized for all border-crossing purposes. Traditional U.S. passport books contain security features including digitized photographs, embossed seals, watermarks, ultraviolet and fluorescent light verification features, security laminations, micro-printing, holograms, and pages for visas and stamps.

U.S. electronic passports or e-passports, which DOS has issued to the public since August 2006, are the same as traditional passports with the addition of a small contactless integrated circuit (computer chip) embedded in the back cover. The chip securely stores the same data visually displayed on the photo page of the passport, and will additionally include a digital photograph. The inclusion of the digital photograph will enable biometric comparison, through the use of facial recognition technology at international borders. The U.S. "e-passport" incorporates additional anti-fraud and security features.

2. Passport Card

DOS published a [notice of proposed rulemaking ("NPRM")] announcing the development and issuance of a card-format passport on October 17, 2006 (71 FR 60928), which would be a secure citizenship and identity document that carries most of the rights and privileges of a traditional U.S. passport, but with validity limited to international travel by land and sea between the United States and Canada, Mexico, the Caribbean or Bermuda.

The passport card would contain security features similar to the passport book, would be issued by DOS, would contain biographical information about the holder, and would be readily authenticated and validated at the border. The passport card will contain a radio frequency identification (RFID) chip, which will link the card, via a manufacturer-generated reference number, to a stored record in secure government databases. Unlike the e-passport, which contains personal data on the RFID chip, there will be no personal information stored on the passport card's RFID chip. The passport card would be particularly useful for citizens in border communities who cross the land border every day. The passport card would satisfy the definition of a passport, and, therefore, it would be specifically authorized in section 7209 of IRTPA.

3. Trusted Traveler Program Documents

Under the proposed rule, U.S. citizens would be permitted to present cards issued for certain DHS Trusted Traveler Programs, such as NEXUS, Free and Secure Trade (FAST), and Secure Electronic Network for Travelers Rapid Inspection (SENTRI), at all lanes at all land and sea ports-of-entry when traveling from contiguous territory or adjacent islands.

These trusted traveler cards contain numerous security features, are issued by either U.S. or Canadian border security agencies, contain biographical information about the holder, and are readily authenticated and validated at the border. These programs are implemented in partnership with the Governments of Canada and Mexico, and many citizens of these countries participate in the programs.

Under the proposed rule, U.S. citizens who arrive by pleasure vessel from contiguous territory would be permitted to show the trusted traveler cards, among other documents, at all ports of entry. Additionally, U.S. citizens who have been pre-screened as part of the NEXUS or Canadian Border Boat Landing Program who arrive by pleasure vessel from Canada would be permitted to report their arrival by telephone or by remote video inspection, respectively.

U.S. citizens who arrive by pleasure vessel from Canada would be permitted to show the NEXUS card in lieu of a passport or passport card along the northern border under the auspices of the remote inspection system for pleasure vessels, such as the Outlying Area Reporting System (OARS). Currently, as NEXUS members, U.S. citizen recreational boaters can report their arrival to CBP by telephone. Otherwise, these pleasure vessel travelers would be required to report in person to a port-of-entry in order to enter the United States. [See 8 CFR 235.1(g)]

*   *   *   *

5. U.S. Military Identification Card

Citizens of the United States currently are not required to possess a valid passport to enter or depart the United States when traveling as a member of the Armed Forces of the United States on active duty under 22 CFR 53.2(d). Because the military identification card is issued to U.S. citizens of the Armed Forces and because U.S. citizen members of the U.S. military traveling under military orders are, without exception, entitled to be admitted to the United States, the Secretary of Homeland Security proposes to determine that a military identification card when traveling under official orders or permit of the U.S. Armed Forces would be an acceptable form of alternative documentation when presented upon arrival at air, sea, and land ports-of-entry.

* * * *

Travel document requirements for spouses and dependents of U.S. citizen members of the U.S. Armed Forces, as well as Department of Defense contractors and civilian employees, will be subject to the same document requirements applicable to other arrivals at sea and land ports-of-entry otherwise specified in this NPRM.

B. *Canadian Citizens and Citizens of Bermuda Arriving by Sea or Land*

1. Canadians

Canadian citizens entering the United States at sea and land ports-of-entry would be required to present, in addition to any applicable visa requirements:

1. A passport issued by the Government of Canada;
2. A valid trusted traveler program card issued by CBSA or DHS as discussed above in Section III.C.1.c, *e.g.,* FAST, NEXUS, or SENTRI; or
3. Alternative Canadian citizenship and identity documents hereafter proposed by Canada and accepted by DHS and DOS.

Additionally, Canadian citizens in the NEXUS program who arrive by pleasure vessel from Canada would be permitted to present a NEXUS membership card in lieu of a passport along the northern border under the auspices of the remote inspection system for pleasure vessels, such as the Outlying Area Reporting System (OARS). Currently, as NEXUS members, Canadian recreational boaters can report their arrival to CBP by telephone. Otherwise, these pleasure vessel travelers would be required to report in person to a port-of-entry in order to enter the United States.

* * * *

2. Bermudians

Under this proposed rule, all Bermudian citizens would be required to present a passport issued by the Government of Bermuda or the United Kingdom when seeking admission to the United States at all sea or land ports-of-entry, including travel from within the Western Hemisphere.

C. *Mexican Nationals Arriving by Sea or Land*

Under this proposed rule, all Mexican nationals would be required to present either (1) A passport issued by the Government of Mexico and a visa when seeking admission to the United States, or (2) a valid Form DSP-150, B-1/B-2 laser visa Border Crossing Card (BCC) when seeking admission to the United States at land ports-of-entry or arriving by pleasure vessel or by ferry from Mexico.

* * * *

1. Border Crossing Card (BCC)

DOS issues BCCs to Mexican nationals who come to the United States on a regular basis. Since 1998, every new BCC contains a biometric identifier, such as a fingerprint, and a machine-readable zone (MRZ). In order to obtain a new BCC, a Mexican traveler must have a passport. Because the BCC is a B-1/B-2 visa, the State Department issuance process is nearly identical to that of other visas, with the attendant background checks and interviews necessary for security purposes.

Mexican nationals who hold a BCC will be allowed to use their BCC for entry at the land border and when arriving by ferry or pleasure vessel in lieu of a passport for travel within 25 miles of the border with Mexico (75 miles for the Tucson, Arizona region) and no longer than a 30-day stay in the United States. . . .

2. Trusted Traveler Program Use

We propose continuing the current practice that Mexican nationals may not use the FAST or SENTRI card in lieu of a passport or BCC. These participants, however, would continue to benefit from expedited border processing.

*   *   *   *

D. Other Approved Documents

DHS and DOS remain committed to considering travel documents developed by the various U.S. States and the Governments of Canada and Mexico in the future that would denote identity and citizenship and would also satisfy section 7209 of IRTPA.

Under this proposed rule, DHS proposes to consider, as appropriate, documents such as State driver's licenses that satisfy the WHTI requirements by denoting identity and citizenship. These documents could be from a State, tribe, band, province, territory, or foreign government if developed in accordance with pilot program agreements between those entities and DHS. In addition to denoting identity and citizenship, these documents will have compatible technology [and] security criteria, and respond to CBP's operational concerns.

*   *   *   *

On March 9, 2007, DHS published in the Federal Register an NPRM concerning minimum standards for State-issued driver's licenses and identification cards that can be accepted for official purposes in accordance with the REAL ID Act.[49] DHS encourages States interested in developing driver's licenses that will meet both the REAL ID and WHTI requirements to work closely with DHS to that end.

*   *   *   *

Section V of the proposed rule set forth special rules for use of other alternative documents by specific groups of travelers: (A) U.S. citizen cruise ship passengers; (B) U.S. and Canadian citizen children; (C) lawful permanent residents of

---

[49] *See* REAL ID NPRM at 72 FR 10819.

the United States; (D) alien members of the U.S. armed forces; (E) members of NATO armed forces; (F) American Indian card holders from Kickapoo Band of Texas and Tribe of Oklahoma; (G) members of U.S. Native American tribes; (H) Canadian Indians; (I) those engaged in sea travel from territories subject to the jurisdiction of the United States; (J) Outer Continental Shelf Employees; (K) International Boundary and Water Commission employees; and (L) individual cases of passport waivers.

b. Card format passports

On December 31, 2007, the Department of State published a final rule on card format passports, described in 1.a. *supra*, and changes to the passport fee schedule, to be effective February 1, 2008. 72 Fed. Reg. 74,169 (Dec. 31, 2007). The proposed rule, published for public comment on October 17, 2006, 71 Fed. Reg. 60,928 (Oct. 17, 2006), is discussed in *Digest 2006* at 11–13.

c. New global passport regulations

On November 19, 2007, the Department of State published an additional final rule, also effective February 1, 2008, that "reorganize[d], restructure[d], and update[d] passport regulations . . . to bring greater clarity to current passport policy and practice and to present it in a less cumbersome way." 72 Fed. Reg. 64,930 (Nov. 19, 2007). The rule was published as a proposed rule on March 7, 2007, for comments. 72 Fed. Reg. 10,095 (Mar. 7, 2007). Excerpts below from the Summary Information section of the March publication explain changes related to passport issuance to minors and felons.

*   *   *   *

Minors. The proposed rule in new § 51.28 makes a number of changes to the current provisions in § 51.27 on Minors. The Department revised its passport regulations in 2001 to implement the provisions of 22 U.S.C. 213n, requiring that both parents consent to the issuance of a passport to minor children under age 14. The Department further amended the regulations in 2004 to require that children under age 14 appear personally when applying for a passport. The proposed rule in § 51.28(a) would extend the two-parent consent and personal appearance requirements to minors under the age of 16. Raising the age requirement for parental consent to passport issuance to minors under 16 is intended to address the troubling issue of runaway children as well as abduction. The change is also consistent with the age requirements in the Hague Convention on the Civil Aspects of International Child Abduction and current passport regulations permitting issuance of a ten-year passport to minors age 16 and above.

A proposed new § 51.28(a)(5)(ii) would amend the "special family circumstances" exceptions to the two-parent consent requirement to include situations in which return of a minor to the jurisdiction of his or her home state or habitual residence is necessary to permit a court of competent jurisdiction to determine custody matters. This change is intended to address the issue of children habitually resident in the United States who are, in effect, wrongfully stranded abroad when an abducting parent or his/her family holds current passports and/or refuses permission for issuance of replacements. The revision would also amend "special family circumstances" to include compelling humanitarian circumstances involving the health, safety or welfare of the minor and ease slightly the standard for "special family circumstances," from the current very stringent "impossible" to "exceptionally difficult."

To further deal with the issue of runaway minors, proposed § 51.28(b) seeks to reaffirm in clearer language the authority of a passport authorizing officer to require a parent, guardian, or person *in loco parentis* to consent to the issuance of a passport for minors age 16 and above. The proposed new § 51.28(c)(4) clarifies the question of access by parents or guardians to passport records of minors.

Denial, Revocation and Restriction of Passports: Proposed new § 51.60(b)(9) revises provisions on denial, revocation, and restriction of passports (currently § 51.70) to permit the Department to deny a passport to applicants who are the subject of outstanding state or local warrants of arrest for a felony. Similarly, new § 51.60(d) would permit the Department to deny passport issuance when the Department has been informed by an appropriate foreign government authority or international organization that the applicant is the subject of a warrant of arrest for a felony. Providing the Department with such authority will enhance U.S. border security and law enforcement cooperation. Proposed new § 51.60(c) clarifies the Department's authority to deny passport issuance to applicants who have not repaid repatriation and other emergency loans extended to them and/or members of their immediate family in a foreign country. This provision is intended to improve the Department's ability to collect unpaid debts to the U.S. Government and to address the problem of dependents of U.S. citizens who are abandoned abroad. Proposed new § 51.60(e) would permit the Department to refuse to issue a passport to a wrongfully removed or retained minor, except a passport limited for direct return to the United States, when return of the minor to the jurisdiction of his or her home state or habitual residence is necessary to permit a court of competent jurisdiction to determine custody matters. This provision would enhance the Department's efforts to protect children against international child abduction and to meet its treaty obligations in that regard.

*   *   *   *

2. Claimed Entitlement to Passport

On September 18, 2007, the U.S. District Court for the Northern District of California dismissed a case brought against the Department of State and other U.S. agencies claiming a right to a passport and money damages due to detention and other actions of various federal agents. *Jibreel v. U.S. Department of State*, Case No. C07-0543 MJJ (N.D. Cal. 2007). In its motion to dismiss, filed February 26, 2007, the United States argued, among other things, that the complaint provided the Court with no cognizable claim:

. . . [Jibreel, formerly known as] Blake complains that the State Department has not issued him a passport, and that he feels he is entitled to one. But the Department of State, which has the sole authority to issue United States passports, 22 U.S.C. 211a, is vested with a discretionary function, not a ministerial one. Because of the legal significance of a passport as a travel document showing the bearer's origin, identity, and nationality, *see* 8 U.S.C. 1101(a)(30), the burden is on the applicant to establish each of the elements or facts required for a passport. *See* 22 C.F.R. part 51 . . . Plaintiff alleges no such facts. . . . [T]he State Department has the discretion to refuse to issue a passport for various reasons, and the courts do not properly second-guess them unless they are unconstitutional.

The full text of the motion to dismiss is available at *www. state.gov/s/l/c8183.htm.*

C. IMMIGRATION AND VISAS

1. Consular Non-Reviewability

On December 20, 2007, the U.S. District Court for the Southern District of New York granted a U.S. motion for summary judgment on a challenge to the exclusion of an alien for providing material support to a terrorist organization. *American Academy of Religion v. Chertoff,* 2007 U.S. Dist. LEXIS 93424 (S.D.N.Y. 2007). The court concluded:

The Court finds that the reason provided by the Government for the exclusion of Professor Ramadan is facially legitimate and bona fide. The Court recognizes the limits on its authority in this case. The question of admissibility of aliens is a political question, a question which is best left to the Legislative and Executive branches. Having articulated a facially legitimate and bona fide reason to exclude Professor Ramadan, [*Kleindienst v. Mandel,* 408 U.S. 753 (1972)] makes clear that the Court

> has no authority to override the Government's consular
> decision. . . .

Excerpts below from the opinion of the court provide a brief
summary of the case and the court's limited First Amendment
review of the decision as an exception to the doctrine of consular non-reviewability because of the "unique circumstances
of the case" (footnotes omitted). For further background, see
Digest 2006 at 18–29. Plaintiffs' appeal to the Second Circuit
was pending at the end of 2007.

———————

In its opinion and order of June 23, 2006, the Court ordered
Defendants Michael Chertoff and Condoleez[z]a Rice, in their
capacities as Secretary of the Department of Homeland Security
and Secretary of State, respectively, (collectively "the Government"),
to issue a final decision on Tariq Ramadan's pending non-immi-
grant visa application within 90 days of the date of the order. On
September 19, 2006, the Government officially denied the visa and
gave its reason: Professor Ramadan had contributed money to an
organization which provided material support to Hamas, a terrorist group. Defendants assert that such contributions were made
in violation of the Immigration and Nationality Act ("INA")
§ 212(a)(3)(B), codified at 8 U.S.C. §1182(a)(3)(B)(iv)(VI), thus
rendering Ramadan inadmissible for providing material support
to a terrorist organization.

After considering the matter for five months, Plaintiffs amended
their complaint and on February 23, 2007, the American Academy
of Religion, the American Association of University Professors, the
PEN American Center, and Tariq Ramadan, (collectively "Plaintiffs"),
moved for summary judgment on dual grounds: (1) that their First
Amendment rights have been, and continue to be, violated by the
Government's actions in the ongoing exclusion of Ramadan, and
(2) that the section of the USA PATRIOT ACT ("Patriot Act")
which provides a basis for excluding any alien from the United
States who "endorses or espouses terrorist activity or persuades
others to endorse or espouse terrorist activity or support a terrorist

organization" is unconstitutional.* 8 U.S.C. § 1182(a)(3)(B)(i)(VII). The Government responded and cross moved for summary judgment on May 21, 2007 on the grounds that it is entitled to exclude Ramadan from the United States as a matter of law under Congress' plenary power to control immigration policy and the delegation of that broad authority to the Executive. . . .

*　　*　　*　　*

IV. The Doctrine of Consular Non-Reviewability

It is well-settled that the decision of a consular official to grant or deny a visa is nonreviewable by courts, absent a Constitutional challenge by a United States citizen. This principle, now firmly rooted in our jurisprudence, has come to be known as the "doctrine of consular nonreviewability." The doctrine of consular nonreviewability provides that when a consular officer decides to negatively exercise the visa authority granted to the Executive by Congress, a court has no jurisdiction to review the exercise of that authority. In other words, the decision of a consular official to deny a visa is final and is not reviewable. . . .

*　　*　　*　　*

V. Consular Nonreviewability and the First Amendment Claim

While the doctrine of consular nonreviewability bars a court from hearing an alien's challenge to a consular decision, a court has jurisdiction over a United States citizen's constitutional claim directly related to a consular decision. *Abourezk v. Reagan*, 785 F.2d 1043, 1051 n.6, 251 U.S. App. D.C. 355 (D.C. Cir. 1986); *Saavedra*, 339 U.S. App. D.C. 78, 197 F.3d 1153, 1163. The court does not exercise jurisdiction over the consular decision denying the alien entry, which is protected by consular nonreviewability, but

---

*　　Editor's note: On this latter claim, the court found that "Ramadan's visa was not denied under this provision. . . . As a result, [i]t would be inappropriate to reach the constitutional merits of any other immigration provisions since a direct application of the 'material support' provision—the provision actually at issue in Ramadan's visa denial—resolves the case."

rather, over the citizen's constitutional claim, which is an exercise of jurisdiction squarely within the court's Article III powers. . . .

*   *   *   *

. . . The Plaintiffs' First Amendment challenge to the consular decision . . . provides an opportunity, but a very limited one, to examine the consular determination. . . . The doctrine of consular nonreviewability still compels judicial deference to consular decisions. But where there is a First Amendment claim, the Supreme Court has applied a separate test. *Kleindienst v. Mandel*, 408 U.S. 753 . . . (1972).

*   *   *   *

. . . The standard is clear: when a consular official denies a visa which implicates a United Sates citizen's First Amendment rights, he or she must have a facially legitimate and bona fide reason for doing so.

*   *   *   *

VI. Analysis

*   *   *   *

The Court does not believe that the consular decision at issue here is beyond its review. It comes to this conclusion based on several factors. First and foremost is the presence of the Plaintiffs' First Amendment rights. The values and freedoms inherent in the First Amendment are at the very core of our constitutional scheme. . . . The Court does not hold that every denial of an alien's visa application would result in a First Amendment claim reviewable by federal courts. That holding would interject the Court into business long allocated to the political branches of government whenever able counsel could devise an ingenious First Amendment argument. It would be an obvious end-run around the doctrine of consular nonreviewability. But there are additional factors here besides Plaintiffs' well-pleaded First Amendment complaint.

Unlike most other cases that are shielded by consular nonreviewability, it is uncontested that the decision at issue here was not made solely by consular officials. Consular nonreviewability is premised, at least in part, on Congress' decision to commit the visa authority exclusively into consular hands. Where other agencies and other officials become involved in the decision to grant or deny a visa, it is not clear that Congress intended the same result to apply.

This Court has previously recognized that consular officials were not in complete control of Professor Ramadan's case. *Am. Acad. of Religion,* 463 F. Supp. 2d at 417–18. DHS was clearly involved, as well. DHS officials made statements to the media regarding Ramadan's exclusion in August 2004, statements now disavowed by the Government. L.A. Times, *supra,* at A23. DHS monitored Ramadan's employment status, as evidenced by its contact with Notre Dame in December 2004 to report that Ramadan's visa application had been revoked because he had resigned his position. Indeed, DHS officials conducted the December 2005 visa interview in which Ramadan revealed his donations to the [Association de Secours Palestinien ("ASP")]. Under these circumstances, where the decision to deny the visa was not made solely by consular officials, it is not apparent that the doctrine of consular nonreviewability should apply with full force.

Finally, given the entire history of this case including the initial grant of the visa, followed by the unexplained (but claimed "prudential") revocation, and then the long, foot-dragging series of inexplicable delays in proceeding, it is appropriate to inquire whether the reason finally offered is satisfactory. Thus, under the unique circumstances of this case, the Court finds that the Government must have a facially legitimate and bona fide reason for excluding Professor Ramadan. The Court now turns to the question of whether the Government's proffered reason is facially legitimate and bona fide.

As this Court has previously noted, while the *Mandel* Court found that the Government had a "facially legitimate and bona fide" reason for excluding the alien, it did not define the term—nor did it explain its source, or instruct lower federal courts how to determine if the standard had been met. Therefore, to conduct the analysis in Ramadan's case, this Court has fashioned a three-part inquiry.

First, the Court inquires whether or not the Government has provided a reason for denial of the visa. The Government has done so: Ramadan's admitted donations to organizations supporting known terrorist organizations. It is noteworthy, in the context of the First Amendment challenge, that this reason is unrelated to

Professor Ramadan's speech. Second, the Court asks whether the Government has a statutory basis for its decision. Here, the Government's reason is based on an appropriate statute, 8 U.S.C. § 1182(a)(3)(B), which permits exclusion when an alien provides material support to individuals or organizations supporting terrorists. Finally, the Court must determine whether the cited provision is properly applied to Professor Ramadan.

Plaintiffs urge that the statute is not properly applied to Professor Ramadan. The Court must resolve two issues: (1) whether the material support provision of the REAL ID Act should be applied retroactively; and (2) whether Ramadan satisfies the knowledge requirement of the statute.

A. Retroactivity

*   *   *   *

The plain meaning of "before" [in the material support provision of the REAL ID Act]* yields an obvious and intended result—the statute applies to events which occurred "before" its effective date.... The language Congress chose evinces a clear Congressional intent for the statute to have retroactive effect. . . .

B. Knowledge

Plaintiffs argue that the Government failed to demonstrate that Ramadan had the requisite statutory knowledge to fall within the material support provision. In support of this argument, Plaintiffs cite to the dual references to "knowledge" in the statute. The material support provision states:

> to commit an act that *the actor knows, or reasonably should know,* affords material support . . . to a terrorist

---

* Editor's note: Section 103(d) of the REAL ID Act provides:
"(d) EFFECTIVE DATE—The amendments made by this section shall take effect on the date of the enactment of this division, and these amendments, and section 212(a)(3)(B) of the Immigration and Nationality Act (8 U.S.C. §1182(a)(3)(B)), as amended by this section, shall apply to . . . acts and conditions constituting a ground for inadmissibility, excludability, deportation, or removal occurring or existing *before, on, or after such date.*" (emphasis added).

organization . . . *unless the actor can demonstrate by clear and convincing evidence that the actor did not know, and should not reasonably have known, that the organization was a terrorist organization.*"

8 U.S.C. § 1182 (a)(3)(B)(iv)(VI)(dd) (emphasis added).

*   *   *   *

Professor Ramadan admits that his 1998–2002 donations benefited ASP. Plaintiffs argue, however, that because ASP was not deemed a Specially Designated Global Terrorist until 2003, he could not have known he was funding terror. . . . Since he knew, the statute then imposes on him the second part of the knowledge requirement. Accordingly, he has the burden to demonstrate "by clear and convincing evidence" that he "did not know, and should not reasonably have known, that the organization was a terrorist organization." The consular official determined that he did not satisfy this burden.

*   *   *   *

The statute imposes a heavy burden: it requires Professor Ramadan to prove a negative, and to do so by clear and convincing proof. But this outcome is the direct result of the language Congress used. It is the Court's role to interpret the language of the statute as written by Congress, not to question Congress' wisdom in drawing the line where it did. Congress has decided to make the alien's burden a high one, and it was well within its power to do so. Given the high standard articulated by Congress, the consular official is then charged with the duty of determining whether the alien has met his or her burden. Once the consular official has made this decision, it is not the Court's role—sitting without the benefit of the subject matter expertise or detailed information on the applicant available to the consular official—to second guess the result.

The Court finds that the Government has satisfied the limited burden imposed by *Mandel*. It has given a reason for the visa denial unrelated to Professor Ramadan's speech, linked the reason to a statutory provision providing the basis for exclusion, and demonstrated that the statute applies to Professor Ramadan. The Plaintiffs' arguments to the contrary are insufficient. Professor Ramadan has not demonstrated by clear and convincing evidence that he lacked knowledge of ASP's illicit activities. The Government has provided a facially legitimate and bona fide reason for Professor Ramadan's exclusion.

*   *   *   *

2. Visas and Temporary Admission for Certain Nonimmigrant Aliens Infected with HIV

On November 6, 2007, the Department of Homeland Security published a notice of proposed rulemaking that would authorize issuance of certain short-term nonimmigrant visas and temporary admission for aliens who are inadmissible solely due to their infection with HIV. 72 Fed. Reg. 62,593 (Nov. 6, 2007).

Excerpts below explain the applicable statutes and the proposed rule.

---

*   *   *   *

II. Intent of the Proposed Rule

This proposed rule, initiated at the direction of the President (*see* White House, *Fact Sheet: World AIDS Day 2006*, December 1, 2006) through the Secretary of State . . . , would establish a more streamlined process for issuance of a nonimmigrant visa and temporary admission to the United States for aliens who are inadmissible to the United States due to HIV infection. DHS is proposing to allow these aliens to enter the United States as visitors (for business or pleasure) for a temporary period not to exceed thirty days, without being required to seek such admission under the more complex (individualized, case-by-case) process provided under the current DHS policy. The proposed rule would provide an additional avenue for temporary admission of these aliens while minimizing costs to the government and the risk to public health. These goals are accomplished by setting requirements and conditions that govern an alien's admission, affect certain aspects of his or her activities while in the United States (*e.g.*, using proper medication when medically appropriate, avoiding behavior that can transmit the infection), and ensure his or her departure after a short stay. Nonimmigrant aliens who do not meet the specific circumstances of these clarifying instructions or who do not wish to consent to the conditions imposed by this rule may still elect a case-by-case determination of their eligibility for a waiver of the nonimmigrant visa requirements for aliens afflicted with HIV.

III. Applicable Law and Regulations

An alien infected with HIV is inadmissible to the United States under section 212(a)(1)(A)(i) of the Immigration and Nationality Act of 1952 (INA), as amended, 8 U.S.C. 1182(a)(1)(A)(i). An inadmissible alien may be temporarily admitted to the United States under INA section 212(d)(3)(A), 8 U.S.C. 1182(d)(3)(A).

DHS may authorize temporary admission to the United States under 8 CFR 212.4(a) or (b). The categorical authorization process proposed in this rule would be added to 8 CFR 212.4 in new paragraph (f).

*   *   *   *

IX. The Proposed Rule

*   *   *   *

B. Specific Conditions of Admission, Control, and Return

The proposed rule includes specific requirements (based in part on criteria discussed above), which are set forth here by type.

(1) *Medical etiology.* A visa applicant, who has tested positive for HIV, must show a controlled state of HIV infection such that there is no anticipated need for additional medical care during the applicant's visit to the United States. A controlled state of HIV infection means that the applicant does not exhibit, at the time of application, symptoms indicative of an active AIDS-related condition that is contagious or that requires urgent treatment.

In cases involving HIV-positive aliens, DHS policy requires that consideration be given to whether: (1) The danger to the public health is minimal, (2) the possibility of the transmission of the infection is minimal, and (3) any cost will be incurred by any level of government agency in the United States (local, state, or federal) without the prior consent of that agency. Consular officers must find (based on evidence provided by the applicant that satisfies reviewing officials) that the former two factors are no more than minimal and that there will not be a cost to an agency absent prior consent.

(2) *Understanding.* The applicant must establish that he or she is aware of, understands, and has been counseled on the nature and severity of his or her medical condition. As part of this process, the applicant also must establish that he or she has been counseled on and is aware of the communicability of his or her medical condition, including the fact that the applicant must not donate blood or blood components.

(3) *Limited potential health danger.* The applicant must establish that his or her admission to the United States for a short duration poses minimal risk of danger to the public health in the United States. The applicant must establish that his or her admission poses a minimal risk of danger of transmission of the infection to any other person in the United States through demonstration of knowledge of the routes of transmission of HIV, including sexual contact, sharing needles, and blood transfusions.

(4) *Continuity of health care.* As with existing policy, admission is contingent upon assurances that the applicant will not impose costs on the health care system of the United States. Accordingly, the applicant must establish that he or she has, or will have access to, an adequate supply of antiretroviral drugs if medically appropriate for the anticipated stay in the United States. The Food and Drug Administration (FDA) has developed enforcement policies under which it may exercise its enforcement discretion not to interdict the importation of unapproved medications for personal use in such circumstances. See *http://www.fda.gov/ora/ compliance_ref/rpm/chapter9/ch9-2.html.*

Moreover, the applicant must establish that he or she possesses sufficient assets or insurance, that is accepted in the United States, that would cover any medical care that the applicant might require in the event of illness at any time while in the United States. These two factors lead to a third factor: The applicant must establish that his or her admission will not create any cost to the United

States, or a state or local government, or any agency thereof, without the prior written consent of that agency.

(5) *Temporary Admission.* The proposed categorical treatment, like the individualized treatment under current DHS policy, is designed only for a temporary admission. Accordingly, the applicant must establish that he or she is seeking admission solely for activities that are consistent with the B-1 (business visitor) or B-2 (visitor for pleasure) nonimmigrant classifications. Travel for tourism only is an activity consistent with this categorical admission. The applicant must understand that because of his or her inadmissibility, he or she is not eligible to seek admission under the Visa Waiver Program. INA section 217, 8 U.S.C. 1187. Under current statutes and regulations, all HIV-positive applicants for admission from Visa Waiver Program countries must apply for and be granted a visa to be admitted to the United States. The applicant must also understand and agree that no single admission to the United States will be for more than thirty days. Because the proposed regulations apply to a specific ground of inadmissibility, the applicant must establish that no other ground of inadmissibility applies. Authorization for admission may not be granted if any other ground of inadmissibility exists. If the applicant requires an additional waiver of inadmissibility, the applicant must use the process described in either 8 CFR 212.4(a) or (b), as applicable.

(6) *Enforcement of the Authorization Agreement.* As this authorization for admission is being granted for a narrow, limited purpose, DHS believes that the applicant must agree to certain conditions. DHS believes that the applicant must understand and agree in writing, once the Department of State issues a waiver form, that he or she, for the purpose of admission pursuant to this waiver, is waiving the opportunity to apply for any extension of nonimmigrant stay, a change of nonimmigrant status, or adjustment of status to that of permanent resident,[1] whether filed affirmatively with DHS or defensively in response to an action for removal. DHS alternatively solicits comments on whether consular

---

[1] Nothing within this proposed rule would prohibit an alien from applying for an immigrant visa before a consular officer abroad.

officers may orally advise or provide written notification to the applicant that he or she has waived the opportunity to apply for any extension of nonimmigrant stay, a change of nonimmigrant status, or adjustment of status to that of permanent resident in lieu of the applicant executing a written waiver of these opportunities. If the applicant chooses not to waive the opportunity to apply for any extension of nonimmigrant stay, a change of nonimmigrant status, or adjustment of status to that of permanent resident, the applicant is not eligible for the streamlined process delineated in this proposed rule. However, the applicant may still elect a case-by-case determination of his or her eligibility for a waiver of the nonimmigrant visa requirements for aliens afflicted with HIV.

Furthermore, under the proposed rule, an applicant must understand and agree that any failure to comply with conditions of admission will make him/her permanently ineligible for authorization for admission under the proposed regulations.

(7) *Duration.* The nonimmigrant visa issued to the applicant will be valid for twelve months or less and may be used for a maximum of two applications for admission. The authorized period of stay will be for thirty calendar days calculated from the initial admission under this visa. The holder of the nonimmigrant visa will be permitted to apply for admission at a United States port of entry at any time during the validity of the visa if he or she is otherwise admissible in B-1 (business visitor) or B-2 (visitor for pleasure) nonimmigrant status.

*   *   *   *

3. Treaty-Investor Visas

On July 17, 2007, Wesley S. Scholz, Director of the Office of Investment Affairs for the Bureau of Economic, Energy and Business Affairs, Department of State, testified in support of a protocol to the U.S.–Denmark Treaty of Friendship, Commerce, and Navigation ("FCN"). As stated in the testimony:

The principal substantive article of the Protocol provides that "[n]ationals of either Contracting Party shall be permitted, subject to the laws relating to the entry and sojourn of aliens, to enter the territories of the other Party and to remain therein for the purpose of developing and directing the operations of an enterprise in which they have invested, or in which they are actively in the process of investing, a substantial amount of capital."

The full text of the testimony, excerpted further below, is available at *http://foreign.senate.gov/testimony/2007/ScholzTestimony070717.pdf.*

* * *

. . . [T]he Protocol to our Treaty of Friendship, Commerce, and Navigation (FCN) with Denmark . . . will establish the legal basis by which the United States may issue treaty-investor visas—also known as "E-2" visas—to qualified nationals of Denmark under the FCN treaty. United States investors interested in investing in Denmark are already eligible for Danish visas that offer comparable benefits to those that would be accorded nationals of Denmark interested in investing in the United States under E-2 visa status.

*   *   *   *

The Protocol will facilitate Danish investment in the United States by making Danish investors, who invest substantial capital in the United States, eligible for consideration to receive treaty-investor visas under the Immigration and Nationality Act (INA). The relevant provision of the INA, section 101(a)(15)(E)(ii), permits issuance of an E-2 visa only to a nonimmigrant who is "entitled to enter the United States under and in pursuance of the provisions of a treaty of commerce and navigation between the United States and the foreign state of which he is a national . . . solely to develop and direct the operation of an enterprise in which he has invested, or of an enterprise in which he is actively in the process of investing, a substantial amount of capital."

*   *   *   *

Although most U.S. FCN treaties contain a provision qualifying the treaty partner's nationals for E-2 visas, the U.S.-Denmark FCN treaty does not. The Protocol is intended to overcome this deficiency.

The Protocol reflects language found in the INA and other U.S. FCN treaties—including more than a dozen modern FCN treaties—and investment treaties generally. European countries whose nationals are already eligible for E-2 visas include, for example, the United Kingdom, Germany, France, Italy, the Netherlands, Belgium, Norway, and Sweden.

*   *   *   *

4. Visa Waiver Program

On August 3, 2007, President George W. Bush signed into law the Implementing Recommendations of the 9/11 Commission Act of 2007, Pub. L. No. 110-53, 121 Stat. 266. Section 711 of the law, "Modernization of the Visa Waiver Program," set forth the Secure Travel and Counterterrorism Partnership Act of 2007. At the time of signing, the President stated: "I . . . appreciate the steps taken to modernize the Visa Waiver Program, particularly the additional security measures, but I will continue to work with Congress to advance our security and foreign policy objectives by allowing greater flexibility to bring some of our closest allies into the program." *See* *www.whitehouse.gov/news/releases/2007/08/20070803-1.html*, 43 WEEKLY COMP. PRES. DOC. 1040 (August 6, 2007). In a statement on June 30, 2007, the President explained his intention to "seek modifications to our Visa Waiver Program that would offer our closest partners in Central and Eastern Europe as well as others, such as the Republic of Korea, an accelerated process for admission to the program as we strengthen the program's security components. . . . It is in our Nation's interest to facilitate travel to the United States and, at the same time, to prevent terrorists from being able to exploit that travel." 43 WEEKLY COMP. PRES. DOC. 896 (July 9, 2007).

A summary of the bill's provisions, prepared to provide information to U.S. posts abroad, is excerpted below.

---

*   *   *   *

4. The new law incorporates security enhancements to the program strongly supported by the Administration. Modernization of the VWP, as the legislation states, will "enhance bilateral cooperation on critical counterterrorism and information sharing initiatives; support and expand tourism and business opportunities to enhance long-term economic competitiveness; and strengthen bilateral relationships." . . .

Enhanced Security Features

5. The legislation . . . adds a number of new or enhanced security measures to the VWP that facilitate the identification of passengers who may pose a threat or are otherwise of interest and are seeking to travel to the United States. Overall, these new security measures will transform the VWP from a program that looks for security threats on a country-by-country basis into one that can screen for security risks on a passenger-by-passenger basis. These measures include:

— An Electronic Travel Authorization (ETA) System: The ETA system will collect basic biographic information about passengers who intend to travel to the United States under the VWP. The Department of Homeland Security (DHS) will use the data to determine whether travelers are eligible to travel under the VWP and whether they are potential threats—e.g., by comparing names against watchlists of known and suspected terrorists. . . . It is important to note that an ETA is not a visa and does not meet the legal requirements to serve as a substitute for a U.S. visa. The ETA system is still under development, but is expected to begin operating in 2008.

— Reporting of Lost and Stolen Passports: . . . The new legislation calls on VWP members to enter into agreements with the United States "to report, or make available through Interpol or other means as designated by the Secretary of Homeland Security, to the United States Government information about the theft or loss of passports within a strict time limit and in a manner specified in the agreement."

— Passenger Information Exchange: Information exchange is an essential component of U.S. counterterrorism policy. The law calls for VWP members to enter into agreements with the United States to share information to assist in determining whether U.S.-bound passengers pose a security threat.

— Repatriation: VWP countries must accept citizens for repatriation no more than three weeks after a U.S. court issues a final order of removal.

6. In the context of determining whether to waive a country into the VWP under the Administration's new waiver authority for countries that do not meet the existing 3 percent statutory visa refusal rate [*see* paras 8–12 below], the new law also specifies that the Secretary of Homeland Security, in consultation with the Secretary of State, shall take into consideration other factors affecting the security of the United States, including:

— Airport Security in the Country: . .

— Whether the Country Assists in the Operation of an Effective Air Marshal Program: . . .

— Standards for Passports and Travel Documents in the Country: Under current law, VWP participants have been required to transition to machine readable biometric passports. Under the new law, DHS could consider the security of travel documents issued by the country. Examples include issuance of passports by central (rather than regional or local) authorities and tougher standards for emergency or temporary passports.

— Other security-related factors, including the country's cooperation with U.S. initiatives to combat terrorism and the country's cooperation with the U.S. intelligence community in sharing information regarding terrorist threats.

*   *   *   *

Exit system

7. The new legislation requires DHS to put in place a system that can verify the departure of at least 97 percent of foreign visitors

who leave the U.S. by air. Initially, the system would be based on biographic data, such as travelers' names and passport numbers. (DHS expects it will be able to achieve the 97 percent target using biographic information within 6–12 months.) Biometric information, such as fingerprints, will be required by June 30, 2009. If this deadline is not met, Administration authority to waive the 3 percent visa refusal rate requirement will be suspended until the Administration certifies that a biometric exit program is in place.

Visa refusal rates

8. The requirement for a visa refusal rate of less than 3 percent remains in the law, but new authority has been added to waive those provisions. This waiver authority is conditioned on a number of factors including adoption of the enhanced security measures, counterterrorism cooperation and sustained reduction of visa refusal rates. The waiver will allow only countries with visa refusal rates of not more than 10 percent in the previous fiscal year to be considered for the waiver, or alternatively, countries with an overstay rate (*see* para 12) below a maximum level to be established by DHS and the Department of State. As noted above, DHS must also meet the air exit standards in the law and have an ETA in place before the waiver authority can be exercised.

9. While a step forward, the waiver provisions in the new law do not provide the degree of flexibility sought to meet the President's goals for expanding membership in the program. The Administration will continue to work with Congress to bring needed flexibility to the VWP.

10. For countries below the 10 percent refusal rate threshhold: Washington is already working with many of the roadmap countries to clarify procedures on the new security requirements. . . .

11. For countries above the 10 percent refusal rate: The Administration is committed to work with Congress to gain additional flexibility on refusal rate criteria. Meanwhile, roadmap countries should seek to implement the new security measures and continue their efforts to reduce refusals and overstays.

12. Overstay rates: As an alternative to the 10 percent visa refusal rate standard, the new legislation allows the Administration to waive the 3 percent visa refusal rate requirement if a country's

visa overstay rate did not exceed the maximum visa overstay rate
to be established by State and DHS. These rates are yet to be established and, according to the conference report, should "reflect a
reasonable expectation" that the country can meet existing statutory criteria for continued participation. Calculation of the overstay rate will require exit data that is not yet available and will be
based on overstays by nationals of the country. . . .

*   *   *   *

5. APEC Business Travel Card

On September 4, 2007, the United States signed an Asia-
Pacific Economic Cooperation ("APEC") Business Travel Card
("ABTC") Certificate "confirm[ing its] participation in the
ABTC scheme and intent to follow the operating procedures
set out in the document, APEC Business Travel Card:
Operating Framework." The certificate, signed by the United
States as a Transitional Member economy and by Australia as
the ABTC Scheme Administrator, is available at *www.state.
gov/s/l/c8183.htm*. APEC welcomed the action of the United
States in a joint statement issued at the conclusion of the
Nineteenth APEC ministerial meeting in Sydney, Australia,
September 5–6, 2007. *See http://aimp.apec.org/Documents/
2007/MM/AMM/07_amm_jms.doc*.

The ABTC was created to expedite travel for business
people within the APEC region. A brief description of the card
from the APEC website explains its use and U.S. participation
as a transitional member, as excerpted below. The full text
is available at *www.apec.org/apec/business_resources/apec_
business_travel0.html*.

Fast and efficient travel for business people within the APEC region
contributes to APEC's goal of free and open trade and investment.
To this end APEC has created an APEC Business Travel Card
(ABTC). The ABTC allows business travelers pre-cleared, facilitated
short-term entry to participating member economies. The ABTC

removes the need to individually apply for visas or entry permits, saving valuable time, and allows multiple entries into participating economies during the three years the card is valid. Card holders also benefit from faster immigration processing on arrival via access to fast-track entry and exit through special APEC lanes at major airports in participating economies. The ABTC also helps to enhance border integrity and security in participating economies as each applicant is checked against 'watch lists' of other participating economies.

*   *   *   *

APEC Member Economies fully participating in the scheme include Australia, Brunei Darussalam, Chile, China, Hong Kong (China), Indonesia, Japan, Korea, Malaysia, New Zealand, Papua New Guinea, Peru, Philippines, Singapore, Chinese Taipei, Thailand, and Viet Nam.

*   *   *   *

In September 2007, the United States became a "transitional member" of the ABTC scheme, with the aim of becoming a full participant within a three-year period. The U.S. currently recognizes the ABTC for expedited visa interview scheduling at U.S. embassies and consulates, and facilitates immigration processing through airline crew lanes upon arrival at U.S. international airports. Cardholders from non-Visa Waiver Program countries still need to present valid passports and obtain U.S. visas as required by United States law. U.S. passport holders are not yet eligible to apply for the ABTC.

*   *   *   *

The APEC Business Mobility Group had amended the ABTC Operating Framework in June 2007 to create the three-year transitional membership category. This category allows participation by an economy that is not able to fully comply with the Operating Framework where (1) the economy meets a majority of the core operating framework principles or expects to do so within one year, and (2) where progress toward meeting all the principles is expected within three years. The text of the Operating Framework is available to APEC member economies on the secure APEC website.

6. Expulsion of Aliens

On October 31, John B. Bellinger, III, Department of State Legal Adviser, addressed the Sixth Committee of the General Assembly on the draft report of the International Law Commission on the Work of its 59th Session. Mr. Bellinger's comments on draft articles addressing the expulsion of aliens are set forth below. The full text of his statement is available at *www.state.gov/s/l/c8183.htm.*

---

*   *   *   *

Expulsion of Aliens is a complex issue that implicates other matters of national concern, including those associated with the formulation of a country's immigration laws, national security, and respect for the rule of law. In light of this complexity, we urge the Commission to bear in mind the need to consider carefully the delicate and unique legal and political issues that this topic presents. In that regard, we note that draft Article 3 on the one hand explicitly recognizes the sovereign right of States to expel aliens and on the other limits on this right under international law.

We appreciate the Special Rapporteur's efforts in formulating draft Articles 1 to 7 and in refining the scope of his study to define more clearly the limits of the Commission's work on this subject. We welcome, in particular, the conclusion of the Special Rapporteur that non-admission and extradition, as well as issues concerning aliens for whom expulsion is governed by special rules, such as diplomats and members of armed forces, fall outside the scope of the topic. We also support the conclusion of the Special Rapporteur that a specific provision relating to migrant workers is not needed, as the situations and rights of migrant workers are encompassed within the general provisions.

We remain concerned, however, that the definition of "territory" suggested by the Special Rapporteur—"the domain in which the State exercises all the powers deriving from its sovereignty"—could be broadly interpreted to encompass more than the Special Rapporteur intends. Accordingly, we propose a more precise definition, such as: "a State's land territory, internal waters, and territorial sea, and its superjacent airspace, in accordance with international law." We also believe that the subject of expulsion of aliens in situations of armed conflict should be excluded from the draft articles.

* * * *

7. Suspension of Entry Under INA Section 212(f)

a. *Threats to Lebanon's sovereignty and democracy*

On June 28, 2007, President Bush issued Proclamation 8158, "Suspension of Entry as Immigrants and Nonimmigrants of Persons Responsible for Policies and Actions That Threaten Lebanon's Sovereignty and Democracy." 72 Fed. Reg. 36,587 (July 3, 2007). Section 212(f) of the INA, 8 U.S.C. § 1182(f), authorizes the President to suspend entry of any aliens or class of aliens if that entry "would be detrimental to the interests of the United States."

In order to foster democratic institutions in Lebanon, to help the Lebanese people preserve their sovereignty and achieve their aspirations for democracy and regional stability, and to end the sponsorship of terrorism in Lebanon, it is in the interest of the United States to restrict the international travel, and to suspend the entry into the United States, as immigrants or nonimmigrants, of aliens who deliberately undermine or harm Lebanon's sovereignty, its legitimate government, or its democratic institutions, contribute to the breakdown in the rule of law in Lebanon, or benefit from policies or actions that do so, including through the sponsorship of terrorism, politically motivated violence and intimidation, or the reassertion of Syrian control in Lebanon.

NOW, THEREFORE, I, GEORGE W. BUSH, President of the United States of America, by the authority vested in me by the Constitution and the laws of the United States, including section 212(f) of the Immigration and Nationality Act of 1952, 8 U.S.C. 1182(f), and section 301 of title 3, United States Code, hereby find that the unrestricted immigrant and nonimmigrant entry into the

United States of persons described in section 1 of this proclamation would, except as provided for in sections 2 and 3 of this proclamation, be detrimental to the interests of the United States.

I therefore hereby proclaim that:

Section 1. The entry into the United States, as immigrants or nonimmigrants, of the following aliens is hereby suspended:

(a) Lebanese government officials, former Lebanese government officials, and private persons who deliberately undermine or harm Lebanon's sovereignty, its legitimate government, or its democratic institutions, or contribute to the breakdown in the rule of law in Lebanon, including through the sponsorship of terrorism, politically motivated violence or intimidation, or the reassertion of Syrian control in Lebanon;

(b) Syrian government officials, former Syrian government officials, and persons who meet the criteria for designation under section 3(a)(i) or (ii) of Executive Order 13338 of May 11, 2004, who deliberately undermine or harm Lebanon's sovereignty, its legitimate government, or its democratic institutions, or contribute to the breakdown in the rule of law in Lebanon, including through the sponsorship of terrorism, politically motivated violence or intimidation, or the reassertion of Syrian control in Lebanon;

(c) Persons in Lebanon who act on behalf of, or actively promote the interests of, Syrian government officials by deliberately undermining or harming Lebanon's sovereignty, its legitimate government, or its democratic institutions, or contribute to the breakdown in the rule of law in Lebanon, including through the sponsorship of terrorism, politically motivated violence or intimidation, or the reassertion of Syrian control in Lebanon;

(d) Persons who, through their business dealings with any of the persons described in subsection (a), (b), or (c) of this section, derive significant financial benefit from, or materially support, policies or actions that deliberately undermine or harm Lebanon's sovereignty, its legitimate government, or its democratic institutions, or contribute to the breakdown in the rule of law in Lebanon, including through the sponsorship of terrorism, politically motivated violence or intimidation, or the reassertion of Syrian control in Lebanon; and

(e) The spouses and dependent children of persons described in subsections (a), (b), (c), and (d) of this section.

Sec. 2. Section 1 of this proclamation shall not apply with respect to any person otherwise covered by section 1 where entry of such person would not be contrary to the interests of the United States.

Sec. 3. Persons covered by section 1 or 2 of this proclamation shall be identified by the Secretary of State or the Secretary's designee, in his or her sole discretion, pursuant to such procedures as the Secretary may establish under section 5 of this proclamation.

Sec. 4. Nothing in this proclamation shall be construed to derogate from U.S. Government obligations under applicable international agreements.

*　*　*　*

b. Burma

On September 28, 2007, the Department of State designated more than three dozen additional Burmese government and military officials and their families under Presidential Proclamation 6925 of October 3, 1996, 61 Fed. Reg. 52,233 (Oct. 7, 1996). The proclamation suspended the entry into the United States under § 212(f) of "persons who formulate, implement, or benefit from policies that impede Burma's transition to democracy and the immediate family members of such persons." *See www.state.gov/r/pa/prs/ps/2007/sep/92960.htm; see also Digest 2003* at 27–29.

D. REFUGEES

1. Territorial Application of Non-Refoulement Obligations

On December 28, 2007, the United States submitted its observations on the UN High Commissioner for Refugees Advisory Opinion on the Extraterritorial Application of *Non-Refoulement* Obligations Under the 1951 Convention Relating to the Status of Refugees and its 1967 Protocol ¶ 15

(Jan. 26, 2007) ("Advisory Opinion" or "Opinion"). The Advisory Opinion is available at *www.unhcr.org/cgi-bin/texis/vtx/refworld/rwmain?docid=470ccbb42*. Excerpts below from the U.S. observations address disagreement with the Advisory Opinion as to "two central points":

> First, the United States disagrees with UNHCR's principal argument that the *non-refoulement* obligation under the 1951 Convention on the Status of Refugees and/or the 1967 Protocol Relating to the Status of Refugees has extraterritorial application. Second, the United States notes that the Advisory Opinion fails to establish many of the propositions it asserts with respect to the secondary topic it addresses, *i.e.*, the nature and scope of customary international law and international treaty law related to *non-refoulement*, both with respect to international refugee law and international human rights law. Most notably in this regard, the United States does not believe that UNHCR has adduced sufficient evidence to support its conclusion that Article 33 of the Refugee Convention has become a rule of customary international law that would be binding on States that are not parties to the Refugee Convention or the 1967 Protocol.

As to other issues, the United States stated:

> Given the broad scope and broad-ranging statements contained in the UNHCR Opinion, it would not be possible for these Observations to address all points in the Opinion with which the United States may not agree. This is particularly the case with respect to the Advisory Opinion's sweeping and largely erroneous assertions regarding international human rights law, an area that falls outside the competence and expertise of UNHCR and that falls under the responsibilities of other organs of the United Nations. To explain more fully its views with respect to certain opinions of the Human Rights Committee regarding the scope of the International Covenant on

> Civil and Political Rights, the United States is attaching hereto its recently issued Observations to the Human Rights Committee's General Comment 31.*

> The full text of the U.S. observations is available at *www. state.gov/s/l/c8183.htm*. As noted in excerpts below, the observations draw on U.S. submissions to the Supreme Court in *Sale v. Haitian Centers Council*, 509 U.S. 155 (1993); *see Digest 1991–1999* at 150–72. For U.S. comments on the absence of a non-refoulement obligation in the ICCPR, *see* Chapter 6.A.2.

* * * *

I. Article 33 of the Refugee Convention Does Not Apply Extraterritorially.

The United States disagrees with UNHCR's opinion that Article 33 of the Refugee Convention imposes obligations on a Contracting State with respect to aliens who are located outside of its territory. Under Article 31(1) of the Vienna Convention on the Law of Treaties ["VCLT"], a provision of a treaty must be interpreted according to the ordinary meaning of the terms employed, in light of their context and in light of the treaty's object and purpose.[1] The Vienna Convention also addresses subsequent practice in the application of the treaty that establishes the agreement of the parties regarding its interpretation, as well as the preparatory work of the treaty in the form of its *travaux preparatoires*. Vienna Convention on the Law of Treaties arts. 31–32, May 23, 1969,

---

* Editor's note: For discussion of the U.S. observations on General Comment 31, *see* Chapter 6.A.2.b.

[1] While the United States has signed but not ratified the treaty, it considers the VCLT to be the "authoritative guide" to treaty law and practice. *See* Letter of Submittal from Secretary of State Rodgers to President Nixon Transmitting the Vienna Convention on the Law of Treaties, October 28, 1971, Ex. L., 92d. Cong. 1st Sess. at 1. In particular, Articles 31 through 33 of the Vienna Convention reflect the preeminent codification of customary international law on the interpretation of treaties.

1155 U.N.T.S. 331 (hereinafter, "Vienna Convention"). As discussed further below, an examination of Article 33 of the Refugee Convention in accordance with these rules indicates that Article 33 applies only with respect to aliens who are inside a Contracting State's territory.[2]

Text and Context of Article 33

Article 33 of the Refugee Convention contains no express statement or other affirmative indication that it was intended to impose obligations on a Contracting State outside its own territory. Paragraph 1 of Article 33 provides that "[n]o Contracting State shall expel or return (*'refouler'*) a refugee in any manner whatsoever to the frontiers of a territory where his life or freedom would be threatened on account of his race, religion, nationality, membership of a particular social group or political opinion." Convention Relating to the Status of Refugees art. 33.1, July 28, 1951, 19 U.S.T. 6259, 189 U.N.T.S. 150 (hereinafter, "Refugee Convention"). The most natural reading of this language is that it expresses a prohibition against removal of a refugee *from* the Contracting State *to* a foreign territory in the specified circumstances, irrespective of the manner in which the removal might be accomplished. "Expel" means "to force or drive *out*." *American Heritage Dictionary* 477 (2d ed. 1991) (emphasis added). Similarly, one meaning for the French word *"refouler"* is "expel (aliens)." *Cassell's French Dictionary* 627 (1978). Under this meaning, "return (*'refouler'*)," like "expel," connotes not merely transfer, but instead ejection of an alien from within the territory of the Contracting State.[3]

---

[2]   The arguments here are largely drawn from the submissions of the United States to the United States Supreme Court in *Sale v. Haitian Centers Council*, 509 U.S. 155 (1993). *See* Brief for the Petitioners at 36-51, *Sale*, 509 U.S. 155 (1993) (No. 92-344); Reply Brief for the Petitioners at 18-29, *Sale*, 509 U.S. 155 (1993) (No. 92-344).

[3]   The United States Supreme Court adopted this interpretation in *Sale*: "'[R]eturn' means a defensive act of resistance or exclusion at a border rather than an act of transporting someone to a particular destination. . . . [B]ecause the text of Article 33 cannot reasonably be read to say anything at all about a nation's actions toward aliens outside its own territory, it does not prohibit such actions." 509 U.S. at 182-83.

As for any suggestion that "return (*'refouler'*)" must have some other meaning (such as transfer from outside a State's territory) in order to avoid redundancy in the terms "expel" and "return (*'refouler'*)," an examination of the two terms indicates that they are not in fact redundant. "Expulsion" in this context typically connotes "the formal process whereby a lawfully resident alien may be required to leave a state, or be forcibly ejected therefrom," as opposed to removal of an individual who is not lawfully resident. Guy Goodwin-Gill, *The Refugee in International Law* 69 (1983). Read in this way, "expel" does not reach all classes of aliens present in a country—it covers only those cases in which the alien's presence is lawful. Accordingly, the term following "expel" in Article 33, "return (*'refouler'*)," rounds out the prohibition by ensuring that aliens whose presence in the country is unlawful are also covered. There is nothing in the text or context to suggest that the use of both "expel" and "return (*'refouler'*)" was meant to encompass individuals within a State's territory as well as individuals outside of a State's territory.

Contrary to UNHCR's position, *see* Advisory Opinion ¶ 28, paragraph 2 of Article 33 confirms that paragraph 1 of Article 33 applies only to aliens inside the territory of a Contracting State. Paragraph 2 states that the benefit of Article 33 may not be claimed by a refugee who is a danger to the security of "the country in which he is." This paragraph, the only reference to territory in the Article, contemplates that a refugee is covered only if he is "in" a "country" of refuge. Accordingly, read as a whole, Article 33 applies only to removal by a Contracting State of a refugee who is within the territory of that Contracting State.

The text and structure of the Convention provide compelling support for this interpretation. The premise that the Convention is limited to the territory of the Contracting State is woven throughout the provisions of the Convention. *See* Refugee Convention arts. 4, 15, 17.1, 18, 19.1, 21, 23, 24, 26, 27, 28, 31.1, 32.1. These other references to the territorial scope are consistent with an overall reading of the instrument that, absent some express provision to the contrary, the Convention applies within the territory of [a] Contracting State. UNHCR reaches a different conclusion regarding these Articles: As support for its extraterritoriality analysis,

UNHCR points out that certain provisions include a requirement that the refugee must be within the territory of the Contracting State, which, according to UNHCR, means that because the territorial scope of Article 33.1 is *not* made explicit as it is in these other Articles, there is no territorial limitation. *See* Advisory Opinion ¶ 28. This is not a natural reading of a treaty text, nor would it be reasonable to impose on treaty drafters a reading that every provision of a treaty would apply extraterritorially absent an express limitation in its text. Such a reading would be particularly illogical where the only express indicators of the drafters' intentions all show the intent that the instrument would not apply extraterritorially. UNHCR's reasoning is flawed because it fails to acknowledge that the provisions that include a requirement that the refugee must be within the territory of the Contracting State demonstrate that the territorial limit of the Convention is evident throughout the Convention. The logical conclusion of the particular Articles that UNHCR cites is not that Article 33.1 does *not* carry any territorial limits; it is, to the contrary, that in context, Article 33.1, like these other provisions in the Convention, is limited to the territory of the Contracting State.

Moreover, further supporting the contextual understanding of the treaty, Article 40.1, entitled "Territorial Application Clause," provides that a State may, at the time of signature, ratification, or accession, "declare that this Convention shall *extend* to all or any of the territories for the international relations of which it is responsible." Refugee Convention art. 40.1 (emphasis added). This provision thus indicates that a Contracting State's obligations under Article 33 do not automatically extend beyond its metropolitan territory, even to its territories or possessions, much less to the high seas and throughout the entire world, as UNHCR contends.

Travaux Preparatoires *of Article 33*

Article 32 of the Vienna Convention provides:

Recourse may be had to supplementary means of interpretation, including the preparatory work of the treaty and the circumstances of its conclusion, in order to confirm the meaning resulting from the application of article 31, or to determine the meaning when the interpretation according to article 31: (a) leaves the meaning ambiguous or obscure; or (b) leads to a result which is manifestly absurd or unreasonable.

Vienna Convention art. 32. Although interpretation of the Refugee Convention under the rules of treaty interpretation set out in Article 31 of the Vienna Convention does not leave the meaning of Article 33 ambiguous or obscure, and the resulting interpretation that Article 33 is limited to individuals within the territory of Contracting States is neither absurd nor unreasonable, the *travaux-preparatoires* of the Convention, and specifically the official minutes of the Conference of Plenipotentiaries, which negotiated the final language of the Convention and adopted Article 33 in the form in which it was ratified, are helpful in reaffirming that Article 33 has no extraterritorial application.

Specifically, the Swiss delegate expressed the view at one session of the Conference that the word "expel" "related to a refugee who had already been admitted to the territory of a country." He distinguished this from the word "return," which related to "refugees who had already entered a country but were not yet resident there." Conference of Plenipotentiaries, Summary Record of the 16th Meeting, U.N. Doc. A/CONF.2/SR.16 at 6 (July 11, 1951). The representatives of France, Belgium, Germany, Italy, the Netherlands, and Sweden agreed. *Id.* at 6, 11–12.

At a subsequent session, the Dutch delegate reiterated the Swiss interpretation of "expulsion" and "return (*'refoulement'*)," and he stated that based on his intervening conversations with other representatives as well, there appeared to be a "general consensus" in favor of the Swiss interpretation. *Id.*, 35th Meeting, U.N. Doc. A/CONF/2/SR.35, at 21 (July 25, 1951). The Dutch delegate then asked to have the record show that the Conference was in agreement with this interpretation, "[i]n order to dispel any possible ambiguity" and to ensure that "mass migrations across frontiers or . . . attempted mass migrations" are "not covered by article 33." *Id.* The President of the Conference noted that there was no objection and ordered that interpretation "placed on record." *Id.* The President further suggested that *"refouler"* be placed in brackets after "return" every place the latter word appeared in the English text, a suggestion that was "adopted unanimously." *Id.* at 21–22; *see also* Goodwin-Gill, *The Refugee in International Law* 74 ("At the 1951 Conference, no formal objection appears to have been raised to the Swiss interpretation of *non-refoulement,* limiting its application to those who have already entered state territory."). Read together, the words "expel" and "return *(refouler)*" in Article 33.1 can thus only be understood to embody a deliberate decision by the Contracting States to incorporate a territorial limitation into the Convention's provision on *non-refoulement.*

UNHCR's arguments from the negotiating record do not contradict this clear indication that the parties drafting the Convention intended to limit Article 33.1 to aliens in the territory of a Contracting State. First, UNHCR quotes a statement of Professor Louis Henkin, then the U.S. representative to the Ad Hoc Committee on Statelessness and Related Problems, expressing that a refugee must not be turned back to a place where his life or freedom would be threatened regardless of whether the refugee was at the frontier or had already crossed the frontier. *See* Advisory Opinion ¶ 30 (quoting Statement of Louis Henkin of the United States ¶¶ 54–55, U.N. Doc. E/AC.32/SR.20 (Feb. 1, 1950)). Professor Henkin expressed this sentiment at the Ad Hoc Committee on Statelessness, a body which prepared the *first draft* of the Convention. His sentiment was not adopted by the Committee (nor was it raised by the U.S. delegate at the later Conference of Plenipotentiaries).

Indeed, the Committee on Statelessness contemporaneously adopted language that intended to restrict Article 33 to aliens within the territory of a Contracting State. A study published by the United Nations in 1949 as a prelude to the Convention had used the term "expulsion" to mean "the juridical decision taken by the judicial or administrative authorities whereby an individual is ordered to leave the territory of the country." U.N. Dep't of Social Affairs, A Study of Statelessness 60, U.N. Doc. E/1112, (Feb. 1, 1949). The study used the term "reconduction," which it regarded as the equivalent of *"refoulement,"* to mean "the mere physical act of ejecting from the national territory a person who has gained entry or is residing therein irregularly." The study explicitly opined that "reconduction" did *not* "signify the act of preventing a foreigner who has presented himself at the frontier from entering the national territory." *Id.* at 60 & n.1. The Committee on Statelessness later replaced the term "reconduction" with "return," which expresses the same sentiment as reconduction—the mere act of ejection without the accompanying judicial process that is implicit in the term "expulsion." The interpretation of these terms by the UN study thus confirms that Article 33 originated in an intention only to bar removal of individuals from within the Contracting State's territory, lending further support to the interpretation of Article 33.1 as a unitary prohibition against a Contracting State's ejection of a refugee *from its territory*. Professor Henkin's vision thus did not advance beyond his proposal at the initial Committee.

UNHCR's analysis is similarly incorrect in its suggestion that, by adopting the particular language that it did, the Conference of Plenipotentiaries must have meant to approve only the Dutch delegate's understanding that a Contracting State would have no obligation to accept a mass migration of refugees across its borders, but not the specific meaning he attached to the terms in the text of Article 33.1 dictating that Article 33.1 related only to refugees who had already entered the territory of the Contracting State. *See* Advisory Opinion n.57; *see also* Principle of *Non-Refoulement* ¶ 28. This argument ignores the rationale of the Dutch delegate's conclusion—that there would be no obligation to accept a mass migration *because* he and the other delegates agreed with the Swiss delegate's underlying interpretation of both "expel" and "return (*'refouler'*)" as applying only to aliens who had already entered the territory of the Contracting State.

UNHCR additionally argues that any interpretation that construes Article 33.1 as not extending to actions taken with respect to aliens outside of a Contracting State's territory "would be fundamentally inconsistent with the humanitarian object and purpose of the 1951 Convention and its 1967 Protocol." Advisory Opinion ¶ 29. The Convention and Protocol undoubtedly sought to achieve humanitarian goals, but the texts and negotiating record reflect that the negotiators of the treaty sought to advance such humanitarian goals with respect to people who had entered the territory of a Contracting State. A retrospective belief, even if true, that the negotiators might have more fully advanced humanitarian goals by extending the reach of the treaty more broadly than they did is not a basis for imposing on the treaty a reading supported neither by its text nor by its negotiating history. Similarly, under long-standing international treaty law, the fact that a treaty may be characterized as generally serving a humanitarian purpose cannot support an effort many years after its entry into force to rewrite the treaty by stretching its terms without limit so long as the final result can be described as serving a humanitarian purpose. Because UNHCR's contemporary vision of the object and purpose of the Convention are fundamentally at odds with its text and negotiating history, it cannot be relied on, without more, to justify UNHCR's interpretation.

Subsequent State Practice

UNHCR additionally claims that Conclusions of the UNHCR Executive Committee and other refugee and human rights instruments are expressions of "subsequent State practice" that indicate that the *non-refoulement* obligation in the Convention and Protocol have extraterritorial application. *See* Advisory Opinion ¶¶ 32–38. UNHCR's citation to these instruments is misguided. The Vienna Convention on the Law of Treaties provides for interpretation of a treaty by reference to its context, including "(a) any agreement relating to the treaty which was made between all the parties in connection with the conclusion of the treaty" or "(b) any instrument which was made by one or more parties in connection with the conclusion of the treaty and accepted by the other parties as an instrument related to the treaty." Vienna Convention art. 31.2. In addition, interpretation of a treaty must take into account, together with the context, "(a) any subsequent agreement between the parties regarding the interpretation of the treaty or the application of its provisions; (b) any subsequent practice in the application of the treaty which establishes the agreement of the parties regarding its interpretation; (c) any relevant rules of international law applicable in the relations between the parties." Vienna Convention art. 31.3. Neither the Conclusions of the Executive Committee nor other human rights and refugee instruments constitute either an "agreement" or actual "practice" or "rules" falling within those categories.

The Conclusions of the Executive Committee are not drafted or agreed to by all parties to the Refugee Convention or the Protocol, do not constitute "agreement" by the parties as to the Convention's interpretation, do not temporally constitute instruments made by the parties in connection with the conclusion of the treaty, and are not "rules" of international law. The Conclusions of the Executive Committee have no conclusive authority in determining the interpretation of the Convention or the Protocol. Indeed, even UNHCR has acknowledged that the conclusions of the Executive Committee have no legal effect. *See* Summary Record of the 41st Meeting at 12, U.N. Doc. A/AC.96/SR.431 (1988) (statement of Mr. Arnaout, Dir., Division of Refugee Law and Doctrine, UNHCR). Instead, they are essentially recommendatory statements of policy, which represent shared policy and program guidance. (In fact, at a 1989 meeting of the Executive Committee, the practice of the United States was to the contrary; it stated that Article 33 "pertained only to persons already in the country and not to those who arrived at the frontier or who were traveling with the intention of entering the country but had not yet arrived at their destination." Summary Record of the 442nd Meeting at 16, U.N. Doc. A/AC.96/SR.442 (1989). No party to the Convention expressed disagreement with this position).

Similarly, the other human rights instruments that UNHCR cites as relevant "State practice"—including the 1969 OAU Convention Governing Specific Aspects of Refugee Problems in Africa, the 1969 American Convention on Human Rights, the non-binding 1984 Cartagena Declaration on Refugees, and the non-binding 1967 Declaration on Territorial Asylum adopted by the General Assembly—are not instructive in interpreting this provision of the Refugee Convention. The OAU Convention and the American Convention are not connected to the conclusion of the Refugee Convention or Protocol, were not made in connection with their conclusion, were not accepted by other parties as related to the Convention or Protocol, and were not made between the parties to the Convention or Protocol regarding the interpretation or application of the provisions of the Convention or Protocol. Accordingly, they do not qualify for consideration under Article 31.2

of the Vienna Convention. As to their significance as "relevant rules of international law" under Article 31.3 of the Vienna Convention, the Conventions simply reflect separate obligations that *some* States—and not *all* parties to the Convention or Protocol—have chosen to undertake in other international instruments. These obligations are distinct from those in the Convention and Protocol and reflect only the obligations of the parties to those instruments. Moreover, the two Declarations to which UNHCR cites are neither "agreements" nor "rules." The existence of those instruments and their territorial scope—even assuming they have the meanings ascribed to them in the Opinion—have no bearing on the interpretation of Article 33. They merely reflect non-legally binding statements of aspiration that some States have chosen to undertake or support in other international instruments.

Relevant Rules of International Law

In addition, UNHCR argues that States are generally obligated "not to return any person over whom they exercise jurisdiction to a risk of irreparable harm," and as a result, interpreting Article 33 as not having extraterritorial application would be inconsistent with relevant rules of international law. *See* Advisory Opinion ¶ 38. In support of this proposition, it cites authorities suggesting that provisions of other treaties have extraterritorial reach. Putting aside the fact, described briefly below, that the interpretations of at least some of these instruments may not be correct, even if those factually unsupported assertions were accurate, the fact that parties to other treaties negotiated provisions with a broader scope of territorial application would say nothing about the territorial scope of the Refugee Convention. Nor does the existence of these other instruments, even if interpreted in the manner asserted by UNHCR, suggest that a proper textual reading of the Refugee Convention could reasonably be read to be in violation of some general principle of international law. Indeed, as described in the following discussion, the United States does not agree with the assertion that there exists some broader legally binding rule on this subject.

As support for its assertions that there is a general principle of international law prohibiting *refoulement* where there is a risk of irreparable harm and that the Refugee Convention should be read to have extraterritorial application, UNHCR cites the statement of the Human Rights Committee in General Comment 31 that "a State party [to the International Covenant on Civil and Political Rights (ICCPR)] must respect and ensure the rights laid down in the [ICCPR] to anyone within the power or effective control of that State Party, even if not situated within the territory of the State Party." Human Rights Committee, General Comment No. 31 on the Nature of the General Legal Obligation on States Parties to the Covenant ¶ 10, U.N. Doc. CCPR/C/21/Rev.1/Add.13 (April 21, 2004). This interpretation disregards accepted modes of treaty interpretation and, as the United States explains in its Observations on General Comment 31, is inconsistent with the plain text of the ICCPR and at odds with the negotiating history of the Covenant. To explain the reasons why it does not agree with this reading of Article 7 of the ICCPR, the United States is pleased to provide its recently issued Observations of the United States on General Comment 31 of the Human Rights Committee for UNHCR's information. (fn. omitted)

In support of its contention that "relevant rules of international law" support extraterritorial application of Article 33 of the Refugee Convention, UNHCR also points to the conclusion of the Committee of the Convention Against Torture and Other Cruel, Inhuman or Degrading Treatment or Punishment (CAT) that the *non-refoulement* obligation in Article 3 of the CAT "applies in any territory under a State party's jurisdiction." Advisory Opinion ¶ 38. As explained in detail in its Reports to the Committee Against Torture and Written Responses to Questions of the Committee Against Torture, the United States disagrees with the notion that Article 3 of the CAT applies to individuals who are outside the territory of a State Party. Neither the text of Article 3, its negotiating history, nor the U.S. record of ratification supports a view that Article 3 of the CAT applies to persons outside the territory of the United States.

Finally, UNHCR's citation to decisions of the European Court of Human Rights and the Inter-American Commission on Human Rights are unpersuasive. *See* Advisory Opinion ¶ 39. In the absence of even any suggestion in the text of the Convention, its negotiating history, or subsequent practice of States that Article 33 of the Convention prohibits *refoulement* not only of individuals within the territory of a Contracting State but also of individuals outside a State's territory, the decisions of these bodies, relating to instruments other than the Refugee Convention, are simply not relevant, much less authoritative or persuasive indicators of the proper interpretation of Article 33.

Conclusion

Although the United States takes the position that Article 33 of the 1951 Refugee Convention applies only with respect to *non-refoulement* of aliens within the territory of the Contracting State, it has been the longstanding policy of the United States to take actions outside the United States consonant with *non-refoulement* obligations that apply to individuals within U.S. territory under the Refugee Convention, as well as under the Convention Against Torture. *See, e.g.,* Foreign Affairs Reform and Restructuring Act of 1998, Pub. L. No. 105-277, div. G., Title XXII, § 2242 ("It shall be the policy of the United States not to expel, extradite, or otherwise effect the involuntary return of any person to a country in which there are substantial grounds for believing the person would be in danger of being subject to torture, regardless of whether the person is physically present in the United States."). Nonetheless, because UNHCR's conclusion that as a matter of treaty law the Refugee Convention's *non-refoulement* obligation applies outside a State's territory is at odds with the text and negotiating history of the Convention, the United States considers it crucial to remind UNHCR of its longstanding interpretation of Article 33, memorialize its fundamental disagreement with UNHCR's interpretation, and explain the clear international law bases for the proposition that Article 33 of the Refugee Convention obligates a State not to "expel or return ('*refouler*') a refugee who is within the territory of the State in any manner whatsoever to the frontiers of territories where his life of freedom would be threatened on account of his race, religion, nationality, membership in a particular social group or political opinion," subject only to the limitations set forth in subsection 2 of that Article.

II. UNHCR Fails to Establish a *Non-Refoulement* Obligation Under Customary International Law.

The Advisory Opinion contains many statements and assertions with respect to the scope of *non-refoulement* obligations under both international refugee law and human rights law. These Observations will focus on the Opinion's principal contentions regarding the status of Refugee Convention Article 33 as a norm of customary international law, but in summary form they will additionally address some of the Opinion's assertions related to international human rights law.

Non-Refoulement *Under Customary International Law*

As discussed above, under Article 33 of the 1951 Convention, to which the United States is bound by virtue of its status as a party to the 1967 Protocol Relating to the Status of Refugees, "[n]o Contracting State shall expel or return ('*refouler*') a refugee in any manner whatsoever to the frontiers of territories where his life or freedom would be threatened on account of his race, religion, nationality, membership of a particular social group or political opinion." Refugee Convention art. 33.1; *see also* Protocol Relating to the Status of Refugees art. 1(1), Jan. 31, 1967, 19 U.S.T. 6223, 606 U.N.T.S. 267. UNHCR argues, however, that a *non-refoulement* obligation exists apart from the Convention or any other instrument, and that "the prohibition of *refoulement* of refugees, as enshrined in Article 33 of the 1951 Convention and complemented by *non-refoulement* obligations under human rights law, . . . constitutes a rule of customary international law" and is therefore binding on all States, including those that are not a party to the 1951 Convention and/or its 1967 Protocol. Advisory Opinion ¶ 15. Although the United States strongly supports and rigorously adheres to the protection against *non-refoulement* that is contained in the Convention, and encourages other States to do the same, the United States believes that in the analysis leading to its conclusion, UNHCR fails to adduce necessary evidence—as opposed to making factually unsubstantiated and conclusory assertions—that would satisfy the standards required to establish that a rule has become customary international law.

As reflected generally in paragraph 14 of the Opinion, a rule becomes a part of customary international law if two elements are established: (1) State practice (*i.e.*, what States actually do) is "both extensive and virtually uniform"; *and* (2) that State practice is followed under a sense of legal obligation, such that there is a "general recognition that a rule of law or legal obligation is involved" (*opinio juris*). *North Sea Continental Shelf* (F.R.G. v. Den.; F.R.G. v. Neth.), 1969 I.C.J. 3, 43 (Judgment of Feb. 20); *see also* Restatement (Third) of Foreign Relations Law of the United States § 102(2) (1986). UNHCR fails to establish either of these two elements.

Paragraph 15 of the Advisory Opinion provides UNHCR's support for its assertion that a customary international norm of *non-refoulement* has developed, but it fails to establish either of the two elements required to elevate a rule to the status of customary international law. First, UNHCR references a 1994 paper in which it initially developed its theory: The Principle of *Non-Refoulement* as a Norm of Customary International Law, Response to the Questions posed to UNHCR by the Federal Constitutional Court of the Federal Republic of Germany in cases 2 BvR 1938/93, 2 BvR 1954/93 (January 31, 1994) (available at *http://www.unhcr.org/home/RSDLEGAL/ 437b6db64.html*) (hereinafter, "Principle of *Non-Refoulement*"). The primary basis for the conclusions of this paper is that UNHCR has interpreted the actions of States that are not parties to the Refugee Convention or the Protocol as indicating acceptance of a rule of *non-refoulement*. UNHCR describes:

> There have . . . been numerous cases in which the High Commissioner has been required to make representations to States which were parties neither to the Convention nor to the Protocol, and it is here that the Office [of the High Commissioner for Refugees] has necessarily had to rely on the principle of *non-refoulement* irrespective of any treaty obligation. In response to such representations of the High Commissioner, the Governments approached have almost invariably reacted in a manner indicating that they accept the principle of *non-refoulement* as a guide for their action. They indeed have in numerous instances sought to explain a case of actual or intended *refoulement* by providing

additional clarifications and/or by claiming that the person in question was not to be considered a refugee.

Principle of *Non-Refoulement* ¶ 5. In the Advisory Opinion, instead of distinguishing between States that are parties to the Convention or the Protocol and those that are not, UNHCR describes its experiences with both categories of States, despite the important difference between the two:

> Moreover, exercising its supervisory function, UNHCR has closely followed the practice of Governments in relation to the application of the principle of *non-refoulement*, both by States Party to the 1951 Convention and/or 1967 Protocol and by States which have not adhered to either instrument. In UNHCR's experience, States have overwhelmingly indicated that they accept the principle of *non-refoulement* as binding, as demonstrated, *inter alia*, in numerous instances where States have responded to UNHCR's representations by providing explanations or justifications of cases of actual or intended *refoulement*, thus implicitly confirming their acceptance of the principle.

Advisory Opinion ¶ 15 (footnotes omitted). Unfortunately, neither the 1994 paper nor the Advisory Opinion provide the specific and verifiable evidence of actual State practice and *opinio juris* that is required to establish the existence of a norm of customary international law.

UNHCR's reasoning is problematic for several reasons. First, in order to establish State practice, UNHCR should identify with specificity particular State practice. Vague references to "numerous" cases in which States acted in some way do not satisfy the burden to establish the practice of States. UNHCR should be able to identify how many and which States are acting in accordance with the articulated rule, and in addition should be able to identify by use of evidence that they are doing so out of any sense of general legal obligation. Instead, UNHCR merely identifies situations in which an unidentified number of unnamed States have, in its opinion, somehow acted "in a matter indicating" acceptance of such a principle "as a guide for their action."

Further, UNHCR fails to consider that the "manner" in which States have responded to UNHCR's expressions of concern might indicate some plausible rationale for their acts other than acceptance of a general legal principle of *non-refoulement*. UNHCR opines that States' offering of clarifications or claims that the person in question was not a refugee "can reasonably be regarded as an implicit confirmation of [those States'] acceptance" of a principle of *non-refoulement*. Principle of *Non-Refoulement* ¶ 5. Perhaps these actions *could be* interpreted in this way. But they also could reasonably be interpreted in many other ways; that they *can* be interpreted as acceptance of a principle of *non-refoulement* does not dictate that they can be interpreted *only* in that way. For example, UNHCR fails to distinguish in the Advisory Opinion between States that are not a party to the Convention or the Protocol (or some other agreement in which it has taken on a relevant *non-refoulement* obligation), and States that are a party to one of those instruments. For States that are a party to an instrument containing an explicit prohibition against *non-refoulement*, the expressions of acceptance of a *non-refoulement* obligation or justifications that suggest acceptance of a *non-refoulement* obligation may be nothing more than the State's awareness that it is bound by the treaty obligation of *non-refoulement*, rather than considering themselves obligated by some general principle of *non-refoulement*.[5]

Moreover, as for the activities of States that are not party to the Convention or Protocol, which UNHCR describes in the 1994 paper, in a situation in which a State responds to the High Commissioner's concerns by pointing out that the person in question was not a refugee, for example, the State could merely be pointing out, regardless of whether the government in question agreed that

---

[5]   The practice of many parties to the Refugee Convention and/or its Protocol applying the *non-refoulement* provisions of Article 33 would not establish the two requirements for the creation of a rule of customary international law, as the practice would exist because of an independent treaty obligation to take such action rather than because of a norm existing under customary international law, while the normative basis for such practice would depend not on the existence of a sense of general legal obligation, but on a particular international treaty obligation to take such action.

such a rule existed, that the rule that the High Commissioner claimed to exist would not apply even if it did exist. Thus, the fact that a State responds with a claim that the person in question is not a refugee does not necessarily indicate that the State not party to the Refugee Convention or its Protocol has accepted the existence of a customary rule of *non-refoulement*. Similarly, the fact that a State provides clarifications in response to the High Commissioner's concerns could simply be a way of responding to the particular matter at hand rather than taking on the much wider issue of the High Commissioner's assumption of the existence of a principle of *non-refoulement* under customary international law. Again, such clarifications might be regarded in a manner indicating acceptance of such a principle, but there are other equally "reasonabl[e]" interpretations.[6] UNHCR fails to provide any specific information—for example, the precise circumstances of these cases or the language or argumentation these States have proffered—that would allow reliance on its claims that these States have justified their behavior because they accept the existence of a rule of *non-refoulement*. *See North Sea Continental Shelf*, 1969 I.C.J. at 44 ("There are many international acts, *e.g.*, in the field of ceremonial and protocol, which are performed almost invariably, but which are motivated only by considerations of courtesy, convenience or tradition, and not by any sense of legal duty.").

Further, UNHCR erroneously relies on a statement of the International Court of Justice to support its contention that explanation by a State that does not comply with a particular customary rule can be evidence of the existence of that customary rule. The Court explains, in language quoted by UNHCR:

> In order to deduce the existence of customary rules, the Court deems it sufficient that the conduct of States should,

---

6   Non-parties to the Convention and/or Protocol might easily interpret demarches by UNHCR as arguments that they should, *as a matter of policy*, apply Article 33, even though they are not legally bound to do so. Indeed, the United States as a matter of policy strongly encourages such non-parties to apply the protective standards contained in Article 33, even while recognizing that such non-parties are not required to do so as a matter of international law.

in general, be consistent with such rules, and that instances of State conduct inconsistent with a given rule should generally have been treated as breaches of that rule, not as indications of the recognition of a new rule. If a State acts in a way *prima facie* incompatible with a recognized rule, but defends its conduct by appealing to exceptions or justifications contained within the rule itself, then whether or not the State's conduct is in fact justifiable on that basis, the significance of that attitude is to confirm rather than weaken the rule.

Military and Paramilitary Activities (Nicar. v. U.S.), 1986 I.C.J. 14 (June 27); *see also* Advisory Opinion ¶ 15. UNHCR only selectively employs the Court's reasoning, however. The Court states that as a threshold matter "the conduct of States should, in general, be consistent with such rules." The requirement that State practice is consistent with the rule in question is thus a *prerequisite* for the applicability of the Court's subsequent guidance that State actions inconsistent with the rule may be treated as confirmation of the rule. UNHCR ignores this prerequisite, and fails to establish by adducing reasonably specific evidence the threshold matter that States' conduct is "in general, . . . consistent with" a rule of *non-refoulement*. Accordingly, UNHCR cannot properly consider as dispositive its unexplained and conclusory experience that States have provided "explanations or justifications of cases of actual or intended *refoulement*." Advisory Opinion ¶ 15. Because there is no clear or definitive evidence of consistent State practice against which to evaluate these States' explanations or justifications of *refoulement*, we cannot assume that their explanations confirm acceptance of the purported rule. That States attempt to justify their deviation from the purported rule may not be construed as confirmation of such a rule, because there is no evidence showing that States that are not party to the Refugee Convention or Protocol generally act consistently with the purported rule, and thus no evidence supporting the notion that the rule exists in the first place.

Finally, UNHCR describes as "extremely rare" cases in which a government has stated that "it is not willing to react positively to [UNHCR's] representations on the simple ground that it does not recognize any obligation to act in accordance with the principle of *non-refoulement*." Principle of *Non-Refoulement* ¶ 6. Again, UNHCR provides no specifics on the identities or even the number of countries that have done so or the circumstances of such statements, nor does it identify any factors that suggest whether "extremely rare" expressions of disagreement with a principle of *non-refoulement* could be consistent with UNHCR's claim that such a principle forms part of customary international law. UNHCR's statement that "[g]overnments of States not parties to the Convention or the Protocol have frequently confirmed to UNHCR that they recognize and accept the principle of *non-refoulement*," Principle of *Non-Refoulement* ¶ 6, is similarly vague—that States have "frequently confirmed" their recognition could mean either that relatively few States confirm their recognition frequently, or that many States have confirmed recognition, or anything in between—and provides no reliable basis for concluding that widespread State practice in conformity with a principle of *non-refoulement* exists due to a sense of legal obligation.

The additional information provided in the Advisory Opinion to buttress the conclusions of the 1994 paper also fails to provide support of State practice or *opinio juris* sufficient to establish a rule of *non-refoulement* under customary international law. First, the Advisory Opinion notes "*inter alia*, the practice of non-signatory States hosting large numbers of refugees, often in mass influx situations," and states in an accompanying footnote, "This is the case, for example, in Bangladesh, India, Pakistan, and Thailand." Advisory Opinion ¶ 15 and n.32. This fact fails to support UNHCR's assertion that customary international law includes a rule of *non-refoulement*. Whether some States that are not parties to the Convention or the Protocol, including the four States that UNHCR names, host refugees, often in mass influx situations, has no bearing on whether State practice is "both extensive and uniform" as to refusal to return individuals to countries where they face persecution. Indeed, UNHCR does not indicate whether Bangladesh, India, Pakistan, and Thailand continue to host refugees in mass influx situations because of a determination that those refugees will face persecution if removed from their territory, or because of some other consideration (e.g., a general policy of concern for people in need). UNHCR's reference to these States similarly does not illuminate whether those States that do refuse to return individuals to such countries do so out of a legal obligation to some generally recognized rule of law.

Finally, UNHCR supports its conclusion that the prohibition of *refoulement* of refugees is part of customary international law with a reference to the Declaration adopted at the December 2001 Ministerial Meeting of States Parties to the Convention and/or its Protocol, in which those parties "[a]cknowledg[ed] the continuing relevance and resilience of this international regime of rights and principles, including at its core the principle of *non-refoulement*, whose applicability is embedded in customary international law." Advisory Opinion ¶ 16 (citing Declaration of States Parties to the 1951 Convention and/or its 1967 Protocol adopted at the Ministerial Meeting of States Parties of 12–13 December 2001, HCR/MMSP/2001/09, January 16, 2002 (available at *http://www. unhcr.org/home/RSDLEGAL/3d60f5557.pdf*). UNHCR's reference to the Declaration again conflates the experience and perspective of parties to the Refugee Convention and Protocol with those of non-parties. The fact that parties to the Convention and/or the Protocol would act as if they had a *non-refoulement* obligation cannot be used as evidence to support State practice sufficient to show a rule of customary international law, as such parties have undertaken an obligation under the international instrument(s) to which they are a party to comply with Article 33. Their statements, including the statement in this Declaration cited by UNHCR, accordingly reflect that treaty obligation, but they do not necessarily indicate anything more than that. The more relevant body of practice consists of the statements and actions of those countries that do not have a treaty obligation, but the Advisory Opinion cites no compelling evidence indicating that such States either follow a rule that they will not *refoule* people or that they have implemented such a rule out of a sense of general legal obligation.

UNHCR additionally argues that its contention that there is a prohibition against *refoulement* under customary international law is supported by the incorporation of a principle of *non-refoulement* in international treaties and by the "reaffirmation" of the principle by the UNHCR Executive Committee. Principle of *Non-Refoulement*

¶¶ 7–8. The international instruments that UNHCR cites and the conclusions of the Executive Committee may state that a principle of *non-refoulement* is, for example, "generally accepted by States," *see* Executive Committee of the U.N. High Comm'r for Refugees, Conclusion No. 6, ¶ 1, 28th Sess. (1977) (cited in Principle of *Non-Refoulement* ¶ 39). In one sense, this is certainly true: Some 147 countries in the world are Contracting States to the Refugee Convention, the 1967 Protocol, or both. *See* U.N. High Comm'r for Refugees, States Parties to the 1951 Convention relating to the Status of Refugees and the 1967 Protocol (available at *http://www. unhcr.org/protect/PROTECTION/3b73b0d63.pdf*). But despite the prevalence of States that commit to a *non-refoulement* obligation because of their treaty obligations, such a statement does not establish extensive and uniform State practice by those who do not have such treaty obligations, much less State practice followed out of a sense of legal obligation. The Conclusions of the Executive Committee that the Advisory Opinion cites are thus similar to the Advisory Opinion in that they provide conclusory statements without any reference to State practice or *opinio juris*. For example, Conclusion No. 3 "[r]eaffirms the fundamental importance of the observance of the principle of *non-refoulement*"; Conclusion No. 17 "[r]eaffirmed the fundamental character of the generally recognized principle of *non-refoulement*"; and Conclusion No. 71 "[c]alls upon States . . . to respect scrupulously the fundamental principle of *non-refoulement*". *See* Executive Committee of the U.N. High Comm'r for Refugees, Conclusion No. 3, 28th Sess. (1977); Conclusion No. 17, 31st Sess. (1980); Conclusion No. 71, 44th Sess. (1994). No Conclusion, however, explains the presumption that there *is* a principle of *non-refoulement* in the first place. Indeed, Conclusion No. 25 "[r]eaffirmed the importance of . . . the principle of *non-refoulement* which was progressively acquiring the character of a peremptory rule of international law," but the Executive Committee proffers no evidence to substantiate that conclusion. *See* Executive Committee of the U.N. High Comm'r for Refugees, Conclusion No. 25, 33rd Sess. (1982).

Moreover, UNHCR fails to mention that the conclusions of the Executive Committee could be read to suggest that State practice on *non-refoulement* might not be extensive and uniform.

Conclusions throughout many years have noted that States were disregarding the purported principle of *non-refoulement*. *See, e.g.*, U.N. High Comm'r for Refugees, Conclusion No. 11, 29th Sess. (1978) (noting that "the principle of *non-refoulement* . . . had, in a number of cases, . . . been disregarded"); Conclusion No. 50, 39th Sess. (1988) (noting that the Executive Committee "expressed deep concern that the fundamental prohibitions against expulsion and *refoulement* are often violated by a number of States"); Conclusion No. 74. 45th Sess. (1994) (expressing concern that "incidents of *refoulement*" had occurred). That throughout several years incidents of *refoulement* had occurred, sometimes on numerous occasions, suggests that States might not operate in conformity with a rule of *non-refoulement* on any extensive or uniform basis, as UNHCR claims, and suggests that States might not consider themselves bound by any general legal principle prohibiting *refoulement*. Of course, without knowing the facts of these cases, it is impossible to draw any conclusion, and as noted by the Advisory Opinion and discussed above, actions in contravention of a rule do not necessarily indicate non-existence of the rule. Nonetheless, as also discussed above, UNHCR fails to establish the existence of a rule in the first place, and thus there is not evidence of a general principle of *non-refoulement* to support inference that these cases of non-compliance are evidence of the purported rule.

Finally, "refer[ence] to" a "principle" of *non-refoulement* in General Assembly resolutions, *see* Principle of *Non-Refoulement* ¶ 43, or inclusion of a *non-refoulement* principle in the Declaration on Territorial Asylum, *see* Principle of *Non-Refoulement* ¶ 46, does not establish State practice—what States actually do as opposed to language upon which they may join consensus at the United Nations—or *opinio juris* sufficient to elevate such a principle to a rule of customary international law. Further, the fact that there are regional treaties that include *non-refoulement* obligations also does not establish that there is [a] norm of customary international law that would apply to non-parties.

As a matter of refugee policy, the United States appreciates UNHCR's desire to see *non-refoulement* from persecution in the refugee context applied generally by States whether or not such

States are obligated to a rule of *non-refoulement* as a matter of fulfilling their treaty obligations under the Refugee Convention or its Protocol or another instrument. As UNHCR correctly states, "[t]he principle of *non-refoulement* constitutes the cornerstone of international refugee protection." Advisory Opinion ¶ 5. For that reason, the United States strongly encourages all countries as a matter of humanitarian policy to take actions consonant with *non-refoulement* as set forth in the Refugee Convention (as well as in the Convention Against Torture), and would support UNHCR using its advocacy role to encourage States that are not bound by a treaty obligation on *non-refoulement* to accede to the 1967 Protocol or apply a rule of *non-refoulement* nonetheless.

What is advisable and highly desirable as a matter of policy, however, does not necessarily rise to the level of an international legal obligation, nor do assertion and restatement of such a desirable principle make it a rule of customary international law. UNHCR has failed to adduce the evidence necessary to establish that *non-refoulement* as set forth in Article 33 of the Refugee Convention has satisfied the requirements necessary to have become a norm of customary international law. The conclusory statements upon which UNHCR relies are based on remarkably thin and unverifiable support and conflation of the experiences of parties and non-parties to the Convention and its Protocol. They are inadequate to establish the existence of such a rule.

Non-Refoulement *Under International Human Rights Law*

These comments will not discuss at length all assertions in the Advisory Opinion relating to the scope of *non-refoulement* under human rights law. The United States notes generally that there are many statements in the Opinion on this subject that are not analytically substantiated and with which it does not agree. For example, the Advisory Opinion fails to support its assertion that customary international law prohibits *refoulement* to a risk of torture and "imposes an absolute ban on any form of forcible return to a danger of torture," much less that these prohibitions are *jus cogens* norms. Advisory Opinion ¶ 21. As discussed in detail above, State practice and *opinio juris* must be established in order to support a conclusion that a rule forms part of customary international law.

UNHCR fails, however, to adduce any evidence of extensive and virtually uniform State practice or of *opinio juris* to support its assertion. The Convention Against Torture, of course, contains a prohibition against *refoulement*, but this obligation applies only to parties to the Convention, and not to non-parties. Moreover, the principle proposed by UNHCR, prohibiting *refoulement* to a "danger of torture" or to a "risk of torture" (UNHCR alternates between these two different formulations), Advisory Opinion ¶ 21, appears broader than the protection afforded by Article 3 of the Convention Against Torture, which prohibits a State from returning an individual from its territory to a State "where there are substantial grounds for believing that he would be in danger of being subjected to torture." Convention Against Torture and Other Cruel, Inhuman or Degrading Treatment or Punishment art. 3, Dec. 10, 1984, S. Treaty Doc. No. 100-20 (1988), 1465 U.N.T.S. 85. UNHCR does not explain the origin of its proposed rule or the basis for its scope. Given that UNHCR fails to establish even that any such rule exists, it is apparent that characterizing such a purported rule a part of customary international law, and beyond that as a *jus cogens* norm, is unsupported as a matter of law.

In addition, the Advisory Opinion fails to support its assertion that there exists an even more expansive rule under customary international law that obligates States "not to send any person to a country where there is a real risk that he or she may be exposed to" "an arbitrary deprivation of life." Advisory Opinion ¶ 21. It is regrettable that the Advisory Opinion would make such a sweeping conclusion in the absence of analytical support, citing only to a statement of the Human Rights Committee regarding reservations practice regarding a particular treaty as evidence for its conclusion regarding the customary international law status of this purported rule. *See* Advisory Opinion ¶ 21 and n.49. Moreover, the United States disagrees with the contention of the Advisory Opinion that the International Covenant on Civil and Political Rights (ICCPR) obligates States "not to extradite, deport, expel or otherwise remove a person from their territory, where there are substantial grounds for believing that there is a real risk of irreparable harm, such as that contemplated by Articles 6 [right to life] and 7 [right to be free from torture or other cruel, inhuman or degrading treatment or punishment] of the Covenant," a position put forward by the Human Rights Committee in General Comment 31. Advisory Opinion ¶ 19. To explain the reasons why it does not agree with this reading of Articles 6 and 7 of the Covenant without further extending these Observations, the United States is pleased to provide its recently concluded Observations of the United States on General Comment 31 of the Human Rights Committee for UNHCR's information.[7]

In this respect, even assuming for the sake of argument that one were to agree with the Human Rights Committee's atextual interpretation of Article 7 of the ICCPR, such an interpretation would not establish that there existed a consistent pattern of State practice or *opinio juris* necessary to establish that such a principal had become a norm of customary international law.

The Advisory Opinion's statement that the prohibition of *refoulement* to a risk of cruel, inhuman or degrading treatment or punishment "is in the process of becoming customary international law, at the very least at regional level" is conclusory and unsubstantiated. Advisory Opinion ¶ 21. Putting aside the fact that debate exists regarding the very existence of regional customary international law,[8] here, as before, the Opinion fails to distinguish between obligations or other commitments that States may assume as *parties* to particular treaties or other instruments—in this case obligations and commitments under the European Convention on

---

[7] As the United States noted during its July 2006 hearing before the Human Rights Committee, the States Parties to the ICCPR have not given the Committee the authority to issue legally binding or authoritative interpretations of that treaty. Moreover, the Committee's interpretation of the Covenant is untenable. Unlike Article 3 of the Convention Against Torture, the Covenant does not impose a *non-refoulement* obligation upon States Parties, and neither Article 6 nor Article 7 of the ICCPR contains any reference to the concept of *non-refoulement*.

[8] *See, e.g.,* S. Sinha Prakash, *Identifying a Principle of International Law Today*, 11 Can. Y.B. Int'l L. 106, 112–116 (1973). Conceding that it is possible to identify different usages and treaty patterns among States of different regions, Prakash argues that because international law operates in the context of one society of States rather than in groupings by region, the international legal system "does not seem to contemplate the creation of its customary rules with reference to any but one society of states."

Human Rights and the European Charter of Fundamental Rights—
and the existence of a consistent pattern of states and *opinio juris*
necessary to establish that a norm has become customary international law *for non-parties* to such instruments. The Advisory
Opinion does not examine, much less establish, "constant and uniform usage, accepted as law," with regard to the alleged rule of
non-refoulement, the requirement the ICJ has set out to establish
regional or local custom.[9] *Asylum Case (Colombia v. Peru)*, 1950
I.C.J. Rep. 266, 277. Instead, the Advisory Opinion cites decisions
of the European Court of Human Rights, as well as the European
Charter of Fundamental Rights and a Council of Europe decision
on the European arrest warrant and surrender procedures between
Member States, none of which provide evidence of "constant and
uniform usage, accepted as law."

Finally, the United States at a broader level questions why
UNHCR has chosen to delve into this area of international human
rights law and to deal with matters that lie outside of its competence and expertise. UNHCR is mandated "to lead and coordinate

---

[9]   Indeed, most scholars hold the view that pursuant to the *Asylum
Case*, the standard of proof required to establish the existence of a regional
custom is *higher* than that required to establish the existence of a general
custom. Whereas general customary law only requires proof of general acceptance among States, a State alleging a "special" customary rule must prove
that "the party against which the rule is invoked has expressly or implicitly
consented to it or recognized it." *See, e.g.*, Malcolm N. Shaw, International
Law 87 (5th ed. 2003). One scholar explains, "While in the case of a general
customary rule the process of consensus is at work so that a majority or a
substantial minority of interested states can be sufficient to create a new custom, a local custom needs the positive acceptance of both or all parties to the
rule." Nancy Kontou, The Termination and Revision of Treaties in Light of
the New Customary International Law 6 (Oxford University Press 1994); *see
also* I. C. MacGibbon, *Customary International Law and Acquiescence*, 33
Brit. Y.B. Int'l L. 115, 117 ("In the case of a general customary right, that is
one which is exercised by the generality of States, the presumption of general
consent or acquiescence is more strongly raised by virtue of the fact of general participation in the practice, than would be the case with regard to an
exceptional customary right exercised by a single State or by a small group of
States."); Shaw, *supra*, at 87 ("Such local customs therefore depend upon a
particular activity by one state being accepted by the other state (or states) as
an expression of a legal obligation or right.").

international action for the worldwide protection of refugees and the resolution of refugee problems." UNHCR, Mission Statement (available at *http://www.unhcr.org/publ/PUBL/4565a5742.pdf*).[10] The United States appreciates and respects the important work of UNHCR on issues within its mandate. The interpretation and breadth of international human rights law, however, fall outside of the work that UNHCR is mandated to do. While human rights violations may result in the *creation* of refugees, they do not integrally relate to protection of refugees. It is regrettable that UNHCR nevertheless has chosen to opine on these matters in this Advisory Opinion and has done so in such an unenlightening and conclusory fashion. That these matters are significant both in terms of their legal interpretation and their practical application makes UNHCR's choice to step beyond the bounds of its expertise even more problematic. The United States urges UNHCR to focus its resources and expertise in the future on matters within its competence and mandate.

As a final observation, returning to the central topic of the UNHCR Advisory Opinion—*non-refoulement* in Article 33 of the Refugee Convention—the United States notes that its analysis in this paper has focused on the legal propositions and assertions in the Opinion. While it is essential to clarify these important legal issues, the United States does not wish to leave the impression that it is necessarily opposed to the policy desire of UNHCR to have the protections in Article 33 applied as widely and by as many countries as possible. Indeed, as noted above, the United States as a matter of policy takes into account such protective principles in its actions outside of its territory and strongly encourages non-parties to the Refugee Convention or Protocol to protect refugees within

---

[10] Since its creation, UNHCR has been asked to expand its activities to include work on behalf of groups other than refugees, including displaced persons, *see* Economic and Social Council (ECOSOC) Resolution 1705, 53rd Sess. (27 July 1972) (calling on UNHCR to extend assistance both to refugees returning then to southern Sudan and "persons displaced within the country"); *see also* ECOSOC Resolution 1655, 52nd Sess. (1 June 1972); G.A. Res. 2958, ¶ 3, U.N. GAOR, 27th Sess., (Dec. 12, 1973), and stateless persons, *see* G.A. Res. 3274, U.N. GAOR, 29th Sess. (Dec. 19, 1974).

their territory in a manner consistent with Article 33. In advancing these policies, the United States believes it is important for the protection and advancement of the rule of law always to be clear in distinguishing those actions that should be done because they are advisable and appropriate from those actions that must be done because they are obligations under international law. In the view of the United States, the blurring of such lines and questionable assertions regarding the content of rules of international law do not in the long run advance our shared interest in the protection and enforcement of international law.

2. Material Support Exemption

a. Legislative amendment

On December 27, 2007, President Bush signed into law the Consolidated Appropriations Act, 2008, Pub. L. No. 110-161. Section 691 of Division J of the act, "Relief for Iraqi, Montagnards, Hmong and Other Refugees Who Do Not Pose a Threat to the United States," amended the Immigration and Nationality Act ("INA") to expand the current authority of the Secretaries of State and Homeland Security to exempt an alien or a group from certain terrorism-related provisions in the INA. As amended, the statute now provides for exemption of aliens from most terrorism-related bars to admission and of groups that otherwise meet the definition from treatment as undesignated terrorist organizations, subject to certain limited exceptions.

Section 691(b) provides that certain ethnic Burmese organizations,* the Tibetan Mustangs, the Cuban Alzados Resistance Fighters, and "appropriate groups affiliated with

---

*   Editor's note: The ethnic Burmese organizations named in the act are the Karen National Union/Karen Liberation Army (KNU/KNLA), the Chin National Front/Chin National Army (CNF/CNA), the Chin National League for Democracy (CNLD), the Kayan New Land Party (KNLP), the Arakan Liberation Party (ALP), and the Karenni National Progressive Party.

the Hmong and the Montagnards shall not be considered to be a terrorist organization on the basis of any act or event occurring before the date of enactment of this section."

Section 691(d) designates the Taliban as a terrorist organization for purposes of § 212(a)(3)(B) of the INA.

b. Discretionary exemptions granted

In January 2007, before enactment of the amendments discussed in 2.a. *supra*, Secretary of State Condoleezza Rice exercised her discretionary authority, following consultations with the Department of Homeland Security and the Attorney General, to determine that, for certain cases, § 212(a)(3)(B)(iv)(VI) of the Immigration and Nationality Act ("INA") "shall not apply with respect to material support" provided by applicants for refugee admission to certain Burmese, Cuban, and Tibetan organizations. These were some of the same groups that were subsequently exempted from treatment as terrorist organizations in Pub. L. No. 110-161. Unlike previous exemptions for certain refugee applicants who provided material support to the KNU/KNLA and CNF/CNA, the January 2007 exemptions were not limited to individuals belonging to specific ethnic groups and/or interviewed in specific locations. *See Digest 2006* at 52–55.

Secretary of Homeland Security Michael Chertoff exercised his same discretionary authority and issued exemptions applicable to all aliens seeking immigration benefits that paralleled those issued by the Secretary of State described above. In October 2007 Secretary Chertoff and Secretary Rice jointly exercised their authority to grant exemptions for certain cases involving material support provided to individuals and groups associated with the Hmong and to the Front Unifié de Lutte des Races Opprimées ("FULRO"). The January and October exemptions are available at *www.state.gov/s/l/c8183.htm.*

In addition, on February 26, 2007, Secretary Chertoff determined that support provided under duress to an undesignated terrorist organization would not be a bar to admissibility, if warranted by the totality of the circumstances. 72 Fed. Reg. 9958 (Mar. 6, 2007). A subsequent exercise by Secretary Chertoff on April 27, 2007, determined that support provided under duress to a designated terrorist organization would also not be a bar to admissibility, if warranted by the totality of the circumstances. 72 Fed. Reg. 26,138 (May 8, 2007). The Federal Register notices of the two determinations explained:

> When determining whether the material support was pro-vided under duress, the following factors, among others, may be considered: whether the applicant reasonably could have avoided, or took steps to avoid, providing material support, the severity and type of harm inflicted or threatened, to whom the harm was directed, and, in cases of threats alone, the perceived imminence of the harm threatened and the perceived likelihood that the harm would be inflicted.
>
> When considering the totality of the circumstances, factors to be considered, in addition to the duress-related factors stated above, may include, among others, the amount, type and frequency of material support provided, the nature of the activities committed by the terrorist organization, the alien's awareness of those activities, the length of time since material support was provided, the alien's conduct since that time, and any other relevant factor.

Cross References

Executive branch authority over foreign state recognition and passports, **Chapter 9.B.**
Efforts to help refugees in conflict situations, **Chapter 18.A.3.**

CHAPTER 2

Consular and Judicial Assistance and Related Issues

A. CONSULAR NOTIFICATION, ACCESS, AND ASSISTANCE

1. Consular Notification

a. *Implementation of ICJ decision:* Medellin

José Ernesto Medellin was convicted and sentenced to death for capital murder in Texas for a crime committed in 1993. He was one of 51 Mexican nationals covered by the 2004 International Court of Justice judgment requiring review and reconsideration of their U.S. state court convictions and death penalty sentences as a remedy for the failure of the competent U.S. authorities to comply with Article 36 of the Vienna Convention on Consular Relations ("VCCR"). *Avena & Other Mexican Nationals (Mexico v. U.S.)*, 2004 I.C.J. 12338 (Mar. 31) ("*Avena*"); *see Digest 2004* at 37–43 and *Digest 2003* at 43–103. On February 28, 2005, President George W. Bush issued a determination that "the United States will discharge its international obligations" under the *Avena* decision "by having State courts give effect to the decision in accordance with general principles of comity" in cases involving any of the Mexican nationals covered by *Avena*.

Following his conviction and sentence in Texas state court in 1994, Medellin unsuccessfully sought habeas relief in Texas state and U.S. federal courts. The courts found among other things that his claim under VCCR Article 36, raised for the first time in his 2001 state court habeas petition, was procedurally

73

defaulted because he had failed to raise it at trial.* In March 2005 Medellin filed a subsequent habeas action in the Court of Criminal Appeals of Texas claiming that the President's memorandum and the *Avena* judgment required the Texas court to grant review and reconsideration of his consular notification claim. At the invitation of the court, the United States filed a brief as *amicus curiae* providing its views that the President's determination required the court to "provide review and reconsideration of Medellin's Vienna Convention claim without regard to the doctrine of procedural default or other state law obstacles" and that neither the Vienna Convention nor *Avena* "gives a foreign national a private, judicially enforceable right to attack his conviction or sentence." On November 15, 2006, the Texas court denied Medellin's habeas writ. *Ex parte Medellin*, 223 S.W. 3d 315 (Tex. Crim. App. 2006). The Texas state court found, among other things, that *Avena* was not binding on it and that the President had exceeded his constitutional authority in issuing the memorandum. *See Digest 2006* at 86–88, *Digest 2005* at 29–59.

On April 30, 2007, the Supreme Court granted a writ of certiorari to the Court of Criminal Appeals of Texas. The United States filed a brief as *amicus curiae* in support of the petition for certiorari in March 2007 (available at *www.usdoj. gov/osg/briefs/2006/2pet/5ami/2006-0984.pet.ami.html*) and at the merits stage in June 2007 (available at *www.usdoj. gov/osg/briefs/2006/3mer/1ami/2006-0984.mer.ami.html*). The Supreme Court heard arguments in the case on October 10, 2007. The case was pending at the end of the year.**

---

* Editor's note: In 2004 the Supreme Court granted a writ of certiorari to the U.S. Court of Appeals for the Fifth Circuit in Medellin's habeas case (543 U.S. 1032 (2004)) but dismissed the writ as improvidently granted following the President's 2005 determination. *Medellin v. Dretke*, 544 U.S. 660 (2005). *See Digest 2004* at 44–47 and *Digest 2005* at 32–33.

** Editor's note: On March 25, 2008, the Supreme Court issued an opinion affirming the Texas Court of Criminal Appeals decision. *Medellin v. Texas*, 128 S. Ct. 1346 (2008). Relevant aspects of the opinion will be discussed in *Digest 2008*.

In its June 2007 brief as *amicus curiae*, the United States argued that the Texas Court of Criminal Appeals decision should be reversed because

> [the Texas court] erred by failing to implement the President's determination to have state courts give effect to *Avena*. While the ICJ's decision in *Avena* is not privately enforceable in its own right, the President's determination that the Nation will comply with *Avena* falls within his authorized power to effectuate our treaty obligations. . . . The President disagrees with the legal interpretations underlying the ICJ's decision, and was faced with a decision whether to comply with the United States' treaty obligations. But the United States has compelling interests in ensuring reciprocal observance of the Vienna Convention by treaty partners who detain U.S. citizens, promoting foreign relations, and reaffirming the United States' commitment to the international rule of law. These competing concerns justified the President in determining to discharge the Nation's obligations under *Avena*, while withdrawing from the Optional Protocol to prevent the ICJ from imposing similar obligations on the United States in the future.

Excerpts follow from the U.S. argument that the ICJ decision is not privately enforceable (footnote and citations to the Petition have been deleted). *See also* web log posting by Department of State Legal Adviser John B. Bellinger, III, "International Obligations and U.S. Law," October 16, 2007, available at *www.state.gov/s/l/rls/93632.htm.*

---

*   *   *   *

II. THE *AVENA* DECISION IS NOT PRIVATELY ENFORCEABLE ABSENT THE PRESIDENT'S DETERMINATION

Petitioner contends that the *Avena* decision is privately enforceable of its own force because the Optional Protocol and the U.N.

Charter obligate the United States to comply with the decision. That contention lacks merit.

. . . [T]he Optional Protocol and the U.N. Charter give the President the authority to decide whether the United States will comply with an ICJ decision, and if so, what measures should be taken to comply. Allowing private enforcement, without the President's authorization, would undermine the President's ability to make those determinations and inappropriately transfer them to the courts. *Cf. Pasquantino v. United States*, 544 U.S. 349, 369 (2005). In the context of this case, it would eliminate non-compliance— which is a possibility contemplated by the U.N. Charter—as an option. Thus, far from being supported by the Optional Protocol and the U.N. Charter, private enforcement of an ICJ decision, without Presidential authorization, conflicts with those treaties.

Moreover, while the Optional Protocol and the U.N. Charter together create an international obligation to comply with an ICJ decision, the text of those treaties forecloses the argument that an ICJ decision is privately enforceable on its own force. *Cf. Sanchez-Llamas*, 126 S. Ct. at 2679. The Optional Protocol provides that "[d]isputes arising out of the interpretation or application of the [Vienna Convention] shall lie within the compulsory jurisdiction of the International Court of Justice and may accordingly be brought before the Court by an application made by any party to the dispute being a Party to the present Protocol." 21 U.S.T. at 326, 596 U.N.T.S. at 488. That provision gives a nation a right to invoke the jurisdiction of the ICJ; it does not give a private individual a right to enforce an ICJ decision in a United States court.

Article 94 of the U.N. Charter provides that "[e]ach member of the United Nations undertakes to comply with the decision of the International Court of Justice in any case to which it is a party." 59 Stat. 1051 (emphasis added). Those words "do not by their terms confer rights on individual citizens; they call upon governments to take certain action." *Committee of United States Citizens Living in Nicar. v. Reagan*, 859 F.2d 929, 938 (D.C. Cir. 1988) (citation and quotation marks omitted).

The text of the ICJ statute, which is incorporated into the U.N. Charter, speaks to the issue even more directly. It makes clear that an ICJ decision is binding only "between the parties" to the case, Art. 59, 59 Stat. 1062, and that only nations "can be parties." Art. 34, 59 Stat. 1059. Accordingly, in the absence of the President's determination, a private party cannot enforce an ICJ decision in court.

Nor does the ICJ decision purport to be privately enforceable of its own force. The ICJ determined that the United States' obligation was "to provide, by means of its own choosing, review and reconsideration of the convictions and sentences of the [affected Mexican nationals.]" Permitting private judicial enforcement in the absence of action from the President or the Congress would deprive the political branches of the very choice of means that the ICJ intended for them to have. Thus, while petitioner is entitled to review and reconsideration by virtue of the President's determination, such review and reconsideration would not be available to petitioner in the absence of the President's determination.

b. Compliance efforts relating to consular notification requirements

On May 11, 2007, by order of the U.S. Court of Appeals for the Second Circuit, the United States filed a letter brief addressing several issues related to efforts undertaken by the Department of State to ensure compliance with the VCCR and the source of the federal government's authority to require state and local law enforcement officials to provide consular notification and access to detained foreign nationals. *Mora v. State of New York*, No. 06-0341opr (2d Cir.); *see also* c.(3) below. Section B of the letter brief provided a summary description of "the extensive steps taken by the State Department to ensure that federal, state, and local law enforcement officials nationwide provide consular notification and access to detained foreign nationals." The full text of the letter brief is available at *www.state.gov/s/l/c8183.htm*. Excerpts addressing the federal government's authority in treaty matters to require action by state and local law enforcement officials are provided in Chapter 4.B.1.

c. Private right of action for money damages against law enforcement officials

(1) Jogi v. Voges

On March 12, 2007, the U.S. Court of Appeals for the Seventh Circuit, on rehearing, withdrew and replaced a 2005 opinion in which it had found that an Indian citizen could enforce the VCCR in U.S. Courts by bringing damages claims against law enforcement officials and that the Alien Tort Statute ("ATS") conferred jurisdiction on a federal court to entertain an alien's claim for alleged violations of Article 36 of the VCCR. *Jogi v. Voges*, 480 F.3d 822 (7th Cir. 2007). *See Digest 2005* at 60–64.

In its 2007 decision, the Seventh Circuit stated:

> In the interest of avoiding a decision on grounds broader than are necessary to resolve the case, especially in an area that touches so directly on the foreign relations of the United States, the panel has re-examined its earlier opinion and has decided to withdraw that opinion and substitute the following one. Briefly put, we are persuaded that it is best not to rest subject matter jurisdiction on the ATS, since it is unclear whether the treaty violation Jogi has alleged amounts to a "tort." . . . Furthermore, rather than wade into the treacherous waters of implied remedies, we have concluded that Jogi's action rests on a more secure footing as one under 42 U.S.C. § 1983.* At bottom, he is complaining about police action, under color of state law, that violates a right secured to him by a federal law (here, a treaty). We can safely leave for another day the question whether the Vienna Convention would directly support a private remedy.

---

*   Editor's note: Section 1983 provides, in relevant part:

Every person who, under color of any statute, ordinance, regulation, custom or usage, of any State or Territory or the District of Columbia, subjects . . . any . . . person . . . to the deprivation of any rights, privileges, or immunities secured by the Constitution and laws, shall be liable to the party injured in an action at law. . . .

The court noted that it was the first court "to be confronted directly with the question whether the Convention creates a private right," and that the "distinction between a private right, on the one hand, and various remedial measures that affect criminal prosecutions, on the other, is an important one."** It concluded that "Article 36 of the Vienna Convention by its terms grants private rights to an identifiable class of persons—aliens from countries that are parties to the Convention who are in the United States—and that its text is phrased in terms of the person benefited."

Quoting the Supreme Court in *Gonzaga University v. Doe*, 536 U.S. 273 (2002), "[o]nce a plaintiff demonstrates that a statute confers an individual right, the right is presumptively enforceable by § 1983," the court explained:

> Nothing in either the Vienna Convention or any other source of law has been presented to us that would rebut this presumption, apart from the argument we have rejected that treaties do not enjoy the same status as statutes. . . .

(2) Cornejo v. San Diego

On June 25, 2007, the U.S. Court of Appeals for the Ninth Circuit affirmed a lower court's dismissal of a § 1983 claim based on alleged violations of Article 36. *Cornejo v. San Diego*, 504 F.3d 853 (9th Cir. 2007). In its analysis the court noted the contrary holding in *Jogi*, (1) *supra*. The majority opinion summarized the case and its holding as excerpted below (footnote omitted). *See Digest 2006* at 86.

** Editor's note: In 2006 the Supreme Court held that, even assuming (without deciding) that the Vienna Convention on Consular Relations creates judicially enforceable rights, "suppression [of a defendant's statements to police] is not an appropriate remedy for a violation of Article 36, and . . . a State may apply its regular rules of procedural default to Article 36 claims." *Sanchez-Llamas v. Oregon*, 548 U.S. 331 (2006). *See Digest 2006* at 63–85.

This appeal requires us to resolve an issue left open in our en banc decision in *United States v. Lombera-Camorlinga*, 206 F.3d 882, 884 (9th Cir. 2000): whether Article 36 of the Vienna Convention on Consular Relations creates judicially enforceable rights that may be vindicated in an action brought under 42 U.S.C. § 1983.

Ezequiel Nunez Cornejo's complaint seeks damages and injunctive relief against the County of San Diego, several deputy sheriffs, and various cities within the county on behalf of a class of foreign nationals who were arrested and detained without being advised of their right to have a consular officer notified as required by Article 36. The district court dismissed the action, concluding that Cornejo could not bring a § 1983 claim for violation of the Convention because it creates no private rights of action or corresponding remedies.

We agree with the district court that Article 36 does not create judicially enforceable rights. Article 36 confers legal rights and obligations on *States* in order to facilitate and promote consular functions. Consular functions include protecting the interests of detained nationals, and for that purpose detainees have the right (if they want) for the consular post to be notified of their situation. In this sense, detained foreign nationals benefit from Article 36's provisions. But the right to protect nationals belongs to *States* party to the Convention; no private right is unambiguously conferred on individual detainees such that they may pursue it through § 1983. Accordingly, we affirm.

*   *   *   *

(3) Other litigation

> On March 2 and September 14, 2007, the United States filed briefs in the Second and Eleventh Circuits respectively as *amicus curiae* in support of affirmance of lower court decisions dismissing claims for damages against law enforcement officials for failure to state a cause of action. *Mora v. New York*, No. 06-03410pr (2d Cir.) and *Gandara v. Bennett*, No. 06-16088 (11th Cir.). The briefs set forth the U.S. view in both cases that (1) Article 36 of the Vienna Convention does not

create judicially enforceable individual rights and (2) Article 36 is not enforceable through a private civil action for money damages. The texts of the briefs are available at *www.state. gov/s/l/c8183.htm*. Both cases were pending at the end of 2007.

2. Social Security Totalization Agreements

The United States enters into bilateral agreements providing benefits for workers who divide their careers between the United States and a foreign country. These agreements eliminate dual social security coverage and contributions, extend protections to prevent gaps in social security protection, and eliminate dual taxation and coverage. In 2007 the United States completed such agreements with Denmark (signed June 13, 2007) and with the Czech Republic (signed September 7, 2007). The text of the agreement with Denmark as a sample is available at *www.state.gov/s///l/c8183.htm*.

3. Consular Assistance: Deaths and Estates

On February 28, 2007, the Department of State published a final rule updating and amending regulations on deaths and estates in 22 C.F.R. pt. 72. 72 Fed. Reg. 8887 (Feb. 28, 2007). The rule, effective March 30, 2007, reflects changes in State Department statutory authority set forth in §§ 234 and 235 of Pub. L. No. 106-113 (2001) and consular practice. As explained in the Supplementary Information section of the Federal Register publication, among other things, the new regulations implement new authorities related to report of presumptive death:

> Section 234 of the Act . . . explicitly authorizes . . . a consular officer to issue a report of presumptive death in the absence of a finding of death by the appropriate local authorities. This latter provision is intended to allow the consular officer to issue a report of presumptive death in

exceptional circumstances where the evidence that the individual has died (e.g., he or she was listed as a passenger on an aircraft that crashed leaving no survivors) is persuasive, but local authorities have not issued and are not likely to issue a finding of death (because e.g., issuance of a local death certificate requires forensic evidence that is not available or there is no local authority that clearly has jurisdiction.)

B. CHILDREN

1. Adoption

a. *Deposit of instrument of ratification*

On December 12, 2007, the United States deposited its instrument of ratification of the 1993 Hague Convention on Protection of Children and Co-operation in Respect of Intercountry Adoption ("Convention" or "Hague Convention"). The date of entry into force for the United States is thus April 1, 2008. For further background, *see Digest 2000* at 141–50 and subsequent annual volumes. A media note issued on December 12 is excerpted below and available at *www.state.gov/r/pa/prs/ ps/2007/dec/97148.htm.*

---

*   *   *   *

The Convention establishes international norms and procedures for processing intercountry adoption cases involving other Hague Convention members. It mandates safeguards to protect the interests of children, birth parents, and adoptive parents. It also provides that member nations recognize adoptions that take place within other Hague Convention countries.

The ratification completed a process begun in 1994, when the United States signed the Convention after participating actively in its negotiation and adoption. In 2000, the Senate consented to ratification and Congress passed implementing legislation, the Intercountry Adoption Act (IAA). The Department of State, with the Department of Homeland Security, promulgated the regulations which govern the immigration and visa processes in a Hague case, developed the standards and procedures for the accreditation of adoption service providers, and took other actions deemed necessary to implement the Convention.

Beginning April 1, 2008, The Hague Convention will govern intercountry adoptions between the United States and other Convention countries. The major changes to the way intercountry adoptions are processed under the Hague Convention are:

- The Department of State, designated as the "Central Authority" for the United States under the Hague Convention and the IAA, is responsible for ensuring that the Hague Convention and IAA requirements are followed.
- Accrediting entities designated by the Department of State must accredit any U.S. adoption service providers that will handle Convention adoption cases.
- The Department of State will maintain a centralized registry to track all adoption cases (both incoming and outgoing cases, in Hague Convention cases and in non-Convention cases), and to receive complaints and comments about accredited adoption service providers involved in Hague Convention cases.
- Outgoing intercountry adoption cases from the United States to other Hague Convention countries, such as Canada or Mexico, must also comply with the Convention and the IAA.

b. Promulgation of implementing regulations

In preparation for the deposit of the U.S. instrument of ratification, during 2007 the Department of State and the Department of Homeland Security adopted additional regulations to implement the Convention and the Intercountry Adoption Act of 2000 ("IAA"), Pub. L. No.106-279, 114 Stat. 825.

On March 6, 2007, the Department of State published a final rule, effective April 5, 2007, to establish a case registry to track intercountry adoptions. 72 Fed. Reg. 9852 (Mar. 6, 2007). The Supplementary Information section of the Federal Register publication explained the final rule as follows:

> . . . The IAA requires the Department and DHS to establish a Case Registry to track all intercountry adoption cases: Convention and non-Convention; emigrating and immigrating* cases. The Department is, with the joint review and approval of DHS, promulgating this final rule to require adoption service providers that provide adoption services in intercountry adoption cases involving a child emigrating from the United States (including governmental authorities who provide such adoption services) to report certain information to the Department for incorporation into the Case Registry.

On October 4, 2007, the Department of Homeland Security published an interim rule governing classification of aliens as children of United States citizens based on intercountry adoptions under the Hague Convention, with a request for public comment. 72 Fed. Reg. 56,832 (Oct. 4, 2007). The interim rule was effective November 5, 2007, pending adoption of the final rule. The Summary section of the Federal Register publication explained:

> . . . First, to facilitate the ratification of the [Adoption] Convention . . . , the rule establishes new administrative procedures for the immigration of children who are habitually resident in Convention countries and who are adopted by U.S. citizens. Second, the rule makes other amendments to DHS regulations relating to the immigration of adopted children to reflect the changes to

---

* Editor's note: Information for the case registry for immigrating cases will be collected through the normal visa process.

those provisions necessary to comply with the Convention. The Senate consented to ratification of the Convention in 2000 conditioned on the adoption of the necessary implementing regulations. Accordingly, this rule is necessary to establish the regulations necessary for the United States to ratify the Convention.

Further brief excerpts from the Background section of the Federal Register explaining the interim rule are set forth below.

---

*   *   *   *

The Immigration and Nationality Act ("the Act"), 8 U.S.C. 1101, et seq., provides three distinct provisions under which an adopted child may be considered, for immigration purposes, to be the child of his or her adoptive parents. Section 101(b)(1)(E) of the Act, 8 U.S.C. 1101(b)(1)(E), relates to adoptions in general, and provides that an adopted child is considered the adoptive parent's child if certain custody and residence requirements are met. Section 101(b)(1)(F) of the Act, 8 U.S.C. 1101(b)(1)(F), facilitates the immigration of aliens who qualify as "orphans", if they are adopted, or are coming to the United States to be adopted, by U.S. citizens. Section 101(b)(1)(G) of the Act, 8 U.S.C. 1101(b)(1)(G), added by section 302 of the Intercountry Adoption Act, Public Law 106-279, governs the immigration of children who are adopted, or are coming to the United States to be adopted, by U.S. citizens under the Convention. . . .

*   *   *   *

C. Convention Adoptions

*   *   *   *

. . . The Hague Conference on Private International Law makes available at http://www.hcch.net the current list of countries that have become Parties to the Convention. According to this Web site, 74 States have become Parties to the Convention. . . .

*   *   *   *

If the Convention is in force between two countries, then any adoption of a child habitually resident in one country by a person habitually resident in the other country must comply with the requirements of the Convention. The objectives of the Convention are:

- To establish safeguards to ensure that intercountry adoptions take place in the best interests of the child and with respect for the child's fundamental rights as recognized in international law;
- To establish a system of cooperation among contracting States to ensure that those safeguards are respected and thereby prevent the abduction, sale of, or traffic in children; and
- To secure the recognition in contracting states of adoptions made in accordance with the Convention.

The Convention also requires all parties to act expeditiously in the processing of intercountry adoptions.

To accomplish its goals, the Convention makes a number of significant modifications to current intercountry adoption practice, including three particularly important changes. First, the Convention mandates close coordination between the governments of contracting countries through a Central Authority in each Convention country. In its role as a coordinating body, the Central Authority is responsible for sharing information about the laws of its own and other Convention countries and for monitoring individual cases. Second, the Convention requires that each country involved make certain determinations before an adoption may proceed. The sending country must determine in advance: That the child is eligible to be adopted; that it is in the child's best interests to be adopted internationally; that the birth parents or other individuals, institutions or authorities who must, under the law of the country of origin, consent to the adoption have freely consented to the adoption in writing; and that the consent of the child, if required, has been obtained. The sending country must also prepare a background study on the child that includes the medical history of the child as well as other background information.

Third, the receiving country must determine in advance: that the prospective adoptive parent(s) are eligible and suited to adopt; that they have received counseling and training, as necessary; and that the child will be eligible to enter and reside permanently in the receiving country. The receiving country must also prepare a home study on the prospective adoptive parent(s). These advance determinations and studies are designed to ensure that the child is protected and that there are no obstacles to completing the adoption.

*   *   *   *

. . . Section 101(b)(1)(G) of the [IAA], which will take effect when the Convention enters into force for the United States, provides for the classification of a Convention adoptee as the child of the U.S. citizen adoptive parent(s). By its terms, the Convention applies to any adoption by a person "habitually resident" in the United States of a child "habitually resident" in another Convention country, if the child "has been, is being or is to be moved" to the United States either after the adoption or for purposes of the adoption. Convention, article 2(1). Under section 101(b)(1)(G) of the Act, however, only a married U.S. citizen whose spouse also adopts the child, or an unmarried U.S. citizen who is at least 25 years old, may file an immigrant visa petition on behalf of a Convention adoptee. For this reason, it will not be possible for anyone who is habitually resident in the United States, but who is not a United States citizen, to bring a child habitually resident in another Convention country to the United States on the basis of a Convention adoption.

Classification as a child under section 101(b)(1)(G) of the Act is somewhat similar to classification as an orphan under section 101(b)(1)(F) of the Act. First, the child's adoption must be sought either by a United States citizen and the United States citizen's spouse, jointly, or by an unmarried United States citizen who is at least 25 years old. The visa petition must be filed before the child's sixteenth birthday. As with orphan cases, the two year legal custody and joint residence requirements of section 101(b)(1)(E) of the Act will not apply to Convention cases. Finally, as with orphans, a Convention adoptee may be adopted abroad, but may also be brought to the United States for the purpose of adoption.

There are, however, some notable differences. First, as a matter of jurisdiction, section 204(d)(2) of the Act, as amended by section 302(b) of the IAA, makes clear that section 101(b)(1)(G) of the Act relates only to adoptions in which the adopting parent is habitually resident in the United States, and the child is habitually resident in another country that is a Party to the Convention. Second, unlike sections 101(b)(1)(E) and (F) of the Act, section 101(b)(1)(G) applies only if the visa petition is filed before a child's sixteenth birthday, with no provision to allow the immigration of an older sibling adopted by the same parent(s). Third, the child does not have to be an "orphan", as defined in 101(b)(1)(F) of the Act. The primary criteria for classification under section 101(b)(1)(G) of the Act are:

- The child's birth parents (or parent, in the case of a child who has one sole or surviving parent because of the death or disappearance of, or the child's abandonment or desertion by, the other parent), or other persons or institutions that retain legal custody of the child, must have freely given their written irrevocable consent to the termination of their legal relationship with the child, and to the child's emigration and adoption; and
- In the case of a child placed for adoption by his or her two living birth parents, the birth parents must be incapable of providing proper care for the child.

The Department notes that section 101(b)(1)(G) of the Act, like sections 101(b)(1)(E) and (F), use the term "natural parents" to describe the individuals to whom an adopted child was born. Adoption professionals generally recommend using the term "birth parents", as some birth and adoptive parents consider "natural parent" offensive or insensitive. . . . Since "birth parent" and "natural parent" are synonymous, this rule uses the term "birth parent".

*   *   *   *

Effective October 30, 2007, the Department of State issued a final rule addressing consular officer processing of immigration petitions, visas, and Convention certificates in cases of children immigrating to the United States in connection with an adoption covered by the Convention. 72 Fed. Reg. 61,301 (Oct. 30, 2007). Excerpts follow from the Supplementary Information provided in the Federal Register.

---

*   *   *   *

. . . To implement the Convention, the IAA makes two significant changes to the Immigration and Nationality Act (INA): (1) It creates a new definition of "child" applicable in Convention adoption cases, found at INA 101(b)(1)(G), that roughly parallels the current definition of "child" in INA 101(b)(1)(F) with respect to an orphan, but that applies only to children being adopted from Convention countries. (2) It incorporates Hague procedures into the immigration process for children covered by INA 101(b)(1)(G), most directly by precluding approval of an immigration petition under this classification until the Department has certified that the child was adopted (or legal custody was granted for purposes of emigration and adoption) in accordance with the Convention and the IAA. Separately, section 301 of the IAA requires all Federal, State, and local domestic entities to recognize adoptions or grants of legal custody that have been so certified by the Department.

*   *   *   *

Summary of the Final Regulation

. . . Although much of the petition and visa processes will be similar to the current orphan case procedures, there are important changes. Perhaps most significantly, United States authorities will perform the bulk of petition and visa adjudication work much earlier than under current practice. This early review will enable United States authorities to make the determination required by Article 5 of the Convention that the child will be eligible to enter and reside permanently in the receiving state prior to the adoption or grant of legal custody. The regulation also provides that, once the country of origin has provided appropriate notification that the adoption or grant of legal custody has occurred, including a copy of the adoption or custody order, the consular officer will issue a certificate to the United States adoptive or prospective adoptive parent(s) if the officer is satisfied that the requirements of the Convention and IAA have been met, and only if so will the consular officer approve the immigration petition and complete visa processing. To streamline the process, the regulation departs from current practice by allowing consular officers to approve petitions for children whose cases are covered by the Convention regardless of whether the petition was originally filed with the Department or DHS.

*   *   *   *

2. Abduction

a. *Efforts to encourage accession to the Hague Abduction Convention*

During 2007 the United States continued efforts to encourage more countries to join the 1980 Hague Convention on the Civil Aspects of International Child Abduction ("Hague Abduction Convention" or "Convention"). In an October 18, 2007, cable providing guidance to U.S. posts abroad on addressing this issue with their host governments, the Department of State explained the importance of broadening membership in the Convention as excerpted below.

_____

*   *   *   *

7. One of the most effective solutions for left-behind parents to reunite their families is the Hague Abduction Convention. Left-behind parents express frustration that foreign courts frequently do not take into account a custody determination made in the country where the child was residing when the abduction took place. The Hague Abduction Convention was negotiated partly because of this frustration. Countries that are party to the Convention have agreed that a child who was living in one Convention country, and who has been removed to or retained in another Convention country in violation of the left-behind parent's custodial rights, shall be promptly returned. Once the child has

been returned, the custody dispute can then be resolved, if necessary, in the courts of that jurisdiction. The Convention does not address who should have custody of the child; it addresses where the custody decision is to be made.

8. The Convention significantly increases the chances that left-behind parents will achieve the return of their children. In FY 2006, 183 children abducted to or wrongfully retained in the United States were returned to their country of origin under the Convention. Also in FY 2006, 65.8 percent of all returns of children who had been abducted from the United States, were returned from U.S. Convention partners. The Hague Permanent Bureau reports that a study of outcomes shows that 70 percent of children were returned to their habitual residence under the Convention.

9. The existence of the Hague Abduction Convention has been an important element in dissuading left-behind parents from taking desperate measures, such as snatch-backs or re-abduction, to secure the return of their children. In countries in which this legal mechanism is not available, the temptation to take extra-legal steps to reunite with children can be great. Such desperate measures traumatize the child and can involve [a U.S. diplomatic or consular] post and the host government in time consuming, heartrending situations that benefit no one, most particularly the child involved.

*   *   *   *

b. Acceptance of accessions

Under the Hague Abduction Convention, a treaty relationship arises automatically between states that were members of the Hague Conference at the time the Convention was concluded and that subsequently become parties to it. Article 38 of the Convention provides a different procedure for acceding countries that were not members of the Hague Conference at that time:

The accession will have effect only as regards the relations between the acceding State and such Contracting States as will have declared their acceptance of the accession. . . .

Such declaration shall be deposited at the Ministry of Foreign Affairs of the Kingdom of the Netherlands. . . .

Before accepting accession under Article 38, the United States assesses whether the acceding state can effectively comply and implement the Convention. Issues reviewed include a general assessment of the country's legal system, including whether the state has designated a Central Authority as required by Article 6 of the Convention, whether the overall legal system is compatible with implementation of the Convention, and whether specific implementing legislation and/or regulations have been adopted if necessary. Then the United States assesses in greater detail how the Convention has been implemented in the country's domestic law, judicial procedures available for adjudication and accessibility to those procedures, and enforcement authorities and mechanisms. Finally, the United States assesses substantive custody and access laws, ability to locate abducted or wrongfully retained children, social services and child protection services, information and training, and Hague Abduction Convention case practice if any. Finally, the United States assesses any potential issues of concern that could either promote or hinder the effective implementation and application of the Convention, including factors that could prevent U.S. courts from ordering a child's return to the country in question.

During 2007 the United States deposited declarations accepting accession by Costa Rica, Guatemala, Paraguay, San Marino, Sri Lanka, and Ukraine. A complete list of countries with which the United States has a treaty relationship under the Hague Abduction Convention is available at *www.travel.state.gov/ family/abduction/hague_issues/hague_issues_1487.html.*

c. *2007 Hague Abduction Convention compliance report*

On May 2, 2007, the Department of State forwarded to Congress the 2007 Report on Compliance with the 1980

Hague Convention on the Civil Aspects of International Child Abduction. The Report, as required by § 2803 of Pub. L. No. 104-277, as amended, 42 U.S.C. § 11611, evaluates each of the countries with which the United States has a treaty relationship for effectiveness in implementing the Hague Abduction Convention with respect to applications for return of or access to children on behalf of parents in the United States. The 2007 report, covering the period October 1, 2005 through September 30, 2006, identified Honduras as "not compliant" with the Convention and cited "patterns of noncompliance" in Brazil, Chile, Colombia, Germany, Greece, Mexico, and Poland.

The 2007 report added a new section entitled "Notable Issues and Cases" in order to provide comment on larger issues that the United States has found to have an impact on compliance. The Issues section discussed concerns related to onerous undertakings imposed in some Convention return orders, the frequency with which Latin American courts apply the UN Convention on the Rights of the Child to abduction cases in order to make determinations on the "best interests" of the child even though the Hague Abduction Convention leaves such determinations to the courts of the child's country of habitual residence, and excessive use of the Mexican *amparo* legal system. It also discussed the use of mediation as a useful tool to reduce litigation in Convention cases.

As explained in the report, the notable cases listed are "precedent-setting, high-profile, egregious in their handling, or emblematic of larger concerns with the country involved. Three of the cases listed remain unresolved for at least 18 months after the filing of the Convention application for return." Notable cases outgoing from the United States described in the 2007 report were to Austria, Germany, Israel, Mexico, Mauritius, New Zealand, and Poland. The report is available at *www.travel.state.gov/pdf/child_abduction_Compliance_Report.pdf.*

C. JUDICIAL ASSISTANCE

1. Hague Apostille Convention

a. *Entry into force*

The Hague Convention Abolishing the Requirement for Legalization of Foreign Public Documents ("The Hague Apostille Convention") entered into force for South Korea, Georgia, and Moldova in 2007, bringing the total number of parties to the convention to ninety-two. A cable sent to American embassies in the three countries explained the effect of the convention as excerpted below. The full text of the cable is available at *www.state.gov/s/l/c8183.htm*.

* * * *

2. WHAT IS THE HAGUE APOSTILLE CONVENTION?

. . . The convention provides a simplification of the series of formalities, which complicate the use of public documents outside of the country from which they emanate. The convention reduces all of the formalities of legalization to the simple delivery of a certificate in a prescribed form, entitled an "apostille," by the designated authorities of the state where the documents originate. The apostille certificate, placed on the document or on a piece of paper attached thereto called an "allonge", is dated, numbered and registered. The verification of its registration can be carried out without difficulty by means of a simple request for information addressed to the authority which delivered the certificate. The effects of the apostille are limited to attestation of the authenticity of the signature, the capacity in which the person signing the document has acted and, where appropriate, the identity of the seal or stamp which it bears. The convention not only serves to lighten the task of the judges before whom foreign documents are produced; it is also of the greatest importance to everyone who wishes to rely abroad on the facts set out in a document emanating from the authorities in his or her own country. Thus, the convention has proved to be very useful for those countries that do not have the practice of requiring legalization in their own legal systems.

3. HOW DOES THE HAGUE APOSTILLE CONVENTION WORK IN THE UNITED STATES?

The United States has three tiers of authorities competent to issue the apostille certificate. The U.S. Department of State authentications office affixes apostilles to documents issued by federal agencies of the United States. The clerks and deputy clerks of the federal courts of the United States issue apostilles on documents issued by those courts. Public documents issued in U.S. states, the District of Columbia and other U.S. jurisdictions may be legalized with an apostille by designated authorities in each jurisdiction, generally the state secretary of state's office. Information about how to contact each of these authorities is available on the Department of State authentications office web page (*http://www.state.gov/m/a/auth/*) and on the web page for The Hague Conference on Private International Law (*www.hcch.net*).

4. U.S. DECLARATION—DO NOT USE APOSTILLES IN EXTRADITION DOCUMENTS

The United States made a declaration at the time of its accession to The Hague Apostille Convention that the convention procedure shall not apply to extradition-related documents due to other requirements of U.S. law. Extradition-related documents for use by the United States must be authenticated by the principal diplomatic or consular officer of the United States in accordance with title 18, United States Code, section 3190.

*   *   *   *

b. Interpretation of requirements

On June 1, 2007, the U.S. embassy in Moscow sent a diplomatic note to the Russian Ministry of Foreign Affairs concerning "an apparent change by the Supreme Court of the Russian Federation in its interpretation of [the Hague Apostille Convention], which has created a serious hardship for American citizens adopting orphans in Russia." The substantive paragraphs of the diplomatic note are set forth below.

The Embassy has learned that four American families who were in Tver to finalize their adoptions on May 29 were told by the court at the last minute that their adoptions could not be approved at that time.

The court told the families that the Supreme Court of Russia had just informed the court that civil documents from other countries submitted in adoption cases, such as marriage records and so on, could not be accepted if the apostilles on the documents did not meet certain standards called for in the Hague Convention of 5 October 1961 Abolishing the Requirement of Legalization of Foreign Public Documents.

The court stated that some of the civil documents from the United States which the families had submitted did not meet those standards.

The court has scheduled another hearing for the families on June 27, and has asked them to submit new documents with apostilles that meet the supposed standards by that time.

As a result, these four families will be returning to the United States for the time being without having completed the adoptions, and therefore without the children they had expected to be providing homes for. This has caused the families a great deal of emotional distress and financial hardship.

In the view of the Embassy, it is extremely unfortunate that the Supreme Court has apparently decided to change the requirements for adopting families without any advance notice to the public.

In addition, the Embassy wishes to bring to the attention of the Ministry the attached report from 2003, by a Special Commission of the Hague Conference on Private International Law, which addresses inconsistencies occurring in some states in the application of the Convention Abolishing the Requirement of Legalization of Foreign Public Documents.

Specifically, in Section II, paragraphs 13 through 18, the report discusses formal requirements for apostilles. In paragraph 13 it states:

> "The SC (Special Commission) underlined the importance of the principle that an Apostille that has been established according to the requirements of the Convention in the

State of issuance must be accepted and produce its effects in any State of production. With a view to further facilitating free circulation of Apostilles, the SC recalled the importance of the Model certificate annexed to the convention. The SC recommended that Apostilles issued by competent authorities should conform as closely as possible to this model. However, variations in the form of an Apostille among issuing authorities should not be a basis for rejection as long as the Apostille is clearly identifiable as an Apostille issued under the Convention."

The Embassy appreciates the efforts of the Tver court to give the families whose adoptions were affected by this new Supreme Court instruction an opportunity to obtain new documents and to complete their adoptions in the near future.

However, the Embassy respectfully requests the assistance of the Ministry of Foreign Affairs in:

— providing the Supreme Court of Russia the attached report by the Special Commission, with specific mention of Section II;
— relaying to the Supreme Court the Embassy's concern about the failure to provide any advance public notice of its new instructions regarding civil documents from other countries;
— relaying to the Supreme Court the severe emotional stress and the financial hardship its decision to suddenly change its interpretation of the convention's requirements has caused these families, who have already made significant sacrifices in order to provide an opportunity for a normal family life to orphaned children; and
— requesting the court to, at a minimum, allow international adoption cases that are already pending to be processed under the requirements that were in place prior to the courts recent change in interpretation of the convention's requirements.

2. U.S. Participation in Judicial Assistance in Ireland

On June 1, 2007, Edward A. Betancourt, Director of the Office of Policy Review and Inter-Agency Liaison in the Directorate of Overseas Citizens Services of the Bureau of Consular Affairs, U.S. Department of State, provided a declaration in *Fidelity International Currency Adviser A Fund, L.L.C. v. United States*, Civil Nos. 05-40151-FDS and 06-40130-FDS(D. Mass.). Excerpts below explain the legal basis for judicial assistance in civil matters between the United States and Ireland and the means by which a U.S. attorney might participate in certain court proceedings before an Irish Court. The full text of the declaration is available at *www.state.gov/s/l/c8183.htm.*

* * * *

3. Judicial assistance in civil matters between the United States and Ireland is governed by the Vienna Convention on Consular Relations (VCCR) 21 UST 77, TIAS 6820, 596 U.N.T.S. 261 and the Hague Convention on the Service Abroad of Judicial and Extra-Judicial Documents in Civil and Commercial Matters, 20 UST 361, to which the United States and Ireland are parties. It is also governed by the U.S.- Ireland Consular Convention, 5 U.S.T. 949 signed at Dublin May 1, 1950, which entered into force June 12, 1954, customary international law; and applicable U.S. and local Irish law, and regulations. Ireland is not a party to the Hague Convention on the Taking of Evidence Abroad in Civil and Commercial Matters, 23 UST 2555.

4. The procedures for obtaining judicial assistance in Ireland are summarized in general in OCS's information circular, 'Judicial Assistance—Ireland' which is available via the Department of State's, Bureau of Consular Affairs' home page on the Internet at *http://www.travel.state.gov/law/info/judicial/judicial_652.html.* General information about preparation of letters rogatory is also available at *http://www.travel.state.gov/law/info/iudicial/iudicial_683.html.*

5. The Department understands that a question has arisen as to whether an Assistant United States Attorney, U.S. Department of Justice attorney, or local Irish legal counsel representing the United States might be permitted to participate in proceedings before an Irish Court considering a letter rogatory from a court in the United States.

6. It has been the general practice in Ireland for Ireland's State Solicitor's office to pose questions in connection with a letter rogatory from a foreign tribunal for compulsion of testimony. On May 23, 2007, the U.S. Embassy in Dublin received a diplomatic note dated May 22, 2007 from the Irish Department of Foreign Affairs in connection with another matter regarding how letters rogatory are executed in Ireland. The note stated "The Department has the honour to inform the Embassy that the State's Law Office has advised that, in order to proceed with the request, either one of two courses of action be adopted. Were a written list of questions to be provided, such questions would be put to (the witness) by an Irish judge and a certified transcript of same would be transmitted to the Embassy. Alternatively a U.S. attorney may travel to Ireland to put questions to (the witness) in court. Should it be preferred to adopt the latter course of action, the State's Law Office has advised that the letter rogatory should be amended so as to expressly request that the examination before the Irish court may be conducted by a named U.S. attorney. The letter rogatory should also set out the attorney's qualifications and memberships. Upon receipt of such an amended letter rogatory, the State's Law Office will make an ex parte application to the High Court seeking an order to the effect that the examination may be conducted by that Attorney. The details of the date and venue of the examination would be communicated to the Embassy."

*   *   *   *

Cross References

International enforcement of child support obligations,
Chapter 15.B.
Judicial assistance for foreign court, **Chapter 15.C.4.**

CHAPTER 3

International Criminal Law

A. EXTRADITION AND MUTUAL LEGAL ASSISTANCE

1. Extradition

a. Judicial reviewability of Secretary of State decision to extradite: Mironescu v. Costner

On March 22, 2007, the U.S. Court of Appeals for the Fourth Circuit ruled that a district court lacked jurisdiction to consider a petition for writ of habeas corpus filed after the petitioner had been found extraditable and the Secretary of State had signed a warrant for his surrender. *Mironescu v. Costner*, 480 F.3d 664 (4th Cir. 2007), *cert. dismissed*, 128 S. Ct. 976 (2008). U.S. pleadings in the case and the district court decision are discussed in *Digest 2006* at 148–55 and *Digest 2005* at 79–89. Excerpts follow from the Fourth Circuit decision finding that the rule of non-inquiry alone would not bar judicial review of the Secretary's extradition decision, but the Foreign Affairs Reform and Restructuring Act ("FARR Act") precludes consideration of the Convention Against Torture ("CAT") and FARR Act claims on habeas review in an extradition case (most footnotes omitted).

* * * *

[I.A.]1. *Extradition Procedure*

* * * *

. . . Once the fugitive is in custody, a district court judge or magistrate judge conducts a hearing to determine whether (1) there is probable cause to believe that the fugitive has violated one or more of the criminal laws of the country requesting extradition; (2) the alleged conduct would have been a violation of American criminal law, if committed here; and (3) the requested individual is the one sought by the foreign nation for trial on the charge at issue. . . . Provided that these requirements are satisfied and that the applicable treaty provides no other basis for denying extradition, the judge certifies to the Secretary of State (the Secretary) that the fugitive is extraditable. *See* 18 U.S.C.A. § 3184. Although a judge's certification of extraditability is not appealable, a fugitive may obtain limited collateral review of the certification in the form of a petition for a writ of habeas corpus. . . . In considering such a habeas petition, the district court generally determines only whether the judge had jurisdiction, whether the charged offense is within the scope of the applicable treaty, and whether there was any evidence supporting the probable cause finding. . . .

Following certification by the district court, the Secretary must decide whether to extradite the fugitive. *See* 18 U.S.C.A. § 3186 (West 2000). . . . In deciding whether to extradite, the Secretary may consider "factors affecting both the individual defendant as well as foreign relations—factors that may be beyond the scope of the . . . judge's review." *Sidali v. INS*, 107 F.3d 191, 195 n.7 (3d Cir. 1997). The broad range of options available to the Secretary includes (but is not limited to) reviewing de novo the judge's findings of fact and conclusions of law, refusing extradition on a number of discretionary grounds, including humanitarian and foreign policy considerations, granting extradition with conditions, and using diplomacy to obtain fair treatment for the fugitive. *See United States v. Kin-Hong*, 110 F.3d 103, 109–10 (1st Cir. 1997).

2. The CAT and the FARR Act

A central issue in this appeal is whether the Secretary's discretion in extradition matters has been constrained by Article 3 of the United Nations Convention Against Torture (CAT) . . . and § 2242 of the Foreign Affairs Reform and Restructuring Act (the FARR Act) of 1998, *see* Pub. L. No. 105-277, div. G, 112 Stat. 2681–822 (codified at 8 U.S.C. § 1231 note). As is relevant here, Article 3 of the CAT provides:

1. No State Party shall expel, return ("refouler") or extradite a person to another State where there are substantial grounds for believing that he would be in danger of being subjected to torture.
2. For the purpose of determining whether there are such grounds, the competent authorities shall take into account all relevant considerations including, where applicable, the existence in the State concerned of a consistent pattern of gross, flagrant or mass violations of human rights.

*　*　*　*

In light of the Senate's determination that the CAT was not self-executing, [136 Cong. Rec. S17486-01, S17492 (1990)] Congress enacted the FARR Act to implement the treaty. The FARR Act provides that "[i]t shall be the policy of the United States not to expel, extradite, or otherwise effect the involuntary return of any person to a country in which there are substantial grounds for believing the person would be in danger of being subjected to torture, regardless of whether the person is physically present in the United States." Section 2242(a). It also directs heads of the appropriate agencies to "prescribe regulations to implement the obligations of the United States under Article 3." Section 2242(b).

The applicable State Department regulations identify the Secretary as "the U.S. official responsible for determining whether to surrender a fugitive to a foreign country by means of extradition." 22 C.F.R. § 95.2(b) (2006). They provide that "to implement the obligation assumed by the United States pursuant to Article 3 of the Convention, the Department considers the question of whether a person facing extradition from the U.S. 'is more likely than not' to be tortured in the State requesting extradition when appropriate in making this determination." *Id.* They further state that in each case in which there is an allegation relating to torture, "appropriate policy and legal offices [shall] review and analyze information relevant to the case in preparing a recommendation

to the Secretary as to whether or not to sign the surrender warrant."
22 C.F.R. § 95.3(a) (2006). And, they provide that "[d]ecisions
of the Secretary concerning surrender of fugitives for extradition
are matters of executive discretion not subject to judicial review."
22 C.F.R. § 95.4 (2006).

B.

*   *   *   *

Upon receiving notification that a warrant to extradite him
had been signed by the Secretary, Mironescu filed the present
habeas petition. Mironescu asserts that the Secretary has a mandatory duty under the CAT and FARR Act not to extradite a fugitive
who is likely to be tortured after his surrender. He further alleges
that he presented substantial evidence to the Secretary that he
would be tortured if extradited to Romania and that the Secretary's
decision to extradite him in the face of such evidence was arbitrary
and capricious. Mironescu submits that the district court possesses
jurisdiction over his habeas petition because he alleges that he is
"in custody in violation of the Constitution or laws or treaties of
the United States." 28 U.S.C.A. § 2241(c)(3). He also asserts that
the district court has jurisdiction to consider his petition under the
Administrative Procedure Act (APA), 5 U.S.C.A. §§ 551–59, 701–06
(West 1996 & Supp. 2006).

*   *   *   *

[II.] A.

The Government maintains that the district court erred in
denying its motion to dismiss Mironescu's petition because claims
that an extradition would violate the CAT or the FARR Act may
not be raised on habeas. Specifically, the Government argues that
the scope of habeas review in extradition cases is limited and the
"rule of non-inquiry" bars such claims.

*   *   *   *

We conclude that the rule of non-inquiry does not warrant a
holding that the district court lacked jurisdiction to review the
Secretary's extradition decision on habeas. Most relevant to our
conclusion is our decision in *Plaster v. United States*, 720 F.2d 340

(4th Cir. 1983). . . . After the court certified Plaster's extraditability, the district court granted a writ of habeas corpus, ruling that extradition would infringe Plaster's due process rights because it would violate the terms of an immunity agreement between him and the United States government. *See id.* at 346.[6]

We affirmed, holding that the district court correctly ruled that it had jurisdiction to enjoin Plaster's extradition when the court determined that his detention was unlawful. *See id.* at 347–51. . . . We explained that the United States must act within the confines of the Constitution when carrying out its treaty obligations, and we noted that "a claim of unconstitutional governmental conduct is within the scope of habeas corpus review mandated by both the Constitution itself and the applicable federal statute." *Id.* . . .

In holding that the district court possessed jurisdiction to review the constitutionality of the extradition, we specifically rejected an argument by the government that the district court lacked jurisdiction because "the extradition power of the United States is *sui generis* and commits the consideration of alleged constitutional violations solely to the Secretary of State and the President." *Plaster*, 720 F.2d at 349. We noted that although the Executive has unlimited discretion to *refuse* to extradite a fugitive, it lacks the discretion to extradite a fugitive when extradition would violate his constitutional rights. *See id.* Additionally, we explained that "unquestionably, it is the province of the judiciary to adjudicate claims that governmental conduct is in violation of the Constitution." *Id.*

Our reasoning in *Plaster* is controlling here. . . .

* * * *

B.

Despite our holding regarding the rule of noninquiry, we nevertheless conclude that the district court erred in denying the Government's motion to dismiss on the basis that § 2242(d) of the FARR Act bars consideration of Mironescu's petition.

* * * *

---

[6] The district court also concluded that the applicable treaty barred extradition because it prohibited extradition when it would violate the relator's constitutional rights. *See id.*

Section 2242(d) states:

Notwithstanding any other provision of law, and except as provided in the regulations described in subsection (b), . . . nothing in this section shall be construed as providing any court jurisdiction to consider or review claims raised under the Convention or this section, or any other determination made with respect to the application of the policy set forth in subsection (a), except as part of the review of a final order of removal pursuant to section 242 of the Immigration and Nationality Act (8 U.S.C. § 1252).

This language plainly conveys that although courts may consider or review CAT or FARR Act claims as part of their review of a final removal order, they are otherwise precluded from considering or reviewing such claims. As Mironescu presents his claim as part of his challenge to extradition, rather than removal, § 2242(d) clearly precluded the district court from exercising jurisdiction.

In reaching the contrary conclusion, the district court suggested that exercising jurisdiction over Mironescu's petition would not be interpreting the FARR Act to "provid[e] any court jurisdiction" to consider the claims insofar as the habeas statute provided the jurisdiction. . . . However, this interpretation of "provid[e] . . . jurisdiction" is squarely at odds with the language in § 2242(d) indicating that the FARR Act may "provid[e] . . . jurisdiction to consider or review" CAT or FARR Act claims only "as part of the review of a final order of removal." . . .

The district court also concluded that *INS v. St. Cyr*, 533 U.S. 289, 121 S. Ct. 2271, 150 L. Ed. 2d 347 (2001), supported its exercise of jurisdiction over Mironescu's petition. . . . In *St. Cyr*, the respondent pleaded guilty to an aggravated felony in 1996 and became subject to deportation and eligible for a discretionary waiver thereof. . . . The Antiterrorism and Effective Death Penalty Act (AEDPA) of 1996, Pub. L. No. 104-132, 110 Stat. 1214, and the Illegal Immigration Reform and Immigrant Responsibility Act (IIRIRA) of 1996, Pub. L. No. 104-208, div. C, 110 Stat. 3009-546, went into effect shortly thereafter. . . . The government maintained that these acts precluded most removal orders from "judicial review" and repealed the discretionary waiver of deportation previously available under § 212(c) of the Immigration and Nationality Act (INA). *See id.* at 293, 297, 310–11. The government argued that the jurisdiction-stripping provisions left St. Cyr with no forum to litigate the question of whether the previously available discretionary waiver was still available. *See id.* at 297. The Court ruled against the government, invoking two presumptions—the "strong presumption in favor of judicial review of administrative action," and the proposition that "[i]mplications from statutory text or legislative history are not sufficient to repeal habeas jurisdiction; instead, Congress must articulate specific and unambiguous statutory directives to effect a repeal." *Id.* at 298–99.

The *St. Cyr* Court concluded that the provisions at issue did not unambiguously repeal habeas jurisdiction in that context. *See id.* at 314. . . . conclud[ing] that in the absence of any "explicit[]" mention[]" of habeas or § 2241 in the statutes, they did not conclusively demonstrate an intent on the part of Congress to preclude habeas review in an immigration context. *St. Cyr*, 533 U.S. at 312.

The Court further reasoned that interpreting the jurisdiction-stripping provisions to bar court review of a "pure question of law" would raise "substantial constitutional questions" in that it could violate the Suspension Clause. *Id.* at 300. *St. Cyr* explained that "at the absolute minimum, the Suspension Clause protects the writ as it existed in 1789" and that the writ in 1789 was available to address errors of law. *Id.* at 301, 302 (internal quotation marks omitted). Thus, because a reading of the statutes that did not preclude habeas was "fairly possible," *id.* at 300 (internal quotation marks omitted), the Court held that habeas jurisdiction remained available to St. Cyr. *See id.* at 314.

We conclude that *St. Cyr* is not dispositive here. Critical to both bases for the *St. Cyr* result was the existence of a plausible reading of the statutes before the Court under which habeas review of the claim at issue was not barred. The same cannot be said for § 2242(d) in this case. Although § 2242(d) resembles two of the statutes before the *St. Cyr* Court, *see* 8 U.S.C. § 1252(a)(2)(C), 8 U.S.C. § 1252(b)(9) (1994 ed., Supp. V), the difference between § 2242(d) and the other two statutes eliminates the ambiguity on which *St. Cyr* was based. . . . Except in the context of immigration proceedings, § 2242(d) flatly prohibits courts from "consider[ing] . . . claims" raised under the

CAT or the FARR Act. This preclusion plainly encompasses consideration of CAT and FARR Act claims on habeas review.

Furthermore, in addition to the critical difference in the statutory language, the fact that Mironescu's claim challenges his extradition rather than his removal is significant. The historical dichotomy in the immigration context between the "limited role played by the courts in habeas corpus proceedings," *St. Cyr*, 533 U.S. at 312, and judicial review in which a court "decid[es] on the whole record whether there is substantial evidence to support administrative findings of fact," *Heikkila*, 345 U.S. at 236 (internal quotation marks omitted), on which the *St. Cyr* Court based its conclusion that the statutes before it did not clearly bar habeas, does not exist with regard to a claim that a fugitive's extradition will result in a violation of his federal rights, *see Plaster*, 720 F.2d at 347–49 (holding that district court on habeas review possessed jurisdiction to resolve constitutional challenge against extradition, including finding facts underlying constitutional claim). Indeed, Mironescu himself has sought review under the APA in the context of a habeas proceeding. Thus, for both of these reasons, § 2242(d) plainly demonstrates Congress' intent to preclude consideration of CAT and FARR Act claims on habeas review of an extradition challenge.

In light of the clear demonstration of Congressional intent here, affirmance would amount to a holding that Congress must always *explicitly* mention habeas or § 2241 in order to bar habeas review. . . . Although *St. Cyr* relied on the fact that the statutes there at issue did not "explicitly mention[]" habeas or § 2241, *St. Cyr*, 533 U.S. at 312, it listed that fact as only one consideration supporting its conclusion that the statutes were not sufficiently clear to bar habeas review. . . . Thus, in light of the absence of any other plausible reading, we interpret § 2242(d) as depriving the district court of jurisdiction to consider Mironescu's claims.

* * * *

b. *Role of Geneva Conventions in extradition:* Noriega v. Pastrana

In 2004 France requested the extradition of Manuel Noriega on charges of engaging in financial transactions with the proceeds of illegal drug trafficking, an offense that corresponds to money laundering under U.S. law. Noriega had been convicted *in absentia* of these crimes but would have an opportunity to challenge that conviction and seek a new trial. On July 17, 2007, the United States filed an initial complaint for extradition based on the French request. Noriega was still serving his sentence for conviction on drug trafficking and related charges in 1992 (*see United States v. Noriega*, 808 F. Supp. 791, 803 (S.D. Fla. 1992)). He filed a Petition for Writs of Habeas Corpus, Mandamus, and Prohibition in that prior criminal case, seeking an order that the magistrate judge immediately cease and desist with any proceedings on the extradition because it would violate his rights as a prisoner of war under the Third Geneva Convention. On August 24, 2007, the court denied the petition for lack of jurisdiction because the statute under which he filed "applies to challenges against the sentence imposed, and [Noriega] has not cited any defect in this Court's sentence . . ." Order Denying Defendant's Petition for Writs of Habeas Corpus, Mandamus, and Prohibition, *United States. v. Noriega*, 2007 U.S. Dist. LEXIS 62488 (S.D. Fla.) While noting that the issue of whether Noriega could succeed on a habeas petition was not before him, Judge Hoeveler in that Order stated that

> in light of the circumstances presented by this case, including the fact of an imminent hearing in the extradition proceeding, and Defendant's planned release from custody in two weeks . . . if the question were before this Court at this time, the Court would find that Defendant has demonstrated no . . . entitlement [to a writ of habeas corpus]. . . .

Judge Hoeveler offered his "observations" on the law and facts leading to this conclusion.

The magistrate judge issued a certificate of extraditability on August 29, 2007. On October 26, 2007, Noriega filed a petition for a writ of habeas corpus challenging the certificate of extraditability, pursuant to 28 U.S.C. § 2241, and petitions for a writ of mandamus and other appropriate relief in the Southern District of Florida. *Noriega v. Pastrana*, Case No. 07-22816-CIV-HUCK (S.D. Fl.). On December 14, 2007, the United States filed its opposition to this petition. Excerpts below from the U.S. opposition explain that Noriega's Geneva Conventions claims were not properly before the court but that the requested extradition would be in full accord with the conventions in any event. The full text of the U.S. December 14 submission, including the attached declaration of Clifton Johnson, is available at *www.state.gov/s/l/c8183.htm*. Resolution of the case remained pending at the end of 2007.

*   *   *   *

II. Noriega's Arguments Based on the Geneva Conventions are not Properly Before this Court. Once a Magistrate Judge issues a certificate of extraditability, the determination of extraditability is not directly appealable. However, a limited collateral review is available through a petition for a writ of habeas corpus. *See Peroff v. Hylton*, 563 F.2d 1099, 1102 (4th Cir. 1977). The district court's review is limited to three issues: (1) did the magistrate court have jurisdiction over the extradition proceeding; (2) was the defendant charged with extraditable offenses under the Treaty; and (3) was there any evidence supporting the finding of probable cause. . . . As Noriega does not advance any of these three grounds for review in his habeas petition, but rather raises a claim under the Geneva Conventions, his habeas petition should be denied by this Court.

Such a claim could only be raised with the Secretary of State. Once a fugitive has been found extraditable by the Judicial Branch, responsibility transfers by the governing statute to the Secretary of State. *See* 18 U.S.C. § 3186. Significantly for this case, that statute commits to the Secretary's sole discretion the decision whether the fugitive will actually be surrendered to the requesting foreign government. . . . The Supreme Court has made clear that, as this statutory provision reflects, the surrender of a fugitive to a foreign government is "purely a national act . . . performed through the Secretary of State," within the Executive's "powers to conduct foreign affairs." *In re Kaine*, 55 U.S. 103, 110 (1852); *see also Plaster v. United States*, 720 F.2d 340, 354 (4th Cir. 1983) . . . For extraditions "[t]he Secretary exercises broad discretion and may properly consider factors affecting both the individual defendant as well as foreign relations—factors that may be beyond the scope of the magistrate judge's review." *Sidali v. INS*, 107 F.3d 191, 195 n.7 (3d Cir. 1997) . . . .

Thus, while the Secretary may consider a broad range of arguments against surrender, habeas review of a certification of extraditability is narrowly circumscribed and does not extend to the arguments Noriega raises here.

The enactment by Congress of the Military Commissions Act of 2006, Pub.L. No. 109-366, § 5(a), Oct. 17, 2006, 120 Stat. 2631,[7] confirms the central role of the Executive Branch here. Section 5(a) of the Military Commissions Act of 2006 has codified the principle that the Geneva Conventions are not judicially enforceable by private parties. In any event, as two courts have already determined in evaluating the same claims, the United States has fully complied with the Geneva Conventions. For the benefit of this Court, the United States reiterates below the reasons that Noriega's Geneva Conventions claims lack merit.

III. The Requested Extradition is in Full Accord with the Geneva Conventions.

Even if Noriega were able to raise it in this proceeding, his argument that the Geneva Conventions prohibit his extradition to France is unavailing. At the outset, it is important to note that, prior to the adoption of the Geneva Conventions, the United States possessed the full panoply of rights and powers inherent in any sovereign nation—including the power to transfer or extradite a prisoner of war to another country. When it became a party to the

---

[7] That provision states: "No person may invoke the Geneva Conventions or any protocols thereto in any habeas corpus or other civil action or proceeding to which the United States, or a current or former officer, employee, member of the Armed Forces, or other agent of the United States is a party as a source of rights in any court of the United States or its States or territories."

Geneva Conventions, the United States agreed to abide by certain express limitations on its pre-existing powers as a sovereign nation. Thus, the relevant question is not whether the Geneva Conventions specifically grant the United States the power to extradite a prisoner of war to another country. The question rather is to what extent the Geneva Conventions expressly limit the United States' pre-existing power to extradite a prisoner of war to face criminal charges in another nation.

A. Article 118 of Geneva III Does Not Bar Noriega's Extradition to France.

The only provision of the Geneva Conventions relied on by Noriega in support of his claim that the requested extradition is barred is Article 118 of Geneva III. Noriega argues that Article 118 "requires that [the] United States repatriate [him] to the Republic of Panama upon his release from the custody of the Bureau of Prisons." This is simply not the case. Article 118 provides that a prisoner of war "shall be released and repatriated without delay *after the cessation of active hostilities*" (emphasis added). Obviously, Noriega was not repatriated to Panama upon the cessation of hostilities, as hostilities ceased nearly two decades ago. That is because Article 118 cannot be read in isolation—as Noriega attempts to do—but rather must be read in accordance with other provisions of the Geneva Conventions. In particular, Article 119 of Geneva III provides, in part:

> Prisoners of war against whom criminal proceedings for an indictable offense are pending may be detained until the end of such proceedings, and, if necessary, until the completion of the punishment. The same shall apply to prisoners of war already convicted of an indictable offense.

This is precisely the provision that allowed the United States to retain custody over Noriega, put him on trial, and confine him during the duration of his federal criminal sentence long after the hostilities in Panama that resulted in his capture had ceased. Indeed, "[t]he Convention clearly sets POWs convicted of crimes apart from other prisoners of war, making special provision for them in Articles 82–108 on 'penal and disciplinary sanctions.'"

United States v. Noriega, 808 F. Supp. 791, 799–800 (S.D. Fla. 1992)(*Noriega I*).

B. Article 119 of Geneva III Provides for the Continued Detention of POWs to Face Criminal Charges.

By the same token, Article 119 of Geneva III allows for the continued detention of Noriega based upon pending "criminal proceedings" for another "indictable offense" in France, and his detention in France may continue "until the completion of the punishment" on the separate and distinct French charges. "[T]he ultimate goal of Geneva III is to ensure humane treatment of POWs," *Noriega I*, 808 F. Supp. at 799; it is not to prevent them from facing justice for crimes they have committed. Nothing in the Geneva Conventions suggests that a prisoner of war cannot be extradited from one Party nation to face criminal charges in another Party nation. To the contrary, the official commentary to Article 119 confirms that Geneva III contemplated detention of prisoners of war for criminal proceedings without specifying that such detention is limited to detention by the nation that originally captured the prisoner of war:

> This amendment was considered necessary since it was not the intention of the drafters of the Convention that a prisoner should be detained because proceedings were being taken against him or because he was summoned to appear before court for neglect of some obligation in civil law; they were thinking only of prisoners of war subject to criminal proceedings. It should be noted that the present provision does not oblige the Detaining Power to detain prisoners under such prosecution or conviction; it is a step which the Detaining Power may take if it wishes.

3 International Committee of the Red Cross, *Commentary on the Geneva Conventions* (J. Pictet, ed., 1960) ("*Commentary*"). As Judge Hoeveler noted: "nothing in the [Geneva III] suggests that honoring a treaty between parties to the Convention concerning extradition for a criminal offense is prohibited." *Noriega II*, 2007 WL 2947572, *3.

C. Article 12 of Geneva III Allows for the Transfer of POWs Between Parties to the Conventions.

The only restrictions placed on the criminal extradition of a POW are specified in Article 12 of Geneva III, which expressly provides for the transfer of POWs between parties to the Geneva Conventions "after the Detaining Power has satisfied itself of the willingness and ability of such transferee Power to apply the Convention." This provision is not a grant of authority to transfer POWs—that authority pre-existed the creation of the Geneva Conventions. It is, instead, a limitation upon that pre-existing authority.

The Commentary to Article 12 makes clear that this provision establishes two, and only two, prerequisites for the transfer of POWs. The first is that "prisoners of war may only be transferred from one Power which is a party to the Convention to another Power which is a party to the Convention." That prerequisite is satisfied here, as both France and the United States are parties to the Conventions. The second prerequisite is that "such transfer may only take place after the transferring Power has satisfied itself of the willingness and ability of the receiving Power to apply the Convention." As explained in more detail in Section IV below, that prerequisite also has been satisfied.

While Article 12 does not expressly define "transfer," as Judge Hoeveler correctly pointed out, Article 45 of the Fourth Geneva Convention, which was adopted the same day as the Third Geneva Convention, "specifically provides that its protections for civilians (as compared to the Convention's protections for POWs) do not constitute an obstacle 'to the extradition, in pursuance of extradition treaties concluded before the outbreak of hostilities, of protected persons accused of offences against ordinary criminal law.'" *Noriega II*, 2007 WL 2947572, *2. As Judge Hoeveler also noted, the commentary to Article 45 makes clear that the definition of the term "transfer" includes "extradition." *Id.* Although the purposes of the Fourth Convention are different from those of the Third, Noriega advances no reason why "transfer" would have different meanings in similar provisions of those Conventions that were adopted the same day, nor can he offer any rationalization as to why the Conventions would allow for Noriega's extradition to

France to face criminal charges if he was a civilian protected person, but not as a POW. Indeed, it is illogical for the Geneva Conventions to provide POWs with greater shielding from criminal prosecutions than civilian protected parties.

Contrary to Noriega's claims, Article 12 is not limited to transfers of a POW between allies to the conflict that originally led to the capture of the POW. As the Commentary to Article 12 makes clear, the need to make provisions in the Geneva Conventions for the protection of POWs who are transferred between nations was highlighted by the fact that transfers of POWs were likely to occur between allies with the creation of "military organizations for collective defence such as the North Atlantic Treaty Organization and the Warsaw Pact," but Article 12 is in no way limited to such circumstances. The unambiguous language of Article 12 cannot be limited by an example in a commentary. Moreover, under Noriega's proposed interpretation of Article 12, the United States could extradite Noriega to France had France taken up arms against Panama, but because France was not a combatant in the conflict between the United States and Panama, he can escape French justice.[10] This suggestion is unreasonable and at odds with the basic principles of the Conventions. . . .

* * * *

. . . [W]hen properly read in conjunction, Articles 12, 118 and 119 of Geneva III provide as follows: a prisoner of war must be repatriated following the cessation of hostilities unless he faces, or has been convicted of, indictable criminal charges in either the Detaining Power or another Party to the Conventions if the Detaining Power has satisfied itself of the other Party's willingness and ability to provide the POW with treatment consistent with his status as a prisoner of war. Given that all of those conditions have been satisfied, the Geneva Conventions do not bar Noriega's extradition to France.

* * * *

---

[10] If Noriega is returned to Panama, he cannot then be extradited to France in light of Article 24 of the 1972 Panamanian Constitution, which prevents the extradition of Panamanian nationals.

IV. The Rule of Non-Inquiry Bars Consideration of the Treatment Noriega Will Receive in France, but Even if it Did Not, the United States Has Complied with Geneva III by Confirming that France will Afford Noriega Treatment Consistent with Judge Hoeveler's Determination that He is a Prisoner of War.

To the extent that Noriega is arguing that France might not accord him proper treatment under the Geneva Conventions once he is extradited, that claim is not only beyond the proper scope of habeas review of a magistrate's decision on extraditability, but also barred by the Rule of Non-Inquiry. . . .

Of considerable importance to this case, "[t]he Secretary may . . . decline to surrender the [defendant] on any number of discretionary grounds, including but not limited to, humanitarian and foreign policy considerations. Additionally, the Secretary may attach conditions to the surrender of the [defendant]. Of course, the Secretary may also elect to use diplomatic methods to obtain fair treatment for the [defendant]." *Kin-Hong*, 110 F.2d at 109–10. One type of condition the Secretary may place on an extradition is a demand that the requesting country provide assurances regarding the individual's proper treatment. *See Jimenez v. United States District Court*, 84 S. Ct. 14, 16–17 n.10 (1963) (Goldberg, J., in chambers) (describing commitments made by foreign government to Department of State as a condition of surrender); *United States v. Baez*, 349 F.3d 90, 92–93 (2d Cir. 2003) (referring to assurances provided by United States upon extradition of fugitive by another country).

Thus, it is within the sole discretion of the Secretary of State to insure that the United States abides by any international commitments relevant to Noriega's extradition to and confinement in France. Even if issues related to Noriega's treatment in France were properly raised in this proceeding, however, the United States, as it explained before Judge Hoeveler, has fully complied with any obligations under Article 12 of Geneva III. Article 12 requires that the transfer of POWs between parties to the Convention "may only take place after the transferring Power has satisfied itself of the willingness and ability of the receiving Power to apply the Convention." As detailed in the attached Declaration of Clifton M. Johnson, Assistant Legal Adviser for Law Enforcement and Intelligence at the Department of State, which was submitted to Judge Hoeveler when this issue was before him, the United States has confirmed that France intends to afford Noriega treatment consistent with the benefits that Noriega enjoyed in prison in the United States, in accordance with this Court's ruling and as specified in Geneva III.

Noriega has advanced no evidence to contradict this declaration. Noriega simply relies on a single sentence from the September 7, 2007 daily press briefing of a spokesman for the French Ministry of Foreign Affairs stating that Noriega could not have the status of a POW in France. Such a statement, however, does not contradict or undermine the specific assurances received by the United States with respect to the actual treatment that Noriega would be accorded in France. . . .

It is important to note that, in full compliance with Judge Hoeveler's order of December 8, 1992, the United States, during the course of Noriega's incarceration in the United States, has treated Noriega in full accordance with the Geneva Conventions' mandates regarding the confinement of a prisoner of war who has been convicted of a criminal offense. *See Noriega I*, 808 F. Supp. 791. Noriega has never alleged otherwise. Prior to filing the extradition complaint, the United States engaged in diplomatic communications with the Government of France to ensure that Noriega would enjoy, upon extradition and incarceration in France, treatment consistent with that which he received in the United States pursuant to Judge Hoeveler's order that he receive the same confinement conditions accorded a prisoner of war. The United States did not ask the Republic of France to declare that Noriega is a prisoner of war. Rather, the United States sought and obtained from the Republic of France specific information regarding the rights to which Noriega will be entitled during his incarceration in France upon his extradition. . . .

* * * *

c. Attempted imposition of unilateral conditions by surrendering country

(1) Benitez v. Garcia

On July 16, 2007, the U.S. Court of Appeals for the Ninth Circuit affirmed a lower court decision refusing to uphold a

unilateral condition on length of sentence imposed by
Venezuela in extraditing Cristobal Rodriguez Benitez to the
United States to stand trial for murder. *Rodriguez Benitez v.
Garcia*, 495 F.3d 640 (9th Cir. 2007). The Ninth Circuit's July
opinion withdrew and replaced a February 2007 opinion by
the same panel concluding that Venezuela's unilateral asser-
tion of a limit on the defendant's sentence was binding on
United States courts.

In its *amicus* brief filed in the Ninth Circuit in March 2007,
seeking rehearing or rehearing en banc of the February opinion, the United States explained the facts of the case as
excerpted below (citations to the record omitted). The full
text of the U.S. *amicus* brief is available at *www.state.gov/sl/
c8183.htm*.

---

*   *   *   *

1. Under the United States-Venezuela Extradition Treaty of 1922,
either nation can request assurances that an extradited person not
be subject to a sentence of death or life imprisonment; while nothing in the Treaty precludes the extradition of a person absent such
assurances, the Executive Authority of the surrendering state can,
if it chooses to do so, decline extradition unless it obtains a satisfactory assurance to this effect. In November 1997, in connection
with Appellant's extradition, the Government of Venezuela asked
for assurances that the death penalty would not be sought; there
was no request for any other assurances. In response, the United
States Embassy sent to Venezuela a diplomatic note dated
November 6, 1997, which stated that, if extradited, Cristobal
Rodriguez Benitez "would not be sentenced to death. . . .
Furthermore, if convicted . . . Rodriguez Benitez would receive a
sentence of incarceration of 25 years to life [and] would have the
right to a parole request after serving the minimum mandatory
prison term of 19 years and 2 months."

On June 4, 1998, the Venezuela Supreme Court issued a decree
granting extradition, but stating that Rodriguez Benitez was not to
receive the "death penalty or life imprisonment or punishment
depriving his freedom for more than thirty years, pursuant to"

Venezuelan law. Notwithstanding the Venezuelan court's statement, and without seeking any additional assurances, Venezuela surrendered Rodriguez Benitez to the United States on August 28, 1998.

Rodriguez Benitez was convicted of murder. In July 1999, after inquiries by the Government of Mexico concerning [Benitez, who was] its citizen, Venezuela notified the United States of its view that a sentence of life imprisonment imposed on Rodriguez Benitez "may" violate the terms of the U.S.-Venezuela extradition treaty and the decree of the Venezuela Supreme Court authorizing the extradition. On August 30, 1999, the day before Rodriguez Benitez's sentencing, the State Department wrote to the District Attorney, stating:

> As was its right under the U.S.-Venezuela extradition treaty, before extraditing Mr. Rodriguez Benitez, the Government of Venezuela sought an assurance that he would not face the possibility of the death penalty if extradited. . . . [T]he United States . . . conveyed an assurance to this effect . . . . In doing so, the United States also advised the Government of Venezuela that Mr. Rodriguez Benitez would face the possibility of life imprisonment . . . . In July 1999, . . . the Government of Venezuela formally advised the United States that in its view Mr. Rodriguez should not receive the death penalty *or* a life sentence. Although the express terms of the U.S.-Venezuela treaty would have allowed Venezuela to seek this additional assurance prior to the extradition, it did not do so, and extradited Mr. Rodriguez Benitez based solely on the death penalty assurance.

The State Department then voiced its recommendation (and that of the Department of Justice) that, because of Venezuela's concerns, it would be in the best interests of the U.S.-Venezuela extradition relationship if Rodriguez Benitez did not receive a life sentence. However, the letter made clear that this recommendation was not based on any international legal or other obligation. Rodriguez Benitez was sentenced to an indeterminate term of 19 years to life imprisonment.

* * * *

Excerpts follow from the Ninth Circuit's July opinion.

*   *   *   *

. . . On June 25, 1997, the United States requested that, pursuant to the U.S.-Venezuela extradition treaty, Venezuela extradite Benitez to face charges in California. The extradition treaty provides:

> [T]he Contracting Parties reserve the right to decline to grant extradition for crimes punishable by death and life imprisonment. Nevertheless, the Executive Authority of each of the Contracting Parties shall have the power to grant extradition for such crimes upon the receipt of satisfactory assurances that in case of conviction the death penalty or imprisonment for life will not be inflicted.

Treaty of Extradition, Jan. 19–21, 1922, U.S.-Venez., Art. IV, 43 Stat. 1698, T.S. No. 675.

*   *   *   *

III. . . . For a writ to issue . . . we must find that the state court's decision was either contrary to or an objectively unreasonable application of "clearly established Federal law, as determined by the Supreme Court of the United States." 28 U.S.C. § 2254(d)(1); . . .

In *United States v. Rauscher*, 119 U.S. 407, 7 S. Ct. 234, 30 L. Ed. 425 (1886), and *Johnson v. Browne*, 205 U.S. 309, 27 S. Ct. 539, 51 L. Ed. 816 (1907), the Supreme Court set forth principles for interpreting extradition treaties and analyzed the effect of limitations on what offenses may be punished by the extraditing country. Benitez fails to establish that the state court's decision was an objectively unreasonable application of *Rauscher's and Browne's* holdings.

Rauscher established the doctrine of specialty, 119 U.S. at 412, which provides that an extradited defendant may not be prosecuted "for any offense other than that for which the surrendering country agreed to extradite." *United States v. Andonian*, 29 F.3d 1432, 1434–35 (9th Cir. 1994) (citations and quotations omitted). In *Rauscher*, the defendant was extradited from Great Britain for the crime of murder but was prosecuted for assault. 119 U.S. at 409–21. The Court held that he could "only be tried for one of the offenses described in [the extradition] treaty, and for the offense with which he is charged in the proceedings for his extradition." *Id.* at 430.

In *Browne*, a defendant who was convicted in the United States of conspiracy to defraud the government fled the country and was extradited from Canada under a treaty which did not cover conspiracy. 205 U.S. at 310–11. Because of the treaty's limitations, Canadian authorities surrendered the defendant for another offense but not for the conspiracy charge. *Id.* at 310–12. The Supreme Court, looking to the agreed-upon terms of extradition and to the relevant treaty language, refused to uphold a reinstated conviction on the conspiracy charge. *Id.*

Rauscher and *Browne* address limitations on charged offenses; here, the extradition decree attempts unilaterally to limit Benitez's sentence. No Supreme Court decision addresses this issue. The state court's decision was not contrary to clearly established federal law since to decide otherwise would have required an extension of the specialty doctrine. . . .

Agreed-upon sentencing limitations are generally enforceable. . . . Though the Supreme Court has not specifically addressed them, *Rauscher* states that "[i]t is unreasonable that the country of the asylum should be expected to deliver up such person to be dealt with by the demanding government without any limitation, implied or otherwise, upon its prosecution of the party." 119 U.S. at 419.

The U.S.-Venezuela extradition treaty expressly provides for extraditions conditioned on sentencing limitations, allowing the extraditing country to extract assurances that "the death penalty or imprisonment for life will not be inflicted." *See* Treaty of Extradition, 43 Stat. 1698, T.S. No. 675. Agreed-upon sentencing limitations should be enforced.

However, *Rauscher* and *Browne* interpret negotiated agreements to extradite, not unilaterally imposed conditions. Venezuela could have refused extradition of Benitez until the United States agreed to the sentencing limitation. Instead, Venezuela relinquished custody. Refusing to extend Supreme Court holdings governing limitations on charged offenses to unilaterally imposed sentencing conditions was not objectively unreasonable, and therefore [the Antiterrorism and Effective Death Penalty Act] requires us to leave the decision of the California court undisturbed. *See Lockyer,* 538 U.S. at 75. Benitez is not entitled to habeas relief.

The court did not address the further argument set forth in the U.S. *amicus* brief, that the February panel's determination that the United States must adhere to unilateral conditions on extradition is inconsistent with the treaty-making and foreign policy prerogatives of the executive branch. That argument is excerpted from the U.S. brief below.

* * * *

The panel's decision interferes with the ability of the Executive Branch to negotiate and enforce extradition treaties. The Supreme Court has made clear that the conduct of our foreign affairs is entrusted to the Executive:

> The President is the constitutional representative of the United States with regard to foreign nations. He manages our concerns with foreign nations and must necessarily be most competent to determine when, how, and upon what subjects negotiation may be urged with the greatest prospect of success.

United States v. Curtiss-Wright Export Corp., 299 U.S. 304, 319 (1936) (quoting Senate Comm. on Foreign Relations, 1816).

Likewise, the Supreme Court has held that the judiciary does not have a role in foreign affairs, explaining that

> the very nature of executive decisions as to foreign policy is political, not judicial. Such decisions are wholly confided by our Constitution to the political departments of the government, Executive and Legislative. They are delicate, complex, and involve large elements of prophecy. They are decisions of a kind for which the Judiciary has neither aptitude, facilities nor responsibility and which has long been held to belong in the domain of political power not subject to judicial intrusion or inquiry.

Chicago & S. Air Lines, Inc. v. Waterman S.S. Corp., 333 U.S. 103, 111(1948). *See also Alperin v. Vatican Bank*, 410 F.3d 532, 560 (9th Cir. 2005).

The panel, in entertaining "the expectations of the extraditing country" about potential sentences, entered this domain. The U.S.-Venezuela Extradition Treaty does not permit the parties to impose any sentencing conditions unilaterally. All that Venezuela could reliably expect with respect to Appellant's sentence is that he would not be sentenced to death. And the only proper channel for establishing those expectations is, through the Executive Branch.

Commitments made in extradition treaties are carefully negotiated and tailored to each individual treaty relationship. As with Article IV of the U.S.-Venezuela Treaty, which notes Venezuela's legal restrictions on death and life-imprisonment ("In view of the abolition of capital punishment and of imprisonment for life by Constitutional provision in Venezuela . . ."), the United States can agree to treaty provisions that provide for the possibility of sentencing assurances, sometimes to accommodate constitutional or other constraints faced by treaty partners. Similarly, the United States might agree in a particular case to limitations sought by a treaty partner even when not contemplated by our bilateral Treaty. But the United States does not always agree to or provide such assurances.

Decisions to give assurances are quintessential Executive Branch decisions, made after consideration of foreign policy factors such as the development of law enforcement cooperation, the impact on diplomatic relations, and reciprocity, as well as of other factors within the sole competence of the Executive, such as prosecutorial discretion and balancing the competing interests of justice. The Executive Branch must be able to make such decisions without fear of judicial imposition of limitations from foreign governments as to which no Executive Branch consideration has occurred (or, worse, which the Executive Branch has determined to reject). *Cf. Prasoprat v. Benov*, 421 F.3d 1009, 1016–17 (9th Cir. 2005), cert. denied, 126 S. Ct. 1335 (2006) (Executive Branch, not court, makes decision on extradition matters involving foreign policy concerns); *Patrickson v. Dole Food Co.*, 251 F.3d 795, 803–04 (9th Cir. 2001), affd in part, 538 U.S. 468 (2003) (court should not engage in foreign policy by evaluating foreign government's view of litigation).

This is more than an academic issue. The United States negotiates extradition treaties that by their terms limit prosecutable offenses (under the rule of specialty), but does not negotiate to permit surrendering nations unilateral control over sentences. Some countries with which the United States has ongoing extradition relationships may refer to expectations limiting sentences in their extradition orders. Absent a specific agreement, however, the United States does not consider itself bound by such unilateral expectations, and in some cases defendants receive sentences that exceed those purported expectations. Nevertheless, our treaty partners continue to honor our bilateral treaties and extradite fugitives to the United States, perhaps after weighing diplomatic or other considerations. The panel's decision threatens this delicate balance, and thereby improperly intrudes into the treaty-making and foreign relations powers reserved to the Executive in its conduct of extraditions with other nations.

*   *   *   *

(2) United States v. Cuevas

Also in July 2007, the U.S. Court of Appeals for the Second Circuit reached the identical conclusion in a similar case involving an extradition from the Dominican Republic. *United States v. Cuevas*, 496 F.3d 256 (2d. Cir.), cert. denied, *Cuevas v. United States*, 128 S. Ct. 680 (2007). The court rejected defendant's assertion that his sentence of 390 months imprisonment violated a decree from the Dominican Republic limiting any sentence to no more than 30 years because the Dominican Republic did not request or secure any assurances regarding the limitation of Cuevas's sentence before surrendering him to the United States. Excerpts follow from the Second Circuit decision (citations to earlier decisions in the case omitted).

———————

*   *   *   *

By Diplomatic Note DEI-99-1349, dated November 29, 1999, the Government of the Dominican Republic acknowledged receipt of the [August 1999 U.S.] extradition request. After some delay, on July 6, 2002, the Dominican Republic transferred custody over

Cuevas to the United States, and Cuevas was subsequently transported to New York. In late July, two weeks after Cuevas's return, the United States received a copy of a decree, signed by the President of the Dominican Republic, authorizing Cuevas's extradition. The decree, dated July 2, 2002, stated in pertinent part: "[I]t is understood that the above-named [defendant] [is] covered by the provisions of Article 4, Paragraph II of Law number 489, dated October 22, 1969, as amended by Law number 278-98 on July 29, 1998." Dom. Rep. Extradition Decree 495-02, July 2, 2002. The referenced provision of the Dominican Republic's Law No. 489 reads: "In extradition treaties signed by the Dominican State with other States, when the extradition of a national is granted, no penalty greater than the maximum established in this country, which at the moment this law enters into force is thirty years, shall be imposed." Dom. Rep. Law No. 489 on Extradition, art. 4, para. II (1969), as amended by Dom. Rep. Law No. 278-98 (1998).

*   *   *   *

. . . The 1909 extradition treaty between the United States and the Dominican Republic contains no limitations on sentencing. *See Banks*, 464 F.3d at 187, 191. Furthermore, the factual record developed on remand establishes that the United States never made any substantive assurances to the Dominican Republic that if extradited and convicted, Cuevas would not be sentenced to a term of more than 30 years' imprisonment. *Cf. Baez*, 349 F.3d at 92 (observing that prior to the extradition, the United States had sent a diplomatic note, "assuring Colombia that should Mr. Restrepo be convicted of the offenses for which extradition has been granted, the United States executive authority, with the agreement of the attorney for the accused, will not seek a penalty of life imprisonment at the sentencing proceedings in this case"); *Campbell*, 300 F.3d at 206 (recounting that the U.S. Department of State had "provided assurances to the Costa Rican government in a diplomatic note . . . stating, *inter alia*, that 'Campbell will not be sentenced to serve a term of imprisonment greater than 50 years'"). While the extradition decree indicates that "officials of the Dominican Republic believed, no doubt based on the domestic law of the Dominican Republic, that [Cuevas's] sentence would be so limited," critically, nothing in the decree "point[s] to any agreement or undertaking made by the United States to limit his sentence." *Banks*, 464 F.3d at 191–92. The Dominican Republic's unilateral belief that Cuevas would be covered by Law No. 489 is insufficient to bind the United States. *See id.* at 192.

*   *   *   *

Here, the Dominican Republic did not make adherence to Law No. 489 a mandatory condition of extradition; indeed, the issue of sentencing was never discussed at any point prior to the transfer of custody. . . .

. . . As the declarations from the Director of the Office of International Affairs and the Assistant Legal Advisor for the State Department establish, when a foreign nation seeks to impose a limitation on a sentence as a condition of granting the extradition of a defendant to the United States, it formally requests assurances from the United States by way of diplomatic note. The DOJ, in consultation with the State Department, determines whether the United States can and should provide the requested assurances, and relays the official position by diplomatic note. The foreign nation then considers the response of the United States in deciding whether to extradite the defendant.

. . . Because the United States never agreed that Cuevas's extradition would be subject to Law No. 489, the District Court was under no obligation to limit Cuevas's sentence to 30 years. . . .

*   *   *   *

d. U.S.–U.K. extradition treaty

The Extradition Treaty between the Government of the United Kingdom of Great Britain and Northern Ireland and the Government of the United States of America signed at Washington on March 31, 2003, entered into force on April 26, 2007. For background on the new treaty, *see Digest 2005* at 69–71, 73–74, and 75–77, and *Digest 2006* at 111–27.

In order to bring the treaty into force in 2007, the two countries exchanged diplomatic notes addressing the issue that the United Kingdom had completed the steps necessary under its law to implement the 2003 treaty in the United Kingdom, and in Jersey, but not in Guernsey or the Isle of Man. Excerpts follow from a note of April 26, 2007, from The Right Honorable the Baroness Scotland QC.

---

* * * *

In order to permit entry into force of the 2003 Treaty without further delay, I have the honour to propose that the United Kingdom and the United States proceed with an early exchange of instruments of ratification. Having regard however to the need to complete the necessary steps in both Guernsey and the Isle of Man, the Government of the United Kingdom is not yet able to apply the 2003 Treaty in respect of those Dependencies. I therefore have the honour to propose that the 2003 Treaty be suspended in its application to Guernsey and the Isle of Man until the Government of the United Kingdom should notify the Government of the United States of America by Diplomatic Note that the steps necessary for its implementation in respect of Guernsey and the Isle of Man have been completed. Notwithstanding any provision to the contrary in the 2003 Treaty, the Extradition Treaty between the Government of the United Kingdom of Great Britain and Northern Ireland and the Government of the United States of America signed at London on 8 June 1972 and the Supplementary Treaty signed at Washington on 25 June 1985, as amended by an Exchange of Notes signed at Washington on 19 and 20 August 1986, will continue to apply to Guernsey and the Isle of Man until such time as the 2003 Treaty is no long suspended with respect to those Dependencies.

If the foregoing proposals are acceptable to the Government of the United States of America, I have the honour to propose that this Note and Your Excellency's reply in that sense shall constitute an agreement between the two Governments concerning the 2003 Treaty.

U.S. Ambassador Robert Tuttle responded in a diplomatic note of the same date, repeating the text of the U.K. note and stating:

I am pleased to confirm that your proposals are acceptable to the Government of the United States of America and that your Note and this reply shall constitute an agreement between the two Governments concerning the 2003 Treaty and that this agreement shall enter into force today.

2. Mutual Legal Assistance and Related Issues: Sharing of Classified Information

On April 30, 2007, the United States and the European Union signed the Agreement between the European Union and the Government of the United States of America on the Security of Classified Information ("Agreement"). The United States has entered into similar agreements over the years with many of the member states of the European Union and is a party to a 1997 agreement on the security of information among the parties to the North Atlantic Treaty. Under the Agreement, each party will follow its own security regulations for classified information, on the basis that they provide no less protection than those of the other party, as well as develop specific agreed arrangements with the other's security authorities. Classified information will be disclosed or released in accordance with the principle of originator control. Each party will determine what information it is willing to share and to whom such information could be distributed by the other party. Any decision on disclosure or release of classified information to recipients other than the parties to the agreement will be made by the receiving party only following the consent of the providing party.

The technical security arrangement required to be established among the U.S. Department of State, the General Secretariat of the Council Security Office, and the European Commission Security Directorate, was approved by the European Council Security Committee on June 29, 2007, as notified to the United States in a diplomatic note to the U.S. Mission to the European Union dated July 2, 2007. At the end of the year the United States had not yet conveyed its formal approval of the security arrangement.

The Agreement, excerpted briefly below, is available at *www.state.gov/s/l/c8183.htm.*

Article 1
Scope

1. This Agreement shall apply to classified information provided or exchanged between the Parties.

2. Each Party shall protect classified information received from the other Party, in particular against unauthorized disclosure, in accordance with the terms set forth herein and in accordance with the Parties' respective laws and regulations.

Article 2
Definitions

* * * *

2. For the purpose of this Agreement "classified information" shall mean information and material subject to this Agreement (i) the unauthorised disclosure of which could cause varying degrees of damage or harm to the interests of the USG, or of the EU or one or more of its Member States; (ii) which requires protection against unauthorized disclosure in the security interests of the USG or the EU; and (iii) which bears a security classification assigned by the USG or the EU. The information may be in oral, visual, electronic, magnetic or documentary form, or in the form of material, including equipment or technology.

* * * *

Article 13
Technical security arrangement

1. In order to implement this Agreement, a technical security arrangement shall be established among the [the U.S. Department of State, the General Secretariat of the Council Security Office, and the European Commission Security Directorate] in order to lay down the standards for the reciprocal security protection of classified information provided or exchanged between the Parties under this Agreement.

* * * *

B. INTERNATIONAL CRIMES

1. Terrorism

a. Country reports on terrorism

On April 30, 2007, the Department of State released the 2006 Country Reports on Terrorism. The annual report is submitted to Congress in compliance with 22 U.S.C. § 2656f, which requires the Department to provide Congress a full and complete annual report on terrorism for those countries and groups meeting the criteria set forth in the legislation. The report is available at *www.state.gov/s/ct/rls/crt/2006*.

b. UN General Assembly

On October 11, 2007, John Sandage, Department of State Bureau of International Organizations, addressed the Sixth Committee of the UN General Assembly on U.S. views on the issue of counterterrorism. Mr. Sandage's statement, excerpted below, is available at *www.state.gov/s/l/c8183.htm*.

―――――――――

*   *   *   *

Global terrorism remains one of our greatest collective challenges. It affects the way we live our lives, raise our families, travel to other nations, carry out business. No geographic region is immune. No individual can feel totally safe from this modern day plague. The vast majority of the victims of terrorism have been innocent civilians. In 2006, the majority of victims were followers of the Islamic faith. . . .

The international community is working together to confront these extremists because they threaten the right of people everywhere to live in peaceful, just, secure neighborhoods and societies. Joined together, through the UN, we have collectively said "enough." The unanimous adoption of the Global Counterterrorism Strategy is a testament to that collective will. And it is one the

United States welcomes. The United States remains strongly committed to supporting the efforts both of the General Assembly, and the Security Council, toward this end.

*   *   *   *

The US strategy to defeat terrorists is structured at multiple levels: a global campaign to counter violent extremism and disrupt terrorist networks; a series of regional collaborative efforts to deny terrorists safe havens; numerous bilateral security and development assistance programs that are designed to build liberal institutions, support law enforcement and the rule of law, to address political and economic injustice and to develop military and security capacity.

But we, the global community, need to do better at galvanizing public opinion to reject violence as an unacceptable means of expressing *any* type of grievance. . . .

Toward this end, I am pleased to be able to share with you that the United States has pledged to the Counterterrorism Strategy Implementation Task Force a voluntary contribution of nearly one-half million dollars to support programs to address the issue of radicalization and extremism, and to protect vulnerable infrastructure. We call on those Member States in a position to do so to respond to the Task Force's call for contributions. . . .

. . . We must continue to work closely together in building and supporting effective multilateral mechanisms for combating terrorism, including the long-pending Comprehensive Convention on International Terrorism. We must ensure the full and effective implementation of the Strategy. And we must continue to cooperate with the Security Council's three counterterrorism committees, to ensure that our obligations under the Charter are fully implemented, and that those Member States having the will, but not the capacity to fulfill these obligations, get the help they need to do so.

c.   *Countries not cooperating fully with antiterrorism efforts*

On May 14, 2007, John D. Negroponte, Deputy Secretary of State, acting on delegated authority, determined and certified to Congress pursuant to § 40A of the Arms Export Control Act, 22 U.S.C. § 2781, and Executive Order 11958, as amended, that Cuba, Iran, North Korea, Syria, and Venezuela were not cooperating fully with U.S. antiterrorism efforts. 72 Fed. Reg. 28,544 (May 21, 2007).

d. International Convention Against the Taking of Hostages: Declaration by Iran

Upon its accession to the International Convention Against the Taking of Hostages (the "Convention") on November 20, 2006, the Government of Iran submitted an interpretive declaration setting forth its belief that "fighting terrorism should not affect the legitimate struggle of peoples under colonial domination and foreign occupation in the exercise of their right of self-determination . . . ." In response, the United States presented a diplomatic note to the United Nations, in its capacity as depositary for the Convention, stating:

> The Interpretive Declaration sets forth Iran's belief that "fighting terrorism should not affect the legitimate struggle of peoples under colonial domination and foreign occupation in the exercise of their right of self-determination . . . ." The United States views this generalized statement as having no effect on the Convention or on application of the Convention between the United States and Iran. Nothing in the Convention provides for or permits any justification, whether political, philosophical, ideological, racial, ethnic, religious, or otherwise for the commission of acts that states parties to the Convention are required to criminalize.

See http://untreaty.un.org/English/CNs/2007/1201_1300/ 1205E.pdf.

e. International Convention for the Suppression of Acts of Nuclear Terrorism

On July 12, 2007, President George W. Bush transmitted the International Convention for the Suppression of Acts of

Nuclear Terrorism, adopted by the UN General Assembly on April 13, 2005, to the Senate for advice and consent to ratification. S. Treaty Doc. No. 110-4 (2007). Both President Bush and Russian President Putin signed the convention on September 14, 2005, the first day it was opened for signature. *See also Digest 2005* at 106–8. The convention entered into force internationally on July 7, 2007.

In his letter transmitting the treaty the Senate, President Bush described its significance as excerpted below.

_____

*   *   *   *

The Convention imposes binding legal obligations upon States Parties either to submit for prosecution or to extradite any person within their jurisdiction who commits terrorist acts involving radioactive material or a nuclear device as set forth in Article 2 of the Convention, threatens or attempts to commit such an act, participates as an accomplice, organizes or directs others to commit such an offense, or in any other way contributes to the commission of such an offense by a group of persons acting with a common purpose, regardless of where the alleged act took place.

States Parties to the Convention will also be obligated to provide one another legal assistance in investigations or criminal or extradition proceedings brought in respect of the offenses set forth in Article 2, in conformity with any treaties or other arrangements that may exist between them or in accordance with their national law. The recommended legislation necessary to implement the Convention will be submitted to the Congress separately.

This Convention is important in the campaign against international terrorism. I recommend, therefore, that the Senate give early and favorable consideration to this Convention, subject to the understandings and reservation that are described in the accompanying State Department report.

Excerpts below from the State Department report, transmitted in S. Treaty Doc. No. 110-4, include one of the understandings and the reservation referred to by the President. In addition, the convention includes important exceptions to the applicability of the convention with respect to "armed conflict" and "activities undertaken by the military forces of a State in the exercise of their official duties, inasmuch as they are governed by other rules of international law," and uses the term "international humanitarian law." The report recommends understandings related to these terms consistent with the understandings proposed for the 2005 SUA and Fixed Platform Protocols and for the Amendment to the Convention on the Physical Protection of Nuclear Material; see Chapter 18.A.6. and A.9.

* * * *

Paragraph 1 of Article 2 describes two categories of principal offenses. First, any person commits an offense under the Convention if that person unlawfully and intentionally possesses radioactive material or makes or possesses a device, as defined in Article 1 above, with the intent either to cause death or serious bodily injury, or to cause substantial damage to property or to the environment. Second, any person commits an offense under the Convention if he or she unlawfully and intentionally uses radioactive material or a device or uses or damages a nuclear facility in a manner that releases or risks the release of radioactive material, with the intent either to cause death or serious bodily injury, or to cause substantial damage to property or to the environment, or to compel a natural or legal person, an international organization, or a State to do or refrain from doing an act.

The Convention also provides for a range of ancillary offenses. Paragraph 2 of Article 2 provides that any person also commits an offense if that person credibly threatens to commit an offense as set forth in Paragraph 1 or demands by credible threat radioactive material, a device, or nuclear facility. The inclusion of "threats" as an ancillary offense is new with this Convention, and is fully warranted by the grave nature of the harm threatened. The threat provision is formulated in a manner that is compatible with threat offenses in U.S. law. There are additional ancillary offenses that are present in the prior counterterrorism conventions. . . . These ancillary offenses will strengthen the ability of the international community to investigate, prosecute, and extradite those who conspire or otherwise contribute to the commission of offenses defined in the Convention.

There is no separate offense for dumping of radioactive waste, if done without the relevant criminal intent specified in Article 2(1) of the Convention. Although a few delegations tried to broaden the offense provisions to include dumping, the United States and other nuclear powers succeeded in resisting this expansion on the grounds that it was better addressed in environmental conventions and that such a provision would be outside the focus on the terrorist acts that form the basis of the Convention.

* * * *

Paragraph 2 of Article 4 contains two important exceptions from the scope of the Convention relating to activities of armed forces and military forces of a State. . . .

* * * *

Paragraph 3 of Article 4 clarifies that nothing in the prior provisions is intended to condone or to make lawful otherwise unlawful acts or to preclude otherwise lawful prosecution. Finally, in a provision that confirms the view of the United States, Paragraph 4 provides that the Convention does not address, nor can it be interpreted as addressing, in any way, the issue of the legality of the use or threat of use of nuclear weapons by States.

* * * *

Article 7 establishes the basis for cooperation between States in the prevention of offenses under the Convention. States Parties must take all practicable measures to prevent and counter preparations in their own territories for an offense under the Convention, including measures to prohibit in their territories illegal activities of persons, groups, and organizations that encourage, instigate, organize, knowingly finance, or knowingly provide technical assistance or information or engage in the perpetration of offenses.

Article 7 also adds significantly to prior counterterrorism conventions in the realm of information sharing. States Parties undertake to exchange accurate and verified information in accordance with their national law, in particular when information is available concerning the commission and preparation of offenses set forth under Article 2, unless doing so would violate national law or jeopardize the security of the concerned State or the physical protection of nuclear material. Paragraph 2 requires States Parties to take steps consistent with their national law to ensure the confidentiality of information received in confidence from another State Party or during an activity carried out to implement the Convention. Each State Party is to inform the Secretary-General of the United Nations of its competent authorities and liaison points responsible for sending and receiving the information referred to in Article 7(4). For the United States, these roles will be performed by the Operations Center of the Department of State.

*   *   *   *

Under the terms of Article 9, States Parties may enact a broad array of jurisdictional bases over the offenses enumerated in Article 2. Of significant interest and value to the United States, which has many government facilities outside of U.S. territory, is the Convention's recognition of jurisdiction over attacks against a State or government facility of that State abroad, including an embassy or other diplomatic or consular premises. This would give the United States internationally recognized jurisdiction based on this Convention to prosecute in U.S. courts the perpetrators and organizers of such attacks on all U.S. Government facilities abroad, as well as military installations. In addition to the foregoing jurisdictional bases, which correspond to those in the Terrorist Bombings Convention, is the provision in Article 9 allowing States Parties to establish jurisdiction over offenses committed in an attempt to compel a State to do or abstain from doing any act. This provision, which is also of significant interest and value to the United States, provides jurisdiction over offenses under this Convention where terrorists seek to coerce State action even where a national or facility of that State is not the target of the attack. Upon becoming a party to the Convention, a State must notify the United Nations Secretary-General of the jurisdiction it has established under its domestic law.

As in the Terrorist Bombings Convention and Terrorism Finance Convention, Article 10 includes provisions relating to alleged offenders arrested or detained for the purpose of extradition or prosecution.

Paragraph 1 of Article 10 requires States Parties to take necessary measures under their national law to investigate any information received that an offense has been committed or is being committed in the territory of a State Party or that the offender or alleged offender may be present in its territory. Paragraph 2 requires the State Party to ensure an alleged offender's presence for the purpose of prosecution or extradition. Paragraph 3 ensures that alleged offenders who are arrested or detained are able to communicate without delay with the appropriate representative of the State of which they are a national, or of a State otherwise entitled to protect them (e.g., a protecting power), or, if they are stateless, the State of habitual residence. The rights set forth in Paragraph 3 must be exercised in conformity with the laws and regulations of the State in the territory of which the offender or alleged offender is present, subject to the provision that the said laws and regulations must enable full effect to be given to the purposes for which the rights accorded under Paragraph 3 are intended. Upon ratification and entry into force, this Convention would supplement other treaties on the same subject, such as the Vienna Convention on Consular Rights or any applicable bilateral agreement on consular relations. These obligations are essentially coterminous except in the case of stateless persons, which the consular treaties do not address.

Article 10, like the Convention as a whole, as well as other similar counterterrorism conventions, is not intended to create judicially enforceable rights. To avoid any unnecessary disputes with our treaty partners, I recommend that an understanding on this point, with respect to both Articles 10 and 12, be included in the United States instrument of ratification. The suggested text of the understanding is set forth following the discussion of Article 12.

In a provision of crucial importance for the Convention and the United States, which is consistent with corresponding provisions in prior counterterrorism conventions, Paragraph 1 of Article 11 declares that a State Party that does not extradite an alleged offender found in its territory shall, "without exception whatsoever and whether or not the offense was committed in its territory," submit the case to its competent authorities for purposes of prosecution, through proceedings in accordance with the laws of that State. Those authorities are obligated to take their decision in the same manner as in the case of any other offense of a grave nature under the law of that State.

Consistent with prior counterterrorism conventions, Paragraph 2 of Article 11 declares that the obligation in Paragraph 1 to extradite or submit for prosecution can be discharged by the temporary transfer of nationals for trial in another country by those States Parties that cannot otherwise extradite their nationals, provided both the Requesting and Requested States agree. Any sentence imposed would be served in the surrendering State. This provision on temporary transfer of nationals for trial is a useful recognition of this practice by the international community in a binding multilateral legal instrument.

Consistent with prior counterterrorism conventions, Article 12 requires States Parties to guarantee to persons taken into custody for the offenses set forth in Article 2 fair treatment, including enjoyment of all rights and guarantees in conformity with the law of the State in the territory of which that person is present and applicable provisions of international law, including international human rights law. Like Article 10 above, this Article is not intended to create judicially enforceable rights. I therefore recommend that the following understanding with respect to Articles 10 and 12 be included in the United States instrument of ratification:

> The United States of America understands that Articles 10 and 12 impose no obligation on the United States to provide any individual remedy within its judicial system for any person who alleges a violation of those articles or any other terms of this Convention.

Consistent with prior counterterrorism conventions, paragraph 1 of Article 13 amends existing extradition treaties between States Parties to include the offenses defined in Article 2 as extraditable offenses and provides that States Parties shall undertake, in subsequent extradition treaties, to include the offenses set forth in Article 2 as extraditable offenses. Paragraph 2 allows States Parties that make extradition conditional on the existence of a treaty providing for extradition between the Parties to utilize the Convention to serve as an independent legal basis for extradition between States Parties without an independent extradition treaty. It is a longstanding United States policy to extradite fugitives only to States with which the United States has a bilateral extradition treaty. Thus, we do not expect that the Convention will serve as an independent legal basis for extradition from the United States.

*   *   *   *

Paragraph 1 of Article 23 provides that disputes between two or more States Parties concerning the interpretation or application of the Convention that cannot be settled through negotiation within a reasonable time shall be submitted at the request of one of them to arbitration, or, failing agreement on the organization of such arbitration, to the International Court of Justice. Paragraph 2 provides that a State may make a declaration excluding this dispute-resolution obligation at the time of signature, ratification, acceptance, approval, or accession. In October 1985, the United States withdrew its declaration under Article 36 of the Statute of the International Court of Justice accepting the compulsory jurisdiction of the Court. Consistent with that action, I recommend that the following reservation to Paragraph 1 of Article 23 be included in the United States instrument of ratification:

(a) Pursuant to Article 23(2) of the Convention, the United States of America declares that it does not consider itself bound by Article 23(1) of the Convention; and

(b) The United States of America reserves the right specifically to agree in a particular case to follow the arbitration procedure set forth in Article 23(1) of the Convention or any other procedure for arbitration.

This reservation would allow the United States to agree to adjudication by a Chamber of the Court in a particular case, if that were deemed desirable. The United States filed similar reservations with respect to the dispute settlement provisions in the Terrorist Bombings Convention and the Terrorism Financing Convention.

*   *   *   *

f. 2005 Protocols to the UN Convention for the Suppression of Unlawful Acts Against the Safety of Maritime Navigation and to its Protocol on Fixed Platforms

As discussed in Chapter 18.A.6., on October 1, 2007, President Bush transmitted to the Senate for advice and consent to ratification the Protocol of 2005 to the Convention for the Suppression of Unlawful Acts Against the Safety of Maritime Navigation ("2005 SUA Protocol") and the Protocol of 2005 to the Protocol for the Suppression of Unlawful Acts Against the Safety of Fixed Platforms Located on the Continental Shelf ("2005 Fixed Platforms Protocol"). S. Treaty Doc. No.110-8 (2007). As described in the President's letter:

> The Protocols are an important component in the international campaign to prevent and punish maritime terrorism and the proliferation of weapons of mass destruction and promote the aims of the Proliferation Security Initiative. They establish a legal basis for international cooperation in the investigation, prosecution, and extradition of those who commit or aid terrorist acts or trafficking in weapons of mass destruction aboard ships at sea or on fixed platforms.
>
> The Protocols establish the first international treaty framework for criminalizing certain terrorist acts, including using a ship or fixed platform in a terrorist activity, transporting weapons of mass destruction or their delivery systems and related materials, and transporting terrorist fugitives. The Protocols require Parties to criminalize these acts under their domestic laws, to cooperate to prevent and investigate suspected crimes under the Protocols, and to extradite or submit for prosecution persons accused of committing, attempting to commit, or aiding in the commission of such offenses. . . .

Excerpts follow concerning the 2005 SUA Protocol from the report of the Department of State transmitted with the President's letter. *See also* proposed understandings concerning definitions of "armed forces" and "international humanitarian law," and the effect of an exception for activities undertaken by military forces, Chapter 18.A.6., and discussion of nonproliferation provisions, Chapter 18.C.6.

---

*   *   *   *

Counterterrorism offenses

Article 3*bis*(1)(a) makes it an offense for a person to unlawfully and intentionally, with the purpose of intimidating a population, or compelling a government or an international organization to do or abstain from doing any act: (i) use against or on a ship or discharge from a ship any explosive, radioactive material or [biological, chemical and nuclear weapon and other nuclear explosive device ("BCN weapon")] in a manner that causes or is likely to cause death or serious injury or damage; (ii) discharge, from a ship, oil, liquefied natural gas, or other hazardous or noxious substance in such quantity or concentration that causes or is likely to cause death or serious injury or damage; (iii) use a ship in a manner that causes death or serious injury or damage; or (iv) threaten to commit any offense set forth in (i)–(iii).

*   *   *   *

Article 6 of the 2005 SUA Protocol makes conforming amendments to Article 6 of the Convention, which requires States Parties to establish jurisdiction over the offenses set forth under the Convention. Each State Party is now required to establish jurisdiction over offenses under Articles 3, 3*bis*, 3*ter*, and 3*quater*. Article 8(1) of the 2005 SUA Protocol makes a similar conforming amendment to Article 8, paragraph 1, of the Convention to permit the master of a ship to deliver to the authorities of any other State Party any person who the master has reasonable grounds to believe has committed an offense under Article 3, 3*bis*, 3*ter*, or 3*quater*. Both provisions simply update the Convention provisions to include the full range of offenses under the Convention as revised by the 2005 SUA Protocol.

Innocent parties

The 2005 SUA Protocol was drafted to ensure that innocent seafarers will not be subject to criminal prosecution under the

Convention simply for being on board a vessel that was engaged in or used for illegal purposes. This is the case even where the seafarer had mere knowledge of the criminal activity.

The offenses enumerated in Article 3*bis*(1)(b) (the transport provisions described above) apply by virtue of the definition of "transport" in Article 2 of the 2005 SUA Protocol (amending Article 1 of the Convention) to those persons who initiate, arrange, or exercise effective control, including decision-making authority, over the movement of a person or item. This definition would exclude from criminal liability seafarers and employees on shore, except in those rare cases where they are actively engaged in the criminal activity.

The individual offenses added by the 2005 SUA Protocol contain subjective elements that would exclude innocent carriers and seafarers from their reach. For example, under the provision that covers certain dual use items (Article 3*bis*(1)(b)(iv)), the transporter must have the intention that the dual use item will be used in the design, manufacture, or delivery of a BCN weapon. In most situations, a seafarer, for example, would not have the requisite general knowledge and intent, let alone the additional specific intent required under this provision. When containers are ordinarily sealed and loaded at port, a seafarer would not know what is in the containers. In order for a seafarer to be held criminally liable, a prosecuting State must prove, for example, that the seafarer (1) knew what the item was, (2) intentionally initiated, arranged, or exercised effective control, including decision-making authority, over the movement of the item by, for example, smuggling the item on board or placing the item in a container to be loaded on the ship, and (3) intended that the item would be used in the design, manufacture, or delivery of a BCN weapon.

*   *   *   *

g. Amendment to the Convention on the Physical Protection of Nuclear Material

On September 4, 2007, President Bush transmitted the Amendment to the Convention on the Physical Protection of Nuclear Material ("Amendment") to the Senate for advice and consent to ratification. S. Treaty Doc. No. 110-6 (2007). The Amendment was adopted at the International Atomic Energy Agency in Vienna on July 8, 2005, by a conference of States Parties to the Convention on the Physical Protection of Nuclear Material, adopted on October 26, 1979. As explained in the report of the Department of State, included in the treaty transmittal, since the time of the convention's adoption,

> the physical protection provisions of the Convention have proven to be too limited in scope, particularly in the face of mounting evidence of increased illicit trafficking in nuclear and other radiological materials in the early 1990s and greater terrorist interest in acquiring weapons-usable nuclear material following the September 11, 2001 terrorist attacks on the United States.

See Chapter 18.C.9.

h. U.S. actions against support for terrorists

(1) Litigation

(i) Humanitarian Law Project v. Mukasey

On December 10, 2007, the U.S. Court of Appeals for the Ninth Circuit issued an opinion addressing constitutional challenges to the statutory prohibition against the provision of "material support" to a designated foreign terrorist organization. *Humanitarian Law Project v. Mukasey*, 509 F.3d 1122 (9th Cir. 2007). For previous developments, *see Digest 2006* at 180–82, *Digest 2005* at 124–28, and *Digest 2004* at 125–26. In its 2007 decision, the court rejected plaintiffs' claims that the statute violated their due process rights and that the terms "scientific [and] technical knowledge" and "personnel" as used in the statute were unconstitutionally vague. The court found unconstitutional, however, the terms "training," "other specialized knowledge," and "service" as used in the statute and enjoined the United States from enforcing provisions relying on these terms. Excerpts from the court's decision explaining its analysis are set forth below (most footnotes omitted).

*   *   *   *

Section 302(a) of AEDPA, Pub. L. 104-132, 110 Stat. 1214 (1996), codified in 8 U.S.C. § 1189, authorizes the Secretary of State (the "Secretary") to designate a group as a "foreign terrorist organization." Section 303(a) makes it a crime for anyone to provide support to even the nonviolent activities of the designated organization. *See* 18 U.S.C. § 2339B(a). . . .

*   *   *   *

Plaintiffs are six organizations, a retired federal administrative law judge, and a surgeon. The Kurdistan Workers Party, a.k.a. Partiya Karkeran Kurdistan ("PKK"), and the Liberation Tigers of Tamil Eelam ("LTTE") engage in a wide variety of unlawful and lawful activities. Plaintiffs seek to provide support only to nonviolent and lawful activities of PKK and LTTE. This support would help Kurds living in Turkey and Tamils living in Tamil Eelam in the Northern and Eastern provinces of Sri Lanka to achieve self-determination.[1]

On October 8, 1997, the Secretary of State designated PKK, LTTE, and twenty-eight other foreign organizations as "foreign terrorist organizations." *See* 62 Fed. Reg. 52, 650, 52,650–51 (Oct. 8, 1997). To this day, both PKK and LTTE remain on the

---

[1]   Plaintiffs who support PKK want: (1) to train members of PKK on how to use humanitarian and international law to peacefully resolve disputes, (2) to engage in political advocacy on behalf of Kurds who live in Turkey, and (3) to teach PKK members how to petition various representative bodies such as the United Nations for relief.

Plaintiffs who support LTTE want: (1) to train members of LTTE to present claims for tsunami-related aid to mediators and international bodies, (2) to offer their legal expertise in negotiating peace agreements between the LTTE and the Sri Lankan government, and (3) to engage in political advocacy on behalf of Tamils who live in Sri Lanka.

designated foreign terrorist organization list. Plaintiffs, fearing that they would be criminally investigated, prosecuted, and convicted under section 2339B(a), have been withholding their support for the PKK and LTTE from the time they were designated as foreign terrorist organizations.

*   *   *   *

On December 17, 2004, . . . Congress passed the Intelligence Reform and Terrorism Prevention Act ("IRTPA") which amended AEDPA. As amended, AEDPA now provides in part:

> Whoever *knowingly* provides material support or resources to a foreign terrorist organization, or attempts or conspires to do so, shall be fined under this title or imprisoned not more than 15 years, or both, and, if the death of any person results, shall be imprisoned for any term of years or for life.

18 U.S.C. § 2339B(a)(1) (emphasis added).

The term "material support or resources" includes:

> any property, tangible or intangible, or *service*, including currency or monetary instruments or financial securities, financial services, lodging, *training, expert advice or assistance*, safehouses, false documentation or identification, communications equipment, facilities, weapons, lethal substances, explosives, *personnel* (1 or more individuals who may be or include oneself), and transportation, except medicine or religious materials.

18 U.S.C. § 2339A(b) (emphasis added).

In enacting IRTPA, Congress amended the definition of "material support or resources" to include an additional ban on providing "service." *See id.* Congress also defined for the first time the terms "training" and "expert advice or assistance," 18 U.S.C. § 2339A(b)(2)-(3), and clarified the prohibition against providing "personnel" to designated organizations, 18 U.S.C. § 2339B(h).

Post-IRTPA, "training" refers to "instruction or teaching designed to impart a specific skill, as opposed to general knowledge." 18 U.S.C. § 2339A(b)(2). "Expert advice or assistance" encompasses "advice or assistance derived from scientific, technical or other specialized knowledge." 18 U.S.C. § 2339A(b)(3). "Personnel" includes "1 or more individuals" who "work under th[e] terrorist organization's direction or control or [who] organize, manage, supervise, or otherwise direct the operation of that organization." 18 U.S.C. § 2339B(h). AEDPA, as amended by IRTPA, narrows the definition of "personnel" by providing that "[i]ndividuals who act *entirely independently* of the foreign terrorist organization to advance its goals or objectives shall not be considered to be working under the foreign terrorist organization's direction or control." *Id.* (emphasis added).

Further, IRTPA provides that AEDPA's prohibition on providing "material support or resources" to a designated foreign terrorist organization includes a mens rea requirement. To violate the statute, a person who provides "material support or resources" to a designated organization must *know* that (1) "the organization is a designated terrorist organization," (2) "the organization has engaged or engages in terrorist activity," or that (3) "the organization has engaged or engages in terrorism." 18 U.S.C. § 2339B(a)(1).

*   *   *   *

III. DISCUSSION
A. *Specific Intent*

*   *   *   *

Here, AEDPA section 2339B(a) already requires the government to prove that the donor defendant provided "material support or resources" to a designated foreign terrorist organization with *knowledge* that the donee organization is a designated foreign terrorist organization, or with *knowledge* that the organization is or has engaged in terrorist activities or terrorism. 18 U.S.C. § 2339B(a). As amended, AEDPA section 2339B(a) complies with the "conventional requirement for criminal conduct—awareness of some wrongdoing." *Staples*, 511 U.S. at 606–07. Thus, a person with such knowledge is put on notice that "providing material support or resources" to a designated foreign terrorist organization is unlawful. Accordingly, we hold that the amended version of section 2339B comports with the Fifth Amendment's requirement of "personal guilt."

*   *   *   *

B. *Vagueness*

* * * *

1. *"Training"*

* * * *

To survive a vagueness challenge, the statute must be sufficiently clear to put a person of ordinary intelligence on notice that his or her contemplated conduct is unlawful. . . . Because we find it highly unlikely that a person of ordinary intelligence would know whether, when teaching someone to petition international bodies for tsunami-related aid, one is imparting a "specific skill" or "general knowledge," we find the statute's proscription on providing "training" void for vagueness. *See HLP I*, 205 F.3d at 1138 (finding the term "training" impermissibly vague because "a plaintiff who wishes to instruct members of a designated group on how to petition the United Nations to give aid to their group could plausibly decide that such protected expression falls within the scope of the term 'training.'"); . . . .

Even if persons of ordinary intelligence could discern between the instruction that imparts a "specific skill," as opposed to one that imparts "general knowledge," we hold that the term "training" would remain impermissibly vague. As we previously noted in HLP I, limiting the definition of the term "training" to the "imparting of skills" does not cure unconstitutional vagueness because, so defined, the term "training" could still be read to encompass speech and advocacy protected by the First Amendment. *See HLP I*, 205 F.3d at 1138 (finding "training" void for vagueness because "it is easy to imagine protected expression that falls within the bounds of this term").

* * * *

2. *Expert Advice or Assistance*

IRTPA defines the term "expert advice or assistance" as imparting "scientific, technical, or other specialized knowledge." 18 U.S.C. § 2339A(b)(3).

* * * *

At oral argument, the government stated that filing an amicus brief in support of a foreign terrorist organization would violate AEDPA's prohibition against providing "expert advice or assistance." Because the "other specialized knowledge" portion of the ban on providing "expert advice or assistance" continues to cover constitutionally protected advocacy, we hold that it is void for vagueness. . . .

The portion of the "expert advice or assistance" definition that refers to "scientific" and "technical" knowledge is not vague. Unlike "other specialized knowledge," which covers every conceivable subject, the meaning of "technical" and "scientific" is reasonably understandable to a person of ordinary intelligence. . . .

3. "Service"

IRTPA amended the definition of "material support or resources" to add the prohibition on rendering "service" to a designated foreign terrorist organization. There is no statutory definition of the term "service."

*   *   *   *

. . . The term "service" presumably includes providing members of PKK and LTTE with "expert advice or assistance" on how to lobby or petition representative bodies such as the United Nations. "Service" would also include "training" members of PKK or LTTE on how to use humanitarian and international law to peacefully resolve ongoing disputes. Thus, we hold that the term "service" is impermissibly vague because "the statute defines 'service' to include 'training' or 'expert advice or assistance,'" and because "'it is easy to imagine protected expression that falls within the bounds' of the term 'service.'" 380 F. Supp. 2d at 1152.

4. "Personnel"

In *HLP I*, we concluded that "personnel" was impermissibly vague because the term could be interpreted to encompass expressive activity protected by the First Amendment. *HLP I*, 205 F.3d at 1137. We stated that, "[i]t is easy to see how someone could be unsure about what AEDPA prohibits with the use of the term 'personnel,' as it blurs the line between protected expression and unprotected conduct." *Id.* We observed that "[s]omeone who advocates the cause of the PKK could be seen as supplying them with personnel . . . . But advocacy is pure speech protected by the First Amendment." *Id.*

. . . Section 2339B(h) clarifies that section 2339B(a) criminalizes providing "personnel" to a foreign terrorist organization only where a person, alone or with others, "[work]s under that terrorist organization's direction or control or . . . organize[s], manage[s], supervise[s], or otherwise direct[s] the operation of that organization." Section 2339B(h) also states that the ban on "personnel" does not criminalize the conduct of "[i]ndividuals who act entirely independently of the foreign terrorist organization to advance its goals or objectives." *Id.*

As amended by IRTPA, AEDPA's prohibition on providing "personnel" is not vague because the ban no longer "blurs the line between protected expression and unprotected conduct." HLP I, 205 F.3d at 1137. Unlike the version of the statute before it was amended by IRTPA, the prohibition on "personnel" no longer criminalizes pure speech protected by the First Amendment. Section 2339B(h) clarifies that Plaintiffs advocating lawful causes of PKK and LTTE cannot be held liable for providing these organizations with "personnel" as long as they engage in such advocacy "entirely independently of th[ose] foreign terrorist organization[s]." 18 U.S.C. § 2339B(h).

Because IRTPA's definition of "personnel" provides fair notice of prohibited conduct to a person of ordinary intelligence and no longer punishes protected speech, we hold that the term "personnel" as defined in IRTPA is not vague.

C. Overbreadth

*   *   *   *

A statute is facially overbroad when its application to protected speech is "substantial, not only in an absolute sense, but also relative to the scope of the law's plainly legitimate applications." *Virginia v. Hicks*, 539 U.S. 113, 119–20, 123 S. Ct. 2191, 156 L. Ed. 2d 148 (2003) (internal quotation marks and citations omitted). The Supreme Court held in *Hicks* that "[r]arely, if ever, will an overbreadth challenge succeed against a law or regulation that is not specifically addressed to speech or to conduct necessarily associated with speech." *Id.* at 124. The Court reasoned that the "concern with chilling protected speech attenuates as the otherwise unprotected behavior that it forbids the State to sanction moves from pure speech toward conduct." *Id.* (internal quotation marks and citations omitted).

*   *   *   *

Section 2339B(a)'s ban on provision of "material support or resources" to designated foreign terrorist organizations undoubtably has many legitimate applications. For instance, the importance of curbing terrorism cannot be underestimated. Cutting off "material support or resources" from terrorist organizations deprives them of means with which to carry out acts of terrorism and potentially leads to their demise. Thus, section 2339B(a) can legitimately be applied to criminalize facilitation of terrorism in the form of providing foreign terrorist organizations with income, weapons, or expertise in constructing explosive devices. *See HLP I,* 205 F.3d at 1133.

*   *   *   *

Thus, because AEDPA section 2339B is not aimed at expressive conduct and because it does not cover a substantial amount of protected speech, we hold that the prohibition against providing "material support or resources" to a foreign terrorist organization is not facially overbroad.

*   *   *   *

(ii) Boim v. Holy Land Foundation for Relief and Development

On December 28, 2007, the U.S. Court of Appeals for the Seventh Circuit vacated partial summary judgments totaling $156 million entered against Holy Land Foundation ("HLF") and others for civil damages based on injury "by reason of an act of international terrorism," as provided by 18 U.S.C. § 2333(a), and remanded to the district court for further proceedings. *Boim v. Holy Land Foundation for Relief and Dev.,* 511 F.3d 707 (7th Cir. 2007). As explained by the court, the lawsuit ha[d] its origins in the murder of David Boim more than ten years ago . . . when he was gunned down while waiting for a bus in the West Bank outside Jerusalem. He was apparently shot at random by gunmen believed to be acting on behalf of the terrorist organization Hamas. . . . .

. . . [Boim's parents brought suit] against not only the two men believed to have shot David, but an array of individuals and organizations in the United States with alleged connections to Hamas. Broadly speaking, the Boims' theory as to the latter group of defendants was that in promoting, raising money for, and otherwise working on behalf of Hamas, these defendants had helped to fund, train, and arm the terrorists who had killed their son. In *Boim v. Quranic Literacy Inst.*, 291 F.3d 1000 (7th Cir. 2002) ("*Boim I*"), we sustained the viability of the Boims' complaint, concluding that liability under section 2333 attached not only to the persons who committed terrorist acts, but to all those individuals and organizations along the causal chain of terrorism.

. . . On remand, the Boims will have to demonstrate an adequate causal link between the death of David Boim and the actions of HLF, Salah, and AMS.

Among other things, the court concluded that the district court erred in holding HLF liable to the Boims by giving collateral estoppel effect to a 2003 decision of the D.C. Circuit finding that HLF knowingly and intentionally provided material support to Hamas by funding its terrorist activities. In the D.C. Circuit case, *Holy Land Found. for Relief & Dev. v. Ashcroft*, 333 F.3d 156 (D.C. Cir. 2003), HLF had challenged its designation as a specially designated terrorist ("SDT") and specially designated global terrorist ("SDGT"). The Seventh Circuit concluded that the holding in that case could not be applied in the Boims' litigation because the issue in the two cases was not the same:

The D.C. Circuit's finding that HLF funded Hamas's terrorist activities was not . . . a finding that HLF engaged in an act of international terrorism within the meaning of section 2333 or that it aided and abetted such an act. . . .

*   *   *   *

. . . In the absence of any discussion of knowledge and intent, the only plausible conclusion is that the D.C. Circuit did not believe that proof of HLF's knowledge and intent in funding Hamas was necessary; so far as it appears, funding *simpliciter* was enough in that court's view to overcome HLF's First Amendment challenge to the blocking order. This, of course, would not suffice to meet the standard for civil liability that we articulated in *Boim I*.

*   *   *   *

The court then examined at length the need to establish knowledge and intent as well as cause in fact to satisfy the requirements of the statute. Excerpts below summarize the court's conclusion in vacating the summary judgments and remanding to the district court.

---

*   *   *   *

Knowledge and intent may seem obvious, given the public face of a group like Hamas, but as we have explained, plaintiffs must nevertheless prove, for each defendant, knowledge and intent that their financial contributions (or other aid) to Hamas would support—directly or indirectly—Hamas's terrorist activities. . . . An assumption that such proof will be easy is no substitute for the real thing. As we emphasized in *Boim I*, aiding and abetting liability can be imposed, in ordinary tort cases just as in this one, only when the alleged aider or abettor knows what it is helping and intends to help bring about the tortious result. . . . As *Boim I* went on to explain, it is proof of knowledge and intent that serves to distinguish the culpable tortfeasor from a party that is merely associating with and expressing its support for Hamas—conduct which, however repugnant, is protected by the First Amendment. . . . However tempting it might be to skip past these requirements where a notorious organization like Hamas is concerned, we cannot do so without setting a precedent that will apply to an untold number of cases in the future.

With respect to cause in fact, we began with the statute, which requires that a plaintiff be "injured . . . by reason of an act of international terrorism." 18 U.S.C. § 2333(a). The only way to read this is as a requirement of proof of cause in fact. . . . Our basic point here has been that the statute does not demand an outright admission of responsibility for David Boim's murder (assuming that the terrorist act in question is that murder) or specific tracing of donations to Hamas or to the assassins (assuming that it is enough to show that the defendants aided and abetted a terrorist organization). Circumstantial evidence will also suffice. . . . So far, however, that step has been skipped. On remand, the plaintiffs must demonstrate how (or show that there are no material issues of fact regarding how) the monetary donations from the defendant organizations supported the activities that grew to include the acts of terrorism. One way to do this, we suggested, would be to show that donations went into a central pool of funds that provided weapons and training for Hamas agents. . . . Plaintiffs would need to show that Hinawi and Al-Sharif were affiliated with Hamas, but they would not otherwise have to show that funds from a particular defendant organization made their way to those two particular Hamas operatives. Another avenue would be to demonstrate that money from the defendant organizations went to Hamas for its charitable endeavors, and thereby freed up funds that Hamas could use for terrorist activities during the time period when David Boim was killed. . . . These examples do not exhaust the possibilities. A comparable showing will, of course, have to be made as to defendant Salah as well. . . . . .

The district court's error was to assume that only proximate causation needed to be proven. And it is indeed necessary in order to ensure that defendants are not held liable for remote risks of misuse of their funds. It is not, however a substitute for cause in fact. . . . Proof of cause in fact (which may in the end be straightforward) and proof that defendants knew and intended to further Hamas's terrorist agenda (which may be less so) will follow the tort model that we found in *Boim I* that Congress intended to adopt. . . . . It will also ensure that liability under this statute will be imposed only through procedures that respect the rule of law. Arguments that proof of knowledge, intent, or cause in fact are too onerous in the context of terrorism are properly addressed to Congress, not us; we could not relieve the plaintiffs of any of these requirements without defying the manifest intent of Congress to incorporate traditional tort principles into section 2333.

*   *   *   *

(2) Sanctions

(i) Amendment to Global Terrorism Sanctions Regulations

Effective January 30, 2007, the Department of the Treasury, Office of Foreign Assets Control ("OFAC") issued a final rule amending the Global Terrorism Sanctions Regulations "to define the term 'otherwise associated with' as used in 31 C.F.R. § 594.201 and to amend an explanatory note accompanying that section." 72 Fed. Reg. 4206 (Jan. 30, 2007). The Background section of the rule explained:

The new section 594.316 defines a person "otherwise associated with" persons whose property and interests in property are blocked pursuant to section 594.201(a)(1), (a)(2), (a)(3), or (a)(4)(i) to include one who: (1) Owns or controls such persons; or (2) attempts, or conspires with one or more persons, to provide financial, material, or technological support, or financial or other services, to such persons. . . . In promulgating this definition, OFAC does not mean to imply any limitation on the scope of section 594.201(a)(1), (a)(2), (a)(3), or (a)(4)(i). Finally, as in all programs OFAC administers, these and other designation criteria in the GTSR will be applied in a manner consistent with pertinent Federal law, including, where applicable, the First Amendment to the United States Constitution.

(ii) Imposition of sanctions

(A) Office of Foreign Assets Control

> During 2007 OFAC made a number of additional designa-
> tions of individuals and entities pursuant to Executive Order
> 13224. Excerpts from the first such designation in 2007
> describe the executive order in the context of designating two
> individuals (Farhad Amed Dockrat and Junaid Ismail Dockrat)
> and one entity (Sniper Africa). 72 Fed. Reg. 4560 (Jan. 31, 2007).

———————

* * * *

On September 23, 2001, the President issued Executive Order 13224 (the "Order") pursuant to the International Emergency Economic Powers Act, 50 U.S.C. 1701–1706, and the United Nations Participation Act of 1945, 22 U.S.C. 287c. In the Order, the President declared a national emergency to address grave acts of terrorism and threats of terrorism committed by foreign terrorists, including the September 11, 2001, terrorist attacks in New York, Pennsylvania, and at the Pentagon. The Order imposes economic sanctions on persons who have committed, pose a significant risk of committing, or support acts of terrorism. The President identified in the Annex to the Order, as amended by Executive Order 13268 of July 2, 2002, 13 individuals and 16 entities as subject to the economic sanctions. The Order was further amended by Executive Order 13284 of January 23, 2003, to reflect the creation of the Department of Homeland Security.

Section 1 of the Order blocks, with certain exceptions, all property and interests in property that are in or hereafter come within the United States or the possession or control of United States persons, of: (1) Foreign persons listed in the Annex to the Order; (2) foreign persons determined by the Secretary of State, in consultation with the Secretary of the Treasury, the Secretary of the Department of Homeland Security and the Attorney General, to have committed, or to pose a significant risk of committing, acts of terrorism that threaten the security of U.S. nationals or the national security, foreign policy, or economy of the United States;

(3) persons determined by the Secretary of the Treasury, in consultation with the Secretary of State, the Secretary of the Department of Homeland Security and the Attorney General, to be owned or controlled by, or to act for or on behalf of those persons listed in the Annex to the Order or those persons determined to be subject to subsection 1(b), 1(c), or 1(d)(i) of the Order; and (4) except as provided in section 5 of the Order and after such consultation, if any, with foreign authorities as the Secretary of State, in consultation with the Secretary of the Treasury, the Secretary of the Department of Homeland Security and the Attorney General, deems appropriate in the exercise of his discretion, persons determined by the Secretary of the Treasury, in consultation with the Secretary of State, the Secretary of the Department of Homeland Security and the Attorney General, to assist in, sponsor, or provide financial, material, or technological support for, or financial or other services to or in support of, such acts of terrorism or those persons listed in the Annex to the Order or determined to be subject to the Order or to be otherwise associated with those persons listed in the Annex to the Order or those persons determined to be subject to subsection 1(b), 1(c), or 1(d)(i) of the Order.

On January 26, 2007, the Secretary of the Treasury, in consultation with the Secretary of State, the Secretary of the Department of Homeland Security, the Attorney General, and other relevant agencies, designated, pursuant to one or more of the criteria set forth in subsections 1(b), 1(c) or 1(d) of the Order, two individuals and one entity whose property and interests in property are blocked pursuant to Executive Order 13224.

*   *   *   *

OFAC issued further designations under the same authority in 2007, as follows:

- 72 Fed. Reg. 8423 (Feb. 26, 2007) (one entity, Jihad Al-Bina).
- 72 Fed. Reg. 34,353 (June 21, 2007) (three individuals, Nur Al-din Al-Dibiski, 'Ali Sulayman Mas'ud 'Abd Al-Sayyid, and Sa'id Yusif Ali Abu Azizah).
- 72 Fed. Reg. 60,714 (Oct. 25, 2007) (three individuals, Fahd Muhammad 'Abd Al'Aziz Al-Khashiban, Abdul

Rahim Al-Talhi, and Muhammad 'Abdallah Salih Sughayr).

- 72 Fed. Reg. 60,715 (Oct. 25, 2007) (two individuals, Ahmad Al-Shami, and Qasim Aliq) and five entities (Al-Qard Al-Hassan Ass'n, Goodwill Charitable Org., Martyrs Foundation, Martyrs Foundation in Lebanon, and Palestinian Martyrs Foundation).
- 72 Fed. Reg. 60,716 (Oct. 25, 2007) (one individual, Ahmad Harb Al-Kurd).
- 72 Fed. Reg. 65,837 (Nov. 23, 2007) (two entities, Bank Saderat and Revolutionary Guard Corps (IRGC)- Qods Force); *see also* Chapter 18.C.4.c.).
- 72 Fed. Reg. 65,838 (Nov. 23, 2007) (one entity, Tamils Rehabilitation Org.).
- 72 Fed Reg. 71,485 (Dec. 17, 2007) (one individual, Rawzi Mutlaq Al-Rawi).
- 72 Fed. Reg. 71,486 (Dec.17, 2007) (one individual, Abdelmalek Droukdel).

In addition to these new designations, on November 14, 2007, OFAC determined that one person and twelve entities "no longer meet the criteria for designation under the Order and are appropriate for removal from the list of Specially Designated Nationals and Blocked Persons." The designations so removed were Ahmed Idris Nasreddin and the following entities: Akida Bank Private Limited; Akida Investment Co. Ltd.; Gulf Center S.R.L.; Miga-Malaysian Swiss, Gulf and African Chamber; Nasco Business Residence Center SAS di Nasreddin Ahmed Idris EC; Nasco Nasreddin Holding A.S.; Nascoservice S.R.L.; Nascotex S.A.; Nasreddin Company Nasco SAS di Ahmed Idris Nasreddin EC; Nasreddin Foundation; Nasreddin Group International Holding Ltd; and Nasreddin International Group Limited Holding.

(B) Secretary of State

As noted in (A) *supra*, Executive Order 13224 authorizes the Secretary of State to designate foreign persons that she determines, in consultation with the Secretary of the Treasury, the Secretary of the Department of Homeland Security, and the Attorney General, "to have committed, or to pose a significant risk of committing, acts of terrorism that threaten the security of U.S. nationals or the national security, foreign policy, or economy of the United States." On August 9, 2007, Secretary of State Condoleezza Rice issued Public Notice 5893, designating "the organization known as Fatah al-Islam" under that authority. 72 Fed. Reg. 45,859 (Aug. 15, 2007).

i.   U.S.–EU information access arrangements

(1) Access to airline passenger name record data

On June 28, 2007, the United States and the European Union concluded negotiations on a Passenger Name Record ("PNR") Agreement. The new agreement replaced an interim agreement concluded in 2006 between the United States and the EU that would have expired on July 31, 2007. See 72 Fed. Reg. 348 (Jan. 4, 2007); see also Digest 2006 at 168–72 and Digest 2004 at 108–16.

The Aviation and Transportation Security Act of 2001, Pub. L. No. 107-71, 115 Stat. 597, as implemented in 19 C.F.R. § 122.49d, requires that all carriers operating passenger flights to or from the United States provide U.S. Customs and Border Protection ("CBP"), Department of Homeland Security, with access to PNR data that is in its automated reservation/departure control system. The U.S.–EU agreement addresses concerns first raised by the European Union in 2002 that the PNR requirement conflicted with its Directive 95/46/EC ("European Data Protection Directive"). The European Data Protection Directive limits the ability of data controllers operating under community law to share personal data with public or private entities in non-EU countries without a demonstration that the receiving entity has adequate data protection standards. The resulting agreement ensures that PNR data may be used by the United States to combat terrorism and serious transnational crime while satisfying the

Europeans' concerns as to protection of the privacy of European citizens. The new agreement also provides air carriers legal certainty that they will not be in potential violation of European privacy law if they comply with U.S. law concerning PNR.

Under the 2007 agreement, the Department of Homeland Security ("DHS") will hold PNR data for seven years as an active file; thereafter, the data will be maintained as a "dormant" file for eight years with limited access. DHS will be able to use this information across its organization, not only within CBP, to prevent terrorism and other serious crimes. Furthermore, under the new PNR agreement, DHS is able to share PNR data with other USG agencies for uses consistent with the defined purposes. At the same time, the agreement ensures that PNR data is not used or shared for purposes other than those for which it is collected, primarily to combat terrorism and serious transnational crime and to protect the vital interests of the individual.

The 2007 agreement is reflected in the terms of the agreement itself and in an exchange of letters between Secretary of Homeland Security Michael Chertoff and Mr. Luis Amado, President of the Council of the European Union, dated July 23 and July 26, 2007, containing related assurances and confirming that, on that basis, the EU considers the level of protection of PNR data in the United States as adequate. In addition, a Declaration on Behalf of the European Union to the 2007 PNR Agreement stated in full:

> This Agreement, while not derogating from or amending legislation of the EU or its Member States, will, pending its entry into force, be implemented provisionally by Member States in good faith, in the framework of their existing national laws.

The 2007 agreement is an executive agreement for the United States but at the end of the year was pending ratification in many member states of the European Union. The full texts of the 2007 agreement and the two letters are available at *www.state.gov/s/l/c8183.htm*.

(2) Financial transaction information

> On October 23, 2007, OFAC published a June 28, 2007, U.S.–
> EU exchange of letters and a document entitled "Terrorist
> Finance Tracking Program Representations of the Department
> of the Treasury" related to financial transaction information
> used in tracking terrorists and their networks. 72 Fed. Reg.
> 60,054 (Oct. 23, 2007). Excerpts below from the Supplementary
> Information section of the Federal Register notice provide
> background on the exchange. The full texts of the letters and
> the U.S. representation are attached to the Federal Register
> notice.

---

*   *   *   *

The Treasury Department initiated the [Terrorist Finance Tracking Program ("TFTP")] shortly after the September 11, 2001 attacks as part of an effort to employ all available means to track terrorists and their networks. Under the TFTP, the Treasury Department's Office of Foreign Assets Control (OFAC) periodically issues administrative subpoenas for terrorist-related data to the U.S. operations center of the Society for Worldwide Interbank Financial Telecommunication (SWIFT), a Belgium-based cooperative that operates a worldwide messaging system used to transmit financial transaction information. These subpoenas require SWIFT to provide the Treasury Department with specified financial transaction records maintained by SWIFT's U.S. operations center in the ordinary course of its business.

After public media disclosure of the TFTP in June 2006, concerns were raised in the European Union (EU) about the TFTP and, in particular, the possibility that the Treasury Department might have access to EU-originating personal data through the SWIFT transaction records. Specifically, questions were raised on the TFTP's consistency with obligations under the Data Protection Directive (Directive 95/46/EC of the European Parliament and of the Council of 24 October 1995 on the protection of individuals with regard to the processing of personal data and on the free movement of such data), as well as Member State laws implementing that Directive.

Treasury Department officials subsequently engaged in a series of discussions with, among others, European Commission and Member State representatives on the operation of the TFTP and its conformity with EU data privacy laws. That dialogue culminated on June 28, 2007, in the "Terrorist Finance Tracking Program Representations of the United States Department of the Treasury" and a related exchange of letters between the Treasury Department and the EU. For the convenience of the user, each of the documents is being included as an appendix to this notice.

The Representations describe, among other things: (1) OFAC's legal authority to obtain and use the SWIFT data; (2) the controls and safeguards that govern the handling, use, and dissemination of the data; (3) the multiple complementary layers of independent oversight of the TFTP; and (4) the U.S. Government's commitment to ongoing counterterrorism cooperation with the EU.

The appended letter from the Treasury Department presents the Representations to the German Finance Minister, whose country then held the rotating EU Presidency, and to the Vice President of the European Commission responsible for Justice, Freedom and Security, whose duties encompass counterterrorism and privacy matters. The European Union's reply letter acknowledges that the Treasury Department has the authority to subpoena SWIFT data, and also states that once SWIFT and the financial institutions making use of its services have completed the necessary arrangements to respect EC law, in particular through the provision of information that personal data will be transferred to the United States and SWIFT's respecting the U.S. Department of Commerce's "Safe Harbor" principles, they will be in compliance with their respective legal responsibilities under European data protection law. In July 2007, SWIFT announced that it had improved the transparency of its contractual documentation relating to the processing of financial messaging data in the context of data protection requirements and that it had joined the Safe Harbor program, which establishes a framework developed with the European Commission on how U.S. organizations can provide "adequate protection" for personal data from Europe.

*   *   *   *

2. Narcotrafficking

a. Majors List certification process

(1) International Narcotics Strategy Report

On March 1, 2007, the Department of State released the 2007 International Narcotics Control Strategy Report ("INCSR"), an annual report submitted to Congress in accordance with § 489 of the Foreign Assistance Act of 1961, as amended, 22 U.S.C. § 2291h(a). The report describes the efforts of key countries to attack all aspects of the international drug trade in Calendar Year 2006. Volume I covers drug and chemical control activities and Volume II covers money laundering and financial crimes. The report is available at *www.state.gov/p/ inl/rls/nrcrpt/2007*. As explained in the introduction to the report:

> This year, pursuant to The Combat Methamphetamine Enforcement Act (CMEA) (The USA Patriot Improvement and Reauthorization Act 2005, Title VII, P.L. 109-177), amending sections 489 and 490 of the Foreign Assistance Act (22 USC 2291h and 2291) section 722, the INCSR has been expanded to include reporting on the five countries that export the largest amounts of methamphetamine precursor chemicals, as well as the five countries importing these chemicals and which have the highest rate of diversion of the chemicals for methamphetamine production. The expanded reporting also includes additional information on efforts to control methamphetamine precursor chemicals: pseudoephedrine, ephedrine, and phenypropanolamine, as well as an economic analysis that estimates legitimate demand for methamphetamine precursors, compared to actual or estimated imports. . . .

(2) Major drug transit or illicit drug producing countries

Presidential Determination 2007-33, Memorandum for the Secretary of State: Presidential Determination on Major Drug Transit or Major Illicit Drug Producing Countries for Fiscal Year 2007, was released September 14, 2007. 43 WEEKLY COMP. PRES. DOC. 1216 (Sept. 24, 2007). In this annual determination, the President named countries meeting the definition of a major drug transit or major illicit drug producing country and determined and identified those that "had failed demonstrably . . . to adhere to their obligations" in fighting narcotrafficking. Excerpts from the President's determination follow.

Pursuant to section 706(1) of the Foreign Relations Authorization Act, Fiscal Year 2003 (Public Law 107-228)(FRAA), I hereby identify the following countries as major drug transit or major illicit drug producing countries: Afghanistan, The Bahamas, Bolivia, Brazil, Burma, Colombia, Dominican Republic, Ecuador, Guatemala, Haiti, India, Jamaica, Laos, Mexico, Nigeria, Pakistan, Panama, Paraguay, Peru, and Venezuela.

A country's presence on the Majors List is not necessarily an adverse reflection of its government's counternarcotics efforts or level of cooperation with the United States. Consistent with the statutory definition of a major drug transit or drug producing country set forth in section 481(e)(2) and (5) of the Foreign Assistance Act of 1961, as amended (FAA), one of the reasons that major drug transit or illicit drug producing countries are placed on the list is the combination of geographical, commercial, and economic factors that allow drugs to transit or be produced despite the concerned government's most assiduous enforcement measures.

Pursuant to section 706(2)(A) of the FRAA, I hereby designate Burma and Venezuela as countries that have failed demonstrably during the previous 12 months to adhere to their obligations under international counternarcotics agreements and take the measures set forth in section 489(a)(1) of the FAA. Attached to this report are justifications for the determinations on Burma and Venezuela, as required by section 706(2)(B). I have also determined, in accordance with the provisions of section 706(3)(A) of the FRAA, that support for programs to aid Venezuela's democratic institutions is vital to the national interests of the United States.

*   *   *   *

(3) Methamphetamines

On February 28, 2007, President Bush determined that

> the top five exporting and importing countries of pseudo-ephedrine and ephedrine in 2005 (Belgium, China, Germany, India, Indonesia, Mexico, Singapore, South Africa, South Korea, Switzerland, Taiwan, and the United Kingdom) have cooperated fully with the United States or have taken adequate steps on their own to achieve full compliance with the goals and objectives established by the United Nations Convention Against Illicit Traffic in Narcotic Drugs and Psychotropic Substances.

Presidential Determination No. 2007-14, 72 Fed. Reg.10,881 (March 9, 2007).

As noted in the INCSR, (1) *supra*, this was the first identification and certification of countries as required by the Combat Methamphetamine Epidemic Act ("CMEA") (2006), Pub. L. No. 109-177. The Presidential Determination is also available, together with the Memorandum of Justification, excerpted below, at *www.state.gov/p/inl/rls/rpt/81222.htm.*

Section 489(a)(8)(A)(I) and (II) of the Foreign Assistance Act of 1961 (FAA) has been amended by Section 722 of the Combat Methamphetamine Epidemic Act of 2005 (CMEA)(Title VII, P.L. 109-177) to require that the annual International Narcotics Control Strategy Report (INSCR) include the identification of the five countries exporting the largest amount of pseudoephedrine, ephedrine, and phenylpropanolamine (including salts, optical isomers or salts of optical isomers, and also including any products or substances containing such chemicals) during calendar year 2006. Section 722 also requires the identification of the five countries importing the largest amounts of the chemicals noted above during calendar year 2006, with the highest rate of diversion of such chemicals for the illicit production of methamphetamine (either in that country or in another country). The statute requires that the identification be based on a comparison of legitimate demand for the chemicals as compared to the actual or estimated amount imported into the country.

Section 490(b) of the FAA has been amended by the CMEA and requires the President to certify that the top five exporting and importing countries have fully cooperated with the United States to prevent these substances from being used to produce methamphetamine or have taken adequate steps on their own to achieve full compliance with the 1988 United Nations Convention against Illicit Traffic in Narcotic Drugs and Psychotropic Substances. Absent a Presidential Determination, fifty percent of the foreign assistance allocated in FY 2007 for the designated countries must be withheld.

In complying with the Section 722 requirements, the Departments of State and Justice have determined that phenylpropanolomine is not a methamphetamine precursor chemical, although it can be used as an amphetamine precursor chemical. In 2000, the Food and Drug Administration issued warnings concerning significant health risks associated with phenylpropanolomine, and as a result, manufacturers voluntarily removed the chemical compound from [their] over-the-counter medicines. The largest U.S. producer ceased production, and today the chemicals are imported only for limited use by veterinarians. The Global Trade Atlas, the source relied upon in this report to determine the top five exporters and importers of ephedrine and pseudoephedrine, does not include data on the export or import of phenylpropanolomine, and no other source of reliable data has been identified. Therefore, it has not been included in this determination. Data on exports and imports of products containing pseudoephedrine and ephedrine are commercial and proprietary and are not available. Data on legitimate demand for these substances are not available at this time. Therefore, this listing of the top five importers does not necessarily demonstrate that these countries have the highest levels of diversion. A U.S. resolution adopted by the March 2006 United Nations Commission on Narcotic Drugs requested countries to provide voluntarily estimates of legitimate demand to the United Nations International Narcotics Control Board, and the estimates should be available for the 2008 determination.

The top five exporters and importers of pseudoephedrine and ephedrine have been identified using 2005 data from the commercially available Global Trade Atlas, which are the latest data available. The top five exporters of pseudoephedrine were Germany, India, China, Switzerland, and Taiwan. The top five exporters of ephedrine in 2005 were India, Germany, Singapore, China, and the United Kingdom. The top five importers of pseudoephedrine in 2005 were the United Kingdom, Mexico, South Africa, Switzerland, and Belgium. The top five importers of ephedrine in 2005 were Singapore, South Korea, Indonesia, South Africa, and the United Kingdom. For purposes of this determination, the United States has been excluded from these lists. Nevertheless, the United States was the largest importer of pseudoephedrine and ephedrine in 2005.

*   *   *   *

b. Interdiction assistance

During 2007 President Bush certified, with respect to Colombia (72 Fed. Reg. 50,035 (Aug. 30, 2007)), and Brazil (72 Fed. Reg. 61,035 (Oct. 26, 2007)), that

> (1) interdiction of aircraft reasonably suspected to be primarily engaged in illicit drug trafficking in that country's airspace is necessary because of the extraordinary threat posed by illicit drug trafficking to the national security of that country; and (2) that country has appropriate procedures in place to protect against innocent loss of life in the air and on the ground in connection with such interdiction, which shall at a minimum include effective means to identify and warn an aircraft before the use of force is directed against the aircraft.

These determinations were made pursuant to section 1012 of the National Defense Authorization Act for Fiscal Year 1995, as amended, 22 U.S.C. § 2291-4. Notwithstanding any other provision of law, during the respective 12 month period following each determination, it is not unlawful for authorized employees or agents of Colombia and Brazil (including members of the armed forces of that country) to interdict or attempt to interdict an aircraft in their country's territory or airspace if that aircraft is reasonably suspected to be primarily engaged in illicit drug trafficking. It is also not unlawful for authorized employees or agents of the United States (including members of the Armed Forces of the United States) to provide assistance for the interdiction actions of Colombia and Brazil during that time period.

3. Trafficking in Persons

a. *Annual reports*

On June 12, 2007, the Department of State released the Trafficking in Persons Report 2007 pursuant to § 119(b)(1) of the Trafficking Victims Protection Act of 2000, Div. A of Pub. L. No. 106-386, 114 Stat. 1464, as amended, 22 U.S.C. § 7107. The report covers the period April 2006 through March 2007. The introduction to the report includes comments on the definition of "severe forms of trafficking" as used in the act and the scope and nature of modern-day slavery as follows. The full text of the report is available at *www.state.gov/g/tip/rls/tiprpt/2007/*.

---

*   *   *   *

The TVPA defines "severe forms of trafficking," as:

    a.   Sex trafficking in which a commercial sex act is induced by force, fraud, or coercion, or in which the person induced to perform such an act has not attained 18 years of age; or

b.   The recruitment, harboring, transportation, provision, or obtaining of a person for labor or services, through the use of force, fraud, or coercion for the purpose of subjection to involuntary servitude, peonage, debt bondage, or slavery.

A victim need not be physically transported from one location to another in order for the crime to fall within these definitions.

*   *   *   *

The common denominator of trafficking scenarios is the use of force, fraud, or coercion to exploit a person for profit. A victim can be subjected to labor exploitation, sexual exploitation, or both. Labor exploitation includes slavery, forced labor, and debt bondage. Sexual exploitation typically includes abuse within the commercial sex industry. In other cases, victims are exploited in private homes by individuals who often demand sex as well as work. The use of force or coercion can be direct and violent or psychological.

*   *   *   *

b.   Presidential determination

Consistent with § 110(c) of the Trafficking Victims Protection Act, as amended, 22 U.S.C. § 7107 nt. (2000), the President annually makes one of four specified determinations with respect to "each foreign country whose government, according to [the annual report]—(A) does not comply with the minimum standards for the elimination of trafficking; and (B) is not making significant efforts to bring itself into compliance." The four determination options are set forth in § 110(d)(1)–(4).

On October 18, 2007, President Bush issued Presidential Determination No. 2008-4 with Respect to Foreign Governments' Efforts Regarding Trafficking in Persons in a memorandum for the Secretary of State. 72 Fed. Reg. 61,037 (Oct. 26, 2007). The Presidential Determination is also available, together with the Memorandum of Justification Consistent with the Trafficking Victims Protection Act of 2000, Regarding Determinations with Respect to "Tier 3" Countries," at *www. state.gov/g/tip/rls/prsrl/07/93704.htm.*

"Tier 3" countries are those countries "whose governments do not fully comply with the minimum standards and are not making significant efforts to do so." The memorandum of justification summarized the determinations made by the President and their effect, as excerpted below; the memorandum also included a separate discussion of each of the named countries.

---

*   *   *   *

. . . The President has determined to sanction Burma, Cuba, the Democratic People's Republic of Korea (DPRK), Iran, Syria, and Venezuela. The United States will not provide funding for participation by officials or employees of the governments of Cuba, the DPRK, or Iran in educational and cultural exchange programs until such government complies with the Act's minimum standards to combat trafficking or makes significant efforts to do so. The United States will not provide certain non-humanitarian, non-trade-related foreign assistance to the governments of Burma, Syria, or Venezuela until such government complies with the Act's minimum standards to combat trafficking or makes significant efforts to do so. Furthermore, the President determined, consistent with the Act's waiver authority, that provision of certain assistance to the governments of the DPRK, Iran, Syria, and Venezuela would promote the purposes of the Act or is otherwise in the national interest of the United States. The President also determined, consistent with the Act's waiver authority, that provision of all bilateral and multilateral assistance to Algeria, Bahrain, Malaysia, Oman, Qatar, Saudi Arabia, Sudan, and Uzbekistan that otherwise would have been cut off would promote the purposes of the Act or is otherwise in the national interest of the United States.

The determinations also indicate the Secretary of State's subsequent compliance determinations regarding Equatorial Guinea and Kuwait. It is significant that two of the sixteen Tier 3 countries took actions that averted the need for the President to make a determination regarding sanctions and waivers. Information highlighted in the Trafficking in Persons report and the possibility of sanctions, in conjunction with our diplomatic efforts, encouraged these countries' governments to take important measures against trafficking.

Section 110(d)(1)(B) of the Act interferes with the President's authority to direct foreign affairs. We, therefore, interpret it as precatory. Nonetheless, it is the policy of the United States that, consistent with the provisions of the Act, the U.S. Executive Director of each multilateral development bank, as defined in the Act, and of the International Monetary Fund will vote against, and use the Executive Director's best efforts to deny any loan or other utilization of the funds of the respective institution to the governments of Burma, Cuba, DPRK, Iran, Syria, and Venezuela (with specific exceptions for Venezuela) for Fiscal Year 2008, until such a government complies with the minimum standards or makes significant efforts to bring itself into compliance, as may be determined by the Secretary of State in a report to the Congress pursuant to section 110(b) of the Act.

*   *   *   *

4. Corruption

On December 7, 2007, U.S. Advisor Brian Young provided an explanation of the U.S. position in joining consensus on the resolution "Globalization and Interdependence: Preventing and combating corrupt practices and laundering of assets of illicit origin and returning such assets, in particular to the countries of origin, consistent with the United Nations Convention against Corruption" in the Second Committee of the General Assembly. The resolution was adopted without a vote by the General Assembly on December 19, 2007. U.N. Doc. A/RES/62/202.

The full text of Mr. Young's statement, explaining U.S. concern with language not consistent with the UN Convention

Against Corruption, is set forth below and available at *www. un.int/usa/press_releases/20071207_363.html.*

The United States is joining consensus on this resolution because we strongly support the goal of preventing and combating corruption. The UN Convention Against Corruption (UNCAC) is a vital tool in the fight against corruption and we support the elements of this resolution that highlight the importance of this Convention. We believe the fight against corruption is a shared problem and that we must work together to find common solutions.

However, we wish to express our disappointment with the title and certain portions of the text, which do not accurately reflect the principles and language of the UNCAC. Specifically, the title and portions of the resolution text repeatedly condemn the "transfer" of assets of illicit origin, and treat the "transfer" of such assets and the laundering of such assets as if they were separate crimes. However, UNCAC requires parties to criminalize the laundering of assets of illicit origin, not the act of transferring assets per se. The resolution text also implies that laundered proceeds of corruption must always be returned to the country of origin. While UNCAC seeks to facilitate and promote return of such proceeds, UNCAC clearly recognizes the principle that assets should be returned to "prior legitimate owners," which can include countries of origin.

UNCAC is the product of over two years of intense negotiations among experts from over 130 countries, and its Chapter V provides a groundbreaking and internationally recognized framework for international cooperation in asset recovery cases. UNCAC enjoys widespread support with 140 Signatories and 104 Parties. The States Parties to the Convention are actively engaged in implementing UNCAC's provisions through the Conference of States Parties and we do not wish to see these efforts or the principles of UNCAC undermined by repeated negotiation of a resolution, particularly one that undercuts UNCAC's framework for asset recovery cooperation, at future sessions of the UN General Assembly. We urge our fellow Member States to respect the primacy of the Conference of States Parties and to not introduce this resolution at the 63rd session of the General Assembly.

5. Money Laundering: Banco Delta Asia

In 2005 the Financial Crimes Enforcement Network ("FinCEN"), Department of the Treasury, found that "reasonable grounds exist for concluding that Banco Delta Asia SARL (Banco Delta Asia) is a financial institution of primary money laundering concern." 70 Fed. Reg. 55,214 (Sept. 20, 2005). At the same time, FinCEN issued a notice of proposed rulemaking to impose sanctions. 70 Fed. Reg. 55,217. *See Digest 2005* at 180–84 for excerpts providing information concerning the basis for the designation and proposed sanction.

On March 19, 2007, FinCEN issued a final rule imposing the fifth special measure against Banco Delta Asia, as provided in the Bank Secrecy Act, 31 U.S.C. § 5318A(b)(1)–(5). 72 Fed. Reg. 12,730 (March 19, 2007). The Federal Register notice stated:

> Available special measures include requiring: (1) Record-keeping and reporting of certain financial transactions; (2) collection of information relating to beneficial ownership; (3) collection of information relating to certain payable-through accounts; (4) collection of information relating to certain correspondent accounts; and (5) prohibition or conditions on the opening or maintaining of correspondent or payable-through accounts. 31 U.S.C. 5318A(b)(1)-(5). For a complete discussion of the range of possible countermeasures, see 68 FR 18917 (April 17, 2003) (proposing to impose special measures against Nauru).

The 2007 final rule explained FinCEN's decision to impose the fifth special measure on the basis of information available in 2005 and an examination of subsequent developments. As to jurisdictional developments, the review found that Macau had "begun to take important steps to address . . . systemic concerns." These included enactment of a new money laundering law and a new law on prevention and repression of terrorism in April 2006 and a set of implementing measures related to the new laws effective November 2006.

The rule concluded that "[w]hile these efforts are important and welcome signs of Macau's overall progress in strengthening its anti-money laundering and combating the financing of terrorism regime, full and comprehensive implementation of these measures in all the covered sectors will need to follow."

As to Banco Delta Asia, following the 2005 finding, "the Macau Monetary Authority appointed a three person 'administrative committee' that temporarily replaced the senior management of the bank to oversee the daily operations of the bank and address the concerns we raised." The final rule reviewed steps taken to address many of the money laundering concerns previously identified. FinCEN concluded, however, that "[d]espite these representations, we continue to have serious concerns regarding the bank's potential to be used, wittingly or unwittingly, for illicit purposes." The final rule noted continuing concerns related to the bank's dealings with "multiple North Korean-related individuals and entities that were engaged in illicit activities."

6. Torture

On July 5, 2007, the U.S. District Court for the Southern District of Florida denied a motion to dismiss an indictment under the federal torture statute, alleging that the statute was unconstitutional on its face and as applied. *United States v. Emmanuel*, 2007 U.S. Dist. LEXIS 48510 (S.D. Fla. 2007).

When the United States became a party to the Convention Against Torture ("CAT"), it enacted the torture statute, 18 U.S.C. §§ 2340 and 2340A, to implement certain obligations under the convention. This case, brought against Mr. Emmanuel, who is the son of Charles McArthur Taylor, the former president of Liberia, is the first indictment under the torture statute in the United States. Excerpts follow from the court's denial of Mr. Taylor's motion.

＊　＊　＊　＊

The Torture Act states that "[w]hoever outside the United States commits or attempts to commit torture shall be fined . . . or imprisoned not more than 20 years, or both, and if death results . . . shall be punished by death or imprisoned for any term of years or for life." Federal courts have jurisdiction if "the alleged offender is a national of the United States; or the alleged offender is present in the United States, irrespective of the nationality of the victim or alleged offender." 18 U.S.C. § 2340A(b). A person who conspires to commit an offense under the Act is subject to the same penalties prescribed for the offense under section 2340A(c).

Under the Torture Act, torture is defined in a slightly different manner from its definition in the Convention. Torture is defined in the Torture Act as "an act committed by a person acting under the color of law specifically intended to inflict severe physical or mental pain or suffering (other than pain or suffering incidental to lawful sanctions) upon another person within his custody or physical control." 18 U.S.C. § 2340(1). "Severe mental pain or suffering" is

> the prolonged mental harm caused by or resulting from—
> (A) the intentional infliction or threatened infliction of severe physical pain or suffering;
> (B) the administration or application, or threatened administration or application, of mind-altering substances or other procedures calculated to disrupt profoundly the senses or the personality;
> (C) the threat of imminent death; or
> (D) the threat that another person will imminently be subjected to death, severe physical pain or suffering, or the administration or application of mind-altering substances or other procedures calculated to disrupt profoundly the senses or personality.

*   *   *   *

. . . Because his father, Charles McArthur Taylor, was president of Liberia, Defendant allegedly had authority to command members of the Liberian Antiterrorist Unit and participated in activities of the Liberian security forces, including the Antiterrorist Unit, a Special Security Service, and the Liberian National Police. During 2002,

Liberia had non-violent groups and armed rebel groups opposed to the presidency of Defendant's father.

Count One of the Indictment charges Defendant with knowingly conspiring with others to commit torture by conspiring with others to commit acts, under the color of law, with the specific intent to inflict severe physical pain and suffering upon a person within their custody and control. The object of the conspiracy was to obtain information from the alleged victim about actual, perceived, or potential opponents of the Taylor presidency by, *inter alia*, committing torture, in violation of Title 18, United States Code, §§ 2340A and 2340(1). . . .

Count Two alleges that Defendant and others, while intending to inflict severe physical pain and suffering, committed and attempted to commit torture, while acting under color of law, by committing acts against the victim, including repeatedly burning the victim's flesh with a hot iron, forcing the victim at gunpoint to hold scalding water, burning other parts of the victim's flesh with scalding water, repeatedly shocking the victim's genitalia and other body parts with an electrical device, and rubbing salt into the victim's wounds, while the victim was within the Defendant's custody and physical control, in violation of 18 U.S.C. §§ 2340A and 2340(1), and 18 U.S.C. § 2.

* * * *

Defendant's Motion to Dismiss challenges the Indictment on several constitutional grounds. The "core problem with this case," according to Defendant, is that "the government seeks to oversee, through the open-ended terms of federal criminal law—the internal and wholly domestic actions of a foreign government." The essence of the challenge to the prosecution is the constitutional infirmity of 18 U.S.C. § 2340A, a law that has been in place for over a decade, and under which Defendant is the first person to be prosecuted.

* * * *

A. Congress' Power to Enact the Torture Act

* * * *

1. Necessary and Proper Clause and the Treaty Power
The undersigned concludes that Congress certainly had the authority to pass the Torture Act under the Necessary and Proper

Clause of Article I, as an adjunct to the Executive's authority under Article II to enter into treaties, with the advice and consent of the Senate. Under Article I, "[t]he Congress shall have Power . . . [t]o make all Laws which shall be necessary and proper for carrying into Execution the foregoing Powers, and all other Powers vested by this Constitution in the Government of the United States, or in any Department or Officer thereof." Const. art. I, § 8, cl. 18. Under Article II, the President "shall have Power, by and with the Advice and Consent of the Senate, to make Treaties, provided two thirds of the Senators concur . . . ." Const. art. II, § 2, cl. 2. Treaties made pursuant to the power contained in Article II, "can authorize Congress to deal with 'matters' with which otherwise 'Congress could not deal.'" *United States v. Lara,* 541 U.S. 193, 201, 124 S. Ct. 1628, 158 L. Ed. 2d 420 (2004) (quoting *Missouri v. Holland,* 252 U.S. 416, 433, 40 S. Ct. 382, 64 L. Ed. 641, 18 Ohio L. Rep. 61 (1920)); *see also United States v. Lue,* 134 F.3d 79, 82 (2d Cir. 1998) (noting that because "Congress's authority under the Necessary and Proper Clause extends beyond those powers specifically enumerated in Article I, section 8, . . . [, it] may enact laws necessary to effectuate the treaty power, enumerated in Article II . . . .") (quotations and citations omitted); *United States v. Ferreira,* 275 F.3d 1020, 1027 (11th Cir. 2001) (quoting *Lue,* 134 F.3d at 82).

A treaty is essentially a contract between two nations. *See Societe Nationale Industrielle Aerospatiale v. United States Dist. Court for S. Dist. of Iowa,* 482 U.S. 522, 533, 107 S. Ct. 2542, 96 L. Ed. 2d 461 (1987). To the extent treaties are self-executing, or if non self-executing, to the extent Congress implements them by legislation and conventions, treaties have the force and effect of legislative enactments, and are the equivalent of acts of Congress. *See* 16 Am. Jur. 2d *Constitutional Law* § 55. "Acts of Congress are the supreme law of the land only when made in pursuance of the Constitution, while treaties are declared to be so when made under the authority of the United States." *Holland,* 252 U.S. at 433.

The treaty in question, the Convention Against Torture, has as its goal to make more effective the struggle against torture and other cruel, inhuman or degrading treatment or punishment throughout the world. It requires that State Parties take effective legislative measures to prevent acts of torture and to make acts of torture offenses under their criminal laws. The Convention further requires that each State Party take measures as may be necessary to establish its jurisdiction over alleged offenders who are either nationals of the State or are present in its jurisdiction.

* * * *

Here, the definition of torture in the Torture Act admittedly does not "track the language of the Convention in all material respects." The statutory definition of torture does, however, parallel the definition found in the Convention, in that both texts define torture to include the intentional infliction of severe pain or suffering by a public official or person acting under color of law. The element missing from the statutory definition, that is, that the torture be inflicted for the purposes of obtaining a confession, for punishment, or for intimidation or coercion, does not take the Torture Act outside the authorization given Congress in the Necessary and Proper Clause. Indeed, the more expansive statutory definition, which captures more acts of torture than does the definition contained in the Convention, is consistent with the international community's near universal condemnation of torture and cruel, inhuman or degrading treatment, and is consistent with repeated calls for the international community to be more "effective [in] the struggle against torture." *Convention Preamble; see also Aldana v. Del Monte Fresh Produce, N.A., Inc.,* 416 F.3d 1242, 1247 (11th Cir. 2005) ("State-sponsored torture, unlike torture by private actors, likely violates international law. . . .") (citation omitted).

* * * *

2. Offences Clause

Alternatively, assuming Defendant was correct, and Congress' more expansive definition of torture took the Torture Act outside the realm of the Necessary and Proper Clause, one additional source of constitutional authority for the Torture Act may be found in Article I, § 8, cl.10 of the Constitution, that is the "offences against the Law of Nations" Clause. That clause gives Congress the power "[t]o define and punish Piracies and Felonies on the high Seas, and Offences against the Law of Nations." Because of the way the clause is written, and contrary to Defendant's proposed interpretation of it, Congress has the power to define and punish offenses against the law of nations, independent of any piracies or felonies that occur on the high seas.

* * * *

The prohibition against official torture has attained the status of a *jus cogens* norm, not merely the status of customary international law. *See id.* at 717 (collecting authorities). In reaching the not surprising conclusion that prohibition of official torture was a *jus cogens* norm, the Ninth Circuit explained:

> [W]e conclude that the right to be free from official torture is fundamental and universal, a right deserving of the highest status under international law, a norm of *jus cogens*. The crack of the whip, the clamp of the thumb screw, the crush of the iron maiden, and, in these more efficient modern times, the shock of the electric cattle prod are forms of torture that the international order will not tolerate. To subject a person to such horrors is to commit one of the most egregious violations of the personal security and dignity of a human being. That states engage in official torture cannot be doubted, but all states believe it is wrong, all that engage in torture deny it, and no state claims a sovereign right to torture its own citizens.

Id. at 717 (citations omitted).

It is beyond peradventure that torture and acts that constitute cruel, inhuman or degrading punishment, acts prohibited by *jus cogens,* are similarly abhorred by the law of nations. *See, e.g., Sosa v. Alvarez-Machain,* 542 U.S. 692, 732, 124 S. Ct. 2739, 159 L. Ed. 2d 718 (2004) ("'[F]or purposes of civil liability, the torturer has become—like the pirate and slave trader before him—*hostis humani generis,* an enemy of all mankind.'") (quoting *Filartiga v. Pena-Irala,* 630 F.2d 876, 890 (2d Cir. 1980)). Certainly the numerous international treaties and agreements, and several domestic statutes that contain varying proscriptions against torture, addressing both civil and criminal reparation, demonstrate the law of nations' repudiation of torture.

Over a century ago, the Supreme Court stated that "if the thing made punishable is one which the United States are required by their international obligations to use due diligence to prevent, it is an offense against the law of nations." *United States v. Arjona,* 120 U.S. 479, 488, 7 S. Ct. 628, 30 L. Ed. 728 (1887). In the present international community, it cannot be said that the Torture Act, legislation that criminalizes acts of torture by U.S. nationals or persons present in the United States, committed outside the United States, does not address an act made punishable by the Government's international obligations under the Convention, and which the Government is required to use due diligence to prevent. Thus, the Torture Act also finds constitutional protection as a law enacted by Congress to punish offences against the law of nations.

B. Congress' Authority to Apply Criminal Laws Extraterritorially

* * * *

1. Extraterritorial Reach of the Torture Act (Counts I and II)

As to Defendant's first argument on the issue of the constitutionality of the extraterritorial reach of the Torture Act, the Indictment alleges that Defendant was born in the United States, and more recently arrived at Miami International Airport. Defendant believes that the Government is of the opinion that he was not a United States citizen when he allegedly committed torture on July 24, 2002, because by that time, Defendant had committed acts that had caused him to lose his citizenship. *See* 8 U.S.C. § 1481(a) (listing acts that result in the loss of U.S. citizenship). Whether or not Defendant is presently a United States citizen, the Indictment alleges he was born here, and *de jure,* it appears he is a citizen. *See* U.S. Const. amend. XIV, § 1 ("All persons born or naturalized in the United States and subject to the jurisdiction thereof, are citizens of the United States . . . ."). And, "[i]t is undisputed that Congress has the power to regulate the extraterritorial acts of U.S. citizens." *Nieman,* 178 F.3d at 1129; *see also United States v. Harvey,* 2 F. 3d 1318, 1329 (3d Cir. 1993) ("No tenet of international law prohibits Congress from punishing the wrongful conduct of citizens, even if some of that conduct occurs abroad.") (citations omitted).

As to Defendant's second argument, that the Torture Act is presumed not to reach conduct that occurred extraterritorially, the argument finds no support from the plain words used in the statute, the starting and ending point here for any inquiry into its extraterritorial reach. . . .

Here, the Court need not search far for Congress' intent to apply the Torture Act extraterritorially. The plain words of the statute, section 2340A(a), state "[w]hoever *outside the United States* commits or attempts to commit torture shall be fined under this title or imprisoned not more than 20 years, or both, ..." (emphasis added). Congressional intent is abundantly clear.

. . . Furthermore, because the substantive provision targets extraterritorial conduct, the conspiracy provision, section 2340A(c) reaches that conduct as well. *See United States v. Layton,* 855 F.2d 1388, 1395 (9th Cir. 1988), *overruled on other grounds, Guam v. Ignacio,* 10 F.3d 608, 612 n.2 (9th Cir. 1993).

*   *   *   *

C. INTERNATIONAL AND HYBRID TRIBUNALS

1. International Criminal Court

> On November 26, 2007, Ambassador Alejandro D. Wolff, U.S. Deputy Permanent Representative to the United Nations, addressed the General Assembly on the draft resolution on the Report of the International Criminal Court. The resolution was adopted by the General Assembly without vote on the same date. U.N. Doc. A/RES/62/12.
>
> Excerpts follow from Ambassador Wolff's explanation of the U.S. position, available in full at *www.un.int/usa/press_releases/20071126_333.html.*

The concerns of the United States about the Rome Statute and the International Criminal Court are well known. They include the

ICC's claimed authority to assert jurisdiction over nationals of states not parties to the Rome Statute, including U.S. nationals, and the lack of adequate oversight of the ICC's Prosecutor, who may initiate cases without first seeking approval of the Security Council. Accordingly, the United States disassociates itself from consensus on this resolution.

In spite of these concerns, the United States made genuine efforts to work with the resolution's sponsors to find common ground. Over the past three years, we have stated clearly, consistently, and repeatedly that we respect the rights of other states to become parties to the Rome Statute, and we have asked in return that other states respect our decision and right not to become a party. Our efforts to find common ground reflect our belief that while parties and non-parties to the Rome Statute have different views about the ICC, they should nonetheless be able to work together in a spirit of mutual respect and cooperation to advance their common interests in promoting accountability for genocide, war crimes, and crimes against humanity.

We are disappointed and surprised to find again this year that the sponsors of this resolution do not appear prepared to move forward in this spirit.

Again this year, the sponsors have declined to include language in the resolution that expresses respect for, or even recognition of, the decisions of some states not to become parties to the Rome Statute. The sponsors of the resolution apparently view such a basic expression of respect as inconsistent with their aspiration of universal membership for the ICC, as if it is, in fact, somehow illegitimate for a state to choose not to become party to the Rome Statute. By their actions, they have made clear that the pragmatic modus vivendi that we have been seeking to promote is simply not working.

As a historical matter, we find some irony in this current emphasis on universality. During the Rome Conference the United States worked tirelessly to convince delegations of the wisdom of an approach to the ICC that would have permitted more states to join the Court. This appeal was rejected in favor of a narrower approach embraced by a smaller group of like-minded states.

As a practical matter, we find this position to be counterproductive. The ICC is unlikely ever to attain universal membership. Yet the same ICC supporters who refuse to express respect for the decisions of non-parties unabashedly seek assistance for the ICC from non-parties, and seek support of non-parties for assistance to the ICC by the United Nations and other international organizations. They seem to think that the relationship with non-parties can be a one-way proposition, in which ICC parties only take and give nothing in return.

*   *   *   *

. . . [W]e are concerned by the suggestion that, as a matter of general principle, it is the responsibility of the United Nations to facilitate the work of the ICC. In this regard, we note the claim of the President of the ICC that the so-called "enforcement pillar" of the Rome Statute, which includes the arrest and surrender of suspects and the protection of victims and witnesses, "has been reserved to States and, by extension, international organizations." This seems to us to misperceive the relationship between the ICC and the United Nations.

It is, of course, true that in some cases the work of the ICC and the work of the United Nations may be complementary. We note in this regard the decision of the Security Council to refer to the ICC the situation in Darfur. But this will not necessarily be true in every case. It is for the Security Council to decide whether there are circumstances in which assisting the ICC in enforcing its decisions will advance the Council's efforts to address threats to international peace and security. In such cases, the relevant question is whether assisting the ICC will advance the Security Council's mandate and interests, not whether such assistance will advance the ICC's mandate and interests. Particularly where assistance sought by the ICC may involve difficult and dangerous tasks that ICC states parties are unwilling or unable to carry out on their own, there will be reasons to question whether the Council should agree that the United Nations should shoulder such burdens.

*   *   *   *

We regret that this resolution has become a source of divisiveness rather than an opportunity to build bridges between parties and non-parties to the ICC. We remain sincere in our desire to develop a cooperative approach to promoting international criminal justice, and in our hope that ICC supporters will join us in such efforts.

> On December 5, 2007, the U.S. Mission to the United Nations released a statement by U.S. Advisor Jeffrey DeLaurentis on the report of the ICC prosecutor Mr. Luis Moreno-Ocampo on Sudan. Mr. DeLaurentis' statement is set forth below and available at *www.un.int/usa/press_releases/20071205_353. html.*

The concerns of the United States about the Rome Statute and the International Criminal Court are well known and have not changed. In spite of these concerns, we appreciate the report of the Prosecutor of the ICC with respect to his work pursuant to UNSCR 1593.

The United States has consistently supported bringing to justice those responsible for crimes, human rights violations and atrocities in Darfur. The violence in Darfur must end, and those who have committed atrocities in Darfur must be brought to account.

We share the Prosecutor's assessment that the ongoing situation in Darfur is alarming, and that justice for crimes against the people of Darfur is needed to enhance security and send a warning to individuals who might resort to criminality as a way of achieving their aims.

The United States is particularly troubled by the Prosecutor's report that the Government of Sudan is still not cooperating and has taken no steps to arrest and surrender the two individuals that are subject to ICC arrest warrants: current Minister of State for Humanitarian Affairs Ahmad Muhammad Harun and the Janjaweed leader known as Ali Kushayb. We call on the Sudanese Government to cooperate fully with the ICC as required by resolution 1593.

As we noted following the Prosecutor's last briefing to the Council on Darfur, the United States has imposed targeted economic sanctions against certain individuals responsible for the violence, a transport company that has moved weapons to the janjaweed militia and government forces, as well as against companies owned or controlled by the Government of Sudan.

We also share the Prosecutor's concern at the increasing number of attacks not only on displaced persons and other innocent civilians, but also on personnel of the African Union, the United

Nations and international aid workers. Violence and criminality against those who came to help the suffering people of Darfur are intolerable, and impunity for such acts must end.

The United States continues to be deeply committed to peace, stability and the provision of humanitarian aid for the people of Sudan. . . .

The United States believes strongly in the need for accountability for acts of genocide, war crimes, and crimes against humanity committed in Darfur. We look forward to continuing to work with other members of the Council on constructive steps to achieve this important objective.

2. International Criminal Tribunals for the Former Yugoslavia and for Rwanda

a. *Statement to Security Council*

> On December 10, 2007, Carolyn Willson, U.S. Legal Advisor to the U.S. Mission to the United Nations, addressed the Security Council on the International Criminal Tribunals for the Former Yugoslavia ("ICTY") and Rwanda ("ICTR"). Ms. Willson's remarks, excerpted below, are available in full at *www.un.int/usa/press_releases/20071210_365.html*.

* * * *

The work of the Tribunals in countering impunity will not be complete . . . without the resolution of the fate of the remaining fugitives and the consolidation of each Tribunal, a legacy.

Nearly twenty fugitives from the ICTY and the ICTR remain at-large. The United States calls on all States to fulfill their legal obligations to cooperate fully with the Tribunals.

* * * *

For the ICTY, Serbia, in particular, must take further steps to fulfill its obligations, especially through the apprehension and transfer of all fugitives who may be on Serbian territory, including Ratko Mladic and Radovan Karadzic. We welcome the improved cooperation of Bosnia and Herzegovina's federal and entity authorities with the ICTY. We are also encouraged by ongoing efforts of the governments of the Western Balkans to share information and evidence to further domestic prosecutions of war crimes cases. We call on these countries to enhance their cooperation in the future. As Prosecutor Del Ponte reports, regional cooperation remains crucial in apprehending and bringing to justice the remaining fugitives.

Concrete action is also needed from The Democratic Republic of the Congo and Kenya to apprehend and transfer all ICTR fugitives within their borders. Evidence continues to mount that top fugitive and alleged genocide financier, Felicien Kabuga, remains in Kenya. As Security Council pressure mounts for the ICTR's successful completion, Kenya must fully cooperate with the ICTR in apprehending Kabuga.

The United States welcomes the November 9 Agreement between the Congolese and Rwandan governments for dismantling the ex-FAR/Interahamwe forces still active in the eastern DRC. We have every confidence that any ICTR fugitive captured during this campaign will be turned over for prosecution.

Mladic, Karadzic, Kabuga, and others are charged with horrific crimes and it is unthinkable that they would escape international justice. They must be immediately captured and prosecuted.

The United States commends the ongoing work of the Tribunals to ensure a lasting positive legacy. Their promotion of domestic capacity within the countries of the former Yugoslavia and Rwanda is central to this legacy. With four ICTR cases currently pending possible transfer to Rwanda, it is imperative that Rwanda's work to improve its judicial system be supported. An enduring legacy also requires that each Tribunal's residual issues be addressed meticulously and pragmatically. The United States will work diligently to ensure these efforts are successful.

*   *   *   *

b. ICTR: Scope of testimony

On July 16, 2007, the Appeals Chamber for the International Criminal Tribunal for Rwanda and the International Criminal

Tribunal for Yugoslavia released its Decision on Interlocutory Appeal Relating to the Testimony of Former United States Ambassador Robert Flaten granting requested conditions. *Prosecutor v. Bizimungu et al.*, Case No. ICTR-99-50-T. On behalf of the United States, on January 20, 2007, Casimir Bizimungu filed a motion requesting that Rule 70 of the Rules of Procedure and Evidence of the Tribunal apply to the testimony of Robert Flaten, U.S. Ambassador to Rwanda between 1990 and 1993, and that the Trial Chamber grant four additional, related conditions for his testimony that would help to protect U.S. information. Specifically the motion requested that the Trial Chamber provide that the following conditions would apply to Ambassador Flaten's testimony:

> (a) Two representatives of the U.S. Government may be present in court during the Witness's testimony for the purpose of monitoring the examination of the Witness and to address the Trial Chamber (should) they object to any question put to the Witness;
> (b) The scope of direct examination shall be limited to that authorised by the U.S. Government and cross-examination of the Witness shall be confined to the scope of direct examination;
> (c) In order to protect the security interests of the U.S. Government, inquiry into matters affecting the credibility of the Witness will be permitted pursuant to Rule 90, provided that the answers are not deemed liable to reveal confidential information provided under Rule 70;
> (d) The discretion of the Trial Chamber to question a witness in order to ascertain the truth under Rule 90 and to permit enquiry into additional matters pursuant to Rule 90 shall be conducted in conformity with Rule 70.

The Appeals Chamber's decision explained:

> . . . [O]n 24 January 2007, the Trial Chamber heard the arguments of the parties on the issue in closed session. Ruling on the Appellant's motion, the Trial Chamber ordered

that Rule 70 apply *mutatis mutandis* to Ambassador Flaten's testimony and granted conditions (a), (c) and (d).[6] It denied condition (b) ("Condition B") on the ground that, "without having received any indication as to the scope of the examination of the topics that have been authorised by the US government, it was not comfortable with granting 'Condition B' at that time."[fn. omitted] The Trial Chamber explained in subsequent decisions that its reasons for denying Condition B were "(i) that it must retain the authority to resolve any disputes as to the proper scope of questioning that may arise during the Witness's testimony, and (ii) that without having received any indication of the scope of the testimony authorized by the U.S. Government, the Chamber could not grant the condition." [fn. omitted]

Following several offers of additional information concerning the scope of Ambassador Flaten's testimony, on April 26, 2007, the Trial Chamber denied the motion "on the basis that while the new information did clarify the subject matter of Ambassador Flaten's testimony, the Appellant did not address the Trial Chamber's concerns about retaining authority over the proceedings. . . . The Trial Chamber reiterated that the concerns of the U.S. Government had been adequately addressed by its prior rulings and recalled that it had granted additional protections." ("Impugned Decision")

On July 16, 2007, the Appeals Chamber ordered the Trial Chamber to grant Condition B. *Prosecutor v. Bizimungu et al.*, Case No. ICTR-99-50-AR73.6 (July 16, 2007). Excerpts from

---

[6] T. 24 January 2007, p. 47 (closed session). *See also* T. 24 January 2007, p. 45 (closed session), recalling the Trial Chamber's Decision on Casimir Bizimungu's Very Urgent Motion for an Order Applying Rule 70 to Specific Information to be Provided to the Defence by the United States Government, 11 December 2006, in which the Trial Chamber stated that "although the ICTR Rule 70 is limited to applications by the Prosecutor, broadening the ambit of that Rule to include applications by the Defence would serve to foster equality of arms between the parties".

the decision follow. The full text is available at *www.state. gov/s/l/c8183.htm.*

---

* * * *

17. The Appeals Chamber recalls that Rule 70 has been incorporated in the Rules to encourage States to fulfill their cooperation obligations under Article 28 of the Statute of the Tribunal. It creates an incentive for such cooperation by permitting information to be shared on a confidential basis and by guaranteeing the providers of such information that the confidentiality thereof, together with its sources, will be protected. Rule 70 operates on the basis that governments showing a genuine interest in protecting the information in their possession may invoke Rule 70 to ensure the protection of such information by requiring limitations on the scope of a witness's testimony or on the dissemination of that witness's testimony. If a Trial Chamber finds that the information has been provided in accordance with Rule 70(B), the information will benefit from the protections afforded under Rules 70(C) and (D). However, the restrictions referred to under Rules 70(C) and (D) will only apply after the Trial Chamber has determined that the restrictions imposed by the government upon the witness's testimony would not undermine the need to ensure a fair trial, and that the need to ensure a fair trial would not substantially outweigh the probative value of the testimony so as to lead to its exclusion. Indeed, Rule 70(F) provides that Rule 70 restrictions shall not "affect a Trial Chamber's power under Rule 89(C) to exclude evidence if its probative value is substantially outweighed by the need to ensure a fair trial."

18. By conducting the balancing exercise under Rule 70(F), a Trial Chamber ensures that the government's legitimate confidentiality concerns are respected, and, at the same time, that the conduct of the trial remains fair and expeditious. While according due weight to legitimate State concerns related to national security and the need for States to safeguard their interests (fn. omitted), the Appeals Chamber adopts the holding of the ICTY Appeals Chamber in the *Milutinović et al.* case that "this deference to States' interests does not go as far as to supersede a Trial Chamber's

authority to maintain control over the fair and expeditious conduct of the trial".

19. In the Impugned Decision, the Trial Chamber denied Condition B on the ground that it had to retain authority over the proceedings. . . .

20. . . . [T]he Appeals Chamber notes that the Trial Chamber had been apprised prior to issuing the Impugned Decision that the U.S. Government would not authorise Ambassador Flaten to testify before the Tribunal unless the Trial Chamber accepted limitations on the scope of his testimony, as had been requested. . . . The Appeals Chamber considers . . . that the U.S. Government's insistence that the Chamber grant Condition B had been counterbalanced by its efforts to clarify the scope of Ambassador Flaten's testimony. The Appeals Chamber concludes that the U.S. Government attempted to cooperate with the Tribunal in good faith, and displayed a genuine interest in protecting the confidential information in its possession.

21. The Appeals Chamber further takes note of the Appellant's argument that Ambassador Flaten would have been able to give evidence directly relevant to some of the charges against him. It finds that the Appellant's perseverance in requesting the Trial Chamber to grant Condition B tends to show that Ambassador Flaten's testimony is important for his defence. . . .

*   *   *   *

25. . . . [T]he extent of the scope of examination authorised by the U.S. Government indicates that the application of Condition B would not have resulted in substantial unfairness to any of the parties. In this regard, the Appeals Chamber points to the observations made by the U.S. Government in the letters it exchanged with the Appellant after the Oral Decision of 24 January 2007. The U.S. Government stated that it was "confident that the broad scope provided will allow for any direct or cross-examination relevant to [the Appellant's] defence." It also stressed that it would be prepared to work with the Prosecution and Defence to resolve expeditiously any dispute arising during Ambassador Flaten's testimony. In light of the U.S. Government's purported flexibility with regard to the limitations imposed under Condition B and its apparent readiness

to solve any disputes arising from these limitations, the Appeals Chamber is persuaded that the application of Condition B would not have precluded the co-accused and the Prosecution from conducting thorough cross-examinations on matters relevant to their cases.

26. Lastly, the Appeals Chamber reiterates that pursuant to Rule 70(F), the Trial Chamber would have been able to exclude the evidence provided by Ambassador Flaten if it found—during the course of his testimony—that the application of Condition B unfairly limited the rights of the co-accused or the Prosecution. . . . The Appeals Chamber finds that such a safeguard in the Rules means that the Trial Chamber would have retained authority over the proceedings even with Condition B applied. Indeed, if the Trial Chamber were to find that the application of Condition B had unfairly limited the rights of the co-accused or the Prosecution to confront the witness during his testimony, the ultimate remedy would be the exclusion of the evidence.

27. The Appeals Chamber considers that the application of Condition B would not have undermined the fairness of the trial, as the Trial Chamber would have ultimately retained authority over the proceedings under Rules 70(F) and 89(C). As a result of the Impugned Decision denying Condition B, the Appellant has been prevented from exercising his right to adduce potentially pro-bative evidence in his defence. Balancing the different interests involved in the case, the Appeals Chamber finds that the Trial Chamber committed a discernible error in the exercise of its dis-cretion when denying the request to Grant Condition B.

*   *   *   *

3. Special Tribunal for Lebanon

On May 30, 2007, the UN Security Council, acting under Chapter VII, adopted Resolution 1757 on the establishment of the Special Tribunal for Lebanon. Speaking in his national capacity, U.S. Permanent Representative Zalmay Khalilzad welcomed the adoption of the resolution and offered the U.S. views on its significance as excerpted below. The full text of

Ambassador Khalilzad's statement is available at *www.un. int/usa/press_releases/20070530_138.html.*

---

* * * *

By adopting this resolution, the Council has demonstrated its commitment to the principle that there shall be no impunity for political assassinations, in Lebanon or elsewhere. Those who killed Rafiq Hariri and so many others will be brought to justice and held responsible for their crimes.

The tribunal will also serve to deter future political assassinations. Those who might be tempted to commit similar crimes will know there will be consequences for perpetuating political violence and intimidation in Lebanon.

We know that it was necessary and right for the Council to act now. The Council approved the tribunal agreement and statute on November 21, 2006. Since that time, the legitimate and democratically-elected Government of Lebanon and the parliamentary majority have tried every possible means to convince the Speaker of Parliament to fulfill his constitutional responsibility to convene parliament so that final action on the tribunal could be taken. But to no avail.

Several influential parties visited Lebanon in an effort to find a framework in which parliament could be convened. These include the Arab League, UN Legal Counsel Nicolas Michel, and the Secretary-General himself. After five months of tireless efforts to reach a solution to the impasse facing his country, Prime Minister Siniora sent the Secretary-General a letter on May 14 asking that the matter be put before the Security Council to take a "binding" decision to establish the Special Tribunal. The Secretary-General endorsed the Prime Minister's request one day later after concluding that all diplomatic efforts had been exhausted.

We would have preferred that the Lebanese ratify the tribunal agreement and statute. But we know that that was not possible. No one can say that the Lebanese Government, the Secretary-General, or the Security Council failed to pursue every possible

option short of Council action on the tribunal. But those opposed
to the tribunal made sure there were no such options available.

*   *   *   *

The agreement was attached to Security Council
Resolution 1664, adopted March 19, 2006, requesting the
Secretary-General to negotiate an agreement with the
Government of Lebanon "aimed at establishing a tribunal of
an international character based on the highest international
standards of criminal justice, taking into account the recommendations of his report and the views that have been
expressed by Council members . . ." The Security Council
approved the tribunal statute on November 21, 2006. U.N.
Doc. S/2006/911. *See Digest 2006* at 272–75.

In Resolution 1757, the Security Council stated that the
United Nations and Lebanon signed the agreement on establishment of the Special Tribunal on January 23 and February 6,
2007, respectively, and referred to a briefing by the UN Adviser
on May 2, 2007 "in which he noted that the establishment of
the Tribunal through the Constitutional process [in Lebanon]
is facing serious obstacles," but noted also that "all parties
concerned reaffirmed their agreement in principle to the
establishment of the Tribunal." The Security Council decided
that the agreement, annexed to Resolution 1757 (with attached
statute), would enter into force on June 10, 2007, unless
Lebanon notified the Council before that date that the legal
requirements for entry into force had been complied with.

On December 5, 2007, Ambassador Khalilzad addressed
the Security Council on the report of the UN International
Investigation Commission on Lebanon. Ambassador
Khalilzad welcomed the appointment of Daniel Bellemare "as
head of the Commission and eventually to become Prosecutor
of the Tribunal." In his statement, Ambassador Khalilzad
urged the Commission and the UN Secretariat "to ensure the
investigation is completed and the Special Tribunal for
Lebanon becomes operational as soon as possible. . . . Action
against the perpetrators is the best deterrent we have to prevent further assassinations." He also called on member

states to make financial contributions to the Tribunal, noting that "[t]he United States has pledged $5 million toward the Tribunal's set-up and first year of operations and is planning additional contributions to support the Tribunal over its lifespan. Other countries also should do their part." The full text of Ambassador Khalilzad's statement is available at *www. un.int/usa/press_releases/20071205_355.html.*

The United Nations and the Netherlands signed a headquarters agreement on December 21, 2007, to enable the seat of the Special Tribunal to be based in The Hague.

Cross References

CHAPTER 4

Treaty Affairs

A. GENERAL

1. U.S. Treaty Practice

On June 6, 2007, U.S. Department of State Legal Adviser John B. Bellinger, III, addressed Dutch and international legal professionals, diplomats, government officials and students in a speech hosted by the Atlantic Commission in The Hague, entitled "The United States and International Law." Excerpts follow on U.S. treaty practice. Excerpts addressing the role of treaties and other international law in U.S. domestic law are set forth in Chapter 5.A.1. The full text of Mr. Bellinger's remarks is available at *www.state.gov/s/l/c8183.htm*.

---

* * * *

. . . [O]ur treaty practice reflects the seriousness with which we take international obligations, not our indifference to them. For example, whenever we consider taking on new obligations, we examine a number of factors—What problem is the treaty designed to address? Is it a problem susceptible to solution through a treaty? Will we be in a position to implement, or will there be complications because of domestic law?

During negotiations, we try to eliminate ambiguities and pin down important questions of policy. This makes it harder to paper over disagreements, and sometimes harder to reach consensus. But we don't do this to be obstructionist. Rather, we want the treaty obligations to be as clear as possible. This is in part a matter of good draftsmanship, and an attempt to head off disputes and promote compliance. But it is also a reflection of the reality in which we operate: We need to explain to our Senate exactly what obligations we are taking on and what the implications of joining a particular treaty are. Important too, is what happens after we join a treaty. More than almost any other state, we are subject to broad and vigorous oversight through private litigation and scrutiny by the press, civil society, and the international community as a whole. If we do not get the words in a treaty exactly right, we will have to answer for the consequences.

This accountability, coupled with the seriousness with which we implement our obligations, also explains why we are so careful from the very start to determine whether we need to subject our ratifications of treaties to any reservations or understandings and why we make sure to line up any implementing legislation in advance. Unlike certain countries, we do not join treaties lightly, as a goodwill gesture, or as a substitute for taking meaningful steps to comply.

Ironically, this rigorous approach is sometimes seen not as a mark of seriousness, but as a sign of hostility. In part, this can be traced to a widespread view that willingness to join a treaty is a litmus test of a country's commitment to international law. Under this view, joining a treaty is good; not joining a treaty, or expressing concerns about its purpose, enforceability, effects, or ambiguity, are the excuses of a nation unwilling to shoulder international responsibilities.

Take, for example, the International Criminal Court. Some critics have interpreted our decision not to become a party as an expression of disdain for international law and international institutions. This is wrong. In fact, for many years, the United States sought to create a permanent tribunal to deal with international crimes. Back in 1990 our Congress called for the creation of such a body—but made clear that its support would hinge on the tribunal's guarantees of due process and fair trial, and its respect for national sovereignty.

In our view, the Rome Statute falls short. We object on principle to the ICC's claim of jurisdiction over persons from non-party states.

And we are particularly concerned by the ICC's power to self-judge its jurisdiction, without any institutional check. We hope that the prosecutor and members of the court will honor their jurisdictional limits, and that the ICC will act only when a state with jurisdiction over an international crime is unable or unwilling to do its duty. But we cannot ignore the chance that a prosecutor might someday assert jurisdiction inappropriately, and the Rome Statute offers no recourse in such a situation. Our attempts to address such concerns during the drafting of the Statute failed—leaving us unable to join.

This decision was in no way, however, a vote for impunity. We share with the parties to the Statute a commitment to ensuring accountability for genocide, war crimes, and crimes against humanity—look, for example, to our unflagging support for the tribunals established to prosecute crimes committed in such disparate places as the former Yugoslavia, Rwanda, and Sierra Leone. We also believe that our domestic system is capable of prosecuting and punishing our own citizens for these crimes.

Moreover, over the past couple of years we have worked hard to demonstrate that we share the main goals and values of the Court. We did not oppose the Security Council's referral of the Darfur situation to the ICC, and have expressed our willingness to consider assisting the ICC Prosecutor's Darfur work should we receive an appropriate request. We supported the use of ICC facilities for the trial of Charles Taylor, which began this week here in The Hague. These steps reflect our desire to find practical ways to work with ICC supporters to advance our shared goals of promoting international criminal justice. We believe it important that ICC supporters take a similarly practical approach in working with us on these issues, one that reflects respect for our decision not to become a party to the Rome Statute. It is in our common interest to find a *modus vivendi* on the ICC based on mutual respect for the positions of both sides.

More recently, we took a drubbing over our objections to the UNESCO Cultural Diversity Convention, accused of being against culture, against diversity, and against treaties. This is silly, and not only because the United States is among the most multicultural nations on earth. In our view, the Convention reflects in part the efforts of some countries to engage in protectionist behavior under the guise of diversity; its ambiguous language can be read to permit the imposition of restrictive trade measures on goods and services defined as "cultural," including books, newspapers, magazines, movies—and perhaps even content available over the internet. This could undermine other international mechanisms, such as the General Agreement on Trade in Services and other WTO agreements, and could, by hindering the free flow of information, raise human rights concerns. One may disagree with the policy judgment not to join. But it hardly shows disrespect for international law to oppose one international legal regime because it threatens to undermine another.

It is also simplistic and misleading to set up ratification of a treaty as a test for whether a state takes the underlying issue seriously. Take the Kyoto Protocol. Is it truly a proxy for whether a state takes climate change seriously? First, a developed country can join Kyoto without necessarily taking on stringent commitments. Indeed, some countries—rather than having to take climate-change measures themselves—will actually be net financial beneficiaries. Second, even when a country has commitments under the Protocol, it will not necessarily implement them. A U.S. push for serious consequences for non-compliance was successfully opposed by other developed countries. As a result, the Protocol lacks bite. Third, developing countries do not have any commitments under Kyoto to limit their emissions, despite the fact that they are generating the highest increase in emissions. These flaws, coupled with anticipated harm to the U.S. economy, were legitimate reasons not to join Kyoto. Our concern for climate change, however, has led us to pursue a host of climate-related measures, both domestically and internationally. Just last week, President Bush expressed support for major country emitters of greenhouse gases and energy consumers to convene and develop, by the end of 2008, a new post-2012 framework on climate change.

Similarly, in the case of the Convention for the Elimination of Discrimination Against Women (CEDAW), we have not been persuaded that the binding international obligations contained in that treaty would add anything to the measures we take domestically. Our law is already highly protective of women's rights. In addition to a constitutional guarantee of equal protection, we have robust federal anti-discrimination laws and the recently reauthorized Violence Against Women Act. Further, the United States is a world leader in promoting women's rights and participation in the political process. We have spent billions of dollars in foreign aid to improve women's political participation, economic status, education, health care, and legal rights. Indeed, our levels of direct assistance for women around the world have increased substantially over the past four years. It cannot seriously be maintained that our decision not to push for ratification of this treaty reflects a lack of respect for, or attention to, women's rights.

Finally, I want to take issue with the notion I sometimes hear that we don't join treaties so that we can avoid compliance. For example, the United States has been abiding by the Law of the Sea Convention since 1983, even though we have not yet joined. The Convention is enormously important: It codifies and clarifies rights and obligations concerning a wide variety of navigational, economic and environmental issues relevant to the use of the world's oceans. Early on, concerns about the deep seabed mining aspects of the Convention kept the United States and others out. An implementing agreement resolved those concerns, and this Administration is a strong supporter of U.S. participation. We have been working with the Senate to move the treaty forward. In fact, although the press has not actively reported it, last month President Bush personally urged the Senate to approve the Convention during this session of Congress. Our strong hope is that we will be able to join the Convention shortly. But in the meantime our conduct has been fully consistent with its obligations.

Some may see our concerns about the potential difficulties in these treaties as excessively scrupulous. Certainly if the U.S. were to take the approach of "join now and worry about complying later," there might be more international law. But would the international law be better? If treaties do not create clear and serious obligations, but only express good intentions, they lose their capacity to encourage states to rely on each other. I believe that our approach results in stronger and more effective international cooperation in the face of real global problems.

*   *   *   *

2. Treaty Priority List

In a letter of February 7, 2007, the Department of State provided the Administration's treaty priority list for the 110th Congress. Letter from Jeffrey T. Bergner, Assistant Secretary of State for Legislative Affairs, to Senator Joseph R. Biden, Chairman, Senate Committee on Foreign Relations. As explained in the letter, the list was divided into three categories:

> (1) treaties currently on the Committee's calendar on which the Administration supports Senate action at this time; (2) treaties currently on the Committee's calendar on which the Administration does not support Senate action at this time; and (3) treaties not yet before the Committee on which the Administration is actively reviewing treaty transmittal packages with a view toward Senate action prior to adjournment of the 100th Congress.

The full text of the list is available at *www.state.gov/s/l/c8183.htm*.

B. CONCLUSION, ENTRY INTO FORCE, RESERVATIONS, APPLICATION, AND TERMINATION

1. Federal Government Authority to Require State and Local Law Enforcement Officials to Comply with U.S. Treaty Obligations

As noted in Chapter 2.A.1.b., on May 11, 2007, by order of the U.S. Court of Appeals for the Second Circuit, the United States filed a letter brief addressing several issues related to efforts undertaken by the Department of State to ensure compliance with the Vienna Convention on Consular Relations and the source of the federal government's authority to require state and local law enforcement officials to provide consular notification and access to detained foreign nationals. *Mora v. State of New York*, No. 06-0341-pr (2d Cir.). The discussion of

the federal authority in treaty matters over state and local officials is excerpted below. The full text of the letter brief is available at *www.state.gov/s/l/c8183.htm.*

For other cases discussing executive branch authority in
making and implementing treaties, *see* Chapter 3.1.A.c.(1)
and B.6.

---

* * * *

C. Authority of the Federal Government To Require State and
Local Law Enforcement Officials To Provide Consular Notification
and Access.

* * * *

. . . [T]he federal government is empowered to require that state or
local law enforcement officials who detain foreign nationals do so
in accordance with the substantive restrictions set out in the
[Vienna Convention on Consular Relations ("Convention")].

Since the earliest days of this country, it has been recognized
that the power of the federal government is supreme in the realm
of foreign affairs. The Framers of our Constitution were acutely
aware of the difficulties resulting from the inability of the Continental
Congress "to 'cause infractions of treaties, or of the law of nations
to be punished,'" with the most notable incidents involving the
treatment of foreign nationals within this country. *Sosa v. Alvarez-
Machain*, 542 U.S. 692, 716 (2004) (quoting J. Madison, Journal
of the Constitutional Convention 60 (E. Scott ed. 1893)). The
importance of national authority in the field of foreign relations,
and the potential danger of state action, are recurring themes in
the Federalist Papers. *See, e.g.,* The Federalist No. 3, at 10–11
(J. Jay) (Gideon ed., 2001) (national government permits uniform
treaty enforcement); The Federalist No. 4, at 14 (J. Jay) (national
government minimizes foreign conflict that could lead to war);
The Federalist No. 22, at 111 (A. Hamilton) (under Articles of
Confederation, "[t]he treaties of the United States * * * are liable
to the infractions of thirteen" States, putting "[t]he faith, the reputation, the peace of the whole union * * * at the mercy of the prej-
udices, the passions, and the interests of every member").

In drafting the U.S. Constitution, the Framers sought to remedy the inadequacies of the Articles of Confederation by vesting in the national government the power to enter into and implement treaties. The U.S. Constitution grants to the President the "Power, by and with the Advice and Consent of the Senate, to make Treaties." U.S. Const., art. II, § 2, cl. 2. In contrast, the Constitution forbids the States from entering into "any Treaty, Alliance, or Confederation," U.S. Const., art. I, § 10, cl. 1, and permits a State to enter into an "Agreement or Compact" with a foreign power only with the approval of Congress. *Id.*, cl. 3. These provisions manifest the broad scope of the political branches' authority in this area and the limited role to be played by the States.

The federal government's authority over foreign relations extends to regulation of the treatment of foreign nationals within this country. As the Supreme Court has recognized, "international controversies of the gravest moment, sometimes even leading to war, may arise from real or imagined wrongs to another's subjects inflicted, or permitted, by a government." *Hines v. Davidowitz*, 312 U.S. 52, 64 (1941). The regulation of aliens is thus a subject "'so intimately blended and intertwined with responsibilities of the national government' that federal policy in this area always takes precedence over state policy." *City of New York*, 179 F.3d at 34 (quoting *Hines*, 312 U.S. at 66); *see also Takahashi v. Fish & Game Comm'n*, 334 U.S. 410, 419 (1948) (contrasting federal government's broad constitutional authority over aliens in this country with States' lack of power). Indeed, the federal government has exercised this broad authority to immunize entirely certain aliens from the regulatory and law enforcement jurisdiction of state and local officials. *See, e.g.,* Vienna Convention on Diplomatic Relations, Arts. 29, 31.

Finally, the President is explicitly authorized by the Constitution to regulate consular relations in the United States and abroad. Under Article II, the President is empowered to "appoint Ambassadors, other public Ministers and Consuls," with the advice and consent of the Senate, U.S. Const., Art. II, § 2, cl. 2, and also to "receive Ambassadors and other public Ministers." U.S. Const., Art. II, § 3. Our Constitution thus reflects an international practice, dating back to the Middle Ages, of sending consular representatives to foreign nations to protect the interests of citizens abroad. *See generally Ross v. McIntyre*, 140 U.S. 453, 462–465 (1891) (describing history of consular relations).

The President exercised his constitutional authority over foreign relations and the conduct of consular relations by entering into the Convention, with the advice and consent of the Senate. The Convention establishes certain requirements for consular notification and access in order "to ensure the efficient performance of functions by consular posts on behalf of their respective States." Preamble. "With a view to facilitating the exercise of consular functions relating to nationals of the sending State," Article 36, ¶ 1, the Convention forbids officials from denying a consular representative access to and the opportunity to communicate with a detained foreign national. Officials are also prohibited from denying a detained foreign national the opportunity to contact consular officials. Finally, officers are required to notify foreign nationals of the opportunity to contact consular officials and, where appropriate, to notify the foreign consulate of the detention. These reciprocal obligations also enable U.S. consular officers to become aware of and assist U.S. nationals detained abroad.

The Convention's requirements of consular notification and access, set forth in a treaty entered into by the Executive with the advice and consent of the Senate, establish supreme law of the land. *See* U.S. Const., art. VI, cl. 2; *Sanchez-Llamas v. Oregon*, 126 S. Ct. 2669, 2680 (2006) ("[I]t is well-established that a self-executing treaty binds the States pursuant to the Supremacy Clause, and that the States therefore must recognize the force of the treaty in the course of adjudicating the rights of litigants."). They are as binding on state and local law enforcement officials as other federal laws. *See Hines*, 312 U.S. at 64–65 (treaties are "binding upon the states as well as the nation"); *American Ins. Ass'n v. Garamendi*, 539 U.S. 396, 413–419 (2003); *see also Reno v. Condon*, 528 U.S. 141, 150–151 (2000) (state departments of motor vehicles must comply with federal restrictions on disclosure of personal information).

Exempting state or local law enforcement officials from the requirements of consular notification and access would make it impossible for the United States to comply with our treaty obligations under the Convention. The refusal of one or a small number of States to provide consular notification and access could provoke foreign governments to refuse those protections to U.S. citizens abroad. But the inability to ensure compliance with international treaties is precisely what the Framers sought to remedy by vesting authority over foreign relations in the federal government, rather than the States. *See Garamendi*, 539 U.S. 396, 413–414 (2003); *see also Chy Lung v. Freeman*, 92 U.S. 275, 279–280 (1875). As Alexander Hamilton explained in The Federalist No. 80, in discussing the federal court's power to adjudicate cases involving foreign litigants, "[t]he Union will undoubtedly be answerable to foreign powers for the conduct of its members," and "the responsibility for an injury, ought ever to be accompanied with the faculty of preventing it."

Furthermore, the inability of the States to enter into treaties, *see* U.S. Const., Art. I, § 10, cl. 1, would mean that, if the federal government could not make reciprocal undertakings with other countries regarding the treatment of detained aliens, no such agreement would be possible. Such a result would be contrary to the Framers' understanding that the federal government possessed the full measure of sovereignty in international affairs. *See, e.g.*, The Federalist No. 42, at 215 (J. Madison) ("If we are to be one nation in any respect, it clearly ought to be in respect to other nations."). The power over international affairs, which passed directly to the Union upon independence, necessarily vested our national government with the authority to effectuate our external sovereignty by exercising rights and powers "equal to the right and power of the other members of the international family." *United States v. Curtiss-Wright Exp. Corp.*, 299 U.S. 304, 316–318 (1936).

It would be particularly anomalous to hold that the federal government lacks authority to enter into binding treaties governing consular relations and the treatment of nationals abroad given a history of such treaties dating back two centuries, to the earliest days of our nation. *E.g., Treaty of Amity, Commerce, and Navigation With Britain (Jay Treaty)*, 12 Bevans 13 (signed Nov. 19, 1794); *Treaty on Functions and Privileges of Consular Officers With France*, 7 Bevans 794 (signed Nov. 14, 1788)

(1788 France Treaty).[7] Notably, a number of early treaties required local officials to take affirmative actions to aid consular officials in their performance of consular duties.[8] A court should not construe the Constitution to deny a power that has been exercised since the founding of our nation and is necessary to protect our own citizens abroad. *See Curtiss-Wright Exp. Corp.*, 299 U.S. at 318; *Missouri v. Holland*, 252 U.S. 416, 433–435 (1920).[9]

---

[7] The index to Charles Bevans' collection of treaties entered into by the United States between 1776 and 1949 lists hundreds of treaties, many dating back to the late 1700s or early 1800s, that address the subject of consular relations. *See* 13 Bevans 29–30.

[8] *E.g.,* 1788 France Treaty, Article 7, 7 Bevans 797 (requiring local authorities to assist with salvage operations); Treaty of May 4, 1850, between Republic of New Granada [Colombia] and United States, Article III (9-11), 6 Bevans 882, 885 (requiring "local authorities" to preserve wrecked vessel until consul's arrival; to secure property of deceased foreigner; and to arrest deserting foreign seamen at consul's request); Treaty of May 8, 1878, between Italy and United States, Articles XI, XIII, XVI, 9 Bevans 91, 94–96 (directing state and local officials to "lend aid to Consular officers" in apprehending deserters from foreign vessels; directing "local authorities" to notify consul of a shipwreck and to "take all necessary measures for the protection of persons and the preservation of property"; and directing local authorities to notify consul of death of foreign national); *see also* A. Mark Weisburd, "International Courts and American Courts," 21 Mich. J. Int'l L. 877, 917 (2000) ("[T]he United States has been entering into treaties imposing duties on state officials since before Washington was inaugurated.").

[9] It is notable, furthermore, that the only affirmative steps called for by the pertinent provisions of the Convention are to notify a foreign national of the opportunity to contact his consulate and, in appropriate cases, to notify the consulate. Like a requirement to provide certain information to the federal government, which Justice O'Connor emphasized in concurrence in *Printz v. United States*, 521 U.S. 898 (1997), would not implicate Tenth Amendment restrictions against "commandeering" state or local officials, *id.* at 936, these requirements involve the purely ministerial provision of information, and at most a *de minimis* burden on state or local officials. *See also id.* at 918 (majority op., emphasizing that Court was not passing on constitutionality of federal requirements to provide information). Even assuming that the federal government's authority to enter into and implement international treaties is subject to constitutional constraints on the imposition of affirmative requirements on state or local officials, the consular notification requirements at issue here are unobjectionable. In any event, because the City of New York has voluntarily decided to provide consular notification and

Indeed, the very breadth of the federal government's power to enlist the aid of state and local officials in satisfying treaty obligations underscores the primary role of the political branches in the context of treaty implementation. That primacy, in turn, highlights the need for judicial caution before construing an international treaty to create privately enforceable rights, much less a remedy of money damages against state or local officials.

2. Self-executing Treaties

On September 20, 2007, President George W. Bush transmitted to the Senate for advice and consent to ratification the Treaty Between the Government of the United States of America and the Government of the United Kingdom of Great Britain and Northern Ireland Concerning Defense Trade Cooperation, done at Washington and London on June 21 and 26, 2007. S. Treaty Doc. No. 110-7 (2007). *See* further discussion in Chapter 18.B.1. The preamble to the treaty states that that the parties understand that "the provisions of this Treaty are self-executing in the United States." An Overview accompanying the Secretary of State's letter submitting the treaty to the President and included in S. Treaty Doc. No. 110-7 explains the significance of the treaty's self-executing status, stating:

> Because the Treaty is self-executing, [the] exemption [from generally applicable licensing requirements under U.S. law] will be created through ratification of the Treaty; no additional legislation will be required to implement the exemption in United States law. Those Implementing Arrangements constituting terms of the exemption are

---

access to arrested foreign nationals, this case presents no occasion to address the federal government's authority to require a State or municipality to provide such information.

authorized by this self-executing Treaty. They will not be submitted for Senate advice and consent to ratification and also require no further legislative action to become a fully effective part of the exemption.

The same language was included in the Overview accompanying transmittal of the similar Treaty with Australia Concerning Defense Trade Cooperation to the Senate, S. Treaty Doc. No. 110-10, on December 3, 2007. For further discussion of the treaties, *see* Chapter 18.B.1.

3. Amendments: World Meteorological Organization

At the Fifteenth World Meteorological Organization ("WMO") Congress, held May 7–25, 2007, in Geneva, the United States voted to approve the adoption of amendments to the preamble to the WMO Convention in accordance with Article 28(c) of the WMO Convention. The WMO Convention was adopted at Washington on October 11, 1947, and entered into force for the United States on March 23, 1950 (1 U.S.T. 281; T.I.A.S. No. 2052; 77 U.N.T.S. 142).

The WMO Convention contains two procedures for amending the treaty. One procedure concerns amendments that result in new obligations on members and requires the deposit of an instrument by member states. The other, set forth in Article 28(c) governing amendments that do not result in new obligations on members, provides an expedited procedure under which such amendments "come into force upon approval by two-thirds of the Members which are States." The 2007 amendments to the preamble were intended to clarify and update the mission statement of the organization. These amendments neither created new obligations for the members nor broadened the mandate of the WMO, and were therefore properly adopted pursuant to Article 28(c). The new amendments entered into force on June 1, 2007.

4. Effect of Armed Conflict on Treaties

On October 31, John B. Bellinger, III, Department of State Legal Adviser, addressed the Sixth Committee of the General Assembly on the report of the International Law Commission on the Work of its 59th Session. Mr. Bellinger's comments on the effects of armed conflicts on treaties are set forth below. The full text of his statement is available at *www.un.int/usa/ press_releases/20071031_280.html.*

---

*   *   *   *

The Commission has made substantial contributions to international law through its work on the law of treaties. The topic of the Effects of Armed Conflict on Treaties is no exception. The Special Rapporteur has tackled many difficult questions in this complex area, while faced with the challenges of identifying relevant State practice and addressing the many views that have been expressed regarding the proper approach to this subject. The Special Rapporteur's third report has been helpful in drawing attention to issues that must be carefully studied before this work is concluded.

We welcome the establishment of the *ad hoc* Working Group and commend it for taking an approach that avoids relying either on the intent of the parties to determine whether a treaty is susceptible to termination or on a list of categories of treaties to determine whether they continue in operation. As a general matter, we support an approach to this subject that preserves the reasonable continuity of treaty obligations during armed conflict, while taking into account particular military necessities, and also provides practical guidance to States by identifying factors relevant to determining whether a treaty should remain in effect in the event of armed conflict.

We caution, however, that many questions have arisen in this complex area. For example, we believe that the effort to give more definition to the term "armed conflict" than exists under the Geneva Conventions is likely to cause confusion and be counterproductive. The wide variety of views that have already been expressed about what the definition should be is evidence of the challenges that such an exercise involves. A better approach would be to make clear in the draft articles that armed conflict refers to armed conflicts covered by common articles 2 and 3 of the Geneva Conventions (*i.e.*, international and non-international armed conflicts). Also, if the decision is made to cover "occupation" together with "armed conflict" within the scope of the draft articles, then the two terms should be referred to separately, as they are not synonymous in the law of armed conflict. These and other issues will continue to require further study and consideration as the Commission's work on this topic progresses.

We have one final comment on a specific textual proposal. We support the suggestion that draft article 6 *bis* be deleted and its subject matter reflected in the Commentaries. We are also of the view that the text should spell out clearly that international humanitarian law is the *lex specialis* that governs in armed conflict.

* * * *

5. Subsequent Agreement and Practice

In his October 31 statement to the Sixth Committee, *supra,* Mr. Bellinger questioned the ILC's proposed topic, "Subsequent agreement and practice with respect to treaties," stating:

This topic has the potential to be large in scope and implicate many subject areas, which leads us to question whether it is sufficiently concrete and suitable for progressive development and codification. Moreover, we are not aware of pressing real-world issues that necessitate the Commission's taking on this topic at this time. Subsequent agreement and practice regarding treaties will necessarily depend on the treaty or treaties at issue, and will require a case-by-case analysis of the particular circumstances.

6. U.S. Conditions on Acceptance of Executive Agreement

a. *Entry into force subject to reservation and understandings*

On January 17, 2007, the Director-General of the World Health Organization circulated a copy of a U.S. diplomatic note informing the WHO member states, associated members, and other states of U.S. acceptance of the International Health Regulations (2005) "subject to the reservation and understandings referred to" in the note. The Director-General informed member states that, "pursuant to paragraph 4 of Article 62, the deadline for the receipt by her of objections [to the reservation] will be six months from the date of the present note verbale, namely, 17 July 2007." The International Health Regulations ("IHRs") entered into force for the United States as an executive agreement on July 18, 2007, subject to the reservation and understandings in the diplomatic note, as set forth below. The full texts of the U.S. note, from the Permanent U.S. Mission to the UN Office and other International Organizations in Geneva, and the WHO transmittal letter are available at *www.state.gov/s/l/c8183.htm.*

* * * *

The Government of the United States of America reserves the right to assume obligations under these Regulations in a manner consistent with its fundamental principles of federalism. With respect to obligations concerning the development, strengthening, and maintenance of the core capacity requirements set forth in Annex 1, these Regulations shall be implemented by the Federal Government or the state governments, as appropriate and in accordance with our Constitution, to the extent that the implementation of these obligations comes under the legal jurisdiction of the Federal Government. To the extent that such obligations come under the legal jurisdiction of the state governments, the Federal Government shall bring such obligations with a favorable recommendation to the notice of the appropriate state authorities.

The Mission, by means of this note, also submits three understandings on behalf of the Government of the United States America. The first understanding relates to the application of the IHRs to incidents involving the natural, accidental or deliberate release of chemical, biological or radiological materials:

In view of the definitions of "disease," "event," and "public health emergency of international concern," as set forth in

Article 1 of these Regulations, the notification requirements of Articles 6 and 7, and the decision instrument and guidelines set forth in Annex 2, the United States understands that States Parties to these Regulations have assumed an obligation to notify to WHO potential public health emergencies of international concern, irrespective of origin or source, whether they involve the natural, accidental or deliberate release of biological, chemical or radionuclear materials.

The second understanding relates to the application of Article 9 of the IHRs:

Article 9 of these Regulations obligates a State Party "as far as practicable" to notify the World Health Organization (WHO) of evidence received by that State of a public health risk occurring outside of its territory that may result in the international spread of disease. Among other notifications that could prove to be impractical under this article, it is the United States' understanding that any notification that would undermine the ability of the U.S. Armed Forces to operate effectively in pursuit of U.S. national security interests would not be considered practical for purposes of this Article.

The third understanding relates to the question of whether the IHRs create judicially enforceable private rights. Based on its delegation's participation in the negotiations of the IHRs, the Government of the United States of America does not believe that the IHRs were intended to create judicially enforceable private rights:

The United States understand that the provisions of the Regulations do not create judicially enforceable private rights.

*   *   *   *

b. *Explanation of federalism reservation*

In a letter of July 10, 2007, to Margaret Chan, Director-General of the World Health Organization, Secretary of Health and Human Services Michael O. Leavitt explained the federalism reservation as excerpted below. Mr. Leavitt's letter is also available at *www.state.gov/s/l/c8183.htm.*

*   *   *   *

The Constitution of the United States establishes a system of Government that distributes the power to govern between the Federal Government and the States; each recognizes the powers of the other while they jointly engage in certain governmental functions. Moreover, in areas of overlapping responsibility, the Constitution limits the manner in which the Federal Government can impose obligations on the States. In particular, there are limits on the power of the Federal Government to direct the use of the resources of State and local governments in instances in which the Federal Government might properly employ its own resources. In the United States, State and local governments—not the Federal Government—have primary responsibility for exercising certain powers necessary to respond to serious public-health emergencies within their borders. Thus, any response to a serious public-health emergency in the United States likely would require cooperation between these levels of Government.

In sum, our Constitution and governmental structure place the authority to carry out many of the provisions of the IHRs at different levels of government within the United States. The United States fully recognizes its obligations under the IHRs, and intends to satisfy those obligations through appropriate Federal, State, and local action in accordance with the U.S. Constitution. In this regard, the Federal Government will exercise every effort to ensure that the provisions of the IHRs are given full effect by the pertinent authorities in the United States. In this sense, our reservation is largely about the internal modalities of fulfilling our obligations under the IHRs.

*   *   *   *

Cross References

Method of accession to Hague Abduction Convention for countries not members of the Hague Conference at time the Convention was concluded, **Chapter 2.B.2.b.**

Presidential implementation of treaty obligations, **Chapter 2.A.1.a.**

Executive branch treaty-making power in negotiating and enforcing extradition treaties and in implementing U.S. obligations under Torture Convention, **Chapter 3.A.1.c.(1)** *and* **B.6.**

U.S.-U.K. exchange of notes concerning applicability of extradition treaty to two U.K. dependencies, **Chapter 3.A.1.d.**

U.S. as party to Protocols to Convention on Rights of the Child but not to the Convention, **Chapter 6.C.1.**

Measures pending entry into force of amendments to World Customs Organization convention, **Chapter 7.C.2.a.**

IMO resolution concerning understanding to ballast water management convention, **Chapter 13.A.2.b.**

CHAPTER 5

Foreign Relations

A. FOREIGN RELATIONS LAW OF THE UNITED STATES

1. Role of International Law in U.S. Domestic Law

On June 6, 2007, U.S. Department of State Legal Adviser John B. Bellinger, III, addressed Dutch and international legal professionals, diplomats, government officials, and students in a speech hosted by the Atlantic Commission entitled "The United States and International Law." Excerpts below address the role of international law in U.S. domestic law; *see also* Chapter 4.A. for discussion of U.S. treaty law practice. The full text of Mr. Bellinger's remarks is available at *www.state.gov/s/l/c8183.htm.*

---

*   *   *   *

. . . I would like to describe in some detail how the U.S. legal system operates to enforce international law. Rather than leaving it to politicians to decide when to comply with our international obligations, our system goes to great lengths to attach serious legal consequences to international rules. My goal here is to clear up some common myths and misperceptions—including that international law is not truly binding in our system.

First, we should start with our Constitution. It declares that treaties are the "supreme law of the land" and assigns to the President the responsibility to take care that the laws are faithfully executed. This duty includes the upholding of such treaties. In addition, in many instances, our courts are authorized to apply and interpret international law. Indeed, our Supreme Court is increasingly confronted with cases involving international law.

In the United States we do, however, recognize a distinction between treaties that can operate immediately and directly in our legal system, without the need for an implementing parliamentary act, and treaties that require the Executive branch and Congress to take further steps to adopt a law. This distinction is not unknown on the continent either. When the European Communities joined the Uruguay Round Agreements, for example, there was an express provision that those obligations would not enter directly into force as European law. Our approach to these agreements is exactly the same.

Let me give an example of how international obligations can be handled in our system. In the case of the Convention Against Torture, our Constitution already prohibited cruel and unusual punishment, which we interpret as encompassing torture. The United States directly enforces our obligations under Article 15 of the CAT by prohibiting the use of statements obtained through torture in legal proceedings, including military commission proceedings. Congress also adopted a statute imposing criminal sanctions on persons who commit torture, consistent with our obligations under the Convention. I should add that contrary to what you might hear from some critics, no one in the United States government has sought to disregard or avoid these obligations.

To take another example, the United States directly enforces the obligations of the Geneva Conventions, including by disciplining military personnel who violate those obligations. Moreover, Congress has enacted laws imposing criminal sanctions on U.S. nationals who commit a grave breach of these Conventions. Our military lawyers receive special training on the Geneva Conventions and work hard to uphold them wherever our forces are engaged in combat. Again, no one in our government has the authority to override these laws. Some critics have argued that even if we regard international law as binding, we don't give it the same stature as our domestic laws. They complain that we don't do enough to open our courts to private claims based on international law. I should note that we also get criticized for exactly the opposite reason: other countries argue that our generous approach to private litigation violates international law, even when the lawsuit itself rests on claims about international law.

Most people would agree that private litigation of international law disputes is a mixed blessing, especially in a legal system like ours. Some issues touch at the heart of foreign policy and are too important to be left to the vagaries of private suits. It therefore is not surprising that no country, to my knowledge, allows unlimited private litigation of international law.

Yet the United States does provide for substantial private enforcement of international law. Let me provide some examples. Our Congress has enacted legislation that allows private persons to sue for specific violations of international law, namely extrajudicial killings and torture. Most other countries limit redress of these international wrongs only to their criminal justice systems. Congress also opened our courts in some circumstances to claims for compensation based on expropriations of property that violate international law. And our courts will allow private parties to raise treaty issues in litigation, if the treaty clearly was intended to achieve this result.

Finally, let me respond briefly to a charge I have sometimes heard—that we hide behind our Constitution to avoid enforcing international law. This is a bit perplexing. After all, the principles of liberty and equality enshrined in our Constitution have helped inspire much of the international law of human rights that has emerged over the last sixty years. Our Constitution has contributed to the progressive development of international law, not held it back.

Still, our Constitution does require us to do certain things by congressionally enacted statutes, rather than by treaties. In particular, it requires a legislative act to impose a tax or create a crime. This reflects the critical role of the House of Representatives, which is more directly accountable to the electorate than the Senate or the President.

In addition, our Supreme Court has made clear that our Constitution protects certain core individual rights, including the right to a fair trial, to free speech, and to equal protection of the laws, from infringement by any legal act, including international rules.

This practice also does not distinguish us from other countries. The German Constitutional Court, for example, in the several "Solange" decisions has upheld exactly the same principle. In those cases, decided over decades, the German Court repeatedly ruled that it, and not the European Court of Justice, has the final authority to determine whether the European treaties comply with the fundamental provisions of the German Constitution. Similarly, our highest court must have the final say when safeguarding the fundamental rights enshrined in our Constitution.

And, as I noted above, far from shielding the United States from international law, our Constitution expressly recognizes treaties as the law of the land. It also authorizes Congress to define and punish offenses against the law of nations. Our Constitution does not prescribe isolationism. To the contrary, it promotes our active participation in the development and enforcement of international law.

In sum, the United States does treat international law as real law, is serious about its international obligations, and, through its legal system, assigns courts to play an important role in international law enforcement.

*   *   *   *

2. Alien Tort Statute

The Alien Tort Statute ("ATS"), also often referred to as the Alien Tort Claims Act ("ATCA"), was enacted in 1789 and is now codified at 28 U.S.C. § 1350. It provides that U.S. federal district courts "shall have original jurisdiction of any civil action by an alien for tort only, committed in violation of the law of nations or a treaty of the United States." The statute was very rarely invoked until *Filartiga v. Pena-Irala*, 630 F.2d 876 (2d Cir. 1980); following *Filartiga*, the statute has been relied upon by plaintiffs and interpreted by the federal courts in various cases raising claims under international law. In 2004 the Supreme Court held that the ATS is "in terms only jurisdictional" but that, in enacting the ATS in 1789, Congress intended to "enable[] federal courts to hear claims in a very limited category defined by the law of nations and recognized at common law." *Sosa v. Alvarez-Machain*, 542 U.S. 692 (2004). By its terms, this statutory basis for suit is available only to aliens.

The Torture Victim Protection Act ("TVPA") was enacted in 1992 and is codified at 28 U.S.C. § 1350 note. It provides a cause of action in federal courts against "[a]n individual . . . [acting] under actual or apparent authority, or color of law, of any foreign nation" for individuals regardless of nationality, including U.S. nationals, who are victims of official torture or extrajudicial killing. The TVPA contains a ten-year statute of limitations.

a. Political question doctrine

(1) Corrie v. Caterpillar

On September 17, 2007, the U.S. Court of Appeals for the Ninth Circuit dismissed claims arising from the Israeli Defense Forces' demolition of homes in the Palestinian Territories using bulldozers manufactured by Caterpillar, Inc., a U.S. corporation. *Corrie v. Caterpillar, Inc.*, 503 F.3d 974 (9th Cir. 2007). The court ruled that because the United States financed the purchase of the bulldozers under a military assistance program for Israel, the case, brought under the Alien Tort Statute and Torture Victim Protection Act, presented a nonjusticiable political question over which the court lacked jurisdiction. Excerpts below provide the court's analysis of the applicability of the political question doctrine. The U.S. *amicus* brief filed in the Ninth Circuit on August 11, 2006, is available as Document 45 for *Digest 2006* at *www. state.gov/s/l/c8183.htm*. Among other things, the United States argued that it would be inappropriate for courts to recognize aiding and abetting liability under the ATS without a congressional directive; the Ninth Circuit did not reach that issue.

*   *   *   *

The political question doctrine first found expression in Chief Justice Marshall's observation that "[q]uestions, in their nature political, or which are, by the constitution and laws, submitted to the executive, can never be made in this court." *Marbury v. Madison*, 5 U.S. (1 Cranch) 137, 170, 2 L. Ed. 60 (1803). The Supreme Court has since explained that "[t]he nonjusticiability of a political question is primarily a function of the separation of powers." *Baker v. Carr*, 369 U.S. 186, 211, 82 S. Ct. 691, 7 L. Ed. 2d 663 (1962). *Baker* outlined six independent tests for determining whether courts should defer to the political branches on an issue:

> Prominent on the surface of any case held to involve a political question is found [1] a textually demonstrable constitutional commitment of the issue to a coordinate political department; or [2] a lack of judicially discoverable and manageable standards for resolving it; or [3] the impossibility of deciding without an initial policy determination of a kind clearly for nonjudicial discretion; or [4] the impossibility of a court's undertaking independent resolution without expressing lack of the respect due coordinate branches of government; or [5] an unusual need for unquestioning adherence to a political decision already made; or [6] the potentiality of embarrassment from multifarious pronouncements by various departments on one question.

Id. at 217.

The Supreme Court has indicated that disputes involving political questions lie outside of the Article III jurisdiction of federal courts. *See Schlesinger v. Reservists Comm. to Stop the War*, 418 U.S. 208, 215, 94 S. Ct. 2925, 41 L. Ed. 2d 706 (1974) . . . .

* * * *

B.

"The conduct of the foreign relations of our government is committed by the Constitution to the executive and legislative [branches] . . . and the propriety of what may be done in the exercise of this political power is not subject to judicial inquiry or decision." *Oetjen v. Cent. Leather Co.*, 246 U.S. 297, 302, 38 S. Ct. 309, 62

L. Ed. 726 (1918). However, it is "error to suppose that every case or controversy which touches foreign relations lies beyond judicial cognizance." *Baker*, 369 U.S. at 211. We will not find a political question "merely because [a] decision may have significant political overtones." *Japan Whaling Ass'n v. Am. Cetacean Soc'y*, 478 U.S. 221, 230, 106 S. Ct. 2860, 92 L. Ed. 2d 166 (1986); *see also Kadic v. Karadzic*, 70 F.3d 232, 249 (2d Cir. 1995).

We "undertake a discriminating case-by-case analysis to determine whether the question posed lies beyond judicial cognizance." *Vatican Bank*, 410 F.3d at 545. Nevertheless, "cases interpreting the broad textual grants of authority to the President and Congress in the areas of foreign affairs leave only a narrowly circumscribed role for the Judiciary." *Id.* at 559 (quotation omitted).

The decisive factor here is that Caterpillar's sales to Israel were paid for by the United States. Though mindful that we must analyze each of the plaintiffs' "individual claims," *id.* at 547, each claim unavoidably rests on the singular premise that Caterpillar should not have sold its bulldozers to the IDF. Yet these sales were financed by the executive branch pursuant to a congressionally enacted program calling for executive discretion as to what lies in the foreign policy and national security interests of the United States. *See* 22 U.S.C. § 2751 (stating that the purpose of the Arms Export Control Act, which authorizes the FMF program, is to support "effective and mutually beneficial defense relationships in order to maintain and foster the environment of international peace and security essential to social, economic, and political progress").

Allowing this action to proceed would necessarily require the judicial branch of our government to question the political branches' decision to grant extensive military aid to Israel. It is difficult to see how we could impose liability on Caterpillar without at least implicitly deciding the propriety of the United States' decision to pay for the bulldozers which allegedly killed the plaintiffs' family members.[7]

---

[7] Plaintiffs cannot plausibly argue that Caterpillar was somehow on notice of IDF policies governing the bulldozers' military utilization while the United States government was not. Much of the "Notice to Caterpillar, Inc."

Several of the six *Baker* tests are implicated by the United States government's role in financing the Caterpillar bulldozer purchases by the IDF. We begin with the first: Whether there is "a textually demonstrable constitutional commitment of the issue to a coordinate political department." 369 U.S. at 217. It is well established that "the conduct of foreign relations is committed by the Constitution to the political departments of the Federal Government; [and] that the propriety of the exercise of that power is not open to judicial review." *Mingtai Fire & Marine Ins. Co. v. United Parcel Serv.*, 177 F.3d 1142, 1144 (9th Cir. 1999) (quoting *United States v. Pink*, 315 U.S. 203, 222–23, 62 S. Ct. 552, 86 L. Ed. 796 (1942)).

Whether to grant military or other aid to a foreign nation is a political decision inherently entangled with the conduct of foreign relations. In *Dickson v. Ford*, Dickson challenged the Emergency Security Assistance Act of 1973, which authorized $ 2.2 billion for military assistance and foreign military sales credit to Israel. 521 F.2d 234, 235 & n.1 (5th Cir. 1975). The Fifth Circuit dismissed the case on political question grounds, noting that both "the Congress and the President have determined that military and economic assistance to the State of Israel is necessary." *Id.* at 236. The court held that "a determination of whether foreign aid to Israel is necessary at this particular time is a 'question uniquely demand[ing] single-voiced statement of the Government's views,'" and is therefore inappropriate for judicial resolution. *Id.* (quoting *Baker*, 369 U.S. at 211); *see also Crockett v. Reagan*, 232 U.S. App. D.C. 128, 720 F.2d 1355, 1356–57 (D.C. Cir. 1983) (per curiam); *Atl. Tele-Network v. Inter-Am. Dev. Bank*, 251 F. Supp. 2d 126, 131 (D.D.C. 2003).

We cannot intrude into our government's decision to grant military assistance to Israel, even indirectly by deciding this challenge to a defense contractor's sales.[8] Plaintiffs' claims can succeed only if a court ultimately decides that Caterpillar should not have sold

---

discussed in the complaint details United Nations resolutions and statements and human rights organization reports dating back to 1967. It is inconceivable that the United States government would not also have been aware of the IDF practice of demolishing Palestinian homes.

[8]   Our holding in *Sarei v. Rio Tinto*, 487 F.3d at 1204, does not provide appellants with shelter from the political question doctrine. The cases are

its bulldozers to the IDF. Because that foreign policy decision is committed under the Constitution to the legislative and executive branches, we hold that plaintiffs' claims are nonjusticiable under the first *Baker* test.

Plaintiffs' action also runs head-on into the fourth, fifth, and sixth *Baker* tests because whether to support Israel with military aid is not only a decision committed to the political branches, but a decision those branches have already made. . . . The executive branch has made a policy determination that Israel should purchase Caterpillar bulldozers. It advances that determination by financing those purchases under a program authorized by Congress. A court could not find in favor of the plaintiffs without implicitly questioning, and even condemning, United States foreign policy toward Israel.

In this regard, we are mindful of the potential for causing international embarrassment were a federal court to undermine foreign policy decisions in the sensitive context of the Israeli-Palestinian conflict. Plaintiffs argue that the United States government has *already* criticized Israel's home demolitions in the Palestinian Territories. They point, for example, to former Secretary of State Powell's statement that "[w]e oppose the destruction of [Palestinian] homes—we don't think that is productive." But that language is different in kind from a declaration that the IDF has systematically committed grave violations of international law, none of which the United States has ever accused Israel of, so far as the record reveals.

---

factually unrelated. *Sarei* involved a dispute between an international mining corporation allied with the then government of Papua New Guinea and local residents opposing the actions of the corporation. The United States was implicated in the litigation only through its filing of a Statement of Interest at the request of the district court. This is a sizable step removed from the current proceedings where the United States is a direct actor, having funded Israel's purchase of the bulldozers in question.

We rejected Rio Tinto's argument in *Sarei* that the first *Baker* factor is satisfied for all ATS claims. However, this should not be understood as accepting the inverse proposition that all ATS claims are *per se* immunized from the first *Baker* factor. Here, the ATS claim runs directly afoul of the first *Baker* factor because our review of the claim would be "inextricable" from a review of a foreign policy decision constitutionally committed to the coordinate political departments. *Baker*, 369 U.S. at 217.

Diplomats choose their words carefully, and we cannot subvert United States foreign policy by latching onto such mildly critical language by the Secretary of State. . . . It is not the role of the courts to indirectly indict Israel for violating international law with military equipment the United States government provided and continues to provide. "Any such policy condemning the [Israeli government] must first emanate from the political branches." *Vatican Bank*, 410 F.3d at 561. Plaintiffs may purport to look no further than Caterpillar itself, but resolving their suit will necessarily require us to look beyond the lone defendant in this case and toward the foreign policy interests and judgments of the United States government itself.

We therefore hold that the district court did not err in dismissing the suit under the political question doctrine. Because we affirm on this ground, we do not reach the other issues raised on appeal.

(2) Matar v. Dichter

> On May 2, 2007, the U.S. District Court for the Southern District of New York dismissed a class action suit against Avraham Dichter, former Director of the Israeli General Security Service, finding him immune from jurisdiction under the FSIA. *Matar v. Dichter*, 500 F. Supp. 2d 284 (S.D.N.Y. 2007). For discussion of the immunity issues and the court's conclusion that the TVPA does not trump the Foreign Sovereign Immunities Act, see Chapter 10.B.2.a.
>
> Excerpts follow from the court's finding that even if Dichter were not immune, it would dismiss the suit as presenting a nonjusticiable political question. Citations to other submissions have been omitted. *See Digest 2006* at 465–76, 479–82, for U.S. submissions on cause of action issues raised under the Alien Tort Statute and the Torture Victim Protection Act.

---

*   *   *   *

III. *Political Question Doctrine*

Even if the FSIA were inapplicable, this Court would dismiss the action pursuant to the political question doctrine. The Supreme

Court in *Baker v. Carr* articulated six situations in which a non-justiciable political question may exist [including]: . . . (4) the impossibility of a court's undertaking independent resolution without expressing lack of respect due coordinate branches of government; . . . or (6) the potentiality of embarrassment from multifarious pronouncements by various departments on one question. *Baker v. Carr,* 369 U.S. 186, 217, 82 S. Ct. 691, 7 L. Ed. 2d 663 (1962); . . . .

The defendant is a high-ranking official of Israel, a United States ally. The Complaint criticizes military actions that were coordinated by Defendant on behalf of Israel and in furtherance of Israeli foreign policy. For this reason, both Israel and the State Department, whose opinions are entitled to consideration, urge dismissal of this action. [fn. omitted] *Sosa v. Alvarez-Machain,* 542 U.S. 692, 733 n.21, 124 S. Ct. 2739, 159 L. Ed. 2d 718 (2004) (noting that in some cases "there is a strong argument that federal courts should give serious weight to the Executive Branch's view of the case's impact on foreign policy"); *Altmann,* 541 U.S. at 702 ("[S]hould the State Department choose to express its opinion on the implications of exercising jurisdiction over *particular* petitioners in connection with *their* alleged conduct, that opinion might well be entitled to deference as the considered judgment of the Executive on a particular question of foreign policy."). Plaintiffs contend that because the administration did not condone the al-Daraj bombing, adjudication of this matter could not exhibit a lack of respect for the political branches. This Court disagrees. The Government has urged the Court to dismiss this action regardless of whether it approved of the attack. Moreover, Plaintiffs do not limit their claims to the Defendant or the al-Daraj bombing. . . .

Furthermore, the Israeli policy criticized in the Complaint involves the response to terrorism in a uniquely volatile region. This Court cannot ignore the potential impact of this litigation on the Middle East's delicate diplomacy. . . . As noted by the Government, the claims asserted by Plaintiffs "threaten to enmesh the courts in policing armed conflicts across the globe—a charge that would exceed judicial competence and intrude on the Executive's control over foreign affairs." Allowing this case to proceed "would undermine the Executive's ability to manage the conflict at issue through diplomatic means, or to avoid becoming entangled in it at all." Consideration of the case against this unique backdrop would impede the Executive's diplomatic efforts and, particularly in light of the Statement of Interest, would cause the sort of intragovernmental dissonance and embarrassment that gives rise to a political question. . . .

Plaintiffs cite a handful of cases in which the courts have adjudicated issues pertaining to the Middle East conflict. . . . However, none of these actions involved claims asserted against a sovereign state, let alone a United States ally, with the unique foreign policy implications presented here.

Neither did these lawsuits elicit a request for dismissal from the Department of State and the government of the foreign state. . . .

Plaintiffs bring this action against a foreign official for implementing the anti-terrorist policy of a strategic United States ally in a region where diplomacy is vital, despite requests for abstention by the State Department and the ally's government. "[T]he character of [such a] claim[] is, at its core . . . peculiarly volatile, undeniably political, and ultimately nonjusticiable." *Doe*, 400 F. Supp. 2d at 112.

*   *   *   *

b. Aiding and abetting liability: Apartheid litigation

On October 12, 2007, the Second Circuit Court of Appeals issued a decision in combined cases raising claims that the corporate and individual defendants "actively and willingly collaborated with the government of South Africa in maintaining a repressive, racially based system known as 'apartheid,' which restricted the majority black African population in all areas of life while providing benefits for the minority white population." *Khulumani v. Barclay National Bank Ltd.*, 504 F. 3d 254 (2d Cir. 2007).* In its Per Curiam opinion, the Second

---

*   Editor's note: The decision below appears under the name *In re S. African Apartheid Litig.*, 346 F. Supp. 2d 538 (S.D.N.Y. 2004). *See Digest 2004* at 354–61 and *Digest 2005* at 400–411.

Circuit found that "a plaintiff may plead a theory of aiding and abetting liability" under the ATS, reversing the district court's dismissal of claims for lack of a cause of action. The court also "declined to affirm the dismissal of plaintiffs' [ATS] claims on the basis of the prudential concerns raised by the defendants," remanding that issue to the district court "to allow it to engage in the first instance in the careful 'case-by-case' analysis that questions of this type require." In remanding the prudential concerns issue, the court stated that the parties "agree that [the Supreme Court's] reference [in *Sosa v. Alvarez-Machain*, 542 U.S. 692, 733 n.21 (2004)] to 'case-specific deference [to the political branches]' implicates either the political question or international comity doctrine," but the Second Circuit did not consider the district court to have resolved the question of those doctrines' application. Finally, the court affirmed the dismissal of claims under the Torture Victims Protection Act.

Defendants filed a petition for writ of certiorari in the Supreme Court that was pending at the end of 2007.

c. *Exhaustion of local remedies:* Sarei v. Rio Tinto

On August 7, 2006, the U.S. Court of Appeals for the Ninth Circuit reversed and remanded a lower court decision dismissing all claims in a case brought under the Alien Tort Statute based on allegations of human rights and other international law violations in Papua New Guinea. *Sarei v. Rio Tinto*, 456 F.3d 1069 (9th Cir. 2006); see *Digest 2006* at 431–36. The defendants in the case filed a petition for rehearing, and the United States filed an *amicus* brief in support of that petition. In its brief, the United States argued, among other things, that the court's analysis of the types of claims that may be asserted under the ATS was significantly flawed and that the court need not have addressed the validity of those claims at the jurisdictional stage in any event. See *Digest 2006* at 436–50. On April 12, 2007, the Ninth Circuit withdrew its 2006 opinion and issued a new opinion. *Sarei v. Rio Tinto*, 487

F.3d 1193 (9th Cir. 2007). The revised opinion accepted the U.S. analysis and reserved the question of the validity of plaintiffs' claims.

Other aspects of the opinion remained unchanged. Defendants again petitioned for rehearing on the court's holding that the claimants were not required to exhaust their local remedies in Papua New Guinea before bringing this case. The United States filed a brief as *amicus curiae* supporting the petition on May 18, 2007. The U.S. arguments that plaintiffs' ATS claims arising in a foreign jurisdiction may be considered, if at all, only after exhaustion of available local remedies, and that the ATS was not intended to be applied to extraterritorial claims, are excerpted below. The full text of the brief is available at *www.state.gov/s/l/c8183.htm*.

On August 20, 2007, the Ninth Circuit vacated the April 12 opinion and granted rehearing en banc. 499 F.3d 923 (9th Cir. 2007). The case was pending at the end of 2007.

* * * *

A. . . .[T]he majority held that, where a claim asserted under the ATS arises abroad, a court should not require exhaustion of foreign remedies, because Congress has not specifically mandated that prerequisite. Slip Op. 4170–71. In so holding, the majority relied on the Supreme Court's admonition in *Sosa* to exercise "judicial caution." *Id.* at 4165. As an initial matter, we do not think it appropriate to construe *Sosa* as counseling against the adoption of an exhaustion requirement. Indeed, the Supreme Court stated that it "would certainly consider this [exhaustion] requirement in an appropriate case." 542 U.S. at 733 n.21.

The majority also erred in focusing on the lack of a clear Congressional statement. . . . Adopting an exhaustion requirement in appropriate cases is fully in keeping with the Supreme Court's instruction that, when exercising common law authority under the ATS, courts should do so in a restrained and modest fashion.

In *Sosa*, the Court questioned whether the courts' limited federal common law power could properly be invoked "at all" in regard to a foreign nation's actions taken abroad. *Sosa*, 542 U.S.

at 727–28 . . . Assuming arguendo, however, that a court could ever do so, it is important that the court show due respect to competent tribunals abroad and mandate exhaustion where appropriate.

As a matter of international comity, "United States courts ordinarily * * * defer to proceedings taking place in foreign countries, so long as the foreign court had proper jurisdiction and enforcement does not prejudice the rights of United States citizens or violate domestic public policy." *Finanz AG Zurich v. Banco Economico S.A.*, 192 F.3d 240, 246 (2d Cir. 1999) (citations and internal quotation marks omitted). Such international comity seeks to maintain our relations with foreign governments, by discouraging U.S. courts from second-guessing a foreign government's judicial or administrative resolution of a dispute or otherwise sitting in judgment of the official acts of a foreign government. *See generally Hilton v. Guyot*, 159 U.S. 113, 163–164 (1895). To reject a principle of exhaustion and proceed to resolve a dispute arising in another country, concerning a foreign government's treatment of its own citizens, is the opposite of the model of "judicial caution" and restraint mandated by *Sosa*.

Moreover, exhaustion is fully consistent with Congress' intent in enacting the ATS. Congress enacted the ATS to provide a mechanism through which certain private insults to foreign sovereigns committed within U.S. jurisdiction could be remedied in federal courts. In the late 18th-century, the law of nations included "rules binding individuals for the benefit of other individuals," the violation of which "impinged upon the sovereignty of the foreign nation." *Sosa*, 542 U.S. at 715. Such violations, "if not adequately redressed[,] could rise to an issue of war." *Ibid*. Violations of safe conducts, infringement of the rights of ambassadors, and piracy came within this "narrow set." *Ibid*. But under the Articles of Confederation, "[t]he Continental Congress was hamstrung by its inability to cause infractions of treaties, or the law of nations to be punished." *Id*. at 716 (quotation marks omitted).

The Continental Congress urged state legislatures to authorize suits "for damages by the party injured, and for the compensation to the United States for damages sustained by them from an injury done to a foreign power by a citizen." *Ibid*. (quotation marks omitted). Most states failed to respond to the Congress' entreaty.

Physical assaults on foreign ambassadors in the United States, and the absence of a federal forum to redress ambassadors' claims, led to significant diplomatic protest. *Id.* at 716–17. After ratification of the Constitution, the First Congress adopted the ATS to remedy this lacuna, thereby reducing the potential for international friction. *Id.* at 717–18.

The whole point of the ATS was thus to *avoid* international friction. The ATS was enacted to ensure that the National Government would be able to provide a forum for punishment or redress of violations for which a nation offended by conduct against it or its nationals might hold the offending party (and, in turn, the United States) accountable. Those animating purposes of the ATS have nothing to do with a foreign government's treatment of its own citizens abroad. Against this backdrop, reinforced by cautions mandated by the Supreme Court in *Sosa* and the prescription against extraterritorial application of U.S. law, courts should be very hesitant *ever* to apply their common law power to apply *U.S. law* to adjudicate a foreign government's treatment of its own nationals. But even assuming that such extraterritorial claims are cognizable under the ATS, an exhaustion requirement manifestly would *further*, not undermine, Congress' intent to minimize the possibility of diplomatic friction by affording foreign states the first opportunity to adjudicate claims arising within their jurisdictions.

Consistent with that result, it is notable that when Congress by statute *has* created a private right for claims that may arise in foreign jurisdictions, it has required exhaustion as a prerequisite to suit. *See, e.g.,* Torture Victim Protection Act of 1991 (TVPA), Pub. L. No. 102-256, § 2(b). And Congress adopted this requirement in the TVPA, in part, because it viewed exhaustion as a procedural practice of international human rights tribunals, as the dissent notes. Slip Op. 4186 (Bybee, J., dissenting) (discussing S. Rep. No. 102-249, pt. 4, at 10 (1991).

B. Finally, we reiterate that the ATS does not encompass claims arising within the jurisdiction of a foreign sovereign, especially where the claims would require a U.S. court to evaluate a foreign sovereign's treatment of its own citizens. As we have noted, the Supreme Court expressly identified—as one of the questions to be considered in demarcating the limited scope of the judge-made law that may be fashioned in accordance with the ATS—whether it would ever be proper for federal courts to project the (common) law of the United States extraterritorially to resolve disputes arising in foreign countries. *See Sosa*, 542 U.S. at 727–28.

The history of the ATS' enactment, described above, shows that Congress enacted the ATS to provide a forum for adjudicating alleged violations of the law of nations occurring within the jurisdiction of the United States and for which the United States therefore might be deemed responsible by a foreign sovereign. There is no indication whatsoever that Congress intended the ATS to apply—or to authorize U.S. courts to apply U.S. law—to purely extraterritorial claims, especially to disputes that center on a foreign government's treatment of its own citizens in its own territory. Indeed, the recognition of such claims would conflict with Congress' purpose in the ATS of reducing diplomatic conflicts.

*   *   *   *

3. Claims Brought Under State Law

a. Foreign policy interests

On May 29, 2007, the United States submitted a Statement of Interest, at the request of the presiding judge of the Superior Court of the State of California, in a case concerning claims by Nigerian nationals alleging violations of California's Business and Professions Code against Chevron Corporation. *Bowoto v. Chevron Corp.*, Case No. CGC 03-417580 (Sup. Ct. Cal. 2007). In a letter to John B. Bellinger, III, Department of State Legal Adviser, the presiding judge invited the United States to provide "its official views, if any, on whether adjudicating this action or granting the relief that plaintiffs seek would adversely affect the diplomatic efforts of the United States, and if so, the nature and significance of such effect."

In a letter of May 25, 2007, attached to the Statement of Interest, Mr. Bellinger explained that grant of one aspect of the requested injunction in the case requiring the defendants to "take all reasonable steps to implement . . . the Voluntary

Principles on Human Rights and Security,"* would be contrary to the foreign policy interests of the United States, as excerpted below. The full texts of the Statement of Interest and Mr. Bellinger's letter are available at *www.state.gov/s/l/c8183.htm*.

The separate federal court action noted in the letter remained pending at the end of the year. *Bowoto v. Chevron Texaco Corp.*, Case No. C-99-2506-SI (N.D. Cal.).

---

*   *   *   *

The claims in California Superior Court assert violations of section 17200 of the California Business and Professions Code based upon alleged unfair business practices and the alleged making of false and/or misleading statements. (As you know, the plaintiffs are separately pursuing a case against Chevron in a federal action in the U.S. District Court for the Northern District of California.) As relief the plaintiffs seek a highly detailed injunction . . . , in addition to restitution, disgorgement of profits, and declaratory relief. The proposed injunctive relief specifically requires, in part, that Defendants "take all reasonable steps to implement . . . the Voluntary Principles on Human Rights and Security." Indeed, in the section heading on page two of the brief entitled "Plaintiffs' Explanation of Proposal Regarding Injunctive Relief," Plaintiffs, referring to the two aforementioned sets of principles, state that "Chevron has promised the U.S. Government to institute responsible corporate security practices in Nigeria, and Plaintiffs' proposed injunction would order Defendants to keep their word."

The Voluntary Principles initiative was established by the Governments of the United States and the United Kingdom in 2000. It now includes the Governments of Norway and the Netherlands and will likely be expanded to include additional governments. The process is the product of a dialogue among these member governments, a number of multinational corporations in the

---

extractive sector, various non-governmental organizations (NGOs), and several observers. As stated on the Voluntary Principles website, "[t]hrough this dialogue, the participants have developed a set of voluntary principles to guide Companies in maintaining the safety and security of their operations within an operating framework that ensures respect for human rights and fundamental freedoms." . . . At a Plenary meeting hosted by the Department of State on May 7–8, 2007, the participants adopted criteria concerning participation in the Voluntary Principles initiative designed to strengthen their implementation and expand membership.

An essential feature of the Voluntary Principles, as the name clearly indicates, is that participation, including adherence to the stated principles, is strictly voluntary. The stakeholders have concluded that this is the most effective way to achieve the objectives underlying the initiative. Moreover, the participation criteria agreed to at the May 7–8 meeting . . . provide, *inter alia:*

> To facilitate the goals of the Voluntary Principles and encourage full and open dialogue, Participants acknowledge that implementation of the Principles is continuously evolving and agree that the Voluntary Principles do not create legally binding standards, and participation in, communications concerning, and alleged failures to abide by the Voluntary Principles shall not be used to support a claim in any legal or administrative proceeding against a Participant.

The plaintiffs in *Bowoto* seek to have a California Superior Court compel Chevron, in order to comply with section 17200 of the California Business and Professions Code, to implement the Voluntary Principles. . . . Such an approach is clearly inconsistent with the delicately balanced voluntary scheme that the U.S. Government has promoted at the international level in order to encourage the active engagement of multinational corporations involved in the extractive sector. Additionally, as a multilateral diplomatic initiative being carried out at the national level of the governments involved, there is no role provided for sub-national government entities. There is a significant risk that an injunctive remedy such as that proposed by the plaintiffs could have a chilling effect on the continued participation of corporate participants in the Voluntary Principles initiative, as well as on U.S. diplomacy in the process, possibly jeopardizing the future of that initiative and other similar corporate social responsibility efforts. Issuing an injunction to compel compliance with the Voluntary Principles would thus interfere with an important foreign policy initiative of the Executive Branch.

*   *   *   *

I wish to note that, in expressing the foreign policy concerns above regarding the injunctive relief sought by the plaintiffs, we are not addressing whether a finding of liability or any relief would be appropriate in this case, including whether there are legal obstacles, such as the Act of State doctrine, to adjudicating the merits of the case. We are also not addressing the propriety of other potential remedies or discounting the possibility that the proposed injunctive relief would be rendered inappropriate by other legal concerns. Finally, we are not expressing a view as to the other issues raised in this case.

The U.S. Statement of Interest to which the letter was attached stated further:

> In evaluating the "facts and circumstances" presented by this case in the exercise of the Court's equitable jurisdiction, the Court "should give serious weight to the Executive Branch's view of the case's impact on foreign policy," *Sosa v. Alvarez-Machain*, 542 U.S. 692, 733 n.21 (2004), and should steer clear of exercising its common law powers in a way that could impinge upon "the discretion of the Legislative and Executive Branches in managing foreign affairs." *Id.* at 727; *accord Republic [of] Austria v. Altmann*, 541 U.S. 677, 702 (2004) (a court should defer to the "considered judgment of the Executive on a particular question of foreign policy."); *see also Sosa*, 542 U.S. at 733 & n.21 (courts should grant "case-specific deference to the political branches"). This is because, under the Constitution, the Federal Government's Executive Branch is the supreme authority in the arena of foreign affairs.

See Am. Ins. Ass'n v. Garamendi, 539 U.S. 396, 420–25 (2003); *Crosby v. Nat'l Foreign Trade Council*, 530 U.S. 363,384–86 (2000); *Japan Line, Ltd. v. County of Los Angeles*, 441 U.S. 434, 447–449 (1979).

Therefore, as the Court considers the equitable relief requested by the plaintiffs here, the United States urges the Court to defer to the United States's view that judicial imposition of the Voluntary Principles would interfere with an important foreign policy initiative of the Executive Branch. . . .

b. Preemption of state laws

On February 8, 2007, the U.S. District Court for the Southern District of Florida denied a motion for a preliminary injunction in a case challenging a Florida law prohibiting certain funds to be used for "activities related to or involving travel to a terrorist state." *Faculty Senate of Florida International University v. Winn*, 477 F. Supp. 2d 1198 (S.D. Fla. 2007). As the court explained (footnotes omitted):

On May 30, 2006, then-Governor Bush signed into law the so-called "Travel Act," which had been passed earlier by the Florida legislature. *See* Act Relating to Travel to Terrorist States, 2006 Fla. Sess. Law Serv. Ch.2006-54 (West), codified at various places in the Florida Statutes, including Fla. Stat. §§ 1005.08 & 1011.90(6). As relevant here, the Act provides that "[n]one of the state or non-state funds made available to state universities may be used to implement, organize, direct, coordinate, or administer, or to support the implementation, organization, direction, coordination, or administration of, activities related to or involving travel to a terrorist state. For purposes of this section, 'terrorist state' is defined as any state, country, or nation designated by the United States Department of State as a state sponsor of terrorism." Fla. Stat. § 1011.90(6). The five countries currently designated by the State Department as state sponsors of terrorism are Cuba, Iran, North Korea, Sudan, and Syria (the "designated countries").

The court found that the motion did not meet the requirements for a preliminary injunction because plaintiffs had not shown a substantial likelihood of success on the merits or irreparable harm. Excerpts follow from the court's discussion of the foreign affairs power and foreign commerce clause of the U.S. Constitution, and its determination that, as a discretionary matter, the preliminary injunction was not warranted. As noted, the United States did not appear in the case.

* * * *

2. THE FOREIGN AFFAIRS POWER

"The exercise of the federal executive authority means that state law must give way where . . . there is evidence of clear conflict between the policies adopted by the two." *Am. Ins. Ass'n v. Garamendi,* 539 U.S. 396, 421, 123 S. Ct. 2374, 156 L. Ed. 2d 376 (2003). Here the plaintiffs have not made a substantial showing of a clear conflict between the Travel Act and the policies of, and sanctions imposed by, the federal government with respect to the designated countries. *Compare, e.g.,* 22 U.S.C. § 6002 *et seq.;* 50 U.S.C. §§ 1701–1707. Although some individuals may elect not to travel to the designated countries if they cannot gain access to state funds to subsidize their trips, the prohibition is merely an "incidental or indirect effect on foreign countries" and does not necessarily render the Act invalid. *See, e.g., Clark v. Allen,* 331 U.S. 503, 517, 67 S. Ct. 1431, 91 L. Ed. 1633 (1947).

In support of their argument based upon the foreign affairs power, the plaintiffs rely principally on *Zschernig v. Miller,* 389 U.S. 429, 432, 88 S. Ct. 664, 19 L. Ed. 2d 683 (1968), *National Foreign Trade Council v. Natsios,* 181 F.3d 38 (1st Cir. 1999), *aff'd on conflict preemption grounds sub nom., Crosby v. Nat'l Foreign Trade Council,* 530 U.S. 363, 120 S. Ct. 2288, 147 L. Ed. 2d 352 (2000), and *Miami Light Project v. Miami-Dade Co.,* 97 F. Supp. 2d 1174 (S.D. Fla. 2000). The laws at issue in those cases, however, are considerably different than the Travel Act, and the plaintiffs have not shown a substantial likelihood of prevailing on the merits.

*   *   *   *

Unlike the laws at issue in these cases, the Travel Act's denial of the use of state funds to subsidize travel to the designated countries has little more than an incidental or indirect effect on those countries. The Act does not discourage or prohibit any person from engaging in business with any of the designated countries, nor does it prevent any professors, educators, or researchers from traveling to any of the designated countries on their own dime.

Furthermore, the countries covered by the Act are designated as sponsors of terrorism by the federal government, so the countries incidentally affected by the Act will always be congruent with the federal government's designations. It therefore cannot be said—at least not convincingly enough to obtain a preliminary injunction— that Florida, through the Travel Act, is countermanding the general views of the federal government with respect to those countries.

3. THE FOREIGN COMMERCE CLAUSE

The plaintiffs also maintain that the Travel Act intrudes on Congress' authority "to regulate Commerce with foreign Nations . . ." U.S. CONST. Art. I, § 8. . . .

The plaintiffs urge me to find that the Act "regulate[s] conduct outside of [the state] and outside of this country's borders." *Natsios*, 181 F.3d at 67. But the Act only prevents individuals from using state funds to travel to the designated countries. The plaintiffs have therefore failed to show that they are substantially likely to succeed on their claim that this prohibition on funding is inconsistent with the Foreign Commerce Clause.

*   *   *   *

C. AS A DISCRETIONARY MATTER, A PRELIMINARY INJUNCTION IS NOT WARRANTED

*   *   *   *

In addition to what I have said above, the federal government was invited to participate in this case, and so far has chosen not to join or support the plaintiffs in their challenge to the Travel Act. I understand, of course, that such lack of participation or involvement is not, in the end, legally dispositive, but it does suggest that the federal government is not too concerned about any obstacles that the Travel Act may pose to the nation's ability to conduct foreign policy with one voice.

This does not mean all questions concerning the Act have been answered. I do not understand, for example, how the Act will be applied to funds donated to state universities by non-state entities or individuals, with certain requirements (or understandings) about how those funds can be used. . . .

These matters, however, go to what may be unintended consequences of the Act. They do not affect the constitutionality of the Act, and do not tip the balance in favor of a preliminary injunction. My task is not to opine on whether the Act is good public policy, but merely to determine whether it violates federal constitutional norms.

*   *   *   *

4. State Secrets Privilege in Litigation

a. Rendition claim

On March 2, 2007, the U.S. Court of Appeals for the Fourth Circuit affirmed a district court order dismissing a case on the ground that it posed an unreasonable risk that privileged state secrets would be disclosed. *El-Masri v. United States*, 479 F.3d 296 (4th Cir. 2007). Khaled El-Masri alleged that he had been arrested in Macedonia and handed over to Central Intelligence Agency ("CIA") officials who then transported him to Afghanistan where he was detained and interrogated by CIA and Afghan officials. The United States intervened as a defendant in the district court, asserting that the action, brought against CIA officials and employees of corporations, could not proceed because of information protected by the state secrets privilege. Excerpts below from the Fourth Circuit opinion provide a brief background and explain the basis for the court's dismissal (citations to submissions and most footnotes omitted).

In September 2007 the United States filed a brief in the Supreme Court opposing a petition for writ of certiorari by El-Masri, arguing that the Fourth Circuit decision was correct and that review by the Supreme Court was not warranted, available at *www.usdoj.gov/osg/briefs/2007/0responses/2006-1613.resp.html*. The Supreme Court denied certiorari on October 9, 2007. 128 S. Ct. 373 (2007).

* * * *

The Complaint alleged three separate causes of action. The first claim was against Director Tenet and the unknown CIA employees, pursuant to *Bivens v. Six Unknown Named Agents of Federal Bureau of Narcotics*, 403 U.S. 388, 91 S. Ct. 1999, 29 L. Ed. 2d 619 (1971), for violations of El-Masri's Fifth Amendment right to due process. Specifically, El-Masri contends that Tenet and the defendant CIA employees contravened the Due Process Clause's prohibition against subjecting anyone held in United States custody to treatment that shocks the conscience or depriving a person of liberty in the absence of legal process. El-Masri's second cause of action was initiated pursuant to the Alien Tort Statute (the "ATS"), and alleged that each of the defendants had contravened the international legal norm against prolonged arbitrary detention. The third cause of action was also asserted under the ATS, and maintained that each defendant had violated international legal norms prohibiting cruel, inhuman, or degrading treatment.

On March 8, 2006, the United States filed a Statement of Interest in the underlying proceedings, pursuant to 28 U.S.C. § 517, and interposed a claim of the state secrets privilege. The then Director of the CIA, Porter Goss, submitted two sworn declarations to the district court in support of the state secrets privilege claim. The first declaration was unclassified, and explained in general terms the reasons for the United States' assertion of privilege. The other declaration was classified; it detailed the information that the United States sought to protect, explained why further court proceedings would unreasonably risk that information's disclosure, and spelled out why such disclosure would be detrimental to the national security (the "Classified Declaration"). . . . On March 13, 2006, the United States formally moved to intervene as a defendant in the district court proceedings. Contemporaneous with seeking to intervene as a defendant, the United States moved to dismiss the Complaint, contending that its interposition of the state secrets privilege precluded the litigation of El-Masri's causes of action.

*   *   *   *

In the period after the district court's dismissal of El-Masri's Complaint, his alleged rendition—and the rendition operations of the United States generally—have remained subjects of public discussion. In El-Masri's view, two additions to the body of public information on these topics are especially significant in this appeal. First, on June 7, 2006, the Council of Europe released a draft report on alleged United States renditions and detentions involving the Council's member countries. This report concluded that El-Masri's account of his rendition and confinement was substantially accurate. Second, on September 6, 2006, in a White House address, President Bush publicly disclosed the existence of a CIA program in which suspected terrorists are detained and interrogated at locations outside the United States. The President declined, however, to reveal any of this CIA program's operational details, including the locations or other circumstances of its detainees' confinement.

II.

El-Masri maintains on appeal that the district court misapplied the state secrets doctrine in dismissing his Complaint without requiring any responsive pleadings from the defendants or permitting any discovery to be conducted. Importantly, El-Masri does not contend that the state secrets privilege has no role in these proceedings. To the contrary, he acknowledges that at least some information important to his claims is likely to be privileged, and thus beyond his reach. But he challenges the court's determination that state secrets are so central to this matter that any attempt at further litigation would threaten their disclosure. As explained below, we conclude that the district court correctly assessed the centrality of state secrets in this dispute. We therefore affirm its Order and the dismissal of El-Masri's Complaint.

A.1. Under the state secrets doctrine, the United States may prevent the disclosure of information in a judicial proceeding if "there is a reasonable danger" that such disclosure "will expose military matters which, in the interest of national security, should not be divulged." *United States v. Reynolds*, 345 U.S. 1, 10, 73 S. Ct. 528, 97 L. Ed. 727 (1953). *Reynolds*, the Supreme Court's leading decision on the state secrets privilege, established the doctrine in its modern form. There, an Air Force B-29 bomber had crashed during testing of secret electronic equipment, killing three civilian observers who were on board. Their widows sued the United States under the Federal Tort Claims Act, and they sought discovery of certain Air Force documents relating to the crash. The Air Force refused to disclose the documents and filed a formal "Claim of Privilege," contending that the plane had been on "a highly secret mission of the Air Force," and that disclosure of the requested materials would "seriously hamper[]national security, flying safety and the development of highly technical and secret military equipment." *Id.* at 4–5.

The Court sustained the Air Force's refusal to disclose the documents sought by the plaintiffs, concluding that the officials involved had properly invoked the "privilege against revealing military secrets." 345 U.S. at 6–7. This state secrets privilege, the Court observed, was "well established in the law of evidence." *Id.* . . .

Although the state secrets privilege was developed at common law, it performs a function of constitutional significance, because it allows the executive branch to protect information whose secrecy is necessary to its military and foreign-affairs responsibilities. *Reynolds* itself suggested that the state secrets doctrine allowed the Court to avoid the constitutional conflict that might have arisen had the judiciary demanded that the Executive disclose highly sensitive military secrets. *See* 345 U.S. at 6. In *United States v. Nixon*, the Court further articulated the doctrine's constitutional dimension, observing that the state secrets privilege provides exceptionally strong protection because it concerns "areas of Art. II duties [in which] the courts have traditionally shown the utmost deference to Presidential responsibilities." 418 U.S. 683, 710, 94 S. Ct. 3090, 41 L. Ed. 2d 1039 (1974). The *Nixon* Court went on to recognize that, to the extent an executive claim of privilege "relates to the effective discharge of a President's powers, it is constitutionally based." *Id.* at 711. Significantly, the Executive's constitutional authority is at its broadest in the realm of military and foreign affairs. The Court accordingly has indicated that the judiciary's role as a check on presidential action in foreign affairs is limited. . . . Moreover, both the Supreme Court and this Court have recognized that the Executive's constitutional mandate encompasses the authority to protect national security information. *See Dep't of the Navy v. Egan*, 484 U.S. 518, 527, 108 S. Ct. 818, 98 L. Ed. 2d 918 (1988) (observing that "authority to protect [national security] information falls on the President as head of the Executive Branch and as Commander in Chief"); *United States v. Marchetti*, 466 F.2d 1309, 1315 (4th Cir. 1972) (" Gathering intelligence information and the other activities of the [CIA], including clandestine affairs against other nations, are all within the President's constitutional responsibility for the security of the Nation as the Chief Executive and as Commander in Chief of our Armed forces."). The state secrets privilege that the United States has interposed in this civil proceeding thus has a firm foundation in the Constitution, in addition to its basis in the common law of evidence.

2. A court faced with a state secrets privilege question is obliged to resolve the matter by use of a three-part analysis. At the outset, the court must ascertain that the procedural requirements for invoking the state secrets privilege have been satisfied. Second, the court must decide whether the information sought to be protected qualifies as privileged under the state secrets doctrine. Finally, if the subject information is determined to be privileged, the ultimate question to be resolved is how the matter should proceed in light of the successful privilege claim.

*   *   *   *

3. . . . [O]ur analysis of the Executive's interposition of the state secrets privilege is governed primarily by two standards. First, evidence is privileged pursuant to the state secrets doctrine if, under all the circumstances of the case, there is a reasonable danger that its disclosure will expose military (or diplomatic or intelligence) matters which, in the interest of national security, should

not be divulged. *See Reynolds*, 345 U.S. at 10. Second, a proceeding in which the state secrets privilege is successfully interposed must be dismissed if the circumstances make clear that privileged information will be so central to the litigation that any attempt to proceed will threaten that information's disclosure. *See Sterling*, 416 F.3d at 348; *see also Reynolds*, 345 U.S. at 11 n. 26; *Totten*, 92 U.S. at 107. With these controlling principles in mind, and being cognizant of the delicate balance to be struck in applying the state secrets doctrine, we proceed to our analysis of El-Masri's contentions.

*   *   *   *

[B. 1.]a. The heart of El-Masri's appeal is his assertion that the facts essential to his Complaint have largely been made public, either in statements by United States officials or in reports by media outlets and foreign governmental entities. He maintains that the subject of this action is simply "a rendition and its consequences," and that its critical facts—the CIA's operation of a rendition program targeted at terrorism suspects, plus the tactics employed therein—have been so widely discussed that litigation concerning them could do no harm to national security. . . . As a result, El-Masri contends that the district court should have allowed his case to move forward with discovery, perhaps with special procedures imposed to protect sensitive information.

El-Masri's contention in that regard, however, misapprehends the nature of our assessment of a dismissal on state secrets grounds. The controlling inquiry is not whether the general subject matter of an action can be described without resort to state secrets. Rather, we must ascertain whether an action can be litigated without threatening the disclosure of such state secrets. Thus, for purposes of the state secrets analysis, the "central facts" and "very subject matter" of an action are those facts that are essential to prosecuting the action or defending against it.

*   *   *   *

. . . [W]e must reject El-Masri's view that the existence of public reports concerning his alleged rendition (and the CIA's rendition program in general) should have saved his Complaint from dismissal.

Even if we assume, arguendo, that the state secrets privilege does not apply to the information that media outlets have published concerning those topics, dismissal of his Complaint would nonetheless be proper because the public information does not include the facts that are central to litigating his action. Rather, those central facts—the CIA means and methods that form the subject matter of El-Masri's claim—remain state secrets. Consequently, pursuant to the standards that El-Masri has acknowledged as controlling, the district court did not err in dismissing his Complaint at the pleading stage.

2. El-Masri also contends that, instead of dismissing his Complaint, the district court should have employed some procedure under which state secrets would have been revealed to him, his counsel, and the court, but withheld from the public. Specifically, he suggests that the court ought to have received all the state secrets evidence in camera and under seal, provided his counsel access to it pursuant to a nondisclosure agreement (after arranging for necessary security clearances), and then conducted an in camera trial. We need not dwell long on El-Masri's proposal in this regard, for it is expressly foreclosed by *Reynolds*, the Supreme Court decision that controls this entire field of inquiry. *Reynolds* plainly held that when "the occasion for the privilege is appropriate, . . . the court should not jeopardize the security which the privilege is meant to protect by insisting upon an examination of the evidence, even by the judge alone, in chambers." 345 U.S. at 10. El-Masri's assertion that the district court erred in not compelling the disclosure of state secrets to him and his lawyers is thus without merit.

C. In addition to his analysis under the controlling legal principles, El-Masri presents a sharp attack on what he views as the dire constitutional and policy consequences of dismissing his Complaint. He maintains that the district court's ruling, if affirmed, would enable the Executive to unilaterally avoid judicial scrutiny merely by asserting that state secrets are at stake in a given matter. More broadly, he questions the very application of the state secrets doctrine in matters where "egregious executive misconduct" is alleged, contending that, in such circumstances, the courts' "constitutional duty to review executive action" should trump the procedural protections traditionally accorded state secrets.

Contrary to El-Masri's assertion, the state secrets doctrine does not represent a surrender of judicial control over access to the courts. As we have explained, it is the court, not the Executive, that determines whether the state secrets privilege has been properly invoked. In order to successfully claim the state secrets privilege, the Executive must satisfy the court that disclosure of the information sought to be protected would expose matters that, in the interest of national security, ought to remain secret. Similarly, in order to win dismissal of an action on state secrets grounds, the Executive must persuade the court that state secrets are so central to the action that it cannot be fairly litigated without threatening their disclosure. The state secrets privilege cannot be successfully interposed, nor can it lead to dismissal of an action, based merely on the Executive's assertion that the pertinent standard has been met.

We have reviewed the Classified Declaration, as did the district court, and the extensive information it contains is crucial to our decision in this matter. El-Masri's contention that his Complaint was dismissed based on the Executive's "unilateral assert[ion] of a need for secrecy" is entirely unfounded. . . .

. . . [W]hen an executive officer's liability for official action can be established in a properly conducted judicial proceeding, we will not hesitate to enter judgment accordingly. But we would be guilty of excess in our own right if we were to disregard settled legal principles in order to reach the merits of an executive action that would not otherwise be before us—especially when the challenged action pertains to military or foreign policy. We decline to follow such a course, and thus reject El-Masri's invitation to rule that the state secrets doctrine can be brushed aside on the ground that the President's foreign policy has gotten out of line.

D. As we have observed in the past, the successful interposition of the state secrets privilege imposes a heavy burden on the party against whom the privilege is asserted. . . . That party loses access to evidence that he needs to prosecute his action and, if privileged state secrets are sufficiently central to the matter, may lose his cause of action altogether. Moreover, a plaintiff suffers this reversal not through any fault of his own, but because his personal interest in pursuing his civil claim is subordinated to the collective interest in national security. . . . [7] In view of these considerations, we recognize the gravity of our conclusion that El-Masri must be denied a judicial forum for his Complaint, and reiterate our past observations that dismissal on state secrets grounds is appropriate only in a narrow category of disputes. *See Sterling*, 416 F.3d at 348; *Fitzgerald*, 776 F.2d at 1241–42. Nonetheless, we think it plain that the matter before us falls squarely within that narrow class, and we are unable to find merit in El-Masri's assertion to the contrary.

* * * *

b. Warrantless surveillance claim

On November 16, 2007, the U.S. Court of Appeals for the Ninth Circuit reversed a district court order that would have allowed the plaintiffs an alternative method of providing evidence determined to be protected by the state secrets privilege. *Al-Haramain Islamic Foundation, Inc. v. Bush*, 507 F.3d 1190 (9th Cir. 2007). As described by the court, the plaintiff in

---

[7] . . . [T]he Executive's authority to protect confidential military and intelligence information is much broader in civil matters than in criminal prosecutions. The Supreme Court explained this principle in *Reynolds*, observing:

> Respondents have cited us to those cases in the criminal field, where it has been held that the Government can invoke its evidentiary privileges only at the price of letting the defendant go free. The rationale of the criminal cases is that, since the Government which prosecutes an accused also has the duty to see that justice is done, it is unconscionable to allow it to undertake prosecution and then invoke its governmental privileges to deprive the accused of anything which might be material to his defense. Such rationale has no application in a civil forum where the Government is not the moving party, but is a defendant only on terms to which it has consented.

345 U.S. at 12. El-Masri's reliance on our decision in *United States v. Moussaoui*, 382 F.3d 453 (4th Cir. 2004), in which we required the United States to grant a criminal defendant substantial access to enemy-combatant witnesses whose very identities were highly classified, is thus misplaced.

the case, Al-Haramain Islamic Foundation, Inc., and two of its attorneys, "claimed that they were subject to warrantless electronic surveillance in 2004 in violation of the Foreign Intelligence Surveillance Act, 50 U.S.C. §§ 1801 et seq. ("FISA"), various provisions of the United States Constitution, and international law." A classified document on which plaintiff relied to show that he had been the subject of surveillance ("Sealed Document") had been inadvertently provided to plaintiff by the government and subsequently recalled.

The Ninth Circuit upheld the district court's conclusion that the general subject matter, *i.e.*, the Terrorist Surveillance Program, was not protected, but that the Sealed Document was protected by the state secrets privilege. The court reversed the district court's order allowing plaintiff to reconstruct the substance of the Sealed Document from memory and remanded the case for a determination whether the Foreign Intelligence Surveillance Act "preempts the common law *state secrets* privilege . . . a question the district court did not reach in its denial of the government's motion to dismiss."

Excerpts follow from the Ninth Circuit decision (footnotes omitted).

Following the terrorist attacks on September 11, 2001, President George W. Bush authorized the National Security Agency ("NSA") to conduct a warrantless communications surveillance program. The program intercepted international communications into and out of the United States of persons alleged to have ties to Al Qaeda and other terrorist networks. Though its operating parameters remain murky, and certain details may forever remain so, much of what is known about the Terrorist Surveillance Program ("TSP") was spoon-fed to the public by the President and his administration.

* * * *

Al-Haramain is a Muslim charity which is active in more than 50 countries. . . . In February 2004, the Office of Foreign Assets Control of the Department of Treasury temporarily froze Al-Haramain's assets pending a proceeding to determine whether to declare it a "Specially Designated Global Terrorist" due to the organization's alleged ties to Al Qaeda. Ultimately, Al-Haramain and one of its directors, Soliman Al-Buthi, were declared "Specially Designated Global Terrorists."

In August 2004, during Al-Haramain's civil designation proceeding, the Department of the Treasury produced a number of unclassified materials that were given to Al-Haramain's counsel and two of its directors. Inadvertently included in these materials was the Sealed Document, which was labeled "TOP SECRET." Al-Haramain's counsel copied and disseminated the materials, including the Sealed Document, to Al-Haramain's directors and co-counsel, including Wendell Belew and Asim Ghafoor. In August or September of 2004, a reporter from *The Washington Post* reviewed these documents while researching an article. In late August, the FBI was notified of the Sealed Document's inadvertent disclosure. In October of 2004, the FBI retrieved all copies of the Sealed Document from Al-Haramain's counsel, though it did not seek out Al-Haramain's directors to obtain their copies. The Sealed Document is located in a Department of Justice Secured Compartmentalized Information Facility.

Al-Haramain alleges that after *The New York Times'* story broke in December 2005 [revealing the program's existence], it realized that the Sealed Document was proof that it had been subjected to warrantless surveillance in March and April of 2004. Though the government has acknowledged the existence of the TSP, it has not disclosed the identities of the specific persons or entities surveilled under the program, and disputes whether Al-Haramain's inferences are correct.

*   *   *   *

II. THE SUBJECT MATTER OF THE LITIGATION IS NOT A STATE SECRET

Based on the various public statements made by the President and members of his administration acknowledging the existence of the TSP, and Al-Haramain's purported knowledge that its members' communications had been intercepted, the district court rejected the government's contention that the subject matter of the litigation is a state secret. *See Al-Haramain*, 451 F. Supp. 2d at 1225. The court found that the government had "lifted the veil of secrecy on the existence of the [TSP] and plaintiffs only seek to establish whether interception of their communications . . . was unlawful." *Id.*

We agree with the district court's conclusion that the very subject matter of the litigation—the government's alleged warrantless surveillance program under the TSP—is not protected by the state secrets privilege. Two discrete sets of unclassified facts support this determination. First, President Bush and others in the administration publicly acknowledged that in the months following the September 11, 2001, terrorist attacks, the President authorized a communications surveillance program that intercepted the communications of persons with suspected links to Al Qaeda and related terrorist organizations. Second, in 2004, Al-Haramain was officially declared by the government to be a "Specially Designated Global Terrorist" due to its purported ties to Al Qaeda. The subject matter of the litigation—the TSP and the government's warrantless surveillance of persons or entities who, like Al-Haramain, were suspected by the NSA to have connections to terrorists—is simply not a state secret. At this early stage in the litigation, enough is known about the TSP, and Al-Haramain's classification as a "Specially Designated Global Terrorist," that the subject matter of Al-Haramain's lawsuit can be discussed, as it has been extensively in publicly-filed pleadings, televised arguments in open court in this appeal, and in the media and the blogosphere, without disturbing the dark waters of privileged information.

* * * *

[Principal Deputy Director for National Intelligence]General Hayden's statements provided to the American public a wealth of information about the TSP. The public now knows the following additional facts about the program, beyond the general contours outlined by other officials: (1) at least one participant for each surveilled call was located outside the United States; (2) the surveillance was conducted without FISA warrants; (3) inadvertent calls involving purely domestic callers were destroyed and not reported; (4) the inadvertent collection was recorded and reported; and (5) U.S. identities are expunged from NSA records of surveilled calls if deemed non-essential to an understanding of the intelligence value of a particular report. These facts alone, disclosed by General Hayden in a public address, provide a fairly complete picture of the scope of the TSP.

Just a month after the President's announcement, on January 19, 2006, the United States Department of Justice joined the succession of government disclosures in a 42-page white paper in which it not only confirmed that President Bush had authorized the interception of international communications into and out of the United States, but also justified the intercepts with a legal analysis. U.S. Department of Justice, Legal Authorities Supporting the Activities of the National Security Agency Described by the President (Jan. 19, 2006), *http://www.usdoj.gov/opa/whitepaper-onnsalegalauthorities.pdf* (last visited Nov. 8, 2007). . . .

* * * *

To be sure, there are details about the program that the government has not yet disclosed, but because of the voluntary disclosures made by various officials since December 2005, the nature and purpose of the TSP, the "type" of persons it targeted, and even some of its procedures are not state secrets. In other words, the government's many attempts to assuage citizens' fears that they have not been surveilled now doom the government's assertion that the very subject matter of this litigation, the existence of a warrantless surveillance program, is barred by the state secrets privilege.

* * * *

[We are not] persuaded by the recent case of *El-Masri*. [discussed in 3a. *supra*] . . .

The Fourth Circuit upheld the government's assertion of the state secrets privilege and dismissed the action. To establish liability, El-Masri would be required to produce "evidence that exposes how the CIA organizes, staffs, and supervises its most sensitive intelligence operations." *Id.* at 309. . . .

The court in *El-Masri* . . . merged the concept of "subject matter" with the notion of proof of a prima facie case. Indeed, in that case, the facts may have counseled for such an approach.

In contrast, we do not necessarily view the "subject matter" of a lawsuit as one and the same with the facts necessary to litigate the case. . . . Because the Fourth Circuit has accorded an expansive meaning to the "subject matter" of an action, one that we have not adopted, *El-Masri* does not support dismissal based on the subject matter of the suit.

* * * *

Al-Haramain's case does involve privileged information, but that fact alone does not render the very subject matter of the action a state secret. Accordingly, we affirm the district court's denial of dismissal on that basis.

III. THE GOVERNMENT'S INVOCATION OF THE STATE SECRETS PRIVILEGE

Although the very subject matter of this lawsuit does not result in automatic dismissal, we must still address the government's invocation of the state secrets privilege as to the Sealed Document and its assertion that Al-Haramain cannot establish either standing or a prima facie case without the use of state secrets. . . .

. . . The parties do not dispute that the procedural requirements for invoking the state secrets privilege have been met. . . .

Next, we must determine whether the circumstances before us counsel that the state secrets privilege is applicable, without forcing a disclosure of the very thing that the privilege is designed to protect. *Id.* at 7–8. . . . The district court held . . . that "because the government has not officially confirmed or denied whether plaintiffs were subject to surveillance, even if plaintiffs know they were, this information remains secret. Furthermore, while plaintiffs know the contents of the [Sealed] Document, it too remains secret." *Al-Haramain*, 451 F. Supp. 2d at 1223.

The district court also concluded that the government did not waive its privilege by inadvertent disclosure of the Sealed Document. *Id.* at 1228. . . . .

* * * *

Having reviewed [the Sealed Document] *in camera*, we conclude that the Sealed Document is protected by the state secrets privilege, along with the information as to whether the government surveilled Al-Haramain. . . . The process of *in camera* review ineluctably places the court in a role that runs contrary to our fundamental principle of a transparent judicial system. It also places on the court a special burden to assure itself that an appropriate balance is struck between protecting national security matters and preserving an open court system. That said, we acknowledge the need to defer to the Executive on matters of foreign policy and national security and surely cannot legitimately find ourselves second guessing the Executive in this arena.

*   *   *   *

We have spent considerable time examining the government's declarations (both publicly filed and those filed under seal). We are satisfied that the basis for the privilege is exceptionally well documented. Detailed statements underscore that disclosure of information concerning the Sealed Document and the means, sources and methods of intelligence gathering in the context of this case would undermine the government's intelligence capabilities and compromise national security. Thus, we reach the same conclusion as the district court: the government has sustained its burden as to the state secrets privilege.

We must next resolve how the litigation should proceed in light of the government's successful privilege claim. . . .

After correctly determining that the Sealed Document was protected by the state secrets privilege, the district court then erred in forging an unusual path forward in this litigation. Though it granted the government's motion to deny Al-Haramain access to the Sealed Document based on the state secrets privilege, the court permitted the Al-Haramain plaintiffs to file *in camera* affidavits attesting to the contents of the document from their memories. *Al-Haramain*, 451 F. Supp. 2d at 1229.

The district court's approach—a commendable effort to thread the needle—is contrary to established Supreme Court precedent. If information is found to be a privileged state secret, there are only two ways that litigation can proceed: (1) if the plaintiffs can prove "the essential facts" of their claims "without resort to material touching upon military secrets," *Reynolds*, 345 U.S. at 11, or (2) in accord with the procedure outlined in FISA. By allowing *in camera* review of affidavits attesting to individuals' memories of the Sealed Document, the district court sanctioned "material touching" upon privileged information, contrary to *Reynolds*. *See* 345 U.S. at 11. Although FISA permits district court judges to conduct an *in camera* review of information relating to electronic surveillance, there are detailed procedural safeguards that must be satisfied before such review can be conducted. *See, e.g.,* 50 U.S.C. § 1806(f). The district court did not address this issue nor do we here.

Moreover, the district court's solution is flawed: if the Sealed Document is privileged because it contains very sensitive information regarding national security, permitting the same information to be revealed through reconstructed memories circumvents the document's absolute privilege. *See Reynolds*, 345 U.S. at 10 (A court "should not jeopardize the security which the privilege is meant to protect by insisting upon an examination of the evidence, even by the judge alone, in chambers."). That approach also suffers from a worst of both world's deficiency: either the memory is wholly accurate, in which case the approach is tantamount to release of the document itself, or the memory is inaccurate, in which case the court is not well-served and the disclosure may be even more problematic from a security standpoint. The state secrets privilege, because of its unique national security considerations, does not lend itself to a compromise solution in this case. The Sealed Document, its contents, and any individuals' memories of its contents, even well-reasoned speculation as to its contents, are completely barred from further disclosure in this litigation by the common law state secrets privilege.

IV. ABSENT THE SEALED DOCUMENT, AL-HARAMAIN CANNOT ESTABLISH STANDING

* * * *

"[E]ven the most compelling necessity cannot overcome the claim of privilege if the court is ultimately satisfied that military secrets are at stake." *Reynolds*, 345 U.S. at 11. Because we affirm the district court's conclusion that the Sealed Document, along with data concerning surveillance, are privileged, and conclude that no testimony attesting to individuals' memories of the document may be admitted to establish the contents of the document, Al-Haramain cannot establish that it has standing, and its claims must be dismissed, unless FISA preempts the state secrets privilege.

* * * *

5. Funding Eligibility Conditions for Organizations Receiving U.S. Federal Funding for Certain Activities Abroad

On February 27, 2007, the U.S. Court of Appeals for the D.C. Circuit upheld a statutory requirement that makes federal funds for international HIV/AIDS programs unavailable "to any group or organization that does not have a policy explicitly opposing prostitution and sex trafficking," with certain specific exceptions. *DKT International Inc. v. USAID*, 477 F.3d 758 (D.C. Cir. 2007). DKT International was denied funds because it did not have the required policy; it brought this action claiming that the requirement violated the freedom of speech clause of the First Amendment. Excerpts below from the court's opinion explain its conclusion that the constraint imposed by the statute did not violate the First Amendment because the government has the right to ensure the clarity of the message it is funding, particularly in matters with foreign policy implications.

The official position of the United States is that eradicating prostitution and sex trafficking is an integral part of the worldwide fight against HIV/AIDS. In awarding grants to private organizations for HIV/AIDS relief efforts, the government—through the U.S. Agency for International Development—only funds organizations that share this view. DKT International refused to certify that it has a policy opposing prostitution and sex trafficking, and therefore did not qualify for a grant. The district court struck down the funding condition on the ground that it violated DKT's freedom of speech under the First Amendment. We reverse.

*　　*　　*　　*

DKT International provides family planning and HIV/AIDS prevention programming in foreign countries, and receives about 16 percent of its total budget from Agency [for International Development] grants. DKT operates as a subgrantee under Family Health International (FHI) in Vietnam, where it distributes condoms and condom lubricant. . . . DKT did not, and does not, have a policy for or against prostitution and sex trafficking. It therefore refused to sign [a] subagreement with the certification requirement [that it certify that it "has a policy explicitly opposing prostitution and sex trafficking"]. FHI then cancelled the grant and informed DKT that FHI was "unable to provide additional funding to DKT."

DKT alleged that it refuses to adopt a policy opposing prostitution because this might result in "stigmatizing and alienating many of the people most vulnerable to HIV/AIDS—the sex workers. . . ." It claims that the certification requirement in § 7631(f) violates the First Amendment because it constrains DKT's speech in other programs for which it does not receive federal funds and because it forces DKT to convey a message with which it does not necessarily agree.

* * * *

Everyone, including DKT, agrees that the government may bar grantees from using grant money to promote legalizing prostitution. But DKT complains that § 7631(f) constrains its speech in other programs, for which it does not receive federal funds. That effect, DKT argues, makes the case like *FCC v. League of Women Voters of California*, 468 U.S. 364, 104 S. Ct. 3106, 82 L. Ed. 2d 278 (1984), and unlike *Rust v. Sullivan* [500 U.S. 173 (1991)] We think the opposite. The restriction struck down in *League of Women Voters* prohibited public broadcasting stations from editorializing. The Court pointed out that a public broadcasting station could not editorialize with its nonfederal funds even if its federal grants amounted to only a small fraction of its income. 468 U.S. at 400. Therefore the restriction did not simply govern the use of federal funds. *Id. Rust*, on the other hand, upheld regulations prohibiting federally funded family planning services from engaging in abortion counseling or in any way advocating abortion as a method of family planning. 500 U.S. at 178.

The difference between the two decisions, as the Court later explained, is that in *Rust* "the government did not create a program to encourage private speech but instead used private speakers to transmit specific information pertaining to its own program. . . ." In this case, as in *Rust*, "the government's own message is being delivered," *Legal Servs. Corp. v. Velazquez*, 531 U.S. 533, 541 (2001).

Under *Rust*, . . . the government may thus constitutionally communicate a particular viewpoint through its agents and require those agents not convey contrary messages. We think it follows that in choosing its agents, the government may use criteria to ensure that its message is conveyed in an efficient and effective fashion. . . . The Supreme Court has also recognized that the government may take "appropriate steps" to ensure that its message is "neither garbled nor distorted." *Rosenberger*, 515 U.S. at 833. This is particularly true where the government is speaking on matters with foreign policy implications, as it is here. *See DKT Mem'l*, 887 F.2d at 289–91. The government's brief summarizes these points: "It would make little sense for the government to provide billions of dollars to encourage the reduction of HIV/AIDS behavioral risks, including prostitution and sex trafficking, and yet to engage as partners in this effort organizations that are neutral toward or even actively promote the same practices sought to be eradicated. The effectiveness of the government's viewpoint-based program would be substantially undermined, and the government's message confused, if the organizations hired to implement that program by providing HIV/AIDS programs and services to the public could advance an opposite viewpoint in their privately-funded operations."

*   *   *   *

B. CONSTITUENT ENTITIES

Republic of the Marshall Islands

On August 2, 2007, the U.S. Court of Federal Claims granted a motion filed by the United States as defendant to dismiss claims related to U.S. nuclear testing from 1946–1958 in the Marshall Islands. *Bikini v. United States*, 77 Fed. Cl. 744 (Ct. Cl. 2007). On the same day, the court also granted the government's motion to dismiss in a companion case, *John v. United States*, 77 Fed. Cl. 788 (Fed. Cl. 2007). For a discussion of the cases, *see Digest 2006* at 316–25.

Excerpts below from the court's analysis in *Bikini* address its conclusion that jurisdiction over these claims was withdrawn by a 1985 agreement between the Republic of the Marshall Islands and the United States pursuant to § 177 of the Compact of Free Association ("Section 177 Agreement") and that the claims should also be dismissed under the political question doctrine.

---

*   *   *   *

During the period June 30, 1946, to August 18, 1958, the United States conducted a series of nuclear tests in the Marshall Islands that included detonation of twenty-three atomic and hydrogen bombs at Bikini Atoll and forty-three atomic and hydrogen bombs at Enewetak Atoll. These tests necessitated removal of the inhabitants and their relocation to other islands and resulted in severe physical destruction at the atolls directly involved, as well as radioactive contamination at other parts of the Marshall [I]sland chain. The effects of the testing program included: annihilation of some islands and vaporization of portions of others; permanent resettlement with substantial relocation hardships to some inhabitants; exposure to high levels of radiation by some inhabitants; and widespread contamination from radioactivity that renders some islands unuseable by man for indefinite future periods.

The Marshall Islands are a part of Micronesia, formerly a United Nations Trust Territory administered by the United States. . . .

*   *   *   *

The United States was designated "administering authority" over the Trust Territory pursuant to an agreement ratified by the United Nations Security Council on April 2, 1947, and approved by Congressional joint resolution on July 18, 1947. 61 Stat. 3301, T.I.A.S. No. 1665. . . .

*   *   *   *

. . . The United States and the Republic of the Marshall Islands ("RMI") signed [a Compact of Free Association] and its related agreements on June 25, 1983. . . .

*   *   *   *

Section 177 of the Compact provides a procedure for the disposition of claims that have resulted from the Nuclear Testing Program. A separate agreement between the United States and the RMI is authorized to provide for the settlement of all such claims (the "Section 177 Agreement"). . . .

Section 177 of the Compact provides:

(a) The Government of the United States accepts the responsibility for compensation owing to citizens of the Marshall Islands, or the Federated States of Micronesia (or Palau) for loss or damage to property and person of the citizens of the Marshall Islands, or the Federated States of Micronesia, resulting from the nuclear testing program which the Government of the United States conducted in the Northern Marshall Islands between June 30, 1946, and August 18, 1958.

(b) The Government of the United States and the Government of the Marshall Islands shall set forth in a separate agreement provisions for the just and adequate settlement of all such claims which have arisen in regard to the Marshall Islands and its citizens and which have not as yet been compensated or which in the future may arise . . . This separate agreement shall come into effect simultaneously with this Compact and shall remain in effect in accordance with its own terms.

(c) The Government of the United States shall provide to the Government of the Marshall Islands, on a grant basis, the amount of $150 million to be paid and distributed in accordance with the separate agreement referred to in this Section, and shall provide the services and programs set forth in this separate agreement, the language of which is incorporated into this Compact.

The Compact [of Free Association Act of 1985] approves Compact Section 177 and, by reference, specifically incorporates the provisions of the Section 177 Agreement into the Compact Act. . . .

*   *   *   *

IV. Withdrawal of jurisdiction

*   *   *   *

1. Withdrawal of jurisdiction in Article X of the Section 177 Agreement

The withdrawal of jurisdiction regarding claims that arise from the Nuclear Testing Program is an unambiguous express provision of the Section 177 Agreement. Article X, Section 1 of the Section 177 Agreement . . . recites:

> This Agreement constitutes the full settlement of all claims, past, present and future, of the Government, citizens and nationals of the Marshall Islands which are based upon, arise out of, or are in any way related to the Nuclear Testing Program. . . .

Article XII of the Section 177 Agreement provides:

> All claims described in Articles X and XI of this Agreement shall be terminated. No court of the United States shall have jurisdiction to entertain such claims, and any such claims pending in the courts of the United States shall be dismissed.

2. Implied-in-fact contract claims and claims based on breach of fiduciary duty

Plaintiffs allege a breach of implied-in-fact contract and breach of fiduciary duties in Counts II, III, IV, and VI, claims that are based upon the conduct of the United States in its treatment and care of the people of the RMI during the Nuclear Testing Program and other subsequent uses of Bikini Atoll. In order to come within the jurisdiction of the Court of Federal Claims, the scope of claims covered by the withdrawal of jurisdiction contained in Article XII of the Section 177 Agreement must not reach these claims.

*   *   *   *

. . . Although the language of plaintiffs' counts carries different connotations, the heart of their dispute with the Government— whether framed as a breach of implied duties or breach of fiduciary duties—relates directly to the Nuclear Testing Program. For example, in Count VI, plaintiffs allege that their cause of action did not accrue until January 24, 2005, when the United States "refused to adequately fund the award issued by the Nuclear Claims Tribunal on March 5, 2001." The NCT determined on March 5, 2001, the amount of award to plaintiffs based on the damages caused by the Nuclear Testing Program. Plaintiffs attempt to mask the essence of their claim by attacking the Compact.

. . . Withdrawal of jurisdiction for a claim based on an implied-in-fact contract or breach of fiduciary duties against the United States, particularly in circumstances that implicate foreign relations, falls squarely within the power of Congress. *See Lynch*, 292 U.S. at 581 ("The rule that the United States may not be sued without its consent is all-embracing.").

Consistent with defendant's argument that all of plaintiffs' claims have been withdrawn, the court notes that the Government attempted to settle fully the claims of the People of Bikini. . . . *See* Pub. L. No. 100-446, 102 Stat. 1774, 1798 (1988). The settlement in Bikini was signed into law on September 27, 1988, and provided, in order to "ful[ly] satis[fy] the obligation of the United States to provide funds to assist in the resettlement and rehabilitation of Bikini Atoll by the People of Bikini, to which the full faith and credit of the United States is pledged pursuant to section 103(l) of Public Law 99-239, [that] the United States shall deposit $ 90,000,000 into the Resettlement Trust Fund for the People of Bikini established pursuant to Public Law 97-257." *Id*. The plain language of this act underscores the finality effected by the withdrawal of jurisdiction. . . .

*   *   *   *

V. Political question

While discussion of the political question doctrine is not essential to decision due to jurisdictional impediments to review of plaintiffs' claims, the court relies, as an alternative ground for dismissal, on application of the political question doctrine to plaintiffs' challenge to the adequacy of relief contained in the Compact and the Section 177 Agreement. Thus, assuming, *arguendo*, that plaintiffs could prosecute a valid claim for review of the adequacy of the alternative relief provided by the Compact and the Section 177

Agreement that was not barred by the statute of limitations, was not subject to collateral estoppel, and would not be subsumed in the withdrawal of jurisdiction, the political question doctrine nevertheless would bar review of their claims.

* * * *

The decision that a question is nonjusticiable is not one courts should make lightly. Although each Baker test [set forth in *Baker v. Carr*, 369 U.S. 186 (1962)]; is independent, *id.*, we must satisfy ourselves that at least one of the six Baker tests is inextricably present in the facts and circumstances in this case before we may conclude that it presents a nonjusticiable political question, *Baker*, 369 U.S. at 217. . . .

* * * *

. . . Resolution of plaintiffs' claims concerning the adequacy of the alternative relief, in contrast, would call for the court to retry plaintiffs' claims before the NCT in order to determine the adequacy of the award as a constitutional measure. Judicial resolution of complex issues of fact to determine whether the NCT's award constitutes just compensation and whether the United States is obligated to pay just compensation (either based on that award or its judicial proxy), would run counter to the final resolution of all plaintiffs' claims embodied in the Compact and the Section 177 Agreement.

The court recognizes "a textually demonstrable constitutional commitment of the issue to a coordinate political department," based upon the factual similarities to the Supreme Court's treatment to the Litinov Assignment in *Belmont*, 301 U.S. at 330, and in *Pink*, 315 U.S. at 229. *See Baker*, 369 U.S. at 217. Review of plaintiffs' claims regarding the adequacy of compensation under the Section 177 Agreement and the NCT would explore the formation of an international agreement and recognition of a foreign government, responsibilities charged to the Executive and Legislative branches of government.

In *Belmont* the Supreme Court reviewed the impact of the political question doctrine upon the challenge to the Litinov Assignment, which "br[ought] about a final settlement of the claims and counterclaims between the Soviet government and the United States;

and it was agreed that the Soviet government would take no steps to enforce claims against American nationals; but all such claims were released and assigned to the United States." 301 U.S. at 326. Similar to the circumstances in this case, "coincident with the assignment set forth in the complaint, the President recognized the Soviet government, and normal diplomatic relations were established between that government and the government of the United States." *Id.* at 330. The Supreme Court's description of the nature of the agreement aids in placing plaintiffs' claims in their proper context:

> The recognition, establishment of diplomatic relations, the assignment, and agreements with respect thereto, were all parts of one transaction, resulting in an international compact between the two governments. That the negotiations, acceptance of the assignment and agreements and understandings in respect thereof were within the competence of the President may not be doubted. Governmental power over internal affairs is distributed between the national government and the several states. Governmental power over external affairs is not distributed, but is vested exclusively in the national government. And in respect of what was done here, the Executive had authority to speak as the sole organ of that government.

Id.

Plaintiffs' objections to the adequacy of the settlement's terms call for an examination of the terms of the "international compact between the two governments" and investigation of complex issues of fact, not a narrow legal issue. *See id.* at 326. In *Ozanic v. United States*, 188 F.2d 228 (2d Cir. 1951), Judge Learned Hand addressed the ability of the President to settle foreign claims arising out of the recognition of the Yugoslav government:

> The constitutional power of the President extends to the settlement of mutual claims between a foreign government and the United States, at least when it is an incident to the recognition of that government; and it would be unreasonable to circumscribe it to such controversies. The continued

mutual amity between the nation and other powers again and again depends upon a satisfactory compromise of mutual claims; the necessary power to make such compromises has existed from the earliest times and been exercised by the foreign offices of all civilized nations.

Id. at 231 (footnote omitted). These factors support the conclusion that plaintiffs' claims impinge on the conduct of foreign affairs that the Constitution delegates to the Executive and Legislative branches. Moreover, the approval of the settlement terms by plebiscite in September 1983 would support a ruling that any dissatisfaction with the terms of the Compact and the Section 177 Agreement should be directed to the government of the RMI, not that of the United States.

* * * *

Among other things, the court also concluded that the claims for additional compensation to fully fund the NTC award are still premature because RMI's effort to obtain funding under the alternative procedure provided in the Compact Act and in Article IX of the Section 177 Agreement was still pending. The court explained:

> The alternative procedure . . . included a Changed Circumstances provision, which allocated to Congress the option to "authorize and appropriate funds" in the event that "loss or damage to property and person of the citizens of the Marshall Islands, resulting from the nuclear testing program arises or is discovered after the effective date" of the Compact Act and Changed Circumstances provision.

The court noted that "the RMI presented a 'Petition Presented to the Congress of the United States of America Regarding Changed Circumstances Arising from U.S. Nuclear Testing in the Marshall Islands' (the 'Changed Circumstances Request') [pursuant to Article IX of the Section 177 Agreement]" and resubmitted it in 2001. Congress had not ruled on that petition.

Cross References

Secretary of State discretionary role in citizenship and passport issues, **Chapter 1.A.** *and* **1.B.2.**

Cases presenting non-justiciable political questions, **Chapters 9. A.2. and B. and 18.A.4.d.(3)(i).**

Presidential statements on signing legislation into law, preserving constitutional powers, **Chapters 13.A.2.d.(1) and 16.A.3.c.**

CHAPTER 6

Human Rights

A. GENERAL

1. Human Rights Reports

On March 6, 2007, the Department of State released the 2006 Country Reports on Human Rights Practices. The document is submitted to Congress annually by the Department of State in compliance with §§ 116(d) and 502B(b) of the Foreign Assistance Act of 1961 ("FAA"), as amended, and § 504 of the Trade Act of 1974, as amended. These reports are often cited as a source for U.S. views on various aspects of human rights practice in other countries. The report is available at *www.state.gov/g/drl/rls/hrrpt/2006/*.

On April 5, 2007, the Department of State submitted its report "Supporting Human Rights and Democracy: The U.S. Record 2006," in compliance with Section 665 of Pub. L. No. 107-228, which requires the Department to report on actions taken by the U.S. Government to encourage respect for human rights. The report and related statements are available at *www.state.gov/g/drl/rls/shrd/2006/*.

2. UN Human Rights Committee

a. Follow-up response: U.S. implementation of the International Covenant on Civil and Political Rights

On October 21, 2005, the United States provided its combined second and third periodic reports to the UN Human Rights Committee concerning implementation of the International Covenant on Civil and Political Rights ("ICCPR" or "Covenant"), available at *www.state.gov/g/drl/rls/55504.htm*. In July 2006 representatives of the United States met with members of the Committee concerning the report. *See Digest 2005* at 258–300 and *Digest 2006* at 346–71. In its Concluding Observations, dated December 18, 2006, the Human Rights Committee requested that the United States provide information pertaining to selected recommendations within a year. U.N. Doc. No. CCPR/C/USA/CO/3/Rev.1. The United States submitted its response on October 10, 2007.

In the 2007 submission, the United States reiterated its position that the Covenant does not apply extraterritorially and that it contains no non-refoulement obligation. Both of these issues are discussed in U.S. comments on the Committee's General Comment 31; *see* 2.b. below. The United States also reiterated its view that such General Comments are non-binding opinions, stating in its discussion of the Committee's non-refoulement claim (footnote omitted):

> As noted in our July 2006 written responses to Committee questions,* the Covenant does not impose a *non-refoulement* obligation upon States Parties. The United States Government is familiar with the Committee's statements in General Comments 20 and 31 regarding Article 7 (stating that such an obligation exists). The non-binding opinions offered

---

*   Editor's note: List of Issues to Be Taken Up in Connection With the Consideration of the Second and Third Periodic Reports of the United States of America—Response of the United States of America, at para. 10, available at *www.state.gov/g/drl/rls/70385.htm*.

by the Committee in General Comments 20 and 31 have no firm legal basis in the text of the treaty or the intention of its States Parties at the time they negotiated or became party to the instrument. Moreover, as the United States explained during its July 2006 appearance, the States Parties under Article 40 of the Covenant did not give the Human Rights Committee authority to issue legally binding or authoritative interpretations of the Covenant. Accordingly, the United States does not consider General Comments 20 and 31 to reflect the "legal obligation" under the Covenant that is claimed by the Committee.

As to specific recommendations concerning treatment of detainees, the October 2007 response stated:

The United States is engaged in an armed conflict with al Qaida, the Taliban, and their supporters. As part of this conflict, the United States captures and detains enemy combatants, and is entitled under the law of war to hold them until the end of hostilities. The law of war, and not the Covenant, is the applicable legal framework governing these detentions.

The United States acknowledged its obligations under the law of war and provided information to the Committee as to its compliance. *See* Chapter 18.A.4.c.(2)

The U.S. response to the Committee's recommendation concerning the aftermath of Hurricane Katrina is set forth below (footnotes omitted). The full text of the U.S. follow-up response is available at *www.state.gov/sl/c8183.htm*.

---

*   *   *   *

Recommendation:
"The State party should review its practices and policies to ensure the full implementation of its obligation to protect life and of the prohibition of discrimination, whether direct or indirect, as well as

of the United Nations Guiding Principles on Internal Displacement, in matters related to disaster prevention and preparedness, emergency assistance and relief measures. In the aftermath of Hurricane Katrina, the State party should increase its efforts to ensure that the rights of the poor, and in particular African-Americans, are fully taken into consideration in the reconstruction plans with regard to access to housing, education and healthcare. The Committee wishes to be informed about the results of the inquiries into the alleged failure to evacuate prisoners at the Parish prison, as well as the allegations that New Orleans residents were not permitted by law enforcement officials to cross the Greater New Orleans Bridge to Gretna, Louisiana."

Response:

The United States Federal Government is aggressively moving forward with implementing lessons learned from Hurricane Katrina, including improving procedures to enhance the protection of, and assistance to, economically disadvantaged members of society. In our July 2006 written responses to Committee questions, the United States provided extensive information on measures taken in the context of the disaster caused by Hurricane Katrina.

Following Hurricane Katrina, which devastated the Gulf Coast region of the United States, there were media reports of alleged ill-treatment perpetrated by law-enforcement personnel. One of the reports included allegations that individuals were not permitted to cross the Greater New Orleans Bridge to Gretna, Louisiana. The Louisiana Attorney General's Office conducted an exhaustive inquiry into that allegation. The investigation currently is under review by the local prosecutor's office. After that office determines whether it will seek any criminal charges in connection with this incident, the Department of Justice's Civil Rights Division will determine whether additional investigation is necessary and whether the facts implicate a violation of any federal statute.

Additionally, in September 2005, the Civil Rights Division requested the FBI to conduct an investigation into allegations that correctional officers did not properly transfer inmates from the Orleans Parish Prison during the aftermath of Hurricane Katrina.

After completing its initial investigation, the FBI forwarded the results of that investigation to the Division. The Division reviewed the results of the initial FBI investigation and concluded that there was insufficient evidence to establish a violation of federal criminal law. Thereafter, the FBI informed the Division that it was pursuing additional leads regarding the treatment of prisoners at the Orleans Parish Prison. Based on that additional information, the Division asked the FBI to continue the investigation. That investigation is ongoing.

In providing assistance to individuals affected by Katrina, the Federal Government is committed to helping all victims, and in particular those who are in the greatest need. In that regard, on February 15, 2006, the Attorney General announced a major new civil rights initiative, Operation Home Sweet Home. This fair housing initiative was inspired by victims of Hurricane Katrina who had lost their homes and were seeking new places to live. This is a concentrated initiative to expose and eliminate housing discrimination in the United States. The initiative will focus on improved targeting of discrimination tests, increased testing, and public awareness efforts. One of the key components of Operation Home Sweet Home is concentrated testing for housing discrimination in areas recovering from the effects of Hurricane Katrina and in areas where Katrina victims have been relocated. In addition, the Division is operating a new website devoted to fair housing enforcement: http://www.usdoj.gov/fairhousing. It has an online mechanism for citizens to submit tips and complaints, as well as obtain information about what constitutes housing-based discrimination.

Further, in the aftermath of Katrina, the U.S. Department of Housing and Urban Development has initiated a number of efforts to prevent discrimination in relocation housing. These include grants of $1.2 million to Gulf Coast Fair Housing groups for outreach to evacuees and investigation of discrimination complaints. The U.S. Department of Health and Human Services has also dedicated substantial resources to help redesign and rebuild Louisiana's health-care system to enhance health care in Louisiana.

The Government of the United States is committed to do what it takes to help residents of the Gulf Coast rebuild their lives in the wake of this disaster and has committed $110.6 billion in federal aid alone for relief, recovery and rebuilding efforts. A partial list of the work Federal agencies have accomplished to help not only get the region back on its feet but also to provide for a stronger and better future for the residents of the Gulf Coast can be found at: http://www.dhs.gov/katrina. We assure the Committee that the needs of the poor and most affected communities, including with respect to "access to housing, education and healthcare," are being taken into account in the government's responses to Katrina.

*   *   *   *

b. Observations on UN Human Rights Committee General Comment 31

On December 27, 2007, the United States submitted to the UN Human Rights Committee the U.S. Observations on Human Rights Committee General Comment 31: Nature of the General Legal Obligation Imposed on States Parties to the Covenant [on Civil and Political Rights], adopted by the Committee on March 29, 2004. In submitting its observations, the United States stated:

> While there are a substantial number of legal statements and conclusions in the General Comment with which the United States does not agree, these Observations address a select number of subjects about which the United States holds fundamentally different views from those apparently held by the Committee. In this paper, the United States sets forth in summary fashion a number of observations concerning this General Comment, without addressing all of the issues or statements in the General Comment with which it may not agree.

The U.S. observations addressed: I. Scope of the ICCPR, II. Obligations Pertaining to Private Conduct, III. Non-Refoulement, IV. International Humanitarian Law, V. Remedies, and VI. *Erga Omnes* Obligations, provided below. *See also Digest 2005* at 296–300 and *Digest* 2006 at 346–49.

The full text of the U.S. observations is available at *www. state.gov/s/l/c8183.htm.* For U.S. views on the proper interpretation of the non-refoulement obligation under the Convention on Refugees, *see* Chapter 1.D.

*   *   *   *

I. *Scope of the ICCPR*

3. General Comment 31, paragraph 10, states that "States Parties are required by article 2, paragraph 1, [of the ICCPR] to respect and to ensure the Covenant rights to all persons who may be within their territory *and to all persons subject to their jurisdiction.* This means that a State Party must respect and ensure the rights laid down in the Covenant to anyone within the power or effective control of that State Party, *even if not situated within the territory of the State Party.*" (Emphases added.)

4. This interpretation, which dispenses with the well-established rules of treaty interpretation, is inconsistent with the plain text of the Covenant as well as its negotiating history. The actual wording of ICCPR Art. 2(1) is as follows: "Each State Party to the present Covenant undertakes to respect and to ensure to all individuals within its territory *and* subject to its jurisdiction the rights recognized in the present Covenant. . . ." (Emphasis added.) Based on the plain and ordinary meaning of its text, this article establishes that States Parties are required to ensure the rights in the Covenant only to individuals who are both within the territory of a State Party *and* subject to that State Party's sovereign authority. Without any analysis or reasoning to support its view, the Committee's interpretation would have the effect of transforming the "and" in Article 2(1) into an "or."

5. Article 2(1) is a foundational provision of the Covenant, as it establishes its scope of application. It is lamentable that the General Comment treats this provision in such a cavalier and inconsistent manner, including the following: "all individuals in their territory and subject to their jurisdiction" (paragraph 3);

"all persons who may be within their territory and to all persons subject to their jurisdiction" (paragraph 10); "persons, who may find themselves in the territory or subject to the jurisdiction of the State Party" (paragraph 10); and, "all persons in their territory and all persons under their control" (paragraph 12). The General Comment's demonstrated indifference to the precise wording of this carefully negotiated text is unfortunate and serves to undermine the Committee's persuasive authority.

6. Because there is no ambiguity in Article 2(1) of the Covenant, there is no need to resort to the *travaux preparatoires* to ascertain the territorial reach of the Covenant. However, resort to the *travaux* serves to underscore the clear intent of the negotiators to limit the territorial reach of obligations of States Parties to the Covenant. In 1950, the draft text of Article 2 then under consideration by the U.N. Commission on Human Rights (the "Commission") would have required that each State Party ensure Covenant rights to everyone "within its jurisdiction." The United States, however, proposed the addition of the requirement that the individual also be "within its territory."[2] Eleanor Roosevelt, the U.S. representative and then-Chairman of the Commission, emphasized that the United States was "particularly anxious" that it not assume "an obligation to ensure the rights recognized in it to citizens of countries under United States occupation."[3] She explained that:

> "The purpose of the proposed addition [is] to make it clear that the draft Covenant would apply only to persons within the territory and subject to the jurisdiction of the contracting states. The United States [is] afraid that without such an addition the draft Covenant might be construed as

---

[2]   *Compilation of the Comments of Governments on the Draft International Covenant on Human Rights and on the Proposed Additional Articles,* U.N. ESCOR Hum. Rts. Comm., 6th Sess. at 14, UN Doc. E/CN.4/365 (1950) (U.S. proposal). The U.S. amendment added the words "territory and subject to its" before "jurisdiction" in Article 2(1).

[3]   *Summary Record of the Hundred and Ninety-Third Meeting,* U.N. ESCOR Hum. Rts. Comm., 6th Sess., 193rd mtg. at 13, 18, U.N. Doc. E/CN.4/SR.193 at 13, 18 (1950) (Mrs. Roosevelt); *Summary Record of the Hundred and Ninety-Fourth Meeting,* U.N. ESCOR Hum. Rts. Comm., 6th Sess., 194rd mtg. at 5, 9, U.N. Doc. E/CN.4/SR.194 (1950).

obliging the contracting states to enact legislation concerning persons, who although outside its territory were technically within its jurisdiction for certain purposes. An illustration would be the occupied territories of Germany, Austria and Japan: persons within those countries were subject to the jurisdiction of the occupying states in certain respects, but were outside the scope of legislation of those states. Another illustration would be leased territories; some countries leased certain territories from others for limited purposes, and there might be question of conflicting authority between the lessor nation and the lessee nation."[4]

7. In the ensuing debate, several states considered that the United States position was the most sound and logical one,[5] and agreed with the view expressed by Mrs. Roosevelt that "it was not possible for any nation to guarantee such rights [e.g., the right to a fair trial in foreign courts] under the terms of the draft Covenant to its nationals resident abroad."[6] At the same time, other delegations spoke against the U.S. amendment, arguing that a nation should guarantee fundamental rights to its citizens abroad as well as at home.[7] Ultimately, the U.S. view prevailed, and the amendment was

---

[4]   *Summary Record of the Hundred and Thirty-Eighth Meeting*, U.N. ESCOR Hum. Rts. Comm., 6th Sess., 138th mtg, at 10, U.N. Doc. E/CN.4/SR.138 (1950) (emphasis added).

[5]   *See, Id.* at 6 (Dr. Carlos Valenzuela, representative of Chile); *Id.* at 8 (E.N. Oribe, representative of Uruguay).

[6]   *Summary Record of the Hundred and Ninety-Fourth Meeting, supra* note 3, at 7 (Mrs. Roosevelt).

[7]   More background on the ensuing debate can be found in Annex I of *Second and Third Periodic Report of the United States of America to the UN Committee on Human Rights Concerning the International Covenant on Civil and Political Rights*, submitted October 21, 2005. Available at http://www.state.gov/g/drl/rls/55504.htm#annex1. It is significant to note even those delegations who unsuccessfully argued for a broader wording of the territorial scope provision than that which was adopted never contemplated that such drafting would have had the Covenant apply with respect to non-nationals of a State Party outside the territory of a State Party, much less to all individuals who may be under the "effective control" of a State Party outside its territory.

adopted at the 1950 session by a vote of 8–2 with 5 abstentions.[8] Subsequently, after similar debates, the United States and others defeated proposals by France to delete the phrase "within its territory" at both the 1952 session of the Commission[9] and the 1963 session of the General Assembly.[10]

8. The position of the United States on this matter is thus fully in accord with the ordinary meaning and negotiating history of the Covenant. It is also the position that the United States has stated publicly since becoming Party to the Covenant. In the course of presenting the Initial Report of the United States in 1995, Conrad Harper, the Legal Adviser of the U.S. Department of State, stated that:

> "[t]he Covenant was not regarded as having extraterritorial application. . . . Article 2 of the Covenant expressly stated that each State Party undertook to respect and ensure the rights recognized 'to all individuals within its territory and subject to its jurisdiction'. That dual requirement restricted the scope of the Covenant to persons under United States jurisdiction and within United States territory. During the negotiating history, the words 'within its territory'

---

[8]   *Id.* at 11.

[9]   *Draft International Convention on Human Rights and Measures of Implementation*, U.N. ESCOR Hum. Rts. Comm., 8th Sess., Agenda Item 4, U.N. Doc. E/CN.4/L.161 (1952) (French amendment); *Summary Record of the Three Hundred and Twenty-Ninth Meeting*, U.N. ESCOR Hum. Rts. Comm., 8th Sess., 329th mtg. at 14, UN Doc. E/CN.4/SR.329 (1952) (vote rejecting amendment). During the debate, France and Yugoslavia again urged deletion of the phrase "within its territory" because states should be required to guarantee Covenant rights to citizens abroad. *Id.* at 13 (P. Juvigny, representative of France); *Id.* at 13 (Branko Jevremovic, representative of Yugoslavia).

[10]   U.N. GAOR 3rd Comm., 18th Sess., 1259th mtg. 30, U.N. Doc. A/C.3/SR.1259 (1963) (rejection of French and Chinese proposal to delete "within its territory"). Several states again maintained that the Covenant should guarantee rights to citizens abroad. *See,* U.N. GAOR 3rd Comm., 18th Sess., 1257th mtg. 1 UN Doc. A/C.3/SR.1257 (1963) (Mrs. Mantaoulinos, representative of Greece); *Id.* at 10 (Mr. Capotorti, representative of Italy); *Id.* at 21 (Mr. Combal, representative of France); U.N. GAOR 3rd Comm., 18th Sess., 1258th mtg. 29, UN Doc. A/C.3/SR.1258 (1963) (Mr. Cha, representative of China); *Id.* at 39 (Antonio Belaunde, representative of Peru).

had been debated and were added by vote, with the clear understanding that such wording would limit the obligations to within a Party's territory."[11]

9. Notwithstanding Article 2's plain text and clear negotiating record, paragraph 10 of General Comment 31 would re-write the Covenant, as it states that Covenant rights are available to "all individuals . . . who may find themselves in the territory *or* subject to the jurisdiction of the State Party" (emphasis added). For the reasons discussed above, the United States considers this interpretation wholly incorrect as a matter of international law on the interpretation of treaties.

II. Obligations Pertaining to Private Conduct

10. General Comment 31, paragraph 8, discusses the extent to which Covenant obligations extend to protection against private acts. In the context of Article 2, the Committee states that a State Party is obligated to protect "not just against violations of Covenant rights by its agents, but also against acts committed by private persons or entities that would impair the enjoyment of Covenant rights in so far as they are amenable to application between private persons or entities." The Committee also refers to the need "to take appropriate measures or to exercise due diligence to prevent, punish, investigate or redress the harm caused by such acts by private persons or entities." (Emphasis added.)

11. While the United States agrees that, in certain areas, the Covenant entails positive obligations that extend to private acts, the Committee's General Comment sweeps too broadly and categorically. As a general matter, with notable exceptions such as slavery, a human rights violation entails state action.[12] Human rights

---

[11] *Summary record of the 1405th meeting: United States of America*, UN ESCOR Hum. Rts. Comm., 53rd Sess., 1504th mtg. at 7, 20, U.N. Doc. CCPR/C/SR 1405 (1995).

[12] Abuses committed by private individuals may constitute human rights violations in certain instances, such as when an abuse is committed at the direction of, or with the acquiescence of the state. *See e.g.*, Article 1 of the Convention Against Torture and Other Cruel, Inhuman or Degrading Treatment or Punishment, which defines torture in a manner that requires pain or suffering to be "inflicted by *or at the instigation of or with the consent*

treaties may contain provisions that clearly and specifically impose obligations upon States Parties to prevent, in certain limited circumstances, particular kinds of misconduct by private parties or non-state actors. Article 2, however, contains no language stating that Covenant obligations extend to private, non-governmental acts, and no such obligations can be inferred from Article 2.

12. The Parties could have decided to negotiate the general obligation found in Article 2 in a manner that extended to the conduct of private parties. For instance, the International Convention on the Elimination of all Forms of Racial Discrimination (CERD) and the Convention on the Elimination of all Forms of Discrimination Against Women (CEDAW) contain specific provisions that do impose limited obligations upon States Parties, in the specific context of preventing discrimination, to prevent discrimination, respectively, "by any persons, group or organization" and "by any person, organization or enterprise" (CERD, Article 2(1)(d); CEDAW, Art. 2(e) (fns omitted)). Importantly, even in the case of CEDAW and CERD, where a State obligation is spelled out regarding prevention of discrimination by non-state actors or private parties, the obligation is carefully circumscribed (e.g., "all appropriate means" or "all appropriate measures") to reflect the limitations on even well-intentioned States Parties to control the actions of non-governmental actors.

13. Parties to the Covenant, however, did not take such an approach, as Article 2 does not refer to private actors. Accordingly, ascertaining whether there is a Covenant obligation relating to non-state actors requires an examination of the Covenant text that pertains to a particular right, rather than recourse to a general proposition to be somehow inferred from Article 2.

14. For instance, the prohibition on slavery imposes an obligation on States Parties to take clear and specific measures on acts of non-state actors. This obligation is not found in the overarching formulation of Article 2, but rather in the nature of slavery itself (which includes private ownership rights or absolute control over a person) and the specific language of Article 8, which states that

---

or *acquiescence of* a public official or other person acting in an official capacity." (Emphasis added.)

"slavery and the slave-trade in all their forms shall be prohibited." The Committee seems to recognize this when it states that "[t]he Covenant itself envisages in some articles certain areas where there are positive obligations on States Parties to address the activities of private persons or entities." Given the fact that the drafters of the Covenant knew how to draft provisions that would address the actions of non-state actors, the absence of any language to this effect in Article 2 reflects a conscious decision not to reach such conduct, which further weakens the Committee's argument that there exists an implicit obligation.

15. For similar reasons, the United States does not agree with the assertion that it is "implicit in article 7 that States Parties have to take positive measures to ensure that private persons or entities do not inflict torture or cruel, inhuman or degrading treatment or punishment on others within their power." Here the Committee seems to be saying that not only is a positive obligation implicit in Article 2, but that analogous obligations exist through imputation in (i.e., non-textual readings of) articles that similarly do not state such application. The Committee offers no evidence or explanation for these assertions of multiple layers of implicit Covenant obligations.

16. Contrary to the assertion of the Committee, it is well established in international law that torture requires state action or affirmative acquiescence. Article 1 of the Convention Against Torture and Other Cruel, Inhuman or Degrading Treatment or Punishment (CAT) defines torture as "any act by which severe pain or suffering, whether physical or mental, is intentionally inflicted . . . when such pain or suffering is inflicted by or at the instigation of or with the consent or acquiescence of a public official or other person acting in an official capacity." Article 16 of the CAT takes the same approach with respect to cruel, inhuman and degrading treatment or punishment (CIDT).

17. The Committee's view on this matter leads to the illogical and unfounded conclusion that, 18 years after the adoption of the Covenant, states adopted a new treaty—the CAT—which contains obligations to prevent torture and CIDT that are *narrower* than those already included in the Covenant. There is simply no obligation—implicit or explicit—in the ICCPR to "ensure that

private persons or entities do not inflict torture or cruel, in-human or degrading treatment or punishment," as claimed by the Committee.

18. Although the United States does not agree with the treaty analysis advanced by the Committee in this respect, it agrees with a more general proposition that States owe a moral and political responsibility to their populations to prevent and protect them from private acts of extreme physical abuse by private individuals. States around the world routinely prohibit and punish such acts under their domestic criminal law, which in some legal systems styles such offenses as crimes such as "aggravated battery." States throughout the world have fulfilled this moral responsibility by enacting and enforcing such criminal laws for many centuries before the Covenant or any other human rights treaty had been written. As a practical matter, there is no need for the Committee to offer an atextual reading of ICCPR Articles 2 or 7 to ensure that governments will protect their populations from private violent acts. For purposes of interpreting the Covenant, it is essential, however, to bear in mind the legal distinction that governmental enforcement in these areas has been and will remain a matter of criminal law in the fulfillment of a state's general responsibilities incident to ordered government, rather than as a requirement derived from their obligations under the Covenant.

III. Non-Refoulement

19. General Comment 31, paragraph 12, states that the Covenant entails an obligation on States Parties "not to extradite, deport, expel or otherwise remove a person from their territory, where there are substantial grounds for believing that there is a real risk of irreparable harm, such as that contemplated by articles 6 and 7 of the Covenant. . . ." General Comment 20 also states the Committee's opinion that the Covenant contains a non-refoulement obligation.

20. The United States fundamentally disagrees with the Committee on this matter. Unlike Article 3 of the Convention Against Torture, Article 7 of the ICCPR contains no reference to the concept of non-refoulement, stating only that "[n]o one shall be subjected to torture or to cruel, inhuman or degrading treatment

or punishment. In particular, no one shall be subjected without his free consent to medical or scientific experimentation."

21. As noted in the July 2006 written responses of the United States to Committee questions, the Covenant does not impose a non-refoulement obligation upon States Parties.[15] Indeed, the adoption of a provision on non-refoulement was one of the important innovations of the later-negotiated Convention Against Torture. States Parties to the Covenant that wished to assume a new treaty obligation with respect to non-refoulement for torture were free to become States Parties to the CAT, and a very large number of countries, including the United States, chose to do so. Accordingly, States Parties to the Convention Against Torture have a non-refoulement obligation under Article 3 of that Convention not to "expel, return ('refouler') or extradite a person to another State where there are substantial grounds for believing that he would be in danger of being subjected to torture." It should be noted that not even the later-in-time CAT contains a provision on non-refoulement that would apply with respect to CIDT or the "irreparable harm" standard suggested by the Committee.

22. In this sense, the non-binding opinions offered by the Committee on this matter in General Comments 31 and 20 have no legal basis in the text of the treaty or the intention of its States Parties at the time they negotiated or became parties to the instrument.

23. The only obligations under international human rights and refugee law that the United States has assumed with respect to non-refoulement are contained in Article 33 of the Convention Relating to the Status of Refugees (applicable to the United States by virtue of its ratification of the Protocol Relating to the Status of Refugees) and in Article 3 of the Convention Against Torture.[16]

---

[15] "List of Issues to Be Taken Up in Connection With the Consideration of the Second and Third Periodic Reports of the United States of America— Response of the United States of America," at para. 10, *available at: http:// www.state.gov/g/drl/rls/70385.htm.*

[16] At the time the United States became a State Party to the CAT, it filed a formal understanding with respect to the scope of the treaty law obligation it was assuming under that article, stating "[t]hat the United States understands

The United States has not assumed obligations with respect to non-refoulement in the human rights and refugee law context other than those referred to in this paragraph and has specifically assumed no such obligation under the ICCPR.

IV. International Humanitarian Law

24. General Comment 31, paragraph 11, states that "the Covenant applies also in situations of armed conflict to which the rules of international humanitarian law are applicable. While, in respect of certain Covenant rights, more specific rules of international humanitarian law may be specially relevant for the purposes of the interpretation of Covenant rights, both spheres of law are complementary, not mutually exclusive."

25. While the United States agrees with the Committee that as a general matter armed conflict does not suspend or terminate a State's obligations under the Covenant within its scope of application, its assertion that the Covenant invariably applies in situations of armed conflict to which the rules of international humanitarian law are applicable sweeps too broadly. As an initial matter, as described in paragraphs 3–9 of these Observations, to the extent that a State Party is engaged in armed conflict *outside* of its territory, the Covenant does not apply, as it does not apply extraterritorially. In addition, as the Committee notes, during armed conflict, international humanitarian law will often serve as the *lex specialis,* thus being the relevant legal standard that would apply to a particular activity. In such instance, it is unclear in what sense or manner the Covenant would "apply," as the law of war provides the relevant legal standard with respect to the conduct in question. As a general matter, a case-by-case inquiry is needed to ascertain the relevant and operative legal rule that is applicable to particular conduct of a particular state during an armed conflict.

26. In paragraph 18 of General Comment 31, the Committee alludes to the Rome Statute and states that "[w]hen committed as

---

the phrase 'where there are substantial grounds for believing that he would be in danger of being subjected to torture,' as used in article 3 of the Convention, to mean 'if it is more likely than not that he would be tortured.'" No State Party has objected to that understanding.

part of a widespread or systematic attack on a civilian population" Covenant violations relating to torture and cruel, inhuman and degrading treatment, summary and arbitrary killing, and enforced disappearances "are crimes against humanity."

27. Such Covenant violations, even in the context described by the Committee, would not in all circumstances constitute crimes against humanity. Without engaging in an extensive analysis of international criminal law, it suffices to say that the Committee's statement is not fully supported by the Covenant, the Rome Statute, or customary international law. Ascertaining whether a crime has occurred would require analyzing the facts and circumstances of a particular case. More fundamentally, the United States does not consider it necessary or appropriate for the Committee to issue statements that purport to define what constitutes international crimes—statements outside the ambit of the Covenant. Instead, mindful of its treaty-based mandate, the Committee might better confine its General Comments to issues related to the ICCPR.

V. Remedies

28. Paragraphs 15–20 of General Comment 31 discuss a range of issues related to remedies. The United States notes that some of the modalities and mechanisms discussed are consonant with and reflected in the "Basic Principles and Guidelines on the Right to a Remedy and Reparation for Victims of Gross Violations of International Human Rights Law and Serious Violations of International Humanitarian Law."[17] The United States was pleased to join consensus on United Nations General Assembly resolution 60/147, which adopted the Basic Principles and Guidelines.[18] As the Basic

---

[17] "Basic Principles and Guidelines on the Right to a Remedy and Reparation for Victims of Gross Violations of International Human Rights Law and Serious Violations of International Humanitarian Law," G.A. Res. 60/147, U.N. GAOR, 60th Session, U.N. Doc. (2005).

[18] *Id.* The Basic Principles and Guidelines are both broader and more limited than the Covenant. They are more limited in that they are directed only at *gross violations* of international human rights law, whereas they are broader in that they are not confined in the human rights sphere to remedies for ICCPR violations and they also address serious violations of international humanitarian law.

Principles and Guidelines note, they "do not entail new international or domestic legal obligations but identify *mechanisms, modalities, procedures and methods for the implementation of existing legal obligations* under international human rights law and international humanitarian law which are complementary though different as to their norms." (Emphasis added.)

29. The United States finds itself in some disagreement with certain Committee views on remedies. Generally, the appropriateness of a particular remedy or remedies is highly context specific. This is reflected in the careful drafting of the Basic Principles and Guidelines, which describe certain flexibilities and contain important caveats and limitations. This level of care and flexibility seems to be lacking in some of the Committee's discussion of remedies.

30. For instance, in paragraph 18, the Committee seems to suggest that a State Party violates its Covenant obligations when it fails to "bring to justice" perpetrators of certain Covenant obligations, particularly those "violations recognized as criminal. . . ." The United States indeed considers itself bound by international obligations to investigate, prosecute, and punish violators in certain instances. For instance, Articles 12 and 16 of the CAT require States Parties to undertake "a prompt and impartial investigation, wherever there is reasonable ground to believe that an act of torture [or cruel, inhuman, or degrading treatment or punishment] has been committed. . . ." Likewise, Article 3 of the CAT requires each State Party to "ensure that all acts of torture are offences under its criminal law."

31. The Committee's statement, however, goes too far and is not grounded in the text of the ICCPR. For instance, it leads to the conclusion that the ICCPR contains obligations to criminalize CIDT—obligations not found in Article 7 or even in the later-negotiated CAT. A plain reading of the ICCPR shows that it contains no such obligations to criminalize CIDT or, for that matter, any particular Covenant violation. Accordingly, the United States does not consider the Committee's interpretations on this matter to accurately describe the Covenant's actual obligations.

32. With respect to remedies, in paragraph 18 the Committee sweepingly states that certain "impediments to the establishment of legal responsibility should also be removed, such as the defense

of obedience to superior orders or unreasonably short periods of statutory limitation in cases where such limitations are applicable." The United States does not consider the mere recognition of a superior orders defense to be inconsistent with the ICCPR.

33. Under United States military law, obedience to superior orders is a defense to charges under the Uniform Code of Military Justice, unless the accused *knew* the order to be unlawful or a person of ordinary sense and understanding *would have known* the orders to be unlawful. Thus, rather than an outright and categorical elimination of the defense, United States law incorporates a *mens rea* requirement. Far from an "impediment" to legal responsibility, the United States considers the limited use of this defense to be appropriate and fair with respect to establishing criminal responsibility of military personnel.

34. The Committee's use of the word "should" suggests to the United States that the Committee does not consider removal of superior orders or statutes of limitations defenses as requirements *per se* of the Covenant, but is perhaps a general policy recommendation. This use of "should" seems appropriate, as neither defense is addressed in the ICCPR, unlike other human rights treaties that do address these issues in specific fashion (*See e.g.*, CAT, Art. 2, with respect to superior orders related to torture; International Convention for the Protection of All Persons from Enforced Disappearance (not yet in force), Art. 8, with respect to statutes of limitations).

35. Overall, the United States strongly agrees with the Committee with respect to the importance of effective remedies under the Covenant. However, the United States considers that some of the Committee's specific views on remedies are not accurate reflections of Covenant obligations.

VI. *Erga Omnes Obligations*

36. General Comment 31, paragraph 2, states that with respect to the Covenant "every State Party has a legal interest in the performance by every other State Party of its obligations. This follows from the fact that the 'rules concerning the basic rights of the human person' are *erga omnes* obligations. . . ."

37. While the United States agrees that, in the context of the Covenant, each State Party has a legal interest in the performance

of obligations by other States Parties, it does not consider that such a conclusion "follows from the fact that the 'rules concerning the basic rights of the human person' are *erga omnes* obligations." Rather, the legal interests of States Parties in the performance of the obligations by other States Parties arise from principles of treaty law and the Covenant itself.

38. The question of which human rights give rise to *erga omnes* obligations is not settled under international law. Similarly, there is no well established method or set of criteria for ascertaining which rights might generate *erga omnes* obligations. Accordingly, the United States cannot identify—and Committee does not explain— the basis for the apparent assertion that all of the rights in the ICCPR constitute "basic rights of the human person" meriting *erga omnes* status.[19] Rather than putting forth a novel legal hypothesis, it may be that the Committee is simply trying to make the broader point that human rights are a common interest of the international community. If this is the case, the United States is in full agreement that States have a profound and shared interest in the protection and promotion of human rights worldwide.

* * *

39. The United States Government concludes these Observations with a statement of its appreciation for the work of the Human Rights Committee. Although the United States does not agree with all of the Committee's recommendations with respect to the application of the Covenant, it fully appreciates the Committee's continuing efforts to advise States Parties on issues related to their implementation of the treaty. The United States looks forward to its continuing dialogue with the Committee on these issues.

---

[19] The Committee seems to reach this view with the aid of the International Court of Justice's opinion in the Barcelona Traction case, which it partially quotes (without reference). *Barcelona Traction, Light and Power Company, Limited*, Second Phase, Judgment, I.C.J. Reports 1970. In this case, the Court posited that erga omnes "obligations derive, for example, in contemporary international law, from the outlawing of acts of aggression, and of genocide, as also from the principles and rules concerning the basic rights of the human person, including protection from slavery and racial discrimination." *Id.*, p. 32, para. 33.

3. Protection of Persons in the Event of Disasters

On October 31, 2007, John B. Bellinger, III, Department of State Legal Adviser, addressed the Sixth Committee of the General Assembly on the report of the International Law Commission on the Work of its 59th Session. Mr. Bellinger's comments welcoming the decision by the ILC to study the topic "Protection of Persons in the Event of Disasters" are set forth below. The full text of his statement is available at *www. state.gov/s/l/c8183.htm.*

*   *   *   *

With respect to the issue of new topics for the Commission's long-term agenda, we strongly support the Commission's criteria for selecting new topics, including placing highest priority on topics that are ripe for development and hold the most promise for addressing the practical needs of States. Consistent with that view, we applaud the Commission's decision to study the topic "Protection of Persons in the Event of Disasters" and congratulate Dr. Eduardo Valencia-Ospina on his appointment as Special Rapporteur. We believe that the Commission's consideration of this topic has the potential to produce practical solutions to pressing problems resulting from natural and other disasters. We hope the Commission will focus its study on areas that will have the most significant practical impact on mitigating the effects of such disasters, including, for example, practical mechanisms to facilitate coordination among providers of necessary disaster assistance and the access of people and equipment to affected areas.

*   *   *   *

4. Human Rights Council

The UN General Assembly adopted a resolution creating the Human Rights Council to replace the Commission on Human Rights on March 15, 2006. U.N. Doc. A/RES/60/251; *see Digest 2006* at 328–43. On November 16, 2007, the United

States voted against adoption of a human rights institution-building package in the General Assembly Third Committee. Ambassador Zalmay Khalilzad, U.S. Permanent Representative to the United Nations, provided an explanation of the U.S. vote, commenting on U.S. disappointment with the Council's first year and concern about procedural irregularities. On December 22, 2007, the UN General Assembly endorsed the Third Committee institution-building package in a resolution entitled "Report of the Human Rights Council." U.N. Doc. A/RES/62/21 (2007).

The full text of Ambassador Khalilzad's statement is set forth below and is available at *www.usunnewyork.usmission.gov/press_releases/20071116_313.html. See also* June 19, 2007 statement by U.S. Department of State Spokesman Sean McCormack, available at *www.state.gov/r/pa/prs/ps/2007/jun/86802.htm.*

Mr. Chairman, the United States is compelled to vote "No" on the institution building package considered by the Committee today.

We cast this vote sadly, because we still believe, as we have always believed, that the protection and promotion of human rights are an important part of the United Nations' reason for being. For at least 60 years—at least since 1948 when the General Assembly unanimously adopted and proclaimed the Universal Declaration of Human Rights—the United Nations has been committed, in the words of the Declaration, to the "recognition of the inherent dignity and the equal and inalienable rights of all members of the human family." And the UN has recognized for all those years, again in the words of the declaration, that "disregard and contempt for human rights have resulted in barbarous acts which have outraged the conscience of mankind."

Mr. Chairman, it was our shared commitment to these principles that inspired Member States to form the Human Rights Council. The Council was intended to be different from and better than its predecessor, the Commission on Human Rights, where political alliances had seemed too often to get in the way of telling the simple truth about human rights violations. Unfortunately, the Council was created with deep structural flaws—particularly the General Assembly's decision not to adopt a provision that would have excluded the world's most serious human rights violators from membership on the Council. Despite our concerns about institutional weaknesses, the United States engaged actively in trying to strengthen the Council during its first year. We had hoped that the "institution building" session would address the deficiencies that had politicized the Council and prevented it from acting as a serious and effective human rights institution.

But the Council's record so far failed to fulfill our hopes. The surprise announcement in Geneva on June 19 that the package now before us had been adopted the night before—although the only thing that had really happened the night before was an announcement that the Council would not act on the package until the next day—was a fitting end to a very bad first year for the Council.

Mr. Chairman, please allow me to itemize some of the things that went wrong during this first year:

First, there was the Council's relentless focus during the year on a single country—Israel.

At the same time, the Council failed during the year to address serious human rights violations taking place in other countries such as Zimbabwe, DPRK, Iran, Belarus, and Cuba.

Key provisions of the institution building package before us today appear likely to compound the Council's institutional weaknesses. It is particularly disappointing that the package prematurely terminates the mandates of the UN Special Rapporteurs charged with monitoring and reporting on two of the world's most active perpetrators of serious human rights violations, the Governments of Cuba and Belarus.

Another disturbing feature of the institution building package is that the Permanent Agenda of the Council contains one and only one item having to do with a specific country. Once again, that country is Israel. This raises serious questions about the Human Rights Council's institutional priorities, its ability to make unbiased assessments of human rights situations, and whether it will take seriously its responsibility to protect and promote human rights around the world with particular attention to the most serious violations of human rights.

Finally, Mr. Chairman, deeply unfair and un-transparent procedures were employed to deny Council members the opportunity
to vote on the package we are now considering. If a tactic like this
had been used in a national election in any country in the world—
announcing that the election would be held on a certain day, and
then telling voters who showed up on the appointed day that the
election had actually been held at midnight the night before—the
world would rightly regard that election as unfree and unfair.

The proceedings of all United Nations bodies should be models of fairness and transparency. This is particularly true of the
Human Rights Council, which was intended to be the world's
leading human rights protection mechanism. The procedure by
which this package was adopted calls into serious question whether
it can ever realize that goal.

Mr. Chairman, we sincerely hope to be proved wrong in our
assessment. In particular, we would be deeply gratified if the
Human Rights Council took several important steps during the
next year:

First, we hope that the process of Universal Periodic Review
will subject the world's worst human rights violators to real scrutiny and perhaps even persuade them to mend their ways. Universal
Periodic Review will be a genuine human rights protection mechanism if it is conducted with seriousness and rigor—with an honest
unbiased focus on the facts on the ground in each country, with
voting on the merits rather than by blocs or alliances, and unhindered by comfortable assertions of cultural relativism and moral
equivalency.

We hope also that the Human Rights Council will be ready to
respond to genuine human rights emergencies—as it did admirably
with respect to Burma this September but had failed to do during
the crisis in Zimbabwe earlier this year.*

---

* Editor's note: On U.S. views that "the recent events in Zimbabwe are
exactly the sort of situation referenced by the General Assembly" in creating
the Human Rights Council, see statement by Ambassador Warren W. Tichenor,
available at *www.us-mission.ch/Press2007/0329StatementonZimbabwe.htm.*

Finally, we hope the Council will pass strong and accurate resolutions about country-specific human rights situations, as it has also done on Burma—and we congratulate the Council for this—but has not yet done with regard to other compelling situations around the world. The Council will be the world's most important human rights mechanism if and only if it consistently focuses on the worst human rights violations in the world—including extrajudicial killing and the use of rape for military and political purposes and imprisonment of people for their political or religious opinions—and calls these acts, which the Universal Declaration called "these barbarous acts which have shocked the conscience of mankind," by their right names.

In short, Mr. Chairman, we hope that the Human Rights Council will stand in solidarity with victims of human rights violations around the world, not with the perpetrators.

5. Legal Status of the UN Committee on Economic, Social and Cultural Rights

On September 7, 2007, the United States responded to an August 17 request by the UN Office of the High Commissioner for Human Rights for U.S. views on the "rectification of the legal status of the Committee on Economic, Social and Cultural Rights":

> As set out in Human Rights Council resolution 4/7, the United States understands that the Council seeks to initiate a process that will place the Committee on Economic, Social and Cultural Rights (the "ESC Committee") "on a par with all other treaty monitoring bodies" and to do so "in accordance with international law, in particular the law of international treaties."

Excerpts follow from the U.S. views that such a change in the ESC Committee would require amendment of or a new optional protocol to the ESC Covenant and that States Parties should "identify and consider whether there are any real, practical problems in the operation of the Committee other than this technical legal difference. . . ." The full text is available at *www.state.gov/s/l/c8183.htm.*

* * * *

2. As the ESC Committee was created by a decision by the United Nations Economic and Social Council ("ECOSOC") rather than being an entity expressly created by the States Parties to the International Covenant on Economic, Social and Cultural Rights ("the ESC Covenant"), it is the view of the United States that if States Parties to the ESC Covenant wished to "rectify . . . the legal status of the [ESC Committee], with the aim of placing the Committee on par with all other treaty monitoring bodies . . . in accordance with international law . . .", then the States Parties should amend the ESC Covenant or adopt a new optional protocol to the Covenant that would accomplish that objective.

3. The ESC Committee was created by ECOSOC resolution 1985/17. As such, it is the only human rights treaty monitoring body that was not created by its respective human rights treaty. Each of the following human rights treaty bodies was created by its respective human rights treaty:

- The Human Rights Committee (International Covenant on Civil and Political Rights, Art. 28),
- The Committee on the Elimination of Racial Discrimination (International Convention on the Elimination of All Forms of Racial Discrimination, Art. 8),
- The Committee on the Elimination of Discrimination Against Women (Convention on the Elimination of All Forms of Discrimination against Women, Art. 17),
- The Committee against Torture (Convention Against Torture and Other Cruel, Inhuman, or Degrading Treatment or Punishment, Article 17),
- The Committee on the Rights of the Child (Convention on the Rights of the Child, Art. 43), and
- The Committee on the Protection of the Rights of All Migrant Workers and Members of Their Families (International

Convention on the Protection of the Rights of all Migrant Workers and Members of their Families, Art. 72).

4. To provide the ESC Committee with a formal legal status equivalent to that of other treaty bodies, it would be necessary to amend the Covenant in such a manner that constitutes the Committee under the Covenant, along the lines of the above-mentioned human rights treaties. Article 29 of the Covenant sets out the appropriate procedure that States Parties are to follow in order to amend the Covenant. The process involves, *inter alia*, the proposal of an amendment by any State Party, the convening of a conference of States Parties by the UN Secretary General, and approval of the amendment by the conference and the General Assembly of the United Nations. Paragraphs 2 and 3 of Article 29 set forth provisions for entry into force of the amendment. Once entered into force, the amendment would be "binding on those States Parties which have accepted [it]" (Covenant, Art. 29). States Parties, of course, could also assume new formal obligations through the negotiation of protocols, which would impose treaty obligations on those states that became parties to such instruments.

5. The initial decision to not establish a treaty body under the ESC Covenant was a reflection by negotiators of the different nature of economic, social, and cultural rights. For example, obligations on a State Party "to undertake steps . . . to the maximum of its available resources, with a view to achieving progressively the full realization of [Covenant] rights. . . ." (Covenant, Art. 2) made it more difficult for an independent body to provide meaningful guidance with respect to treaty implementation. Furthermore, unlike the International Covenant on Civil and Political Rights (ICCPR) and its Optional Protocol, the ESC Covenant contains no inter-state or individual complaint procedures that require administration and oversight by an independent body. Thus, instead of creating a treaty monitoring body, the drafters opted to utilize, where appropriate, existing institutional structures such as the Economic and Social Council.

6. Notwithstanding the initial decision by the negotiators of the ESC Covenant not to establish a committee in the Covenant, the international community subsequently decided that there would be benefit in creating such a committee. Having been created by an

ECOSOC resolution, the ESC Committee as a practical matter monitors implementation of the ESC Covenant in a manner similar to the Human Rights Committee's monitoring of the ICCPR. For instance, both bodies receive and examine the reports of States Parties, as well as express their concerns and recommendations to States Parties (through "concluding observations"). Both bodies publish their non-binding opinions and legal interpretations of the provisions of their respective Covenants (through "general comments"). The Committees each maintain dialogues with States Parties to the respective Covenants as well as with civil society. Likewise, both Committees are comprised of independent experts that serve in their personal capacities.

7. There are two substantive differences between the competencies of the Human Rights Committee and the ESC Committee, although these differences are of little or no consequence with respect to a proposed "rectification" process. First, the ICCPR's first Optional Protocol gives the Human Rights Committee competence to examine individual complaints with regard to alleged violations of Covenant rights by States Parties to the Protocol. There is, of course, a separate exercise underway to consider whether the ESC Covenant might have an individual complaint procedure that would expand the ESC Committee's competencies.[1] Second, Article 41 of the ICCPR provides that the Human Rights Committee may consider inter-state complaints with respect to those States Parties that have made a declaration that they recognize the competence of that Committee to receive and consider such communications. While there is no corresponding provision in the ESC Covenant, so far as the United States is aware, no State Party to any human rights treaty has ever availed themselves of such inter-state complaint

---

[1] Indeed, Article 1 of the draft Optional Protocol would "recognize[] the competence of the Committee to receive and consider communications and to conduct inquiries as provided for by the provisions of the present Protocol." Draft Optional Protocol to the International Covenant on Economic, Social and Cultural Rights, Open-ended Working Group on an Optional Protocol to the International Covenant on Economic, Social and Cultural Rights, Fourth session, Geneva, 16-27 July 2007. Doc. No. A/HRC/6/WG.4/2 (Apr. 23, 2007) (Hereinafter "Draft Optional Protocol").

procedures under the major UN human rights treaties containing such provisions. Thus, apart from individual complaints, while there is a technical difference in the potential duties of the two treaty bodies, there does not seem to be a meaningful practical difference in their general operations.

8. Accordingly, when considering whether it is necessary or worthwhile to address any differences in the legal status of the ESC Committee, it would be useful for States Parties to the ESC Covenant to identify what practical goals, if any, they seek to achieve. As discussed above, the way to give the ESC Committee a legal status that is identical to other treaty monitoring bodies would be to formally create the entity as a matter of treaty law, either by amending the Covenant or by concluding an optional protocol to the ESC Covenant. However, if this and nothing more is the goal, then there would be a strong argument that it would probably not be worth such labor intensive and costly efforts that such a process would entail.

9. On the other hand, if the goal of States Parties to the ESC Covenant is to create substantial changes in the authorities of the Committee—for example, creating an inter-state complaint procedure—then the rationale for adoption of such a provision by treaty would be strengthened. But even this particular change would not seem to justify amending the ESC Covenant. The Draft Optional Protocol to the ESC Covenant, which is currently under negotiation, proposes an inter-state complaint procedure that would include new ESC Committee competencies.(fn. omitted). . . .

*　　*　　*　　*

B. DISCRIMINATION

1. Race

a. *Periodic Report on International Convention on the Elimination of All Forms of Racial Discrimination*

In April 2007 the United States submitted its Periodic Report to the UN Committee on the Elimination of Racial Discrimination Concerning the International Convention on the Elimination of All Forms of Racial Discrimination ("CERD"). As explained in its introduction, the report is submitted pursuant to article 9 of the CERD and follows guidelines adopted by the Committee in August 2000 (CERD/C/70/Rev.5) and May 2006 (HRI/GEN/2/Rev3). The United States submitted its initial, second, and third periodic reports as a single document in September 2000 ("Initial U.S. Report" or "Initial Report") and met with the Committee on August 3 and 6, 2001. *See Digest 2000* at 347–50 and *Digest 2001* at 247–67. The 2007 report, constituting the fourth, fifth, and sixth periodic reports, updates relevant information since the submission of the Initial Report and, as stated in the report, "takes into account the concluding observations of the Committee (CERD/A/56/18, paragraphs 380–407), published on August 14, 2001, as well as relevant general Committee recommendations and other Committee actions." Excerpts below address legal issues in U.S. implementation of CERD since 2001. The full text of the report, with three annexes (Annex I: Examples of State Civil Rights Programs; Annex II: Background on Matter Raised by Certain Western Shoshone Descendants, and Annex III: Domestic Laws), is available at *www.state.gov/g/drl/rls/cerd_report/83404.htm.*

PART I. GENERAL

A. Background

*   *   *   *

6. In this consolidated report, the United States has sought to respond to the Committee's concerns as fully as possible. In this regard, the United States notes the discussion of U.S. reservations, understandings, and declarations to the Convention contained in paragraphs 145 through 173 of the Initial U.S. Report. The United States maintains its position with regard to these reservations, understandings, and declarations, and with respect to other issues as discussed in this report.

*   *   *   *

D. General Legal Framework

41. The basic Constitutional and legal framework through which U.S. obligations under the Convention are implemented remains the same. The Constitution provides for equal protection of the laws and establishes a carefully balanced governmental structure to administer those protections. Among other factors:

- Under the Fifth and Fourteenth Amendments, all persons are equal before the law and are equally entitled to constitutional protection. All states are equal, and none may receive special treatment from the federal government. Within the limits of the Constitution, each state must give "full faith and credit" to the public acts, records, and judicial proceedings of every other state. State governments, like the federal government, must be republican in form, with final authority resting with the people;
- The Constitution stands above all other laws, executive acts, and regulations, including treaties;
- Powers not granted to the federal government are reserved to the states or the people.

42. In addition to the civil rights protections of the federal Constitution, laws, and courts—state constitutions, laws, and courts play an important role in civil rights protections. In this regard, state constitutions and laws must, at a minimum, meet the basic guarantees of the U.S. Constitution. Moreover, in keeping with the federal system of government, in many cases state laws actually afford their citizens greater protections than the federal Constitution requires. *See, e.g., Locke v. Davey,* 540 U.S. 712, 724 n. 8 (2004) (noting that, "at least in some respects," Washington State's constitution provides greater protections than the Federal Free Exercise Clause).

* * * *

F. Factors Affecting Implementation

52. As noted in the Initial U.S. Report, the United States has made significant progress in the improvement of race relations over the past half-century. . . .

53. Nonetheless, significant challenges still exist. Subtle, and in some cases overt, forms of discrimination against minority individuals and groups continue to plague American society, reflecting attitudes that persist from a legacy of segregation, ignorant stereotyping, and disparities in opportunity and achievement. . . .

54. In addition, two subjects of concern have been particularly acute in the years since 2000. The first involves the increase in bias crimes and related discriminatory actions against persons perceived to be Muslim, or of Arab, Middle Eastern, or South Asian descent, after the terrorist attacks of 9/11. The second involves the impacts of the changing demographic caused by high rates of immigration into the United States—both legal and illegal. The continuing legacies described above, in addition to these more recent issues, create on-going challenges for the institutions in the United States that are charged with the elimination of discrimination. Thus, despite significant progress, numerous challenges still exist, and the United States recognizes that a great deal of work remains to be done.

PART II. INFORMATION RELATING
TO ARTICLES 2 TO 7 OF THE CONVENTION

*   *   *   *

Article 2

A. Information on the legislative, judicial, administrative, or other measures that give effect to the provisions of article 2, paragraph 1, of the Convention.

*   *   *   *

85. Department of Justice. Shortly after 9/11, the Department of Justice Civil Rights Division reviewed and assessed existing laws and practices and spearheaded a special Initiative to Combat Post 9/11 Discriminatory Backlash. This initiative reflected a commitment by the U.S. government to combat violations of civil rights laws against Arab, Muslim, Sikh, and South-Asian Americans by: (1) ensuring that processes were in place for individuals to report violations and that cases were handled expeditiously; (2) implementing proactive measures to identify cases involving bias crimes and discrimination being prosecuted at the state level that might

merit federal action; (3) conducting outreach to affected communities to provide information on how to file complaints; (4) working with other offices and agencies to ensure accurate referral, effective outreach, and comprehensive provision of services to victims of civil rights violations; and (5) appointing two senior Department of Justice attorneys to focus on post 9/11 backlash issues—a Special Counsel for Post 9/11 National Origin Discrimination and a Special Counsel for Religious Discrimination. More in-depth descriptions of the programs carried out under this initiative appear under the discussion of article 5, Right to Security of Person and Protection by the State against Violence or Bodily Harm, below.

* * * *

111. *Racial Profiling.* The mission of the Justice Department Civil Rights Division includes combating racial profiling. The current Administration was the first to issue racial profiling guidelines for federal law enforcement officers and remains committed to the elimination of unlawful racial profiling by law enforcement agencies. *See Guidance Regarding the Use of Race by Federal Law Enforcement Agencies.* Specifically, racial profiling is the invidious use of race or ethnicity as a criterion in conducting stops, searches, and other law enforcement investigative procedures, based on the erroneous assumption that a particular individual of one race or ethnicity is more likely to engage in misconduct than any particular individual of another race or ethnicity. Specifically, the Civil Rights Division enforces the Violent Crime Control and Law Enforcement Act of 1994, 42 U.S.C. 14141, the Omnibus Crime Control and Safe Streets Act of 1968, 42 U.S.C. 3789d, and Title VI of the Civil Rights Act, 42 U.S.C. 2000d. The Civil Rights Division receives and investigates allegations of patterns or practice of racial profiling by law enforcement agencies. If a pattern or practice of unconstitutional policing is detected, the Division will typically seek to work with the local agency to revise its policies, procedures, and training protocols to ensure conformity with the Constitution and federal laws.

112. [I]n in June of 2003 the Department of Justice issued policy guidance to federal law enforcement officials concerning racial profiling. The guidance bars federal law enforcement officials from

engaging in racial profiling, even in some instances where such profiling would otherwise be permitted by the Constitution and laws. Federal law enforcement officers may continue to rely on specific descriptions of the physical appearance of criminal suspects, if a specific suspect description exists in that particular case. However, when conducting investigations of specific crimes, federal law enforcement officials are prohibited from relying on generalized racial or ethnic stereotypes. Under the new policy, a federal law enforcement agent may use race or ethnicity only in extremely narrow circumstances—when there is trustworthy information, relevant to the locality or time frame at issue, that links persons of a particular race or ethnicity to an identified criminal incident, scheme, or organization. In the national and border security context, race and ethnicity may be used, but only to the extent permitted by the applicable laws and the Constitution. On June 1, 2004, then-DHS Secretary Tom Ridge formally adopted the DOJ June 2003 guidance and directed all DHS components to develop agency-specific racial profiling training materials, in concert with the DHS Office for Civil Rights and Civil Liberties. That Office is responsible for implementing the DOJ guidance on racial profiling and continues to work with all DHS components to update and strengthen racial profiling training of law enforcement personnel.

*   *   *   *

B. Information on the special and concrete measures taken in the social, economic and cultural and other fields to ensure the adequate development and protection of certain racial groups or individuals belonging to them, for the purpose of guaranteeing them the full and equal enjoyment of human rights and fundamental freedoms, in accordance with article 2, paragraph 2 of the Convention.

*   *   *   *

127. The United States acknowledges that article 2 (2) requires States parties to take special measures "when circumstances so warrant" and, as described below, the United States has in place numerous such measures. The decision concerning when such measures are in fact warranted is left to the judgment and discretion of

each State Party. The decision concerning what types of measures should be taken is also left to the judgment and discretion of each State Party, and the United States maintains its position that, consistent with the Convention, special measures taken for the sole purpose of securing adequate advancement of certain racial or ethnic groups or individuals requiring such protection may or may not in themselves be race-based. For example, a "special measure" might address the development or protection of a racial group without the measure itself applying on the basis of race (e.g., a measure might be directed at the neediest members of society without expressly drawing racial distinctions).

128. A substantial number of existing federal ameliorative measures could be considered "special and concrete measures" for the purposes of article 2 (2). These include the panoply of efforts designed to promote fair employment, statutory programs requiring affirmative action in federal contracting, race-conscious educational admission policies and scholarships, and direct support for historically Black colleges and universities, Hispanic-serving institutions, and Tribal colleges and universities. Some provisions are hortatory, such as statutory encouragement for recipients of federal funds to use minority-owned and women-owned banks. Others are mandatory; for example, the Community Reinvestment Act, 12 U.S.C. 2901, requires federally chartered financial institutions to conduct and record efforts to reach out to under-served communities, including, but not limited to, minority communities.

* * * *

131. Any affirmative action plan that incorporates racial classifications must be narrowly tailored to further a compelling government interest, *see, e.g., Adarand Constructors, Inc., v. Pena*, 515 U.S. 200 (1995). The United States Supreme Court recently addressed the use of racial classifications in university admissions. In *Grutter v. Bollinger*, 539 U.S. 306 (2003), and *Gratz v. Bollinger*, 539 U.S. 244 (2003), the Court recognized a compelling interest that permits the limited consideration of race to attain a genuinely diverse student body, including a critical mass of minority students, at universities and graduate schools. Specifically, the Court held that the University of Michigan Law School's interest in "assembling a class

that is . . . broadly diverse" is compelling because "attaining a diverse student body is at the heart of [a law school's] proper institutional mission." *Grutter*, 539 U.S. at 329. In so doing, the Court deferred to the Law School's educational judgment that student-body diversity was essential to its educational mission. In *Grutter*, the Court further found the Law School's program to be narrowly tailored to achieve this mission because it applied a flexible goal rather than a quota, because it involved a holistic individual review of each applicant's file, and because it did not "unduly burden" individuals who were not members of the favored racial and ethnic groups. The Court also held that "race-conscious admissions policies must be limited in time," and expressed an expectation that "25 years from now, the use of racial preferences will no longer be necessary to further the interest approved today." *Id.* At 342–43. At the same time, however, in *Gratz v. Bollinger*, the Court struck down the admissions policies of the University of Michigan's undergraduate program, which automatically awarded points to an applicant's diversity score depending on the applicant's race, because it operated as a mechanical quota that was not "narrowly tailored" to meet the university's objective. *See id.* at 270.

132. To date, the Court has not recognized the goal of achieving broad diversity as compelling outside of the educational settling. Moreover, whether the goal of achieving simple racial diversity is a compelling interest that would permit the use of racial classifications in an education setting has yet to be determined. In its current term, the Supreme Court is expected to decide whether elementary and secondary schools may use race as a deciding factor in making student assignment decisions in order to achieve (or maintain) racially diverse schools. *See Parents Involved in Community Schools v. Seattle School District No. 1, 05-908; Meredith v. Jefferson County Board of Education, 06-915.*

*   *   *   *

134. Based on the Equal Educational Opportunities Act of 1974 (EEOA) and Title VI of the Civil Rights Act of 1964, courts have also continued to uphold the responsibility of states and local school districts to take affirmative steps to rectify the language deficiency of children with limited English proficiency, as required

by the landmark decision of *Lau v. Nichols*, 414 U.S. 563 (1974). For example, in *Flores v. Arizona*, 405 F. Supp. 2d 1112 (D. Ariz. 2005), the federal district court in Arizona, pursuant to the EEOA, found the State of Arizona's funding of its limited English Proficiency (LEP) programs so inadequate that it enjoined the state from requiring LEP students to pass a particular standardized test as a requirement for graduation from high school until funding was restored to an adequate level.

＊　＊　＊　＊

Article 4

A. Information on the legislative, judicial, administrative or other measures that give effect to the provisions of article 4 of the Convention, in particular measures taken to give effect to the undertaking to adopt immediate and positive measures designed to eradicate all incitement to, or acts of, racial discrimination, in particular:

1. *To declare an offence punishable by law all dissemination of ideas based on racial superiority or hatred, incitement to racial discrimination, as well as all acts of violence or incitement to such acts against any race or group of persons of another colour or ethnic origin, and also the provision of any assistance to racist activities, including the financing thereof;*
2. *To declare illegal and prohibit organizations, and also organized and all other propaganda activities, which promote and incite racial discrimination, and to recognize participation in such organizations or activities as an offence punishable by law;*
3. *Not to permit public authorities or public institutions, national or local, to promote or incite racial discrimination.*

136. The American people reject all theories of the superiority of one race or group of persons of one color or ethnic origin, as well as theories that attempt to justify or promote racial hatred and discrimination. It is government policy to condemn such theories, and none is espoused at any level of government. . . .

137. The United States reiterates that, for the reasons described in paragraphs 147 through 156 of the Initial U.S. Report, its ability to give effect to these requirements is circumscribed by the protections provided in the United States Constitution for individual freedom of speech, expression, and association. . .

138. In the United States, speech intended to cause imminent violence may constitutionally be restricted, but only under certain narrow circumstances. In 1992, the U.S. Supreme Court struck down a municipal ordinance making it a misdemeanor to "place on public or private property a symbol, object, appellation, characterization, or graffiti, including, but not limited to, a burning cross or Nazi swastika, which one knows or has reasonable grounds to know arouses anger, alarm or resentment in others on the basis of race, color, creed, religion or gender" on the grounds that it unconstitutionally restricted freedom of speech on the basis of its content, *R.A.V. v. City of St. Paul*, 505 U.S. 377 (1992). A more recent Supreme Court decision, however, upheld a statute that prohibited cross-burning with the intent of intimidating any person or group of persons, *Virginia v. Black*, 538 U.S. 343 (2003). Although the Virginia Supreme Court had struck down the statute as unconstitutional on the basis that it singled out a type of speech based on content and viewpoint, the U.S. Supreme Court held that the protections of the first amendment are not absolute, and that cross-burning with the intent to intimidate is in the nature of a true threat—a type of speech that may be banned without infringing the First Amendment, whether or not the person uttering the threat actually intends to carry it out, *see Watts v. United States*, 394 U.S. 705 (1969). In the Court's view, because cross-burning is such a particularly virulent form of intimidation, the First Amendment permits Virginia to outlaw cross-burning with the intent to intimidate.

139. Thus, consistent with the limitations of the U.S. Constitution, the United States can, and does, give effect to article 4 in numerous areas. For example:

140. *Hate Crimes.* The Civil Rights Division of the U.S. Department of Justice enforces several criminal statutes that prohibit acts of violence or intimidation motivated by racial, ethnic, or religious hatred and directed against participation in certain activities. Those crimes include: 18 U.S.C. 241 (conspiracy against rights);

18 U.S.C. 245 (interference with federally protected activities); 18 U.S.C. 247(c) (damage to religious property); 42 U.S.C. 3631 (criminal interference with right to fair housing); and 42 U.S.C. 1973 (criminal interference with voting rights). In addition, 47 of the 50 U.S. states enforce state laws prohibiting hate crimes, and organizations to combat hate crimes exist in a number of states.

141. Enforcement against hate crimes—including particular efforts devoted to prosecution of post 9/11 hate crimes targeting Arab Americans and Muslim Americans—is a high priority. Statistics concerning the breakdown of racial and ethnic groups involved in hate crimes cases, as well as specific examples of cases, are set forth in the section on article 5, Security of Person, below.

142. *Hate Crimes on the Internet.* The U.S. Supreme Court has made it clear that communications on the internet receive the same constitutional protections under the First Amendment that communications in other media enjoy, *Reno v. ACLU*, 521 U.S. 844 (1997). Nonetheless, when speech contains a direct, credible threat against an identifiable individual, organization, or institution, it crosses the line to criminal conduct and loses that constitutional protection. *See, e.g., Planned Parenthood of the Col[u]mbia/ Willamette, Inc. v. American Coalition of Life Activists*, 290 F. 3d 1058 (9th Cir. 2002), *cert denied*, 539 U.S. 958 (2003); *see also Virginia v. Black*, 538 U.S. 343 (2003).

*   *   *   *

A. The right to equal treatment before the tribunals and all other organs administering justice.

149. The right to equal treatment before courts in the United States is provided through the operation of the Equal Protection Clause of the Fourteenth Amendment to the U.S. Constitution. This provision is binding on all governmental entities at all levels throughout the United States. The constitutional provision has not changed since 2000.

*   *   *   *

167. *Capital Punishment.* At the time of the Initial U.S. Report, the federal government and 38 states imposed capital punishment for crimes of murder or felony murder, generally only when aggravating

circumstances were present, such as multiple victims, rape of the victim, or murder-for-hire. However, since 2000, the law in New York has been declared unconstitutional under the state constitution, and executions in Illinois and New Jersey have been suspended. Kansas's law was also declared unconstitutional, but that decision was overturned by the U.S. Supreme Court, *Kansas v. Marsh*, 126 S. Ct. 2516 (2006). All criminal defendants in the United States, especially those in potential capital cases, enjoy numerous procedural guarantees, which are respected and enforced by the courts. These include, among others: the right to a fair hearing by an independent tribunal; the presumption of innocence; the right against self-incrimination; the right to access all evidence used against the defendant; the right to challenge and seek exclusion of evidence; the right to review by a higher tribunal, often with a publicly funded lawyer; the right to trial by jury; and the right to challenge the makeup of the jury.

168. Two major Supreme Court decisions since 2000 have narrowed the categories of defendants against whom the death penalty may be applied. In *Roper v. Simmons*, 543 U.S. 551 (2005), the Court held that the execution of persons who were under the age of eighteen when their capital crimes were committed violates the Eighth and Fourteenth Amendments. *Atkins v. Virginia*, 536 U.S. 304 (2002), held that the execution of mentally retarded criminal defendants constituted cruel and unusual punishment in violation of the Eighth and Fourteenth Amendments. The Supreme Court has repeatedly refused to consider the contention that a long delay between conviction and execution constitutes cruel and unusual punishment under the Eighth Amendment, *see, e.g., Foster v. Florida*, 537 U.S. 990 (2002), leaving in place numerous decisions by lower federal courts rejecting such a claim, *see, e.g., Knight v. Florida*, 528 U.S. 990 (1999) (Thomas, J., concurring in denial of certiorari). However, in June of 2006 the Supreme Court decided that death row inmates may, under civil rights laws, challenge the manner in which death by lethal injection is carried out, *Hill v. McDonough*, 126 S. Ct. 2096 (2006). The underlying constitutional question—whether lethal injection violates the Eighth Amendment prohibition on cruel and unusual punishment—was not addressed by the Supreme Court, but will be decided in the

first instance by lower courts in specific cases. In June of 2006, the Supreme Court also ruled that new evidence, including DNA evidence concerning a crime committed long ago, raised sufficient doubt about who had committed the crime to merit a new hearing in federal court for a prisoner who had been on death row in Tennessee for 20 years, *House v. Bell*, 126 S. Ct. 2064 (2006). Five states have authorized the death penalty for sexual assault of a child—Louisiana, Florida, Montana, Oklahoma, and South Carolina, with the last two doing so in 2006. The courts have not yet ruled on the constitutionality of these laws.

169. Both the number of prisoners under sentence of death and the number of executions have declined since 2000. In 2000, 37 states and the federal government held 3,601 prisoners under death sentence. By the end of 2005, this number had decreased to 3,254—a reduction of 9.6 percent. Likewise, while there were 85 executions in 2000, the number of executions fell to 53 in 2006. In 2004, the number of inmates who were put on death row (128) was the lowest since 1973. This was the third consecutive year such admissions had declined. Of the inmates in prison under sentence of death, 56 percent were white and 42 percent were African American. Of the inmates whose ethnicity was known, 13 percent were Hispanic.

*   *   *   *

C. Political rights—Information on the means for guaranteeing these rights, and on their enjoyment in practice.

199. U.S. law guarantees the right to participate equally in elections, to vote and stand for election on the basis of universal and equal suffrage, to take part in the conduct of public affairs, and to have equal access to public service. Under the Voting Rights Act, the Department of Justice brings suits in federal court to challenge voting practices or procedures that have the purpose or effect of denying equal opportunity to minority voters to elect their candidates of choice. The Department also reviews changes with respect to voting in certain specially covered jurisdictions. In July of 2006, Congress extended the Voting Rights Act for another 25-year period.

200. *Voting.* To address problems with balloting in the 2000 election, Congress passed the Help America Vote Act of 2000 (HAVA),

Pub. L. No. 107-252. That legislation seeks to improve the administration of elections in the United States in three ways: (1) creation of a new federal agency, the Election Assistance Commission, to serve as a clearinghouse for election administration information; (2) provision of funds to states to improve election administration and replace outdated voting systems; and (3) creation of minimum standards for states to follow in several key areas of election administration. The Attorney General enforces the nationwide standards and requirements established by Section III of the Act. These include, for example, standards for voting systems, including alternative language accessibility; availability of provisional voting; standards for provisional voting; requirements for each state to create a single, interactive, computerized statewide voter registration list; and standards for absentee balloting.

201. The Department of Justice has pursued its enforcement responsibilities through litigation and non-litigation guidance. In 2003, after enactment of the Act, the Attorney General sent letters to the chief election officials, governors, and attorney generals in each of the 50 states, the District of Columbia, Guam, America Samoa, the U.S. Virgin Islands, and Puerto Rico describing the requirements and required timelines for compliance under HAVA and offered the Civil Rights Division's assistance in efforts to comply with the requirements of Title III. Each year, the Justice Department has also advised specific states and territories on actions needed to meet the Act's standards. In early 2004, the Justice Department sent informal advisories to six states raising specific concerns about their ability to comply with HAVA in time for the 2004 federal elections. After that round of elections in February and March of 2004, Justice also conducted a state-by-state analysis of compliance and wrote to three states raising compliance concerns noted by monitors. In 2004 and 2005, respectively, the Justice Department filed the first HAVA lawsuits against San Benito County, California and Westchester County, New York. Both suits involved the failure of poll officials to post required voter information. San Benito County also failed to have a system allowing provisional voters to find out whether their ballots were accepted and counted. Consent agreements were reached in both cases. In 2006, the Department filed lawsuits against the States of Alabama, Maine, New Jersey,

and New York, and Cochise County, Arizona. As of March 2007, the Justice Department had filed one HAVA lawsuit, against Cibola County, New Mexico.

202. In addition to enforcement of HAVA, the Justice Department continues to enforce other voting legislation, including the Voting Rights Act of 1965, as amended, the Uniformed and Overseas Citizen Absentee Voting Act of 1986 (UOCAVA), and the National Voter Registration Act of 1993. . . . .

* * * *

206. Under section 2 of the Voting Rights Act, 42 USC 1973(b), it is unlawful to re-draw voting districts for purposes of federal elections if the re-districting results in political processes that are not as equally open to members of a racial group as they are to other members of the electorate. In *League of United Latin American Citizens v. Perry*, 126 S. Ct. 2594 (2006), the United States Supreme Court found a violation of the Voting Rights Act in one Texas congressional district, district 23, but found no violations of the Constitution or the Voting Rights Act in the remaining 31 of the state's 32 congressional districts. The Court's decision left the Texas redistricting plan largely intact and left it to the state to determine how to remedy the problem identified as to congressional district 23. The majority's decision as to district 23 was founded on a new principle, under Section 2 of the Voting Rights Act, that the creation of an offsetting majority-minority district may not remedy the loss of a majority-minority district in the same part of the state, if the new district is not compact enough to preserve communities of interest.

* * * *

208. *Disenfranchisement of Convicted Criminals.* The Fourteenth Amendment to the U.S. Constitution explicitly recognizes the right of states to bar an individual from voting "for participation in rebellion, or other crime." . . .

209. Criminal disenfranchisement is a matter of continuing scrutiny in the states of the United States, and changes have occurred in a number of states since 2000. In 2001, New Mexico repealed the state's lifetime voting ban for persons with felony convictions.

In 2003, Alabama enacted a law that permits most felons to apply for a certificate of eligibility to register to vote after completing their sentences. In March 2005, the Nebraska legislature repealed the lifetime ban on all felons and replaced it with a two-year-post-sentence ban. In 2006, Iowa (by Executive Order) restored voting rights to persons who have completed felony sentences, and voters in Rhode Island approved a ballot measure restoring voting rights to persons released from prison on probation or parole. Policy changes that lower barriers to voting for ex-felons have also been enacted in Connecticut, Delaware, Kentucky, Maryland, Nevada, Pennsylvania, Virginia, Wyoming, and Washington.

210. In September 2005, the National Commission on Federal Election Reform, chaired by former Presidents Carter and Ford, recommended that all states restore voting rights to citizens who have fully served their sentences. While there is a lively debate within the United States on the question of voting rights for persons convicted of serious crimes pursuant to due process of law, the longstanding practice of states within the United States does not violate U.S. obligations under the Convention.

*   *   *   *

Article 6

*   *   *   *

D. Information in connection with general recommendation XXVI on article 6 of the Convention (2000).

289. General recommendation XXVI suggests that to meet the needs of victims of discrimination, courts and other competent authorities should consider awarding financial compensation for damage—material or moral—to victims, when appropriate, rather than limiting remedies solely to punishment of the perpetrator. As noted above, remedies to assist victims are available in the United States in private suits, civil suits, and administrative proceedings. In those cases settlement may include monetary relief, punitive damages, injunctive relief (prohibiting the perpetrator from taking certain actions with regard to the victim), or mandamus (requiring the perpetrator to do something affirmative with regard to the victim). Furthermore, in 2004 Congress enacted the Crime Victims'

Rights Act, P.L. 108-405, which provides a number of additional rights to the victims of criminal activity. The Department of Justice Office of Victims of Crime maintains a full program of grants and other activities designed to assist the victims of crime. Among other activities, this office provides funding to the National Victim Assistance Academy and to state victim's assistance academies, which conduct annual training sessions throughout the United States.

* * * *

Conclusion

308. The United States is aware of the challenges brought about by its historical legacy of racial and ethnic discrimination as well as other more recent challenges, and it continues to work toward the goal of eliminating discrimination based on race, ethnicity, or national origin. As a vibrant, multi-racial, multi-ethnic, and multi-cultural democracy, the United States, at all levels of government and civil society, continually re-examines and re-evaluates its successes and failures in this regard, recognizing that more work is to be done. The United States looks forward to discussing its experiences and this report with the Committee.

Committee Comments and Recommendations

309. This section addresses the concerns and recommendations set forth in the Committee's concluding observations on the Initial U.S. Report, A/56/18, paras. 380–407, 14/08/2001.

This Committee, concerned by the absence of specific legislation implementing the provisions of the Convention in domestic laws, recommends that the State party undertake the necessary measures to ensure the consistent application of the provisions of the Convention at all levels of government (paragraph 390).

310. The United States has taken, and continues to take, necessary measures to ensure the application of the provisions of the Convention at all levels of government, consistent with the U.S. constitutional structure. This commitment is set out in the understanding adopted with respect to the Convention:

> "[T]he United States understands that this Convention shall be implemented by the Federal Government to the extent that it exercises jurisdiction over the matters covered therein,

and otherwise by the state and local governments. To the extent that state and local governments exercise jurisdiction over such matters, the Federal government shall, as necessary, take appropriate measures to ensure the fulfillment of this Convention."

311. The ways in which the Convention is implemented by the federal government, by the respective state governments, and in U.S. territories are described throughout this report.

The Committee emphasizes its concern about the State party's far-reaching reservations, understandings and declarations entered at the time of ratification of the Convention. The Committee is particularly concerned about the implication of the State party's reservation on the implementation of article 4 of the Convention. In this regard the Committee recalls its general recommendations VII and XV, according to which the prohibition of dissemination of all ideas based upon racial superiority or hatred is compatible with the right to freedom of opinion and expression, given that a citizen's exercise of this right carries special duties and responsibilities, among which is the obligation not to disseminate racist ideas. The Committee recommends that the State party review its legislation in view of the new requirements of preventing and combating racial discrimination, and adopt regulations extending the protection against acts of racial discrimination, in accordance with article 4 of the Convention (para 391).

312. The United States supports the goals of the Convention and believes that its reservations, understandings, and declarations are compatible with the objects and purposes thereof.

313. As the United States has previously noted, its Constitution contains extensive protections for individual freedoms of speech, expression, and association, which (absent a reservation, understanding, or declaration) might be construed in tension with articles 4 and 7. The United States believes that its constitutional protections are fully consistent with the goals of the Convention. The purpose of the First Amendment is to preserve an uninhibited marketplace of ideas in which truth will ultimately prevail. See, *e.g., Abrams v. United States*, 250 U.S. 616 (1919) (dissenting opinion of Oliver Wendell Holmes, Jr., in which Justice Brandeis concurred).

Through freedom of expression, ideas can be considered and allowed to stand or fall of their own weight. As the late Gerald Gunther, one of the foremost constitutional law scholars in the history of the United States, explained: "The lesson I have drawn from my childhood in Nazi Germany and my happier adult life in this country is the need to walk the sometimes difficult path of denouncing the bigot's hateful ideas with all my power, yet at the same time challenging any community's attempt to suppress hateful ideas by force of law." *See also Virginia v. Black*, 538 U.S. 343, 367 (2003) (quoting Professor Gunther). To be sure, the Supreme Court has upheld the suppression of particularly hateful and dangerous speech under certain circumstances. *See, e.g., id.* (upholding a ban on cross-burning with intent to intimidate). In general, however, the United States believes that the goal of eliminating racial discrimination is, in fact, better served by application of the principles of freedom of expression and association than by the application of greater restrictions on those freedoms.

314. The Initial U.S. Report and the sections covering article 4 and article 5 (security of persons) in this report describe in greater detail the U.S. constitutional limitations on implementation of article 4, as well as the activities that may constitutionally be restricted. In addition, it should be noted that in cases such as hate crimes, the racial element of the crime may yield more severe punishment. The United States enforces against all such crimes to the fullest extent of the law, and numerous examples of such enforcement actions are described in this report.

The Committee also notes with concern the position of the State party with regard to its obligation under article 2, paragraph 1 (c) and (d), to bring to an end all racial discrimination by any person, group or organization, that the prohibition and punishment of purely private conduct lie beyond the scope of governmental regulation, even in situations where the personal freedom is exercised in a discriminatory manner. The Committee recommends that the State party review its legislation so as to render liable to criminal sanctions the largest possible sphere of private conduct that is discriminatory on racial or ethnic grounds (para 392).

315. Although the civil rights protections of the Fourteenth Amendment of the U.S. Constitution reach only "state action,"

private conduct may be regulated on several other constitutional bases. First, the Thirteenth Amendment's prohibition against slavery and involuntary servitude encompasses both governmental and private action and serves as the basis for several civil rights statutes. *See, e.g.,* 42 U.S.C. 1981, 1982. . . . In addition, the commerce power of Article 1 of the Constitution underlies Title II and Title VII of the 1964 Civil Rights Act, which prohibit private entities from discriminating in public accommodations and employment. The authority of Congress over commerce also serves as the basis for the Fair Housing Act, which prohibits private parties from discrimination in housing. The spending powers of Article 1 as well as Section 5 of the Fourteenth Amendment serve as the basis for Title VI of the 1964 Civil Rights Act, which prohibits discrimination by public and private institutions that receive federal funds. This report sets forth numerous examples of enforcement action against private persons with regard to activities such as those noted above.

316. In the U.S. view, it is unclear whether the term "public life" in the definition of "racial discrimination" in the Convention is synonymous with the permissible sphere of governmental regulation under U.S. law. Thus, the United States felt it prudent in acceding to the Convention to indicate through a formal reservation that U.S. undertakings in this regard are limited by the reach of constitutional and statutory protections under U.S. law as they may exist at any given time:

> "[T]he Constitution and laws of the United States establish extensive protections against discrimination, reaching significant areas of non-governmental activity. Individual privacy and freedom from governmental interference in private conduct, however, are also recognized as among the fundamental values which shape our free and democratic society. The United States understands that the identification of the rights protected under the convention by reference in article 1 to fields of "public life" reflects a similar distinction between spheres of public conduct that are customarily the subject of governmental regulation, and spheres of private conduct that are not. To the extent, however, that the Convention calls for a broader regulation of

private conduct, the United States does not accept any obligation under this Convention to enact legislation or take other measures under paragraph (1) of article 2, sub-paragraphs (1) (c) and (d) of article 2, article 3 and article 5 with respect to private conduct except as mandated by the Constitution and laws of the United States."

The Committee draws the attention of the State party to its obligations under the Convention and, in particular, to article 1, paragraph 1, and general recommendation XIV, to undertake to prohibit and to eliminate racial discrimination in all its forms, including practices and legislation that may not be discriminatory in purpose, but in effect. The Committee recommends that the State party take all appropriate measures to review existing legislation and federal, State and local policies to ensure effective protection against any form of racial discrimination and any unjustifiably disparate impact (para. 393).

317. The United States recognizes and supports the importance of prohibiting and eliminating racial discrimination in all its forms. Under U.S. law, claims that seemingly neutral laws, procedures, or practices are having disparate impacts or effects on persons or groups of a particular race, color, or national origin may be brought under the Voting Rights Act of 1965, as amended, Title VII of the 1964 Civil Rights Act, and the federal regulations implementing Title VI of the 1964 Civil Rights Act.

318. General Recommendation XIV, which is recommendatory in nature, states that "in seeking to determine whether an action has an effect contrary to the Convention, [the Committee] will look to see whether that action has an unjustifiable disparate impact upon a group distinguished by race, colour, descent, or ethnic origin." The term "unjustifiable disparate impact" indicates the view of the Committee that the Convention reaches only those race-neutral practices that both create statistically significant racial disparities and are unnecessary, i.e., unjustifiable. This reading of article 2 (1) (c) tracks the standards for litigating disparate impact claims under Title VII and the Title VI regulations in U.S. law. It is also consistent with the standards used in litigation of equal protection claims under the Fifth and Fourteenth Amendments of the U.S. Constitution,

for which statistical proof of racial disparity, particularly when combined with other circumstantial evidence, is probative of the discriminatory intent necessary to make out a claim. In the view of the United States, article 1 (1) (c) does not impose obligations contrary to existing U.S. law.

*   *   *   *

With regard to affirmative action, the Committee notes with concern the position taken by the State party that the provisions of the Convention permit, but do not require States parties to adopt affirmative action measures to ensure the adequate development and protection of certain racial, ethnic or national groups. The Committee emphasizes that the adoption of special measures by States parties when the circumstances so warrant, such as in the case of persistent disparities, is an obligation stemming from article 2, paragraph 2, of the Convention (para. 399).

334. It appears from the text of its conclusion and recommendation that the Committee may have misinterpreted the United States Government's position. As described in the section concerning article 2 (2), above, the United States acknowledges that article 2 (2) requires States parties to take special measures "when circumstances so warrant" and, as described in this report, the United States has in place a number of such measures. The decision concerning when such measures are in fact warranted is left to the judgment and discretion of each State Party. The determination of the precise nature and scope of such measures is also left to the judgment and discretion of each State Party, and the United States maintains its position that, consistent with the Convention, special measures taken for the sole purpose of securing adequate advancement of certain racial or ethnic groups or individuals requiring such protection may or may not in themselves be race-based. For example, a "special measure" might address the development or protection of a racial group without the measure itself applying on the basis of race (e.g., a measure might be directed at the neediest members of society without expressly drawing racial distinctions).

*   *   *   *

It is noted that the State party has not made the optional declaration provided for in article 14 of the Convention, and the

Committee recommends that the possibility of such a declaration be considered (para 404).

355. In submitting the Convention to the United States Senate for ratification, President Carter recognized that if the Senate gave its advice and consent to ratification, the President would then have the right to decide whether to make a declaration, pursuant to article 14 of the Convention, recognizing the competence of the Committee on the Elimination of Racial Discrimination to consider communications from individuals. If such a declaration were contemplated, he noted that it would be submitted to the Senate for consent to ratification. The United States remains aware of the possibility of making the optional declaration under article 14, but has not made any decision to do so.

The Committee recommends that the State party ratify the amendments to article 8, paragraph 6 of the Convention, adopted on 15 January 1992 at the Fourteenth Meeting of States Parties to the Convention (para 405).

356. It is the general policy of the United States that the financial obligations of treaty bodies should be funded by the States parties to the particular treaty at issue. The United States believes that the costs of the CERD Committee should be funded under the Convention itself by the parties thereto, as required by the Convention in its original form, and thus does not support the amendment to article 8, paragraph 6.

* * * *

b. UN General Assembly: Elimination of racism and racial discrimination

On November 28, 2007, the United States voted against a resolution on elimination of racism and racial discrimination in the UN General Assembly Third Committee. The resolution, entitled "Global efforts for the total elimination of racism, racial discrimination, xenophobia and related intolerance and the comprehensive implementation of and follow-up to the Durban Declaration and Programme of Action," was adopted by vote by the General Assembly on December 22, 2007. U.N. Doc. A/RES/62/220.

Ambassador Grover Joseph Rees, Acting U.S. Representative to the UN Economic and Social Council, explained the U.S. vote based on concerns regarding follow-up to the 2001 World Conference in Durban, as excerpted below. The full text of Ambassador Rees's statement is available at *www.usunnew york.usmission.gov/press_releases/20071128_344.html.*

The United States is opposed to racism, racial discrimination, xenophobia, and related intolerance. Our record of domestic legislation and policies to combat vigorously such activities and attitudes demonstrates our commitment. The United States has long been a party to the Convention on the Elimination of Racial Discrimination (CERD).

Although we supported the stated objectives of the World Conference held in Durban in 2001—and we continue to support these objectives—the outcomes of the conference were deeply flawed and divisive. The resolution now before us endorses that flawed outcome and is therefore itself seriously problematic.

We believe that Durban follow-up activities are duplicative of the work done by the CERD committee, as well as of the Human Rights Committee for the International Covenant on Civil and Political Rights and of the work related to the ILO conventions that address workers rights. In a time of limited resources and many great needs, we do not support the continuation of such duplicative work.

For these reasons, and as we have stated before, we do not believe the Human Rights Council should act as a preparatory committee for the Durban Review Conference. Rather, that body should dedicate itself to the role for which it was created: addressing human rights situations around the world, particularly emerging situations. . . .

Each country must have a legal framework in place to protect individuals from discrimination and to preserve other individual rights and fundamental freedoms including freedom of expression, freedom of association, and freedom of religion.

At this time States should be focusing on implementation of existing commitments, rather than on the follow-up of a flawed instrument or the creation of new instruments. The essential elements in multilateral efforts to combat contemporary forms of racism are universal ratification and effective implementation of the existing Convention on the Elimination of Racial Discrimination. . . .

*   *   *   *

2. Gender

a. *Violence against women*

(1) *UN Human Rights Council*

On March 20, 2007, Amy Ostermeier, member of the U.S. Observer Delegation, addressed the Human Rights Council on violence against women. Ms. Ostermeier's statement, excerpted below, is available at *www.us-mission.ch/Press2007/0321 ViolenceAgainstWomen.html.*

*   *   *   *

The United States is deeply concerned that in recent conflicts, rape has been used as a weapon by governments during wartime to target women and children. In Darfur, the conflict has had a devastating impact on Sudanese women and girls due to sexual and gender-based violence perpetrated by the janjaweed and Sudanese Government soldiers. In the early stages of the conflict, women and girls were brutalized as a tool of war as they were driven out of their homes. Now, as part of more than two million internally displaced persons, they remain vulnerable in the course of their daily lives.

The disturbing use of rape, violence, torture and forced labor of the women of Burma's Karen State are of equal concern to my government. These human rights abuses occur as part of a strategy designed to terrorize and subjugate the Karen people. We highlight the Special Rapporteur's observation that "the failure to investigate, prosecute and punish those responsible for rape and sexual violence has contributed to an environment conducive to the perpetuation of violence against women and girls in Myanmar." We call on the Burmese regime to step up to the responsibility of protecting its own people from these heart-wrenching crimes.

Finally, we have a question for the Special Rapporteur. The U.S. Government believes that prostitution and related activities are inherently harmful and dehumanizing, and contribute to the phenomenon of trafficking in persons. We fear that legalizing prostitution increases the number of trafficking victims. In your experience, to what degree does the legalization of prostitution lead to this form of violence against women and girls?

*   *   *   *

(2) UN General Assembly

On November 15, 2007, the UN General Assembly Third Committee adopted a resolution entitled "Eliminating rape and other forms of sexual violence in all their manifestations, including as instruments to achieve political objectives." The United States welcomed consensus on the resolution, of which it was an original co-sponsor. Excerpts follow from the statement of Ambassador Rees, explaining the U.S. views, including the U.S. belief that stronger emphasis should be placed on the issue of the use of rape to attain political and military objectives. The General Assembly adopted the resolution on December 18, 2007, without a vote. U.N. Doc. A/RES/62/134. The full text of Ambassador Rees's statement is available at *www.usunnewyork.usmission.gov/press_releases/ 20071115_314.html.*

———————

*   *   *   *

We believe it is important that the Committee has adopted the resolution and that the General Assembly do so as well. As the resolution makes clear, rape under any circumstances is an atrocious act, and all of us, including but not limited to states and the United Nations, must intensify our efforts to eliminate it. The resolution also makes clear that rape and other forms of sexual violence in conflict and related situations, whether it be a random act by soldiers or an attack by government forces, rebel groups, or other State or non-State actors, are reprehensible acts that cry out for scrutiny and for accountability.

Mr. Chairman, contrary to [what] some have suggested, this resolution never said there were "two kinds of rape." Unfortunately, Mr. Chairman, there are many kinds of rape and sexual violence. As you know, the resolution as originally proposed was focused primarily on the particularly outrageous situation in which a state condones the use of systematic mass rape by its own forces or surrogate militias [in] order to advance their military or political objectives. Governments have a responsibility to protect their citizens. When governments become perpetrators rather than protectors, their citizens have no recourse within their country. The United States and other co-sponsors have accepted numerous additions and changes throughout the process that has resulted in today's consensus. But it is no secret that we would have strongly preferred the final wording to place stronger emphasis on the use of rape to attain political and military objectives. The U.S. proposed this resolution with the intent of calling attention to this problem, and above all to help the victims.

We are gratified that the resolution contains a strong paragraph on impunity and suggests concrete ways that states and other actors can assist victims. We are happy that the resolution still calls special attention to the situation of rape in conflict situations and to rape and other sexual violence committed in order to achieve political or military objectives, and we are particularly happy that the resolution contains a number of provisions that are particularly relevant to cases in which rape is used or condoned by those in authority. The resolution's reporting requirement will help identify situations in which rape is being used to advance political and military objectives, in order to spur the international community to act to stop this practice.

(3) UN Security Council

On October 23, 2007, Ambassador Alejandro D. Wolff, Deputy U.S. Permanent Representative to the United Nations,

addressed the Security Council in its open debate to assess
progress in the implementation of Resolution 1325 (2000),
"Women, Peace and Security."

Excerpts from Ambassador Wolff's remarks below stress
the importance of the General Assembly resolution *supra* and
address the need for investigation and follow-up action in
cases of sexual exploitation and abuse by UN peacekeeping
personnel. The full text is available at *www.usunnewyork.
usmission.gov/press_releases/20071023_254.html.*

* * * *

Sexual violence against women is reprehensible in any context, but
it is especially heinous when it is used by political or military leaders as a tool to achieve political or military objectives. It is with
this in mind that the United States and others have introduced a
resolution in the Third Committee of the General Assembly entitled "Eliminating the Use of Rape and Other Forms of Sexual
Violence to Achieve Political or Military Objectives."

This resolution condemns the use by states and by non-state
actors of rape, typically systematic mass rape, to achieve military
or political objectives. This would be the first UN resolution to
focus specifically on this particularly egregious form of violence
against women. It calls for states to end impunity by prosecuting
and punishing those who use rape as a military or political tool; to
protect and support victims; and for states, for appropriate UN
officers and agencies, and for civil society to develop and implement
comprehensive strategies on prevention and prosecution of rape.
We ask member states to support and to consider co-sponsoring
the text, which will be addressed under the Agenda Item on
"Advancement of Women."

. . . Given the special vulnerability of the civilian population
during conflicts which threaten the peace and security of their
nations, it is particularly abhorrent when those charged with
restoring peace and stability become the perpetrators of sexual
exploitation and abuse of women and children. The Council has
addressed this issue in past statements, reiterating its condemnation

of all acts of sexual exploitation and abuse by all categories of personnel in UN peacekeeping missions and urging troop contributing countries to take appropriate preventive action, including the conduct of pre-deployment awareness training, and to take disciplinary and other action to ensure full accountability in cases of misconduct involving their personnel. The United Nations, as we heard from Under-Secretary-General Guéhenno earlier this morning, has made considerable and laudable efforts to enforce a zero-tolerance policy toward sexual exploitation and abuse by personnel assigned to UN peacekeeping operations, and has made considerable progress in providing appropriate training as well as improved oversight of conduct and discipline. We underscore the need for all allegations to be investigated properly and for appropriate follow-up action to be taken.

b. Fourth World Conference on Women and the Beijing Declaration and Platform for Action

On November 27, 2007, Ambassador Rees provided an explanation of the U.S. decision to disassociate from consensus on certain paragraphs of the resolution "Follow-Up to the Fourth World Conference on Women and Full Implementation of the Beijing Declaration and Platform for Action and the Outcome of the Twenty-Third Special Session of the General Assembly" in the Third Committee. The resolution was adopted by the General Assembly on December 18, 2007. U.N. Doc. A/RES/62/137.

Ambassador Rees's statement is set forth below and is available at *www.usunnewyork.usmission.gov/press_releases/ 20071127_337.html.*

The United States must dissociate itself from consensus with respect to certain paragraphs of this resolution. We do this with some reluctance, because we do support appropriate follow-up and implementation of the Beijing Declaration and Platform for Action. But we must dissociate from consensus with respect to certain paragraphs, and we have explanatory comments on other paragraphs:

For OP 2.

The U.S. understands that references to the Beijing Declaration and Platform for Action and their five and ten year reviews do not create any rights and, in particular, do not create or recognize a right to abortion. They cannot be interpreted to constitute support, endorsement, or promotion of abortion.

For OP 3.

OP 3 of the resolution "welcomes the contributions of the Committee on the Elimination of Discrimination Against Women." We regard this as an acknowledgment of the CEDAW Committee's efforts on Beijing implementation rather than an endorsement of specific pronouncements or recommendations.

For OP 5.

OP 5 calls upon States Parties to CEDAW, *inter alia*, "to take into consideration the concluding comments as well as the general recommendations of the Committee." While the U.S. acknowledges the important work of the CEDAW Committee in some areas, we have serious concerns about the Committee's recommendations in other areas.

For OP 7(h) and OP 7(i).

The U.S. understands that there is international consensus that the term "sexual and reproductive health" does not include abortion or constitute support, endorsement, or promotion of abortion or the use of abortifacients.

However, the wording in OP 7(h) also contains a variant of the phrase "reproductive health services." The U.S. cannot accept this term because there is ambiguity in its meaning.

c.   Women in development

William A. Heidt, Counselor for Economic and Social Affairs, commented on a draft resolution "Women in Development" in the UN Second Committee on December 7, 2007. The resolution was adopted by the UN General Assembly on December 19, 2007. U.N. Doc. A/RES/62/206. The full text of

Mr. Heidt's remarks is available at *www.usunnewyork.usmission.gov/press_releases/20071207_359.html.*

The U.S. understands that there is international consensus that none of the wording in this resolution creates any rights and, in particular, does not create or recognize a right to abortion. The wording cannot be interpreted to constitute support, endorsement, or promotion of abortion or the use of abortifacients.

The U.S. understands that PP 11 does not imply that States must implement obligations under human rights instruments to which they are not a Party. Of course, the U.S. joins in the call for full and urgent implementation by States of obligations under instruments to which they are Parties.

*   *   *   *

OP 21 reiterates the language of subparagraph 57(g) of the World Summit Outcome Document. Unfortunately, the UN Secretariat has sometimes attempted to define implementation of this and other such commitments without the agreement of all Member States.

The U.S. understands that there is an international consensus that the language in OP 21 does not create, recognize, or support a new goal, target, or indicator within the internationally agreed goals known as the Millennium Development Goals. This language is identical to language in the World Summit Outcome Document, a carefully negotiated and well crafted document that sought to balance strongly held views. Therefore, it is of the utmost importance to ensure that respect for this delicate balance be maintained. To this end, it is important to reaffirm that the objective set forth in subparagraph 57(g) of the World Summit Outcome Document was seen as a means of achieving the goal of reducing maternal mortality and other MDG goals, rather than being a goal in and of itself.

There are many elements that will be necessary to achieve the goals of reducing maternal mortality, increasing maternal health, reducing child mortality, promoting gender equality, combating HIV/AIDS, and eradicating poverty. For instance, increased attention must also be paid to preventable and/or treatable conditions such as malaria, tuberculosis, upper respiratory infections, and immunizable diseases.

While neither these objectives nor the health objective in OP 21 constitutes a goal, target, or indicator in the context of the MDGs, all are important to achieving the goals aimed at reducing maternal mortality, increasing maternal health, reducing child mortality, promoting gender equality, combating HIV/AIDS, and eradicating poverty.

3. Religion

a. Annual Report on International Religious Freedom

On September 14, 2007, the Department of State released the 2007 Annual Report on International Religious Freedom covering the period July 1, 2006 through June 30, 2007, transmitted to Congress pursuant to § 102(b) of the International Religious freedom Act of 1998, 22 U.S.C. § 6412(b). The report is available at *www.state.gov/g/drl/rls/irf/2007*. Statements to the press on the release of the report by Secretary of State Rice and by John V. Hanford III, Ambassador at Large for International Religious Freedom, are available at *www.state. gov/secretary/rm/2007/09/92113.htm* and at *www.state. gov/g/drl/rls/rm/2007/92101.htm*, respectively.

b. Report on combating defamation of religions

In July 2007 the United States responded to a request from the UN Office of the High Commissioner for Human Rights for contributions to a report on combating defamation of religions. In its general introduction, the United States explained that, because of U.S. constitutional protections of free speech, "an approach such as 'defamation of religions' entails a slippery slope, and endangers the very freedom of expression that international human rights treaties are designed to protect and that is essential in a democratic society." Excerpts below provide U.S. views on the need to protect peaceful free expression while also protecting individuals against discrimination and violence. The full text is available at *www.state. gov/s/l/c8183.htm.*

In response to Queries 1 and 2 concerning actions to prohibit discrimination based on religion and faith as well as legal and constitutional guarantees "aimed at protecting against discrimination based on religion and faith, acts of hatred and violence, xenophobia and related intolerance, intimidation and coercion resulting from defamation of religions," the United States stated as follows.

---

a. The First Amendment of the U.S. Constitution guarantees the right to freedom of religion. It prohibits the federal government from making any law that establishes a national religion (Establishment Clause) or prohibits free exercise of religion (Free Exercise Clause). The Free Exercise Clause as interpreted includes the right to freedom of belief and worship, and the freedom to not believe in any faith.

b. The First Amendment also prohibits the federal legislature from making laws that infringe on freedom of speech, freedom of the press, the right to assemble peacefully, and to petition the government.

c. The 14th Amendment extends these protections against encroachment by state as well as federal officers.

d. Additionally, many state constitutions have Bills of Rights which guarantee freedom of religion at the state level.

e. The Religious Freedom Restoration Act, passed by Congress in 1993, aims to prevent laws which substantially burden a person's free exercise of religion.

f. The freedom of speech clause protects individual expression relating to views on religion, even if these views may be perceived by some as negative, insulting, or offensive. Freedom of speech is one of the fundamental freedoms in the country, and the United States rejects the concept of "defamation of religion."

1. Human rights law vests rights in individuals, not in groups, ideologies, or beliefs, including religions.

2. "Defamation" carries a particular legal meaning and application in the United States and indeed elsewhere which makes the term wholly unsuitable in the context of "religions" as a term of use in multilateral fora. Because one defense to a charge of defamation is the truth, and merely issuing an opinion about something cannot be verified one way or another as true, this term is simply not appropriate.

3. The United States has voted against every United Nations resolution on Defamation of Religion since the inception of this notion in Pakistan's 1999 "Defamation of Islam" resolution, which was altered to a "Defamation of Religions" resolution. The United States does not believe it should be illegal to express an opinion on a particular religion, including those which are highly critical. These resolutions carve out a special status for Islam, above concerns for other religions, and infringe on basic freedom of speech rights, such as the right to state opinions, publish books and articles, and freely express views in other ways which may be critical of religions. The U.S. Constitution would not permit any international agreement or treaty purporting to prohibit unpopular opinions and viewpoints to have legal effect in the United States.

4. The United States does not outlaw statements or expressions such as Holocaust denial, and allows groups that are considered racist, xenophobic or otherwise intolerant to congregate peacefully. Of course any acts of *violence* are not protected under the U.S. Constitution and may be criminally punished. It is *peaceful* worship, belief, and speech that are afforded the widest protections under the U.S. Constitution.

5. The United States believes that the issues of concern for Muslims described in the UN Defamation of Religions resolutions *in toto* are better dealt with under the auspices of the International Covenant for Civil and Political Rights (ICCPR) and the International Convention on the Elimination of All Forms of Discrimination Based on Race (ICERD), rather than in this new *sui generis* and deeply-flawed concept of "defamation of religions."

6. The United States is deeply concerned with the use of the concept of "defamation of religions" to justify torture, imprisonment, abuse, and even issu[ing] execution orders against individuals and religious groups who do not subscribe to a particular "state" religion, or who wish to convert to another religion according to their conscience. The defamation of religions concept has also been promulgated into national legal systems in order to halt any public comment or dissent against political figures, and is now being promoted at the international level to promote and justify blasphemy laws in some countries. The United States believes that the employment of this concept jeopardizes freedom of religion, expression, assembly, association, and press.

g. The United States has significant legislation in place which prohibits discrimination based on religion in several contexts. The Civil Rights Act of 1964 has many protections against discrimination. Title II outlaws discrimination in places of public accommodation and amusement, including hotels, motels, restaurants, and theaters. Title III prohibits state and municipal governments from denying access to public facilities on the grounds of race, religion or ethnicity. Title IV prohibits discrimination on the basis of race, religion, or ethnicity by public schools, colleges, and universities. Title VII prohibits discrimination in the employment context based on race, color, religion, sex or national origin. Public and private employers, with certain exceptions including the federal government and small private businesses, may not discriminate based on the above categories. Executive Order 11246, as amended, prohibits most federal contractors and subcontractors and federally assisted contractors and subcontractors from discriminating in employment decisions on the basis of "race, color, sex, religion or national origin." The Fair Housing Act, 42 U.S.C. § 3601, prohibits discrimination based on "race, color, religion, sex, national origin, handicap, and familial status" in activities relating to the sale, rental, financing, and advertising of housing. These laws are vigorously enforced. The Religious Land Use and Institutionalized Persons Act of 2000 protects the religious rights of persons in institutions such as prisons or mental institutions, and protects houses of worship and religious schools from abuses by local zoning authorities.

h. Additionally, hate crime laws establish prohibitions on actions which are motivated by hatred towards individuals of a particular social group. Crimes against individuals because they are of a particular religion are outlawed as hate crimes as well as common crimes.

i. The U.S. Supreme Court has ruled on numerous cases upholding the free exercise of religion. As just one example, the Court ruled that unemployment compensation may not be denied to a beneficiary who is unwilling to accept employment that would require working on his or her Sabbath (*Sherbert v. Verner*). The beneficiary's beliefs need not be based on the tenets of an established religious sect, if his or her belief is a sincere religious one (*Frazee v. Illinois Department of Employment*).

j. The separation of church and state has, in part, been preserved by the judicial doctrine that when there is a dispute within a religious order or organization, courts will not inquire into religious doctrine, but will defer to the decision-making body recognized by the church and give effect to whatever decision is officially and properly made.

k. These broad statutory and constitutional protections are implemented in practice. Criminal investigations and prosecutions can be initiated against any person exercising the authority of any local, state or federal government who violates the civil rights of individuals, including freedom of religion. Investigations and prosecutions can be undertaken at the federal level, state level, or sometimes both.

l. The Civil Rights Division (CRD) of the U.S. Department of Justice has primary authority over prosecutions for violations of federal criminal civil rights laws. The CRD welcomes complaints from members of the public, which are reviewed to determine whether the facts warrant a criminal investigation. If an investigation develops sufficient evidence to prove a case beyond a reasonable doubt, a federal prosecution can be brought.

m. In February 2007, the U.S. Attorney General launched an initiative to increase enforcement of federal laws protecting against religious discrimination and religious hate crimes. He also released a report detailing the Department of Justice's successes in these areas in the past six years. The report is available at the initiative's website, www.FirstFreedom.gov, which also describes the various facets of the initiative.

n. Where there are allegations of constitutional violations pervading an institution or department, private citizens can file a class action lawsuit using federal civil rights statutes, including 42 U.S.C. § 1983.

> In response to Queries 3 and 4 concerning measures adopted to prohibit dissemination of racist and xenophobic ideas and material aimed at any religion or its followers that constitute incitement to discrimination, hostility, or violence, and to ensure that physical attacks and assaults related to religion are offences punishable by law, the United States explained as follows.

---

a. In accordance with the 1st and 14th Amendments to the U.S. Constitution which protect freedom of speech, the United States may not criminalize racist and xenophobic ideas, expressed either in conversation or in published materials. The concept of free speech is very important in the U.S. and protects individuals with diverse ideas, including prejudicial ones. The Constitution provides broad protection for speech that may be considered objectionable by most of society. Courts have carved out narrow categories, such as libel, obscenity, fighting words and threats of injury, in which an individual's statements may not be protected by the First Amendment. *See Chaplinsky v. New Hampshire*, 315 U.S. 569, 572 (1942); *New York Times v. Sullivan*, 376 U.S. 254, 270 (1964).

b. Accordingly, the United States has made reservations, understandings, and declarations to certain provisions in international treaties that prohibit the dissemination of racist ideas or otherwise restrict freedom of expression. For example, when the United States ratified the ICCPR and ICERD, it attached reservations, understandings, and declarations concerning provisions insofar as they are inconsistent with the U.S. Constitution. These cover, *inter alia*, ICCPR Article 20(2), which requires Parties to "prohibit advocacy of national, racial or religious hatred that constitutes incitement to discrimination, hostility or violence," and ICERD Article 4, which condemns propaganda and organizations which promote racial hatred or discrimination, and requires parties to punish dissemination of "ideas based on racial superiority."

c. U.S. law does allow for suppression of or legal sanctions against harmful *conduct* motivated by racism and other forms of social intolerance. Racist conduct that incites violence or itself inflicts injury has been characterized as outside of First Amendment protections, and is therefore punishable. Under the U.S. Constitution, hateful speech can be criminalized only if it is intended to incite "imminent lawless action" (*Brandenburg v. Ohio*). Some courts/states require for a conviction of incitement to violence, that the person must not only have made speech which advocates unlawful action, but that the circumstances must indicate that there was some likelihood that the unlawful action would actually occur.

d. Hate crimes in the U.S. exist at both the federal and state levels. Laws vary from state to state, but 45 states and the District of Columbia have statutes criminalizing various types of hate crimes—examples include laws prohibiting assault, murder or other violent crimes perpetrated against a person because of one's race, color, religion, sex and other categories. Thirty-one (31) states allow a civil cause of action for hate crimes, in addition to a criminal penalty.

e. Many states' laws allow hate crimes—crimes motivated by hate due to religion and other factors—to have more severe punishments than the comparable crime not stirred by such motivations, and this is constitutionally permissible. The U.S. Supreme Court considers punishing prejudice as a motive for conduct that is already criminal to be different than punishment for abstract beliefs, which would not be constitutional.

f. The federal law goes even further. The Hate Crime Sentencing Enhancement Act of 1994 requires the U.S. Sentencing Commission to increase penalties for crimes committed on the basis of actual or perceived race, color, religion, national origin, ethnicity, and other factors. This act only applies to federal crimes.

g. 18 U.S.C. Sec. 245, also known as the 1969 law (federal) permits federal prosecution of an individual who "by force or threat of force willfully injures, intimidates or interferes with . . . any person because of his race, color, religion or national origin and because he is or has been" attempting to engage in one of six types of federally protected activities, including voting or going to school. To date, this law has been upheld in the courts.

h. Laws which prohibit racist conduct which stops short of clearly inciting violence or inflicting injury are fairly likely to be held unconstitutional. In a seminal Supreme Court case, (*R.A.V. v. City of St. Paul, Minnesota*, 505 U.S. 377 (1992)), the Court held that a city hate speech ordinance (which made it a misdemeanor [minor crime] to place on public or private property a symbol, graffiti, object or other expression which reasonably arouses anger or resentment in others on the basis of religion and other factors) was unconstitutional.

i. Laws are in place to ensure that any destruction of another's property is an offense punishable by law. These laws will generally suffice to punish those who physically attack and assault businesses, cultural centers and places of worship.

j. Under the Hate Crimes Sentencing Enhancement Act, if the destruction of a building was motivated by religious hatred, the sentence for the crime would increase.

k. Targeting of religious symbols accompanied by violence or destruction of property is similarly punishable.

> Query 6 concerned action undertaken "to ensure that the print, audio-visual and electronic media, including the Internet, and any other means do not incite acts of violence, xenophobia or related intolerance and discrimination against Islam or any other religion." The United States responded as follows.

a. The free speech guarantee of the First Amendment has been interpreted by the U.S. Supreme Court to extend to speech advocating illegal conduct, and regulation of such speech is permissible only in narrow circumstances: "the constitutional guarantees of free speech and free press do not permit a State to forbid or proscribe advocacy of the use of force or of law violation, except where such advocacy is directed to inciting or producing imminent lawless actions and is likely to incite or produce that action"

(*Brandenburg v. Ohio*). Notwithstanding the First Amendment limitations on the regulation of speech, speech that is tantamount to conduct—or that is simply the means of effecting conduct—may itself be legitimately proscribed, punished, or regulated incidentally to the constitutional enforcement of generally applicable statutes.

b. A number of U.S. statutes criminalize speech-related conduct in certain circumstances, including general laws criminalizing the solicitation to commit acts of violence, conspiracy, and aiding and abetting. More specific laws forbid such acts as seditious conspiracy; advocating the overthrow of the government; conspiring within the jurisdiction of the United States to kill, kidnap, or maim any individual outside the United States or in a foreign country with which the United States is at peace; mailing material that incites murder, assassination, or arson; and providing material support to designated terrorist organizations or in support of terrorist acts.

c. The U.S. material support laws are broad-based charging statutes that provide an important vehicle for prosecuting terrorists' recruitment, training, and fundraising efforts, which is sometimes conducted by terrorists online. Material support may include actions such as providing funding, training, expert advice or assistance, personnel, or providing communications equipment (which could include ISPs and other web services, among other things). The material support provisions, however, either require proof that the defendant knew or intended that the support was to be used in the preparing or carrying out of a terrorist activity, or proof that the defendant knowingly provided material support to a designated foreign terrorist organization, regardless of whether the defendant knew that the support would be used for a terrorist activity. Additionally, U.S. law also prohibits certain financial transactions with certain designated foreign states or individuals.

d. Depending on the specific facts and circumstances, these criminal laws and other civil (non-criminal) tools may be applicable to unlawful conduct that occurs on a U.S. website, and could be used to close U.S. terrorist used or related websites. However, prosecution for speech-related conduct on the Internet would face significant First Amendment, due process, and other statutory challenges.

C. CHILDREN

1. Optional Protocols to the Convention on the Rights of the Child

In May 2007 the United States submitted initial reports to the UN Committee on the Rights of the Child concerning two protocols to the Convention on the Rights of the Child: (1) the Optional Protocol on the Involvement of Children in Armed Conflict ("Armed Conflict Protocol") and (2) the Optional Protocol on the Sale of Children, Child Prostitution and Child Pornography ("Sale of Children Protocol"). Although it is not a party to the Convention on the Rights of the Child, the United States became party to the two protocols on December 24, 2002. *See* S. Treaty Doc. No. 106-37 (2000) for U.S. transmittal of the protocols to the Senate for advice and consent to ratification; *see also Digest 2002* at 183–86 and 293–300 and *Digest 2000* at 356–64.

a. Optional Protocol on the Involvement of Children in Armed Conflict

See C.2.a. below.

b. Optional Protocol on the Sale of Children, Child Prostitution and Child Pornography

Excerpts follow from the report on the Sale of Children Protocol, prepared in accordance with article 12 of the protocol and organized following the General Guidelines of the Committee on the Rights of the Child, adopted April 4, 2002. U.N. Doc. CRC/OP/SA/1.* Two annexes, Annex I—U.S. Instrument Of

---

* Editor's note: Although the Committee adopted Revised Guidelines on November 3, 2006 (U.N. Doc. CRC/C/OPSC/2), a footnote to the report explained that "[b]ecause most of the preparation and drafting of this initial report predates the Revised Guidelines," the report follows the 2002 guidelines.

Ratification and Annex II—Principal U.S. Statutes Cited In This Report, are available with the report at *www.state.gov/g/drl/rls/c22156.htm.*

I. Introduction

*   *   *   *

3. Prior to U.S. ratification of the Protocol, U.S. federal and state law satisfied the substantive requirements of the Protocol. Accordingly, no new, implementing legislation was required to bring the United States into compliance with the substantive obligations that it assumed under the Protocol, although a technical legal lacuna caused the United States to enter a reservation with respect to offenses committed on board a ship or aircraft registered in the United States. The provisions of the Protocol are not self-executing under U.S. domestic law, with one exception. That exception is Article 5, discussed below, which permits States Parties to consider the offenses covered by Article 3(1) as extraditable offenses in any existing extradition treaty between States Parties.

II. Information on Measures and Developments Relating to the Implementation of the Protocol

*   *   *   *

Article 3(1)(a)(i)a—Sexual Exploitation

15. The requirement to criminalize the sale of a child for purposes of sexual exploitation largely overlaps with the requirement to criminalize acts concerning child prostitution and child pornography. The term "sexual exploitation" is not defined, but it was generally understood during the negotiations that the term means prostitution, pornography, or other sexual abuse in the context of the sale of children.

16. In the United States, the Federal and State Governments have enacted criminal laws to protect children from sexual exploitation by adults. For example, federal and state laws prohibiting child sexual abuse and statutory rape laws are used to prosecute adults who sexually exploit children for the above-described purposes. Moreover, as set forth in detail in the analysis of Article 3(1)(b)

and 3(1)(c), federal and state law prohibit exploitation of children for purposes of prostitution and pornography. Additionally, federal law prohibits trafficking in children for sexual purposes. 18 U.S.C. § 1591, which was passed as part of the Trafficking Victims Protection Act of 2000, criminalizes all sex trafficking of children, regardless of whether fraud, force or coercion was used in the offense. There is no requirement that the sex trafficking cross state lines, provided it can be shown that the conduct is in or affecting interstate or foreign commerce. In addition, under 18 U.S.C. § 2423(a), it is prohibited to transport in interstate commerce any individual under age 18 with the intent that the "individual engage in prostitution or in any sexual activity for which any person can be charged with a criminal offense." Attempts to do so are prohibited by 18 U.S.C. § 2423(e). . . .

Article 3(1)(a)(i)b—Transfer of Organs of the Child for Profit

17. During the negotiations, States limited the scope of the Protocol with respect to organ trafficking to situations where (1) the sale of a child occurred and (2) the organs of that child were subsequently extracted and sold for a profit.

18. U.S. federal law contains comprehensive protections against trafficking in the organs of a child. U.S. federal law criminalizes acquiring, receiving, or otherwise transferring any human organ for valuable consideration for use in human transplantation if the transfer affects interstate commerce. 42 U.S.C. § 274e (National Organ Transplant Act of 1984, as amended). The federal proscription is limited to transfers affecting interstate commerce because "laws governing medical treatment, consent, definition of death, autopsy, burial, and the disposition of dead bodies are exclusively State law." S.Rep. 98-382, 98th Cong., 2nd Sess. 1984. Nonetheless, the phrase "affecting interstate commerce" is generally interpreted broadly by U.S. courts.

19. While U.S. state law may not always criminalize the sale of organs per se, the situation addressed in the Protocol would inevitably fall within the scope of one or more criminal state statutes. Since the transfer of organs of a child must be within the context of the sale of a child, situations involving the lawful consent of a child to donate an organ in which the transfer does not involve

valuable consideration are not prohibited. Accordingly, depending on the nature of the crime and state law, the conduct prohibited by the Protocol would constitute assault, and might also be battery, maiming, child abuse or criminal homicide.

20. Consequently, to clarify the scope of the obligation to criminalize the transfer of organs in Article 3 the United States expressed the following understanding in its instrument of ratification:

> The United States understands that the term "transfer of organs for profit" as used in Article 3(l)(a)(i) of the Protocol, does not cover any situation in which a child donates an organ pursuant to lawful consent. Moreover, the United States understands that the term "profit", as used in Article 3(1)(a)(i) of the Protocol, does not include the lawful payment of a reasonable amount associated with the transfer of organs, including any payment for the expense of travel, housing, lost wages, or medical costs.

Article 3(1)(a)(i)c—Engagement of the Child in Forced Labor

21. The Protocol requires States Parties to criminalize the conduct of both the seller and buyer of a child in the context of a sale, i.e., (1) acts of arranging for a buyer of a child (seller's conduct), (2) delivering the child pursuant to a sale (the seller's conduct or the conduct of his/her agent), and (3) accepting the child pursuant to the sale (the buyer's conduct). Since "offering, delivering or accepting" a child for the purpose of forced labor must take place in the context of a sale, criminal penalties are required under Article (3)(1)(a)(i)c where the transaction has been completed.

22. U.S. federal law, consistent with the requirements of Article 3(1)(a)(i)c, criminalizes the sale of a child for the purpose of engagement in forced labor. Forced labor is specifically prohibited by 18 U.S.C. § 1589, which was passed as part of the Trafficking Victims Protection Act of 2000. Section 1589 criminalizes providing or obtaining the labor or services of a person by (1) threats of serious harm to, or physical restraint against, that person or another person; (2) by means of any scheme, plan, or pattern intended to cause the person to believe that, if the person did not perform such labor or services, that person or another person

would suffer serious harm or physical restraint, or (3) by means of the abuse or threatened abuse of the law or the legal process. . . . In addition to the forced labor statute, other provisions of the U.S. Code provide criminal penalties for peonage, enticement into slavery, involuntary servitude, and trafficking with respect to peonage, slavery, involuntary servitude, or forced labor, sex trafficking, as discussed above, and unlawful conduct with respect to documents in furtherance of trafficking, peonage, slavery, involuntary servitude, or forced labor. *See* 18 U.S.C. §§ 1581, 1583, 1584, 1590, 1591, and 1592. Attempts to commit such crimes are penalized under 18 U.S.C. § 1594. These laws reach any such conduct that takes place anywhere in the United States. Federal law further criminalizes interstate kidnapping (18 U.S.C. § 1201). The kidnapping statutes punish individuals who kidnap others, including minors, across state lines. . . .

23. The provisions of 18 U.S.C. § 241, the federal civil rights conspiracy statute, prohibits conspiracies to violate the Thirteenth Amendment. The Thirteenth Amendment prohibits slavery and involuntary servitude and has been interpreted very broadly. . . . Furthermore, under the Thirteenth Amendment, Congress may reach conduct by private individuals as well as governments.

24. Finally, a person who "aids, abets, counsels, commands, induces or procures" the commission of one of these federal offenses is punishable as a principal under 18 U.S.C. § 2. Accordingly, those who take part in a portion of the transaction resulting in the sale of a child for the purpose of forced labor will also be subject to punishment under U.S. anti-trafficking laws in combination with § 2. Such conduct when involving two or more persons could also incur conspiracy liability under 18 U.S.C. § 371.

* * * *

Article 3(1)(b)—Child Prostitution

30. Child prostitution is not legal anywhere in the United States. Under U.S. federal law, the Mann Act, 18 U.S.C. § 2421, prohibits transporting a person across foreign or state borders for the purpose of prostitution. In addition to this general prohibition, federal law specifically prohibits transportation across foreign or state borders of any individual under age 18 with the intent that

the "individual engage in prostitution or in any sexual activity for which any person can be charged with a criminal offense." 18 U.S.C. § 2423. Federal laws further prohibit enticing, persuading, inducing, etc., any person to travel across a state boundary for prostitution or for any sexual activity for which any person may be charged with a crime, 18 U.S.C. § 2422, and travel with intent to engage in any sexual act with one under age 18, 18 U.S.C. § 2423(b). The newest federal legal tool in the fight against child prostitution is 18 U.S.C. § 1591, which prohibits sex trafficking of children. Sex trafficking is defined as causing a person to engage in a commercial sex act through force, fraud, or coercion, or where the victim is under 18. The term "commercial sex act" means any sex act, on account of which anything of value is given to or received by anyone. For offenses involving persons under the age of 18, there is no requirement of force, fraud, or coercion. There are additional penalties if the victim is younger than 14. Furthermore, unlike the Mann Act, there is no requirement that any person be transported across foreign or state borders.

31. In addition, all 50 states prohibit prostitution activities involving minors under the age of 18. State child prostitution statutes specifically address patronizing a child prostitute, inducing or employing a child to work as a prostitute, or actively aiding the promotion of child prostitution. See, e.g., NMSA [New Mexico] 1978, § 30-6A (4), Sexual Exploitation of Children by prostitution; in Utah, child prostitution is a second-degree felony punishable by 1 to 15 years in prison. Section 76-10-1306, Utah Code Annotated.

Article 3(1)(c)—Child Pornography

32. U.S. federal and state criminal laws also prohibit the child pornography activities proscribed by Article 3(1)(c).

33. Federal law prohibits the production, distribution, receipt, and possession of child pornography, if the pornographic depiction was produced using any materials that had ever been transported in interstate or foreign commerce, including by computer, or if the image was transported interstate or across a U.S. border. 18 U.S.C. §§ 2251–2252A. Conspiracy and attempts to violate the federal child pornography laws are also chargeable federal offenses. Thus, federal law essentially reaches all the conduct proscribed by this Article.

* * * *

Article 4—Jurisdiction

46. Article 4 provides that each State Party shall take measures as may be necessary to establish jurisdiction over criminal conduct identified in Article 3(1) concerning the sale of children, child prostitution, and child pornography when the offense is committed in its territory or on board a ship or aircraft registered in that State (Article 4(1)). Each State Party is also required to establish jurisdiction when the alleged offender is present in its territory and it does not extradite him to another State Party on the ground that the offense has been committed by one of its nationals (Article 4(3)). Article 4 further provides that each State Party may, but is not obligated to, establish jurisdiction in the following cases: (1) when the alleged offender is a national of that State or has his habitual residence in that country (Article 4(2)(a)) and (2) when the victim is a national of that State (Article 4((2)(b)).

47. The general nature of the U.S. obligations under the Protocol was clarified by the following U.S. understanding:

> The United States understands that the Protocol shall be implemented by the Federal Government to the extent that it exercises jurisdiction over the matters covered therein, and otherwise by the State and local governments. To the extent that State and local governments exercise jurisdiction over such matters, the Federal Government shall, as necessary, take appropriate measures to ensure the fulfillment of the Protocol.

Article 4(1)—Territorial, Ship, and Aircraft Jurisdiction

* * * *

49. Federal laws criminalizing the offenses described in the Protocol confer jurisdiction over such offenses committed on U.S. territory. Additionally, U.S. laws extend special maritime and territorial criminal jurisdiction (18 U.S.C § 7) over crimes involving (among others) sexual abuse, (18 U.S.C. §§ 2241–2245), child pornography (18 U.S.C. §§ 2252 and 2252A), assault (18 U.S.C. § 113), maiming (18 U.S.C. § 114), murder (18 U.S.C. § 1111), and manslaughter (18 U.S.C. § 1112). Special maritime and territorial

jurisdiction extends to any vessel or aircraft belonging in whole or in part to the United States, or any citizen or corporation thereof, while such vessel or aircraft is on or over the high seas or any other waters within the admiralty or maritime jurisdiction of the United States and out of the jurisdiction of any particular State. Special maritime jurisdiction also extends to any place outside of the jurisdiction of any nation with respect to an offense by or against a national of the United States. Additionally, federal law extends special aircraft jurisdiction over the following crimes (among others) if committed on aircraft registered in the United States (49 U.S.C. §§ 46501, 46506): assault (18 U.S.C. § 113), maiming (18 U.S.C. § 114), murder (18 U.S.C. § 1111), manslaughter (18 U.S.C. § 1112), and attempts to commit murder or manslaughter (18 U.S.C. § 1113). For cases not covered by special aircraft or special maritime and territorial jurisdiction, U.S. law extends jurisdiction in other ways. U.S. law extends jurisdiction over transportation in foreign commerce of any individual who has not attained the age of 18 years with the intent to cause the person to be used to produce child pornography and the transportation in foreign commerce of child pornography images (18 U.S.C. §§ 2251, 2252, and 2252A). U.S. law also prohibits travel with intent to engage in illicit sexual conduct (defined as a commercial sex act with a person under 18 or a sexual act with a person under 18 that would be in violation of federal law had it happened in the special maritime and territorial jurisdiction of the United States) (18 U.S.C. § 2423(b), or engaging in illicit sexual conduct in foreign places (18 U.S.C. § 2423(c)). U.S. law also applies extraterritorially to child pornography offenses where there is an intent to import the images to the United States (18 U.S.C. § 2260). U.S. law also broadly extends criminal jurisdiction over vessels used in peonage and slavery (18 U.S.C. §§ 1582, 1585–1588), while the statute outlawing child sex trafficking applies in cases in or affecting foreign commerce as well (18 U.S.C. § 1591).

50. Accordingly, while U.S. law provides a broad range of bases on which to exercise jurisdiction over offenses covered by the Protocol that are committed "on board a ship or aircraft registered in" the United States . . . , U.S. jurisdiction in such cases is not uniformly stated for all crimes covered by the Protocol, nor is

it always couched in terms of "registration" in the United States. Therefore, the reach of U.S. jurisdiction may not be co-extensive with the obligation contained in this Article. This is a minor technical discrepancy. As a practical matter, it is unlikely that any case would arise which could not be prosecuted due to the lack of maritime or aircraft jurisdiction. The United States did not, therefore, delay ratification of the Protocol for this reason, but instead entered a reservation at the time of ratification that suspended the obligation that the United States establish jurisdiction over any covered offenses that may fall within this technical gap until the United States has enacted the necessary legislation to establish such jurisdiction. Accordingly, the following reservation accompanied the U.S. instrument of ratification:

> Subject to the reservation that, to the extent that the domestic law of the United States does not provide for jurisdiction over an offense described in Article 3(1) of the Protocol if the offense is committed on board a ship or aircraft registered in the United States, the obligation with respect to jurisdiction over that offense shall not apply to the United States until such time as the United States may notify the Secretary-General of the United Nations that United States domestic law is in full conformity with the requirements of Article 4(1) of the Protocol.

* * * *

Article 8—Protection of Child Victims

* * * *

67. During the negotiations, delegations generally recognized that the protections to be afforded children under Article 8(1) are necessarily a matter of discretion under national law. As described below, federal and state law provides extensive protection for child victims in the criminal justice process as contemplated by Article 8(1).

68. With regard to Article 8(1)(a), U.S. law at both the federal and state levels recognizes the special needs of child victims and witnesses. For example, in federal cases, 18 U.S.C. § 3509(b) provides

various alternatives for live, in-court testimony when it is determined that a child cannot or should not testify. Additionally, all states provide special accommodation for child victims and witnesses, including the use of videotaped or closed-circuit testimony, child interview specialists, and developmentally-appropriate questioning. . . . In addition, nationwide, there are over 600 Child Advocacy Centers (CACs) supported by various combinations of federal, state, and local funds that use a similar approach. In order to reduce the need for multiple child-interviews by the various disciplines involved in a case, which can be traumatic to the child, CACs utilize a multidisciplinary approach, with one key interviewer observed and provided questions by the rest of the team in one interview. The Federal Government also aids states in reducing the trauma to child sexual abuse victims through funding to states under the Children's Justice Act, established in the Victims of Crime Act (VOCA), and the Child Abuse Prevention and Treatment Act (CAPTA) (42 U.S.C. § 5101 et seq; 42 U.S.C. § 5116 et seq).

*   *   *   *

75. Also, the immigration laws of the United States bear important protections for child victims of trafficking. For example, the Immigration and Nationality Act, as amended by section 107 of the Trafficking Victims Protection Act of 2000, provides for a "T visa" that allows victims of severe forms of trafficking in persons to remain in the United States and to receive certain kinds of public assistance to the same extent as refugees. See 8 U.S.C. § 1101(a)(15)(T); 8 CFR 214.11. After three years in T status, victims of human trafficking may apply for permanent residency. In addition, subject to some limitations, eligible child victims of trafficking may apply for lawful immigration status for their parents. The immigration laws also provide that a child victim of trafficking may not be removed from the United States based solely on information provided by the trafficker and sets forth robust confidentiality protections for child trafficking victims. See 8 U.S.C. § 1367.

76. Furthermore, administered by the Office of Refugee Resettlement (ORR) in the U.S. Department of Health and Human Services, the Unaccompanied Refugee Minors (URM) program was developed in 1979 to address the needs of thousands of children

from Southeast Asia who entered the United States as refugees without a parent or a guardian to care for them. Since 1980, over 12,000 minors have entered the URM program. . . .

77. Each child in the care of this program is eligible for the same range of child-welfare benefits as non-refugee children. Depending on their individual needs, minors are placed in home foster care, group care, independent living, or residential treatment. The URM program assists unaccompanied minors in developing appropriate skills to enter adulthood and to achieve economic and social self-sufficiency. Services provided through the program include English language training, career planning, health/mental needs, socialization skills/adjustment support, family reunification, residential care, education/training, and ethnic/religious preservation. Individuals must be under the age of 18 in order to qualify for the program, but can in most cases remain in the program until age 20 or 21, depending on state guidelines for emancipation.

*　*　*　*

Article 9—Prevention

*　*　*　*

84. The United States meets the requirements of Article 9. With respect to Articles 9(1) and 9(2), it is a priority commitment for the United States at both the federal and state levels to strengthen and implement laws to prevent the offenses prohibited by the Protocol. It is also a policy priority for the United States to create a climate through education, social mobilization, and development activities to ensure that parents and others legally responsible for children are able to protect children from sexual exploitation. . . .

85. With respect to measures to ensure appropriate assistance to victims, including their full social integration and full physical and psychological recovery, a wide range of federal and state programs satisfy the standards set forth in Article 9(3). The Federal Government provides many types of aid to such agencies and comparable organizations that serve children. . . .

*　*　*　*

89. With regard to the requirement under Article 9(4) that States Parties ensure access by child victims to adequate procedures

for seeking compensation, there is mandatory restitution for victims in these cases under federal law. 18 U.S.C. § 1593 provides for mandatory restitution for any trafficking offense, including the crimes of forced labor and sex trafficking. In addition, 18 U.S.C. § 2259 provides for mandatory restitution for any offense involving the sexual exploitation of children, including selling and buying of children. There are also civil remedies available to victims of trafficking and sexual exploitation. See 18 U.S.C. §§ 1595 and 2255. . . .

90. Consistent with the provisions of Article 9(5), U.S. law contains certain restrictions on advertising that are appropriate under our legal system. For example, 18 U.S.C. § 2251 proscribes advertising child pornography when the child pornography actually exists for sale or distribution. Advertising or promoting child prostitution could, in some circumstances, be punished under federal law if it aids and abets child prostitution or constitutes a conspiracy to violate child prostitution laws.

*   *   *   *

Article 10—International Cooperation and Assistance

*   *   *   *

94. With regard to Article 10(1), the United States regularly engages in bilateral and multilateral efforts to deter and prevent the increasing international traffic in children for labor and sexual exploitation. . . .

95. Additionally, pursuant to bilateral and multilateral legal assistance treaties with foreign governments, the United States regularly cooperates with law enforcement agencies of other countries to counteract child prostitution, pornography, and sale of children, as well as sex tourism. The United States funds training for law enforcement and consular officials of foreign countries in the areas of trafficking in persons, child sex tourism, and sexual exploitation of women and children. The United States also supports deterrent programs that encourage innovative partnerships among governments, labor, industry groups, and NGOs to end the employment of children in hazardous or abusive conditions. . . .

*   *   *   *

105. The United States is also a Party to the UN Protocol to Prevent, Suppress and Punish Trafficking in Persons, Especially Women and Children. The United States signed the Protocol on December 13, 2000, and it entered into force for the United States on December 3, 2005. The Protocol calls for information exchange in certain circumstances (Art. 10). The general provisions of the Transnational Organized Crime Convention, to which the United States is also a Party, apply to the Protocol and contain provisions on extradition (Art. 16) and mutual legal assistance (Art. 18).

106. Additionally, since the Trafficking Victims Protection Act (TVPA) was passed in 2000, the United States has submitted annual Trafficking in Persons Reports to the U.S. Congress on foreign governments' efforts to eliminate severe forms of trafficking in persons. The Report is a major tool for advancing international cooperation to combat human trafficking and raising global awareness on the issue. . . .

2. Children and Armed Conflict

a. *Optional Protocol on the Involvement of Children in Armed Conflict*

Excerpts follow from the initial report on the Optional Protocol to the UN Convention on the Rights of the Child on the Involvement of Children in Armed Conflict ("Armed Conflict Protocol") (*see* C.1. *supra*). The report was prepared in accordance with article 8 of the protocol and organized following the General Guidelines of the Committee on the Rights of the Child, adoptaed October 12, 2001. U.N. Doc. CRC/OP/AC/1. Three annexes, Annex I—U.S. Instrument Of Ratification, Annex II—U.S. Declaration under Article 3(2), and Annex III— U.S. Military Service Plans, are included with the report at *www.state.gov/g/drl/rls/c22156.htm.*

* * * *

II. Information on Measures and Developments Relating to the Implementation of the Protocol

Article 1—Direct Participation in Hostilities

7. The Protocol requires States Parties to "take all feasible measures" to ensure that members of their armed forces under age 18 do not take "a direct part in hostilities." At the time the United States deposited its instrument of ratification, it expressed the following understanding of the meaning of the terms "feasible" and "direct part in hostilities:"

> With respect to Article 1, the United States understands that the term "feasible measures" means those measures that are practical or practically possible, taking into account all the circumstances ruling at the time, including humanitarian and military considerations. The United States understands the phrase "direct part in hostilities" to mean immediate and actual action on the battlefield likely to cause harm to the enemy because there is a direct causal relationship between the activity engaged in and the harm done to the enemy. The phrase "direct participation in hostilities" does not mean indirect participation in hostilities, such as gathering and transmitting military information, transporting weapons, munitions and other supplies, or forward deployment. The United States further understands that any decision by any military commander, military personnel, or any other person responsible for planning, authorizing, or executing military action, including the assignment of military personnel, shall only be judged on the basis of that person's assessment of the information reasonably available to the person at the time the person planned, authorized, or executed the action under review, and shall not be judged on the basis of information that comes to light after the action under review was taken.

8. This understanding is based upon the negotiating history of Article 1 of the Protocol. The language in Article 1 is drawn from Article 38(2) of the Convention on the Rights of the Child, and Article 77(2) of the Protocol Additional to the Geneva Conventions

of 12 August 1949, relating to the Protection of Victims of International Armed Conflicts (Protocol 1), which both require that States Parties take all "feasible measures" to ensure that children under the age of 15 do not take a "direct part in hostilities."

9. The terminology used in Article 1 of the Protocol recognizes that in exceptional cases it will not be "feasible" for a commander to withhold or prevent a soldier under the age of 18 from taking a part in hostilities. The term "feasible" is understood in the law of armed conflict to mean that which is "practicable or practically possible taking into account all circumstances ruling at the time, including humanitarian and military considerations." This is the definition used in Article 3(10) of the Protocol to the 1980 Conventional Weapons Convention Concerning the Use of Mines, Booby-Traps and Other Devices (Protocol II), adopted at Geneva October 10, 1980. It is also the generally accepted meaning of the term in Protocol I to the Geneva Conventions. Indeed, a number of States (e.g., Canada, Germany, Ireland, Italy, Netherlands, and Spain) included such a definition of "feasible" in understandings that accompanied their instruments of ratification to Protocol I to the Geneva Conventions.

10. The standard set out in Article 1 also recognizes that there is no prohibition concerning indirect participation in hostilities or forward deployment. The term "direct" has been understood in the context of treaties relating to the law of armed conflict (including International Committee of the Red Cross (ICRC) commentaries on the meaning of the provisions of Protocol I to the Geneva Conventions) to mean a direct causal relationship between the activity engaged in and the harm done to the enemy at the time and place where the activity takes place.

11. Throughout negotiations of Article 77(2) of Protocol I to the Geneva Conventions, Article 38(2) of the Convention on the Rights of the Child, and Article 1 of this Protocol, some delegations, as well as the ICRC, repeatedly attempted to replace "all feasible measures" with "necessary" or a variant thereof and to remove the reference to "direct." However, other delegations, including the United States, insisted that there should be no deviation from existing treaties using the same terminology.

* * * *

14. At the final session of negotiations, just before adoption of the Protocol, the U.S. delegation made a statement regarding its understanding of Article 1 that the U.N. Working Group summarized as follows:

> As for participation in hostilities, the terms in Article 1, with their roots in international humanitarian law and the law of armed conflict, were clear, well understood and contextually relevant. The United States of America would take all steps it feasibly could to ensure that under-18-year-old service personnel did not take a direct part in hostilities. While the standard recognizes that, in exceptional cases, it might not be feasible for a commander to withhold or remove such a person from taking a direct part in hostilities, the United States believed that it was an effective, sensible and practical standard that would promote the object that all sought: protecting children and ensuring that the protocol had the widest possible adherence and support.

Working Group on Involvement of Children in Armed Conflict, Report on Its Sixth Session, UN Doc. E/CN.4/2000/74, para. 131.

15. In contrast, other delegations expressed disappointment that the Protocol did not bar "indirect" participation in hostilities and that the discretionary power granted to States through use of the term "feasible measures" weakened the Protocol. Id. At paras. 106, 116, 121–22, 135, 143, 148 (statements by the ICRC, Italy, Belgium, Ethiopia, the Russian Federation, and Portugal). The Russian delegation acknowledged that since States were not required to prohibit participation, but only called on to take "all feasible measures" to prevent such participation, the Protocol left States open to the possibility in any emergency of involving persons under 18 years of age in hostilities. Id. At para. 131.

*   *   *   *

17. To implement the terms of Article 1 of the Protocol, U.S. Military Services have adopted an implementation plan. The implementation plans have been tailored to meet the unique mission requirements of each Service. The implementation plans went

into effect in January 2003. The plans relate to the date (not year) of birth of the individual. . . .

* * * *

Article 2—Forced or Compulsory Recruitment

18. Article 2 prohibits States Parties from forcibly or compulsorily recruiting into military service anyone under 18. The United States does not permit compulsory recruitment of any person under 18 for any type of military service. While inactive, the U.S. selective service system remains established in law and provides for involuntary induction at and after age 18. *See* The Military Selective Service Act, 50 U.S.C. App. §§ 451 et seq. By law, the Selective Service System is an independent agency, separate from the Department of Defense.

19. The general scope of Article 2 of the Protocol is substantially identical to Article 3 of the Convention (No. 182) for Elimination of the Worst Forms of Child Labor, adopted by the International Labor Conference on June 17, 1999, which, *inter alia*, requires that States Parties take immediate and effective measures to secure the elimination of forced or compulsory recruitment of children under the age of 18 for use in armed conflict. ILO Convention No. 182 entered into force with respect to the United States on December 2, 2000.

Article 3—Voluntary Recruitment

20. Article 3(1) obliges States Parties to raise the minimum age for voluntary recruitment into their national armed forces from 15 years, which is the minimum age provided in Article 38(3) of the Convention on the Rights of the Child and in Article 77(2) of Protocol I to the Geneva Conventions. The United States expressed the following understanding in order to clarify the nature of the obligation it assumed under Article 3(1):

> The United States understands that Article 3 obliges States Parties to raise the minimum age for voluntary recruitment into their national armed forces from the current international standard of age 15.

21. Article 3(1) states that in raising the age for voluntary recruitment States Parties shall "take account" of the "principles"

contained in Article 38(3) of the Convention on the Rights of the Child and recognize that persons under the age of 18 are entitled to special protection. In this regard, Article 38(3) states that "[i]n recruiting among those persons who have attained the age of fifteen years but who have not attained the age of eighteen years, States Parties shall endeavour to give priority to those who are oldest." This provision is compatible with the long-standing U.S. practice of permitting 17-year-olds, but not those who are younger, to volunteer for service in the Armed Forces. The Department of Defense goal is that at least 90% of new recruits should have high school diplomas, but many enlistment contracts are signed with high school seniors who may be as young as 17. While waiting for graduation, these individuals are placed in the Delayed Entry Program. Most of these individuals turn 18 before graduating from high school and shipping to basic training. Of the nearly 175,000 new enlistees each year, only about 7,500 (just over 4%) are 17 when they ship to basic training, and nearly all of those (80%) will turn 18 while in training. At no time since 1982 has the percentage of 17-year-old recruits into the Armed Forces exceeded 8%. Qualified 17-year-olds will remain an integral part of the U.S. military's recruiting efforts into the foreseeable future, but it is not expected that their numbers will fluctuate significantly, or dominate the Armed Forces' recruiting pool. No one under age 17 is eligible for recruitment, including for participation in the Delayed Entry Program.

22. Article 3(2) provides that each State Party effects the increase in minimum age by depositing a binding declaration to that effect upon ratification, and by providing a description of the safeguards it maintains to ensure that such recruitment is not forced or coerced. The United States submitted the following declaration in conjunction with the deposit of its instrument of ratification of the Protocol:

> Pursuant to Article 3(2) of the Protocol, the United States declares that the minimum age at which the United States permits voluntary recruitment into the Armed Forces of the United States is 17 years of age. The United States has established safeguards to ensure that such recruitment is

not forced or coerced, including a requirement in section 505(a) of title 10, United States Code, that no person under 18 years of age may be originally enlisted in the Armed Forces of the United States without the written consent of the person's parent or guardian, if the parent or guardian is entitled to the person's custody and control. . . . Moreover, each person recruited into the Armed Forces of the United States receives a comprehensive briefing and must sign an enlistment contract that, taken together, specify the duties involved in military service. All persons recruited into the Armed Forces of the United States must provide reliable proof of age before their entry into the military service.

* * * *

Article 4—Non-governmental Actors

27. Article 4(1) provides that armed groups, distinct from the armed forces of a State, "should" not recruit or use in hostilities persons under the age of 18. Article 4(2) requires that States Parties take "all feasible measures" to prevent in their territory the recruitment and use in hostilities of persons under the age of 18 by "armed groups, distinct from the armed forces of a State," including by the enactment of legislation to ensure that such recruitment and use is punishable as a criminal offense under their national laws. Additionally, Article 4(3) provides that "the application of the present article under this Protocol shall not affect the legal status of any party to an armed conflict."

28. In order to clarify the nature of the obligation assumed under Article 4, the United States submitted the following understanding with its instrument of ratification of the Protocol:

> The United States understands that the term "armed groups" in Article 4 of the Protocol means nongovernmental armed groups such as rebel groups, dissident armed forces, and other insurgent groups.

29. Consistent with Article 4, U.S. law already prohibits insurgent activities by nongovernmental actors against the United States, irrespective of age. *See* 18 U.S.C. § 2381, et seq. U.S law

also prohibits the formation within the United States of insurgent groups, again irrespective of age, which have the intent of engaging in armed conflict with foreign powers. *See* 18 U.S.C. § 960.

*   *   *   *

Article 7—International Cooperation and Assistance

33. Article 7(1) obliges States Parties to undertake to cooperate in the implementation of the Protocol, including in the prevention of any act contrary to the Protocol and in the demobilization, rehabilitation, and social reintegration of persons who are victims of acts contrary to the Protocol through, *inter alia*, technical cooperation and financial assistance. Article 7(2) specifies that States Parties "in a position to do so" shall provide financial, technical or other assistance through existing multilateral, bilateral or other programs.

34. The United States has contributed substantial resources to international programs aimed at preventing the recruitment of children and reintegrating child ex-combatants into society and is committed to continue to develop rehabilitation approaches that are effective in addressing this serious and difficult problem. The United States applies a definition of child ex-combatants in keeping with the Cape Town Principles of 1997, which cover any child associated with fighting forces in any capacity, whether or not he or she ever bore arms. In this regard, United States programming adopts a broad approach by seeking to include all children affected by armed conflict rather than singling out for separate services former child combatants. It also espouses the principle that family reunification and community reintegration are both goals and processes of recovery for former child combatants. United States programming aimed at assisting children affected by war addresses the disarmament, demobilization, rehabilitation and integration into civilian society of former child combatants; the prevention of recruitment of children; and the recovery and rehabilitation of children affected by armed conflict, including activities to identify separated children, protect them from harm, provide appropriate interim care, carry out tracing for family reunification, arrange alternate care for children who cannot be reunited, reform their legal protections and facilitate community reintegration. The Protocol

serves as a means for encouraging such programs and constitutes an important tool for increasing assistance to children who are affected by armed conflict.

*   *   *   *

Article 8—Reporting

37. Article 8 provides that States Parties shall submit, within two years following the entry into force of the Protocol for that State Party, a report to the Committee on the Rights of the Child providing comprehensive information on the measures it has taken to implement the provisions of the Protocol.

38. Initial U.S. reporting under Article 8 is limited to reporting on the measures the United States has taken to implement the provisions of the Protocol. The United States has no obligation to comply with any additional reporting requirements contained in Article 44 of the Convention on the Rights of the Child, nor is the Committee on the Rights of the Child competent to request information from the United States on any matter other than implementation of the Protocol.

*   *   *   *

40. The Protocol grants the Committee on the Rights of the Child no authority other than receiving reports and requesting additional information as set forth above. During the negotiations, States rejected proposals that would have permitted the Committee, *inter alia*, to hold hearings, initiate confidential inquiries, conduct country visits, and transmit findings to the State Party concerned.

41. This report is submitted in accordance with U.S. obligations under Article 8 of the Protocol.

Article 9—Signature and Ratification

42. Article 9 provides that the Protocol is subject to ratification or open for accession by any State, i.e., it is not limited to parties to the Convention on the Rights of the Child. During the negotiations of the Protocol, the United Nations Legal Counsel provided a legal opinion which confirmed that under the rules of the law of treaties there was no legal impediment to an instrument which is entitled "optional protocol" being open to participation by States that had not also established, or which did not also establish,

their consent to be bound by the convention to which that instrument was said to be an optional protocol. . . .
UN Office of Legal Affairs, 18 January 2000. . . .

43. Consistent with the fact that the Protocol is an independent international agreement, the following understanding was attached to the U.S. instrument of ratification:

> The United States understands that the Protocol constitutes an independent multilateral treaty, and that the United States does not assume any obligations under the Convention on the Rights of the Child by becoming a party to the Protocol.

*   *   *   *

b.   Child soldiers and victims in Burma

At the 11th meeting of the Security Council Working Group on Children and Armed Conflict, established pursuant to Security Resolution 1612 (2005), Acting U.S. Representative to the UN Economic and Social Council Ambassador Grover Joseph Rees provided the views of the United States on the report of the Secretary General entitled "Children and Armed Conflict in Myanmar." The full text of Ambassador Rees's statement of December 6, 2007, excerpted below, is available at *www.usunnewyork.usmission.gov/press_releases/20071206_357.html*. For further information on the working group, *see www.un.org/children/conflict/english/securitycouncilwg.html*.

*   *   *   *

The United States is deeply concerned about the continuing recruitment and use of child soldiers in Burma. According to the UN and the various NGOs operating in the area, the Tatmadaw Kyi recruits and uses children as young as 12 years old, as do certain non-state actors. The United States condemns this unlawful practice and calls upon the Burmese regime and the non-state actors active in Burma to end immediately all unlawful child recruitment and their use in the armed forces and in armed groups. Furthermore, the U.S. strongly urges the State Peace and Development Council and the non-state actors to assist in reuniting former child soldiers with their families.

The United States notes the establishment of various mechanisms by the regime to address the problem of child soldiers in the national army, but also notes with deep concern the inability of the UN or the NGO community to verify any progress by the State Peace and Development Council on the issue of Children and Armed Conflict due to the Burmese regime's failure to comply with its commitment to provide unfettered access to the UN Country Team.

The United States calls on the State Peace and Development Council to provide to the UN Country Team free and confidential access to relevant people and areas, which include timely freedom to travel for the purpose of verifying information without the presence of regime officials. Only when the UN has the freedom to travel independently and without advance notice to recruiting stations, military barracks, and to meet with all non-state actors will the world be able to know the truth about children in armed conflict in Burma.

* * * *

According to the Secretary-General's report, the Burmese regime incarcerates children for up to five years in prison if they are convicted of desertion from their military posts. The United States agrees wholeheartedly with paragraph 11 of the report which states, "International practice and principles stipulate that children who have been unlawfully recruited or used by armed forces should not be treated as deserters."

The United States also notes with deep concern paragraph 36 of the Secretary General's report that states the UN received credible reports indicating that during 2006–2007 government armed forces in Kayin state attacked villagers, which resulted in the death and injury of children. The United States is equally disturbed by what the UN categorized, in paragraph 39, as "credible but unverified" reports of rapes perpetrated by regime forces and armed groups, not just due to the heinous nature of these crimes, but because the Burmese regime refuses to allow the UN to investigate and verify these reports.

The United States calls on the State Peace and Development Council to lift all restrictions on access to conflict-affected areas and to allow international and humanitarian organizations access to these areas for the delivery of humanitarian services. Mr. Chairman, if the Burmese government is correct in saying that there are no longer any conflict areas in the country, then there is even less reason to deny access to these areas. We also call on the military regime to work with the UNCT to codify guarantees of security for victims, monitors, and individuals reporting cases of child recruitment and to facilitate the provision of visas, in-country travel authorizations, unhindered access, confidentiality and security of the UN Country Team in all aspects of its operations.

*   *   *   *

c. Conference on children and armed conflict

During 2007 France and UNICEF jointly hosted two conferences on children and armed conflict. Meeting in Paris in February 2007, France and UNICEF introduced two documents: (1) the Paris Principles and Guidelines on Children Associated With Armed Forces or Armed Groups ("Paris Principles") and (2) the Paris Commitments to protect children from unlawful recruitment by armed forces or armed groups ("Paris Commitments"). On October 1, 2007, France and UNICEF jointly hosted a second conference at the United Nations in New York. The aim of the meeting was to solicit additional support for the Paris Principles and Paris Commitments.

As explained in the U.S. statement at the October meeting, the United States did not attend the Paris conference because it was told that participation in that meeting would "amount[] to an endorsement" of the two Paris documents. Excerpts follow from the U.S. statement explain its substantive and procedural concerns with the documents.

The full text of the U.S. statement is available at *www. state.gov/s/l/c8183.htm*. For more information on the February and October conferences and the two Paris documents, *see www.un.org/children/conflict/english/parisprinciples.html.*

*   *   *   *

The United States is deeply committed to addressing issues important to the welfare of children, including protecting children from the scourges of war. . . .

The United States is pleased that France has taken an active leadership role on children and armed conflict issues. Under France's leadership in the Security Council Working Group on Children and Armed Conflict, we have worked intently this year to address a number of serious situations around the world. We look forward to continuing to work with France, other members of the Security Council, and the Special Representative to the Secretary General on Children and Armed Conflict to address these and other situations where children are, often tragically, both participants in and victims of armed conflict.

However, with respect to the Paris Principles and the Paris Commitments, the United States is not able to endorse these documents. I would like to take this opportunity to briefly [explain] why this is the case.

Although we strongly support the overall aim of the documents, our review identified a number of legal and policy concerns, in particular some significant inconsistencies between the document and international legal norms governing the issue of children in armed conflict. We fully believe that our concerns could have been addressed through further discussions and negotiations. Unfortunately, there was no opportunity for Member States to have such discussions or to provide their input into those documents before the Paris Conference last February at which these documents were presented.

Since we were told that participation in the Paris Conference amounted to an endorsement of the documents, we were not in a position to attend. For this reason, regrettably, we cannot support the objective, as outlined in this meeting's Concept Paper, to "ensure both the Principles and the Commitments are referred to as standards in the UN." We believe that documents can only become "UN standards" following a full process of discussion among Member States. We also believe that any decision to create a new standard should only be taken after a decision by Member States that the current international law on the subject is unclear or otherwise requires the creation of new standards.

Our views on this matter are principled, and are not in any way a reflection on our commitment to seriously confront the issue of children and armed conflict.

The United States would be pleased to engage with France, other Member States, and UNICEF on the application of current legal standards so that we end the tragedy of the unlawful recruitment and use of child soldiers and further promote the welfare of children in armed conflict situations.

3. UN General Assembly: Rights of the Child

On November 27, 2007, Robert Hagen, Deputy U.S. Representative to the Economic and Social Council, addressed the UN General Assembly Third Committee to explain the U.S. vote against adoption of a resolution entitled "Rights of the Child." The resolution was adopted on December 18, 2007, by the UN General Assembly. U.N. Doc. A/RES/62/141.

The full text of Mr. Hagen's statement, excerpted below, is available at *www.usunnewyork.usmission.gov/press_releases/20071127_335.html.*

* * * *

We are committed to ensuring that the protection of the rights of children is fully integrated into American foreign policy. It is for this reason that the United States supports many of the principles underlying this resolution. For example, the United States has ratified the two Optional Protocols to the Convention of the Rights of the Child relating to the Involvement of Children in Armed Conflict, and to the Sale of Children, Child Pornography, and Prostitution.

However, the United States has repeatedly made clear that the Convention on the Rights of the Child raises a number of concerns. In particular, the convention conflicts with the authority of parents, and the provisions of state and local law in the United States. Many of the activities covered by the convention in areas such as education, health, and criminal justice are primarily the responsibility of state and local governments in the United States. In addition, the convention, in some cases—such as the degree to which children should participate in decisions affecting themselves, or have the right to choose actions independent of parental control—sets up a tension between the rights of children and parental authority. United States laws generally place greater emphasis on duties of parents to protect and care for children, and apportion rights between adults and children in a manner different from the convention. At the same time, the convention contains many positive principles and standards, which the United States applies in practice.

*   *   *   *

Nevertheless, we cannot accept this resolution's overemphasis on the Convention on the Rights of the Child and the assertion that the Convention "must constitute the/the standard in the promotion and protection of the rights of the child." While the convention may touch upon most issues confronting children, other international instruments address particular problems in a far more comprehensive and effective manner.

Apart from the Convention, this draft resolution contains problematic language in paragraphs too numerous to mention in a brief Explanation of Vote.

We continue to maintain that the process of dealing with this resolution needs to change. In particular, what is needed is a text that is shorter and targeted on specific issues of critical importance to children, as well as one that concentrates on matters not addressed in other resolutions.

In summary, my delegation will vote NO on this draft resolution because it once again contains unacceptable language from past resolutions that my delegation has repeatedly requested the co-sponsors to eliminate, address elsewhere, revise, or amend, as well as new problematic language.

D. ECONOMIC, SOCIAL, AND CULTURAL ISSUES

1.   Water and Human Rights

In June 2007 the United States responded to a request for information by the UN Office of the United Nations High Commissioner for Human Rights on "human rights obligations related to equitable access to safe drinking water and sanitation." The U.S. submission included three parts: "Part I describes the United States' views on the issue of water as a human right. Part II provides a broad overview of U.S. water law and policy. Part III describes the U.S. approach to international development assistance on water issues." Part I is set forth below; the full text is available at *www.state.gov/s/l/c8183.htm.*

---

*   *   *   *

I. Water and Human Rights

3. The United States notes that water is increasingly referred to as a human right. References to water as a human right take various forms, including the following:

- right to clean water,[1]
- right to water,[2]
- right to water and sanitation,[3]

---

[1]   *See* General Assembly Resolution 54/175. "The right to development." A/RES/54/175, 15 February 2000. OP 12: The General Assembly "*Reaffirms* that, in the full realization of the right to development, *inter alia*: (a) The rights to food and clean water are fundamental human rights . . . ."

[2]   *See* Committee on Economic, Social and Cultural Rights, General Comment 15. E/C.12/2002/11 20 January 2003. Paragraph 1 ("The human right to water is indispensable for leading a life in human dignity. It is a prerequisite for the realization of other human rights."). *See also The Right to Water*, World Health Organization, 2003.

[3]   *See* Sub-Commission on the Promotion and Protection of Human Rights, "Realization of the right to drinking water and sanitation." Report of the Special Rapporteur, El Hadji Guissé. E/CN.4/Sub.2/2005/25 at 2. 11 July 2005.

- right to drinking water and sanitation,[4]
- right to sufficient supplies of water,[5]
- right to a sufficient quantity of clean water for personal and domestic uses,[6]
- right to have access to adequate and safe sanitation,[7]
- right to "access to safe water,"[8] and
- right to "access to water for life."[9]

The right to water, in its various formulations, is often described as a human right that is "critical," "fundamental," or "basic" in nature.

4. The United States does not share the view that a "right to water"—in any of the above formulations—exists under international human rights law. This view is informed by a review of the relevant instruments of international human rights law. Such a review demonstrates that there is no internationally agreed "right to water." Neither the Universal Declaration of Human Rights (UDHR) nor the International Covenant on Economic, Social, and Cultural Rights (ICESCR) mentions water at all.

5. Two core international human rights treaties mention "water," but neither establishes nor even alludes to a legal "right" to water. First, the Convention on the Elimination of all Forms of Discrimination Against Women (CEDAW) requires Parties to "take all appropriate measures to eliminate discrimination against women in rural areas . . . and, in particular, [to] ensure to such women the right . . . [t]o enjoy adequate living conditions, particularly *in relation to* housing, sanitation, electricity and *water supply*,

---

[4] Id. at 1–5.

[5] Id. at 5.

[6] Id.

[7] Id.

[8] U.N. Secretary General, as quoted in United Nations Development Programme, *Human Development Report 2006: Beyond Scarcity: Power, Poverty and the Global Water Crisis*, United Nations, 2006 at 4; WHO, 2003, *supra* note 2 at 6. ("Access to safe water is a fundamental human need and, therefore, a basic human right.")

[9] UNDP, 2006, *supra* note 8 at v. ("Access to water for life is a basic human need and a fundamental human right.")

transport and communications." CEDAW, Art. 14(2)(h). (Emphases added.)

6. Second, the Convention on the Rights of the Child says that state parties shall "pursue full implementation" of the "right of the child to the enjoyment of the highest attainable standard of health" by taking "appropriate measures" to "combat disease and malnutrition, including within the framework of primary health care, through, *inter alia*, the application of readily available technology and through the provision of adequate nutritious foods and *clean drinking-water. . . .*" CRC, Art. 24(2)(c). (Emphasis added.)

7. Thus, although the word "water" appears in CEDAW and the CRC, neither instrument establishes a "right to water" in any of the formulations listed in paragraph 3 above.

8. The Committee on Economic, Social and Cultural Rights has asserted that a right to water exists in its General Comment 15 (GC 15). We have not identified a legal basis for this conclusion and therefore disagree with it. General Comment 15 is perhaps the most elaborate and most cited treatment of the "right to water" and therefore merits discussion here, with respect to both its legal reasoning and status.

9. General Comment 15 begins by stating "Water is a limited natural resource and a public good fundamental for life and health. The human right to water is indispensable for leading a life in human dignity." While the United States agrees that water is fundamental for the life and good health of all human beings and that there is a profound duty as a matter of policy for governments to take responsible actions to ensure that their citizens have proper access to water and to other resources needed for people to live healthy and productive lives, this responsibility is not of a legal nature. In this sense, the manifest importance and indispensability of water do not in themselves create legally binding international obligations on States.

10. In paragraphs 2–7 the Committee attempts to describe the "legal bases of the right to water." The Committee relies most heavily on Article 11(1) of the ICESCR. This article states in part: "The States Parties to the present Covenant recognize the right of everyone to an adequate standard of living for himself and his

family, including adequate food, clothing and housing, and to the continuous improvement of living conditions."

11. From this, the Committee concludes that "use of the word 'including' indicates that this catalogue of rights was not intended to be exhaustive." GC 15, para 3. While it is apparent enough that this provision of the Covenant does not create an open-ended "catalogue of rights," any doubt is dispelled by the following sentence which states: "The States Parties will take appropriate steps to ensure the realization of *this right* . . . ." ICESCR, Art. 11(1) (Emphasis added). The reference to "this right" makes it manifestly clear that governments negotiating this agreement intended to create one right in Article 11(1), namely the right to an adequate standard of living which has a number of different elements identified in the Covenant.

12. The fact that the provision of a particular good or service may be essential to the realization of a Covenant right does not make that good or service itself the subject of a distinct international human right. Where one right "includes" another right, it can be expressed in the text of the treaty. This is the case in Article 6 of the Covenant, which states that "the right to work . . . *includes the right* of everyone to the opportunity to gain his living by work which he freely chooses or accepts. . . ." ICESCR, Art. 6. (Emphasis added.)

13. As legal bases for the right to water, the Committee also relies on the provisions in CEDAW and the CRC discussed above. These provisions, as noted, plainly do not contain a right to water. In addition, according to the Committee, two of the Geneva Conventions and their Protocols Additional recognize the "right to water." These instruments create certain legal obligations for State Parties during times of armed conflict or occupation. They do not, of course, recognize or create a "right to water" under international human rights law.

14. The United States also notes that General Comments, including those of the Committee on Economic, Social and Cultural Rights, are not legally binding or authoritative. Under international treaty law, it is the duty and responsibility of parties to treaties—which are the subjects of international law—to interpret and apply treaties in good faith. As a matter of international law,

treaty body committees enjoy only those authorities granted to them by parties to those instruments. The United States respects the Committee and similar committees established under other human rights treaties. States sometimes agree with the opinions and interpretations offered by such committees. In other instances states do not agree, and there is nothing in the Covenant or elsewhere suggesting that the views of treaty bodies are legally binding or authoritative.

15. As noted above, while there is no "right to water" under international law, as a matter of policy and good government it is manifest that water is essential for the life and all individuals, and indeed for all life on earth. Safe and accessible water supplies further the realization of certain human rights, such as the right to a standard of living adequate for the health and well-being of all individuals. UDHR, Art. 25. The provision of safe and accessible water supplies may also be appropriate or even necessary for the furthering of certain other "economic, social and cultural rights indispensable for [one's] dignity and the free development of [one's] personality." UDHR, Art. 22. Similarly, the intentional deprivation of water by a state based on prohibited grounds of discrimination (e.g., on the basis of race) may also involve violations of international human rights law.

*   *   *   *

2. Corporate Social Responsibility

See the discussion of the Voluntary Principles on Human Rights and Security in Chapter 5.A.3.a.

3. Protection of Migrants

On November 28, 2007, Ambassador Grover Joseph Rees, Acting U.S. Representative to the UN Economic and Social Council, addressed the Third Committee on a resolution concerning the protection of migrants. Ambassador Rees's statement, explaining the U.S. decision to join consensus and certain remaining concerns, is set forth below and is available at *www.usunnewyork.usmission.gov/press_releases/ 20071128_343.html.*

The resolution was adopted by the General Assembly without vote on December 18, 2007. U.N. Doc. A/RES/62/156.

The United States has joined consensus on this resolution after substantial negotiations among many delegations. We regret that during those negotiations a number of proposed revisions—which might have improved the resolution—were never reflected in revised texts which were distributed for consideration. Moreover, as late as last night revisions were introduced to this text without an adequate opportunity for discussion or negotiation.

Regarding PP 8, we understand this paragraph as recalling the obligation of States to provide consular notification pursuant to article 36 of the Vienna Convention.[*]

---

[*]   Editor's note: The language of the referenced paragraphs is as follows:

PP8: *Taking note also* of the Judgment of the International Court of Justice of 31 March 2004 in the case concerning Avena and Other Mexican Nationals, and recalling the obligations of States reaffirmed therein

*   *   *   *

OP 10: *Urges* States to ensure that repatriation mechanisms allow for the identification and special protection of persons in vulnerable situations and take into account, in conformity with their international obligations and commitments, the principle of best interest of the child and family reunification;

*   *   *   *

OP 19: *Also requests* the Secretary-General to report on the implementation of the present resolution at its sixty-third session and to include in that report an analysis of the ways and means to promote the human rights of migrants, including through the use of data and statistics on the contribution of migrants to recipient countries, taking into account the views of the Special Rapporteur of the Human Rights Council on the human rights of migrants, and decides to examine the question further under the item entitled "Promotion and protection of human rights".

Regarding OP 10, the United States notes that repatriation mechanisms must be consistent not only with international obligations but also with domestic legislation.

Regarding language in OP 19 which was added to the final draft after negotiations concluded, the United States is confident that the Secretary General will give strong considerations only to those parts of the Special Rapporteur's report that address the human rights of migrants rather than those which treat other policy issues.

This resolution also lacks a number of proposed points which could have strengthened it, most notably a paragraph that would have reaffirmed "the sovereign rights of States to enforce national migration legislation and control migration to their territory in a manner consistent with their obligations under international law." The missing paragraph, proposed by one of the negotiators, would have also affirmed the obligation of all States "to respect the rights of migrants to return to their country of citizenship and of all States to accept the return of their nationals."

The above passages from the missing paragraph are not controversial. States, of course, do have the sovereign right to determine who enters their country and under what conditions. States also have the important responsibility of protecting the human rights of migrants present within their territories, and of accepting the return of their nationals.

The United States values legal, orderly and humane migration, and we continue to believe that effective migration management will allow all states, as well as individual migrants, to harness the benefits of migration and reduce its challenges. It is for this reason that all UN member states must endeavor for sound migration policies, including those that protect the human rights of migrants.

An important element in the protection of the human rights of migrants is to reduce the vulnerabilities that are inherent when migrants travel to or reside in destination countries in an irregular manner. Therefore, all States have the obligation to work to reduce illegal migration and to accept the return of their nationals who were found to be residing illegally in another country.

The United States is a nation of immigrants. We welcome legal immigrants and properly-documented temporary visitors, including workers and students, and we are committed to protecting the human rights of migrants within our borders.

Mr. Chairman, more than one million American citizens currently live outside our borders. The United States urges its own citizens to observe all local laws when moving to or working in another country. We expect the citizens of other countries who come to the United States to do the same—beginning with our immigration laws.

4. Right to Development

On November 28, 2007, the United States requested a vote and voted against a resolution on the right to development in the UN General Assembly Third Committee. In an explanation of position, Ambassador Rees stated:

> . . . Our position on this resolution is well-known—the United States understands the term "right to development" to mean that each individual should enjoy the right to develop his or her intellectual or other capabilities to the maximum extent possible through the exercise of the full range of civil and political rights.
> . . . [T]he resolution before us contains the same initiatives that we have found objectionable in years past, such as a discussion of a possibly legally binding instrument on the Right to Development.
> The United States will continue our long-standing commitment to international development and maintain, as a major goal of our foreign policy, helping nations achieve sustainable economic growth. Our delegation, however, does not believe this resolution helps to advance these goals and will therefore vote "no" and encourages others to join us.

The text of Ambassador Rees's statement is available at *www.usunnewyork.usmission.gov/press_releases/ 20071128_342.html.* Following adoption by the Third Committee, the resolution was adopted by the General Assembly on December 18, 2007. U.N. Doc. A/RES/62/161. *See also* statement on Women in Development, B.2.c. *supra.*

E. INDIGENOUS PEOPLE

On September 13, 2007, the UN General Assembly adopted by vote the United Nations Declaration on the Rights of Indigenous Peoples, U.N. Doc. A/RES/61/1295 (2007). Robert Hagen, U.S. Advisor, provided an explanation of the U.S. vote against adoption of the declaration and described U.S. efforts to promote indigenous rights domestically and internationally. The full text of Mr. Hagen's statement is available at *www. usunnewyork.usmission.gov/press_releases/20070913_ 204.html,* with an accompanying document entitled "Observations of the United States with Respect to the Declaration on the Rights of Indigenous Peoples," both reproduced in major part below. The Third Committee had delayed a vote on the declaration during 2006; *see Digest 2006* at 394–401 for statements delivered by New Zealand and Australia on behalf of the United States and those two countries expressing concerns with the draft declaration and related issues.

Thank you Mr. President, we regret that we must vote against the adoption of the declaration on the rights of indigenous peoples. We worked hard for 11 years in Geneva for a consensus declaration, but the document before us is a text that was prepared and submitted after the negotiations had concluded. States were given no opportunity to discuss it collectively. It is disappointing that the Human Rights Council did not respond to calls we made, in partnership with Council members, for States to undertake further work to generate a consensus text. This declaration was adopted by the Human Rights Council in a splintered vote. This process was unfortunate and extraordinary in any multilateral negotiating exercise and sets a poor precedent with respect to UN practice.

The declaration on the rights of indigenous peoples, if it were to encourage harmonious and constructive relations, should have been written in terms that are transparent and capable of implementation. Unfortunately, the text that emerged from that failed process is confusing, and risks endless conflicting interpretations and debate about its application, as already evidenced by the numerous complex interpretive statements that were issued by States at its adoption at the Human Rights Council. We cannot lend our support to such a text.

Mr. President, our views with respect to the core provisions of the text can be found in a separate document entitled Observations of the United States with respect to the Declaration on the Rights of Indigenous Peoples,. . . . Because the flaws in this text run through its most significant provisions, the text as a whole is rendered unacceptable.

Although we are voting against this flawed document, my government will continue its vigorous efforts to promote indigenous rights domestically. Under United States domestic law, the United States government recognizes Indian tribes as political entities with inherent powers of self-government as first peoples. In our legal system, the federal government has a government-to-government relationship with Indian tribes.

In this domestic context, this means promoting tribal self-government over a broad range of internal and local affairs, including determination of membership, culture, language, religion, education, information, social welfare, maintenance of community safety, family relations, economic activities, lands and resources management, environment and entry by non-members, as well as ways and means for financing these autonomous functions.

At the same time, the United States will continue its work to promote indigenous rights internationally. In its annual human rights report, the United States Department of State reports on the situation of indigenous persons and communities throughout the world. In our diplomatic efforts, we will continue our opposition to racial discrimination against indigenous individuals and communities and continue to press for full indigenous participation in democratic electoral processes throughout the world. We will also continue with out international assistance programs involving indigenous peoples.

*   *   *   *

OBSERVATIONS OF THE UNITED STATES WITH RESPECT TO THE DECLARATION ON THE RIGHTS OF INDIGENOUS PEOPLES

The United States was an active participant throughout the long history of the negotiations to draft a declaration on the rights of indigenous peoples. Many other countries did not, however, participate in these negotiations in Geneva and may not be fully aware of what participants intended in its drafting. We can, therefore, provide an understanding of the intent of participating States on the core issues:

Nature of the Declaration:

With respect to the nature of the declaration, it was the clear intention of all States that it be an aspirational declaration with political and moral, rather than legal, force. Its persuasiveness and usefulness to the international community therefore critically depends upon the extent to which it enjoys unqualified support among States. This text contains recommendations regarding how States can promote the welfare of indigenous peoples. It is not in itself legally binding nor reflective of international law.

The United States rejects any possibility that this document is or can become customary international law. We have continually expressed our rejection of fundamental parts of the former Subcommission text, and of this text, as have numerous other States. As this declaration does not describe current State practice or actions that States feel obliged to take as a matter of legal obligation, it cannot be cited as evidence of the evolution of customary international law. This declaration does not provide a proper basis for legal actions, complaints, or other claims in any international, domestic, or other proceedings.

Self-Determination:

The right of self-determination is addressed in Article 1 of both the International Covenant on Civil and Political Rights and the International Covenant on Economic, Social and Cultural Rights. This common Article 1 right of self-determination is understood by some to include the right to full independence under certain circumstances. Under existing common Article 1 legal obligations, indigenous peoples generally are not entitled to independence nor any right of self-government within the nation-state. It was not the mandate of the Working Group (nor was it within its power) to qualify, limit, or expand the scope of the existing legal obligations set forth in common Article 1, and it was never the intent of States to do so.

Instead the mandate of the Working Group was to articulate a new concept, i.e., self-government within the nation-state. It is not the same concept as the right contained in common Article 1. It is therefore confusing that Article 3 of the declaration reproduces the language of common Article 1 when the intention of the States was (i) not to afford indigenous peoples the right to independence or permanent sovereignty over resources; and (ii) not to modify retroactively the scope of existing legal obligations in common Article 1 to include self-government within the nation-state. During the negotiations in the Working Group, many States therefore resisted reproducing the text of common Article 1 in Article 3 of the declaration.

Despite the provisions that limit the scope of Article 3 of the declaration (e.g., Article 4 and Article 46), we are unable to associate ourselves with this text because of the wholly inappropriate approach of reproducing common Article 1 in Article 3 of the text with no intention that Article 3 mean the same thing as common Article 1, nor that it be considered to explain or modify the scope of existing common Article 1 legal obligations. We find such an approach on a topic that involves the foundation of international relations and stability (i.e., the political unity and territorial integrity of nation-states) to be ill advised and likely to result in confusion and disputes.

Simply put, given that the clear intent of the States in the Working Group was to develop aspirational principles dealing with the concept of self-government within the framework of the nation-state, the declaration should have used clear and understandable language to express that goal and to avoid confusion with the common Article 1 right. We also note that preambular paragraphs 2 and 16 as well as Article 2 were not intended to imply that the existing right of self-determination is automatically applicable to indigenous peoples per se or to indicate that indigenous peoples automatically qualify as "peoples" for purposes of common Article 1.

Lands, Resources, & Redress:

The provisions on lands and resources are phrased in a manner that is particularly unworkable. The language is overly broad and inconsistent. For example, Article 26 appears to require recognition of indigenous rights to lands without regard to other legal rights existing in land, either indigenous or non-indigenous. Clearly the intent of the Working Group was not to ignore contemporary realities in most countries by announcing a standard of achievement that would be impossible to implement.

The intention of States in the Working Group was to encourage the establishment of mechanisms at the national level for the full legal recognition and protection of the lands, territories and resources indigenous peoples possess by reason of traditional ownership, occupation, or use, as well those which they have otherwise acquired. Furthermore, it was intended that such recognition should take into account the customs, traditions, and land tenure systems of the indigenous peoples concerned. Similarly, many of the declaration's provisions involving redress are set forth in a confusing manner and are equally unacceptable. Again, the goal of the States in the Working Group was to encourage just, transparent and effective mechanisms for redress for actions taken by States after endorsing the declaration.

The text also could be misread to confer upon a sub-national group a power of veto over the laws of a democratic legislature by requiring indigenous peoples' free, prior and informed consent before passage of any law that "may" affect them (e.g., Article 19). We strongly support the full participation of indigenous peoples in democratic decision-making processes, but cannot accept the notion of a sub-national group having a "veto" power over the legislative process.

Collective Rights: There was discussion within the Working Group regarding whether or not the collective indigenous rights set forth in the declaration were collective human rights. The intent of States participating in the Working Group was clear that, as has always been the case, human rights are universal and apply in equal measure to all individuals. This principle is fundamental to international human rights, and means that one group cannot have human rights that are denied to other groups within the same nation-state.

Moreover, if a collective entity or group—as opposed to individuals—could hold and exercise human rights, individuals within those groups would be extremely vulnerable to potential violations of their human rights by the collective. In addition, if groups and individuals could each hold human rights, it would be difficult to reconcile disputes over which human rights should prevail. As preambular paragraph 22 makes clear, the rights set forth in this declaration are collective rights of indigenous peoples as first peoples and are in a distinct category from human rights, which are held by all individuals. Article 46 also makes clear that human rights are not to be violated in the exercise of collective rights.

General Welfare: The aspirational principles and collective rights described in the declaration are typically written in extremely general and absolute terms. It was recognized by the States in the Working Group that it would not be possible to implement such broadly expressed provisions and that debating the restrictions on the exercise of each provision was not feasible given time constraints. It was therefore decided that the ability of democratic States to govern for the good of all their citizens be recognized at the end of the declaration (Article 46) and that such a clause would apply to all the principles and collective rights set forth in this declaration. Article 46 provides individual States with the flexibility needed to design domestic programs to preserve the unique characteristics of indigenous culture, and to ensure the continued integrity of indigenous communities, without disenfranchising other citizens of the State.

There are other provisions in the declaration that are unacceptable, including the article on the repatriation of human remains. The provisions on this important right have been misconstrued by some countries as allowing them to maintain their holdings of indigenous remains and artifacts. Even more fundamental and debilitating to the effective application and implementation of the declaration is its failure to define the phrase "indigenous peoples." This obvious shortcoming will subject application of the declaration to endless debate, especially if entities not properly entitled to such status seek to enjoy the special benefits and rights contained in the declaration.

The flaws in this text run through all of its most significant provisions. Because these provisions are fundamental to interpreting all of the provisions in text, the text as a whole is rendered unworkable and unacceptable. Our position on this declaration does not, however, mean that we shall in any way withdraw from continuing to pursue the recognition of rights of indigenous individuals and peoples, internationally or domestically.

F. TORTURE AND OTHER CRUEL, INHUMAN, OR DEGRADING TREATMENT OR PUNISHMENT

The United States submitted its second periodic report on May 6, 2005, and met with the UN Committee Against Torture during its May 2006 session. *See Digest 2005* at 341–71 and *Digest 2006* at 403–21 and 1124–37. The Committee's conclusions and recommendations are available as U.N. Doc. CAT/C/USA/CO/2 (July 25, 2006).

On July 25, 2007, the United States transmitted its response to specific recommendations as requested by the Committee Against Torture in its conclusions and recommendations in relation to the Second Periodic Report of the United States. Excerpts follow from the U.S. response concerning treatment of women and children in detention, and the response to Hurricane Katrina. On Hurricane Katrina, *see also* U.S. response in follow-up report on implementation of ICCPR, A.2.a. *supra*. Issues related to detainees are provided in Chapter 18.A.4.c.(3). The full text of the U.S. response, including Annex I, Declaration of Clint Williamson, Ambassador-at-Large for War Crimes Issues at the Department of State, is available at *www.state.gov/s/l/c8183.htm*.

* * * *

Paragraph 33
Recommendation:
"The State party should adopt all appropriate measures to ensure that women in detention are treated in conformity with international standards."

Response:
The United States provided the Committee with information about its efforts to ensure appropriate treatment of women in detention facilities, including action taken against gender-based violence and sexual abuse.[21] As the United States told the

---

[21]   *See, e.g.*, Second Periodic Report, *supra* note 3, at ¶¶ 87–94, 96–101, 120; Response to List of Issues, *supra* note 2, at 101–05.

Committee,[22] incidents of shackling of female detainees during childbirth are extremely rare and are not a standard procedure. It also provided the information on these issues in response to other questions from members of the Human Rights Committee.[23]

In its written reply to the Committee's List of Issues, the United States provided Bureau of Prisons statistics regarding enforcement actions for sexual abuse against prisoners.[24] These figures were for calendar year 2004, the latest year for which statistics were available at the time. Updated figures are provided below [omitted in these excerpts].

*   *   *   *

Paragraph 34
Recommendation:
"The State party should ensure that detained children are kept in facilities separate from those for adults in conformity with international standards. The State party should address the question of sentences of life imprisonment of children, as these could constitute cruel, inhuman or degrading treatment or punishment."

Response:
As the United States explained to the Committee,[25] juveniles are not regularly held in federal prison with the adult prison population. Federal law prohibits juvenile offenders held in the custody of federal authorities from being housed in correctional institutions or detention facilities in which they could have regular contact with adults. As a general rule, the state prison populations do not include "juveniles" as that term is defined by the applicable state law.

The Convention does not prohibit the sentencing of juveniles to life imprisonment without parole. The United States, moreover, does not believe that the sentencing of juveniles to life imprisonment

---

22   *See* Response to List of Issues, *supra* note 2, at 100.

23   *See* List of Issues to be Taken up in Connection with the Second and Third Periodic Reports of the United States of America, available at *http://www.usmission.ch/ICCPRAdvanceQ&A.pdf* (July 17, 2006).

24   *See* Response to List of Issues, *supra* note 2, at 102–03.

25   *See* Second Periodic Report, *supra* note 3, at ¶¶114–17; Response to List of Issues, *supra* note 2, at 97–99.

constitutes cruel, inhuman or degrading treatment or punishment as defined in United States obligations under the Convention. In this context, it is significant to recall the specific treaty obligations of the United States under Article 16 in light of the formal reservation the United States took with respect to that provision at the time it became a State Party to the Convention. Specifically, that reservation stated "[t]hat the United States considers itself bound by the obligation under article 16 to prevent 'cruel, inhuman or degrading treatment or punishment,' only insofar as the term 'cruel, inhuman or degrading treatment or punishment' means the cruel, unusual and inhumane treatment or punishment prohibited by the Fifth, Eighth, and/or Fourteenth Amendments to the Constitution of the United States." United States courts have considered such sentences on numerous occasions and ruled that juvenile life imprisonment does not violate the United States Constitution. Accordingly, such sentences do not violate U.S. obligations under the Convention with respect to cruel, inhuman or degrading treatment or punishment.

A prohibition of juvenile life imprisonment without parole is an important provision in the later-negotiated Convention on the Rights of the Child (CRC). States that wished to assume new treaty obligations with respect to juvenile sentencing were free to become States Parties to the CRC, and a very large number of countries chose to do so. Accordingly, States Parties to the CRC have an obligation under Article 37 of that Convention to ensure that "neither capital punishment nor life imprisonment without possibility of release shall be imposed for offences committed by persons below eighteen years of age." However, the United States has not become a State Party to the CRC [fn. omitted] and, accordingly, is under no obligation to prohibit the sentencing of juveniles to life imprisonment without the opportunity for parole.

Paragraph 42

*   *   *   *

Recommendation #3:

"The Committee also requests the State party to provide information on investigations into the alleged ill-treatment perpetrated by law-enforcement personnel in the aftermath of Hurricane Katrina."

Response:

For the Committee's information, a partial list of the work done by Federal agencies in response to Hurricanes Katrina and Rita, including enhanced law enforcement operations in the Gulf Coast region, is attached at Annex 6 and is available at *http:// www.dhs.gov/xprepresp/programs/gc_1157649340100.shtm.*

Since the Committee has not provided the United States with specific information about the allegations of ill-treatment it mentions, the United States is unable to provide a detailed response to any specific allegations the Committee may have in mind.

That said, U.S. law prohibits brutality and discriminatory actions by law enforcement officers. The Civil Rights Division of the Department of Justice, with the aid of United States Attorney's Offices and the FBI, actively enforces those laws. In addition, states have laws and/or other mechanisms that protect individuals from mistreatment by law enforcement officers.

* * * *

G. GENOCIDE, CRIMES AGAINST HUMANITY, AND RELATED ISSUES

1. U.S. Criminal Law

On December 21, 2007, President George W. Bush signed into law the Genocide Accountability Act, Pub. L. No. 110-151, 121 Stat. 1821. The act amended 18 U.S.C. § 1091(d) to provide jurisdiction over persons who commit genocide in three circumstances not previously included in the law, set forth in new subsections (d)(3)–(5):

> (d) Required Circumstance for Offenses.— . . .
> (1) the offense is committed in whole or in part within the United States;
> (2) the alleged offender is a national of the United States (as that term is defined in section 101 of the Immigration and Nationality Act (8 U.S.C. 1101));

(3) the alleged offender is an alien lawfully admitted for permanent residence in the United States (as that term is defined in section 101 of the Immigration and Nationality Act (8 U.S.C. 1101));

(4) the alleged offender is a stateless person whose habitual residence is in the United States; or

(5) after the conduct required for the offense occurs, the alleged offender is brought into, or found in, the United States, even if that conduct occurred outside the United States.

See also Chapter 3.C. concerning international and hybrid criminal tribunals.

2. Holocaust Denial

On January 26, 2007, the General Assembly adopted without vote a resolution introduced by the United States condemning any denial of the Holocaust as a historical event. U.N. Doc. A/RES/61/255. Ambassador Alejandro D. Wolff, then Acting U.S. Permanent Representative to the United Nations, provided a statement explaining U.S. support of the resolution, set forth below in full and available at *www.usunnewyork.usmission.gov/press_releases/20070126_011.html.*

———————

The United States strongly supports this Resolution that condemns without reservation any denial of the Holocaust. This Assembly should be proud of adopting today's Resolution by consensus. It is shameful that one country decided to reject that consensus.

Tomorrow will be the 62nd anniversary of the liberation of Auschwitz, a Nazi death camp where over 1 million people were murdered. To this day, Auschwitz serves as a powerful symbol of what can happen when tyranny and oppression go unchecked. As we mourn those who lost their lives, we must, as Secretary-General Ban Ki-moon noted, "reassert our commitment to human rights" which was "desecrated at Auschwitz and by genocides and atrocities since."

The United States introduced and sponsored this important Resolution, not as a rhetorical exercise, but because of the implications of Holocaust denial in the world today. Some experts on the topic have noted that, "Every genocide is followed by denial." Despite the undeniable truth about the Holocaust, we are now witnessing so-called scholars, even world leaders, attempting to revise history, masking a more dangerous agenda.

This Resolution is not about countering free speech or intellectual thought; it is about avoiding future disasters. One observer put it simply and powerfully when he stated that "The black hole of forgetting is the negative force that results in future genocides."

A little over a month ago, people around the world marked International Human Rights Week and renewed the solemn pledge of the Universal Declaration on Human Rights, which was drafted in the wake of the atrocities of World War II.

We take note that this esteemed body adopted by consensus in 2005 a Resolution unequivocally rejecting the denial of the Holocaust as an historical event. We call upon all Member States to follow through on that and today's Resolution to include measures in their educational systems that underscore the importance of never denying the Holocaust. As Kofi Annan remarked at the end of his tenure, "some of the rhetoric used in connection with the issue implies a refusal to concede the very legitimacy of Israel's existence, let alone the validity of its security concerns. . . .Today, Israelis are often confronted with words and action that seem to confirm their fear that the goal of their adversaries is to extinguish their existence as a state, and as a people."

Indeed, the words and actions of some, in direct violation of the UN Charter, underscore why this Resolution is so important. Just last month, the Iranian regime sponsored a conference questioning the historical fact of the atrocities of the Holocaust. Iranian President Ahmadi-Nejad has also called for the state of Israel to be "wiped off the map." That same regime is under UN Security Council sanctions right now to prevent it from developing nuclear weapons, in direct violation of its obligations under the Nuclear Nonproliferation Treaty. The confluence of these three forces cannot be viewed abstractly or in isolation of each other. They create a cauldron of conflict that cannot be ignored.

Some will cloak their hatred and hidden agenda by invoking the right to free speech and academic freedom. There is a categorical difference between free speech and speech which willfully and maliciously ignores recognized historical facts in order to advance an ulterior agenda. Conferences like those sponsored by Iran are designed solely to polarize and incite hatred. If successful, they can then use that hatred as a catalyst to justify genocide. It is also specious to diminish the Holocaust by making false comparisons— as we heard earlier this morning by some delegations. As Kofi Annan powerfully noted, "What was done to Jews and others by the Nazis remains an undeniable tragedy, unique in human history."

The United States stands firmly opposed to any attempts to deny the Holocaust. This Resolution reinforces that message and we encourage all Member States to take concrete steps to make that message heard. To deny the events of the Holocaust is tantamount to the approval of genocide in all its forms. Today we stand together saying to the world that we will not allow that to happen.

3. Holocaust-era Archives Agreement

On November 28, 2007, two protocols related to the International Tracing Service ("ITS") entered into force: (1) the Protocol on the Amendment of the Agreement Constituting an International Commission for the International Tracing Service and (2) the Protocol Amending the Agreement on the Relations between the International Commission for the International Tracing Service and the International Committee of the Red Cross.

The two underlying agreements are referred to collectively as the Bonn Agreements; both were concluded in Bonn on June 6, 1955. As explained on the ITS website:

. . . On June 6, 1955, the governments of Belgium, France, Federal Republic of Germany, Greece, Israel, Italy, Luxembourg, Netherlands, the United Kingdom and the USA signed an agreement to set up an International Commission to supervise the ITS. The Federal Republic of Germany undertook financial responsibility for the ITS.

The International Commission, now consisting of eleven member states, monitors the activities of the ITS. On foundation the ITS was given the humanitarian tasks of providing information about the fate of those persecuted by the Nazi regime and reuniting families torn apart by the war. The ITS is under the direction and management of the International Commission of the Red Cross (ICRC) [pursuant to the second Bonn Agreement, entered into between the International Commission and the ICRC]. . . .

See *www.its-arolsen.org/en/about_its/funding_and_legal_basis/index.html.*

The protocols, agreed to on May 16, 2006, amended the Bonn Agreements to provide access for research purposes to Holocaust-era archives preserved by ITS "both on site and through copies of the archives and documents." New Article 8*bis* set forth in Article III of the first protocol provides:

a. Each Government shall receive upon request a single copy of the archives and documents of the International Tracing Service.

b. Each Government may make these archives and documents accessible for research on the premises of an appropriate archival repository in its territory, where access shall be granted in accordance with the relevant national law and national archival regulations and practices.

The texts of the protocols are available at *www.its-arolsen.org/en/about_its/funding_and_legal_basis/index.html.*

A media note issued by the Department of State welcoming the agreement is set forth below and is available at *www.state.gov/r/pa/prs/ps/2007/nov/95836.htm.*

We welcome the entry into force today of an agreement opening the extensive Holocaust-era archives of the International Tracing Service (ITS) to survivors, their families and to researchers.

Established at the end of World War II at Bad Arolsen, Germany, the ITS has drawn on its archive of 50 million documents concerning 17.5 million people to assist family reunification efforts and to support claims by survivors and heirs for pensions and other forms of compensation.

On May 16, 2006, the International Commission approved two amendments to the 1955 Bonn Agreements to enable the ITS to make its holdings more readily available to the public. Each of the member states of the International Commission will be eligible to receive an electronic copy of the entire archive. The ITS plans to complete digitization of its holdings in 2011.

The United States Holocaust Memorial Museum in Washington, D.C. will administer the U.S. copy of the archive. Once the documents are formatted to the museum's computer system, the Museum will facilitate access to the documents for survivors and their families. The copy of the archives will also be a valuable source of information for researchers. The formatting process is now underway and is expected to take several months.

H. JUDICIAL PROCEDURE, PENALTIES, AND RELATED ISSUES*

1. Capital Punishment Moratorium

On November 15, 2007, U.S. Advisor Robert Hagen responded to a draft resolution in the UN General Assembly Third Committee on capital punishment as follows, stating:

> The United States recognizes that the supporters of this resolution hold principled positions on the issue of the death penalty. Nonetheless, it is important to recognize that international law does not prohibit capital punishment. In fact, the International Covenant on Civil and Political Rights specifically recognizes the right of countries

---

*   Editor's note: Discussion of litigation under the Alien Tort Statute ("ATS"), previously included under this heading, has been moved to Chapter 5: Foreign Relations, in recognition of the fact that claims under the ATS are not limited to those claiming human rights violations and that much recent litigation has focused on the scope of the application of the statute.

to impose the death penalty for the most serious crimes carried out pursuant to a final judgment rendered by a competent court and in accordance with appropriate safeguards and observance of due process. In this respect, the United States urges all governments that employ the death penalty to do so in conformity with their international human rights obligations and to ensure that it is not applied in an extrajudicial, summary or arbitrary manner.

The statement is available at *www.usunnewyork.usmission. gov/press_releases/20071115_309.html.* The resolution, "Moratorium on the Death Penalty," was adopted by the UN General Assembly on December 18, 2007. U.N. Doc. A/RES/ 62/149.

2. Juvenile Life Sentencing

In April 2007 the United States responded to a request from the Inter-American Commission on Human Rights regarding the sentencing of juveniles to life imprisonment without parole in the United States. The issue arose in a petition filed against the United States and the state of Michigan by a number of U.S. citizens convicted of serious crimes committed when they were under 18 years of age and sentenced to life imprisonment without the opportunity for parole. Petition No. P-161-06. As stated in the U.S. response, "[t]he essence of Petitioners' claim is that the sentencing of juveniles without the opportunity for parole violates the American Declaration, the International Covenant on Civil and Political Rights, various other international legal instruments, and customary international law."

In its response, the United States requested that the Commission "declare the petition inadmissible with respect to alleged violations of the American Declaration of Rights and

---

[1]　The American Declaration of the Rights and Duties of Man ("American Declaration") is a non-binding instrument and does not itself create rights or impose duties on OAS member states.

Duties of Man ('American Declaration').'" The grounds for inadmissibility under the Commission Rules of Procedure, each applicable to some or all of the petitioners, included failure to exhaust domestic remedies (Article 31); failure to file a timely petition (Article 32); failure to show a breach of a duty under the American Declaration (Article 34); failure to state a valid claim; and improper inclusion of a non-OAS member (the state of Michigan). Excerpts below provide the U.S. views on the failure to show a breach and the improper inclusion of the state of Michigan. The full text of the U.S. response is available at *www.state.gov/s/l/c8183.htm.* See also F. *supra,* discussion of paragraph 34.

* * * *

IV. Failure to Show a Breach of a Duty under the American Declaration

Under Article 34 of the Commission's Rules, a petition must state facts that tend to establish a violation of the American Declaration. If it does not, the Commission must find the petition inadmissible. Moreover, a petition cannot merely allege general complaints about a state's law, but must state facts that show actual harm suffered by a petitioner. This petition states no set of facts that constitute a violation of the American Declaration.

In deciding upon claims, the Commission may not, as Petitioners suggest, apply international law outside of the Inter-American system. The Commission Statute explicitly provides that in relation to non-States Parties to the American Convention on Human Rights, for purposes of the Statute, human rights are understood to be only the rights set forth in the American Declaration. Commission Statute, Article 1(2)(b). Further, Petitioners' repeated reference to and reliance upon decisions and opinions of the Inter-American Court as binding upon the United States are factually and legally incorrect as the United States is not subject to the jurisdiction of that body. The petition is likewise replete with references to treaties to which the United States is not party and other instruments that are not binding upon the United States, including the American Convention on Human Rights, the European Convention on Human Rights, and the Convention on the Rights of the Child.

Although Petitioners allege violations of Articles I, VII, XVIII, XXIV, XXV, and XXVI of the American Declaration, their allegations are based on an erroneously expansive interpretation of those articles. These assertions are unsupported by the text of those articles and rely on a systematically flawed analysis of relevant international law.

A. Petitioners' criminal sentences do not violate Article VII of the American Declaration

Article VII of the American Declaration states, "all children have the right to special protection, care and aid." From this language, Petitioners find and assert two "fundamental rights."

First, Petitioners claim that Article VII of the Declaration includes "the right to be incarcerated for the shortest possible duration." Petition at 25–6. The second "fundamental right" that Petitioners claim emanates from Article VII is the "right to rehabilitation." Petition at 26–7. Petitioners' life imprisonment sentences, it is argued, constitute violations of these fundamental rights.

This reasoning has no basis in the text, history, or structure of Article VII of the American Declaration. Rather, Petitioners base their argument on other international instruments, including the Convention on the Rights of the Child (CROC). A State that wishes to assume international legal obligations with respect to juvenile sentencing is free to become a Party to the CROC, and a very large number of countries have chosen to do so. Accordingly, States Parties to the CROC have an obligation to ensure that "neither capital punishment nor life imprisonment without possibility of release shall be imposed for offences committed by persons below eighteen years of age." CROC, Article 37. However, the U.S. has not joined the CROC and, accordingly, is under no obligation to prohibit the sentencing of juveniles to life imprisonment without the opportunity for parole. Rather, the citizens of many U.S. states (including Michigan) have decided, through democratic processes, that serious crimes may warrant life imprisonment, even when committed by persons under the age of eighteen.

To further support their argument, Petitioners cite Article 14(4) of the International Covenant on Civil and Political Rights (ICCPR) which states, *inter alia*, that "[i]n the case of juvenile persons, the [criminal] procedure shall be such as will take account of their age and the desirability of promoting their rehabilitation."

First, Petitioners' reliance on the ICCPR is not appropriate, as the Commission does not have the authority to decide upon ICCPR obligations, even for States Parties. Second, any interpretation by the Commission of the ICCPR would need to take into account the relevant U.S. reservation, which clarifies that the United States "reserves the right, in exceptional circumstances, to treat juveniles as adults, notwithstanding . . . paragraph 4 of article 14." ICCPR, United States of America: Reservations, para. 5. The history of this reservation shows that it was intended to permit the trial of juveniles as adults and the incarceration of juveniles and adults in the same prison facilities. Moreover, in the case of the Petitioners, exceptional circumstances exist: the five individual Petitioners have been convicted of serious violent crimes, including first-degree murder. These are precisely the kind of circumstances that the United States included within its reservation.

Accordingly, the United States is not bound by any international law rule prohibiting sentencing of juveniles to life imprisonment, nor is the United States bound by the "fundamental rights" that Petitioners intuit from Article VII. Overall, Petitioners improperly and atextually conjure specific and "fundamental" rights from the otherwise general prescription of Article VII.

B. Petitioners' criminal sentences do not violate the right to life, liberty and security (Article I) or constitute cruel, infamous, or unusual punishment (Article XXVI)

Petitioners' claim that the United States Government violated Article I (right to life, liberty, and security) and Article XXVI (right not to receive cruel, infamous or unusual punishment) is incorrect. Article I of the American Declaration states that everyone has the right to life, liberty and security. The United States respects this right fully as evidenced by the fact that a sentence of life without parole can only occur in accordance with due process of law and stringent procedural safeguards guaranteed by the U.S. Constitution and relevant state constitutions. The right to life, liberty and security is in no way a prohibition on the sentencing of juveniles to life imprisonment.

Petitioners further attempt to characterize sentences of life imprisonment without parole for those under 18 years of age as cruel, infamous or unusual punishment in violation of Article XXVI of the American Declaration. This characterization is without merit, as the United States Constitution prohibits cruel and unusual punishment. U.S. Const. amend. VIII. When the United States becomes party to treaties, it does so only with the understanding that prohibitions of cruel, infamous, or unusual treatment or punishment (or similar language) are coextensive with the United States' constitutional prohibitions. *See, e.g.*, Convention against Torture and Other Cruel, Inhuman or Degrading Treatment or Punishment, Declarations and Reservations of the United States: Reservation I(1).[3] It would be fundamentally improper for the Commission to interpret the analogous provisions of the American Declaration as establishing protections for U.S. citizens that exceed those guaranteed by the Fifth, Eighth, and/or Fourteenth Amendments of the U.S. Constitution. As discussed in Section II, and readily admitted by Petitioners, none of the Petitioners has challenged the Constitutionality of their sentences in the United States judicial system.

Petitioners fail to allege a valid claim under Articles I or XXVI and United States law is fully consistent with the American Declaration. The Commission should find Petitioners' claims to be without merit.

C. The United States has not violated the due process provisions of the American Declaration (Articles XVIII, XXIV, XXV and XXVI)

Petitioners claim that Michigan law violates Article XVIII (right to fair trial), XXIV (right to submit respectful petitions to any competent authority), Article XXV (right to liberty and humane treatment), and XXVI (right to an impartial and public hearing). These claims, too, are without merit. As is well known, the United States Constitution affords all defendants extensive due

---

[3] This reservation reads: "The United States considers itself bound by the obligation under article 16 to prevent 'cruel, inhuman or degrading treatment or punishment', only insofar as the term 'cruel, inhuman or degrading treatment or punishment' means the cruel, unusual and inhumane treatment or punishment prohibited by the Fifth, Eighth, and/or Fourteenth Amendments to the Constitution of the United States."

process protections. This is evidenced in part by Petitioners' extensive trials, appeals, and subsequent habeas proceedings. Overall, Petitioners offer only a generalized grievance with respect to Michigan law and do not present facts sufficient to support a claim that any particular right of any particular Petitioner has been violated.

D. A sentence of life imprisonment without parole for a juvenile does not violate customary international law

As a preliminary matter, the Commission is not empowered to consider the question of whether the United States laws violate customary international law since this is beyond the scope of its jurisdiction. Commission Statute, Art. 20. Nevertheless, Petitioners' claim that the United States has violated customary international law is unfounded.

A rule of customary international law may be formed where state practice is "both extensive and virtually uniform" and where States act under a sense of legal obligation (*opinio juris*). *North Sea Continental Shelf* (F.R.G. v. Den; F.R.G. v. Neth), 1969 I.C.J. at ¶ 74 (Merits—Judgment of Feb. 20). In this case, there is neither the uniformity of state practice, nor the required *opinio juris*. Even if one were to assert, as Petitioners do, that a customary international law rule forbids the sentencing of juveniles to life imprisonment without parole, no such rule could bind the United States. A State that *persistently objects* to an alleged customary rule cannot be bound by it. *See, e.g., Ian Brownlie, Principles of Public International Law* at 10 (1998). Indeed, the Commission in *Domingues* stated that "a norm of customary international law binds all states with the exception of only those states that have persistently rejected the practice prior to its becoming law." *Domingues*, Case 12.285, Oct. 22, 2002 (IACHR) at para. 48.

The United States has persistently maintained its right to sentence juveniles who have committed serious crimes to life imprisonment without parole and has done so for over a century. *See, e.g., List of Issues To Be Taken Up in Connection With the Consideration of the Second and Third Periodic Reports of the United States of America.*[4] The United States has never accepted the prohibition of this

---

[4]   Available online at *http://www.state.gov/g/drl/rls/70385.htm.*

practice and explicitly objects (and has persistently objected, as a historical matter) to any suggestion of its status as a rule of customary international law. Further, the United States has not ratified the CROC, and regularly cites Article 37 of the treaty—which prohibits the sentencing of juveniles to life imprisonment without parole—as one of its justifications for its lack of support. Considering the clear and long-standing objections of the United States, the United States cannot be held to any such rule prohibiting life sentences without parole for juveniles.

Overall, the policies and practices of the United States, including those of the State of Michigan, concerning life imprisonment without parole are fully consistent with U.S. obligations under international law.

* * * *

V. Improper Inclusion of a non-OAS Member

Petitioners bring this petition "against the United States of America *and the State of Michigan*." Petition at 3, emphasis added. According to its Rules of Procedure, the Commission is to consider petitions alleging violations of human rights "with respect to the *Member States of the OAS*." Rules of Procedure, Art. 27, emphasis added. The procedures for reviewing, considering, processing, and admitting petitions involve only petitioners, the Commission, and States. Rules of Procedure, Arts. 26–30. Furthermore, the Commission has authority under its statute to examine petitions only "in relation to . . . member states of the Organization. . . ." Commission Statute, Art. 20.

The state of Michigan is not a member of the Organization of American States, and the Commission's rules do not allow for a petition to be considered with respect to a sub-national entity such as Michigan. Accordingly, the United States requests that the Commission declare this petition inadmissible *in toto* with respect to the state of Michigan.

I. RULE OF LAW AND DEMOCRACY PROMOTION

On October 25, 2007, Elizabeth Wilcox, Deputy Legal Advisor, U.S. Mission to the United Nations, addressed the Sixth

Committee of the UN General Assembly on its consideration of the rule of law. Excerpts below from the U.S. statement describe its support for international rule of law development and commitment to the rule of law domestically and internationally, and provide suggestions for subtopics that might be considered by the International Law Commission. The full text of Ms. Wilcox's statement is available at *www.state.gov/s/l/c8183.htm.*

* * * *

The United States strongly advocates the rule of law at both the international and national levels. International law has a critical role in world affairs, and it is vital to the resolution of conflicts and the coordination of cooperation. We believe that international law can and should play a role in ensuring accountability and justice, and a key aspect of our diplomacy rests on our conviction that international law is a vital and powerful force in the search for freedom. The United States helps develop international law, relies on international law, and abides by it.

At the international level, we have strongly supported international legal institutions. For example, the United States supports the work of the International Court of Justice, and we are glad that President Higgins once again will meet with the Sixth Committee next week. We also support the Security Council's use of legal mechanisms and institutions to promote international peace and security, including by ensuring accountability for genocide, war crimes, crimes against humanity, and terrorism. The United States has initially pledged $5 million to support the start up costs of the Special Tribunal for Lebanon, and we encourage other countries to contribute as well. This new tribunal is essential to support Lebanon's work to hold accountable all those involved in the terrorist bombing that killed former Lebanese Prime Minister Rafiq Hariri and others. We also have contributed over a half a billion dollars in strong support of the International Criminal Tribunals for the Former Yugoslavia and Rwanda and the Special Court for Sierra Leone. Finally, we follow with great interest the activities of the Extraordinary Chambers in the Courts of Cambodia.

We also support the targeted sanctions regimes the Security Council has established, which, by imposing important international obligations, contribute to the development of international law. We should continue to recognize that sanctions remain an important, measured tool for the maintenance of international peace and security, and that targeted sanctions can be important in minimizing the adverse impact of sanctions upon innocent civilians. These regimes play a crucial role in combating international terrorism and the proliferation of weapons of mass destruction, as well as efforts to end violence and establish stability in countries including Sudan, Somalia, Côte d'Ivoire, Liberia, and the Democratic Republic of the Congo. It also is noteworthy that past concerns about the need for fair and clear procedures for the Security Council and its sanctions committees to de-list persons subject to Security Council sanctions have been addressed, including through Security Council Resolution 1730 of December 2006.

Aside from the Security Council, other parts of the UN system also have an important role in promoting the rule of law. In particular, we are pleased at the work of the UN Commission on International Trade Law with respect to commercial and economic law reform. UNCITRAL has played a key role in promoting international legal regimes that can enhance commerce in all geographic regions and for States at all levels of development. We also applaud the important efforts of the UN Office of Drugs and Crime's Terrorism Prevention Branch, which is playing a lead role in helping States become parties to and implement the international conventions and protocols relating to terrorism.

Mr. Chairman, International law has an important role in our nation's Constitution and domestic law. The United States Constitution declares that treaties are the "supreme law of the land" and assigns to the President the responsibility to take care that the laws are faithfully upheld and executed. In addition, in many instances, our courts are authorized to apply and interpret international law. We entered into over 400 international agreements and treaties in 2006 alone, and we negotiate and conclude hundreds of international agreements and treaties every year. The Administration has asked our Senate to take priority action on about 35 treaties during the current session of Congress. The United States also serves as a depositary for approximately 200 multilateral treaties, including the North Atlantic Treaty, the Antarctic Treaty, the Treaty on the Non-Proliferation of Nuclear Weapons, and the Biological Weapons Convention. Finally, the State Department's Treaty Office increasingly promulgates important information about U.S. treaties on a public webpage (*www.state.gov/s/l/treaty*), including depositary information, answers to frequently asked questions, and the *Treaties in Force* publication, which details the over 10,000 U.S. treaties and international agreements in force as of a certain date during each year.

Also at the national level, the commitment of the United States to advancing the rule of law is demonstrated by the extensive efforts and resources we devote to assisting other States in their efforts to strengthen their legal, judicial, and law enforcement institutions and to combat the production and trafficking of illicit drugs. In addition, the UN Convention against Transnational Organized Crime and the UN Convention against Corruption represent the first legally binding global instruments to target transnational organized crime and corruption. The United States is committed to promoting ratification and implementation of these treaties, which serve as new tools for enhancing international cooperation, including mutual legal assistance.

In order to achieve a more holistic approach to developing justice institutions, U.S. Government organizations collaborate to deliver integrated and strategically focused rule of law assistance. These include the State Department's Bureau of International Narcotics and Law Enforcement (INL) and the U.S. Agency for International Development (USAID). . . .

U.S. technical assistance in the rule of law area is wide-ranging. For instance, we have provided assistance to States' efforts to train police, implement criminal justice reforms and human rights protection, improve court administration, promote judicial reform, train judges and lawyers, modernize legal education, create bar associations, and improve access to justice. We are increasing our efforts to incorporate policing projects into our rule of law and human rights programs, and have a solid track record of community-based policing programs in Africa and Central America. We are also examining closely the role of traditional legal systems, such as indigenous community law, Sha'ria law, and tribal law, in contributing to the rule of law.

These U.S. programs, along with parallel efforts undertaken by the United Nations and by other States, make significant contributions to advancing the rule of law. In this vein, we would like to comment briefly on the Secretary-General's report (A/61/636-S/2006/280) on enhancing UN support for the rule of law. We welcome the practical recommendations it makes for increasing coherence and coordination among the many players within the UN system that provide rule of law-related assistance. The establishment of the Rule of Law Coordination and Resource Group, as well as the Rule of Law Assistance Unit are also promising developments, although we wish to stress that the Unit should be funded from existing resources. More specifically, the idea of enhancing quality control over UN documentation in the rule of law area is worth considering. We do note with concern, however, the report's reference to rule of law assistance by "non-UN actors." We wish to reiterate the importance of bilateral assistance in the rule of law area and to emphasize the need for the UN to coordinate its rule of law activities with bilateral donors.

Moving now to the broader issue of what sub-topic or subtopics the Sixth Committee should consider next fall, we continue to believe that the Committee's future work on this agenda item should have a practical focus. The United States is concerned that some of the topics that delegations have suggested, including ones reflected in the Secretary-General's report on views received from States (A/62/121 and A/62/121/Add. 1), are not sufficiently focused to allow the Committee to provide a basis for constructive work. Instead, we believe it would be particularly useful to focus our discussions in the next session on ways in which the UN's existing rule of law assistance programs could be better coordinated and made more effective. In this regard, the Sixth Committee can use as a starting point the Secretary-General's final report on the inventory of current activities of parts of the UN system devoted to the promotion of the rule of law at the national and international levels. Alternatively, the Sixth Committee could consider a focus on transitional justice at the national level, which is an essential issue for societies seeking to emerge from conflict.

* * * *

J.   HUMAN RIGHTS AND COUNTERTERRORISM

1.   UN Special Rapporteur

On November 22, 2007, the Special Rapporteur on the Promotion and Protection of Human Rights and Fundamental Freedoms While Countering Terrorism, Professor Martin Scheinin, issued a report on his country visit to the United States. U.N. Doc. A/HRC/6/17/Add.3, available at *http://daccessdds.un.org/doc/UNDOC/GEN/G07/149/55/PDF/G0714955.pdf?OpenElement*. The summary of the report explained, in part:

> The Special Rapporteur on the promotion and protection of human rights and fundamental freedoms while countering terrorism, Martin Scheinin, visited the United States of America from 16 to 25 May 2007, during which he met with senior officials of the Government, members of Congress and their staff, academics and non-governmental organizations, as well as with the Inter-American Commission on Human Rights. The objective of the visit was to undertake a fact-finding exercise and a legal assessment of United States law and practice in the fight against terrorism, measured against international law. His visit also aimed at identifying and disseminating best practice in the countering of terrorism.

During an oral presentation to the Human Rights Council on December 12, 2007, Mr. Scheinin also briefly described his observations upon attending military commission hearings at Guantanamo at the invitation of the United States, earlier that month.

In a statement to the Human Rights Council on December 12, 2007, Melanie Khanna, Deputy Legal Adviser to the U.S. Mission in Geneva, provided the U.S. response to the November report and the rapporteur's oral presentation. Ms. Khanna's statement, set forth below, is available at *www.usmission.ch/Press2007/1212ScheininReport.html*. A more detailed response to the Special Rapporteur's report, referred to in her statement, is available at *http://geneva.usmission.gov/Press 2007/Scheinin-Response-HRC.pdf*.

I appreciate this opportunity to respond to Professor Scheinin's presentation on the United States.

During the Special Rapporteur's country visit to the United States from May 16th to 25th, my government was pleased to offer access to senior officials from many different United States government agencies, including the Departments of State, Justice, Defense, and Homeland Security, the Central Intelligence Agency, and the Office of the Director of National Intelligence, as well as the opportunity to attend the trial of Jose Padilla and others in Miami.

We were also pleased to offer the Special Rapporteur the opportunity just last week to visit Guantanamo Bay to observe proceedings in the military commission trial of Salim Hamdan for the war crimes of conspiracy and material support to terrorism. We appreciate the Special Rapporteur's observation that the military judge was doing his utmost to ensure fair and orderly proceedings. Given the complexity of the cases and the fact that the commission is still in the process of determining whether it has jurisdiction over the proceedings, it is perhaps not surprising that there were certain logistical challenges, challenges that we believe could occur in any domestic criminal system in any country.

We further appreciate that during his visit, Professor Scheinin took advantage of the opportunity to receive a briefing from the detention facility command on the measures in place to ensure that detainees at Guantanamo are treated humanely.

We were, however, disappointed that the Special Rapporteur declined an offer to tour the detention facility on the same terms as a number of international observers, including representatives from the parliaments of two members of this Council as well as the Parliamentary Assembly of the Organization for Security and Cooperation in Europe. We believe such a tour would have enabled him to provide the Council with a valuable perspective on the facility.

In addition, we regret that Mr. Scheinin's oral presentation about his Guantanamo visit is in part misleading about the facts of the process and revisits well-worn, ill-informed criticisms about military commissions hearings rather than bringing to the Council's attention fresh information about the military commissions process.

As to the Special Rapporteur's report on his country visit, we appreciate that the report contains a number of positive aspects. For example, the report acknowledges United States leadership in the international fight against terrorism, and pays tribute to the respect for the rule of law and the system of self-correcting mechanisms that are the hallmark of our system of government.

We also note his identification of a number of best practices in United States counter-terrorism law and practice in such diverse areas as compensation of terrorism victims, community outreach, the rejection of racial profiling, and respect for freedom of the press.

In other ways, however, we were extremely disappointed at the report. The report missed a number of opportunities to deepen the ongoing international discussion of how democracies might best deal with the current threats posed by armed combatant terrorist groups.

The unfortunate fact is that a large part of the report again repeats unfair and oversimplified criticisms of the United States. This is particularly true in the sections dealing with the legal framework for the armed conflict with Al Qaida. These sections simply catalogue well-known criticisms and fail even to acknowledge that there are multiple ways of approaching the difficult issues discussed, something that other international observers have highlighted.

This approach duplicates the work of other special procedures, in particular the 2006 report on Guantanamo by five mandate holders—the very duplication of work that this mandate was supposed to avoid.

My government has prepared a detailed response to this report that is now available on my Mission's website.

In conclusion, while the United States supports the extension of this mandate, we hope that in future work the Special Rapporteur proceeds differently. In particular, we hope he will focus less on well-worn arguments under discussion elsewhere and more on practical solutions to common problems faced by the international community.

2. Right of Reply to Cuba

On March 14, 2007, Velia De Pirro, Counselor for Political and Specialized Agency Affairs, delivered the U.S. right of reply to statements made by Cuba to the Human Rights Council. Ms. De Pirro's statement is set forth below in full and is available at *www.us-mission.ch/Press2007/0314Rightof Reply.html.*

Yesterday the Minister of Foreign Affairs of the Republic of Cuba, Mr. Felipe Perez Roque, made several references to the United States and attributed certain positions to us. I would like to set the record straight.

Terrorism is real. Every country here has been affected by it. All civilized countries need to pull together to fight terrorism. Within the framework of democracy and rule of law, the United States Government has adopted policies to fulfill its responsibility to protect its citizens and its territory.

The United States thoroughly addressed its policy on the detention of enemy combatants in reports to the Committee Against Torture and Human Rights Committee. I reiterate: torture is prohibited by all U.S. personnel in all locations at all times.

The United States' commitment to the Special Procedures mechanism is well-known; we have welcomed the visits of dozens of mandate holders over the years. My government was particularly struck by Cuba's new-found support in yesterday's statement for a range of civil and political thematic mandates, including those on Freedom of Opinion and Expression, Torture, and the Working Group on Arbitrary Detention. This is great news. My government sincerely hopes this new support from the government of Cuba will soon lead to invitations from Cuba to these mandate-holders to visit Cuba, for the first time in their history.

Cross References

Protection of civilians in armed conflict, **Chapter 18.A.3.**
Refugee issues, **Chapter 1.D.**
Trafficking in persons, **Chapter 3.B.3.**
International and hybrid tribunals, **Chapter 3.C.**
Relationship between human rights law and law of war, **Chapter 18.A.1.b. and A.4.c.(1).**

CHAPTER 7

International Organizations

A. GENERAL: RESPONSIBILITY OF INTERNATIONAL ORGANIZATIONS

On October 31, John B. Bellinger, III, Department of State Legal Adviser, addressed the Sixth Committee of the UN General Assembly on the report of the International Law Commission on the Work of its 59th Session. Mr. Bellinger's comments on the draft articles concerning the responsibility of international organizations are set forth below. The full text of his statement is available at *www.state.gov/s/l/c8183. htm.* The draft articles discussed here are available in the fifth report on responsibility of international organizations, U.N. Doc. A/CN.4/583.

---

* * * *

The United States appreciates the Commission's desire to generate a common set of articles on the responsibility of international organizations. We remain concerned, however, about the methodology that underlies the Commission's work. As noted in our previous statements on this topic, we have reservations regarding the assumption that the Commission's articles on State Responsibility establish a good template for articles on the responsibility of international organizations. States and international organizations are fundamentally different. The fact that both have international legal personalities does not in and of itself mean they should be subject to the same basic rules under international law. Unlike States, which share a fundamental set of qualities, there is great diversity in the structure, functions, and interests of international organizations both as they relate to States and to each other. In addition, many of the interests of States that underpin the articles on State Responsibility—such as those related to sovereignty, citizenship, and territorial integrity—do not exist in the case of international organizations. Such differences make applying the Commission's articles on State Responsibility to international organizations problematic.

The draft articles raise additional concerns, some of which I would like to bring to your attention. We question whether the principle embedded in draft Article 35, which is drawn from the articles on State responsibility, is applicable to international organizations. Draft Article 35 would preclude an international organization from relying on its constituent instruments and other rules to justify failure to comply with its obligations, unless the rules of the organization specifically provide that it may do so for relations between the organization and its Member States. Yet those rules, unlike the internal rules of States, clearly operate as law at the international level, and thus raise additional questions about the obligations of particular international organizations across the range of situations they may face. In view of such complexities, we believe that additional analysis would be useful before drawing a firm conclusion that an international organization cannot rely on its constituent instruments and other rules to justify its conduct.

With respect to draft Article 36, we note that it may be that the obligations of an international organization may depend on considerations beyond those listed in the draft article, including for example, the character and the content of a particular organization's constituent instruments.

With respect to draft Article 43, we question the appropriateness of including such a provision and are concerned that it may prove to be confusing. For example, we could imagine questions being raised about the meaning of the phrase "in accordance with the rules of the organization," or the call for implementation of all "appropriate" measures. In the final analysis, the extent to which a principle on this topic applies may depend on the nature of the organization and duties at issue in a particular case.

Draft Articles 44 and 45 deal with the issue of "serious breaches of obligations under peremptory norms of general international law." We question the decision to draw a distinction between "serious breaches" and other breaches. We do not believe that the "seriousness" of a breach is a distinction in kind in the manner suggested by this provision, and this draft article should be deleted. Also with respect to these provisions, we appreciate the explanation that these articles are not intended to vest international organizations with functions outside their competencies, but are concerned the text of the articles may not be sufficiently clear on this point.

*   *   *   *

B. UNITED NATIONS

1. UN Reform

a. *Security Council*

On May 3, 2007, Ambassador Zalmay Khalilzad, U.S. Permanent Representative to the United Nations, addressed the Open-Ended Working Group on the question of equitable representation on the Security Council, an increase in its membership, and other matters related to the Security Council. Ambassador Khalilzad's statement, including U.S. views on Security Council expansion, is excerpted below; the full text of his remarks is available at *www.usunnewyork. usmission.gov/press_releases/20070503_102.html. See also* statement of Ambassador Alejandro D. Wolff, U.S. Deputy Permanent Representative, on Security Council Reform, to the Open-Ended Working Group, December 14, 2007, available at *www.usunnewyork.usmission.gov/press_releases/ 20071214_374.html.*

---

*   *   *   *

We recognize that the world has changed dramatically since the founding of the United Nations. This means that for the organization to be relevant, legitimate, effective, and efficient, it must adapt by focusing on the relevant issues, ensuring that it reflects the diversity of the world, being as effective as possible in terms of decision making and implementation capabilities, and getting the most out of its resources. Thus, there is an imperative to adapt.

This imperative is leading our own deliberations on reform at all levels, including the Security Council, the Secretariat, peace-keeping operations, UN agencies, and others. Comprehensive improvement will result if we address the whole range of issues from personnel selection, ethics oversight and management processes, mandate reform, to the professionalism and discipline among peace-keeping forces.

*   *   *   *

Regarding reform of the Security Council, we can support expansion of the Council that preserves its ability to carry out its Charter-mandated responsibilities to maintain international peace and security, while recognizing the emergence since 1945 of other states capable of assuming the global responsibilities of permanent membership, in particular Japan and perhaps others.

Also, the expansion of the Council should move forward in a way that will secure not only the legally required support for implementation but also, as the facilitators rightly note, "the widest possible political acceptance by the membership."

This report indicates that wide differences remain among the Member States with respect to the specifics of how expansion might be pursued. Undoubtedly, it will take time for us to develop a common understanding.

We recognize the logic of need for Security Council expansion. At the same time, it is important to pursue efforts to improve the capabilities and effectiveness of other organizations and processes of the United Nations. Because all countries would benefit from improving the ability of the United Nations to advance its diverse missions, we should accelerate the implementation of changes in these areas in order to create an environment conducive to Security Council reform.

*   *   *   *

A fact sheet issued September 20, 2007, by the Department of State Bureau of Public Affairs listed UN reforms secured through U.S. diplomatic engagement since 2005 and U.S. priorities for continued reform, including:

- Institutionalizing a system-wide approach to enforcing ethical conduct;
- Strengthening the UN's internal oversight body to better identify, obtain, and deploy the resources to accomplish its mandate;
- Enhancing transparency and accountability through procurement reform;
- Increasing the UN's effectiveness and efficiency through results-based management.

The full text of the fact sheet is available at *www.state.gov/r/pa/scp/92622.htm.*

b. Internal justice system

On October 8, 2007, Rodger Young, U.S. public delegate, addressed the UN General Assembly on issues related to efforts to redesign the UN internal justice system. *See* press release of that date, excerpted below and available at *www.usunnewyork.usmission.gov/press_releases/20071008_231.html.*

---

* * * *

The United States supports efforts to create a more effective and efficient internal justice system for the United Nations, and we are pleased that this Committee is continuing to discuss the reform of that system. We welcome the progress the Sixth Committee made during its resumed session last spring but note that there are a number of significant issues on which delegations did not reach consensus.

Among the issues requiring further discussion within this Committee include basic questions about the appropriate scope of the jurisdiction and powers of a new system of administration of justice for the UN, how, if at all, that system should apply to non-UN staff members, and what the appropriate role of the relevant staff associations should play in relation to the system. We look forward to the opportunity during this session to discuss these issues further.

We welcome the report of the Secretary-General. . . .

Included in the report are elements for draft statutes for the new UN Dispute Tribunal and for the new UN Appeals Tribunal, as well as draft elements of the rules for both new bodies. My delegation believes it is premature at this stage for the working group to begin detailed consideration of language for the new statutes of the formal judicial system. In our view, broader agreement is needed on the basic principles underlying the new formal system of justice before productive discussions on potential statutes will be possible.

. . . As our discussions in this Committee proceed, we should bear in mind that budget considerations will influence the General Assembly's ultimate decisions on this topic, and that recommendations from this Committee that are divorced from budgetary realities will be of limited practical value.

The task we are undertaking of designing a new system of administration of justice for the UN is both enormously important and enormously complex. . . . My delegation would like to take this opportunity to highlight our views on some of the more significant issues which remain unresolved from the Committee's prior discussions on this topic, noting that many other important issues must be considered.

We remain deeply concerned with the recommendation to extend the justice system beyond UN staff to cover non-staff members (consultants, individual contractors, and daily paid workers). The UN's obligations to staff members and non-staff members are not the same, and the dispute resolution mechanisms for each should remain separate. We do recognize that contractors and others may need access to a more flexible dispute resolution system than they currently receive, but we remain convinced that any such system must remain separate from the one focusing on UN staff. Even if the General Assembly could develop such a system to cover contractors and others, it is important to note that the General Assembly cannot by its own force alter the dispute settlement provisions of service contracts currently in place between the UN and the UN's various categories of non-staff.

We also remain concerned about proposals to permit staff associations to bring claims either in their own names or on behalf of their members. We believe staff associations have a valuable role to play in assisting individual employees in understanding their rights and in helping them pursue remedies that may be available to them. We do not support expanding this role to permit staff associations to participate in litigation as parties. Doing so is unnecessary and will likely lead to litigation of institution-wide issues that should be resolved politically.

On a related issue, we do not support proposals that the United Nations establish a new office with full-time lawyers to provide staff with direct legal representation in pursuing their claims. Aside from the pro bono assistance available under the current system, we believe legal assistance provided by the organization should be limited to providing information about the process and procedures of the UN's administration of justice system. Although we accept that the UN's current system for assisting staff could be strengthened, the legal assistance provided by the organization should not involve advocacy in a particular case. Such advocacy would displace the appropriate role of a staff association as an advisor and would inappropriately encourage litigation by creating an office with a built-in incentive to file claims against the organization to insure the office's relevance. We note that no other international organization of which we are aware provides advocacy assistance to staff before administrative tribunals.

We further note that the asserted examples of such assistance from national jurisdictions cited in the Secretary General's report, which appear to be limited to military justice systems, are not relevant here, as they involve assistance to persons in defending themselves against disciplinary actions being brought against them by their government, not assistance in pursuing affirmative claims for relief. Although charges against soldiers affect their employment status, and a court-martial could result in a soldier losing his or her job, the military justice system is quite different even from administrative disciplinary systems for public-sector civilian workers. In the United States, for example, federal agencies do not provide counsel for employees facing disciplinary charges, let alone for employees who want to sue their employer. It is our strong view that UN staff members should look to relevant staff associations only for assistance in pursuing claims against the organization.

Among other things, we remain concerned about the recommendation to eliminate the cap on compensatory damage awards, common in many systems, and believe that any adjustment of the current cap should only be considered following careful analysis. In addition, we do not think it would be consistent with modern principles of justice to allow issues of both law and fact to be heard at both levels of the justice system. We note further that modern principles of justice also do not require more than one judge to hear cases at the trial level, i.e., cases to be heard by the UN Dispute Tribunal. Moreover, having more than one judge at the trial level could reduce the efficiency of these proceedings, undermining a key goal of the reform process. We also believe that there is a need for greater clarity in the types of claims staff members may pursue in the system, in particular to make clear that such claims are limited to allegations of violations of the written terms of the UN Staff Regulations and Rules.

*   *   *   *

2. Charter Committee

On October 16, 2007, Mr. Young addressed the UN General Assembly Sixth Committee concerning the role of the UN Charter Committee, primarily in proposals related to the committee's involvement in sanctions; see Chapter 16.A.8. Excerpts below address other issues. The full text of the statement is available at *www.state.gov/s/l/c8183.htm*.

The United States welcomes the Report of the Charter Committee (A/62/33), and appreciates the opportunity to express our views on some of the issues addressed in the report.

We commend the Secretary-General's ongoing efforts to reduce the backlog in preparing the *Repertory of Practice of United*

Nations Organs and the *Repertoire of the Practice of the Security Council.* Both publications provide a useful resource on the practice of United Nations organs, and we appreciate the Secretariat's hard work on them.

*   *   *   *

We also note with interest proposals of several Member States regarding new subjects that might warrant consideration by the Special Committee. With respect to the proposal mentioned in the Special Committee's report concerning "Consideration of the legal aspects of the reform of the United Nations," we agree that, as appropriate, the Committee could have a technical role to play in the matters relating to the implementation of any decisions to amend the Charter of the United Nations, at the appropriate time. It would be helpful to receive additional detail about this proposal before the Charter Committee meets next spring.

Finally, we do not support the proposal discussed in the Committee that the General Assembly request from the International Court of Justice an advisory opinion on the use of force, which in our view is adequately and clearly set forth in the UN Charter.

C. OTHER INTERNATIONAL ORGANIZATIONS

1. Reorganization of International Hydrographic Organization

On October 23, 2007, President George W. Bush transmitted to the Senate for advice and consent to ratification the Protocol of Amendments to the Convention on the International Hydrographic Organization, done at Monaco on April 14, 2005. S. Treaty Doc. No. 110-9 (2007). The underlying convention was done at Monaco on May 3, 1967, and entered into force for the United States on September 22, 1970 (21 U.S.T. 1857; T.I.A.S. 6933; 751 U.N.T.S. 41). Excerpts follow from the President's letter of transmittal and from the report by the Department of State accompanying Secretary of State Condoleezza Rice's letter submitting the Protocol to the President.

Letter of Transmittal

*   *   *   *

The Protocol will facilitate the reorganization of the International Hydrographic Organization (IHO). The IHO, which is a technical and consultative international organization head-quartered in Monaco, facilitates safe and efficient maritime navigation throughout the world. It accomplishes these objectives by facilitating the coordination of the activities of national hydrographic offices, promoting uniformity in the nautical charts and documents generated by such offices, encouraging the adoption of reliable surveying methods, and fostering the development of the science of hydrography. Reorganization of the IHO will result in a more flexible, efficient, and visible organization.

Ratification of the Protocol would serve important U.S. interests. United States commercial shipping, the United States Navy, and the scientific research community rely heavily on hydrographic information collected and shared under the auspices of the IHO. The United States plays an important leadership role in the IHO and as a result enjoys expeditious and economical access to this information. Moreover, the United States has committed more resources than any other country to research, development, and evaluation of hydrographic instruments and therefore stands to benefit significantly from the efficiencies generated by this reorganization.

*   *   *   *

Report of the Department of State

*   *   *   *

. . . Rapidly changing technologies and increasing demands from the maritime community for up-to-date hydrographic instruments led States that are members of the IHO to push for its reform. In April 2002, the XVIth Conference of the IHO established the Strategic Planning Working Group (SPWG) to study the structure and processes of the IHO and develop appropriate recommendations on reform, including revisions to the Convention. At the direction of the Conference, the SPWG developed a series of recommendations intended to make the organization's decision-making process more efficient, streamline the membership application process to increase membership, and increase the visibility of the organization. The United States actively participated in the SPWG. Throughout the negotiations, the U.S. delegation had one key objective—adoption of recommendations that would facilitate a cost-effective reorganization of the IHO.

In April 2005, the Third IHO Extraordinary Conference adopted a series of recommendations to reorganize the organization to address weaknesses identified in the current organization. . . . The reorganization is intended to make the organization more responsive to Member States' needs by, inter alia, providing for faster decision-making through more regularly scheduled Conferences in which all Member States participate and annual meetings of a smaller, more dynamic representative body, the Council, through which Member States can oversee the organization between Conferences. Reorganization will consolidate the committee structure, which will result in improved communication mechanisms and better defined organizational goals and operating guidelines. Relationships with other intergovernmental organizations, such as the International Maritime Organization, and non-governmental associations, industry, and professional institutions will be expanded and improved to facilitate better understanding of the mission and goals of the IHO and ways through which the IHO can interact with, and support efforts of, other organizations with similar objectives.

Implementation of some of the recommendations requires amendments to the Convention. The Protocol of Amendments will amend the Convention by, inter alia, clarifying the respective functions of the organs of the organization, including those of the principal organ, the Conference (to be referred to as the "Assembly"); establishing a new organ, the Council, with responsibility for coordinating the activities of the organization during the period between two Assemblies; shortening the period between meetings of the Assembly from five years to three years to enable the organization to address significant policy concerns on a more timely basis; and streamlining the process by which States can become members, thereby facilitating increased Member State participation in the organization, greater worldwide chart coverage, and, as a result, improved safety of global navigation. These amendments do not change the fundamental technical and consultative nature of the organization.

* * * *

2. European Community

a. World Customs Organization

At its 109th/110th Sessions, held in June 2007, the World Customs Organization ("WCO") Policy Council adopted a recommendation to amend Articles VIII and XVIII of its convention in order to enable customs or economic unions to become contracting parties to the convention and thereby members of the WCO. At the same session, the WCO adopted a decision addressing the fact that the amendment was initiated by a request for membership by the European Communities ("EC") and noting that the amendment procedure is "likely to be a rather slow process since, in accordance with Article XX(c) of the Convention, an amendment cannot come into force until three months after the Belgian Ministry of Foreign Affairs has received notification of acceptance of the amendment from all of the Contracting Parties to the Convention."

In the decision, the WCO decided "that pending the entry into force of an amendment permitting Customs or Economic Unions to accede to the Convention, the European Communities shall, as an interim measure, be granted rights akin to those enjoyed by WCO Members, subject to [certain specified] special arrangements and conditions."

At a meeting of the WCO Policy Commission in Almaty, Kazakhstan in December 2007, the head of the U.S. delegation explained U.S. concerns with efforts to give the EC rights "akin to" membership in the WCO pending entry into force of the amendments. The Policy Commission accepted the U.S.

offer to provide a paper "outlining its legal concerns and suggesting a possible way forward" to providing the EC with a
substantial role in the WCO. A summary of the U.S. intervention is excerpted in major part below as included in the final
report of the meeting, available at *www.state.gov/sl/c8183.
htm.*

---

1. The Delegate from the United States intervened under this item
regarding the recent Council Decision regarding participation of
the European Community in the WCO. He noted that in June
2007, the WCO Council took action in an attempt to confer rights
"akin to" membership on the European Community (EC) on an
interim basis pending formal amendment of the WCO Convention.

2. The United States Delegate expressed that the United States
believes that the Council exceeded its authority under the current
text of the WCO Convention when it purported to grant rights
"akin to" membership to the EC. It is the United States position
that the "akin to" resolution (ATR) has no legal effect. The United
States acknowledges, however, that the ATR reflects the desire of
the WCO Membership, including the desire of the United States,
that the EC should have a substantial role in the WCO. The United
States, therefore, is prepared to accept as a political statement of
the WCO Membership those parts of the ATR that are consistent
with the WCO Convention and the Rules of Procedure. In addition, the United States considers that the meaning of draft amendment to Article VIII of the WCO Convention to permit EC
Membership must be formally clarified.

3. Accordingly, the United States urges the Secretariat to prepare a resolution for the June Policy Commission's consideration
and Council's adoption that includes a statement of the Parties'
intent and makes clear the Council's understanding that the proposed amendment to Article VIII allows the Council to make special provisions (a) affecting the vote both of Customs and Economic
Unions that have become parties to the WCO Convention (and
thus Members of the WCO), and of States that are parties to the
WCO Convention (and thus Members of the WCO) that are also
members of such Unions; and (b) that, where a Customs and

Economic Union becomes a party to the WCO Convention and votes, States parties that are also members of such a Union cannot exercise their right to vote.

*   *   *   *

b. International Coffee Organization

In September 2007 the International Coffee Organization ("ICO") concluded negotiation of a new International Coffee Agreement ("ICA 2007"). *See* Chapter 11.D.3. During the negotiations the United States worked to revise provisions on ICO membership and distribution of votes. Article 40(4) provides for the EC to join as a single member, on behalf of the 27 Member States of the EU, upon a declaration by the EC that it has exclusive legal competence in the areas covered by the Agreement. Article 12(5) allocates votes to the EC in the same manner as other members (five basic votes and additional votes based on import volume). The new approach eliminated the current, anomalous practice of allocating votes to member states of the EU as individual ICO members, who also had been represented as a block by the EC, including in voting.

Cross References

World Meteorological Organization amendments, **Chapter 4.B.3.**
Role of Human Rights Council, **Chapter 6.A.4.**
Legal status of ESC Committee, **Chapter 6.A.5.**
Immunities of international organizations, **Chapter 10.E.**
International Coffee Organization amendments, **Chapter 11.D.3.**

CHAPTER 8

International Claims and State Responsibility

A. GOVERNMENT TO GOVERNMENT CLAIMS: INTERNATIONAL LAW COMMISSION

1. Draft Articles on State Responsibility

On February 1, 2007, the United States submitted comments to the UN Secretary-General concerning the International Law Commission's draft articles on state responsibility, at the invitation of the General Assembly (U.N. Doc. A/RES/59/35 (2004)). The full text of the U.S. submission is set forth below as reproduced in U.N. Doc. A/62/63/Add.1.

---

*   *   *   *

II. Comments on any future action regarding the articles on responsibility of States for internationally wrongful acts

United States of America

1. The United States of America once again extends its congratulations to the International Law Commission for completing in 2001 its important project on the topic of the responsibility of States for internationally wrongful acts and its appreciation to the five Special Rapporteurs who contributed significantly to the completion of the project.

2. The Sixth Committee and the General Assembly have considered the future of the draft articles on two occasions. In 2001, the General Assembly welcomed the draft articles in Resolution 56/83,

which contained the text of the draft articles as an annex, and "commend[ed] them to the attention of Governments without prejudice to the question of their future adoption or other appropriate action". In 2004, the General Assembly postponed further consideration of the final form of the draft articles in the General Assembly until the sixty-second session in 2007.

3. The United States believes that the action of the General Assembly in 2001 in commending the draft articles to the attention of Governments was the right course of action to adopt.

4. There is a large body of well-established state practice pertaining to many of the issues covered by the draft articles. The draft articles have shown themselves to be useful in their current, non-binding form, as a guide to States and other international actors on either what the law is or how the law might be progressively developed. It is difficult to see what would be gained by the adoption of a convention. Indeed, the negotiation of a convention would risk undermining the very important work that has been undertaken by the Commission on this topic, particularly if a significant number of States did not ratify the resulting convention. For these reasons, the United States believes that no further action need be taken on this topic.

III. Information on State Practice regarding the articles on responsibility of States for internationally wrongful acts

United States of America

The following table provides information on decisions of United States courts referring to the draft articles on state responsibility since October 2001:

U.S. Court of Appeals	*Compagnie Noga d'Importation et d'Exportation S.A. v. Russian Federation*	361 F.3d 676, U.S. App. LEXIS 4983 (2d Cir. N.Y. 2004)	p. 619 and note 13	Article 4 and commentary, para 4 (conduct of organ of a State)
U.S. District Court	*Villeda Aldana v. Fresh Del Monte Produce, Inc.*	305 F. Supp. 2d 1285 (S.D. Fla. 2003)	p. 1303	Article 8 (conduct directed or controlled by a State)

2. Draft Articles on Diplomatic Protection

In May 2007 the United States submitted comments to the UN Secretary-General concerning the International Law Commission's draft articles on diplomatic protection, at the invitation of the General Assembly (U.N. Doc. A/RES/61/35 (2006)). The full text of the U.S. submission is set forth below as reproduced in U.N. Doc. A/62/118 at 8–12. The text of the draft articles is reprinted in Chapter IV of the Report of the International Law Commission on its Fifty-eighth session (2006), U.N. Doc. A/61/10, available at *http://untreaty.un. org/ilc/reports/2006/2006report.htm.*

* * * *

The Government of the United States of America appreciates the work of the members of the International Law Commission, in particular the Special Rapporteur, Professor John Dugard, for their valuable contribution to the realm of diplomatic protection. The subject is an important one and we welcome the adoption on second reading by the International Law Commission of the draft articles of diplomatic protection and the commentaries thereto.

The United States does not believe that it would be advisable to attempt to adopt a binding instrument on this topic. There is a large body of well-established State practice pertaining to many of the issues covered by the draft articles. In light of this, our comments will only highlight a few key issues.

The United States welcomes the changes made by the Commission over the past year to a number of the provisions in preliminary drafts of the articles to reflect more accurately customary international law and to clarify expressly that some articles, such as article 8, represent a progressive development of the law.[4] For example, we think it is useful that paragraph 8 of the commentary on draft article 1 makes clear that diplomatic protection does not include

---

[4] Article 8 is not reflected in customary international law, particularly in terms of its definition of "refugee", which is without any legal foundation.

demarches or other diplomatic action that do not involve the invocation of the legal responsibility of another State, such as informal requests for corrective action. We also note that paragraph 2 of the commentary to draft article 2 reaffirms that a State is under no obligation to exercise diplomatic protection, since the question of whether to espouse claims is a sovereign prerogative, the exercise of which necessarily implicates other considerations of national interest.

The United States is pleased that the formulation by the draft articles of the principle of exhaustion of remedies, taking into account the commentary, is in substantial conformity with the customary law rule. Specifically, the United States takes the position that under customary international law local remedies do not have to be exhausted where the local remedies are obviously futile or manifestly ineffective, a formulation that conveys the same substance as draft article 15(a). Moreover, paragraph 4 of the commentary correctly elaborates that neither a low possibility of success nor the difficulties and costs of further appeals are sufficient and that the test is not whether a successful outcome is likely or possible but whether the municipal system of the respondent State is reasonably capable of providing effective relief. Draft article 15(d) provides that local remedies do not have to be exhausted where the injured person is manifestly precluded from pursuing local remedies. Paragraph 11 of the commentary makes clear that this is an exercise in progressive development that must be narrowly construed, with the burden of proof on the injured person to show not merely that there are serious obstacles and difficulties in the way of exhausting local remedies, but that he is "manifestly" precluded from pursuing such remedies. Paragraph 14 of the commentary to draft article 14 on exhaustion of domestic remedies also clarifies that exhaustion of local remedies may result from the fact that another person has submitted the substance of the same claim before a court of the respondent State.

The United States believes that certain other provisions of the articles deviate from the State practice representing customary international law without a sufficient public policy rationale. Our comments on these provisions are grouped into four categories: continuous nationality and the *dies ad quem*; extinct corporations;

protection of shareholders; and draft article 19 on "recommended practice."

Continuous Nationality and the *dies ad quem*

The draft articles honour the established principle of continuity of nationality[5] as a prerequisite to the exercise of diplomatic protection on behalf of natural and corporate persons in articles 5 and 10 and, by implication, in articles 7 and 8. We note that this continuity of nationality between two dates is required by customary international law, not a progressive development of the law as stated in paragraph 2 of the commentary to draft article 5. What is a progressive development of the law, however, is setting the date of the official presentation of the claim as the *dies ad quem*. This approach diverges from customary international law in that it does not extend the requirement of continuity of nationality beyond the date of official presentation of the claim to the date of resolution, except in cases where, subsequent to presentation, the injured person acquires the nationality of the respondent State or, as stated in the commentary, acquires the nationality of a third State in bad faith. Our view is that the customary international law rule is that reflected in the clear record of state practice and in the most recent articulation of the rule that appears in the award of the arbitral tribunal in the case of *The Loewen Group Inc. v. United States of America*. The Tribunal in that case stated, "[i]n international law parlance, there must be a continuous national

---

[5]   Some of the limitations on claiming nationality for purposes of diplomatic protection are set forth in the commentaries. For example, paragraph 13 of the commentary to article 2 provides that, if the injured person has in bad faith retained that nationality until the date of presentation and thereafter acquired the nationality of a third State, equity would require that the claim be terminated. Although article 5(2) provides that a State may exercise diplomatic protection under certain circumstances in respect of a person who was not its national at the date of injury, paragraph 10 of the commentary makes clear that this exception will not apply where the person has acquired a new nationality for commercial reasons connected with the bringing of the claim. Paragraph 1 of the commentary to article 10 notes that corporations generally change nationality only by being re-formed or reincorporated in another State, in which case the corporation assumes a new personality, thereby breaking the continuity of nationality of the corporation.

identity from the date of the events giving rise to the claim . . . through the date of the resolution of the claim . . .". The commentary cites no convincing authority that nationality at both the date of injury and the date of official presentation of the claim is sufficient, but instead finds that requiring nationality to be maintained to the date of resolution of the claim "could be contrary" to the interests of the person suffering the injury. It thereby treats the date of the official presentation of the claim as the *dies ad quem* as a policy decision, not one grounded in customary international law.

Extinct corporations

Draft article 10(3) provides for a State to exercise diplomatic protection in respect of a corporation which was its national at the date of injury and which, as the result of the injury, has ceased to exist according to the law of the State of incorporation. Draft article 11 creates two exceptions to the general rule that only the State of incorporation may exercise diplomatic protection in respect of claims of that corporation, one of which is for an injury to an extinct corporation. Specifically, draft article 11(a) would allow the States of nationality of shareholders to exercise diplomatic protection with respect to claims arising from injuries to a corporation where "the corporation has ceased to exist according to the law of the State of incorporation for a reason unrelated to the injury". As we explained in our comments of 28 December 2005 on the draft articles,[6] the United States has reservations about articles 10(3) and 11(a). First, the articles neither reflect customary international law nor have a rational basis for their existence. For example, although the commentary to draft article 10(3) characterizes the issue as one that troubled four judges in the *Barcelona Traction* case, other than the separate opinion of Judge Gros, the opinions do not address the issue of the State of incorporation's right to pursue a claim on behalf of a defunct corporation.[7]

---

[6]   *See* A/CN.4/561.

[7]   Jessup sep. op. at 193 (opining that a State may extend diplomatic protection to shareholders who are its nationals where the State of incorporation has liquidated or wound up the corporation after the injury was inflicted by some third State; does not address the rights of the State of incorporation); Gros sep. op. at 277 ("[I]f the company's State had started an

Furthermore, Judge Gros does not suggest that the State's right of espousal should last in perpetuity, as contemplated by draft article 10(3). Further, despite the suggestions to the contrary in paragraphs 2–7 of the commentary to article 11, the International Court of Justice left the questions set forth in draft article 11 very much undecided in its Judgment of February 5, 1970 in the *Barcelona Traction* case, since the circumstances for their consideration did not arise in the case.

Second, the articles expand the rights of succession beyond those provided for in the law of the state of incorporation. For example, draft article 11(a) creates the anomalous situation of granting States of shareholders a greater right to pursue claims of a corporation than the State of incorporation itself provides to the shareholders. Furthermore, draft article 10(3) undermines the benefits of finality inherent in municipal survival and corporate wind-up statutes. Third, not only may the articles result in a change in the nationality of the claim after a corporation becomes extinct, depending on whether draft article 10(3) or draft article 11(a) is operative, but draft article 11(a) could result in multiple States of shareholders espousing the same injury to the corporation.

Protection of Shareholders

Draft article 12 restates the customary international law rule that a State of nationality of shareholders can exercise diplomatic protection on their behalf when they have suffered direct losses. Although the commentary to draft article 11 provides in paragraph 1 that only "where the act complained of is aimed at the direct right of the shareholders does the shareholder have an independent right of action", citing to paragraph 47 of the *Barcelona Traction* case, that sentence (read in the context of paragraph 47)

---

action it could not be nonsuited through the disappearance of the company. And even if such action had been instituted after the disappearance of the company, it is difficult to see why the State of the company should be unable to make a claim in respect of the unlawful act which was the root cause of the disappearance."); Fitzmaurice sep. op. at 101–02 (questioning need for continuity of nationality after date of injury); Riphagen dissent (demise of corporation irrelevant since right of diplomatic protection of shareholders is independent right).

is setting forth one example of a type of action that would result in infringement of a right of the shareholder. Paragraph 47 makes it clear that intent is not necessarily a prerequisite to a direct infringement of a right of the shareholders. Rather, the correct standard is the one articulated in draft article 12 itself: whether the shareholders have suffered direct losses. Shareholders may suffer direct losses even when the action is not "aimed" at their direct rights.

The United States does not believe that draft article 11(b) reflects customary international law. Article 11(b) provides for the State of nationality of shareholders to espouse corporate claims where the corporation has the nationality of the State causing injury to it, and incorporation under the law of that State is required as a precondition for doing business there. As explained in our comments of 28 December 2005, the commentary does not provide persuasive authority for this proposition. All of the cases provided by the commentary as evidence for this exception were based on a special agreement between two States granting a right to shareholders to claim compensation, or an agreement between the injuring State and its national corporation granting compensation to the shareholders. Not only was the issue not before the court in *Barcelona Traction*, but the case concerning Electronica Sicula, S.p.A. (ELSI) involved a claim under a treaty that expressly provided for indirect claims by shareholders and thus cannot be read to support the proposition that this exception is an element of customary international law, notwithstanding the commentary's description in paragraph 11.

Article 19 on "recommended practice"

We are concerned with inclusion of article 19 on "recommended practice" which is not appropriately placed in the articles since, as acknowledged in paragraph 1 of the commentary, they have not acquired the status of customary rules nor are they susceptible to transformation into rules of law in the progressive development of the law.[8] The fact that the commentary argues that

---

[8]   Although paragraph 1 of the commentary confirms that draft article 19 is recommendatory and not prescriptive language and paragraph 3 confirms that a State is not obliged under international law to exercise diplomatic protection, article 19(a) and (b) provide that a State entitled to exercise diplomatic

they are "desirable practices" does not render it appropriate to place them in the text of the articles.

In conclusion, the draft articles deviate from settled customary international law on a limited set of issues. Nonetheless, it is doubtful that the expense and other burdens of a diplomatic conference are warranted. The negotiation of a convention would risk undermining the very important work that has been undertaken by the Commission on this topic, particularly if a significant number of States did not ratify the resulting convention. Instead, the United States believes that the General Assembly should adopt a resolution, in which it notes the draft articles, with the text to be annexed to the resolution. This would allow States and other bodies to draw on the draft articles in their present form, giving due account as to whether a draft article correctly codifies customary international law or constitutes an appropriate progressive development of the law.

B. CLAIMS OF INDIVIDUALS: NAZI ERA

1. *Gross v. German Foundation*

On August 16, 2007, the U.S. District Court for the District of New Jersey dismissed claims brought by beneficiaries of the German Foundation "Remembrance, Responsibility, and the Future" ("Foundation") for interest owed on German company contributions to the Foundation. *Gross v. German Foundation Industrial Initiative*, 499 F. Supp. 2d 606 (2007), as amended.

---

protection should give due consideration to that possibility and take into account, wherever feasible, the views of injured persons with regard to resort to diplomatic protection and the reparation to be sought. Article 19(c) provides that a State should transfer to the injured person any compensation obtained for the injury from the responsible State subject to any reasonable deductions, although paragraph 5 of the commentary confirms that the protecting State has no obligation to do so, and in any event that it would not be inappropriate for that State to make reasonable deductions from the compensation transferred, such as to recoup the costs of State efforts to obtain compensation for its nationals, or to recover the costs of goods or services provided by the State to them.

> *See Digest 2006* at 507–17 for discussion of the Third Circuit
> opinion reversing the prior decision of the district court
> (which had dismissed the claims as presenting nonjusticiable
> political questions) and remanding. The Third Circuit found
> that "there is a difference between a suit for reparations and
> a suit to enforce an alleged contract for 'interest.'"
>   In dismissing the case on remand, the district court con-
> cluded that there was no contractual basis for the claims and,
> in the alternative, if the Joint Statement were found to create
> contractual obligations, it did not require the German com-
> panies to pay more than the DM 5.1 billion that they had
> already paid. Excerpts follow from the introduction to the opin-
> ion summarizing the key facts and the court's conclusions.

* * * *

July 17, 2000, was the occasion of one of the most remarkable
diplomatic achievements since the end of World War II. The efforts
of two extraordinary diplomats, Secretary Stuart E. Eizenstat, representing the United States, and Count Otto Lambsdorff, representing the Federal Republic of Germany, had, after approximately
19 months of negotiations, secured the signing of two documents
that would lead to the creation of the Foundation, "Remembrance,
Responsibility and Future" (the "Foundation"), to compensate the
victims for wrongs against them committed by German companies
during the Nazi-era and to provide an exclusive forum in which
the victims could assert their claims.

The documents were i) the Joint Statement on Occasion of the
Final Plenary Meeting Concluding International Talks on the Pre-
paration of the Foundation, "Remembrance, Responsibility, and
the Future" (the "Joint Statement") and ii) Agreement between the
Government of the Federal Republic of Germany and the Government of the United States of America concerning the Foundation
"Remembrance, Responsibility and the Future" (the "Executive
Agreement"). Shortly thereafter, the German Bundestag enacted a
Law on the Creation of a Foundation "Remembrance, Responsibility and Future" (the "Foundation Law") that, among other things,
established the Foundation as a German sovereign instrumentality

and as the "exclusive remedy and forum" for resolution of claims against German companies arising out of the Nazi-era and World War II. . . .

. . . The Joint Statement provided, among other significant provisions, that DM 10 billion contributed by the German Government and German companies was to be distributed to former National Socialist slave and forced laborers, for other personal injury, for damages to property and for a Future Fund to fund ongoing projects to prevent religious and ethnic intolerance in Germany.

The Joint Statement provided that the DM 5 billion contribution of the German companies "shall be due and payable to the Foundation and payments from the Foundation shall begin once all lawsuits against German companies arising out of the National Socialist era and World War II pending in U.S. courts . . . are finally dismissed with prejudice by the courts.". . . Para. 4(d) of the Joint Statement concluded: "German company funds will continue to be collected on a schedule and in a manner that will ensure that the interest earned thereon before and after their delivery to the Foundation will reach at least 100 million DM."

* * * *

The German Government made its payments in a timely manner. On various occasions after the May 30, 2001 Bundestag announcement [that adequate legal security had been achieved], the German companies paid, according to [the German Economy Foundation Initiative ("GEFI")] (but disputed by Plaintiffs), DM 5.1 billion to the Foundation. . . .

. . . [A] dispute has arisen between the Plaintiffs in the two cases pending before the Court, who are victims entitled to compensation from the Foundation, and the German companies that were the members of GEFI. Plaintiffs contend that the German companies have failed to comply with their obligations under Para. 4, and, in particular, to pay to the Foundation the interest specified in that paragraph. It is the Plaintiffs' contention that this language contains no ceiling and requires the companies to pay interest on all funds the Initiative collected from the time of their receipt of those funds until payment to the Foundation, or in the alternative, to pay interest on the companies' share from December, 1999.

*   *   *   *

The German companies contend that the additional DM 100 million was a fixed amount to be added to the DM 10 billion cap to enable the representatives of the victims to reach agreement on the allocation of the DM 10 billion capped amount.

Having reviewed the full record submitted in connection with the pending motions as well as the briefs and arguments of counsel, the court concludes as follows:

1. The Joint Statement is a political document that does not confer upon the signatories, or any portion of them, contractual rights which can be enforced in United States courts. Consequently, Defendants' motion to dismiss each of these cases should be granted.

2. In the alternative, were the Joint Statement found to create contractual obligations between Plaintiffs and the Defendants, enforceable in United States courts, Para. 4(d) concerning interest is ambiguous, requiring resort to the history of the negotiations to determine its meaning.

3. The history of the negotiations . . . establishes, as the Defendants contend, i) in December, 1999, the negotiating parties reached an understanding that the German Government and the German companies would pay into the Foundation a capped amount of DM 10 billion in exchange for "legal peace" with no agreement to pay interest; ii) in March, 2000, the negotiating parties reached an understanding that GEFI would pay an additional DM 100 billion denominated as "interest" in order to enable the victim groups to reach agreement on the allocation of the DM 10 billion, but there was no other commitment on the part of the German companies to pay interest in addition to the DM 100 million; between March, 2000, and July 17, 2000, when the Joint Statement was executed, Secretary Eizenstat and the Plaintiffs' attorneys made repeated demands that the German companies pay interest on their DM 5 billion share of the DM 10 [m]illion total sum. All of these demands were rejected, and as a consequence Para. 4(d) of the Joint Statement cannot

be construed as requiring the German companies to pay to the Foundation more than DM 5.1 billion.

4. If this court has authority under the Joint Statement to do so, it would construe the Joint Statement as not requiring the German companies to pay the Foundation more than DM 5.1 billion and deny the summary judgment motions of the . . . Plaintiffs and grant summary judgment to the Defendants, dismissing both complaints on the merits.

*   *   *   *

The very title of the instrument—Joint Statement—negates the creation of a legally binding agreement. In international practice, governments may make "joint statements" or "declarations" that summarize a conference and express mutual intentions but do not establish legal obligations enforceable in any domestic court. The United States has signed numerous such documents that have been described as "not a treaty or agreement. . . ." The International Law Commission, when developing the Vienna Convention on the Law of Treaties, excluded such documents from its definition of "treaty" because they are non-binding. See Report of the International Law Commission to the General Assembly, 1958 Y.B. Int'l Law Comm. 96–97 (1959). Note may be made of the fact that the Executive Agreement was signed by officials of the United States and German Governments accredited to enter into agreements binding on their governments. At the same signing ceremony, the United States and Germany had the Joint Statement signed by other people who were not so accredited.

That the Joint Statement speaks the language of diplomatic expectations is further evidenced by the fact that its Para. 4(b) provides that the United States and German Governments "will sign an Executive Agreement . . . and [s]uch agreement contains the obligation undertaken by the United States to assist in achieving all-embracing and enduring legal peace for German companies." Other paragraphs of the Joint Statement provide for the execution of the Executive Agreement, and still other paragraphs impose obligations upon Central and Eastern European States and Israel. In all this, there is nothing to suggest that the private lawyer signatories can extract from the comprehensive Joint Statement selected provisions for judicial enforcement.

The language of the Joint Statement is not that used to create enforceable obligations. The signatories are "participants," not "parties." After the Preamble, the signatories "declare" rather than "undertake" or "agree." . . .

Defendants contrast the language of the Executive Agreement with that of the Joint Statement. Unlike the Joint Statement, which avoids all "agreement" language, the Executive Agreement is replete with language of "agreement" from its title to constant use of the terms "parties," "agree," and "agreed."

*   *   *   *

2. *Mandowsky v. Dresdner Bank, AG*

On July 20, 2007, the Third Circuit Court of Appeals affirmed the decision of the U.S. District Court for the District of New Jersey denying plaintiffs' motion to set aside a prior voluntary dismissal of their case that they had requested in order to seek compensation from the Foundation "Remembrance, Responsibility, and the Future." The Third Circuit issued its decision in a brief non-precedential opinion, explaining that

In this case . . . we have concluded that neither a full memorandum explanation nor a precedential opinion is necessary. Judge Bassler's ruling [in the district court] is a thorough statement of his reasoning and fully supports his order. No further refutation of the Appellants' allegations of error is necessary.

In re: Nazi Era Cases Against German Defendants Litigation, 240 Fed. Appx. 980 (3d Cir. 2007), *cert. denied, Mandowsky v. Dresdner Bank,* 128 S. Ct. 887 (2008). *See Digest 2006* at 517–21 for discussion of Judge Bassler's opinion in 236 F.R.D. 231 (D.N.J. 2006) and the U.S. brief as *amicus curiae* in the Third Circuit.

Cross References

Cases presenting non-justiciable political questions, **Chapter 5.**
   A.2.a and B *and* **Chapter 9.A.2. and B.**
Differences between responsibility of states and of international
   organizations, **Chapter 7.A.**
Claims under NAFTA, **Chapter 11.B.**
Claims under WTO dispute settlement, **Chapter 11.C.**
Arbitration with Canada re compliance with Softwood Lumber
   Agreement before London Court of International
   Arbitration, **Chapter 11.D.6.**

CHAPTER 9

Diplomatic Relations, Succession, and Continuity of States

A. STATUS ISSUES

1. Kosovo

On December 10, 2007, John B. Bellinger, III, Department of State Legal Adviser, addressed the World Legal Forum at The Hague on the topic of peaceful settlement of disputes. Mr. Bellinger discussed the U.S. involvement in efforts to resolve the status of Kosovo as excerpted below. The full text of the address is available at *www.state.gov/s/l/c8183.htm*; *see also* Chapter 17.A.1.

* * * *

Finally, and perhaps most important at this moment, the United States has consistently demonstrated its commitment to working toward a peaceful settlement in Kosovo. Kosovo's status remains in urgent need of resolution. NATO took action in 1999 to respond to a tragic crisis. The UN Security Council, recognizing the distinct threat that the Kosovo situation posed to international peace and security, immediately followed by adopting Resolution 1244. That resolution set in motion a political process aimed toward establishing a lasting peace. For over fifteen months, the UN's Special Envoy, Martii Ahtisaari, led an intensive effort designed to resolve Kosovo's final status, culminating in March 2007 in the submission of the Ahtisaari plan and its recommendation for supervised independence. This was followed by prolonged negotiations in New York last spring and summer that failed to produce an agreement in the Security Council. Last Friday, the EU-U.S.-Russia Troika, which had facilitated high-level discussions between Kosovo and Serbia during a further 120-day period that began last August, submitted a report on its work to the UN Secretary General. Through all this, the United States has worked closely with our European partners, and has strongly supported the UN process and the efforts of the Troika.

All of us, of course, would have preferred for the parties to reach agreement on the future status of Kosovo. But at this point, after intensive engagement by the Troika, it is now clear that there is no realistic chance of such an agreement. We therefore believe that the Ahtisaari Plan offers the best way forward. By its terms, existing Resolution 1244 remains in effect, and the resolution provides a solid basis for the international community to proceed. The United States will continue to engage in consultations with the European Union during the next month on how best to achieve a durable solution for Kosovo as we enter 2008.

*   *   *   *

In a press statement also dated December 10, 2007, Gonzalo Gallegos, Department of State Director of Press Relations, noted that the mandate of the U.S.–EU–Russia Troika ended with submission of its report and stated: "We continue to believe that implementation of the Ahtisaari Plan will promote stability in the region and enable both Serbia and Kosovo to move forward on the Euro-Atlantic path. . . . The people of Kosovo and the region urgently need clarity about their future." The press statement is available at *www. state.gov/r/pa/prs/ps/2007/dec/96625.htm*.

As indicated in Mr. Bellinger's remarks, the Troika submitted its report to UN Secretary General Ban Ki-moon on December 4, 2007. The Secretary General transmitted the report to the Security Council by letter of December 10. U.N. Doc. S/2007/723. Excerpts follow from the report's summary and conclusions. Other key documents from the period of the Troika's negotiations beginning August 1, 2007, are provided as annexes to the report.

Summary

1. We, a Troika of representatives from the European Union, the United States and the Russian Federation, have spent the last four months conducting negotiations between Belgrade and Pristina on the future status of Kosovo. Our objective was to facilitate an agreement between the parties. The negotiations were conducted within the framework of Security Council resolution 1244 (1999) and the guiding principles of the Contact Group [France, Germany, Italy, Russia, the United Kingdom, and the United States] (see S/2005/709). In the course of our work, the parties discussed a wide range of options, such as full independence, supervised independence, territorial partition, substantial autonomy, confederal arrangements and even a status silent "agreement to disagree"

2. The Troika was able to facilitate high-level, intense and substantive discussions between Belgrade and Pristina. Nonetheless, the parties were unable to reach an agreement on the final status of Kosovo. Neither party was willing to cede its position on the fundamental question of sovereignty over Kosovo. This is regrettable, as a negotiated settlement is in the best interests of both parties.

* * * *

Conclusions

11. Throughout the negotiations both parties were fully engaged. After 120 days of intensive negotiations, however, the parties were unable to reach an agreement on Kosovo's status. Neither side was willing to yield on the basic question of sovereignty.

12. Nevertheless, despite this fundamental difference on status, which the Troika was unable to bridge, we believe this process served a useful purpose. We gave the parties an opportunity to find a solution to their differences. Under our auspices, the parties engaged in the most sustained and intense high-level direct dialogue since hostilities ended in Kosovo in 1999. Through this process, the parties discovered areas where their interests aligned. The parties also agreed on the need to promote and protect multi-ethnic societies and address difficult issues holding back reconciliation, particularly the fate of missing persons and the return of displaced persons. Perhaps most important, Belgrade and Pristina reaffirmed the centrality of their European perspective to their future relations,

with both sides restating their desire to seek a future under the common roof of the European Union.

13. While differences between the parties remain unchanged, the Troika has nevertheless been able to extract important commitments from the parties. In particular, both parties have pledged to refrain from actions that might jeopardize the security situation in Kosovo or elsewhere and not use violence, threats or intimidation (see [Troika assessment of negotiations: principal conclusions,] annex VII). They made these commitments without prejudice to their positions on status. Both parties must be reminded that their failure to live up to these commitments will affect the achievement of the European future that they both seek.

14. We note that Kosovo and Serbia will continue to be tied together due to the special nature of their relationship, especially in its historical, human, geographical, economical and cultural dimensions. As noted by Contact Group Ministers at their meeting in New York on 27 September, [2007, *see* Annex III] the resolution of Kosovo's status is crucial to the stability and security of the Western Balkans and Europe as a whole. We believe the maintenance of peace in the region and the avoidance of violence is of paramount importance and therefore look to the parties to stand by their commitments. We, furthermore, strongly believe that the settlement of Kosovo's status would contribute to the fulfillment of the European aspirations of both parties.

> In a statement to the Security Council concerning the future of Kosovo on December 19, 2007, Ambassador Zalmay Khalilzad, U.S. Permanent Representative to the United Nations, reiterated U.S. support for adoption of the Ahtisaari proposal and its basis in international law, as excerpted below. The full text of Ambassador Khalilzad's statement is available at *www.usun newyork.usmission.gov/press_releases/20071219_381.html.*
> At the end of 2007 the Security Council had taken no action.

---

*   *   *   *

Our discussion today takes place against the backdrop of the last remaining unresolved conflict in the Balkans, and a source of continuing instability in Europe. Kosovo is a unique situation—it is a land that used to be part of a country that no longer exists and that has been administered for eight years by the United Nations with the ultimate objective of definitely resolving Kosovo's status. This issue is, as several colleagues have pointed out, sui generis and therefore, any solution to this problem is not a precedent for any other conflict or dispute.

It is important to consider this issue in its recent historical context. The policies of ethnic cleansing that the Milosevic government pursued against the Kosovar people forever ensured that Kosovo would never again return to rule by Belgrade. This is an unavoidable fact and the direct consequence of those barbaric policies. And it places the Kosovo issue in a fifteen-year history of recent Balkan conflicts that resulted in the independence of every other constituent part of the former Yugoslavia.

*   *   *   *

. . . The status quo in Kosovo is unsustainable and threatens to spark new regional instability. We must swiftly act on the one proposal on the table: the plan of the UN Special Envoy Martti Ahtisaari. In doing so, we shall act in accordance with international law and Security Council Resolution 1244. 1244 provides an appropriate legal framework to reach a sustainable final status for Kosovo, as well as the EU and NATO presences to enable that outcome.

2. U.S. Relations with Taiwan

As discussed in Chapter 1.A.1., on April 5, 2007, the United States filed a motion to dismiss a case brought by individuals residing in Taiwan seeking a declaratory judgment that they were United States nationals. *Lin v. United States,* Civil Action No. 06-1825(RMC)(D.D.C.). The United States argued that the Immigration and Nationality Act did not provide a basis for the claims because the United States is not sovereign over Taiwan, and therefore the plaintiffs had no claim as U.S. nationals. Sections of the U.S. motion demonstrating that the United States does not exercise sovereignty over Taiwan, and that determinations of sovereignty are reserved to the executive branch and are nonjusticiable political questions, are excerpted below (footnotes and citations to the complaint omitted). The case was pending at the end of 2007.

The full text of the U.S. submissions is available at *www. state.gov/s/l/c8183.htm.*

* * * *

As a matter of law, the relationship between the United States and Taiwan derives solely and exclusively from Exec. Order No. 13014 of August 15, 1996, 61 Fed. Reg. 42963 (superseding Exec. Order No. 12143 of June 22, 1979, 44 Fed. Reg. 37191), and the Taiwan Relations Act of 1979, 22 U.S.C. 3301, et seq. That intricate relationship does not involve the United States exercising sovereignty over Taiwan.

Prior to 1979, the United States recognized the government of the Republic of China ("ROC") and considered Taiwan to be part of the ROC, belying plaintiffs' assertion that "Taiwan has been an occupied territory of the United States" since the end of World War II. The Mutual Defense Treaty signed between the United States and the ROC in 1954 specified that the ROC included the territory of Taiwan. *See* Mutual Defense Treaty, Article VI, Treaties and International Acts Series 3178 (1955) ("the terms 'territorial' and 'territories' shall mean in respect of the Republic of China, Taiwan and the Pescadores; and in respect of the United States of America, the inland territories in the West Pacific under its jurisdiction"). In 1979, President Carter terminated the Mutual Defense Treaty, *see* U.S. Department of State Bulletin, Vol. 79 (1979), No. 2023 at 25, but that does not negate the fact that prior to 1979, it was the policy of the United States that the ROC included Taiwan. Significantly, prior to 1979, the United States negotiated with the ROC, in the capacity as sovereign, numerous other international agreements that applied to Taiwan. *See generally Treaties in Force* (2006) at 361, 362.

On December 30, 1978, President Carter issued a memorandum maintaining that the "United States has announced that on January 1, 1979, it is recognizing the government of the People's

Republic of China as the sole legal government of China and is terminating diplomatic relations with the Republic of China." 44 Fed. Reg. 1075. President Carter further stated that the "[e]xisting international agreements and arrangements in force between the United States and Taiwan shall continue in force." *Id*. (emphasis added). Besides continuing the international agreements that the United States entered into with Taiwan prior to January 1, 1979, President Carter's memorandum stated that "[a]s President of the United States, I have constitutional responsibility for the conduct of the foreign relations of the nation." 44 Fed. Reg. 1075; *see also Banco Nacional de Cuba v. Sabbatino*, 376 U.S. 398, 410 (1964) ("[p]olitical recognition [of a government] is exclusively a function of the Executive"). In his memorandum, President Carter also stressed that the "American people will maintain commercial, cultural, and other relations with the people on Taiwan without official government representation and without diplomatic relations." 44 Fed. Reg. 1075. In executive orders in 1979 and 1996, the Executive further spelled out the manner in which the United States is to maintain unofficial relations with the people of Taiwan. *See* Exec. Order No. 13014 (August 15, 1996); Exec. Order No. 12143 (June 22, 1979). That 1996 Executive Order also specified that the "[a]greements and arrangements referred to in paragraph (B) of President Carter's memorandum of December 30, 1978, entitled 'Relations With the People on Taiwan' (44 FR 1075) shall, unless otherwise terminated or modified in accordance with law, continue in force." Exec. Order No. 13104 (August 15, 1996).

Besides issuing executive orders and presidential memorandums concerning the status of Taiwan, the United States also issued a series of joint communiqués between 1972 and 1982 with the People's Republic of China ("PRC"). Those communiqués included discussion of the status of Taiwan. In the February 28, 1972, Communiqué, the United States acknowledged "that all Chinese on either side of the Taiwan Strait maintain there is but one China and that Taiwan is a part of China." *See* United States of America–People's Republic of China Joint Communiqué of Feb. 27, 1972 [The Shanghai Communiqué]—U.S. Department of State Bulletin, Vol. 66 (1972), No. 1708, at 435 (attached as Exhibit 1). In 1979, the two countries issued another Joint Communiqué regarding the establishment of diplomatic relations between the PRC and the United States. *See* United States of America–People's Republic of China Joint Communiqué of January 1, 1979 on Establishment of Diplomatic Relations—U.S. Department of State Bulletin, Vol. 79 (1979), No. 2022, at 25 (attached as Exhibit 2). In that Communiqué, the United States again acknowledged the "Chinese position that there is but one China and Taiwan is part of China." *Id*. In a third Communiqué in 1982, the United States agreed that "[r]espect for each other's sovereignty and territorial integrity and non-interference in each other's internal affairs constitute the fundamental principles guiding United States China relations." *See* United States of America-People's Republic of China Joint Communiqué of Aug. 17, 1982—Weekly Compilation of Presidential Documents (August 23, 1982), at 1039 (attached as Exhibit 3). The United States and the PRC also "agreed that the people of the United States would continue to maintain cultural, commercial, and other unofficial relations with the people of Taiwan." *Id*.

The political branches have also charted the United States' relationship with Taiwan through the Taiwan Relations Act of 1979, 48 U.S.C. § 3301, which was passed by Congress and signed into law by the President. Congress found that the enactment of this statute was "necessary—(1) to help maintain peace, security, and stability in the Western Pacific; and (2) to promote the foreign policy of the United States by authorizing the continuation of commercial, cultural, and other relations between the people of the United States and the people of Taiwan." *See* 22 U.S.C. § 3301(a). Furthermore, it declared that the policy of the United States is, *inter alia*, "to make clear that the United States decision to establish diplomatic relations with the People's Republic of China rests upon the expectation that the future of Taiwan will be determined by peaceful means." 22 U.S.C. § 3301(b)(3). Congress specifically stated in the Taiwan Relation Act that it approved "the continuation in force of all treaties and other international agreements, including multilateral conventions, entered into by the United States and the governing authorities on *Taiwan recognized by the United States as the Republic of China prior to January 1, 1979*, and in force between them on December 31, 1978, unless and until terminated in accordance with law." *See* 22 U.S.C. § 3303(c) (emphasis added). The United States now exercises nonofficial relations with Taiwan through the American Institute in Taiwan, a "nonprofit corporation incorporated under the laws of the District of Columbia." *See* 22 U.S.C. §§ 3305, 3310a ("[t]he American Institute of Taiwan shall employ personnel to perform duties similar to those performed by personnel of the United States and Foreign Commercial Service.").

*   *   *   *

B. EXECUTIVE BRANCH CONSTITUTIONAL AUTHORITY OVER FOREIGN STATE RECOGNITION AND PASSPORTS

On September 19, 2007, the U.S. District Court for the District of Columbia dismissed, for lack of subject matter jurisdiction, a lawsuit brought by a U.S. citizen child (by his parents and guardians) challenging the Department of State's refusal to grant his request to list "Israel" (rather than "Jerusalem") as the place of birth in his U.S. passport and Consular Report of Birth Abroad ("CRBA"). *Zivotofsky v. Sec. of State*, 511 F. Supp. 2d 97 (D.D.C. 2007). The court, acting on remand from the D.C. Circuit Court of Appeals, found that the case presented a nonjusticiable political question. For prior history in the case *see Digest 2006* at 530–47, *Digest 2004* at 452–54, and *Digest 2003* at 485–501.

Excerpts follow from the district court's analysis of the political question doctrine as it applied to the issues concerning recognition of states and passports (footnotes omitted).

---

*   *   *   *

The final political status of Jerusalem has been in dispute since 1948 as a result of the long-standing Arab-Israeli conflict. Since the Truman Administration, the executive branch has pursued a policy of encouraging the parties to that conflict to settle all outstanding issues, including the final status of Jerusalem, through peaceful negotiations between the parties with the support of the broader international community. Therefore, the executive branch of the United States government does not acknowledge the sovereignty of any state over Jerusalem.

State Department passport policy reflects the executive branch's policy with regard to the status of Jerusalem. The State Department's *Foreign Affairs Manual* requires that citizens born in Jerusalem after May 14, 1948 shall have their place of birth listed as "Jerusalem." Declaration of JoAnn Dolan, Sept. 29, 2006 ("Dolan Decl."), Ex. 2 (7 FAM § 1383.1(b) & Part II: Other Countries & Territories). The *Manual* makes clear that "Israel" should not be entered on the passports of United States citizens born in Jerusalem. *Id.*

On September 30, 2002, Congress enacted the Foreign Relations Authorization Act for Fiscal Year 2003. Pub. L. No. 107-228, 116 Stat. 1350 (2002). Section 214 is titled "United States policy with respect to Jerusalem as the capital of Israel." *Id.* at 1365. Subsection (a), which is not at issue here, "urges the President" to relocate the United States Embassy in Israel from Tel Aviv to Jerusalem. *Id.* Subsection (d) provides

> RECORD OF PLACE OF BIRTH AS ISRAEL FOR PASSPORT PURPOSES.—For purposes of the registration of birth, certification of nationality, or issuance of a passport of a United States citizen born in the city of Jerusalem, the Secretary shall, upon the request of the citizen or the citizen's legal guardian, record the place of birth as Israel.

Id. at 1366.

The President signed the Act into law on the same day, and made the following statement:

> Section 214, concerning Jerusalem, impermissibly interferes with the President's constitutional authority to conduct the Nation's foreign affairs and to supervise the unitary executive branch. Moreover, the purported direction in section 214 would, if construed as mandatory rather than advisory, impermissibly interfere with the President's constitutional authority to formulate the position of the United States, speak for the Nation in international affairs, and determine the terms on which recognition is given to foreign states. U.S. policy regarding Jerusalem has not changed.

Statement by President George W. Bush Upon Signing H.R. 1646, 2002 U.S.C.C.A.N. 931, 932 (Sept. 30, 2002).

Following the enactment of Section 214(d), a State Department cable to its overseas posts noted that the "media and public in many Middle Eastern and Islamic states continue to believe that the State Authorization Bill signals a change in U.S. policy towards Jerusalem." Dolan Decl., Ex. 3 (DOS 001791). The cable clarified that, despite the enactment of Section 214, United States policy regarding Jerusalem had not changed, that the status of Jerusalem "must be resolved through negotiations between the parties," and that the United States opposed actions by any party that would prejudice those negotiations. *Id.* (DOS 001792).

*   *   *   *

The courts lack jurisdiction over "political questions that are by their nature 'committed to the political branches to the exclusion of the judiciary.'" *Schneider v. Kissinger*, 366 U.S. App. D.C. 408, 412 F.3d 190, 193 (D.C. Cir. 2006) (quoting *Antolok v. United States*, 277 U.S. App. D.C. 156, 873 F.2d 369, 379 (D.C. Cir. 1989) (separate opinion of Sentelle, J.)). Thus, "[t]he nonjusticiability of a political question is primarily a function of the separation of powers." *Baker v. Carr*, 369 U.S. 186, 210, 82 S. Ct. 691, 7 L. Ed. 2d 663 (1962).

In *Baker*, the Supreme Court laid out the six factors that characterize a non-justiciable political question. . . . 369 U.S. at 217. The presence of any one factor indicates that the case presents a non-justiciable political question. *Schneider*, 412 F.3d at 194.

*   *   *   *

. . . When we apply these factors of the *Baker* analysis to this case, we see that it raises a quintessential political question which is not justiciable by the courts.

A. The Text of the Constitution Commits Foreign Policy Questions to the Political Branches of the Government

The first *Baker* factor requires the Court to determine if there is "a textually demonstrable constitutional commitment of the issue to a coordinate political department." 369 U.S. at 217.

"The conduct of the foreign relations of our Government is committed by the Constitution to the Executive and Legislative— 'the political'—Departments of the Government, and the propriety of what may be done in the exercise of this political power is not subject to judicial inquiry or decision." *Schneider*, 412 F.3d at 194 (quoting *Oetjen v. Cent. Leather Co.*, 246 U.S. 297, 302, 38 S. Ct. 309, 62 L. Ed. 726 (1918)).

*　*　*　*

The grant of power to the President in Article II to receive ambassadors, which has been construed by the courts to include the power to recognize the sovereignty of foreign governments over disputed territory, demonstrates a constitutional commitment of this issue to the executive branch of the Government.

Plaintiff argues that this case does not require the Court to determine the status of Jerusalem but only to interpret and apply the provisions of Section 214. Plaintiff is wrong. Resolving his claim on the merits would necessarily require the Court to decide the political status of Jerusalem. The case law makes clear that the Constitution commits that decision to the executive branch. The first *Baker* factor is therefore present in this case.

B. The Court Lacks Judicially Manageable Standards for Resolving Foreign Policy Questions

The second *Baker* factor examines whether there is "a lack of judicially discoverable and manageable standards for resolving" the question before the Court. 369 U.S. at 217.

*　*　*　*

As the Government correctly argues, the Court cannot resolve Plaintiff's claim without considering current United States policy regarding the status of Jerusalem and weighing the possible consequences of changes in that policy.

In the State Department's judgment, an order by this Court that Plaintiff's passport record "Israel" as his place of birth

> would signal, symbolically or concretely, that [the United States] recognizes that Jerusalem is a city that is located within the sovereign territory of Israel [and] would critically compromise the ability of the United States to work with

Israelis, Palestinians and others in the region to further the peace process, to bring an end to violence in Israel and the Occupied Territories, and to achieve progress on the Roadmap. The Palestinians would view any United States change with respect to Jerusalem as an endorsement of Israel's claim to Jerusalem and a rejection of their own. It would be seen as a breach of the cardinal principle of U.S. foreign policy barring any unilateral act(s) that could prejudge the outcome of future negotiations between the contending parties and cause irreversible damage to the credibility of the United States and its capacity to facilitate a final and permanent resolution of the Arab-Israeli conflict.

Dolan Decl., Ex. 1 (Def.'s Interrogatory Response No. 5). Moreover, the destabilizing impact of any Court order would be felt regardless of whether the place of birth for citizens born in Jerusalem was recorded as "Israel" or "Jerusalem, Israel." *Id.*

* * * *

The political situation in the Middle East is enormously complex, volatile, and long-standing. Indeed, "it is hard to conceive of an issue more quintessentially political in nature than the ongoing Israeli-Palestinian conflict, which has raged on the world stage with devastation on both sides for decades." *Doe I v. State of Israel*, 400 F. Supp. 2d 86, 111–12 (D.D.C. 2005).

There are no judicially discoverable or manageable standards for the Court to apply in considering this fundamental and extraordinarily weighty question of U.S. foreign policy. As our Court of Appeals held in *Schneider*, the courts lack the policy advisors, intelligence sources, and other institutional resources to even begin to resolve a foreign policy issue of this magnitude. 412 F.3d at 196. Nor has the Plaintiff suggested any judicially discoverable or manageable standards that could be applied in this case. Accordingly, the second *Baker* factor is also present here.

C. Resolution of this Case Would Be Impossible Without Expressing Lack of Respect to Coordinate Branches of Government

The fourth *Baker* factor is triggered by "the impossibility of a court's undertaking independent resolution without expressing lack of the respect due coordinate branches of government." 369 U.S. at 217.

* * * *

. . . [A] decision by the Court would run the risk of "justifiably offending" one or both of the political branches. Since the Truman Administration, the executive branch has pursued a policy of not recognizing the sovereignty of any state over Jerusalem, pending the outcome of negotiations between the parties to the Arab-Israeli dispute. Congress apparently sought to alter this policy through the enactment of Section 214, which is titled "United States policy with respect to Jerusalem as the capital of Israel." The President views Section 214, if construed as mandatory, as impermissibly interfering "with the President's constitutional authority to formulate the position of the United States, speak for the Nation in international affairs, and determine the terms on which recognition is given to foreign states." 2002 U.S.C.C.A.N. at 932.

This conflict between the political branches could be avoided if, as the Secretary urges, Section 214(d) could be construed as advisory, and not mandatory. But it is difficult to construe Section 214(d) as anything but mandatory. . . . Therefore, a decision by this Court on the merits would risk offending either, or both, the legislative and executive branches, which are at loggerheads over United States policy regarding Jerusalem. Such conflicts are best resolved through political means, by the two political branches themselves. *Goldwater v. Carter*, 444 U.S. 996, 1003, 100 S. Ct. 533, 62 L. Ed. 2d 428 (1979) (Rehnquist, J., concurring). Thus, the fourth *Baker* factor is also present in this case.

D. Resolution of this Case Involves the Potentiality of Embarrassment from Multifarious Pronouncements by Various Departments on One Question

The sixth *Baker* factor involves "the potentiality of embarrassment from multifarious pronouncements by various departments on one question." 369 U.S. at 217.

The effect of conflicting pronouncements by coordinate branches on the political status of Jerusalem is already apparent. Congress' enactment of Section 214 created outrage among Palestinians and was subject to criticism by foreign governments. A State Department cable regarding Section 214 stated that "[d]espite our best efforts to get the word out that U.S. policy on Jerusalem has not changed, the reservations contained in the President's signing statement have been all but ignored, as Palestinians focus on what they consider the negative precedent and symbolism of an American law declaring that Israel's capital is Jerusalem." Dolan Decl., Ex. 4 (DOS 001867).

Should this Court add its voice to those of the President and Congress on the subject of Jerusalem's status, a controversial reaction is virtually guaranteed. Such a reaction can only further complicate and undermine United States efforts to help resolve the Middle East conflict. Therefore, the sixth *Baker* factor is also present here.

*   *   *   *

CHAPTER 10

Privileges and Immunities

A. OVERVIEW

During the period January 10 through January 25, 2007, Department of State Legal Adviser John B. Bellinger, III, participated as a guest blogger on the weblog *Opinio Juris*. In one of his postings Mr. Bellinger addressed "some of the immunity issues that confront [the Office of the Legal Adviser ("L")] on a regular basis." Excerpts from that posting follow. Other postings, related to law-of-war issues, are discussed in Chapter 18. A.1.a. and A.4.a.(2).

Mr. Bellinger's postings and postings by others in response are available at *www.opiniojuris.org/posts/chain_1169503291.shtml*. Mr. Bellinger's postings are also available at *www.state.gov/s/l/c8183.htm*.

. . . I would like to . . . address some of the immunity issues that confront L on a regular basis. Most of you are familiar with the Foreign Sovereign Immunities Act (FSIA), 28 U.S.C. 1330, 1602 et seq., which codified the restrictive theory of the immunity of states and established procedures for bringing suits and enforcing judgments against foreign states (including their political subdivisions and agencies and instrumentalities). A principal purpose of the FSIA was to provide courts with the tools to determine when immunity would apply in suits against foreign states, obviating the need for the Executive Branch to file suggestions of immunity on behalf of foreign states. But L, in conjunction with the Department of Justice, continues to play an important role in providing guidance to our courts on the various immunity issues they confront.

The immunity of foreign government officials is one example. The FSIA does not by its express terms address the immunity of such officials. Several Executive Branch officials who worked on the formulation of the FSIA wrote that it did not deal with such officials when they published a review of pre-FSIA sovereign immunity decisions in the Department of State's 1977 Digest of International Practice. And, the House Report on the FSIA stated that it would have no effect on diplomatic or consular immunity. Nevertheless, in *Chuidian v. Philippine National Bank*, 912 F.2d 1095 (1990), the Ninth Circuit concluded that the FSIA should apply to foreign government officials as "agencies," so as to prevent an "end run" around state immunity. In that case, this approach produced the same result—immunity—advocated by the Executive Branch, but on a theory—applicability of the FSIA— that the Executive Branch did not advance. The point is not academic, because the FSIA treats "agencies" differently than other components of a state and would not, for example, accord immunity to officials for commercial activities undertaken while merely carrying out normal governmental functions. Since 1990, some other circuits have adopted the *Chuidian* reading of the FSIA, such as the D.C. Circuit in *El-Fadl v. Cent. Bank of Jordan*, 75 F.3d 668 (1996) and the 6th Circuit in *Keller v. Cent. Bank of Nigeria*, 277 F.3d 811 (2002). Just this past November, at the request of Judge Pauley of the Southern District of New York, the Executive Branch reiterated the position it advanced in *Chuidian*—that the immunities of foreign government officials generally derive from federal common law as informed by international custom, rather than the FSIA, in a Statement of Interest filed in *Matar v. Dichter*, S.D.N.Y. 05 Civ. 10270 (WHP). This approach avoids some of the obvious problems of the *Chuidian* approach and is more consistent with the position taken by the United States on behalf of its own officials when they are sued abroad.

In addition, certain categories of foreign officials are accorded immunity by more specific legal regimes. Diplomatic and consular officers enjoy immunities under the Vienna Conventions on Diplomatic and on Consular Relations, respectively, bilateral treaties with certain countries, and in some instances customary international law. These sources reflect some of the oldest principles of international law, which recognize the importance of facilitating a sovereign state's unimpeded representation within each other's jurisdictions. The Executive Branch does not necessarily play a role in cases involving the immunities of such officers, because we expect the states or officers involved to retain private counsel for the officers' representation. The State Department does, however, certify the status of diplomatic and consular officers and may work with the Department of Justice to file a statement of interest addressing issues in a case. For example, we have filed to address whether a particular type of action by a consular officer should be regarded as performance of a consular function falling within the scope of a consular officer's immunity for official acts. We also, when necessary, advise arresting officers and prosecutors of the applicable criminal immunities of diplomatic and consular officers. This advisory practice significantly reduces the need for criminal immunity issues to be litigated in court.

Another basis for foreign government officials' immunity that is independent of the FSIA is the doctrine of head-of-state immunity. When applicable, it entails full personal immunity from the jurisdiction of U.S. courts. The Executive Branch has a longstanding practice of affirmatively "suggesting" head-of-state immunity to our courts when a person who enjoys the immunity has been served with judicial process. The practice dates at least to the mid-1960s, when such suggestions were made with respect to the South Korean Foreign Minister (1963) and King Faisal of Saudi Arabia (1965). Since then, we have suggested head-of-state immunity in some thirty cases which have dealt with heads of state, heads of government, the spouse of a head of state, and foreign ministers. The doctrine of head-of-state immunity recognizes the unique role played by government leaders and the special sensitivities of exposing them to civil litigation in foreign courts, particularly while they are still in office.

Another immunity that may be accorded to foreign officials is special mission immunity, which is also grounded in customary international law and federal common law (Like most countries, the United States has not joined the Special Missions Convention.).

The doctrine of special mission immunity, like diplomatic immunity, is necessary to facilitate high level contacts between governments through invitational visits. The Executive Branch has made suggestions of special mission immunity in cases such as one filed against Prince Charles in 1978 while he was here on an official visit. *Kilroy v. Charles Windsor, Prince of Wales*, Civ. No. C-78-291 (N.D. Ohio, 1978). This past summer, in response to a request for views by the federal district court for the D.C. Circuit, the Executive Branch submitted a suggestion of special mission immunity on behalf of a Chinese Minister of Commerce who was served while attending bilateral trade talks hosted by the United States, in *Li Weixum v. Bo Xilai*, D.C.C.Civ. No. 04-0649 (RJL).

Our suggestions of immunity normally respond to requests from a foreign government made after its official has been served with a complaint in a civil action. We usually ask that the request be conveyed through a diplomatic note, with all relevant information and documents, including of course the summons and complaint. If we agree that a suggestion of immunity should be filed, the Justice Department submits one to the court on behalf of the Executive Branch. These filings are typically very short because, once we have determined that an official enjoys immunity, we expect the court to defer to that decision, in accordance with well-established judicial doctrines tracing back to *The Schooner Exchange v. McFaddon*, 11 U.S. (7 Cranch) 116 (1812).

Our immunity practice also encompasses international organizations (IOs). Here the governing standard is usually the International Organizations Immunities Act (IOIA) rather than the FSIA. If IOs are sued in our courts we normally expect them, like foreign governments, to appear in court to assert their own immunity. The United Nations is an exception, however. Under Section 2 of the UN Convention on Privileges and Immunities, the UN has complete immunity from suit in the US, including "from every form of legal process." Officials of IOs generally have official acts immunity, but a small number of officials of the UN and the Organization of American States have full diplomatic immunity pursuant to our headquarters agreements with them.

Finally, back to the FSIA. While it ended the Department of State's practice of suggesting immunity on behalf of sovereign states, it by no means ended the Department's participation in litigation against foreign states. Along with the Department of Justice, L works to ensure that the FSIA is interpreted and applied properly, bearing in mind its purpose and the reciprocity and foreign policy issues that could arise from the decisions of our courts. We do not keep track of all of the many cases in our courts that involve FSIA issues, but we participate as amicus when our views are requested by the courts and occasionally on our own initiative or in response to a request by parties to the litigation. Most recently, for example, in response to a Supreme Court request for views with respect to two petitions for certiorari (Nos. 05-85 and 05-584), the Executive Branch argued that the Court should address two 9th Circuit decisions involving whether a Canadian entity—Powerex Corporation—is an "organ" of British Columbia and, therefore, an "agency or instrumentality" of a foreign state under the FSIA.

The sovereign and official immunity rules the United States applies domestically have important implications for how the United States and its officials are treated abroad. Thus immunity outcomes in our courts are relevant not merely because of the potential immediate foreign policy consequences of U.S. exercises of jurisdiction. In cases in which immunity precludes litigation, whether in the United States against foreign states and their officials or abroad against the United States and its officials, we may also—in appropriate cases—look for other ways to help resolve the underlying dispute. In addressing immunity questions we carry out research and analysis of treaties and international practice with the goal of establishing principles that will benefit all countries. . . .

*   *   *   *

In his final wrap-up session on *Opinio Juris,* Mr. Bellinger responded to a comment on criminal immunity of heads of state as follows:

[T]he Legal Adviser's office is not aware of any criminal charges having been brought against a sitting head of state by United States federal or state prosecutors. No U.S. court has squarely addressed the immunity from criminal charges of a *former* head of state in the face of an assertion of immunity by the relevant state, but we have had at least one case in which a prosecution proceeded after a waiver: Pavel Lazarenko, former Ukrainian Prime Minister and Member of Parliament, was prosecuted successfully by the United States for violations of various U.S. laws after the Ukrainian parliament voted to remove his immunity.

B.   FOREIGN SOVEREIGN IMMUNITY

1.   Foreign Sovereign Immunities Act

The Foreign Sovereign Immunities Act ("FSIA"), 28 U.S.C. §§ 1330, 1602–1611, provides that, subject to international agreements to which the United States was a party at the time of enactment in 1976, a foreign state is immune from the jurisdiction of courts in the United States unless one of the specified exceptions in the statute applies. A foreign state is defined to include its agencies and instrumentalities. The FSIA provides the sole basis for obtaining jurisdiction over a foreign state in U.S. courts. *Argentine Republic v. Amerada Hess Shipping Corp.*, 488 U.S. 428 (1989); *Saudi Arabia v. Nelson*, 507 U.S. 349 (1993). For a number of years before enactment of the FSIA, courts abided by "suggestions of immunity" from the State Department. When no suggestion was filed, however, the courts made the determination.

In the FSIA Congress codified the "restrictive" theory of sovereign immunity, under which a state is entitled to immunity with respect to its sovereign or public acts, but not those that are private or commercial in character. The United States had previously adopted the restrictive theory in the so-called "Tate Letter" of 1952, reproduced at 26 Dep't State Bull. 678 at 984–85 (1952). *See Alfred Dunhill of London, Inc. v. Cuba*, 425 U.S. 682, 711–15 (1976).

From the beginning the FSIA has provided certain other exceptions to immunity, such as by waiver or commercial activity. Over time, amendments to the FSIA incorporated additional exceptions, including one enacted in 1996 for acts of terrorism in certain circumstances. The FSIA's various statutory exceptions, set forth at 28 U.S.C. §§ 1605(a)(1)–(7), have been subject to significant judicial interpretation in cases brought by private entities or persons against foreign sovereigns. Accordingly, much of U.S. practice in the field of sovereign immunity is developed by U.S. courts in litigation to which the U.S. Government is not a party and participates, if at all, as *amicus curiae*.

The following items represent a selection of the relevant decisional material during 2007.

a. Scope of application

The FSIA (28 U.S.C. § 1603(a)) defines the term "foreign state" to include "an agency or instrumentality of a foreign state," which, in turn, is defined to mean

any entity—(1) which is a separate legal person, corporate or otherwise, and (2) which is an organ of a foreign state or political subdivision thereof, or a majority of whose shares or other ownership interest is owned by a foreign state or political subdivision thereof, and (3) which is neither a citizen of a State of the United States as defined in section 1332(c) and (d) of this title, nor created under the laws of any third country.

28 U.S.C. § 1603(b). *See also* cases discussed in B.1.d.(1)(ii) and 2.(ii), below.

(1) Agency or instrumentality: Powerex v. Reliant Energy Services, Inc.

On June 18, 2007, the Supreme Court vacated in part a decision by the Ninth Circuit Court of Appeals that Powerex was not a foreign state for purposes of the FSIA because it did not meet the "organ" prong of the FSIA's definition of "agency or instrumentality." The Court vacated on the ground that the Ninth Circuit did not have jurisdiction to consider the issue, without deciding whether Powerex was an "organ" of the Canadian Government. *Powerex Corp. v. Reliant Energy Services, Inc.*, 127 S. Ct. 2411 (2007).

In this case, California and others had brought suit in California state court alleging that various companies in California's energy market had conspired to fix prices in violation of California state law. Two Canadian entities, BC Hydro (a crown corporation wholly owned by British Columbia) and Powerex (a Canadian corporation wholly owned by BC Hydro) filed notices removing the case from state to federal district court pursuant to the FSIA, 28 U.S.C. § 1441(d), as well as 1442(a)(1). Section 1441(d) allows removal to federal court by a "foreign state" as defined by the Foreign Sovereign Immunities Act, 28 U.S.C. § 1603.

The federal district court remanded the case to California state court. As to the Canadian entities, the district court concluded that Powerex was not entitled to remove the case from state court because it did not come within the FSIA definition of "agency or instrumentality." It specifically rejected Powerex's claim to be an "organ" of British Columbia and thus to be within the "organ prong" of the FSIA's "agency or instrumentality" definition. (Powerex had not claimed immunity, but only foreign sovereign status entitling it to a federal forum.) The Ninth Circuit affirmed. The United States filed a brief as *amicus curiae* in response to an invitation from the Supreme Court in November 2006. *See Digest 2006* at 550–58.

In its decision the Supreme Court found that appellate review was barred by 28 U.S.C. § 1447(d). Excerpts below from the majority opinion provide its analysis in rejecting the argument that § 1447(d) was not applicable to suits removed under the FSIA and concluding that any change must be made by Congress. Citations to submissions by the parties in the case have been omitted. The dissent would have found the decision below reviewable and would have agreed with the U.S. position that Powerex was an "organ" of the Canadian government, thus entitling Powerex to removal to federal court.

* * * *

. . . [P]etitioner [Powerex] contends, with no textual support, that § 1447(d) is simply inapplicable to a suit removed under the FSIA. It asserts that "§ 1447(d) must yield because Congress could not have intended to grant district judges irrevocable authority to decide questions with such sensitive foreign-relations implications." We will not ignore a clear jurisdictional statute in reliance upon supposition of what Congress *really* wanted. See *Connecticut Nat. Bank v. Germain*, 503 U.S. 249, 253–254, 112 S. Ct. 1146, 117 L. Ed. 2d 391 (1992). Petitioner's divination of congressional intent is flatly refuted by longstanding precedent. . . .

We are well aware that § 1447(d)'s immunization of erroneous remands has undesirable consequences in the FSIA context. A foreign sovereign defendant whose case is wrongly remanded is denied not only the federal forum to which it is entitled (as befalls all remanded parties with meritorious appeals barred by § 1447(d)), but also certain procedural rights that the FSIA specifically provides foreign sovereigns only in federal court (such as the right to a bench trial, see 28 U.S.C. § 1330(a); § 1441(d)). But whether that special concern outweighs § 1447(d)'s general interest in avoiding prolonged litigation on threshold nonmerits questions, see *Kircher* [*v. Putnam Funds Trust*, 547 U.S. 633(2006)], at __ 126 S. Ct. 2145, 165 L. Ed. 2d 92 (slip op., at 5), is a policy debate that belongs in the halls of Congress, not in the hearing room of this Court. As far as the Third Branch is concerned, what the text of § 1447(d) indisputably does prevails over what it ought to have done. (fn. omitted)

✻   ✻   ✻   ✻

Section 1447(d) reflects Congress's longstanding "policy of not permitting interruption of the litigation of the merits of a removed case by prolonged litigation of questions of jurisdiction of the district court to which the cause is removed." *Rice, supra*, at 751, 66 S. Ct. 835, 90 L. Ed. 982. Appellate courts must take that jurisdictional prescription seriously, however pressing the merits of the appeal might seem. We hold that § 1447(d) bars appellate consideration of petitioner's claim that it is a foreign state for purposes of the FSIA. We therefore vacate in part the judgment of the Ninth Circuit and remand the case with instructions to dismiss petitioner's appeal for want of jurisdiction.

(2) Organ: Peninsula Asset Management v.
Hankook Tire Co., Ltd.

On January 30, 2007, the U.S. Court of Appeals for the Second
Circuit addressed the issue of the term "organ" under the
FSIA that was not reached by the Supreme Court in *Powerex,
supra. Peninsula Asset Management v. Hankook Tire Co., Ltd.,*
476 F.3d 140 (2d Cir. 2007). The court concluded, as excerpted
below, that the Financial Supervisory Service of the Republic
of Korea ("FSS") was an organ of the government of Korea;
as a result, the court below lacked jurisdiction to compel FSS
compliance with a subpoena served on it by Peninsula Asset
Management in the underlying litigation.

---

*   *   *   *

. . . Absent a statutory or treaty exemption, the FSIA grants foreign
states immunity from the jurisdiction of any court of the United
States. 28 U.S.C. § 1604. . . . An agency or instrumentality of a
foreign state is considered a foreign state for FSIA purposes. 28
U.S.C. § 1603(a). . . .

Here, the dispute focuses solely on whether FSS is an "organ"
of the Korean government. Although this Court has no definitive
test to determine whether an entity is a government "organ," we
consider:

(1) whether the foreign state created the entity for a national
purpose; (2) whether the foreign state actively supervises
the entity; (3) whether the foreign state requires the hiring
of public employees and pays their salaries; (4) whether the
entity holds exclusive rights to some right in the [foreign]
country; and (5) how the entity is treated under foreign
state law.

Filler, 378 F.3d at 217 (quoting *Kelly v. Syria Shell Petroleum Dev.
B.V.,* 213 F.3d 841, 846–47 (5th Cir. 2000))(alteration in original).

We find that FSS provided sufficient evidence to satisfy four of the
Filler factors, thereby establishing a prima facie case for foreign

sovereign immunity. Because Peninsula has put forward no argument or evidence showing that one of the FSIA exceptions applies, FSS is entitled to foreign sovereign immunity. First, Korea created FSS for the national purpose of examining, supervising, and investigating Korean financial institutions. Second, the Korean government actively supervises FSS by, *inter alia*: (1) appointing its governor and auditor; (2) acting through a related agency, FSC; and (3) regulating the inspection fees that FSS can collect. Third, FSS has the exclusive right to receive monthly business reports from the solvent financial institutions it oversees. Finally, the Korean government informed the State Department and the district court that it treats FSS as a government entity.

Only one factor weighs against finding sovereign immunity: the Korean government neither requires the hiring of public employees for FSS positions, nor directly pays the salaries of FSS employees. Nonetheless, in light of the four other factors, this is insufficient to deny FSS sovereign immunity.

We reached a similar conclusion as to the Korean Deposit Insurance Corporation ("KDIC") in *Filler.* 378 F.3d at 217. As with KDIC, FSS is an organ of a foreign state because it: (1) was formed by statute and presidential decree; (2) performs traditional government functions; (3) has directors appointed by the Korean government; and (4) has many of its operations overseen by the Korean government. *Cf. id.*

As an agency or instrumentality of a foreign state under the FSIA, FSS is immune from the present subpoena. Thus, we affirm the denial of the contempt motion.

* * * *

b. Exceptions to immunity

(1) Rights in immovable property: Permanent Mission of India to the United Nations v. City of New York

On June 14, 2007, the U.S. Supreme Court held that the FSIA does not immunize a foreign sovereign "from a lawsuit to declare the validity of tax liens on property held by the sovereign for the purpose of housing its employees." *Permanent Mission of India to the United Nations v. City of New York*, 127 S. Ct. 2352 (2007). Initially, the City of New York sought a declaratory judgment against the Permanent Mission of India to the United Nations and the Permanent Representative of Mongolia to the United Nations affirming the validity of tax liens against real property India and Mongolia used to house their UN mission staffs. The Court found jurisdiction pursuant to 28 U.S.C. § 1605(a)(4), which provides an exception to immunity under the FSIA where "rights in immovable property situated in the United States are in issue." The United States filed a brief in the case as *amicus curiae* in December 2006 supporting the petition for a writ of certiorari filed by the governments of India and Mongolia seeking reversal of lower court decisions that had found jurisdiction on that basis. *See Digest 2006* at 592–603.

Excerpts follow from the Court's decision, interpreting § 1605(a)(4) to mean that courts in the United States have jurisdiction over a lawsuit to establish the validity of a tax lien on real property owned by a foreign sovereign and concluding that this interpretation was consistent with "two well-recognized and related purposes of the FSIA: adoption of the restrictive view of sovereign immunity and codification of international law at the time of the FSIA's enactment." The Court noted that it was addressing only the jurisdictional issue, leaving "merits-related arguments" to the lower courts. The Court also noted that its ruling did not affect the government's immunity from foreclosure:

> The City concedes that even if a court of competent jurisdiction declares the liens valid, petitioners are immune from foreclosure proceedings. . . . The City claims, however, that the declarations of validity are necessary for three reasons. First, once a court has declared property tax liens valid, foreign sovereigns traditionally concede and pay. Second, if the foreign sovereign fails to pay in the face of a valid court judgment, that country's foreign aid may be reduced by the United States by 110% of the

outstanding debt. See Foreign Operations, Export Financing, and Related Programs Appropriations Act, 2006, § 543(a), 119 Stat. 2214...; Consolidated Appropriations Act of 2005, § 543(a), 118 Stat. 3011. ... Third, the liens would be enforceable against subsequent purchasers. 5 Restatement of Property § 540 (1944).

Citations to submissions in the case have been omitted.

---

* * * *

[I] The Permanent Mission of India to the United Nations is located in a 26-floor building in New York City that is owned by the Government of India. Several floors are used for diplomatic offices, but approximately 20 floors contain residential units for diplomatic employees of the mission and their families. The employees—all of whom are below the rank of Head of Mission or Ambassador—are Indian citizens who receive housing from the mission rent free.

Similarly, the Ministry for Foreign Affairs of the People's Republic of Mongolia is housed in a six-story building in New York City that is owned by the Mongolian Government. Like the Permanent Mission of India, certain floors of the Ministry Building include residences for lower level employees of the Ministry and their families.

Under New York law, real property owned by a foreign government is exempt from taxation if it is "used exclusively" for diplomatic offices or for the quarters of a diplomat "with the rank of ambassador or minister plenipotentiary" to the United Nations. N. Y. Real Prop. Tax Law Ann. § 418 (West 2000). But "[i]f a portion only of any lot or building . . . is used exclusively for the purposes herein described, then such portion only shall be exempt and the remainder shall be subject to taxation. . . ." *Ibid.*

For several years, the City of New York (City) has levied property taxes against petitioners for the portions of their buildings used to house lower level employees. Petitioners, however, refused to pay the taxes. By operation of New York law, the unpaid taxes eventually converted into tax liens held by the City against the two properties. As of February 1, 2003, the Indian Mission owed about $16.4 million in unpaid property taxes and interest, and the Mongolian Ministry owed about $2.1 million.

*   *   *   *

II

. . . . At issue here is the scope of the exception [to immunity under the FSIA] where "rights in immovable property situated in the United States are in issue." § 1605(a)(4). Petitioners contend that the language "rights in immovable property" limits the reach of the exception to actions contesting ownership or possession. The City argues that the exception encompasses additional rights in immovable property, including tax liens. Each party claims international practice at the time of the FSIA's adoption supports its view. We agree with the City.

[A.] We begin, as always, with the text of the statute. . . . The FSIA provides: "A foreign state shall not be immune from the jurisdiction of courts of the United States . . . in any case . . . in which . . . rights in immovable property situated in the United States are in issue." 28 U.S.C. § 1605(a)(4). Contrary to petitioners' position, § 1605(a)(4) does not expressly limit itself to cases in which the specific right at issue is title, ownership, or possession. Neither does it specifically exclude cases in which the validity of a lien is at issue. Rather, the exception focuses more broadly on "rights in" property. Accordingly, we must determine whether an action seeking a declaration of the validity of a tax lien places "rights in immovable property . . . in issue."

At the time of the FSIA's adoption in 1976, a "lien" was defined as "[a] charge or security or incumbrance upon property." Black's Law Dictionary 1072 (4th ed. 1951). "Incumbrance," in turn, was defined as "[a]ny right to, or interest in, land which may subsist in another to the diminution of its value. . . ." *Id.*, at 908; *see also id.*, at 941 (8th ed. 2004) (defining "lien" as a "legal right or interest that a creditor has in another's property"). New York law defines "tax lien" in accordance with these general definitions. See N. Y. Real Prop. Tax Law Ann. § 102(21) (West Supp. 2007) ("'Tax lien' means an unpaid tax . . . which is an encumbrance of real property . . . "). This Court, interpreting the Bankruptcy Code, has also recognized that a lienholder has a property interest, albeit a "nonpossessory" interest. *United States v. Security Industrial Bank*, 459 U.S. 70, 76, 103 S. Ct. 407, 74 L. Ed. 2d 235 (1982).

The practical effects of a lien bear out these definitions of liens as interests in property. A lien on real property runs with the land and is enforceable against subsequent purchasers. See 5 Restatement of Property § 540 (1944). As such, "a lien has an immediate adverse effect upon the amount which [could be] receive[d] on a sale, . . . constitut[ing] a direct interference with the property. . . ." *Republic of Argentina v. New York*, 25 N. Y. 2d 252, 262, 250 N.E.2d 698, 702, 303 N.Y.S.2d 644 (1969). A tax lien thus inhibits one of the quintessential rights of property ownership—the right to convey. It is therefore plain that a suit to establish the validity of a lien implicates "rights in immovable property."

[B.] Our reading of the text is supported by two well-recognized and related purposes of the FSIA: adoption of the restrictive view of sovereign immunity and codification of international law at the time of the FSIA's enactment. Until the middle of the last century, the United States followed "the classical or virtually absolute theory of sovereign immunity," under which "a sovereign cannot, without his consent, be made a respondent in the courts of another sovereign." Letter from Jack B. Tate, Acting Legal Adviser, U.S. Dept. of State, to Acting U.S. Attorney General Phillip B. Perlman (May 19, 1952) (Tate Letter), reprinted in 26 Dept. of State Bull. 984 (1952), and in *Alfred Dunhill of London, Inc. v. Republic of Cuba*, 425 U.S. 682, 711, 712, 96 S. Ct. 1854, 48 L. Ed. 2d 301 (1976) (App. 2 to opinion of the Court). The Tate Letter announced the United States' decision to join the majority of other countries by adopting the "restrictive theory" of sovereign immunity, under which "the immunity of the sovereign is recognized with regard to sovereign or public acts *(jure imperii)* of a state, but not with respect to private acts *(jure gestionis)*." *Id.*, at 711, 96 S. Ct. 1854, 48 L. Ed. 2d 301. In enacting the FSIA, Congress intended to codify the restrictive theory's limitation of immunity to sovereign acts. *Republic of Argentina v. Weltover, Inc.*, 504 U.S. 607, 612, 112 S. Ct. 2160, 119 L. Ed. 2d 394 (1992); *Asociacion de Reclamantes v. United Mexican States*, 237 U.S. App. D.C. 81, 735 F.2d 1517, 1520 (CADC 1984) (Scalia, J.).

As a threshold matter, property ownership is not an inherently sovereign function. See *Schooner Exchange* v. *M'Faddon*, 7 Cranch 116, 145, 11 U.S. 116, 3 L. Ed. 287 (1812) ("A prince, by acquiring private property in a foreign country, may possibly be considered as subjecting that property to the territorial jurisdiction, he may be considered as so far laying down the prince, and assuming the character of a private individual"). In addition, the FSIA was also meant "to codify . . . the pre-existing real property exception to sovereign immunity recognized by international practice." *Reclamantes, supra*, at 1521 (Scalia, J.). Therefore, it is useful to note that international practice at the time of the FSIA's enactment also supports the City's view that these sovereigns are not immune. The most recent restatement of foreign relations law at the time of the FSIA's enactment states that a foreign sovereign's immunity does not extend to "an action to obtain possession of or establish a property interest in immovable property located in the territory of the state exercising jurisdiction." Restatement (Second) of Foreign Relations Law of the United States § 68(b), p. 205 (1965). As stated above, because an action seeking the declaration of the validity of a tax lien on property is a suit to establish an interest in such property, such an action would be allowed under this rule.

Petitioners respond to this conclusion by citing the second sentence of Comment *d* to § 68, which states that the rule "does not preclude immunity with respect to a claim arising out of a foreign state's ownership or possession of immovable property but not contesting such ownership or the right to possession." *Id.,* at 207. According to petitioners, that sentence limits the exception to cases contesting ownership or possession. When read in context, however, the comment supports the City. Petitioners ignore the first sentence of the comment, which reemphasizes that immunity does not extend to cases involving the possession of or "interest in" the property. *Ibid.* And the illustrations following the comment make clear that it refers only to claims incidental to property ownership, such as actions involving an "injury suffered in a fall" on the property, for which immunity would apply. *Id.,* at 208. By contrast, for an eminent-domain proceeding, the foreign sovereign could not claim immunity. *Ibid.* Like the eminent-domain proceeding, the City's lawsuits here directly implicate rights in property.

In addition, both parties rely on various international agreements, primarily the Vienna Convention on Diplomatic Relations, Apr. 18, 1961, [1972] 23 U.S.T. 3227, T.I.A.S. No. 7502, to identify pre-FSIA international practice. Petitioners point to the Vienna Convention's analogous withholding of immunity for "a real action relating to private immovable property situated in the territory of the receiving State, unless [the diplomatic agent] holds it on behalf of the sending State for the purposes of the mission." *Id.,* at 3240, Art. 31(1)(a). Petitioners contend that this language indicates they are entitled to immunity for two reasons. First, petitioners argue that "real action[s]" do not include actions for performance of obligations "'deriving from ownership or possession of immovable property.'" Brief for Petitioners 28 (quoting E. Denza, Diplomatic Law: A Commentary on the Vienna Convention on Diplomatic Relations 238 (2d ed. 1998); emphasis deleted). Second, petitioners assert that the property here is held "'on behalf of the sending State for purposes of the Mission. . . .'"

But as the City shows, it is far from apparent that the term "real action"—a term derived from the civil law—is as limited as petitioners suggest. See *Chateau Lafayette Apartments, Inc.* v. *Meadow Brook Nat. Bank,* 416 F.2d 301, 304, n. 7 (CA5 1969). Moreover, the exception for property held "on behalf of the sending State" concerns only the case—not at issue here—where local law requires an agent to hold in his own name property used for the purposes of a mission. 1957 Y. B. Int'l L. Comm'n 94–95 (402d Meeting, May 22, 1957); *see also Deputy Registrar Case,* 94 I. L. R. 308, 313 (D. Ct. The Hague 1980). Other tribunals construing Article 31 have also held that it does not extend immunity to staff housing. See *id.,* at 312; cf. *Intpro Properties (U.K.) Ltd.* v. *Sauvel,* [1983] 1 Q. B. 1019, 1032–1033.

In sum, the Vienna Convention does not unambiguously support either party on the jurisdictional question.[2] In any event,

---

[2] The City offers several other arguments against immunity based on the Vienna Convention, but those arguments ultimately go to the merits of the case, *i.e.,* whether petitioners are actually responsible for paying the taxes. Because the only question before us is one of jurisdiction, and because the text and historical context of the FSIA demonstrate that petitioners are not immune from the City's suits, we leave these merits-related arguments to the lower courts.

nothing in the Vienna Convention deters us from our interpretation of the FSIA. Under the language of the FSIA's exception for immovable property, petitioners are not immune from the City's suits.

Because the statutory text and the acknowledged purposes of the FSIA make it clear that a suit to establish the validity of a tax lien places "rights in immovable property . . . in issue," we affirm the judgment of the Court of Appeals and remand the case for further proceedings consistent with this opinion.

*   *   *   *

On June 29, 2007, Secretary of State Condoleezza Rice sent a circular diplomatic note to all chiefs of mission in the United States informing them of the Court's decision. After summarizing the holding of the Court, the note explained:

> The Supreme Court decision concerned only immunity from jurisdiction. The decision did not address the merits of the underlying question, which is whether property taxes are owed on the real properties at issue. That tax question may now be addressed by the federal district court.

On a more general level, the note provided the following information on litigation in which the FSIA is at issue:

> The Secretary reiterates the Department of State's previous guidance that, under the FSIA, decisions on sovereign immunity are made exclusively by the courts. In the event a lawsuit is filed against a foreign state in a court in the United States, the foreign state should retain private counsel and address jurisdictional and other defenses, including claims of sovereign immunity, to the court. It is the responsibility of the foreign state, together with its legal counsel, to assert immunity or otherwise to defend the action in court.

The full text of the circular note is available at *www.state.gov/s/l/c8183.htm.*

(2) Commercial activity

Section 1605(a)(2) of the FSIA provides that a foreign state is not immune from suit in any case "in which the action is based upon a commercial activity carried on in the United States by the foreign state; or upon an act performed in the United States in connection with a commercial activity of the foreign state elsewhere; or upon an act outside the territory of the United States in connection with a commercial activity of the foreign state elsewhere and that act causes a direct effect in the United States." *See also* discussion of "commercial activity" in the context of the immunity of assets to attachment, B.1.d. below, and of the inapplicability of FSIA precedent on commercial activity to a case involving a claim of diplomatic immunity, C.1. below.

In *Kensington Int'l Ltd. v. Itoua*, 505 F.3d 147 (2d Cir. 2007), the U.S. Court of Appeals for the Second Circuit reversed a district court decision finding jurisdiction under the commercial activity definition. The Second Circuit concluded that the activities cited by the plaintiffs to establish jurisdiction were not "based upon a commercial activity carried on in the United States" by the foreign state defendant, as that concept was defined by the FSIA. Excerpts follow from the Second Circuit decision as to the immunity of Société Nationale des Pétroles du Congo ("SNPC"). *See also* discussion of SNPC's immunity in the U.S. letter brief, filed at the invitation of the court of appeals, available at *www.state.gov/s/l/c8183.htm*. For the facts of the case, and discussion of the immunity of the second defendant, Bruno Jean Richard Itoua, *see* B.2.b. below.

* * * *

In this case, the district court determined that Section 1605(a)(2) applied to SNPC based on the following alleged acts: (1) the sale of at least eleven shipments of "stolen" oil totaling 9,210,221 barrels to United States purchasers; and (2) multi-million dollar premium payments to the New York branch of BNP. The district court further concluded that because Itoua was chairman and managing director of SNPC during the relevant time, SNPC's acts were imputed to him and thus his conduct also satisfied the commercial activities exception. In reaching this conclusion, the district court assumed without deciding that the FSIA applied to individual officials like Itoua. The district court noted that this was an open question, but found it unnecessary to decide the issue because even if Itoua could invoke the immunity provisions of the FSIA, the district court found that the commercial activities exception abrogated any immunity to which he was entitled.

*   *   *   *

We conclude that the district court did not properly apply the statutory requirements that Kensington's cause of action be "based upon" SNPC's alleged commercial activity in the United States, or "based . . . upon" an act in the United States in connection with commercial activity elsewhere, or "based . . . upon" SNPC's act or commercial activity abroad that is alleged to have had a "direct effect" in the United States. The absence of these elements renders the commercial activities exception inapplicable, and therefore SNPC is immune from suit under the FSIA.

1. Whether Kensington's cause of action is "based upon" SNPC's alleged commercial activity in the United States

The first prong of the commercial activities exception applies if the plaintiff's action is "based upon a commercial activity carried on in the United States by the foreign state." 28 U.S.C. § 1605(a)(2). The Supreme Court has found that the phrase "based upon" in the first prong of Section 1605(a)(2) is "read most naturally to mean those elements of a claim that, if proven, would entitle a plaintiff to relief under his theory." [*Saudi Arabia v.*] *Nelson*, 507 U.S. [349 (1993)] at 357. The term "calls for something more than a mere connection with, or relation to, commercial activity." *Id.* at 358. The Court clarified, however, that it did not "mean to suggest that the first clause of § 1605(a)(2) necessarily requires that each and every element of a claim be commercial activity." *Id.* at 358 n. 4. In *Transatlantic Shiffahrtskontor GmbH v. Shanghai Foreign Trade Corp.*, 204 F.3d 384 (2d Cir. 2000), we analyzed the phrase "based upon" in conjunction with the third prong of Section 1605. We explained:

> What does 'based upon' mean? At a minimum, that language implies a causal relationship. Thus, at the least, the 'act that caused a direct effect in the United States' ('the Act') must be a 'but for' cause of the judgments that are the ground of this suit. That is, it must be true that without the Act, there would be no judgments on which to sue. But this is not enough. . . . '[B]ased upon' requires a degree of closeness between the acts giving rise to the cause of action and those needed to establish jurisdiction that is considerably greater than common law causation requirements.

Id. at 390. We further explained in *Reiss v. Societe Centrale du Groupe des Assurances Nationales,* 235 F.3d 738 (2d Cir. 2000), that "based upon" requires "a significant nexus . . . between the commercial activity in this country upon which the exception is based and a plaintiff's cause of action." *Id.* at 747 (internal quotation marks omitted; emphasis added); *see also Garb v. Republic of Poland,* 440 F.3d 579, 586 (2d Cir. 2006) ("As a threshold step in assessing plaintiffs' reliance on the 'commercial activity' exception, we must identify the act of the foreign sovereign State that serves as the basis for plaintiffs' claims."). . . .

Kensington dismisses *Transatlantic* as "plainly inapposite" because *Transatlantic* involved the third prong of the commercial activities exception and any attempt to apply its construction of "based upon" to other prongs "finds no support whatsoever in the decisions of this Court." We find no merit in Kensington's attempt to distinguish *Transatlantic.* Absent any indication from Congress to the contrary, we do not believe that the phrase "based upon" has distinct meanings in different parts of the same provision of the statute. . . . *Transatlantic's* interpretation of the phrase "based upon" applies equally to all three prongs of the commercial activities exception, and we must follow its guidance in evaluating whether the required nexus exists here.

Citing the statement of the *Nelson* Court that it "did not mean . . . to suggest that the first clause of § 1605(a)(2) necessarily requires that each and every element of a claim be commercial activity by a foreign state," 507 U.S. at 358 n.4, Kensington contends that it has satisfied the "based upon" element because it need only show that one of the elements of its cause of action is established by the commercial activity in the United States. Thus, Kensington argues, because the RICO statute requires as one of its elements that the stolen property be transported in interstate or foreign commerce, SNPC's alleged shipment of allegedly stolen oil in the United States establishes an element of the RICO claim. As support for this contention, Kensington relies on various cases from other circuits. . . .

Applying the principles of *Transatlantic, Reiss, Garb,* and *Nelson,* we cannot agree with Kensington's position that its action is "based upon" the alleged acts in the United States merely because those acts satisfy the interstate commerce element of the RICO statute. As *Transatlantic* makes clear, the "based upon" element requires a "degree of closeness between the acts giving rise to the cause of action and those needed to establish jurisdiction that is *considerably greater* than common law causation requirements." 204 F.3d at 390 (emphasis added). This "degree of closeness" must exist between the commercial activity and the gravamen of the plaintiff's complaint. *See Garb,* 440 F.3d at 586; *see also Nelson,* 507 U.S. at 358 (rejecting argument that plaintiffs' suit was based upon commercial acts in the United States because "[w]hile these activities led to the conduct that eventually injured the Nelsons, they are not the *basis* for the Nelsons' suit") (emphasis added).

The requisite nexus does not exist between SNPC's commercial activity in the United States—the shipment of oil and the premium payments—and the gravamen of Kensington's complaint. These acts in the United States had no bearing on Kensington's ability or inability to recover the money owed by Congo under the loan agreements. As Kensington's complaint makes clear, its claims arise from the alleged scheme to use "excessive over collateralized" oil loans to thwart legitimate creditors for the financial benefit of government officials. The gravamen of Kensington's complaint therefore is SNPC's entering into the prepayment agreements with BNP. It is these agreements that are at the core of the alleged scheme to hide assets and prevent oil revenues from being used to satisfy debts held by legitimate creditors. This scheme would have the same alleged effect on Kensington's ability to collect on its debt even if all of the oil shipments had been to destinations outside the

United States or if the premium payments had been made through BNP's Paris office instead of its New York branch. Kensington has failed to show how the oil shipments and premium payments, rather than the execution of the prepayment agreements themselves, form the basis of its action.

Furthermore, it is clear that the prepayment agreements themselves have no connection to the United States. Kensington has therefore failed to show that its cause of action is "based upon a commercial activity carried on in the United States by the foreign state," 28 U.S.C. § 1605(a)(2). Accordingly, the first prong of the commercial activities exception does not apply here.

2. Whether Kensington's cause of action is "based . . . upon" any alleged act performed by SNPC in the United States in connection with its commercial activity abroad

The second prong of the commercial activities exception applies if the plaintiff's action is "based . . . upon *an act performed in the United States* in connection with a commercial activity of the foreign state elsewhere." 28 U.S.C. § 1605(a)(2) (emphasis added). . . . Here, Kensington has not argued that any non-commercial acts performed by SNPC in the United States allegedly formed the basis of its complaint. Accordingly, this prong of the commercial activities exception is also inapplicable.

3. Whether SNPC's alleged activity abroad had a "direct effect" in the United States

The third prong of the commercial activities exception applies when the plaintiff's action is "based . . . upon an act outside the territory of the United States in connection with a commercial activity of the foreign state elsewhere *and that act causes a direct effect in the United States.*" 28 U.S.C. § 1605(a)(2) (emphasis added). Here, Kensington's action may properly be characterized as "based . . . upon" the execution of the prepayment agreements, which can constitute "an act outside the territory of the United States in connection with a commercial activity of the foreign state elsewhere." However, in order to abrogate sovereign immunity under this provision, Kensington must also show that this act caused a "direct effect" in the United States.

"[A]n effect is direct if it follows as an immediate consequence of the defendant's . . . activity." *Republic of Argentina v. Weltover,*

Inc., 504 U.S. 607, 618, 112 S. Ct. 2160, 119 L. Ed. 2d 394 (1992) (internal quotation marks omitted; alteration in original). The effect need not be substantial or foreseeable, *id.*, but it must be something more than trivial or incidental. "Congress did not intend to provide jurisdiction whenever the ripples caused by an overseas transaction manage eventually to reach the shores of the United States." *Virtual Countries, Inc. v. Republic of South Africa*, 300 F.3d 230, 236 (2d Cir. 2002) (internal quotation marks omitted). Here, the record does not support a finding that SNPC's execution of the prepayment agreements caused a "direct effect" in the United States.

Accepting as true Kensington's allegation that SNPC executed an elaborate scheme to thwart legitimate creditors from collecting on debts owed by Congo by "stealing" oil and engaging in "straw men" transactions to keep the oil revenue away from creditors, we cannot conclude that these actions had a "direct" or "immediate" consequence in the United States. The record does not indicate that the prepayment agreements required performance in the United States. . . . Nor does the record indicate that Kensington has suffered harm felt in the United States. Kensington is a foreign corporation and thus any alleged injury it suffered occurred outside the United States. In *Rafidain Bank*, we held that the "direct effect in the United States" standard was not met where the loss was suffered by a foreign corporation. . . . Thereafter, we held that "the fact that an American individual or firm suffers some financial loss from a foreign tort cannot, standing alone, suffice to" satisfy the "direct effect" prong of the commercial activity exception. *Antares Aircraft, L.P. v. Fed. Republic of Nigeria*, 999 F.2d 33, 36 (2d Cir. 1993). . . . A fortiori, the financial losses allegedly suffered by Kensington, a foreign corporation that is not present in the United States, do not meet the "direct effect in the United States" standard.

On appeal, Kensington does not attempt to defend the district court's analysis on this point. Rather, Kensington raises a new argument in support of its view that SNPC's actions caused a "direct effect" in the United States. Kensington contends that the "direct effect" in the United States is the interference with a judgment obtained by Kensington in another lawsuit in the United States District Court for the Southern District of New York—against the Republic of the Congo—which recognized the validity of the foreign judgment Kensington had obtained in London. See *Kensington*

Int'l Ltd. v. Republic of Congo, 461 F.3d 238, 240 (2d Cir. 2006) ("On September 30, 2004, Judge Preska granted summary judgment to Kensington on its claim for recognition of the English judgment."). Kensington argues that a judgment is essentially like a contract and the "place of performance" of a judgment is the jurisdiction in which it is entered. Thus, according to Kensington, SNPC has "breached" a "contract" requiring "performance" in New York.

We find several flaws in this argument. First, it is procedurally improper because it is raised for the first time on appeal. . . .

Moreover, even if we were to exercise our discretion to consider this waived argument, . . . we do not find it persuasive. We reject Kensington's assertion that the legal judgment at issue here is equivalent to a private contract that requires performance in New York. This judgment does not have a "place of performance." There is no requirement that repayment of this debt be made in New York. Payment could come from anywhere and take any form. In addition, the judgment is against the Republic of the Congo, not SNPC or Itoua. The New York judgment placed no obligations or responsibilities on SNPC or Itoua to perform any act, let alone one in the United States. . . .

Furthermore, the prepayment agreements were negotiated in 1999 and the alleged unlawful transactions under the agreements occurred between 1999 and 2004. The complaint further alleges that the "latest" known act of alleged racketeering activity occurred in January 2004. The New York judgment was entered at the earliest on September 30, 2004, months after the alleged racketeering activity. Kensington does not explain how this scheme had the "direct effect" of interfering with a judgment that did not yet exist.

Finally, accepting Kensington's rationale would substantially narrow the scope of the FSIA. The threshold for recognition of a foreign judgment is not high. See, e.g., N.Y.C.P.L.R. §§ 5302–5304 (subject to narrow exceptions, foreign judgments that are "final, conclusive and enforceable" in the country where rendered are deemed conclusive between the parties and enforceable by U.S. courts). Under Kensington's theory, the mere recognition of a foreign judgment by a United States court would be sufficient to abrogate sovereign immunity regardless of how insubstantial the connection was between the acts underlying that judgment and the United

States. We do not believe such a narrow view of sovereign immunity corresponds with the statutory language. . . .

* * *

For these reasons, we find that the commercial activities exception does not apply to SNPC. We therefore hold that SNPC is immune from suit under the FSIA. Accordingly, the district court's decision with respect to SNPC is reversed with instructions to dismiss SNPC from the case. . . .

*   *   *   *

(3) Acts of terrorism

See B.1.d. (1) below discussing execution of judgments obtained under the exception to immunity for acts of terrorism.

c. Effect of dismissal on grounds of immunity in case to settle ownership of assets: Republic of Philippines v. Pimentel

In October 2007, at the invitation of the Supreme Court, the United States filed a brief as *amicus curiae* supporting a petition by the Philippines and others for writ of certiorari to the U.S. Court of Appeals for the Ninth Circuit. *Republic of the Philippines v. Pimentel* (No. 06-1204) and *Roxas v. Pimentel* (No. 06-1039), available at *www.usdoj.gov/osg/briefs/2007/ 2pet/6invit/2006-1039.pet.ami.inv.html*.

As explained in the U.S. brief, this interpleader action

was brought to settle ownership of certain assets allegedly misappropriated by Ferdinand Marcos when he was President of the Republic of the Philippines. The assets are claimed by several parties, including the Philippines (which under Philippine law is the owner of property acquired through the misuse of public office by Philippine officials), a class of judgment creditors of the Marcos estate, and a judgment creditor of Marcos's wife, Imelda.

The assets at issue were held in the name of Arelma S.A., created by Marcos in 1972, in an account with Merrill,

Lynch, Pierce, Fenner & Smith, Inc. ("Merrill Lynch") in New York.

In September 2000 Merrill Lynch commenced the interpleader action to settle competing claims to the Arelma account's assets, including the claims of the Philippines and the Philippine Commission on Good Governance ("PCGG"), and deposited the account's assets with the court. The Philippines and the PCGG asserted sovereign immunity under the FSIA and moved to dismiss the interpleader action because they were necessary parties to the litigation under U.S. rules for compulsory joinder. The lower court found that the Philippines and the PCGG were entitled to immunity and were necessary parties, but denied the motion to dismiss on the ground that they were not indispensable and in 2004 awarded the bulk of the Arelma assets to the Pimentel claimants.

Excerpts below from the U.S. brief provide its view that the Court should grant the petition in order to review the relevance of the Philippines' immunity from suit in deciding whether its presence was indispensable. Citations to other pleadings in the case have been omitted.

The Supreme Court granted the petition for certiorari on December 3, 2007, on the question "Whether a foreign sovereign that is a necessary party to a lawsuit under Fed. R. Civ. P. 19(a) and has successfully invoked sovereign immunity is, under Rule 19(b), an indispensable party to an action brought in the courts of the United States to settle ownership of assets claimed by that sovereign." 128 S. Ct. 705 (2007). The Court also instructed the parties to address whether the Philippines and the PCCG had the right to appeal the lower courts' decisions, given that they had been dismissed based on their successful assertion of sovereign immunity.*

* * * *

---

* Editor's note: On June 12, 2008, as this volume of the *Digest* was going to press, the Supreme Court reversed the Ninth Circuit decision and remanded to the district court with instructions to order dismissal of the interpleader action. *Philippines v. Pimentel*, 2008 U.S. Lexis 4889 (2008). The court found that it did not need to rule on the right to appeal issue.

I. THE COURT OF APPEALS' APPLICATION OF RULE 19(b) WITH RESPECT TO IMMUNE ABSENT PARTIES WARRANTS THIS COURT'S REVIEW

Federal Rule of Civil Procedure 19 provides for mandatory joinder of persons "needed for just adjudication." Rule 19(a) describes persons who must be joined in an action if feasible. For example, under Rule 19(a)(2)(i), if a person "claims an interest relating to the subject of the action" and "disposition of the action in the person's absence may * * * as a practical matter impair or impede the person's ability to protect that interest," that person must be joined.

If a person described in Rule 19(a) cannot be made a party for some reason, the court must determine, under Rule 19(b), "whether in equity and good conscience the action should proceed among the parties before it or should be dismissed, the absent party thus being thus regarded as indispensable. . ."

*   *   *   *

A. The Immunity Of An Absent Party Is A Very Significant Consideration In The Analysis Under Rule 19(b)

This Court has recognized the importance of sovereign immunity to the Rule 19 analysis in cases where the United States is the absent party. See *California* v. *Arizona*, 440 U.S. 59 (1979); *Mine Safety Appliances Co.* v. *Forrestal*, 326 U.S. 371, 375 (1945); *Minnesota* v. *United States*, 305 U.S. 382, 386–388 (1939). . . .

Similarly, a number of courts of appeals have held that an absent party's sovereign status is entitled to special weight under Rule 19(b). For example, in dismissing a suit where the absent party was an Indian Tribe, the D.C. Circuit stated: "This is not a case where some procedural defect such as venue precludes litigation of the case. Rather the dismissal turns on the fact that society has consciously opted to shield Indian tribes from suit without congressional or tribal consent." *Wichita & Affiliated Tribes* v. *Hodel*, 788 F.2d 765, 777 (1986); see *Fluent* v. *Salamanca Indian Lease Auth.*, 928 F.2d 542, 548 (2d Cir.) (recognizing the "paramount importance accorded the doctrine of sovereign immunity under [r]ule 19"), cert. denied, 502 U.S. 818 (1991); *Enterprise Mgmt. Consultants, Inc.* v. *United States*, 883 F.2d 890, 894 (10th Cir. 1989) (where "a necessary party under Rule 19(a) is immune from suit, there is very little room for balancing of other factors set out in Rule 19(b), because immunity may be viewed as one of those interests compelling by themselves") (internal quotation marks omitted).

That is not to suggest that an immune sovereign is automatically indispensable. For instance, in some cases the interests of the absent sovereign may be properly and adequately protected by the parties remaining in the suit, and in others relief may be structured so as not to prejudice the absent party. . . . But even though the Philippines' and PCGG's immunity was not in itself outcome determinative under Rule 19(b), it should have received far greater weight than it did. Indeed, the court of appeals recognized that its analysis conflicts with the approach of other courts of appeals on this issue.

B. The Court Of Appeals' Rule 19(b) Analysis Was Flawed In Other Respects As Well

1. Central to the court of appeals' reasoning concerning the first factor in Rule 19(b) was its conclusion that the Philippines and PCGG would not be prejudiced by a judgment rendered in their absence because they had "no practical likelihood of obtaining the Arelma assets." The court found that any claim by the Philippines to the assets would be barred by New York's six-year statute of limitations for misappropriation of public funds. *Id.* at 8a–9a (citing N.Y. C.P.L.R. 213 (McKinney Supp. 2007)). By resting its analysis so heavily on its assessment of the merits of the Philippines' and PCGG's claims, the court in effect deprived them of the benefit of their sovereign immunity.

While this Court has not ruled out consideration of the underlying merits of a claim in the course of determining the extent of prejudice to an absent party from adjudication without his participation, . . . it is particularly problematic for a court to assess the merits of an absent party's own claim when the party's absence is due to its sovereign immunity from the court's jurisdiction. The immune party would either have to participate in the litigation (despite its immunity) in order to argue the merits of its claim, or risk the possibility that the court will, as here, underestimate the strength of the party's interest and evaluate the absent sovereign's claim based on the arguments of the present and hardly disinterested other litigants. In this case, moreover, the lower courts' assessment of the strength of the immune parties' interests was mistaken. Contrary to the court of appeals' assumption that the Philippines would have to sue Merrill Lynch in New York court to litigate its claim that Marcos obtained the assets illegally, that claim by the Philippines can properly be litigated in a Philippine court. The Philippines' claim to Arelma and its assets is based on Philippine law providing that property misappropriated by public officers through abuse of their office is forfeited to the Philippines from the moment it is obtained. A special Philippine court—the Sandiganbayan—is vested with authority to adjudicate disputes under that statute. Indeed, the Philippines and PCGG are presently seeking forfeiture of the Arelma shares and Arelma's assets in that court, and a fully briefed motion for summary judgment with respect to those assets is pending before it.

*   *   *   *

. . . It is unnecessary for this Court to decide whether a court in the United States would *always* be bound by a foreign court's judgment of forfeiture. It is sufficient to recognize that the court's categorical rule that United States courts would *never* enforce a foreign judgment of forfeiture relating to assets located in the United States is erroneous.

There are without question instances in which a foreign judgment of forfeiture relating to assets located in the United States may be recognized and enforced by a court here. Indeed, a federal statute specifically provides for enforcement of foreign judgments of forfeiture in certain circumstances. See 28 U.S.C. 2467(c) (upon certification by the Attorney General, "the United States may file an application on behalf of a foreign nation in [a] district court of the United States seeking to enforce the foreign forfeiture or confiscation judgment as if the judgment had been entered by a court in the United States"). Further, the Treaty on Mutual Legal Assistance in Criminal Matters (MLAT), Nov. 13, 1994, U.S.-Phil., Art. 16, S. Treaty Doc. No. 18, 104th Cong., 1st Sess. (1995), and chapters IV and V of the United Nations Convention Against

Corruption, G.A. Res. 4 (LVIII), U.N. Doc. A/RES/58/4, at 22, 32 (2003), contemplate cooperation by the two countries on proceedings related to asset forfeiture.

The MLAT, for example, generally requires the parties, as permitted by their domestic law, to assist each other when the object of a forfeiture proceeding in one country is located within the other country. The MLAT presupposes the existence of jurisdiction of Philippine courts over assets located in the United States, and vice versa. And, in fact, courts in the United States do sometimes exercise jurisdiction in civil forfeiture proceedings over property located outside the United States. See 28 U.S.C. 1355(b)(2) ("Whenever property subject to forfeiture under the laws of the United States is located in a foreign country, * * * an action or proceeding for forfeiture may be brought as provided in paragraph (1), or in the United States District [C]ourt for the District of Columbia.") (footnote omitted).[4]

Moreover, even assuming arguendo that the Philippine courts could not adjudicate ownership of the actual assets held in the Merrill Lynch account, it is undisputed that the Philippine courts have jurisdiction to determine the ownership of Arelma itself, as the share certificates are being held in escrow in the Philippines. If ownership of Arelma were awarded to the Philippines by the Sandiganbayan, there is no reason to assume, as the court of appeals did, that a court in the United States would refuse to recognize that judgment.

The court of appeals' analysis of the first Rule 19(b) factor also failed to take into account the logical priority of the Philippines' and PCGG's claims over those of the Pimental claimants. The Pimentel claimants do not assert that they are the rightful owners of the assets in Arelma account. Rather, as holders of a judgment against the Marcos estate, the Pimentel claimants ask the court to ascribe the Arelma assets to the Marcos estate through "'reverse piercing' of the corporate veil," and then to award those assets to

---

[4] If the Philippine judgment did not qualify for enforcement under Section 2467(c), there would be a further question whether the judgment would qualify for recognition under principles of international comity. See *Hilton* v. *Guyot*, 159 U.S. 113, 163–164 (1895).

them in partial satisfaction of their judgment against the Marcos estate. Thus, the Pimental claimants' claim depends upon a determination that the assets are really Marcos assets. If the Sandiganbayan determines that Arelma and its assets are forfeited under Philippine law, it would mean that those assets have been owned by the Philippines since the time Marcos first obtained them. The claims of the Pimentel claimants against those assets would thereby be vitiated. They would then be seeking to execute a judgment that they possess vis-a-vis *Marcos* against assets of the *Philippines*.

* * * *

C. The Court Of Appeals' Decision Threatens To Impair The Nation's Foreign Policy Interests

The court of appeals' decision threatens to undermine significant interests of the United States. The United States has a strong interest in the proper application of principles of foreign sovereign immunity, a matter of great sensitivity in foreign relations both because of its impact on foreign states and because of the United States' own interests relating to reciprocity. See *The Schooner Exchange* v. *McFaddon*, 11 U.S. (7 Cranch) 116, 137 (1812). More particularly, the United States has an interest in ensuring that property to which it has a significant claim will not be awarded to others by a foreign court that has no jurisdiction over the United States because of sovereign immunity. And the United States has an interest in cooperating with foreign governments in their efforts to repatriate assets misappropriated by their former leaders.

This case itself reflects such international cooperation in the agreement of the Swiss government and courts to transfer Marcos-related assets in Switzerland, including the Arelma bearer share certificates, to PNB to hold in escrow pending a determination by a Philippine court whether those assets are ill-gotten, and therefore forfeited. For a court in the United States, in effect, to nullify those proceedings by transferring the Arelma assets to Marcos creditors, without awaiting a determination whether the assets are, in fact, assets of the estate or of the Philippine government, frustrates the cooperative efforts of the Philippine and Swiss governments for an orderly procedure to repatriate the wealth stolen from the Philippines by its former leader. Indeed, the Swiss and Philippine governments have each expressed concern that the court of appeals' decision will undermine multilateral anticorruption cooperation. Those concerns provide additional reason for this Court to review the court of appeals' decision.

* * * *

d. Execution of judgments

(1) Attachments under the Terrorism Risk Insurance Act of 2002

(i) Property of Iranian Ministry of Defense

On July 17, 2007, the U.S. Circuit Court of Appeals for the Ninth Circuit issued an opinion finding that the holder of a wrongful death default judgment against the Iranian Ministry of Defense could enforce that judgment against certain property of the Ministry of Defense under the terms of the Terrorism Risk Insurance Act of 2002 ("TRIA"), Pub. L. No. 107-297, 28 U.S.C. § 1610 note. *Ministry of Def. & Support v. Cubic Def. Sys.,* 495 F.3d 1024 (9th Cir. 2007).

The case came before the court of appeals after the Supreme Court vacated the Ninth Circuit's previous decision, finding that the Ninth Circuit had failed to address the distinction in the FSIA between immunity from attachment against property belonging to a foreign state and immunity from attachment of property belonging to an agent or instrumentality of a foreign state. *Ministry of Defense v. Elahi,* 546 U.S. 450 (2006). *See Digest 2006* at 612–21; *see also Digest 2005* at 549–55 and *Digest 2004* at 516–17.

In its 2007 opinion, the Ninth Circuit held that the Iranian property at issue—a $2.8 million judgment obtained in a contract dispute against an American company—satisfied the criteria for attachment under TRIA § 201(a). Although not relevant to its analysis concerning attachment under TRIA, the court also reviewed the status of the Ministry of Defense ("MOD") under the FSIA as instructed by the Supreme Court. The Ninth Circuit determined that the MOD was a foreign state rather than an agent or instrumentality thereof, and thus was subject to more limited bases for attachment under the FSIA. In the absence of TRIA, the court found that the assets would have been protected from attachment under the FSIA. At the end of 2007, Iran's petition for writ of certiorari, filed November 7, 2007, was pending in the Supreme Court.

Excerpts from the court's opinion providing its analysis on these topics follow (footnotes omitted).

---

*   *   *   *

On remand, we requested two rounds of supplemental briefing and permitted the United States to appear as *amicus curiae*. As a result of this supplemental briefing, two additional issues have emerged. First, the parties agree that in 2003, Elahi applied for and received payment of $2.3 million from the United States Treasury in partial satisfaction of his $11.7 million compensatory damages award against Iran. In receiving this payment, Elahi signed a declaration in which he relinquished some, but not all, of his rights to pursue the remainder of his default judgment against Iran. Specifically, he relinquished his right to punitive damages and his right to "execute against or attach property that is at issue in claims against the United States before an international tribunal." Office of Foreign Assets Control, Department of Treasury, *Payment to Persons Who Hold Certain Judgments Against Cuba or Iran*, 68 Fed. Reg. 8,077, 8,081 (Feb. 19, 2003); *see also* Victims of Trafficking and Violence Protection Act of 2000 ("Victims Protection Act"), Pub. L. No. 106-386, § 2002(a)(2)(D) (as amended by TRIA, § 201(c)(4)).

The Ministry and the United States both argue that by accepting this payment Elahi waived his right to attach the Cubic judgment. They contend that the Cubic judgment is currently "at issue" in Claim B/61 before the Iran-U.S. Claims Tribunal in The Hague in which Iran is attempting to recover, from the United States, *inter alia*, any value of the Cubic contracts in excess of the ICC award.

The second new issue is Elahi's contention that he may attach the Cubic judgment under TRIA § 201, which created an alternative avenue of attachment for certain judgment creditors of "terrorist part[ies]."

DISCUSSION

1. Elahi's purported waiver pursuant to his receipt of payment under the Victims Protection Act

In the fall of 2000, Congress directed the Secretary of the Treasury to make available to certain judgment creditors of Iran payments equal to the creditors' compensatory damages awards. Victims Protection Act, § 2002(a)(1). Under this statute, a person is eligible to receive payment for certain judgments against Iran for harms caused by state-sponsored terrorism . . . .

In 2002, Congress amended the Victims Protection Act in several ways, three of which we highlight here. *See* TRIA § 201. First, it expanded the class of judgment creditors eligible to receive payment under the Victims Protection Act to include certain creditors who had filed suit against Iran before October 28, 2000 based on claims of state-sponsored terrorism. Victims Protection Act, § 2002(a)(2)(A)(ii) (as amended by TRIA § 201(c)(1)). This amendment made Elahi eligible to receive payment under the Victims Protection Act, as he had filed suit before October 28, 2000. *See Elahi v. Islamic Republic of Iran*, 124 F. Supp. 2d at 99–100 (noting entry of default judgment on August 14, 2000). Second, based on Congress's recognition of the limited funds available to pay victims with judgments against Iran, the amended Victims Protection Act authorized the Secretary of the Treasury to make pro rata payments on compensatory damages awards. Victims Protection Act, § 2002(d)(1) (as amended by TRIA § 201(c)(4)). Finally, the statute requires a person who accepts a pro rata payment to relinquish certain rights, including the right to execute against or attach "property that is at issue in claims against the United States before an international tribunal" or that is the subject of awards by such tribunal. *Id.* § 2002(a)(2)(D) (as amended by TRIA § 201(c)(4)). Elahi concedes that he waived this right by accepting a pro rata payment under the Victims Protection Act.

Iran has brought a claim against the United States in the Iran-U.S. Claims Tribunal, Claim B/61, for damages based on the non-export of contracted-for goods, including the ACMR that was the subject of the Cubic contract, by United States companies who breached contracts following the Iranian Revolution. Related to the [Air Combat Maneuvering Range ("ACMR")], Iran contends in its brief to the Claims Tribunal that the $ 2.8 million [International Chamber of Commerce ("ICC")] award (which became the Cubic judgment) did not fully compensate it for Cubic's non-delivery of goods, and it seeks to recoup the difference from the United States. In that filing, Iran distinguished between the Cubic judgment and its claim before the Claims Tribunal, stating, "[t]he subject-matter of this case, at variance with the ICC action, is the losses suffered by Iran as a result of the United States' non-export of Iranian properties." In other words, the Cubic judgment itself already adjudicated in the ICC action is not "at issue" in Iran's claim that it has not been fully compensated by the United States.

We find this concession persuasive in distinguishing between the contractual obligations resolved through the Cubic judgment and the United States' obligations that will be addressed before the Claims Tribunal. In essence, Claim B/61 addresses what liability the United States incurred by failing to restore frozen Iranian assets, including the ACMR, as required under the Algiers Accords. In contrast, the Cubic judgment had resolved Cubic's liability to Iran for nondelivery of the ACMR.

Nonetheless, Iran argues that the Cubic judgment is "at issue" before the Claims Tribunal because Iran has offered to offset from its demand against the United States in Tribunal Case B/61 any proceeds it receives from the Cubic judgment. This argument ignores Iran's presentation of its claims against Cubic to the ICC and its resulting judgment against Cubic. Having arbitrated this dispute before the ICC and secured a judgment against Cubic for its breach, Iran has fully adjudicated its claim against Cubic for non-delivery of the ACMR. Further, as noted *supra*, the Tribunal has no jurisdiction over claims against private parties, having jurisdiction only to hear counterclaims against such parties. The question of whether Elahi can attach the Cubic judgment is a separate matter from Iran's claim against the United States. Iran's claim against Cubic has been addressed by a tribunal, resolved by the $2.8 million arbitration award against Cubic, and further reduced to a judgment in the Southern District of California.

We hold that the Cubic judgment is not "at issue" before the Claims Tribunal and therefore that Elahi did not waive his right to attach the Cubic judgment by accepting a pro rata payment under the Victims Protection Act.

2. Attachment under TRIA § 201(a)

On remand, Elahi advances the alternative claim that he may attach the Cubic judgment under TRIA § 201(a). We agree that Congress created, in passing TRIA, a method of attachment for creditors such as Elahi who hold final judgments for harms caused by terrorism. *See* TRIA § 201(a) (incorporating by reference 28 U.S.C. § 1605(a)(7)).

Under TRIA, these creditors may attach "the blocked assets of [a] terrorist party." *Id.* Specifically, TRIA § 201(a) provides:

(a) In general.—Notwithstanding any other provision of law, and except as provided in subsection (b) [of this note], in every case in which a person has obtained a judgment against a terrorist party on a claim based upon an act of terrorism, or for which a terrorist party is not immune under section 1605(a)(7) of title 28, United States Code, the blocked assets of that terrorist party (including the blocked assets of any agency or instrumentality of that terrorist party) shall be subject to execution or attachment in aid of execution in order to satisfy such judgment to the extent of any compensatory damages for which such terrorist party has been adjudged liable.

TRIA § 201(a) (alteration in original).

Elahi's claim for relief under TRIA § 201(a) turns on two factors: (1) whether Iran is a "terrorist party" under that statute and (2) whether the Cubic judgment is a "blocked asset." The first factor is easily answered. TRIA includes within its definition of "terrorist party" a foreign state "designated as a state sponsor of terrorism" by the Secretary of State. TRIA § 201(d)(4). Iran is subject to this definition, having been designated by Secretary of State George Shultz as a state sponsor of terrorism. *See* Secretarial Determ. 84-3, 49 Fed. Reg. 2836-02 (January 23, 1984).

We therefore turn to the second factor, whether the Cubic judgment fits within TRIA's definition of a blocked asset. TRIA defines "blocked asset" to mean "any asset seized or frozen by the

United States . . . under sections 202 and 203 of the International Emergency Economic Powers Act [("IEEPA")] (50 U.S.C. §§ 1701, 1702)." TRIA § 201(d) (2)(A). The IEEPA grants the President broad authority to regulate foreign assets when faced with "an unusual and extraordinary threat" related to a declared national emergency. 50 U.S.C. § 1701(b). Following the hostage crisis in 1979, President Carter exercised his authority under IEEPA to freeze Iranian assets in the United States:

> I hereby order blocked all property and interests in property of the Government of Iran, its instrumentalities and controlled entities and the Central Bank of Iran which are or become subject to the jurisdiction of the United States or which are in or come within the possession or control of persons subject to the jurisdiction of the United States.

Exec. Order No. 12,170, 44 Fed. Reg. 65,729 (Nov. 14, 1979). . . .

Following release of the hostages, the United States unblocked most Iranian assets and lifted the trade embargo. *See* Exec. Order Nos. 12,276–12,283, 46 Fed. Reg. 7913–7929 (Jan. 19, 1981); Iranian Assets Control Regulations, 46 Fed. Reg. 14330–14337 (Feb. 26, 1981) (codified at 31 C.F.R. pt. 535). However, military goods such as the ACMR remained blocked. *See* 22 U.S.C. §§ 2751 *et seq.*; Exec. Order No. 12,170, 44 Fed. Reg. 65729 (Nov. 14, 1979); International Traffic in Arms Regulations, 22 C.F.R. §§ 120–30; OFFICE OF FOREIGN ASSETS CONTROL, DEP'T. OF TREAS., FOREIGN ASSETS CONTROL REGULATIONS FOR EXPORTERS AND IMPORTERS 23 (2007). . . .

*   *   *   *

In sum, we find that the Cubic judgment is a "blocked asset" under TRIA because it represents Iran's interest in an asset "seized or frozen by the United States . . . under sections 202 and 203 of the International Emergency Economic Powers Act." TRIA § 201(d)(2)(A). Because TRIA § 201(a) waives attachment immunity for such blocked assets, we hold that Elahi may attach the Cubic judgment.

3. MOD's status under FSIA

The Supreme Court's remand order asks us to determine the status of MOD. We answer that question although it is relevant only if our determination, either that the Cubic judgment is a blocked asset or that Elahi did not waive his right to attach the judgment under the Victims Protection Act, is in error.

All parties agree that, at a minimum, MOD is a "foreign state" for purposes of FSIA and that, as such, its assets would be subject to attachment under the narrow set of circumstances set forth in § 1610(a). The disputed question is whether MOD is an "agency or instrumentality" whose property is subject to attachment under the broader set of exceptions contained in § 1610(b). The answer turns on whether the entity, here the Ministry, is a "separate legal person." 28 U.S.C. § 1603(b).

In answering this question, some courts have created a "characteristics" test, asking whether, under the law of the foreign state where it was created, the entity can sue and be sued in its own name, contract in its own name, and hold property in its own name. . . . On the other hand, circuit courts have adopted a "core functions" test, asking whether the defendant is "an integral part of a foreign state's political structure" or, by contrast, "an entity whose structure and function is predominantly commercial." . . . The United States, in its briefing as *amicus curiae*, urges us to adopt the core functions test.

* * * *

We adopt the "core functions" test as the appropriate benchmark for deciding whether an entity should be viewed as a "foreign state" or as an "agency or instrumentality." This analysis has been adopted by each of our sister circuits which has considered the issue . . . and it is consistent with the purpose and structure of FSIA.

The question thus becomes whether MOD is inherently a part of the political state or a commercial actor. As the D.C. Circuit observed in *Transaero*, "the powers to declare and wage war" are so intimately connected to a state's sovereignty that "it is hard to see what would count as the 'foreign state' if its armed forces do not." 30 F.3d at 153. We find this reasoning persuasive, although we decline to adopt the D.C. Circuit's categorical rule that the armed forces will always be a part of the foreign state itself. *See id.* It is possible to imagine situations in which a state would "subcontract" its defense to paramilitary groups or mercenary forces that would not properly count as part of the state but rather as "separate legal person[s]." However, we adopt a strong presumption that the armed forces constitute a part of the foreign state itself, and that presumption has not been rebutted here.

Here, Elahi has presented no evidence that MOD is a "separately constituted legal entity" distinct from the Iranian state. *First Nat. City Bank v. Banco Para El Comercio Exterior De Cuba (Bancec),* 462 U.S. 611, 624, 103 S. Ct. 2591, 77 L. Ed. 2d 46 (1983). He has not established that MOD is "primarily responsible for its own finances," that it is run as a "distinct economic enterprise," that it operates with "independence from close political control," or that it exhibits any of the traits—other than the capacity to sue and be sued—that the Court has identified as characteristic of a "separately constituted legal entity." *Id.* As such, Elahi has failed to overcome the presumption that MOD constitutes an inherent part of the state of Iran.

A. Attachment of the property of a foreign state.

Although MOD is a "foreign state," Elahi asserts that he may still attach the Cubic judgment under 28 U.S.C. § 1610(a)(7). Under this provision, Elahi must satisfy two conditions. First, his judgment against Iran must "relate[ ] to a claim" brought "against a foreign state for personal injury or death that was caused by an act of . . . extrajudicial killing." *See id.* (incorporating by reference 28 U.S.C. § 1605(a)(7)). Elahi asserts, and MOD has no choice but to concede, that he has satisfied this requirement. Second, the property in dispute, *i.e.,* the Cubic judgment, must be "property . . . used for a commercial activity in the United States." *Id.* § 1610(a). The parties dispute whether Elahi has satisfied this second requirement.

Section 1610(a) provides that, under certain circumstances, "the property in the United States of a foreign state . . . used for a commercial activity in the United States, shall not be immune from attachment in aid of execution . . . upon a judgment entered by a court of the United States." 28 U.S.C. § 1610(a). Focusing on whether Iran's contract with Cubic constituted commercial activity, Elahi argues that the Cubic judgment was "used for commercial activity in the United States" because it "arose out of MOD's commercial activity." This analysis begs the question. Even assuming the Cubic contract constituted a commercial contract for sale of military goods and services, we are still faced with the question posed by § 1610(a) on the use to which MOD has put the judgment. The source of the property is not determinative and "the mere fact that the property has a nexus or connection to a commercial activity in the United States is insufficient." . . .

To satisfy § 1610(a), MOD must have used the Cubic judgment for a commercial activity in the United States, and this it has not done. We have recently stated that "property is 'used for a commercial activity in the United States' when it is put into action, put into service, availed or employed *for* a commercial activity, not *in connection* with a commercial activity or *in relation* to a commercial activity." *Af-Cap Inc.*, 475 F.3d at 1091(emphasis in original). Cautioning that "FSIA does not contemplate a strained analysis of the words 'used for' and 'commercial activity,'" we instructed courts to "consider[ ] the use of the property in question in a straightforward manner." *Id.* The Ministry has not used the Cubic judgment as security on a loan, as payment for goods, or in any other commercial activity. Instead, Iran intends to send the proceeds back to Iran for assimilation into MOD's general budget. Because repatriation into a ministry's budget does not constitute commercial activity, we hold that the Cubic judgment is not subject to attachment under § 1610(a).

*　　*　　*　　*

(ii) Assets of Iranian banks held in accounts with the Bank of New York: Bank of New York v. Rubin

On April 11, 2007, the U.S. Court of Appeals for the Second Circuit affirmed in part a district court decision determining that assets of three Iranian banks held in accounts with the Bank of New York were not subject to attachment under TRIA.

Bank of New York v. Rubin, 484 F.3d 149 (2d Cir. 2007). The court held that

> assets blocked pursuant to Executive Order 12170, 44 Fed. Reg. 65,729 (Nov. 14, 1979), and its accompanying regulations, *see* 31 C.F.R. Part 535, that are also subject to the general license of 31 C.F.R. § 535.579, are not blocked assets under the TRIA and therefore are not subject to attachment under that statute.

The court noted further, however, that the United States "notified the court prior to oral argument that the Department of the Treasury has recently frozen the assets of . . . Bank Sepah Iran ('Bank Sepah') because of its role as the 'financial linchpin of Iran's missile procurement network.' "[*] Therefore, the court vacated the judgment of the district court as to Bank Sepah and remanded in part to the U.S. District Court for the Northern District of Illinois "so that the district court may determine whether the Rubin defendants may now attach Bank Sepah's assets. . . ."

In an order of July 16, 2007, on remand, the district court ordered Bank Sepah's funds to be turned over to the Rubin defendants and Bank Saderat Iran's funds to be returned to the Bank of New York, for return to Bank Saderat Iran. *Bank of New York v. Rubin*, 2007 U.S. Dist. LEXIS 50827 (S.D.N.Y. 2007).

(iii) Former residence of Consul General of Iran: Rubin v. Islamic Republic of Iran

On December 13, 2007, the United States filed a Statement of Interest expressing its view that the district court should deny an application of judgment creditors for an order appointing their counsel as a receiver authorized to sell real property formerly used as the residence of the Iranian Consul General in New York. *Rubin v. Islamic Republic of Iran*, No. M19-63 (S.D.N.Y).

---

[*]   Editor's note: The order freezing Bank Sepah's assets is discussed in Chapter 18.C.4.c.

Excerpts below provide the U.S. argument that the property is not subject to attachment because it is not a blocked asset within the meaning of TRIA § 201. The full texts of the U.S. Statement of Interest and attached Declaration of Claude J. Nebel, Deputy Assistant Secretary of the Office of Foreign Missions of the United States Department of State ("OFM"), are available at *www.state.gov/s/l/c8183.htm.*

———

*   *   *   *

TRIA § 201(a) permits plaintiffs with certain judgments against a terrorist party to attach a "blocked asset" of the terrorist party in order to satisfy the compensatory damages portion of a judgment. TRIA, however, excludes from its definition of "blocked asset" any property "subject to the . . . Vienna Convention on Consular Relations ["VCCR"] . . . [that] is being used exclusively for diplomatic or consular purposes." TRIA § 201(d)(2)(B)(ii), 116 Stat. at 2340. Because the Consular Property is subject to the VCCR and is being used exclusively for diplomatic or consular purposes, it is not a blocked asset under TRIA and thus is not subject to attachment under that statute.

A. The Consular Property Is Subject to the VCCR

As plaintiffs admit, the Consular Property "was used as the residence of the [Consul] General of Iran in New York." . . . The VCCR definition of "consular post" includes "any consulate-general, consulate, vice-consulate or consulate agency". VCCR Art. 1(1)(a). The United States interprets "property of the consulate post" in Article 27(1)(a) to include real property such as the Consular Property at issue here. *See* Nebel Dec. ¶¶ 9, 15.[3]; *see also Hegna v. Islamic Republic of Iran*, 376 F.3d at 494 (finding that VCCR covers former residence of Consul [General] of Iran in Houston, Texas).

———

[3]   This view is entitled to substantial deference because the Executive Branch is charged by the Constitution with conducting the foreign policy of the United States, including negotiating treaties. *See, e.g., Sumitomo Shoji America, Inc. v. Avagliano*, 457 U.S. 176, 184–85 (1982); *Kolovrat v. Oregon*, 366 U.S. 187, 194 (1961).

Under the VCCR, the United States is required to "respect and protect the consular premises, together with the property of the consular post and the consular archives." VCCR Art. 27(1)(a). Thus, the VCCR mandates that the United States protect the Consular Property from an order of execution against it. The "respect and protect" obligation under VCCR Art. 27(l)(a) applies not just to the United States' treatment of property in this country owned by Iran, but also to the Iranian government's treatment of United States consular property in Iran. Accordingly, an order of execution against the Consular Property could impair the ability of the United States to obtain reciprocal compliance from Iran. . . .

B. The Property Is Being Used Exclusively for a Diplomatic or Consular Purpose

To fall under TRIA's exemption from the definition of "blocked asset," a foreign state's property subject to the VCCR must be "used exclusively for diplomatic or consular purposes." (fn. omitted) By renting Iran's consular property and using the proceeds to maintain the properties the United States is fulfilling its obligation under VCCR Art. 27(l)(a) to "respect and protect" Iran's consular properties. (*See* Nebel Dec. ¶¶ 11–15 (State Department's determination that "to fulfill the U.S. obligation under the Vienna Conventions . . . the real properties could not be adequately maintained over any significant period of time if not occupied. . . . [and] that rental . . . would provide a source of funds for essential maintenance and repairs"); *id.* (State Department's determination that "actions in connection with the maintenance and rental of Iran's diplomatic and consular property have been and continue to be taken exclusively for diplomatic and consular purposes, as such actions are in furtherance of obligations of the United States, as the receiving State, to protect the property pursuant to the Vienna Conventions")).

Because rental of the Consular Property has served—and was intended—to provide funds to maintain and repair the property in an effort to comply with the United States' "respect and protect" obligations under the VCCR, the United States' use of the property is exclusively for diplomatic or consular purposes. *See Hegna v. Islamic Republic of Iran*, 376 F.3d at 494 (holding that United

States has used Iranian consular property in Houston solely for diplomatic purpose by renting it in order to further its treaty obligations); *Hegna v. Islamic Republic of Iran*, 287 F. Supp. 2d 608, 610 (D. Md. 2003) ("[T]he goal of assuring that the United States is in compliance with its treaty obligations is quintessentially 'diplomatic.'"), *aff'd on other grounds*, 376 F.3d 226 (4th Cir. 2004).[5]

(2) Attachment under FSIA

(i) Property used for commercial activity: Af-Cap v. Chevron

On January 25, 2007, the Ninth Circuit Court of Appeals addressed whether certain property owned by the Republic of Congo was "used for commercial activity in the United States" and thus subject to attachment under the FSIA. *Af-Cap v. Chevron, 475 F.3d 1080 (9th Cir. 2007)*. The court concluded that that the assets in question were protected from attachment

---

[5] Plaintiffs rely exclusively on TRIA as a basis to execute against the Consular Property. There is no other source of law that would allow Plaintiffs to sell the Consular Property, and indeed, the Consular Property is specifically exempted from attachment or execution under both the FSIA and the [Foreign Missions Act ("FMA")]. Under the FSIA, property in the United States of a foreign state is presumptively immune from attachment, 28 U.S.C. § 1609. An exception from immunity may arise where the foreign state uses the property "for a commercial activity in the United States." 28 U.S.C. 1610(a); *see Republic of Argentina v. Weltover. Inc.*, 504 U.S. 607, 614 (1992) (operative test under FSIA is whether use by foreign state constitutes commercial activity). Because the Iranian Government used the Consular Property as the residence of the Consul General of Iran in New York and not for a "commercial activity," the Consular property is immune from execution or attachment under the FSIA.

The FMA, in turn, specifically prohibits attachment of mission property being held by the Department of State. 22 U.S.C. § 4308(f) ("assets of or under the control of the Department of State, wherever situated, which are used by or held for the use of a foreign mission shall not be subject to attachment, execution, injunction, or similar process, whether intermediate or final"). [The Department of State Office of Foreign Missions] currently has custody over Iran's diplomatic and consular property under 22 U.S.C. § 4305. Nebel Dec. ¶¶ 4, 14. Therefore, the Consular Property is immune from attachment under the FMA.

under the FSIA. Excerpts from this part of the decision—
which was then relied on in *Cubic,* discussed in (1)(i) *supra*—
follow (most footnotes omitted).

———————

In this consolidated action, Af-Cap Inc. (Af-Cap), the judgment
creditor, appeals the district court's judgment dissolving and vacating garnishments and liens filed against any property of the Republic
of Congo (the Congo), the judgment debtor, held by third party
ChevronTexaco Corporation (CT Corp) and domestic Chevron-
Texaco subsidiaries (collectively ChevronTexaco), and dismissing
Af-Cap's writ of execution action filed against ChevronTexaco,
three ChevronTexaco foreign subsidiaries, and the Congo, a sovereign country.

The Congo asserts a sovereign immunity defense against Af-
Cap's attempted execution of its judgment against the Congo's
property allegedly held by ChevronTexaco. The property sought
to be garnished includes intangible obligations of ChevronTexaco
owed to the Congo for various bonuses, taxes, and royalties related
to the extraction of hydrocarbons, oil, and other of the Congo's
natural resources. Because these obligations were not "used for a
commercial activity in the United States," they are protected from
execution or collection under the Foreign Sovereign Immunity Act
(FSIA) codified at 28 U.S.C. § 1610(a). We therefore affirm the
dismissal of this garnishment action.

*   *   *   *

In sum, we adopt in principle the test articulated by the Fifth
Circuit in [*Connecticut Bank of Commerce v. Republic of Congo,*
309 F.3d 240 (5th Cir. 2002) ("*CBC*")] to determine whether
property was "used for a commercial activity in the United States,"
as that term is used in the FSIA. Like the Fifth Circuit, we conclude
that property is "used for a commercial activity in the United
States" when the property in question is put into action, put into
service, availed or employed *for* a commercial activity, not *in connection* with a commercial activity or *in relation* to a commercial activity.

The FSIA does not contemplate a strained analysis of the
words "used for" and "commercial activity," and neither do we.

See Corporacion Mexicana, 89 F.3d at 655 (instructing that the FSIA provisions should be narrowly construed). Rather, we anticipate that this determination will be made by considering the use of the property in question in a straightforward manner, with a proper appreciation of the fact that the further removed the property is from the referenced commercial transaction, the less likely it is that the property was used *for* that transaction. *See id.*

We expressly decline, however, to incorporate the Fifth Circuit's articulated "reservations about defining property use as commercial in nature solely by reference to past single and/or exceptional commercial uses." *Af-Cap,* 383 F.3d at 369. In our view, attempting to quantify the number of commercial uses associated with the property, or to embark upon characterizing property use as exceptional or unexceptional, would unnecessarily complicate the determination to be made under § 1610(a).

C. Application Of § 1610(a) To The Obligations.

*   *   *   *

1. Af-Cap's Global Argument Regarding The Obligations At Issue.

Af-Cap first argues that all the obligations at issue were used for a commercial activity in the United States because the Congo and SNPC pledged the obligations as security for [a] 1984 Loan Agreement. However, Af-Cap's reliance on the 1984 Loan Agreement is misplaced. That Loan Agreement was between the Congo and a bank located in the Bahamas for the financing and construction of a highway in the Congo, to be managed by an English contractor. None of the obligations presently at issue and purportedly used for a commercial activity in the United States was in existence in 1984. . . .

2. The Obligations Used To Offset Prepayments Made By Chevron Texas To The Congo.

Based on a "Participation Agreement" between the parties, COCL is obligated to pay certain bonuses to the Congo because the Congo selected it to develop an oil field. A separate agreement between the Congo and [Chevron Overseas Congo Ltd ("COCL")]—a "$25 Million Prepaid Crude Oil Sales Contract"—provided that COCL would make a prepayment to the Congo for oil in the amount of $25 million, and also specified that: (1) "[t]he value of cargoes lifted by [COCL would] be credited by [COCL] against the outstanding Prepayment Amount," and (2) "in the event a participation bonus [was] payable by [COCL to the Congo], the amount of such participation bonus [would be] . . . applied as a credit against the [Congo's] obligation to reimburse the [$25 million] Prepayment Amount."

Af-Cap maintains that the obligation of COCL to pay bonuses to the Congo is the Congo's property, which the Congo used as collateral for the $25 million "loan" from COCL, an entity that the district court presumed was present in the United States for purposes of the dispositive motion. Relying on *CBC*, Af-Cap postulates that this obligation was therefore used for a commercial activity in the United States. *See id.* at 259 ("[T]he royalty and tax obligations would be used for a commercial activity in the United States if the Congo used them as collateral for loans obtained from United States banks.").

* * * *

Regardless of whether the obligation was previously used as collateral for the $25 million prepayment, when the $25 Million Prepaid Oil Sales Contract was consummated, the obligation was transferred to COCL and became the property of COCL up to the prepayment amount, which had not yet been satisfied. Given the unique structure of this transaction, which among other things allowed for other companies owing participation bonuses to the Congo to put their payments into COCL's designated bank account rather than paying the Congo directly, the district court did not clearly err in finding that the obligation is COCL's property. *See United States v. Perez-Lopez*, 348 F.3d 839, 845 (9th Cir. 2003) . . . Because only "[t]he property in the United States *of a foreign state*" is subject to garnishment, 28 U.S.C. § 1610(a) (emphasis added); *CBC*, 309 F.3d at 251 ("Under the FSIA, courts may attach *only a foreign state's property* . . .") (emphasis added) (internal quotation marks omitted), Af-Cap cannot garnish the obligation to pay bonuses or the bonus payments up to the prepayment amount.

Af-Cap also contends that the operator bonus was used for a commercial activity in the United States as "COCL paid the bonus to the Congo . . . by wire transferring funds from COCL's Citibank New York account. . . ." However, the method of payment is not determinative. The appropriate inquiry is whether the property in question was used for a commercial activity in the United States. . . . [I]in order to satisfy § 1610(a), the property must have been "used"; the mere fact that the property has a "nexus or connection to a commercial activity in the United States" is insufficient. *CBC*, 309 F.3d at 254.

3. CTGEI's $7 Million Payment To The Congo For The Acquisition Of SCLOG.

According to Af-Cap, CTGEI's obligation "to make payments of over $7 million to the Congo in exchange for 25% of the shares in the commercial joint venture" was "integral to the commercial activity" and, therefore, used for it. Af-Cap also declares that the joint venture was formed as a result of "substantial activities" in the United States and that substantial activities pertaining to the operation of the joint venture took place in the United States.

We reject Af-Cap's contention that the joint venture, located entirely in the Congo, constitutes commercial activity in the United States. Property that is "integral to" but not "used for" commercial activity in the United States does not meet the requirements of § 1610(a). . . . [W]hether the joint venture was formed as a result of substantial activities in the United States or whether substantial activities involving the operation of the joint venture took place in the United States is of no import.

4. $2 Million Payable by COPCL Directly To Third-Party Contractors For Social Programs Within The Congo.

Af-Cap argues that the obligations to pay for social programs, or the payments themselves, constitute Congolese property used for a commercial activity in the United States because under the agreement, "the obligations were paid for the benefit of, and at the direction of, the Congo." This argument is not convincing.

Assuming, without deciding, that the obligations or payments are Congolese property, "there was no commercial activity separate from the transaction that generated the property in the first place," *Walker Int'l Holdings Ltd.*, 395 F.3d at 236, and, as we have held, *supra*, how that property was generated is irrelevant. . . . The decisive point is that Af-Cap has presented no evidence that the Congo put the obligations or payments in the service of a commercial activity in the United States. . . .

D. The "Used For a Commercial Activity" Immunity Standard Applies to Property of SNPC as the Congo's Stipulated Alter Ego.

Af-Cap asserts that as an instrumentality of the Congo, SNPC's immunity from execution is governed by the standard prescribed in 28 U.S.C. § 1610(b), providing an exception from immunity for the property of an "instrumentality of a foreign state *engaged in* a commercial activity in the United States," rather than the more restrictive standard of § 1610(a), excepting from immunity only property of a sovereign "*used for* a commercial activity in the United States."

Af-Cap's contention is unavailing because, as part of the dispositive motion procedure, the parties stipulated that SNPC was an alter ego of the Congo, and an alter ego is not a "separate legal entity."

(ii) Assets of foreign central banks and distinction between foreign state and agent or instrumentality under FSIA: EM Ltd. v. Republic of Argentina

In an amended decision issued January 22, 2007, the U.S. Court of Appeals for the Second Circuit held that funds in an account of the Banco Central de la Republica Argentina ("BCRA") at the Federal Reserve Bank of New York ("FRBNY") were immune from attachment under the FSIA. *EM Ltd. v. Republic of Argentina*, 473 F.3d 463 (2d Cir. 2007). The court rejected arguments that the funds lost their FSIA immunity because the President of Argentina issued decrees giving the Republic authority to use BCRA funds for repayment of the Republic's debts to the International Monetary Fund ("IMF"). The court held that "the Decrees did not create an attachable interest on the part of the Republic in the FRBNY Funds, and that [FSIA] Section 1610's provision allowing attachment of property of a foreign state 'used for a commercial activity'

would not permit attachment of the FRBNY Funds even if
they were attachable assets of the Republic." Most footnotes
have been omitted from the excerpts that follow.

---

*   *   *   *

A. General Principles

*   *   *   *

The FSIA's protections against attachment and execution extend to
the instrumentalities of a foreign state such as BCRA, although the
protections applicable to assets of instrumentalities vary from those
applicable to the assets of the foreign states themselves. . . . Under
subsections 1610(a) and (d), assets of a foreign state can be attached
only *if the assets sought to be attached* are "used for a commercial
activity in the United States." But under subsection 1610(b), which
concerns agencies and instrumentalities of foreign states, creditors
may attach "*any property in the United States* of an agency or
instrumentality of a foreign state engaged in commercial activity in
the United States," 28 U.S.C. § 1610(b)(emphasis added). . . .

The FSIA provides additional protection to assets of foreign
central banks. *See* 28 U.S.C. § 1611(b)(1), note 7, *ante.* Congress
developed 28 U.S.C. § 1611(b)(1) to shield from attachment the
U.S. assets of foreign central banks, many of which might be
engaged in commercial activity in the United States while managing reserves and engaging in financial transactions, and to provide
an incentive for foreign central banks to maintain their reserves in
the United States:

> Section 1611(b)(1) provides for the immunity of central
> bank funds from attachment or execution. It applies to
> funds of a foreign central bank or monetary authority
> which are deposited in the United States and "held" for the
> bank's or authority's "own account"—i.e., funds used or
> held in connection with central banking activities, as dis-
> tinguished from funds used solely to finance the commer-
> cial transactions of other entities or of foreign states. If
> execution could be levied on such funds without an explicit

waiver, deposit of foreign funds in the United States might be discouraged. Moreover, execution against the reserves of foreign states could cause significant foreign relations problems.

H.R. Rep. No. 94-1487 ("FSIA House Report") at 31, *as reprinted in* 1976 U.S.C.C.A.N. 6604, 6630; *see also* Paul L. Lee, *Central Banks and Sovereign Immunity*, 41 Colum. J. Transnat'l L. 327, 376 (2003) (noting that Section 1611(b)(1) appears to have been developed in order to avoid the "potential difficulties" that central banks would be faced with if their assets were subject to attachment under the provisions of Section 1610(b) applicable to other instrumentalities).

Plaintiffs' reliance on the attachment provisions applicable to foreign states—§ 1610(a) and its prejudgment counterpart, § 1610(d)—rather than on the attachment provisions applicable to foreign agencies and instrumentalities set forth in § 1610(b), makes clear that their arguments are premised on a threshold determination that the FRBNY Funds are an attachable interest of *the Republic*, not of BCRA.

B. The Decrees Did Not Convert the FRBNY Funds Into an Attachable Interest of the Republic

Although plaintiffs hold or seek judgments against the Republic, the FRBNY Funds that plaintiffs seek to attach are held in BCRA's name. . . .

*　*　*　*

We conclude that (1) the Decrees did not alter property rights with respect to the FRBNY Funds—the assets that are the subject of the present appeal—but merely reflect the Republic's ability to exert control over BCRA itself, and (2) plaintiffs have not availed themselves of any arguments that would allow attachment of the FRBNY Funds based on the Republic's control over BCRA.

1. Control Over the FRBNY Funds

Plaintiffs' arguments concerning ownership of, and control over, the FRBNY Funds are not supported by the Decrees. The record is barren of any evidence that ownership or control over the FRBNY Funds was transferred to the Republic upon issuance of the Decrees, or that the Decrees required BCRA to use the FRBNY Funds, as opposed to other reserves, to repay the IMF. Rather than transferring funds to the Republic from BCRA, the Decrees and Resolution No. 49 directed BCRA to make reserves available to repay the IMF, and then to repay the IMF using those funds, leaving the decision of which specific funds would be used to BCRA's discretion. *See, e.g.,* Reply Br. of Appellant NML 13-14 n. 9 (acknowledging that "the Decrees fail to specify particular assets as Unrestricted Reserves").

While the Decrees may have manifested the Republic's ability and willingness to control BCRA, and to direct BCRA to use its assets for the benefit of the Republic, they did not cause control of BCRA's assets to change from BCRA to the Republic. To conclude otherwise would be to allow creditors of a foreign state to attach all of the assets of the state's central bank any time the foreign state issues directives affecting the central bank's reserves.[12] . . .

2. Control over BCRA

To the extent that plaintiffs' claim on the FRBNY Funds is based on the Republic's control over BCRA, as demonstrated by the Decrees, . . . plaintiffs have failed to avail themselves of well-established legal principles that might permit attachment. In [*First Nat. City Bank v. Banco Para El Comercio Exterior De Cuba* ("*Bancec*"), 462 U.S. 611 (1983)], the Supreme Court stated that "government instrumentalities established as juridical entities distinct and independent from their sovereign should normally be treated as such." 462 U.S. at 626–27. According to the Court,

---

[12] As the FRBNY points out, plaintiffs' theory could expose to attachment the assets of a majority of the world's central banks because national governments customarily retain the ability to direct their central banks to take actions with respect to the central banks' foreign exchange reserves. *See, e.g.,* M.H. de Kock, *Central Banking* 34–37, 312–18 (4th ed. 1974). Under plaintiffs' theory, for example, all of the assets of the United States Federal Reserve system would be treated as attachable interests of the United States (absent otherwise-applicable sovereign immunity protections) because the United States has exercised the power to direct the Federal Reserve Banks to transfer their "surplus funds" to the U.S. Treasury for use by the federal government. *See, e.g.,* 12 U.S.C. § 289(b)(1) . . . .

[f]reely ignoring the separate status of government instrumentalities would result in substantial uncertainty over
whether an instrumentality's assets would be diverted to
satisfy a claim against the sovereign, and might thereby
cause third parties to hesitate before extending credit to a
government instrumentality without the government's
guarantee. As a result, the efforts of sovereign nations to
structure their governmental activities in a manner deemed
necessary to promote economic development and efficient
administration would surely be frustrated.

Id. at 626 (footnote omitted).

*   *   *   *

In *Bancec*, the Court held that the "presumption that a foreign
government's determination that its instrumentality is to be
accorded separate legal status will be honored," *id.* at 628, could
be overcome under certain circumstances, including where the
instrumentality is "so extensively controlled by its owner that a
relationship of principal and agent is created," *id.* at 629, and
where recognizing the instrumentality's separate juridical status
would "work fraud or injustice," *id.* (quoting *Taylor v. Standard
Gas Co.*, 306 U.S. 307, 322, 59 S. Ct. 543, 83 L. Ed. 669 (1939))
(internal quotation mark omitted). . . .

*   *   *   *

We reject plaintiffs' effort to circumvent *Bancec* and our
decisions in [*Letelier v. Republic of Chile*, 748 F.2d 790, 794
(2d Cir. 1984)] and [*LNC Invs., Inc. v. Republic of Nicaragua*,
115 F. Supp. 2d 358 (S.D.N.Y. 2000), *aff'd sub nom. LNC Invs.,
Inc. v. Banco Central de Nicaragua*, 228 F.3d 423 (2d Cir. 2000)]
by characterizing the Republic's ability and willingness to control
BCRA as a transfer of property rights sufficient to give the Republic
an attachable interest in the FRBNY Funds. Under *Bancec* and its
progeny, plaintiffs bear the burden of overcoming the presumption
that the FRBNY Funds are not available to satisfy a judgment
against the Republic. *Bancec* indicates two circumstances in which
the presumption may be overcome—if BCRA were proven to be
the alter ego of the Republic, or if disregarding BCRA's separate

juridical status were necessary to avoid fraud or injustice. Plaintiffs chose not to argue that either of these circumstances existed here, even though the Republic's alleged misdeeds cited in plaintiffs' briefs might have lent some credence to these arguments. *Bancec* forecloses any argument that all of BCRA's $26.8 billion in reserves are "attachable interests" of the Republic merely because the Republic hypothetically *could have* ordered (but in the Decrees did not order) BCRA to assign or transfer the FRBNY Funds. . . .

C. Use of Funds To Repay the IMF Is Not a "Commercial Activity"

Even if we agreed that the Decrees effectively converted all of BCRA's reserves—including the reserves held in the FRBNY Account—into attachable assets of the Republic, we could not authorize the pre- or postjudgment attachment of the FRBNY Funds unless we found that the account had become property of the Republic "used for a commercial activity in the United States." 28 U.S.C. §§ 1610(a) & (d); *see* note 6, *ante* (quoting relevant portions of § 1610). Plaintiffs essentially concede as much by arguing that the Unrestricted Reserves are attachable because they were "used for a commercial activity.". . .

Plaintiffs contend that the Republic's use of the FRBNY Funds constituted "a commercial activity in the United States" under 28 U.S.C. § 1610(a) because the funds could have been used to repay the Republic's debt to the IMF. They rely on *Republic of Argentina v. Weltover, Inc.*, 504 U.S. 607, 112 S. Ct. 2160, 119 L. Ed. 2d 394 (1992), in which the Supreme Court held that Argentina's issuance of commercial bonds constituted "commercial activity" under the FSIA, *see id.* at 615–17, to argue that a repayment of debt *always* constitutes "commercial activity" within the meaning of the FSIA. Under this reasoning, the Republic engaged in "commercial activity" when BCRA repaid the Republic's debt to the IMF.

We disagree with plaintiffs' argument on two separate and independent grounds. First, we hold that the Republic's relationship with the IMF is not "commercial" in nature; thus, use of Unrestricted Reserves to repay the IMF did not constitute "commercial activity." Second, even if we assumed that the Republic's relationship with the IMF was "commercial" in nature, plaintiffs have failed to show on the present record that any of the FRBNY Funds were to be "used" to pay the IMF.

The FSIA's definition of "commercial activity" states that "[t]he commercial character of an activity shall be determined by reference to the nature of the course of conduct or particular transaction or act, rather than by reference to its purpose." 28 U.S.C. § 1603(d). According to the Supreme Court in *Weltover*, "[a] foreign state engaging in 'commercial' activities 'do[es] not exercise powers peculiar to sovereigns'; rather, it 'exercise[s] only those powers that can also be exercised by private citizens.'" 504 U.S. at 614 (second and third alterations in original) (quoting *Alfred Dunhill of London, Inc. v. Republic of Cuba*, 425 U.S. 682, 704, 96 S. Ct. 1854, 48 L. Ed. 2d 301 (1976) (plurality opinion)). This led the Court to conclude that "when a foreign government acts, not as regulator of a market, but in the manner of a private player within it, the foreign sovereign's actions are 'commercial' within the meaning of the FSIA. . . . [T]he issue is whether the particular actions that the foreign state performs (whatever the motive behind them) are the *type* of actions by which a private party engages in 'trade and traffic or commerce.'" *Id.* (quoting Black's Law Dictionary 270 (6th ed. 1990)). The Court concluded in *Weltover* that Argentina engaged in "commercial activity" within the meaning of the FSIA when it issued commercially-available debt instruments, because the instruments were "in almost all respects garden-variety debt instruments: They may be held by private parties; they are negotiable and may be traded on the international market (except in Argentina); and they promise a future stream of cash income." *Id.* at 615.

The Republic's borrowing relationship with the IMF, and the repayment obligations assumed thereunder, are not similarly "commercial" for several reasons. First, when the Republic borrows from the IMF, it "exercise[s] powers peculiar to sovereigns." *Id.* at 614. The IMF is a unique cooperative international institution established by treaty—the Bretton Woods Agreement—following the end of the Second World War. . . . The Republic is one of 184 sovereign nations that are members of the IMF. *See* IMF, *Members' Quota and Voting Power*, http://www.imf.org/external/np/sec/memdir/members.htm.

Second, the IMF's borrowing program is part of a larger regulatory enterprise intended to preserve stability in the international monetary system and foster orderly economic growth. *See* IMF Agreement art. IV § 1, 29 U.S.T. at 2208. . . . The Republic's borrowing relationship with the IMF is regulatory in nature because the IMF's provision of foreign currency or IMF-specific assets in exchange for domestic currency, *see post* (discussing unique nature of IMF loan arrangements), generally requires regulatory action by the Republic. *See Fact Sheet-IMF Lending*, http://www.imf.org/external/np/exr/facts/howlend.htm ("An IMF loan is usually provided under an 'arrangement,' which stipulates the specific policies and measures a country has agreed to implement to resolve its balance of payments problem."); . . . . The Republic agreed to many economic policy and regulatory reform measures in exchange for the IMF loans that were ultimately repaid in 2005. *See* IMF Independent Evaluation Office, *The IMF and Argentina, 1991–2001* 17–38 (2004) (describing and evaluating IMF's efforts to influence Argentina's exchange rate and fiscal policies, and to encourage structural reforms, in exchange for providing Argentina access to IMF capital); . . . .[21]

Third, the terms and conditions of the Republic's borrowing relationship with the IMF are not governed by a "garden-variety debt instrument[]," *id.* at 615, but instead by the Republic's treaty obligations to the international organization, as supplemented by the terms and conditions contained in agreements associated with individual loans. If the Republic failed to comply with these obligations, it would be in breach of the IMF Agreement and as a result could lose its rights to use IMF borrowing facilities, participate in IMF governance, and ultimately, remain a member of the IMF. *See* IMF Agreement art. V § 5, 29 U.S.T. at 2213; *id.* art. XXVI § 2, 29 U.S.T. at 2254. The vehicle for enforcing the Republic's obligations to the IMF is diplomatic and thus sovereign, not commercial. . . .

---

[21] We do not mean to imply that a loan becomes non-"commercial" any time a sovereign debtor agrees to take regulatory actions in connection with the receipt of the loan—for example, in order to become more attractive to potential lenders, or in order to satisfy terms and conditions of the loan. . . . We merely point out that the relationship between the Republic and the IMF, a multilateral organization, is non-commercial in a way that the Republic's relationship with commercial lenders cannot be because of the unique role that the IMF plays in regulating the international monetary system by intervening in the economies of its members.

Fourth, IMF loans are structured in a manner unique to the international organization, and are not available in the commercial market. Instead of obtaining currency in exchange for debt instruments, IMF debtors purchase "Special Drawing Rights" ("SDRs") or other currency from the IMF *in exchange for their own currency*. *See* IMF Agreement art. V § 2(a), 29 U.S.T. at 2210 . . . *id.* art. XVII §§ 2–3, 29 U.S.T. at 2239–40. . . . Because a nation state's borrowing relationship with the IMF takes place outside of the commercial marketplace, it cannot be considered "commercial" in nature. *Compare Weltover*, 504 U.S. at 617 (holding that Argentina "participated in the bond market in the manner of a private actor" when it issued bonds).

Even if we were to regard repayment of IMF debts as "commercial activity" within the meaning of §§ 1610(a) and (d), we would be required to hold that, on the present record, the FRBNY Funds are not available for attachment under § 1610 because the FRBNY Funds were never *"used for* commercial activity," and plaintiffs presented no evidence to the District Court that the Republic or BCRA intended the FRBNY Funds to be so designated. . . . The mere fact that the FRBNY Funds *could have* been used to repay the Republic's debts to the IMF after the Decrees does not, standing alone, render those funds attachable. . . . Even if actual use were not required, at least specific designation for such use would be necessary. . . .

Here, though, the Decrees made *all* BCRA funds *potentially* available for the repayment of the Republic's debts, and never specified which funds would be used to back the monetary base and which funds would be designated Unrestricted Reserves. Accordingly, plaintiffs cannot demonstrate on the basis of the Decrees alone that the FRBNY Funds were intended to be "used for" repaying the IMF.

D. The FRBNY Funds Are Immune From Attachment Even Without Reference to Section 1611(b)(1)

The parties have offered a variety of interpretations of 28 U.S.C. § 1611(b)(1)'s provision granting immunity from attachment for property "of a foreign central bank . . . held for its own account," provided that the central bank's immunity is not "explicitly waived."

28 U.S.C. § 1611(b)(1). But because the FRBNY Funds have remained assets of BCRA that cannot be used to satisfy a judgment against the Republic, we need not decide which interpretation of § 1611(b)(1)'s "held for its own account" language is correct in order to resolve this appeal. Section 1611(b)(1) provides a central bank with special protections from a judgment creditor who would otherwise be entitled to attach *the central bank's funds* under 28 U.S.C. § 1610. *See* 28 U.S.C. § 1611(b)(1) (protecting from attachment assets of a central bank "[n]otwithstanding the provisions of section 1610"). We have already held that plaintiffs have not established their right to attach the FRBNY Funds. Thus, even assuming *arguendo* that the FRBNY Funds were not "held for [BCRA's] own account," or that the Republic explicitly waived BCRA's immunity from attachment, plaintiffs would remain unable to attach the FRBNY Funds.

Our interpretation of Section 1611(b)(1) is in accord with the district court's opinion in *LNC Investments*, which found persuasive the Nicaraguan central bank's argument that its assets could not be attached to satisfy a judgment against Nicaragua even if Nicaragua waived the central bank's immunity from attachment:

> [a]lthough a parent government may waive the immunity of its central bank pursuant to § 1611, nothing in the clear language of § 1611 remotely suggests that such a waiver automatically renders a central bank liable for a judgment entered against its parent government. Section 1611 simply demonstrates that the assets of a foreign bank can be attached and executed to satisfy a judgment entered *against that foreign central bank* when, and only when, the central bank or its parent government has made an explicit waiver of the bank's immunity.

LNC Invs., Inc. v. Republic of Nicaragua, 115 F. Supp. 2d 358, 362–63 (S.D.N.Y. 2000) (alteration and emphasis in original), *aff'd sub nom. LNC Invs., Inc. v. Banco Central de Nicaragua*, 228 F.3d 423 (2d Cir. 2000); *see also* Paul L. Lee, *Central Banks and Sovereign Immunity*, 41 Colum. J. Transnat'l L. 327, 395 (2003) ("[W]hether or not the central bank has explicitly waived immunity and whether or not the funds constitute funds held for the central bank's own account, property of the central bank will be subject to attachment or execution only for claims against the central bank and not for claims that pertain only to the government or its other agencies and instrumentalities.").

*   *   *   *

2. Foreign Officials

In two cases in 2007 courts considered whether foreign officials are immune from jurisdiction under the FSIA or under longstanding common law immunity that the FSIA did not replace.

a. Matar v. Dichter

On May 2, 2007, the U.S. District Court for the Southern District of New York dismissed a class action suit against Avraham Dichter, former Director of the Israeli General Security Service, after finding him immune from jurisdiction under the FSIA. *Matar v. Dichter*, 500 F. Supp. 2d 284 (S.D.N.Y. 2007). In so holding, the court reached a result urged by the United States in a Statement of Interest filed in November 2006, but on different grounds. The court did not accept the U.S. view that foreign officials such as Dichter enjoy immunity from suit for their official acts pursuant not to the FSIA but to "longstanding common law that the FSIA did not displace." *See Digest 2006* at 629–52; *see also Digest 2006* at 465–76, 479–82, for U.S. arguments that it would be an improper exercise of the court's discretion to create a cause of action to cover the claims in this case, arising from Dichter's role in an Israeli military attack in the Gaza Strip in July 2002, under the Alien Tort Statute or the Torture Victim Protection Act ("TVPA").

Excerpts follow from the court's analysis of Dichter's immunity under the FSIA, and its conclusion that the TVPA does not trump the FSIA's immunity. For discussion of the court's view that even if Dichter were not immune, the suit should be dismissed as presenting a nonjusticiable political question, *see* Chapter 5.A.2.a.(2). Citations to other submissions have been omitted.

---

* * * *

The Complaint alleges that since the fall of 2000, Israel has systematically committed "targeted killings" of suspected terrorists. The targeted killings are allegedly performed with knowledge that civilians may be killed or injured. Since September 29, 2000, 327 suspected terrorists and 174 bystanders have died in targeted killing attacks.

* * * *

Dichter allegedly authorized, planned and directed [the bombing of an apartment building in al-Daraj in the Occupied Palestinian Territory]. More generally, the Complaint alleges that Dichter "developed, implemented, and escalated" Israel's targeted killing policy, and that the al-Daraj attack was "part of a pattern and practice of systematic human rights violations designed, ordered, implemented and directed with the participation of Defendant and carried out by military personnel acting at his direction."

* * * *

This Court must first consider whether foreign officials such as Dichter are eligible for immunity under the FSIA as "agencies or instrumentalities" of a foreign state. Plaintiffs contend that they are not. However, "[t]he Court is mindful that foreign sovereigns are legal fictions to the extent that they can only act through their individual officers." *Doe v. Israel*, 400 F. Supp. 2d 86, 104 (D.D.C. 2005); . . . . To allow "unrestricted suits against individual foreign officials acting in their official capacities . . . would amount to a blanket abrogation of foreign sovereign immunity by allowing litigants to accomplish indirectly what the [FSIA] barred them from doing directly." *Chuidian v. Phil. Nat'l Bank*, 912 F.2d 1095, 1102 (9th Cir. 1990).

Although the Second Circuit "has not clearly addressed" the issue of whether the FSIA applies to individuals, . . . numerous courts have found that "immunity under the FSIA extends also to agents of a foreign state acting in their official capacities . . ." *In re Terrorist Attacks,* 392 F. Supp. 2d at 551 . . .[2] On the other hand, "[a]n individual employed by a foreign state enjoys no FSIA immunity for acts that are 'beyond the scope' of her official responsibilities," i.e., acts that are "personal and private in nature." *Leutwyler,* 184 F. Supp. 2d at 287 (quoting *Cabiri v. Assasie-Gyimah,* 921 F. Supp. 1189, 1197 (S.D.N.Y. 1996)); . . .

*   *   *   *

B. *Application of the FSIA*

Plaintiffs unquestionably sue Dichter in his official capacity. Nothing in the Complaint permits an inference that Dichter's alleged conduct was "personal and private in nature." *Leutwyler,* 184 F. Supp. 2d at 287 . . . The caption in this action identifies Dichter as "former Director of Israel's General Security Service," and the body of the Complaint alleges that Dichter participated in formulating and implementing Israel's official anti-terrorist strategy. *See Doe,* 400 F. Supp. 2d at 105 (individual Israeli defendants, including Dichter, were immune from suit when "plaintiffs challenge[d] the conduct of the Israeli occupation activities in the West Bank—something that is an official policy of the sovereign State of Israel").

Furthermore, the State of Israel has represented to this Court that Dichter's actions were taken "in the course of [his] official duties,

---

[2]   In light of the cited precedent, this Court is unpersuaded by the Government's contention that the FSIA does not apply to individuals and, in its place, the Court should apply the common law that was operative prior to the FSIA's enactment. *See Republic of Austria v. Altmann,* 541 U.S. 677, 701, 124 S. Ct. 2240, 159 L. Ed. 2d 1 (2004) ("[I]nterpretation of the FSIA's reach [is] a pure question of statutory interpretation" that is "well within the province of the Judiciary," meaning the Government's views on the subject "merit no special deference.") "No authority supports the continued validity of the pre-[FSIA] common law" as applied to individuals who are not heads of state. *Chuidian,* 912 F.2d at 1103.

and in furtherance of official policies of the State of Israel." . . .
Courts assign "great weight" to the opinion of a sovereign state
regarding whether one of its officials was acting within his official
scope. *See In re Terrorist Attacks,* 392 F. Supp. 2d at 551; . . .
Dichter is entitled to sovereign immunity under the FSIA because
he is "being sued solely for actions taken in his official capacity."
Belhas, 466 F. Supp. 2d at 130; *see also In re Terrorist Attacks,*
392 F. Supp. 2d at 553 (foreign officials entitled to sovereign
immunity for official acts); *Leutwyler,* 184 F. Supp. 2d at 288–89
(same).(fn. omitted)

C. *Scope of Lawful Authority*

Plaintiffs allege that the extrajudicial killings alleged in the
complaint violate *jus cogens* principles of international law. On this
basis, Plaintiffs argue that the FSIA does not apply to Dichter because
jus cogens violations are necessarily beyond the scope of an official's
lawful authority. This Court disagrees. Plaintiffs cite several cases
in which a foreign official alleged to have violated *jus cogens* principles was denied immunity under the FSIA. However, these officials did not act in their official capacity. None of the cases cited by
Plaintiffs involved a situation where, as here, the foreign government had expressly ratified the defendant's actions and affirmed
that the defendant was acting pursuant to his official duties. . . .

. . . Indeed, courts have analyzed whether *jus cogens* violations
implicate FSIA Section 1605(a)(1), which provides that a foreign
state "shall not be immune from the jurisdiction of courts in the
United States [if] the foreign state has waived its immunity either
explicitly or by implication." 28 U.S.C. § 1605(a)(1). The courts
have held that "*jus cogens* violations, without more, do not constitute an implied waiver of FSIA immunity" for individuals acting in
their official capacity. . . .

D. *TVPA*

The TVPA provides that "an individual who, under actual
or apparent authority, or color of law, of any foreign nation . . .
(2) subjects an individual to extra judicial killing" shall be liable for
damages. 28 U.S.C. § 1350 Note, at § 2(a). Plaintiffs assert that
the TVPA trumps the FSIA as it applies to individuals, such that an
individual's immunity under the FSIA is forfeited when the official's

conduct falls within the TVPA. In *Belhas*, the court rejected an identical argument, explaining:

> Because a foreign official is an agency or instrumentality of the foreign state, and agencies and instrumentalities of foreign states are included within the definition of foreign state in the FSIA, the Court concludes that there is no basis in this case to treat individual officials differently from foreign states themselves under the FSIA.

Belhas, 466 F. Supp. 2d at 131 (internal quotations and citations omitted). This Court agrees. . . .

Plaintiffs contend that immunizing individuals acting in their official roles would conflict with the language of the TVPA, which expressly provides liability for those acting under "actual" authority of a foreign nation. This Court perceives no such conflict, because not all individuals acting in their official capacity will be immune under the FSIA. "In a case where an FSIA exception applies, a foreign state official acting in his official capacity could be sued under the TVPA." *Belhas*, 466 F. Supp. 2d at 131. Plaintiffs offer no compelling reason why statutory immunity should be abrogated in favor of the TVPA. The facts of this case do not warrant such an outcome.

*   *   *   *

b. Kensington v. Itoua

On October 18, 2007, the U.S. Court of Appeals for the Second Circuit remanded a case to the Southern District of New York for consideration of the immunity of Bruno Jean-Richard Itoua, a foreign official. *Kensington Int'l Ltd. v. Itoua and Société Nationale des Pétroles du Congo*, 505 F.3d 147 (2d Cir. 2007). The court also reversed the district court's finding that another defendant, Société Nationale des Pétroles du Congo ("SNPC"), was not immune under the FSIA under the commercial activity exception. *See* B.1.b.(2) *supra*. The court described Kensington, Itoua, and SNPC as follows:

> Kensington International Limited ("Kensington") is a Cayman Islands corporation that buys and sells debt and

equity instruments held by domestic and foreign entities. . . . Defendant-appellant SNPC is the principal state-run oil company of the Republic of the Congo. SNPC was created by statute on April 23, 1998, and its shares are fully held by the Republic of the Congo. SNPC's purpose, as defined in the statute, is to carry out all operations and transactions relating to Congo oil production and distribution. Defendant-appellant Itoua was the chairman and managing director of SNPC at the time of the acts alleged in the complaint and has since become the Minister for Energy and Hydraulics in the Congolese government.

Kensington filed its claim for damages under the Racketeer Influenced and Corrupt Organizations Act, 18 U.S.C. § 1961 et seq. As explained by the court,

> Kensington alleges that defendants engaged in a complex scheme to "divert oil revenues from the Republic of Congo into the pockets of powerful Congolese public officials, while at the same time protecting both the oil and the oil revenues from seizure by legitimate creditors."

Excerpts below provide the court's discussion of the source of Itoua's immunity and its decision to remand for consideration of that immunity. Citations to other submissions in the case have been omitted.

---

* * * *

. . . [I]t is an open question in this circuit whether individual officials enjoy sovereign immunity under the FSIA. The FSIA applies to foreign states. 28 U.S.C. § 1604. For purposes of the FSIA, a "foreign state" includes a "political subdivision of a foreign state or an agency or instrumentality of a foreign state." . . . On their face, these provisions do not expressly include or exclude individual officials.

The United States, which submitted an amicus brief in this case at the request of the Court, contends that the definitions [of agency or instrumentality] do not encompass individual officials, and thus Itoua is not entitled to invoke the protections of the FSIA. The United States argues that the FSIA was not intended to displace common law immunity, and therefore common law principles govern the question of whether individual officials like Itoua are immune from suit. The Ninth Circuit was the first circuit court to address this issue, and it rejected the government's position. *See Chuidian v. Philippine Nat'l Bank*, 912 F.2d 1095, 1100–03 (9th Cir. 1990) (holding that the FSIA applies to individuals acting in their official capacity on behalf of a foreign sovereign). . . . This circuit has yet to address the question. . . .

The district court recognized that ordinarily it would need to first determine whether Itoua can invoke the immunity provisions of the FSIA, but found it unnecessary because it concluded that even if Itoua were entitled to sovereign immunity under the FSIA, the commercial activities exception abrogated that immunity. As we explained above, that conclusion was erroneous. Thus, if the FSIA applies to Itoua, then, like SNPC, he is immune from this suit and should be dismissed from the case. Accordingly, we vacate the district court's decision with respect to Itoua and remand the case to the district court to address in the first instance (1) under what circumstances, if any, the FSIA applies to individuals; and (2) whether Itoua has demonstrated the existence of such circumstances. (fn. omitted) In determining whether Itoua is a "foreign state" for purposes of the FSIA, we note that the burden rests squarely on Itoua. . . .

*   *   *   *

In a letter brief filed May 23, 2007, at the request of the Second Circuit, the United States set forth its analysis of the common law immunity applicable to government officials as excerpted below. The full text of the U.S. letter brief is available at *www.state.gov/s/l/c8183.htm*. The U.S. Statement of Interest in *Matar v. Dichter*, referred to here and in 1.a.(iii) *supra*, is available as Document 67 on the *Digest 2006* List of Documents at *www.state.gov/s/l/c24878.htm*.

---

*   *   *   *

1. Common Law, Not the FSIA, Governs the Question Whether Defendant Itoua Has Immunity.

The parties' contentions concerning defendant Itoua's immunity have centered on the FSIA. Itoua argues that he qualifies as an "instrumentality" of a foreign sovereign and thus is entitled to immunity according to the FSIA's terms. Plaintiff argues in turn that the FSIA's "agency or instrumentality" definition, 28 U.S.C. § 1603(b), does not encompass individual officials. See Pl. Br. 43–44. Neither party has considered, however, whether Itoua may claim immunity from a source other than the FSIA, in particular the common law. Yet that is the question that should control.

As explained in a Statement of Interest filed by the government in a recently decided case in the Southern District of New York, *Matar v. Dichter*, 05 Civ. 10270 (WHP), 2007 WL 1276960 (S.D.N.Y. May 2, 2007), attached hereto and summarized below, the immunity of individual foreign officials is not governed by the FSIA. Rather, the immunity available to such officials stems from longstanding common law that the FSIA did not displace. While a number of courts, following the Ninth Circuit's decision in *Chuidian v. Philippine National Bank*, 912 F.2d 1095 (9th Cir. 1990), have construed the FSIA to extend to individuals, this construction is unsound and yields problematic results. Thus, the Court should reject Itoua's argument that he is immune as an instrumentality under the FSIA and, at the same time, remand for the district court to consider the question whether Itoua may claim immunity under pre-FSIA common law, as this question has not been raised or briefed by the parties on this appeal.

The *Dichter* Statement of Interest covers in detail how American jurisprudence has long recognized individual officials of foreign sovereigns to be immune from civil suit with respect to their official acts—as reflected, for example, in opinions of the Attorney General dating from the early years of the Republic. See *Dichter* Statement of Interest [hereinafter *Dichter* Statement] at 4–7. This immunity remained in place even as the law of sovereign immunity evolved over time. See *id.* at 7–10. Thus, in the years following the State Department's adoption of the "restrictive" theory of immunity in 1952, leading up to the codification of the theory in the FSIA, the State Department continued to recognize the immunity of individual officials for their official acts—as did the courts, following the Executive's lead. *See, e.g., Heaney v. Government of Spain,* 445 F.2d 501, 504 (2d Cir. 1971); *Greenspan v. Crosbie,* No. 74 Civ. 4734 (GLG), 1976 WL 841, at *2 (S.D.N.Y. Nov. 23, 1976); *Waltier v. Thomson,* 189 F. Supp. 319, 320–21 (S.D.N.Y. 1960).

Notably, in at least one of these pre-FSIA cases, *Greenspan v. Crosbie,* individual foreign officials were found to be immune notwithstanding that their conduct fell within the restrictive theory's exception to immunity for commercial activity. There, plaintiffs sued the Province of Newfoundland and three of its individual officials for alleged violations of U.S. securities laws. 1976 WL 841, at *1. Even though the Department of State determined that the province was not immune since the suit involved commercial activity, the Department filed a suggestion of immunity for the individual defendants, reasoning that they had participated in this activity only in their official capacities. The court dismissed the individual defendants from the suit on this basis, while retaining jurisdiction over the province itself. *Id.* at *2. Thus, the State Department recognized, and the court accepted, that the individuals were immune from suit even though the foreign state itself was not.[2]

Following the enactment of the FSIA in 1976, the Ninth Circuit in *Chuidian* was the first circuit court to consider whether the statute had any application to individual officials. The court found that it did; specifically, the court held that individual officials fall within the statute's definition of an "agency or instrumentality of a foreign state" and so possess the same immunity afforded to such entities under the statute. 912 F.2d at 1103. In reaching this holding, the court unnecessarily and erroneously rejected the government's position—which was the same position the government recently asserted in *Dichter*—that immunity for foreign officials is instead rooted in the common law. *Id.* at 1102–03. A number of

---

[2]   This differential treatment is analogous to the protection given federal employees under the Federal Tort Claims Act (FTCA). As amended by the Westfall Act, the FTCA permits suits against the government for the acts of its employees within the scope of their employment, see 28 U.S.C. § 1346(b)(1), but immunizes the employees themselves from liability for the same conduct, see 28 U.S.C. § 2679(b)(1).

other courts have followed *Chuidian* in this respect, though without significant analysis, and without the benefit of briefing by the government. *See, e.g., Velasco v. Gov't of Indonesia*, 370 F.3d 392, 399 (4th Cir. 2004); *Keller v. Cent. Bank of Nigeria*, 277 F.3d 811, 815 (6th Cir. 2002); *Byrd v. Corporacion Forestal*, 182 F.3d 380, 388 (5th Cir. 1999); *El Fadl v. Cent. Bank of Jordan*, 75 F.3d 668, 671 (D.C. Cir. 1996); *but see Enahoro v. Abubakar*, 408 F.3d 877 (7th Cir. 2005) (rejecting *Chuidian*'s holding that the FSIA applies to individuals, yet failing to consider the possibility of common law immunity for individual officials). The district court in *Dichter* perfunctorily followed the *Chuidian* line of precedent as well, without any attempt to address the government's criticism of the decision. *See Dichter*, 2007 WL 1276960, at *4 n.2.

The Court should reject that approach here. For while *Chuidian*'s outcome was correct to the extent that it preserved some form of immunity for individual foreign officials, its statutory interpretation is misguided. The *Chuidian* court based its holding on the flawed rationale that "a bifurcated approach to sovereign immunity was not intended by the Act"—i.e., that Congress intended the FSIA to be a "comprehensive" statute governing all sovereign immunity determinations, regardless of the nature of the defendant. *See Chuidian*, 912 F.2d at 1102. But this reading of the statute is inconsistent with its text and legislative history. The statutory text speaks only to the immunity of "foreign states," their political subdivisions, and any "agency or instrumentality of a foreign state," 28 U.S.C. §§ 1603(a)–(b), terms that do not naturally describe individuals. Likewise, the legislative history's only reference to any type of individual official—diplomatic or consular representatives—clarifies that the FSIA does not govern their immunity since the statute "deals only with the immunity of foreign states." H.R. Rep. No. 94-1487, at 21 (1976) ("FSIA House Report"), 1976 U.S.C.C.A.N. 6604, 6620.

Moreover, contrary to *Chuidian*'s premise, courts have followed "a bifurcated approach to sovereign immunity" in other contexts where the FSIA is silent. As numerous courts have held, because the FSIA does not address the immunity of heads of state, their immunity continues to be governed by common law as it was pre-FSIA. *See Dichter* Statement at 16 & n.12 (collecting cases);

see also Tachiona v. United States, 386 F. 3d 205, 220–21 (2d Cir. 2004) (expressing doubt that the FSIA "was meant to supplant" common-law immunity for heads of state, given that the statute and legislative history make no reference to individual officials). The same reasoning applies to the immunity of individual officials other than heads of state: the FSIA did not address their immunity, and so did not supplant it as it previously existed at common law.

Chuidian's mistaken analysis on this point is not of mere academic interest. By stretching the FSIA's terms to cover individual officials, the holding generates problematic implications. Most important, it implies that individual officials are subject to the same exceptions to immunity laid out in the FSIA for states and their agencies and instrumentalities—such that if an individual foreign official were sued, for example, over commercial transactions undertaken in an official capacity, the official would not be immune from suit and could be held personally liable for the conduct at issue. *See Chuidian*, 912 F.2d at 1103–6 (considering, after finding individual official's immunity to be governed by the FSIA, whether any of the FSIA's exceptions were met). There is no indication that Congress intended any such result—which, significantly, diverges from the common law as it existed at the time of the FSIA's enactment. As reflected in *Greenspan v. Crosbie, supra*, the immunity then recognized for foreign officials acting in their official capacity did not merely match, but rather exceeded, that of the state: even if the state could be sued for an official's acts under the restrictive theory, the official himself could not be. Thus, by subjecting the immunity of individual officials to the same limits applicable to the immunity of states and their agencies or instrumentalities, the *Chuidian* court's construction leaves foreign officials with less immunity than they enjoyed before the FSIA's enactment.

Furthermore, *Chuidian*'s interpretation of the FSIA's "agency or instrumentality" definition as encompassing individual officials would imply that an individual official's personal property qualifies as property of a state agency or instrumentality, making it subject to attachment according to the rules set forth in FSIA § 1610. Yet § 1610 was clearly intended to apply only to state-owned assets. *See* FSIA House Report at 27–30, 1976 U.S.C.C.A.N. at 6626–29. Notably, § 1610 affords litigants broader attachment rights with respect to property of state agencies or instrumentalities compared to property of the state itself: so long as an agency or instrumentality is "engaged in commercial activity in the United States," any of its property in the United States can be attached to satisfy any claim as to which it lacks immunity from suit. *See* 28 U.S.C. § 1610(b); *see also De Letelier v. Republic of Chile*, 748 F.2d 790, 798–99 (2d Cir. 1984). Another important difference is that an agency or instrumentality of a foreign state is subject to punitive damages under the FSIA, whereas the foreign state itself is not. *See* 28 U.S.C. § 1606. Thus, were the FSIA's "agency or instrumentality" definition read to encompass individual officials, litigants in any FSIA action would have an obvious incentive to name as many individual foreign officials as possible as defendants, in order to maximize the potential for recovery and to circumvent the FSIA's limitations on attachment and punitive damages that apply to a suit against the state itself. It defies common sense to believe that Congress intended these consequences.

For all of these reasons, the Court should decline Itoua's invitation to hold that he is immune under the FSIA as an "agency or instrumentality" of a foreign state. To the extent Itoua can claim immunity from suit, such immunity would have to rest on common law rather than any provision of the FSIA. By so holding, the Court would effectively preserve immunity for individual foreign officials while avoiding the conceptual difficulties and problematic implications of the *Chuidian* approach.

As to whether Itoua is ultimately entitled to claim common law immunity here, the Court should remand the case for the district court to decide that issue in the first instance, as it turns on potentially complex questions that have not been raised or briefed by the parties and that are not addressed in the United States' Statement of Interest in *Dichter*. In particular, while common law immunity clearly extends to the official acts of traditional government ministers, such as the internal security minister sued in the *Dichter* case, it is not clear whether (and if so, to what extent) this immunity applies to corporate officers of a state owned commercial enterprise, such as Itoua. Moreover, even if common law immunity did extend to such individuals, there would still remain the question whether Itoua's allegedly corrupt conduct should be regarded as official or private in nature, *see Dichter* Statement at 24, a question that has received only cursory treatment here.

The government may wish to submit views on these and other relevant questions on remand.

*   *   *   *

c. Immunity of foreign officials from criminal jurisdiction

On October 31, John B. Bellinger, III, Department of State Legal Adviser, addressed the Sixth Committee of the General Assembly on the report of the International Law Commission on the Work of its 59th Session. Mr. Bellinger noted the ILC's decision to include the topic "Immunity of State officials from foreign criminal jurisdiction" in its program of work, stating: "The criminal prosecution of foreign officials raises complex issues of domestic and international law. We look forward to contributing to the Commission's work on this topic." The full text of Mr. Bellinger's statement is available at *www.state. gov/s/l/c8183.htm.*

C. DIPLOMATIC IMMUNITY

1. Employment Relationship: *Gonzalez v. Vila*

On March 29, 2007, the U.S. District Court for the District of Columbia ruled that a diplomat and his wife were immune from a suit by an employee alleging wage and employment violations. *Gonzalez v. Vila*, 479 F. Supp. 2d 187 (D.D.C. 2007). Excerpts below provide the court's analysis in rejecting arguments that the employment contract between the diplomat and his wife on the one hand and the domestic worker on the other constituted "commercial activity" exempted from the protection of diplomatic immunity by the Vienna Convention on Diplomatic Relations, and that "commercial activity" analysis under the FSIA was relevant to diplomatic immunity. Citations to submissions in the case have been omitted.

*   *   *   *

The Vienna Convention on Diplomatic Relations provides in relevant part that a "diplomatic agent shall . . . enjoy immunity from [the receiving state's] civil and administrative jurisdiction. . . ." VCDR, Article 31(1). There are three exceptions set forth in the Convention, including an exception "in the case of . . . (c) an action relating to any professional or commercial activity exercised by the diplomatic agent in the receiving State outside his official functions." *Id.* The Convention also provides that the "members of the family of a diplomatic agent forming part of his household shall, if they are not nationals of the receiving State, enjoy the privileges and immunities specified in Articles 29 to 36." VCDR, Article 37. Finally, the VCDR provides that a diplomatic agent "shall not in the receiving State practise for personal profit any professional or commercial activity." VCDR, Article 42.

. . . As the defendants have moved to dismiss on the grounds of diplomatic immunity, the only question before the Court is whether defendants are immune under the terms of the Vienna Convention, or whether, as plaintiff contends, they are excepted from immunity under Article 31(1)(c) thereof. If the Court concludes that defendants are immune, it must dismiss the action pursuant to 22 U.S.C. § 254d.

* * * *

Plaintiff made her first argument—that defendants did not present any evidence supporting their assertion of diplomatic immunity—before the letter from the Embassy of Argentina arrived and was filed on the docket of the Court. That letter, and the letter from the United States Department of State included with it certifying the defendants' status as diplomatic agent and family member thereof, render plaintiff's first argument moot. The process by which the defendants in this case have documented their diplomatic status was appropriate. As the D.C. Circuit has explained, "[i]t is enough that [the diplomat] has requested immunity, that the State Department has recognized that the person for whom it was requested is entitled to it, and that the Department's recognition has been communicated to the court. The courts are disposed to accept as conclusive of the fact of the diplomatic status of an individual claiming an exemption, the views thereon of the political department of their government." *Carrera v. Carrera*, 84 U.S. App. D.C. 333, 174 F.2d 496, 497 (D.C. Cir. 1949) (internal quotation and citation omitted). . . .

With respect to plaintiff's second argument, there are few published decisions of United States courts interpreting the "commercial activity" exception found within Article 31(1)(c) of the Vienna Convention.[5] Judge Ellis in the Eastern District of Virginia was faced with a case involving similar allegations and defenses in *Tabion v. Mufti*, 877 F. Supp. 285 (E.D.Va. 1995), aff'd 73 F.3d at 539. As Ms. Gonzalez and *amici* do in this case, the plaintiff in *Tabion* argued that her employment relationship with the defendants was itself a commercial activity with respect to which the defendants should not be diplomatically immune. *See id.* at 287. Both Judge Ellis and the Fourth Circuit concluded that this argument was incorrect. The Fourth Circuit explained:

> When examined in context, the term "commercial activity" [as used in the Vienna Convention on Diplomatic Relations] does not have so broad a meaning as to include occasional service contracts as [plaintiff] contends, but rather relates only to trade or business activity engaged in for personal profit. Accepting the broader meaning fails to take into account the treaty's background and negotiating

---

[5]   The Court rejects the suggestion of the plaintiff and *amici* that case law interpreting and applying the phrase "commercial activity" under the Foreign Sovereign Immunities Act should inform the interpretation of the commercial activity exception to diplomatic immunity under the VCDR, largely for the reasons carefully explained by the Fourth Circuit in *Tabion*. *See Tabion v. Mufti*, 73 F.3d at 539 n.7. In sum: the Vienna Convention is a multilateral treaty—a contract between many sovereign nations—rather than a domestic American statute; it was written well before the FSIA was enacted; and there is evidence that Congress specifically did not intend for the FSIA to change the meaning of existing international agreements. *See id.* . . .

In a Statement of Interest filed by the United States pursuant to 28 U.S.C. § 517, the United States Department of State expressed a similar position—it agrees that "the case law interpreting the term 'commercial activity' under the FSIA should not be used to interpret the same term under the Diplomatic Relations Convention." This Court also agrees, and therefore will not consider any cases under the FSIA in its analysis of this case.

history, as well as its subsequent interpretation. It also ignores the relevance of the remainder of the phrase—"outside his official functions."

Tabion v. Mufti, 73 F.3d at 537. The State Department filed a Statement of Interest in *Tabion* (as it has in this case), which concluded that "the term 'commercial activity' as used in the exception 'focuses on the pursuit of trade or business activity; it does not encompass contractual relationships for goods and services incidental to the daily life of the diplomat and his family in the receiving State.'" *Tabion v. Mufti*, 73 F.3d at 538 (quoting a Statement of Interest of the United States).

Similarly, the Statement of Interest filed by the United States in this case concluded that "[w]hen diplomats enter into contractual relationships for personal goods or services incidental to residing in the host country, including the employment of domestic workers, they are not engaging in 'commercial activity' as that term is used in the Diplomatic Relations Convention." The Supreme Court has held that "although not conclusive, the meaning attributed to treaty provisions by the Government agencies charged with their negotiation and enforcement is entitled to great weight." *United States v. Stuart*, 489 U.S. 353, 369, 109 S. Ct. 1183, 103 L. Ed. 2d 388 (1989) (citing *Sumi[tom]o Shoji America, Inc. v. Avagliano*, 457 U.S. 176, 184–85, 102 S. Ct. 2374, 72 L. Ed. 2d 765 (1982) (internal quotations and citations omitted)). Accordingly, the Statement of Interest filed by the United States, while not dispositive, is entitled to great deference. . . . The Court finds no reason to disagree with the conclusion of the Department of State—and the Fourth Circuit—that a contract for domestic services such as the one at issue in this case is not itself a "commercial activity" within the meaning of Article 31(1)(c) of the Vienna Convention on Diplomatic Relations.

Plaintiff also argues that because Ms. Nielsen was pursuing academic studies—a pursuit facilitated by Ms. Gonzalez's provision of domestic help—this case is "an action relating to any professional . . . activity exercised by the diplomatic agent in the receiving State outside his official functions" under Article 31(1)(c) of the VCDR. This argument, while creative, also is without merit.

Even if the Court were to conclude—which it does not—that the pursuit of academic studies is a professional activity under the Convention, plaintiff's argument would fail. To conclude that the pursuit of academic study by a diplomat's wife is "related to" the provision of domestic services within the meaning of the exception to immunity is to read the treaty too broadly. . . . The Court cannot conclude that this lawsuit is "an action related to" a professional activity within the meaning of the Convention simply because having domestic services would be helpful while one is pursuing an L.L.M.

*   *   *   *

Plaintiff's final argument is that "diplomatic immunity should not extend to those who, like defendants in this case, obtained entry into the United States based on misrepresentations and deceit." Plaintiff may be correct that it "should" not—but that is a policy argument more appropriately directed at either Congress or the Department of State, not at this Court. The Department of State certified the defendants' diplomatic status, and it is not for this Court to revoke or question it, but rather only to determine if an exception to diplomatic immunity set forth in the Convention applies. As noted, "the courts are disposed to accept as conclusive of the fact of the diplomatic status of an individual claiming an exemption, the views thereon of the political department of their government." *Carrera v. Carrera*, 174 F.2d at 497 (internal quotation and citation omitted). Fraud is not an exception recognized within the Vienna Convention itself, so—in this forum at least—plaintiff's third argument must fail. *See* VCDR, Article 31(1).

*   *   *   *

In upholding defendants' claim of diplomatic immunity from suit, the Court recognizes that it is leaving plaintiff without recourse—at least within the United States and at this time. Again, the Fourth Circuit eloquently described the phenomenon:

Here, as in most cases invoking sovereign immunity, there may appear to be some unfairness to the person against whom the invocation occurs. But it must be remembered that the outcome merely reflects policy choices already made.

Policymakers in Congress and the Executive Branch clearly have believed that diplomatic immunity not only ensures the efficient functioning of diplomatic missions in foreign states, but fosters goodwill and enhances relations among nations. Thus, they have determined that apparent inequity to a private individual is outweighed by the great injury to the public that would arise from permitting suit against the entity or its agents calling for application of immunity.

Tabion v. Mufti, 73 F.3d at 539. The conduct of foreign relations is not entrusted to the judiciary, and in the cases that come before it the Court may only apply the treaties (and related statutes) that the President has signed and that Congress has ratified. And the law that binds this Court states that "[a]ny action or proceeding brought against an individual who is entitled to immunity with respect to such action or proceeding under the Vienna Convention on Diplomatic Relations . . . *shall be dismissed*." 22 U.S.C. § 254d (emphasis provided); *but see supra* at 2 n.2. Accordingly, defendants' motion to quash service of process and dismiss the complaint will be granted. This action will be dismissed without prejudice.

*　*　*　*

2. Diplomatic Pouch

On January 23, 2007, the International Civil Aviation Organization ("ICAO") Working Group on the Diplomatic Pouch (a subgroup of ICAO's Aviation Security Panel of Experts) completed work to update the seventh edition of the Security Manual for Safeguarding Civil Aviation Against Acts of Unlawful Interference (Document 8973). ICAO Contracting States have obligations under the Chicago Convention to implement ICAO Global Standards and Recommended Practices, and the Security Manual provides the guidelines for fulfilling those obligations with respect to aviation security.

In December 2007 ICAO posted selected portions of Volume I and Volume IV of the revised edition to a restricted website, available to governmental authorities with the appropriate password at *www.icao.int/icaonet*. Those selections include Appendix 1 to Volume I (National Organization and Administration), concerning in-flight security officers, and sections of Volume IV (Preventive Measures) entitled "Diplomatic Personnel/VIPs," "Royalty and Heads of State," and "Diplomatic Bags/Pouches."

The United States was actively engaged in negotiations leading to the adoption of the revised manual and served as chair of a working group on guidelines concerning the diplomatic pouch. Among other issues, the United States welcomed ICAO's adoption of language for the seventh edition of the Security Manual clarifying that the screening of hold baggage does not require nor authorize the screening of diplomatic bags by X-ray or any other method inconsistent with the Vienna Convention on Diplomatic Relations.

D. HEAD OF STATE IMMUNITY

On November 23, 2007, the United States filed a Suggestion of Immunity in the U.S. District Court for the Eastern District of New York suggesting the immunity of Keith Mitchell, Prime Minister of Grenada, from the jurisdiction of the court. *Howland v. Resteiner*, Civ No. 07-2332 (ILG)(SMG). A letter from U.S. State Department Legal Adviser John B. Bellinger, III, attached to the Suggestion of Immunity, stated:

> The Department of State recognizes and allows the immunity of Prime Minister Mitchell from this suit. Under the rules of customary international law, recognized and applied in the United States, Prime Minister Mitchell, as the sitting head of government of a foreign state, is immune from the jurisdiction of the United States courts. . . .
>
> This letter recognizes the particular importance attached by the United States to obtaining the prompt dismissal of the proceedings against Prime Minister Mitchell in view of the significant foreign policy implications of such an action against the head of a foreign government.

Excerpts below from the Suggestion of Immunity provide the views of the United States on the law applicable to head of state immunity in U.S. courts. The full texts of the Suggestion of Immunity and the attached letter from Mr. Bellinger are available at *www.state.gov/sl/c8183.htm*.

* * * *

2. Under customary rules of international law, recognized and applied in the United States, the head of a foreign government is immune from the jurisdiction of United States courts under the doctrine of head-of-state immunity. *See Lafontant v. Aristide*, 844 F. Supp. 128, 133 (E.D.N.Y.), *appeal dismissed*, No. 94-6026 (2d Cir. 1994); *Saltany v. Reagan*, 702 F. Supp. 319, 320 (D.D.C. 1988), *rev'd in part on other grounds*, 886 F.2d 438 (D.C. Cir. 1989). The head-of-state immunity doctrine serves to protect the dignity of foreign leaders and reflects the principle that conflicts with sovereign nations are often best handled through diplomacy rather than litigation. *See Ex parte Peru*, 318 U.S. 578, 588–89 (1943). The doctrine traces its roots to the Supreme Court's decision in *The Schooner Exchange v. M'Faddon*, 11 U.S. (7 Cranch) 116 (1812). Although that case held merely that an armed ship of a friendly state is exempt from U.S. jurisdiction, it has come "to be regarded as extending virtually absolute immunity to foreign sovereigns." *Verlinden B.V. v. Cent. Bank of Nigeria*, 461 U.S. 480, 486 (1983). Over time, the absolute immunity of the state itself has been diminished through the widespread acceptance of the restrictive theory of sovereign immunity, a theory reflected in the 1976 passage of the Foreign Sovereign Immunities Act ("FSIA"), 28 U.S.C. § 1602 et seq. Nevertheless, U.S. courts have held that the FSIA's limitations on immunity do not apply to heads of state. As the Seventh Circuit recently explained,

> The FSIA does not . . . address the immunity of foreign heads of states. The FSIA refers to foreign states, not their leaders. The FSIA defines a foreign state to include a political subdivision, agency or instrumentality of a foreign state but makes no mention of heads of state. Because the FSIA

does not apply to heads of states, the decision concerning the immunity of foreign heads of states remains vested where it was prior to 1976—with the Executive Branch.

Wei Ye v. Jiang Zemin, 383 F.3d 620, 625 (7th Cir. 2004) (citations and footnotes omitted); *see also United States v. Noriega*, 117 F.3d 1206, 1212 (11th Cir. 1997) ("Because the FSIA addresses neither head-of-state immunity, nor foreign sovereign immunity in the criminal context, head-of-state immunity could attach . . . only pursuant to the principles and procedures outlined in *The Schooner Exchange* and its progeny."). Indeed, as another judge of this Court has concluded, the FSIA does not disturb the traditional procedures governing head-of-state immunity: "The language and legislative history of the FSIA, as well as case law, support the proposition that the pre-1976 suggestion of immunity procedure survives the FSIA with respect to heads-of-state." *Lafontant*, 844 F. Supp. at 137 (fn. omitted).

3. The Legal Adviser of the U.S. Department of State has informed the Department of Justice that the government of Grenada has requested that the United States Government suggest the immunity of Prime Minister Mitchell in this action. The Legal Adviser has further informed the Department of Justice that the Department of State recognizes Prime Minister Mitchell as the sitting head of government of Grenada and "allows the immunity of Prime Minister Mitchell from this suit." Letter from John B. Bellinger, III, to Peter D. Keisler (Nov. 1, 2007). . . .

4. The Supreme Court has mandated that the courts of the United States are bound by suggestions of immunity, such as this one, submitted by the Executive Branch. *See Republic of Mexico v. Hoffman*, 324 U.S. 30, 35–36 (1945); *Ex parte Peru*, 318 U.S. at 588–89. *In Ex parte Peru*, the Supreme Court, without further scrutinizing the Executive Branch's immunity determination, declared that the Executive Branch's suggestion of immunity "must be accepted by the courts as a conclusive determination by the political arm of the Government" that the retention of jurisdiction would jeopardize the conduct of foreign relations. *Ex parte Peru*, 318 U.S. at 589; *see also Hoffman*, 324 U.S. at 35 ("It is . . . not for the courts to deny an immunity which our government has

seen fit to allow. . . ."). Accordingly, where, as here, immunity has been recognized by the Executive Branch and a suggestion of immunity has been filed, it is the "court's duty" to surrender jurisdiction. *Ex parte Peru*, 318 U.S. at 588; *see also Hoffman*, 324 U.S. at 35–36.[3]

5. The courts of the United States have applied these principles in numerous cases to dismiss actions against foreign heads of state upon the Executive Branch's suggestion of immunity. . . .

6. Judicial deference to the Executive Branch's suggestion of immunity is predicated on compelling considerations arising out of the Executive Branch's authority to conduct foreign affairs under the Constitution. First, "[s]eparation-of-powers principles impel a reluctance in the judiciary to interfere with or embarrass the executive in its constitutional role as the nation's primary organ of international policy." *Spacil [v. Crowe*, 489 F.2d 614 (5th Cir. 1974)] at 619 (citing *United States v. Lee*, 106 U.S. 196, 209 (1882)); *see also Ex parte Peru*, 318 U.S. at 588; *Rich*, 295 F.2d at 26. Second, the Executive Branch's institutional resources and expertise in foreign affairs make it peculiarly well situated to weigh the implications of immunizing a foreign leader from suit. By comparison, "the judiciary is particularly ill-equipped to second-guess" how the Executive Branch's determinations may affect the Nation's interests. *Spacil*, 489 F.2d at 619; *see also Wei Ye*, 383 F.3d at 627. Finally, and "[p]erhaps more importantly, in the chess game that is diplomacy only the executive has a view of the entire board and an understanding of the relationship between isolated moves." *Spacil*, 489 F.2d at 619.

*   *   *   *

---

[3] Just as the FSIA does not disturb traditional head-of-state immunity procedures, neither does it alter the binding nature of the Executive Branch's suggestion of immunity. Before enactment of the FSIA, the Executive Branch filed suggestions of immunity with respect to both heads of state and foreign states themselves. The FSIA transferred responsibility for determining the immunity of foreign states from the Executive Branch to the Judicial Branch. It did not, however, alter the Executive Branch's authority to suggest head-of-state immunity for foreign leaders or change the conclusive effect of such suggestions. *See Wei Ye*, 383 F.3d at 624–25; *Noriega*, 117 F.3d at 1212.

On December 5, 2007, the district court dismissed the claims against Dr. and Mrs. Mitchell, stating:

> In this civil action alleging a single cause of action against three defendants, including Dr. Keith Mitchell, the current prime minister of Grenada, and Dr. Mitchell's wife Marietta Mitchell, the Government has submitted a Suggestion of Immunity asserting head-of-state immunity from this Court's jurisdiction on behalf of Prime Minister Mitchell. The plaintiff concedes that Dr. Mitchell is entitled to immunity and consents to the dismissal of his claims against both Dr. and Mrs. Mitchell, but asks that such dismissal be without prejudice so that he may revive his claims at some point in the future when Dr. Mitchell is no longer the head of a sovereign state. The defendants oppose this request, arguing that dismissal should be with prejudice.

Howland v. Resteiner, 2007 U.S. Dist. LEXIS 89593 (E.D.N.Y. 2007).

The court noted that "the essential legal question on which the parties disagree is whether head-of-state immunity applies to former heads of state for actions taken while in office." After reviewing U.S. cases that have addressed former head-of-state immunity and also noting the possibility of a waiver of immunity, the court granted dismissal without prejudice. In a footnote the court explained that it was not deciding the question of former head-of-state immunity:

> To be clear, this Court cannot hold that head-of-state immunity does or does not apply to former heads of state because that issue is not yet ripe; Dr. Mitchell is the *current* head of the nation of Grenada and as such there is no doubt that he is entitled to immunity from this Court's jurisdiction at the present time. If the plaintiff renews his claim against the Mitchells at a point in the future when Dr. Mitchell is no longer the Prime Minister of Grenada, the issue will then be ripe and this opinion shall not

preclude or estop *de novo* review of the question whether head-of-state immunity applies to former heads of state against civil actions arising from their private acts while in office. . . .

E. INTERNATIONAL ORGANIZATIONS

1. African Union and Holy See

On March 7, 2007, President George W. Bush issued Executive Order 13427, extending to the African Union Mission to the United States of America, and to its members, "the privileges and immunities enjoyed by diplomatic missions accredited to the United States, and by members of such missions, subject to corresponding conditions and obligations." 72 Fed. Reg. 10,879 (Mar. 9, 2007).

In Executive Order 13444 of September 12, 2007, President Bush extended to the Permanent Observer Mission of the Holy See to the United Nations in New York and its members, "the privileges and immunities enjoyed by the diplomatic missions of member states to the United Nations, and members of such missions, subject to corresponding conditions and obligations." 72 Fed. Reg. 52,745 (Sept. 14, 2007).

In so doing, the President relied on his constitutional authority and U.S. laws, including § 7 of the Department of State Authorities Act of 2006 (Pub. L. No. 109-472). Both executive orders also stated that the action was "not intended to abridge in any respect privileges or immunities that [the respective organization] and its members otherwise may have acquired or may acquire by law."

2. ITER International Fusion Energy Organization

On November 19, 2007, President Bush issued Executive Order 13451, designating the ITER International Fusion Energy Organization as a "public international organization entitled to enjoy the privileges, exemptions, and immunities provided by the International Organizations Immunities Act," 22 U.S.C. § 288 et seq. 43 Weekly Comp. Pres. Doc. 1526 (Nov. 26, 2007).

Cross References

Cultural property protected under 22 U.S.C. § 2459 and FSIA immunity, **Chapter 14.B.**
Act of state, **Chapter 14.B.**

Chapter 11

Trade, Commercial Relations, Investment, and Transportation

A. TRANSPORTATION BY AIR

1. Open Skies Agreements and Related Issues

a. United States–European Union agreement

On April 25 and 30, 2007, the United States and the European Community and Member States signed a comprehensive, first-stage air transport agreement. The new agreement will replace existing bilateral agreements between the United States and EU member states and establish an expanded open skies framework between the United States and all 27 EU Member States. The agreement is to be provisionally applied beginning March 30, 2008. A declaration to the United States by the Presidency, on behalf of the European Community and its Member States, upon signing of the Air Transport Agreement, stated that the agreement "will be applied on a provisional basis until its entry into force by the Member States in good faith and in accordance with the provisions of domestic law in force." The declaration is available at *www.state.gov/e/eeb/rls/othr/2007/85602.htm*.

The agreement also calls for U.S.–EU negotiations on a second stage of aviation liberalization to commence within two months of March 30, 2008. *See* fact sheet issued by the Department of State on April 30, excerpted below and available at *www.state.gov/r/pa/prs/ps/2007/apr/83982.htm*. The text of the agreement is available at *www.state.gov/e/eeb/rls/othr/2007/84475.htm.*

---

*   *   *   *

Valuable Open Skies Benefits: The Agreement will authorize every U.S. and every EU airline to:

- fly between every city in the European Union and every city in the United States;
- operate without restriction on the number of flights, aircraft, and routes;
- set fares according to market demand; and
- enter into cooperative arrangements, including codesharing, franchising, and leasing.

In addition, the Agreement will foster enhanced regulatory cooperation in areas as diverse as competition law, government subsidies, the environment, consumer protection, and security. It establishes a consultative Joint Committee through which the U.S. and the EU can resolve questions and further develop areas of cooperation.

Investment Measures: Under the Agreement:

- U.S. investors are allowed to invest in a European Community airline, as long as the airline is majority owned and effectively controlled by a member state and/or nationals of member states.
- The Agreement makes clear that, under U.S. law, EU investors may hold up to 49.9 percent of the total equity in a U.S. airline and, on a case-by-case basis, even more, provided that foreign nationals do not own more than 25% of the voting stock and the airline is under the actual control of U.S. citizens.
- The Agreement also opens the possibility for EU investors to own or control airlines from Switzerland, Liechtenstein, members of the European Common Aviation Area (ECAA), Kenya, and America's Open Skies partners in Africa without putting at risk such airlines' rights to operate to the United States.

- Finally, the grant of new traffic rights to EU carriers opens the door to cross-border airline mergers and acquisitions within the EU, which is possible today only if airlines are prepared to place their international operating rights in legal jeopardy.

Other Benefits: The Agreement erects a pro-growth, pro-competitive, pro-consumer framework that:

- Eliminates outmoded restrictive arrangements affecting London Heathrow airport, where U.S.–UK service is now limited to four airlines.
- Allows EU airline transport of non-DOD USG passengers (employees and civilian-agency-funded contractors) and cargo on scheduled and charter flights between two foreign points and on all U.S.–EU routes not covered by a GSA "city pair" contract.
- Allows EU airline transport of cargo between the United States and all third (non-EU) countries, and transport of passengers between the United States and members of the ECAA as of the date of signature of the Agreement.

* * * *

b. Other instruments

The texts of all U.S. open skies and air transport agreements and related information, by country, are available at *www.state.gov/e/eeb/tra/c661.htm*. During 2007 the United States engaged in negotiations with a number of countries, as summarized here.

The United States and Canada signed an Air Transport Agreement on March 12, 2007, which entered into force on that date.

The United States and Georgia signed an Air Transport Agreement on June 21, 2007; it entered into force with an exchange of notes on December 6, 2007.

On July 9, 2007, the United States and China signed an Air Transport Agreement amending their bilateral air services agreement "to allow significantly expanded air service" between them. *See* fact sheet of May 23, 2007, available at *www.state.gov/r/pa/prs/ps/2007/may/85432.htm.*

On September 28, 2007, the United States and Colombia exchanged diplomatic notes updating their Air Transport Agreement of 1956.

The United States and Japan met in Tokyo from September 11–14, 2007, to discuss matters relating to further development of the aviation relations between the two countries and initialed a Record of Discussions. Paragraph 10 of the document recorded that the two delegations' aeronautical authorities "intend to implement provisionally upon signature of this Record of Discussions on the basis of comity and reciprocity the proposed amendments to the 1998 MOU" set forth in the document.

The United States and Argentina exchanged diplomatic notes on July 3, 2007, to amend their 1985 Air Transport Services Agreement.

The United States and Liberia entered into an Air Transport Agreement on February 15, 2007, effective on signature and superseding their 1978 Air Transport Agreement.

B. NORTH AMERICAN FREE TRADE AGREEMENT

1. Free Trade Commission Joint Statement

On August 14, 2007, U.S. Trade Representative Susan C. Schwab, Canadian Minister of International Trade David Emerson, and Mexican Secretary of Economy Eduardo Sojo issued a joint statement following the meeting of the NAFTA Free Trade Commission in Vancouver, Canada. The full text of the joint statement, excerpted below, is available at *www.ustr.gov/ Document_Library/Press_Releases/2007/August/Joint_ Statement_on_2007_NAFTA_Commission_Meeting.html.*

*   *   *   *

As the NAFTA concludes the complete elimination of duties within North America, we must look for new and creative ways of further promoting trade and new business opportunities. We must build upon our initial success, and continue to strengthen our regional competitiveness with a view not only of intra-NAFTA trade, but considering other regions as potential destinations for our exports and an important source of imports.

In keeping with our collective commitment to increasing market efficiencies, economic growth, prosperity and innovation in all three countries for the benefit of our citizens, we engaged in a constructive discussion of what we can do to achieve these goals. Thus, we have agreed to:

— develop a work plan to respond to the ever increasing pressures on North American competitiveness. The plan—which will address the key issues that impact our trade and identify the most effective means to facilitate it—will be presented for review at our next meeting so we can develop a strong and competitive North American platform that increases the welfare and the prosperity of all our citizens;

— facilitate trade in specific sectors in order to foster stronger more competitive North American value chains. To this end, we have instructed officials to move ahead on the following sectors: swine, steel, consumer electronics, and chemicals. We also tasked our officials to identify a second set of sectors. We look forward to receiving progress reports on the first set of sectors, as well as reviewing work plans for the second set of sectors, at our next FTC meeting; and

— conduct an analysis of the free trade agreements that each country has negotiated subsequent to the NAFTA, beginning with those in the western hemisphere. This work will focus on identifying specific, meaningful differences between agreements, especially those related to trade facilitation and transparency.

*   *   *   *

We also reaffirmed our commitment to cooperate in other regional and global fora:

— We are committed to multilateral trade liberalization and to successfully concluding the WTO Doha Round of negotiations. We urge all WTO Members to demonstrate renewed energy and flexibility in the negotiations based on the Chairs' texts in agriculture and non-agricultural market access, and put the Doha Development Agenda on a path toward a balanced and ambitious overall outcome that results in meaningful improvements in global trading conditions.

— At the same time, we reaffirm our commitments undertaken at our last meeting of APEC Ministers Responsible for Trade, held in July 2007 in Cairns, Australia. To this end, we reiterated our commitment to examine the prospect of a Free Trade Area of the Asia-Pacific (FTAAP).

We are also pleased with significant progress on rules of origin. In 2003, the NAFTA Working Group on Rules of Origin set out to liberalize the requirements for obtaining NAFTA duty-free treatment.

*   *   *   *

We also commend our officials for having completed the technical rectifications to align the NAFTA rules of origin with the Parties' updated tariff schedules resulting from the World Customs Organization's amendments to the nomenclature of the Harmonized Commodity Description and Coding System that came into force on January 1, 2007. We are pleased to note that the NAFTA Working Group on Rules of Origin will soon consult with officials from Chile to share experiences with issues of common interest.

We recognize the concept of cumulation of origin as an important mechanism for creating new business opportunities by strengthening the competitiveness of North American products globally. The Commission intends to instruct the Working Group on Rules of Origin to study further appropriate opportunities for cumulation.

We take note of the agreement reached by the Chapter 19 Operation Working Group on proposed amendments to the NAFTA Chapter 19 Rules of Procedure. We commend the Working Group for its efforts to improve the functioning of Chapter 19 panels. We refer the proposals developed by the Working Group to the State Parties to complete any internal review procedures, with a view to having the Commission adopt an agreed package of amendments to the Rules of Procedure by November 15, 2007.

We are pleased to accept the Mutual Recognition Agreement that has been signed by the architecture professions of Canada, Mexico and the United States. We hereby encourage our respective competent authorities to implement it in a manner consistent with the NAFTA. This agreement will facilitate the recognition of credentials within the three NAFTA countries. By facilitating the cross-border trade in services, this type of agreement contributes to achieving the objectives of NAFTA, and we encourage other bodies of professionals to complete the agreements that are being negotiated to develop mutually acceptable standards and criteria for licensing and certification of professional service providers.

* * * *

2. Investment Dispute Settlement Under Chapter 11

a. *Expropriation and minimum standard of treatment:* Glamis Gold, Ltd. v. United States

On March 15, 2007, the United States filed its Rejoinder in *Glamis Gold, Ltd. v. United States.* Glamis Gold, Ltd., a publicly held Canadian corporation engaged in the mining of precious metals, submitted a claim on behalf of Glamis Gold, Inc. and Glamis Imperial Corporation for alleged injuries relating to a proposed gold mine in Imperial County, California. Glamis claimed that certain federal and California state regulatory measures imposed on mining operations resulted in the expropriation of its investments in violation of Article 1110 and denied its investments the minimum standard of treatment under international law in violation of Article 1105. *See Digest 2006* at 709–26. The tribunal held hearings on the merits in August and September. Transcripts for the periods August 12–17 and September 17–19 are available, as are submissions and orders in the case, at *www.state. gov/s/l/c10986.htm*. At the end of 2007 a decision was pending with the arbitral tribunal.

Excerpts below from the U.S. Rejoinder (confidential information redacted) address preexisting limitations on property rights and reasonable investment-backed expectations in the context of expropriation and minimum standard of treatment under customary international law (most footnotes omitted). In sections II B, C, and D of the Rejoinder, not excerpted here, the United States elaborated on its arguments (1) that the international minimum standard of treatment reflected in Article 1105(1) does not contain a transparency obligation; (2) that mere frustration of a foreign investor's expectations does not give rise to State responsibility under customary international law; and (3) in response to Glamis's claims of allegedly arbitrary actions, that imperfect legislation or regulation does not give rise to State responsibility under customary international law. Under each topic, the U.S. Rejoinder also demonstrated that Glamis's arguments of lack of transparency, frustrated expectations, and arbitrary actions failed in any event. *See Digest 2006* at 723–25.

---

*   *   *   *

Glamis's Imperial Project, as it was proposed, would have involved mining for gold by digging pits hundreds of feet deep, leaving a gaping, mile-wide hole, and piling the excavated land into stockpiles measuring approximately 300 feet high. This would have been done in the environmentally sensitive California Desert Conservation

Area ("CDCA") on federally-owned land that was sacred to the neighboring Quechan Tribe. At the conclusion of its mining operations, Glamis proposed to simply leave this massive scar and these enormous piles, permanently damaging the environment and preventing the Quechan—or any member of the public—from ever using the area again.

That the federal and state governments took action to address concerns generated by Glamis's plan is hardly surprising. Indeed, in light of the history of increasing environmental regulation and the known harms stemming from unreclaimed open-pit mines in California, it would have been surprising if the government *had not* acted to prevent even more mining companies from leaving publicly-owned lands in a state of devastation after they had extracted the desired minerals from them.

*   *   *   *

I. Glamis's Expropriation Claim Should be Denied

*   *   *   *

2. The California Measures Could Not Have Expropriated Glamis's Investment Because They Do Not Interfere With Any Property Right Owned By Glamis

Both the United States and Glamis agree that when considering a claim of expropriation under international law, a first step in that analysis is the review of domestic law to determine the scope of the property interest at issue. Glamis also agrees with the United States that property rights are subject to legal limitations existing at the time the property rights are acquired, and any subsequent burdening of property rights by such limitations cannot be expropriatory. As Professor Sax noted in his first Report, where there is no property interest, there is no taking.

In this case the scope of Glamis's property interest is narrowed by three limitations that predate Glamis's acquisition of its unpatented mining claims: *first*, the principle of religious accommodation under the First Amendment of the U.S. Constitution and Article I of the California Constitution; *second*, the prohibition on causing irreparable damage to Native American sacred sites absent a showing of necessity under the Sacred Sites Act, enacted in 1976; and *third*, the requirement that mined lands be reclaimed to a "usable condition" and pose no danger to public health and safety under SMARA, enacted in 1975.

The California measures challenged by claimants implemented the above preexisting limitations. [California Senate Bill 22 ("SB 22")] implemented both the Constitutional principle of religious accommodation and the Sacred Sites Act's prohibition on irreparably damaging Native American sites. The [California Mining and Geology Board ("SMGB")] regulations implemented [the Surface Mining and Reclamation Act of 1975 ("SMARA")]'s reclamation standard. Because property rights are acquired subject to the limitations in then-existing laws and regulations, the implementation of pre-existing limitations on property rights cannot be expropriatory.

Although Glamis contends that the above pre-existing principles do not apply to its unpatented mining claims, its arguments in support of that proposition do not withstand scrutiny. First, Glamis errs in asserting that states lack the authority to limit property interests granted by the federal government under the Mining Law. Second, Glamis's assumption that the [California] Sacred Sites Act does not apply to federal lands is plainly wrong. And third, Glamis's contention that the pre-existing limitations in this case cannot limit property rights because they are not sufficiently specific is legally unsound. As demonstrated below, Glamis did not have any property right that was affected by the California measures, and, therefore, its expropriation claim challenging those measures should be denied.

a. The Federal Mining Law Does Not Prohibit California From Imposing Its Reclamation Requirements On Federal Land

Glamis's unpatented mining claims are located on federal land, and are governed by the Mining Law. The locator of an unpatented mining claim holds only a possessory interest in the land on which its claims are located. The United States retains title to the land, and substantial regulatory powers over the claims. This possessory interest gives a mining claimant the right to enter onto the land and extract minerals. It does not give the mining claimant the right to extract those minerals in a particular manner, nor does it include the right to leave the land unreclaimed after mining is complete.

Indeed, a mining claimant may not proceed with its operations until it obtains a permit to do so. To obtain such a permit, a claimant must have a plan of operations approved by the relevant federal, state and local governments, and that plan of operations must contain a reclamation plan.

Because it cannot refute the United States' arguments on their terms, Glamis argues that it "need not possess nor assert any such rights"—*i.e.*, a right to engage in mining activities free from state reclamation requirements—because "that the actions of the Respondent are legitimate or lawful or in compliance with the law from the standpoint of the Respondent's domestic laws does not mean that they conform to the Agreement or to international law." Glamis ignores the threshold issue that must be determined *before* it can be decided whether the actions violated international law: whether it had a property right to engage in the activity that was prohibited by the challenged measures.

Whether something constitutes a property right is determined by the relevant domestic law of the State where the property is located—not international law. But the question, in any event, is not, as Glamis frames it, whether Glamis has a property right in its mining claims—the United States has never disputed that it does—but rather whether that property right includes the right to be free from California's reclamation requirements.

*   *   *   *

Glamis maintains that the background principles of state property law at issue here, specifically, California's constitutional authority to accommodate Native American religious practices, its authority under the Sacred Sites Act to prevent irreparable harm to Native American sacred sites, and its authority under SMARA to ensure that mined lands are fully reclaimed cannot "prevail" over its "federal-law property interest" in its mining claims. This is a consistent undercurrent throughout Glamis's Reply—*i.e.*, that state regulations are somehow implicitly preempted, and, as such, a state background principle cannot narrow a property interest acquired pursuant to federal law. Glamis's argument is meritless. First, preemption is purely a question of municipal law, and therefore not a valid ground for decision before an international tribunal.

Second, under U.S. law, neither SMARA nor the Sacred Sites Act is preempted.

As an initial matter, the Tribunal should not engage in an inquiry into whether SMARA or the Sacred Sites Act is preempted. It is a basic principle of international law that States have broad discretion to decide how to structure their internal political systems, and the particular allocation of power between the states and the federal government in the United States is a matter that falls within this realm of exclusive domestic authority. While international tribunals look to municipal law to determine the scope of a claimant's property right, they do not have the power to opine on the internal *validity* of rules of national law. International arbitration is simply not the proper forum for deciding whether, as a matter of municipal law, the Sacred Sites Act or SMARA are valid. Therefore, the Tribunal should disregard Glamis's suggestion that the Sacred Sites Act and SMARA are preempted by federal law, and instead should accept the internal validity of the laws at issue.

In any event, neither the Sacred Sites Act nor SMARA is preempted by federal law. . . .

*   *   *   *

b. California's Sacred Sites Act Applies To The Land On Which Glamis's Unpatented Mining Claims Are Located

*   *   *   *

There is nothing in either the plain language of the Sacred Sites Act, or its legislative history, which suggests that the California Legislature intended that its provisions should not be applied on federal lands. . . .

*   *   *   *

3. Neither SB 22 Nor The SMGB Regulation Have Effected An Indirect Expropriation of Glamis's Investment

*   *   *   *

b. The California Measures Could Not Have Frustrated An Investor's Reasonable Investment-Backed Expectations

Given the regulatory climate in California at the time Glamis made its investments, including SMARA, Glamis could have had no reasonable expectation that the SMGB would not amend its regulations to require complete backfilling of open-pit metallic mines. And, even assuming arguendo that the Quechan's sacred sites had not been discovered until after Glamis had made its investments in the Project, Glamis could not have had a reasonable expectation that California would not legislate in the form of SB 22 to protect those sites.

i. An Investor's Expectations Must Be Informed By The Regulatory Framework Existing At The Time Of The Investment

Glamis's analysis of whether its expectations were reasonable is premised on a fundamental misunderstanding of the proper legal question. Glamis phrases the issue as "whether Glamis was reasonable in its view, informed by the applicable law and regulations, that such measures would not result in the full devaluation of its property rights." Glamis also states that "there was no way for even the most prudent of investors to recognize that so-called cultural-resource protection would yield an expropriation of Glamis's Imperial mining claims." These statements, of course, beg the question. The analysis of whether an investor's expectations were reasonable does not ask whether an investor could have expected its property to be expropriated. Rather, the issue is whether the claimant can show that it acquired its property "in reliance on the non-existence of the challenged regulation," and the extent to which further regulation was foreseeable. The inquiry into an investor's expectations is an objective one, and Glamis's "subjective expectations are irrelevant to the reasonableness of the expectations." Glamis's claims that its expectations were "reasonable based on its understanding as to the Quechan Tribe's position on the Imperial Project area," and its understanding of the applicable federal and state requirements is therefore inapposite.

Consideration of whether an industry is highly regulated is a standard part of the legitimate expectations analysis, and Glamis does not contest this. "[T]he regulatory regime in place at the time the claimant acquires the property at issue helps to shape the reasonableness of [the investor's] expectations." Glamis's claim that the United States is trying to "create an exception to its NAFTA obligations" by noting mining's regulated nature is mistaken. The United States does not contend that "expropriations are somehow excusable where an industry is regulated." Rather, where an industry is already highly regulated, reasonable extensions of those regulations are foreseeable. In such circumstances, the reasonable expectations prong of the analysis weighs against a finding of expropriation.

*   *   *   *

Examples abound in international and U.S. law of regulatory and legislative action that were found to be reasonably foreseeable extensions of preexisting rules. . . .

*   *   *   *

II. Glamis's Minimum Standard Of Treatment Claim Should Be Denied

The question before this Tribunal with respect to Glamis's Article 1105 claim is whether the United States' treatment of Glamis fell below the customary international law minimum standard of treatment incorporated therein. The answer is clear from the record before the Tribunal: Glamis has simply failed to show that the minimum standard of treatment incorporated in Article 1105 prohibits any of the United States' actions.

Below, the United States establishes as a threshold matter that Glamis misconstrues the nature of customary international law and thus proffers an analysis of the legal standard under Article 1105 that is gravely flawed. This confusion, moreover, proves fatal to each of the premises of Glamis's Article 1105 claim. As a result, Glamis fails to meet its burden of establishing the existence of the three rules that it purports to be part of the customary international law minimum standard of treatment, namely, that customary international law requires (i) notice and comment of proposed regulatory actions; (ii) the fulfillment of investors' legitimate expectations; and (iii) flawlessness in legislative and regulatory action. Finally, in any event, Glamis fails to show that the United States acted contrary to these alleged rules. Glamis's Article 1105 claim should, therefore, be denied.

A. Glamis's Analysis Of Article 1105's Requirements Is Seriously Flawed

Although Glamis pays lip service to several basic tenets of customary international law, it proceeds to ignore them throughout its analysis pertaining to its Article 1105 claim. To begin, there is no dispute between the parties that Article 1105 prescribes the customary international law minimum standard of treatment. The NAFTA Free Trade Commission's 2001 Note of Interpretation confirms as much. The parties here also agree that Glamis bears the burden of proving the existence of an alleged rule of customary international law and its violation by the United States. Nor is there any debate that such a rule must be based upon the practice of States followed by them from a sense of legal obligation. Establishing the existence of a rule of customary international law, however, is no small task. The International Court of Justice ("ICJ") has stated that to establish a rule of customary international law, it is "an indispensable requirement" to demonstrate that

> State practice, including that of States whose interests are specially affected, should have been both extensive and virtually uniform in the sense of the provision invoked;—and should moreover have occurred in such a way as to show a general recognition that a rule of law or legal obligation is involved.[568]

Yet, as the proponent of several supposed rules of customary international law, Glamis has failed to show in each case that State practice has coalesced to achieve the requisite density "in terms of uniformity, extent and representativeness."

Glamis further errs in several additional respects. *First,* Glamis misconstrues the nature of customary international law; *second,* Glamis assumes that Article 1105 is the same as "autonomous" fair and equitable treatment clauses in other treaties; and *third,* Glamis erroneously asserts that a new rule of customary international law can be proved based solely on arbitral decisions that do not

---

[568] *North Sea Continental Shelf Cases (F.R.G. v. Den.; F.R.G. v. Neth.),* 1969 I.C.J. 3, 43 (Judgment of Feb. 20).

demonstrate, through State practice and *opinio juris*, the existence of such a rule. These fundamental errors prove fatal to Glamis's Article 1105 claim.

1. Glamis Misapprehends Both Its Burden And The Fundamental Nature Of The International Minimum Standard Of Treatment

Glamis's theories about Article 1105 find no support in customary international law. In its Reply, Glamis relies on the proposition, attributed to the *Mondev* tribunal, that "there is an overwhelming body of treaty law establishing states' practice of providing fair and equitable treatment to foreign investors." However, the fact that treaty practice establishes the repeated inclusion of fair and equitable treatment provisions in bilateral investment treaties ("BITs") proves nothing in and of itself. As the *Mondev* tribunal itself noted, the central question in a Chapter Eleven case still remains: "what is the *content* of customary international law providing for fair and equitable treatment . . .?" Only a handful of such investment treaties can be said to provide any guidance. Moreover, as demonstrated below, there are significant textual differences among various fair and equitable treatment provisions, which indicates that their meanings are not uniform across agreements. Thus, the existence of thousands of BITs calling for fair and equitable treatment does not by itself provide any basis for Glamis's claims under Article 1105. Because Glamis has failed to establish the content of any customary international law rule that would be violated by the treatment it allegedly received from the United States, Glamis's claim should be denied.

Glamis also argues that the minimum standard of treatment varies—indeed, "requires better conduct" in some cases—depending on the level of development of the legal system in the State in question. This argument is fundamentally flawed. It is axiomatic that any rule forming part of the customary international law minimum standard of treatment of aliens must be based on *international* law, not *domestic* law: "[I]t is international law and international law alone which is the determining factor of the status of the alien."[574]

---

[574] Andreas H. Roth, The Minimum Standard of International Law Applied to Aliens 81 (1949). . . .

Glamis's view of Article 1105, however, would tie the minimum standard of treatment to the domestic legal system of the respondent in each case.

Such a proposition—in addition to being wholly unsupported by State practice—ignores the very essence of the international minimum standard. The standard, by definition, sets a minimum. But Glamis nonetheless argues that a country with a highly developed respect for the rule of law, like the United States, should be held to a higher standard. This argument not only disregards the fact that the minimum standard is based on the "common standard of conduct" observed by States, but it also measures the minimum standard according to a domestic law yardstick, essentially turning it into a national treatment standard. Such an interpretation cannot stand:

> The international minimum standard is a norm of customary international law which governs the treatment of aliens, by providing for a minimum set of principles which States, *regardless of their domestic legislation and practices*, must respect when dealing with foreign nationals and their property.[577]

As the *Genin* tribunal observed, "[w]hile the exact content of this standard is not clear, the Tribunal understands it to require an 'international minimum standard' that is separate from domestic law, but that is, indeed, a *minimum* standard."[578] Likewise, according to the *Saluka* tribunal, the customary minimum standard:

> provides a minimum guarantee to foreign investors, even where the State follows a policy that is in principle opposed to foreign investment; in that context, the minimum standard

---

[577] OECD, *Fair and Equitable Treatment Standard in International Investment Law*, Working Papers on International Investment (2004), at 8 n. 32 (emphasis added) (citing ROTH, THE MINIMUM STANDARD, *supra* n. 575, at 127; BROWNLIE, PRINCIPLES OF PUBLIC INTERNATIONAL LAW, *supra* n. 45, at 502; CHARLES ROUSSEAU, DROIT INTERNATIONAL PUBLIC 46 (1970)).

[578] *Genin v. Republic of Estonia*, ICSID Case No. ARB/99/2, Award ¶ 367 (June 25, 2001) (emphasis in original).

of 'fair and equitable treatment' may in fact provide no more than 'minimal' protection.[579]

In short, the Tribunal should reject Glamis's meritless suggestion that the customary international law minimum standard of treatment requires the United States, based on its level of development, to accord foreign investments a higher standard of treatment than it requires of other countries.

The Tribunal should also reject Professor Wälde's invitation for it to follow in the footsteps of other tribunals that have "frequently used [fair and equitable treatment] as a fall-back solution when they find it too difficult to determine an 'indirect expropriation.'" Creating legal principles in order to justify pre-desired results approximates deciding *ex aequo et bono*, an authority tribunals clearly lack absent explicit consent of the disputing parties. What *is* required is for tribunals to measure State conduct against the standard alleged to be breached. Neither Glamis nor Professor Wälde has presented any evidence that the NAFTA Parties intended Article 1105 to give rise to liability in circumstances when a State's conduct does not rise to the level of an expropriation under Article 1110, *i.e.*, as if Article 1105 provided protection for some kind of "expropriation lite."

Moreover, such a "fall-back" relationship, where State responsibility would arise under customary international law despite the lack of an unlawful expropriation, is belied by history. Although the proscription against uncompensated expropriation has long been a well-recognized part of customary international law, its history has been marked by significant debate and conflicting State practice. It is simply untenable to suggest that in the last few years there has been a general and consistent recognition among States that international responsibility could arise from something far less than an unlawful expropriation.

---

[579] *Saluka Invs. BV v. Czech Republic*, UNCITRAL, Partial Award ¶ 292 (Mar. 17, 2007) ("*Saluka* Partial Award"). It is in this sense that the United States argued that the standard sets an absolute minimum floor of treatment. . . .

Rather, the historical origin of the minimum standard of treatment demonstrates that the obligation was intended to fill any potential gaps left by domestic law. As the *S.D. Myers* tribunal explained, minimum standard provisions are a necessary "floor" of protection for aliens to "avoid what might otherwise be a gap" when States fail to accord their own nationals a level of treatment that meets international standards. In this light, this Tribunal must reject any notion of Article 1105 as catch-all provision to find liability when government action does not rise to the level of an expropriation.

2. Article 1105 Cannot Be Interpreted As If It Were The Same As An "Autonomous" Fair And Equitable Treatment Provision

As is well-established, the minimum standard of treatment required by Article 1105 is the customary international law minimum standard of treatment. Consequently, there can be no debate that Article 1105 differs from bilateral investment treaties and other agreements that either contain no fair and equitable treatment provision or contain such a provision that lacks a reference to international law or to the minimum standard of treatment. In fact, the majority of fair and equitable treatment clauses in international investment agreements do not include any reference to international law. This is not to argue, as Glamis suggests the United States does, that Article 1105 is *sui generis*. It is not. There are certainly other agreements in force with provisions similar to Article 1105. But that does not mean, however, that all fair and equitable treatment provisions are the same.

*   *   *   *

3. Glamis Cannot Meet Its Burden By Relying Solely On Arbitral Decisions That Do Not Examine State Practice

Moreover, as the United States demonstrates below, even those cases cited by Glamis that do purport to opine on a customary international law minimum standard are of little assistance because none of those cases identifies any State practice in support of the alleged rule of customary international law. There is no dispute between the parties that rules of customary international law are formed through the general and consistent practice of States from a sense of legal obligation. Likewise, as a part of customary international law, "[t]he minimum standard is the expression of the *common standard of conduct* which civilized States have observed and still are willing to observe with regard to aliens[.]"

Thus, in order to prove a rule of customary international law, Glamis must show consistent State practice. The declarations of arbitral tribunals are insufficient. As Judge Shahabuddeen of the I.C.J. observed, "development of customary international law depends on State practice." Standing alone, decisions of international tribunals cannot evidence—let alone create—new rules of customary international law, because "decisions of international courts . . . do not constitute State practice." Judge Shahabuddeen explained:

> It is difficult to regard a decision of the Court [or an international tribunal] as being in itself an expression of State practice. . . . A decision made by it is an expression not of the practice of the litigating States, but of the judicial view taken of the relations between them on the basis of legal principles which must necessarily exclude any customary law which has not yet crystallised. The decision may recognise the existence of a new customary law and in that limited sense it may no doubt be regarded as the final stage of development, but, *by itself, it cannot create one.* It lacks the element of repetitiveness so prominent a feature of the evolution of customary international law.

*   *   *   *

. . . Glamis provides this Tribunal with no evidence of extensive State practice to support the principles it contends are part of customary international law. Instead, Glamis relies on a series of very recent arbitral decisions to support the existence of the specific customary rules that it alleges the United States violated here. Customary international law, however, does not evolve every time a new decision is issued by an arbitral tribunal; its evolution—if any— depends on evidence of a general practice or custom among States.

*   *   *   *

b. *Allocation of costs:* Tembec v. United States

On July 19, 2007, the arbitral tribunal established pursuant to NAFTA Article 1126 in the Softwood Lumber Consolidated Proceeding issued its Joint Order on the Costs of Arbitration and for the Termination of Certain Arbitral Proceedings ("Joint Order"). Three claims were originally filed under Article 1120 and consolidated in the proceeding by a consolidation tribunal order issued September 7, 2005: *Canfor Corp. v. United States, Tembec Inc. et al. v. United States,* and *Terminal Forest Products Ltd. v. United States. See Digest 2005* at 602–5. In December 2005 Tembec requested that the tribunal terminate the consolidated proceeding as to it and filed a motion to vacate the consolidation order in the U.S. District Court for the District of Columbia. On January 10, 2006, the arbitral tribunal established in the consolidated case terminated the proceedings as to Tembec, except for issues concerning the costs of arbitration. The tribunal issued its Decision on the Preliminary Question on June 6, 2006. *See Digest 2006* at 702–9. On September 12, 2006, the United States and Canada signed the Softwood Lumber Agreement ("SLA"), which entered into force on October 12, 2006. That agreement was intended to settle the long-standing softwood lumber dispute between the Parties and also terminated several, but not all, actions in other fora concerning the dispute.* *See Digest 2006* at 762–63. Submissions and orders in the consolidated arbitral proceeding are available at *www.state.gov/s/l/c14432. htm.*

In its 2007 Joint Order, the arbitral tribunal terminated the proceedings as to the remaining claimants, Canfor and Terminal Forest Products, and addressed the allocation of

---

* Editor's note: On March 30, 2007, the United States requested formal consultations with Canada regarding compliance with several provisions and subsequently requested arbitration on two matters concerning implementation of the SLA before the London Court of International Arbitration. *See* D.6. below.

costs with respect to all three of the original claimants. The Tribunal determined that Tembec must bear the costs of arbitration and legal fees claimed by the United States. Finding that the "the costs as claimed by the United States are . . . reasonable by any standard," the tribunal ordered Tembec to pay $271,844.24 to the United States (Joint Order at ¶ 188). Excerpts below from the tribunal's analysis address the effect of Tembec's unilateral withdrawal as a claimant from the Article 1126 proceedings (footnotes omitted).

In October 2007 Tembec filed a challenge to the order of costs in the District Court for the District of Columbia. That suit was pending at the end of 2007.

*   *   *   *

148. . . . When Tembec availed itself of the dispute resolution mechanism of NAFTA Chapter Eleven for its claim against the United States, Article 1126 of the NAFTA concerning consolidation was part and parcel of the mechanism. Tembec disagreed with the outcome of the United States' request for consolidation, but such a disagreement does not entitle a claimant to withdraw unilaterally without consequences, and in particular cost consequences.

149. The UNCITRAL Arbitration Rules do not address expressly the issue of a unilateral withdrawal by a claimant. However, the issue can be resolved on the basis of an interpretation of the UNCITRAL Rules. Accordingly, the Tribunal interprets the reference to "the unsuccessful party" in Article 40(1) of the UNCITRAL Rules to include a party that unilaterally withdraws its claim. It triggers also the general principle of "costs follow the event," which, according to this Tribunal, is the guiding principle for the application of Article 40(2) of the Rules. The rule that a claimant is liable for the costs of the proceedings when that claimant unilaterally withdraws from the proceedings is in accord with many national legal systems. The Tribunal recognizes that the rule may not be applicable in exceptional circumstances, which, however, are not present in the instant case.

150. Tembec did unilaterally seek to withdraw from the proceedings by its letter of 7 December 2005. The Tribunal's 10 January 2006 Termination Order meant that Tembec had indeed withdrawn its claims under Chapter Eleven of the NAFTA (save for the costs of

arbitration). As it is explained in the Consolidation Order, in the case of an order for consolidation under Article 1126(2), the Article 1126 Tribunal takes over the proceedings, in the capacity of an arbitral tribunal, to hear and determine the disputes from the respective Article 1120 Tribunals. Thus, this Tribunal took over the jurisdiction from the *Tembec* Article 1120 Tribunal to hear and determine Tembec's NAFTA Chapter Eleven claim. Accordingly, when Tembec "remove[d] its Statement of Claim from these Article 1126 arbitration proceedings," it withdrew its NAFTA Chapter Eleven claim altogether, and this is so even though the Tribunal's Order of 10 January 2006 was neither with nor without prejudice to the question of reinstatement.

151. Tembec advances one further argument, which is that it is singled out by the United States, motivated by retribution for Tembec's challenge of the Consolidation Order, while the United States treated Canfor and Terminal differently. That argument is of no avail to Tembec either. Pursuant to the applicable UNCITRAL Arbitration Rules, the United States is entitled to seek the costs of arbitration from Tembec, and, in the absence of an abuse of right, motive for the use of a right is irrelevant when an arbitral tribunal exercises its discretion in awarding costs. Moreover, the situation of Tembec differs from that of Canfor and Terminal. Tembec unilaterally withdrew from the proceedings, while Canfor and Terminal continued the proceedings. When Tembec did so, the United States made it clear that it would seek costs from Tembec.

152. Consequently, Tembec shall have to bear the costs of arbitration referred to in Articles 38 and 39 of the UNCITRAL Arbitration Rules insofar as it concerns the Article 1120 and Article 1126 proceedings between it and the United States.

*   *   *   *

c. Investment in claimant's own state

(1) Bayview Irrigation District v. United Mexican States

On June 19, 2007, the arbitration panel established to decide the NAFTA claim brought by Bayview Irrigation District and others against Mexico issued an Award finding that it lacked jurisdiction over claims by Texan claimants that alleged harm as a result of Mexico's failure to release a certain volume of water from the Rio Grande to the United States. *Bayview Irrigation District et al. v. United Mexican States*, ICSID Case No. ARB (AF)/ 05/01, available at *http://icsid.worldbank.org/ICSID/Front Servlet?requestType=CasesRH&actionVal=showDoc&docId =DC653_En&caseId=C246*. The tribunal concluded (¶ 122):

> In the view of the Tribunal it has not been demonstrated that any of the Claimants seeks to make, is making or has made an investment *in Mexico*. That being the case, the Tribunal does not have the jurisdiction to hear any of these claims against Mexico because the Claimants have not demonstrated that their claims fall within the scope and coverage of NAFTA Chapter Eleven, as defined by NAFTA Article 1101.

In *Bayview*, the United States had filed a submission under NAFTA Article 1128 stating its view that "all of the protections afforded by the NAFTA's investment chapter extend only to investments that are made by an investor of a NAFTA Party in the territory of another NAFTA Party, or to investors of a NAFTA Party that seek to make, are making, or have made an investment in the territory of another NAFTA Party." The full text of the U.S. Article 1128 submission, filed November 27, 2006, is available at *www.state.gov/s/l/c20028.htm*.

In finding that it lacked jurisdiction over the claims in *Bayview*, the tribunal specifically agreed with the U.S. analysis, stating in ¶ 100 of the Award:

> The USA Government submission, dated 27 November 2006, stated that:
>
>> "The aim of international investment agreements is the protection of *foreign* investments, and the investors who make them. This is as true with respect to the investment provisions of free trade agreements (FTAs) as it is for agreements devoted exclusively to investment protection,

such as bilateral investment treaties (BITs). NAFTA Chapter Eleven is no different in this regard. One of the objectives of the NAFTA, expressly set forth in Article 102(1)(c) is to "increase substantially investment *opportunities* in the territories of the Parties" which refers to, and can only sensibly be considered as referring to, opportunities for *foreign* investment in the territory of each Party made by investors of another Party. . . ."

In the view of the Tribunal, this is the clear and ordinary meaning that is borne by the text of NAFTA Chapter Eleven.

(2) In Re NAFTA Chapter 11/UNCITRAL Cattle Cases

On May 7, 2007, the United States filed a Reply on the Preliminary Issue in *In Re NAFTA Chapter 11/UNCITRAL Cattle Cases*, which consolidated several claims by Canadian claimants alleging that the United States violated NAFTA Chapter Eleven by closing the border to the importation of Canadian cattle after the discovery in 2003 of a case of bovine spongiform encephalopathy ("BSE" or "mad cow disease") in a cow in Alberta, Canada. The Reply elaborated on U.S. positions set forth in its December 1, 2006, Memorial, in particular (as in *Bayview, supra*) that NAFTA Chapter Eleven does not provide for investor-State arbitration where claimants have invested solely in their own country. *See also Digest 2006* at 693–701. The tribunal held hearings on the jurisdictional issue on October 9 and 10, 2007, and decision was pending at the end of the year.

Excerpts below from the U.S. Reply address the "claimants' suggestion that the NAFTA parties, *sub silentio*, derogated from their habitual practice concerning an important treaty principle [on extraterritoriality]." The full texts of the Reply and transcripts of the hearing on October 9 and 10, 2007, as well as other submissions and orders in the case, are available at *www.state.gov/s/l/c14683.htm*.

* * * *

It is well-accepted that when States intend to depart from common, habitual past practice, they express their intentions clearly. Thus, absent clear language to the contrary, treaties should be construed in accordance with the "common habitual pattern adopted by previous treaties." Claimants here, however, brush aside the entire history of investor-State arbitration in the United States (and, indeed, in the rest of the world). They argue that the NAFTA is unique, and that, through the absence of a few words in 1101(1)(a), the United States has agreed to be sued for money damages by Canadian "investors" concerning their investments in Canada. The common habitual pattern adopted in other investment treaties is that private parties lack standing to bring claims against States for money damages absent actual investment (or, in some circumstances at least, an investment sought to be made) in the territory of the host State.

International courts and tribunals recognize that a State's intention to deviate from a well-established treaty principle "would naturally have found direct expression in the [treaty] itself and would not have been left to doubtful interpretation." The *Loewen* NAFTA Chapter Eleven tribunal thus concluded that "[a]n important principle of international law should not be held to have been tacitly dispensed with by international agreement, in the absence of words making clear an intention to do so." "Such an intention," the tribunal observed, "may be exhibited by express provisions which are at variance with the continued operation of the relevant principle of international law." "It would be strange indeed," therefore, "if sub silentio the international rule were to be swept away."

Here, there is no direct expression in the NAFTA of the NAFTA Parties' intent to discard decades of consistent and habitual treaty practice and, suddenly, allow suits against them for money damages by "investors" who never actually invested in their respective territories. Nor is there any express provision in the NAFTA indicating that the Parties sought to expand the habitual meaning and scope of the national treatment protection contained in Chapter Eleven beyond their habitual practice. It would be unreasonable to conclude that the NAFTA Parties *unwittingly* effected the revolution in investor-State arbitration that Claimants endorse. As the International Court of Justice observed in the *Oil Platforms* case, if the treaty provision at issue "impose[d] actual obligations on the Contracting Parties, obliging them to maintain long-lasting peaceful and friendly relations," then "the Parties would have been led to point out its importance during the negotiations or the process of ratification."

The need for clear indications by the Parties of a departure from habitual practice is especially pronounced where the departure is as radical and far-reaching as that which would result from Claimants' interpretation. Under Claimants' interpretation, not only would the national treatment obligation be extended to investments outside the territorial jurisdiction of the Parties, but every cross-border trade dispute could trigger the investor-State dispute resolution mechanism. Every enterprise that engages in the export of goods and services is an investor in its home country and could suffer losses with respect to its home-country investment as a result of barriers to trade imposed by another State. The international community, however, has negotiated elaborate and carefully designed State-to-State dispute resolution mechanisms for resolving such disputes. It cannot reasonably be argued that the NAFTA Parties created such a mechanism for trader-State arbitration without any record of their consciously doing so.

Clearly, if the NAFTA's obligations had been intended to extend extraterritorially, as Claimants contend, each Party's internal deliberations concerning the NAFTA would have reflected this. This is particularly true with regard to the United States, because domestic U.S. law governing the interpretation of treaties requires the clear expression of any intent to assume extra-territorial obligations. It is a fundamental principle of U.S. domestic law that a "treaty cannot impose uncontemplated extraterritorial obligations on those who ratify it."

*   *   *   *

Just as Claimants have failed to provide any evidence of the NAFTA Parties' affirmative intent to depart from their past habitual practice of protecting only investors that have made or seek to make investments in the territory of another treaty partner, Claimants have provided no evidence of any intent on the part of the United States to undertake obligations with respect to investors that have made investments outside its territory. The mere *absence* of a few words from a few sub-provisions of the NAFTA cannot, consistent with international and U.S. law, be presumed to signal the NAFTA Parties' affirmative intent to be sued for money damages by "investors" concerning their investments outside of the Parties' respective territories.

* * * *

3. Implementation of Obligations Related to Cross-Border Trucking with Mexico

On February 23, 2007, U.S. Secretary of Transportation Mary E. Peters and Mexico Secretary of Communications and Transportation Luis Téllez Kuenzler announced a demonstration project to implement the cross-border long haul trucking provisions of NAFTA . See *www.dot.gov/affairs/cbtsip/peters 022307.htm*. On May 1, the Federal Motor Carrier Safety Administration ("FMCSA"), U.S. Department of Transportation, published a notice of the demonstration project, with request for comments, in the Federal Register. 72 Fed. Reg. 23,883 (May 1, 2007). On May 25, 2007, President George W. Bush signed into law Public Law No. 110-28. Section 6901 of that act imposed certain new technical requirements on the demonstration project and required that "simultaneous and comparable authority to operate within Mexico" be "made available" to U.S. carriers. FMCSA published a further notice to comply with the new statutory requirements. 72 Fed. Reg. 31,877 (June 8, 2007). On August 17, 2007, FMCSA provided notice of its intent to proceed with the demonstration project. 72 Fed. Reg. 46,263 (Aug. 17, 2007). On September 6, 2007, the Secretary of Transportation announced the start of the demonstration project and granted operating authority to the first Mexico-domiciled carrier. See *www.fmcsa.dot.gov/about/news/news-releases/2007/090707.htm*.

Two actions were filed seeking an emergency stay of the demonstration project. The Sierra Club filed a petition for review and emergency stay in the Ninth Circuit Court of Appeals on August 29, 2007. The Ninth Circuit denied the stay on August 31, 2007. *Sierra Club v. U.S. Department of Transportation,* Order of August 31, 2007, No. 07-73415 (9th Cir. 2007). On September 7, 2007, the Owner-Operator Independent Drivers Association ("OOIDA") filed a petition for review and emergency stay of the demonstration project in the District of Columbia Circuit Court of Appeals. The D.C. Circuit denied the stay. *Owner-Operator Independent Drivers Association v. Federal Motor Carrier Safety Administration,* Order of September 7, 2007, No. 07-1355 (D.C. Cir. 2007). The two cases were consolidated in the Ninth Circuit.

On November 19, 2007, the United States filed its brief for respondents on the petition for review. Excerpts below provide the history of issues related to U.S.–Mexico cross-border trucking, including efforts under NAFTA to resolve those issues that resulted in the February 2007 U.S.–Mexico agreement on the demonstration project. For further information on the dispute resolution procedures initiated by Mexico under NAFTA Chapter 20 mentioned here, *see Digest 2002* at 666–70. The full text of the brief is available at *www.state.gov/s/l/c8183.htm.*

* * * *

Until 1982, Mexico- and Canada-domiciled motor carriers could operate in the United States provided that they qualified for U.S. operating authority under Interstate Commerce Commission regulations. *See Department of Transp. v. Public Citizen,* 541 U.S. 752, 759 (2004) (*"Public Citizen"*). Prompted by complaints that U.S. motor carriers were not allowed the same access to Mexican and Canadian markets that carriers from those nations enjoyed in this country (*id.*), Congress imposed a moratorium on the issuance of new grants of operating authority to motor carriers domiciled in Canada or Mexico, or owned or controlled by persons of those countries. *See* Bus Regulatory Reform Act of 1982, Pub. L. No. 97-261, § 6(g), 96 Stat. 1102, 1107.

While the disagreement with Canada was quickly resolved, the issue of trucking reciprocity with Mexico was not. *Public Citizen*, 541 U.S. at 759. As a result, since 1982, most Mexican carrier operations within the United States have been limited to the commercial zones adjacent to the U.S.–Mexico borders. Mexico-domiciled trucks and buses cross into those commercial zones about 4.5 million times yearly. 72 Fed. Reg. 46,263, 46,264 (Aug. 17, 2007). Data collected from the border zones suggest that Mexican carriers are as safe (or perhaps even safer) than their American counterparts. *See* 70 Fed. Reg. 50,277, 50,283 (Aug. 26, 2005) . . . ; 72 Fed. Reg. at 46,269. . . .

In NAFTA, which entered into force on January 1, 1994, the United States agreed to phase out the moratorium on licensing Mexico-domiciled motor carriers to operate beyond the border zones. *See Public Citizen*, 541 U.S. at 759. Based on concerns relating to the adequacy of Mexican motor carrier safety regulation, however, the United States announced in late 1995 an indefinite delay in opening the border to long-haul Mexican commercial motor vehicles. *Public Citizen*, 541 U.S. at 760.

Mexico filed complaints against the United States under NAFTA's dispute resolution provisions, challenging the delay. An arbitration panel issued a report in February 2001 concluding that the blanket refusal to process applications of Mexico-domiciled long-haul carriers breached NAFTA. *Id.* After the President responded to the arbitration panel decision by announcing the United States' intent to resume the process for implementing NAFTA, Congress enacted section 350 [of the Department of Transportation and Related Agencies Appropriations Act for Fiscal Year 2002, Pub. L. No. 107-87, 115 Stat. 833, 864 ("section 350"), which . . . imposed threshold conditions to be met before the Secretary could authorize any Mexico-domiciled motor carriers to operate beyond the border commercial zones. Several of those conditions were satisfied by a rule published by FMCSA in March 2002, establishing a new application process for Mexico-domiciled long-haul carriers and mandating pre-authorization safety audits for all such carriers. *See* 67 Fed. Reg. 12,702 (Mar. 19, 2002). At the same time, the agency published a rule implementing a safety monitoring system for Mexico-domiciled carriers operating in the U.S. 67 Fed. Reg. 12,758 (Mar. 19, 2002).

Satisfying another requirement of section 350, the Secretary certified in November 2002 that operations by Mexico-domiciled carriers beyond the border commercial zones would not pose an unacceptable safety risk to the American public. The President subsequently modified the 1982 moratorium to permit such operations. 67 Fed. Reg. 71,795 (Nov. 27, 2002). Ongoing litigation over the validity of FMCSA's implementing regulations prevented the President's action from immediately taking effect, however. Those regulations were vacated by this Court in January 2003 but reinstated after the Supreme Court's *Public Citizen* decision in June 2004. 541 U.S. at 752.

Thereafter, and following consultations with Mexico over details of implementing reciprocal long-haul carrier access in each country, the U.S. Secretary of Transportation and Mexico's Secretary of Communications and Transportation announced on February 23, 2007 a Demonstration Project to implement the trucking provisions of NAFTA. The Project's purpose is to demonstrate both the ability of Mexico-domiciled motor carriers to comply with U.S. laws and regulations and the effectiveness of DOT's monitoring and enforcement mechanisms, which together ensure that Mexican carriers operating in the United States can maintain the same level of highway safety as U.S.–based carriers.

*   *   *   *

The November 2007 U.S. brief argued that under U.S. domestic law (1) "[n]either Sierra Club nor OOIDA has demonstrated the injury in fact necessary to establish Article III standing, because neither has shown that its members face any particularized harms resulting from the Demonstration Project"; (2) "Congress has enacted multiple statutes containing preconditions for any test of opening the border to long-haul operations by Mexico-domiciled trucks. In extensive Federal Register notices, FMCSA has explained how the Demonstration Project challenged here meets each of those preconditions"; and (3) "None of the generally applicable statutes concerning commercial vehicles and their operation upon which petitioners rely poses any impediment to continuation of the Demonstration Project. . . ."

Although the focus of the two challenges on appeal was whether FCMSA had complied with U.S. domestic law in setting up the demonstration project, the United States was also concerned that interruption of the project would be a setback in the U.S. course of implementing the NAFTA trucking obligations. A declaration of Reuben Jeffery III, Under Secretary of State for Economic, Energy, and Agricultural Affairs, dated August 30, 2007, and attached to the FMCSA submission opposing the motion for stay in the Ninth Circuit in *Sierra Club*, provided the U.S. views on the significance of the demonstration project as an important step in U.S. implementation of its obligations under NAFTA in the U.S.–Mexico relationship. The full text of Mr. Jeffery's declaration, excerpted below, is available at *www.state.gov/s/l/c8183.htm*. A similar declaration by Mr. Jeffery, dated September 13, 2007, was attached to the FMCSA Opposition to Petitioner's Emergency Motion for Stay and Affirmative Motion for Transfer in *OOIDA*.

---

*   *   *   *

4. The U.S.–Mexico relationship is one of the most important bilateral relationships for the United States. The North American Free Trade Agreement (NAFTA), which entered into force in 1994, has helped build a dynamic trading system by liberalizing trade in goods and services, thereby promoting growth and improving competitiveness in the United States, Mexico and Canada. Farmers, workers and manufacturers benefit from the removal of arbitrary and discriminatory trade restrictions, while consumers enjoy lower prices and more choices. Under NAFTA, U.S.–Mexico trade in goods grew to over USD 332 billion in 2006, aided by low tariffs, coordinated border procedures, and key infrastructure investment— all outgrowths of NAFTA implementation.

5. Initiation of the Demonstration Project is an important interim step toward fulfilling U.S. obligations under the North American Free Trade Agreement (NAFTA), and has been repeatedly delayed before. The issue of cross-border trucking is one of the last matters to be resolved before the final phase of NAFTA implementation in January 2008. Mexican President Calderon's administration has

committed to implementing the final tariff cuts and quota elimination on January 1, 2008,* in keeping with the NAFTA schedule, but faces substantial domestic opposition to doing so. Lack of U.S. progress on the cross-border trucking issue may affect Mexico's planned grant of enhanced market access in those key sectors.

6. Moreover, U.S. compliance with our NAFTA obligations is seen by Mexico as a bellwether of the level of the U.S. commitment to the bilateral relationship overall. Additional delay on cross-border trucking could aggravate U.S.–Mexico bilateral relations, slow progress on other issues, and reinforce Mexico's concerns over the U.S. commitment to comply with its NAFTA obligations.

7. Initiation of the Demonstration Project will also lead to increased operations by U.S.–domiciled motor carriers in Mexico, improving the efficiency of our own transportation networks. It is expected that expanding our southern border operations to include cross-border long-haul trucking will promote American competitiveness and market access, and thereby lead to job creation and lower costs for American consumers. Additional delay on cross-border trucking would mean postponement of such benefits. The Department of State and the Administration remain fully committed to implementing the Demonstration Project, which is a key element in the NAFTA partners' efforts to improve global competitiveness for North American manufacturers, farmers and workers.

* * * * *

Jeffrey N. Shane, Under Secretary for Policy of the U.S. Department of Transportation, also filed a declaration in the FMCSA Opposition in *OOIDA*, and a similar filing in *Sierra Club*, elaborating on the transportation-related issues under NAFTA, as excerpted below. The full text of Mr. Shane's declaration is available at *www.state.gov/s/l/c8183.htm*.

* * * * *

4. United States compliance with NAFTA's cross-border motor carrier provisions related to Mexican trucks has been long delayed.

---

* Editor's note: *See www.fas.usda.gov/info/factsheets/NAFTA.asp.*

Under NAFTA, the phase-in of those provisions was to have begun in December 1995, and was to have been completed in January 2000. . . .

5. Since the 2001 NAFTA panel decision [described in excerpts from the November 2007 U.S. brief *supra*] DOT has diligently worked to implement NAFTA's cross-border motor carrier provisions in a manner that ensures safety. Additionally, the Department has worked to comply with substantial new statutory prerequisites to implementation and has defended litigation that delayed implementation. Throughout this period, the Government of Mexico has refrained from imposing trade sanctions on the United States based on the arbitration panel's findings, beyond barring grants of operating authority to U.S. motor carriers. Instead, the Government of Mexico has diligently, patiently, and cooperatively worked with DOT to bring about reciprocal implementation of NAFTA's cross-border motor carrier provisions in a manner that is consistent with each country's laws, and that ensures the safety of each country's citizens. This has been particularly true during preparations for the Demonstration Project announced earlier this year.

6. On September 6, 2007, FMCSA commenced the Demonstration Project. A halt to the Project would cause further delay in complying with our NAFTA motor carrier commitments and thus would cause considerable harm to our relationship with Mexico, an important trading and diplomatic partner, especially in light of Mexico's substantial efforts to cooperate with DOT to ensure the safe implementation and operation of the Demonstration Project. Among other consequences, Mexico would likely postpone reciprocal grants of authority to U.S. motor carriers, thereby continuing a prohibition that has frustrated U.S. long-haul truckers from expanding their operations into Mexico. A halt to the Project would also serve to frustrate other significant trade and commercial objectives intended by NAFTA. Finally, a halt to the Project could have a negative impact on the wide range of other transportation-related issues that are currently the subject of consultations or negotiations between the United States and the Government of Mexico.

C. WORLD TRADE ORGANIZATION

1. Dispute Settlement

U.S. submissions in WTO dispute settlement cases are available at *www.ustr.gov/Trade_Agreements/Monitoring_ Enforcement/Dispute_Settlement/WTO/Section_Index. html.*

The discussion that follows of a selection of WTO disputes involving the United States is drawn from Chapter II, "World Trade Organization," of The President's 2007 Annual Report on the Trade Agreements Program ("2007 Annual Report"), available at *www.ustr.gov/Document_Library/ Reports_Publications/2008/2008_Trade_Policy_Agenda/ Section_Index.html.*

a. *Disputes brought by the United States*

The United States requested consultations with China on three matters during 2007. Excerpts below from the 2007 Annual Report at 67–69 describe the status of the three disputes.

(1) China—Measures Affecting the Protection and Enforcement of Intellectual Property Rights (WT/DS362)

In April 2007 the United States requested consultations with China related to intellectual property rights, as follows.

On April 10, 2007, the United States requested consultations with China regarding certain measures pertaining to the protection and enforcement of intellectual property rights in China. The issues of concern included: (1) the thresholds that must be met in order for certain acts of trademark counterfeiting and copyright piracy to be subject to criminal procedures and penalties; (2) the disposal by Chinese customs authorities of goods that infringe intellectual property rights and that have been confiscated by those authorities, in particular, the disposal of such goods following removal of their infringing features; (3) the denial of copyright and related rights protection and enforcement to creative works of authorship, sound recordings, and performances that have not been authorized for publication or distribution within China; and (4) the scope of coverage of criminal procedures and penalties for unauthorized reproduction or unauthorized distribution of copyrighted works. The Chinese measures at issue appear to be inconsistent with China's obligations under several provisions of the *Agreement on Trade-Related Aspects of Intellectual Property Rights* (the TRIPS Agreement).

The United States and China held consultations on June 7–8, 2007, but they did not resolve the dispute. On August 13, 2007, the United States requested the establishment of a panel with respect to issues (1) through (3) in the consultation request, and a panel was established on September 25, 2007. . . .

(2) China—Measures Affecting Trading Rights and Distribution Services for Certain Publications and Audiovisual Entertainment Products (WT/DS363)

On the same day, the United States requested consultations with China regarding measures related to imported publications, films for theatrical release, sound recordings, and audiovisual entertainment products, as explained below.

On April 10, 2007, the United States requested consultations with China regarding certain measures related to the import and/or distribution of imported films for theatrical release, audiovisual home entertainment products (*e.g.*, video cassettes and DVDs), sound recordings, and publications (*e.g.*, books, magazines, newspapers, and electronic publications). On July 10, 2007, the United States requested supplemental consultations with China regarding certain measures pertaining to the distribution of imported films for theatrical release and sound recordings.

Specifically, the United States is concerned that certain Chinese measures: (1) restrict trading rights (such as the right to import goods into China) with respect to imported films for theatrical release, audiovisual home entertainment products, sound recordings, and publications; and (2) restrict market access for, or discriminate against, imported films for theatrical release and sound recordings in physical form and foreign service providers seeking to engage in the distribution of certain publications, audiovisual home entertainment products, and sound recordings. The Chinese measures at issue appear to be inconsistent with several WTO provisions, including provisions in the *General Agreement on Tariffs and Trade 1994* (GATT 1994) and *General Agreement on Trade in Services* (GATS), as well as specific commitments made by China in its WTO accession agreement.

The United States and China held consultations on June 5–6, 2007 and July 31, 2007, but they did not resolve the dispute. On October 10, 2007, the United States requested the establishment of a panel, and on November 27, 2007 a panel was established.

(3) China—Prohibited Subsidies (WT/DS358)

In a case concerning subsidies, the United States and China reached agreement at the end of 2007, as described below, requiring China to take certain actions that, if completed, could form the basis for settlement of the dispute.

On February 2, 2007 and April 27, 2007, the United States requested consultations and supplemental consultations, respectively, with China regarding subsidies provided in the form of refunds, reductions, or exemptions from income taxes or other payments. Because they are offered on the condition that enterprises purchase domestic over imported goods or on the condition that enterprises meet certain export performance criteria, these subsidies appear to be inconsistent with several provisions of the WTO Agreement, including Article 3 of the *Agreement on Subsidies and Countervailing Measures*, Article III: 4 of the *General Agreement on Tariffs and Trade 1994* and Article 2 of the *Agreement on Trade-Related Investment Measures*, as well as specific commitments made by China in its WTO accession agreement. Mexico also initiated a dispute regarding the same subsidies.

Because consultations did not resolve the disputes, the WTO Dispute Settlement Body, at the request of the United States and

Mexico, established a single dispute settlement panel on August 31, 2007, to hear both disputes.

On December 19, 2007, the United States and China informed the DSB that they had reached an agreement with respect to this matter and circulated a copy of the agreement. The agreement calls for China to take certain steps, including the revision and repeal of certain existing measures as well as the adoption of new measures that would eliminate the import substitution and export subsidies challenged by the United States by January 1, 2008. The agreement also commits China to not re-introduce those subsidies or establish import substitution or export subsidies under its new income tax law that went into effect on January 1, 2008. Mexico reached a similar agreement with China with respect to Mexico's dispute on the same subsidies.

b. Disputes brought against the United States

(1) United States—Measures Affecting the Cross-Border Supply of Gambling and Betting Services (DS285)

In 2005 the WTO Dispute Settlement Body adopted panel and Appellate Body reports finding no breach of Article XVI (Market Access) of the GATS in a dispute concerning gambling and betting services and also finding that three U.S. federal gambling laws at issue "fall within the scope of 'public morals' and/or 'public order'" exceptions under Article IV of the GATS. To meet the requirements of the Article XVI chapeau, however, the United States needed to clarify an issue concerning internet gambling on horse racing. At a DSB meeting on April 21, 2006, the United States informed the DSB that it was in compliance with the DSB's recommendations and rulings. Following consultations requested by Antigua regarding U.S. compliance, Antigua requested the DSB to establish a panel pursuant to Article 21.5 of the Dispute Settlement Understanding. The panel was established on July 19, 2006. Developments in 2007 are described below; see 2007 Annual Report at 84–85.

*　　*　　*　　*

The report of the Article 21.5 panel, which was circulated on March 30, 2007, found that the United States had not complied with the recommendations and rulings of the DSB in this dispute. The DSB adopted the report of the Article 21.5 panel on May 22, 2007.

On June 21, 2007, Antigua submitted a request, pursuant to Article 22.2 of the DSU, for authorization from the DSB to suspend the application to the United States of concessions and related obligations of Antigua under the GATS and the TRIPS. On July 23, 2007, the United States referred this matter to arbitration under Article 22.6 of the DSU. The arbitration was carried out by the three panelists who served on the Article 21.5 panel.

On December 21, 2007, the Article 22.6 arbitration award was circulated. The arbitrator concluded that Antigua's annual level of nullification or impairment of benefits is $21 million and that Antigua may request authorization from the DSB to suspend its obligations under the TRIPS Agreement in this amount.

(2) Zeroing

In 2006 a panel established at the request of Japan found that the U.S. practice of "zeroing" in connection with average-to-average comparisons in antidumping investigations was inconsistent with the Antidumping Agreement but that zeroing in transaction-to-transaction comparisons in investigations was not. *United States—Measures Relating to Zeroing and Sunset Reviews (DS322)*. The panel also expressly rejected the Appellate Body's reasoning in *United States—Laws, Regulations and Methodology for Calculating Dumping Margins ("zeroing") (DS294)* to find that zeroing in assessment proceedings was also not inconsistent with the Antidumping Agreement. Japan appealed, and the United States cross-appealed. These panel findings were reversed in 2007:

In a report circulated January 9, 2007, the Appellate Body upheld the panel's findings that the United States maintains a single "zeroing procedures" measure applicable to investigations and administrative reviews. The Appellate

Body reversed the panel's findings regarding zeroing in transaction-to-transaction comparisons in investigations, and it also reversed the panel's findings concerning zeroing in assessment proceedings. The DSB adopted the Appellate Body report and the panel report, as modified by the Appellate Body, on January 23, 2007. On February 20, 2007, the United States informed the DSB of its intention to implement the recommendations and rulings of the DSB in connection with this matter. On May 4, 2007, the United States and Japan informed the DSB that they had agreed that the reasonable period of time for the United States to implement the recommendations and rulings of the DSB would end on December 24, 2007.

See 2007 Annual Report at 86–87.

In 2007 the WTO also established panels in two disputes brought by the European Union on the U.S. use of zeroing at the request of the European Communities. In *United States— Laws, Regulations and Methodology for Calculating Dumping Margins ("zeroing") (DS294)*, the WTO established a compliance panel, and in *United States—Continued Existence and Application of Zeroing Methodology (Zeroing II) (DS350)*, the WTO established a panel following consultations requested in 2006. See 2007 Annual Report at 85 and 88, respectively.

In June 2007 the United States submitted a proposal to the WTO Negotiating Group on Rules to address the zeroing issue, noting its strong disagreement with the recent dispute settlement findings by the WTO Appellate Body on zeroing. As described in the 2007 Annual Report:

With respect to zeroing, the Chairman's text addressed important aspects of the U.S. proposal, by providing that zeroing would be permitted in reviews and in transaction-to-transaction and "targeted dumping" comparisons in antidumping investigations, but also provided, contrary to the U.S. proposal, that zeroing would not be permitted in average-to-average comparisons in investigations.

At the December Rules Group meeting, the United States expressed its preliminary views about the text, and voiced specific concerns about the text's treatment of such issues as sunset reviews and zeroing in investigations. A number of Members, with Japan and India being the most vocal, submitted a joint statement at the December meeting expressing their unhappiness that the Chair's text addressed the U.S. zeroing proposal at all and urged that zeroing should not be permitted.

See 2007 Annual Report at 10–11.

3. Doha Development Agenda

On February 7, 2007, WTO Director-General Pascal Lamy, in his report to the WTO General Council, stated that "we have resumed our negotiations fully across the board . . . political conditions are now more favourable for the conclusion of the Round than they have been for a long time." *See www.wto. org/english/news_e/news07_e/gc_dg_stat_7feb07_e.htm.*

a. UN Conference on Trade and Development

On October 8, 2007, Deputy U.S. Representative to the WTO David Shark addressed the UN Conference on Trade and Development's 54th Trade and Development Board on the Post-Doha Work Program. The full text of Mr. Shark's statement, excerpted below, is available at *www.usmission.ch/Press 2007/1008UNCTAD.htm.*

*   *   *   *

II. Achieving a Successful Doha Outcome

- The Doha negotiations are at a critical juncture.
- In July, the Chairs of the negotiating groups on agriculture and non-agricultural market access (NAMA) tabled their best judgment on the outlines of a possible deal.

- Our gratitude goes out to the Chairs for their efforts to narrow differences among us. The ranges in the texts cut along the razor's edge and push everyone well into their discomfort zones.
- As recognized by the APEC Leaders—representing over 50% of global trade—in September, these texts—and the ranges therein—are our best, and possibly our only, chance to take the negotiations forward in the coming months.

*   *   *   *

- The United States has clearly signaled our willingness to negotiate on the basis of the texts, and recently reaffirmed this willingness with regard to the agriculture text's ranges for overall trade distorting support—provided others are willing to commit to negotiate on the basis of the current ranges and flexibilities in the Agriculture and NAMA texts.
- Consensus is possible, but only on the ranges and flexibilities in the texts that provide for a "real and substantial" market access outcome in agriculture and NAMA.
- In agriculture, the challenge is to find the right balance between tariff reduction formulas and flexibilities contained in the text that are intended to address individual countries' sensitivities and concerns.
- One concern—shared by many exporting countries, developed and developing—is to ensure that the operation of these flexibilities do not disrupt existing trade opportunities and do not hinder the important goal of creating new market openings.
  — For example, during the negotiations, groups of developing countries identified concerns about the possible impact of further liberalization on their farmers. The concept of Special Products emerged as a way to address the food security, livelihood security and rural development concerns of these countries.
  — Negotiators have been working on a way to ensure appropriate indicators and treatment for Special Products that respects the rationale for this flexibility but at the same

time complies with the Doha Mandate for substantial improvements in market access.

— Likewise, the concept of a Special Safeguard Mechanism has also been agreed to help provide comfort to those developing countries concerned about the possible negative consequences of unforeseen impacts of further trade liberalization. All Members, however, agree that the operation of this measure should not be applied in a way that is disruptive to normal trade.

• In NAMA, the challenge is to build from the Chair's draft text an agreement on NAMA modalities that will truly open markets and enable trade to grow worldwide. At the end of the day, it is the new tariff rates that our businesses will be paying that will determine whether we have a worthwhile outcome.

• This is simply a practical, commercial and political reality: we need a result that provides meaningful new market access for our workers and manufacturers. Without such a result, we would be kidding ourselves that we have concluded a pro-development Round—as manufacturing represents 75 percent of global merchandise trade.

* * * *

• In services, a robust outcome is essential in a final package. As one of the three core pillars of the market access negotiations, the services group must achieve significant progress in terms of closing the gap between current practice and trade commitments and in going beyond current practice to provide for new competitive opportunities, particularly in key infrastructure sectors like financial services and telecommunications where significant trade impediments remain.

* * * *

b. *Initiative to prohibit harmful fisheries subsidies*

On March 21, 2007, U.S. Trade Representative Susan C. Schwab announced that the United States had submitted an extensive proposal for new rules on fisheries subsidies in the WTO as part of the Doha Development Round. As described in a press release of that date, the proposal "calls for disciplines on subsidies that contribute to substantial global overcapacity in the fishing sector and the overexploitation or depletion of many commercially important fish stocks." The press release is available at *www.ustr.gov/Document_Library/Press_Releases/2007/March/Section_Index.html*.

The introduction to and explanation of the U.S. proposal are set forth below. The full text of the proposal, including proposed text for a fisheries subsidies annex to the WTO Agreement on Subsidies and Countervailing Measures with draft annexes, is available in full at *www.ustr.gov/assets/Trade_Sectors/Environment/asset_upload_file520_10878.pdf*.

Introduction

1. Worldwide fishing capacity is substantially above sustainable levels, and many commercially significant fish populations face overexploitation or depletion. A number of Members have experienced first hand the social and economic consequences that result when the level of exploitation tips over into overexploitation and leads to the collapse of particular fisheries stocks. The Rules Negotiating Group has therefore been given a mandate to clarify and improve the disciplines on subsidies that contribute to overcapacity and overfishing. Only an ambitious outcome pursuant to this mandate will deliver an outcome that is a win for trade, a win for development and a win for the environment.

2. As we have stated previously (TN/RL/W/196), the United States believes that a broad prohibition addressing all elements that contribute most directly to overcapacity and overfishing would be the most effective means to fulfill our mandate. Both New Zealand (TN/RL/GEN/100 and TN/RL/GEN/141) and Brazil (TN/RL/GEN/79/Rev.3) have offered legal text for framework proposals based on such an approach. In contrast, the alternative proposals from Japan, Korea and Chinese Taipei (TN/RL/GEN/114/Rev.1), the European Communities (TN/RL/GEN/134) and Norway (TN/RL/GEN/144) would fall short of that result. We note that much

of the technical work in the Group over the last year, including the identification of appropriate exceptions and the discussions of Argentina's proposal for special and differential treatment for developing countries (TN/RL/GEN/138/Rev.1), has been premised on a broad prohibition as the backbone of new disciplines.

3. Now that negotiations have resumed, the United States offers a framework proposal that we believe would achieve an ambitious, pragmatic result sufficiently flexible to address the concerns we have heard from other Members. While remaining sensitive to the unique challenges of fisheries, we have sought to draft text that is grounded in familiar WTO rules and concepts to the maximum extent possible. The proposed text is attached to this paper. For ease of review, we have also attached an annotated version of the text as an annex to this proposal.

Explanation of the Proposal

4. *A broad prohibition on subsidies to the harvesting of marine wild capture fisheries.* There is broad agreement that the focus of improved rules should be on subsidies to the harvesting sector of marine wild capture fisheries. For these purposes, subsidies would be those included within the meaning of Article 1 of the existing Agreement on Subsidies and Countervailing Measures (ASCM), and that meet the criteria for specificity set out in the existing Article 2 of the ASCM.[1]

5. *Effective disciplines for programs that are not included in the prohibition.* The United States and others have contributed to identification of programs that do not normally promote overcapacity

---

[1] Aquaculture would be treated along the lines suggested in the Brazil and New Zealand proposals, *i.e.*, subsidies to aquaculture would remain under the existing ASCM disciplines because these disciplines are generally adequate to address them; however, subsidies to associated wild capture activities (*e.g.*, the harvesting of juveniles to raise in pens or farms, or the harvesting of wild stocks to use as feed) would be covered by the prohibition. Similarly, subsidies to non-marine (inland) fisheries activities would not be included in the prohibition, as in Brazil's proposal (TN/RL/GEN/79/Rev.3); however, species that spend part of their life cycle in the marine environment would be considered "marine" for purposes of the prohibition.

and overfishing, and are therefore appropriate exceptions to a prohibition. The proposals by New Zealand (TN/RL/GEN/141) and Brazil (TN/RL/GEN/79/Rev.3) show substantial convergence on the scope of these exceptions. We have drawn upon these proposals in developing our exceptions text.[2] In addition, we have expanded upon the appropriate treatment of arrangements under which a Member acquires fishing rights for its distant water fleet to fisheries resources in the exclusive economic zone of another country. We recognize the sensitivity of this issue to developing countries and look forward to a further discussion.

6. To avoid loopholes, and to retain Members' rights under the existing ASCM, exceptions to the prohibition should remain actionable. As Members have recognized, however, the current rules on serious prejudice (Article 6 of the ASCM) have not been fully effective in the fisheries context. New rules should include some appropriate customization of the serious prejudice criteria to make those rules more operational. We have proposed two such customized criteria. In addition to the current Article 6.3, serious prejudice would arise if a Member could show that the effect of the subsidy is either: (i) to increase the capacity of the subsidizing Member to produce the like product; or (ii) to increase the subsidizing Member's relative share of the like product as compared to non-subsidized production over a representative period (*cf.* ASCM article 6.4). We look forward to further discussion of this issue in the Group.[3]

---

[2] We have also clarified that there should be an exception for government assistance to establish "rights-based" management systems, such as individual or group limited access privileges or other exclusive quotas. As explained in the United States' earlier paper (TN/RL/GEN/41), such systems are a promising approach to addressing the fundamental problem of the "race for fish," because they allow fishermen to fish at their own pace instead of racing to harvest the fish before someone else does. Several Members already have such systems in place and others (including the United States) are actively developing them.

[3] We are also interested in exploring further the possibility of additional new disciplines on subsidies to on-shore processing, in light of suggestions that overcapacity in the processing sector may have some link to overcapacity in the harvesting sector. One possibility would be to consider a "dark amber" category for such subsidies, modeled on the expired ASCM

7. *Some elements of flexibility for small programs.* Additionally, Members may have small programs that, by virtue of the small benefits conferred, do not contribute to overcapacity or overfishing, but might nevertheless be inconsistent with a prohibition. In our view, this consideration should not prevent adoption of a high level of ambition for the core discipline. Therefore, Members should consider flexibility to address such programs, bearing in mind that developing such a provision raises technical issues that will need to be addressed and that such flexibility must not create a loophole that could undermine the core discipline. Any exception for small programs should be subject to the serious prejudice and notification requirements. We have not proposed text for such a provision, but are interested in exploring it with the Group. Further technical work also needs to be done on artisanal subsidies.

8. *Notifications and transparency.* We share the views of others that transparency and notification procedures in the fisheries sector need to be strengthened while remaining workable and not unduly burdensome. We have sought to make the notifications more useful in light of the objectives of new fisheries disciplines (requiring information concerning the fisheries benefiting from the subsidy, as well as information concerning how any conditions specified for the applicable exceptions have been or will be met). To further promote transparency, we also propose that each Member establish an inquiry point to respond to reasonable enquiries from other Members and interested parties in other Members concerning its fisheries management system, including measures in place to address fishing capacity and fishing effort and the biological status of managed stocks. This kind of mechanism has worked well in the Agreement on Technical Barriers to Trade (*see* TBT Agreement, Article 10.1). It would be one way of ensuring that Members receive relevant fisheries management-related information of particular interest, while avoiding the burden of requiring lengthy submissions of information in the notifications that may

---

Article 6.1; however, we have not proposed text for such a provision at this time. We note that proposals have been made to the Group concerning reinstatement of Article 6.1 as part of the general subsidies disciplines.

or may not be useful. In addition, we have been carefully considering proposing additional incentives to notify, but note that there are some practical considerations to be accounted for in implementing such an approach. We therefore have not made a proposal on this issue, but would like to explore it further.

9. *Special and differential treatment.* Special and differential treatment should address the practical problems developing countries may face in implementing stronger rules while not undermining the objectives of the negotiations. Further work needs to be done in this area to assure this balance. We continue to be interested in developing Argentina's proposal (TN/RL/GEN/138/Rev.1), and we have already had some valuable discussions concerning how to make the sustainability and fisheries management criteria referred to in the proposal workable within the structure of WTO rules. We also believe that some aspects concerning the limits of special and differential treatment need to be more explicitly spelled out. For example, given that fishing vessels are a mobile capital asset with a useful life of thirty years or more, we have questions about how such vessels would be treated once the capacity of the fishery builds up to the level to exploit maximum sustainable yield.

10. *Other provisions.* Our proposal also contains provisions on anti-circumvention (similar to that proposed by Brazil), review, fisheries expertise and transitional arrangements. The provisions on review and expertise reflect some minor revisions to our initial proposal (TN/RL/GEN/127) in light of the discussion in the Group. Concerning transition periods, Members might also consider provision for negotiating individualized country phase-out schedules for specified programs. This could provide an additional element of flexibility to the transition to stronger rules, as well as a further element of transparency. While we have not provided explicit text, we are interested in exploring this concept further.

c.   Environmental goods and services

On November 30, 2007, U.S. Trade Representative Susan C. Schwab announced that the United States and the European Union had submitted proposals for new climate initiatives for the WTO Doha Development agenda, including a new environmental goods and services agreement. The full text of the USTR press release, excerpted below, is available at *www.ustr. gov/Document_Library/Press_Releases/2007/November/ Section_Index.html.*

. . . U.S. Trade Representative Susan C. Schwab announced today that the United States and EU have submitted a ground-breaking proposal as part of the Doha Round negotiations to increase global trade in and use of environmental goods and services. The initiative would place priority action on technologies directly linked to addressing climate change and energy security.

*   *   *   *

The proposal lays the foundation for an innovative new environmental goods and services agreement (EGSA) in the WTO and would include a commitment by all WTO Members to remove barriers to trade to a specific set of climate-friendly technologies. The [proposal] was prompted by President Bush's initiative earlier this year to seek an agreement with major economies on a new international climate agreement. The proposal underscores the importance of liberalizing trade in environmental goods and services in parallel by recognizing, for the first time, how the market works in this sector—how goods are bundled with services. For example, designing more energy efficient buildings can require consulting, design and construction services, as well as solar panels for heating.

The United States, joined by the European Union, proposes to eliminate tariff and non-tariff barriers to environmental technologies and services through a two-tiered approach: 1) A first-ever in the WTO agreement on worldwide elimination of tariffs on a specific list of climate friendly technologies recently identified by the World Bank; and 2) A higher level of commitment on the part of developed and the most advanced developing countries to eliminate barriers to trade across a broader range of other environmental technologies and an array of environment-friendly services.

*   *   *   *

A summary of the proposal, linked to the press release and available at *www.ustr.gov/assets/Document_Library/Reports _Publications/2007/asset_upload_file479_13638.pdf*, explained:

> Paragraph 31 (iii) of the WTO Doha Declaration calls for the "reduction or, as appropriate, elimination of tariff and non-tariff barriers to environmental goods and services." Liberalization of environmental goods and services can result in substantial benefits to Members as they pursue their environmental policy objectives, including addressing climate change.
>
> . . . Trade liberalisation can and should support the fight against climate change, notably by contributing to the necessary deployment of climate-friendly goods and technologies as well as services, thereby complementing and supporting the objectives of and the process under the United Nations Framework Convention on Climate Change (UNFCCC).
>
> We propose that WTO Members make a substantial and concrete contribution to support global and national climate objectives. Our proposal builds upon a recent report from the World Bank titled, "International Trade and Climate Change: Economic, Legal, and Institutional Perspectives,"[1] which concludes that eliminating tariff and non-tariff barriers to clean energy technologies could result in a 7–14 percent increase in trade volumes in these goods and that these technologies "also confer local environmental benefits and general efficiency improvements in the production process."
>
> Our proposal seeks to contribute to climate goals as a priority, but goes further to address a broader set of global and domestic environmental challenges. In order to address the broader set of environmental issues, we propose to

---

[1]   The International Bank for Reconstruction and Development/World Bank, 2007, *www.worldbank.org*.

negotiate in the WTO a ground-breaking and innovative Environmental Goods and Services Agreement (EGSA) involving market access commitments on a wide range of goods and services that contribute to environmental protection.

An attached summary chart indicated, among other things, that negotiations as to goods would be based on a set of more than 150 environmental goods outlined in a WTO submission of April 27, 2007, by Canada, the European Communities, Japan, Korea, New Zealand, Norway, Chinese Taipei, Switzerland, and the United States. WTO document Job(07)54. 2.

D. OTHER TRADE AGREEMENTS AND RELATED ISSUES

1. Bipartisan Agreement on Trade Issues

On May 10, 2007, U.S. Trade Representative Susan C. Schwab welcomed a bipartisan agreement between the Administration and the U.S. Congress on trade issues, stating:

> Today we have seized an historic opportunity to restore the bipartisan consensus on trade with a clear and reasonable path forward for congressional consideration of Free Trade Agreements with Peru, Colombia, Panama and Korea. The new trade policy template also opens the way for bipartisan work on Trade Promotion Authority.

See www.ustr.gov/Document_Library/Press_Releases/2007/May/Statement_from_Ambassador_Susan_C_Schwab_on_US_trade_agenda.html

Among other things, the new agreed approach called for certain new labor and environmental provisions to be included in the four free trade agreements. On May 11, 2007, USTR issued fact sheets describing various components of the bipartisan agreement, namely those addressing issues of the environment, labor, investment, intellectual property, government procurement, and port security. The fact sheets are available at *www.ustr.gov/Document_Library/Fact_Sheets/2007/Section_Index.html.*

a. Environment

USTR's fact sheet on environmental issues is excerpted below.

- The Administration and Congress have agreed to incorporate a specific list of multilateral environmental agreements (MEAs) in our FTAs.
- The list includes (with abbreviated titles) the Convention on International Trade in Endangered Species (CITES), Montreal Protocol on Ozone Depleting Substances, Convention on Marine Pollution, Inter-American Tropical Tuna Convention (IATTC), Ramsar Convention on Wetlands, International Whaling Convention (IWC), and Convention on Conservation of Antarctic Marine Living Resources (CCAMLR).

*   *   *   *

- We have also agreed to alter the non-derogation obligation for environmental laws from a "strive to" to a "shall" obligation, with allowance for waivers permitted under law as long as it does not violate the MEA. For the United States, this obligation is limited to federal laws and should not affect our implementation of these laws.
- Finally, we have agreed that all of our FTA environmental obligations will be enforced on the same basis as the commercial provisions of our agreements—same remedies, procedures, and sanctions. Previously, our environmental dispute settlement procedures focused on the use of fines, as opposed to trade sanctions, and were limited to the obligation to effectively enforce environmental laws.
- In connection with the Peru FTA, we have agreed to work with the Government of Peru on comprehensive steps to address illegal logging, including of endangered mahogany,

and to restrict imports of products that are harvested and traded in violation of CITES.

b. *Labor*

USTR's fact sheet on labor aspects of the bipartisan agreement is excerpted below.

- Enforceable reciprocal obligation for the countries to adopt and maintain in their laws and practice the five basic internationally-recognized labor principles, as stated in the ILO Declaration on Fundamental Principles and Rights at Work.
  o Freedom of association;
  o The effective recognition of the right to collective bargaining;
  o The elimination of all forms of forced or compulsory labor;
  o The effective abolition of child labor and a prohibition on the worst forms of child labor; and
  o The elimination of discrimination in respect of employment and occupation.
- The obligation refers only to the ILO Declaration on Fundamental Principles and Rights at Work. . . .
- Enforceable obligation to effectively enforce labor laws; five basic internationally-recognized labor principles from the 1998 Declaration, plus acceptable conditions of work.
- Violation requires showing that non-enforcement of labor obligations occurred through a sustained or recurring course of action or inaction.
- A violation must occur in a manner affecting trade or investment between the parties.
- The agreement does not change the current definition of labor laws in our FTAS and thus applies only to federal labor laws.
- Only a government can invoke dispute settlement against the other government for a labor violation under an FTA.
- Labor obligations subject to the same dispute settlement procedures and remedies as commercial obligations. Available

remedies are fines and trade sanctions, based on amount of trade injury.
• As with commercial provisions, panel decisions are not self-executing. That is, they would not alter U.S. law.

*   *   *   *

c. **Investment**

USTR's fact sheet on investment stated that a "preamble provision would recognize that foreign investors in the United States will not be accorded greater substantive rights with respect to investment protections than United States investors in the United States."

d. **Intellectual property**

USTR's fact sheet on intellectual property is excerpted below.

———————

*   *   *   *

• . . . [T]he agreement with the Congressional leadership entails the following elements related to intellectual property, medicines, and health:
  ○ Clarification that the period of protection for test data for pharmaceuticals by developing country FTA partners will generally not extend beyond the period that such protection is available for the same product in the United States, coupled with a provision that will encourage our partners to process marketing approval applications for innovative drugs in a timely manner.
  ○ Clarification that developing country FTA partners may implement exceptions to normal rules for protecting test data if necessary to protect public health.
  ○ A more flexible approach, for developing country partners, to restoring patent terms to compensate for processing delays.

This flexibility is accompanied by new provisions stipulating that trading partners will make best efforts to process patent and marketing approval applications expeditiously.

- o More flexibility in terms of the types of procedures that developing country partners may implement to prevent the marketing of patent-infringing products.
- o Integration within the intellectual property chapter of a recognition that nothing in the chapter affects the ability of our FTA partners to take necessary measures to protect public health by promoting access to medicines for all, and a statement affirming mutual commitment to the 2001 Doha Declaration on the TRIPS Agreement and Public Health.

- While the agreement on pending FTAs with developing countries incorporates various flexibilities with respect to pharmaceutical-related IPR provisions, the intellectual property chapters of these agreements continue to represent an enhancement of IPR protection for pharmaceutical products in those markets, compared to the status quo situation. In particular, these FTAs:

- o Contain provisions protecting against unfair commercial use of test and other data submitted in connection with product approval. These provisions, even as modified by the Administration-Congress agreement, provide assurances that our developing country FTA partners will satisfy their obligations under the TRIPS Agreement.
- o Require the establishment of procedures through which patent holders can effectively enforce their rights against pharmaceutical products that infringe patents. While the nature of these procedures is more flexibly defined than in the original negotiated FTA text, it remains the case that the IP chapters establish a firm basis for preventing the marketing of patent-infringing products.
- o Limit grounds for patent revocation, and improve other important patent rules and procedures.
- o Require FTA partners to join major international agreements in such areas as patent and trademark procedure, protection of new plant varieties, and deposit of microorganisms and industrial designs.

o Require FTA partners to make best efforts to process patents and marketing approvals expeditiously, and retain the option that patent term extension may be applied in cases of unreasonable delays.

o Establish trademark-related obligations that will contribute to effective efforts to combat production of and trade in counterfeit drugs.

o Establish civil, criminal, and border enforcement disciplines that will also contribute to combating trade in fake drugs.

e. Government procurement

As to government procurement, USTR's fact sheet stated that the agreement "clarif[ies] that FTA parties may insert requirements in their government contracts that suppliers must comply with core labor laws in the country where the good is produced or the service is performed."

f. Port security

USTR's fact sheet on port security stated that "[a] new FTA provision would clarify that the agreement's 'essential security' exception, which can be invoked to override any FTA obligation, including on port services, is not subject to challenge."

2. Free Trade Agreements

On December 14, 2007, President Bush signed the United States–Peru Trade Promotion Agreement Implementation Act, Pub. L. No. 110-138, approving the United States–Peru Free Trade Agreement signed in April 2006. As explained in a fact sheet issued by the White House on that date, the United States–Peru Agreement incorporated the "enforceable labor and environmental provisions" discussed in D.1.a. and b. *supra*.

In comments with President Garcia of Peru at the time of signing, and in the fact sheet, the President urged Congress also to enact legislation for free trade agreements with Colombia (signed on November 22, 2006), Panama (signed on June 28, 2007), and South Korea (signed on June 30, 2007). Like the agreement with Peru, each of these agreements also had been drafted or, in the case of Colombia, amended, to include the environmental, labor, and other elements of the May 10, 2007, bipartisan agreement discussed in D.1. *supra.* Those agreements remained pending at the end of 2007. *See* remarks on signing the United States–Peru legislation, available at 43 Weekly Comp. Pres. Doc. 1588 (Dec. 17, 2007) and White House fact sheet, available at *www.whitehouse.gov/news/releases/2007/12/ 20071214-7.html.*

3. International Coffee Agreement

In September 2007 the International Coffee Organization ("ICO") concluded negotiation of a new International Coffee Agreement ("ICA 2007"). U.S. Trade Representative Susan C. Schwab welcomed the new agreement in a press release issued by the Office of the U.S. Trade Representative ("USTR") on October 2, 2007. A background section of the release described the ICO and the U.S. relationship with it:

> The International Coffee Agreement (ICA) is a commodity trade agreement that establishes the International Coffee Organization (ICO), an intergovernmental forum to discuss coffee matters. The new agreement is the seventh ICA since the agreement was first concluded in 1962. The ICO brings together exporting and importing Member countries to tackle the challenges facing the world coffee sector through international cooperation. . . .
>
> The United States was a founding member of the ICO in the 1960s, but eventually left the organization in the 1990s because of continuing concerns that the ICO was primarily focused on manipulating coffee prices through restrictions on production and trade. In 2005, the United States resumed membership after ICO Members agreed

to remove all vestiges of market manipulation from the organization's activities. Since rejoining, the United States has been an advocate for efforts to rejuvenate and reform the ICO, with strong support from the U.S. private sector and non-governmental organizations. The new agreement reflects many of the specific changes proposed by the United States.

Excerpts below from the press release explain the U.S. support for ICA 2007. The full text is available at *www.ustr. gov/Document_Library/Press_Releases/2007/October/ Section_Index.html*. See also Chapter 7.B.2.b. on the role of the European Community in ICA 2007.

*   *   *   *

Since rejoining the ICO in February 2005, the United States has stressed the need for structural and operational reforms to create new relevancy for the organization and provide an example of the potential role of international commodity organizations in facilitating international trade and sustainable development in economic, social and environmental terms and in a manner consistent with market principles. Renegotiation of the agreement began in January of this year and concluded at the September meeting of the International Coffee Council at the headquarters of the organization in London.

The new agreement is designed to enhance the ICO's role as a forum for intergovernmental consultations, increase its contributions to meaningful market information and market transparency and ensure that the organization plays a unique role in developing innovative and effective capacity building in the coffee sector, including promoting sustainable approaches to coffee production and enhancing the value of production for small-scale farmers in key developing country trading partners.

The new agreement establishes a first-ever "Consultative Forum on Coffee Sector Finance" to promote the development and dissemination of innovations and best practices that can enable coffee producers to better manage financial aspects of the inherent volatility and risks associated with competitive and evolving markets.

Other notable changes include: expanding the organization's work in providing relevant statistical and market information; strengthening efforts to develop, review and implement capacity building projects; and strengthening the Council through the elimination of an Executive Board.

*   *   *   *

4. Import Safety

a. *Interagency Import Safety Working Group Action Plan*

On July 18, 2007, President Bush established the Interagency Import Safety Working Group ("IISWG") chaired by Secretary of Health and Human Services Mike Leavitt to conduct a comprehensive review of the U.S. import system and identify ways to further increase the safety of imports entering the United States. Executive Order 13439, 72 Fed. Reg. 40,051 (July 20, 2007). On September 10, the IISWG presented a report to the President entitled "Protecting the American Consumer Every Step of the Way: A strategic framework for import safety" and an Immediate Actions Memorandum. *See* White House Press release at *www.whitehouse.gov/news/releases/2007/09/20070910-1.html.*

On November 6, 2007, the IISWG submitted its "Action Plan for Import Safety: A roadmap for continual improvement" ("Action Plan") to President Bush, available with related information at *www.importsafety.gov.* In comments to the press on the Action Plan, the President noted that his creation of the working group resulted from the fact that "[u]nfortunately, in recent months Americans have seen imports from toys to toothpaste to pet food recalled because of safety concerns." *See* 43 WEEKLY COMP. PRES. DOC. 1463 (Nov. 12, 2007).

The Action Plan contains 14 broad recommendations and 50 action steps that provide a roadmap for better protecting American consumers and enhancing the safety of the increasing volume of imports entering the United States. The Action Plan is the product of extensive coordination among Federal agencies, months of information-gathering, and feedback and suggestions from the private sector.

The Action Plan notes that certification can be a powerful tool to foster compliance with U.S. safety standards while facilitating trade. For example, the Action Plan recommends that the Food and Drug Administration ("FDA") should have the authority to require that producers of certain high-risk foods in a particular country, under an agreement with that country, be certified as meeting FDA standards as a condition for importing those products into the United States. This is viewed as helping to "shrink the haystack" and better target resources on the greatest threats. In addition, voluntary certification should be encouraged for other products and, as an incentive to participate in voluntary certification programs, products certified as meeting U.S. safety standards could receive expedited entry.

The Action Plan recommends the Federal government work with the importing community to develop good importer practices. These practices should be developed as guidelines, be risk-based, and provide concrete guidance to the importing community for evaluating imported products and to foreign suppliers for compliance with U.S. safety requirements and implementation of effective supply-chain management systems. Names of certified producers and importers of record could be made public so that distributors and retailers could identify importers that only handle imported products from certified producers, and consumers could make more informed decisions about the products they buy.

The Action Plan calls for the importing community, U.S. Customs and Border Protection, and other Federal agencies to exchange real-time product and compliance data on each import transaction to better inform decisions to clear or reject import shipments. It also recommends that strategic information-sharing agreements be concluded with key foreign governments, in order to facilitate the exchange of import and recall data, and that product safety should be a guiding principle of U.S. cooperative agreements with foreign governments.

The Action Plan emphasizes the importance of providing training and other technical assistance to foreign regulatory agencies to build and improve their capacity to ensure the safety of products exported to the United States. In addition, it mentions that the presence of U.S. safety officials abroad and working with foreign governments and manufacturers will help ensure compliance with U.S. safety standards.

The Action Plan calls for Federal departments and agencies with jurisdiction over imported products to work with industry and the public to strengthen U.S. safety standards, where needed and appropriate, particularly for products determined to be high-risk. It also recommends that, to hold both foreign and domestic entities accountable and to discourage the sale of unsafe products, the Federal government should take steps to strengthen penalties against entities that violate U.S. laws, thus providing a significant incentive to comply with U.S. requirements.

b. China-related instruments

The Third U.S.–China Strategic Economic Dialogue, co-chaired by U.S. Treasury Secretary Henry M. Paulson, Jr., and Chinese Vice Premier Wu Yi, met in Beijing, December 12–13, 2007. A fact sheet released by the U.S. Department of the Treasury summarized the result of talks between the two countries, including those related to product quality and food safety, as excerpted below. The full text of the fact sheet is available at *www. ustreas.gov/press/releases/hp732.htm*. *See also* USTR fact sheet, available at *www.ustr.gov/assets/Document_Library/Fact_Sheets/2007/asset_upload_file675_13697.pdf.* The texts of the two December 11 agreements on food and feed and on drugs and medical devices are available at *http://globalhealth.gov/news/agreements/ia121107a.html* and *http://globalhealth.gov/news/agreements/ia121107b.html*, respectively.

* * * *

In product quality and food safety, the United States and China committed to expand their dialogue and information sharing to enhance the infrastructure of laws, policies, programs and incentives that allow for effective government oversight of exports of food, drugs, medical products, and consumer goods. To this end, the two countries signed memorandums in eight areas intended to improve the safety of exports. These included:

- *Food and feed*: Memorandum of agreement between the U.S. Department of Health and Human Services (HHS) and China's General Administration of Quality Supervision, Inspection, and Quarantine (AQSIQ), signed on December 11, 2007;
- *Drugs and medical products*: Agreement between the U.S. Department of Health and Human Services (HHS) and China's State Food and Drug Administration (SFDA), signed on December 11, 2007;
- *Environmentally compliant exports/imports*: Memorandum of understanding signed between the U.S. Environmental Protection Agency (EPA) and China's AQSIQ;
- *Food safety*: The U.S. Department of Agriculture (USDA) and China's AQSIQ agree to upgrade their food safety memorandum of cooperation to a ministerial-level;
- *Alcohol and tobacco products*: Memorandum of understanding between the U.S. Department of the Treasury and China's AQSIQ, signed on December 11, 2007; and,
- *Additional areas*: Toys, fireworks, lighters, and electrical products; motor vehicle safety; and pesticides tolerance and trade.

*   *   *   *

5. Most-Favored Nation Clause

On October 31, John B. Bellinger, III, Department of State Legal Adviser, addressed the Sixth Committee of the UN General Assembly on the report of the International Law Commission on the work of its 59th Session. Mr. Bellinger commented on the inclusion of the topic "Most-Favored-Nation clause" in the ILC's long-term work program, stating:

MFN provisions are principally a product of treaty formation and tend to differ considerably in their structure, scope and language. They also are dependent on other provisions in the specific agreements in which they are located and, as a result, resist easy categorization or study. In light of these observations, we question the utility of the Commission taking on this topic.

The full text of Mr. Bellinger's statement is available at *www.state.gov/s/l/c8183.htm.*

6. Arbitration Arising from the Softwood Lumber Agreement

As noted in B.2.b *supra,* on September 12, 2006, the United States and Canada agreed to the Softwood Lumber Agreement ("SLA" or "Agreement") that was intended to settle issues concerning trade between the two countries in softwood lumber that had given rise to arbitration under the North American Free Trade Agreement. The text of the SLA, which entered into force on October 12, 2006, is available at *www. ustr.gov/assets/World_Regions/Americas/Canada/asset_ upload_file847_9896.pdf.* Amendments to Articles II–IV and X, as well as associated annexes, are available at *www. ustr.gov/assets/World_Regions/Americas/Canada/asset_ upload_file667_9897.pdf.*

a. U.S. request for formal consultations

Pursuant to the dispute settlement provisions set forth in SLA Article XIV, on March 30, 2007, the United States requested formal consultations with Canada regarding compliance with several provisions. *See* letter from U.S. Trade Representative Susan Schwab to David Emerson, Canadian Minister for International Trade, March 30, 2007, available at *www.ustr. gov/Trade_Agreements/Monitoring_Enforcement/2006_ Softwood_Lumber_Agreement/Arbitration_on_Export_ Measures/Section_Index.html.* The letter identified two issues on which consultation was sought: "The Annex 7D, Paragraph 14 Adjustment to Expected U.S. Consumption" and "Certain Provincial and Federal Assistance Programs."

In a press release of the same date, the Office of the U.S. Trade Representative described the U.S. request as excerpted below. The full text of the press release is available at *www.ustr.gov/Document_Library/Press_Releases/2007/March/Section_Index.html.*

---

*   *   *   *

One concern identified in the consultation request involves Canada's application of certain adjustments to export levels based on differences between expected and actual conditions in the U.S. market. Because the Agreement contemplates that these adjustments should already have been made, Canada should have collected additional export taxes on lumber exports from interior British Columbia to the United States in January. Further, lumber exports from Ontario in February should have been lower.

A second concern identified in the request is the assistance programs maintained by Quebec and Ontario and the Canadian federal government. These programs provide benefits, such as grants, loans, loan guarantees, and tax credits, to the Canadian forest products sector in excess of C\$2 billion and raise questions under the Agreement. The consultations will assist the United States in obtaining clarification from Canada concerning the operation of these programs.

*   *   *   *

U.S. officials have expressed their concerns regarding these Canadian programs on several occasions over the last several months. Most recently, U.S. and Canadian officials discussed these issues at the February 22–23 meeting of the bilateral Softwood Lumber Committee, which also saw the establishment of several technical working groups and have begun work to resolve various data discrepancies relating to softwood lumber exports from Canada.

Under the Agreement, consultations are to be held within 20 days. If the matter is not resolved within 40 days of the request for consultations, either party may refer the matter to arbitration under the rules of the London Court of International Arbitration.

If the matter is referred to arbitration, there is an approximately two-month process to select the arbitrators, and the arbitral tribunal will endeavor to issue its award within six months of its appointment.

b. U.S. request for arbitration on export measures

On August 13, 2007, the United States filed a Request for Arbitration with the London Court of International Arbitration on the export measures issue, stating:

> In the Agreement, Canada agreed to impose certain export charges upon exports from certain Canadian regions to the United States, when exports exceeded the agreed-upon share of the United States market. Canada also agreed to limit the volume of certain exports from other regions when the United States price dropped below a certain level. Canada has failed to impose the agreed-upon export charges, and it has failed to limit the volume of exports in a timely manner. Accordingly, Canada has breached the Agreement.

United States of America v. Canada, LCIA, Case No. 7941. Pursuant to the tribunal's procedural order of October 15, 2007, ordering that proceedings in the arbitration be bifurcated, the United States submitted its Statement of the Case on October 19, 2007, limited to issues of liability. The United States filed its Rebuttal Memorial, in response to Canada's statement of defense, on November 28, 2007. The texts of the U.S. submissions in the case are available at *www.ustr. gov/Trade_Agreements/Monitoring_Enforcement/2006_ Softwood_Lumber_Agreement/Arbitration_on_Export_ Measures/Section_Index.html*. The arbitration panel held a hearing in December 2007. A decision was pending at the end of the year.

In its Statement of the Case, the United States explained the basis of its claim that "Canada has breached the SLA by failing to apply timely the calculation of Expected U.S. Consumption and by failing to apply completely the calculation to Option A and Option B," as excerpted below. Footnotes and references to other submissions in the case have been omitted.

* * * *

2. This case concerns Canada's breach of the 2006 Softwood Lumber Agreement ("SLA" or "Agreement"), an international trade agreement between the United States and Canada, which resolved a longstanding trade dispute regarding Canadian exports of softwood lumber to the United States. *See* Exhibit A (SLA); Exhibit B (Amendments). After years of painstaking negotiations, the United States agreed in the SLA to forgo the imposition of antidumping and countervailing duties in favor of a mechanism for Canada to impose, when certain market conditions prevail, export measures designed to avoid adverse effects to the United States from continuing Canadian lumber practices. Canada now rejects this mechanism, even though the United States already has fulfilled its obligations under the Agreement by (a) refunding to Canada approximately five billion US dollars in previously-collected duties, and (b) terminating antidumping and countervailing duty orders that had helped address these continuing Canadian practices. After extensive discussions and formal consultations did not resolve the dispute, the United States commenced this arbitration.

* * * *

A. The Export Measures

14. The export measures to which Canada agreed give Canada's different lumber producing regions a choice between two options, Option A and Option B. SLA, art. VII.* Both options involve export

---

*   Editor's note: SLA, art. VII ¶1, provides:

By the Effective Date, each Region shall elect to have Canada apply the measures in either Option A or Option B to exports of Softwood Lumber Products to the United States from the Region. Option A is an Export Charge collected by Canada, the rate of which varies

charges and volume limits. Under both options, export charges are imposed when the United States price is at or below US$355, and the charges increase as the price declines. SLA, art. VII, ¶ 2. Under Option A, an additional export charge—50 percent of the existing export charge—is imposed on all exports from that region if the region's exports exceed the region's "trigger" volume by more than one percent. SLA, art. VIII, ¶ 1(b). Under Option B, in addition to the export charge, a quota volume (or volume restraint) is applied to each region, which limits the volume that region may export.

15. Thus, Option A accommodates those Canadian regions whose producers export large volumes of lumber and would prefer to be subject to increasing export charges rather than strict volume restraints. Option B accommodates those Canadian regions whose producers export less lumber and, therefore, can easily remain within the Agreement's pre-set, proportional volume restraints as a percentage of expected United States consumption in the Agreement.

*　*　*　*

23. Pursuant to Annex 7D, monthly expected United States consumption is equal to the average United States consumption for the 12-month period ending three months before the month for which expected consumption is being calculated (United States consumption for the latest, available 12-month period divided by 12) multiplied by an assigned seasonal adjustment factor. SLA, Annex 7D, ¶¶ 12 and 13. Further, if actual United States consumption during a quarter differs by more than five percent from expected United States consumption during that quarter, the calculation of expected United States consumption for the following quarter for which quotas are being determined is to be adjusted to minimize any divergence between expected United States consumption and actual United States consumption . . . SLA, Annex 7D, ¶ 14.

---

based on the Prevailing Monthly Price, as provided in the table in paragraph 2. Option B is an Export Charge with a volume restraint, where both the rate of the Export Charge and the applicable volume restraint vary based on the Prevailing Monthly Price, also as provided in the table in paragraph 2. The Export Charge shall be levied on the Export Price. The Prevailing Monthly Price is defined in Annex 7A.

24. This provision is designed to prevent the calculation of expected United States consumption under the Agreement from becoming a systematically inaccurate estimate under the circumstances of a rapid change in the level of United States consumption. In the absence of such an adjustment, the use of a 12-month moving average as the basis for the estimate would result in an estimate that lags behind such movements in actual United States consumption. In providing for the calculation of expected United States consumption, Annex 7D neither mentions nor distinguishes between Option A and Option B, or trigger volumes and quota volumes.

25. In short, the parties agreed upon an approach for calculating a fair and accurate value for expected United States consumption that provides for continual adjustment to minimize any divergence between expected United States consumption and actual United States consumption, and that approach applies equally when calculating both Option A trigger volumes and Option B quota volumes.

*   *   *   *

Excerpts below from the introduction to the November 28 Rebuttal summarize the U.S. legal analysis. References to other submissions in the arbitration and most footnotes have been omitted.

---

*   *   *   *

2. The parties agree that only two issues are before the Tribunal: (1) whether the 2006 Softwood Lumber Agreement ("SLA" or "Agreement") requires Canada to apply the complete calculation of "Expected U.S. Consumption" to all exporting regions, that is, to Option A regions in addition to Option B regions; and (2) whether Canada was required to begin to apply the complete calculation as of the Agreement's effective date. The parties agree further that there are no factual disputes, that Articles 31 and 32 of the Vienna Convention apply, and that the Tribunal may resolve both issues by determining the correct interpretation of the Agreement.

3. Canada has breached the Agreement, and continues to breach the Agreement, by refusing to apply the complete calculation of Expected U.S. Consumption to all regions. Canada refuses to acknowledge that the Agreement contains only one definition of Expected U.S. Consumption. Rather than addressing the Agreement's ordinary meaning or offering a competing interpretation that might account for Canada's position, Canada focuses almost exclusively upon the use of the undefined word "quota," in what Canada concedes is only a subordinate clause on timing. Canada proffers an ungrammatical interpretation of "quota" at the expense of the entirety of the Agreement's text and, therefore, fails to support its position. The ordinary meaning of the text supports the United States' position.

4. Additionally, Canada breached the Agreement by failing to apply timely the export measures. Nothing in the text of the Agreement delays Canada's obligation to apply the complete calculation of Expected U.S. Consumption from the effective date of the Agreement. Nonetheless, Canada appears to read words into the text of the Agreement that are not there, purportedly to allow it to avoid implementing the complete calculation for nine consecutive months. There is no basis in the Agreement for such a grace period.

5. Rather than respond to the core of the United States' arguments, which are firmly grounded in the text of the Agreement, Canada expends considerable effort in its statement of defence selectively focusing upon side issues in an apparent attempt to cast doubt regarding the central questions of this dispute. Canada distorts the United States' unremarkable observation that a primary purpose of the provision at issue is to enhance the accuracy of the calculation and similarly misconstrues the United States' argument concerning the Agreement's object and purpose.

6. Canada's interpretation of the Agreement is inconsistent with the ordinary meaning of the text, read in its context and in light of the object and purpose. In sections I and II, the United States addresses the ordinary meaning of the Agreement in its context. In section III, the United States addresses why its interpretation in both cases is consistent with the SLA's object and purpose.

* * * *

E. COMMUNICATIONS: WORLD RADIOCOMMUNICATION CONFERENCE 2007

The World Radiocommunication Conference 2007 was held in Geneva, October 22–November 16, 2007. In a press briefing on the first day of the conference, Ambassador Richard M. Russell, U.S. Representative to the World Radiocommunication Conference, highlighted issues of particular interest to the United States, stating:

> The World Radiocommunication Conference occurs roughly every four years. The purpose of it is to review and revise the treaty that governs the use of spectrum globally. That includes both terrestrial and satellite spectrum. Obviously, as a general rule what is most important is looking at the implications of the use of technology, both space technology and ground-based technology that implicates border areas in particular. The whole point of having an international organization to review spectrum policy is to make sure that you don't have harmful interference, but in addition to ensuring that you avoid harmful interference or that people's individual systems can work, you also can create some very significant synergies, which reduce the cost of technology and promote the rapid deployment of new technologies and services. And that is one of the main themes of this year's conference, the 2007 World Radiocommunication Conference.

The full text of Ambassador Russell's briefing is available at *www.usmission.ch/Press2007/1022RussellTranscipt.html*. On November 16, 2007, the Conference adopted an international treaty to meet the global demand for radio-frequency spectrum, setting the future course for wireless communication. *See www.itu.int/newsroom/press_releases/2007/36. html*.

F.　INVESTMENT AND OTHER ISSUES

1.　President Bush's Open Economies Statement

On May 10, 2007, President Bush issued an Open Economies Policy Statement reaffirming encouragement of foreign direct investment in the United States. This was the first Presidential statement on foreign direct investment since December 26, 1991. *See Cumulative Digest 1991–1999* at 1461–63.

The President's Open Economies Policy Statement is set forth below in full and available at *www.whitehouse.gov/ news/releases/2007/05/20070510-2.html. See also* White House press release available at 43 Weekly Comp. Pres. Doc. 608 (May 14, 2007).

In advancing open markets, the United States will:

- Reinforce the principle that a domestic climate conducive to foreign investment strengthens national security. Meeting the challenges of a post-9/11 world need not require securing one at the expense of the other. The United States recognizes that growing inflows of foreign investment are necessary to expand levels of employment, innovation, and competitiveness in this country. Only those safeguards that are clearly necessary to protect our national security should be maintained.
- Actively target unreasonable and discriminatory barriers to investment. The United States encourages a broad acceptance of the national-treatment principle in all countries and places a premium on the protection of U.S. investments abroad. The United States opposes measures that distort international investment flows, including trade-related or other performance requirements, discriminatory treatment of foreign investment, and expropriation without compensation. In turn, when countries promise to protect investment and eliminate such distortions, investors must have the ability to enforce

those binding promises in neutral international settings that are free from the political intervention of governments. Further, countries need to be responsive to the needs of investors for access to innovative cross-border financial services. The United States will continue to allow foreign investors open and fair access to investment opportunities under our statutes and regulations and in accordance with international law, and will continue to welcome investment through programs such as the Invest in America initiative.

• Work with our partners in the WTO to strengthen the rules-based trading system so that it continues to promote open markets, trade reform and new opportunities for development and growth. My Administration is committed to completing the Doha Development Round with an agreement that opens markets for goods and services, ensures reform of agriculture and strengthens WTO rules, including in key areas such as trade facilitation. The predictability, certainty, and transparency of the system enhance opportunities for international investment by building investor confidence.

• Promote an international environment in which international investment can make the greatest contribution to the development process. The United States has initiated the Millennium Challenge Account, which assists developing countries that create and maintain sound policy environments, including governing justly, investing in people, and encouraging economic freedoms. Through our bilateral and multilateral economic assistance programs, the United States will continue to explore ways to increase both public and private capital flows and support international investment in the developing world. As countries continue to adopt free market principles and democratic reforms, international investment is necessary to nurture market-oriented development and reduce debt service burdens. Economic freedom is one of the single greatest antidotes to poverty worldwide, and a positive link exists between the liberalization of investment flows and greater international trade.

2. Committee on Foreign Investment in the United States

On July 26, 2007, President Bush signed into law the Foreign Investment and National Security Act of 2007 ("FINSA"), Pub. L. No. 110-49 (2007), enacted "[t]o ensure national security while promoting foreign investment and the creation and maintenance of jobs, to reform the process by which such investments are examined for any effect they may have on national security, to establish the Committee on Foreign Investment in the United States, and for other purposes." Effective October 4, 2007, FINSA amended § 721 of the Defense Production Act of 1950, under which the President and the Committee on Foreign Investment in the United States ("CFIUS") conduct national security reviews of foreign acquisitions of control of U.S. businesses. Among other things, the legislation statutorily established CFIUS, originally established by Executive Order No. 11858 (May 7, 1975), to oversee the national security implications of foreign investment in the U.S. economy.

In a press statement of July 26, Secretary of the Treasury Henry M. Paulson, Jr., commented as follows on the new law. The full text of Mr. Paulsen's press statement is available at *www.ustreas.gov/press/releases/hp509.htm*.

---

*   *   *   *

I commend Congress, especially the Senate Banking and the House Financial Services Committee, for their successful efforts to reach bipartisan agreement. These efforts resulted in a law that will accomplish our mutual goals of ensuring that the Committee on Foreign Investment in the U.S., CFIUS, can continue to address national security imperatives while also reaffirming that America welcomes foreign investment.

The CFIUS process applies only when a transaction may be related to national security, and that is a very small percentage of foreign investment. The vast majority are mergers, acquisitions and investments, and don't receive a CFIUS review. Last year, and historically, only 10 percent of foreign direct investments were reviewed by CFIUS, and the vast majority of those received a review which was resolved without controversy. Importantly, the new law maintains CFIUS' narrow focus on transactions that raise national security concerns.

President Bush, through his open economies statement on May 10, 2007, and the Congress, through their actions on this bill, have reaffirmed that the U.S. continues to welcome foreign investment.

* * * *

On October 11, 2007, the Department of the Treasury published a notice of inquiry and notice of an October 23, 2007, public meeting seeking public comments on regulations being developed to implement the new legislation. 72 Fed. Reg. 57,900 (Oct. 11, 2007). The notice provided background information on FINSA, as excerpted below.

---

* * * *

Background: On May 10, 2007, President Bush issued an Open Economies statement reaffirming the United States' longstanding policy of welcoming international investment. He noted that, while continuing "to take every necessary step to protect national security, my Administration recognizes that our prosperity and security are founded on our country's openness." In that context, on July 26, 2007, President Bush signed into law the Foreign Investment and National Security Act of 2007 ("FINSA") (Pub. L. 110-49), which amends section 721 of the Defense Production Act of 1950 (50 U.S.C. 2170 et seq.) ("section 721"), to codify the structure, role, process, and responsibilities of CFIUS. The principal provisions of the new legislation are described below.

CFIUS Membership: FINSA establishes CFIUS in statute and specifies its membership to include the Secretaries of the Departments of the Treasury, State, Defense, Commerce, Energy, and Homeland Security, and the Attorney General. Additionally, the Secretary of Labor and the Director of National Intelligence are ex officio, non-voting members of CFIUS, with the latter serving as an independent advisor to CFIUS on intelligence matters. In addition to certain officials in the Executive Office of the President, the President may also appoint the head of any other executive department, agency, or office whom he deems appropriate to serve as a CFIUS member. Current executive orders specify twelve CFIUS members, including certain officials in the Executive Office of the President.

FINSA specifies that the Secretary of the Treasury shall serve as Chairperson of CFIUS and, as appropriate, shall designate a CFIUS member or members to be the "lead" agency or agencies for each covered transaction reviewed by CFIUS and for the monitoring of completed transactions.

Review and Investigation Process: FINSA requires that, upon receipt by Treasury of written notification of a "covered transaction" (*i.e.,* a merger, acquisition, or takeover by or with any foreign person that could result in foreign control of any person engaged in interstate commerce in the United States), the President, acting through CFIUS, shall review the transaction within 30 days to determine its effects on national security, based on any relevant factors, including several new factors FINSA added to an illustrative list contained in section 721. The term "national security" is clarified to include those issues relating to "homeland security," including its application to "critical infrastructure", which is also defined in the new legislation.

If, during its review, CFIUS determines that (1) the transaction threatens to impair U.S. national security and the threat has not yet been mitigated, (2) the lead agency recommends an investigation and CFIUS concurs, (3) the transaction would result in foreign government control, or (4) the transaction would result in the control of any U.S. critical infrastructure that could impair U.S. national security and the threat has not yet been mitigated, then CFIUS must conduct and complete within 45 days an investigation of the transaction. The latter two grounds for an investigation do not mandate an investigation if the Secretary or Deputy Secretary of the Treasury and the equivalent lead agency counterparts jointly determine that the transaction will not impair U.S. national security.

FINSA also authorizes the President or CFIUS, if approved at the Under Secretary level or above, to review unilaterally any covered transaction that is proposed or pending after August 23, 1988, and that has not previously been reviewed, or a previously reviewed transaction if false or inaccurate information was submitted to CFIUS during the review or investigation of the transaction or a mitigation agreement resulting from the review or investigation was intentionally and materially breached.

Risk Mitigation and Tracking of Withdrawn Cases: FINSA provides that CFIUS or a lead agency designated by the Secretary of the Treasury may, on behalf of CFIUS, enter into, modify, monitor, and enforce agreements with any party to a covered transaction to mitigate national security risk posed by the transaction. Any mitigation agreement must be based on transaction-specific, risk-based analysis. FINSA also requires that CFIUS establish a method of tracking transactions withdrawn from the review or investigation process, as well as a process for establishing interim protections to address any national security concerns raised by withdrawn transactions that have not yet been refiled.

Actions by the President: FINSA authorizes the President to suspend or prohibit any covered transaction when (1) there is credible evidence that the foreign interest might take action that threatens to impair national security, and (2) provisions of law other than section 721 and the International Emergency Economic Powers Act do not provide adequate and appropriate authority to protect national security in the matter before the President. The President must decide whether to take such action within 15 days of the completion of an investigation, based on all relevant factors, including, as appropriate, an illustrative list of factors contained in section 721, which has been expanded by FINSA.

Regulations: FINSA requires the President to direct the issuance of implementing regulations. These regulations shall impose civil penalties for violations of section 721, including those relating to mitigation agreements. Proposed regulations will be published in the Federal Register and be subject to notice and comment before final regulations are published. Treasury must also publish in the Federal Register guidance on the types of transactions that CFIUS has reviewed and that have presented national security considerations. Treasury plans to do so separately from the regulations that will be published under section 721.

Request for Comment: The purpose of issuing this notice of inquiry and convening a public meeting is to obtain a wide array of views of businesses active in international mergers and acquisitions on several broad topics, in order to inform regulatory development. Topics of particular interest to Treasury include, but are not limited to:

(i) Procedural issues relating to the review process, including pre-filing, filing of voluntary notice, unilateral initiation of review by CFIUS, withdrawal of notice, refiling of notice, and notice to filers of the results of a review or investigation;

(ii) Definitional issues, including the definitions of "control", "foreign person", "person engaged in interstate commerce in the United States", "critical infrastructure", and "critical technologies";

(iii) Mitigation agreements, including determinations of the need for risk mitigation, scope of provisions, compliance monitoring, modification, and enforcement, including civil penalties and other remedies for breach;

(iv) Confidentiality issues;

(v) Collection of information from filers, including personal identifier information and information to aid CFIUS in determining jurisdiction and whether the transaction raises national security considerations; and

(vi) Emerging trends in international investment and their relevance to the CFIUS process, including legal structures for effecting acquisitions of U.S. businesses.

Treasury would also be interested in hearing views on other topics of interest to the private sector that relate to the CFIUS review process or FINSA.

*   *   *   *

3. Intellectual Property: Special 301 Report

On April 30, 2007, the Office of the U.S. Trade Representative announced the results of the 2007 Special 301 report on the adequacy and effectiveness of intellectual property protection by U.S. trading partners. The report explained the Special 301 process, summarized particular concerns with China and Russia, and identified countries whose performance had improved in 2007, as excerpted below. The full text of the report is available at *www.ustr.gov/assets/Document_Library/ Reports_Publications/2007/2007_Special_301_Review/ asset_upload_file230_11122.pdf.*

* * * *

Pursuant to Section 182 of the Trade Act of 1974, as amended by the Omnibus Trade and Competitiveness Act of 1988 and the Uruguay Round Agreements Act (enacted in 1994) ("Special 301"), under Special 301 provisions, USTR must identify those countries that deny adequate and effective protection for IPR or deny fair and equitable market access for persons that rely on intellectual property protection. Countries that have the most onerous or egregious acts, policies, or practices and whose acts, policies, or practices have the greatest adverse impact (actual or potential) on the relevant U.S. products must be designated as "Priority Foreign Countries."

Priority Foreign Countries are potentially subject to an investigation under the Section 301 provisions of the Trade Act of 1974. USTR may not designate a country as a Priority Foreign Country if it is entering into good faith negotiations or making significant progress in bilateral or multilateral negotiations to provide adequate and effective protection of IPR.

USTR must decide whether to identify countries within 30 days after issuance of the annual National Trade Estimate Report. In addition, USTR may identify a trading partner as a Priority Foreign Country or remove such identification whenever warranted.

USTR has created a "Priority Watch List" and "Watch List" under Special 301 provisions. Placement of a trading partner on the Priority Watch List or Watch List indicates that particular problems exist in that country with respect to IPR protection, enforcement, or market access for persons relying on intellectual property. Countries placed on the Priority Watch List are the focus of increased bilateral attention concerning the problem areas.

Additionally, under Section 306, USTR monitors a country's compliance with bilateral intellectual property agreements that are the basis for resolving an investigation under Section 301. USTR may apply sanctions if a country fails to satisfactorily implement an agreement. The interagency Trade Policy Staff Committee, in advising USTR on the implementation of Special 301, obtains information from and holds consultations with the private sector, U.S. embassies, foreign governments, and the U.S. Congress, among other sources.

*   *   *   *

The Administration's top priorities this year continue to be addressing weak IPR protection and enforcement, particularly in China and Russia. Although this year's Special 301 Report shows positive progress in many countries, rampant counterfeiting and piracy problems have continued to plague China and Russia, indicating a need for stronger IPR regimes.

With respect to Russia, the Special 301 Report describes the Bilateral Market Access Agreement between the United States and Russia, concluded in November 2006, which includes a letter setting out important commitments that will strengthen IPR protection and enforcement in Russia. Under the terms of the agreement, Russia will take action to address piracy and counterfeiting and further improve its laws on IPR protection and enforcement. The agreement sets the stage for further progress on IPR issues in ongoing multilateral negotiations concerning Russia's bid to enter the WTO. This year's Special 301 Report also continues heightened scrutiny of Russia by maintaining Russia on the Priority Watch List and announcing plans for an Out-of-Cycle Review.

With respect to China, this year's Special 301 Report describes the United States' plan to maintain China on the Priority Watch List and to continue Section 306 monitoring, as well as to pursue World Trade Organization (WTO) dispute settlement with China on a number of IPR protection and enforcement issues. In addition, the United States is reporting on IPR protection and enforcement in China in the section entitled "Special Provincial Review of China," following an unprecedented special provincial review conducted over the past year. The United States will be monitoring closely China's and Russia's IPR activities throughout the coming year.

In addition to China and Russia, the Special 301 Report sets out significant concerns with respect to such trading partners as Argentina, Chile, Egypt, India, Israel, Lebanon, Thailand, Turkey, Ukraine, and Venezuela. In addition, the report notes that the United States will consider all options, including, but not limited to, initiation of dispute settlement consultations in cases where countries do not appear to have implemented fully their obligations under the WTO Agreement on Trade-Related Aspects of Intellectual Property Rights (TRIPS Agreement).

In this year's review, USTR devotes special attention to the need for significantly improved enforcement against counterfeiting and piracy. In addition, USTR continues to focus on other critically important issues, including Internet piracy, counterfeit pharmaceuticals, transshipment of pirated and counterfeit goods, requiring authorized use of legal software by government ministries, proper implementation of the TRIPS Agreement by developed and developing country WTO members, and full implementation of TRIPS Agreement standards by new WTO members at the time of their accession.

*   *   *   *

Positive Developments

Several countries made significant positive progress on IPR protection and enforcement in 2006. For example, Vietnam joined the WTO in January 2007. As part of its accession efforts, Vietnam enacted a comprehensive intellectual property law and implementing regulations to create a modern legal framework for IPR protection and enforcement. Taiwan also made significant strides in its IPR enforcement efforts and passed legislation to create a specialized IPR court. China recently joined the two key World Intellectual Property Organization (WIPO) treaties for copyright protection, and Russia has made strong commitments to improve intellectual property protection and enforcement as part of the path towards WTO accession.

In addition, USTR is pleased to announce that the following countries are having their status improved or are being removed entirely from the Watch List because of progress on IPR issues this past year:

- Bahamas has been removed from the Watch List due to improvements in IPR enforcement efforts. The United States continues to urge the Government of the Bahamas to implement the amendments to its copyright law.

- Belize has been moved from the Priority Watch List to the Watch List due to improvements in IPR enforcement efforts in response to heightened engagement with the United States.
- Brazil has been moved from the Priority Watch List to the Watch List due to improvements in IPR enforcement efforts and the United States will conduct an Out-of-Cycle Review.
- Bulgaria has been removed from the Watch List due to improvements in IPR enforcement efforts and passage of IPR legislation in response to heightened engagement with the United States.
- Croatia has been removed from the Watch List due to improvements in IPR enforcement and passage of IPR legislation in response to heightened engagement with the United States.
- The European Union (EU) has been removed from the Watch List, principally as a result of the EU's adoption of new regulations concerning geographical indications (GIs) following an adverse ruling by the WTO Dispute Settlement Body in April 2005. While the United States maintains certain concerns with respect to the EU's implementation of the revised GI rules, these will continue to be addressed outside the Special 301 context. The United States looks forward to continued cooperation with the EU on this and other intellectual property matters, including EU border enforcement and other IP initiatives.
- Latvia has been removed from the Watch List at the conclusion of an Out-of-Cycle Review in recognition of Latvia's improvements in IPR enforcement.

The United States commends this positive progress by our trading partners. The United States will continue to work with these and other countries to achieve further improvements in IPR protection and enforcement during the coming year.

*   *   *   *

A USTR press release of the same date provided a summary of countries identified in the 2007 report as excerpted below. The full text of the press release is available at *www.ustr.gov/*

*Document_Library/Press_Releases/2007//April/SPECIAL_
301_Report.html.*

---

* * * *

This year's Special 301 report places 43 countries on the Priority Watch
List (PWL), Watch List (WL) or the Section 306 monitoring list.

Countries on the Priority Watch List do not provide an adequate level of IPR protection or enforcement, or market access for
persons relying on intellectual property protection. In addition to
China and Russia, 10 countries are on the PWL in this year's
report: Argentina, Chile, Egypt, India, Israel, Lebanon, Thailand,
Turkey, Ukraine, and Venezuela. In announcing the elevation of
Thailand to the Priority Watch List, the report cites a range of
intellectual property concerns, including deteriorating protection
for patents and copyrights. Priority Watch List countries will be
the subject of particularly intense engagement through bilateral
discussion during the coming year.

Thirty trading partners are on the lower level Watch List, mer-
iting bilateral attention to address the underlying IPR problems.
The Watch List countries are: Belarus, Belize, Bolivia, Brazil, Canada,
Colombia, Costa Rica, Dominican Republic, Ecuador, Guatemala,
Hungary, Indonesia, Italy, Jamaica, Korea, Kuwait, Lithuania,
Malaysia, Mexico, Pakistan, Peru, Philippines, Poland, Romania,
Saudi Arabia, Taiwan, Tajikistan, Turkmenistan, Uzbekistan, and
Vietnam.

Paraguay will continue to be subject to Section 306 monitoring
under a bilateral Memorandum of Understanding that establishes
objectives and actions for addressing IPR concerns in that country.

The implementation of Free Trade Agreements negotiated with
the United States constitutes an important element in IPR improvements. FTA partner countries, including those in Central America
and the Dominican Republic, have undertaken important improvements in IPR legal frameworks in keeping with the obligations
reflected in the FTAs. Our most recent FTAs also reflect these high
standards and we welcome the commitments made to improve
intellectual property protection and enforcement by future FTA
trading partners, including Colombia, Korea, Panama and Peru.

Despite some encouraging developments, the detailed country discussions in the Special 301 report make clear that numerous IPR problems persist around the world. Trade in counterfeit pharmaceuticals is a particularly grave concern, in light of the risks to human health and safety. Unabated piracy of CDs, DVDs and CD-ROMS, and the widespread counterfeiting of trademark-protected consumer and industrial goods will also remain important focuses of U.S. IPR trade policy efforts in the coming year.

Cross References

Treaty-investor visas, **Chapter 1.C.3.**
APEC Business Travel Card, **Chapter 1.C.5.**
Commercial private international law, **Chapter 15.A.**
International civil litigation in U.S. courts, **Chapter 15.C.**
Economic sanctions, **Chapter 16.**

CHAPTER 12

Territorial Regimes and Related Issues

A. LAW OF THE SEA AND RELATED BOUNDARY ISSUES

1. UN Convention on the Law of the Sea

On October 31, 2007, the Senate Committee on Foreign Relations ("SFRC") voted to report the 1982 United Nations Convention on the Law of the Sea ("Convention") and the 1994 Agreement relating to the Implementation of Part XI of the Convention ("1994 Agreement") to the full Senate with a recommendation that the Senate provide advice and consent to U.S. accession to the Convention and ratification of the 1994 Agreement. S. Exec. Rep. No. 110-9 (2007).

A press release from the Department of State of November 5, 2007, welcomed the SFRC action and stated:

> This treaty was a victory for U.S. diplomacy—the one chapter that President Reagan disliked was modified in 1994 to overcome all his objections. It would serve both our national security interests, as countless current and former U.S. military officials have stated, by assuring navigational rights of our vessels worldwide, as well as our economic and energy interests, as a wide array of U.S. industries have stated. The treaty would secure U.S. sovereign rights over extensive offshore natural resources, including substantial oil and gas resources in the Arctic. The extended continental shelf areas we stand to gain under the treaty are at least twice the size of California.

Joining the Convention is the only viable means of protecting and maximizing our ocean-related interests and the Senate should approve U.S. accession without delay.

The SFRC held hearings on the Convention on September 27 and October 4, 2007. On September 27, Deputy Secretary of State John Negroponte, Deputy Secretary of Defense Gordon England, and U.S. Navy Vice Chief of Naval Operations Admiral Patrick M. Walsh, testified in support of Senate advice and consent.

The SFRC and other committees had previously held hearings on the Convention and 1994 Agreement in 2003 and 2004. In 2004 the SFRC reported the Convention and the 1994 Agreement to the Senate recommending advice and consent to accession and ratification. S. Exec. Rep. No. 108-10 (which includes testimony from the 2003 hearings). When the full Senate did not vote on advice and consent before the end of the 108th Congress, the two treaties were returned to the SFRC. See Digest 2003 at 715–54, Digest 2004 at 671–96, and Digest 2005 at 675–82.

Excerpts from Deputy Secretary Negroponte's written testimony follow. The full texts of the witness statements are available at *www.senate.gov/~foreign/hearing2007.html*. Testimony of administration witnesses is also available at *www.state.gov/s/l/c8183.htm*.

----

*   *   *   *

At my confirmation hearing earlier this year, I reminded the Committee that the Senate confirmed me 20 years ago as Assistant Secretary for Oceans and International Environmental and Scientific Affairs. Shortly thereafter, under the first President Bush, we began to work on revising the deep seabed mining section of the Convention to address the flaws President Reagan had correctly identified, so that we could join the Convention. That effort succeeded, resulting in the 1994 Agreement overhauling the deep seabed mining regime, as I will explain in greater detail.

Since my first involvement with the Law of the Sea Convention, I have had the privilege to serve the United States in other assignments that have only strengthened my support for this treaty. As Ambassador to the United Nations, I learned that other countries look to the United States for leadership on oceans issues such as maritime security—a role that is lessened without U.S. accession to the Convention. As Ambassador to Iraq, I saw first-hand the importance of navigational freedoms for deploying and sustaining our forces in combat zones, and how the Convention serves as a foundation for our partnerships in the Proliferation Security Initiative. Most recently, as Director of National Intelligence, I was reminded how the Convention strengthens our ability to carry out intelligence activities that other countries might seek to restrain.

Mr. Chairman, these experiences compel me to endorse—most enthusiastically and emphatically—the President's urgent request that the Senate approve the Convention, as modified by the 1994 Agreement. As the President said in his May 15 statement,* joining will serve the national security interests of the United States, secure U.S. sovereign rights over extensive marine areas, promote U.S. interests in the environmental health of the oceans, and give the United States a seat at the table when the rights essential to our interests are debated and interpreted.

HISTORY

. . . Due to flaws in the deep seabed mining chapter—Part XI of the Convention—President Reagan decided not to sign the 1982 Convention. However, the other aspects of the treaty were so favorable that President Reagan, in his Ocean Policy Statement in 1983, announced that the United States accepted, and would act in accordance with, the Convention's balance of interests relating to traditional uses of the oceans—everything but deep seabed mining. He instructed the Government to abide by, or as the case may be,

---

*   Editor's note: President Bush's "Statement on Advancing U.S. Interests in the World's Oceans," "urg[ing] the Senate to act favorably on U.S. accession to the United Nations Convention on the Law of the Sea during this session of Congress," is available at 43 WEEKLY COMP. PRES. DOC. 635 (May 21, 2007).

to enjoy the rights accorded by, the other provisions, and to encourage other countries to do likewise.

*   *   *   *

JOINING IS A WIN-WIN

Joining is a win/win proposition. We will not have to change U.S. laws or practices, or give up rights, and we will benefit in a variety of ways. The United States already acts in accordance with the Convention for a number of reasons:

- First, we are party to a group of 1958 treaties that contain many of the same provisions as the Convention.
- Second, the United States heavily influenced the content of the 1982 Convention, based on U.S. law, policy, and practice.
- Finally, the treaty has been the cornerstone of U.S. oceans policy since 1983, when President Reagan instructed the Executive Branch to act in accordance with the Convention's provisions with the exception of deep seabed mining.

Thus, we are in the advantageous position in the case of this treaty that U.S. adherence to its terms is already time-tested and works well.

At the same time, the United States would gain substantial benefits from joining the Convention—these can be summarized in terms of security, sovereignty, and sustainability.

Security. As the world's foremost maritime power, our security interests are intrinsically linked to freedom of navigation. We have more to gain from legal certainty and public order in the world's oceans than any other country. Our forces are deployed throughout the world, and we are engaged in combat operations in Central and Southwest Asia. The U.S. Armed Forces rely on the navigational rights and freedoms reflected in the Convention for worldwide access to get to the fight, sustain our forces during the fight, and return home safely, without permission from other countries.

In this regard, the Convention secures the rights we need for U.S. military ships and the commercial ships that support our forces to meet national security requirements in four ways:

- by limiting coastal States' territorial seas—within which they exercise the most sovereignty—to 12 nautical miles;

- by affording our military and commercial vessels and aircraft necessary passage rights through other countries' territorial seas and archipelagoes, as well as through straits used for international navigation (such as the critical right of submarines to transit submerged through such straits);
- by setting forth maximum navigational rights and freedoms for our vessels and aircraft in the exclusive economic zones of other countries and in the high seas; and
- by affirming the authority of U.S. warships and government ships to board stateless vessels on the high seas, which is a critically important element of maritime security operations, counter-narcotic operations, and anti-proliferation efforts, including the Proliferation Security Initiative.

The United States has had a certain amount of success in promoting these provisions internationally as reflective of customary international law, as well as in enforcing them through operational challenges. However, these tools alone are not adequate to ensure the continued vitality of these rights. Customary law is not universally accepted and, in any event, changes over time—in this case, potentially to the detriment of our interests. There are increasing pressures from coastal States around the world to evolve the law of the sea in ways that would unacceptably alter the balance of interests struck in the Convention. Operational challenges are inherently risky and resource-intensive. Joining the Convention would put the navigational rights reflected in the Convention on the firmest legal footing. We would have treaty rights rather than have to rely solely upon the acceptance of customary international law rights by other states or upon the threat or use of force. Securing these treaty rights, and obtaining a seat at the table in treaty-based institutions, would provide a safeguard against changes in State practice that could cause customary law to drift in an unfavorable direction. Moreover, joining would promote the willingness of other countries to cooperate with us on initiatives of great security importance, such as the Proliferation Security Initiative.

Sovereignty. Joining the Convention would advance U.S. economic and resource interests. Recent Russian expeditions to the Arctic have focused attention on the resource-related benefits of being a party to the Convention. Because so much is at stake in vast areas of continental shelf beyond 200 nautical miles, I will explain in some detail the Convention's provisions that govern these areas and why being a party would put the United States in a far better position in terms of maximizing its sovereign rights.

The Convention recognizes the sovereign rights of a coastal State over its continental shelf, which extends out to 200 nautical miles—and beyond, if it meets specific criteria. These rights include sovereign rights for the purpose of exploring the continental shelf and exploiting its natural resources, including oil, gas, and other energy resources. U.S. interests are well served not only by the Convention's detailed definition of the shelf (in contrast to the 1958 Convention's vague standard), but also by its procedures for gaining certainty regarding the shelf's outer limits. Parties enjoy access to the expert body whose technical recommendations provide the needed international recognition and legal certainty to the establishment of continental shelf beyond 200 nautical miles.

Following such procedures, Russia made the first submission (in 2001) to that expert body, the Commission on the Limits of the Continental Shelf.[*] The Commission found that Russia needed to collect additional data to substantiate its submission. Russia has announced that the data it collected this year support the claim that its continental shelf extends as far as the North Pole. Setting aside its recent flag planting, which has only symbolic value, Russia's continuing data collection in the Arctic reflects its commitment to maximizing its sovereign rights under the Convention over energy resources in that region.

Currently, as a non-party, the United States is not in a position to maximize its sovereign rights in the Arctic or elsewhere. We do not have access to the Commission's procedures for according international recognition and legal certainty to our extended shelf. And we have not been able to nominate an expert for election to the Commission. Thus, there is no U.S. commissioner to review the detailed data submitted by other countries on their shelves.

---

[*] Editor's note: See *Digest 2002* at 732–37 and *Digest 2003* at 731–32 for discussion of the U.S. response to the Russian claim with the Commission on the Limits of the Continental Shelf.

Norway has also made a submission to support its extended continental shelf in the Arctic, and Canada and Denmark are conducting surveys there to collect data for their submissions. The Commission has already made recommendations on submissions by Brazil and Ireland and is considering several other submissions. Many more are expected in the coming months.

The United States has one of the largest continental shelves in the world; in the Arctic, for example, our shelf could run as far as 600 miles from the coastline. However, as noted, we have no access to the Commission, whose recommendations would facilitate the full exercise of our sovereign rights—whether we use them to explore and exploit natural resources, prevent other countries from doing so, or otherwise. In the absence of the international recognition and legal certainty that the Convention provides, U.S. companies are unlikely to secure the necessary financing and insurance to exploit energy resources on the extended shelf, and we will be less able to keep other countries from exploiting them.

Joining the Convention provides other economic benefits: it also gives coastal States the right to claim an exclusive economic zone ("EEZ") out to 200 nautical miles. That gives the United States, with its extensive coastline, the largest EEZ of any country in the world. In this vast area, we have sovereign rights for the purpose of exploring, exploiting, conserving, and managing living and non-living natural resources.

Sustainability. The Convention also supports U.S. interests in the health of the world's oceans and the living resources they contain. It addresses marine pollution from a variety of sources, including ocean dumping and operational discharges from vessels. The framework appropriately balances the interests of the coastal State in protection of the marine environment and its natural resources with the navigational rights and freedoms of all States. This framework, among other things, supports vital economic activities off the coast of the United States. Further, the United States has stringent laws regulating protection of the marine environment, and we would be in a stronger position as a party to the Convention as we encourage other countries to follow suit.

The Convention also promotes the conservation of various marine resources. Indeed, U.S. ocean resource-related industries strongly support U.S. accession to the Convention. U.S. fishermen, for example, want their government to be in the strongest possible position to encourage other governments to hold their fishermen to the same standards we are already following, under the Convention and under the Fish Stocks Agreement that elaborates the Convention's provisions on straddling fish stocks and highly migratory fish stocks.

Joining the Convention provides other important benefits that straddle the security, sovereignty, and sustainability categories. For example, its provisions protect laying and maintaining the fiber optic cables through which the modern world communicates, for both military and commercial purposes; for that reason, the U.S. telecommunications industry is a strong supporter of the Convention.

WE NEED TO JOIN NOW

Some may ask why, after the Convention has been in force for thirteen years, there is an urgent need to join. There are compelling reasons why we need to accede to the Convention now. Although the first several years of the Convention's life were fairly quiet, its provisions are now being actively applied, interpreted, and developed. The Convention's institutions are up and running, and we—the country with the most to gain and lose on law of the sea issues—are sitting on the sidelines. For example, the Commission on the Limits of the Continental Shelf (which is the technical body charged with addressing the continental shelf beyond 200 nautical miles) has received nine submissions and has made recommendations on two of them, without the participation of a U.S. commissioner. Recommendations made in that body could well create precedents, positive and negative, on the future outer limit of the U.S. shelf. We need to be on the inside to protect our interests. Moreover, in fora outside the Convention, the provisions of the Convention are also being actively applied. Our position as a non-Party puts us in a far weaker position to advance U.S. interests than should be the case for our country.

We also need to join now to lock in, as a matter of treaty law, the very favorable provisions we achieved in negotiating the Convention. It would be risky to assume that we can preserve *ad infinitum* the situation upon which the United States currently relies. As noted, there is increasing pressure from coastal States to augment their authority in a manner that would alter the balance of interests struck in the Convention. We should secure these favorable treaty rights while we have the chance.

DEEP SEABED MINING

One part of the Convention deserves special attention, because, in its original version, it kept the United States and other industrialized countries from joining. Part XI of the Convention, now modified by the 1994 Implementing Agreement, establishes a system for facilitating potential mining activities on the seabed beyond the limits of national jurisdiction—specifically, the deep seabed beyond the continental shelf of any nation. The Convention, as modified, meets our goal of guaranteed access by U.S. industry to deep seabed minerals under reasonable terms and conditions.

Specifically, the Convention sets forth the process by which mining firms can apply for and obtain access and exclusive legal rights to deep seabed mineral resources. The International Seabed Authority is responsible for overseeing such mining; it includes an Assembly, open to all Parties, and a 36-member Council. The Authority's role is limited to administering deep seabed mining of mineral resources in areas beyond national jurisdiction; it has no other authority over uses of the oceans or over other resources in the oceans. The Council is the primary decision-making body, with responsibility for giving practical effect to the requirement for non-discriminatory access to deep seabed minerals and for adopting rules for exploration and development.

The 1994 Agreement, which contains legally binding changes to the 1982 Convention, fundamentally overhauls the deep seabed mining provisions in a way that satisfies each of the objections of the United States, as stated by President Reagan, and of other industrialized countries. . . .

. . . Specifically, the Agreement:

- deletes the objectionable provisions on mandatory technology transfer;
- ensures that market-oriented approaches are taken to the management of deep seabed minerals (e.g., by eliminating

production controls), replacing the original Part XI's central-ized economic planning approach;

- scales back the deep seabed mining institutions and links their activation and operation to actual development of interest in deep seabed mining;
- guarantees the United States a permanent seat on the Council, where substantive decisions are made by consensus—the effect of which is that any decision that would result in a substan-tive obligation on the United States, or that would have finan-cial or budgetary implications, would require U.S. consent;
- ensures that the United States would need to approve the adoption of any amendment to the Part XI provisions and any distribution of deep seabed mining revenues accumu-lated under the Convention; and
- recognizes the seabed mine claims established on the basis of the exploration already conducted by U.S. companies and provides assured equality of access for any future qualified U.S. miners.

The deep seabed is an area that the United States has never claimed and has consistently recognized as being beyond the sov-ereignty and jurisdiction of any nation. As reflected in U.S. law (the Deep Seabed Hard Mineral Resources Act of 1980), it has long viewed deep seabed mining as an activity appropriate for international administration. The United States asked for changes to the 1982 Convention's deep seabed mining provisions and got them. As George P. Shultz, Secretary of State to President Reagan, said recently in a letter to Senator Lugar: "The treaty has been changed in such a way with respect to the deep sea-beds that it is now acceptable, in my judgment. Under these circumstances, and given the many desirable aspects of the treaty on other grounds, I believe it is time to proceed with ratification."

WHY STAY OUT?

Given all the valuable benefits of joining and the substantial costs of not joining, is there a persuasive argument why the United States should remain a non-party? I do not think there is one.

*   *   *   *

Certain arguments against U.S. accession are simply inaccurate. And other arguments are outdated, in the sense that they may have been true before the deep seabed mining provisions were fixed and thus are no longer true. I would like to address some of these "myths" surrounding the Convention:

Myth: Joining the Convention would surrender U.S. sovereignty.

Reality: On the contrary. Some have called the Convention a "U.S. land grab." It expands U.S. sovereignty and sovereign rights over extensive maritime territory and natural resources off its coast, as described earlier in my testimony. It is rare that a treaty actually increases the area over which a country exercises sovereign rights, but this treaty does. The Convention does not harm U.S. sovereignty in any respect. As sought by the United States, the dispute resolution mechanisms provide appropriate flexibility in terms of both the forum and the exclusion of sensitive subject matter. The deep seabed mining provisions do not apply to any areas in which the United States has sovereignty or sovereign rights; further, these rules will facilitate mining activities by U.S. companies. And the navigational provisions affirm the freedoms that are important to the worldwide mobility of U.S. military and commercial vessels.

* * * *

Myth: The International Seabed Authority (ISA) has the power to regulate seven-tenths of the Earth's surface.

Reality: The Convention addresses seven-tenths of the earth's surface; the ISA does not. First, the ISA does not address activities in the water column, such as navigation. Second, the ISA has nothing to do with the ocean floor that is subject to the sovereignty or sovereign rights of any country, including that of the United States. Third, the ISA only addresses deep seabed mining. Thus, its role is limited to mining activities in areas of the ocean floor beyond national jurisdiction. It has no other role and no general authority over the uses of the oceans, including freedom of navigation and overflight.

Myth: The Convention gives the UN its first opportunity to levy taxes.

Reality: Although the Convention was negotiated under UN auspices, it is separate from the UN and its institutions are not

UN bodies. Further, there are no taxes of any kind on individuals or corporations or others. Concerning oil/gas production within 200 nautical miles of shore, the United States gets exclusive sovereign rights to seabed resources within the largest such area in the world. There are no finance-related requirements in the EEZ. Concerning oil/gas production beyond 200 nautical miles of shore, the United States is one of a group of countries potentially entitled to extensive continental shelf beyond its EEZ. Countries that benefit from an Extended Continental Shelf have no requirements for the first five years of production at a site; in the sixth year of production, they are to make payments equal to 1% of production, increasing by 1% a year until capped at 7% in the twelfth year of production. If the United States were to pay royalties, it would be because U.S. oil and gas companies are engaged in successful production beyond 200 nautical miles. But if the United States does not become a party, U.S. companies will likely not be willing or able to engage in oil/gas activities in such areas, as I explained earlier.

Concerning mineral activities in the deep seabed, which is beyond U.S. jurisdiction, an interested company would pay an application fee for the administrative expenses of processing the application. Any amount that did not get used for processing the application would be returned to the applicant. The Convention does not set forth any royalty requirements for production; the United States would need to agree to establish any such requirements.

In no event would any payments go to the UN, but rather would be distributed to countries in accordance with a formula to which the United States would have to agree.

* * * *

Deputy Secretary of Defense Gordon England stated:

> The legal framework that the Convention establishes is essential to the mission of the Department of Defense, and the Department of Homeland Security concurs that it is also essential for their mission. For that reason, Secretary Gates, the Joint Chiefs of Staff, the Military Department Secretaries, all of the Combatant Commanders, and the Commandant of the Coast Guard join me in asking

the Senate to give its swift approval for U.S. accession to the Law of the Sea Convention and ratification of the 1994 Agreement.

Further excerpts from his testimony follow.

———————

*   *   *   *

In our judgment, the bar should be set very high for the United States to decide to join a major multilateral treaty, such as this Convention. Therefore, before the President issued his statement of support for the Convention on May 15, the Administration thoroughly reviewed the benefits and challenges. As I will explain further below, the benefits to joining this Convention are significant, and they substantially and unquestionably outweigh any perceived risks.

*   *   *   *

. . . The navigation and overflight rights and high seas freedoms codified in the Convention are essential for the global mobility of our Armed Forces and the sustainment of our combat forces overseas. We are a nation at war, and we require a great sacrifice of the men and women in uniform who go into harm's way on our behalf. Joining this Convention will make our nation stronger and will directly support our men and women in uniform.

As the world's foremost maritime power, our security interests are intrinsically linked to freedom of navigation. America has more to gain from legal certainty and public order in the world's oceans than any other country. By joining the Convention, we provide the firmest possible legal foundation for the rights and freedoms needed to project power, reassure friends and deter adversaries, respond to crises, sustain combat forces in the field, and secure sea and air lines of communication that underpin international trade and our own economic prosperity. Specifically, the legal foundation of this Convention:

- Defines the Right of Innocent Passage, whereby ships may continuously and expeditiously transit the territorial seas of foreign States without having to provide advance notification or seek permission from such States.

- Establishes the Right of Transit Passage through, under, and over international straits and the approaches to those straits. This right, which may not be suspended, hampered or infringed upon by coastal States, is absolutely critical to our national security. This is the right that underpins free transit through the critical chokepoints of the world, such as the Strait of Hormuz, the Straits of Singapore and Malacca, and the Strait of Gibraltar.
- Establishes the Right of Archipelagic Sealane Passage, which, like Transit Passage, helps ensure free transit through, under, and over the sealanes of archipelagic nations, such as Indonesia.
- Secures the right to exercise High Seas Freedoms in exclusive economic zones, the 200 nautical mile-wide bands of ocean off coastal shores. The Department's ability to position, patrol, and operate forces freely in, below, and above those littoral waters is critical to our national security.
- Secures the right of U.S. warships, including Coast Guard cutters, to board stateless vessels on the high seas, which is a critically important element of maritime security operations, counter-narcotic operations, and anti-proliferation efforts, including the Proliferation Security Initiative.

If the United States is not a Party to the Convention, then our current legal position is reduced to President Reagan's oceans policy statement of March 1983 and several 1958 Conventions on the seas that remain in force but are, in our judgment, no longer adequate. President Reagan accepted that the navigation and overflight provisions of the Convention—as well as those relating to other traditional uses of the oceans—reflected customary international law and state practice. Further, President Reagan directed the United States Government to adhere to those provisions of the Convention while he, and successive Presidents, worked to fix the Deep Seabed Mining provisions of the Convention.

* * * *

Although reliance on customary international law has been relatively effective for us as an interim measure, neither customary international law nor the 1958 Conventions are adequate in the long-term. U.S. assertions of rights under customary international law carry less weight to States than do binding treaty obligations. By its very nature, customary international law is less certain than convention law, as it is subject to the influence of changing State practice. In addition, the 1958 Conventions are inadequate for many reasons, including their failure to establish a fixed limit to the breadth of territorial seas, silence regarding transit passage and archipelagic sea lanes passage, and absence of well-defined limits on the jurisdictional reach of coastal states in waters we now recognize as exclusive economic zones. If the United States remains outside the Convention, it will not be best positioned to interpret, apply, and protect the rights and freedoms contained in the Convention.

Becoming a Party to the Law of the Sea Convention directly supports our National Strategy for Maritime Security. As the President noted in the opening pages of the Strategy: "We must maintain a military without peer—yet our strength is not founded on force of arms alone. It also rests on economic prosperity and a vibrant democracy. And it rests on strong alliances, friendships, and international institutions, which enable us to promote freedom, prosperity, and peace in common purpose with others." That simple truth has been the foundation for some of our most significant national security initiatives, such as the Proliferation Security Initiative. As the leader of a community of nations that are Parties to the Convention, more than 150 in total, the United States will be better positioned to work with foreign air forces, navies, and coast guards to address jointly the full spectrum of 21st Century security challenges.

Before closing, I would like to address some of the opposing views. Critics of the Convention argue that an international tribunal will have jurisdiction over our Navy and that our intelligence and counter-proliferation activities will be adversely affected. In the judgment of the Department, these concerns have been more than adequately addressed within the terms of the Convention.

- Our intelligence activities will not be hampered by the Convention. This matter was fully addressed in a series of open and closed hearings in 2004. Just recently, the Defense Department, State Department, and Office of the Director of National Intelligence confirmed the accuracy of the testimony provided in those hearings.
- The Senate can ensure that international tribunals do not gain jurisdiction over our military activities when we join this Convention. In 2003, the Administration worked closely with the Committee to develop a proposed Resolution of Advice and Consent—which we continue to support—that contains a declaration regarding choice of procedure for dispute resolution. The United States rejected the International Court of Justice and the International Tribunal for the Law of the Sea and instead chose arbitration. That choice-of-procedure election is expressly provided for in the Convention itself. In addition, and again in accordance with the express terms of the Convention, the draft Resolution of Advice and Consent completely removes our military activities from the dispute resolution process. Furthermore, each State Party, including the United States, has the exclusive right to determine which of its activities constitutes a military activity, and that determination is not subject to review.
- Regarding our counter-proliferation efforts, which include interdiction activities at sea and in international airspace, I strongly endorse the position of the Vice Chief of Naval Operations, Admiral Walsh, who served as the Commander of all U.S. and Coalition maritime forces in the Persian Gulf, North Arabian Sea, Horn of Africa, and Red Sea from 2005 to 2007. There is no better authority on maritime interception operations than Admiral Walsh, and he correctly points out that not only does the Convention enhance our interdiction authorities, but not joining the Convention is detrimental to our efforts to expand the number of countries that support the Proliferation Security Initiative.
- And, as all recognize, this Convention does not affect the United States' inherent right and obligation of self defense. Further, as Mr. Negroponte has explained in detail, joining

the Convention gives us the opportunity to extend our sovereign rights dramatically and advance our energy security interests by maximizing legal certainty and international recognition for our extended continental shelf off Alaska and elsewhere.

*   *   *   *

In a letter to the editor of the *Washington Times* dated October 31, 2007, Department of State Legal Adviser John B. Bellinger, III, responded to points raised in a letter arguing against ratification of the LOS Convention. Mr. Bellinger explained, among other things, that the previous writer was "wrong that 'environmental activists' would be empowered to enforce the Kyoto Protocol against us." He explained:

> The U.S. would not be committed to implement Kyoto standards. Also, if another country were to bring such a claim (and nongovernmental activists could not), there would be no jurisdiction. Regarding marine pollution from land, the treaty includes very general obligations to limit such pollution; however, as we have explained to the Senate, it does not provide for dispute settlement unless there are specified international standards applicable to the U.S., which there are not. Finally, as a non-self-executing treaty, the agreement would not provide for any private rights of action in U.S. courts.

In conclusion Mr. Bellinger stated:

> People need to read the treaty. If they do, they will see the treaty's enormous national security and economic advantages to the United States, including clear legal rights of navigation for our military through and over the world's oceans and economic sovereign rights over the enormous oil, gas and other resources on the U.S. continental shelf in the Arctic, the Gulf of Mexico and elsewhere. As Russia and other countries rush to stake their claims to Arctic resources, it would be folly for the Senate to follow

Mr. Feulner's advice and give up sovereign rights to this vast wealth.

The full text of Mr. Bellinger's letter to the editor is available at *www.state.gov/s/l/c8183.htm.*

2. Arctic Continental Shelf

On September 15, 2007, the Department of State, the National Oceanic and Atmospheric Administration's Office of Coast Survey, the University of New Hampshire's Joint Hydrographic Center, and the National Science Foundation concluded an expedition to map the ocean floor on the northern Chukchi Borderland, a large underwater shelf in the Arctic Ocean. An October 11, 2007, release by the Department of State Bureau of Oceans and International Environmental and Scientific Affairs explained the venture's purpose:

> The scientists explored this relatively uncharted seafloor to better understand its form and structure. The data collected during the cruise provided valuable information to map sea floor processes and fisheries' habitat and define our continental shelf. The data also provided input into climate and circulation models that will help scientists predict future conditions in the Arctic.

The full text of the October 11 release is available at *www.state.gov/r/pa/ei/pix/b/sat/93321.htm.*

3. Piracy

a. *U.S. Piracy Policy*

On June 14, 2007, President George W. Bush issued for immediate implementation the Policy for the Repression of Piracy and Other Criminal Acts of Violence at Sea ("Piracy Policy"). The full texts of the President's memorandum and the attached Piracy Policy are available at *www.whitehouse.gov/ news/releases/2007/06/20070614-3.html*. Excerpts follow from the Piracy Policy, which is to be appended to the National Strategy for Maritime Security as Annex B. The National Strategy is available at *www.whitehouse.gov/homeland/4844-nsms. pdf* and *www.dhs.gov/xlibrary/assets/HSPD13_Maritime SecurityS?trategy.pdf*.

I. PURPOSE

This document establishes United States Government policy and implementation actions to cooperate with other states and international and regional organizations in the repression of piracy and other criminal acts of violence against maritime navigation.[1]

II. BACKGROUND

Piracy is any illegal act of violence, detention, or depredation committed for private ends by the crew, or the passengers, of a private ship and directed against a ship, aircraft, persons, or property on the high seas or in any other place outside the jurisdiction of any state. Piracy also includes inciting or facilitating an act of piracy, and any act of voluntary participation in the operation of a ship with knowledge of facts making it a pirate ship. Piracy is a universal crime, and all states are obligated to cooperate to the fullest possible extent in the repression of piracy.[2]

Piracy threatens U.S. national security interests and the freedom and safety of maritime navigation throughout the world, undermines economic security, and contributes to the destabilization of weak or failed state governance. The combination of illicit activity and violence at sea might also be associated with other maritime challenges, including illegal, unlawful, and unregulated fishing, international smuggling, and terrorism.

---

[1]   The National Security Strategy (2006) and the National Strategy for Maritime Security identify these maritime threats.

[2]   Articles 14–15, Convention on the High Seas (1958), and Articles 100–101, Law of the Sea Convention (1982).

Criminal and terrorist activities not defined as piracy also occur at sea and similarly threaten U.S. economic and national security interests. These acts of violence endanger the safety of maritime navigation and may involve weapons of mass destruction. The prevention, interdiction, and punishment of those acts occurring in territorial seas are generally the responsibility of the coastal state. Prevention and punishment of acts occurring in international waters likely will require international cooperation and adequate domestic legal systems, most recently reflected in the 2005 Protocols to the 1988 Convention for the Suppression of Unlawful Acts against the Safety of Maritime Navigation and the Protocol for the Suppression of Unlawful Acts against the Safety of Fixed Platforms located on the Continental Shelf.

The policy set forth in this annex fosters both increased interagency coordination and international cooperation and is consistent with, supports, and builds upon existing maritime security efforts for piracy repression.

III. POLICY

The United States strongly supports efforts to repress piracy and other criminal acts of violence against maritime navigation. The physical and economic security of the United States—a major global trading nation with interests across the maritime spectrum—relies heavily on the secure navigation of the world's oceans for unhindered legitimate commerce by its citizens and its partners. Piracy and other acts of violence against maritime navigation endanger sea lines of communication, interfere with freedom of navigation and the free flow of commerce, and undermine regional stability.

*   *   *   *

Piracy repression should include diplomatic, military, intelligence, economic, law enforcement, and judicial actions. Effectively responding to piracy and criminal activity sends an important deterrent message and requires coordination by all departments and agencies of the U.S. Government in order to ensure that those responsible are brought to justice in a timely manner.

It is the policy of the United States to repress piracy, consistent with U.S. law and international obligations, and to cooperate with other nations in repressing piracy through the following actions:

- Prevent pirate attacks and other criminal acts of violence against U.S. vessels, persons, and interests;
- Interrupt and terminate acts of piracy consistent with international law and the rights and responsibilities of coastal and flag states;
- Reduce the vulnerability of the maritime domain to such acts and exploitation when U.S. interests are directly affected;
- Ensure that those who commit acts of piracy are held accountable for their actions by facilitating the prosecution of suspected pirates and ensure that persons suspected of committing acts of violence against maritime navigation are similarly held accountable by flag and littoral states and, in appropriate cases, the United States;
- Preserve the freedom of the seas, including high seas freedoms;
- Protect sea lines of communication; and
- Continue to lead and support international efforts to repress piracy and other acts of violence against maritime navigation and urge other states to take decisive action both individually and through international efforts.

Responses to these threats will vary according to geographic, political, and legal environments. The scope of the mission and the defined nature of the threat also will affect the choice of response.

*   *   *   *

Among other things, the implementation section of the memorandum included a mandate to "review existing U.S. laws against or relating to piracy and prepare for consideration such amendments as may be necessary to enhance our ability to prosecute pirates in U.S. courts.[3]"

---

[3]   U.S. Constitution, Article I, Section 8; 18 USC 7(1) (Special Maritime and Territorial Jurisdiction of the United States); 18 USC 111 (Assault on Federal Officials); 18 USC 113 (Assault on the high seas); 18 USC 371 (Conspiracy); 18 USC 844(i) (Use of explosive against property used in foreign commerce of the United States or against any property used in an activity

b. IMO resolution

At the meeting of the 25th Session of the IMO Assembly in London from November 17–29, 2007, the Assembly adopted a resolution on piracy and armed robbery against ships in waters off the coast of Somalia. The United States introduced several amendments to the draft resolution, including language to: (1) clarify that the resolution did not apply to warships and other sovereign immune vessels; (2) include direct reference to the Convention for the Suppression of Unlawful Acts against the Safety of Maritime Navigation for other relevant acts of violence outside the precise definition of piracy in the LOS Convention; and (3) incorporate a role for states located outside the region. The amendments were accepted by the Assembly. IMO Doc. A25/Res.1002. For further information see *www.imo.org/Newsroom/mainframe.asp?topic_id=1472& doc_id=8751.*

4. Freedom of Navigation

a. *Excessive air space claims*

(1) *Venezuela*

In January 2007 the United States protested action by Venezuela advising that a U.S. military aircraft could not enter a flight information region ("FIR") administered by Venezuela, known as the Maiquetia Flight Information Region, without overflight clearance. In May 2007 the United States protested similar actions by Burma and India concerning FIRs administered by those countries.

---

affecting foreign commerce of the United States); 18 USC 1651 (Piracy on the high seas); 18 USC 1659 (plundering a ship); 18 USC 2111 (Robbery on high seas); 18 USC 2280(a)(1)(A),(B), and/or (H) (Maritime violence/hijacking of a ship); 18 USC 2232 (Assaults on U.S. nationals overseas); 18 USC 2232a (Use of WMD against U.S. nationals outside of the U.S.)

In November 2006 a U.S. Air Force squadron mission planned to transit the FIRs administered by Burma and India, known as the Yangon (Rangoon) and Chennai (Madras) FIRs, respectively. The planned routes would have had the aircraft transit the FIRs through international airspace only, without ever entering the territorial airspace of Burma or India, so that diplomatic clearance was not necessary. Notwithstanding the right to operate in international airspace, the U.S. aircraft were denied entry to both the Yangon and Chennai FIRs.

There had been instances in the past in which U.S. officials had unnecessarily requested diplomatic clearance for transit in international airspace, and the United States voluntarily files flight plans in many instances. In these circumstances, the United States determined that it was necessary to establish clearly the applicable legal framework.

In May 2007 the U. S. Department of State provided information, excerpted below, for use by U.S. embassies in Rangoon and New Delhi in addressing the issue with their respective governments.

* * * * *

Customary international law, as reflected in the 1982 United Nations Convention on the Law of the Sea, authorizes a state to claim a twelve (12) mile territorial sea and corresponding airspace, measured from baselines drawn consistent with international law (normally the low-water mark).

Beyond the territorial sea, all state aircraft, including military aircraft, enjoy high seas freedoms of navigation and overflight.

A coastal state may establish a FIR in international airspace consistent with the requirements of the 1944 Convention on International Civil Aviation (Chicago Convention), to which your country is a party; however, under Article 3 of that convention, FIR rules do not apply to state aircraft, including military aircraft.

State aircraft, including military aircraft, operating in international airspace (whether within or outside a FIR) are free to operate without the consent of or notice to coastal state authorities and are not subject to the jurisdiction or control of the ATC authorities of those states.

No notice to, clearance from, or approval of a coastal state is required to exercise such freedoms of navigation and overflight.

The United States reaffirms its navigation and overflight rights in international airspace.

Regular flights through the (Yangon or Chennai) FIR in international airspace can be expected to continue.

The United States requests that your government review this matter, prevent a recurrence, and ensure that the freedoms and rights guaranteed to all nations under international law are protected.

The United States is willing to send experts from Washington to explain further its position if that would be of help to your government.

The U.S. will continue to request diplomatic clearance for state aircraft if entry into the sovereign airspace of your country is planned.

*   *   *   *

Additional Information.

A Flight Information Region, or FIR, is simply an area over which a civil aviation authority has responsibility for provision of flight information services. FIRs are allocated to coastal states by the International Civil Aviation Organization (ICAO) to facilitate the safety of civil aviation. Some FIRs encompass both national and international airspace. Civil aviation authorities may confuse responsibility for and authority over civil aviation in a FIR for sovereignty over the area.

*   *   *   *

Article three of the Chicago Convention only requires state aircraft, including military aircraft, to exercise "due regard for the safety of civil aircraft."

It is USG policy that U.S. military aircraft operating in international airspace will observe ICAO flight procedures when practicable and compatible with the mission. When they do so, for example by filing flight plans, this is entirely voluntary and does not prejudice the continued right to fly in international airspace, exercising "due regard for the safety of civil aircraft."

Due to changing international conditions and/or operational requirements it is not possible to predict in advance which flights may choose to observe ICAO procedures and which may not observe ICAO procedures but simply fly in international airspace exercising "due regard."

(2) Iran

On October 23, 2006, the Ministry of Foreign Affairs of the Islamic Republic of Iran delivered a note to the U.S. Interests Section with the Embassy of Switzerland in Tehran protesting alleged flights of American planes. The note stated that "American planes have on five occasions passed the FIR of the Islamic Republic of Iran and flown over its territorial waters . . . contradict[ing] international law and the 1982 Convention on sea laws. . . . A second note of the same date alleged that "a small American battleship has embarked on inspecting an Iranian fishing boat . . . at 25/39 north and 53/56 east of the Persian Gulf waters." Iran protested this "illegal measure which contradicts international regulations and free shipping, and calls for preventing the repetition of such accidents."

The United States responded to both notes on March 12, 2007, asserting the lawfulness of its flights and disputing the boarding incident, as set forth below.

In reference to your diplomatic notes No. 642/1630 and 642/1632 of October 23, 2006, concerning U.S. military operations in the Persian Gulf on June 21 and 24, and July 3 and 28, 2006, we have carefully reviewed each allegation and found that all flight and naval operations were conducted in international airspace and waters and in accordance with international law. Specifically:

- With respect to your Note No. 642/1630, aircraft were operating more than 12 nautical miles from low water line of

Iran, consistent with the baseline provisions of the UN Convention on the Law of the Sea (1982). The International Court of Justice, in paragraph 212 of its judgment on the merits of the Case Concerning Delimitation and Territorial Questions between Qatar and Bahrain, 16 March 2001, . . . observed that "the method of straight baselines, which is an exception to the normal rules for the determination of baselines, may only be applied if a number of conditions are met. This method must be applied restrictively. Such conditions are primarily that either the coastline is deeply indented and cut into, or that there is a fringe of islands along the coast in its immediate vicinity." Iran's straight baselines are not drawn in accordance with those conditions. The United States Government has a long-standing position to support the customary international law norms and other provisions embodied in the Law of the Sea Convention. All U.S. operations mentioned by Iran were conducted consistent with the Convention and the international law supporting OPERATION IRAQI FREEDOM operations to protect Iraq's equities in the Northern Arabian Gulf.

• With respect to your Note No. 642/1632, the United States Government has no record of this boarding having taken place as reported in the note. All United States and Coalition air operations in Iraq and neighboring air and maritime regions are executed in accordance with international law and ICAO procedures.

b. Straits

(1) Head Harbor Passage

On June 13, 2007, the Department of State delivered a diplomatic note to the Canadian Embassy in Washington, D.C. concerning the right of innocent passage of vessels, including liquefied natural gas tankers, through Head Harbor Passage. The diplomatic note is set forth below in full.

The Department of State informs the Embassy Legation of Canada in Washington of its concerns regarding Head Harbor Passage. In reference to Head Harbor Passage, the Department of State recalls the Aide-Memoire to the Government of Canada dated March 12, 1975 and American Embassy Ottawa Notes No. 28 of January 29, 1982, and No.49 of February 19, 1982, concerning the navigational rights that vessels proceeding to or departing from United States ports through the waters of Head Harbor Passage enjoy under international law, and refers to the navigational regime applicable in Head Harbor Passage that is now codified in the UN Convention on the Law of the Sea, to which Canada is party and which reflects customary international law.

It is indisputable that:

- Head Harbor Passage is a strait used for international navigation;
- Head Harbor Passage is a natural, and the only suitable, outlet to the high seas from Eastport, Maine, and other U.S. seaports on Passamaquoddy Bay and the St. Croix River; and
- ships entering and exiting Passamaquoddy Bay, whether on the Canadian or United States side of the international boundary in the Bay, bound to or from the Atlantic Ocean, including the Grand Manan Channel and the Bay of Fundy, navigate through Head Harbor Passage.

Subparagraph (1)(b) of Article 45 of the UN Convention on the Law of the Sea provides: "The regime of innocent passage, in accordance with Part II, section 3, shall apply in straits used for international navigation . . . between a part of the high seas or an exclusive economic zone and the territorial sea of a foreign State."

Subparagraph (2) of Article 45 provides: "There shall be no suspension of innocent passage through such straits."

Article 17 of the UN Convention on the [Law of the] Sea provides that "ships of all States enjoy the right of innocent passage through the territorial sea" All ships includes warships and liquefied natural gas (LNG) tankers. Moreover, all ships enjoy the right of innocent passage through the territorial sea regardless of, for example, cargo, armament, means of propulsion, flag, origin, destination, or purpose.

Article 34, paragraph 1, of the UN Convention on the Law of the Sea provides: "The regime of passage through straits used for international navigation established in this Part [III] shall not in other respects affect the legal status of the waters forming such straits or the exercise by the States bordering the strait of their sovereignty or jurisdiction over such waters and their air space, sea, and subsoil." Paragraph 2 of Article 34 provides: "The sovereignty or jurisdiction of the States bordering the straits is exercised subject to this Part and to other rules of international law."

The waters of Head Harbor Passage are part of the territorial sea of Canada. As noted in the Reply of the United States in the [ICJ] Case Concerning Delimitation of the Maritime Boundary in the Gulf of Maine (volume 5, at page 484 n.4), the United States has not in the past accepted, and continues not to accept, any claim by Canada that the waters of the Bay of Fundy are historic internal waters of Canada. Canada has not met the strict requirements for a claim of historic waters status for those waters.

Therefore, it is clear that all ships have the right of innocent passage through Head Harbor Passage, a right which may not be suspended.

Accordingly, the Government of the United States of America cannot accept the assertion by the Government of Canada purporting to prohibit the passage of LNG tankers through Head Harbor Passage, and reaffirms and reserves its rights and the rights of its nationals in that regard, including the right of nonsuspendable innocent passage through Head Harbor Passage.

(2) Torres Strait

The 25th Session of the Assembly of the International Maritime Organization, meeting in London from November 17–29, 2007, considered again the nature of pilotage in the Torres Strait as documented in resolution MEPC.133(53), adopted July 22, 2005. Singapore, supported by the United States, emphasized that, contrary to Australia's assertion, the 2005 resolution provided no international legal basis for mandatory pilotage in the Torres Strait, or in any other strait used for international navigation. Australia repeated its assertion that pilotage should be mandatory. The Assembly recalled the debate on the matter at previous sessions of MEPC, and taking into consideration the overwhelming majority of delegations expressing their support for the position of Singapore and the United States, reaffirmed the decision reached at MEPC 55 that the resolution is recommendatory in nature. IMO Doc. A 25/5(b)/2, paras 54–58, available at *www.state.gov/s/l/c8183. htm. See also Digest 2006 at 810–12; Digest 2005 at 686–87.*

c. Archipelagic state

In a diplomatic note delivered October 18, 2007, the embassies of the United States and the United Kingdom informed the Ministry of Foreign Affairs of the Dominican Republic that they did not accept the definition of the Dominican Republic as an Archipelagic State and contested certain other claims enumerated in a May 22, 2007, law. The substantive paragraphs of the diplomatic note are set forth below in full.

The Embassies of the United Kingdom of Great Britain and Northern Ireland and the United States of America present their compliments to the Ministry of Foreign Affairs and refer to Law No. 66-07 of May 22, 2007, by which the Dominican Republic

a) declared itself an Archipelagic State,

b) drew straight baselines connecting a number of turning points on certain banks and keys,

c) claimed certain bodies of waters as internal waters and others as historic bays,

d) sets out the coordinates of the outer limits of its claimed exclusive economic zone (EEZ),

e) purported to limit the right of innocent passage through its archipelagic waters and territorial sea (and overflight) to those ships and aircraft not carrying cargoes of radioactive substances or highly toxic chemicals,

f) does not recognize the right of archipelagic sea lanes passage, and

g) claimed rights over old shipwrecks within its EEZ.

The governments of the United States and Great Britain do not accept the definition of the Dominican Republic as an Archipelagic State and contest the claims enumerated in Law No. 66-07, including navigational rights, the exclusive economic zone, internal waters and historic byways.

Archipelagic States

The Embassies recall that articles 46 and 47 of Part IV of the United Nations Convention on the Law of the Sea (the Convention) establish the criteria by which a State may be considered an archipelagic State and may draw archipelagic baselines. One of those criteria is that the turning points of straight archipelagic baselines may only join the outermost islands and drying reefs of the archipelago, and may not be drawn to or from low-tide elevations except in two enumerated circumstances.

The information available to the governments of the United Kingdom and the United States do not show that the turning points set out in Law No. 66-07 are all above water at high tide, or that they qualify for either of the exceptions in article 47, suggesting that they do not qualify as turning points under article 47, paragraph I, of the Convention, and that the Dominican Republic does not meet the other requirements of article 47 to be an archipelagic State.

The governments of the United Kingdom and the United States would be grateful if the Ministry could provide to their Embassies documentation regarding the status of these turning points as islands or drying reefs that are above water at high tide, or that they otherwise meet the requirements of article 47.

Navigational rights

If the Dominican Republic qualifies as an archipelagic State, which the governments of the United Kingdom and the United States do not accept, the Embassies note that Articles 11 and 12 of Law No. 66-07 do not recognize the right of archipelagic sea lanes passage set out in article 53 of the Convention. The Embassies would be grateful if the Dominican Republic would clarify this.

Whether or not the Dominican Republic qualifies as an archipelagic State, the governments of the United Kingdom and the United States cannot accept as being consistent with the law of the sea the limitations on the exercise of innocent passage set out in article 12 of Law No. 66-07. All ships, regardless of cargo, means of propulsion, or armament, enjoy the right of innocent passage through the territorial sea.

Exclusive Economic Zone (EEZ)

The Embassies note that article 14 of Law No. 66-07 sets out a series of coordinates purporting to delimit the outer limit of the Dominican Republic's EEZ. The Embassies note that portions of the claimed EEZ impinge on the rights of the United Kingdom in respect of the Turks and Caicos Islands and of the United States in respect of Puerto Rico.

The Embassies further note that the paragraph following article 14 appears to claim rights to old shipwrecked vessels in its claimed EEZ, rights which are not accorded to coastal States in Part V of the Convention.

Internal waters and historic bays

The Embassies also note that articles 6 and 7 of Law No. 66-07 claim certain bodies of waters as internal waters and historic bays. Pending examination of those claims, the governments of the United Kingdom and the United States cannot accept these claims as valid under international law.

Reservation of rights

Accordingly, the governments of the United Kingdom and the United States reserve their rights and those of their territories and citizens.

d. Exclusive economic zone

(1) U.S. exclusive economic zone generated by Howland and Baker Islands

On December 28, 2007, the United States filed its Opposition to Defendant's Motion to Dismiss for Lack of Subject Matter and In Rem Jurisdiction in a case contesting the existence of the U.S. exclusive economic zone ("EEZ") around the Howland and Baker Islands. *United States v. Marshalls 201,* Civil Case No. 06-00030 (D. Guam) in the U.S. District Court for the Territory of Guam. In this case, the U.S. Coast Guard observed and arrested the defendant in September 2006 on charges of fishing illegally in the EEZ generated by Howland and Baker Islands. On October 10, 2006, the United States initiated this action by filing a complaint for forfeiture of the vessel *Marshalls 201,* registered in the Republic of the Marshall Islands, and its catch. Fishing within the U.S. EEZ by a foreign fishing vessel without authorization of the National Oceanic and Atmospheric Administration is prohibited by the Magnus-Stevens Fishery Conservation and Management Act, Pub. L. No. 94-265, 16 U.S.C. § 1857(2); pursuant to 16 U.S.C. § 1860(a), an offending vessel "shall be subject to forfeiture of the United States."

As explained in the U.S. Opposition,

> The EEZ adjacent to Howland and Baker Islands is well defined, with geographic coordinates published in the Federal Register. . . . 60 Fed. Reg. 43,829 (Aug. 23, 1995). The Federal Register provides a list of 15 geographic coordinates such that the exact EEZ location can be accurately charted by any vessel either manually or using electronic instruments such as GPS and charting devices. . . .

The defendant asserted that Howland and Baker Islands are "rocks" within the definition of article 121(3) of the Law of the Sea Convention, and therefore that the United States may not establish an EEZ around them. Article 121(3) provides: "Rocks which cannot sustain human habitation or economic life of their own shall have no exclusive economic zone or continental shelf." The U.S. submission refuted this argument, first on the ground that the defendant had no standing to dispute the EEZ of the United States because "[r]ights under international law, including the law of the sea, accrue to sovereign nations. Allegations of inconsistency with international law are matters of international affairs, not judicial redress." The United States noted that it is not a party to the Convention on the Law of the Sea on which the defendant relied, and even if it were, the convention would not be self-executing nor would it create a private right of action or other enforceable individual legal rights in U.S. courts.

Second, the United States argued that "[i]t is simply incorrect to assert that Howland and Baker Islands may not generate an EEZ." Excerpts follow addressing this latter argument (citations to other submissions omitted). The full text of the U.S. submission and attached declaration of J. Ashley Roach are available at *www.state.gov/s/l/c8183.htm*. The case remained pending at the end of 2007.

———————

*   *   *   *

Defendant concludes that Howland and Baker are "rocks" as that term is used in paragraph 3 of article 121. For several reasons, Defendant's radical reading of Article 121(3) is wrong, not least because his reading conflicts with the plain meaning of the words of Article 121. First, the Defendant and its expert, Professor Van Dyke, think that if there is no present human habitation on an island, then it "cannot sustain human habitation" and is thus a rock under Article 121(3). The Defendant and Professor Van Dyke take the view that even if there had been habitation on an island in the past, if there is no habitation on the island today, then it is necessarily a rock. In the professional opinion of J. Ashley Roach, the State Department's expert on law of the sea, this is not a correct interpretation of Article 121(3) and is contrary to the plain language of Article 121(3). Article 121(3) uses the formulation "cannot sustain human habitation," not "do not support human habitation." The question posed by Article 121(3) is whether the feature at issue is habitable. Robert Smith, who as the nation's former chief maritime geographer, has had direct experience with States establishing EEZs adjacent to presently uninhabited islands (including those of Kiribati and many other Pacific Island nation States), agrees with the present Department of State position, as expressed by Mr. Roach. . . . A review of the history of Howland

and Baker shows that both islands have had periods of habitation in the relatively recent past and they have played a role in various economic ventures. Further, there is no evidence in the record that they will be uninhabited in the future or have no economic life. Significantly, the Department of State does not view either island as a rock under Article 121(3). . . .

Second, the Defendant and Professor Van Dyke rely heavily on what they assert is "State practice" showing that Howland and Baker are rocks under Article 121(3). . . . As noted by Mr. Roach, State practice refers to the subsequent practice in the application of a treaty text which establishes the agreement of the parties regarding its application. It refers to the way a text is actually applied by the parties. If the practice is consistent and is common to, or accepted by, the parties, the subsequent practice is usually a good indication of what the parties understand the text to mean. Anthony Aust, Modern Treaty Law and Practice 194 (Cambridge University Press, 2000). . . . Defendant misleadingly mischaracterizes and distorts State practice in support of its view, which is in fact unsupportable.

Third, as Mr. Roach attests, State practice supports the U.S. view that Howland and Baker are not rocks under Article 121(3). There are many examples of relatively small, uninhabited features around or from which countries have established Exclusive Economic Zones. . . .

*   *   *   *

Finally, the Court should consider the implications of Defendant's argument that an uninhabited island necessarily is a rock under Article 121(3). Under Defendant's reasoning, a country would lose jurisdiction if it decided—as the United States has done—to make outlying islands a nature preserve and not to develop the land for residential, industrial or commercial use. This would not only be bad policy, but could not have been the intent of the drafters of Article 121(3)—for many of the other provisions of the Convention are specifically designed to protect and preserve the marine environment.

*   *   *   *

(2) Military survey activities: Marine scientific researched distinguished

(i) China

> On January 18, 2007, the United States provided an aide memoire to officials of the People's Republic of China concerning military survey activities in the Exclusive Economic Zone ("EEZ"), which China asserts requires its prior consent. The text of the aide memoire is set forth below in full. *See also Digest 2001* at 698–99 and *Digest 2003* at 727, 738.

The United States is pleased to provide the following explanation of why military survey activities do not require either prior notification to or the consent of the coastal state. The U.S. Government exercises its high seas freedoms with respect to military survey activities in the EEZ of coastal states worldwide, consistent with international law, and as described in this aide-memoire. The United States has conducted military survey activities in more than 85 different EEZs, including China's, without notice to, or consent of, those coastal states.

Customary international law, as it is reflected in the 1982 United Nations Convention on the Law of the Sea (LOS Convention) authorizes coastal states to claim limited rights and jurisdiction in an EEZ. The limited jurisdictional rights relate to the exploration, exploitation, and conservation of natural resources, marine scientific research (MSR), and protection and preservation of the marine environment. Furthermore, as reflected in Article 56 of the LOS Convention, customary international law requires coastal states to exercise their limited, resource-related rights in their EEZs with "due regard" for the rights of other states. Notwithstanding coastal state resource rights, high seas freedom of navigation and overflight apply seaward of the outer edge of a coastal state's lawfully delimited territorial sea. Moreover, the LOS Convention does not purport in any manner to restrict the military activities of a state in the EEZ.

The United States recognizes that a coastal state may require anyone seeking to conduct MSR in the coastal state's EEZ to obtain approval in advance. However, international law, as reflected in the LOS Convention, distinguishes between MSR and survey activities, and is reflected in articles 19(2) (j), 21 (1) (g), 40, 54 and in article 246(1) of the LOS Convention.

Beyond the territorial sea (in which the coastal state enjoys full sovereignty, subject only to the rights of transit passage, innocent passage, assistance entry, and safe harbor), all states enjoy the high seas freedoms of navigation and overflight and other related uses of the sea within the EEZ, provided that they do so with due regard to the rights of the coastal state and other states.

The conduct of surveys in the EEZ is an exercise of the high seas freedoms of navigation and other internationally lawful uses of the sea related to those freedoms, such as those associated with the operation of ships, which international law, as reflected in article 58(1) of the LOS Convention, guarantees to all states. Appropriate activities include launching and landing of aircraft, operating military devices, formation steaming, intelligence collection, weapons exercises, and military surveys. Coastal states must show "due regard" for such lawful uses.

The United States therefore reserves the right to engage in military surveys anywhere outside lawfully delimited foreign territorial seas, international straits, and archipelagic waters. As a high seas freedom, United States military surveys within foreign EEZS are entitled to "due regard" from coastal states under international law, as reflected in the LOS Convention, and we expect China to fulfill its obligation in this regard. Additionally, when encountering U.S naval auxiliaries off the coast of China, PRC vessels are obligated to comply with the navigational requirements of the 1972 International Regulations for Preventing Collisions at Sea (COLREGS). The United States expects China to comply fully with the COLREGS navigational rules.

(ii) India

On May 3, 2007, the United States responded to a diplomatic note from the Indian Ministry of External Affairs asserting that the U.S. Naval Ship *Mary Sears* had been conducting marine scientific research in the exclusive economic zone of

India without permission. The U.S. diplomatic note explained that the USNS *Mary Sears* was "not engaged in marine scientific research (MSR) . . . [but rather] in lawful military activities in international waters, in full compliance with international law." The substantive paragraphs of the note are set forth below in full.

The United States recalls that coastal state jurisdiction in the EEZ is limited to resource-related matters. While Article 56 of the United Nations Convention of the Law of the Sea (UNCLOS) recognizes coastal state exclusive resource rights, as well as jurisdiction over off-shore installations, MSR and protection of the marine environment, in the EEZ, Article 58 of the Convention specifically provides that all states enjoy in the zone the traditional high seas freedoms of navigation and overflight and other internationally lawful uses of the sea related to those freedoms. Military operations, exercises, and activities have always been regarded as internationally lawful uses of the sea. Consistent with international law, the mission of the USNS MARY SEARS is to collect marine data at various locations for military, not scientific, purposes. Accordingly, the conduct of military survey operations within a nation's EEZ is not MSR and does not require permission from or prior notification of the coastal state. We follow the same policy in our own EEZ, requiring neither notification nor consent for foreign military survey activities in the U.S. EEZ.

The United States also takes this opportunity to reaffirm its protest of those provisions of the Maritime Zones of India Act of 1975, which purport to assert jurisdiction over the EEZ in a manner that is contrary to international law as reflected in UNCLOS. Insofar as the 1976 Act is applied to foreign military vessels engaged in military activities in the EEZ, to include military surveys and hydrographic surveys, a requirement for prior permission from India authorities is contrary to customary international law and UNCLOS. Accordingly, the Government of the United States rejects the claim to require consent for military activities in the EEZ. The United States considers it fully consistent with international law to conduct military surveys in a foreign EEZ without coastal state consent and we reserve the right to engage in such surveys anywhere in the world outside foreign territorial seas, international straits and archipelagic waters. The United States calls on India to respect the freedoms and rights guaranteed to all nations under international law for uses of the sea and airspace.

5. Entry into Ports Under *Force Majeure*

On January 22, 2007, the Department of Homeland Security, U.S. Coast Guard, issued a press release reporting:

> The 485-foot Chinese-flagged cargo ship *Tong Cheng* has requested authorization for an unscheduled entry into the port of Honolulu to effect repairs to a crack in its hull below the waterline.

> * * * *

> A team of technical experts from the USCG Salvage Engineering Response Team (SERT), U.S. Navy Mobile Diving Salvage Unit One (MDSU ONE), and commercial entities conducted a thorough assessment of the vessel's structural integrity while offshore. Based on that assessment the vessel was granted permission to enter the Captain of the Port (COTP) Honolulu zone to effect repairs. The Coast Guard will continue to monitor repairs, and the vessel will receive a safety inspection prior to its departure from Honolulu.

See *www.uscghawaii.com/go/doc/800/142470/*.

In the view of the United States, under the *force majeure* doctrine there is a clear customary law right of entry into ports by ships in distress in order to preserve human life. A ship does not have an absolute right to enter foreign ports or internal waters in order to save its cargo, where human life is not at risk, if the gravity of the ship's situation is outweighed by the probability, degree, and kind of harm to the coastal State that would arise were the ship allowed to enter. It appears to be a well-settled rule of customary international law that a ship entering a foreign port by reason of *force majeure* or distress is not subject to the jurisdiction of the port State in connection with actions to relieve the distress. A paper collecting sources on which the U.S. view is based is available at *www.state.gov/s/l/c8183.htm*.

A letter of January 21, 2007, from V. B. Atkins, Captain, U.S. Coast Guard, to an attorney representing the M/V *Tong Cheng*, set forth the terms on which entry into port was granted. Substantive paragraphs are set forth below in full. As noted below, there was a concern that the *Tong Cheng* carried cargo destined for Cuba, which would implicate U.S. statutes prohibiting a ship from proceeding from a U.S. port to Cuba.

The U.S. government will grant the request of the Tong Cheng's master to enter the Port of Honolulu, Hawaii to effect emergency repairs, subject to the application of reasonable measures to mitigate environmental and navigational consequences in the United States arising from the damage to the ship. The U.S. government has also made the government of the People's Republic of China aware of these measures.

In view of the ship's urgent need for assistance in port, the U.S. government will not subject the vessel, cargo, or persons on board to prohibitions, duties or taxes arising from entry into the port, except as herein noted.

The U.S. government intends to examine the vessel, cargo, and persons on board for the purpose of ensuring the health and safety of the port. For safety purposes, all cargo will be examined to ensure alignment with manifests provided by the shipping interests.

— The Chinese shipping interests shall ensure that any and all cargo bound for Cuba, to the extent that it is appropriately manifested, shall be returned to China in due course.
— Given the damage suffered to the Tong Cheng, the U.S. government understands that the temporary repairs will have to be effected in the United States. Thereafter, the vessel will proceed to China for more thorough repairs or other disposition. The vessel will not proceed from Hawaii to Cuba.

The cargo originally bound for Cuba must be returned to China. All other cargo may proceed to manifested destinations through any viable means at the shipping interests' discretion. . . .

On January 25, 2007, as the *Tong Cheng* was being prepared for entry into port, the Department of State provided guidance to the U.S. Embassy in Beijing concerning treatment of cargo on the vessel.

* * * *

4. . . . [T]he Tong Cheng now remains at anchor off Honolulu for dewatering and temporary repairs prior to port entry. These operations are expected to continue for most of Wednesday, January 24. The ship is expected to transit to a pier late Wednesday or on Thursday. Cargo off loading is expected to begin Friday, January 26.

5. The Coast Guard (USCG) remains concerned about potential discrepancies between the manifest and actual cargo, which will remain unconfirmed until the vessel arrives pier side. USOG intends to conduct routine non-intrusive, external inspections of the containers with gamma ray scanners and radiation portal monitors to ensure the health and safety of the port. USCG notes Chinese assurance that the containers manifested as containing ammunition contain, in fact, cloth wrappings for ammunition. The external inspections will confirm the accuracy of the manifest.

6. In the event of an anomaly in the cargo manifest identified by non-intrusive inspection, the Honolulu Port Director has the authority to open the specific container in order to ensure that it can be handled and stored safely. Examination of the open container would be limited to those steps reasonably necessary to safely resolve the anomaly. Examinations will be documented by video-recorder and representatives of the owner will be offered the opportunity to observe the examination, unless it would be unsafe to do so. The Coast Guard will report to Embassy Beijing the findings of any examination.

Captain Wei Jiafu, Group President and CEO of China Ocean Shipping Co. thanked the United States for its assistance to his crew and vessel in a letter to Clark T. Randt,

U.S. Ambassador to The People's Republic of China, dated March 19, 2007. In his letter Captain Wei explained that the M/V *Tong Cheng* had departed Honolulu on March 17, 2007, and was "heading back towards China for complete repair." The full text of Captain Wei's letter is available at *www.state. gov/s/l/c8183.htm*.

6. Wreck Removal

In May 2007 the International Maritime Organization International Conference on the Removal of Wrecks, meeting in Nairobi, Kenya, adopted the Convention on the Removal of Wrecks. On May 17, the United States provided a statement recording its views on the adopted text, explaining:

> The United States has participated in the development of the Convention on the Removal of Wrecks with a view to adoption of a text that is widely acceptable.
>
> Because there are no summary records of the proceedings and the records of decisions of the Conference have been limited in scope, as others have said in the Conference, there will be no historical record that explains the important substantive actions and decisions taken here in Nairobi this past week.
>
> To fill that gap for the United States and perhaps for those Member States who have not participated in this Conference, we wish to place on the record of this Conference our understanding of these actions and decisions, and are grateful that this statement has been circulated as a document of the Conference.

The remainder of the U.S. statement, published as IMO Doc. LEG/CONF.16/18, is set forth below and available at *www.state.gov/s/l/c8183.htm*. The text of the convention is available in IMO Doc. LEG/CONF.16/19 and is reprinted in 46 I.L.M. 694 (2007), with an introduction by Captain Charles D. Michel, Chief of the Office of Maritime and International

Law, U.S. Coast Guard Headquarters, and head of the U.S. delegation.

*   *   *   *

It is important to recognize that the Convention imposes significant duties and responsibilities on flag States and grants new rights to coastal and port States, but not *vice versa*. This imbalance continues to be of concern. We believe that the absence of a tonnage requirement in the entry into force article does not reflect the need for international acceptance by flag States of these significant new obligations. To the extent major flag States have not consented to be bound by the Convention, their ships will not be required to carry the insurance called for in Article 12 except as required as a condition of entry into ports of States Parties.[*]

We note that all of those delegations that spoke agreed that this treaty does not apply to States that have not consented to be

---

[*]   Editor's note: As explained by Captain Michel, "The United States repeatedly objected to the purported application of the Convention to non-Party States, particularly where such application is inconsistent with customary international law as reflected in UNCLOS, such as requiring their flag vessels to carry insurance while in innocent passage through the territorial sea of a State Party." 46 I.L.M. at 695. As adopted, paragraphs 1 and 12 of Article 12 provide as follows concerning port state authority:

> 1. The registered owner of a ship of 300 gross tonnage and above and flying the flag of a State Party shall be required to maintain insurance or other financial security, such as a guarantee of a bank or similar institution, to cover liability under this Convention in an amount equal to the limits of liability under the applicable national or international limitation regime, but in all cases not exceeding an amount calculated in accordance with article 6(1)(b) of the Convention on Limitation of Liability for Maritime Claims, 1976, as amended.

*   *   *   *

> 12. Subject to the provisions of this article, each State Party shall ensure, under its national law, that insurance or other security to the extent required by paragraph 1 is in force in respect of any ship of 300 gross tonnage and above, wherever registered, entering or leaving a port in its territory, or arriving at or leaving an offshore facility in its territorial sea.

bound by its terms and their commitment that as States Parties they will not seek to do so except as a condition of entry into their ports. We will rely on those representations.

We wish to draw the Conference's attention [to the fact] that the text is not clear as to the rights and duties of States Parties *inter se* in their territorial sea, straits used for international navigation, and archipelagic waters. In particular, it is unclear what a State Party, that has opted to apply the Convention to its territory, may do in respect of ships of States Parties that have not opted to apply the Convention to their territory that are exercising the rights of innocent passage, transit passage, and archipelagic sea lanes passage in the waters of a State Party that has applied the Convention in its territory. We understand that, in the absence of mutuality of consent by States Parties, a State Party will not seek to apply the Convention to ships of State Parties that have not consented except as a condition of port entry.

We believe that Article 16, Relationship to other conventions and international agreements, is not legally correct. The text reads:

> "Nothing in this Convention shall prejudice the rights and obligations of any State under the United Nations Convention on the Law of the Sea, 1982, and under the customary international law of the sea."

We note that the Convention substantively alters the rights and obligations of States Parties under the law of the sea and thus Article 16 is incorrect.

For example, the Convention permits States Parties to intervene in their exclusive economic zone in circumstances that the law of the sea does not presently permit. Hence the rights of coastal States are expanded and the rights of flag States are diminished.

It is evident thus that the Convention does prejudice the balance of rights and duties of coastal and flag States in the law of the sea as is permitted by article 311 of the Law of the Sea Convention. In our view, this provision should have stated that "Except as provided in this Convention, nothing in this Convention shall prejudice the rights and obligations of any State under" the law of the sea.

We would also note for the record that if, as one delegate mentioned, any wreck poses a danger to the environment satisfying the criteria of article 221 of the Law of the Sea Convention, which incorporates the standards of the Intervention Convention—"major harmful consequences"—there would have been no need for the public international law provisions of this Convention.

Finally, with regard to Article 15 on the settlement of disputes between States Parties, I wish to make four points.

- My delegation objected to the inclusion of paragraphs 2 to 5 at LEG 92 on procedural grounds. We continue to have those concerns.
- We note that the May 30, 2006, judgment by the Grand Chamber of the European Court of Justice in the case of *Commission v. Ireland*,[1] indicates those provisions, incorporating dispute settlement provisions contained in Part XV of the Law of the Sea Convention, may not be invoked by one member State of the EU in a dispute with another EU member State.
- As there is no provision in Article 15 for a State to opt out of compulsory dispute settlement, as was done in the 1988 SUA Convention [and Protocol] and is the norm in many conventions, States wishing to consent to be bound by the Convention still have the right to reserve as to the application of paragraphs 2 to 5 to them.
- The inclusion of these provisions from the Law of the Sea Convention on compulsory dispute settlement is unprecedented in IMO conventions resulting from the work of the Legal Committee. The United States does not accept that the inclusion of such provision in this Convention, particularly one without an opt-out provision and adopted under improper procedures, is a precedent for future IMO Conventions developed by the Legal Committee.

---

[1]   Case C-459/03, available at *http://curia.europa.eu/jurisp/cgi-bin/ form.pl?lang=en&newform=newform&jurcdj=jurcdj&alldocrec=alldocrec &docj=docj&docor=docor&docop=docop&docav=docav&docsom=docso m&docinf=docinf&typeord=ALLTYP&numaff=&ddatefs=30&mdatefs=0 5&ydatefs=2006&ddatefe=&mdatefe=&ydatefe=&nomusuel=Commission +v.+Ireland&domaine=&mots=&resmax=100&Submit=Submit.*

The United States remains committed to the development by the Organization and the Legal Committee of international solutions to shared concerns. We look forward to continuing to work with the IMO and its Member States to reach these solutions.

7. International Maritime Crew Issues

a. *Crew list exemption*

In a diplomatic note dated April 11, 2007, the Indian Ministry of External Affairs proposed to exempt American Navy ships visiting Indian ports from a requirement to furnish crew lists. The note stated in its substantive paragraphs:

> ... [R]ecognising the long standing and excellent relations between the US Navy and the Indian Navy, the Government of India has decided to exempt, on a reciprocal basis, the visiting Naval ships of US Navy from the requirement of furnishing particulars of the crew as contemplated under Section 6 of our Foreigners Act, 1946 (31 of 1946) when visiting ports in India.
>
> (2) This exemption would come into effect on confirmation by the US Government through a diplomatic note stating that the same exemptions would be available to Indian Naval Ships visiting US ports.

The United States responded with a diplomatic note of May 2, 2007, quoting the Indian note in its entirety and stating:

> The Embassy confirms that the procedures set forth in the Ministry's Note are consistent with international law and acceptable to the Government of the United States of America and that the same exemptions are available to sovereign immune Indian vessels visiting U.S. ports, pursuant to Title 19, United States Code of Federal Regulations, section 4.7b.

b. *Transportation Worker Identification Credential*

Section 104 of the Security and Accountability for Every Port Act of 2006 ("SAFE Port Act"), Pub. L. No. 109-347 (2006), amended requirements for transportation security cards under § 102 of the Maritime Transportation Security Act ("MTSA"), 46 U.S.C. § 70105. As explained in the final rule discussed below, § 102

> requires [the Department of Homeland Security ("DHS")] to issue regulations to prevent individuals from entering secure areas of vessels or MTSA-regulated port facilities unless such individuals hold transportation security cards issued under section 102 and are authorized to be in the secure areas. An individual who does not hold the required transportation security card, but who is otherwise authorized to be in the secure area in accordance with the facility's security plan, must be accompanied by another individual who holds a transportation security card.

Among other things, § 104 of the SAFE Port Act required the Transportation Security Administration and the Coast Guard to "concurrently process an application from an individual for merchant mariner's documents." Section 106 prohibited issuance of transportation security cards to individuals found guilty or not guilty by reason of insanity of a felony involving treason, espionage, sedition, or "a crime listed in chapter 113B of title 18, United States Code ["Terrorism"], a comparable State law, or conspiracy to commit such crime."

On January 25, 2007, Department of Homeland Security published a final rule, effective March 26, 2007, with request for comments, to implement the new Transportation Worker Identification Credential ("TWIC"). 72 Fed. Reg. 3492 (Jan. 25, 2007). The Summary of the final rule explained:

> The Department of Homeland Security (DHS), through the Transportation Security Administration (TSA) and the

United States Coast Guard (Coast Guard), issues this final rule to further secure our Nation's ports and modes of transportation. This rule implements the Maritime Transportation Security Act of 2002 and the Security and Accountability for Every Port Act of 2006. Those statutes establish requirements regarding the promulgation of regulations that require credentialed merchant mariners and workers with unescorted access to secure areas of vessels and facilities to undergo a security threat assessment and receive a biometric credential, known as a Transportation Worker Identification Credential (TWIC). After DHS publishes a notice announcing the compliance date for each Captain of the Port (COTP) zone, persons without TWICs will not be granted unescorted access to secure areas at affected maritime facilities. Those seeking unescorted access to secure areas aboard affected vessels, and all Coast Guard credentialed merchant mariners must possess a TWIC by September 25, 2008. This final rule will enhance the security of ports by requiring such security threat assessments of persons in secure areas and by improving access control measures to prevent those who may pose a security threat from gaining unescorted access to secure areas of ports.

With this final rule, the Coast Guard amends its regulations on vessel and facility security to require the use of the TWIC as an access control measure. The Coast Guard also amends its merchant mariner regulations to incorporate the requirement to obtain a TWIC. . . .

On November 13, 2007, the Transportation Security Administration published a notice that initial enrollment for the TWIC for the ports of Houston, Texas, and Providence, Rhode Island, would begin on November 14, 2007, and enrollment for the ports of Chicago, Illinois; Port Arthur, Texas and Savannah, Georgia, would begin on November 15, 2007. 72 Fed. Reg. 63,919 (Nov. 13, 2007).

c. Marine Casualty Code

The IMO Maritime Safety Committee held its 83rd session in Copenhagen, Denmark, from October 3–12, 2007. Among other things, the committee decided to make the Code of the International Standards and Recommended Practices for a Safety Investigation into a Marine Casualty or Marine Incident ("Casualty Code") mandatory under the Safety of Life at Sea Convention ("SOLAS"). The U.S. delegation indicated that, after careful review of the existing text of the draft code, the United States had identified significant areas of substantive and procedural concern that would currently prevent it from allowing the amendments to enter into force for the United States. The United States suggested that the draft Code be referred back to the Subcommittee on Flag State Implementation for further consideration to remove individual legal rights and legal process requirements, which the United States believed to be contrary to the purpose of SOLAS, and to prevent inconsistencies with the Joint IMO/ILO Guidelines for the Fair Treatment of Seafarers in the Event of a Maritime Accident, and their ongoing review by other bodies. The Committee did not agree with the U.S. proposal and approved the draft Code along with draft amendments to SOLAS chapter XI-I making the Code mandatory for adoption at MSC 84. The United States reserved its position on the action taken by the Committee. The text of the draft code is set forth in FSI 15/18/Add.1, Annex 2, June 18, 2007, and the draft resolution at Annex 5. Both are available at *www.state.gov/sl/c8183.htm*.

B. OUTER SPACE

1. U.S. National Space Policy

Mark Simonoff, Attorney Adviser in the Office of the Legal Adviser, participated in the December 6, 2007, 2nd Eilene Galloway Symposium on Critical Issues in Space Law, entitled "International Civil Space Cooperation: Obstacles and Opportunities."

In addressing the U.S. perspective, Mr. Simonoff observed that the National Space Policy, issued on August 31, 2006, included a provision requiring that all actions undertaken by departments and agencies in implementing the policy shall be, among other things, consistent with U.S. law and regulations, treaties and other agreements to which the United States is a party, applicable international law, and U.S. foreign policy. For further discussion of the National Space Policy, see *Digest 2006* at 840–42. *See also* B.4.a. below.

2. UN Register for Space Objects

On December 17, 2007, the United States joined consensus on a UN General Assembly resolution entitled "Recommendations on enhancing the practice of states and international intergovernmental organizations in registering space objects." U.N. Doc. A/RES/62/101 (2007). In a statement before the Legal Subcommittee of the UN Committee on the Peaceful Uses of Outer Space ("COPUOS") in March 2007, Mark Simonoff, U.S. representative to the committee, reiterated U.S. support on this issue:

> Since the establishment of the UN Register for space objects, activities in space have dramatically increased and changed in nature to include increasing commercial activities. We are pleased with the progress that has been made on this agenda item, and think that the practical suggestions that have been developed will be beneficial to all nations. We look forward to finalizing the proposed text of a possible UN General Assembly Resolution on this issue during this session.

The full text of the statement is available at *www.state.gov/s/ l/c8183.htm*.

3. Space Debris Mitigation Guidelines

On June 15, 2007, COPUOS adopted a report to the General Assembly which included the voluntary Space Debris Mitigation Guidelines. *See* Report of the Committee on Peaceful Uses of Outer Space, U.N. Doc. A/62/20 (2007), available at *www. unoosa.org/pdf/gadocs/A_62_20E.pdf*. The text of the Space Debris Mitigation Guidelines is attached as an annex to the report. The UN General Assembly endorsed the guidelines on December 22, 2007. U.N. Doc. A/RES/62/217. Paragraphs 27 and 28 of UNGA Resolution 62/217 stated that the General Assembly:

> 27. *Agrees* that the voluntary guidelines for the mitigation of space debris reflect the existing practices as developed by a number of national and international organizations, and invites Member States to implement those guidelines through relevant national mechanisms; [and]
> 28. *Considers* that it is essential that Member States pay more attention to the problem of collisions of space objects, including those with nuclear power sources, with space debris, and other aspects of space debris, calls for the continuation of national research on this question, for the development of improved technology for the monitoring of space debris and for the compilation and dissemination of data on space debris, also considers that, to the extent possible, information thereon should be provided to the Scientific and Technical Subcommittee, and agrees that international cooperation is needed to expand appropriate and affordable strategies to minimize the impact of space debris on future space missions. . . .

In a statement to the Fourth Committee on October 24, 2007, concerning adoption of the COPUOS Report, U.S. Public Delegate to the UN General Assembly Kelly Knight welcomed the adoption of the guidelines and explained U.S. concern with recent Chinese actions in this context.

The full text of Ms. Knight's statement, excerpted below, is available at *www.usunnewyork.usmission.gov/press_releases/20071024_258.html.*

*   *   *   *

The Scientific and Technical Subcommittee (STSC) had another highly productive session. We would particularly like to note the Subcommittee's success in reaching consensus on a set of space debris mitigation guidelines that are based on the Inter-Agency Space Debris Coordination Committee (IADC) Space Debris Mitigation Guidelines. This is a highly significant achievement that demonstrates the relevancy of the work of COPUOS to the global space community.

The United States views these guidelines as solid, technically-based measures that should be adopted by all space-faring nations and implemented through appropriate national mechanisms. The U.S. Government had previously endorsed the Interagency Debris Coordination Committee (IADC) orbital debris mitigation guidelines, and our domestic agencies are well along in implementing debris mitigation practices that are consistent with the IADC guidelines and the guidelines endorsed by the STSC this year.

This positive development has been tarnished by the intentional destruction of a satellite by the Government of China on January 11th of this year. While the United States has separately expressed it[s] concerns about this event to the Government of China, we think it is appropriate to comment about the January 11th event in this forum due to the long-standing interest of Member States in the mitigation of space debris. The U.S. has confirmed through its space tracking sensors that the January 11th event has created thousands of pieces of large space debris, the majority of which will remain in orbit for more than 100 years. A much larger number of smaller, but still hazardous, debris was also created.

The United States is concerned about the increased risk to human spaceflight and space infrastructure as a result of this action, a risk that is shared by all space-faring nations. As we have discussed many times, technological advances have increased the global importance of the use of space systems. The United States and many other nations have satellites in space in conformance with international agreements that provide for their national security, foreign policy and economic interests.

We note with concern the contradiction between China's efforts within COPUOS, and within the IADC, related to the mitigation of space debris, and its action taken on January 11th. The avoidance of intentional creation of long-lived space debris is one of the guidelines that we have included in the set of guidelines. The creation of thousands of pieces of debris through an act that could have been avoided makes it even more important that we conclude our work on the space debris mitigation guidelines this year. These guidelines will not prevent the intentional creation of space debris, but they will serve to provide a clear and unambiguous set of mitigation measures that can be implemented by all space-faring nations, and they will make it clear that intentional creation of long-lived debris is not in the best interests of the world community.

*   *   *   *

4. Weapons and Outer Space

a. Conference on Disarmament: Prevention of an Arms Race in Outer Space

On February 13, 2007, Ambassador Christina Rocca, U.S. Permanent Representative to the Conference on Disarmament ("CD"), addressed the CD on U.S. space policy, particularly as related to the CD topic "Prevention of an Arms Race in Outer Space." The full text of Ambassador Rocca's remarks, excerpted below, is available at *www.us-mission.ch/Press 2007/0213PAROS.html.*

I take the floor today to contribute to the discussion on the issue of Prevention of an Arms Race in Outer Space (PAROS). Let me begin by saying a few words about United States space policy, about which much has been said—much of it inaccurate—and how U.S. space policy relates to efforts on the part of a few to prevent an arms race that does not exist. The United States' space policy articulates a number of substantive objectives: the primary one is to ensure that we maintain and enable free access to and use of space for peaceful purposes for the United States and all nations of the world and for the benefit of all mankind. Our policy also mandates the pursuit of programs and capabilities to ensure that our space assets are protected. Put simply, these assets are vital to our national security, including our economic interests, and must be defended. Similar concerns have been raised by our colleagues here yesterday.

As a number of our colleagues have pointed out, there already exists a number of treaties and conventions that establish a regime for the peaceful use of outer space. We note that many nations represented here within the CD itself have not signed on to all these conventions. We believe universalization of these conventions is a much more practical and effective step towards guaranteeing the peaceful use of outer space.

*   *   *   *

The January 11 test of an anti-satellite (or ASAT) weapon [by China] reminds us that a relatively small number of countries are exploring and acquiring capabilities to counter, attack, and defeat vital space systems, including those of the United States. These capabilities include jamming satellite links or blinding satellite sensors, which can be disruptive or can temporarily deny access to space-derived products. Kinetic or conventional ASAT weapons— or electro-magnetic pulse weapons—can permanently and irreversibly damage or destroy a satellite and create vast amounts of orbital debris.

Just as the United States reserves the right to protect its infrastructures and resources on land, so too do we reserve the right to protect our space assets. This principle was first established for the United States by President Eisenhower and is also enshrined in the 1967 Outer Space Treaty. Consistent with this principle, the United States views the purposeful interference with its space systems as an infringement on our rights, just as we would view interference with U.S. naval and commercial vessels in international waters as an infringement on our rights.

I emphasize that, by maintaining the right of self-defense, the United States is not out to claim space for its own or to weaponize it. Our policy is not about establishing a U.S. monopoly of space, as some have asserted. Even a cursory reading of our new space policy statement demonstrates just the opposite. There is significant emphasis on international cooperation throughout our National Space Policy. International cooperation is identified as both a U.S. space policy principle and goal. International cooperation is also emphasized in the other related policy directives, such as President Bush's Commercial Remote Sensing Space Policy and the January 2004 Vision for Space Exploration. . . .

Critics, however like to claim that our National Space Policy ignores or downplays U.S. international legal obligations and that the Administration's opposition to space arms control may spur an arms race in space. Let me state it clearly and to the point: the President's space policy does not advocate, nor direct the development or deployment of weapons in space.

Nonetheless, we are told that there must be a ban to prevent weapons in space. We have some experience in that regard. For many years the U.S. engaged in such talks with the Soviet Union to no avail, largely because no one then, or now for that matter, could formulate an agreed definition of what is meant by "space weapon." What is often meant is whatever the U.S. may be exploring in terms of ballistic missile defenses in space, but not weapons on the ground that would attack satellites in space. And without a definition, one is left with loopholes and meaningless limitations that endanger national security.

Some assert that the recent test of an ASAT weapon, which has drawn so much international attention and concern, constitutes a further reason to pursue outer space arms control, as some have proposed. The U.S. submits that they have drawn the wrong conclusion. It is regrettable that some countries' attempts to link important issues like the Fissile Material Cutoff Treaty and PAROS have contributed to tying up movement in the CD for years. It is also regrettable that China has conducted this ASAT demonstration, endangering hundreds of satellites with the resulting debris.

And it is regrettable that China continues to call for an arms control arrangement which, if its recent behavior is any indication, would not ban its ASAT activities nor address the fears its actions have stoked. The system that was tested January 11 was not based in space, but launched from the ground. PAROS, as we have usually discussed it in this Conference, would not ban such a weapon. Indeed, China has claimed that this ASAT weapon test was consistent with long-standing support for PAROS. Despite the ASAT test, we continue to believe that there is no arms race in space, and therefore no problem for arms control to solve.

* * * *

Central to the existing legal regime is the Outer Space Treaty, drafted almost 40 years ago. A quick look at some of the Treaty's key provisions shows that, with the advent of commercial space activities, this document has become even more applicable today than when it was first drafted. Encompassed within the Outer Space Treaty are the guiding principles for space operations by which all nations should conduct themselves.

These principles include, for instance, that space shall be free for all to explore and use; space activities shall be carried out in accordance with international law, including the Charter of the United Nations, which guarantees the right of self defense; and States Party bear responsibility for the activities carried on by governmental and nongovernmental entities. The Treaty also prohibits placing weapons of mass destruction in orbit and prohibits the parties from interfering with the assets of other parties. We note in particular the importance of this non-interference provision in light of the recent ASAT weapon test.

Beyond the Outer Space Treaty, the United States is also Party to a number of conventions designed to provide for cooperation in space and to promote an understanding of the responsibilities associated with being a space-faring nation. These include: the Convention on International Liability for Damage Caused by Space Objects; the Convention on Registration of Objects Launched into Outer Space; the Agreement on the Rescue of Astronauts, the Return of Astronauts, and the Return of Objects Launched into Outer Space; and the Hague Code of Conduct against Ballistic Missile Proliferation (HCOC).

Despite this long-standing and effective international space treaty regime, centered on the Outer Space Treaty, there are those who advocate negotiating new multilateral agreements that we believe to be unnecessary and counterproductive. We do not need to enter into new agreements. Rather, we should be seeking to gain universal adherence to, and compliance with, existing agreements.

We should focus our efforts on ensuring free access to space for peaceful purposes and deterring and dissuading the misuse of space, seeking universal adherence to the existing treaties and conventions to which not all members have signed up to. This is precisely what the U.S. National Space Policy states. We believe this approach will have more of a deterrent and dissuasion effect than an additional set of international constraints—constraints that would be unverifiable, protect no one, and constrain only those who comply and not those who cheat.

In closing, let me say that our interest is to continue to expand the use of space for peaceful purposes. Our advances in space in the fields of communication, medicine, and transportation, as well as many other areas, have come to benefit all of mankind, including citizens of countries that have not yet ventured into space. For the United States, that means continuing our tradition of pursuing diplomatic efforts to gain the broadest possible appreciation for the benefits that all nations receive from the peaceful uses of outer space.

b. UN General Assembly First Committee: Outer Space (Disarmament Aspects)

On October 22, 2007, former New York Governor George Pataki, Public Delegate to the 62nd UN General Assembly, addressed the Thematic Debate on "Outer Space (Disarmament Aspects)" in the General Assembly First Committee. Mr. Pataki stressed the U.S. commitment to "the principle of free access to and the use of space by all nations for peaceful purposes," stating:

> [T]he United States stands ready to work with other nations to extend the benefits of space, to enhance space

exploration, and to use space to protect and promote freedom around the world. All we ask in return is that other nations demonstrate similar transparency regarding their own intentions in space.

Excerpts below from Mr. Pataki's statement explain U.S. views that negotiation of a treaty on arms control in outer space would be counterproductive. The full text of Mr. Pataki's statement is available at *www.usmission.ch/Press2007/1022 PatakiFC.html.*

---

*   *   *   *

Since the 1970s, five consecutive U.S. administrations have come to the same conclusions on the impossibility of achieving an effectively verifiable and militarily meaningful space arms control agreement. Indeed, separate negotiations during the administrations of Presidents Jimmy Carter and Ronald W. Reagan failed for a variety of reasons, including the inability to agree on the scope of coverage, and the impossibility of identifying effective means to verify compliance with any such agreement. It is time for the international community to move beyond unnecessary and counterproductive discussions over the merits of unverifiable treaties and space arms control regimes designed to forestall this chimerical "arms race" in outer space.

In simple terms, Mr. Chairman, any object orbiting or transiting through outer space can be a weapon if that object is placed intentionally on a collision course with another space object. This makes treaty verification impossible. Given the commonality of technology, the only way to distinguish a co-orbital satellite interceptor from a non-threatening autonomous servicing vehicle is to determine the operator's intent. The best way to determine intent is for national authorities to have a clear understanding of each other's policies and strategies for space activities.

Mr. Chairman, the United States categorically rejects the premise that transparency and confidence-building measures are useful only in the context of preventing the so-called "weaponization" of outer space. In fact, there are a number of such measures already in place.

The United States also supports non-binding bilateral measures to enhance stability and reduce uncertainty in the conduct of military space operations. In addition to dialogues on national and defense space policies, bilateral confidence-building activities can occur at the working level. One such example are the forthcoming exchanges between American and Russian space launch and military satellite movement control specialists, which are occurring as part of a broader set of military-to-military activities under the U.S.-Russia Interoperability Work Plan.

It is therefore with regret, Mr. Chairman, that I must note our disappointment that we were unable to reach agreement this year with Russia on a draft General Assembly resolution to examine the feasibility of new voluntary TCBMs. We had hoped that such a resolution could build upon the concrete proposals recently advanced by Russia and the European Union, as well as thoughtful suggestions from technical experts in the commercial space sector. Unfortunately, we could not reach agreement on a resolution that removes what the United States believes is a false and unacceptable linkage between expert assessments of pragmatic TCBMs and efforts to begin pointless negotiations on unverifiable space arms control agreements.

. . . [W]e shall welcome new opportunities for substantive discussions on outer space TCBMs with Russia, with other established and emerging space-faring nations, and with experts from civil society.

Mr. Chairman, the United States is a leader in the exploration of outer space, and we believe in strengthening international cooperation for the further use of and continued exploration of outer space. We are always prepared to discuss constructive proposals for measures that protect the outer space environment and protect free access to and use of space for the benefit of all. . . .

5. U.S.–France Framework Agreement

On January 23, 2007, the United States and France signed the Framework Agreement for Cooperative Activities in the Exploration and Use of Outer Space for Peaceful Purposes.

Article 1, "Scope of Activities," is set forth below. The full text of the framework agreement is available at *www.state.gov/s/l/c8183.htm*.

_____

1. The Parties shall identify areas of mutual interest and seek to develop cooperative activities in the exploration and peaceful uses of outer space and shall work closely together to this end.

2. These cooperative activities may be undertaken, as mutually agreed and subject to the provisions of this Framework Agreement (hereinafter "Agreement"), and the specific terms and conditions of Implementing Arrangements set forth pursuant to Article 2, in the following areas:

A. Exploration systems;
B. Space operations;
C. Earth observation and monitoring;
D. Science and space research; and
E. Other relevant areas as agreed between the Parties.

3. These cooperative activities may be implemented using:

A. Spacecraft and space research platforms;
B. Scientific instruments onboard spacecraft and space research platforms;
C. Sounding rocket and scientific balloon flights and campaigns;
D. Aircraft flights and campaigns;
E. Ground-based antennas for tracking and data acquisition;
F. Ground-based space research facilities;
G. Exchanges of scientific personnel;
H. Exchanges of scientific data;
I. Education and public outreach activities and;
J. Other forms of cooperation as agreed between the Parties.

4. These cooperative activities may take place on the surface of the Earth, in air space, or in outer space. The Parties intend that the activities will be performed on a cooperative basis involving no exchange of funds.

5. All cooperative activities under this Agreement shall be conducted in a manner consistent with the respective laws and regulations of each Party and in accordance with applicable international law.

6. This Agreement shall not apply to activities undertaken pursuant to the IGA or any subsequent agreement that modifies, or is concluded, pursuant to the IGA.

Cross References

Protocol to International Hydrographic Organization
        Convention, **Chapter 7.C.1.**
Transboundary harm, **Chapter 13.A.1.b.**

CHAPTER 13

Environment and Other Transnational Scientific Issues

A. ENVIRONMENT AND CONSERVATION

1. Land and Air Pollution and Related Issues

a. *Climate change*

(1) *Meeting of major economies*

On May 31, 2007, President George W. Bush announced U.S. support for an effort to develop a new framework on climate change to follow the 2012 goals of the Kyoto Protocol, to which the United States is not a party. As explained in a fact sheet released by the White House on May 31, 2007, concerning the President's proposed plan:

> . . . The plan recognizes that it is essential that a new framework include both major developed and developing economies that generate the majority of greenhouse gas emissions and consume the most energy, and that climate change must be addressed in a way that enhances energy security and promotes economic growth.
>
> Under the President's proposal, the United States will convene the major emitters and energy consumers to advance and complete the new framework by the end of 2008.

- The U.S. remains committed to the UN Framework Convention on Climate Change, and we expect the new framework to complement ongoing UN activity.
- The President's proposal breaks new ground in advancing areas of common interest between developed countries and the major emerging economies.
- The effort will build on and advance U.S. relations with the Asia-Pacific Partnership on Clean Development and Climate and other technology and bilateral partnerships.

The President's proposal is based on the principle that climate change must be addressed by fostering both energy security and economic security, by accelerating the development and deployment of transformational clean energy technologies.

- The participants will develop parallel national commitments to promote key clean energy technologies.
- The proposal seeks to bring together the world's top greenhouse gas emitters and energy consumers.
- In creating a new framework, the major emitters will work together to develop a long-term global goal to reduce greenhouse gasses.
- Each country will work to achieve this emissions goal by establishing its own ambitious mid-term national targets and programs, based on national circumstances.
- They will ensure advancement towards the global goal with a review process that assesses each country's performances.

*   *   *   *

The full text of the fact sheet is available at *www.state.gov/g/oes/rls/or/85843.htm*.

On September 28, 2007, the Department of State hosted the first major economies meeting on energy security and climate. A statement by President Bush at the meeting, excerpted below, is available at 43 WEEKLY COMP. PRES. DOC. 1261 (Oct. 1, 2007).

A fact sheet released by the White House on the same date is available at *www.whitehouse.gov/news/releases/2007/09/20070928-1.html.*

---

* * * *

Energy security and climate change are two of the great challenges of our time. The United States takes these challenges seriously. The world's response will help shape the future of the global economy and the condition of our environment for future generations. The nations in this room have special responsibilities. We represent the world's major economies, we are major users of energy, and we have the resources and knowledge base to develop clean energy technologies.

Our guiding principle is clear: We must lead the world to produce fewer greenhouse gas emissions, and we must do it in a way that does not undermine economic growth or prevent nations from delivering greater prosperity for their people. We know this can be done. Last year America grew our economy while also reducing greenhouse gases. Several other nations have made similar strides.

. . . With the work we begin today, we can agree on a new approach that will reduce greenhouse gas emissions, strengthen energy security, encourage economic growth and sustainable development, and advance negotiations under the United Nations Framework Convention on Climate Change.

* * * *

Th[e] growing demand for energy is a sign of a vibrant, global economy. Yet it also possesses—poses serious challenges, and one of them, of course, is energy security. Right now much of the world's energy comes from oil, and much of the oil comes from unstable regions and rogue states. This dependence leaves the global economy vulnerable to supply shocks and shortages and manipulation, and to extremists and terrorists who could cause great disruptions of oil shipments.

Another challenge is climate change. Our understanding of climate change has come a long way. A report issued earlier this year by the U.N. Intergovernmental Panel on Climate Change concluded both that global temperatures are rising and that this is caused largely by human activities. When we burn fossil fuels we release greenhouse gases into the atmosphere, and the concentration of greenhouse gases has increased substantially.

For many years those who worried about climate change and those who worried about energy security were on opposite ends of the debate. It was said that we faced a choice between protecting the environment and producing enough energy. Today we know better. These challenges share a common solution: technology. By developing new low-emission technologies, we can meet the growing demand for energy and at the same time reduce air pollution and greenhouse gas emissions. As a result, our nations have an opportunity to leave the debates of the past behind, and reach a consensus on the way forward. And that's our purpose today. . . .

*   *   *   *

This new approach must involve all the world's largest producers of greenhouse gas emissions, including developed and developing nations. We will set a long-term goal for reducing global greenhouse gas emissions. By setting this goal, we acknowledge there is a problem. And by setting this goal, we commit ourselves to doing something about it.

By next summer, we will convene a meeting of heads of state to finalize the goal and other elements of this approach, including a strong and transparent system for measuring our progress toward meeting the goal we set. This will require concerted effort by all our nations. Only by doing the necessary work this year will it be possible to reach a global consensus at the U.N. in 2009.

Each nation will design its own separate strategies for making progress toward achieving this long-term goal. These strategies will reflect each country's different energy resources, different stages of development, and different economic needs.

There are many policy tools that nations can use, including a variety of market mechanisms, to create incentives for companies and consumers to invest in new low-emission energy sources. We will also form working groups with leaders of different sectors of our economies, which will discuss ways of sharing technology and best practices.

Each nation must decide for itself the right mix of tools and technologies to achieve results that are measurable and environmentally effective. While our strategies may be differentiated, we share a common responsibility to reduce greenhouse gas emissions while keeping our economies growing.

* * * *

We must also work to make [clean energy] technologies more widely available, especially in the developing world. So today I propose that we join together to create a new international clean technology fund. This fund will be supported by contributions from governments from around the world, and it will help finance clean energy projects in the developing world. I've asked Treasury Secretary Hank Paulson to coordinate this effort, and he plans to begin exploratory discussions with your countries over the next several months.

At the same time, we also must promote global free trade in energy technology. The most immediate and effective action we can take is to eliminate tariff and non-tariff barriers on clean energy goods and services.

As we work to transform the way we produce energy, we must also address another major factor in climate change, which is deforestation. The world's forests help reduce the amount of greenhouse gases in the atmosphere by storing carbon dioxide. But when our forests disappear, the concentration of greenhouse gas levels rise in the atmosphere. Scientists estimate that nearly 20 percent of the world's greenhouse gas [e]missions are attributable to deforestation.

We're partnering with other nations to promote forest conservation and management across the world. We welcome new commitments from Australia, Brazil, with China and Indonesia. The United States remains committed to initiatives such as the Congo Basin Forest Partnership and the Asian Forest Partnership. We will continue our efforts through the Tropical Forest Conservation Act, which helps developing nations redirect debt payments toward forest conservation programs. So far my administration has concluded 12 agreements, [covering] up to 50 million acres of forest lands.

America's efforts also include an $87-million initiative to help developing nations stop illegal logging. These efforts will help developing nations save their forests, and combat a major source of greenhouse gas emissions.

The United States is also taking steps to protect forests in our own country. . . .

*   *   *   *

We have seen what happens when we come together to work for a common cause, and we can do it again. And that's what I'm here to urge you. The United States will do our part. We take this issue seriously. And we look forward to bringing a spirit of cooperation and commitment to our efforts to confront the challenges of energy security and climate change. By working together, we will set wise and effective policies. . . .

*   *   *   *

(2) UN Framework Convention on Climate Change: Conference of the Parties

The United States participated in the Thirteenth Session of the Conference of the Parties to the UN Framework Convention on Climate Change in Bali, Indonesia, December 3–14, 2007. In a December 3 statement to the press on behalf of the U.S. delegation, Dr. Harlan L. Watson, Senior Climate Negotiator and Special Representative and Alternate Head of the U.S. Delegation, addressed the U.S. position at the outset of the conference as excerpted below. The full text of Dr. Watson's remarks is available at *www.state.gov/g/oes/rls/rm/2007/96155.htm*.

. . . First, I want to say that the United States is committed to advancing negotiations and developing a "Bali Roadmap" that will guide the negotiations on a new post-2012 global climate change regime that is environmentally effective and economically sustainable. We are also committed to the successful completion of these negotiations by the end of 2009.

What do we mean by a new post-2012 global climate change regime that is environmentally effective and economically sustainable?

First, emissions are global and the response, to be environmentally effective, will need to be global. It needs to include the United States and all the world's largest producers of greenhouse gas emissions, developed and developing countries alike, while respecting national circumstances.

Second, the new regime must be economically sustainable and promote, not inhibit, the legitimate aspirations of nations and people everywhere for sustainable economic growth, energy security, and clean air. Energy is a key driver of economic growth and global energy demand is anticipated to rise by more than 50 percent by 2030, with most of that increase coming from the developing world as nations build infrastructure and improve the economic welfare of their citizens. We need to accelerate cost-effective development and adoption of advanced technologies that could fundamentally alter the way we produce and consume energy—such as carbon capture and storage, nuclear power, biofuels, and others—by providing incentives and by making large investments in technology. The United States and Japan lead the world in this effort and we need other countries to do the same.

*   *   *   *

I also want to highlight three other issues—forestry, adaptation, and technology access—that are key issues to be discussed here in Bali.

Avoided deforestation is a priority for Indonesia and many other developing countries, and it will be a focus of discussions in Bali. The United States is an international leader in promoting forest conservation. . . .

Adaptation is an increasing priority both at home and internationally, and we are promoting effective planning as part of broader development strategies. The United States is also leading efforts such as the Global Earth Observation System of Systems, which gives communities early warning of natural disasters, and improves decision-making for agriculture, coastal development and other economic sectors that are affected by climate variability and change.

And, to accelerate the uptake of clean energy technologies around the world, President Bush has proposed a new international clean technology fund. Secretary of the Treasury Paulson is working with international partners in developing a new approach for spurring investments in the global energy infrastructure that reduce greenhouse gas emissions.

*   *   *   *

Question: You said you had to include developed and developing countries. Could you please elaborate on that? Are you pushing for mandatory cuts from developing countries?

Dr. Watson: No, we realize that developing countries have to grow their economies in order to lift millions, hundreds of millions of people around the world out of poverty, and of course, provide the general economic growth that all countries require. We need economic growth to afford the very expensive technologies. We really need to revamp our entire global energy system. And that is going to require hundreds of billions of dollars—trillions, over the coming years. And so in order to afford that, we are obviously going to have to have economic growth worldwide. We certainly respect all countries' need to have economic growth, particularly in developing countries. That is going to require energy . . . obviously increased energy use, given that we are fossil fuel-based at this time and do not have alternative technologies yet in place. That is definitely going to mean that emissions are going to grow from developing countries in order to maintain their economic growth. We accept that. What we would like is to work with developing countries to help them to make that transition so at least they can bend over their emissions pathway. We fully expect that their emissions are going to increase over the coming years, but again, we hope to first slow down that growth and, as in the United States, hopefully stop it and then reverse. That is simply the path that the world is going to have to take.

*   *   *   *

On December 6, 2007, James Connaughton, Chairman of the White House Council on Environmental Quality, and Paula Dobriansky, Under Secretary of State for Democracy and Global Affairs, held a press briefing before their departure for the Bali meeting. Brief excerpts follow; the full text is available at *http://fpc.state.gov/fpc/96485.htm*.

*   *   *   *

Under Secretary Dobriansky: . . . We want a successful outcome in Bali. The United States is committed to developing a new global post-2012 framework that is environmentally effective and economically sustainable. And toward that end, in Bali we will work with our partners to reach a consensus on a Bali road map that will advance negotiations on a post-2012 framework under the UN Framework Convention on Climate Change. And we're recommitted to concluding these negotiations by 2009.

At a recent pre-Bali ministerial that was held in Bogor, Indonesia, the ministers assembled and talked about the areas to be addressed in the post-2012 framework, and I'd like to share those with you.

In four substantive areas there was a consensus that emerged around what we'd like to see in a Bali road map, including mitigation, adaptation, financing, and technology. We support all of these four areas. In fact adaptation is a particular priority for the United States.

During these pre-discussions, many developing countries spoke to this issue and their strong desire to have not only adaptation discussed, but also to have specific efforts, initiatives, programs that would support adaptation. These are efforts, I will give you one example, like the United States has put forward the Global Earth Observation System of Systems in which, with over some 70 countries, we have tried to advance technologies, standardized ways of forecasting climatic change and dealing with climate change.

Just recently, a few days ago, there was a meeting in Cape Town, South Africa, specifically of the Global Earth Observation System of Systems, and which the intent was to come forward with some recommendations to feed into Bali.

We also will work to advance discussions on forestry, together with land use, which accounts for some 20 percent of greenhouse gas emissions.

*   *   *   *

Mr. Connaughton: Bali will be, we hope, the start of a very intensive negotiating process. We are planning a very significant series of meetings following Bali to advance the effort and fill out the details of the elements that the participants in Bali agree to as far as a negotiating agenda. One of the tools will be the major economies process which started in September of this year over at the State Department in Washington, and this is the bringing together of leader representatives, my counterparts in other governments, to see if we can reach agreement on the major components of a new framework going forward, and begin to think through some of the content of that in order to bring a more substantial package of recommendations and ideas into the UN process. So we'll be doing that pretty aggressively through the early part of next year.

We're pleased that [Executive Secretary of UN Framework Convention on Climate Change] Yvo de Boer . . . featured the major economies process in his speech at the beginning of the Bali conference as one of the significant developments of 2007, the opportunity it will bring to help contribute to the UN negotiating process. . . .

*   *   *   *

Just so you know what's on our agenda in the major economies, we're trying to work toward agreement on a long-term global goal for reducing emissions. We want to draw forward national plans to include mid-term goals and specific national strategies for achieving mid-term goals. We anticipate those would include binding components, market-based components, incentives, and other policy measures.

We want a global effort on the key priorities for addressing emissions. They are coal, cars, and forests. They are efficiency, nuclear power, and renewable power. Six big categories of activity that require global focus.

We are also committed to enhanced financing for the investment in clean energy technologies, and that has two pieces. Secretary of Treasury Hank Paulson has already begun discussions with other countries on the creation of an International Clean Energy Fund. I think there will be further discussion of how to shape that in Bali and beyond. And then U.S. Trade Representative Schwab has already delivered a proposal to the WTO in partnership with the EU on the elimination of tariff barriers and non-tariff barriers for climate change and clean energy-related technologies and services. We hope that that will also receive some significant discussion in Bali, so those are well under development.

With respect to forestry, we have a package of initiatives that are currently part of our 2008 budget. We're waiting on Congress to give us that budget as we are now approaching well into the fiscal year for 2008. Then we'll be discussing issues related to adaptation, a broad agenda on adaptation, and we will also be discussing a lot of ideas about a broad agenda for a future framework that focuses on key sectors. . . .

Question: . . . I was wondering what you think the appropriate forum . . . would be for the actual negotiation. . . . Do you think we actually need a major economies meeting, or a new ad hoc working group, or something else?

Mr. Connaughton: The United Nations is the appropriate forum for negotiations on climate change. These related activities are all in support of that process. Quite typical in a UN negotiation, smaller groups get together on particular views to try to advance the agenda and do some of the early work that is then brought to all the parties.

We are part of the UN Framework Convention on Climate Change. It's a treaty we've ratified and we have been fulfilling our obligations under that treaty. That's a common platform for all of us.

Under Secretary Dobriansky: . . . There have been other mechanisms which will assist and contribute to the advancement of these negotiations and that's where, for example, the [major] [e]conomies meeting comes in and also in the G8. Specifically targeting and addressing different issues that need to be developed further and discussed in greater detail.

*   *   *   *

On December 15, 2007, the United States joined consensus on the Decision of the Conference of the Parties for proceeding with negotiations, referred to as the Bali Plan of Action. A statement released on the same date by the White House Press Secretary provided the views of the United States on the decision, including certain concerns related to the principle of common but differentiated responsibilities. The full text of the press statement is available at *www.whitehouse. gov/news/releases/2007/12/20071215-1.html.*

* * * *

The United States joins the consensus Decision of the Conference of the Parties in Bali that is a critical first step in assuring that the UN negotiation process moves forward toward a comprehensive and effective post-2012 arrangement.

There are many features of the Decision that are quite positive, including those provisions recognizing the importance of developing clean technologies, financing the deployment of those technologies in the developing world, assisting countries in adapting to climate change, exploring industry sector agreements on emissions, and addressing deforestation.

The United States does have serious concerns about other aspects of the Decision as we begin the negotiations. Notably, the United States believes that, in three important ways, we have not yet fully given effect to the principle of common but differentiated responsibilities that is a pillar of the UN Framework Convention on Climate Change.

First, the negotiations must proceed on the view that the problem of climate change cannot be adequately addressed through commitments for emissions cuts by developed countries alone. Major developing economies must likewise act. Just as the work of the IPCC has deepened our scientific understanding of the scope of the problem and action required, so too empirical studies on emission trends in the major developing economies now conclusively establish that emissions reductions principally by the developed world will be insufficient to confront the global problem effectively.

Second, negotiations must clearly differentiate among developing countries in terms of the size of their economies, their level of emissions and level of energy utilization, and sufficiently link the character or extent of responsibility to such factors. We must give sufficient emphasis to the important and appropriate role that the larger emitting developing countries should play in a global effort to address climate change.

Third, the negotiations must adequately distinguish among developing countries by recognizing that the responsibilities of the smaller or least developed countries are different from the larger, more advanced developing countries. In our view, such smaller and less developed countries are entitled to receive more differentiated treatment so as to more truly reflect their special needs and circumstances.

Accordingly, for these negotiations to succeed, it is essential that the major developed and developing countries be prepared to negotiate commitments, consistent with their national circumstances, that will make a due contribution to the reduction of global emissions. A post-2012 arrangement will be effective only if it reflects such contributions. At the same time, the United States believes that any arrangement must also take into account the legitimate right of the major developing economies and indeed all countries to grow their economies, develop on a sustainable basis, and have access to secure energy sources.

We have seen what can be accomplished when we come together to work for a common cause. Only by doing the necessary work this year will it be possible to reach a global consensus under the Convention in 2009. The United States looks forward to participating in the negotiations envisioned in the Bali Roadmap, in the Major Economies Process, in the G8 and in other appropriate channels in order to achieve a global and effective post-2012 arrangement.

b. Transboundary harm

(1) International Law Commission

On October 23, 2007, U.S. delegate James Donovan addressed the UN General Assembly Sixth Committee on Consideration of Prevention of Transboundary Harm from Hazardous Activities and Allocation of Loss in the Case of Such Harm in the report of the International Law Commission. The statement is set forth below and is available at *www.state.gov/s/l/c8183.htm.*

The United States welcomes the completion of the ILC's work on the prevention of transboundary harm and the allocation of loss from such harm.

As we stated last year, we believe that the principles on allocation of loss are a positive step toward encouraging states to establish mechanisms to provide prompt and adequate compensation for victims of transboundary harm. They incorporate progressive ideas such as the responsibility of operators, the desirability of backup financial security measures, the importance of prompt response measures, and broad concepts of compensable harm. They also stress the importance of national, bilateral, regional and sectoral arrangements to carry out these ideas.

Similarly, we believe that the draft articles on prevention are a positive step toward encouraging states to establish mechanisms to address such issues as notification in specific national and international contexts.

We continue to believe, however, that both the draft articles and draft principles go beyond the present state of international law and practice. It is therefore appropriate that the principles take the form of non-binding standards of conduct and practice and that the work on prevention was formulated as draft articles. We believe that both documents were designed to encourage national and international action in specific contexts, rather than form the basis of a global treaty. Thus, the United States opposes any efforts to reflect the draft principles on allocation of loss as mandatory or to convert them into a draft convention. For the same reasons, the United States opposes the elaboration of a global convention on prevention of transboundary harm.

In sum, the United States believes that the General Assembly should take note of the work on these topics and encourage states to use the articles and principles in context specific situations.

(2) Litigation concerning transboundary water pollution: Teck Cominco

In July 2006 the U.S. Court of Appeals for the Ninth Circuit denied a motion to dismiss a citizen suit seeking enforcement of a 2003 U.S. Environmental Protection Agency ("EPA") order against Teck Cominco Metals, Ltd. ("Teck"), a Canadian corporation. *Pakootas v. Teck Cominco Metals, Ltd.*, 452 F.3d 1066 (9th Cir. 2006). The order, under the Comprehensive Environmental Response, Compensation, and Liability Act ("CERCLA"), 42 U.S.C. §§ 9601–9675, directed Teck to conduct a remedial investigation/feasibility study of a section of the Columbia River in the United States where hazardous substances disposed of by Teck in Canada have come to rest. Among other things, the Ninth Circuit rejected Teck's allegation that CERCLA had been applied extraterritorially in the case, finding the EPA to have applied the statute domestically "even though the original source of the hazardous substances is located in a foreign country." The court also found that although the EPA and Teck had entered into a settlement agreement in 2006 in which the EPA agreed to withdraw the order at issue, the agreement did not render the action moot because neither Pakootas nor the State of Washington were party to the agreement. *See Digest 2006* at 855–60 for further discussion of the court of appeals decision and the settlement.

Teck filed a petition for writ of certiorari with the Supreme Court, and the Supreme Court invited the views of the United States. 127 S. Ct. 2930 (2007). In its brief as *amicus curiae* filed in November 2007, the United States argued that the Supreme Court should not grant review of the case for two reasons: (1) further proceedings on remand could shed significant light on the validity of respondents' claims because EPA's withdrawal of the administrative order pursuant to the settlement agreement rendered moot the claims that had been considered, and additional claims recently added should be heard in the first instance by the lower courts; and (2) the questions presented did not merit review because the issue was one of first impression, and the comity concerns invoked by the petitioner were unusually weak.

Further excerpts below summarize CERCLA and provide the U.S. views on its applicability in these circumstances (most citations to other submissions have been omitted). The full text of the *amicus* brief is available at *www.usdoj.gov/osg/ briefs/2007/2pet/6invit/2006-1188.pet.ami.inv.html.*

On January 7, 2008, the Supreme Court denied certiorari. *Teck Cominco Metals, Ltd. v. Pakootas*, 127 S. Ct. 2930 (2008).

*   *   *   *

STATEMENT

1. . . . A party is generally liable under CERCLA if there was a release or threatened release of a hazardous substance from a facility and the defendant falls within the definition of an owner or operator, past owner or operator, arranger, or transporter. 42 U.S.C. 9607(a).

2. Petitioner is a Canadian corporation that operates the world's largest zinc and lead smelter in Trail, British Columbia, approximately ten miles north of the United States border. For 90 years, from 1906 until 1995, petitioner's smelter discharged up to 145,000 tons of slag annually (13 million tons total) into the Columbia River. That river flows directly into the United States. Pet. App. 4a–5a, 72a.

*   *   *   *

DISCUSSION

*   *   *   *

Even setting aside the procedural impediments to this Court's review, the petition presents a question of first impression that should be permitted to percolate in the lower courts and that lacks sufficient importance to warrant this Court's review at this time.

1. Petitioner does not assert a conflict among the circuits on the first question presented (involving international comity), and indeed does not identify any other decisions addressing that question. The fact that the comity question in this case is apparently arising now for the first time, notwithstanding the decades-old potential for disputes concerning cross-border pollution, strongly suggests that it lacks the recurring importance that petitioner attributes to it.

As a practical matter, the United States has dealt with international pollution issues in a variety of ways. First, as it did here, the United States often attempts to achieve diplomatic solutions to transborder pollution issues.[2] Second, in disputes with Canada, the United States has discretion to seek advice or dispute resolution under the Treaty Between the United States and Great Britain Relating to Boundary Waters Between the United States and Canada, Jan. 11, 1909, Arts. IX, X, 36 Stat. 2448, 2452, 2453, and has sought such advice jointly with Canada in the past, though the treaty does not require the United States to do so. See *Ohio v. Wyandotte Chems. Corp.*, 401 U.S. 493, 507 (1971) (Douglas, J., dissenting). Third, there has been some litigation of transborder pollution disputes in the United States courts. See, e.g., *Her Majesty the Queen in Right of Ont. v. United States EPA*, 912 F.2d 1525 (D.C. Cir. 1990); *Michie v. Great Lakes Steel Div., Nat'l Steel Corp.*, 495 F.2d 213 (6th Cir.), cert. denied, 419 U.S. 997 (1974).

In practice, therefore, issues have been resolved satisfactorily in various ways, without the need for a definitive resolution of the comity question. The order issued to petitioner represents the only time in the 27 years since CERCLA's enactment that EPA has sought to compel a foreign party to take a response action with respect to domestic pollution resulting from actions in a foreign country, and EPA has now withdrawn that order. The United States is aware of only one other effort (by private parties) to apply CERCLA in an international setting, and the Ninth Circuit correctly rejected that effort because the facility was outside of the United States. See *ARC Ecology v. United States Dep't of the Air Force*, 411 F.3d 1092 (2005).

2. The court of appeals' decision does not "threaten[ ] to disrupt our ties with Canada." Because this case involves a direct and compelling United States interest, an assertion of jurisdiction to prescribe law would be consistent with considerations of international comity. Indeed, the Province of British Columbia recognizes that, "to the extent [petitioner] is responsible for polluting the

---

[2] EPA attempted to negotiate with Canada regarding a study of cross-border pollution on the Columbia River, but negotiations broke down. The United States also involved Canada in developing the settlement agreement with petitioner, and agreed to give Canada an enhanced consultative role in the remedial investigation process. A representative of the Canadian government has been actively participating in technical discussions related to that process.

Columbia River, it may be required to contribute to the cleanup costs." While Canada and British Columbia would prefer to resolve this dispute through diplomatic channels and negotiation rather than litigation in United States courts—a preference the United States strongly shares—Canada correctly "recognizes the possibility that some cases involving transboundary pollution may appropriately be resolved in the domestic courts of Canada or the United States."

Canada argues that the court of appeals erred by "not even acknowledg[ing], let alone analyz[ing], the relevant factors for determining whether a state may reasonably prescribe laws with respect 'to a person or activity having connections with another state.'" Can. Amicus Br. 13 (quoting Restatement (Third) of Foreign Relations Law of the United States § 403(1), at 244 (1987) (Restatement)). Assuming *arguendo* that the Restatement analysis is relevant, however, it only confirms that comity concerns would not preclude an assertion of jurisdiction to prescribe in the circumstances of this case. According to the Restatement, "a state has jurisdiction to prescribe law with respect to * * * conduct outside its territory that has or is intended to have substantial effect within its territory." *Id.* § 402(1)(c) at 227–228. The Restatement provides, however, that a state may not exercise such jurisdiction in situations where it would be "unreasonable" to do so. *Id.* § 403(1), at 244. The Restatement illustrates its approach by explaining that assertion of jurisdiction based on domestic effects is "not controversial with respect to acts such as shooting * * * across a boundary." *Id.* § 402 cmt. d at 239. Indeed, "[t]he traditional example" is that "when a malefactor in State *A* shoots a victim across the border in State *B*, State *B* can proscribe the harmful conduct." *Laker Airways Ltd.* v. *Sabena, Belgian World Airlines*, 731 F.2d 909, 922 (D.C. Cir. 1984).

Here, petitioner's deliberate, 90-year discharge of millions of tons of hazardous substances into a river just upstream from the United States directly and foreseeably caused harmful effects in the United States. Petitioner's conduct could arguably be analogized in some respects to firing a gun across the border, because it was inevitable that the river would carry the pollution directly into the United States. Moreover, the slag at the bottom and on the beaches of the Columbia River is clearly identifiable and directly attributable to petitioner's actions.[3]

Petitioner contends that the court of appeals' decision paves the way for suits over trans-oceanic pollution such as acid rain or mercury from Asia. Distant sources that contribute to widespread and diffuse air pollution, however, present a much different case from this one, and are in no way analogous to the "traditional example" (*Laker Airways*, 731 F.2d at 922) of a gun being fired across a border. Thus, it would not necessarily follow from the assertion of jurisdiction in this case that the courts of the United States would exercise jurisdiction in the cases posited by petitioner. Moreover, this Nation's courts might lack personal jurisdiction in those cases. . . .

*   *   *   *

c. Mercury contamination

On February 6, 2007, Daniel A. Reifsnyder, Deputy Assistant Secretary of State for Environment, addressed the Committee of the Whole Governing Council, United Nations Environment Programme meeting in Nairobi, Kenya. In discussing the proposals concerning the risk associated with mercury contamination globally, Mr. Reifsnyder commented as follows concerning U.S. opposition to consideration of a new treaty on the issue. The full text is available at *www.state.gov/g/oes/ rls/rm/2007/87656.htm*.

*   *   *   *

My delegation has long opposed efforts to negotiate a legally-binding agreement on mercury for several elemental reasons:

First, we believe that partnerships, if properly supported, are both more welcome and more effective than legally binding mandates

---

3   The position of the United States is that the reasonableness test set forth in the Restatement does not restrict the United States' jurisdiction to prescribe. Nonetheless, that test, which Canada invoked, confirms that considerations of comity would not preclude an assertion of jurisdiction to prescribe in the circumstances of this case.

and better reflect that many problems remain unsolved, not because of a lack of will, but because of a lack of means, both technical and financial, to tackle them.

Partnerships enable us to take action now in cooperation with countries across the globe to make specific, near-term progress, actually reducing mercury uses and releases to the environment in real time.

Second, there has been much concern with the proliferation of multilateral environmental agreements and with the problems many countries, particularly developing countries and economies in transition, have experienced with an increasing multitude of treaties, each with its own meeting schedule, reporting requirements and drain on scarce expert resources. Some have suggested that these resources could be better spent at home addressing real problems on the ground.

Third, a legally-binding instrument on mercury would necessarily create an entirely new international superstructure to address a single chemical—we do not believe that this is an efficient approach, notwithstanding our very real concerns about the risks of this chemical.

Fourth, we believe that calls to include other chemicals, such as lead and cadmium in such an effort ignore the very real differences between mercury on the one hand, for which there is an established problem of global transport, and lead and cadmium on the other hand for which there is not. In our view, there are other, more effective ways to address concerns about these chemicals such as through national or regional actions.

And fifth, if it is proposed not to create a new stand-alone MEA to address mercury but instead to amend existing ones, then this—the UNEP Governing Council— is not the forum in which to have that discussion.

*   *   *   *

d. Aviation emission controls

On April 6, 2007, the United States, Australia, Canada, China, Japan, and South Korea transmitted a joint letter to the

European Union urging EU Member States and EU representatives to "reconsider the [European] Commission's unilateral proposal" to include international civil aviation in the EU Emission Trading Scheme. The text of the letter is set forth below and available at *www.state.gov/s/l/c8183.htm.*

Our governments share with the Member States of the European Union an interest in finding approaches to limit the impact of aviation greenhouse gas emissions on global climate. As you know, the member states of the International Civil Aviation Organization (ICAO), including the EU Member States, agreed to broad goals in this area at the triennial ICAO Assembly in 2004. We believe that success in addressing this matter lies in constructive consultation with international partners, a foundation of the international aviation system.

From this point of view, we want to convey our deep concern and strong dissatisfaction with the December 20, 2006, European Commission proposal to include international civil aviation in the European Union (EU) Emission Trading Scheme (ETS). Inclusion of our airlines in the EU scheme without the consent of our governments would potentially violate EU Member State international obligations under the Convention on International Civil Aviation, as well as bilateral aviation agreements.

Moreover, the proposal runs counter to the international consensus that ICAO should address international aviation emissions. ICAO is in fact doing so now. The ICAO Assembly in 2004 urged "States to refrain from unilateral environmental measures" and the ICAO Council echoed this in November 2006, urging Contracting States to "refrain from unilateral action to implement an emissions trading system." We are disappointed that the Commission has ignored the strong objections from the international community and is bypassing ICAO by issuing this proposal.

We support ICAO's current work to develop guidance on emissions trading for use by countries that wish to pursue this market-based approach based on mutual consent. We also believe real opportunities for addressing emissions exist in broader cooperative approaches to aviation operations including energy efficiency and traffic management. In addition, some developing countries believe that the EU's unilateral inclusion of developing country airlines is also of concern in relation to the Framework Convention's principle of common, but differentiated, responsibilities and respective capabilities. Obviously, Europe is free to include emissions from European aircraft in its trading system. However, the Commission proposal to include third-country carriers unilaterally would significantly undercut rather than support international efforts to carry out improvements to better manage the impact of aviation emissions. We urge you to consider fully the concerns of the international community and to exclude operations of non-European aircraft from the scope of the EU Emission Trading Scheme, unless they are included on the basis of mutual consent. If the EU insists on moving forward unilaterally, we reserve our rights to take appropriate measures under international law.

We ask EU Member States and EU representatives to participate continuously and constructively toward finalizing ICAO guidelines on aviation emissions and to reconsider the Commission's unilateral proposal. It is our hope that by these efforts we can move forward in a manner that will lead to a successful global solution to address aviation emissions.

> On September 22, 2007, Andrew Steinberg, U.S. Assistant Secretary of Transportation for Aviation and International Affairs, addressed the ICAO Executive Committee on agenda item 17, concerning aviation emissions, stating that the United States supported a comprehensive approach to addressing aircraft emissions and the issuing of guidance on emissions trading systems based on the mutual consent of the countries concerned. The full text of Mr. Steinberg's statement, excerpted below, is available at *http://useu.usmission. gov/Dossiers/AviationSep2207_Steinberg_ICAO.asp*   and *www.state.gov/s/l/c8183.htm*.

---

* * * *

. . . [W]e all recognize the need to address international aviation's contribution to greenhouse gas emissions. The question at hand is not if, but how we go about doing so—whether we do so in a way consistent with ICAO's mission and international law, based on sound science, and with tangible and measurable results that allow aviation to grow.

*   *   *   *

The U.S. pioneered emissions trading as a way to deal with pollution. But we have decided that emissions trading does not make sense for our domestic aviation sector, partly because we know that any scheme that raises ticket prices will drive passengers away from the airlines and onto the highways in their cars, which is far worse for the environment. . . .

*   *   *   *

Any system that appoints the regulators of one state as the administrators of a charging scheme affecting operators in another state is, of course, inherently subject to competitive manipulation. Under the EU plan, each non-EU airline's participation will be regulated by the so called "administering state," which is wherever it flies the most. . . .

*   *   *   *

. . . Let me be clear. The U.S. has no desire to prevent the EU or any other entity from choosing its own policies, including emissions trading, for its own domestic industry. We welcome the European commission first implementing [a] trading scheme for its carriers in domestic markets and then bringing any lessons back into ICAO.

But the United States, like the vast majority of states assembled here, has repeatedly said that emissions trading schemes covering international aviation can only proceed with the consent of the states involved. That is why in 2004 the assembly decided that states should refrain from unilateral action. This is an issue of state rights under the Chicago Convention. It is not something that should be traded away for political reasons. That convention is clear on this point: no state may condition the right of transit over or entry into or exit from its territory of any aircraft of another state on their operator's payment of fees, dues, or other charges. That is precisely what a mandatory program of emissions permits does.

It has been suggested that developing countries need not be concerned about the EU ETS plan because they will be protected by the notion of "common but differentiated responsibilities." This is misleading. There is no way an emissions trading scheme that exempts developing countries can be applied under the Chicago Convention without violating its principle of non-discrimination. The Chicago Convention and [UN Framework Convention on Climate Change ("UNFCCC")] are separate legal instruments, and one does not prevail over the other. Thus agreeing to accept the unilateral imposition of such a scheme on the hope that it will never apply to you is wishful thinking at best.

* * * *

We recognize the importance of acknowledging "common but differentiated responsibilities" under the Kyoto protocol and UNFCCC. While doing so, we must also ensure strong international opposition to unilateral action.

Mr. President, the U.S. is committed to finding a way forward on this issue based on collaboration, pragmatism, and factual information. The U.S. supports this assembly adopting the proposed resolution providing a comprehensive approach to addressing emissions. We strongly support the issuance of guidance on emissions trading requiring mutual consent and we look forward to productive conversations over the coming days. We believe multilateral action is the best path toward finding solutions that will facilitate sustainable aviation growth.

> At its 36th meeting, in Montreal, September 18–28, 2007, the ICAO Assembly adopted Resolution A36-22, "Consolidated statement of continuing ICAO policies and practices related to environmental protection." In Appendix L to Resolution A36-22, "Market-based measures, including emissions trading," the Assembly, among other things, requested the Council to "finalize and keep up-to-date . . . the guidance developed by ICAO for incorporating emissions from international aviation into Contracting States' emissions trading schemes consistent with the UNFCCC process." It also "[u]rge[d] Contracting States to refrain from unilateral implementation of greenhouse gas emissions charges" and "not to implement an emissions

trading system on other Contracting State[s'] aircraft operators except on the basis of mutual agreement between those
States." The full text of the Resolutions Adopted by the
Assembly is available at *www.icao.int/icao/en/assembl/a36/
docs/A36_res_prov_en.pdf.*

e. Ozone depletion

The 19th meeting of the parties to the Montreal Protocol on
Substances That Deplete the Ozone Layer ("Montreal
Protocol") took place in Montreal from September 17–21,
2007. In negotiations on the issue of an accelerated freeze
and phase-out of hydrochlorofluorocarbons ("HCFCs") as an
adjustment to the protocol, the United States strongly advocated for an aggressive schedule of reductions. At the conclusion of the meeting, the parties agreed to a reduction although
it was not as aggressive as that proposed by the United States.
See fact sheet on the adjustment providing a comparison of
old and new commitments, available at *http://ozone.unep.org/
Ratification_status/2007_Montreal_adjustments_on_
hcfcs.shtml.* The text of the U.S. proposal is set forth in UNEP/
OzL.Pro.SG.1/27/8/Rev.2 (March 16, 2007), pp. 12–15, available at *http://ozone.unep.org/Meeting_Documents/oewg/
27oewg/OEWG-27-8Rv2E.pdf.*
    A statement for the press described the results as
excerpted below. The full text is available at *http://ozone.unep.
org/Publications/PressReleaseFinal-22Sept2007.pdf. See also*
fact sheet on the adjustment providing a comparison of old
and new commitments, available at *http://ozone.unep.org/
Ratification_status/2007_Montreal_adjustments_on_
hcfcs.shtml.*

*   *   *   *

The decision, including an agreement that sufficient funding will
be made available to achieve the strategy, follows mounting evidence that HCFCs contribute to global warming.

HCFCs emerged as replacement chemicals in the 1990s for [use] in air conditioning, some forms of refrigeration equipment and foams following an earlier decision to phase out older and more ozone-damaging chemicals known as CFCs or chlorofluorocarbons. Governments meeting in the Canadian city agreed at the close to freeze production of HCFCs in 2013 and bring forward the final phase-out date of these chemicals by ten years.

The acceleration may also assist in restoring the health of the ozone layer—the high flying gas that filters out damaging levels of ultra violet light—by a few years too. Achim Steiner, UN Under-Secretary General and UNEP Executive Director, praised the decision taken at the 20th anniversary celebrations of the Montreal Protocol calling it an 'important and quick win' for combating climate change.

"Historic is an often over-used word but not in the case of this agreement made in Montreal. Governments had a golden opportunity to deal with the twin challenges of climate change and protecting the ozone layer—and governments took it. The precise and final savings in terms of greenhouse gas emissions could amount to several billions of tonnes illustrating the complementarities of international environmental agreements," he said.

* * * *

The Agreement on HCFCS

HCFCs, which also damage the ozone layer but less than CFCs, were always planned as interim substitutes and were due to be phased out in 2030 by developed countries and in 2040 by developing ones.

However in recent years and months mounting evidence has emerged on the growth in HCFCs and the potentially significant benefits arising in terms of combating climate change and ozone loss if an accelerated freeze and accelerated phase-out could be achieved.

Experts estimate that without this week's agreement, production and consumption of HCFCs may have doubled by 2015 adding to the dual challenges of ozone depletion and climate change.

* * * *

The final agreement is a combination of the various options proposed by Argentina and Brazil; Norway and Switzerland; the

United States; Mauritania, Mauritius and the Federated States of Micronesia. Under the agreement, productions of HCFCs are to be frozen at the average production levels in 2009–2010 in 2013.

Developed countries have agreed to reduce production and consumption by 2010 by 75 per cent and by 90 per cent by 2015 with final phase out in 2020.

Developing countries have agreed to cut production and consumption by 10 per cent in 2015; by 35 per cent by 2020 and by 67.5 per cent by 2025 with a final phase-out in 2030.

It was also agreed that a small percentage of the original base line amounting to 2.5 per cent will be allowed in developing countries during the period 2030–2040 for 'servicing' purposes.

Essentially this means that some equipment, coming towards the end of its life such as office block air conditioning units, could continue to run on HCFCs for a few more years if needed.

The 191 Parties to the Montreal Protocol—190 countries plus the European Commission—also made an agreement on financing.

The Protocol's financial arm—the Multilateral Fund—which to date has spent over $2 billion to assist developing country reductions comes up for replenishment next year. The new agreement takes into account the need for 'stable and sufficient' funds and the fact that there may be 'incremental costs' for developing countries under the accelerated HCFC freeze and phase out.

Governments agreed here to commission a short study by experts to fully assess the likely costs of the acceleration. They will report back early in 2008 and inform parties on the suggested sums required for the new replenishment.

*   *   *   *

2. Protection of Marine Environment and Marine Conservation

a. *Marine pollution from dumping of wastes and other matter*

On September 4, 2007, President Bush transmitted the 1996 Protocol to the Convention on the Prevention of Marine Pollution by Dumping of Wastes and Other Matter ("London Convention"), done in London on November 7, 1996. The United States signed the protocol on March 31, 1998, and it entered into force internationally on March 24, 2006. President Bush's letter explained the importance of the protocol to the United States as excerpted below.

*   *   *   *

The Protocol represents the culmination of a thorough and intensive effort to update and improve the London Convention. The London Convention governs the ocean dumping and incineration at sea of wastes and other matter and was a significant early step in international protection of the marine environment from pollution caused by these activities.

Although the Protocol and the London Convention share many features, the Protocol is designed to protect the marine environment more effectively. The Protocol moves from a structure of listing substances that may not be dumped to a "reverse list" approach, which prohibits ocean dumping of all wastes or other matter, except for a few specified wastes. This approach is combined with detailed criteria for environmental assessment of those materials that may be considered for dumping and potential dumping sites.

The Protocol would be implemented through amendments to the Marine Protection, Research, and Sanctuaries Act (MPRSA), which currently covers London Convention obligations. There will not be any substantive changes to existing practices in the United States, and no economic impact is expected from implementation of the Protocol. I recommend that the Senate give early and favorable consideration to this Protocol and give its advice and consent to ratification with the declaration and understanding contained in Articles 3 and 10 respectively in the accompanying report of the Department of State.

Excerpts follow from the report of the Department of State, submitted to the President by Secretary of State Condoleezza Rice on April 2, 2007, and included in S. Treaty Doc. No.110-5, addressing Articles 4 and 10. The proposed conditions on ratification noted above concern dispute resolution aspects of those articles.

*   *   *   *

Article 4 (Dumping of Wastes and Other Matter)
Like Article IV of the London Convention. Article 4 implements
one of the core purposes of the Protocol, namely that Contracting
Parties are to prohibit the dumping of wastes or other matter without a permit. The London Convention and the Protocol differ,
however, in approach. Article IV of the London Convention
embodies what has come to be known as the "black list/gray list"
approach. Under this approach, wastes or other matter listed in
the London Convention's Annex I (the "black list") may not be
dumped except in emergency or *force majeure* situations; wastes
or other matter listed on Annex H (the "gray list") may only be
dumped if a special permit has been issued prior to dumping; and
wastes or other matter not listed in either of these two Annexes
require a general permit prior to dumping. Any permits for ocean
dumping may be issued only after careful consideration of the
factors listed in Annex III of the London Convention. Article 4
of the Protocol works differently in that a substance must be
included on, rather than excluded from, the Protocol's Annex I
list (the "reverse list") before issuance of a dumping permit may
be considered, Under paragraph 1.2, Parties are obliged to adopt
administrative or legislative measures to ensure that the issuance
of permits and permit conditions complies with the provisions
of Annex 2, which establishes a framework for evaluating the
acceptability of dumping material on the reverse list at Annex I.
There are currently eight types of wastes or other matter listed in
Annex I. It should be noted that the Parties to the Protocol, through
a process also involving observer States (including the United
States), adopted an addition to the Annex I list to permit sub-
seabed sequestration of carbon dioxide streams from carbon
dioxide capture processes. This amendment entered into force in
February 2007.

Article 4.2 of the Protocol provides that Parties to the Protocol
may prohibit the dumping of even those wastes or other matter
included on the reverse list at Annex I. This is similar to Article IV(3)
of the London Convention. Although sewage sludge is one of
the materials that may be considered for dumping under Annex I
of the Protocol, the MPRSA currently does not allow the ocean
dumping of sewage sludge from wastewater treatment plants.

The Executive branch will not seek to change this prohibition in the MPRSA.

Although Article 4 will not affect U.S. ocean dumping practice, amendments to the MPRSA will be sought to clarify that, except in emergency situations, only materials on the reverse list may be considered for dumping. The administrative and legislative measures already in place for ocean dumping permit applications in the United States implement the assessment criteria set forth in Annex 2.

*   *   *   *

Article 10 (Application and Enforcement)

Article 10 specifies the vessels, aircraft, and platforms or other man-made structures to which each Party is obliged to apply the measures required to implement the Protocol. It further clarifies the extent of each Party's responsibility to prevent and, if necessary, punish acts contrary to the Protocol. This article also addresses the Protocol's application to and enforcement against vessels and aircraft entitled to sovereign immunity under international law.

In large measure Article 10 repeats the provisions of Article VII of the London Convention although it builds on the coastal State authorities reflected in Articles 210(5) and 216 of the LOS Convention. Thus, Article 10.1.3 obliges coastal State Parties to apply the measures required to implement the Protocol to all vessels, aircraft, and platforms or other man-made structures believed to be engaged in dumping or incineration at sea in areas within which it is entitled to exercise jurisdiction in accordance with international law. Moreover, the "appropriate" enforcement measures to which Article 10.2 refers are to be determined in accordance with international law (e.g., as reflected in the LOS Convention). Thus, the MPRSA will have to be amended to include all covered dumping or incineration activity in the Exclusive Economic Zone and continental shelf. Currently, dumping by non-US vessels transporting material from outside the United States is regulated only when dumping material into the territorial sea or into the contiguous zone, to the extent that the dumping affects the territorial sea or the territory of the United States. Ocean dumping by vessels transporting material from the United States, or by vessels owned by or registered in the United States, will continue to be regulated wherever the dumping occurs (*see* MPRSA Section 101(a), 33 U.S.CA. § 1411(a)).

Like Article VII of the London Convention, Article 10.3 states that Parties agree to co-operate in the development of procedures for effective application of the Protocol in areas beyond national jurisdiction (i.e., the high seas), including procedures for the reporting of vessels and aircraft observed dumping or incinerating at sea in contravention of the Protocol.

Article 10.4, repeating verbatim Article VII(4) of the London Convention, exempts vessels and aircraft entitled to sovereign immunity under international law from coverage of the Protocol and provides that Parties take appropriate measures that such vessels and aircraft act in a manner consistent with the purpose of the Protocol. Further, a new provision, Article 10.5, allows a State to declare, at the time of ratification or accession or at any time thereafter, that it will apply the Protocol to its sovereign immune vessels and aircraft, recognizing that only that State may enforce the provisions of the Protocol with respect to such vessels and aircraft.

I do not recommend a formal declaration under Article 10.5, but the United States should make clear its understanding that the Protocol's dispute settlement procedures under Article 16 do not apply to the obligation to take appropriate measures to ensure that sovereign immune vessels and aircraft act in a manner consistent with the object and purpose of this Protocol. I therefore recommend that the United States notify the Secretary-General of the following understanding upon deposit of its instrument of ratification:

> The United States understands, in light of Article 10.4 of the Protocol, which provides that the Protocol "shall not apply to those vessels and aircraft entitled to sovereign immunity under international law," that disputes regarding the interpretation or application of the Protocol in relation to such vessels and aircraft are not subject to Article 16 of the Protocol.

*   *   *   *

b. Ballast water management convention

The International Convention for the Control and Management of Ships' Ballast Water and Sediments, adopted by the International Maritime Organization in 2004, includes Regulation B-3.3, which requires ships constructed in or after 2009 with a ballast water capacity of less than 5,000 cubic meters to conduct ballast water management in a way that at least meets a standard described in the Convention (Regulation D-2). Concerns were raised during 2007 that type-approved ballast water treatment technologies necessary for compliance with this regulation would not be immediately available for ships constructed in 2009, which in turn raised concerns that the potential lack of availability of technology would create an obstacle to ratification. Because the convention had not yet entered into force, its amendment procedure was not available to accommodate these concerns. The United States joined consensus in adopting a resolution in the IMO Assembly, "Application of the International Convention for the Control and Management of Ships' Ballast Water and Sediments, 2004," in order to remove the obstacles to ratification that such concerns presented. This resolution recommended that States henceforth ratifying, accepting, approving, or acceding to the Convention accompany their instrument of ratification, acceptance, approval, or accession as appropriate with a declaration, or otherwise notify the Secretary-General of their intention to apply the Convention, on the basis of the following understanding:

> A ship subject to regulation B-3.3 constructed in 2009 will not be required to comply with regulation D-2 until its second annual survey, but no later than 31 December 2011.

The resolution also recommended that Contracting States to the Convention make such a declaration or otherwise notify the Secretary-General of their intention to apply the Convention in accordance with the above understanding. The resolution recommended further that "following the entry into force of the Convention, Parties to the Convention ensure that ships affected by the understanding . . . comply with either regulation D-1 or D-2 until such time as regulation D-2 is enforced." The resolution is attached as Annex 5 to the Report of the Technical Committee to the Plenary, November 29, 2007, IMO Doc. A 25/5(b)2, available at *www.state.gov/s/l/ c8183.htm*

c. *Specially protected areas*

On May 15, President Bush issued a "Statement on Advancing U.S. Interests in the World's Oceans." President Bush stated that he was "acting to advance U.S. interests in the world's oceans in two important ways." His first action urged Senate advice and consent to accession to the Convention on the Law of the Sea and ratification of the 1994 Agreement, as discussed in Chapter 12.A.1. The President's statement continued:

> Second, I have instructed the U.S. delegation to the International Maritime Organization (IMO) to submit a proposal for international measures that would enhance protection of the Papahānaumokuākea Marine National Monument, the area including the Northwestern Hawaiian Islands.
>
> Last June, I issued a proclamation establishing the Monument, a 1,200-mile stretch of coral islands, seamounts, banks, and shoals that are home to some 7,000 marine species. The United States will propose that the IMO designate the entire area as a Particularly Sensitive Sea Area (PSSA)—similar to areas such as the Florida Keys, the Great Barrier Reef, and the Galapagos Archipelago—which will alert mariners to exercise caution in the ecologically important, sensitive, and hazardous area they are entering. This proposal, like the Convention on the Law of the Sea, will help protect the maritime environment while preserving the navigational freedoms essential to the security and economy of every nation.

The full text of the President's statement is available at 43 Weekly Comp. Pres. Doc. 635 (May 21, 2007).

d. Fish and marine mammals

(1) Magnuson-Stevens Fishery Conservation and Management Reauthorization Act of 2006

On January 12, 2007, President Bush signed into law the Magnuson-Stevens Fishery Conservation and Management Reauthorization Act of 2006, Pub. L. No. 109-479 (2007). A fact sheet released on the day of the signature stated that, by signing the bill, "the President reaffirmed our commitment to protect America's fisheries and keep our commercial and recreational fishing communities strong. This Act will end over-fishing in America, help us replenish our Nation's fish stocks, and advance international cooperation and ocean stewardship."

Further excerpts from the fact sheet describing the act follow; the full text is available at 43 Weekly Comp. Pres. Doc. 31 (Jan. 15, 2007). *See also* A.2.d.(3) and A.2.f. below for provisions of the act implementing U.S. treaty obligations.

*   *   *   *

The Signing Of The Magnuson-Stevens Act Completes A Goal From The Administration's 2004 Ocean Action Plan—And Caps Two Years Of Accomplishment In Ocean Conservation. In 2004, the Administration released its Ocean Action Plan to promote an ethic of responsible use and stewardship of our ocean and coastal resources. Since its release, the plan has produced good results. . . .

*   *   *   *

The Magnuson-Stevens Act Builds On The Administration's Progress Implementing Its Ocean Action Plan

1. **The Act Sets A Firm Deadline To End Over-Fishing In America By 2011.** Over-fishing occurs when more fish from a species are caught than is sustainable, endangering the species' long-term existence. This Act directs Regional Fishery Management Councils to establish annual quotas in Federally-managed fisheries to end over-fishing by 2010 for fish stocks currently undergoing over-fishing and by 2011 for all other Federally-managed fish stocks.

2. **The Act Uses Market-Based Incentives To Replenish America's Fish Stocks.** The Act will help us double the number of limited-access privilege programs by the year 2010. Limited-access privilege programs assign specific shares of the annual harvest quota to eligible fishermen, fishing communities, and regional fishery associations. Increasing the number of these programs will end the race for fish, improve the quality of catches, and protect those who earn their livelihood from fishing.

3. **The Act Strengthens Enforcement Of America's Fishing Laws.** Under the Act, those who break the law can lose their individual fishing quotas. The Act also expands cooperation between State and Federal officials to ensure our fishing laws are fully enforced, and it encourages the use of the latest technology in vessel-monitoring to aid in the real-time tracking of fishing boats.

4. **The Act Improves Information And Decisions About The State Of Ocean Ecosystems.** The Act creates several programs to improve the quality of information used by fishery managers and establishes regional registries for recreational fishermen. It also provides for improved assessment of the effects of proposed fishery management actions through timely, clear, and concise analysis that is useful to decision makers and more effectively involves the public.

The Act Provides New Tools To Improve The Administration's Cooperative Conservation Efforts. The President believes that to meet the environmental challenges of the 21st century we must bring together conservationists, fishermen, sportsmen, and business leaders in a spirit of cooperation, and we must continue to listen to the needs of States, communities, and local citizens. This Act promotes community-based efforts to restore local fish habitats by helping Federal agencies partner with State and local organizations.

Section 403 of the Act amended Title VI of the High Seas Driftnet Fishing Moratorium Act (16 U.S.C. § 1826d et seq.) ("HSDFMA") to add a number of new requirements relating to efforts to address illegal, unreported, and unregulated ("IUU") fishing. In particular, new HSDFMA § 607 requires the Secretary of Commerce to compile a biennial report that provides information on a range of international fisheries issues, including, inter alia, identification of nations whose fishing vessels have been engaged in IUU fishing, progress made by regional fishery management organizations to end IUU fishing, and steps taken by the United States at the international level to adopt international measures to reduce impacts of fishing on protected living marine resources.

Section 403 also added a new § 609 to the HSDMFA that requires the Secretary of Commerce to initiate a process to identify nations whose vessels engage in IUU fishing and to notify and initiate consultations with such nations to encourage corrective action; ultimately the Secretary may impose sanctions under the HSDFMA against such nations in certain circumstances. New § 610 provides for a similar process with regard to bycatch of protected living marine resources.

In a statement issued at the time of signing, the President commented as follows on implementation of the act consistent with constitutional and treaty requirements. The full text of the signing statement is available at *www.whitehouse. gov/news/releases/2007/01/20070112-3.html*.

* * * *

The executive branch shall construe provisions of the Act that purport to direct or burden the conduct of negotiations by the executive branch with foreign governments or international organizations in a manner consistent with the President's constitutional authority to conduct the Nation's foreign affairs, including the authority to determine which officers shall negotiate for the United States with a foreign country, when, in consultation with whom, and toward what objectives, and to supervise the unitary executive branch. Such provisions include subsections 609(c) and 610(b) of the High Seas Driftnet Fishing Moratorium Protection Act, as enacted by section 403 of the Act; section 408 of the Act; and section 505 of the Marine Mammal Protection Act of 1972, as enacted by section 902 of the Act.

Subsection 505(a) of the Marine Mammal Protection Act of 1972, as enacted by section 902 of the Act, purports to condition the authority granted to the President to make appointments upon prior consideration of recommendations from particular sources and purports to limit the qualifications of the pool of persons from whom the President may select appointees in a manner that rules out a large portion of those persons best qualified by experience and knowledge to fill the positions. Also, provisions of the Act, such as section 303A(c)(6)(D)(i) of the Magnuson-Stevens Fishery Conservation and Management Act, as enacted by section 106 of the Act, purport to give significant governmental authority of the United States to individuals who are not appointed in accordance with the Appointments Clause of the Constitution. The executive branch shall construe these provisions in a manner consistent with the Appointments Clause.

The executive branch shall construe section 510 of the Act, relating to notifications regarding certain entry and transit of specified portions of the United States Exclusive Economic Zone, in a manner consistent, to the maximum extent permissible, with treaties to which the United States is a party and other international obligations of the United States.

(2) Conservation of Antarctic marine living resources: Bottom fishing

The Commission for the Conservation of Antarctic Marine Living Resources ("CCAMLR") held its 26th meeting in Hobart, Tasmania, from October 22 to November 2, 2007. Among other things, CCAMLR adopted Conservation Measure 22-06, a binding conservation measure ("CM") proposed by the United States to protect vulnerable marine ecosystems from the destructive impacts of bottom fishing in high seas areas within the geographic scope of the Convention on Antarctic Marine Living Resources. The report of the 26th meeting is available at *www.ccamlr.org/pu/E/e_pubs/cr/07/toc.htm*; the text of CM 22-6 is published in the Schedule of Conservation Measures in Force 2007/08, available at *www.ccamlr.org/pu/e/e_pubs/cm/07-08/22-06.pdf*.

In a proposal submitted to CCAMLR on October 22, 2007, the United States described UN General Assembly Resolution 61/105 to which the CM responded. The full text of the U.S. proposal, excerpted below, is available at *www.state. gov/s/l/c8183.htm*.

* * * *

1. On December 8, 2006, the United Nations General Assembly (UNGA) adopted, by consensus, its resolution 61/105, which contains detailed provisions calling on States, both individually and collectively through regional fisheries management organizations (RFMOs) with the competence to regulate bottom fisheries, and the Food and Agriculture Organization (FAO) to take specific actions to protect vulnerable marine ecosystems (VMEs)[1] from bottom fishing activities that would have significant adverse impacts on such ecosystems [fn. omitted].

* * * *

4. In UNGA Resolution 61/105, all UN Members (including all CCAMLR Members) made a number of commitments that are not currently reflected in [CCAMLR] Conservation Measures 22-04 and 22-05 [2006]. . . .

* * * *

6. UNGA Resolution 61/105 calls upon CCAMLR and other RFMOs with the competence to regulate bottom fisheries to adopt specific measures for regulating bottom fisheries to protect VMEs

---

[1]   For the purposes of this measure, "vulnerable marine ecosystems" include seamounts, hydrothermal vents, cold water corals and sponge fields.

by 31 December 2008. In particular, if CCAMLR has not taken action to adopt conservation and management measures in respect of areas where VMEs are known to occur or are likely to occur, based on the best available scientific information, to prevent significant adverse impacts to such ecosystems, the UNGA Resolution calls for the closure of those areas and for States to cease authorization of such fishing. Thus, all CCAMLR Members have a strong incentive to work diligently on this issue and consider how to ensure that CCAMLR fully implements the provisions of UNGA Resolution 61/105.

*   *   *   *

The provisions adopted by the Commission as CM 22-06 limit bottom fishing activities during the 2007/2008 season strictly to areas where bottom fishing was approved in the 2006/2007 fishing season, offering temporary protection to bottom VMEs such as seamounts, hydrothermal vents, cold water corals, and sponge fields. The measure applies to any activities utilizing gear that interacts with the bottom. Beginning December 1, 2008, all proposed bottom fishing activities will be required to undergo an assessment to determine if they would have significant adverse impacts on VMEs. If impacts are anticipated, then such activities should be managed accordingly or not authorized to proceed. The measure calls for the closure of areas where VMEs are known to occur or are likely to occur. An encounter clause is also in effect, where fishing vessels must cease their activities in any location where evidence of VMEs is encountered during the course of fishing operations. Provisions for monitoring, research, and data sharing are also included. The Scientific Committee ("SC") will play a prominent role under this CM. This includes the release of guidelines for the submission of information on VMEs by interested parties, the preparation of assessments on proposed bottom fishing activities, and the review of mitigation measures proposed to prevent significant adverse impacts on VMEs. The SC will provide advice to the Commission on the known and anticipated impacts of bottom fishing activities on VMEs, and recommend mitigation measures, including ceasing fishing operations if needed, when evidence of a VME is encountered in the course of bottom fishing operations.

(3) Western and Central Pacific Fish Stocks Convention

On November 18, 2005, the Senate gave advice and consent to ratification of the Western and Central Pacific Fish Stocks Convention, signed by the United States on September 5, 2000, in Honolulu, and entered into force internationally in June 2004. Implementing legislation, the "Western and Central Pacific Fisheries Convention Implementation Act," was included as Title V, §§ 501–511, of the Magnuson-Stevens Fishery Management and Conservation Reauthorization Act of 2006 (Pub. L. No. 109-479), signed into law on January 12, 2007. The U.S. embassy in Wellington, New Zealand, delivered the U.S. instrument of ratification to the Government of New Zealand, as depositary, on June 27, 2007. As explained in a media note released by the Department of State on June 28, 2007, "The U.S. submission to the Depository also included a declaration authorizing the participation of American Samoa, Guam and the Northern Mariana Islands in the work of the Commission as Participating Territories." The convention entered into force for the United States on July 27, 2007, at which time the United States also became a member of the Western and Central Pacific Fisheries Commission. As further explained by the media note,

> Through the work of the Commission, various nations, including Australia, Canada, China, Japan, New Zealand and Pacific Island States of the Forum Fisheries Agency, work together to implement a comprehensive conservation and management program with the goal of ensuring the long-term conservation and sustainable use of highly migratory fish stocks in the west and central Pacific. While the Commission focuses mainly on tuna species, it also works to reduce the inadvertent catch of sea birds and sea turtles in commercial fisheries and has adopted measures

to improve compliance with, and enforcement of, fisheries regulations.

The United States has been a key player during the past decade in the efforts to establish the Commission. The United States continues to strongly support the mission of [the] Commission and as a Contracting Party, looks forward to increased involvement and participation in the upcoming Commission meetings.

The full text of the media note is available at *www.state.gov/ r/pa/prs/ps/2007/jun/87537.htm.*

(4) *South Pacific Regional Fisheries Management Organization treaty negotiations*

The United States strongly supported an initiative launched in 2005 by the governments of Australia, New Zealand, and Chile to establish a multilateral regional fisheries management organization ("RFMO") in the South Pacific Ocean. The purpose of the new RFMO is to ensure the long-term conservation and sustainable use of non–highly migratory fishery resources and in so doing to safeguard the marine ecosystems in which those resources occur. The second session of negotiations toward this objective was held in Reñaca, Chile, from April 30 to May 4, 2007. In addition to discussing the draft treaty text, the meeting was expected to adopt precautionary non-binding interim measures for the fisheries and ecosystems in the proposed convention area, which the participants were unable to do at the first negotiation session in November 2006. The United States was actively involved in negotiations leading to adoption of interim measures for bottom fishing at this session, consistent with UN General Assembly sustainable fisheries resolution 61/105 (2006), discussed in d.(2) *supra.* On May 4, 2007, the meeting adopted a comprehensive set of voluntary, non-binding interim measures that covers both pelagic and bottom fisheries in the proposed RFMO convention area, and which are fully consistent with the provisions of UNGA resolution 61/105.

The text of the interim measures can be found at *www.*
southpacificrfmo.org/assets/Third%20International%20M
eeting/SPRFMO%20Interim%20Measures_Final.doc.

(5) *North Western Pacific regional fisheries management*
arrangements

In January 2007 the United States participated in consultations to establish a fisheries management arrangement for
the North Western Pacific that adopted an interim measure
for bottom fisheries on the Emperor Seamounts, consistent
with UN General Assembly 61/105, discussed in d.(2) *supra*.

(6) *Sustainable fisheries*

On December 18, 2007, the UN General Assembly adopted a
resolution entitled "Sustainable fisheries, including through
the 1995 Agreement for the Implementation of the Provisions
of the United Nations Convention on the Law of the Sea of 10
December 1982 relating to the Conservation and Management
of Straddling Fish Stocks and Highly Migratory Fish Stocks
["UN Fish Stocks Agreement"], and related instruments."
U.N. Doc. A/RES/62/177 (2007). In a statement to the General
Assembly on December 10, 2007, Kelly Knight, U.S. Public
Delegate to the United Nations, provided the views of the
United States in support of the sustainable fisheries resolu-
tion as set forth below. *See www.usunnewyork.usmission.*
gov/press_releases/20071210_364.html.

* * * *

As we have noted in the past, the United States places great importance on ensuring freedom of navigation, safety of navigation, and
the rights of transit passage, archipelagic sea lanes passage, and
innocent passage in accordance with international law, in particular the [UN Law of the Sea] Convention. In this context, we note
with appreciation the recent conclusions and discussions at the
Assembly of the International Maritime Organization.

This year's resolution on sustainable fisheries contains important provisions to address such critical issues as control of illegal, unregulated and unreported fishing; reduction of fishing capacity; implementation of the UN Fish Stocks Agreement; regulation of destructive fishing practices; and other important matters. Perhaps the most notable aspect of this year's resolution are the provisions for the regulation of shark fisheries, including those calling for strengthened implementation of existing measures and consideration of a range of new measures to manage these stocks comprehensively and effectively. In this year's resolution, the United States, along with many other countries, sought strong results to address critical gaps in oceans governance that currently exist with respect to many fisheries. We view the provisions contained in the resolution as another in a series of welcome and positive steps forward. We will continue to work to advance these issues bilaterally, through the relevant regional fisheries management organizations and arrangements, or RFMOs, and in negotiations to establish new regional organizations where they do not currently exist.

The resolution also establishes other steps for the international community, including a resumption of consultations of the States Party to the UN Fish Stocks Agreement. The United States reaffirms its view of the significance of the Agreement and welcomes the impressive number of recent accessions to the Agreement in 2007, which we see as a positive sign in the endeavor to achieve sustainable fisheries. We urge all States that have not yet become Party to the Agreement to do so. We also believe that the Agreement must continue to be the foundation for negotiations to establish new regional agreements, including agreements for the management of discrete high seas stocks, such as the negotiations currently underway in the South Pacific and the Northwestern Pacific. The Agreement's basic principles should also be applied to discrete high seas stocks by all flag States, including in areas where no competent RFMO currently exists to manage such fisheries.

Reducing the excess capacity of the world's fishing fleets continues to be a high priority for the United States. We are therefore pleased that this year's resolution urges States "to commit to urgently reducing the capacity of the world's fishing fleets to levels commensurate with the sustainability of fish stocks." We will push for full implementation of this language as we have for similar language in past resolutions.

Regarding illegal, unregulated, and unreported fishing, the resolution recognizes continuing efforts over the past year to address this problem, but we must make further progress in this area. The upcoming negotiation of a legally binding port States regime provides a valuable opportunity to develop stronger controls. In that exercise, which is taking place under the auspices of the UN Food and Agriculture Organization, we want to see port States take stronger measures to prevent the landing and transshipment in their ports of fish caught in contravention of existing regulatory regimes.

Mr. President, we continue to see that the annual sustainable fisheries resolution remains a relevant instrument through which the international community can highlight issues of concern and articulate ways to address such issues. However, much work remains if we are to ensure the sustainability of global fish stocks. It is the various RFMOs themselves, as those bodies with direct regulatory responsibility for the management of the fisheries under their purview, that must carry out this work and, in so doing, implement the guidance provided to the international community through the General Assembly Resolutions. We urge all RFMOs to take timely and concrete actions to realize the calls from this body to ensure effective conservation and management of target stocks, to minimize by-catch of non-target species and to mitigate the adverse impacts of fishing activities on the broader marine environment.

*   *   *   *

(7) Sea turtle conservation and shrimp imports

On May 3, 2007, the Department of State issued its annual certifications related to conservation of sea turtles. The full text of a media note from the Department of State Spokesman is set forth below and available at *www.state.gov/r/pa/prs/ps/2007/may/84238.htm*.

On May 1, the Department of State certified 40 nations and one economy as meeting the requirements set by Section 609 of P.L. 101-162 for continued importation of shrimp into the United States. Section 609 prohibits importation of shrimp and products of shrimp harvested in a manner that may adversely affect sea turtle species. This import prohibition does not apply in cases where the Department of State certifies annually to Congress, not later than May 1, that the government of the harvesting nation has taken certain specific measures to reduce the incidental taking of sea turtles in its shrimp trawl fisheries—or that the fishing environment of the harvesting nation does not pose a threat to sea turtle species. Such certifications are based in part on verification visits made to countries by teams of experts from the State Department and the U.S. National Marine Fisheries Service.

The chief component of the U.S. sea turtle conservation program is a requirement that commercial shrimp boats use sea turtle excluder devices (TEDs) to prevent the accidental drowning of sea turtles in shrimp trawls. The sixteen nations meeting this standard are: Belize, Colombia, Costa Rica, Ecuador, El Salvador, Guatemala, Guyana, Honduras, Madagascar, Mexico, Nicaragua, Nigeria, Pakistan, Panama, Suriname, and Venezuela.

Twenty-four nations and one economy were certified as having fishing environments that do not pose a danger to sea turtles. Of these, eight nations and one economy—the Bahamas, China, the Dominican Republic, Fiji, Hong Kong, Jamaica, Oman, Peru and Sri Lanka—harvest shrimp using manual rather than mechanical means to retrieve nets, or use other fishing methods not harmful to sea turtles. Sixteen nations have shrimp fisheries only in cold waters, where the risk of taking sea turtles is negligible. They are: Argentina, Belgium, Canada, Chile, Denmark, Finland, Germany, Iceland, Ireland, the Netherlands, New Zealand, Norway, Russia, Sweden, the United Kingdom, and Uruguay.

Importation of shrimp from all other nations will be prohibited unless harvested by aquaculture methodology (fish-farming), in cold-water regions where sea turtles are not likely found, or by specialized fishing techniques that do not threaten sea turtles. . . .

(8) Dolphin-safe tuna: Earth Island Institute v. Hogarth

On July 13, 2007, the U.S. Court of Appeals for the Ninth Circuit found that the U.S. Secretary of Commerce had not complied with statutory mandates in making a final finding that the use of purse-seine nets in catching yellowfin tuna did not have a significant adverse impact on dolphins and affirmed a district court mandate directing the Secretary to vacate the finding. *Earth Island Institute v. Hogarth*, 494 F.3d 757 (9th Cir. 2007). The court concluded that the scientific studies relied on by the Secretary did not meet statutory requirements and that the final finding was improperly influenced by international political concerns. The court explained:

> This means as a practical matter that pursuant to the current statute, there will be no change in tuna labeling standards absent new Congressional directive. The label of "dolphin safe" will continue to signify that the tuna was harvested in compliance with the requirements of 16 U.S.C. § 1385.

Excerpts below from the court's opinion provide the factual and legislative background to the litigation.

See also *Cumulative Digest 1991–1999* at 1745–54 for a history of developments in dolphin conservation during that period; *Digest 2001* at 748–52 for the Ninth Circuit opinion rejecting the Secretary of Commerce's initial finding that "there is insufficient evidence that chase and encirclement by the tuna purse seine fishery 'is having a significant adverse impact' on depleted dolphin stocks in the ETP"; *Digest 2002* at 794–96 for announcement of the final finding "that the intentional deployment on or encirclement of dolphins with purse seine nets is not having a significant adverse impact on depleted dolphin stocks in the ETP"; and *Digest 2004* at 757–62 for the district court decision affirmed by the court of appeals here.

* * * *

In the Eastern Tropical Pacific Ocean (the "ETP"), off the west coast of South America, schools of yellowfin tuna tend to congregate underneath pods of dolphin. In the late 1950s, fishermen started throwing large nets, called purse-seine nets, around the dolphin pods to capture the tuna below. This method of fishing is known as "setting" because the fishermen use explosives, chase boats, and helicopters to drive the dolphins into the center of large nets, which then close like a purse around all that is trapped inside. It is not disputed that the technique has caused the death of more than six million dolphins. By 1993, the extensive use of fishing with purse-seine nets depleted the stock of three species of dolphins—the northeastern offshore spotted dolphin, the eastern spinner dolphin, and the coastal spotted dolphin—to levels below their optimum sustainable population, which is the number of animals which will result in the maximum productivity of the population or the species. Today, these species of dolphin are struggling to recover. Experts estimate that their populations in the ETP are "growing" at a slow rate of anywhere between –2% and 2% annually.

Congress has long been concerned with the high mortality rate of ETP dolphins. In 1972, it enacted the Marine Mammal Protection Act ("MMPA"), which was designed to "protect marine mammals from the adverse effects of human activities." *See* 16 U.S.C. § 1371 *et seq.*; H.R. Rep. No. 105-74(I) at 12 (1997). The Act was subsequently amended to ban the importation of tuna that failed to meet certain conditions regarding dolphin mortality. 16 U.S.C. §§ 1371(a)(2)(B), 1411 *et seq.* In 1990, Congress passed the Dolphin Protection Consumer Information Act ["IDPCA"], which barred tuna sellers from labeling their products as "dolphin-safe" if the tuna was caught by intentionally encircling dolphins with purse-seine nets. 16 U.S.C. § 1385.

Given the choice of whether to purchase dolphin-safe tuna or to purchase tuna not labeled dolphin-safe, American consumers overwhelmingly chose to purchase tuna that was labeled dolphin-safe. As a result, foreign tuna sellers who did not adjust their fishing methods were quickly forced out of the market. . .

. . . [The MMPA and the IDCPA together] directed the Secretary of Commerce to determine whether the "intentional deployment on or encirclement of dolphins with purse seine nets" is "having a significant adverse impact on any depleted dolphin stock in the [ETP]." 16 U.S.C. § 1385(g); *see also* 16 U.S.C. § 1414a. IDCPA directed the Secretary to make an Initial Finding by March 31, 1999 and a Final Finding by December 31, 2002. 16 U.S.C. § 1385(g)(1),(2). The amended MMPA enumerated three studies the NOAA had to conduct in making its determination . . . 16 U.S.C. § 1414a(a)(3).

*   *   *   *

(9) Whales

(i) International Whaling Commission

The International Whaling Commission ("IWC") held its 59th annual meeting in Anchorage, Alaska, May 28–31, 2007. *See www.iwcoffice.org/meetings/meeting2007.htm*. The United States succeeded in obtaining renewal of authorization for scientifically defensible aboriginal subsistence whaling. At the meeting, the Commission renewed by consensus a five-year block catch limit of 280 bowhead whales for the Bering-Chukchi-Beaufort Sea ("BCB"), shared by U.S. and Russian native communities for the years 2008–2012. The Commission also agreed by consensus to extend for 2008–2012 the current five-year catch limit of 620 gray whales for the eastern North Pacific stock, hunted by Russian Chukotkan natives and potentially the Makah tribe in Washington State. Issues related to Makah tribe whaling are discussed below.

Japan offered but then withdrew a proposal and resolution to resume limited commercial whaling in its coastal waters after significant opposition, including by the United States. The Commission adopted Resolution 2007-4, "Resolution on Convention on International Trade in Endangered Species," which affirmed that the moratorium on commercial whaling remained in place.

The United States also opposed Japan's plan to hunt humpback whales for claimed research purposes. While the

United States recognized Japan's right to conduct research whaling under the Convention, it viewed the legality of any given hunt as depending on the exact circumstances of the hunt and noted that non-lethal research techniques were available to provide nearly all relevant data on whale populations. On December 21, 2007, the U.S. Department of State issued a media note welcoming an announcement from Japan "that it will suspend its plan to target humpback whales during this year's whaling program that is underway in the seas off Antarctica." The media note continued:

> The decision follows several rounds of talks between the U.S. chairman and Japanese vice-chairman of the International Whaling Commission (IWC). The IWC announced the agreement publicly today, and the Department of State has supported the U.S. chairman's dialog with his Japanese counterparts since June. Japanese ships left for Antarctica on November 18.
>
> "Japan's decision will promote global efforts to protect the endangered humpback whale," said Assistant Secretary Claudia McMurray. "It also is an important step in fostering continued cooperation through the IWC."
>
> Japanese officials told the U.S. Commissioner and IWC chairman Bill Hogarth they would postpone the harvest of humpback whales at least until after the next meeting of the International Whaling Commission slated for June. This year, Japan had planned to target 50 humpback whales for the first time in its Antarctic program along with 50 fin whales and up to 935 minke whales.

The media note is available at *www.state.gov/r/pa/prs/ps/2007/dec/97931.htm. See also* December 20, 2007, Circular Communication to Commissioners and Contracting Governments IWC.CCG.657, issued by Dr. William T. Hogarth, Chair of the International Whaling Commission, reporting Japan's agreed delay, available at *www.state.gov/s/l/c8183.htm.*

The United States had also urged restraint and measured approaches from all sides in any protest activity that might have been planned against Japanese whaling vessels. The 59th Annual Meeting adopted Resolution 2007-2, declaring that "the Commission and its Contracting Governments do not condone *and in fact condemn* any actions that are a risk to human life and property in relation to the activities of vessels at sea" and "urge[d] Contracting Governments to take actions, in accordance with relevant rules of international law and respective national laws and regulations, to cooperate to prevent and suppress actions that risk human life and property at sea and with respect to alleged offenders" and to "cooperate in accordance with UNCLOS and other relevant instruments in the investigation of incidents at sea including those which might pose a risk to life or the environment." *See www.iwcoffice.org/meetings/resolutions/resolution2007. htm#res2.*

(ii) Subsistence whaling by U.S. Makah tribe

In August 2007 a representative of the National Marine Fisheries Service of the National Oceanic and Atmospheric Administration ("NOAA"), provided information on the Makah whaling issue to a meeting of the U.S. Marine Mammal Commission.[*] *See www.nwr.noaa.gov/Marine-Mammals/Whales-Dolphins-Porpoise/Gray-Whales/upload/Makah_MMC_pres. pdf.* Among other things, the presentation explained that 20 of the 620 gray whales in the 2007 IWC aboriginal limit were allocated to the United States on behalf of the Makah Tribe. The Whaling Convention Act ("WCA"), 16 U.S.C. §§ 916a–916l, implements the International Convention for the Regulation of Whaling in the United States and bans commercial whaling;

---

[*]   Editor's note: The Marine Mammal Commission is an independent agency of the U.S. government, established under Title II of the Marine Mammal Protection Act to provide independent oversight of the marine mammal conservation policies and programs being carried out by federal regulatory agencies. *See www.mmc.gov.*

the aboriginal subsistence whaling quotas set by the International Whaling Committee must be allocated under WCA regulations. The Marine Mammal Protection Act, 16 U.S.C. §§ 1361–1423h, imposes a moratorium on the take of all marine mammals, with certain exceptions, but the Secretary of Commerce may waive the moratorium under certain circumstances.

In September 2007 the Makah tribe of the state of Washington killed a gray whale off the coast of Washington. A posting on the website of the National Marine Fisheries Service of the NOAA described the history of whaling by the Makah tribe and the September incident as excerpted below. *See www.nwr.noaa.gov/Marine-Mammals/Whales-Dolphins-Porpoise/Gray-Whales/Makah-Whale-Hunt.cfm.*

The Makah Indian Tribe is seeking to continue limited treaty-right hunting of eastern North Pacific gray whales (*Eschrichtius robustus*). The right of whaling at usual and accustomed grounds is a Makah tradition secured by the 1855 Treaty of Neah Bay. Makah whaling dates back at least 1,500 years, but was halted in the 1920s because the eastern North Pacific gray whale population was severely reduced by commercial whaling.

With international and national legal protections, the eastern North Pacific gray whale distinct population segment recovered. The whales were removed from the Endangered Species list by NOAA Fisheries Service in 1994. The Makah hunted one eastern North Pacific gray whale in 1999, but have since been prevented from exercising treaty hunting rights by litigation.

The Ninth Circuit Court ruled in 2004 that the Makah, to pursue any treaty rights for whaling, must comply with the process prescribed in the Marine Mammal Protection Act (MMPA) for authorizing take of marine mammals otherwise prohibited by a moratorium. [*Anderson v. Evans*, 371 F.3d 475 (9th Cir. 2004)] (*Take* means to or attempt to, harass, hunt, capture, or kill any marine mammal.) On Feb. 14, 2005, NOAA Fisheries Service received a request from the Makah for a limited waiver of the

MMPA's take moratorium, including issuance of regulations and any necessary permits.[*]

*   *   *   *

Several Makah tribal members shot and killed a gray whale on Sept. 8, without any NOAA Fisheries Service authorization or permit, or any apparent formal tribal authorization. Fisheries Enforcement is investigating, and NOAA is assessing how to proceed with processing the tribe's MMPA waiver request.

e.   Land-based sources and activities, Wider Caribbean Region

On February 16, 2007, President Bush transmitted the Protocol Concerning Pollution from Land-based Sources and Activities ("Protocol") to the Convention for the Protection and Development of the Marine Environment of the Wider Caribbean Region ("Cartagena Convention"), with Annexes, done at Oranjestad, Aruba, on October 6, 1999. S. Treaty Doc. No. 110-1 (2007). The United States signed the Protocol on October 6, 1999.

President Bush's transmittal letter is set forth in major part below.

---

*   *   *   *

The Convention for the Protection and Development of the Marine Environment of the Wider Caribbean Region (the "Cartagena Convention") is a regional framework agreement negotiated under the auspices of the Regional Seas Program of the United Nations Environment Program (UNEP). It sets out general legal obligations to protect the marine environment of the Gulf of Mexico, Straits of

---

[*]   Editor's note: Although the NMFS is in the process of considering the Makah request for a waiver submitted in 2005—*see* 70 Fed. Reg. 49,911 (Aug. 25, 2005), 70 Fed. Reg. 57,860 (Oct. 4, 2005), and 71 Fed. Reg. 9781 (Feb. 27, 2006)—this process is ongoing, and no action had been taken at the end of 2007.

Florida, Caribbean Sea, and immediately adjacent areas of the Atlantic Ocean—collectively known as the Wider Caribbean Region. The United States became a Party to the Cartagena Convention in 1984. The Cartagena Convention envisions the development of protocols to further elaborate certain of its general obligations and to facilitate its effective implementation.

Negotiated with the active participation and leadership of the United States, the Protocol addresses one of the most serious sources of marine pollution in the Wider Caribbean Region. It is estimated that 70 to 90 percent of pollution entering the marine environment emanates from land-based sources and activities. Among the principal land-based sources of marine pollution in the Caribbean are domestic wastewater and agricultural nonpoint source runoff. Such pollution contributes to the degradation of coral reefs and commercial fisheries, negatively affects regional economies, and endangers public health, recreation, and tourism throughout the region.

The Protocol and its Annexes list priority source categories, activities, and associated contaminants that affect the Wider Caribbean Region, and set forth factors that Parties will be required to apply in determining prevention, reduction, and control strategies to manage land-based sources of pollution. In particular, the Parties are required to ensure that domestic wastewater discharges meet specific effluent limitations, and to develop plans for the prevention and reduction of agricultural nonpoint source pollution. The Protocol is expected to raise standards for treating domestic wastewater throughout the region to levels close to those already in place in the United States.

The United States would be able to implement its obligations under the Protocol under existing statutory and regulatory authority.

The Protocol is the first regional agreement to establish effluent standards to protect one of our most valuable resources, the marine environment. It differs markedly from other, similar regional agreements in its conceptual approach and the specificity of its obligations. As such, the Protocol is expected to set a new standard for regional agreements on this subject. Early ratification will demonstrate our continued commitment to global leadership and to the protection of the marine environment of the Wider Caribbean Region.

I recommend that the Senate give early and favorable consideration to the Protocol and its Annexes, with the declaration described in the accompanying report of the Secretary of State, and give its advice and consent to ratification.

In her May 17, 2005, letter submitting the Protocol to the President, Secretary of State Condoleezza Rice stated further:

> From the U.S. perspective, the Protocol's major attribute is its framework for the development of source-specific controls on land-based sources of marine pollution. Two specific, mandatory annexes were negotiated with, and will enter into force at the same time as, the Protocol. Of particular importance is Annex III, which establishes quantitative and measurable effluent standards for domestic wastewater discharges in the Region. Implementation of Annex III would result in significant progress toward addressing a major source of pollution in the Wider Caribbean Region. As more countries in the Region take actions to protect the marine environment, benefits will accrue to the health of people and ecosystems in the Gulf of Mexico, Straits of Florida, and the Caribbean. Those waters are interconnected across the region through circulation patterns and shared biological resources. It will also result in benefits to local economies, commercial and recreational fisheries, tourism, and biodiversity throughout the region.
>
> U.S. waters adjacent to the following U.S. states and territories fall within the geographic scope of the Protocol: Texas, Louisiana, Mississippi, Alabama, Florida, the Commonwealth of Puerto Rico, and the Territory of the U.S. Virgin Islands. Officials in these states and territories were consulted throughout the negotiating process and following conclusion of the Protocol in 2000.

The attached Report of the Secretary of State included the following discussion of Articles XVII and XVIII of the Protocol, including the declaration referred to in the President's letter.

* * * *

Article XVII (Adoption and Entry into Force of New Annexes and Amendments to Annexes)

Article XVII described procedures for the adoption and entry into force of new annexes and of amendments to existing annexes. The Protocol generally incorporates the amendment process for annexes set out in the Cartagena Convention, i.e., following adoption by a three-fourths majority of the Parties, an amendment will enter into force for all Parties except those that indicate that they object to the amendment within ninety days of its adoption. An objecting Party may later agree to be bound by such an amendment. In the event that an annex amendment were adopted that was of such a nature that it needed to be sent to the Senate for advice and consent in order for the United States constitutionally to be bound by it, the executive branch would take the necessary steps to ensure that such an amendment did not enter into force for the United States absent such advice and consent.

The Protocol differs from the Cartagena Convention in that paragraph 2 allows the Parties to decide at the time of the adoption of a particular amendment that it is of such importance that it will bind only those Parties that have affirmatively consented to be bound and will enter into force only once three-fourths of the Parties have so consented.

Further, with respect to the adoption of new annexes, the Protocol gives a Party the option to make entry into force for it of a new annex subject to its express consent to be bound. I recommend that the United States include the following declaration at the time of deposit of its instrument of ratification:

> *In accordance with Article XVIII, the United States declares that, with respect to the United States, any new annexes to the Protocol shall enter into force only upon the deposit of its instrument of ratification, acceptance, approval or accession with respect thereto.*

Article XVIII (Ratification, Acceptance, Approval and Accession)

Article XVIII provides that the provisions of the Cartagena Convention regarding ratification, acceptance, approval or accession apply to the Protocol. As noted above, each Party must accept the original four annexes in its consent to be bound by the Protocol, but may choose not to accept any additional annexes.

*   *   *   *

f. U.S.–Russia Agreement on the Conservation and Management of the Alaska-Chukotka Polar Bear Population

The United States signed the Agreement on the Conservation and Management of the Alaska-Chukotka Polar Bear Population on October 16, 2000, and the Senate gave its advice and consent to ratification on July 31, 2003. *See* S. Treaty Doc. No. 107-10 transmitting the agreement to the Senate, discussed in *Digest 2002* at 800–805. Section 902 of the Magnuson-Stevens Fishery Management and Conservation Reauthorization Act of 2006 (Pub. L. No. 109-479), amended the Marine Mammal Protection Act of 1972 (16 U.S.C. §§ 1361–1423h) by adding a new Title V to that act, §§ 501–509, to implement the agreement. The treaty entered into force on September 23, 2007.

As explained by Assistant Secretary of State for Oceans, International Environment, and Science Claudia A. McMurray in her remarks on wildlife in 3.b. below,

> [the treaty] will protect females with cubs and cubs less than one year old to help ensure the health of the breeding population. The commission created by the treaty will also recommend measures for the bear's habitat protection.

See www.state.gov/g/oes/rls/rm/2007/94157.htm.

3. Other Conservation Issues

a. Antarctica

The Antarctic Treaty Consultative Meeting ("ATCM"), held in New Delhi, India, from April 30 to May 11, 2007, adopted, among other things, Resolution 4, "Ship-based Tourism in the Antarctic Treaty Area." Resolution 4 recommended that

Parties, consistent with their national law,

1. discourage or decline to authorize tour operators that use vessels carrying more than 500 passengers from making any landings in Antarctica; and
2. encourage or require tour operators to:
   a) coordinate with each other such that not more than one tourist vessel is at a landing site at any one time;
   b) restrict the number of passengers on shore at any one time to 100 or fewer, unless otherwise specified in applicable ATCM Measures or Resolutions; and
   c) maintain a minimum 1:20 guide-to-passenger ratio while ashore, unless otherwise specified in applicable ATCM Measures or Resolutions.

The full text of Resolution 4 is available in Annex C to the ATCM Final Report Part II, available at *http://30atcm.ats.aq/ 30atcm/Documents/Docs/fr/Atcm30_fr002_e.doc.*

Excerpts below from the ATCM Final Report at 21 summarize the U.S. views in introducing the resolution. The full text of the ATCM Final report is available at *http://30atcm. ats.aq/30atcm/Documents/Docs/fr/Atcm30_fr001_e.doc.*

---

*   *   *   *

The US introduced WP 6 *Approaches to Tourism Policy*, which contained a number of concrete proposals for action on the issue of tourism, as well as a draft resolution for consideration by ATCPs. It first proposed, based on a UK proposal introduced in Edinburgh, to establish a policy to limit landings by ships carrying 500 passengers or more, and also proposed a non-binding statement of policy endorsing for use by all tour operators a series of regulations that have proven necessary and successful for IAATO. The US also outlined a proposal to seek advice from appropriate expert bodies regarding issues related to vessels and necessary maritime standards to ensure passenger safety and minimize potential adverse effects of maritime activities on the Antarctic environment.

In addition, the US encouraged Parties to take necessary steps to approve Measure 4 (2004) and for Parties to fulfill the provisions of the related Resolution 3 (2004) that was also adopted by the 27th ATCM at Cape Town. The US encouraged Parties and vessel operators to improve communications systems as a means for promoting safety of passengers and crew on tour and other vessels in Antarctica.

The US believed that it was important that the ATCM underscore the importance of the Protocol in regulating tourism and suggested that the ATCM call on all Parties to implement their obligations fully, including through ensuring that sufficient resources are available for government oversight.

* * * *

b. Wildlife trafficking

On October 10, 2007, Assistant Secretary of State Claudia A. McMurray addressed the Rosenstiel School of Marine and Atmospheric Science on the coalition against wildlife trafficking. The full text of Ms. McMurray's remarks, excerpted below, is available at *www.state.gov/g/oes/rls/rm/2007/94157.htm*.

---

* * * *

. . . I'd like to talk about our work to stop illegal wildlife trafficking. It is common knowledge that animal species are endangered around the world, and most of the time what people attribute the problem to is loss of habitat, loss of land, and human pressures that cause them.

But what people really don't know as much about, and we're talking about today, is that animal species are threatened by the bounty on their head. The illegal trade in wildlife and wildlife products poses an even greater threat in some cases than the loss of natural habitat. And the numbers are really quite staggering. I can't give you every statistic this evening but I'll give you a few.

First of all, the conservative estimate that we have is that the trade amounts to about $10 billion a year globally. Some estimates put it closer to $20 billion—only behind drugs and maybe weapons.

*   *   *   *

. . . [G]iven the challenges we face and the fact that they're not limited by national borders, I think we're going to be increasingly reliant on these partnerships in the future. That's why the U.S. put together a partnership to fight wildlife trafficking, the Coalition Against Wildlife Trafficking. It was created and launched here in the United States with the World Wildlife Fund, Conservation International, Wildlife Conservation Society, and Wild Aid. Today, we have 19 partners, including the governments of Australia, Canada, Chile, India, and the United Kingdom.

Since the founding of CAWT, we've helped create an enforcement network in the Association of South East Asian Nations, the ASEAN countries, that has helped them bring together their customs, their police, and their wildlife officials in a cooperative way.

In the past two years, the enforcement network has already won several victories in the fight against trafficking. One of the Network's first cooperative efforts involved the governments of Thailand, Indonesia and Malaysia working together to successfully return to Indonesia 48 orangutans who had been illegally smuggled into Thailand from their native habitat. We are trying to expand our reach into other regions. You have all probably read about the tragic and brutal slaughter of the mountain gorillas in the Virunga National Park, Africa's oldest national park, in the Democratic Republic of the Congo.

The U.S. Government recently provided half a million dollars in new funds to improve enforcement against the criminal activity by helping rangers better protect endangered wildlife in the Virunga. The United States is also committed to protecting sharks. The U.S. is working through regional fisheries management organizations and international organizations such as the Convention on International Trade in Endangered Species (CITES) to secure shark management and conservation.

Earlier this year, we successfully proposed several species of critically endangered sawfish for listing on Appendix 1 of CITES.

This effectively bans all trade in sawfish parts and fins. We also supported proposals by Germany to list spiny dogfish and porbeagle shark. At the United Nations General Assembly meeting starting today, the United States will be taking a leadership role and asking other countries to do more to protect sharks and to end the practice of shark finning. Most of the U.S. actions I have spoken about are designed to cut off the supply of these illegal products by improving enforcement. Now I want to talk about what you and others can do to stop the demand. Unfortunately, we have a problem right here in America, we are the second largest market, after China, for these illegal products. . . .

The high U.S. demand for these products seems to be coming largely from a lack of knowledge of what is legal and what isn't— the tourist who can't resist the black and red coral necklace or the turtle hair clip; the cowboy who just can't resist the snake-skin boots, not knowing they are from an endangered species; or the aquarium enthusiast who just has to have the rarest of the rare reef fish for his tank.

To give you an idea of the scope of the problem, the total annual declared value for U.S. wildlife imports and exports was approximately $1.6 billion for 2000–04. During that period, the U.S. processed approximately 135,000 wildlife shipments (approximately 34,000 per year). In those shipments, enforcement officials found violations in approximately 3,500 shipments per year, roughly 10%.

*   *   *   *

c. Forest conservation

(1) Debt-for-nature

On November 7, 2007, the United States and Costa Rica entered into agreements to protect Costa Rican forests, financed by relief from debt owed the United States and contributions from two non-governmental organizations, Conservation International and The Nature Conservancy. A statement by David Henifen, Chargé d'Affaires, U.S. Embassy Costa Rica, is excerpted below and available at *www.state.gov/g/oes/rls/rm/2007/94714.htm.*

---

*   *   *   *

. . . The Tropical Forest Conservation Act (TFCA) was enacted by the U.S. Congress in 1998 to offer eligible developing countries options to relieve certain official debt owed the U.S. Government while at the same time generating funds to support tropical forest conservation activities. The TFCA is intended to strengthen civil society by creating local foundations to support small grants to NGOs and local communities. To date, most of the agreements, like Costa Rica's, have also included funds raised by U.S.-based NGOs.

With this agreement, Costa Rica joins other neighbors in the region—Belize, Colombia, Guatemala, El Salvador, Jamaica, Paraguay, and Panama—that have made use of this instrument to help protect their countries' forests. Globally, the U.S. invested nearly USD 95 million in 13 TFCA agreements with countries from the Americas, Africa, and Asia. Together, these agreements will generate more than USD 163 million.

Our agreement today is made possible by a more than USD 12 million donation from the U.S. government and a more than 2 million contribution from Conservation International and The Nature Conservancy. It is expected to generate approximately USD 26 million through 2024. Its Board will include representatives from the two governments, Conservation International, The Nature Conservancy, and civil society, and will make decisions on supporting activities that will help conserve Costa Rica's tropical forests and the species that depend upon them.

This support will ultimately be measured not by dollar amounts but by what this investment achieves. The funds will be used to protect the Talamanca forests that shelter most of Costa Rica's indigenous peoples; the Nicoya forests that provide water to Nicoya's farming communities and tourist havens; the forests north of Rincon de la Vieja that provide buffers for species adapting to a changing climate; and the forests that host macaws and other endangered species in Maquenque, Tortuguero, and Osa.

Our agreement today builds on Costa Rica's impressive commitment to protecting biodiversity. GRUAS, for example, is a joint effort by the Costa Rican government, academic and research institutions and NGOs like Conservation International and The Nature Conservancy to identify gaps in the protection of Costa Rican ecosystems; this joint analysis guided our choice of regions on which to focus our resources. We are pleased to be able to provide concrete backing to elements of President Arias' Peace with Nature Initiative, and hope that our joint efforts on TFCA will bolster other Costa Rican policy priorities in the service of sustainable development.

*   *   *   *

(2) Illegal logging

On December 12, 2007, the United States and China announced the conclusion of a non-binding memorandum of understanding on illegal logging and associated trade. A Department of State media note described the action and the more detailed bilateral agreement to follow as excerpted below. The full text is available at *www.state.gov/r/pa/prs/ps/2007/dec/97147.htm*.

. . . This is the first-ever commitment between the two countries to focus on addressing the devastating problem of illegal logging and the trade in illegally harvested timber. The Understanding was reached at this week's meeting of the U.S.-China Strategic Economic Dialogue.

"This joint Understanding clearly demonstrates that we and China recognize our shared responsibilities as the world's largest timber producers, consumers and traders," said Assistant Secretary of State for Oceans, Environment and Science Claudia A. McMurray. Action under the Understanding should help conserve forests and their wildlife and reduce deforestation—a major factor in the global effort to address climate change. Nearly 20 percent of global greenhouse gas emissions results from deforestation and other land use changes.

The Memorandum of Understanding establishes a Bilateral Forum between the two countries to identify joint work promoting both sustainable forest management and trade in legally-sourced forest products, as well as encourage public-private partnerships. Through the Forum, the United States and China will pursue a more detailed bilateral agreement to be concluded at the next round of economic talks in the Spring of 2008 in Washington, DC.

(3) Non-Legally Binding Instrument on All Types of Forests

On December 17, 2007, the UN General Assembly adopted the Non-Legally Binding Instrument on All Types of Forests. U.N. Doc. A/RES/62/98 (2007). The United States was actively involved in the negotiations of the instrument in the UN Forum on Forests, adopted at its seventh session, meeting in New York, April 16–27, 2007. The agreed principles are set forth below. Of particular legal significance was the inclusion of a savings clause in the preamble noting that the provisions of this instrument do not prejudice the rights and obligations of Member States under international law.

---

*   *   *   *

II. Principles
2. Member States should respect the following principles, which build upon the Rio Declaration on Environment and Development and the Rio Forest Principles:

(a)   The instrument is voluntary and non-legally binding;

(b)   Each State is responsible for the sustainable management of its forests and for the enforcement of its forest-related laws;

*   *   *   *

(f)   International cooperation, including financial support, technology transfer, capacity-building and education, plays a crucial catalytic role in supporting the efforts of all countries, particularly developing countries as well as countries with economies in transition, to achieve sustainable forest management.

*   *   *   *

(4) International Tropical Timber Agreement

On April 27, 2007, the United States signed the International Tropical Timber Agreement ("ITTA") 2006, adopted on January 27, 2006, by a conference convened under the UN Conference on Trade and Development. The full text of the agreement is available at *http://untreaty.un.org/English/not-publ/XIX_46_english.pdf*. This commodity agreement is the third ITTA and will replace ITTA 1994, which is currently in force. The ITTA is implemented through the International Tropical Timber Organization ("ITTO"), which provides the only international forum in which producer and consumer countries can engage in efforts to address all aspects of the world tropical timber economy. ITTA 2006 increases the focus on promoting trade from sustainably managed and legally harvested tropical forests, streamlines the operations of the ITTO, expands ITTO's statistical work and member reporting obligations, and provides for a more balanced distribution of costs between consumers and producers. The 2006 agreement has positive implications for tropical forest conservation, as well as for economies that benefit from trade in tropical timber.

B. MEDICAL AND HEALTH ISSUES

1. Pandemic Influenza Preparedness

On May 23, 2007, the World Health Assembly adopted Resolution WHA60.28, "Pandemic influenza preparedness: sharing of influenza viruses and access to vaccines and other benefits," available at *www.who.int/gb/ebwha/pdf_files/WHA60/*

A60_R28-en.pdf. Dr. John O. Agwunobi, Assistant Secretary
of Health, U.S. Department of Health and Human Services,
delivered a statement welcoming the adoption of the resolution and commenting on the legal obligations to share data
and virus samples. The need to address the sharing issue
was prompted by Indonesia's decision in February 2007 to
discontinue sharing with the WHO samples of avian influenza A (H5N1) strains appearing in Indonesia. Dr. Agwunobi's
statement, excerpted below, is available at *http://Geneva.
usmission.gov/Press2007/0523WHAbirdflu.html.*

While the world engages in preparations for a possible global pandemic, no nation can go it alone and all nations must cooperate.
As the late Dr. J.W. Lee reminded us in the remarks he had prepared
to deliver to this Assembly before his unfortunate death exactly
one year ago, "We are—and we must remain—alert to every hint
that the virus may be changing its behavior." All nations have a
responsibility under the revised International Health Regulations
(IHRs) to share data and virus samples on a timely basis and without preconditions. The United States wishes to be clear that our
view is that withholding influenza viruses from the Global Influenza
Surveillance Network greatly threatens global public health, and
will violate the legal obligations we have all agreed to undertake
through our adherence to the IHRs.

The United States is pleased the resolution before us makes
clear Member States must continue to share specimens and viruses
with WHO Collaborating Centers to ensure the continuance of
critical risk-assessment and response activities. We understand
such response activities include the development and production
of pandemic-influenza vaccines.

While we acknowledge the preambular language on each
State's sovereign rights over its biological resources, all nations
need to recognize the distinctive nature of influenza viruses. Viruses
with pandemic potential represent a global health threat. Influenza
viruses spread freely across international borders through the
movement of people and animals. Our goal is not to conserve such

influenza viruses for sustainable use, but to combat them and the sickness and death that they cause.

This resolution asks the Director-General to commission an expert report on the potential patent issues related to influenza viruses and their genes. The United States urges the Director-General to collaborate closely with other international organizations with expertise in intellectual property rights, particularly the World Intellectual Property Organization and the World Trade Organization, to address any issues related to intellectual property rights that could arise in the context of the Global Influenza Surveillance Network.

*   *   *   *

2. International Health Regulations (2005)

On July 18, 2007, the International Health Regulations (2005) entered into force for the United States subject to one reservation and three understandings. *See* Chapter 4.B.6. The regulations are discussed in *Digest 2006* at 891–92 and *Digest 2005* at 768–71.

Cross References

International Health Regulations, **Chapter 4.B.6.**
Doha Development Agenda, **Chapter 11.C.3.**
Environmental provisions in U.S. trade agreements,
      Chapter 11.D.1.a.

CHAPTER 14

Educational and Cultural Issues

A. CULTURAL PROPERTY: IMPORT RESTRICTIONS

In 2007 the United States extended agreements or memoranda of understanding with Guatemala, Mali, Cyprus, and Peru to protect the cultural heritage of those countries by restricting the importation of specified cultural property into the United States. In each case the action was based on a determination by the Bureau of Educational and Cultural Affairs, U.S. Department of State, that the cultural heritage of the named country "continues to be in jeopardy from pillage of archaeological materials."

The United States took these steps pursuant to the 1970 UNESCO Convention on the Means of Prohibiting and Preventing the Illicit Import, Export and Transfer of Ownership of Cultural Property ("Convention"), which the United States ratified in 1983 and implements through the Convention on Cultural Property Implementation Act. *See* Pub. L. No. 97-446, 96 Stat. 2329, 19 U.S.C. §§ 2601–2613. If the requirements of 19 U.S.C. § 2602 are satisfied, the President has the authority to enter into agreements to apply import restrictions for up to five years on archaeological or ethnological material of a nation which has requested such protections and which has ratified, accepted, or acceded to the Convention. The President may also impose import restrictions on cultural property in an emergency situation pursuant to 19 U.S.C. §§ 2603 and 2604.

Further information and links to related documents are available at *http://exchanges.state.gov/culprop*.

1. Guatemala

Effective September 29, 2007, the United States and Guatemala extended their memorandum of understanding ("MOU") concerning the imposition of import restrictions on archaeological objects and materials from the pre-Columbian cultures of Guatemala, originally agreed to on September 29, 1997 (62 Fed. Reg. 51,771 (Oct. 3, 1997)), for an additional five years. 72 Fed. Reg. 54,538 (Sept. 26, 2007), previously extended at 67 Fed. Reg. 61,259 (Sept. 30, 2002). A 2007 revision to Article II of the memorandum of understanding is available at *http://exchanges.state.gov/culprop/gt07extaIIeng.pdf*.

2. Mali

Effective September 19, 2007, the United States and the Republic of Mali extended their bilateral agreement, with certain changes. 72 Fed. Reg. 53,414 (Sept. 19, 2007). The original agreement, entered into in September 1997, concerned the imposition of import restrictions on certain archaeological material in Mali from the region of the Niger River Valley and the Bandiagara Escarpment (Cliff). *See* 62 Fed. Reg. 49,594 (Sept. 23, 1997), extended at 67 Fed. Reg. 59,159 (Sept. 20, 2002).

To reflect expansion of coverage in 2007, the agreement was renamed "Agreement between the Government of the United States of America and the Government of the Republic of Mali Concerning the Imposition of Import Restrictions on Archaeological Material from Mali from the Paleolithic Era (Stone Age) to approximately the Mid-Eighteenth Century." As explained in the 2007 Federal Register,

Newly threatened archaeological sites include, but are not limited to those located in and near: The Tilemsi Valley;

the Boucle du Baoule; the Bura Band; Tondidarou; Teghaza; Gao; Menaka; Karkarichinkat; Iforas Massif (Adrar des Iforas); Es-Souk; and Kidal. These sites represent a continuum of civilizations from the Paleolithic Era (Stone Age) to the colonial occupation of the 18th century, and lend an archaeological significance to the region.

3. Cyprus

Effective July 16, 2007, the United States and Cyprus extended their bilateral agreement for an additional five years and created a new subcategory of protected material. 72 Fed. Reg. 38,470 (July 13, 2007). The agreement was originally entered into in 2002, 67 Fed. Reg. 47,447 (July 19, 2002), amended in 2006, 71 Fed. Reg. 51,724 (Aug. 31, 2006). As explained in the 2007 Federal Register publication,

> The Designated List of articles that are protected pursuant to the bilateral agreement, as extended, on Pre-Classical and Classical Archaeological Objects and Byzantine Period Ecclesiastical and Ritual Ethnological Material from Cyprus has been revised and is published below. We note that the subcategory Coins of Cypriot Types has been added to the category entitled Metal, pursuant to 19 U.S.C. 2604. This addition comes in response to a request from the Government of the Republic of Cyprus to amend the Designated List. Coins constitute an inseparable part of the archaeological record of the island, and, like other archaeological objects, they are vulnerable to pillage and illicit export.

4. Peru

Effective June 9, 2007, the United States and Peru extended their memorandum of understanding to continue the import restrictions on pre-Columbian archaeological artifacts and Colonial ethnological materials from all areas of Peru, for an additional term of five years. 72 Fed. Reg. 31,176 (June 6, 2007).

The original MOU was agreed in June 1997, 62 Fed. Reg. 31,713 (June 11, 1997), previously extended at 67 Fed. Reg. 38,877 (June 6, 2002).

On June 13, 2007, the U.S. Department of Homeland Security returned more than 300 Peruvian archaeological objects to the custody of Peru that had been unearthed from gravesites and smuggled into the United States. The objects were forfeited and repatriated following the successful prosecution of a smuggler in Miami, Florida. *See http://exchanges. state.gov/culprop/whatsnew.html.*

B. IMMUNITY OF ART AND OTHER CULTURAL OBJECTS

On June 27, 2007, the U.S. District Court for the District of Columbia held that works of art temporarily loaned to museums in the United States by the City of Amsterdam under immunity protection afforded pursuant to 22 U.S.C. § 2459 for works "of cultural significance" could serve as the basis for jurisdiction under the expropriation exception to the Foreign Sovereign Immunities Act, 28 U.S.C. § 1605(a)(3). *Malewicz v. Amsterdam*, 517 F. Supp. 2d 322 (D.D.C. 2007). After reviewing the terms of the loan agreement, visits by representatives to the United States in connection with the loan, and consideration offered by the American museums, the court concluded that "the City's contact with the United States in connection with the loan of the Malewicz artwork was substantial." As a result, the court found that the "property is present in the United States 'in connection with a commercial activity carried on in the United States by the foreign state'" as required by § 1605(a)(3).

In an opinion issued in March 2005, the district court had denied the City's motion to dismiss for lack of jurisdiction, finding that the status of the artworks did not deprive the court of jurisdiction under the expropriation exception even though they were immunized from judicial process under 22 U.S.C. § 2459. The United States filed a Statement of Interest and Supplemental Statement of Interest in support of the

City of Amsterdam's immunity in 2004 and 2005; *see Digest 2004* at 792–96 and *Digest 2005* at 776–77.

Among other things, the court in 2007 also rejected the City's argument that it should dismiss based on the act of state doctrine. The court's analysis on that issue is excerpted below. Appeal of the 2007 decision by the City of Amsterdam to the U.S. Court of Appeals for the District of Columbia Circuit was pending at the end of 2007.

----

*   *   *   *

The City argues that this case falls within the act of state doctrine because its acquisition of the Malewicz paintings was an "official act of the City." City's Mem. at 30. It further argues that the policies underlying the doctrine—that courts should not interfere with matters that could complicate foreign relations and should defer to the executive branch in the area of foreign policy—are implicated here because a decision against the City would chill future cultural exchanges such as the one at issue in this case. *Id.* at 31–32. . . .

A review of the cases reveals that the City's attempt to cast its acquisition of the Malewicz artwork as an "official act" stretches the meaning of that phrase—and hence the act of state doctrine—too far. The cases reveal that the key question is whether the act in question is truly a *sovereign* act—that is, an act " *jure imperii*," an act that is taken "by right of sovereignty." *Black's Law Dictionary* 854 (7th ed. 1999). . . .

*   *   *   *

. . . [T]he City's acquisition of the Malewicz paintings . . . in 1956 was not the type of sovereign act that receives protection under the act of state doctrine. The acquisition may have been an "official" act in the sense that it was done by an employee of the City of Amsterdam . . . acting in his capacity as such. But it was not an "official action by a foreign sovereign" as that phrase has been used in the relevant case law because it was not an action taken "by right of sovereignty"; any private person or entity could have purchased the paintings for display in a public or private museum. *Cf. Alfred Dunhill of London, Inc. v. Republic of Cuba,*

425 U.S. 682, 697–98, 96 S. Ct. 1854, 48 L. Ed. 2d 301 (1976) (opinion of White, J.) ("[Courts] are in no sense compelled to recognize as an act of state the purely commercial conduct of foreign governments. . . ."). In other words, there was nothing *sovereign* about the City's acquisition of the Malewicz paintings, other than that it was performed by a sovereign entity. Moreover, the fact that the initial acquisition of the Malewicz paintings took place in Germany, not in the Netherlands, further illustrates that it was not an "official action" within the scope of the City's sovereign authority. . . .

Further, this Court's application of international law to the City's acquisition of the Malewicz paintings would do nothing to "frustrate the conduct of foreign relations by the political branches of the government." *First Nat'l City Bank v. Banco Nacional de Cuba*, 406 U.S. 759, 767–68, 92 S. Ct. 1808, 32 L. Ed. 2d 466 (1972). The City's argument that this lawsuit could chill further cultural exchanges again overreads the case law. The loan of the artwork from the City to the American Museums was not a matter touching upon "foreign relations," as that phrase is used by the relevant authorities. *See id.* It was a private transaction, admittedly with an altruistic public purpose, that had no far-reaching national or international implications. Essentially, the City has done nothing more than show that paintings were acquired by an employee of the Stedelijk under the authority of the City, which is itself a political subdivision of the Netherlands. That alone is insufficient to make the acquisition an "act of state." The Court must therefore reject the City's argument that the act of state doctrine applies in this case.

* * * *

CHAPTER 15

Private International Law

A. COMMERCIAL LAW

1. Consumer Protection

During 2007 the United States continued to engage with representatives of other members of the Organization of American States ("OAS") in drafting instruments focusing on consumer protection to be considered at the next Inter-American Specialized Conference on Private International Law ("CIDIP VII"). A paper prepared by Michael Dennis of the Office of Private International Law, Department of State Office of the Legal Adviser, and head of the U.S. delegation to CIDIP VII, discussed the challenges to the existing legal framework, particularly from e-commerce, and proposals being developed for the conference by the United States, Canada, and Brazil. Excerpts below provide the U.S. positions being developed; the full text of Mr. Dennis's paper is available at *www.state.gov/s/l/c8183.htm* and published as Michael Dennis, Developing a Practical Agenda for Consumer Protection in the Americas, XXXIV CCURSO DE DERECHO INTERNACIONAL (2007) (forthcoming).

* * * *

[I.][B.]1.Proposals

Three proposals have been put forward by states on consumer protection for CIDIP VII:

- *United States.* The United States has proposed a draft legislative guide and model laws and rules on redress mechanisms designed to assist consumers recover monetary damages suffered in consumer transactions. The United States proposal includes: (1) a model law on government consumer protection authority to provide redress and cooperation across borders against fraudulent and deceptive commercial practices; (2) a draft model law on simplified tribunals for small consumer claims; (3) a draft legislative guide for collective and/or representational dispute resolution and redress for common injuries to consumers; and (4) model rules for electronic arbitration of small [business to consumer ("B2C")] cross-border claims.[13]

- *Brazil.* Brazil has introduced a draft convention on the law applicable to B2C cross-border transactions. The draft convention generally provides that consumer contracts will be governed by the law where the consumer resides (if there is no choice of law in the contract) or the law most favorable to the consumer (if there is a choice of law provision in the contract).[14]

- *Canada.* Canada has introduced a model law on jurisdiction and choice of law. The Canadian proposal focuses on electronic

---

[13]   For documents relating to the proposal of the United States, including earlier versions of the draft legislative guide, *see http://www.oas.org/dil/ CIDIP-VII_topics_cidip_vii_consumerprotection_monetaryrestitution.htm.*

[14]   For documents relating to the Brazilian proposal, including an earlier version of the draft convention, *see http://www.oas.org/dil/CIDIP-VII_ topics_cidip_vii_proposal_consumerprotection_applicablelaw_brazil_17dec2004. htm. See also* Claudia Lima Marques, *Insufficient Consumer Protection in the Provisions of Private International Law, The Need for an Inter-American Convention (CIDIP) on the Law Applicable to Certain Contracts and Consumer Relations,* available at *http://oas.org/dil/AgreementsPDF/Inglesdo cumento%20de%20apoyo%20a%20la%20convencion%20propuesta%20 por%20br%E2%80%A6.pdf,* for a helpful discussion of the background of the Brazilian proposal.

B2C cross-border transactions and would generally apply a country of destination approach to choice of court and choice of law.[15]

* * * *

II. Consumer Remedies for Deceptive Practices

The United States has proposed that CIDIP VII adopt a model law that would assist OAS member states in establishing competent consumer protection authorities, and vest them with the power to obtain redress for consumers and enable them to cooperate with their foreign counterparts. The draft Model Law also aims to facilitate the enforcement of certain judgments for consumer redress across borders.

In the United States, the Federal Trade Commission ["FTC"] can obtain a court order for consumer redress for . . . unfair and deceptive practices under U.S. laws and regulations. . . . The FTC has also entered into enforcement cooperation arrangements with consumer protection agencies in Australia, Canada, Costa Rica, Ireland, Mexico, and the United Kingdom.

A number of OAS member states have established consumer protection authorities. However, many state laws do not vest the consumer protection entity with authority to obtain redress for consumers or enable them to cooperate with their foreign counterparts.

Consumers in cross-border transactions in the Americas need to be protected from fraudulent, deceptive, and unfair practices. . . .

The problem is not limited to the Americas. . . .

The recently approved Organization for Economic Cooperation and Development (OECD) Recommendations on Consumer Dispute Resolution and Redress specifically recommend that national consumer protection agencies have legal authority to obtain and facilitate redress on behalf of consumer victims. They also recommend that the consumer protection authority be able to cooperate with

---

15 For documents relating to the Canadian proposal, including earlier versions of the draft model law, *see http://www.oas.org/dil/CIDIP-VII_topics_ cidip_vii_consumerprotection_jurisdiction.htm.*

similar entities in other states.[23] Representatives from the OAS itself, Argentina, Brazil, Canada, Chile, Mexico and the United States participated in the OECD conference on dispute resolution and redress that led up to development of the recommendations.[24]

III. Judicial Disposition of Consumer Disputes

Traditionally, consumer disputes have been addressed by national courts. However, . . . B2C e-commerce poses challenges to the existing legal framework. Given the small value of most consumer complaints, it does not appear that resolving cross-border claims through traditional court mechanisms is practical.

[An] EU study on consumer protection . . . reports that a relative majority of European consumers do not perceive resolving arguments with sellers/providers in court to be easy. . . .

The issue is, of course, even more complicated in B2C cross-border e-commerce disputes. For example, from a practical standpoint, how would most consumers enforce a judgment against a vendor located in another country? The United States has taken the position that practical proposals that simplify and facilitate the judicial resolution of *domestic* consumer disputes have value.

A. Small Claims Tribunals

The United States has proposed that CIDIP VII adopt a model law for providing monetary consumer redress through low cost expedited small claims tribunals. The U.S. proposal, entitled Model Law on Small Claims, provides sample legislative language for implementing a small claims procedure. Member states, in particular those with no current small claims procedures or those with

---

[23]   OECD Recommendation on Consumer Dispute Resolution and Redress, July 12, 2007, at 10–11, available at *http://www.oecd.org/dataoecd/43/50/38960101.pdf.* Similar recommendations were contained in the OECD Guidelines for Protecting Consumers from Fraudulent and Deceptive Practices Across Borders, June 2003, available at *http://www.oecd.org/dataoecd/24/33/2956464.pdf.*

[24]   The report is available at *http://www.oecd.org/dataoecd/9/26/34431531.pdf.* OECD member states include the United States, Canada, and Mexico. In 2007 the OECD initiated membership talks with Chile and decided to strengthen OECD cooperation with Brazil, through enhanced engagement or as a full member.

procedures that are less developed, could make appropriate use of such provisions in light of their particular needs and existing legal systems. The draft Model Law on Small Claims omits detailed sections regarding topics such as choice of court, venue, service of process, and motions to vacate judgments; member states can include such sections as best fit within their own overall legal frameworks.

The United States and some OAS member states already have in place viable low cost small claims tribunals for consumer claims. [fn. omitted] These procedures vary significantly from country to country in terms of type of procedure; type of dispute and claim that may be heard; monetary thresholds; financial costs to parties; and overall accessibility to consumers. These low cost expedited small claims tribunals offer consumers access to monetary redress at a cost and burden not disproportionate to the amount of their claim. The new OECD Recommendations on Consumer Dispute Resolution and Redress also call for states to establish simplified court procedures for small claims, which offer consumers the opportunity to obtain a judicial determination of their disputes through less formal and expedited procedures rather than those used in traditional court proceedings. [fn. omitted] Even more recently, the European Parliament adopted a regulation establishing common small claims procedures for simplified and accelerated cross-border litigation on consumer claims.[28]

B. Collective Actions

The U.S. proposed legislative guide on redress and dispute resolution for CIDIP VII includes a section calling for states to provide for some form of collective or representational legal actions for common consumer injuries, that is fair to both consumers and business. The U.S. proposal provides general principles for collective dispute resolution. It contemplates that the specific laws providing for collective actions may vary substantially from state to state, depending on the overall legal framework.

Collective or class actions have not existed in most civil law countries, including in Latin America and Europe. On the other

---

[28] Regulation No. EC 861/2007, May 22, 2007, available at *http:// register.consilium.europa.eu/pdf/en/07/st03/st03604.en07.pdf.*

hand, class actions have long been recognized in common law countries, such as the United States. In the United States each state has procedures available allowing collective action lawsuits to be filed by groups of private consumers who have suffered similar harm as a result of the wrongful actions of the vendor or provider.

Collective actions provide consumers with access to remedies in cases where they could not afford to act individually. These procedures are particularly useful where large numbers of consumers have each suffered small losses. In such cases, although the cost to each individual consumer may be small, the aggregate cost and the impact on consumer welfare is large.

The key idea is to reduce the cost of litigation to the point that the total remedy, and administrative cost of distributing the remedy collected to all the individual claimants, is substantially greater than the cost of bringing the claim. The goal then is to reduce the cost of bringing all the claims by eliminating the redundancy of litigating each claim individually. When consumers can pool their claims together into one large case, it has the effect of reducing the per unit costs of bringing each individual claim to a much lower cost than if each claim were prosecuted separately.

The EU study on consumer protection reported that 74% of European citizens polled would be more willing to defend their rights in court, if they could join other consumers complaining about the same thing. [fn. omitted] Additionally, the new OECD Recommendations on Consumer Dispute Resolution and Redress specifically call for states to establish mechanisms that provide for collective resolution of consumer disputes that are fair to both consumers and businesses. [fn. omitted]

C. Jurisdiction and Choice of Law

The Canadian and Brazilian proposals focus on cross-border resolution of consumer disputes and deal with the theory of jurisdiction and choice of law. As discussed above, the creation of the Internet has raised complex jurisdiction and choice of law issues. Traditionally, disputes are settled within the physical territory where the property or disputants are located, or where the performance takes place. With e-commerce, however, consumers and vendors may be located anywhere in the world. Moreover, the disputes raise challenging jurisdictional issues. For example, what is the place of performance where a vendor sells software to the consumer and the consumer downloads the software from the Internet? Legal systems vary widely in the resolution of this issue.

*   *   *   *

3. CIDIP V—Mexico City Convention

[In addition to other concerns outlined by the United States], [t]he Brazilian and Canadian approaches also conflict with the approach taken by OAS member states when they earlier addressed choice of law issues during CIDIP V in Mexico City in 1994. CIDIP V produced the Inter-American Convention on the Law Applicable to International Contracts,[47] which is applicable inter alia to consumer contracts. Article 7 of that Convention provides that the contract is governed by the law chosen by the parties. Article 11 of the Convention further provides that the provisions of the law of the forum shall necessarily be applied when they are mandatory requirements. Article 11 also grants the forum court discretion to apply the mandatory provisions of the law of another state with which the contract has close ties.

The CIDIP V Mexico City Convention approach to autonomy of contract in consumer matters is comparable to the approach taken by the European Union in its Rome Convention on the Law Applicable to Contractual Obligations.[48] Article 3 of the Rome Convention recognizes that the contract is governed by the law chosen by the parties. Moreover, the Rome Convention also provides for the application of mandatory rules in certain cases involving transactions with consumers. [fn. omitted] The CIDIP V Mexico City Convention approach to autonomy of contract is also generally consistent with

---

[47] The Convention entered into force on December 15, 1996 and it has been ratified by Mexico and Venezuela and signed by Bolivia, Brazil, and Uruguay. It is likely that other OAS member states, including the United States, will consider ratification of the treaty concerning its application in cross-border transactions. *See* Articles 22–23 of the Convention providing that states are not obliged to apply the Convention to conflicts between the legal systems in force in its territorial units. The Convention is available at *http://www.oas.org/dil/CIDIPV_convention_international contracts.htm.*

[48] The text of the Rome Convention is available at *http://www.rome-convention.org/instruments/i_conv_orig_en.htm.*

the approach taken in the United States. While U.S. state law varies from jurisdiction to jurisdiction, it generally supports autonomy of contract in consumer transactions, subject to some limitations.

In short, a serious question exists as to whether CIDIP VII will actually harmonize the approach of states to choice of law/choice of court in cross-border consumer transactions in the Americas. Indeed, if CIDIP VII were to consider the proposals in their current form, it would likely result in three different approaches to choice of law/choice of court in consumer transactions: (1) the CIDIP V Mexico City Convention requirement recognizing autonomy of contract; (2) the Canadian country of destination option, and (3) the Brazilian law most favorable to the consumer alternative. The direct conflict between the policies of the Mexico City Convention and the Canadian and Brazilian proposals should be addressed and resolved first in the CIDIP VII negotiations. The most useful form for any new instrument might be a protocol to the Mexico City Convention addressing specific concerns relating to consumers.[50]

In all events, it does not appear that resolving cross-border consumer claims through traditional court mechanisms is practical. A dispute over a few hundred dollars is not, as a practical matter, the stuff of international litigation.

IV. Arbitration of Cross-border B2C e-Commerce Disputes

The United States proposal also includes Draft Model Rules for Electronic Arbitration of Small Cross-Border Consumer Claims. The rules are intended to provide practical procedures for resolution of certain common types of small consumer disputes that are simple, economical, effective, fast, and fair. The term "arbitration" is used in the model rules and this paper as a general term covering non-judicial dispute procedures, and does not necessarily entail the applicability to these procedures of laws governing formal arbitration.

Electronic arbitration of B2C e-commerce disputes is widely regarded as holding great promise for the low-cost and efficient

---

[50] The protocol might for example, consistent with U.S. law, permit the parties to select the law of a domestic or foreign jurisdiction to govern their rights and duties with respect to an issue in the contract if the transaction bears a reasonable relationship to the selected jurisdiction.

resolution of consumer disputes, especially cross-border disputes. The new OECD Guidelines on Consumer Dispute Resolution and Redress call on states to establish online dispute resolution by which consumers and businesses engage in an out of court process utilizing the active intervention of a neutral third party who imposes solutions or alternatively, agency-based mechanisms, by which consumers submit their claim to a public agency for investigation and finding. [fn. omitted]

* * * *

It is also contemplated that the CIDIP VII process may produce a model implementation arrangement for electronic arbitration of cross-border disputes. The U.S. proposal notes that consideration might be given to including mechanisms such as maintaining a list of arbitrators to handle claims and arranging to refer such claims to arbitrators. The Model Rules could also be used in conjunction with any model implementation agreement.

States may also wish to separately consider how to establish practical incentives for compliance with such arbitral awards. Possibilities include:

- promoting a voluntary seal program that vendors can join only on condition that they satisfy all resulting arbitral awards;
- arranging for vendors joining the program to post a bond or other guarantee for amounts in dispute; and,
- developing an arrangement whereby vendors would consent to the reversal of charges on their merchant bank accounts to reflect arbitral awards involving a credit card transaction.

Payment cardholder protections sometimes referred to as charge backs can play an important role for consumer redress in cases of fraudulent, unauthorized, or otherwise disputed charges on payment cards. However, protections for non-conforming or non-delivery of goods and services vary greatly and these protections may not be available at all for cross-border transactions.

Consideration could be given to whether or not the award is enforceable under the OAS Panama Convention on Commercial Arbitration or the New York Convention on the Recognition and

Enforcement of Foreign Arbitral Awards. However, given the small size of most consumer claims, use of these treaties would not be cost-effective in the typical case.

Another issue is whether consumers can be required to submit to binding ADR, either before or after the dispute has arisen. OAS member states have a mixed approach as to whether to permit pre-dispute binding arbitration in consumer contracts. In the United States, consumers are generally free to consent to be bound by ADR, but a court may consider general contract law defenses such as fraud, undue influence or unconscionability to strike down such a contractual clause. These differences in theoretical approach would not preclude developing practical rules for arbitration of B2C cross-border disputes, at least for post-dispute agreements to such arbitration.[54]

*   *   *   *

2. UN Commission on International Trade Law

a. Review of work

On October 23, 2007, James Donovan, Counselor, U.S. Mission to the United Nations, addressed the UN General Assembly Sixth Committee in support of the work of the

---

[54]   A 2003 joint statement of Consumers International and Global Business Dialogue on Electronic Commerce (GBDe) on alternate dispute resolution guidelines provides as follows concerning binding arbitration:

Merchants should generally avoid using arbitration that is binding on consumers because it may impair consumer confidence in electronic commerce. Arbitration that is binding on merchants as an obligation of membership in a trustmark program, on the other hand, serves to promote consumer confidence in electronic commerce. Arbitration that is binding on consumers should only be used in limited circumstances, and where it clearly meets the criteria of impartiality, transparency and public accountability. Consumer decisions to engage in binding arbitration must be fully informed, voluntary, and made only after the dispute has arisen.

Available at *http://www.gbde.org/IG/CC/Consumers_Internationa_GBDe Joint_Statement_Nov03.pdf*. Thus, the differing approaches do not preclude post dispute binding arbitration.

Commission on International Trade Law ("UNCITRAL"). The
text of the U.S. statement is set forth below and available at
www.state.gov/s/l/c8183.htm.

The United States is pleased again to be able to support the work
of the Commission on International Trade Law. The Commission
has continued its technical and non-politicized approach to commercial and economic law reform, and has focused on promotion
of commerce in all geographic regions and for states at all levels of
development. The Commission and its Working Groups throughout their work in 2006 continued to recognize that, despite liberalization of trade through international agreements, the failure to
also upgrade commercial laws has meant that trade liberalization
is less effective and its benefits do not reach as many sectors as it
might. The Commission's work continues to help close that gap and
reflects the practical achievements possible within the UN system.

The principal achievement at the 2006 Plenary session was
partial approval of the draft Legislator's Guide on secured finance
reform. The remainder of the Guide is expected to be concluded at
a second meeting of the Plenary Session scheduled for mid-
December of this year in Vienna. The Guide will have over 200
legislative recommendations, which is a very significant achievement in an area considered by many international financial institutions to be the front-line area for law reform to boost economic
development in less developed and emerging states.

We also support the continued progress in the other Working
Groups, including upgrading procurement practices for electronic
commerce; modernizing commercial arbitration rules; and seeking
solutions to the treatment of corporate groups and promoting
protocols on cross-border cooperation in bankruptcy cases. The
Commission's Working Group III is moving toward finalizing
a multilateral treaty on carriage of goods which offers an opportunity to harmonize an area of trade law that has lacked that
for over eighty years. In that regard, we think it very important
to maintain the Working Group's decision to allow certain
parties the right to freely negotiate terms of carriage so as to both
mirror existing maritime practices and reflect modern commercial law.

We note that at this year's UN treaty event, additional states have signed the Commission's Convention on electronic commerce, which will promote modern laws to enhance the growth of internet commerce and other areas of electronic commerce. The US supports the Convention's provisions and its market-based approach to laws enabling e-commerce without overly regulating the field.

Coordination remains an important focus, and we support the continuing work in cross-border business insolvency law toward a merger of the insolvency legislative recommendations concluded by this Commission and approved by the UNGA and parallel recommendations prepared by the World Bank with the goal of producing a single standard to be adopted by the Bank and the International Monetary Fund.

The United States welcomes the Commission's continued efforts concerning the growing problem of commercial fraud in a number of sectors, such as banking and finance, cross-border bankruptcy, maritime cargo documentation, and other sectors. This work which does not fall conveniently into the core area of activity of any existing UN body should continue to be undertaken in coordination with UNODC and other UN bodies as appropriate.

Finally, we note that the Commission, while doubling the number of its active Working Groups and projects, enhancing its outreach through innovative websites, and upgrading its technical assistance programs has remained within its existing budget. We support the efficiency and management approach that has made that possible. In line with that, we support the ongoing discussion of ways to clarify the Commission's working methods, and support the substantial majority who welcome guidelines but wish to avoid overly detailed rules.

*   *   *   *

b. Rules of procedure and methods of work

At the first part of its 40th session, meeting in Vienna from June 25 to July 12, 2007, UNCITRAL considered a proposal to modify its working methods. At the conclusion of the session, the Commission "requested the Secretariat to prepare a compilation of procedures and practices established by UNCITRAL itself or by the General Assembly in its resolutions regarding the work of the Commission, and present it for consideration by the Commission. . . ." *See* UNCITRAL rules of procedure and methods of work, Note by the Secretariat, U.N. Doc. A/CN.9/638 (Oct.17, 2007) and Add 1-Add 6. As explained in the Secretariat's note:

> The United Nations Commission on International Trade Law (UNCITRAL or the "Commission"), at the first part of its fortieth session (Vienna, 25 June–12 July 2007), considered observations and proposals by France on UNCITRAL's working methods, set out in document A/CN.9/635. In the general discussion of the observations and proposals, it was widely felt that, while the current UNCITRAL's working methods had demonstrated their efficiency, a comprehensive review of the working methods of the Commission might be timely, particularly in view of the recent increase in membership of the Commission and the number of topics being dealt with by the Commission and its six full-membership working groups to which also non-member States were invited. It was agreed that the guiding principles for such a comprehensive review should be those of inclusiveness, transparency and flexibility. . . .

At the conclusion of the final meeting of the plenary session, held in Vienna from December 10 to 14, 2007, UNCITRAL reached a decision by consensus that the next step should be a clarification of existing rules. This result was largely in line with U.S. views opposing the proposal to require more formal rules:

> In light of the clarification provided in the Secretariat's Note, drafting an entire new set of procedural rules is not necessary. Such a revision would be time-consuming, difficult to negotiate, and divert attention from UNCITRAL's important substantive work.

U.S. Observations on UNCITRAL's Rules of Procedure and Methods of Work, U.N. Doc. A/CN.9/639 (Nov. 22, 2007) (Annex). Further excerpts from the U.S. position paper follow (footnotes omitted). The UN documents for the UNCITRAL 40th session are available at *www.uncitral.org/uncitral/en/commission/sessions/40th.html#second.*

1. For 40 years UNCITRAL has served as a highly effective UN body working to provide the world the framework to support global trade and business. Member and observer states can be proud of their contributions over the decades in the development of international commercial practices in the context of model laws, legislative guides, treaties and other international legal texts. Many of these instruments have been adopted or are serving as models for legal developments around the world.

2. The Commission's rules of procedure and work methods are very clearly explained in the Secretariat's Note, which is available on the Commission's web site. This paper should be the basis for any review of UNCITRAL rules of procedure and working methods. It demonstrates that the Commission's rules of procedure and work methods work well and have been a significant contributing factor in producing UNCITRAL's distinguished track record.

3. This Note reviews various proposed changes to the Commission's rules of procedures and methods of work in light of the Secretariat's Note. It offers modest suggestions concerning possible ways in which the Commission's methods of work might be improved.

II. UNCITRAL Rules of Procedure

4. Contrary to the suggestion by some, UNCITRAL does operate under the Rules of Procedure of the General Assembly. The Secretariat paper gives a thorough commentary of how these rules have evolved to suit the specific needs of the Commission. At the first session of UNCITRAL in 1968, States decided on the basis of rule 161 of the Rules of Procedure of the General Assembly that the rules of procedure of Committees (now rules 96–133) as well as rules 45 and 60, would apply to UNCITRAL, since it is a subsidiary organ of the General Assembly. The Commission further decided

that it would be guided by the general principle that the rules of procedure of the GA would apply *mutatis mutandis* to the Commission, as appropriate for the performance of its functions. Since that time the Commission and its working groups have followed these general procedural rules, subject to decisions by the Commission to alter specific rules.

* * * *

III. Decision Making

6. Most states have welcomed the fact that UNCITRAL decisions have been made without the need for a formal vote. The General Assembly has repeatedly commended UNCITRAL for having reached its decisions by consensus. By seeking to find solutions that are generally acceptable, UNCITRAL has avoided politicization and entrenched disagreement, remained technically focused, and established itself as an effective standard setting organization. This method of work has benefited countries in all economic stages, especially developing and emerging states.

7. The Secretariat's paper includes a comprehensive commentary on decision making within UNCITRAL and the General Assembly generally, and should provide helpful clarification for those States that are new members of the Commission or are not familiar with the practices of the Commission.

8. At its first session in 1968, States expressed the general view that every effort should be made to reach all decisions by consensus. Since that time the Commission has consistently followed this view. Indeed, there has been only one formal vote in the entire history of the Commission (on a procedural matter concerning the move of the Secretariat to Vienna in 1973).

9. UNCITRAL's use of consensus is consistent with the long established and common practice of the General Assembly, its Committees, subsidiary organs, and plenipotentiary conferences. The opinions of the United Nations Office of Legal Affairs (quoted in the Secretariat paper) conclude that there is no definitive or authoritative interpretation of consensus and it is somewhat difficult to arrive at an exact definition of the term. The Office of Legal Affairs has concluded that a decision may be considered as having been made "by consensus" if the decision was "arrived at as a

result of a collective effort to achieve a generally acceptable text and consequently the participating delegations are considered to be more closely associated with the decision."

10. The legal opinions of the UN Office of Legal Affairs stress that consensus should not be confused with unanimity. The Commission records demonstrate that in a number of instances, subsidiary organs have adopted decisions on the basis of consensus, despite reservations or opposition regarding some aspects of the decision. It is a well-established custom within the UN and UNCITRAL that in such situations, any reports clearly reflect any dissents to decisions that have been made by consensus.

11. The UN legal opinions also underscore that consensus cannot be imposed on any member state of a subsidiary organ. Any member may insist on its Charter given right to exercise its vote and if a member formally requests that a vote be taken, such a vote must be taken.

IV. Participation of Observers

12. UNCITRAL is a technical body that does not operate in the political realm, but instead brings together the best legal minds from member and non-member countries as well as expert observers to facilitate discussion. The Secretariat's Note provides a very important discussion of the decisions that have been taken by the Commission and the General Assembly concerning the participation of observers in the work of UNCITRAL.

13. General Assembly Resolution 2205 (XXI), which established UNCITRAL, provided that the Commission may establish working relationships with nongovernmental organizations concerned with the progressive harmonization and unification of the law of international trade. At its inception UNCITRAL adopted a workable method (administered by the Secretariat in consultation with Member States) for identifying those non-state entities with particular knowledge, expertise, or experience in the subjects under consideration. The Secretariat has sent invitations to nongovernmental organizations for each session of the Commission and its Working Groups. The Secretariat has generally only issued invitations to organizations with specific expertise on the issues under consideration. The Commission has repeatedly recognized

that the participation of nongovernmental organizations with international expertise is critical to the quality of texts formulated by the Commission, as well as its program of work. The General Assembly has also on several occasions affirmed the practices of the Commission, as well as the importance of the participation of observers from interested organizations with international expertise at the sessions of the Commission and its working groups.

14. The concerns raised about the participation of NGOs can be resolved by simply clarifying existing rules, rather than introducing new rules. Such clarifications should include:

(a) having the relevant standards and expectations about participation of non-member states, international governmental organizations, specialized agencies, and non-governmental organizations restated in the letter of invitation to the observer delegation or in the Commission's report;

(b) handling participation by non-governmental observers according to two categories of nongovernmental observers, i.e., those with a "general interest for international commerce" which can be granted a permanent status, and those with "special expertise" in one of the topics discussed, which should not be admitted beyond the duration of the particular subject in which they have expertise;

(c) continuing to remind observer organizations of their role as contributors of technical information, information on practices of an affected economic or commercial sector, and other relevant information, and that they do not participate as decision makers.

15. Like many technical UN bodies, the work of UNCITRAL cannot be done effectively without expert observer participation. Limiting this participation could jeopardize UNCITRAL's relevance and could ultimately take the discussion of these important private international law issues wholly out of the UN.

V. Languages

16. Member states have welcomed the fact that UNCITRAL is the only UNGA organization whose entire website is available in

all six official UN languages. Some states have raised the issue of whether UNCITRAL should provide language services at informal governmental and intercessional expert group meetings. The proposal, however, has substantial resource implications.

*   *   *   *

VI. Public and Private Meetings

19. Another issue raised by some States concerns the possibility of closing working group meetings, as is done in some political bodies of the UN. As the Secretariat's Note explains, the general principles of the General Assembly concerning public and private meetings are set forth in rules 60 of the Rules of Procedure of the General Assembly. That rule provides that: "The meetings of the General Assembly and its Main Committees shall be held in public unless the organ concerned decides that exceptional circumstances require that the meeting be held in private. Meetings of other committees and subcommittees shall also be held in public unless the organ concerned decides otherwise."

20. For this Commission to remain effective and relevant, all Commission and working group meetings should continue to be held, as they have for the past 40 years, in public. One of the hallmarks of the Commission's successful work methods has been its open and public process. Transparency and participation by knowledgeable and affected groups, including international and non-governmental organizations and private sector representatives, in working group meetings are key to UNCITRAL's success.

VII. Methods of Work

21. The Secretariat's Note also contains a comprehensive explanation of UNCITRAL's method of work. It demonstrates that the current methods are sound and should be continued.

*   *   *   *

3.   Investment Securities

In a memorandum prepared for the American Bar Association, dated July 30, 2007, Harold Burman of the Office of the Legal Adviser, Office of Private International Law, provided a review of recent developments on two securities law projects in the International Institute for the Unification of Private Law ("UNIDROIT"). The full text of the memorandum, excerpted below, is available at *www.state.gov/s/l/c8183.htm*. *See also Digest 2006 at 936–38.*

. . . The two securities law projects discussed below are the first multilateral efforts to seek harmonization of private transactional law in the field of cross-border securities practice. One, the 2006 Hague Convention on law applicable to intermediated securities, has been concluded and we are examining possible US ratification. The second, the draft Unidroit convention on transactional securities law may be concluded in the fall 2008. It is not very likely that a third international project in this field may emerge for some years.

Both projects reflect the need for greater certainty in globalizing markets, and each can boost liquidity in markets, transactional commerce and trade, promote effective securities practices, and lower both market and systemic risks. Since both projects in the U.S. rest on uniform state law, state securities law interests as well as federal have been fully involved, along with the ABA and securities and market associations. Federal and public agency participation has included primarily SEC, Treasury, the New York Federal Reserve Bank, CFTC, State Department.

THE HAGUE CONVENTION

. . . [T]he United States together with Switzerland signed the Convention in 2006 and the ABA has adopted a policy endorsing US ratification. Its provisions cover rules to determine applicable law, treatment of pre and post-convention interests, multi-unit states such as the U.S., etc. . . .

As securities trades and transfers as collateral or otherwise rose to very high volumes through computerized means, especially in countries employing intermediation, the inability of traditional property-based securities laws to effectuate the tracing of rights and interests in a timely manner, sufficient to permit current valuation or prevent significant systemic risk, became clear. The Convention's principal effect is to set out a means of rapidly determining law applicable to intermediated securities as they move from point to point, largely tracking [Uniform Commercial Code ("UCC")] 8-110.

Notwithstanding the treaty, several countries primarily in the EU continue to question allowing party choice of law governing account agreements to play an important role in determining applicable law. We expect to continue exploring with the EU options to resolve the concerns expressed. We anticipate that with US and Swiss ratification, important securities market countries, other than those within the EU, may join the new treaty system.

THE DRAFT UNIDROIT CONVENTION

Following conclusion of the Hague Convention . . ., the second round on securities treaties was started at UNIDROIT as an effort to harmonize relevant areas of substantive transactional law. As cross-border transfers become increasingly common, and accounts increasingly hold securities from differing country origins, the uncertainties of what interests are actually effectively transferred have become significant issues for the international capital markets, and that is one point of focus of this draft second convention. Other important aspects include recognition of rules of securities settlement and clearing entities, and special rules on collateral transactions, closeout netting, etc. The objectives of the financial community on this project range from achieving a text that the U.S. can affirmatively seek to ratify, to being satisfied with a text that brings disparate securities systems closer together, or with a text that facilitates cross-border transactions regardless of differences remaining in underlying securities laws.

A Diplomatic Conference is expected to be set during 2008 to finalize the Convention; many financial community participants in the U.S. support that. . . . While it is of course not certain that sufficient agreement will be found or can result in a treaty text that makes substantial progress, this is likely to be the last international project on this area of law for some years (see comment on the OAS below).

It became clear during 2007 negotiations that gaining wider support for the draft treaty also meant bringing within its provisions so-called "directly-held" systems as well as intermediated systems (early drafts were limited to the latter). The existence of directly-held systems (such as those in China, Brazil, Finland, Spain, Greece and others), while significantly different amongst themselves, often involve requirements incompatible with US-style intermediated systems, such as matching debits and credits, traceability and limited scope of actions for intermediaries. The draft convention was altered at the recent May 2007 meeting so as to accommodate such systems where possible.

It also became clear that the world was not at this stage going to move robustly toward U.S. style intermediation, which in turn affected the nature of changes and amendments sought by the U.S. Indeed, a number of views have been expressed that fully developed intermediated systems if implemented in countries lacking strong securities regulation and other protective mechanisms, could pose risk. Thus the focus now on the treaty is to find as much common ground as is feasible, clarify what types of interests result from cross-border transfers, the extent of [bona fide] acquirer's rights, the extent of intermediaries' protection, etc.

REGIONAL DEVELOPMENTS

Various regional developments need to be taken into account. Canada is currently moving closer to the UCC 8 framework, which might affect changes at some point in Mexico as well so there is a harmonized North American securities market. Both conventions discussed, whether or not ratified, can play a role in that process. An earlier proposal by the U.S., supported by some Central and South American countries, to develop a new treaty on securities transactional law amongst the OAS states, was unsuccessful, in part because of the concurrent effort at UNIDROIT. Once UNIDROIT has concluded, the prospects for supplementary work within the OAS may be reexamined. . . .

*   *   *   *

4. Railway Rolling Stock Finance Protocol

At the conclusion of a diplomatic conference held at Luxembourg, February 12–23, 2007, UNIDROIT adopted a protocol ("Luxembourg Protocol") to the UNIDROIT Mobile Equipment

Convention ("Cape Town Convention") on railway rolling stock finance. See *www.unidroit.org/english/conventions/mobile-equipment/main.htm*. A memorandum prepared by government members of the U.S. delegation, Harold Burman, Department of Transportation General Counsel Peter Bloch, and U.S. Export-Import Bank structured finance counsel Louis Emery, provided U.S. views on the protocol, as excerpted below. The full text of the delegation memorandum is available at *www.state.gov/s/l/c8183.htm*. For further background on the Cape Town Convention and its protocols to date, *see* annual volumes of the *Digest* beginning with 2002.

———

Over 40 States participated representing all regions, plus the World Bank, the Hague Conference, the Southern African Development Community (SADAC), the European Investment Bank, the European Commission, and industry-based NGOs including the Unidroit-sponsored Railroad Working Group (RWG), the International Rail Transport Committee, the International Union of Railways, and others. The negotiation concluded . . . a four-year project to bring to railroad finance the benefits we have already secured for aircraft and air transportation under the new UNIDROIT treaty system (the "Cape Town Convention") for international equipment finance.

The principal effects expected of the Luxembourg Protocol, consistent with US objectives going into the final negotiation, are: (a) significant enhancement in global financing of rail equipment and increase of exports of rail equipment, (b) boosting domestic rail improvements, and especially capacity of developing countries to obtain modern rail facilities, (c) boosting potential regional rail development where geography and political circumstances permit, (d) reaffirming the trend toward modern US-style secured finance laws and economics, begun in 2001 with the UNIDROIT Cape Town Convention and the concurrently negotiated UNCITRAL Convention on assignments financing, and (e) protecting the North American (US, Canada, Mexico) rail system so that it would only come under the Protocol's new international finance registry system if North American rail industry interests (rail operators, manufacturers, financers and regulators) agree to that.

The 2001 Cape Town Convention, which established the framework for the Luxembourg Protocol, requires a separate protocol for each type of equipment. The first protocol to that Convention cover[ing] aircraft, aircraft engines and helicopters, came into force in 2006, and is already covering over fifty (50) percent of the worldwide aircraft transaction market, a major achievement. The circumstances of the two international industries, aircraft and rail, are substantially different and the dynamics of the negotiations therefore were quite different.

First, the international organizational framework was different. All protocols to the Cape Town Convention are negotiated under UNIDROIT auspices, a small intergovernmental body headquartered in Rome which is highly productive in the private transactional law field, and which in some cases partners with other international bodies in each relevant sector. For aircraft, that was an obvious connection with ICAO (International Civil Aviation Organization, a UN specialized agency) which now serves as the Supervisory Authority for the new aircraft transaction registry system, and the USG as a member of the ICAO Council is adequately positioned there. Rail however has no comparable UN body or other organization which has jurisdiction over transportation. The largest multilateral rail transportation body is the Bern, Switzerland-based OTIF (Intergovernmental Organization for International Carriage by Rail), which has taken an active role in the process and was selected to become the Secretariat for the new Registry system as well as the Preparatory Commission of 20 states that will establish the rail registry. While we have no issue at this juncture with how OTIF manages its affairs, it remains a regional body, largely composed of European states, with some additional membership from North Africa and the Middle East (its role in this rail protocol is expected to expand its membership). Neither the US, Canada or Mexico are parties to OTIF, thus making the optional carve-out for national or regional rail systems vis-a-vis the new registry system an important US objective, which was met.

In addition, the markets themselves are different. US rail markets already benefit from UCC asset-based finance law (which the treaty incorporates) and are already largely integrated in the three NAFTA states, whereas European markets lack both an equally modern commercial law and sufficient integration of their practices to achieve efficiencies. US rail is largely freight-based and largely private sector, unlike European and some other systems which rely more on passenger service and are more often government-related, which is reflected in differing financing and registration practices. For the cost of a new international finance registry to be reasonably amortized, air finance needed the entry of the US aircraft markets into that system to avoid substantial delay. The opposite may be true for rail, where either European rail interests or a combination of large developing countries with significant rail service can result in sufficient transactional filings to amortize such costs. Moreover, it is expected that at least in the near term US rail may seek a carve-out from the new registry system even if the US ratifies the Protocol. . . .

* * * *

. . . [M]ore milestones need to be met following the negotiation for the US to consider ratification. First, private commercial law treaties require, unlike most public law treaties, very specific language carefully interwoven as to all parties' rights and interests, each provision of which is then assessed closely by capital markets analysts and international credit risk raters as to the effect in transactions (a process that sets credit and transaction costs up front). This leads to extended informal negotiations, after conclusion of the protocol treaty text, as to the wording of an official commentary on the text, which fills in a number of factors important to transactions and credit ratings.

Assuming that is concluded satisfactorily, detailed negotiations are required (and are already planned to be underway later in 2007) to work out the technical and policy issues surrounding the setting up of a new international computer-based finance registry for rail interests. This type of transparent system, built into the Convention itself, tracks market-tested concepts in the Uniform Commercial Code (UCC) in force in all states of the US and comparable to law in all provinces of Canada. . . .

Only when these next two phases are complete can the potential value and benefit for US rail interests and US export and development assistance programs be assessed. . . .

* * * *

Following the successful conclusion of this second equipment protocol under the new Cape Town treaty system, it is expected that negotiations will be restarted on a third protocol on outer space commercial asset finance, with a focus on financing of satellites and space-based commercial services.

B. FAMILY LAW

1. Convention on International Recovery of Child Support and Other Forms of Family Maintenance

On November 23, 2007, the United States joined 67 other states and the European Community in signing the Final Act of the fifth session of the Special Commission on Maintenance of the Hague Conference on Private International Law, meeting from November 5 to 23, 2007. The Final Act adopted the final text of the Convention on International Recovery of Child Support and other Forms of Family Maintenance.

On the same date, the United States became the first country to sign the convention itself. A statement by U.S. Assistant Secretary of State for Consular Affairs Maura Harty at the time of signature is set forth below and is included in the Hague Conference on Private International Law press release of November 23, available at *www.hcch.net/upload/press 20071123e.pdf*. The text of the convention is available at *www. hcch.net/index_en.php?act=conventions.text&cid=131*. For further information on the convention, *see Digest 2006* at 938–42 and other annual volumes beginning in 2002.

The United States is delighted to sign the new Hague Convention on the International Recovery of Child Support, which we believe represents a major step forward in the development of a global system for enforcement of child support obligations in transnational cases. Every child deserves the support of both the child's parents. And yet recovering child support when the child and one parent are in one country and the other parent is in another is difficult and often impossible. The legal and practical obstacles often mean that little or no support ever reaches the parent and child. Given the importance of this topic to U.S. families, and because the number of transnational cases will continue to increase, the United States has been an active participant in this negotiation. This new convention is necessary to modernize and improve the existing international system, which is outdated and does not meet the needs of an increasingly global world.

As stated in the Preamble of the new Convention, what is needed is a system which produces results, and is accessible, prompt, efficient, cost-effective, responsive and fair. The Convention is designed to achieve those goals. In particular, the Convention establishes a comprehensive system of cooperation among child support authorities, which we believe will result in more children receiving more support more quickly.

We are pleased to have signed the Convention, and we hope that other States, from every region of the world, will quickly join us. We look forward to working with other States and the Hague Conference on the important work of implementing this Convention in the United States and all around the world.

> Prior to the November session, the United States submitted extensive proposals and comments on the Draft Explanatory Report being prepared to accompany the convention. The U.S. comments are available, with comments from other states and regional organizations, in Prel. Doc. No. 35 (October 2007), at *www.hcch.net/index_en.php?act=publications.details &pid=4143&dtid=35*.

2. Bilateral Arrangements for Enforcement of Family Support Obligations

> On July 11, the Department of State issued a notice amending and supplementing a 2004 notice providing a list of reciprocating countries for the enforcement of family support obligations. 72 Fed. Reg. 39,127 (July 17, 2007). The notice explained the reciprocating-country status as excerpted below.
>
> As reflected in the notice, during 2007 new arrangements were completed with El Salvador (June 21, 2007), Hungary

(Jan. 22, 2007), and two Canadian Provinces: Saskatchewan (Jan. 24, 2007) and Yukon (May 22, 2007). As of the date of the notice, reciprocity agreements had been signed, but were not yet in effect, with Costa Rica and Finland. Subsequently, parallel unilateral declarations of reciprocity were exchanged between the United States and the United Kingdom, and the United Kingdom was declared a reciprocating country on December 17, 2007.

* * * *

Section 459A of the Social Security Act (42 U.S.C. 659A) authorizes the Secretary of State with the concurrence of the Secretary of Health and Human Services to declare foreign countries or their political subdivisions to be reciprocating countries for the purpose of the enforcement of family support obligations if the country has established or has undertaken to establish procedures for the establishment and enforcement of duties of support for residents of the United States. These procedures must be in substantial conformity with the standards set forth in the statute. The statutory standards are: Establishment of child support orders, including the establishment of paternity if necessary to establish the order; enforcement of child support orders, including collection and distribution of payments under such orders; cost-free services (including administrative and legal services), as well as paternity testing; and the designation of an agency as Central Authority to facilitate enforcement.

Once such a declaration is made, support agencies in jurisdictions of the United States participating in the program established by Title IV-D of the Social Security Act (the IV-D program) must provide enforcement services under that program to such reciprocating countries as if the request for service came from a U.S. State.

The declaration authorized by the statute may be made "in the form of an international agreement, in connection with an international agreement or corresponding foreign declaration, or on a unilateral basis." The Secretary of State has authorized either the Legal Adviser or the Assistant Secretary for Consular Affairs to make such a declaration after consultation with the other.

As of this date, the following countries (or Canadian provinces or territories) have been designated foreign reciprocating countries: [Australia, El Salvador, Czech Republic, Hungary, Ireland, Netherlands, Norway, Poland, Portugal, Slovak Republic, Switzerland, and Canadian Provinces or Territories: Alberta, British Columbia, Manitoba, New Brunswick, Northwest Territories, Nunavut, Newfoundland/Labrador, Nova Scotia, Ontario, Saskatchewan, and Yukon].

Information

Each of these countries (or Canadian provinces or territories) has designated a Central Authority to facilitate enforcement and ensure compliance with the standards of the statute. . . .

*   *   *   *

The law also permits individual states of the United States to establish or continue existing reciprocating arrangements with foreign countries when there has been no Federal declaration. Many states have such arrangements with additional countries not yet the subject of a Federal declaration. Information as to these arrangements may be obtained from the individual State IV-D Agency.

C. INTERNATIONAL CIVIL LITIGATION

1. Concurrent and Related Proceedings in Foreign Courts

a. *Comity-based abstentions:* Dependable Highway Express v. Navigators Ins. Co.

On August 22, 2007, the U.S. Court of Appeals for the Ninth Circuit reversed and remanded a lower court order staying a domestic contract dispute in U.S. court pending resolution of arbitration proceedings in England. *Dependable Highway Express v. Navigators Ins. Co.*, 498 F.3d 1059 (9th Cir. 2007). In this case Dependable brought suit in the United States against its indemnity insurer Navigators seeking reimbursement resulting from two cargo thefts. Subsequent to Dependable's initial filing, Navigators commenced court proceedings in the High

Court of Justice, Queen's Bench Division, Commercial Court, to restrain Dependable from proceeding in U.S. court, arguing that an arbitration clause in the parties' contract required them to arbitrate the dispute. The English court granted an injunction enjoining Dependable from proceeding with its U.S. litigation and assessed court fees against Dependable in March 2005. The U.S. district court granted a motion for a stay filed by Navigators, "pending the resolution of the London proceedings, including arbitration." Dependable appealed.

The court first found that the district court's stated grounds for issuing the stay were erroneous under U.S. law, and then considered "whether the stay nevertheless should be upheld under principles of international comity." Excerpts follow from the court's conclusion that application of international comity "would be inappropriate on the inadequate record" in this case where the existence of arbitration and forum selection clauses designating London remained in issue, and the action was brought in the United States in the first instance.

---

*　*　*　*

IV

*　*　*　*

Comity is "the recognition which one nation allows within its territory to the legislative, executive or judicial acts of another nation." *Hilton v. Guyot*, 159 U.S. 113, 164, 16 S. Ct. 139, 40 L. Ed. 95 (1895). The term "summarizes in a brief word a complex and elusive concept—the degree of deference that a domestic forum must pay to the act of a foreign government not otherwise binding on the forum." *Laker Airways Ltd. v. Sabena Belgian World Airlines*, 235 U.S. App. D.C. 207, 731 F.2d 909, 937 (D.C. Cir. 1984). Comity "is neither a matter of absolute obligation, on the one hand, nor of mere courtesy and good will, upon the other." *Hilton*, 159 U.S. at 163–64. Indeed,

there are limitations to the application of comity. When the foreign act is inherently inconsistent with the policies underlying comity, domestic recognition could tend either to legitimize the aberration or to encourage retaliation, undercutting the realization of the goals served by comity. No nation is under an unremitting obligation to enforce foreign interests which are fundamentally prejudicial to those of the domestic forum.

Laker Airways, 731 F.2d at 937.

* * * *

More recently, we addressed the comity doctrine in *E. & J. Gallo Winery v. Andina Licores S.A.*, 446 F.3d 984 (9th Cir. 2006), which involved a contract dispute between a California winery and its Ecuadorian distributor. *Id.* at 987. Following a series of disagreements concerning the parties' contract, Andina filed suit in Ecuador, alleging the violation of a decree that was issued by an Ecuadorian military dictatorship in 1976 and later repealed in 1997. *Id.* In response, Gallo filed suit in California pursuant to the contract's forum selection clause, seeking declaratory and injunctive relief, and damages. *Id.* at 988. After Andina removed the domestic action to federal court, the district court denied Gallo's request for a preliminary injunction restraining Andina's action in Ecuador and relying heavily on considerations of comity. *Id.*

On appeal, we held that the district court abused its discretion when it declined to grant a preliminary injunction. Highlighting the strong domestic policy favoring enforcement of forum selection clauses, and noting that neither party disputed the validity of the contract's clause naming California as the forum, we concluded that "[a]n anti-suit injunction is the only way Gallo can effectively enforce the forum selection clause." *Id.* In doing so, we rejected the district court's application of the comity doctrine. Although the Ecuadorian action was filed first, the parties had "previously agreed to litigate their disputes" in California, and thus respecting the Ecuadorian proceedings would frustrate "United States policy favoring the enforcement of forum selection clauses." *Id.* at 994. We therefore declined to extend comity to a foreign action instituted solely in an effort to "evade the enforcement of an otherwise valid forum selection clause." *Id.*

In light of the principles applied in *Laker Airways* and *E. & J. Gallo*, we conclude that invoking the international comity doctrine would be inappropriate on the inadequate record before us. Dependable filed suit in a U.S. forum before Navigators brought its anti-suit injunction action in the English court. The English court thus had the "initial opportunity to exercise comity," *Laker Airways,* 731 F.2d at 939, but elected not to. Moreover, the clear thrust of Navigators' English action was to halt Dependable's domestic proceedings—a tactic frowned upon in *Laker Airways*. *Cf. id.* at 938. . . . Indeed, the express purpose of an anti-suit injunction, be it offensive or defensive, is to block litigation in a separate forum. Comity is not required where the British action was filed after the U.S. action for the sole purpose of interfering with the U.S. suit.

To be sure, Navigators' actions are far less egregious than those of the defendants in *Laker Airways* and *E. & J. Gallo*. . . . The record now before us contains no evidence that Navigators has acted in bad faith or sought deliberately to circumvent the terms of the agreement with Dependable (whatever the district court may find them to be on remand). On the contrary, Navigators claims it has acted in accordance with the terms of a forum selection clause that it believed to have been part of the insurance contract. Despite Navigators' purportedly good intentions, however, the practical effect of its action in English court was to interfere with the domestic forum's ability to adjudicate the dispute.

If the record were clear that the parties agreed to foreign arbitration, or if the district court made such a determination, we would have little trouble upholding the stay on grounds of international comity. *See Mitsubishi Motors Corp. v. Soler Chrysler-Plymouth, Inc.,* 473 U.S. 614, 629, 105 S. Ct. 3346, 87 L. Ed. 2d 444 (1985). . . . The English court would not have been bound by principles of comity in the first instance, and the district court's stay would have simply recognized the validity of the parties' forum selection clause. *See E. & J. Gallo,* 446 F.3d at 994 ("[W]here private parties have previously agreed to litigate their disputes in a certain forum, one party's filing first in a different forum would not implicate comity at all [in the second forum]."). Central to the dispute before us, however, is the parties' disagreement over the very existence of arbitration and forum selection clauses designating London as the site of the arbitration and English law as the sole means of settling insurance coverage disputes. *Cf. id.* (noting that "the contract clearly contains a California choice-of-law clause"). Where, as here, the record does not even contain a copy of the original insurance contract, it would be improper to invoke international comity based on the mere possibility of upholding a disputed forum selection or arbitration clause.

In sum, because the district court never addressed the parties' dispute over the substance of the contract—specifically, the contested arbitration clause—we decline Navigators' invitation to defer to the English anti-suit injunction obtained in Dependable's absence. *See Laker Airways,* 731 F.2d at 934 (noting that a forum with jurisdiction over a particular dispute is not obligated to "stay its own proceedings in response to an anti-suit injunction").

V

We hold that the district court's indefinite . . . stay was an abuse of discretion. Furthermore, upholding the stay under the doctrine of international comity would be inappropriate at this stage based on the limited record before us. We remand so the district court can develop the record in order to determine whether Dependable and Navigators agreed to arbitrate disputes arising from the insurance contract. *See Nagrampa v. MailCoups, Inc.,* 469 F.3d 1257, 1268 (9th Cir. 2006) (en banc) (reiterating that a district court is obligated to answer threshold issues of arbitrability).

b. Anti-suit injunctions

(1) Goss International Corp. v. Man Roland Druckmaschinen Aktiengesellschaft

On June 18, 2007, the U.S. Court of Appeals for the Eighth Circuit vacated a district court preliminary anti-suit injunction and remanded for dismissal of Goss International Corp.'s request for a permanent injunction. *Goss International Corp. v.*

Man Roland Druckmaschinen Aktiengesellschaft, * 491 F.3d 355 (8th Cir. 2007). In this case, the court explained that Goss International Corp. ("Goss") had obtained a judgment for more than $35 million against Japanese defendant Tokyo Kikai Seisusho ("TKS") under the Antidumping Act of 1916 ("the 1916 Act"), 15 U.S.C. § 72, "which made it unlawful for foreign persons to sell imported articles within the United States at a price substantially less than the actual market value or whole-sale price at the time of exportation, with the intent of destroy-ing or injuring an industry in the United States." In 2004 Congress repealed the 1916 Act prospectively following a WTO decision that the 1916 Act violated WTO rules. Shortly thereafter, Japan enacted the Special Measures Law, under which Japanese corporations and/or Japanese nationals could sue in Japanese courts to recover any judgment awarded under the 1916 Act.

The Eighth Circuit affirmed the $35 million judgment in January 2006 and, in June of that year, TKS notified Goss of its intent to file suit in Japan under the Special Measures Law. The district court subsequently granted Goss's request for a preliminary injunction restraining TKS from proceeding in Japan, TKS paid the judgment in full, and the district court entered a satisfaction of judgment; subsequently the court terminated TKS's supersedeas bond. The background of the litigation and the district court preliminary injunction issued in 2006 are discussed in *Digest 2006* at 958–63.

TKS appealed the preliminary injunction. Excerpts from the Eighth Circuit opinion set forth below describe a split in the circuit courts concerning the deference afforded to inter-national comity in determining the appropriateness of an anti-suit injunction and provide the court's conclusion that Goss was not entitled to injunctive relief in light of changed

---

* Editor's note: Man Roland Druckmaschinen Aktiengesellschaft, a German company, was originally a party to the litigation and one of three companies with which Goss reached settlement agreements before judgment was rendered in the case.

circumstances. Goss filed a petition for writ of certiorari in the Supreme Court that remains pending.

---

*   *   *   *

The propriety of issuing a foreign antisuit injunction is a matter of first impression for our circuit. Other circuits having decided the issue agree that "federal courts have the power to enjoin persons subject to their jurisdiction from prosecuting foreign suits." *Kaepa, Inc. v. Achilles Corp.*, 76 F.3d 624, 626 (5th Cir. 1996). . . . The circuits are split, however, on the level of deference afforded to international comity in determining whether a foreign antisuit injunction should issue.

The First, Second, Third, Sixth, and District of Columbia Circuits have adopted the "conservative approach," under which a foreign antisuit injunction will issue only if the movant demonstrates (1) an action in a foreign jurisdiction would prevent United States jurisdiction or threaten a vital United States policy, and (2) the domestic interests outweigh concerns of international comity. . . . Under the conservative approach, "[c]omity dictates that foreign antisuit injunctions be issued sparingly and only in the rarest of cases." *Gau Shan Co.*, 956 F.2d at 1354 (citing *Laker Airways Ltd. v. Sabena, Belgian World Airlines*, 731 F.2d 909, 927 (D.C. Cir. 1984). . . .

In contrast, the Fifth and Ninth Circuits follow the "liberal approach," which places only modest emphasis on international comity and approves the issuance of an antisuit injunction when necessary to prevent duplicative and vexatious foreign litigation and to avoid inconsistent judgments. *See Kaepa, Inc.*, 76 F.3d at 627–28. . . .

Under either the conservative or liberal approach, "[w]hen a preliminary injunction takes the form of a foreign antisuit injunction, [courts] are required to balance domestic judicial interests against concerns of international comity." *Karaha Bodas Co.*, 335 F.3d at 366. We agree with the observations of the First Circuit that the conservative approach (1) "recognizes the rebuttable presumption against issuing international antisuit injunctions," (2) "is more respectful of principles of international comity," (3) "compels an inquiring court to balance competing policy considerations," and (4) acknowledges that "'issuing an international antisuit injunction is a step that should 'be taken only with care and great restraint' and with the recognition that international comity is a fundamental principle deserving of substantial deference." *Quaak [v. Klynveld Peat Marwick Goerdeler Bedrijfsrevisoren]*, 361 F.3d 11, 18 (1st Cir. 2004). . . . Likewise, we agree with the Sixth Circuit's observation the liberal approach "conveys the message, intended or not, that the issuing court has so little confidence in the foreign court's ability to adjudicate a given dispute fairly and efficiently that it is unwilling even to allow the possibility." *Gau Shan Co.*, 956 F.2d at 1355.

Although comity eludes a precise definition, its importance in our globalized economy cannot be overstated. . . . Indeed, the "world economic interdependence has highlighted the importance of comity, as international commerce depends to a large extent on 'the ability of merchants to predict the likely consequences of their conduct in overseas markets.'" *See Quaak*, 361 F.3d at 19. . . . We also note, the Congress and the President possess greater experience with, knowledge of, and expertise in international trade and economics than does the Judiciary. The two other branches, not the Judiciary, bear the constitutional duties related to foreign affairs. For these reasons, we join the majority of our sister circuits and adopt the conservative approach in determining whether a foreign antisuit injunction should issue.

* * * *

The district court's obvious purpose in issuing the antisuit injunction was to constrain TKS from undermining six years of litigation by seeking recovery under the newly promulgated Japanese Special Measures Law. At the time the district court issued the injunction, TKS had not paid its judgment and the district court had not lifted the stay on TKS's performance bond. Given the status of the case at the time the injunction issued, the district court maintained ancillary enforcement jurisdiction to preserve the judgment and pursue collection. Thus, we need not decide whether the district court abused its discretion in issuing the preliminary antisuit injunction at that juncture. However, the jurisdictional circumstances and comity considerations have changed because there is no longer an outstanding judgment to protect. Given the criteria for granting a foreign antisuit injunction set forth and discussed herein, we conclude, under the facts of this case, the maintenance of the antisuit injunction on a satisfied judgment cannot be justified.

*   *   *   *

(2) Karaha Bodas Co., L.L.C. v. Perusahaan Pertambangan Minyak Dan Gas Bumi Negara

On September 7, 2007, the U.S. Court of Appeals for the Second Circuit affirmed, with minor modifications, an antisuit injunction issued by a district court that

> enjoin[ed] appellant Perusahaan Pertambangan Minyak Dan Gas Bumi Negara ("Pertamina") from pursuing foreign litigation that would undermine federal judgments enforcing a foreign arbitral award that appellee Karaha Bodas Company, L.L.C. ("KBC") had obtained in Switzerland and enforced in the United States pursuant to the Convention on the Recognition and Enforcement of Foreign Arbitral Awards, *opened for signature* June 10, 1958, 21 U.S.T. 2517, 330 U.N.T.S. 38 ("New York Convention" or "Convention"), *implemented at* 9 U.S.C. §§ 201–208. *See Karaha Bodas Co. v. Perusahaan Pertambangan Minyak Dan Gas Bumi Negara*, 465 F. Supp. 2d 283 (S.D.N.Y. 2006) (*"District Court Opinion"*). . . .

Karaha Bodas Co., L.L.C. v. Perusahaan Pertambangan Minyak Dan Gas Bumi Negara, 500 F.3d 111 (2d Cir. 2007). The Second Circuit explained that the lower court "issued the anti-foreign-suit injunction upon learning that Pertamina had initiated a suit in the Cayman Islands that sought, inter alia, to 'vitiate' the foreign arbitral award and obtain return of funds that had been paid over pursuant to the award."

As explained by the Second Circuit, this case concerned a joint venture entered into in 1994 by KBC, a Cayman Islands company owned by American power companies and other investors, and Pertamina, an oil and gas company owned and controlled by the Republic of Indonesia. Subsequently, the Indonesian government suspended the project, and in 1998 KBC initiated arbitration proceedings in Switzerland as the parties had agreed for settlement of disputes. In December 2000 the arbitral panel awarded KBC more than $261 million plus interest. A challenge to the award by Pertamina was dismissed by the Supreme Court of Switzerland. In an action initiated by KBC, the U.S. District Court for the Southern District of Texas confirmed KBC's award pursuant to the New York Convention in 2001 and temporarily restrained Pertamina from pursuing injunctive relief in Indonesian courts.

Pertamina appealed to the Fifth Circuit and, despite the restraining order, filed an action in Jakarta, Indonesia, seeking to collaterally attack the award and enjoin KBC from enforcing it. The Fifth Circuit affirmed the Texas district court's confirmation of KBC's award but vacated the lower court's temporary injunction. Pertamina prevailed in the Indonesian trial court proceeding, but in March 2004 the Indonesian Supreme Court vacated the trial court's order annulling the award and its issuance of an anti-suit injunction. Both the Indonesian Supreme Court and the Fifth Circuit concluded that only a Swiss court could annul the award under the New York Convention. KBC registered and confirmed the Texas judgment in the U.S. District Court for the Southern District of New York and commenced execution proceedings against Pertamina's assets there, which were ultimately successful.

The Second Circuit affirmed the district court order for payment by Pertamina from funds in New York bank accounts in March 2006. *Karaha Bodas Co., L.L.C. v. Bank of Indon.*, 2006 U.S. App. LEXIS 5932 (2d Cir. 2006), *cert. denied* 127 S. Ct. 129 (2006). Following the Supreme Court's denial of certiorari, Pertamina paid the arbitral judgment amount to KBC. In the meantime, however, Pertamina filed a new action in the Cayman Islands seeking restitution of all sums received pursuant to the arbitral award as well as an injunction prohibiting KBC from disposing of any funds obtained pursuant to the award.

The Southern District of New York granted KBC an anti-suit injunction prohibiting Pertamina from maintaining the Cayman Islands action, or any similar action anywhere, 465 F. Supp. 2d 283 (S.D.N.Y. 2006), and this appeal to the Second Circuit followed.

Excerpts follow from the Second Circuit's analysis in concluding (1) that the test set forth in *China Trade & Development Corp. v. M.V. Choong Yong*, 837 F.2d 33 (2d Cir. 1987) was applicable to the anti-suit injunction in this case where a judgment had already been entered in a U.S. federal court and that the injunction was justified under that test, and (2) that the scope of the district court injunction should be modified "to clarify that the injunction does not prohibit foreign confirmation proceedings contemplated by the New York Convention." (Most footnotes have been omitted.) The court also concluded that the district court maintained jurisdiction to protect the federal judgments even after the money judgment against Pertamina was satisfied because "[w]ere we to vacate the District Court's injunction, Pertamina would be free to engage in vexatious proceedings that . . . are intended to undermine or vitiate federal judgments. . . ." (Footnotes have been omitted.)

Pertamina filed a petition for writ of certiorari in the Supreme Court that remains pending.

---

*   *   *   *

B. The *China Trade* Test Applies to, and Supports Entry of, the Anti-Suit Injunction

1. The *China Trade* Test

In *China Trade*, we adopted a test governing the circumstances under which a federal district court could issue an anti-foreign-suit injunction. Under the *China Trade* test, an anti-suit injunction against foreign litigation may be imposed only if two threshold requirements are met: "(A) the parties are the same in both matters, and (B) resolution of the case before the enjoining court is dispositive of the action to be enjoined." *Paramedics [Electro-medicina Comercial, Ltda. v. GE Med. Sys. Info. Techs., Inc.*, 369 F.3d 645, 652 (2d Cir. 2004)], (citing *China Trade*, 837 F.2d at 35). If these two threshold requirements are satisfied, "courts are directed to consider a number of additional factors," *id.*, including whether the parallel litigation would:

> (1) frustrat[e] . . . a policy in the enjoining forum; (2) . . . be vexatious; (3) . . . threat[en] . . . the issuing court's in rem or quasi in rem jurisdiction; (4) . . . prejudice other equitable considerations; or (5) . . . result in delay, inconvenience, expense, inconsistency, or a race to judgment.

Ibeto Petrochemical Industries Ltd. v. M/T Beffen, 475 F.3d 56, 64 (2d Cir. 2007) (quoting *China Trade*, 837 F.2d at 35). *China Trade* instructed that two of these factors should be accorded "greater significance": whether the foreign action threatens the enjoining forum's jurisdiction or its "strong public policies." 837 F.2d at 36. However, we have reiterated that *all* of the additional factors should be considered when determining whether an anti-suit injunction is warranted. *See Ibeto Petrochemical*, 475 F.3d at 64 (disagreeing with courts and commentators that "have erroneously interpreted *China Trade* to say that we consider *only* these two [more significant] factors"). *China Trade* also states that "principles of comity counsel that injunctions restraining foreign litigation be 'used sparingly' and 'granted only with care and great restraint.'" *Paramedics*, 369 F.3d at 652 (quoting *China Trade*, 837 F.2d at 36).

2. The *China Trade* Test Applies to the Anti-Suit Injunction

China Trade involved an anti-suit injunction prohibiting a foreign defendant from pursuing a parallel proceeding in a foreign forum *while a proceeding was pending* in the Southern District of New York. The District Court, noting that judgment had already been entered in American courts, did not apply the *China Trade* test. Relying on *dicta* in a district court decision that had been affirmed by our Court in a brief published *per curiam* opinion, the District Court concluded that a "more lenient standard" applied to injunctions intended to prevent an abusive effort to evade a domestic judgment. . . .

In the instant case, Pertamina argues that the District Court committed legal error . . . not[ing] that the *China Trade* test has been applied by our Court for twenty years, and that we applied the *China Trade* test to an anti-foreign-suit injunction in *Paramedics* even though a "judgment ha[d] been rendered" in that case. . . .

We agree with Pertamina that, pursuant to our decision in *Paramedics*, the *China Trade* test applies to anti-foreign-suit injunctions intended to protect federal judgments. We note, however, that as discussed in *Paramedics*, the discretionary *China Trade* factors will tend to weigh in favor of an anti-foreign-suit injunction that is sought to protect a federal judgment. . . . We also concluded that while "[p]rinciples of comity weigh heavily in the decision to impose a foreign anti-suit injunction . . . where one court has already reached a judgment—on the same issues, involving the same parties—considerations of comity have diminished force." [*Paramedics*] at 654–55.

3. The *China Trade* Test Is Satisfied

Despite the District Court's legal error in not applying the *China Trade* test, we do not think it necessary to vacate the injunction and remand for further proceedings given the particular circumstances of the instant case. The principal difference between the "more lenient" test applied by the District Court and the *China Trade* test lies in the threshold requirements that a party must surmount to obtain an injunction under the latter. Based on the extensive record developed in the District Court and in other United States and foreign courts, we conclude as a matter of law that those threshold requirements are met. Turning to the discretionary factors under *China Trade*, we find that the District Court properly considered these factors, albeit under a different rubric, and found them supportive of injunctive relief.

a. The Threshold Requirements Are Met

It is undisputed that the first threshold requirement of *China Trade* is satisfied; the parties are the same in both the proceedings before the District Court and in the Cayman Islands action. Application of the second threshold requirement of *China Trade*—that resolution of the case before the enjoining court is dispositive of the action to be enjoined, *see* 837 F.2d at 35—requires further analysis. First, we must determine the substance of the "case before the enjoining court." KBC obtained (1) a judgment from the Texas District Court confirming the Award and (2) judgments from the Southern District of New York enforcing the Texas District Court's judgment (collectively, the "federal judgments"). . . .

. . . When KBC registered the Texas District Court's judgment confirming the arbitration award in the Southern District of New York, that judgment had the same effect, and was entitled to the same protection, as if it had been entered in the Southern District of New York in the first instance. . . . The Southern District of New York was therefore empowered to take any action to protect the judgment confirming the Award that the Texas District Court could have taken. . . . Thus, we conclude that the "case before the enjoining court" includes all of the federal judgments related to the case, including (1) the Texas District Court judgment confirming the Award and (2) the judgments entered by the Southern District of New York enforcing the Texas District Court's judgment.

. . . We agree with KBC that the federal judgments satisfy the *China Trade* requirement because the Award, and the federal judgments confirming and enforcing it, actually decided the claims raised in the Cayman Islands action. We also conclude that the New York Convention permits the federal judgments to be treated as "dispositive" of the Cayman Islands action.

*　*　*　*

Pertamina argues that the Cayman Islands action is a proceeding "separate and independent of the arbitration proceedings and award." We, however, conclude that this characterization is inconsistent with the nature of the Cayman Islands action. Beyond seeking to vitiate the Award, the Cayman Islands action seeks a (1) determination that the District Court wrongfully ordered almost $319 million to be paid to KBC pursuant to the federal judgments confirming and enforcing the Award, and (2) return of all funds obtained by KBC "pursuant to the Arbitral Award (and its enforcement)." Although Pertamina makes new factual allegations in support of its claim that the Award should not have been enforced against it, these new factual allegations are not sufficient to undermine the preclusive effect of several earlier federal court decisions that (1) the Award should be enforced and (2) KBC is entitled to Pertamina's New York funds in an amount sufficient to satisfy the Award. . . .

We also conclude that, under the New York Convention, the federal judgments to be protected are "dispositive" of the Cayman Islands action. Pertamina essentially argues that the federal judgments could not be dispositive because (1) the federal courts involved in confirming and enforcing the Award within the United States were only acting as "secondary-jurisdiction court[s] under the Convention," . . . and (2) secondary jurisdictions, under the New York Convention, are not entitled to protect judgments related to a foreign arbitral award from foreign interference. . . .

We agree . . . that federal courts should not attempt to protect a party seeking enforcement of an award under the New York Convention "from *all* the legal hardships" associated with foreign litigation over the award. But it does not follow, as Pertamina would have us hold, that a federal court cannot protect a party who is the beneficiary of a federal judgment enforcing a foreign arbitral award from *any* of the legal hardships that a party seeking to evade enforcement of that judgment might seek to impose. Federal courts in which enforcement of a foreign arbitral award is sought cannot dictate to other "secondary" jurisdictions under the New York Convention whether the award should be confirmed or enforced in those jurisdictions. But federal courts *do* have inherent power to protect *their own* judgments from being undermined or vitiated by vexatious litigation in other jurisdictions. . . . [T]he New York Convention does not divest federal courts of this inherent power. *See Fifth Circuit Injunction Opinion*, 335 F.3d at 365 ("Given the absence of an express provision [in the New York Convention], we discern no authority for holding that the New York Convention divests the district court of its inherent authority to issue an antisuit injunction.").

In this case, the federal judgments reached a dispositive determination that KBC should be paid $319 million of Pertamina's funds, held in New York bank accounts, pursuant to the Award. This determination is entitled to protection from Pertamina's attempts to vitiate it through the Cayman Islands action. . . .

*   *   *   *

. . . [T]he Cayman Islands has no arguable basis for jurisdiction to adjudicate rights and obligations of the parties with respect to the Award. Cayman Islands courts have no power to modify or annul the Award under the Convention; and Pertamina does not even attempt to argue that the Cayman Islands action is one that would be contemplated by the Convention. We conclude that in these circumstances the District Court had power to prevent Pertamina from engaging in litigation that would tend to undermine the regime established by the Convention for recognition and enforcement of arbitral awards. "[C]oncerns of international comity, respect for the capacities of foreign and transnational tribunals, and sensitivity to the need of the international commercial system for predictability in the resolution of disputes require that we enforce . . . agreement[s]" to submit disputes to binding international arbitration. *Mitsubishi Motors Corp. v. Soler Chrysler-Plymouth, Inc.*, 473 U.S. 614, 629, 105 S. Ct. 3346, 87 L. Ed. 2d 444 (1985). These considerations also require us to protect the regime established by the Convention for enforcement of international arbitral awards, if necessary by enjoining parties from engaging in foreign litigation that would undermine it.

b. The Additional *China Trade* Factors Support Issuance of an Injunction

As discussed above, where an anti-foreign-suit injunction is sought to protect a federal judgment, the additional *China Trade* factors will often favor issuance of an anti-suit injunction when the threshold *China Trade* requirements are met. Despite adopting a "more lenient" test, the District Court considered the discretionary factors set forth in *China Trade* and determined they warranted an injunction. *See District Court Opinion*, 465 F. Supp. at 295–301. We agree.

We turn first to the two additional factors that have been described as having "greater significance," *China Trade*, 837 F.3d at 36—namely, whether the foreign action threatens the jurisdiction or the strong public policies of the enjoining forum. . . . Here, an injunction is necessary because the Cayman Islands action threatens to undermine the federal judgments confirming and enforcing the Award against Pertamina, and may also undermine federal jurisdiction to determine whether prior federal judgments should be invalidated on the basis of the fraud alleged by Pertamina. . . . The injunction is also supported by strong public policy considerations. We have noted "the strong public policy in favor of international arbitration," and the need for proceedings under the New York Convention "to avoid undermining the twin goals of arbitration, namely, settling disputes efficiently and avoiding long and expensive litigation." *Encyclopaedia Universalis S.A. v. Encyclopaedia Britannica, Inc.,* 403 F.3d 85, 90 (2d Cir. 2005) (internal quotation marks omitted). These important objectives would be undermined were we to permit Pertamina to proceed with protracted and expensive litigation that is intended to vitiate an international arbitral award that federal courts have confirmed and enforced.

We also conclude that one of the three remaining additional *China Trade* factors—whether the foreign action would be vexatious—counsels strongly in favor of the injunction. . . . Here, the District Court . . . concluded that the subsequent litigation in this case, being aimed at the recovery by KBC in the federal courts, was entirely vexatious. . . .

Finally, we note that comity considerations, though important, have "diminished force" when a court has already reached a judgment involving the same issues and parties. *Paramedics,* 369 F.3d at 655. Comity concerns have particular importance under the Convention; a federal court should be wary of entering injunctions that may prevent parties from engaging in post-award enforcement or annulment proceedings that are contemplated by the Convention. But comity concerns under the Convention have no bearing on our consideration of the Cayman Islands action, which is not a proceeding contemplated by the Convention and is, moreover, intended to undermine federal judgments. As we have stated, "orders of foreign courts are not entitled to comity if the litigants who procure them have 'deliberately courted legal impediments' to the enforcement of a federal court's orders." *Motorola Credit Corp. v. Uzan,* 388 F.3d 39, 60 (2d Cir. 2004) . . . Accordingly, comity concerns do not weigh against entry of an anti-suit injunction in this case.

* * * *

(3) Ibeto Petrochemical Industries Ltd v. M/T Beffen

> As noted in b.(2) *supra*, the Second Circuit had earlier addressed the issue of anti-suit injunctions in January 2007, affirming in part and modifying in part a 2005 lower court order granting motions by *M/T Beffen* and others to stay the U.S. action brought by Ibeto, compel arbitration in London pursuant to the applicable arbitration clause, and enjoin an action brought by defendants in Nigerian court. The Order also denied Ibeto's motion for voluntary dismissal and defendant's motion to limit Ibeto's recovery." *Ibeto Petrochemical Industries Ltd. v. M/T Beffen*, 475 F.3d 56 (2d Cir. 2007). The 2005 order at issue is discussed in *Digest 2005* at 831–32.
>
> Excerpts follow from the Second Circuit's review of the anti-suit injunction enjoining court proceedings in Nigeria, concluding that it met the *China Trade* test but that the injunction must be amended to clearly apply only to the parties in the case and only pending resolution of other proceedings.

---

*   *   *   *

Underlying its Order enjoining further proceedings in Nigeria was the District Court's determination that the controversy between the parties ought to proceed by way of arbitration and that "[p]ermitting the Nigeria litigation to continue may frustrate the general federal policy of promoting arbitration." *Ibeto*, 412 F. Supp. 2d at 292–93. Defendants contend that the anti-foreign suit injunction was not warranted because Ibeto did not contractually agree to arbitration with [a party to the Charter Party containing the arbitration provision] in the first place.

*   *   *   *

In the case before us, the Charter Party was specifically identified by date (December 31, 2003) and by the parties thereto (Chemlube as Charterer, Bryggen as Owner). That was more than sufficient to identify the relevant Charter Party (including the documents referred to in the Charter Party Fixture) and therefore to give effect to the incorporation of the arbitration clause under the provision incorporating "all conditions and exceptions whatsoever." The District Court's analysis comports with the general rule that "[w]here terms of the Charter Party are specifically incorporated by reference in the bill of lading, the Charter Party terms alone are to be looked to for the contract of the parties." 80 C.J.S. SHIPPING § 89. And, although the District Court's direction to proceed with arbitration in London is not appealable (nor is the stay of this action pending that arbitration), *see* 9 U.S.C. § 16(b)(1), (b)(2), we here note our agreement with the District Court's direction in light of Ibeto's challenge to arbitration as a basis for the anti-foreign suit injunction.

[B.] Ibeto's challenge to the appropriateness of the District Court's injunction in regard to the action pending in Nigeria is properly before this Court. *See* 28 U.S.C. § 1292(a)(1). (fn. deleted) Ibeto's contention that the injunction was inappropriate under the circumstances revealed in this case properly was rejected by the District Court. In issuing the injunction, the District Court carefully applied the test, set forth in *China Trade & Dev. Corp. v. M.V. Choong Young*, 837 F.2d 33, 35–36 (2d Cir. 1987), for injunctions against suits in foreign jurisdictions.

* * * *

The "threshold" [*China Trade* test] is clearly met in this case, for the parties are the same in this matter and in the Nigerian proceeding and the resolution by arbitration of the case before the District Court is dispositive of the Nigerian proceeding. . . .

In the *China Trade* case, we found that the [additional] factors having "greater significance" there were threats to the enjoining forum's jurisdiction and to its strong public policies. *Id.* at 36. Finding no such threats, we determined that the equitable factors of that case were "not sufficient to overcome the restraint and caution required by international comity." *Id.* at 37. Some courts and commentators have erroneously interpreted *China Trade* to say that we consider *only* these two factors. . . .

Applying all the factors, the District Court found that the general federal policy favoring arbitration might be frustrated by the Nigerian litigation; widely disparate results might obtain because the Nigerian Courts would not apply the provisions of COGSA; a race to judgment could be provoked by the disparity; equitable considerations such as deterring forum shopping favor the injunction; and "it is likely that adjudication of the same issues in two separate actions would result in inconvenience, inconsistency, and a possible race to judgment." *Ibeto*, 412 F. Supp. 2d at 293. The District Court foresaw "considerable inconvenience" in the movement of witnesses between the two venues. *Id.* The District Court determined, however, that the threat to jurisdiction factor did not apply since "both courts have in personam jurisdiction over the parties." *Id.* We agree with the foregoing analysis of the District Court in applying the *China Trade* factors and add our observation that the policy favoring arbitration is a strong one in the federal courts. *See Paramedics*, 369 F.3d at 654. Accordingly, the injunction is fully justified in this case. We note, however, that the District Court's application of the principle that "'an anti-suit injunction may be proper where a party initiates foreign proceedings in an attempt to sidestep arbitration,'" *Ibeto*, 412 F. Supp. 2d at 289 (quoting *LAIF X SPRL v. Axtel, S.A. de C.V.*, 390 F.3d 194, 199 (2d Cir. 2004)), is not warranted here, where the proceeding in Nigeria was first in time.

The foregoing having been said, we reiterate our understanding that due regard for principles of international comity and reciprocity require a delicate touch in the issuance of anti-foreign suit injunctions, that such injunctions should be used sparingly, and that the pendency of a suit involving the same parties and same issues does not alone form the basis for such an injunction. *See China Trade*, 837 F.2d at 36. Having these caveats in mind, we think that the injunction in this case cuts much too broadly.

The learned District Court wrote only that "defendants' motion to enjoin the Nigerian action is granted." *Ibeto*, 412 F. Supp. 2d at 293. The injunction should be directed specifically to the parties, for it is only the parties before a federal court who may be enjoined from prosecuting a suit in a foreign country. *See* 13 CHARLES ALAN WRIGHT, ARTHUR R. MILLER & EDWARD H. COOPER, FEDERAL PRACTICE & PROCEDURE: JURISDICTION § 3523 (2d ed. 1984). Moreover, there is no need for the permanent injunction that the District Court seems to have issued. The parties need to be enjoined from proceeding in the courts of Nigeria only until the conclusion of the London arbitration and the consequent resolution of the still-pending case in the District Court. The District Court should modify its injunction with a specificity consonant with this determination.

*   *   *   *

(4) Canon Latin America, Inc. v. Lantech (CR), S.A.

On November 21, 2007, the U.S. Court of Appeals for the Eleventh Circuit vacated an anti-suit injunction issued by the U.S. District Court for the Southern District of Florida because it determined that the claimant in U.S. district court "ha[d] not shown that the resolution of its claims in the district court would actually dispose of [the defendant's] claim in Costa Rica." *Canon Latin America, Inc. v. Lantech (CR), S.A.*, 508 F.3d 597 (11th Cir. 2007). Excerpts below from the decision provide the court's analysis in reaching this conclusion (footnotes omitted).

---

*   *   *   *

I. Background

In 1996, [Canon Latin America, Inc. ("Canonlat")], a Florida corporation headquartered in Miami, entered into an agreement with [Lantech (CR), S.A. ("Lantech")], a Costa Rican corporation, to distribute Canon brand products in Costa Rica. In 2003, the parties entered into a superseding distribution agreement ("the Agreement"). Under the Agreement, Canonlat appointed Lantech "as a non-exclusive authorized distributor of the CANON(R) brand products" for the territory of Costa Rica. The Agreement also included a forum selection and choice of law clause in favor of Florida. The parties negotiated the original and superseding agreements at arm's length and entered into both agreements voluntarily.

In March 2004, Canonlat notified Lantech that it was seeking to appoint an additional distributor. The following month, over Lantech's objections, Canonlat appointed Santa Barbara Technology,

S.A. ("SB Technology") as an additional distributor beginning in July 2004. At the time of SB Technology's appointment, Lantech had fallen behind on its payments and owed Canonlat $247,653.20.

In November 2004, without informing Canonlat, Lantech filed suit in Costa Rica against Canonlat and SB Technology for violating Costa Rica Public Law 6209 ("Law 6209"), entitled "Representatives of Foreign Companies Act." Lantech sought indemnity in excess of $6 million on grounds that Canonlat unlawfully terminated Lantech as an "exclusive" distributor. In December 2004, without prior notice to Canonlat, a Costa Rican court required Canonlat to post a $1 million bond or discontinue importing goods to Costa Rica. After SB Technology informed Canonlat of the lawsuit in January 2005, Canonlat posted the bond and sought unsuccessfully to dismiss the Costa Rican action for lack of jurisdiction. Later, in March 2005, Canonlat formally notified Lantech by letter that the Agreement was terminated for non-payment of goods.

After learning of the Costa Rican action, Canonlat filed this suit in February 2005 against Lantech in the Southern District of Florida for declaratory and injunctive relief, seeking to bar Lantech from proceeding with its suit in Costa Rica. The district court granted the requested permanent anti-suit injunction. In reaching its decision, the district court rejected Lantech's argument that the parties in the two actions were not identical and that the action in the enjoining court was not similar to or dispositive of the action in the foreign court. The district court concluded instead that the parties and claims were sufficiently similar to meet the threshold requirements for issuing an anti-suit injunction. Lantech now appeals the district court's order.

* * * *

III. Discussion

It is well-established among the courts of appeals that federal courts have some power to enjoin foreign suits by persons subject to federal court jurisdiction. See, e.g., *Quaak v. Klynveld Peat Marwick Goerdeler Bedrijfsrevisoren*, 361 F.3d 11, 16 (1st Cir. 2004); *China Trade & Dev. Corp. v. M.V. Choong Yong*, 837 F.2d 33, 35 (2d Cir. 1987). Lantech challenges the injunction at issue here, however, on grounds that the threshold requirements for issuing an anti-suit injunction are not satisfied. Because we agree with Lantech that this case does not meet at least one of the threshold requirements, we vacate the injunction.

As an initial matter, a district court may issue an anti-suit injunction only if: (1) "the parties are the same in both [the foreign and domestic lawsuits]," and (2) "resolution of the case before the enjoining court is dispositive of the action to be enjoined." *Paramedics*, 369 F.3d at 652; *see also E. & J. Gallo Winery v. Andina Licores S.A.*, 446 F.3d 984, 991 (9th Cir. 2006). . . .

Lantech contends that the claims in the district court are not dispositive of the claim in the Costa Rican court because the actions involve different substantive issues. For instance, the only substantive issue in the Costa Rican action is a claim arising from Law 6209 for unlawful termination of an exclusive distributorship. No claim under Law 6209 is before the district court. Instead, the only substantive issues before the district court are common law contract and quasi-contract claims for non-payment of goods.

*   *   *   *

IV. Conclusion

While we agree with Canonlat that the two actions are somewhat similar, Canonlat has not shown that the resolution of its claims in the district court would actually dispose of Lantech's claim in Costa Rica. The district court conceded as much in its discussion of the issue by concluded nevertheless that the cases were "sufficiently similar" to justify an anti-suit injunction because "the effect and enforceability of the Agreement [were] placed directly at issue in the Costa Rican action." Whether or not the cases are similar is not the legal standard, however. On the contrary, the standard, even according to *Gallo* upon which the district court mostly relied, is "whether or not the first action is *dispositive* of the action to be enjoined." *Gallo*, 446 F.3d at 991 (internal quotation marks omitted) (emphasis added). That the district court regarded the "dispositive" requirement as merely an "additional factor" in some courts, and not as a prerequisite, is therefore legal error that constitutes an abuse of discretion. Because we conclude that the second threshold requirement is not satisfied, the permanent injunction is improper. Accordingly, we vacate the injunction and remand the case for dismissal of Counts I and II in accordance with this opinion.

2. Confirmation and Enforcement of Foreign Arbitral Award

See Karaha Bodas Co., L.L.C. v. Perusahaan Pertambangan Minyak Dan Gas Bumi Negara, 500 F.3d 111 (2d Cir. 2007), discussed in C.1.b.(2) *supra.*

3. *Forum Non Conveniens*

On March 5, 2007, the U.S. Supreme Court issued a decision holding that a U.S. district court was not required to definitively establish jurisdiction over a case before dismissing on grounds of *forum non conveniens. Sinochem International Co. Ltd. v. Malaysia Int'l Shipping Corp.,* 127 S. Ct. 1184 (2007). In 2003 Sinochem International Company Ltd., a Chinese state-owned importer, filed a complaint in the Guangzhou Admiralty Court against Malaysia International Shipping Corporation, a Malaysian company, and others. The suit alleged that the Malaysian company had falsely backdated a bill of lading resulting in unwarranted payment by Sinochem for the purchase of steel coils from Triorient Trading, Inc., a U.S. corporation not party to the litigation.

In the same year Malaysia International filed the suit at issue here against Sinochem in the U.S. District Court for the Eastern District of Pennsylvania, asserting that Sinochem's submissions to the Guangzhou court contained misrepresentations and seeking compensation for losses resulting from the delay caused by the arrest of its ship by the Guangzhou court in response to a petition by Sinochem for interim relief. The district court dismissed on the basis of *forum non conviens.* In doing so it determined that it had subject-matter jurisdiction but did not definitively determine whether it had personal jurisdiction over the suit. In 2006 the Third Circuit reversed the lower court's decision, holding that the district court should have determined whether it had personal jurisdiction before dismissing on *forum non conveniens* grounds. The United States submitted a brief as *amicus curiae* in support of Sinochem's petition for writ of certiorari to the Supreme Court. *See Digest 2006* at 963–65.

As summarized by the Supreme Court:

> This case concerns the doctrine of *forum non conveniens*, under which a federal district court may dismiss an action on the ground that a court abroad is the more appropriate and convenient forum for adjudicating the controversy. We granted review to decide a question that has divided the Courts of Appeals: "Whether a district court must first conclusively establish [its own] jurisdiction before dismissing a suit on the ground of *forum non conveniens?*" Pet. for Cert. i. We hold that a district court has discretion to respond at once to a defendant's *forum non conveniens* plea, and need not take up first any other threshold objection. In particular, a court need not resolve whether it has authority to adjudicate the cause (subject-matter jurisdiction) or personal jurisdiction over the defendant if it determines that, in any event, a foreign tribunal is plainly the more suitable arbiter of the merits of the case.

Excerpts follow from the Court's analysis in reaching this conclusion and declining to decide whether a court conditioning a *forum non conveniens* dismissal on the waiver of certain defenses in the foreign forum must first determine its own jurisdiction.

-----

*   *   *   *

II

A federal court has discretion to dismiss a case on the ground of *forum non conveniens* "when an alternative forum has jurisdiction to hear [the] case, and . . . trial in the chosen forum would establish . . . oppressiveness and vexation to a defendant . . . out of all proportion to plaintiff's convenience, or . . . the chosen forum

[is] inappropriate because of considerations affecting the court's own administrative and legal problems." *American Dredging Co. v. Miller,* 510 U.S. 443, 447–448, 114 S. Ct. 981, 127 L. Ed. 2d 285 (1994). . . . Dismissal for *forum non conveniens* reflects a court's assessment of a "range of considerations, most notably the convenience to the parties and the practical difficulties that can attend the adjudication of a dispute in a certain locality." *Quackenbush v. Allstate Ins. Co.,* 517 U.S. 706, 723, 116 S. Ct. 1712, 135 L. Ed. 2d 1 (1996) (citations omitted). We have characterized *forum non conveniens* as, essentially, "a supervening venue provision, permitting displacement of the ordinary rules of venue when, in light of certain conditions, the trial court thinks that jurisdiction ought to be declined." *American Dredging,* 510 U.S., at 453, 114 S. Ct. 981, 127 L. Ed. 2d 285; cf. *In re Papandreou,* 139 F.3d, at 255 (*forum non conveniens* "involves a deliberate abstention from the exercise of jurisdiction").

The common-law doctrine of *forum non conveniens* "has continuing application [in federal courts] only in cases where the alternative forum is abroad," *American Dredging,* 510 U.S., at 449, n. 2, 114 S. Ct. 981, 127 L. Ed. 2d 285, and perhaps in rare instances where a state or territorial court serves litigational convenience best. . . . For the federal-court system, Congress has codified the doctrine and has provided for transfer, rather than dismissal, when a sister federal court is the more convenient place for trial of the action. . . .

A defendant invoking *forum non conveniens* ordinarily bears a heavy burden in opposing the plaintiff's chosen forum. When the plaintiff's choice is not its home forum, however, the presumption in the plaintiff's favor "applies with less force," for the assumption that the chosen forum is appropriate is in such cases "less reasonable." *Piper Aircraft Co.,* 454 U.S., at 255–256, 102 S. Ct. 252, 70 L. Ed. 2d 419.

*   *   *   *

IV

A *forum non conveniens* dismissal "den[ies] audience to a case on the merits," *Ruhrgas,* 526 U.S., at 585, 119 S. Ct. 1563, 143 L. Ed. 2d 760; it is a determination that the merits should be adjudicated elsewhere. See *American Dredging*, 510 U.S., at 454, 114 S. Ct. 981, 127 L. Ed. 2d 285; *Chick Kam Choo* v. *Exxon Corp.*, 486 U.S. 140, 148, 108 S. Ct. 1684, 100 L. Ed. 2d 127 (1988). The Third Circuit recognized that *forum non conveniens* "is a non-merits ground for dismissal." 436 F.3d, at 359. Accord *In re Papandreou*, 139 F.3d at 255; *Monde Re*, 311 F.3d at 497–498. A district court therefore may dispose of an action by a *forum non conveniens* dismissal, bypassing questions of subject-matter and personal jurisdiction, when considerations of convenience, fairness, and judicial economy so warrant.

*   *   *   *

Of course a court may need to identify the claims presented and the evidence relevant to adjudicating those issues to intelligently rule on a *forum non conveniens* motion. But other threshold issues may similarly involve a brush with "factual and legal issues of the underlying dispute." *Biard*, 486 U.S., at 529, 108 S. Ct. 1945, 100 L. Ed. 2d 517. For example, in ruling on the non-merits threshold question of personal jurisdiction, a court may be called upon to determine whether a defendant's contacts with the forum relate to the claim advanced by the plaintiff. . . . The critical point here, rendering a *forum non conveniens* determination a threshold, nonmerits issue in the relevant context, is simply this: Resolving a *forum non conveniens* motion does not entail any assumption by the court of substantive "law-declaring power." See *id.*, at 584–585. . . .

Statements in this Court's opinion in *Gulf Oil Corp.* v. *Gilbert*, 330 U.S. 501, 67 S. Ct. 839, 91 L. Ed. 1055 (1947), account in large part for the Third Circuit's conclusion that *forum non conveniens* can come into play only after a domestic court determines that it has jurisdiction over the cause and the parties and is a proper venue for the action. . . .

*   *   *   *

. . . *Gulf Oil* did not present the question we here address: whether a federal court can dismiss under the *forum non conveniens* doctrine before definitively ascertaining its own jurisdiction. Confining the statements we have quoted to the setting in which they were made, we find in *Gulf Oil* no hindrance to the decision we reach today.

The Third Circuit expressed the further concern that a court failing first to establish its jurisdiction could not condition a *forum non conveniens* dismissal on the defendant's waiver of any statute of limitations defense or objection to the foreign forum's jurisdiction. Unable so to condition a dismissal, the Court of Appeals feared, a court could not shield the plaintiff against a foreign tribunal's refusal to entertain the suit. 436 F.3d, at 363, and n 21. Accord *In re Papandreou*, 139 F.3d, at 256, n 6. Here, however, Malaysia International faces no genuine risk that the more convenient forum will not take up the case. Proceedings to resolve the parties' dispute are underway in China, with Sinochem as the plaintiff. Jurisdiction of the Guangzhou Admiralty Court has been raised, determined, and affirmed on appeal. We therefore need not decide whether a court conditioning a *forum non conveniens* dismissal on the waiver of jurisdictional or limitations defenses in the foreign forum must first determine its own authority to adjudicate the case.

V

This is a textbook case for immediate *forum non conveniens* dismissal. The District Court's subject-matter jurisdiction presented an issue of first impression in the Third Circuit, see 436 F.3d, at 355, and was considered at some length by the courts below. Discovery concerning personal jurisdiction would have burdened Sinochem with expense and delay. And all to scant purpose: The District Court inevitably would dismiss the case without reaching the merits, given its well-considered *forum non conveniens* appraisal. Judicial economy is disserved by continuing litigation in the Eastern District of Pennsylvania given the proceedings long launched in China. And the gravamen of Malaysia International's complaint—misrepresentations to the Guangzhou Admiralty Court in the course of securing arrest of the vessel in China—is an issue best left for determination by the Chinese courts.

If, however, a court can readily determine that it lacks jurisdiction over the cause or the defendant, the proper course would be to dismiss on that ground. In the mine run of cases, jurisdiction "will involve no arduous inquiry" and both judicial economy and the consideration ordinarily accorded the plaintiff's choice of forum "should impel the federal court to dispose of [those] issue[s] first." *Ruhrgas*, 526 U.S., at 587–588, 119 S. Ct. 1563, 143 L. Ed. 2d 760. But where subject-matter or personal jurisdiction is difficult to determine, and *forum non conveniens* considerations weigh heavily in favor of dismissal, the court properly takes the less burdensome course.

4. Judicial Assistance for Foreign Court: *In re Clerici*

On March 21, 2007, the U.S. Court of Appeals for the Eleventh Circuit affirmed a district court order denying a motion to vacate a previous order directing the defendant to give sworn answers to written questions for use in a Panamanian court. *In re Clerici*, 481 F.3d 1324 (11th Cir. 2007), *cert. denied*, 128 S. Ct. 1063 (2008). In this case NoName, a Panamanian business, obtained a judgment against a Panamanian citizen Patricio Clerici, who resides in Miami, Florida. Subsequently, at the request of NoName, the Panamanian court issued a letter rogatory to a Florida court requesting assistance with obtaining answers to questions proposed by NoName regarding Clerici's assets and other financial matters. Pursuant to 28 U.S.C. § 1782, the U.S. District Court for the Southern District of Florida issued an order appointing an Assistant U.S. Attorney as commissioner for the purpose of obtaining the evidence requested and the commissioner requested that Clerici sit for a deposition. The district court denied Clerici's motion to vacate.

Excerpts follow from the Eleventh Circuit opinion affirming that decision (most footnotes deleted). The court also noted that the Panamanian judgment against Clerici had not been domesticated and was not enforceable in Florida but found that irrelevant to the enforcement of the order under 28 U.S.C. § 1782.

* * * *

A district court has the authority to grant an application for judicial assistance if the following statutory requirements in § 1782(a) are met: (1) the request must be made "by a foreign or international tribunal," or by "any interested person"[7]; (2) the request must seek evidence, whether it be the "testimony or statement" of a person or the production of "a document or other thing"; (3) the evidence must be "for use in a proceeding in a foreign or international tribunal"; and (4) the person from whom discovery is sought must reside or be found in the district of the district court ruling on the application for assistance. 28 U.S.C. § 1782(a). If these requirements are met, then § 1782 "authorizes, but does not require, a federal district court to provide assistance. . . ." *Intel,* 542 U.S. at 255, 124 S. Ct. at 2478. . . .

Here, Clerici does not dispute that the Panamanian Court is a foreign tribunal or that he resides within the Southern District of Florida. Therefore, the first and fourth requirements for a proper request under § 1782 are met.

As to the second statutory requirement—that the request must seek evidence—Clerici argues that the Panamanian Court is not seeking evidence, but rather is attempting to enforce its judgment through a § 1782 request. We disagree because the Panamanian Court asked for assistance in obtaining only Clerici's sworn answers to questions regarding his assets and other financial matters. The district court recognized this key distinction and properly concluded that the request for assistance was limited to seeking evidence from Clerici, and therefore, was proper under § 1782. Unlike the requests for judicial assistance in the cases cited in Clerici's brief, . . . the Panamanian Court never requested that the district court sequester, levy on, or seize control of Clerici's assets or otherwise help enforce NoName's judgment. The Panamanian Court requested only assistance in obtaining evidence—sworn answers from Clerici to written questions—and this is the primary purpose of § 1782. Therefore, the second requirement for a proper request under § 1782 is met.

---

[7] A request for judicial assistance from a foreign tribunal can be, but is not required to be, made through the issuance of a letter rogatory. *See* 28 U.S.C. § 1782(a).

As to the third statutory requirement, we reject Clerici's contention that the requested evidence was not "for use in a proceeding" before the Panamanian Court. Here, there is a proceeding currently pending before the Panamanian Court that allows NoName or the Panamanian Court to question Clerici under oath about his properties, rights, credits, sustenance means, and other sources of income from the date of his court-ordered obligation. Had Clerici been residing in Panama, NoName or the Panamanian Court would have been able to interrogate Clerici directly with the questions proposed by NoName. Because Clerici was residing in Florida, however, the Panamanian Court issued a letter rogatory seeking international assistance in order to obtain this evidence. The Panamanian Court's letter rogatory itself stated that this evidence "will be used in the civil process before this court." Such a request is clearly within the range of discovery authorized under § 1782 and comports with the purpose of the statute to provide assistance to foreign tribunals.

Given the pending proceeding before the Panamanian Court, Clerici is reduced to arguing that a "proceeding" means an adjudicative proceeding, and thus, NoName's post-judgment petition regarding a judgment that already has been rendered is not a "proceeding" within the meaning of the statute. This argument is also without merit for several reasons. First, § 1782 only states that the evidence must be "for use in a proceeding," and nothing in the plain language of § 1782 requires that the proceeding be adjudicative in nature. See 28 U.S.C. § 1782(a). In fact, the statute specifically provides that the evidence obtained through § 1782 can be used in "criminal investigations conducted *before* formal accusation," even though such investigations are not adjudicative proceedings. *Id.* (emphasis added).

Second, the Supreme Court has recognized the "broad range of discovery" authorized under § 1782 and has held that § 1782 is not limited to proceedings that are pending or imminent. . . . Here, the proceeding actually was filed before the letter rogatory was even issued, and the third statutory requirement for a proper request under § 1782 is satisfied.

Because all four statutory requirements are met, the Panamanian Court's request for assistance in obtaining Clerici's sworn answers for use in the proceeding in Panama was proper under § 1782. 12 Accordingly, the district court had authority to grant the § 1782 discovery application.

Even so, " a district court is not required to grant a § 1782(a) discovery application simply because it has the authority to do so." *Intel*, 542 U.S. at 264, 124 S. Ct. at 2482–83. . . . Once the prima facie requirements are satisfied, the Supreme Court in *Intel* noted these factors to be considered in exercising the discretion granted under § 1782(a): (1) whether "the person from whom discovery is sought is a participant in the foreign proceeding," because "the need for § 1782(a) aid generally is not as apparent as it ordinarily is when evidence is sought from a nonparticipant"; (2) "the nature of the foreign tribunal, the character of the proceedings underway abroad, and the receptivity of the foreign government or the court or agency abroad to U.S. federal-court judicial assistance"; (3) "whether the § 1782(a) request conceals an attempt to circumvent foreign proof-gathering restrictions or other policies of a foreign country or the United States"; and (4) whether the request is otherwise "unduly intrusive or burdensome." *Id.* at 264–65, 124 S. Ct. at 2483. The Supreme Court in *Intel* added that "unduly intrusive or burdensome requests may be rejected or trimmed." *Id.* at 265, 124 S. Ct. at 2483.

Our review of the *Intel* factors reveals that none of the factors favors Clerici, and that the district court did not abuse its discretion in granting the § 1782 application.

As to the first *Intel* factor, because Clerici is a party in the foreign proceeding, this factor normally would favor Clerici and suggest that § 1782 assistance is not necessary. *See Intel*, 542 U.S. at 264. . . . In this case, however, the first factor does not favor Clerici because Clerici has left Panama and the Panamanian Court cannot enforce its order against Clerici directly while Clerici is in the United States. Given the particular factual circumstances in this case, the first *Intel* factor does not favor Clerici.

As to the second and third *Intel* factors, there is nothing in the record to suggest that the district court should have declined to grant the § 1782 application based on the nature of the foreign tribunal or the character of the proceedings in Panama, or that the Panamanian Court's request is merely an attempt to circumvent foreign proof-gathering restrictions. Rather, these factors all support the district court's decision to grant the § 1782 application given that the foreign tribunal here is the Panamanian Court and the Panamanian Court itself issued the letter rogatory requesting assistance due to Clerici's presence in the United States.

Finally, as to the fourth *Intel* factor—whether the § 1782 request is unduly intrusive—the district court's order granting the § 1782 application specifically indicated that if Clerici wished to pursue his "unduly intrusive" argument, Clerici should file a motion to limit discovery. Clerici never did so and instead chose to appeal the grant of any discovery whatsoever. On appeal, as in the district court, Clerici does not identify the terms of the written request that are overly broad or assert how the scope of the request should be narrowed. Thus, we, like the district court, have no occasion to address the scope of the Panamanian Court's discovery request.

In sum, the district court had authority to grant the § 1782 application, and Clerici has not shown that the district court abused its discretion in doing so.

*   *   *   *

Cross References

International adoption and child abduction, **Chapter 2.B.**
Judicial assistance, **Chapter 2.C.**
Comity issues in Alien Tort Statute case, **Chapter 5.A.2.c.**
Comity issues in cross-border water pollution case, **Chapter 13. A.1.b.(2).**

CHAPTER 16

Sanctions

A. IMPOSITION OF SANCTIONS

1. Threats to Lebanon's Sovereignty and Democracy

On August 1, 2007, President George W. Bush issued Executive Order 13441, "Blocking Property of Persons Undermining the Sovereignty of Lebanon or its Democratic Processes and Institutions." 72 Fed. Reg. 43,499 (Aug. 3, 2007). Acting under authority of the Constitution and U.S. laws including the International Emergency Economic Powers Act ("IEEPA"), the National Emergencies Act, and 3 U.S.C. § 301, the President declared a national emergency to deal with the threat to the national security and foreign policy of the United States, based on his determination that

> the actions of certain persons to undermine Lebanon's legitimate and democratically elected government or democratic institutions, to contribute to the deliberate breakdown in the rule of law in Lebanon, including through politically motivated violence and intimidation, to reassert Syrian control or contribute to Syrian interference in Lebanon, or to infringe upon or undermine Lebanese sovereignty contribute to political and economic instability in that country and the region and constitute an unusual and extraordinary threat to the national security and foreign policy of the United States . . .

Section one of the executive order blocked property and interests of certain persons, as set forth below. *See also* 72 Fed. Reg. 65,835 (Nov. 23, 2007), publishing the November 5, 2007, designation by the Secretary of the Treasury in consultation with the Secretary of State of four individuals pursuant to Executive Order 13441, effective November 5, 2007.

---

* * * *

Section 1. (a) Except to the extent provided in section 203(b)(1), (3), and (4) of IEEPA (50 U.S.C. 1702(b)(1), (3), and (4)), or in regulations, orders, directives, or licenses that may be issued pursuant to this order, and notwithstanding any contract entered into or any license or permit granted prior to the date of this order, all property and interests in property that are in the United States, that hereafter come within the United States, or that are or hereafter come within the possession or control of any United States person, including any overseas branch, of the following persons are blocked and may not be transferred, paid, exported, withdrawn, or otherwise dealt in:

(i) any person determined by the Secretary of the Treasury, in consultation with the Secretary of State:

(A) to have taken, or to pose a significant risk of taking, actions, including acts of violence, that have the purpose or effect of undermining Lebanon's democratic processes or institutions, contributing to the breakdown of the rule of law in Lebanon, supporting the reassertion of Syrian control or otherwise contributing to Syrian interference in Lebanon, or infringing upon or undermining Lebanese sovereignty;

(B) to have materially assisted, sponsored, or provided financial, material, or technological support for, or goods or services in support of, such actions, including acts of violence, or any person whose property and interests in property are blocked pursuant to this order;

(C) to be a spouse or dependent child of any person whose property and interests in property are blocked pursuant to this order; or

(D) to be owned or controlled by, or acting or purporting to act for or on behalf of, directly or indirectly, any person whose property and interests in property are blocked pursuant to this order.

(b) I hereby determine that the making of donations of the type of articles specified in section 203(b)(2) of IEEPA (50 U.S.C. 1702(b)(2)) by, to, or for the benefit of any person whose property and interests in property are blocked pursuant to paragraph (a) of this section would seriously impair my ability to deal with the national emergency declared in this order, and I hereby prohibit such donations as provided by paragraph (a) of this section.

(c) The prohibitions in paragraph (a) of this section include but are not limited to (i) the making of any contribution or provision of funds, goods, or services by, to, or for the benefit of any person whose property and interests in property are blocked pursuant to this order, and (ii) the receipt of any contribution or provision of funds, goods, or services from any such person.

* * * *

See also suspension of entry under INA § 212(f), Chapter 1.C.7.a.

2. Government of Burma

In addressing the UN General Assembly on September 25, 2007, President Bush announced that the United States would impose additional sanctions on Burma. *See* 43 WEEKLY COMP. PRES. DOC. 1245, 1246 (Oct. 1, 2007), excerpted in Chapter 17.A.2.b. Effective September 27, 2007, the Department of the Treasury, Office of Foreign Assets Control ("OFAC"), published the names of fourteen newly-designated individuals whose property and interests in property are blocked pursuant to Executive Order 13310, including members of the regime and individuals who actively support it, 72 Fed. Reg. 56,437 (Oct. 3, 2007), and on October 19, 2007, designated eleven more individuals under Executive Order 13310. 72 Fed. Reg. 60,713 (Oct. 25, 2007).

On September 28, 2007, the Department of State designated more than three dozen additional government and military officials and their families as ineligible to receive visas to travel to the United States. *See www.state.gov/r/pa/prs/ps/2007/sep/92960.htm.*

On October 19, 2007, President Bush issued Executive Order 13448, "Blocking Property and Prohibiting Certain Transactions Related to Burma." 72 Fed. Reg. 60,223 (Oct. 23, 2007). The President acted "in order to take additional steps with respect to the Government of Burma's continued repression of the democratic opposition in Burma," relying on the Burmese Freedom and Democracy Act of 2003 (Public L. No. 108-61, 117 Stat. 864, as amended, 50 U.S.C. § 1701 note), as well as authorities cited in the action related to Lebanon, A.1 *supra.* Effective October 19, seven individuals and five entities were designated in the annex to Executive Order 13448. Excerpts from Executive Order 13448 follow. *See also* suspension of entry under INA § 212(f), Chapter 1.C.7.b.

* * * *

I, GEORGE W. BUSH, President of the United States of America, hereby expand the scope of the national emergency declared in Executive Order 13047 of May 20, 1997, and relied upon for additional steps taken in Executive Order 13310 of July 28, 2003, finding that the Government of Burma's continued repression of the democratic opposition in Burma, manifested most recently in the violent response to peaceful demonstrations, the commission of human rights abuses related to political repression, and engagement in public corruption, including by diverting or misusing Burmese public assets or by misusing public authority, constitute an unusual and extraordinary threat to the national security and foreign policy of the United States, and I hereby order:

Section 1. Except to the extent provided in section 203(b)(1), (3), and (4) of IEEPA (50 U.S.C. 1702(b)(1), (3), and (4)), the Trade Sanctions Reform and Export Enhancement Act of 2000 (title IX, Public Law 106-387), or regulations, orders, directives, or licenses that may be issued pursuant to this order, and notwithstanding any contract entered into or any license or permit granted prior to the effective date of this order, all property and interests in property of the following persons that are in the United States, that hereafter come within the United States, or that are or hereafter come within the possession or control of United States persons, including their overseas branches, are blocked and may not be transferred, paid, exported, withdrawn, or otherwise dealt in:

(a) the persons listed in the Annex attached and made a part of this order; and

(b) any person determined by the Secretary of the Treasury, after consultation with the Secretary of State:

(i) to be a senior official of the Government of Burma, the State Peace and Development Council of Burma, the Union Solidarity and Development Association of Burma, or any successor entity to any of the foregoing;

(ii) to be responsible for, or to have participated in, human rights abuses related to political repression in Burma;

(iii) to be engaged, or to have engaged, in activities facilitating public corruption by senior officials of the Government of Burma;

(iv) to have materially assisted, sponsored, or provided financial, material, logistical, or technical support for, or goods or services in support of, the Government of Burma, the State Peace and Development Council of Burma, the Union Solidarity and Development Association of Burma, any successor entity to any of the foregoing, any senior official of any of the foregoing, or any person whose property and interests in property are blocked pursuant to Executive Order 13310 or section 1(b)(i)-(v) of this order;

(v) to be owned or controlled by, or to have acted or purported to act for or on behalf of, directly or indirectly, any person whose property and interests in property are blocked pursuant to Executive Order 13310 or section 1(b)(i)-(v) of this order; or

(vi) to be a spouse or dependent child of any person whose property and interests in property are blocked pursuant to this order or Executive Order 13310.

* * * *

Effective October 24, 2007, the Department of Commerce, Bureau of Industry and Security, issued a final rule amending the Export Administration Regulations ("EAR") consistent with Executive Order 13448. 72 Fed. Reg. 60,248 (Oct. 24, 2007). Excerpts from the Federal Register notice follow.

---

* * * *

. . . Consistent with Executive Orders 13310 and 13448, and the Trade Sanctions Reform and Export Enhancement Act (Title IX of Pub. L. 106-387), this final rule amends the EAR to impose a license requirement for exports, reexports or transfers of items subject to the EAR to persons listed in or designated pursuant to Executive Orders 13310 or 13448, except for agricultural commodities, medicine, or medical devices classified as EAR99* and destined for entities listed in or designated pursuant to those orders. All persons listed in or designated pursuant [to] these Executive Orders are identified with the reference [BURMA] on OFAC's list of Specially Designated Nationals and Blocked Persons set forth in Appendix A to 31 CFR Chapter V and on OFAC's Web site at *http://www.treas.gov/OFAC*. This rule creates a new § 744.22 to set forth this new license requirement.

Further, in part 740 of the EAR (License Exceptions), this rule moves Burma from Computer Tier 1 to Computer Tier 3, restricting access to high-performance computers and related technology and software under License Exception APP (Section 740.7). In Supplement No. 1 to part 740 (Country Groups), this rule moves Burma from Country Group B (countries raising few national security concerns) to Country Group D:1 (countries raising national security concerns), which further limits the number of license

---

*   Editor's note: "EAR99 is a designation for dual-use goods that are covered by the EAR but are not specifically listed on the Commerce Control List. EAR99 items can be shipped without a license to most destinations under most circumstances. In fact, the majority of commercial exports from the United States fall into this category. Exporters of most consumer goods, for instance, may find their product listed under EAR 99." *See www.export. gov/regulation/exp_001498.asp*.

exceptions available for exports to Burma. Burma will remain in Country Group D:3 (countries raising proliferation concerns related to chemical and biological weapons).

*   *   *   *

3. Government of Sudan

a. *New designations*

On May 29, 2007, OFAC imposed new economic sanctions on two Sudanese Government officials, a Darfur rebel leader, 30 companies owned or controlled by the Government of Sudan, and one company that violated the arms embargo in Darfur. See *www.treas.gov/offices/enforcement/ofac/actions/20070529.shtml*. A fact sheet released by the Department of State on that date describing the new sanctions and U.S. efforts to obtain additional UN sanctions is excerpted below and available at *www.state.gov/r/pa/prs/ps/2007/may/85597.htm*.

---

*   *   *   *

The sanctions, administered by the U.S. Treasury Department, are intended to increase pressure on the Government of Sudan to end the violence in Darfur. At the same time, the Treasury Department will use enhanced enforcement techniques to crack down on violators of new and existing sanctions.

The U.S. sanctions targeted Ahmad Muhammed Harun, Sudan's State Minister for Humanitarian Affairs, Awad Ibn Auf, head of Sudan's Military Intelligence and Security, and Khalil Ibrahim, leader of the Justice and Equality Movement (JEM), a rebel group. The Azza Air Transport Company was also sanctioned under Executive Order 13400 for transferring small arms, ammunition and artillery to Sudanese government forces and Janjaweed militia in Darfur.

The individuals named have widespread involvement in Darfur, and have been linked to violence, atrocities and human rights abuses in the region. Khalil Ibrahim has also worked to obstruct the ongoing peace process.

Of the 30 companies owned or controlled by the Government of Sudan, five are in the petrochemical sector. These companies have been added to a list of over 100 other Sudanese companies currently sanctioned by the United States. They were designated pursuant to Executive Orders 13067 and 13412.

At the United Nations, the United States is proposing a draft resolution to widen the scope of existing UN sanctions against the Government of Sudan. Such a draft resolution, which we have already discussed with the United Kingdom, France and other partners on the Security Council, would expand the UN's existing arms embargo against the Government of Sudan and ban military flights over Darfur. The U.S. will also seek to build a coalition of countries to join us in imposing similar bilateral sanctions on Sudan.

Sanctions underscore continued U.S. efforts to end the suffering of the millions of Darfuris affected by the crisis. The United States, the single largest donor of humanitarian, development and reconstruction assistance to the people of Sudan, is committed to providing life-saving humanitarian assistance to the people of Darfur and seeking a politically negotiated peace settlement.

b. Amendments to Sudanese Sanctions Regulations

On October 13, 2006, President Bush signed into law the Darfur Peace and Accountability Act of 2006, Pub. L. No. 109-344, 120 Stat. 1869 and signed Executive Order 13412, "Blocking Property of and Prohibiting Transactions with the Government of Sudan." *See Digest 2006* at 978–83. Effective October 31, 2007, OFAC issued a final rule amending the Sudanese Sanctions Regulations ("SSR") to include several new provisions implementing Executive Order 13412. 72 Fed. Reg. 61,513 (Oct. 31, 2007). Excerpts below from the Background section of the rule explain the action taken. The Background section also explained the legislation and executive order.

* * * *

. . . Paragraph (a) of new § 538.210 prohibits all transactions by United States persons relating to the petroleum or petrochemical industries in Sudan, including, but not limited to, oilfield services and oil or gas pipelines. Paragraph (b) of § 538.210 prohibits the facilitation by a United States person of any transaction relating to Sudan's petroleum or petrochemical industries.

Second, OFAC is adding an exemption to newly renumbered § 538.212. Paragraph (g)(1) of § 538.212 provides that, except for the provisions of. §§ 538.201–203, 538.210, and 538.211, and except as provided in paragraph (g)(2) of § 538.212, the prohibitions contained in the SSR do not apply to activities or related transactions with respect to the Specified Areas of Sudan. This provision means that, subject to the new interpretive sections set forth below, activities and related transactions with respect to the Specified Areas of Sudan are no longer prohibited, unless they involve any property or interests in property of the Government of Sudan or relate to Sudan's petroleum or petrochemical industries. In addition, paragraph (g)(2) of § 538.212 states that the exemption does not apply to the exportation or reexportation of agricultural commodities, medicine, and medical devices. Section 906 of the Trade Sanctions Reform and Export Enhancement Act of 2000 (Pub. L. 106-387) continues to impose licensing requirements on these transactions, regardless of the intended destination in Sudan. These licensing requirements are implemented in §§ 538.523, 538.525, and 538.526.

Third, OFAC is revising the definition of the term Government of Sudan contained in § 538.305 to exclude the regional government of Southern Sudan, as set forth in section 6(d) of E.O. 13412.

Fourth, OFAC is adding a new definitional section to identify the areas of Sudan that were exempted in section 4(b) of E.O. 13412 from the prohibitions contained in section 2 of E.O. 13067. New § 538.320 defines the term Specified Areas of Sudan to mean Southern Sudan, Southern Kordofan/Nuba Mountains State, Blue Nile State, Abyei, Darfur, and marginalized areas in and around Khartoum. This section also defines the term "marginalized areas in and around Khartoum" to refer to four official camps for internally displaced persons.

Fifth, OFAC is adding interpretive § 538.417 to clarify that all of the prohibitions in the SSR apply to shipments of goods, services, and technology that transit areas of Sudan other than the Specified Areas of Sudan. Section 538.417(a) provides that an exportation or reexportation of goods, technology, or services to the Specified Areas of Sudan is exempt under § 538.212(g) only if it does not transit or transship through any area of Sudan other than the Specified Areas of Sudan. Section 538.417(b) provides that an importation into the United States of goods or services from, or originating in, the Specified Areas of Sudan is exempt under § 538.212(g) only if it does not transit or transship through any area of Sudan other than the Specified Areas of Sudan. Thus, imports and exports to or from the Specified Areas of Sudan that do not transit or transship non-exempt areas of Sudan are not prohibited, provided that the Government of Sudan does not have an interest in the transaction and the transaction does not relate to Sudan's petroleum or petrochemical industries. However, imports and exports to or from the Specified Areas of Sudan that involve the transiting of, or transshipment through, non-exempt areas of Sudan, e.g., Khartoum and Port Sudan, require authorization from OFAC.

OFAC is also adding interpretive § 538.418 to explain the prohibitions on financial transactions in Sudan. Financial transactions are no longer prohibited by the SSR if: (1) The underlying activity is not prohibited by the SSR; (2) the financial transaction involves a third-country depository institution, or a Sudanese depository institution not owned or controlled by the Government of Sudan, that is located in the Specified Areas of Sudan; and (3) the financial transaction is not routed through a depository institution that is located in the non-exempt areas or that is owned or controlled by the Government of Sudan, wherever located. However, any financial transactions that involve, in any manner, depository institutions that are located in the non-exempt areas of Sudan, e.g., Khartoum, remain prohibited and require authorization from OFAC.

For example, if a financial transaction involves a branch of a depository institution in the Specified Areas of Sudan, but that depository institution is headquartered in Khartoum and requires all financial transactions to be routed through the headquarters or another branch located in the non-exempt areas of Sudan, that transaction is prohibited and requires authorization from OFAC.

Finally, OFAC is amending the SSR to add three new general licenses, which are set forth in §§ 538.530, 538.531, and 538.532. Paragraph (a) of § 538.530 provides that all general licenses issued pursuant to E.O. 13067 are authorized and remain in effect pursuant to E.O. 13412. Paragraph (b) of § 538.530 provides that all specific licenses and all nongovernmental organization registrations issued pursuant to E.O. 13067 or the SSR prior to October 13, 2006, are authorized pursuant to E.O. 13412 and remain in effect until the expiration date specified in the license or registration, or if no expiration date is specified, June 30, 2008. OFAC urges all license and nongovernmental organization registration holders to take note of this potentially new expiration date, which applies to all licenses and registrations that do not otherwise contain an expiration date, regardless of when they were originally issued.

The second general license, new § 538.531, authorizes otherwise prohibited official activities of the United States Government and international organizations. Subject to certain conditions and limitations, paragraph (a)(1) of § 538.531 authorizes all transactions and activities otherwise prohibited by the SSR or E.O. 13412 that are for the conduct of the official business of the United States Government by contractors or grantees thereof. Employees who engage in transactions for the conduct of the official business of the United States Government already are exempt from these prohibitions. See § 538.212(e) and section 5(a) of E.O. 13412. Paragraph (a)(2) of § 538.531 authorizes, subject to the same conditions and limitations as paragraph (a)(1), all transactions and activities otherwise prohibited by the SSR or E.O. 13412 that are for the conduct of the official business of the United Nations, or United Nations specialized agencies, programmes, and funds, by employees, contractors, or grantees thereof. Paragraphs (b), (c), and (d) of § 538.531 set forth conditions and limitations on the authorizations described in paragraph (a).

The third general license, § 538.532, authorizes humanitarian transshipments of goods, technology, or services through non-exempt areas of Sudan to or from Southern Sudan and Darfur. This license will be subject to review on an annual basis. Upon completion of the annual review, OFAC may revoke the general license through the issuance of a notice in the Federal Register. If OFAC does not take any action, this license will remain in force.

c. Sudan Accountability and Divestment Act of 2007

On December 31, 2007, President Bush signed into law the Sudan Accountability and Divestment Act of 2007, Pub. L. No. 110-174, 121 Stat. 2516 (2007). The act included a number of provisions expressing the sense of Congress on relevant issues. In addition, it prohibited U.S. government contracts with "business operations in Sudan that include power production activities, mineral extraction activities, oil-related activities, or the production of military equipment," with certain exceptions (Section 6). It also requires the Secretary of State and Secretary of the Treasury to submit reports assessing the effectiveness of sanctions imposed with respect to Sudan under specified statutory authority (Section 10). Section 3 of the act addressed divestment of state and local government assets, providing:

> Notwithstanding any other provision of law, a State or local government [of the United States] may adopt and enforce measures that meet [certain specified] requirements . . . to divest the assets of the State or local government from, or prohibit investment of the assets of the State or local government in, persons that the State or local government determines, using credible information available to the public, are conducting or have direct investments in business operations in Sudan that include power production activities, mineral extraction activities, oil-related activities, or the production of military equipment [with certain exceptions].

State and local governments are required to notify the Attorney General of any such measures adopted.

Section 12 provides that enumerated sections, including the three summarized here, will terminate after a Presidential certification that the Government of Sudan "has honored its commitments to—

(1) abide by United Nations Security Council Resolution 1769 (2007);

(2) cease attacks on civilians;

(3) demobilize and demilitarize the Janjaweed and associated militias;

(4) grant free and unfettered access for delivery of humanitarian assistance; and

(5) allow for the safe and voluntary return of refugees and internally displaced persons."

In signing the bill into law, President Bush stated that his Administration "will continue its efforts to bring about significant improvements in the conditions in Sudan through sanctions against the Government of Sudan and high-level diplomatic engagement and by supporting the deployment of peacekeepers in Darfur." 44 WEEKLY COMP. PRES. DOCS 1645 (Jan. 4, 2008). The President also stated that he would construe the legislation consistent with his constitutional authority over foreign relations, particularly as it relates to powers of State and local governments:

This Act purports to authorize State and local governments to divest from companies doing business in named sectors in Sudan and thus risks being interpreted as insulating from Federal oversight State and local divestment actions that could interfere with implementation of national foreign policy. However, as the Constitution vests the exclusive authority to conduct foreign relations with the Federal Government, the executive branch shall construe and enforce this legislation in a manner that does not conflict with that authority.

4. Stabilization Efforts in Iraq

On July 17, 2007, President Bush issued Executive Order 13438, "Blocking Property of Certain Persons Who Threaten Stabilization Efforts in Iraq." 72 Fed. Reg. 39,719 (July 19, 2007). Excerpts follow from the order, which takes additional steps with respect to the national emergency originally declared in Executive Order 13303 of May 22, 2003.

By the authority vested in me as President by the Constitution and the laws of the United States of America, including the International Emergency Economic Powers Act, as amended (50 U.S.C. 1701 et seq.)(IEEPA), the National Emergencies Act (50 U.S.C. 1601 et seq.)(NEA), and section 301 of title 3, United States Code,

I, GEORGE W. BUSH, President of the United States of America, find that, due to the unusual and extraordinary threat to the national security and foreign policy of the United States posed by acts of violence threatening the peace and stability of Iraq and undermining efforts to promote economic reconstruction and political reform in Iraq and to provide humanitarian assistance to the Iraqi people, it is in the interests of the United States to take additional steps with respect to the national emergency declared in Executive Order 13303 of May 22, 2003, and expanded in Executive Order 13315 of August 28, 2003, and relied upon for additional steps taken in Executive Order 13350 of July 29, 2004, and Executive Order 13364 of November 29, 2004. I hereby order:

Section 1. (a) Except to the extent provided in section 203(b)(1), (3), and (4) of IEEPA (50 U.S.C. 1702(b)(1), (3), and (4)), or in regulations, orders, directives, or licenses that may be issued pursuant to this order, and notwithstanding any contract entered into or any license or permit granted prior to the date of this order, all property and interests in property of the following persons, that are in the United States, that hereafter come within the United States, or that are or hereafter come within the possession or control of United States persons, are blocked and may not be transferred, paid, exported, withdrawn, or otherwise dealt in: any person determined by the Secretary of the Treasury, in consultation with the Secretary of State and the Secretary of Defense,

(i) to have committed, or to pose a significant risk of committing, an act or acts of violence that have the purpose or effect of:
   (A) threatening the peace or stability of Iraq or the Government of Iraq; or
   (B) undermining efforts to promote economic reconstruction and political reform in Iraq or to provide humanitarian assistance to the Iraqi people;
(ii) to have materially assisted, sponsored, or provided financial, material, logistical, or technical support for, or goods or services in support of, such an act or acts of violence or any person whose property and interests in property are blocked pursuant to this order; or
(iii) to be owned or controlled by, or to have acted or purported to act for or on behalf of, directly or indirectly, any person whose property and interests in property are blocked pursuant to this order.

(b) The prohibitions in subsection (a) of this section include, but are not limited to, (i) the making of any contribution or provision of funds, goods, or services by, to, or for the benefit of any person whose property and interests in property are blocked pursuant to this order, and (ii) the receipt of any contribution or provision of funds, goods, or services from any such person.

Sec. 2. (a) Any transaction by a United States person or within the United States that evades or avoids, has the purpose of evading or avoiding, or attempts to violate any of the prohibitions set forth in this order is prohibited.

(b) Any conspiracy formed to violate any of the prohibitions set forth in this order is prohibited.

* * * *

Sec. 4. I hereby determine that the making of donations of the type specified in section 203(b)(2) of IEEPA (50 U.S.C. 1702(b)(2)) by, to, or for the benefit of, any person whose property and interests in property are blocked pursuant to this order would seriously impair my ability to deal with the national emergency declared in Executive Order 13303 and expanded in Executive Order 13315, and I hereby prohibit such donations as provided by section 1 of this order.

Sec. 5. For those persons whose property and interests in property are blocked pursuant to this order who might have a constitutional presence in the United States, I find that, because of the ability to transfer funds or other assets instantaneously, prior notice to such persons of measures to be taken pursuant to this order would render these measures ineffectual. I therefore determine that for these measures to be effective in addressing the national emergency declared in Executive Order 13303 and expanded in Executive Order 13315, there need be no prior notice of a listing or determination made pursuant to section 1(a) of this order.

*   *   *   *

On December 6, 2007, OFAC designated six individuals who were senior officials in the former regime of Saddam Hussein under Executive Order 13315, "Blocking Property of the Former Iraqi Regime, Its Senior Officials and Their Family Members, and Taking Certain Other Actions." 72 Fed. Reg. 71,484 (Dec. 17, 2007).

5. Liberia: Regime of Former President Charles Taylor

Effective May 23, 2007, OFAC issued a final rule implementing Executive Order 13348 of July 22, 2004, "Blocking Property of Certain Persons and Prohibiting the Importation of Certain Goods from Liberia." 72 Fed. Reg. 28,855 (May 23, 2007). For a discussion of Executive Order 13348 and OFAC's initial actions, *see Digest 2004* at 919–22. Excerpts follow from the Background section of the final rule describing the regulations adopted.

*   *   *   *

These regulations are promulgated in furtherance of the sanctions set forth in Executive Order 13348, which are targeted sanctions directed at the regime of former President Charles Taylor. The sanctions are not directed against the country of Liberia, the Government of Liberia, or the Central Bank of Liberia. They do not generally prohibit the provision of banking services to the country of Liberia, including the maintenance of correspondent banking relationships with Liberian banks, unless the bank in question, or any other person engaged in the transaction, is a person whose property and interests in property are blocked pursuant to § 593.201(a). In addition, the importation into the United States of rough diamonds from Liberia is governed by the Rough Diamonds Control Regulations, 31 CFR part 592.

Subpart B of the Regulations implements the prohibitions contained in Sections 1, 2, and 3 of the Order. See §§ 593.201, 593.205, and 593.206. Appendix A to 31 CFR chapter V has previously been amended to incorporate the names of persons set forth in the Annex to the Order. Persons identified in the Annex to the Order or designated by or under the authority of the Secretary of the Treasury pursuant to the Order are referred to throughout the Regulations as "persons whose property and interests in property are blocked pursuant to § 593.201(a)". Their names are or will be published on OFAC's Specially Designated Nationals and Blocked Persons List, which is accessible via OFAC's Web site, announced in the Federal Register, and incorporated on an ongoing basis into appendix A to 31 CFR chapter V, which lists persons who are the targets of various sanctions programs administered by OFAC.

* * * *

Section 593.205 sets forth the prohibition contained in Section 2 of the Order with respect to the importation into the United States of round logs or timber products from Liberia. However, in Resolution 1689 of June 20, 2006, the United Nations Security Council decided to lift the multilateral prohibition on importation of round logs and timber products set forth in paragraph 10 of Resolution 1521. In accordance with the decision of the Security

Council in Resolution 1689,* OFAC is issuing § 593.510, a general license authorizing the importation into the United States of round logs and timber products originating in Liberia.

Subpart C of part 593 defines key terms used throughout the Regulations, and subpart D sets forth interpretive sections regarding the general prohibitions contained in subpart B. Transactions otherwise prohibited under part 593 but found to be consistent with U.S. policy may be authorized by one of the general licenses contained in subpart E or by a specific license issued pursuant to the procedures described in subpart E of 31 CFR part 501.

* * * *

By Notice of July 19, 2007, President Bush extended the national emergency with respect to the former Liberian regime of Charles Taylor, stating:

> Today, Liberia is engaged in a peaceful transition to a democratic order under the administration of President Ellen Johnson-Sirleaf. The regulations implementing Executive Order 13348, clarify that the subject of this national emergency has been and remains limited to the former Liberian regime of Charles Taylor and specified other persons and not the country, citizens, Government, or Central Bank of Liberia.
>
> Charles Taylor is today standing trial in The Hague by the Special Court for Sierra Leone. However, stability in Liberia is still fragile. The actions and policies of Charles Taylor and others have left a legacy of destruction that still has the potential to undermine Liberia's transformation and recovery.

72 Fed. Reg. 40,057 (July 20, 2007).

---

*   Editor's note: In Resolution 1689, adopted June 20, 2006, the Security Council, acting under Chapter VII of the UN Charter, among other things, decided "not to renew the measure in paragraph 10 of resolution 1521 (2003) that obligates Member States to prevent the import into their territories of all round log and timber products originating in Liberia."

6. Political Repression in Belarus

Effective November 13, 2007, OFAC designated Belneftekhim and Belneftekhim USA, Inc. under Executive Order 13405 (2006), which targets individuals and entities who are either undermining the democratic processes or institutions or are responsible for human rights violations related to political repression in Belarus. 72 Fed. Reg. 65,132 (Nov. 19, 2007). Effective February 27, 2007, OFAC designated six Belarusian Government officials who have played important roles in the oppressive regime of Alexander Lukashenka under Executive Order 13405. 72 Fed. Reg. 13,556 (Mar. 22, 2007).

7. Conflict in the Democratic Republic of the Congo

Effective March 30, 2007, Treasury/OFAC designated 10 persons (seven entities and three individuals) under Executive Order 13413 (2006), which targets, among others, individuals and entities determined to have supplied arms contributing to the conflict in the Democratic Republic of the Congo (DRC) or having provided support to armed militias or the leaders of foreign armed groups operating in the DRC. *See www.treas. gov/press/releases/hp334.htm*. Nine of the 10 persons designated have also been designated by the UN Security Council Committee established pursuant to resolution 1533. *See www. un.org/sc/committees/1533/*.

8. Role of UN Charter Committee

On October 16, 2007, Rodger Young, U.S. public delegate, addressed the UN General Assembly Sixth Committee concerning the role of the UN Charter Committee, primarily on proposals related to the committee's involvement in sanctions. The full text of the statement, excerpted below, is available at *www.state.gov/s/l/c8183.htm*.

The United States welcomes the Report of the Charter Committee (A/62/33), and appreciates the opportunity to express our views on some of the issues addressed in the report.

*   *   *   *

The Charter Committee's report notes the Committee's discussions on various proposals relating to sanctions. As we have said previously, we do not believe that the Charter Committee should aim to devise norms concerning the design and implementation of sanctions. The Committee should not pursue activities in this area that would be duplicative or inconsistent with the roles of the principal organs of the United Nations as set forth in the Charter, in particular Article 24.

As noted at prior sessions of the Sixth Committee and the Charter Committee, some Member States continue to assert that Article 50 of the Charter requires the Security Council to take some sort of action to assist "third States" affected by the imposition of sanctions. We would like to reiterate our long-held view that while Article 50 consultations provide a mechanism to discuss the effects of sanctions on third States, it does not require the Council to take any specific action.

In that regard, we welcome the Secretary-General's report (A/62/206), which informed Member States of the fact that, in the period under review, none of the sanctions committees had been approached by Member States to express concerns about special economic problems resulting from the imposition of sanctions. We believe this is the result of concerted Council efforts to impose targeted measures that minimize unintended economic problems for States and applaud the Council's work in that regard. Since targeted sanctions have substantially minimized unintended economic consequences for States, we see no reason for Member States to consider actively the establishment of a fund financed from assessed contributions or other UN-based financial arrangements to address an abstract concern.

We also note that the Secretary-General's report observes that the Security Council has taken steps to mitigate economic burdens on targeted individuals arising from the implementation of Security Council assets freezes. The Secretary-General's report observes that in every case in which the Security Council has decided that States shall freeze the assets owned or controlled by designated individuals and entities, the Council has also adopted exceptions by which States can signal to the relevant sanctions committee their intention to authorize access to frozen funds for a variety of basic and extraordinary expenses, which can include payment for legal services.

It also is noteworthy that concerns that have been expressed in the past about the need for fair and clear procedures for the Security Council to de-list persons subject to Security Council sanctions have been addressed and therefore proposals relating to this subject are no longer timely or relevant. It is a priority of the United States to make the lists of individuals and entities that the Security Council targets for sanctions as accurate as possible and to make the process fair and clear. In this regard we welcome in particular the adoption of Security Council Resolution 1730 of 2006, under which a focal point has been established in the Secretariat to receive de-listing requests.

* * * *

B. REMOVAL OR MODIFICATION OF SANCTIONS

1. Palestinian Authority

In March 2006 a new elected government of the Palestinian Authority ("PA") formed by Hamas was sworn in. Because Hamas is subject to a number of terrorism-related sanctions in the United States, OFAC revised terrorism-related regulations to clarify that transactions with the PA would be prohibited without a license and issued six general licenses authorizing certain actions in connection with the PA. 71 Fed. Reg. 27,199 (May 10, 2006). On December 1, 2006, President Bush signed into law the Palestinian Anti-Terrorism Act of 2006, Pub. L. No. 109-446, limiting assistance to the Palestinian Authority and for the West Bank and Gaza under the Foreign Assistance Act of 1961, as amended. *See Digest 2006* at 990–95.

Following the appointment of a new prime minister and the entry into the PA government of ministers not affiliated with Hamas, on June 20, 2007, OFAC issued a general license authorizing "U.S. persons . . . to engage in all transactions otherwise prohibited by 31 C.F.R. pts 594, 595, and 597 with the Palestinian Authority." The general license is available at *www.treas.gov/offices/enforcement/ofac/programs/terror/gls/gl7.pdf.* On October 23, 2007, OFAC published this general license in the Federal Register, excerpted below. 72 Fed. Reg. 61,517 (Oct. 31, 2007).

*   *   *   *

HAMAS is a target of each of these sanctions programs, resulting in the blocking of its property and interests in property that are in the United States or within the possession or control of a U.S. person. In the case of the FTOSR, U.S. financial institutions are required to retain possession or control of any funds of HAMAS and report the existence of such funds to Treasury. These restrictions effectively prohibit U.S. persons from dealing in property or interests in property of HAMAS. Following the 2006 parliamentary elections in the West Bank and Gaza, which resulted in HAMAS members forming the majority party within the Palestinian Legislative Council and holding positions of authority within the government, OFAC determined that HAMAS had a property interest in the transactions of the Palestinian Authority. That determination remains in place. Accordingly, pursuant to the TSR, the GTSR, and the FTOSR, U.S. persons are prohibited from engaging in transactions with the Palestinian Authority unless authorized. On April 12, 2006, OFAC issued six general licenses authorizing U.S. persons to engage in certain transactions in which the Palestinian Authority may have an interest.

Based on foreign policy considerations resulting from recent events in the West Bank and Gaza, including the appointment of Salam Fayyad as the new Prime Minister of the Palestinian Authority and of other ministers not affiliated with HAMAS, OFAC is revising the TSR, GTSR, and FTOSR to add a new general license as TSR § 595.514, GTSR § 594.516, and FTOSR § 597.512.

Paragraph (a) of new §§ 595.514, 594.516, and 597.512 authorizes U.S. persons to engage in all transactions with the Palestinian Authority. Paragraph (b) of these sections defines the term Palestinian Authority, for purposes of the authorization in paragraph (a), as the Palestinian Authority government of Prime Minister Salam Fayyad and President Mahmoud Abbas, including all branches, ministries, offices, and agencies (independent or otherwise) thereof. Transactions with HAMAS, or in any property in which HAMAS has an interest, not covered by the general license remain prohibited.

* * * *

2. Southern Sudan

On January 2, 2007, Secretary of State Condoleezza Rice determined, pursuant to the Darfur Peace and Accountability Act, Pub. L. No. 109-344, that

. . . the provision of non-lethal military equipment and related defense services (hereafter "assistance") to the Government of Southern Sudan for the purpose of constituting a professional military force is in the national security interests of the United States . . .

and authorized the provision of such non-lethal assistance for fiscal years 2007 and 2008, notwithstanding any other provision of law. 72 Fed. Reg. 2326 (Jan. 18, 2007).

See also Amendments to Sudanese Sanctions Regulations in A.3. above.

C. U.S. SANCTIONS ENFORCEMENT

1. Enhanced Penalties for Violations of Sanctions Imposed Under the International Emergency Economic Powers Act

On October 16, 2007, President Bush signed into law the International Emergency Economic Powers Enhancement Act, Pub. L. No. 110-96. The act amended the International

Emergency Economic Powers Act ("IEEPA") to increase civil
and criminal penalties for violations of economic sanctions
imposed under IEEPA. The new sanctions are set forth in
amended IEEPA § 206, 50 U.S.C. § 1705:

> (a) Unlawful Acts.—It shall be unlawful for a person to
> violate, attempt to violate, conspire to violate, or cause a
> violation of any license, order, regulation, or prohibition
> issued under this title.
> (b) Civil Penalty.—A civil penalty may be imposed on any
> person who commits an unlawful act described in sub-
> section (a) in an amount not to exceed the greater of—
>> (1) $250,000; or
>> (2) an amount that is twice the amount of the transac-
>> tion that is the basis of the violation with respect to
>> which the penalty is imposed.
> (c) Criminal Penalty.—A person who willfully commits,
> willfully attempts to commit, or willfully conspires to com-
> mit, or aids or abets in the commission of, an unlawful
> act described in subsection (a) shall, upon conviction, be
> fined not more than $1,000,000, or if a natural person,
> may be imprisoned for not more than 20 years, or both.

2. OFAC Denial of License Related to Trademark Renewal for Cuban Company

On September 27, 2007, the U.S. District Court for the District
of Columbia granted summary judgment for defendant Office
of Foreign Assets Control ("OFAC") in part and remanded to
OFAC to supplement the administrative record in a case seeking to invalidate OFAC's denial of an application necessary for
renewal of the trademark HAVANA CLUB by a Cuban company. *Empresa Cubana Exportadora de Alimentos y Productos
Varios d/b/a Cubaexport v. United States Department of Treasury,
Office of Foreign Assets Control*, 516 F. Supp. 2d 43 (D.D.C.
2007). For discussion of the case and the U.S. memorandum

in support of its motion to dismiss or for summary judgment and related documents, *see Digest 2006* at 1006–15.

The court described the basic regulatory structure at issue as follows.

* * * *

Prior to 1998, the CACR included a general license for trademark registration and renewal by Cuban nationals: "Transactions related to the registration and renewal in the United States Patent and Trademark Office . . . of . . . trademarks . . . in which the Government of Cuba or a Cuban national has an interest are authorized." 31 C.F.R. § 515.527(a) (1996). On October 21, 1998, however, . . . Congress exempted a defined class of transactions from that general license. Omnibus Consolidation and Emergency Supplemental Appropriations Act, Pub. L. No. 105-277, § 211, 112 Stat. 2681 (1998). The operative provision, Section 211, states

> Notwithstanding any other provision of law, no transaction or payment shall be authorized or approved pursuant to [the general license] with respect to a mark, trade name, or commercial name that was used in connection with a business or assets that were confiscated unless the original owner of the mark, trade name, or commercial name, or the bona fide successor-in-interest[,] has expressly consented.

Id. § 211(a). Thus, a Cuban national who wished to renew a trademark registration was now required to seek a specific license from OFAC if: 1) the mark had been used in connection with property expropriated by the Cuban government; and 2) the mark's original owner or bona fide successor-in-interest had neither consented nor received compensation.[1] *See id.*; 31 C.F.R. § 515.336 (2007) (defining "confiscated").

* * * *

---

[1] According to defendant Szubin, OFAC's director, after Section 211's enactment, OFAC retained "the authority to issue a specific license, should facts and circumstances and current U.S. foreign policy militate in favor of authorizing a transaction that does not qualify for the general license." . . .

The court awarded summary judgment on the first and third of three claims by Cubaexport under the Administrative Procedure Act, in one instance finding OFAC's action "both reasonable and fully warranted by the facts," and in the other that the action was committed to agency discretion by law. As to the second APA claim, the court found that "neither the Administrative Record nor the Szubin declaration clearly articulates the reasoning process [OFAC] followed [in making] its determination that 'renewal of the HAVANA CLUB trademark . . . would be prohibited unless specifically licensed. . . .'" Specifically, it found that "nowhere in the Administrative Record does OFAC explicitly state that the general license was inapplicable or that it believed Section 211 and 31 C.F.R. section 515.527(a)(1) compelled such a conclusion." Therefore the court granted summary judgment to neither party but "order[ed] defendant OFAC to supplement the Administrative Record with evidence elucidating the contemporaneous reasons" for that determination.

The court did not reach Cubaexport's claims of violations under the Fifth Amendment to the U.S. Constitution for deprivation of property without due process and taking of a protected property interest without compensation. The court noted that Cubaexport's constitutional claims "all assume, as an antecedent fact, that OFAC actually applied Section 211 and 31 C.F.R. § 515.527(a)(2) to Cubaexport." Given its action on the second APA claim, requiring OFAC to address the relevance of these authorities, the court declined to rule on the constitutional claims as an exercise of judicial restraint.

The U.S. reply brief, filed on April 13, 2007, is available at *www.state.gov/s/l/c8183.htm.*

3. Criminal Charges for Cuban Travel Restriction Violations

On February 22, 2007, Adam J. Szubin, Director of the Office of Foreign Assets Control, Department of the Treasury, announced that criminal charges had been brought against two individuals for conspiracy to violate restrictions on travel to Cuba and against one of them with making materially false statements in applications to obtain religious travel licenses to Cuba. The full text of the press release, excerpted below, is available at *www.treas.gov/press/releases/hp274.htm*.

. . . The criminal complaint unsealed today marks an important step in stopping fraud involved in facilitating violations of restrictions on travel to Cuba.

OFAC issues hundreds of licenses each year to individuals and groups seeking to engage in legitimate religious activities and programs in Cuba. Those who fraudulently obtain or traffic in such licenses not only commit a crime, but also undermine the good works of legitimate religious groups traveling to Cuba.

The Cuban Sanctions Enforcement Task Force, headed by the U.S. Attorney for the Southern District of Florida, is moving aggressively to stop such violations, pursuing criminal investigations against those involved in unlicensed dealings with Cuba, whether travel, remittances, or other prohibited activities. I commend the Task Force's efforts to halt this abuse and OFAC will continue to support its activities. OFAC investigators played a key role in uncovering the activity that is being exposed today. OFAC has detected abuse among religious license applicants and the travel providers who service them, including fabricated religious organizations, ministers, and programs of religious activity.

As today's action demonstrates, OFAC takes the integrity of U.S. sanctions programs very seriously and will continue to work to safeguard these sanctions programs against abuse. Those who seek to evade sanctions laws face serious penalties, both civil and criminal.

* * * *

Cross References

Suspension of entry to the United States, **Chapter 1.C.7.**
Counternarcotics sanctions, **Chapter 3.B.2.a.**

Trafficking in persons sanctions, Chapter 3.B.3.b.
Money laundering sanctions, Chapter 3.B.5.
Terrorism sanctions, Chapter 3.B.1.c. and B.1.h.
Rule of law statement on Security Council targeted sanctions,
     Chapter 6.I.
Nonproliferation sanctions, Chapter 18.C.3.b., C.4.c., and C.11.

CHAPTER 17

International Conflict Resolution and Avoidance

A. PEACE PROCESS AND RELATED ISSUES

1. General

On December 10, 2007, Department of State Legal Adviser John B. Bellinger, III, addressed the World Legal Forum in The Hague on the importance of peaceful and effective international dispute resolution. Excerpts follow from his prepared remarks. For further discussion of international and hybrid criminal tribunals, see Chapter 3.C.; of Israeli-Palestinian peace efforts, see A.3. below; of Security Council actions concerning nuclear issues in North Korea and Iran, see Chapter 18.C.3. and 4. The full text is available at *www.state.gov/s/l/rls/96686. htm.*

. . . It is particularly fitting to discuss the topic of dispute resolution on the centennial of the Hague Peace Conference of 1907. That conference and the one before it in 1899 were animated by the belief that international disputes could be settled by arbitration and law. The diplomats who attended the 1907 conference faced, much as the world today does, a pressing set of international issues— how to establish mechanisms for peaceful settlement of international conflict, how to address a troubling increase in arms expenditures, and how to make war more humane. The conference concluded a number of conventions addressing these issues, including the Convention for the Pacific Settlement of International Disputes.

The then-American Secretary of State Elihu Root called the conference "the greatest advance ever made at any single time toward the reasonable and peaceful regulation of international conduct."

Some of the problems addressed at the 1907 conference are still problems with us. We still seek ways of avoiding conflict and humanizing war. But we also face new challenges in managing a world that is tied together more tightly and in more complex ways than before. As the number of connections has grown, so too have the potential sources of disputes. We all have a shared interest in resolving those disputes peacefully and permanently.

The United States has particular reasons to seek peaceful and effective international dispute settlement. Few if any international disputes do not have an impact on our security, humanitarian, and economic interests. Thus, we rely heavily on international institutions and international law to find peaceful and effective resolutions to conflicts and disagreements.

But we also believe that successful dispute resolution requires that states be active and politically engaged in seeking a settlement. That is where I want to focus my remarks today. It is not enough to turn over a problem to international organizations and hope that after a time, a solution will emerge. Such formal resolution mechanisms have a vital role to play, and can be a decisive factor in resolving disputes. But especially in the most serious crises, there is no substitute for the application of political will and energy by states.

With respect to dispute resolution mechanisms, the United States has typically taken a pragmatic approach—using such mechanisms where they fit the problem and can advance the parties toward a resolution. Moreover, no one mechanism of dispute resolution is inherently superior to another. The United States has made use of a wide range of mechanisms—some within existing institutional frameworks, others wholly ad hoc—to try to address the critical peace and security problems of our time. In this respect, we have wholeheartedly embraced the perspective of Article 33 of the UN Charter, which suggests an array of resolution mechanisms to disputing parties.

Consistent with this approach, the United States has resorted to international courts and tribunals where they are likely to be most effective—for example, where they are tasked with enforcing a fairly specific set of obligations. This is evident in the United States' strong support for the World Trade Organization, which has a dispute settlement mechanism tailored to address trade issues. In the last dozen years, the US and the EU have managed to resolve a number of trade disputes through the WTO—some affecting critical industries and involving billions of dollars, without resort to a damaging trade war. Courts or tribunals can also be tailored to address specific political or security problems. Indeed, the very act of establishing a tribunal can take a particular issue off the table and make resolution of a broader dispute easier. The Iran-US Claims Tribunal, based here in The Hague, was created as part of an arrangement that resolved a major crisis and led to the release of the U.S. hostages. In a different vein, the Permanent Court of Arbitration, also here in The Hague, has provided a mechanism for states to reduce conflict by allowing resolution of disputes on an ad hoc basis.

More recently, the United States has firmly backed the Special Tribunal created, in accordance with UN Security Council Resolution 1757, to bring to justice those responsible for the murder of former Lebanese Prime Minister Rafik Hariri and others. Although deference to a state's internal legal process is the norm, this was a case where that process was itself subverted by threats of violence and terrorism. We strongly hope that the Tribunal will ultimately punish those responsible for the assassinations and put to rest the resulting civil discord. And we also owe a note of thanks to the Dutch, who have kindly agreed to host the Special Tribunal.

By contrast, we have found it more difficult to reach political consensus for a single tribunal covering all manner of international law disputes. The International Court of Justice was meant to serve as the ultimate arbiter of most international law issues affecting the UN Charter. Although it has not achieved this lofty and difficult aspiration, we believe the court can play a constructive role in resolving international disputes. To be sure, the United States—like many countries—does not accept the mandatory jurisdiction of the ICJ. But we have nevertheless turned to the ICJ to address a number of disputes, including a longstanding boundary issue with Canada and Iran's takeover of our embassy in Tehran in 1979.

These cases allowed the ICJ to do what it does best: resolve a concrete dispute in light of well-developed international law.

We believe, however, that some look to courts and tribunals for more than they realistically can deliver, because they somehow regard them as the most authentic source of international law. Efforts to lure international courts and tribunals into choppier political waters can often prove embarrassing to those bodies. Justice Holmes of our Supreme Court once said, "Great cases, like hard cases, make bad law." This is especially true of inherently political cases, which can strain the legitimacy of international legal institutions and undermine the capacity of those institutions to contribute to effective dispute settlement. A notable example is the ICJ's advisory opinion process, which allows the court to opine on matters without full participation by all disputing parties and tends to cast the court in the role of arbitrating political conflict.

Despite these concerns, the United States believes that an effective ICJ is invaluable to advancing the rule of law and encouraging the peaceful settlement of international disputes. That commitment is evident in the *Avena* case, which President Bush has determined to enforce by instructing our states to provide new hearings to the 51 foreign nationals covered by the ICJ order. This has been deeply controversial in the affected states, and there has been strong resistance to the President's actions. But we remain committed to complying with the ruling, and have asked our Supreme Court to give full effect to the President's decision.*

But I want to leave international courts and tribunals to the side for now, and focus my remaining time on other mechanisms of dispute settlement. Most international disputes do not end up in court. Instead, they are managed by the international community, and often resolved, through many other formal and informal mechanisms. One such mechanism is the process of consultation and confidence-building that can prevent mutual suspicion from developing into full blown disputes. Another is the ongoing monitoring and negotiation, which can help resolve a dispute that has already taken concrete shape. The distinctions between these mechanisms

---

*   Editor's note: *See* Chapter 2.A.1.a.

of dispute settlement are not always clean: a single international institution might engage in each of these forms of dispute settlement, depending on the nature of the problem. But we believe these various mechanisms are different tools in the lawyer and policymaker's toolbox, and which one is best typically depends on the problem to be solved.

The United States strongly supports the role of international institutions in preventing disputes from ever taking shape. This work of heading off real trouble is the everyday work of valuable international institutions, such as the OECD and OSCE, for example, which in their respective areas host regular intergovernmental and promote appropriate reporting and consultation mechanisms.

The United States has been particularly supportive of the role of the UN Security Council in helping to prevent disputes from escalating into dangerous conflict. In recent years, the United States has been an active participant in the Security Council process. In fact, over the last several years, the United States has been among the leaders in pressing for Security Council action to deal with threats that have emerged to international peace and security.

We believe this engagement has moved serious international disputes closer to resolution. With respect to Iran, the United States has pressed the Council to take robust action to address the serious concerns surrounding that country's nuclear program. The Council unanimously adopted two sanctions resolutions, requiring Iran to take certain steps to allow for negotiations toward a long-term agreement. The measures imposed in the resolutions have also reinforced the efforts of EU High Commissioner Solana— on behalf of China, France, Germany, Russia, the UK and the US—and those of the IAEA to secure Iran's compliance with its obligations. This targeted, multilateral approach is increasing the costs to the Iranian regime of its behavior and maintaining pressure necessary to persuade Iran to help find a negotiated solution. For this approach to succeed, however, the international community must intensify pressure on Iran to suspend its enrichment program—most importantly by adopting a new UN Security Council sanctions resolution. We continue to insist that Iran provide a full account of its past and present nuclear activities, and we must ensure that Iran's nuclear weapons program remains halted.

International disputes can be handled through formal or informal frameworks of negotiation and mediation. The United States supports many organizations that offer formal frameworks for resolving disputes at an early stage. US border issues with Canada and Mexico have long been managed by international commissions, which address not only issues related to the actual borders, but also water use, navigation, and environmental disputes. In addition, the United States has supported the work of the NAFTA Free Trade Commission in addressing trade-related disputes through non-binding mechanisms before those disputes reach arbitration.

But we believe that informal negotiation and mediation—where states must engage and real political effort must be expended—are often the best way to address the most serious international disputes. Such disputes never invite neat solutions, and effective settlement is mainly a political problem.

In this vein, the United States has played, and continues to play, a leading role to help bring peace to the Middle East. We do not act alone by any means—the participation of some 50 ministerial level delegations at the President's recent Annapolis conference shows how broad international support is for peacefully resolving the Arab-Israeli dispute. Amr Moussa was there, and the United States was honored by his attendance. I know Amr has worked tirelessly for the peaceful resolution of disputes in the Middle East for many years.

As Secretary Rice noted, the issue of Middle East peace is "an issue of conscience that . . . stir[s] us all." We have joined with the other members of the so-called international Quartet—Russia, the EU and the UN—to help Israelis and Palestinians progress on their path to a two-state solution. But it is the United States to which the parties have turned for most hands-on help in resolving their differences.

As a result of Annapolis, as the President announced, Israelis and Palestinians are launching permanent status talks to end their conflict. At our urging, these negotiations will be continuous and deal with all the core issues, including borders, security arrangements, refugees, Jerusalem, water and settlements. Moreover, the parties committed themselves at Annapolis to make every effort to conclude an agreement before the end of 2008. This is an ambitious goal, so Palestinian President Abbas and Israeli Prime Minister Olmert have also agreed to meet on a bi-weekly basis to oversee the negotiations. The United States will continue to be deeply engaged in supporting these efforts, as you will see by high-level visits to the region in the upcoming days and weeks.

In parallel to their political negotiations, the Israelis and Palestinians also asked the United States at Annapolis to develop a trilateral mechanism to monitor and judge implementation of their prior commitments to improve conditions on the ground. Too often, hopeful signs of progress on the political track have been compromised by acts eroding confidence in the ability to achieve a mutually satisfactory outcome through negotiations. In recognition of that risk, the parties are looking to us as an outside party to help them avoid these lapses. This will be a sensitive task since our mutual goal is progress in meeting obligations not recriminations over shortcomings. If we are successful, it will be an excellent illustration of how a creative approach to dispute-resolution can blend diplomacy, monitoring, and informal adjudication to address issues as explosive as the Arab-Israeli conflict.

The United States has also strongly promoted negotiation and mediation to address the problem of North Korea's nuclear program. We have insisted that those negotiations include all the major interested parties in the region—South Korea, North Korea, Japan, China, Russia and the United States. The goal of these Six-Party Talks is the "verifiable denuclearization of the Korean peninsula in a peaceful manner." A September 2005 joint statement contains the ingredients for resolution of many sources of conflict that undermine security and stability in Northeast Asia. First and foremost, North Korea committed to abandoning all nuclear weapons and existing nuclear programs and returning to the nuclear non-proliferation treaty and to IAEA safeguards. The joint statement also charted a path by which the North can be integrated into the international community—through economic cooperation in the fields of energy, trade and investment, and through eventual normalization of relations between North Korea and both the United States and Japan.

The negotiations regarding North Korea, as reflected in the joint statement, look to the past, and to the future. No peaceful settlement agreement has ever been reached to replace the provisional armistice that halted the Korean war more than 50 years ago. The joint statement committed certain "directly related parties" to negotiate one. In addition, the Six Parties committed themselves to joint efforts toward lasting peace and stability in Northeast Asia and toward long-term mechanisms to address security issues in the region.

These negotiations are now bearing some fruit, and the parties are completing negotiations in coordinated steps, as envisioned by the joint statement. At the request of the other parties, the United States is leading a team to disable specified facilities by December 31st. North Korea is to provide a complete declaration. The implementation of the 2005 consensus has not been without bumps in the road. But it continues to produce very positive results, and there is reason to hope it can lead to the eventual denuclearization of the Korean Peninsula, and to a stable and peaceful North East Asia.

Finally, and perhaps most important at this moment, the United States has consistently demonstrated its commitment to working toward a peaceful settlement in Kosovo.* . . .

*   *   *   *

In closing, I wish to reiterate that the United States is firmly committed to UN Charter principles for resolving international disputes peacefully. We are not wedded to any particular theory of how that should be done. Instead, we believe in a pragmatic approach, and believe in the need to rely upon whatever mechanism can best reduce, manage, or resolve disputes. International law— the Charter in particular, with its purpose of "maintain[ing] international peace and security"—expects states to do exactly this.

2. Burma

a. U.S. efforts in the Security Council

On January 12, 2007, the UN Security Council failed to adopt a resolution offered by the United States calling on the military regime in Burma to work with UN special representative

---

*   Editor's note: *See* Chapter 9.A.1.

Ibrahim Gambari and take concrete steps to allow full freedom of expression, association, and movement. Acting Permanent Representative of the United States to the United Nations Alejandro Wolff addressed the Security Council to express U.S. disappointment following the vote in which two permanent members voted no. The full text of Ambassador Wolff's statement, excerpted below, is available at *www.usunnewyork.usmission.gov/press_releases/20070112_005.html.*

The United States is deeply disappointed by the failure of the Council to adopt this resolution.

This resolution would have been a strong and urgently needed statement by the Security Council about the need for change in Burma, whose military regime arbitrarily arrests, tortures, rapes and executes its own people, wages war on minorities within its own borders, and builds itself new cities, while looking the other way as refugee flows increase, narcotics and human trafficking grow, and communicable diseases remain untreated.

The deteriorating humanitarian and political situation in Burma affects, first and foremost, the people of Burma, and today the United States reiterates its support for them. However, we also believe that the situation in Burma does pose a risk to peace and security beyond its borders.

*   *   *   *

This resolution would have contributed to stability in the region by providing its clear support for the Secretary General's "good offices" mission, which is intended to provide a framework for constructive dialogue between the UN and the Burmese regime leading to concrete progress. Under Secretary General Gambari specifically asked this body for our support, and we are disappointed that today we have been unable to respond to his request.

However, while Council members may have disagreed over whether this body should address the situation in Burma, there is no disagreement over the urgent, compelling need for tangible change in Burma. We agree on the importance of the Secretary General's "good offices" mission in promoting peaceful change in

Burma, and the need for the Burmese regime to take prompt, concrete action on the requests made by Under Secretary General Gambari in his two visits to Burma, specifically: the initiation of an inclusive national political dialogue representing all parties and ethnic groups; the release of all political prisoners, including Daw Aung San Suu Kyi; the cessation of military violence against ethnic minorities; and, the loosening of restrictions on the work of international humanitarian organizations in Burma.

*   *   *   *

In a meeting with the press following the Security Council action, Ambassador Wolff responded to a question from a reporter concerning the basis for Security Council involvement:

> *Reporter:* What's the threat to international peace and security, sir, in the Myanmar case?
>
> *Ambassador Wolff:* If you read the draft resolution and you hear . . . the statements made by a number of delegations, including mine, the cross-border refugee flows, the threats from communicable disease, the internally displaced persons, all of these things in today's era, as other members of the council have said, reflect the type of contemporary threat that the council and the international community needs to address before they become imminent, immediate, irremedial threats to international peace and security. The charter allows for this, and this was the right thing to do.

On October 11, 2007, the Security Council issued a Presidential Statement, "Situation in Myanmar." S/PRST/2007/37. Ambassador Khalilzad commented on the statement as follows:

> . . . We've had a statement from the Security Council that the United States finds acceptable. It is a statement that has the key elements that we have been focused on. To strongly deplore what has happened; the statement does that. To call for the release of all detainees, demonstrators who are detained, as early as possible; it does that.

It calls for the release of political prisoners, those who were held before; and it does that. And it strongly endorses national reconciliation and a transition to democracy, and supports the role of Mr. Gambari. It strengthens his hand as he gets ready to go there again. And, it also, for the first time, brings the Security Council together to speak unanimously on the situation with regard to Burma and commits the Security Council to remain focused on this issue. . . .

The full text of Ambassador Khalilzad's statement to the press is available at *www.usunnewyork.usmission.gov/press_releases/20071011_236.html*.

b. President Bush: Address to the General Assembly

In his address to the UN General Assembly on September 25, 2007, President George W. Bush discussed the need for further action concerning Burma, as follows:

. . . Americans are outraged by the situation in Burma, where a military junta has imposed a 19-year reign of fear. Basic freedoms of speech, assembly, and worship are severely restricted. Ethnic minorities are persecuted. Forced child labor, human trafficking, and rape are common. The regime is holding more than 1,000 political prisoners—including Aung San Suu Kyi, whose party was elected overwhelmingly by the Burmese people in 1990.

. . . This morning, I'm announcing a series of steps to help bring peaceful change to Burma. The United States will tighten economic sanctions on the leaders of the regime and their financial backers. We will impose an expanded visa ban on those responsible for the most egregious violations of human rights, as well as their family members. We'll continue to support the efforts of humanitarian groups working to alleviate suffering in Burma. And I urge the United Nations and all nations to use their diplomatic and economic leverage to help the Burmese people reclaim their freedom.

The full text of President Bush's address is available at 43 Weekly Comp. Pres. Doc. 1245, 1246 (Oct. 1, 2007). The imposition of further U.S. sanctions is discussed in Chapter 16.A.2.

3. Israeli-Palestinian Conflict

a. *Mecca agreement and formation of new Palestinian Authority national unity government*

On February 8, 2007, Palestinian representatives, in a meeting in Mecca hosted by the government of Saudi Arabia, adopted an agreement that provided the basis for movement toward a Palestinian national unity government. On February 21, 2007, representatives of the United States, Russia, the United Nations, and the European Union, referred to as the Quartet, stated that the Quartet had "expressed its appreciation for the role of King Abd[u]llah of Saudi Arabia and the cessation of violence among Palestinians." *See www.state.gov/r/pa/ prs/ps/2007/february/80838.htm.*

The Palestinian Authority established the new national unity government on March 17, 2007, with Ismail Haniyeh as prime minister and other ministers not affiliated with Hamas. The Quartet welcomed the developments, as set forth below. *See www.state.gov/r/pa/prs/ps/2007/mar/82019.htm.*

---

*   *   *   *

The Quartet reiterated its respect for Palestinian democracy and the agreement reached in Mecca on 8 February 2007, which laid the foundation for Palestinian reconciliation. The Quartet expressed hope that the establishment of a new government on 17 March 2007 would help end intra-Palestinian violence and ensure calm. The Quartet reaffirmed its previous statements with regard to the need for a Palestinian government committed to nonviolence, recognition of Israel and acceptance of previous agreements and obligations, including the Roadmap, and encouraged progress in this direction. The Quartet agreed that the commitment of the new government in this regard will be measured not only on the basis of its composition and platform, but also its actions. The Quartet expressed its expectation that the unity government will act responsibly, demonstrate clear and credible commitment to the Quartet principles, and support the efforts of President Abbas to pursue a two-state solution to the Israeli-Palestinian conflict, thereby achieving the peace, security, and freedom the Israeli and Palestinian people desire and deserve.

* * * *

The Quartet expressed its strong support for Secretary Rice's efforts to further facilitate discussions with President Abbas and Prime Minister Olmert with the aim of defining more clearly the political horizon for the establishment of a Palestinian state and an end to the Israeli-Palestinian conflict. The Quartet agreed to meet in the region soon to review developments and discuss the way ahead.

b. Escalation of violence and break-up of Hamas-led Palestinian Authority

On May 30, 2007, reacting to the escalation of violence in Gaza and attacks on Israel and other events in the region, the Quartet met and issued a statement urging restraint on both sides. The full text of the statement, excerpted below, is available at *www.state.gov/r/pa/prs/ps/2007/may/85784.htm.*

* * * *

The Quartet expressed its deep concern over recent factional violence in Gaza. It called for all Palestinians to immediately renounce all acts of violence and respect the ceasefire. It called upon the Palestinian Authority government, in cooperation with President Abbas and regional actors, to do everything necessary to restore law and order, including the release of kidnapped BBC journalist Alan Johnston.

The Quartet strongly condemned the continued firing of Qassam rockets into Southern Israel as well as the buildup of arms

by Hamas and other terrorist groups in Gaza. It endorsed PA
President Abbas' call for an immediate end to such violence, and
called upon all elements of the PA government and all Palestinian
groups to cooperate with President Abbas to that end. The Quartet
called for the immediate and unconditional release of Israeli
Corporal Gilad Shalit. The Quartet urged Israel to exercise restraint
to ensure that its security operations avoid civilian casualties or
damage to civilian infrastructure. It noted that the detention of
elected members of the Palestinian government and legislature
raises particular concerns and called for them to be released. The
Quartet noted its support for the May 30th Security Council Press
Statement on the breakdown of the ceasefire in the Gaza Strip.

The Quartet welcomed continued dialogue between Prime
Minister Olmert and President Abbas, including bilateral summits,
and expressed support for U.S. efforts to effect progress on security and movement and access issues. The Quartet agreed that
movement and access are essential and in this regard called on
both parties to implement fully the Movement and Access
Agreement of 15 November 2005. The Quartet urged the parties
to work positively and constructively in order to build confidence
and to create an environment conducive to progress on the political horizon for Palestinian statehood, consistent with the Roadmap
and relevant UN Security Council resolutions, which should also
be addressed in these bilateral discussions. Palestinians must know
that their state will be viable, and Israelis must know a future state
of Palestine will be a source of security, not a threat.

*   *   *   *

The Quartet welcomed the [March 29, 2007] re-affirmation of
the Arab Peace Initiative,* noting that the initiative is recognized in

---

*   Editor's note: On March 29, 2007, Arab leaders issued the Riyadh
Declaration, which stated, among other things, that the leaders "[a]ffirm the
option of just and comprehensive peace as a strategic option for the Arab
nation; in accordance with the Arab peace initiative that draws the right path
for reaching a peaceful settlement for the Arab-Israeli conflict based on the
principles and resolutions of international legitimacy, and the land for peace
formula."

the Roadmap as a vital element of international efforts to advance regional peace. The Arab Peace Initiative provides a welcome regional political horizon for Israel, complementing the efforts of the Quartet and of the parties themselves to advance towards negotiated, comprehensive, just and lasting peace. The Quartet noted its positive meeting with members of the Arab League in Sharm al-Sheikh on May 4, and looked forward to continued engagement with the Arab states. It welcomed the intention of the Arab League to engage Israel on the initiative, and Israeli receptiveness to such engagement. Recalling elements of the April 18 decision by the Arab League Follow-up Committee, the Quartet urged all involved to demonstrate their seriousness and commitment to making peace. In that context, the Quartet reiterated the need for a Palestinian Government committed to nonviolence, recognition of Israel, and acceptance of previous agreements and obligations, including the Roadmap, and reaffirmed its willingness to support such a government. The Quartet encouraged continued and expanded Arab contacts with Israel, and Israeli action to address concerns raised in the April 18 Arab League decision, including a cessation of settlement expansion and the removal of illegal outposts, as called for in the Roadmap.

*   *   *   *

In June 2007 Hamas illegally seized control of Gaza, and President Abbas dissolved the Palestinian Authority cabinet, replacing it with an emergency government without Hamas members, and outlawed the militia forces of Hamas. On June 16, 2007, the Quartet issued a statement expressing "deep concern over the welfare and security of all Palestinians— especially those in Gaza, whose lives have been most seriously affected by the ongoing crisis." Further,

> The Quartet expressed understanding and support for President Abbas' decisions to dissolve the Cabinet and declare an emergency, given the grave circumstances. The Quartet recognized the necessity and legitimacy of these decisions, taken under Palestinian law, and welcomed President Abbas' stated intention to consult the Palestinian

people at the appropriate time. The Quartet noted its continuing support for other legitimate Palestinian institutions.

See www.state.gov/r/pa/prs/ps/2007/jun/86596.htm. In a
special press briefing on June 18, 2007, Secretary of State
Condoleezza Rice stated as follows on the changes in the
government and U.S. reaction. The full text of Secretary Rice's
briefing is available at www.state.gov/secretary/rm/2007/06/
86750.htm.

. . . This morning President Bush spoke with Palestinian Authority
President Abbas. He told him that the United States supports his
legitimate decision to form an emergency government of responsible Palestinians, and he welcomed the appointment of Salam
Fayyad as Prime Minister. The President pledged the full support
of the United States for the new Palestinian Government.

I delivered this same message this morning in a phone call to
Prime Minister Fayyad. I congratulated him on his new post, and
I told him that the United States would resume full assistance to the
Palestinian Government and normal government-to-government
contacts. I told the Prime Minister that we want to work with his
government and support his efforts to enforce the rule of law and
to ensure a better life for the Palestinian people.

A fundamental choice confronts the Palestinians, and all people in the Middle East, more clearly now, than ever. It is a choice
between violent extremism on the one hand and tolerance and
responsibility on the other. Hamas has made its choice. It has
sought to attempt to extinguish democratic debate with violence
and to impose its extremist agenda on the Palestinian people in
Gaza. Now, responsible Palestinians are making their choice and it
is the duty of the international community to support those
Palestinians who wish to build a better life and a future of peace.

. . . I am working with my Quartet colleagues on ways that the
international community can deliver support to the new Palestinian
Government. In the meantime, the United States is taking some immediate actions of its own. We intend to lift our financial restrictions on
the Palestinian Government, which has accepted previous agreements

with Israel and rejects the path of violence. This will enable the American people and American financial institutions to resume normal economic and commercial ties with the Palestinian Government.

*   *   *   *

On June 20, 2007, the United States Department of the Treasury, Office of Foreign Assets Control, issued a general license to authorize transactions with the Palestinian Authority, and amended its terrorism regulations to the same effect in October. *See* Chapter 16.B.1.

c. *Appointment of former Prime Minister Tony Blair as Quartet representative*

On June 27, 2007, the Quartet announced the appointment of former U.K. Prime Minister Tony Blair as the Quartet Representative. A statement released on that date explained the action as excerpted below. The full text of the June 27 statement is available at *www.state.gov/r/pa/prs/ps/2007/jun/87431.htm.*

---

*   *   *   *

As Quartet Representative, [Mr. Blair] will:

- Mobilize international assistance to the Palestinians, working closely with donors and existing coordination bodies;
- Help to identify, and secure appropriate international support in addressing, the institutional governance needs of the Palestinian state, focusing as a matter of urgency on the rule of law;
- Develop plans to promote Palestinian economic development, including private sector partnerships, building on previously agreed frameworks, especially concerning access and movement; and
- Liaise with other countries as appropriate in support of the agreed Quartet objectives.

*   *   *   *

d. Annapolis Conference

On November 27, 2007, President Bush hosted a conference in Annapolis, Maryland, attended by Israeli Prime Minister Ehud Olmert, Palestinian Authority President Mahmoud Abbas, and representatives of more than forty countries. As noted by the President in opening remarks, "[t]he broad attendance at this conference by regional states and other key international participants demonstrates the international resolve to seize this important opportunity to advance freedom and peace in the Middle East." See *www.whitehouse.gov/news/releases/20 07/11/20071123.html.*

Later in the day, President Bush read a joint understanding reached between Prime Minister Olmert and President Abbas, as set forth below and available at 43 Weekly Comp. Pres. Doc. 1532 (Dec. 3, 2007).

*   *   *   *

PRESIDENT BUSH: The representatives of the government of the state of Israel and the Palestinian Liberation Organization, represented respective[ly] by Prime Minister Ehud Olmert, and President Mahmoud Abbas in his capacity as Chairman of the PLO Executive Committee and President of the Palestinian Authority, have convened in Annapolis, Maryland, under the auspices of President George W. Bush of the United States of America, and with the support of the participants of this international conference, having concluded the following joint understanding.

We express our determination to bring an end to bloodshed, suffering and decades of conflict between our peoples; to usher in a new era of peace, based on freedom, security, justice, dignity, respect and mutual recognition; to propagate a culture of peace and nonviolence; to confront terrorism and incitement, whether committed by Palestinians or Israelis. In furtherance of the goal of two states, Israel and Palestine, living side by side in peace and security, we agree to immediately launch good-faith bilateral negotiations in order to conclude a peace treaty, resolving all outstanding issues, including all core issues without exception, as specified in previous agreements.

We agree to engage in vigorous, ongoing and continuous negotiations, and shall make every effort to conclude an agreement before the end of 2008. For this purpose, a steering committee, led jointly by the head of the delegation of each party, will meet continuously, as agreed. The steering committee will develop a joint work plan and establish and oversee the work of negotiations teams to address all issues, to be headed by one lead representative from each party. The first session of the steering committee will be held on 12 December 2007.

President Abbas and Prime Minister Olmert will continue to meet on a bi-weekly basis to follow up the negotiations in order to offer all necessary assistance for their advancement.

The parties also commit to immediately implement their respective obligations under the performance-based road map to a permanent two-state solution to the Israel-Palestinian conflict, issued by the Quartet on 30 April 2003—this is called the road map—and agree to form an American, Palestinian and Israeli mechanism, led by the United States, to follow up on the implementation of the road map.

The parties further commit to continue the implementation of the ongoing obligations of the road map until they reach a peace treaty. The United States will monitor and judge the fulfillment of the commitment of both sides of the road map. Unless otherwise agreed by the parties, implementation of the future peace treaty will be subject to the implementation of the road map, as judged by the United States.

* * * *

Excerpts follow from further remarks by President Bush. The full text of his remarks is available at 43 WEEKLY COMP. PRES. DOC. 1534 (Dec. 3, 2007).

---

* * * *

For these negotiations to succeed, the Palestinians must do their part. They must show the world they understand that while the borders of a Palestinian state are important, the nature of a Palestinian state is just as important. They must demonstrate that a Palestinian state will create opportunity for all its citizens, and govern justly, and dismantle the infrastructure of terror. They must show that a Palestinian state will accept its responsibility, and have the capability to be a source of stability and peace—for its own citizens, for the people of Israel, and for the whole region.

The Israelis must do their part. They must show the world that they are ready to begin—to bring an end to the occupation that began in 1967 through a negotiated settlement. This settlement will establish Palestine as a Palestinian homeland, just as Israel is a homeland for the Jewish people. Israel must demonstrate its support for the creation of a prosperous and successful Palestinian state by removing unauthorized outposts, ending settlement expansion, and finding other ways for the Palestinian Authority to exercise its responsibilities without compromising Israel's security.

Arab states also have a vital role to play. Relaunching the Arab League initiative and the Arab League's support for today's conference are positive steps. All Arab states should show their strong support for the government of President Abbas—and provide needed assistance to the Palestinian Authority. Arab states should also reach out to Israel, work toward the normalization of relations, and demonstrate in both word and deed that they believe that Israel and its people have a permanent home in the Middle East. These are vital steps toward the comprehensive peace that we all seek.

Finally, the international community has important responsibilities. Prime Minister Fayyad is finalizing a plan to increase openness and transparency and accountability throughout Palestinian society—and he needs the resources and support from the international community. With strong backing from those gathered here, the Palestinian government can build the free institutions that will support a free Palestinian state.

The United States will help Palestinian leaders build these free institutions—and the United States will keep its commitment to the security of Israel as a Jewish state and homeland for the Jewish people.

*   *   *   *

On December 17, 2007, the Quartet issued a statement on developments at the end of the year, as set forth below and available at *www.state.gov/r/pa/prs/ps/2007/dec/97671. htm.*

---

*   *   *   *

The Quartet lauded the success of the November 27 Annapolis Conference, which resulted in agreement to launch bilateral Israeli-Palestinian negotiations in order to conclude a peace treaty and demonstrated broad regional and international support for Israeli-Palestinian and comprehensive Arab-Israeli peace. The Quartet welcomed the commencement of Israeli-Palestinian negotiations to resolve all outstanding issues, including all core issues, and looked forward to vigorous, ongoing and continuous negotiations. The Quartet reaffirmed its commitment to remain closely involved and to support the parties' efforts in the period ahead as they make every effort to conclude an agreement before the end of 2008.

*   *   *   *

Quartet Principals noted the continuing importance of improving conditions on the ground and creating an environment conducive to the realization of Israeli-Palestinian peace, and the establishment of a Palestinian state living side by side with Israel in peace and security. In this regard, the Quartet expressed concern over the announcement of new housing tenders for Har Homa/Jabal abu Ghneim. Principals called for all sides to refrain from steps that undermine confidence, and underscored the importance of avoiding any actions that could prejudice the outcome of permanent status negotiations. The Quartet called on both parties to make progress on their Phase One Roadmap obligations, including an Israeli freeze on settlements, removal of unauthorized outposts, and opening of East Jerusalem institutions, and Palestinian steps to end violence, terrorism, and incitement.

The Quartet condemned the continued rocket fire from Gaza into Israel and called for an immediate cessation of such attacks.

The Quartet gave its strong support to the projects developed by Quartet Representative Blair and commended the constructive support of the Government of Israel and the Palestinian Authority for their implementation.

The Quartet reiterated its deep concern over the humanitarian conditions facing the population of the Gaza Strip and emphasized the importance of continued emergency and humanitarian assistance without obstruction. The Quartet called for the continued provision of essential services, including fuel and power supplies. It expressed its urgent concern over the continued closure of major crossing points given the impact on the Palestinian economy and daily life. The Quartet encouraged contacts between Israel and the Palestinian Authority to consider ideas such as Prime Minister Salam Fayyad's proposal for the PA to assume responsibility for the Palestinian side of the Gaza crossings in order to improve operations and oversight for the passage of goods and people.

Recognizing the crucial role that Arab states must play in support of the peace process, and the importance of the Arab Peace Initiative, the Quartet commended the broad and constructive Arab participation at Annapolis and called for their political and financial support for the Palestinian Authority government and institutions. Principals looked forward to their meeting with Arab foreign ministers, to be hosted by the Portuguese Foreign Minister, which would present an opportunity to discuss the way ahead. The Quartet agreed to meet regularly in 2008, to review progress and provide support for the parties' efforts. Envoys will meet to follow up and discuss how best to harness international support for progress towards peace.

The Quartet reaffirmed its commitment to a just, lasting, and comprehensive peace in the Middle East based on UNSCRs 242 and 338.

4.   Middle East Regional Stability

On July 31, 2007, the foreign ministers of the Gulf Cooperation States, Egypt, Jordan, and the United States issued a joint statement following a meeting in Sharm El-Sheikh, Egypt, to promote regional peace and prosperity. The full text of the statement, set forth below, is available at *www.state.gov/r/pa/prs/ps/2007/89855.htm.*

The Foreign Ministers of the Gulf Cooperation Council (GCC), Egypt, Jordan, and the United States met today in Sharm El-Sheik to consult as partners and friends and to coordinate their efforts to promote regional peace and security. The participants reaffirmed their shared vision of a stable, peaceful, and prosperous Middle East and their commitment to work together to achieve this common goal. This meeting follows the meetings previously held in New York, Cairo, at the Dead Sea and in Kuwait [C]ity.

The participants emphasized the importance of dialogue and diplomacy and affirmed that disputes among states should be settled peacefully and in a manner consistent with international law, including the Charter of the United Nations, and that relations among all countries should be based on mutual respect for the sovereignty and territorial integrity of all states, and on the principle of noninterference in the internal affairs of other nations. The participants expressed their steadfast support to any Gulf states in facing external threats to its sovereignty and territorial integrity. Agreeing that the peace and security of the Gulf region are critical to the health of the global economy and international stability and the need to continue the stability of the Gulf as a vital national interest for all, the participants resolved to continue their long-standing cooperation against such threats.

Agreeing on the importance of a just, comprehensive peace to the prosperity, stability and security of the Middle East, the Foreign Ministers reiterated their commitment to the two-state solution to the Israeli-Palestinian conflict and noted that the foundation for such an outcome includes UN Security Council resolutions 242, 338, 1397, and 1515, and the Arab Peace Initiative, to end the occupation since 1967 and establish a Palestinian state that is viable and contiguous and living in peace and security with all its neighbors. They also emphasized the work of the International Quartet in this context.

The participants expressed deep concern about the humanitarian conditions of the Palestinian people, particularly in Gaza, and affirmed the necessity of continuing assistance and support to the Palestinian people and the Palestinian Authority under the leadership of President Abbas and his government. Participants denounced all acts of violence and called for law and order under the Palestinian Authority in the West Bank and Gaza.

The participants urged Israel and the Palestinians to meet all previous commitments. They undertook to support efforts to create an environment conducive to progress on the bilateral tracks for a just and comprehensive settlement and in that context welcomed the joint visit by the Egyptian and Jordanian Foreign Ministers to Israel on July 25, 2007, to discuss the Arab Peace Initiative as mandated by the Arab League's Arab Peace Initiative Follow-up Committee.

The participants welcomed the commitment expressed by U.S. President George W. Bush in his July 16, 2007, speech to strengthen political and diplomatic efforts to achieve peace between Israel and the Palestinians and the establishment of a viable and contiguous Palestinian state, and promised to support efforts to this end.

The participants reaffirmed the sovereignty; territorial integrity, political independence, and national unity of Iraq; the inviolability of Iraq's internationally recognized borders; and their adherence to the principle of noninterference in Iraq's internal affairs. To this end, participants confirmed their commitment to full implementation of United Nations Security Council resolutions 1511, 1546, 1618, 1637 and 1723, urged all of Iraq's neighbors to also fully [implement] these resolutions, and called for an end to all interference in Iraq, including supply of arms and training to the militia and extra-governmental armed groups.

While calling on the government of Iraq to respect its commitments, the participants underlined the urgency and importance of implementing the principles agreed upon in Sharm El-Sheikh during the May 2007 Ministerial Conference of the Neighbouring Countries of Iraq and Egypt with the Permanent Members of the UN Security Council and the G-8, and reiterated their commitment to prevent the transit of terrorists to Iraq, arms for terrorists and financing that would support terrorists and for strengthening cooperation in this regard, and called on all of Iraq's neighbors to take all necessary steps to interdict such transit, and call on Iraq and its neighbors to exchange information regarding the fight against terrorism.

Acknowledging that a unified, democratic, and stable Iraq that is at peace with its neighbors and itself is a shared, critical objective, the participants pledged to continue to support Iraq, and expand their financial and political support. The participants agreed that the international community also must demonstrate its support for Iraq, including through the International Compact with Iraq, and that all of these efforts must supplement Iraq's own efforts.

Underscoring that every political community leader in Iraq has a role to play in national reconciliation efforts, the ministers called on all Iraqis to work together through the political process to build a brighter common future. They reiterated to the Iraqi government the need to undertake national reconciliation efforts by ensuring a fair and inclusive political process that engages all Iraqis, fosters economic reform, and provides security and services to all Iraqis. The participants called for the disbanding of all militia immediately in order for Iraqi security forces to grow stronger and for an immediate cessation of all acts of terrorism and sectarian violence in Iraq that exacerbate the suffering of the Iraqi people and undermine regional security and stability. Participants encouraged the Arab League and the United Nations to continue their effort to work with the Government of Iraq and the Iraqi people to help Iraq's leaders forge a common national vision that will advance Iraqi national reconciliation.

Recognizing the grave threat [posed] to regional and global security by the proliferation of weapons of mass destruction, and wishing to avoid a destabilizing nuclear arms race in the region, the participants concur that it is important to achieve the universality of the Nuclear Non-Proliferation Treaty, and for all parties to comply with it fully, and with all relevant resolutions of the United Nations Security Council, including resolutions 1737 and 1747. The participants recognize the goal of a zone free of nuclear weapons in the Middle East.

With regard to Iran's nuclear activities, the participants reiterated their strong support for international diplomatic efforts and called on Iran to comply with international diplomatic efforts and called on Iran to comply with all its NPT obligations, including its safeguards obligations. They hope that the talks between the IAEA and the government of Ira[n] will be positively pursued. The participants also reiterated the rights of all the parties to the Treaty to use nuclear energy for peaceful purposes in conformity with the nonproliferation obligations in Articles I, II, and III of the Treaty.

The participants reiterated their condemnation of terrorism in all its forms and manifestations, resolved to maintain a united front against the terrorist elements that have targeted the Middle East and threaten the states and peoples of the region, and reaffirmed the United Nations Security Council's declaration on the global effort to combat terrorism, adopted by resolution 1377, including its "unequivocal condemnation of all acts, methods, and practices of terrorism as criminal and unjustifiable, regardless of all their motivation, in all their forms and manifestations, whenever and by whomever committed." The ministers also endorsed the March 2007 Riyadh Declaration's call to "promote the culture of moderation, tolerance, dialogue, and openness, and reject all forms of terrorism, fanaticism, and extremism, as well as all forms of exclusionist racism, the campaigns of hatred and distortion, and attempts to cast doubt on our humanitarian values or harm the religious beliefs and sacred places, and warn against the use of sectarianism for political ends with the aim of dividing the nation, driving a wedge between its states and peoples, and igniting destructive civil strife and conflicts in them".

The participants reaffirmed their support for a sovereign democratic, and prosperous Lebanon, and for Lebanon's [l]egitimate government, headed by Prime Minister Siniora. They encouraged the Lebanese parties to support the efforts towards resuming national dialogue and noted the imperative of full implementation of relevant U.N. Security Council resolutions, particularly resolutions 1559, 1680, 1701, and 1757. They also took note of the recent report of the U.N.'s border assessment team. They called on all Lebanese factions and regional parties to respect the legitimate political process and to refrain from any activities to destabilize this process. The participants strongly condemned all terrorist attacks in Lebanon, including the recent assassination of Lebanese Member of Parliament Walid Eido. Participants lauded the efforts of the Lebanese Armed Forces in its fight against violent armed groups, such as Fatah al-Islam, which are determined to spread terror, and undermine Lebanese stability. Finally, the participants called for the respect of the Lebanese constitution including the holding of free and fair presidential elections held on-time, and the establishment of Lebanese national unity behind a constitutional process to elect a new president.

5. Lebanon

On January 23, 2007, the Department of State issued a press statement condemning violence in Lebanon and its effect on restoring peace, stating:

> The United States is deeply concerned about developments today in Lebanon. Lebanese factions allied with Syria are blocking roads, preventing people from reaching their jobs and schools, and obstructing the work of the security services. These factions are trying to use violence, threats, and intimidation to impose their political will on Lebanon. They also seek to distract attention from the Paris III conference to be held later this week, where international donors will demonstrate their strong support for the people and government of Lebanon. Especially given the dangers of sectarian clashes, the United States calls on all parties to use peaceful and constitutional means to debate the political issues before them, and to exercise restraint. Lebanon is a democracy with a strong parliamentary system and a tradition of national dialogue. The United States hopes that Lebanon's leaders will return immediately to the Parliament, or resume a national dialogue, in order to resolve political differences peacefully.

See www.state.gov/r/pa/prs/ps/2007/79195.htm. On December 12, 2007, in a further press statement, Department of State Spokesman Sean McCormack condemned the assassination of Lebanese Brigadier General Francois al-Hajj:

> Today's heinous attack comes at a crucial time for the future of the Lebanese people when a minority in Lebanon's

opposition is blocking the holding of presidential elections.
The international community has called for the Lebanese
to hold, without delay, a free and fair presidential election
in conformity with the Lebanese constitutional rules, without foreign interference or influence and with full respect
for Lebanon's democratic institutions.

See *www.state.gov/r/pa/prs/ps/2007/dec/97143.htm*. See also
B.4. below concerning peacekeeping forces in Lebanon, discussion of the Lebanon Special Tribunal in Chapter 3.C.3. and
discussion of sanctions in Chapters 1.C.7.a. and 16.A.1.

6. Sudan

In a statement on the report of the ICC prosecutor on
Sudan, on December 5, 2007, U.S. Advisor Jeffrey DeLaurentis
stated:

> The United States continues to be deeply committed to
> peace, stability and the provision of humanitarian aid for
> the people of Sudan. Presidential Special Envoy Natsios
> and Deputy Secretary Negroponte have both visited
> Sudan in the past year to consult with all parties to stress
> our continued support for the Darfur Peace Agreement
> (DPA) and the Comprehensive Peace Agreement (CPA),
> and the deployment of the UN-AU hybrid peacekeeping
> force, UNAMID, as mandated by Resolution 1769. We
> also continue to urge those who have not signed the DPA
> or agreed to participate in the peace process led jointly by
> the UN and the AU to do so quickly so that efforts to
> rebuild Darfur may accelerate.

Mr. DeLaurentis's statement is available in full at *www.usun-
newyork.usmission.gov/press_releases/20071205_353.
html*. *See also* B.3. below concerning the UN-AU hybrid peacekeeping force, and Chapter 16.A.3. concerning sanctions.

7. Great Lakes Region

On December 5, 2007, Secretary of State Condoleezza Rice
met with the presidents of Burundi, Rwanda, and Uganda,
and the foreign minister of the Democratic Republic of the
Congo in a Tripartite Plus Joint Commission member states
meeting, facilitated by the United States. Secretary Rice
announced that the countries had agreed on a joint communiqué and additional steps, as excerpted below from the transcript of a joint press availability on that date. The full text is
available at *www.state.gov/secretary/rm/2007/12/96505.htm.*
A more detailed summary of conclusions of the meeting is
available at *www.state.gov/r/pa/prs/ps/2007/dec/96318.htm.*

* * * *

Secretary Rice: . . . I will briefly summarize. In addition to the joint
communiqué, out of the, as President Museveni put it conclave,
that we held among the heads of state, they decided to take the
following steps. First of all, to commit to the rapid strengthening
of, particularly, security institutions of the DROC and to ask for
international help in doing so. I think that everyone believes that
the strengthening of the security institutions of the DROC is a prerequisite for the long term solution to the problems of the Congo
and to the problems that are therefore affecting the entire Great
Lakes region. Secondly, they committed again not to harbor negative
forces—the illegal groups, militias and armed groups that are causing destabilization—and there was a promise not to harbor. And
third, to recommit to all existing agreements including the Nairobi
Accord, as well as to ask their officials to seek additional measures
that might deal with the near-term problem as well as the long terms
problem. There was also a long discussion of how to make the joint
verification mechanism more effective and to renew that mechanism, but to renew it with a new set of rules and a new set of measures that could be taken and to perhaps seek third-party help in
the joint verification mechanism. Those were the conclusions, in
addition to those conclusions that are in the joint communiqué. . . .

Question: Can each of you explain what diplomatic action you've used to remove the negative forces—the LRA, General Nkunda, and the FDLR? And have these diplomatic actions come up short and you're really now faced with a military solution, and what kinds of military solutions do you envision? Would the U.S. Government be supporting with the equipment and training and other ways?

Secretary Rice: Well, perhaps I can speak to the U.S. Government part of this. The United States has long supported first of all the efforts of the DROC, or the transitional government to go then to an elected government and now the strengthening of the security institutions of the DRC, which is going to be a large part of the answer here. Also, we are very involved in the evaluation and restructuring of the mandate of MONUC. There was a representative of MONUC here who spoke about the importance of the international effort until the DROC forces are capable on their own. I would just say that I think the diplomatic efforts are still underway and I might note that there are also UN Security Council sanctions against some of these leaders of these irregular groups and perhaps more can be looked at there, but the efforts have to be for greater diplomacy for greater consequences for the illegals and for very strong efforts so that they cannot be harbored and supported in any way, and that was the context of our discussion. Anyone else wish to comment?

*　　*　　*　　*

The Democratic Republic of Congo and Rwanda signed a joint communiqué (referred to above as the Nairobi Accord) on November 10, 2007, with representatives of the European Union, the United Nations, and the United States, signing as witnesses. A Department of State press release of November 13, 2007, welcomed the communiqué, stating that it

creates a new opportunity to end the armed presence in eastern Democratic Republic of Congo of former Rwandan Armed Forces (ex-F[AR]) and rebel Interahamwe implicated in Rwanda's 1994 genocide.

We call on both parties to implement the provisions of the communiqué immediately. As a friend of both countries, we will work with them and the international community to support implementation. We condemn continuing attacks on innocent civilians in eastern Congo, especially by illegal armed groups such as the forces of renegade Congolese General Laurent Nkunda, as well as the ex-FAR and Interahamwe.

See *www.state.gov/r/pa/prs/ps/2007/nov/95083.htm*. The full text of the communiqué is available at *www.state.gov/s/l/c8183.htm*.

8. Somalia

Also on December 5, 2007, Secretary of State Rice discussed the need to restore lasting peace and stability in Somalia. Secretary Rice's statement is set forth below and available at *www.state.gov/secretary/rm/2007/12/96290.htm*. *See also* address, "U.S. Policy in Somalia," by James Swan, Deputy Assistant Secretary for African Affairs, April 21, 2007, available at *www.state.gov/p/af/rls/rm/83935.htm*.

Today, I met with key regional leaders, representatives of Somalia's Transitional Federal Government (TFG), as well as representatives from the African Union and United Nations to discuss the regional strategy to help restore lasting peace and stability in Somalia, including efforts to support the full and timely deployment of the African Union Mission in Somalia (AMISOM) and progress towards national elections in 2009.

During today's meeting, I encouraged the TFG, following the appointment of Prime Minister Nur "Adde" Hassan Hussein, to renew and revitalize efforts towards a lasting political solution based on the Transitional Federal Charter. I hope Prime Minister Hussein will draw on his humanitarian background to help facilitate delivery of much-needed humanitarian aid. A cease-fire agreement with key stakeholders, such as clan and business leaders, would be an important step in helping to facilitate delivery of humanitarian assistance, and would reduce the level of violence and create the conditions for longer term security sector reform. I also encouraged Prime Minister Hussein to develop a timeline for the remainder of the transitional process by early January, including the drafting of a new constitution and electoral law, as the first step in this process.

9. Belarus

Additional designations of "persons undermining democratic process or institutions in Belarus" were made during 2007 under Executive Order 13405. *See* 16.A.6.

B. PEACEKEEPING AND RELATED ISSUES

1. Criminal Accountability in UN Peacekeeping Missions

On October 25, 2007, James Donovan, Counselor, U.S. Mission to the United Nations, addressed the Sixth Committee of the UN General Assembly on promotion of accountability for crimes committed by UN staff and experts on mission. Excerpts below provide the U.S. views that additional information is needed before considering negotiation of a convention on this issue. The full text of Mr. Donovan's comments is available at *www.state.gov/s/l/c8183.htm*.

The United States regards abuses by personnel participating in UN peacekeeping missions, who are sent to areas in conflict and need to help those in dire distress, as a violation of trust. We applaud the efforts that Member States and the Secretary-General have invested in recent years to address this problem. We all recognize that there is a great deal that remains to be done.

My delegation welcomed the opportunity to address these important issues during last spring's ad hoc session on this agenda item. During that session, we offered our preliminary views on the

Report of the Group of Legal Experts. While we welcomed that report, we felt that it left a number of important questions unanswered, particularly in respect of its proposal regarding the possible negotiation of a multilateral convention with respect to criminal accountability for UN staff and experts on mission.

The report begins from the assumption that there are theoretical gaps in accountability mechanisms that could preclude accountability for crimes committed by UN staff and experts on mission in particular cases. But more information is needed on what practical problems, if any, are actually arising in efforts to investigate and prosecute crimes committed by these categories of personnel and whether a convention would actually address such problems. During the discussions in the spring, we requested additional information on these questions to help us assess the utility of a convention. Other delegations indicated that they had similar questions and echoed these requests for further information.

Answers to these questions are important because the negotiation of a convention would require the dedication of significant resources, time, and political capital. As we noted last spring, the United States could not support commencing such a significant effort without being sure that such a convention is likely to be an effective solution to whatever problems currently exist in ensuring accountability for crimes committed by this category of personnel. A convention might be of some use if the problem to be solved is the lack of a legal basis for states to cooperate with each other in investigating or prosecuting such crimes or for states to prosecute their own nationals for crimes they commit abroad. The proposed convention would not, however, address other possible barriers to accountability, such as national definitions of crimes, such as rape, that make it difficult to prove guilt or to prosecute sexual conduct involving adolescents. We also note that a convention can only bind those states that become party to it, and thus that the proposed convention will only have practical value to the extent that states that are likely to host peacekeeping operations and the states of nationality of relevant staff and experts on mission choose to become parties. Our preference is to address these questions in practical terms, by identifying effective solutions to actual problems, rather than by addressing theoretical gaps for their own sake.

We had hoped that in the period between last spring's session and our current meetings we would receive additional information on what practical impediments, if any, are actually being encountered in efforts to ensure accountability for crimes by UN staff and experts on mission in order to advance our discussions. We regret that the Secretariat's additional written input on this topic did not address these questions and instead took the unusual form of a paper purporting to express the "support" of the Secretariat for particular proposals that are the subject of active discussions among Sixth Committee members. In the absence of such information, we do not expect to be in a position during the course of this week's discussions to support a proposal to proceed with negotiation of a convention. Instead, we believe this working group's efforts would be best devoted to considering more practical measures to promote accountability for crimes committed by UN staff and experts on mission. Such measures might include work on a statement calling on states to take stronger action domestically, work on "model laws" that states could pass at the national level to address such cases, increased effort by the Secretariat to monitor efforts by states to investigate and prosecute cases, and the naming and shaming of states that fail to take appropriate action.

*   *   *   *

2. Appropriate Use of Peacekeeping Forces

In a statement to the Security Council on the Secretary-General's Report on the Protection of Civilians in Armed Conflict, Ambassador Jackie Wolcott, U.S. Alternate Representative to the United Nations, addressed the appropriate use of peacekeeping forces, stating:

. . . [T]he United States applauds the Secretary-General's report on the protection of civilians in armed conflict, and looks forward to reviewing and considering the report's recommendations. At this time, however, we note the importance of the Security Council—when faced with particular situations threatening international peace and security—being able and willing to craft responses that deal with the particularity of the threat at hand. It follows from this that adoption of a "one-size-fits-all" approaches—for example, statements that the Security Council should in all cases adopt provisions of a certain type—may not represent the most effective way for the Security Council to proceed.

As an example, while we agree with the report that disputes over land tenure can lead to armed conflict and abuse when civilians are driven from their homes and their properties are appropriated, it is less clear to us that UN peacekeeping missions should in all cases be mandated to deal with these issues in the manner specified in the report.

The full text of Ambassador Wolcott's statement is available at *www.usunnewyork.usmission.gov/press_releases/2007 1120_322.html.*

3. Darfur

On July 31, 2007, the UN Security Council adopted Resolution 1769, in which it decided to "authorize and mandate the establishment . . . of an [African Union]/UN Hybrid operation in Darfur (UNAMID)." Acting under Chapter VII of the UN Charter, the Security Council

(a) *decide[d]* that UNAMID is authorised to take the necessary action, in the areas of deployment of its forces and as it deems within its capabilities in order to:
    (i) protect its personnel, facilities, installations and equipment, and to ensure the security and freedom of movement of its own personnel and humanitarian workers,
    (ii) support early and effective implementation of the Darfur Peace Agreement, prevent the disruption of its implementation and armed attacks, and protect civilians, without prejudice to the responsibility of the Government of Sudan. . . .

Ambassador Zalmay Khalilzad, U.S. Permanent Representative, explained the U.S. vote supporting the adoption of the hybrid force in a statement to the Security Council. The full text of Ambassador Khalilzad's statement, excerpted below, is available at *www.usunnewyork.usmission.gov/press_releases/20070731_184.html.*

The formal transfer of authority from the African Union-led peacekeeping force in Sudan ("AMIS") to UNAMID occurred on December 31, 2007. *See* Department of State press statement by Tom Casey, Deputy Spokesman, welcoming the transfer, available at *www.state.gov/r/pa/prs/ps/2007/dec/98152.htm.*

*   *   *   *

The hybrid operation represents a new and unique form of cooperation between the UN and the African Union, and the passage of this resolution is the culmination of intense efforts by many in the international community over the past several months. It must now be implemented without delay.

*   *   *   *

This resolution gives UNAMID full authority under Chapter VII to use force to prevent armed attacks, to protect civilians, and to prevent any disruption of the implementation of the Darfur Peace Agreement.

In passing this resolution, the Council is entrusting UNAMID, its force commander, and its personnel to do their utmost to protect the civilian population of Darfur and we expect UNAMID to achieve this central objective.

It is imperative that the signatories to the Agreement, including the Government of Sudan, comply fully with their commitments. Among other things, the Darfur Peace Agreement prohibits all attacks, harassment, abduction, intimidation and injury to civilians, impeding humanitarian assistance or the protection of civilians, restriction on the free movement of people and goods, and all hostile propaganda and incitement to military action, and includes among its stated aims ensuring that civilians are not subject to violence, intimidation or threats.

Parties must comply with the requirements of this resolution, which, in turn, demands compliance with relevant agreements, including the Darfur Peace Agreement. We call on the Government of Sudan and all other parties to the conflict in Darfur to cooperate fully with the implementation of this resolution and all other relevant resolutions; to cease attacks against civilians immediately; to permit full and unhindered access for humanitarian assistance; and to engage fully in the political process led by the UN and the AU to promote peace. The United States will continue its efforts to promote a broadly supported and inclusive political settlement that is the only long-term solution to the crisis in Darfur.

We call on President Bashir to provide maximum cooperation with the deployment of the new peacekeeping force. We hope his acceptance of the force marks a new chapter in his cooperation with the international community. If Sudan does not comply with the Darfur Peace Agreement, and if Sudan does not comply with this resolution, the United States will move for the swift adoption of unilateral and multilateral measures.

*   *   *   *

4. Lebanon

On August 24, 2007, the UN Security Council adopted Resolution 1773 to extend the mandate of the UN Interim Force in Lebanon ("UNIFIL"). Ambassador Alejandro D. Wolff, Deputy U.S. Permanent Representative, explained the U.S. vote in support of the resolution as set forth below and available at *www.usunnewyork.usmission.gov/press_releases/20070824_195.html. See also* remarks to the press following adoption of the resolution, available at *www.usunnewyork.usmission.gov/press_releases/20070824_196.html.*

The United States welcomes the unanimous adoption of resolution 1773 to extend the mandate of UNIFIL for one year. This vote is a clear signal of the Council's support for the UN peacekeepers on the ground in south Lebanon and of its commitment to the full implementation of resolution 1701.

Although the primary aim of this technical resolution is to extend the mandate of UNIFIL, it also reaffirms the Council's resolutions on Lebanon, including 1559, 1680, and 1701, as well as the three Presidential Statements on Lebanon adopted since last summer.

We commend the progress that has been achieved since the adoption of resolution 1701 last summer. The Lebanese Armed Forces have deployed throughout the country for the first time in 30 years. Together with the reinforced UNIFIL, the LAF has helped to create a new strategic reality in south Lebanon.

At the same time, the deadly June 24 attack against UNIFIL and the June 17 rocket attack against Israel demonstrate that there are unauthorized armed elements and weapons in south Lebanon and that they pose a danger both to regional stability and the safety of UN personnel. In this regard, we reiterate our condolences to the families, colleagues and governments of those peacekeepers killed in the line of duty.

We welcome UNIFIL's intention to redouble its efforts to carry out its mandate in response to these attacks, especially in terms of coordination with the Lebanese Armed Forces. We urge UNIFIL and the LAF to move quickly to establish joint patrols and co-located checkpoints, particularly along the Litani River, to ensure that no unauthorized weapons are transferred into south Lebanon. We look forward to hearing more from the Secretary-General on these efforts in his next report.

These and other threats to peace, as well as the violence perpetrated by Fatah al-Islam in the north of Lebanon, underscore the need to fully implement the provisions of the Taif Accords and resolution 1559 calling for the disbanding and disarmament of all Lebanese and non-Lebanese militia. Peace will never be fully secured until this call is met.

We also reiterate our deep concern about continued illegal weapons transfers across the Syrian-Lebanese border in violation of resolution 1701. These weapons transfers directly threaten both the stability of Lebanon and the safety of UN peacekeepers. We join the Secretary-General in calling, yet again, on Syria and Iran to honor their obligations under the arms embargo established under resolution 1701.

Mr. President, one year has now passed since the cessation of hostilities between Israel and Hizballah and the adoption of resolution 1701. While we are pleased by the progress that has been achieved, we deplore the fact that the cause of this conflict, namely Hizballah's abduction of the two Israeli soldiers, has not been resolved. This Council must not relent in demanding progress on this issue, as well as all the others required for a cease-fire and long-term solution between Israel and Lebanon, in order to fulfill the promise of the resolution we adopted last summer.

Cross References

CHAPTER 18

Use of Force, Arms Control and Disarmament, and Nonproliferation

A. USE OF FORCE

1. Overview

a. *Legal Adviser web logs*

In January 2007 Department of State Legal Adviser John B. Bellinger, III, participated as a guest commentator, or blogger, on the web log *Opinio Juris*. Mr. Bellinger's six postings, from January 10 through January 25, included (1) The Work of the Office of the Legal Adviser; (2) Armed Conflict With Al Qaida?; (3) The Meaning of Common Article Three; (4) Armed Conflict with Al Qaida: A Response; (5) Unlawful Enemy Combatants; (6) Immunities; and two wrap-up discussions. These postings and postings by others in response are available at *www.opiniojuris.org/posts/chain_1169503291. shtml.* Mr. Bellinger's postings are also available at *www. state.gov/s/l/c8183.htm.*

In Mr. Bellinger's final wrap-up posting on January 25, he noted that "[t]here is a growing international acceptance that the legal framework applicable to international terrorism is complex and unclear." Mr. Bellinger stated:

Although I think it is premature to attempt to negotiate a new Geneva Convention—especially in light of the strides that we have made in developing the specific rules and regulations governing the detention, interrogation and trial of unlawful enemy combatants in the Military Commissions Act and recent DOD directives—I do agree that further work needs to be done to examine how to deal with the problem of international terrorists who may be beyond the reach of our criminal laws and yet who are not part of the armed forces of a party to the Geneva Conventions.

Excerpts follow from postings 2 and 4 on armed conflict with Al Qaida. For excerpts from topics 3 and 5, see A.4.a.(2) and b.(1) below. Topic 6 on immunities is discussed in Chapter 10.A.1.

. . . I know that many people have objected passionately to some of the Administration's policies and legal positions relating to detainees. I have heard many assertions that U.S. detainee policies violate international law, and I must say that I think many of the criticisms are based on an inaccurate understanding of applicable international law or on aspirational statements of international law as critics wish it were, rather than as it now exists. I am not going to try in this limited space to rebut or discuss every one of these criticisms. I want instead to describe in detail our legal thinking on three specific matters. My purpose is not to persuade readers to agree with Administration policies. But I would ask readers to engage in serious legal analysis. If you question our approach, I would ask you to consider whether a different approach is actually legally required or simply preferable as a matter of policy. Did a realistic alternative approach exist, and how would that approach have worked better in practice?

I want to begin by addressing two related issues that have come up frequently in my discussions with my European colleagues. The first issue is whether the law of war is an appropriate legal framework in which to respond to terrorist attacks. The second issue is whether a state can be in an armed conflict with a non-state actor outside that state's territory.

The phrase "the global war on terror"—to which some have objected—is not intended to be a legal statement. The United States does not believe that it is engaged in a legal state of armed conflict at all times with every terrorist group in the world, regardless of the group's reach or its aims, or even with all of the groups on the State Department's list of Foreign Terrorist Organizations. Nor is military force the appropriate response in every situation across the globe. When we state that there is a "global war on terror," we primarily mean that the scourge of terrorism is a global problem that the international community must recognize and work together to eliminate. Having said that, the United States does believe that it is in an armed conflict with al Qaida, the Taliban, and associated forces.

*   *   *   *

Some critics agree that we were in a war with the Taliban and al Qaida in Afghanistan in 2001–02, and that our detention of at least some of the detainees was justified under the law of war. But they argue that the conflict ended in June 2002 with the establishment of Afghanistan's new government and that our legal basis for holding any detainees ended at that time. But this assertion is not consistent with the facts on the ground, because the Taliban continues to fight U.S. and coalition forces in Afghanistan. We see the Afghanistan conflict as a continuing conflict that began in 2001, and believe that the United States is not obligated to release any Taliban detainees we currently hold in Afghanistan or Guantanamo, only to see them return to kill U.S. and coalition forces. Anybody who questions whether this conflict continues should consider that combat operations over the past few months have resulted in the deaths of several hundred Taliban fighters and a number of U.S., European, and Canadian forces.

Equally important, however, we believe that the United States was and continues to be in an armed conflict with al Qaida, one that is conceptually and legally distinct from the conflict with the Taliban in Afghanistan. It cannot reasonably be argued that the conflict with al Qaida ended with the closure of al Qaida training camps and the assumption of power by a new government in Afghanistan. Al Qaida's operations against the United States and its allies continue not only in and around Afghanistan but also in other parts of the world. And because we remain in a continued state of armed conflict with al Qaida, we are legally justified in continuing to detain al Qaida members captured in this conflict.

Let me respond to two arguments I often hear as to why it is not correct to characterize this conflict as a war. First, some argue that a legal state of armed conflict can only occur between two nation states and that a state may not use force against a non-state entity. This contention is incorrect. The international rules regarding the right to use force, including those reflected in Article 51 of the UN Charter, do not differentiate between an armed attack by a state and an armed attack by another entity. This makes logical sense: The principle of self-defense permits a state to take armed action to protect its citizens against external uses of force, regardless of the source. It is true that most past wars were between states, or existed within the territorial limits of a single state, but this is an historical fact, not a legal limitation on the concept of armed conflict.

Over a century of state practice supports the conclusion that a state may respond with military force in self defense to attacks by a non-state actor from outside the state's territory, at least where the harboring state is unwilling or unable to take action to quell the attacks. This includes the famous 1837 case of the *Caroline*, in which British forces in Canada entered the United States and set fire to a vessel that had been used by private American citizens to provide support to Canadian rebels, killing two Americans in the process. Even law of war treaties that govern the treatment of detainees in armed conflict contemplate conflicts between state and non-state actors across national borders. Common Article 3 of the Geneva Conventions expressly contemplates armed conflicts between a state party and non-state actors. And any country that is party to Additional Protocol I of the Geneva Conventions, which contains additional rules applicable to international armed conflicts and also applies to certain conflicts with groups engaged in wars of national liberation, has acknowledged implicitly that a state may be in an international armed conflict with a non-state actor.

For an explanation of how U.N. Security Council resolutions and the U.N. Charter also contemplate States engaging in armed conflict with non-state actors, please see Thomas Franck's article

"Terrorism and the Right of Self Defense" [95 Am. J. Int'l L. 839 (2001)].

The second argument I hear is that the United States may have been justified in using force against, and detaining members of, al Qaida in Afghanistan, but it is not lawful for us to use military force against or detain members of al Qaida who were picked up outside Afghanistan. This argument seems more motivated by a fear of the implications about the possible scope of the conflict than by actual legal force or logic. We would all be better off if al Qaida limited itself to the territory of Afghanistan, but unfortunately, that is not the reality we face. No principle of international law limits to a single territory a state's ability to act in self-defense, when the threat comes from areas outside that territory as well. This is not to suggest that, because the United States remains in a state of armed conflict with al Qaida, the United States will use military force against al Qaida in any state where an al Qaida terrorist may seek shelter. The U.S. military does not plan to shoot terrorists on the streets of London. As a practical matter, though, a state must prevent terrorists from using its territory as a base for launching attacks. As a legal matter, where a state is unwilling or unable to do so, it may be lawful for the targeted state to use military force in self-defense to address that threat.

One reason critics vigorously refuse to acknowledge that we have been and continue to be in a legal state of war with al Qaida is that they fear such an acknowledgement would give the United States a blank check to act as it pleases in combating al Qaida. However, recognizing a state's right to take certain actions in self-defense is not to give a state carte blanche in responding to the terrorist threat. A state acting in self-defense must comply with the UN Charter and fundamental law of war principles. And whether a state legitimately may use force will necessarily require a careful review of the relevant law and specific facts, and will depend on a variety of factors, including the nature and capabilities of the non-state actor; the patterns of activity of that non-state actor; and the level of certainty a state has about the identity of those it plans to target. It also will depend on the state from which a non-state actor is launching attacks—specifically, whether that state consents to self-defense actions in its territory, or whether the state is willing and able to suppress future attacks. Rather than suggest that the use of force against al Qaida, including the detention of al Qaida operatives, is illegitimate, it makes more sense to examine the conditions under which force and detention may be used.

Let me close by emphasizing that I am not suggesting that military force and the laws of war are the ONLY appropriate or legal approach to dealing with international terrorism generally or al Qaida in particular. We recognize that other countries, like the UK, Germany, and Spain, may choose to use their criminal laws to prosecute members of al Qaida. Indeed, the United States itself continues to use its criminal laws to prosecute members of al Qaida, like Zacharias Moussaoui, who find their way inside our own territory in appropriate cases. But we do believe that it was—and continues to be—legally permissible to use military force and apply the laws of war, rather than rely on criminal laws, to deal with members of al Qaida in certain cases, such as those fighting or detained by U.S. military personnel outside the United States.

Responses to other bloggers

*   *   *   *

[In response to suggestions that criminal law should be used to prosecute al Qaida operatives found outside Afghanistan:] As I have noted, we have used criminal law to prosecute some al Qaida operatives found in the United States, such as Zacharias Moussaoui, but I would ask you to consider—in addition to the legal arguments underpinning wartime detention—the practical difficulties of prosecuting an al Qaida member not found in the United States. To begin with, our criminal courts simply do not have extraterritorial jurisdiction over many of these individuals or many of their activities. Some of them had never set foot in the United States or planned specific criminal acts in violation of our federal criminal statutes. One thing that all of our countries have learned since September 11th is that we are facing a different kind of terrorism than we used to face, and we have to expand the reach of our criminal laws. There has been a flurry of activity in the United States and other countries to do just that. But the current effort to expand our criminal laws cannot be made retroactive. Therefore, in many cases there would have been no legal basis to try al Qaida operatives in our courts for violations of our domestic criminal laws. Moreover, in many instances the evidence against these operatives was obtained on the battlefield, even where the detainees themselves were captured elsewhere. Our federal courts require a chain of custody to be presented for all evidence introduced at trial, and this could pose a great deal of difficulty for our forces. Ultimately, we think we are not legally obligated to try al Qaida combatants under the laws of war, but have set up military commissions to prosecute those who have committed the most serious violations of the laws of war.

[In response to a question as to what is as stake in the argument about the applicability of international law to the conflict with al Qaida:] Fundamentally, what is at stake is the reputation of the United States as a nation that takes international law seriously and that does not bend the law to meet our immediate needs. It is true that when novel situations present themselves, governments have some flexibility in how they adapt traditional rules to new realities. But [the] United States cannot regard international law as something to be completely redone whenever a new challenge presents itself, and must care about the implications down the road of the positions that it decides to defend today. A reputation for consistency and reasonableness in its approach to its international obligations is valuable to the United States. Without that, other countries will be less willing to cooperate with us and live up to their own international law commitments. Even though international law constraints are sometimes limited, they are nevertheless real and substantive and we cannot maintain that we are a nation that abides by law if we say we have the choice of disregarding international law. As lawyers, we must take into account not just the texts and decisions that make up the building blocks of international law, but also the quality and integrity of the arguments we make and the analogies we draw in framing our positions on international law. It is in the broader interests of the United States not to let these arguments become merely a matter of convenience.

Turning now to how we will know when the war with al Qaida is over. This is an important question. Of course, in any war, you don't know how long the war is going to go on. There have been wars that have gone on for five years, ten years, thirty years, one hundred years. But the fact that a particular conflict with an enemy may go on indefinitely does not mean we should simply release all members of the enemy we are holding so long as that conflict is continuing. There is a reason that under customary principles of international law, you may hold the people until the end of a conflict, and that is to keep dangerous people off the battlefield.

Nevertheless, we recognize that the conflict with al Qaida is not a traditional conflict that will end with an armistice agreement on a battleship. We could reach the point where we have so decimated al Qaida that there may be so few operatives left that we don't think they are actually engaged in a major war with us. But as a practical matter, with respect to the people we are holding in Guantánamo, we have added an annual administrative review process to determine whether an individual detainee continues to pose a threat to the United States or its allies. In a sense, we ask if the war is over with respect to that person. Even if al Qaida continues to be fighting us, if an individual can credibly say, "I want to stop fighting, I want to just go back and join my community," and in fact the community will credibly commit, "We will take responsibility for this person, and make sure that he doesn't go back to fighting," then we will release people. We have released or agreed to release, subject to their countries' taking them back, more than one hundred people pursuant to that process. Thus, the [Administrative Review Boards] balance our authority to detain fighters so they do not come back to fight us again against our desire not to hold anyone any longer than necessary.

*   *   *   *

[In response to comments] about my discussion of the *Caroline* case—that case involved private persons on the American side of the US-Canadian border supporting insurrectionist efforts in Canada, then retreating back to sanctuaries on the American side of the border in upstate New York, where they were attacked by the British. The case involved two issues relevant here: first, whether acts by private actors (as opposed to acts by state militaries) could trigger a right of self-defense where the government of the host state was unable or unwilling to take action; and, second, whether the threat posed by those private actors satisfied the conditions of necessity, proportionality and immediacy so that the British action would be justified. But there was no question that the acts of private actors could trigger the right of self-defense where the host government was unable or unwilling to deal with the situation. Secretary Webster may not have accepted that the facts were right to legally justify the use of force in the *Caroline* case, but the British and Americans both accepted the underlying principle.

With respect to immediacy, or what is usually referred to as imminence, the longstanding US view has been that a state need not wait until it is actually attacked before using force in self-defense, and that view has been more strongly embraced than ever in recent years, including for example by the UN Secretary-General in his In Larger Freedom report in 2005. The US continues to accept the importance of the distinction between imminent and non-imminent threats, but—in the face of the threats now posed by terrorism and proliferation of weapons of mass destruction—the principles of self-defense must be understood and applied in the security environment in which the US and other states now find themselves. But it is also important to note that, insofar as the conflict with al-Qaida is concerned, imminence is not a "live" issue, as the United States has been subject to actual—as opposed to anticipated—attack.

b.　Oxford Leverhulme Programme on the Changing Character of War

On December 10, 2007, Mr. Bellinger presented a lecture at the University of Oxford as part of the Oxford Leverhulme Programme on the Changing Character of War. The full text of the lecture is set forth below and is available at *www.state. gov/s/l/c8183.htm.*

_____

As many of you may be aware, I have been engaged over the last three years in extensive bilateral and multilateral efforts to discuss

developing a common legal approach regarding combating transnational terrorism. As part of this effort, I have traveled to a dozen
countries, engaged in seven rounds of discussions with the legal
advisers of the 27 EU countries, and held additional discussions
with the legal advisers of the member states of the Council of
Europe. I have also participated in numerous panels and roundtable discussions on the matter with legal experts in this area.

Some of my work has been retrospective, in which I have tried
to explain to our allies the actions we took after the September
11th attacks. I have acknowledged that one of the mistakes the
United States made after 9/11 was not discussing with our allies
the reasoning and legal basis behind the steps we took to combat
al Qaida. A little more than a year ago, I gave a speech at the
London School of Economics in which I gave a comprehensive
public explanation of our legal views and policy decisions with
respect to the detention and treatment of terrorists, as these have
evolved in the United States since September 11th.* In that speech
I explained the legal basis for various decisions the United States
took after 9/11, and then asked critics to consider what realistic
alternatives existed to our approach, and whether those alternatives are legally mandated or are simply among the acceptable
alternative options available to policy makers. In retrospect, we
might well have handled some matters differently as a matter of
policy, but that does not mean our approach was flawed as a matter of law. The bottom line, as an increasing number of legal experts
now acknowledge, is that the legal framework for conflicts with
transnational terrorists like al Qaida is not clear.

Rather than continue to look back, however, tonight I would
like to focus more prospectively on whether international humanitarian law in general, and the Geneva Conventions in particular,
provide a satisfactory set of rules for contemporary conflicts. I am
not advocating that we discard existing rules, which serve a critical
role in dealing with the situations for which we developed them.
Nor am I straining to find gaps in the existing legal framework in
order to place detained persons in a legal black hole. The gaps are

---

*   Editor's note: *See Digest 2006* at 1104–17.

real, and recognizing this fact does not mitigate the obligation of States to comply with international law, nor does it justify placing persons beyond the protection of the law. My key point tonight is that the Geneva Conventions were designed for traditional armed conflicts between States and their uniformed military forces, and do not provide all the answers for detention of persons in conflicts between a State and a transnational terrorist group.

Common Article 2 of the Conventions restricts the scope of applicability of most of the Conventions' provisions to conflicts between High Contracting Parties. But as we are seeing throughout the world, contemporary conflicts often do not have more than one High Contracting Party to the Conventions involved. Some of these conflicts occur within the boundaries of a country, like Sri Lanka's conflict with the Tamil Tigers. But more and more the conflicts cross national boundaries, like Israel and Hezbollah or the ongoing conflict between the U.S., its allies and al Qaida. In cases such as these, we are left in a situation where Common Article 3, and depending on a State's treaty obligations and the nature of the non-state actor, Additional Protocol II, provide the only treaty-based rules governing detention of unprivileged combatants.

I must note here that it was not always clear to our government that Common Article 3 applied as a treaty-law matter to a conflict between a State and non-state actors that transcended national boundaries. While the U.S. Supreme Court decision in *Hamdan v. Rumsfeld* [548 U.S. 557 (2006)] held that the conflict with al Qaida, as one not between States, is a non-international conflict covered by Common Article 3, I think many international legal scholars would question that conclusion. Textually the provision is limited to armed conflict "not of an international character" occurring "in the territory of *one* of the High Contracting Parties," suggesting the scope of the provision is limited to conflicts occurring in the territory of a single state. Indeed, other states, such as Israel, have concluded that conflicts with terrorist organizations outside the State's borders are international armed conflicts not falling within the scope of Common Article 3. I make these points not to re-litigate the *Hamdan* case, or to disregard the view of many that Common Article 3 is customary international law, but rather to note that in some cases, not even Common Article 3 may apply as a treaty-law matter to conflicts with transnational terrorist groups.

But even assuming that Common Article 3 does cover contemporary transnational conflicts of this sort, I think it is striking just how little guidance Common Article 3 in fact provides. The one area where Common Article 3 does provide good detail is with respect to the treatment of detainees once in custody. Treatment protections include the prohibition against torture and cruel, humiliating and degrading treatment, and a requirement that those criminally tried in relation to the conflict be provided judgment by "a regularly constituted court affording all the judicial guarantees considered essential by civilized peoples." Depending on a State's treaty-law obligations these treatment protections can be supplemented in certain circumstances by Additional Protocol II. Many would also argue that Article 75 of Additional Protocol I provides other relevant protections as customary international law applicable in non-international armed conflict.

But quite clearly, the meaning of particular treatment protections may be subject to different interpretations. Common Article 3 was not designed with the precision of a criminal statute. Indeed, the International Criminal Tribunal for the Former Yugoslavia acquitted a defendant of violation of Common Article 3's prohibition on "violence to life and person" because the term lacked a sufficiently precise definition under international law. The U.S. has also wrestled with how to implement this article in our criminal law, especially since the *Hamdan* court ruled it governs our operations in the conflict with al Qaida. For example, "outrages upon personal diginity" is defined in Pictet's Commentary on CA3 . . . as capturing only those acts that "world public opinion finds particularly revolting." But reasonable people can and do differ about what behavior that phrase captures. It was this concern that led the Administration and Congress to agree in the Military Commissions Act to amend the War Crimes Act to clarify which specific violations of Common Article 3 are criminally sanctionable.

More important, though, Common Article 3 does not address at all four central questions that I believe must be answered with respect to conflicts with non-state groups. I want to discuss each of those questions this evening. First, who may a State detain in a conflict with a global non-state actor? Second, what processes must a State provide detainees to determine whether they can be detained? Third, when are hostilities over in armed conflict with a non-state group? And fourth, what legal obligations do States have in connection with repatriating detainees at the end of the conflict?

The Gaps Are Not Already Filled

A response I have frequently heard to these questions is that we are looking in the wrong place for their answers. Critics respond that other treaties or customary international law fill these gaps. It is not clear, however, that they do.

First, some argue that 1977's Additional Protocol II of the Geneva Conventions was designed to address the limited scope of Common Article 3 by providing additional rules for non-international armed conflict. President Reagan submitted Additional Protocol II to the Senate seeking advice and consent to ratification in 1987, but the Senate has not acted on the treaty to date, meaning its provisions do not bind the United States as a treaty law matter. But even for States that have become party to AP II, such as the United Kingdom, the Protocol does not provide a satisfactory answer to the questions I just posed. While AP II expands on the treatment protections provided in Common Article 3, it has a more limited scope of application defined in Article 1, and its provisions do not squarely address any of my four questions.

Second, some have suggested that customary international law can be used to fill gaps in treaty law. As I just explained, the conclusion that Article 75 of Additional Protocol I is customary international law applicable in all armed conflicts would add to the treatment protections in non-international armed conflict provided by Common Article 3. But as a general matter, States need to be careful to adhere to proper methodology before describing particular provisions of treaty law as custom. Many commentators assert customary international law as they would like it to be, rather than as it actually is. The U.S. Government sent a letter to the ICRC President Dr. Kellenberger noting concerns with the methodology employed by the ICRC IHL Customary International Law Study in deeming treaty provisions customary international law.

Although it may seem attractive as a policy matter to import rules developed in international armed conflict to other situations, we must be careful not to describe rules as custom when there is an insufficient basis to do so. Providing unprivileged combatants the same or greater protections and rights as those provided prisoners of war risks rewarding illegal actions, ultimately placing innocent civilians at greater risk.

Third, human rights groups and some European states argue that human rights law fills the gap wherever IHL is insufficiently specific to address a particular situation. It is important to remember here that States have different obligations under different treaties. U.S. obligations under the International Covenant on Civil and Political Rights only apply in U.S. territory, while European States are parties to human rights instruments with protections that extend outside national borders. So when we talk about human rights law, we need to be sure we are taking into account different national circumstances.

But even where States do have human rights obligations, it is fair to ask proponents of this approach what particular human rights provisions they would apply to activities arising in the conduct of armed conflict, and how they would apply them in practice. For example, Article 9 of the ICCPR requires States to provide anyone detained the right to bring their case before a judge without delay to determine the legality of the detention. Would it be practical to expect States detaining tens of thousands of unprivileged combatants in a non-international armed conflict to bring them before a judge without delay? This is not something States must do even for prisoners of war under the Third Geneva Convention. If the answer is that the State should derogate from Article 9 if the exigencies of a civil war so demand, then what contribution has human rights law made to answering questions regarding the procedures owed combatants in non-international armed conflict? Some rights deemed non-derogable by the ICCPR, such as the right to life, would be clearly displaced by more specific law of war rules that govern as the lex specialis.

In the end, I think the gaps I have identified in the rules regarding detention of combatants in non-international armed conflict are real, and that simply labeling international armed conflict rules custom in non-international armed conflict or importing human rights law does not satisfactorily resolve these difficulties. Through the course of my dialogue, more and more Europeans have been willing to acknowledge that the existing rules were not designed for, and are in fact not well-suited for, the threat posed by transnational terrorism. For example, earlier this year the Foreign Affairs Committee of the UK House of Commons wrote that the Geneva Conventions dealt inadequately with the problems posed by transnational terrorism, and called on the British government to work with other States and the ICRC on updating these Conventions for modern problems. Although I think it is premature to talk about negotiating a new international instrument, I am pleased to see that more people are beginning to think about whether the challenges terrorism poses to the law of war requires more than just calling for more robust implementation of existing rules.

Detention Scope and Procedures

Having established that the issues I have identified with Common Article 3 are not easily resolved by resort to other treaties or customary international law, I want to explore each of the four major unaddressed issues in turn. These issues are not an exhaustive list of areas where further dialogue and legal development are needed, but are perhaps the most important issues I have faced as Legal Adviser. The first question is how States should define the category of persons that can be detained in non-international armed conflict. With respect to combatants, traditional international armed conflict has a relatively easy answer: a State detains enemy forces, who usually wear uniforms, are in clear command and control structures, and conduct their operations in accordance with the laws of war. But in the contemporary conflicts we are discussing tonight, determining the legal contours of the category of "combatant" can be extremely difficult.

Clearly, Taliban militants captured on the battlefield in Afghanistan, as many of those at Guantanamo were, would fall within the scope of persons that can be detained for the duration of hostilities. So too would an al Qaida terrorist in Iraq with a strapped-on suicide vest headed to a civilian area to detonate. But what about the person who made the explosive-laden vest?

The financier whose money laundering for al Qaida made the suicide operation possible? The religious leader who knowingly inspired the suicide bomber to embark on his mission? This issue has been a difficult one for the United States with regards to al Qaida, and has been a source of tension with our European allies, some of whom are concerned that our definition of combatant is over-inclusive. But where exactly to draw the line here is unclear. Although it may seem reasonable to say that only those like the suicide bomber or vest maker should be detained as combatants, it may be the financier's broad operations that in fact pose the greatest threat to a State.

Of course, the law of war envisions that a State will detain both combatants and civilians during armed conflict. The laws of war have long permitted the detention of supporters of hostile forces during armed conflict, including civilians connected to armies such as laborers, messengers, guides, scouts, and civilians transporting military supplies and equipment in proximity to the battlefield. Article 42 of the Fourth Geneva Convention clearly contemplates security internment of protected persons, "where the security of the Detaining Power makes it absolutely necessary." The Israeli Supreme Court in the *Public Committee against Torture* case concluded that combatants not in regular armies or militias that meet the requirements of Article 4(A)(2) of the Third Convention were in fact civilians, who lost their comprehensive protections against attacks, "for such time as they take a direct part in hostilities."

It's worth noting here that the term "direct part in hostilities" in Article 51, paragraph 3, of Additional Protocol I, has been a difficult phrase to define. For years, a group of forty law-of-war experts have grappled with this issue in a series of expert meetings co-organized by the ICRC and the TMC Asser Institute. Although the experts' work is not finished, I am aware that it delves into these difficult questions, and I look forward to reviewing the report. More centrally though, query what the relevant differences are between categorizing some as unprivileged combatants (e.g., al Qaida) and other civilians who may be the object of direct attack but only for such time as they take a direct part in hostilities. In each case, a State can detain these persons for the duration of the conflict, and must treat individuals involved in a non-international armed conflict consistently with Common Article 3.

This question of whom a State may detain relates to the second major question I want to discuss: what procedures must a State use before deciding someone may be detained in non-international armed conflict. In international armed conflict, normally no process is used to determine whether or not soldiers from the opposing army may be detained. Such detained combatants, usually prisoners of war, who are not criminally charged are not entitled to counsel or judicial review. After 9/11, we took the view that Taliban and al Qaida militants we picked up on the battlefield were subject to detention under the law of war. As with traditional conflicts, these combatants were not provided lawyers nor afforded judicial review of the legality of their detention. But while this practice may make sense with respect to clearly identifiable soldiers, how should a State decide whether to detain non-state actors who often lack identifiable indicia of being a combatant? Is it sufficient to treat them as the law of war treats traditional combatants, or does something about their non-traditional status make further process necessary?

The U.S. Supreme Court clearly felt uncomfortable with applying the traditional rules to these unprivileged combatants. In its *Hamdi* decision in 2004, the Court ruled that US citizens picked up on the battlefield and detained in the United States are entitled to an administrative review process to determine whether they are in fact combatants. And in the companion *Rasul* decision, the Court extended statutory habeas corpus rights to alien detainees held at Guantanamo. The issue in last week's *Boumediene* argument was whether the right to common law habeas corpus protected by the Suspension Clause extends to the Guantanamo detainees. Ultimately, the United States appears to have arrived at a place where it is unquestioned, as a general matter, that administrative review of combatant status, and often subsequent judicial review of the legality of detention, accompanies extended detention in non-traditional conflicts.

It may be that we may have arrived at rules not that different from the rules set out for internment of civilian Protected Persons in Article 43 of the Fourth Geneva Convention. That article states in part, "Any protected person who has been interned or placed in assigned residence shall be entitled to have such action reconsidered as soon as possible by an appropriate court or administrative board designated by the Detaining Power for that purpose." We are following this procedure in Iraq, where we adhere to the Fourth Convention as a policy matter with civilian security internees. But we also meet this standard with combatants who are detained at Bagram in Afghanistan or Guantanamo. While I continue to question whether it makes sense to classify al Qaida members as civilians as opposed to unprivileged combatants, as the Israeli Supreme Court and others have suggested, the added procedural protections afforded interned or detained civilians may provide a model for appropriate rules for the detention of unprivileged combatants.

End of the Conflict?

Along with these two questions surrounding initiation of detention, Common Article 3 and other applicable IHL do not provide clear answers to two questions regarding termination of detention in contemporary conflicts. Even if one acknowledges that al Qaida militants may be lawfully detained as unprivileged enemy combatants, when must detained persons be released? Again, traditional IHL principles provide a simple answer: upon the cessation of active hostilities. In traditional conflicts it is obvious why this is the case. Could anyone imagine Allied forces during World War II releasing before the end of the conflict German soldiers who could return to the fight? And in the U.S. conflict in Viet Nam, captured U.S. military personnel were held by the North Vietnamese for up to nine years without any idea as to when they might be released or repatriated. At the same time this answer seems deeply unsatisfactory to some in the current conflict with al Qaida. Critics ask fair questions when they query how the United States will identify the end of hostilities. Although it would have been difficult for those living in Blitz London to identify when hostilities would have ended, at least there was a sense of what an end to the conflict might look like. It is highly unlikely this conflict will end with the signing of a formal surrender document on a battleship.

But what are the consequences of the conclusion that it will be difficult to identify when the conflict may end? Does this mean we should just release everyone we are holding now? This option is unpalatable given that many of the people we would release would immediately return to the fight. The Defense Department believes that more than 30 released Guantanamo detainees have already returned to the fight. Presumably, releasing the more dangerous individuals still detained at Guantanamo would result in an even greater number of recidivists. Or could it mean that . . . after some period of time States must release the detainees or subject them to trial? I have in the past given lengthy explanations of the difficulties Western legal systems have faced in criminally prosecuting terrorists—from the challenges posed by extraterritorial and retroactive legislation to difficulties in collecting admissible evidence in battlefield and intelligence settings.

The better answer may be to conceptualize the end of the conflict differently, possibly looking to principles found in the Fourth Geneva Convention. Article 43 of the Fourth Convention contemplates twice-yearly reviews of security internment of protected persons by a court or administrative board. In situations where the end of the conflict is as uncertain as it is with our conflict with al Qaida, administrative reviews could be used to determine whether the conflict has ended as to a particular detainee. Two leading legal experts, Curt Bradley and Jack Goldsmith, have written on this point, arguing that the unique characteristics of the war on terrorism require an individualized determination on end of the conflict. They suggested that such a determination could take into account the detainee's past conduct, level of authority within al Qaida, statements and actions during confinement, age and health, and psychological profile.

At Guantanamo, we have implemented annual Administrative Review Boards, or ARBs, in which a panel of military officers considers whether an individual detainee can be released or transferred in a manner that would not threaten the security of the United States or its allies. In a sense, this is an assessment of whether or not the conflict . . . can be viewed as having been ended with respect to the detainee in question. Perhaps we should consider what changes to the ARB process might be warranted to pursue this concept further.

The fourth and final question I want to address this evening is what should be done with detainees we no longer have a reason to hold in these non-traditional conflicts. Common Article 3 does not answer this question. The Third Geneva Convention offers a simple answer with respect to Prisoners of War. Article 118 states, "Prisoners of war shall be released and repatriated without delay after the cessation of active hostilities." Traditional state practice has been to return these detainees to their States of nationality. But although this traditional rule has been easier to apply in conflicts involving a limited number of States, it becomes far more challenging to apply when there are nationals of many States involved in the conflict. At Guantanamo, for example, we have detained nationals from more than forty countries. This has raised numerous practical problems. Rather than negotiate one bulk repatriation, as envisioned in Article 118, we have been forced to negotiate separate agreements with every country whose nationals we detain in the conflict. Needless to say, this has delayed the repatriation process significantly.

This problem grows in magnitude when the detainees we wish to repatriate express fears of mistreatment or persecution upon return. Although this is not a new problem, Article 118 is conspicuously silent on what States should do when those they wish to return do not wish to go back due to their concerns about treatment upon return. In World War II many thousands of Soviet nationals who had taken up arms for Germany, and who expressed fears of returning to the Soviet Union were forcibly repatriated by the US and UK in compliance with the 1945 Yalta Agreement. Christine Shields Delessert's good book on this topic details the brutal treatment these prisoners received after being returned to Soviet custody, including relocation to forced labor camps in Siberia and in some cases execution. In Korea and again in the first Gulf War, Allied forces used a different approach with prisoners not wishing to be repatriated, eschewing forcible repatriation in favor of third-country resettlement. In the current conflict with al Qaida, the United States has looked to human rights law as a nonbinding guide for determining when to repatriate prisoners to third countries, establishing the firm policy not to turn over detainees where it is more likely than not they will be tortured. This policy, central as it is to Western values, has meant that dozens of detainees who cannot be repatriated, such as the Uighurs to China, have remained at Guantanamo for years after we have wished to transfer them. This is an area where the U.S. has asked for assistance from its European partners and other allies to assist in the humanitarian resettlement of these individuals.

I would suggest that this problem is only likely to grow. In the conflict with al Qaida, for example, the majority of detainees are nationals of countries with poor human rights records. The problem is even more acute than in traditional armed conflict, because these governments are often harshest towards the very group of citizens that are being detained—people considered to be terrorists. This is less true when those being repatriated are a State's own soldiers. Exacerbating the problem is the lack of available third countries to resettle those detainees expressing credible fears. Unlike in previous conflicts when those detained may have had no ideological disagreement with the detaining power beyond the current conflict, and who may be expected to live peaceful lives once resettled, terrorists such as those at Guantanamo have the training and ideological desire to pose a continuing threat once resettled. Not surprisingly, third countries, including the United States, have not been willing to accept this risk.

Ultimately, I would posit that the solution is going to require a greater pragmatism in approaching this question. Although groups like Human Rights Watch have argued against the use of diplomatic assurances as the basis for repatriations, I would posit that such groups need to think about what alternative tools exist to manage humane treatment concerns in States that mistreat their citizens. Not only can assurances be effective when properly obtained and monitored, but taking a principled stand against assurances results in detainees being marooned in detention facilities years after they might otherwise have been released. For those detainees who come from countries where even assurances do not sufficiently mitigate the risk of mistreatment, the West is going to need to consider what realistic options exist to allow for third-country resettlement.

Conclusion

As we move forward then, I hope I have demonstrated that Common Article 3 and other applicable international legal rules do not answer important questions related to both the initiation and termination of detention in armed conflict with transnational terrorist groups. While there may be a range of reasonable policy answers, none are dictated by international law. I hope that the scholarly debate in this area will move beyond assertions that all that is needed is better implementation of existing law, and instead work will begin in earnest on addressing the difficult challenges I have identified. It is very easy for all of us to agree that the fight against transnational terrorism must be conducted in accordance with the rule of law, but it is much harder to say what the law exactly is, and how it should be applied in this context. As I continue my dialogue with other governments, I will continue to encourage them to work towards a common approach in dealing with these issues. I look forward to a good discussion this evening and for the rest of the conference of the way forward on these issues. Thank you.

c.   International Conference of the Red Cross and Red Crescent

The 30th International Conference of the Red Cross and Red Crescent met in Geneva, November 27–30, 2007. Legal Adviser John B. Bellinger, III, head of the U.S. delegation, addressed the opening session on behalf of the United States, stating:

We are . . . pleased that today presents another opportunity to reaffirm our commitment to international law. As we all know, the years since the tragic attacks of September 11th, 2001 have highlighted the challenges the international legal system faces in combating international terrorism. The U.S. Government has been engaged in an active dialogue with the international community regarding these challenges. The ICRC has been an important voice in defending the integrity of international humanitarian law while combating terrorism, and we look forward to continuing our work together in this area.

The full text of Mr. Bellinger's remarks is available at *www.us-mission.ch/Press2007/1127BellingerRCRCStatement.html*.

A press release issued by the U.S. Mission to the UN in Geneva on November 30, 2007, reiterated U.S. support for the "initiatives taken at the conference to support international humanitarian law and disaster preparedness." The statement continued:

> The U.S. is also pleased to sign a number of pledges to support international humanitarian action, in particular a pledge to protect the activities of journalists in situations of armed conflict. Mr. Bellinger said, "the United States is committed to protecting the rights—and the lives—of civilian journalists working in armed conflicts around the world."

Cooperative arrangements between the newly participating Palestine Red Crescent Society and Magen David Adom are discussed in A.5. below. The full text of the press release is available at *www.us-mission.ch/Press2007/1130RCRCFinal.html*.

2. Convention on Conventional Weapons

a. *Ratification of CCW-related instruments*

On August 15, 2007, Deputy Secretary of State John Negroponte and Deputy Secretary of Defense Gordon England wrote to the U.S. Senate Committee on Foreign Relations stating that their Departments "strongly support [five pending treaties dealing with the law of armed conflict] and encourage their prompt ratification." As explained in the letter,

> Four [of the five treaties pending before the committee] relate to the Convention on Certain Conventional Weapons

(CCW). Three of those are protocols to the CCW on incendiary weapons, blinding lasers, and explosive remnants of war, and the fourth is an amendment to the Convention itself to extend its scope to non-international armed conflicts. The fifth treaty is the Convention for the Protection of Cultural Property in the Event of Armed Conflict, done in 1954 at The Hague.

The treaties had been transmitted to the Senate for advice and consent to ratification in previous years. On January 7, 1997, President William J. Clinton transmitted to the Senate for advice and consent to ratification the Protocol on Prohibitions or Restrictions on the Use of Incendiary Weapons ("CCW Protocol III"), adopted at Geneva on October 10, 1980, and the Protocol on Blinding Laser Weapons ("CCW Protocol IV"), adopted at Geneva on May 3, 1996. S. Treaty Doc. No. 105-1 (1997). *See Cumulative Digest 1991–1999* at 2192–94. On June 20, 2006, President George W. Bush transmitted the CCW Protocol on Explosive Remnants of War ("CCW Protocol V") and the CCW Amendment to Article 1 ("CCW Amendment"), S. Treaty Doc. No. 109-10 (2006). *See Digest 2006* at 1094–100.

President Clinton transmitted the Hague Convention for the Protection of Cultural Property in the Event of Armed Conflict, concluded on May 14, 1954, and entered into force on August 7, 1956, 249 U.N.T.S. 240, on January 6, 1999. S. Treaty Doc. No. 106-1 (1999). *See Cumulative Digest 1991–1999* at 2197–206.

At the end of 2007 the Senate had not acted on the treaties.

b. San Remo International Institute on Humanitarian Law Roundtable on the Conduct of Hostilities

On September 7, 2007, Ronald Bettauer, Deputy Legal Adviser, U.S. Department of State, addressed the San Remo International Institute on Humanitarian Law Roundtable on the

Conduct of Hostilities, Session V, Working Group III. The full text of Mr. Bettauer's presentation, excerpted below, is available at *www.state.gov/s/l/c8183.htm.*

---

*   *   *   *

I would like to address briefly: (1) Protocol V to the Convention on Certain Conventional Weapons ("CCW"), on explosive remnants of war ("ERW"); (2) anti-vehicle mines ("AVM" or "MOTAPM"); and (3) cluster munitions.

*   *   *   *

Before starting, let me make clear [the U.S. view] on anti-personnel mines. For the United States, the relevant instrument is the Amended Mine Protocol ("APII") of the CCW (requirements concerning (1) the detectability of such mines and equipping such mines with effective self-destruction or self-neutralization mechanisms and back-up self-deactivation features; (2) recording information on minefields; and (3) the removal of such mines, among other provisions). Protocol V deals with ERW other than that already covered by APII.

Protocol V

First, let me address how Protocol V addresses the ERW problem.

The period immediately following the conflict is when civilians are most likely to interact with ERW. Rapid and effective implementation of Protocol V's provisions will provide substantial protection to the civilian population.

Protocol V requires each Party to mark and clear, remove, or destroy ERW in affected territories under its control. The Party that used the munitions which have become ERW on territory it does not control is obligated to assist "to the extent feasible." Users of munitions are obligated to record and retain information on use/abandonment of munitions "to the extent feasible and as far as practicable." They are also to transmit such information to the party in control of the territory. The Parties to an armed conflict are obligated to take steps, to the extent feasible, in the territory under their control, to protect civilians and civilian objects, as well as humanitarian missions and organizations, from ERW. In addition, Protocol V contains provisions on cooperation and assistance as well as non-binding guidelines on a variety of topics, including recording and release of information on ERWs, risk education in affected areas, and measures to increase the reliability/functioning rate of munitions.

The First Conference of Parties on Protocol V will consider guidelines and informal mechanisms aimed at facilitating rapid and effective implementation of these provisions, including: (1) the establishment of a database on ERW incorporating information from national reports and subsequent updates on locations of ERW, status of clearance efforts and measures taken to provide warning; (2) measures for recording, retaining, and transmitting information called for under the Protocol; and (3) an informal mechanism for consultations to connect countries needing assistance with ERW with countries able to provide that assistance.

Although not yet a State Party to Protocol V, I note that the United States is committed to reducing the humanitarian impact of ERW and looks forward to these discussions. The United States has provided more than $1 billion in assistance to 52 countries since 1993 for clearance of ERW, more than any other country or international organization.

Anti-Vehicle Mines

I now turn briefly to AVM, also an important area.

There was intensive work from 2002 to 2006 to develop a protocol on anti-vehicle landmines. Non-detectable, long-lived anti-vehicle mines can pose threats to civilians and civilian vehicles long after a conflict is over. The irresponsible use of such anti-vehicle mines poses a serious humanitarian problem that is not adequately addressed by existing instruments. Although the number of civilian casualties associated with anti-vehicle mines is less than those associated with antipersonnel mines, there are major humanitarian effects in terms of denial of assistance and post-conflict reconstruction.

In 2005 and 2006 there was near unanimous agreement on a text, but a few states blocked consensus last November at the Third CCW Review Conference. In the face of that, we and 24 other countries stated our intention to follow the policies set out in a Declaration on Anti-Vehicle Mines. The declaration is in Document WP.16 and can be found on the Geneva UN CCW website.[6] It states the intention of countries, as a matter of policy:

- Not to use any anti-vehicle mine outside of a perimeter-marked area if that mine is not detectable.
- Not to use any anti-vehicle mine outside of a perimeter-marked area that does not incorporate a self-destruction or self-neutralization mechanism.
- To prevent the transfer of any anti-vehicle mine unless the mine meets the detectability and active life standards and unless the transfer is to a state that has also adopted this policy.

The November 2007 meeting of CCW states parties reserved up to 2 days to discuss AVM. Speaking for the United States, if positions were to change and consensus appeared to be possible, we would be prepared to return to this matter.

Cluster Munitions

Finally, let me turn to cluster munitions. The U.S. views on cluster munitions were set forth in detail at the June CCW Group of Government Experts meeting; there is only time now to make some brief comments.

First, the United States considers cluster munitions to be legitimate weapons when employed properly and in accordance with existing international humanitarian law. It is wrong to say such munitions are inherently unreliable; militaries want weapons that function as intended and will not be a hazard for civilians or themselves.

In certain situations, cluster munitions provide military capabilities that cannot be provided by other weapons systems. Cluster munitions provide advantages against a range of target-types. They allow commanders to attack multiple stationary or moving targets within specific areas, either engaging the enemy over broad areas

---

6   *http://www.unog.ch/80256EE600585943/(httpPages)/1DB747 088014E6D7C12571C0003A0818?OpenDocument*

that they are occupying or narrowly engaging specific targets. There are different types of cluster munitions for different uses, and they are scalable to different target areas.

In many instances, cluster munitions result in much less collateral damage than unitary weapons would if used for the same mission. If the use of cluster munitions was restricted, certain missions would require our forces to fire many times more non-cluster projectiles to achieve the objectives.

Cluster munitions are well suited to attack area targets when time is of the essence. Because they can attack various types of targets quickly and simultaneously, they can also reduce the exposure of our forces to enemy fire. Their absence from the arsenal would also have serious logistics and cost implications. Cost and economy of force are certainly legitimate military considerations.

We believe that the law of war already covers cluster munitions both during and after their use, and a study published under CCW auspices reached the same conclusion, noting that strict compliance with existing rules is key.[7] . . . [W]e believe these weapons *can* be used in accordance with the law.

The key applicable law of war rules are those of proportionality and distinction. The rule of proportionality requires that a military commander wishing to use cluster munitions assess whether a particular attack may be expected to cause loss of civilian life, injury to civilians, damage to civilian objects, or a combination thereof that would be excessive in relation to the concrete and direct military advantage anticipated. Of course a commander needs to take into account what he knows about the reliability of the munitions he uses. He also is entitled to anticipate that his adversary will comply with its obligations concerning ERW, for example, those contained in Protocol V.

The rule of distinction requires that cluster munitions, like other weapons, only be used against military objectives. A commander may use cluster munitions only if he judges, in the particular circumstances, that the munition in question can be directed at

---

[7] Timothy L.H. McCormack, Paramdeep B. Mtharu, and Sarah Finnin, *Report on States Parties' Responses to the Questionnaire, International Humanitarian Law & Explosive Remnants of War*, at 49 (March 2006).

a military objective and will not strike military objectives, civilians, and civilian objects without distinction. The presentations by our military experts at the June CCW meeting demonstrated that cluster munitions can be used consistent with this requirement.

Protocol V to the CCW, which I have already discussed, addresses the issue of unexploded cluster munitions primarily in the post-conflict stage. There is really no need to duplicate the measures in Protocol V in a separate instrument on cluster munitions.

[As to] the humanitarian impact of cluster munitions, [t]he impacts are limited in scope, scale and duration as compared to other ERW. There is no country—except one (Laos)—where cluster munitions constitutes the principal ERW threat. And we are unaware of any unmet request for assistance in clearing cluster munitions. By 2008, only Laos will have a need for assistance dedicated specifically to cluster munitions. I don't have time to go into the details that support these points, but you will find them carefully set out in Richard Kidd's remarks at the June CCW meeting.[8]

Despite this, due to the importance of the issue, concerns raised by other countries, and our own concerns about the humanitarian implications of these weapons, the United States has concluded that it makes sense to initiate negotiations on a new instrument on cluster munitions within the framework of the CCW. We have taken no position as to the outcome of the negotiations, but we do believe this issue is best addressed in the CCW framework, which is most likely to achieve a result that balances humanitarian concerns with military utility and is, therefore, likely to have a more substantial impact than a result that fails to garner the support of many military powers. In June Government experts recommended that the November meeting of states parties to the CCW decide how best to address cluster munitions in the framework of the CCW.

c. Meeting of states parties

The states parties to the Convention on Certain Conventional Weapons convened in Geneva on November 7, 2007. Mr. Bettauer's opening statement on November 7, 2007,

---

8   *http://www.ccwtreaty.com/press/0620CCWGGE.htm*

is excerpted below. The full text is available at *www.state. gov/s/l/c8183.htm. See also* U.S. statements at the June 2007 CCW Group of Government Experts meeting in Geneva, including statement by Mr. Bettauer concerning negotiation on cluster munitions within the CCW framework, available at *www.state.gov/t/pm/rls/rm/87087.htm* and statement of Richard G. Kidd IV, Director of the Office of Weapons Removal and Abatement, on humanitarian impacts of cluster munitions, available at *www.ccwtreaty.com/press/0620CCWGGE.html.* A fact sheet entitled "United States Clearance of Unexploded Cluster Munitions," dated February 23, 2007, is available at *www.state.gov/r/pa/prs/ps/2007/february/81000.htm.* The Declaration on Anti-Vehicle Mines referred to here and in 2.b. *supra* is discussed in *Digest 2006* at 1089–91.

---

*   *   *   *

How to deal with the issue of cluster munitions is the most important topic at this meeting. As you are all aware, the United States changed its view on how to address the main humanitarian concerns raised by the use of cluster munitions. We took this step due to the importance of the issue, concerns raised by other countries, and our own concerns about the humanitarian implications of these weapons, and based on an internal review. . . .

What has not changed, however, is the view of the United States that cluster munitions continue to be legitimate weapons when employed properly and in accordance with existing international humanitarian law. In many instances, cluster munitions result in much less collateral damage than unitary weapons would if used for the same mission. If the use of cluster munitions were banned or unreasonably restricted, certain missions would require our forces to fire many times more non-cluster projectiles to achieve the objectives, potentially causing greater civilian casualties and damage to infrastructure.

*   *   *   *

The United States believes achieving agreement to begin negotiation is important because we believe that the issue of cluster munitions should be addressed within the framework of the CCW. We favor working within this framework because it ensures the widest participation of states, including all the major military powers and the key producers and potential users of cluster munitions. An instrument developed within this framework is more likely to have a meaningful, practical effect; is more likely to be widely adhered to; and is more likely to lead to widely accepted rules of international humanitarian law. It is important that we demonstrate we are up to the challenge of starting a negotiation that will find a balance between humanitarian objectives and military requirements in this area. We urge our colleagues here to work with us and each other in a spirit of cooperation and compromise to obtain agreement at this meeting on a negotiating mandate on cluster munitions.

One of the other important topics we will address at these meetings is anti-vehicle landmines, or MOTAPM. It should be no surprise to anyone here that the U.S. delegation worked hard, along with many other delegations, to develop the text of a protocol on MOTAPM. . . . In order that the humanitarian steps that would have been achieved by such a protocol not be lost, we were pleased to join with 24 other states in stating our intention to follow the policies set out in the Declaration on Anti-Vehicle Mines. The declaration is contained in Document WP.16.

* * * *

The declaration was an important step but it is not the end of the story for us or for others who have signed up to it. We would still like to see a protocol adopted. We stand ready, if positions have changed and it appears possible that consensus may be achieved, to restart the work immediately on a new protocol dealing with anti-vehicle landmines building on the work done between 2001 and 2006. However, the discussion at the June government experts meeting suggested that positions have not changed, and the United States has not seen any indications since last November that makes it appear that consensus is now possible. If this is the case, we see no reason to have a fruitless repetition of many prior discussions this year. If there is no chance of agreement, we should save the time and money and move directly to other agenda items, as we agreed we would last year.

Before closing, I would like to note that the United States is actively pursuing ratification of amended Article I and Protocols III, IV and V. The Administration supported expeditious Senate action on these treaties in its Treaty Priority List for the current session of Congress. The Deputy Secretaries of State and Defense sent the Chairman and Ranking Minority member of the Senate Foreign Relations Committee letters stating support for ratification without delay. And this summer the American Bar Association passed a resolution supporting ratification of these treaties. We will continue to work to achieve advice and consent to ratification of these instruments and hope that by this by this time next year the United States will have ratified them all.

> In a decision taken on November 13, 2007, the states parties adopted a "mandate which tasks a Group of Governmental Experts to negotiate a proposal to address urgently the humanitarian impact of cluster munitions, while striking a balance between military and humanitarian considerations." See www.unog.ch/80256EDD006B9C2E/(httpNewsByYear _en)/73D70D0349367C99C125739300334440?Open Document.
>
> Mr. Bettauer's closing statement, excerpted below, is available at www.state.gov/sl/c8183.htm.

* * * *

The United States believes that the humanitarian impact of cluster munitions is an important issue that should be addressed. . . . The language of the decision taken today is clear and direct; there can be no doubt that it represents agreement of all the states parties to the CCW, by consensus, to initiate negotiations on an urgent basis next year. The United States thinks the decision is a good one, and we are pleased with the result. It demonstrates that the states parties to the CCW can come to consensus on an urgent issue rapidly, and it means that an issue considered important by most states and their publics will be addressed in the appropriate framework.

States are responsible for protecting their citizens but under international humanitarian law the right to use force is not unlimited—

humanitarian and military considerations are both important. Our decision affirms the importance of the CCW as a framework for balancing these considerations in the interest of mitigating the effects of weapons on civilian populations. The CCW is the only framework that brings together the users and producers of munitions and those concerned with their humanitarian impact, and that can achieve results that are meaningful and will result in real humanitarian progress.

There are significant differences among States Parties on what to include in a new instrument addressing the issue of cluster munitions. These differences will need to be worked out through the negotiating process. . . . We welcome the decision to start the negotiations with an initial meeting of government experts in January and we believe that the process will be significantly enhanced by the support of military experts.

*   *   *   *

3. Protection of Civilians in Armed Conflict

On November 20, 2007, Ambassador Jackie Wolcott, U.S. Alternate Representative to the United Nations, addressed the Security Council on the Secretary-General's Report on the Protection of Civilians in Armed Conflict. Excerpts below address the issues of preventing sexual violence in conflicts and the humanitarian impact of cluster munitions. The full text of the statement is available at *www.un.int/usa/press_ releases/20071120_322.html.*

---

*   *   *   *

The Secretary-General, in his most recent Report on the Protection of Civilians in Armed Conflict, reminded us all that "the protection of civilians is a human, political and legal imperative that recognizes the inherent dignity and worth of every human being. It is a cause that unites us all in the responsibility to protect civilians from abuse, to mitigate the impact of warfare and to alleviate their suffering."

In that spirit, I would like to comment on some of the challenges raised in the Secretary-General's report.

*   *   *   *

Second—Preventing Sexual Violence in Conflict.

The United States condemns sexual violence as an instrument of policy and calls on all Member States to end this gross injustice. We applaud the recent adoption of the General Assembly resolution calling on states to end impunity by prosecuting and punishing those who rape and use other sexual violence to advance military or political objectives, to protect and support victims, and to develop and implement comprehensive strategies on prevention and prosecution of rape.

The United States has responded in many ways to the intolerable widespread violence against civilians. At the behest of Secretary Rice, the Department of State and the U.S. Agency for International Development are implementing an initiative to target five key strategic areas to help address the issue of gender-based violence including: access to justice, human rights monitoring efforts, access to accurate information, and humanitarian protections to include clinical care. The U.S. Department of State also supports programs which focus on prevention and response to gender-based violence for Darfur Sudanese refugees in Chad. The United States urges all Member States to take similar concrete steps to end impunity for perpetrators and the use of rape as an instrument of war.

*   *   *   *

Fifth—Addressing the humanitarian impact of cluster munitions.

With respect to the issue of cluster munitions, it is important to highlight the decision of the meeting of States Parties to the Convention on Certain Conventional Weapons last week in Geneva to instruct government experts to "negotiate a proposal to address urgently the humanitarian impact of cluster munitions, while striking the right balance between military and humanitarian considerations." The United States believes that the CCW is the right framework to take up this issue, because it is uniquely well-placed to strike this balance between humanitarian and military considerations. However, the U.S. believes that cluster munitions continue to be legitimate weapons when employed properly and in accordance with existing international humanitarian law.

*   *   *   *

4. Detainees

a. Overview

In his lecture at Oxford University on December 10, 2007, Legal Adviser Bellinger examined the existing legal framework to demonstrate his "key point . . . that the Geneva Conventions were designed for traditional armed conflicts between States and their uniformed military forces, and do not provide all the answers for detention of persons in conflicts between a State and a transnational terrorist group." *See* A.1.b. *supra.* Additional statements by Mr. Bellinger during 2007 are excerpted below as to other issues related to detainees. *See also* A.1.a. *supra* on the nature of the armed conflict with al Qaida.

(1) Helsinki Commission testimony

On June 21, 2007, Mr. Bellinger testified before the Commission on Security and Cooperation in Europe (often referred to as the Helsinki Commission*), in a hearing entitled "Guantanamo: Implications for U.S. Human Rights Leadership." Excerpts from Mr. Bellinger's testimony follow. The full text is available at *www.state.gov/s/l/c8183.htm.*

---

*   *   *   *

The legal authority to detain enemy combatants dovetails with a practical reality: many of the people we have captured in this

---

* Editor's note: The commission is an independent U.S. government agency created in 1976 to monitor and encourage compliance with the Helsinki Final Act and other OSCE commitments. Act of June 3, 1976, Public Law No. 94-304, 90 Stat. 661, codified as amended at 22 U.S.C. 3001–3009. For additional information, *see www.csce.gov.*

conflict are extremely dangerous individuals who by their past actions have proven their ruthlessness, destructive intent, and flagrant disregard for universally accepted norms of armed conflict. These include the architects of 9/11, the Bali bombings, the attacks on the U.S.S. Cole, and the Embassy bombings in Africa. It is not reasonable or responsible to suggest that these individuals should simply be released to rejoin the fight, where they could further harm our nation or our allies.

Despite this general recognition that the United States acted lawfully in detaining the Taliban and al Qaida combatants incident to the armed conflict in Afghanistan, and is justified in continued detention of dangerous terrorists like Khalid Sheikh Mohammed and Abu Zubaydah, the Administration understands fully that the detention facility at Guantanamo Bay has been a lightning rod for international and domestic criticisms. Many of these criticisms stem from misperceptions about the conditions at Guantanamo Bay. While critics continue to imagine orange-jump suited detainees in cages, visitors to Guantanamo, such as Madame Lizin who will speak after me, have recognized that the true conditions there mirror, and in some respects improve upon, those of high security prisons in Europe and the United States. And the horrifying images of detainee abuse at Abu Ghraib caused many to conclude that widespread detainee abuse takes place at Guantanamo, when in fact U.S. and international groups have found no evidence of ongoing detainee abuse there. The Detainee Treatment Act, the Department of Defense Detainee Directive, and the revised Army Field Manual on interrogation collectively provide detainees at Guantanamo a robust set of treatment protections that are fully consistent with, and in some respects exceed, our international obligations, including Common Article 3 of the Geneva Conventions.

Other criticisms stem from a sense that detainees at Guantanamo are in a "legal black hole," because they are not being prosecuted domestically. It is simply incorrect to suggest that the detainees have no legal protections absent criminal prosecution. All detainees at Guantanamo have received Combatant Status Review Tribunals confirming that they are properly detained as enemy combatants, and under the Detainee Treatment Act detainees have the opportunity to challenge that determination in the U.S. Court of Appeals for the D.C. Circuit. To our knowledge, these procedural protections are more extensive than those used by any other nation to determine a combatant's status.

And the Administration remains committed to trying by military commission those who have violated the laws of war or committed other serious offences under the MCA. After the Supreme Court in *Hamdan* [*v. Rumsfeld*, 548 U.S. 557 (2006)] set aside the original system of military commissions, we worked with the Congress to create a new set of military commission procedures that are fully consistent with U.S. law and Common Article 3 of the Geneva Conventions. While the Department of Defense can describe to you the latest developments regarding military commissions, it remains important as a matter of international law that we hold those responsible for serious war crimes to account.

Although we may disagree with many of the charges leveled against U.S. detention policies, the Administration recognizes the need to address the concerns that we have heard. As the President said on September 6th of last year, "we will work with the international community to construct a common foundation to defend our nation and protect our freedoms." Secretary Rice has made dialogue with our allies on these difficult issues a priority. We demonstrated continued American commitment to international human rights instruments by leading large interagency delegations presenting reports on U.S. compliance with the Convention Against Torture and International Covenant on Civil and Political Rights last year in Geneva, and we are currently working on a one-year follow up report to both treaty bodies on our actions in response to their recommendations.[*]

At the Secretary's instruction, I have undertaken extensive bilateral and multilateral efforts to discuss a common approach to counterterrorism policies. I have traveled to a dozen countries to speak with government officials, legal scholars and academics, and the media to answer questions they have about U.S. detention laws and policies and to emphasize the importance the United States

---

[*] Editor's note: The follow-up reports are discussed in A.4.c.(2) and (3) below and Chapter 6.A.2.a.

attaches to complying with our international legal obligations. I have also engaged in seven rounds of discussions with the legal advisers of the 27 EU countries, and held additional discussions with the legal advisers of the member states of the Council of Europe, with the intention of moving towards a common approach to the international legal issues posed by the conflict with al Qaida.

. . . We have also facilitated visits to Guantanamo by international groups including the OSCE, led by the Special Rapporteur for Guantanamo, Anne Marie Lizin, the U.K. Foreign Affairs Committee of the House of Commons, and a group of EU parliamentarians, as well as members of the international media. These visits have led to positive contributions to the international dialogue, and we will continue to work with the Department of Defense to facilitate future visits.

Although differences remain, I believe there is a growing international recognition that the threat posed by al Qaida does not neatly fit within existing legal frameworks. Madame Lizin's report from last July recognized that "there is incontestably some legal haziness" regarding the legal status of members of international terrorist organizations. Indeed, she recommended the formation of an international commission of legal experts to examine the question. Likewise, at last year's U.S.-E.U. summit, then-Austrian Chancellor Wolfgang Schussel acknowledged that we face "legal gray areas" regarding detention of terrorists. Most recently the Foreign Affairs Committee of the U.K. House of Commons wrote that the Geneva Conventions dealt inadequately with the problems posed by international terrorism, and called on the U.K. government, in connection with state parties to the Geneva Conventions and the International Committee of the Red Cross to work on updating these Conventions for modern problems. Although we do not—and will not—always see eye to eye with our European allies, I am encouraged that we have reached some degree of common ground, and that there is a growing acknowledgment that international terrorist organizations like al Qaida do not fit neatly into the existing international legal system.

Progress on this front aside, the President has stated that he would like to move towards the day when we can eventually close the detention facility at Guantanamo Bay.* . . . Moving forward, it is critical that the international community recognize, as the UK Foreign Affairs Committee recently did, that many of the detainees at Guantanamo pose a threat not just to the United States but to its allies, and that the longer-term solution to Guantanamo, including resettlement of detainees who cannot be repatriated, is a responsibility shared between the United States and those allies.

. . . We recognize that many people around the world view Guantanamo as inconsistent with U.S. values. We have worked hard to address those concerns, both through dialogue and changes to our policies. We will continue to work hard to take the steps necessary to protect Americans and the international community, while at the same time respecting our commitment to the rule of law. I look forward to answering any questions that you might have.

(2) Unlawful enemy combatants

As noted in A.1.a. *supra,* during January 2007 Legal Adviser John Bellinger posted web log entries on *Opinio Juris.* In one entry, Mr. Bellinger addressed the suggestion that the United States "invented" the concept of unlawful enemy combatants, as excerpted below. The full text is available at *www.state. gov/s/l/c8183.htm* and at *www.opiniojuris.org/posts/chain_ 1169503291.shtml,* which also includes postings from those responding to Mr. Bellinger.

––––––––

In this post I would like to take issue with the suggestion that the United States invented the concept of "unlawful enemy combatants" to avoid providing protections under the Geneva Conventions to al Qaida and Taliban detainees. I frequently hear the charge in Europe and elsewhere that this term has no basis in national or international law, and I fear that this has become conventional wisdom among critics of U.S. policy. In fact, the distinction between lawful and unlawful enemy combatants (also referred to as "unprivileged belligerents") has deep roots in international humanitarian

––––––––

* Editor's note: For a more detailed discussion of the challenge of closing Guantanamo, *see* A.4.c.(3) below.

law, preceding even the 1949 Geneva Conventions. The Hague Regulations of 1899 and 1907 contemplated distinctions between lawful and unlawful combatants, and this distinction remains to this day. As Professor Adam Roberts told the Brookings Speakers Forum in March 2002, "There is a long record of certain people coming into the category of unlawful combatants—pirates, spies, saboteurs, and so on. It has been absurd that there should have been a debate about whether or not that category exists."

I frequently hear the question, "Why not consider all captured belligerents, lawful or unlawful, 'prisoners of war'?" It is not immediately clear why some advocate such a move. Prisoners of war can be held until the cessation of hostilities, and, ironically, many of those advocating for POW status for Taliban and al Qaida forces object to that basic principle. Moreover, I question whether those who insist that the Taliban and al Qaida be treated as POWs have thought through the practical consequences. Do proponents of POW status for al Qaida detainees expect them to be provided with all the benefits accorded to POWs under the Third Convention, despite their failing to follow the laws and customs of war?

More critically, though, the drafters of the Third Geneva Convention were aware that they were not drafting the treaty in a way that would ensure that everyone who took up weapons on a battlefield would receive POW status. To begin with, Common Article 2 of the Conventions limits the application of the vast majority of provisions, including protections to be provided to POWs, to armed conflicts between two or more High Contracting Parties. Thus, POW status is limited to belligerents engaged in international armed conflict. The U.S. Supreme Court has decided that the U.S. conflict with al Qaida is governed by Common Article 3. Because the Court has found that the conflict with al Qaida is not one between nations, but instead a Common Article 3 conflict, al Qaida detainees are not entitled to POW protections under the Third Convention. . . .

Moreover, Article 4 of the Third Convention affirms the longstanding distinction between lawful and unlawful combatants because it limits "prisoner of war" status to lawful combatants, such as members of the regular armed forces of a Party to the Convention. The underlying concept here is simple—unlawful combatants should not be provided combatant immunity during wartime, and should be held criminally accountable for their acts of war. By contrast, AU Professor Robert Goldman explains that lawful combatants have combatants' privilege, which "immunizes members of armed forces from criminal prosecution by their captors for violent acts that do not transgress the laws of war, but might otherwise be crimes under domestic law."

An examination of the nature of al Qaida and its members results in the conclusion that they are not entitled to POW status under Article 4. Al Qaida members are not members of the armed forces of a party to the Geneva Conventions, meaning that they are not entitled to protection under Article 4(A)(1). Al Qaida has also failed to adhere even to the most fundamental tenets of the laws of war—including the critical need to maintain distinction between civilian objects and military objectives—and have blended into the general population, deliberately choosing not to wear fixed distinctive signs or carry arms openly. Under such circumstances, the United States is correct in denying al Qaida fighters the protections owed prisoners of war.

Although most international legal scholars agree that al Qaida detainees are not entitled to POW status, I recognize there is more debate regarding the status of the Taliban detainees. The Taliban did not display the indicia of regular "armed forces of a party" for purposes of Article 4(A)(1). The armed forces of Afghanistan ceased to exist as such with the dissolution of former President Mohammad Najibullah's armed forces in the mid-nineties, and were replaced by a patchwork of rival armies. Although the Taliban were the most powerful of these rival armies at the time of the U.S. invasion, it does not appear that they ever rose to the level of the official armed forces of Afghanistan. Nor were they "regular armed forces who profess allegiance to a government or an authority not recognized by the Detaining Power," entitled to POW protection under Article 4(A)(3). The Taliban do not possess the attributes of regular armed forces, as they do not distinguish themselves from the general population, or conduct their operations in accordance with the laws and customs of war.

The Taliban is better conceptualized as a militia belonging to a Party to the conflict, which would be eligible for POW protection under Article 4(A)(2) if they used a command hierarchy; wore a uniform or distinctive sign; carried arms openly; and observed the laws and customs of war. The Taliban, however, fail to meet at least two of these conditions: specifically, the Taliban do not distinguish themselves from the general population, nor do they obey the laws and customs of war. Contemporary news reports from the Allied invasion of Afghanistan indicate that the Taliban dressed like civilians, and in fact used this similar dress to blend into the civilian population to evade capture. Worse still, they have targeted and continue to target civilians as such in violation of the laws of war, having adopted suicide bombing techniques similar to those used by al Qaida. These types of transgressions explain why the United States believes that Taliban detainees do not enjoy POW status under the Third Convention.

Assuming that the Taliban were the armed forces of Afghanistan, however, they still do not qualify for POW status because they fail to meet many of the fundamental criteria for POW status under the Third Convention; specifically, the Taliban lacked the command structure, distinctive uniforms, and compliance with the laws and customs of war which characterize regular military forces. Some have argued that these additional factors would not preclude POW status under Article 4(A) (1) because that provision omits the list of requirements found in Article 4(A) (2). This is a difficult question, but as Jean Pictet's commentary on the Third Convention explains, it seems the drafters of the Convention had an expectation that the armed forces of a party would generally meet the requirements contained in Article 4(A)(2), and it's unlikely they envisioned granting POW status to groups that openly flout these requirements.

In separating lawful and unlawful combatants, the Third Convention creates a basic bargain for those engaged in an international armed conflict. Engage lawfully in combat and, if captured, you will receive the comprehensive treatment protections of the Convention. Ignore the laws of war, and you cannot seek the status given to lawful combatants. POW status is perhaps best seen then as an incentive to follow the rules in armed conflict. It also is a way to protect civilians more effectively: when combatants masquerade as civilians to mislead the enemy and avoid detection, civilian suffering increases as a tragic consequence of the failure of these combatants to adhere to the fundamental law of war principle of distinction between combatants and the civilian population.

Long before the war against al Qaida began, the United States forcefully insisted that this incentive to follow the rules remain strong by limiting these extensive treatment protections to those who generally follow the rules of warfare. President Reagan decided not to submit Additional Protocol I of the Geneva Conventions to the Senate for ratification in part because he feared that the treaty contained a disincentive to follow the laws of war by extending combatant status in certain cases to those who do not follow the rules. As former Department of State Legal Adviser Abe Sofaer explained, "Inevitably, regular forces would treat civilians more harshly and with less restraint if they believed that their opponents were free to pose as civilians while retaining their right to act as combatants and their POW status if captured."

I believe that the bargain of the Third Convention works: follow the laws of war to gain their robust protections and privileges. Those who believe in the rules should insist that incentives to follow those rules not be weakened.

I wanted to add a final thought about the recent Israeli Supreme Court decision in Public Committee against Torture in Israel v. Israel, where it has been reported that the Court concluded there was no category of individuals labeled unlawful enemy combatants. That is not quite what the court held. Instead, the Court held that combatants not in regular armies or militias meeting the requirements of Article 4(A)(2) of the Third Convention were in fact civilians, who lost their comprehensive protections against attacks, "for such time as they take a direct part in hostilities."

To begin with, it's important to stress that the Israeli Court largely agreed with our views regarding treatment of terror groups like al Qaida. We agree with the Court that these types of combatants were not entitled to protection from attack regardless of their categorization, nor were they entitled to prisoner of war status if detained. The Court did conclude that Article 51(3) of Additional Protocol I was customary international law, which limited the circumstances in which a "civilian combatant" could be considered a legitimate military target. While we agree that there is a general principle of international law that civilians lose their immunity from attack when they engage in hostilities, we disagree with the contention that the provision as drafted in AP I is customary international law. In fact, the Israeli Court's opinion appears to recognize that point inadvertently by highlighting the lack of international consensus regarding the meaning of both "for such time" and "direct part in hostilities."

More centrally, though, most of the sources cited by the Court support our contention that "unlawful enemy combatant" is a category of combatant, distinct from civilians, recognized under international law. Kenneth Watkin, Richard Baxter, Jason Callen, Robert K. Goldman, and Michael Hoffman, all of whom the Court cites, agree that unlawful combatants exist as a legal category, although they may disagree somewhat with us and each other about who qualifies for membership in such a group, and what the legal consequences are, such as whether unlawful combatants are entitled to protection under the Fourth Convention. My point here is that even those that disagree with us as to the legal framework for detaining al Qaida and Taliban detainees should acknowledge that we are on legally firm ground in using this construct as the basis for our framework.

In closing, my sense is that the insistent opposition to our use of the term "unlawful combatant," despite its clear lineage in international law, is motivated by a fear that acknowledging this category might place the detainees in a legal black hole. While it certainly could be the subject of a policy debate whether we should grant POW status to detainees not legally entitled to it, saying that the Taliban and al Qaida detainees are not criminals on the one hand, nor POWs or protected persons on the other does not mean they do not have significant legal protections. Following the Supreme Court's decision in Hamdan [v. Rumsfeld, 548 U.S. 557 (2006)], all detainees in the conflict against al Qaida and the Taliban must be treated in accordance with Common Article 3 of the Geneva Conventions. They are also protected by the blanket prohibitions on torture and cruel, inhuman or degrading treatment or punishment found in U.S. law. And the Department of Defense recently promulgated a new directive on detention operations and a field manual governing interrogation that provide clear direction to the U.S. Armed Forces regarding compliance with these important norms. Nevertheless, critics prefer to strain to force the detainees to fit into the more traditional legal categories of common criminals or POWs. I am more inclined to agree with the conclusions of the OSCE Rapporteur on Guantanamo, Anne-Marie Lizin, the President of the Belgian Senate, that there is "incontestably some legal haziness" regarding the legal status of individuals captured in the course of military operations against international terrorists and that further legal work needs to be done to clarify the status of these kinds of combatants.

b. Interpretation of Common Article 3

(1) Comments by Legal Adviser

In his January 2007 participation in the *Opinio Juris* web log discussed in A.1.a. *supra*, Mr. Bellinger addressed issues concerning the interpretation of Common Article 3 as excerpted below. The full text of Mr. Bellinger's posting is available at *www.state.gov/s/l/c8183.htm* and at *www.opiniojuris.org/posts/chain_1169503291.shtml*, which includes postings from persons responding to Mr. Bellinger's posting. *See also* discussion in Mr. Bellinger's lecture in A.1.b. *supra*.

---

* * * *

I've heard lots of questions and concerns about why the President wanted to define in greater detail the terms of CA3 [as codified in the Military Commissions Act, Pub. L. No. 109-366 (2006)]. Some say, "The military has been able to train to the standards of CA3 for years. How can it be vague?" Others suggest that efforts to define the terms of the article are simply an effort by the Administration to walk back from its binding treaty obligations.

Let me say several things in response to those concerns. First, the U.S. military trains to standards higher than the minimum standards of CA3; it trains to the standards that apply to the detention and treatment of prisoners of war. Thus, it has not had to grapple with precisely what CA3 requires.

Second, some of CA3's terms are not sufficiently clear about which acts are prohibited and which are permitted. Murder, hostage taking, and torture are quite clear. But which acts constitute "outrages upon personal dignity, in particular humiliating and degrading treatment"? Pictet's Commentary on CA3 states that the drafters intended to capture only those acts that "world public opinion finds particularly revolting." Reasonable people can and do differ about what behavior that phrase captures. While this ambiguity may be understandable given the purposes of CA3, a clear definition of what conduct is prohibited was particularly important to us after the *Hamdan* decision concluded that CA3 applied to the conflict with al Qaida. Because Congress had criminalized violations of CA3 in its 1999 amendments to the War Crimes Act, it was essential that what was criminally sanctionable under federal law be carefully delineated, to provide clarity to both prosecutors and potential defendants as to what conduct was criminal. Thus, the Administration chose to ask Congress to criminalize certain acts that it believed clearly fell within the CA3 prohibitions—such as rape and sexual assault. The Military Commissions Act, which emerged from the Administration's draft bill, now provides clear guidance on which violations of CA3 are criminal offenses.

Incidentally, the Administration and Congress are not the only entities to have determined that terms in CA3 are vague. The International Criminal Tribunal for the Former Yugoslavia acquitted defendant Mitar Vasiljevic, who was accused of killing five Muslim men, of the offense of "violence to life and person" because the term lacked a sufficiently precise definition under international law.

Some have argued that we are undercutting or violating our international law obligations by not criminalizing each provision in CA3. But the Geneva Conventions do not require High Contracting Parties to criminalize all such violations. Instead, they require Parties to criminalize all violations listed in the Conventions as "grave breaches" (such as those violations in Article 130 of the Third Convention and Article 147 of the Fourth) when committed against "persons or property protected by" that Convention. And, of course, the United States has complied with this obligation. Pictet's Commentary makes clear that the reference to "persons protected by" in Article 130 and 147 means those individuals defined in Article 4 of the Third and Fourth Conventions, respectively (prisoners of war and protected persons).

The U.S. Government took a different approach in 1995 in its amicus brief in the *Tadic* appeal in the ICTY, arguing in favor of the view that "grave breaches" of the Geneva Convention should be interpreted broadly to include acts committed in internal conflicts covered by CA3. But the ICTY expressly rejected this argument, noting that "State parties to the 1949 Geneva Conventions did not want to give other States jurisdiction over serious violations of international humanitarian law committed in their internal armed conflicts—at least not the mandatory universal jurisdiction involved in the grave breaches system." The panel concluded that the grave breach provisions such as those found in Article 130 of the Third Convention "do not include persons or property coming within the purview of CA3 of the four Geneva Conventions."

We believe the approach reflected in the [Military Commissions Act]—criminalizing as serious violations of CA3 those acts committed during internal armed conflict that represent serious violations of that provision—reflects a good faith interpretation of our obligations under the Geneva Conventions that is consistent with approaches taken by others in the international community. The Article on its face does not require us to criminalize any of its prohibitions; nothing in the negotiating history suggests that the provision was intended to create such an obligation. Even the ICC statute does not criminalize all violations of CA3, but rather criminalizes what it calls "serious violations" of CA3. In this context, we thought it was important and appropriate to be as clear and specific as possible about what prohibited acts trigger criminal liability.

It is true that, before this new law, the War Crimes Act criminalized any conduct that constituted a violation of CA3. But the statute never defined the specific conduct that would have constituted a criminal act, and was arguably, therefore, overly vague. Our review of CA3 led us to the view that certain of the Article's prohibitions—including the vague prohibition against "outrages upon personal dignity"—were simply too poorly defined and understood to provide a basis for prosecution. Indeed, it is difficult to imagine Congress enacting a federal offense to make it a crime to subject a federal inmate to an "outrage on personal dignity"—but the War Crimes Act, before its amendment, had a comparable effect in armed conflict scenarios. Perhaps because of the absence of clarity, the U.S. government never prosecuted anyone under that statute, even those who committed war crimes against U.S. forces. By providing clear definitions of criminal conduct, we have made the War Crimes Act a more effective tool for prosecuting war crimes in the future.

Of course, any activity that violates CA3, including "outrages upon personal dignity" and the prohibition against the passing of a sentence without previous judgment pronounced by a regularly constituted court, even if not a war crime, still is prohibited, may violate other criminal laws, and would be subject to administrative or other penalties. The Military Commissions Act confirms that cruel, inhuman, and degrading treatment is a violation of CA3, which is absolutely prohibited under U.S. law, and contemplates that the President may issue further interpretations of what constitutes violations of that provision. The Act therefore does not alter our treaty obligations in any way.

Finally, just a word about the Supreme Court's decision in *Hamdan* as it relates to CA3. I think the Court's decision took a number of international lawyers by surprise in holding that CA3 applied to the conflict with al Qaida as a matter of treaty law. Had the Court concluded that CA3 applied as a matter of customary international law, it might have been less surprising, as many commentators have reached this conclusion (although, such a finding probably would not have been dispositive in the *Hamdan* litigation itself). But given the text of the Article, it was reasonable for the President to have determined in February 2002 that, as a treaty law matter, CA3, which applies to armed conflict "not of an international character" occurring "in the territory of one of the High Contracting Parties," applied only to armed conflicts that occurred in the territory of a single state. Indeed, the Israeli Supreme Court has just concluded in the *Public Committee against Torture* case that Israel's conflict with terrorist organizations—that is, a conflict that is not literally between nations—nevertheless is an international armed conflict, not a conflict to which CA3 applies. Pictet too describes the conflicts referred to in CA3 as armed conflicts that are "in many respects similar to an international war, but take place within the confines of a single country." The conflict with al Qaida, which has taken place both inside and outside the United States, does not meet that description. The United States, of course, has complied and will continue to comply with the Supreme Court's decision in *Hamdan*, but I raise this simply to note that, before that decision, many believed that CA3 applied as a treaty law matter only to internal armed conflicts.

(2) Executive Order: Central Intelligence Agency program

> On July 20, 2007, President Bush issued Executive Order 13440, "Interpretation of the Geneva Conventions Common Article 3 as Applied to a Program of Detention and Interrogation Operated by the Central Intelligence Agency." 72 Fed. Reg. 40,707 (July 24, 2007). A press statement issued by the White House on that date explained:

> > . . . The Order interprets the meaning and application of Common Article 3 with respect to . . . the Central Intelligence Agency's detention and interrogation program whose purpose is to question captured Al Qaeda terrorists who have information on attack plans or the whereabouts of the group's senior leaders.

> > *   *   *   *

> > Last September, the President explained how the CIA's program had disrupted attacks and saved lives, and that it must continue on a sound legal footing. The President has insisted on clear legal standards so that CIA officers involved in this essential work are not placed in jeopardy for doing their job—and keeping America safe from attacks. This Order was signed after an extensive interagency process of review and coordination. By providing these clear rules, the Order has clarified vague terms in Common Article 3, and its interpretation is consistent with the decisions of international tribunals applying

> Common Article 3, including the International Criminal
> Tribunal for the Former Yugoslavia.
>
> The press statement is available at *www.whitehouse.gov/
> news/releases/2007/07/20070720-5.html*. The text of the
> order is set forth in full below.

By the authority vested in me as President and Commander in
Chief of the Armed Forces by the Constitution and the laws of the
United States of America, including the Authorization for Use of
Military Force (Public Law 107-40), the Military Commissions
Act of 2006 (Public Law 109-366), and section 301 of title 3,
United States Code, it is hereby ordered as follows:

Section 1. *General Determinations.* (a) The United States is
engaged in an armed conflict with al Qaeda, the Taliban, and associated forces. Members of al Qaeda were responsible for the attacks
on the United States of September 11, 2001, and for many other
terrorist attacks, including against the United States, its personnel,
and its allies throughout the world. These forces continue to fight
the United States and its allies in Afghanistan, Iraq, and elsewhere,
and they continue to plan additional acts of terror throughout the
world. On February 7, 2002, I determined for the United States
that members of al Qaeda, the Taliban, and associated forces are
unlawful enemy combatants who are not entitled to the protections that the Third Geneva Convention provides to prisoners of
war. I hereby reaffirm that determination.

(b) The Military Commissions Act defines certain prohibitions
of Common Article 3 for United States law, and it reaffirms and
reinforces the authority of the President to interpret the meaning
and application of the Geneva Conventions.

Sec. 2. *Definitions.* As used in this order:

*   *   *   *

(c) "Cruel, inhuman, or degrading treatment or punishment"
means the cruel, unusual, and inhumane treatment or punishment
prohibited by the Fifth, Eighth, and Fourteenth Amendments to
the Constitution of the United States.

Sec. 3. *Compliance of a Central Intelligence Agency Detention
and Interrogation Program with Common Article 3.* (a) Pursuant

to the authority of the President under the Constitution and the laws of the United States, including the Military Commissions Act of 2006, this order interprets the meaning and application of the text of Common Article 3 with respect to certain detentions and interrogations, and shall be treated as authoritative for all purposes as a matter of United States law, including satisfaction of the international obligations of the United States. I hereby determine that Common Article 3 shall apply to a program of detention and interrogation operated by the Central Intelligence Agency as set forth in this section. The requirements set forth in this section shall be applied with respect to detainees in such program without adverse distinction as to their race, color, religion or faith, sex, birth, or wealth.

(b) I hereby determine that a program of detention and interrogation approved by the Director of the Central Intelligence Agency fully complies with the obligations of the United States under Common Article 3, provided that:

(i) the conditions of confinement and interrogation practices of the program do not include:

(A) torture, as defined in section 2340 of title 18, United States Code;

(B) any of the acts prohibited by section 2441(d) of title 18, United States Code, including murder, torture, cruel or in-human treatment, mutilation or maiming, intentionally causing serious bodily injury, rape, sexual assault or abuse, taking of hostages, or performing of biological experiments;

(C) other acts of violence serious enough to be considered comparable to murder, torture, mutilation, and cruel or in-human treatment, as defined in section 2441(d) of title 18, United States Code;

(D) any other acts of cruel, inhuman, or degrading treatment or punishment prohibited by the Military Commissions Act (subsection 6(c) of Public Law 109-366) and the Detainee Treatment Act of 2005 (section 1003 of Public Law 109-148 and section 1403 of Public Law 109-163);

(E) willful and outrageous acts of personal abuse done for the purpose of humiliating or degrading the individual in a manner so serious that any reasonable person, considering the circumstances, would deem the acts to be beyond the bounds of human decency, such as sexual or sexually indecent acts undertaken for the purpose of humiliation, forcing the individual to perform sexual acts or to pose sexually, threatening the individual with sexual mutilation, or using the individual as a human shield; or

(F) acts intended to denigrate the religion, religious practices, or religious objects of the individual;

(ii) the conditions of confinement and interrogation practices are to be used with an alien detainee who is determined by the Director of the Central Intelligence Agency:

(A) to be a member or part of or supporting al Qaeda, the Taliban, or associated organizations; and

(B) likely to be in possession of information that:

(1) could assist in detecting, mitigating, or preventing terrorist attacks, such as attacks within the United States or against its Armed Forces or other personnel, citizens, or facilities, or against allies or other countries cooperating in the war on terror with the United States, or their armed forces or other personnel, citizens, or facilities; or

(2) could assist in locating the senior leadership of al Qaeda, the Taliban, or associated forces;

(iii) the interrogation practices are determined by the Director of the Central Intelligence Agency, based upon professional advice, to be safe for use with each detainee with whom they are used; and

(iv) detainees in the program receive the basic necessities of life, including adequate food and water, shelter from the elements, necessary clothing, protection from extremes of heat and cold, and essential medical care.

(c) The Director of the Central Intelligence Agency shall issue written policies to govern the program, including guidelines for Central Intelligence Agency personnel that implement paragraphs (i)(C), (E), and (F) of subsection 3(b) of this order, and including requirements to ensure:

(i) safe and professional operation of the program;

(ii) the development of an approved plan of interrogation tailored for each detainee in the program to be interrogated, consistent with subsection 3(b)(iv) of this order;

(iii) appropriate training for interrogators and all personnel operating the program;

(iv) effective monitoring of the program, including with respect to medical matters, to ensure the safety of those in the program; and

(v) compliance with applicable law and this order.

Sec. 4. *Assignment of Function.* With respect to the program addressed in this order, the function of the President under section 6(c)(3) of the Military Commissions Act of 2006 is assigned to the Director of National Intelligence.

Sec. 5. *General Provisions.* (a) Subject to subsection (b) of this section, this order is not intended to, and does not, create any right or benefit, substantive or procedural, enforceable at law or in equity, against the United States, its departments, agencies, or other entities, its officers or employees, or any other person.

(b) Nothing in this order shall be construed to prevent or limit reliance upon this order in a civil, criminal, or administrative proceeding, or otherwise, by the Central Intelligence Agency or by any individual acting on behalf of the Central Intelligence Agency in connection with the program addressed in this order.

c. Responses to UN bodies

(1) Addendum to Report of Human Rights Council Special Rapporteur

As noted in Chapter 6.J.1., on December 12, 2007, the United States responded to an addendum to the Report of the Human Rights Council Special Rapporteur on the promotion and protection of human rights and fundamental freedoms while countering terrorism. In its detailed response to the report, the United States addressed the relationship between human rights law and law of war, stating:

The report invokes the "well-established principle that regardless of issues of classification, international human rights law continues to apply in armed conflict." While the report does not directly characterize the United States position on this question, the implication is that the United States position is at odds with that of the Special Rapporteur.

The United States does not argue that human rights treaties cease to apply as a categorical matter during times of armed conflict. There will be circumstances in which the two bodies of law are mutually exclusive—as in peacetime, when the law of war is inapplicable—and circumstances in which they may not be—as in an armed conflict occurring in one's own territory. Thus, whether international human rights law applies to the conduct of a particular state during an armed conflict is a case-by-case inquiry. This is the concept of *lex specialis*. For example, as stated above, the United States has never argued that every action taken against terrorism would entail the application of the law of armed conflict to the exclusion of human rights law. What it has argued in the specific context of detention operations at Guantanamo, for example, is that where the law of armed conflict is applicable—as in the conflict with al Qaida, the Taliban, and associated forces—international law dictates that the law to be applied is the specific body of law—in this case the law of armed conflict rules governing detention.

The full text of the detailed response, which addresses a number of other issues also discussed in this chapter, is available at *http://geneva.usmission.gov/Press2007/Scheinin-Response-HRC.pdf.*

(2) One-year follow-up report on U.S. implementation of ICCPR

As explained in Chapter 6.A.2.a., on October 10, 2007, the United States filed a follow-up report responding to certain recommendations by the UN Human Rights Committee following its review of the U.S. combined second and third periodic reports on implementation of the ICCPR, and meetings with the Committee in 2006.

The U.S. response to a question concerning interrogation techniques is excerpted below. The full text of the U.S. follow-up response is available at *www.state.gov/s/l/c8183.htm.*

* * * *

Paragraph 13

Recommendation:

"The State party should ensure that any revision of the Army Field Manual only provides for interrogation techniques in conformity with the international understanding of the scope of the prohibition contained in article 7 of the Covenant; the State party should also ensure that the current interrogation techniques or any revised techniques are binding on all agencies of the United States Government and any others acting on its behalf; the State party should ensure that there are effective means to [bring] suit against abuses committed by agencies operating outside the military structure and that appropriate sanctions be imposed on its personnel who used or approved the use of the now prohibited techniques; the State party should ensure that the right to reparation of the victims of such practices is respected; and it should inform the Committee of any revisions of the interrogation techniques approved by the Army Field Manual."

Response:

As noted elsewhere in this submission, the United States is engaged in an armed conflict with al Qaida, the Taliban, and their supporters. As part of this conflict, the United States captures and detains enemy combatants, and is entitled under the law of war to hold them until the end of hostilities. The law of war, and not the Covenant, is the applicable legal framework governing these detentions. There are, of course, many analogous protections under the law of war, which the United States fully respects.

For instance, international humanitarian law prohibits torture of detainees in international or non-international armed conflict. Consistent with international humanitarian law, there is a statutory prohibition in U.S. criminal law against the torture of anyone in the custody or under the physical control of the United States Government outside the territory of the United States. In addition, cruel, inhuman, and degrading treatment or punishment of anyone in the custody or under the physical control of the United States Government is prohibited both within and outside of the territory of the United States.[9] All detainee interrogations are conducted in a manner consistent with these prohibitions, as well with Common Article 3 of the Geneva Conventions.[10]

In September 2006, following the U.S. presentation of its report to the Committee, the Department of Defense released the updated detainee program Directive 2310.01e ("The Department of Defense Detainee Program") and the Army released its revised Field Manual on interrogation. These documents are attached in Annexes 1 and 2, respectively. They provide guidance to military personnel to ensure compliance with the law, including Common Article 3 of the Geneva Conventions.

For instance, the revised Army Field Manual states that "[a]ll captured or detained personnel, regardless of status, shall be treated humanely, and in accordance with the Detainee Treatment Act of 2005 and DOD Directive 2310.[0]1E . . . and no person in the custody or under the control of DOD, regardless of nationality or physical location, shall be subject to torture or cruel, inhuman, or degrading treatment or punishment, in accordance with and as defined in U.S. law."[11] The Field Manual also provides specific guidance, including a non-exclusive list of actions—such as "waterboarding" and placing a hood or sack over the head of a detainee, among others—that are prohibited when used in conjunction with interrogations.[12] Finally, the Field Manual provides guidance to be

---

[9] Detainee Treatment Act of 2005, Pub. L. No. 109-148, Title X (Dec. 30, 2005).

[10] *See e.g.*, Geneva Convention Relative to the Protection of Civilian Persons in Time of War, August 12, 1949, art. 3, 75 UNTS 135.

[11] Army Field Manual 2-22.3, Human Intelligence Collector Operations, para. 5-74.

[12] *Id.* at para. 5-75.

used while formulating interrogation plans for approval. For example, the Field Manual states:

> "In attempting to determine if a contemplated approach or technique should be considered prohibited . . . consider these two tests before submitting the plan for approval:
>
> • If the proposed approach technique were used by the enemy against one of your fellow soldiers, would you believe the soldier had been abused?
> • Could your conduct in carrying out the proposed technique violate a law or regulation? Keep in mind that even if you personally would not consider your actions to constitute abuse, the law may be more restrictive.
>
> If you answer yes to either of these tests, the contemplated action should not be conducted."[13]

We would also note that U.S. law provides several avenues for the domestic prosecution of United States Government officials and contractors who commit torture and other serious crimes overseas. For example, section 2340A of title 18 of the United States Code authorizes the prosecution of any U.S. national who commits torture outside of the United States, while section 2441 does the same for serious violations of Common Article 3. Similarly, under the provisions of the Military Extraterritorial Jurisdiction Act ("MEJA"),[14] persons employed by or accompanying the Armed Forces outside the United States may be prosecuted domestically if they commit a serious criminal offense overseas. MEJA specifically covers all civilian employees and contractors directly employed by the Department of Defense and, as amended in October 2004, also those employed by other United States Government agencies, to the extent that such employment relates to supporting the mission of the Department of Defense overseas.

---

[13] *Id.* at paras. 5-76, 5-77.

[14] Military Extraterritorial Jurisdiction Act of 2000, Pub. L. No. 106-523, codified at 18 U.S.C. § 3261 *et seq.*

In addition, U.S. nationals who are not currently covered by MEJA are still subject to domestic prosecution for certain serious crimes committed overseas if the crime was committed within the special maritime and territorial jurisdiction of the United States defined in section 7 of title 18 (e.g., U.S. diplomatic and military missions overseas). These crimes include murder under section 1111 of title 18, assault under section 113, and sexual abuse under section 2241.

Finally, in 2006 the Uniform Code of Military Justice ("UCMJ") was amended so that it now includes within its scope of application, "[i]n time of declared war or a contingency operation, persons serving with or accompanying an armed force in the field."[3] This amendment broadens the coverage of the UCMJ to provide court-martial jurisdiction over these individuals not only during conflicts where the United States has issued a declaration of war, but also during certain other significant military operations.

*   *   *   *

(3) One-year follow-up report on U.S. implementation of Convention Against Torture

As discussed in Chapter 6.F., on July 25, 2007, the United States transmitted its response to specific recommendations as requested by the Committee Against Torture in its conclusions and recommendations in relation to the Second Periodic Report of the United States. *See also Digest 2005* at 341–71 (submission of Second Periodic Report) and *Digest 2006* at 403–21 and 1124–37 (U.S. meeting with Committee Against Torture on the report). The Committee's conclusions and recommendations are available as U.N. Doc. CAT/C/USA/CO/2 (July 25, 2006).

Excerpts follow from the 2007 U.S. follow-up report concerning certain issues related to military detainees. Other issues are discussed in Chapter 6.F. The full text of the U.S. response, including the declaration of Clint Williamson,

---

[3]   Uniform Code of Military Justice, Art. 2(a); 10 U.S.C. § 802(a).

Ambassador-at-Large for War Crimes Issues at the Department of State, is available at *www.state.gov/s/l/c8183.htm*.

---

*   *   *   *

Paragraph 16

Recommendation:

"The State party should register all persons it detains in any territory under its jurisdiction, as one measure to prevent acts of torture. Registration should contain the identity of the detainee, the date, time and place of the detention, the identity of the authority that detained the person, the ground for the detention, the date and time of admission to the detention facility and the state of health of the detainee upon admission and any changes thereto, the time and place of interrogations, with the names of all interrogators present, as well as the date and time of release or transfer to another detention facility."

Response:

As an initial matter it should be noted that the Convention Against Torture and other Cruel, Inhuman or Degrading Treatment or Punishment (hereinafter referred to as "the Convention") has no provision requiring the registration of prisoners.

Although there is no unified national policy governing the registry of persons detained in territory subject to the jurisdiction of the United States, relevant individual federal, state, and local authorities, including military authorities, as a matter of good administrative practice generally maintain appropriate records on persons detained by them.[2] Such records would generally include the information mentioned in the Committee's recommendation.

---

2 For further information on such records, *see* List of Issues to Be Examined During the Consideration of the Second Periodic Report of the United States of America—Response of the United States of America, *available at http://www.usmission.ch/Press2006/CAT-May5.pdf* at 13 (May 5, 2006) [hereinafter referred to as "Response to List of Issues"].

Paragraph 20

Recommendation:

"The State party should apply the *non-refoulement* guarantee to all detainees in its custody, cease the rendition of suspects, in particular by its intelligence agencies, to States where they face a real risk of torture, in order to comply with its obligations under article 3 of the Convention. The State party should always ensure that suspects have the possibility to challenge decisions of *refoulement*."

Response:

There are two issues that appear to be raised in this conclusion and recommendation. The first issue is the *evidentiary standard* that would trigger application of CAT Article 3. As the United States described to the Committee,[3] pursuant to a formal understanding the United States filed at the time it became a State Party to the Convention, the United States determines whether it is more likely than not that a person would be tortured, rather than whether a person faces a "real risk" of torture.

The second issue addresses the *territorial scope* of Article 3. Although the United States and the Committee hold differing views on the applicability of the non-refoulement obligation in Article 3 of the Convention outside the territory of a State Party, as the United States explained to the Committee at length,[4] with respect to persons outside the territory of the United States as a matter of policy, the United States government does not transfer persons to countries where it determines that it is more likely than not that they will be tortured. This policy applies to all components of the government, including the intelligence agencies.[5] Although there is no requirement under the Convention that individuals should have the possibility to challenge refoulement, United States practice in

---

[3]   *See, e.g.,* Second Periodic Report of the United States of America to the Committee Against Torture, *available at http://www.state.gov/g/drl/ rls/45738.htm* at ¶ 30 (May 6, 2005) [hereinafter referred to as "Second Periodic Report"]; Response to List of Issues at 37–38.

[4]   *See, e.g.,* Response to List of Issues, *supra* note 2, at 32–37.

[5]   *See id.* at 49.

the different areas in which this provision comes into play is designed to ensure that any torture concerns, whenever raised by the individual to be transferred, are taken into account. For example, in the context of immigration removals from the United States, as noted in the United States periodic report,[6] there are procedures for alleging torture concerns and procedures by which those claims can be advanced.

Paragraph 21

Recommendation:

"When determining the applicability of its non-refoulement obligations under article 3 of the Convention, the State party should only rely on "diplomatic assurances" in regard to States which do not systematically violate the Convention's provisions, and after a thorough examination of the merits of each individual case. The State party should establish and implement clear procedures for obtaining such assurances, with adequate judicial mechanisms for review, and effective post-return monitoring arrangements. The State party should also provide detailed information to the Committee on all cases since 11 September 2001 where assurances have been provided."

Response:

As explained to the Committee,[7] the United States undertakes a thorough, case-by-case analysis of each potential transfer where diplomatic assurances are involved. This analysis takes into account all relevant factors, including all available information about the compliance of the potential receiving state with its international obligations, including those under the Convention, and the merits of each individual case.

The United States would like to emphasize to the Committee, as it did on other occasions,[8] that diplomatic assurances are used sparingly but that assurances may be sought in order to be satisfied

---

[6] *See* Second Periodic Report, *supra* note 3, at ¶ 32–38; Response to List of Issues, *supra* note 2, at 27–30.

[7] *See, e.g.,* Second Periodic Report, *supra* note 3, at ¶ 30; Response to List of Issues, *supra* note 2, at 45–48.

[8] *See, e.g.,* Response to List of Issues, *supra* note 2, at 45.

that it is not "more likely than not" that the individual in question will be tortured upon return. It is important to note that diplomatic assurances are only a factor that may be considered in appropriate cases and are not used as a substitute for a case-specific assessment as to whether it is not more likely than not that a person will be tortured if returned.

Procedures for obtaining diplomatic assurances vary according to the context (e.g., extradition, immigration removal, or military custody transfer) and have been made available to the Committee.[9] For example, the United States report provides information regarding regulatory procedures for consideration of diplomatic assurances in the immigration removal context, which provide for the opportunity to allege torture and advance such claims.[10] In addition, attached in Annex 1 is a declaration by Clint Williamson, Ambassador-at-Large for War Crimes Issues at the Department of State, dated June 8, 2007, and filed in United States federal court. This declaration explains in detail the process for obtaining and considering diplomatic assurances for detainees to be transferred from Guantanamo. It supersedes the declaration by former Ambassador Pierre Prosper that was provided to the Committee as part of the Second Periodic Report.[11] For the Committee's information, [w]ith regard to post-return monitoring arrangements, the United States agrees that follow-up following return is important. Indeed, the United States has requested and obtained information about the situation of individuals who have been transferred to other countries subject to assurances. As explained to the Committee, the United States would pursue any credible report and take appropriate action if it had reason to believe that those assurances would not be, or had not been, honored.

The United States does not unilaterally make public the specific assurances provided to it by foreign governments. Reasons for this policy were articulated in the materials provided to the Committee,[12]

---

[9]   *See* Second Periodic Report, *supra* note 3, at ¶ 33 (immigration removal) and ¶ 40 (extradition); Annex I, Part One, Section II.E (military transfers).

[10]   *See* Second Periodic Report, *supra* note 3, at ¶ 33.

[11]   *See id.*, Annex I, Tab. 1.

[12]   *See id.*

including the fact that unilaterally making assurances public might make foreign governments reluctant in the future to communicate frankly with the United States concerning important concerns related to torture or mistreatment.

Paragraph 22

Recommendation:

"The State party should cease to detain any person at Guantánamo Bay and close this detention facility, permit access by the detainees to judicial process or release them as soon as possible, ensuring that they are not returned to any State where they could face a real risk of being tortured, in order to comply with its obligations under the Convention."

Response:

Among the actions purported by the Committee to be governed under the Convention—including, for example, (1) closing Guantanamo; (2) permitting judicial access by enemy combatant detainees in that facility; or (3) not returning individuals who face "a real risk" of being tortured—the first two lack an arguable textual basis in the Convention, while the third issue is discussed at length in materials provided to the Committee[13] as well as in the response to the Committee's recommendation in paragraph 20 above.

As the United States explained to the Committee,[14] the United States is in an armed conflict with al-Qaida, the Taliban, and their supporters. As part of this conflict, the United States captures and detains enemy combatants, and is entitled under the law of war to hold them until the end of hostilities. The law of war, and not the Convention, provides the applicable legal framework governing these detentions.

Without going into further detail about its legal disagreements with the Committee's sweeping legal assertions regarding the scope

---

[13] *See, e.g.,* Second Periodic Report, *supra* note 3, at ¶ 30; Response to List of Issues, *supra* note 2, at 37–38.

[14] *See, e.g.,* Second Periodic Report, *supra* note 2, Annex I, Part One, Section I.

of the Convention—which are addressed in other responses[15]—the United States has made it clear in many different settings that it does not want to be the world's jailer. Although the Committee calls for the closure of Guantanamo, it does not appear to take into account the consequences of releasing dangerous terrorist combatants detained there or explain where those who cannot be repatriated due to humane treatment concerns might be sent. The United States will continue to look to the international community for assistance with resettlement of those detainees approved for transfer or release.

The United States does permit access by Guantanamo detainees to judicial process. Every detainee in Guantanamo is evaluated by a Combatant Status Review Tribunal (CSRT), which determines whether the detainee was properly classified as an enemy combatant and includes a number of procedural guarantees. A CSRT decision can be directly appealed to a United States domestic civilian court, the Court of Appeals for the District of Columbia Circuit. Providing such an opportunity for judicial review exceeds the requirements of the law of war and is an unprecedented and expanded protection available to all detainees at Guantanamo. These procedural protections are more extensive than those applied by any other nation in any previous armed conflict to determine a combatant's status.

After a CSRT determination, each enemy combatant not charged by a Military Commission receives an annual review to determine whether the United States needs to continue detention. An Administrative Review Board (ARB) conducts this review.

Since the Committee's consideration of the United States report in May 2006, approximately 120 detainees have departed Guantanamo. This process is ongoing. Updates are available at *http://www.defenselink.mil/news/nrdgb.html*.

These transfers are a demonstration of the United States' desire not to hold detainees any longer than necessary. It also underscores the processes put in place to assess each individual and make a determination about their detention while hostilities are ongoing—an unprecedented step in the history of warfare.

---

[15] *See supra* at 2–3.

At present, approximately 375 detainees remain at Guantanamo, and approximately 405 have been released or transferred. The Department of Defense has determined—through its comprehensive review processes—that approximately 75 additional detainees are eligible for transfer or release. Departure of these detainees is subject to ongoing discussions between the United States and other nations.

Paragraph 24

Recommendation:

"The State party should rescind any interrogation technique, including methods involving sexual humiliation, "waterboarding", "short shackling" and using dogs to induce fear, that constitutes torture or cruel, inhuman or degrading treatment or punishment, in all places of detention under its de facto effective control, in order to comply with its obligations under the Convention."

Response:

As an initial matter, as the United States has informed the Committee,[16] the United States is in an armed conflict with al-Qaida, the Taliban, and their supporters. As part of this conflict, the United States captures and detains enemy combatants, and is entitled under the law of war to hold them until the end of hostilities. The law of war, and not the Convention, is the applicable legal framework governing these detentions. Moreover, as the Committee is aware,[17] the United States disagrees with the Committee's contention that "de facto effective control" is equivalent to territory subject to a State party's jurisdiction for the purposes of the Convention.

Leaving aside interpretive issues arising under the Convention, as a matter of United States law, there is a ban on torture of anyone under the custody or physical control of the United States Government. . . .*

* * * *

---

[16] *See, e.g.,* Second Periodic Report, *supra* note 3, Annex I, Part One, Section I.

[17] *See* Response to List of Issues, *supra* note 2, at 87.

* Editor's note: For more detailed discussion of this issue, *see* c.(2) *supra*.

d. Litigation in U.S. courts

(1) Guantanamo detainees

(i) Boumediene v. Bush

On February 20, 2007, the U.S. Court of Appeals for the District of Columbia Circuit dismissed for lack of jurisdiction consolidated cases brought by alien detainees held on Guantanamo seeking writs of habeas corpus. *Boumediene v. Bush*, 476 F.3d 981 (D.C. Cir. 2007). The D.C. Circuit in *Boumediene* had before it two decisions consolidated on appeal. In eleven detainee habeas cases, Judge Green of the U.S. District Court for the District of Columbia determined in January 2005 that "the petitioners have stated valid claims under the Fifth Amendment and that the [Combatant Status Review Tribunal] procedures are unconstitutional for failing to comport with the requirements of due process." Judge Green found further that "Taliban fighters who have not been specifically determined to be excluded from prisoner of war status by a competent Article 5 tribunal have also stated valid claims under the Third Geneva Convention." *Guantanamo Detainee Cases*, 355 F. Supp. 2d 443 (D.D.C. 2005); *see Digest 2005* at 995–1008. In two other detainee habeas cases, including *Boumediene*, Judge Leon of the same court, also in January 2005, concluded that "no viable legal theory exits by which [the court] could issue a writ of habeas corpus" under the circumstances presented by the case. *Khalid v. Bush*, 355 F. Supp. 2d 311 (D.D.C. 2005); *see Digest 2005* at 1008–16.

In June 2006 the Supreme Court ruled that the procedures for the military commissions established to try Guantanamo detainees accused of crimes violated the requirements of the Uniform Code of Military Justice and Common Article 3 of the Geneva Conventions, *Hamdan v. Rumsfeld*, 548 U.S. 557 (2006). In 2004 the Supreme Court had ruled that the U.S. habeas statute applied to the detainees at Guantanamo and that the detainees could bring habeas petitions in

U.S. courts. *Rasul v. Bush*, 542 U.S. 466 (2004). *See Digest 2006* at 1138–55; *Digest 2004* at 995–1001.

In response to the *Hamdan* decision, on October 27, 2006, Congress enacted the Military Commissions Act ("MCA"), Pub. L. No. 109-366, 120 Stat. 2600 (2006). *See Digest 2006* at 1168–77. On October 18, 2006, the D.C. Circuit granted leave to the parties to file supplemental briefs on the significance of the MCA in the pending appeal. *See* U.S. Supplemental Reply Brief Addressing the Military Commissions Act, *Digest 2006* at 1179–83.

In its February 20, 2007 decision, the D.C. Circuit concluded that "[f]ederal courts have no jurisdiction in these cases" because (1) the MCA amendment to the habeas corpus statute precluded jurisdiction over the habeas petitions at issue, filed by aliens held on Guantanamo and (2) the MCA does not violate the Suspension Clause of the Constitution because the writ of habeas corpus would not have been available at the time of the Constitution to aliens without presence or property in the United States and, as aliens outside U.S. sovereign territory, the detainees have no constitutional rights under the Suspension Clause. The court also rejected a request by the United States to treat the habeas appeals as requests for review of the merits under the Detainee Treatment Act, finding that "even if [the court had] authority to convert the habeas appeals over the petitioners' objections, the record does not have sufficient information to perform the review the DTA allows. Our only recourse is to vacate the district courts' decisions and dismiss the cases for lack of jurisdiction."

Following an initial denial of a petition for certiorari to the D.C. Circuit on April 2, 2007, 127 S. Ct. 1478 (2007), the Supreme Court on rehearing granted certiorari on June 29. 127 S. Ct. 3067 and 3078 (2007). The Supreme Court heard arguments in the case on December 5, 2007, and a decision was pending at the end of the year.*

---

  * Editor's note: On June 12, 2008, as this volume of the *Digest* was going to press, the Supreme Court reversed the D.C. Circuit, holding that

The United States filed its brief in the Supreme Court in support of affirmance of the D.C. Circuit court decision in October 2007. In its brief the United States argued that "protection afforded by the Suspension Clause does not extend to overseas detentions of aliens in the first place," that the common law writ in 1789 extended only to sovereign territory and did not make habeas available to enemy combatants, and that "[p]etitioners, along with the other enemy combatants being held at Guantanamo Bay, enjoy more procedural protections than any other captured enemy combatants in the history of warfare." Thus, "even if petitioners could show a historical precedent for habeas corpus in the extraordinary circumstances here, Congress has afforded them a constitutionally adequate substitute for challenging their detention." As to the merits, the United States argued:

> . . . [I]f the Court does review the merits of petitioners' detention in this case, it should hold that their detention is lawful. Congress has authorized the President to use "all necessary and appropriate force" against those "organizations" that "he determines" committed the terrorist attacks of September 11, 2001. Al Qaeda is such an organization, and this Court squarely held in *Hamdi* that detention is part and parcel of the force authorized by Congress. *See* 542 U.S. at 518 (plurality opinion). Petitioners are properly detained because they have been determined by a military tribunal to be "part of or supporting Taliban or al Qaida forces." Petitioners may challenge that determination under the procedures authorized by Congress, but they have provided no basis for upsetting that determination at this preliminary stage.

---

petitioners had a constitutional right to habeas review and that the DTA did not provide an adequate substitute. The court stated that it did not address "whether the President has authority to detain these petitioners nor do we hold that the writ must issue. These and other questions regarding the legality of the detention are to be resolved [on remand] in the first instance by the District Court." 2008 U.S. LEXIS 4887 (2008). Relevant aspects of the Supreme Court decision will be discussed in *Digest 2008*.

Excerpts from the U.S. brief addressing the basis for detention follow. The full text of the brief is available at 2007 U.S. S. Ct. Briefs LEXIS 1280. (Footnotes and citations to the Appendix have been omitted.)

---

*   *   *   *

II. PETITIONERS' DETENTION IS LAWFUL

A. The AUMF Authorizes The Detention of Enemy Combatants As Defined By The CSRT Process Petitioners argue that the AUMF does not authorize their detention. That argument rests on a misreading of the AUMF, is directly contradicted by this Court's construction of the AUMF in *Hamdi,* and misunderstands the law of armed conflict.

*   *   *   *

. . . [P]etitioners assert that "support" for al Qaeda or the Taliban is not sufficient to authorize detention; instead, to be properly detained, an individual must "take a direct part in hostilities." Br. 39 (citations omitted). In support of that claim, they rely on *Hamdi,* which upheld the President's authority to detain individuals who were "part of or supporting forces hostile to the United States" and who had themselves "engaged in an armed conflict against the United States." 542 U.S. at 516 (plurality opinion). Nothing in *Hamdi* even remotely suggests, however, that the AUMF encompasses *only* those individuals.

Nor does the law of armed conflict suggest such an implied limitation. To the contrary, the laws of war—including the Geneva Convention—have long permitted the detention of members or supporters of hostile forces. See, *e.g.,* [W. Winthrop, *Military Law and Precedents* 789 (2d ed. 1920)] ("class of persons" subject to detention includes "civil persons * * * in immediate connection with an army, such as clerks, telegraphists, aeronauts, teamsters, laborers, messengers, guides, scouts, and men employed on transports and military railways"); Adjutant Gen.'s Off., War Dep't, *General Orders No. 100, Instructions for the Government of Armies of the United States in the Field,* 7 (1863) (Art. 15) ("Military necessity * * * allows of the capturing" of "every armed enemy" and, in addition, "every enemy of importance to the hostile government, or of peculiar danger to the captor."); J. Baker & H. Crocker, *The Laws of Land Warfare Concerning the Rights and Duties of Belligerents as Existing on August 1, 1914*, at 35 (1919) ("Persons belonging to the auxiliary departments of an army * * * such as commissariat employees, military police, guides, balloonists, messengers, and telegraphists * * * are still liable to capture."); Geneva Convention Art. 4(A)(4), 6 U.S.T. at 3320, 75 U.N.T.S. at 138 (prisoners of war include "[p]ersons who accompany the armed forces without actually being members thereof, such as * * * war correspondents, supply contractors, members of labour units or of services responsible for the welfare of the armed forces"); *id.* Art. 33, 6 U.S.T. at 3344, 75 U.N.T.S. at 162 (permitting the retention of "medical personnel and chaplains").

Thus, the laws of war allow for detention not only of uniformed members of an armed force, but also of those persons supporting the enemy. See *Eisentrager,* 339 U.S. at 765 (noting petitioners' allegation that "their employment * * * was by civilian agencies of the German Government" but concluding that their "exact affiliation is * * * for our purposes immaterial"); *Miller,* 78 U.S. (11 Wall.) at 312 ("[N]o recognized usage of nations excludes from the category of enemies those who act with, or aid or abet and give comfort to enemies, whether foreign or domestic."). That rule has always been sensible; today, it is essential. Congress has authorized a war against an international terrorist organization with no uniformed soldiers, and the detention of its members and supporters is a critical component of any such war.

Petitioners cite certain rules of engagement governing the targeting of civilians in war zones for violent attack. But the capture and detention of enemy combatants is a fundamental incident of warfare. Thus, as petitioners concede, the military may clearly detain an enemy soldier even in circumstances where the use of deadly force might not be appropriate because, for example, he has surrendered. Likewise, if a member or supporter of al Qaeda is not brandishing a weapon, the rules of engagement might preclude the use of lethal force against that person, but they do not bar his detention as an enemy.

Ultimately, much of petitioners' argument rests on the flawed premise that they are "civilians." But a member or supporter of an entity engaged in armed conflict against the United States is not, in any relevant sense, a "civilian." Al Qaeda is unquestionably such an entity—as recognized by Congress, see AUMF § 2(a), 115 Stat. 224; the President, see *Military Order of Nov. 13, 2001,* 3 C.F.R. 918 (2001); America's allies, see, *e.g.,* Statement of Lord Robertson, NATO Sec'y Gen. (Oct. 2, 2001) <http://www.nato.int/docu/speech/2001/s011002a.htm> (describing the September 11 attack as an "armed attack" under Article 5 of the North Atlantic Treaty, Apr. 4, 1949, 63 Stat. 2241, 2244, 34 U.N.T.S. 243, 246); and al Qaeda itself, see, *e.g.,* World Islamic Front, *Jihad Against Jews and Crusaders* (Feb. 23, 1998) <http://www.fas.org/irp/world/para/docs/980223-fatwa.htm>. The AUMF plainly authorizes petitioners' detentions.

*   *   *   *

(ii) Bismullah v. Gates

In granting the petition for writ of certiorari in *Boumediene v. Bush supra,* the Supreme Court noted that "it would be of material assistance to consult any decision in *Bismullah, et al. v. Gates,* No. 06-1197, and *Parhat, et al., v. Gates,* No. 06-1397, currently pending in the United States Court of Appeals for the District of Columbia Circuit. . . ." 127 S. Ct. 3078 (2007). Those cases, consolidated in the D.C. Circuit, concern the scope of the record from a determination of enemy combatant status by a Combatant Status Review Tribunal ("CSRT") on review by the D. C. Circuit pursuant to § 1005(e)(2)(A) of the Detainee Treatment Act, Pub. L. No. 109-148, Title X (2005).

On July 20, 2007, the D.C. Circuit issued an opinion and order addressing procedural motions filed by the United States and petitioners. 501 F.3d 178 (D.C. Cir. 2007) (*"Bismullah I"*). On October 3, 2007, the D. C. Circuit denied a U.S. petition for rehearing or rehearing en banc. 503 F.3d 137 (D.C. Cir. 2007). The court explained that the petition for rehearing addressed "two distinct aspects of *Bismullah I*: the scope of the record on review before the court; and the extent to which the Government must disclose that record to the petitioners' counsel."[*]

(2) Detainees held at Bagram Air Force Base in Afghanistan: Ruzatullah v. Gates

During 2007 the U.S. District Court for the District of Columbia examined two cases concerning alien detainees held in the U.S. detention facility at Bagram Air Force Base in Afghanistan. *Ruzatullah v. Gates*, No. 06-CV-01707 (GK). On April 20, 2007, the United States filed its Reply to Petitioners' Reply and Opposition to Respondents' Motion to Dismiss the Second Amended Petition. The United States argued that

> ... In their opening brief, [U.S.] respondents demonstrated that this Court has no jurisdiction to hear the present habeas petition because the petition, filed by two alien enemy combatants detained at Bagram Airfield in Afghanistan, falls squarely within the jurisdiction-limiting provision of the Military Commissions Act of 2006 ("MCA"), Pub. L. No. 109-366, 120 Stat. 2600 (2006). Respondents also demonstrated that petitioners do not have a constitutional right to habeas relief because under *Johnson v. Eisentrager*, 339 U.S. 763 (1950), aliens detained abroad, such as petitioners, who have no significant voluntary connections with this country, cannot invoke protections under the Constitution.

In its April submission, the United States noted the D.C. Circuit's decision in *Boumediene v. Bush*, discussed in d.(1)(i) *supra*, confirming these arguments as to detainees on Guantanamo. The United States also argued that even the holding in *Rasul v. Bush* finding habeas jurisdiction under the habeas statute as it then existed for aliens held on Guantanamo

---

[*]   On June 23, 2008, as this volume of the *Digest* was going to press, the Supreme Court granted certiorari and vacated and remanded *Bismullah I* to the D.C. Circuit "for further consideration in light of *Boumediene v. Bush*." *Gates v. Bismullah*, 2008 U.S. LEXIS 5081 (2008).

would not be applicable to these cases because of the differences between Bagram and Guantanamo. That section of the U.S. response is excerpted below (citations to other submissions in the case omitted); the full text is available at *www.state.gov/s/l/c8183.htm.*

---

*   *   *   *

B. The Degree of the United States' Control Over Bagram Airfield Does Not Affect the Interpretation of the Habeas Statute Both Before and After the Statute's Amendment.

In their opening brief, respondents showed that even had Congress not amended the federal habeas statute, the logic of the Supreme Court's decision in *Rasul* would not extend to Bagram. Unlike Cuba, which has expressly consented to the United States' "complete jurisdiction and control" over Guantanamo, *see Rasul*, 542 U.S. at 471, the Government of Afghanistan has made no similar concession regarding Bagram. In response, petitioners maintain that *Rasul* is controlling on the statutory question because the United States' control over Bagram Airfield is similar, if not greater, than its control over Guantanamo. According to petitioners, as to both Bagram and Guantanamo, the host nation exercises no legal jurisdiction over the base, nor has the host nation entered into a Status of Force Agreement ("SOFA") with the United States.

Petitioners are wrong. First, their arguments rest on the false premise that the MCA's jurisdiction-limiting provision is inapplicable to them because they allegedly have not been determined by the United States to be properly detained as enemy combatants. In fact, the United States has made such a determination, and the plain language of the amended habeas statute precludes this Court's jurisdiction, wherever petitioners may be detained. *See* MCA § 7. Given that the MCA clearly applies here and that it is also intended to overrule *Rasul* even as to Guantanamo, this Court need not, and should not, reach the issue of the United States' control over Bagram, nor can petitioners advance their case by arguing that Bagram is just like Guantanamo.

Second, even if the United States had not determined petitioners to be enemy combatants, the pre-amended habeas statute was not intended to be, nor has it ever been, extended beyond the United States, except in the unique circumstance of Guantanamo. Bagram is not like Guantanamo, however, other than that neither is a sovereign territory of the United States. The United States' presence at Bagram Airfield is necessitated by the war against al Qaeda, the Taliban, and their affiliates and supporters. *See* Miller Decl. ¶ 4; Letter from the President to the Speaker of the House of Representatives and the President Pro Tempore of the Senate (Sept. 19, 2003), *available at* http://www.whitehouse.gov/news/releases/2003/09/20030919-1.html. The United States began combat efforts in Afghanistan in October 2001, and the military continues to fight in this area. As a result of the United States' presence in the area, and contrary to petitioners' representation, the United States did execute a SOFA in 2002 with the Government of Afghanistan regarding the United States' activities in Afghanistan, including Bagram Airfield. *See* Diplomatic Note 202, attached hereto as Exhibit 4. The agreement, effected through an exchange of diplomatic notes, recognizes that United States personnel "may be present in Afghanistan in connection with cooperative efforts in response to terrorism, humanitarian and civic assistance, military training and exercises, and other activities." *Id.* at 1. The agreement further ensures, among other things, that such personnel be accorded a status equivalent to that accorded to American embassy administrative and technical staff. *See id.* Importantly, under the SOFA, the United States' jurisdiction in Afghanistan extends only to U.S. personnel:

> The Government of Afghanistan recognizes the particular importance of disciplinary control by United States military authorities over United States personnel and, therefore, Afghanistan authorizes the United States Government to exercise criminal jurisdiction over United States personnel. The Government of Afghanistan and the Government of the United States of America confirm that such personnel may not be surrendered to, or otherwise transferred to, the custody of an international tribunal or any other entity or state without the express consent of the Government of the United States.

Id. at 3. In other words, common crimes committed by Afghan citizens at Bagram would be prosecuted by the Government of

Afghanistan, not the United States, and the Government of Afghanistan in that respect has legal jurisdiction over Bagram.

The lease agreement between the two governments regarding Bagram Airfield is not to the contrary. Far from granting the United States "complete jurisdiction and control" as is the case in Guantanamo, the Bagram lease is silent about U.S. jurisdiction over the Airfield. While the lease speaks in terms of "exclusive use" and "exclusive, peaceable, undisturbed and uninterrupted possession" of the premises and gives the United States the right to assign the lease, Miller Decl. Ex., 1 at ¶¶ 1, 9, that is no different from an ordinary commercial lease. The lease simply does not give the United States jurisdiction over the Airfield because the issue of jurisdiction is governed by the SOFA. What the lease does warrant is that the Government of Afghanistan "is the sole owner of the Premises and/or has the right, without any restrictions, to grant the use of the Premises" to the United States. *See* Miller Decl., Ex. 1 at ¶ 8. Indeed, consistent with that ownership, the Government of Afghanistan agrees that all claims arising out of the United States' possession of the premises may be directed to the Government of Afghanistan for processing and payment, if any. *See id.*

As for petitioners' protestation that "Bagram is not a battlefield and the United States does not treat Bagram as a temporary, battlefield facility," it is indisputable that Bagram is located in a theater of active military operations, even if the Airfield itself is secured by U.S. and multinational forces. That petitioners and other enemy combatants captured in Afghanistan (and allegedly elsewhere) have been detained there long term is due to the fact that the war is on-going and the detention is necessary for reasons of military necessity. As explained in Colonel Miller's declaration,

> The detention of these enemy combatants [at Bagram] prevents them from returning to the battlefield and engaging in further armed attacks against innocent civilians and U.S. and coalition forces. Detention also serves as a deterrent against future attacks by denying the enemy the fighters needed to conduct war. Interrogations during detention enable the United States to gather important intelligence to prevent future attacks.

See Miller Decl. ¶ 8; *see also Hamdi v. Rumsfeld*, 542 U.S. 507, 531 (2004) (noting the "weighty and sensitive governmental interests in ensuring that those who have in fact fought with the enemy during a war do not return to battle against the United States;" and "[t]he purpose of detention is to prevent captured individuals from returning to the field of battle and taking up arms once again").

*   *   *   *

(i) Mootness

On July 6, 2007, the United States informed the court that it had relinquished custody of Ruzatullah and transferred him to the custody and control of the Government of Afghanistan. Respondents' Supplement to Motion to Dismiss, with attached declarations, is available at *www.state.gov/s/l/c8183.htm*. "Because Ruzatullah is no longer within the legal or physical custody of the United States, there is no case or controversy before this Court regarding him," and therefore, the United States argued, "his petition should be dismissed as moot."

On September 5, 2007, the United States responded to Ruzatullah's argument that the United States might have constructive custody of him, as excerpted below. The full text of the U.S. reply in support of its motion to dismiss is available in full at *www.state.gov/s/lc/8183.htm*.

_____

*   *   *   *

I. THE UNITED STATES DOES NOT HAVE CONSTRUCTIVE CUSTODY OF PETITIONER RUZATULLAH

The federal habeas statute confers jurisdiction on the district courts if, among other things, the habeas petitioner is "in custody under or by the color of the authority of the United States." 28 U.S.C. § 2241(c). Even if this provision is applicable to petitioner, which it is not, petitioner cannot meet this standard because he is in the exclusive custody and control of the [Islamic Republic of Afghanistan ("IRoA")] and the United States does not have constructive custody over him. "A [habeas petitioner] is in the constructive custody of the United States when he is in the actual, physical custody of some person or entity who cannot be deemed the United States, but is being held under the authority of the United States or on its behalf." *Mohammed v. Harvey*, 456 F. Supp. 2d 115, 122 (D.D.C. 2006). Clearly, the United States has no authority over the IRoA, which is a foreign sovereign.

Nor is the IRoA's detention of petitioner at the behest, or under the ongoing supervision, of the United States. The U.S. military's presence in Afghanistan is to "establish security, deter the re-emergenc[e] of terrorism, and enhance the sovereignty of Afghanistan." *See* Declaration of Rose M. Miller ["Miller Decl."], ¶ 2 . Consistent with that mission and pursuant to diplomatic arrangements reached with the IRoA, the United States expects to transfer a significant percentage of the Afghan detainees at Bagram Airfield to the exclusive custody and control of the IRoA. *Id.* ¶ 15. The IRoA, in turn, has provided assurances that it would treat individuals transferred to its custody, such as Ruzatuallh, humanely and in accordance with the laws and international obligations of the IRoA. *See* Declaration of Colonel Anthony Zabek (attached hereto), ¶ 4. It also agrees to accept responsibility for ensuring, consistent with its laws, that the detainees will not pose a continued threat to the United States and its allies. *Id.* The implementation and enforcement of any specific measure, however, is committed to the IRoA's exclusive discretion and not within the control of the United States. *Id.*

Thus, as the attached declaration of Colonel Anthony Zabek demonstrates, the release, continued detention, and/or prosecution of the transferred detainees is within the IRoA's exclusive control. *Id.* ¶ 5. The Afghan Detainee Review Board, which is led by the Afghan Office of the National Security Council under the exclusive jurisdiction and control of the IRoA, is the entity charged with determining whether to release a detainee. *Id.* Specifically, the Board will release a detainee from the [Afghan National Detention Center in Pol-e-Charki ("ANDF")] if it determines that such release is appropriate under Afghan law. *Id.* For example, on 16 August 2007, a detainee the United States had recently transferred to the IRoA was released after it concluded there was insufficient evidence to prosecute the detainee under Afghan law. *Id.* The United States has no control over any of the Board's decisions. *Id.*

Petitioner Ruzatullah was transferred pursuant to the process described above, and the IRoA is detaining him at the ANDF pursuant to Afghan law. *Id.* ¶ 6. His future status is a matter within the sole discretion of the IRoA and the processes that exist under Afghan law. *Id.* The United States retains no control over his current detention or future status, and thus, does not have constructive custody of him. As for petitioner's speculation that the ANDF is operated by the United States military, he is wrong. The ANDF is the former block IV of the Pol-e-Charki prison. *Id.* ¶ 2. Pursuant to a diplomatic arrangement with the IRoA, the United States refurbished the ANDF in order to facilitate the transfer of Afghan detainees and to ensure an Afghan detention capability that meets international standards. *See* Miller Decl. ¶ 15. The ANDF, however, is owned by the IRoA, controlled by the Afghan Ministry of Defense, and operated by the Afghan National Guard Force. . . . Thus, petitioner's argument that he is in the constructive custody of the United States because of U.S. Military presence at the ANDF has no merit.

* * * *

(ii) Thirty-day notice

On August 10, 2007, a second detainee in *Ruzatullah*, Haji Rohullah, filed a motion for an order requiring the United States to provide 30 days' advance notice of any proposed transfer from Bagram. The United States filed its opposition to the motion on August 24, 2007. The United States argued (1) that the motion should be denied because the court had no power to grant the requested relief since it lacks subject matter jurisdiction over the petitioner's case for the reasons set forth in the April 20 submission *supra*, and (2) that despite the fact that in the interim the Supreme Court had granted certiorari in *Boumediene,* the D.C. Circuit opinion remained binding law of the Circuit and precluded a grant of the petitioner's motion. In addition, the U.S. submission argued:

. . . Even if the Supreme Court were to reverse the Court of Appeals' holding that section 7 of the MCA eliminates federal jurisdiction over petitions for habeas corpus by alien enemy combatants, another aspect of the MCA would nevertheless preclude this Court from granting an order enjoining a transfer of petitioner from Bagram absent prior notice. A holding by the Supreme Court in *Boumediene* that the MCA's removal of federal court jurisdiction over alien enemy combatants' habeas petitions is unconstitutional would not affect the independent provision of the MCA which expressly bars any claims by such aliens regarding, inter alia, transfer. *Compare* 28 U.S.C. § 2241(e)(1) (added by MCA 7(a)) ("No court, justice, or judge shall have jurisdiction to hear or consider an application for a writ of habeas corpus filed by or on behalf of an alien detained by the United States who has been determined by the United States to have been properly detained as an enemy combatant or is awaiting such determination.") *with* 28 U.S.C. § 2241(e)(2) (added by MCA 7(a)) ("[with the exception of Detainee Treatment Act proceedings initiated in the Court of Appeals,] no court, justice, or judge shall have jurisdiction to hear or consider *any other action* against the United States or its agents relating to any aspect of the detention, *transfer*, treatment, trial, or conditions of confinement [of alien enemy combatant detained by the United States]") (emphasis added). Separate from the question of whether petitioner's habeas case could proceed, therefore, the MCA expressly prohibits this Court from granting an injunction in connection with a transfer of petitioner. Thus, while affirmance of *Boumediene* would constitute validation of even the aspect of the MCA under which district courts lack jurisdiction over habeas claims asserted by alien enemy combatants, reversal of that decision would not constitute a holding as to the legitimacy or applicability of the MCA provision denying district court jurisdiction over those detainees' transfer claims.

The United States also argued that Rohulla's alleged potential irreparable harm, the basis for his request for notice "is speculative at best, and therefore insufficient to warrant preliminary relief." Excerpts examining the balancing of interests follow. The full text of the August submission is available at *www.state.gov/s/l/c8183.htm*.

————

*   *   *   *

Here, petitioner is a citizen of Afghanistan, who was captured in Afghanistan and has been detained on Afghan soil. *See* Gray Decl. ¶ 5. His potential transfer to his own government, whether for release or for detention and prosecution under Afghan law, clearly is beyond the purview of this Court. *See Worldwide Minerals, Ltd. v. Republic of Kazakhstan*, 296 F.3d 1154, 1164–65 (D.C. Cir. 2002) ("The act of state doctrine precludes the courts of this country from inquiring into the validity of the public acts of a recognized foreign sovereign power committed within its own territory.") (internal quotation marks and citation omitted). *Cf., e.g., Matter of Requested Extradition of Smyth*, 61 F.3d 711, 714 (9th Cir. 1995) (discussing "rule of noninquiry" which has to do with "the notion that courts are ill-equipped as institutions and ill-advised as a matter of separation of powers and foreign relations policy to make inquiries into and pronouncements about the workings of foreign countries' justice systems"). This is particularly so because such transfers implicate not only the Executive's conduct in foreign relations, but also the additional, weighty concern of the Executive's war-making powers. And "[w]ithout doubt, our Constitution recognizes that core strategic matters of war-making belong in the hands of those who are best positioned and most politically accountable for making them." *See Hamdi v. Rumsfeld*, 542 U.S. 507, 531 (2004) (plurality opinion). There is also "no doubt that decision-making in the fields of foreign policy and national security is textually committed to the political branches of the government." *Schneider*, 412 F.3d at 194. *See also Joo v. Japan*, 413 F.3d 45, 52–53 (D.C. Cir. 2005) (adjudication that "would undo" Executive's judgment in foreign policy "would be imprudent to a degree beyond our power"); *Schneider v. Kissinger*, 412 F.3d 190, 197 (D.C. Cir. 2005) ("pass[ing] judgment on the policy-based decision of the executive" in foreign policy "is not the stuff of adjudication").

The potential harm to the public and the United States if an order is entered to prohibit the Government from transferring a Bagram detainee absent 30 days' advance notice is sufficient to tip the scale against issuance of the injunction. As respondents have discussed in their motion to dismiss, the United States' presence in Afghanistan was necessitated by its ongoing war against al Qaeda, the Taliban and their affiliates and supporters. *See* Miller Decl. ¶ 4. The mission of the U.S. military in Afghanistan is to join with multinational forces and the Afghans to "establish security, deter the re-emergenc[e] of terrorism, and enhance the sovereignty of Afghanistan." *Id.* ¶ 2. While the United States has detained some Afghan citizens at Bagram so as to prevent those enemy combatants from returning to the battlefield, *see id.* ¶ 8, the United States has no interest in detaining them indefinitely. Thus, as the respondents noted in their motion to dismiss, the United States has transferred some Afghan detainees at Bagram to the Government of Afghanistan pursuant to a national reconciliation program, which is designed to allow combatants who are ready to put down their weapons to join in their country's progress by living peaceful and productive lives. . . . Those detainees are returned by the Government of Afghanistan to their village elders for reintegration into society. *Id.*

Moreover, pursuant to a diplomatic arrangement reached with the Government of Afghanistan, the United States expects to transfer a significant percentage of the Afghan detainees at Bagram to the Government of Afghanistan. *See id.* at 8. And, as noted before, pursuant to that arrangement, the United States funded the renovation of the Afghan National Detention Center and is providing other aid to the Government of Afghanistan regarding the operation of that prison, both to facilitate these transfers and to ensure that the detention facility would meet international standards. *See* Miller Decl. ¶ 8.

The harm stemming from an order conditioning the transfer of Afghan detainees at Bagram is twofold. First, the injunction would undermine the President's constitutional authority as Commander-in-Chief to capture individuals in armed conflict, detain them as enemy combatants, and upon determining that their release or transfer to another country is otherwise appropriate, to so transfer or release them. . . .

Second, the injunction would infringe on the President's power to conduct foreign relations. If the Court were to place conditions on repatriation or removal of Afghan citizens from Bagram, it would insert itself into the most sensitive of diplomatic matters and undermine the Government's ability to interact effectively with the Government of Afghanistan. This is particularly true in light of the existing United States' military presence in Afghanistan and its diplomatic arrangements with the Government of Afghanistan, including any cooperative efforts in the military campaign to establish security, deter the re-emergence of terrorism, and enhance the sovereignty of Afghanistan. At the very least, the very prospect of judicial review, exemplified by an advance notice requirement, would undermine the ability of the Executive Branch to speak with one voice in its dealings with that country. *See Crosby v. National Foreign Trade Council*, 530 U.S. 363, 381 (2000) (expressing disapproval of acts that "compromise the very capacity of the President to speak for the nation with one voice in dealing with other governments"). An advance notice requirement, after all, would make the results of diplomatic dialogue between the Executive Branch and a foreign government regarding repatriations or transfers inherently contingent because the effective acquiescence of another Branch (i.e., the Judiciary) would be required for the transfer or repatriation to be effected. This type of intrusion clearly would pose significant harm to the public interest. As one Judge of this Court has held:

> [T]here is a strong public interest against the judiciary needlessly intruding upon the foreign policy and war powers of the Executive on a deficient factual record. Where the conduct of the Executive conforms to law, there is simply no benefit—and quite a bit of detriment—to the public interest from the Court nonetheless assuming for itself the role of a guardian ad litem for the disposition of these detainees. *See People's Mojahedin Org. v. Dep't of State*, 182 F.3d 17, 23 (D.C. Cir. 1999) ("[I]t is beyond the judicial function for a court to review foreign policy decisions of the Executive Branch.").

Al-Anazi v. Bush, 370 F. Supp. 2d 188, 199 (D.D.C. 2005) (Bates, J.).

On October 2, 2007, the court granted Rohullah's motion
for 30 days' advance notice. The court's unpublished opinion
is excerpted below. The full text is available at *www.state.
gov/s/l/c8183.htm*.

* * * *

On July 7, 2007, the Government informed the Court that it had
transferred Ruzatullah from Bagram to a national security wing
of Policharky Prison outside of Kabul, Afghanistan, where the
Government asserts he is under the custody of the Afghan Government.[1] Rohullah alleges that at least 56 detainees have been transferred from Bagram to Policharky since the national security wing
opened in April 2007. He argues that the recent transfer of
Ruzatullah and others indicates a significant risk that he also will
be transferred to Policharky.

If Rohullah is transferred, his habeas claim may be eliminated.
See Al Marri v. Bush, No. 04-2035, 2005 U.S. Dist. LEXIS 6259,
at *13 (D.D.C. Apr. 4, 2005) (noting that "it is unclear at this
point whether transferring [the detainee] would strip this Court of
jurisdiction."). Since the dissolution of the Afghan National Security
Court, it is possible that no other court in that country would have
jurisdiction to hear his claims. Apart from the potential consequences
of transfer to his legal claims, Rohullah has also presented evidence
that he would face a serious threat of torture in Policharky. . . .

On June 29, 2007, the Supreme Court granted certiorari to review
the merits of our Court of Appeals' decision in *Boumediene v. Bush*,
476 F.3d 981 (D.C. Cir. 2007) ("*Boumediene*"). *Boumediene v.
Bush*, 127 S. Ct. 3078, 2007 WL 1854132 (2007); *Al Odah v.
United States*, 127 S. Ct. 3067, 2007 WL 681992 (2007). The
petitions for certiorari challenge, inter alia, the Court of Appeals'
decision that aliens captured or detained by the United States
outside of the United States do not have a constitutional or common law right to challenge their detentions via habeas corpus

---

[1] Petitioners argue that although Ruzatullah has been transferred to an
Afghan prison, he remains under the United States' constructive custody.

petitions. . . . The resolution of that question is likely to directly affect the outcome of the instant case.

*   *   *   *

It is well-settled that this Court has jurisdiction to determine its own habeas jurisdiction. *See Hamdan v. Rumsfeld*, 126 S. Ct. 2749 (2006); *Rasul v. Bush*, 542 U.S. 466 (2004);. . . .

Respondents' Opposition emphasizes the consequences of an injunction against transfer, which it characterizes as "an injunction barring the Executive from acting in spheres in which it has been vested by the Constitution to act." The relief Rohullah seeks in this Motion, however, is much narrower. He requests only an order requiring Respondents to provide notice of a potential transfer. Therefore, there is no need to address Respondents' legal arguments at this time.

Nor does the fact that Rohullah is incarcerated at Bagram, not Guantanamo, require denial of the Motion. The Court cannot predict the Supreme Court's resolution of the jurisdictional issues raised in its review of *Boumediene*. "[T]he Supreme Court could issue a broad[] decision in favor of the detainees, one whose reasoning applies not just to Guantanamo, but to Bagram and other locations as well." *Al Maqaleh*, 2007 WL 2059128, at *1.

*   *   *   *

(3) Multinational Force-Iraq detainees: Challenges to transfers to Iraqi government

During 2007 the U.S. Court of Appeals for the District of Columbia Circuit affirmed decisions in two cases considering jurisdiction over petitions for writs of habeas corpus brought by U.S. citizens being held by the Multinational Force-Iraq ("MNF-I") in Iraq. MNF-I was established pursuant to UN Security Council Resolutions 1546 and 1637. In *Omar v. Harvey*, 479 F.3d 1 (D.C. Cir. 2007), the court of appeals affirmed the district court's holding that it had jurisdiction for purposes of granting a preliminary injunction against transfer to Iraqi custody. In *Munaf v. Geren*, 482 F.3d 582 (D.C. Cir. 2007),[*] the court of appeals affirmed the district court's ruling that it had no habeas jurisdiction, on the alternative grounds that his conviction by an Iraqi court deprived the federal courts of jurisdiction. The district court opinions and background of the cases are discussed in *Digest 2006* at 1194–213.

On December 7, 2007, the Supreme Court granted certiorari in both cases and consolidated them. *Geren v. Omar*, and *Munaf v. Geren*, 128 S. Ct. 741 (2007).[**]

(i) Omar v. Harvey

In *Omar v. Harvey*, 479 F.3d 1 (2007), the D. C. Circuit affirmed a district court order granting a preliminary injunction enjoining the transfer of Shawqi Omar, a dual American-Jordanian citizen, from Camp Cropper, a detainee facility operated by the MNF-I in Iraq, to the custody of the Government of Iraq for possible prosecution for criminal offenses committed in Iraq. 416 F. Supp. 2d 19 (D.D.C. 2006); *see Digest 2006* at 1195–204. In issuing the preliminary injunction, the lower court stated that the jurisdictional issue would be revisited in a later stage of the litigation.

In its opinion, excerpted below, the D.C. Circuit held that

> . . . [N]either *Hirota* [*v. MacArthur*, 338 U.S. 197 (1948)] nor the political question doctrine deprives the district court of jurisdiction to entertain Omar's petition for a writ of habeas corpus. Because transfer would not afford Omar all the relief

---

[*] Editor's note: Prior to the decision in *Munaf*, Pete Geren, Acting Secretary of the U.S. Army, was substituted for Secretary of the Army Francis J. Harvey in the two cases.

[**] Editor's note: On June 12, 2008, as this volume of the *Digest* was going to press, the U.S. Supreme Court vacated the judgments in both cases and an injunction issued by the lower court in Omar, finding jurisdiction under the habeas statute and concluding that the petitioners stated no claim for which relief could be granted. Munaf v. Geren, 2008 U.S. LEXIS 4888 (2008). Relevant aspects of the Supreme Court opinion will be discussed in *Digest* 2008.

he could obtain through a writ of habeas corpus and because the district court's preliminary injunction properly preserves its jurisdiction to entertain his petition, we affirm.

(ii) Munaf v. Geren

In the second case, on April 6, 2007, the D.C. Circuit "[c]on-strained by precedent," concluded that the district court was correct in holding that it lacked jurisdiction. *Munaf v. Geren*, 482 F.3d 582 (D.C. Cir. 2007). The court found dispositive under *Hirota* and *Flick* [*v. Johnson*, 338 U.S. 940 (1950)] that Munaf, unlike Omar, had been convicted of a crime by the Central Criminal Court of Iraq ("CCCI"), a tribunal that was "not a tribunal of the United States." The court stated:

> . . . In holding that the district court lacks jurisdiction, we do not mean to suggest that we find the logic of *Hirota* especially clear or compelling, particularly as applied to American citizens. In particular, *Hirota* does not explain why, in cases such as this, the fact of a criminal convic-tion in a non-U.S. court is a fact of jurisdictional signifi-cance under the habeas statute. And as we acknowledged in *Omar*, the Supreme Court's recent decisions in *Hamdi v. Rumsfeld*, [542 U.S. 507 (2004)] and *Rasul v. Bush* [542 U.S. 466 (2004)], are grounds for questioning *Hirota*'s continued vitality. *Omar*, 2007 U.S. App. LEXIS 2891 at *12. But we are not free to disregard *Hirota* simply because we may find its logic less than compelling. . . .

(iii) Petitions for certiorari

Both Munaf in *Munaf v. Geren* and the United States in *Geren v. Omar* filed petitions for certiorari to the Supreme Court. The United States petition in *Omar* answered in the negative two questions presented in the case:

1. Whether the United States courts have jurisdiction to entertain a habeas corpus petition filed on behalf of an

individual such as respondent challenging his detention by the multinational force.

2. Whether, if such jurisdiction exists, the district court had the power to enjoin the multinational force from releasing respondent to Iraqi custody or allowing respondent to be tried before the Iraqi courts.

Excerpts from the factual statement and the U.S. argument on the second question are set forth below (citations to the Appendix deleted.) The full text of the U.S. brief is available at *www.usdoj.gov/osg/briefs/2007/2pet/7pet/2007-0394.pet. aa.html.*

---

*　*　*　*

STATEMENT

1. a. The Multinational Force-Iraq (MNF-I) is an internationally authorized entity consisting of forces from approximately 27 nations, including the United States. It operates in Iraq at the request of the Iraqi government and under a United Nations (U.N.) Security Council resolution authorizing it "to take all necessary measures to contribute to the maintenance of security and stability in Iraq." Res. 1546, U.N. SCOR, at 4, U.N. Doc. S/Res. 1546 (2004). The MNF-I is charged with, among other tasks, deterring and preventing terrorism and detaining individuals where necessary for imperative reasons of security. Pursuant to its U.N. mandate, the MNF-I operates under the "unified command" of United States military officers, *id.* at 74a, but the multinational force is legally distinct from the United States, has its own insignia, and includes high-ranking officers from other nations (for example, the second in command is a British officer).

b. The Central Criminal Court of Iraq (CCCI) is an Iraqi court under Iraqi governance, staffed by Iraqi judges who apply Iraqi law. . . .

Under the authority of the U.N. Security Council resolutions, the Government of Iraq and the MNF-I have determined that the

MNF-I should maintain physical custody of many individuals suspected of criminal activity in Iraq pending investigation and prosecution in Iraqi courts, because, inter alia, many Iraqi prison facilities have been damaged or destroyed in connection with the hostilities in Iraq.

2. Respondent is an American-Jordanian citizen who voluntarily traveled to Iraq. In October 2004, he was captured by MNF-I forces in a raid of his Baghdad home targeting associates of Abu Musab al-Zarqawi, the former Al-Qaeda leader in Iraq. . . .

* * * *

REASONS FOR GRANTING THE PETITION

* * * *

B. The Court Of Appeals' Ruling Upholding The District Court's Injunction Warrants This Court's Review

Because the court of appeals held that it possessed jurisdiction over this habeas action, this case presents a second—and complementary—question concerning the limits on the appropriate exercise of such jurisdiction. That question is of fundamental importance and likewise necessitates this Court's review. Indeed, the divided court of appeals held that—in order to "preserve[]" its jurisdiction over this action—the district court had the power to enjoin the multinational force from transferring respondent to Iraqi custody, sharing with the Iraqi government details concerning any decision to release respondent, and allowing respondent to appear before the Iraqi courts to answer for alleged crimes committed in Iraq. That ruling disregards the traditional limits on habeas relief, conflicts with this Court's precedent recognizing that foreign sovereigns have exclusive jurisdiction to try and punish individuals for offenses committed within their borders, and impermissibly intrudes on the Executive's military and foreign policy powers.

* * * *

[1.]a. There is no legal basis for enjoining the MNF-I from transferring respondent—within Iraq—to Iraqi custody. As Judge Brown recognized [in her dissent to the D.C. Circuit opinion], respondent's transfer to Iraqi authorities would not be an extradition, because respondent traveled to Iraq voluntarily and has been within the sovereign territory of Iraq at all relevant times. Moreover, "[w]here, as is true here, the prisoner is physically in the territory of the foreign sovereign that seeks to make the arrest, release is tantamount to transfer, and thus the logic underlying stays on extradition does not apply." The court of appeals did not attempt to identify a legal basis for blocking respondent's transfer to Iraqi custody. Instead, the court reasoned that it is an open question whether the United States would need treaty or statutory authorization to transfer respondent within Iraq to Iraqi custody, and then refused to consider that question in upholding the district court's injunction on transfer. That ruling is mistaken and conflicts with this Court's precedent.

This Court has long recognized that a "sovereign nation has exclusive jurisdiction to punish offenses against its laws committed within its borders, unless it expressly or impliedly consents to surrender its jurisdiction." *Wilson v. Girard*, 354 U.S. 524, 529 (1957); *see Reid v. Covert*, 354 U.S. 1, 15 n.29 (1957) (plurality opinion) ("[A] foreign nation has plenary criminal jurisdiction, of course, over all Americans * * * who commit offenses against its laws within its territory."); *Schooner Exch. v. M'Fadden*, 11 U.S. (7 Cranch) 116, 136 (1812) (Marshall, C.J.) ("The jurisdiction of the nation within its own territory is necessarily exclusive and absolute."). A foreign sovereign's "plenary" authority (*Reid*, 354 U.S. at 15 n.29) is not just the power to punish after conviction; it is also the power to arrest a suspect within its own sovereign territory, charge that suspect, and try that suspect in its courts.

In *Wilson*, this Court reversed a district court injunction against the transfer of an American soldier (Girard) serving in Japan from the custody of the United States Army to Japanese authorities in Japan to face trial for the alleged shooting of a civilian during a training exercise. 354 U.S. at 525-526. The Court held that Japan has "exclusive jurisdiction to punish offenses against its laws committed within its borders, unless it expressly or impliedly consents to surrender its jurisdiction." *Id.* at 529. Because Japan had not surrendered that jurisdiction, a unanimous Court found "no constitutional or statutory barrier" to the Army's transfer of Girard to Japanese authorities to face trial. *Id.* at 530. Because Iraq has not surrendered its jurisdiction over criminal offenses committed within Iraq, and because there is no treaty or statute that bars his transfer to Iraqi authority, *Wilson* controls here and requires that the injunction on transfer be set aside.(fn. omitted)

Indeed, this case presents a more compelling situation than *Wilson* for setting aside the injunction on respondent's transfer to Iraqi authorities to answer for his conduct within Iraq. Unlike Girard, who was stationed in Japan when he committed the alleged offense, respondent voluntarily traveled to Iraq and committed alleged criminal offenses there. Moreover, unlike Girard, respondent was apprehended by a multinational force in a foreign combat zone, and bringing him to justice in Iraqi courts implicates vital military and foreign relations matters. Respondent was captured in an active combat zone and while harboring an Iraqi insurgent and four Jordanian fighters and while possessing weapons and Improvised Explosive Device-making materials. The decision to detain respondent was made for the safety and security of MNF-I troops in Iraq, as well as for the safety and security of the government and people of Iraq, and any decision to transfer respondent to Iraqi authorities to face trial would be consistent with the MNF-I's U.N. mandate to protect and assist Iraq's government institutions—including its criminal justice system.(fn. omitted)

There is no dispute that the MNF-I forces who apprehended respondent could have immediately handed him over to Iraqi authorities without approval by a court in the United States. The fact that a habeas petition has been filed on behalf of respondent does not deprive the MNF-I of its discretion to transfer respondent to the custody of Iraq. Nor does it in any way diminish Iraq's "exclusive jurisdiction to punish offenses against its laws committed within its borders." *Wilson*, 354 U.S. at 529.[8]

---

[8] The authority of United States forces to operate in Iraq, and to hold security internees on behalf of the Government of Iraq, necessarily includes any authority needed to transfer detainees to Iraqi authorities. That is particularly true where, as here, such a transfer would be carrying out a U.N. mandate and at the request of the Government of Iraq. *See Munaf*, 482 F.3d at 586 (Randolph, J., concurring in judgment) (citing Authorization for Use of Military Force Against Iraq Resolution of 2002, Pub. L. No. 107-243, 116 Stat. 1498; Res. 1637, U.N. SCOR, U.N. Doc. S/Res. 1637 (2005); and Res. 1546, U.N. SCOR, U.N. Doc. S/Res. 1546 (2004)).

Nor can the injunction be sustained based on allegations that respondent may be deprived of due process by Iraqi authorities. As this Court long ago held, "[w]hen an American citizen commits a crime in a foreign country, he cannot complain if required to submit to such modes of trial and to such punishment as the laws of that country may prescribe for its own people, unless a different mode be provided for by treaty stipulations between that country and the United States." *Neely*, 180 U.S. at 123. Even in the extradition context, therefore, "under what is called the 'rule of non-inquiry' * * * courts in this country refrain from examining the penal systems of requesting nations, leaving to the Secretary of State determinations of whether the defendant is likely to be treated humanely." *Lopez-Smith v. Hood*, 121 F.3d 1322, 1327 (9th Cir. 1997); *see United States v. Kin-Hong*, 110 F.3d 103, 110-111 (1st Cir. 1997). The separation-of-powers concerns embodied in the rule of non-inquiry are even stronger here than in the typical extradition case because respondent is already voluntarily in Iraq, and the United States is working closely with the Government of Iraq to restore order to that country, in part by working to build respect for Iraq's vital governmental institutions, including its courts.[9]

Significantly, the court of appeals declined to consider the government's arguments on this point, considering them irrelevant to the courts' jurisdiction. But the court of appeals affirmed the district court's injunction as well as its jurisdictional finding, and in doing so it simply ignored the relevance of those arguments to respondent's likelihood of success on the merits of his challenge to a potential transfer to Iraqi custody. Thus, the court of appeals affirmed the district court's unprecedented injunction against respondent's transfer only by assuming, incorrectly, that respondent could prevail on the merits of such a challenge.

---

[9]   To be clear, the United States would object to the MNF-I's transfer of respondent to Iraqi custody if it believed that he would be tortured. Under the rule of non-inquiry discussed above, however, that is fundamentally a foreign affairs determination, based in part on the Executive's assessment of the foreign country's legal system and the Executive's ability to obtain assurances it considers reliable. See App., infra, 37a n.6 (Brown, J., dissenting).

b. The other aspects of the district court's unprecedented injunction are even more problematic under the principles discussed above and underscore the extent to which the courts have intruded on core Executive responsibilities and international comity. In addition to blocking respondent's transfer to Iraqi custody, the court of appeals ruled that the MNF-I may not release respondent after providing Iraqi authorities with information that would enable them to arrest respondent upon his release. However, as Judge Brown observed, "information sharing among sovereigns regarding the location of persons subject to arrest is a common and desirable practice, particularly in a situation like that in present-day Iraq, where the United States military is cooperating with Iraqi authorities to secure the country."

Under the court of appeals' decision, the MNF-I could evidently release respondent in Iraq only if it gave him a head start before notifying Iraqi authorities that it had released someone that those authorities believed to be a dangerous criminal. As Judge Brown noted, the upshot of the court of appeals' decision is therefore that "a single unelected district court judge can enjoin the United States military from sharing information with an allied foreign sovereign in a war zone and may do so with the deliberate purpose of foiling the efforts of the foreign sovereign to make an arrest on its own soil, in effect secreting a fugitive to prevent his capture. The trespass on Executive authority could hardly be clearer."

Significantly, however, United States courts lack authority to interfere with the efforts of a foreign sovereign to arrest an individual within its territory who had voluntarily traveled there. *See Republic of the Philippines v. Westinghouse Elec. Corp.*, 43 F.3d 65, 79 (3d Cir. 1995). "When an American citizen commits a crime in a foreign country he cannot complain if required to submit to such modes of trial and to punishment as the laws of the country may prescribe for its own people." *Neely*, 180 U.S. at 123. That concern is especially pronounced here, where the MNF-I detained respondent precisely because he is a confirmed security threat in an active combat zone. Simply releasing him in an area of ongoing conflict, without advance notice to the local sovereign, could have grave diplomatic and practical consequences. Even if the injunction against respondent's transfer were sustainable, therefore, the injunction against communication among sovereigns concerning a potential arrest by Iraqi authorities in Iraq would remain an impermissible intrusion on the Executive's war powers and foreign affairs responsibilities, as well as on Iraq's sovereignty.

The court of appeals compounded its error by directing that respondent not be brought before the CCCI for trial, even if he remained in MNF-I custody. Even if the United States courts could prevent Iraq from assuming custody of respondent, there would be no justification for preventing the Iraqi courts from adjudicating respondent's guilt or innocence while he remained within the custody of the MNF-I. As long as respondent remains in MNF-I custody, the jurisdiction of the United States courts (if any) to review that custody would be unaffected. The court of appeals' unfounded speculation that Iraq might seize respondent from the MNF-I is refuted by the government's declaration explaining that he would remain in MNF-I custody during proceedings before the CCCI, and in any event provides no basis for interfering with a foreign sovereign's "exclusive jurisdiction to punish offenses against its laws committed within its borders." *Wilson*, 354 U.S. at 529.

2. While the injunction at issue suffers the specific defects discussed above, it likewise runs afoul of the political question doctrine. By interfering with core military determinations in a zone of active combat, and also with sensitive national security and foreign relations matters related to the rebuilding of Iraqi political and judicial institutions, the district court's injunction violates fundamental separation-of-powers principles.

As discussed above, this case and the relief approved by the court of appeals directly implicate sensitive decisions made by the Executive in the conduct of a multinational force abroad. In the current volatile atmosphere in Iraq, a judicial order demonstrating a lack of respect for the Executive Branch's determinations to hold a security internee to permit the Iraqi legal system to prosecute him could have unsettling consequences. As Justice Jackson observed in *Hirota*:

> For this Court now to call up these cases for judicial review under exclusively American law can only be regarded as a

warning to our associates in the trials that no commitment of the President or of the military authorities, even in matters such as these, has finality or validity under our form of government until it has the approval of this Court. And since the Court's approval or disapproval cannot be known until after the event—usually long after—it would substantially handicap our country in asking other nations to rely upon the word or act of the President in affairs which only he is competent to conduct.

Hirota v. MacArthur, 335 U.S. 876, 878 (1948) (statement respecting oral argument). The unprecedented injunction in this case barring the MNF-I from releasing respondent to the custody of Iraq, sharing information with the Iraqi authorities over the handling of respondent, or allowing the Iraqi authorities to prosecute respondent for offenses committed in Iraq underscores the continuing wisdom of Justice Jackson's observation.

As Judge Brown explained, the injunction in this case "substantial[ly] impair[s] * * * the Executive's ability to prosecute the war efficiently and to make good on its commitments to our allies." Such an extraordinary exercise of American judicial power over the conduct of important and sensitive foreign and military affairs abroad warrants this Court's review.

＊   ＊   ＊   ＊

In its response to Munaf's petition for certiorari, the United States argued, among other things, that Munaf was not entitled to the relief he sought:

This habeas petition amounts to an impermissible collateral attack on petitioner's conviction by an Iraqi court based on serious criminal conduct that petitioner—a dual Iraqi citizen—committed in Iraq in violation of Iraqi law. The United States courts lack authority to accommodate such attacks.

The full text of the U.S. response, excerpted below, is available at *www.usdoj.gov/osg/briefs/2007/0responses/2006-1666.*

resp.html. (Citations to other submissions and footnotes deleted).

---

*   *   *   *

3. The . . . separation-of-powers and international-comity concerns are even more pronounced in this case than in *Omar* because petitioner is a dual Iraqi-United States citizen who has already been tried and convicted by an Iraqi court. Petitioner's Iraqi citizenship distinguishes this case and heightens the comity concerns inherent in preventing Iraq from punishing him for crimes he committed in that country.

Even setting petitioner's Iraqi citizenship to the side, his habeas petition amounts to an impermissible collateral attack on his foreign conviction. A "sovereign nation has exclusive jurisdiction to punish offenses against its laws committed within its own borders." *Wilson*, 354 U.S. at 529. Thus, as petitioner concedes, "it is axiomatic that an American court does not provide collateral review of the proceedings in a foreign tribunal."[6]

Petitioner's contention that he is not attacking his Iraqi conviction is contradicted by the record. In his filings below, petitioner argued that he had been convicted and sentenced "by an Iraqi court operating under glaring procedural deficiencies and the direct manipulation of U.S. military personnel." . . . In this Court, petitioner continues to assert that those proceedings were improperly influenced by the United States—a contention the United States vigorously denies, but that strongly confirms that petitioner is attacking his Iraqi conviction and sentence.

Any doubt that petitioner is trying to use this habeas action to evade the jurisdiction of the Iraqi courts and to prevent his sentence from being carried out is eliminated by the relief he seeks, including an injunction barring respondents from transferring

---

[6] Respondents agree with petitioner . . . that the jurisdiction of the United States courts under *Hirota* does not depend on whether an individual has been convicted by a foreign tribunal. . . . As explained in the text, however, petitioner's conviction by the Iraqi court nevertheless provides further support for the conclusion that his claims are non-justiciable.

petitioner to Iraqi custody and instead requiring respondents to transport petitioner to the United States. . . .[7]

*   *   *   *

(4) Detainee held in the United States: Al-Marri v. Wright

> On June 11, 2007, the U.S. Court of Appeals for the Fourth Circuit ordered the release from military custody of an alien held as an enemy combatant in the United States pursuant to a Presidential determination. *Al-Marri v. Wright*, 487 F.3d 160 (4th Cir. 2007). The Fourth Circuit concluded that the habeas-stripping language of the Military Commissions Act did not apply to al-Marri and remanded to the district court with instructions to issue a writ of habeas corpus. In conclusion, the court noted that "[t]he Government can transfer al-Marri to civilian authorities to face criminal charges, initiate deportation proceedings against him, hold him as a material witness in connection with grand jury proceedings, or detain him for a limited time pursuant to the Patriot Act. But military detention of al-Marri must cease."
>
> Excerpts below provide the court's analysis in concluding that it had jurisdiction over al-Marri's habeas petition and that the habeas writ should issue. The Fourth Circuit granted the government's petition for rehearing en banc, and at year's end the case remained under submission following oral argument on October 27, 2007.

---

*   *   *   *

---

[7] Petitioner asserts that, in addition to challenging the Iraqi proceedings and his potential transfer within Iraq to Iraqi custody, he also challenges his custody by United States forces acting as part of the MNF-I. But petitioner's challenge to his MNF-I custody would be mooted by his transfer to Iraqi custody (which he seeks to block). Thus, this action boils down to an attempt by petitioner to evade the jurisdiction of the Iraqi courts and to prevent his conviction from being given effect.

Al-Marri, a citizen of Qatar, lawfully entered the United States with his wife and children on September 10, 2001. . . . [O]n December 12, 2001, FBI agents arrested al-Marri at his home in Peoria as a material witness in the Government's investigation of the September 11th attacks. Al-Marri was imprisoned in civilian jails in Peoria and then New York City.

In February 2002, al-Marri was charged . . . with the possession of unauthorized or counterfeit credit-card numbers with the intent to defraud. A year later, in January 2003, he was charged in a second, six-count indictment, with two counts of making a false statement to the FBI, three counts of making a false statement on a bank application, and one count of using another person's identification for the purpose of influencing the action of a federally insured financial institution. . . .

. . . [On] June 23, [2003, while the criminal charges were pending,] the Government moved *ex parte* to dismiss the indictment based on an order signed that morning by the President.

In the order, President George W. Bush stated that he "DETERMINE[D] for the United States of America that" al-Marri: (1) is an enemy combatant; (2) is closely associated with al Qaeda; (3) "engaged in conduct that constituted hostile and warlike acts, including conduct in preparation for acts of international terrorism;" (4) "possesses intelligence . . . that . . . would aid U.S. efforts to prevent attacks by al Qaeda;" and (5) "represents a continuing, present, and grave danger to the national security of the United States." The President determined that al-Marri's detention by the military was "necessary to prevent him from aiding al Qaeda" and thus ordered the Attorney General to surrender al-Marri to the Secretary of Defense, and the Secretary of Defense to "detain him as an enemy combatant."

The federal district court in Illinois granted the Government's motion to dismiss the criminal indictment against al-Marri. In accordance with the President's order, al-Marri was then transferred to military custody and brought to the Naval Consolidated Brig in South Carolina.

Since that time (that is, for four years) the military has held al-Marri as an enemy combatant, without charge and without any indication when this confinement will end. . . .

[Following dismissal in 2003 of a petition for writ of habeas corpus on jurisdictional grounds in the Central District of Illinois,] al-Marri's counsel filed the present habeas petition on al-Marri's behalf in the District of South Carolina. On September 9, 2004, the Government answered al-Marri's petition, citing the Declaration of Jeffrey N. Rapp, Director of the Joint Intelligence Task Force for Combating Terrorism, as support for the President's order to detain al-Marri as an enemy combatant.

*   *   *   *

. . . [W]e conclude that the MCA does not apply to al-Marri. . . .

. . . The MCA eliminates habeas jurisdiction under § 2241 only for an alien who "has been determined by the United States to have been properly detained as an enemy combatant or is awaiting such determination." MCA § 7(a). . . .

*   *   *   *

. . . [T]he plain language of the MCA does not permit the Government's interpretation—i.e., that the President's initial order to detain al-Marri as an enemy combatant constitutes both a decision to detain al-Marri and a determination under the MCA that al-Marri has been properly detained as an enemy combatant. The MCA requires both to eliminate our jurisdiction.

*   *   *   *

III.

Al-Marri premises his habeas claim on the Fifth Amendment's guarantee that no person living in this country can be deprived of liberty without due process of law. He maintains that even if he has committed the acts the Government alleges, he is not a combatant but a civilian protected by our Constitution, and thus is not subject to military detention. Al-Marri acknowledges that the Government can deport him or charge him with a crime, and if he is convicted in a civilian court, imprison him. But he insists that neither the Constitution nor any law permits the Government, on the basis of the evidence it has proffered to date—even assuming all of that evidence is true—to treat him as an enemy combatant and subject him to indefinite military detention, without criminal charge or process.

The Government contends that the district court properly denied habeas relief to al-Marri because the Constitution allows detention of enemy combatants by the military without criminal process, and according to the Government it has proffered evidence that al-Marri is a combatant. The Government argues that the Authorization for Use of Military Force (AUMF), Pub. L. No. 107-40, 115 Stat. 224 (2001), as construed by precedent and considered in conjunction with the "legal background against which [it] was enacted," empowers the President on the basis of that proffered evidence to order al-Marri's indefinite military detention as an enemy combatant. Alternatively, the Government contends that even if the AUMF does not authorize the President to order al-Marri's military detention, the President has "inherent constitutional power" to do so.

* * * *

. . . Both parties recognize that it does not violate the Due Process Clause for the President to order the military to seize and detain individuals who "qualify" as enemy combatants for the duration of a war. They disagree, however, as to whether the evidence the Government has proffered, even assuming its accuracy, establishes that al-Marri fits within the "legal category" of enemy combatants. The Government principally contends that its evidence establishes this and therefore the AUMF grants the President *statutory* authority to detain al-Marri as an enemy combatant. Alternatively, the Government asserts that the President has inherent *constitutional* authority to order al-Marri's indefinite military detention. Al-Marri maintains that the proffered evidence does not establish that he fits within the "legal category" of enemy combatant and so the AUMF does not authorize the President to order the military to seize and detain him, and that the President has no inherent constitutional authority to order this detention. . . .

B.
　　The Government's primary argument is that the [Authorization for Use of Military Force], as construed by precedent and considered against the "the legal background against which [it] was enacted," i.e. constitutional and law-of-war principles, empowers

the President to order the military to seize and detain al-Marri as an enemy combatant. . . .

*   *   *   *

. . . [W]e note that American courts have often been reluctant to follow international law in resolving domestic disputes. In the present context, however, they, like the Government here, have relied on the law of war—treaty obligations including the Hague and Geneva Conventions and customary principles developed alongside them. The law of war provides clear rules for determining an individual's status during an international armed conflict, distinguishing between "combatants" (members of a nation's military, militia, or other armed forces, and those who fight alongside them) and "civilians" (all other persons). *See, e.g.,* Geneva Convention Relative to the Treatment of Prisoners of War (Third Geneva Convention) arts. 2, 4, 5, Aug. 12, 1949, 6 U.S.T. 3316, 75 U.N.T.S. 135; Geneva Convention Relative to the Protection of Civilian Persons in Time of War (Fourth Geneva Convention) art. 4, Aug. 12, 1949, 6 U.S.T. 3516, 75 U.N.T.S. 287. American courts have repeatedly looked to these careful distinctions made in the law of war in identifying which individuals fit within the "legal category" of "enemy combatants" under our Constitution. *See, e.g., Hamdi,* 542 U.S. at 518; *Quirin,* 317 U.S. at 30–31 & n.7; *Milligan,* 71 U.S. at 121–22; *Padilla,* 423 F.3d at 391.

*   *   *   *

. . . [T]he holdings of *Hamdi* and *Padilla* share two characteristics: (1) they look to law of war principles to determine who fits within the "legal category" of enemy combatant; and (2) following the law of war, they rest enemy combatant status on affiliation with the military arm of an enemy nation.

ii.

. . . [U]nlike *Hamdi* and *Padilla,* al-Marri is not alleged to have been part of a Taliban unit, not alleged to have stood alongside the Taliban or the armed forces of any other enemy nation, not alleged to have been on the battlefield during the war in Afghanistan, not alleged to have even been in Afghanistan during the armed conflict there, and not alleged to have engaged in combat with United States forces anywhere in the world. . . .

*   *   *   *

. . . [B]oth Hamdi and Padilla upheld the President's authority pursuant to the AUMF to detain as enemy combatants individuals (1) who affiliated with and fought on behalf of Taliban government forces, (2) against he armed forces of the United States and its allies, (3) on the battlefield in Afghanistan. . . .

*   *   *   *

. . . [T]he Supreme Court's most recent terrorism case provides an additional reason for rejecting the contention that al-Marri is an enemy combatant. In *Hamdan*, the Court held that because the conflict between the United States and al Qaeda in Afghanistan is not "between nations," it is a "'conflict not of an international character'"—and so is governed by Common Article 3 of the Geneva Conventions. See 126 S. Ct. at 2795. . . . Common Article 3 and other Geneva Convention provisions applying to non-international conflicts (in contrast to those applying to international conflicts, such as that with Afghanistan's Taliban government) simply do not recognize the "legal category" of enemy combatant." *See* Third Geneva Convention, art. 3, 6 U.S.T. at 3318. As the International Committee of the Red Cross—the official codifier of the Geneva Conventions—explains, "an 'enemy combatant' is a person who, either lawfully or unlawfully, engages in hostilities for the opposing side in an *international* armed conflict;" in contrast, "[i]n non-international armed conflict combatant status *does not exist.*" Int'l Comm. of the Red Cross, Official Statement: The Relevance of IHL in the Context of Terrorism, at 1, 3 (Feb. 21, 2005), *http:// www.icrc.org/Web/Eng/siteeng0.nsf/htmlall/terrorismihl-210705* (emphasis added).

*   *   *   *

. . . [S]ince the legal status of "enemy combatant" does not exist in non-international conflicts, the law of war leaves the detention of persons in such conflicts to the applicable law of the detaining country. In al-Marri's case, the applicable law is our Constitution.

Thus, even if the Supreme Court should hold that the Government may detain indefinitely Hamdan and others like him, who were captured *outside* the United States and lacked substantial and voluntary connections to this country, that would provide no support for approving al-Marri's military detention. For not only was al-Marri seized and detained *within* the United States, he also has substantial connections to the United States, and so plainly is protected by the Due Process Clause.

*   *   *   *

In sum, the Government has not offered, and although we have exhaustively searched, we have not found, any authority that permits us to hold that the AUMF empowers the president to detain al-Marri as an enemy combatant. If the Government's allegations are true, and we assume they are for present purposes, al-Marri, like Milligan [*see Ex Parte Milligan*, 71 U.S. (4 Wall.) 2 (1866)], is a dangerous enemy of this nation who has committed serious crimes and associated with a secret enemy organization that has engaged in hostilities against us. But, like Milligan, al-Marri is still a civilian: he does not fit within the "permissible bounds of" "[t]he legal category of enemy combatant." *Hamdi*, 542 U.S. at 522 n.1. Therefore, the AUMF provides the President no statutory authority to order the military to seize and indefinitely detain al-Marri.

C.

Accordingly, we turn to the Government's final contention. The Government summarily argues that even if the AUMF does not authorize al-Marri's seizure and indefinite detention as an enemy combatant, the President has "inherent constitutional authority" to order the military to seize and detain al-Marri. The Government maintains that the President's "war-making powers" granted him by Article II "include the authority to capture and detain individuals involved in hostilities against the United States." In other words, according to the Government, the President has "inherent" authority to subject persons legally residing in this country and protected by our Constitution to military arrest and detention, without the benefit of any criminal process, if the President believes these individuals have "engaged in conduct in preparation for acts of international terrorism." *See* Rapp Declaration.

This is a breathtaking claim, for the Government nowhere represents that this "inherent" power to order indefinite military detention extends only to aliens or only to those who "qualify" within the "legal category" of enemy combatants.

*   *   *   *

In light of al-Marri's due process rights under our Constitution and Congress's express prohibition in the Patriot Act [§ 412] on the indefinite detention of those civilians arrested as "terrorist aliens" within this country, we can only conclude that in the case at hand, the President claims power that far exceeds that granted him by the Constitution.

We do not question the President's wartime authority over enemy combatants; but absent suspension of the writ of habeas corpus or declaration of martial law, the Constitution simply does not provide the President the power to exercise military authority over civilians within the United States. . . .

*   *   *   *

e. Military commissions

(1) Manual and regulation

On January 18, 2007, the Department of Defense transmitted the Manual for Military Commissions to Congress in accordance with the Military Commissions Act of 2006. The full text of the manual is available at *www.defenselink.mil/news/commissionsmanual.html*. *See also* U.S. response to UN Human Rights Committee recommendations on U.S. implementation of its ICCPR obligations, discussed in A.4.c.(2) *supra*, response to paragraph 20 (requesting information on U.S. implementation of Supreme Court decision in *Hamdan v. Rumsfeld*), available at *www.state.gov/s/l/c8183.htm*.

On April 27, 2007, the Department of Defense released the Regulation for Trial by Military Commissions implementing the Manual. The full text of the Regulation is available at *www.defenselink.mil/news/commissionsmanual.html*.

(2) Charges against Guantanamo detainees

On February 2, 2007, the Department of Defense announced that charges had been sworn against three Guantanamo detainees who could face trial by military commission in accordance with the Military Commissions Act. The three individuals charged, David M. Hicks, Omar Khadr, and Salim Ahmed Hamdan, were among the first group of terrorists under Department of Defense control that the President determined were to be tried by Military Commissions, before the Supreme Court decision in *Hamdan v. Rumsfeld* and the subsequent enactment of the Military Commissions Act. On October 10, 2007, charges were brought against Mohammed Jawad, and on December 20, 2007, charges were brought against Ahmed Mohammed Ahmed Haza al Darbi. For copies of the sworn charges *see www.defenselink.mil/news/ commissionspress.html*. A fact sheet on military commissions under the Military Commission Act is available at *www. defenselink.mil/news/d2007OMC%20Fact%20Sheet%20 08%20Feb%2007.pdf.*

On March 30, 2007, the Department of Defense announced that Hicks had been convicted of material support to terrorism in the first trial by military commission under the Military Commissions Act of 2006, based on a guilty plea. Hicks was repatriated to Australia, where he served a nine-month sentence. *See www.defenselink.mil/releases/release.aspx? releaseid=10678.* Proceedings against Khadr and Hamdan were pending at the end of 2007, as discussed below.

(3) Determination of status as "alien unlawful enemy combatant"

(i) Omar Khadr

On June 4, 2007, the military judge presiding over Khadr's military commission dismissed all charges against him, finding that the commission, established under the MCA, lacked personal jurisdiction. *See www.defenselink.mil/news/news-article.aspx?id=46281.* On September 24, 2007, the U.S. Court of Military Commission Review ("CMCR"), established under § 950f of the MCA, reversed. *United States v. Khadr*, CMCR 07-001, available at *www.defenselink.mil/news/Copy %20 of %20CMCRKHADR.html*. The CMCR opinion described the issue as excerpted below (footnote omitted).

In this appeal by the Government (hereinafter Appellant) we are called upon to interpret for the first time the jurisdictional provisions contained in the Military Commissions Act of 2006 (hereinafter M.C.A.) as they relate to the trial by military commission of a Canadian citizen, Omar Ahmed Khadr, Appellee (hereinafter Mr. Khadr). Mr. Khadr was captured on the battlefield in Afghanistan in 2002, is currently detained in Guantanamo Bay, Cuba, and was pending trial upon charges that were referred for trial before a military commission. . . .

The basis for the military judge's ruling was Appellant's failure to properly determine Mr. Khadr's status as an "alien unlawful enemy combatant" before his Combatant Status Review Tribunal (C.S.R.T.), which the judge ruled was an indispensable prerequisite to the military commission's ability to exercise personal jurisdiction under the M.C.A. The military judge further ruled that "the military commission is not the proper authority, under the provisions of the M.C.A., to determine that Mr. Khadr is an unlawful enemy combatant in order to establish initial jurisdiction for this commission to try Mr. Khadr." . . .

*   *   *   *

On September 7, 2004, a three-member C.S.R.T. unanimously determined that Mr. Khadr was properly classified as an "enemy combatant" and an individual who was "a member of, or affiliated with al Qaeda," as defined by a memorandum issued by the Deputy Secretary of Defense on July 7, 2004. *See* Report of C.S.R.T. (AE 11 at 6).

*   *   *   *

The CMCR agreed with the military judge that "Mr. Khadr's 2004 C.S.R.T. classification as an 'enemy combatant' failed to meet the M.C.A.'s jurisdictional requirements in that it did not establish that Mr. Khadr was in fact an '*unlawful* enemy combatant' to satisfy the jurisdictional prerequisite [under the MCA] for trial by military commission." In reaching this conclusion, the CMRC explained:

> . . . Critical to [our] analysis is the understanding that— unlike the White House and Wolfowitz memoranda,* both of which declared "enemy combatant" status solely for purposes of continued detention of personnel captured during hostilities and applicability of the Geneva Conventions—Congress in the M.C.A. was carefully and deliberately defining status for the express purpose of specifying the *in personam* criminal jurisdiction of military commission trials. In defining what was clearly intended to be limited jurisdiction, Congress also prescribed serious criminal sanctions for those members of this select group who were ultimately convicted by military commissions.

The CMRC held further, however, that "the military judge erred in two respects: first, in not affording Appellant the opportunity to present evidence in support of its position on the jurisdictional issue before the military commission; and second, in concluding that a C.S.R.T. (or another competent tribunal) determination of "unlawful enemy combatant" status was a prerequisite to referral of charges to a military commission, and that the military commission lacked the power to independently consider and decide this important

---

* Editor's note: Footnotes 15 and 16 to the CMCR opinion identify these documents as follows:

15 *See* White House Memorandum, Humane Treatment of al Qaeda and Taliban Detainees 2 (February 7, 2002), fact sheet available at *www.whitehouse.gov/news/releases/2002/02/20020207-13.html.* . .

16 *See* Deputy Secretary of Defense Memorandum, Order Establishing C.S.R.T. 1 (July 7, 2004), available at *http://www.globalsecurity. org/security/library/olicy/dod/d20040707review.pdf.*

jurisdictional matter under the M.C.A." The opinion explained (footnote omitted):

> The text, structure, and history of the M.C.A. demonstrate clearly that a military judge presiding over a military commission may determine both the factual issue of an accused's 'unlawful enemy combatant status' and the corresponding legal issue of the military commission's *in personam* jurisdiction. . . . This interpretation is consistent with the requirements of both the M.C.A. and with international law. *See Murray v. Schooner Charming Betsy*, 6 U.S. (2 Cranch) 64, 118 (1804) (acts of Congress will generally be construed in a manner so as not to violate international law, as we presume that Congress ordinarily seeks to comply with international law when legislating).

Excerpts below from the CMCR opinion discuss the significance of the terms used in describing Khadr's status under international law and the MCA and its conclusion that "[d]etermining lawful and unlawful combatant status under existing international treaties, customary international law, case law precedent (both international and domestic), and the M.C.A. is a matter well within the professional capacity of a military judge." (most footnotes omitted).

* * * *

The determination of whether an individual captured on the battlefield is a "lawful" or "unlawful" enemy combatant carries with it significant legal consequences (both international and domestic) relating to the treatment owed that individual upon capture and ultimate criminal liability for participating in war-related activities associated with the armed conflict. The Third Geneva Convention Relative to the Treatment of Prisoners of War (GPW III)—signed in 1949 and entered into force in 1950 following battlefield atrocities occurring during World War II—sought to carefully define "lawful combatant" for all signatory nations. Geneva Convention Relative to the Treatment of Prisoners of War, August 12, 1949,

6 U.S.T. 3316, T.I.A.S. No. 3364, 75 U.N.T.S. 135, Art. 4. *See also* Hague Convention No. IV Respecting the Laws and Customs of War on Land, October 18, 1907, 36 Stat. 2277, T.S. No. 539 (Hague Regulations).

* * * *

This critical determination of "lawful" or "unlawful" combatant status is far more than simply a matter of semantics. Without any determination of lawful or unlawful status, classification as an "enemy combatant" is sufficient to justify a detaining power's continuing detention of an individual captured in battle or taken into custody in the course of ongoing hostilities. However, under the well recognized body of customary international law relating to armed conflict, and specific provisions of GPW III, lawful combatants enjoy "combatant immunity" for their pre-capture acts of warfare, including the targeting, wounding, or killing of other human beings, provided those actions were performed in the context of ongoing hostilities against lawful military targets, and were not in violation of the law of war. . . . Lawful enemy combatants enjoy all the privileges afforded soldiers under the law of war, including combatant immunity and the protections of the Geneva Conventions if wounded or sick, and while being held as prisoners of war (POWs).[6] Additionally, lawful enemy combatants facing judicial proceedings for any of their actions in warfare that violate the law of war, or for post-capture offenses committed while they are POWs, are entitled to be tried by the same courts, and in accordance with the same procedures, that the detaining power would utilize to try members of its own armed forces (i.e., by court-martial for lawful enemy combatants held by the United States). *See* Arts. 84, 87 and 102, GPW III.

Indeed, GPW III codified many existing principles of customary international law and added numerous additional provisions, all aimed at protecting lawful combatants from being punished for

---

[6] *Lindh,* 212 F. Supp. 2d at 553–54; *see also* U.S. Army Judge Advocate General's Legal Center and School, Dept. of the Army, Operational Law Handbook 16 (2006)(hereinafter Army Op. Law Handbook).

their hostile actions prior to capture;[7] ensuring that POWs were treated and cared for humanely upon capture; and seeking to guarantee the general welfare and well-being of POWs during the entire period they remained in captivity. . . . At the conclusion of the armed conflict, lawful combatants who are held as POWs are entitled to be safely and expeditiously repatriated to their nation of origin.[8]

Unlawful combatants, on the other hand, are not entitled to "combatant immunity" nor any of the protections generally afforded lawful combatants who become POWs. Unlawful combatants remain civilians and may properly be captured, detained by opposing military forces, and treated as criminals under the domestic law of the capturing nation for any and all unlawful combat actions. *Lindh*, 212 F. Supp. 2d at 554 (citing *Ex parte Quirin*, 317 U.S. at 30–31); *see* Army Op. Law Handbook 17.

> By universal agreement and practice, the law of war draws a distinction between the armed forces and the peaceful populations of belligerent nations and also between those who are lawful and unlawful combatants. Lawful combatants are subject to capture and detention as prisoners of war by opposing military forces. Unlawful combatants are likewise subject to capture and detention, but in addition they are subject to trial and punishment by military tribunals for acts which render their belligerency unlawful.

Ex parte Quirin, 317 U.S. at 30. M.C.A. § 948b(f) addresses Common Article 3's application, stating, "A military commission established under this chapter is a regularly constituted court, affording all the necessary 'judicial guarantees which are recognized

---

[7] *See e.g.*, GPW III, Article 87 ("[POWs] may not be sentenced by the military authorities and courts of the Detaining Power to any penalties except those provided for in respect of members of the armed force of the said Power who have committed the same acts.") and Article 99 ("No [POW] may be tried or sentenced for an act which is not forbidden by the law of the Detaining Power or by international law, in force at the time the said act was committed."). These two Articles, when read together, have been interpreted to "make clear that a belligerent in war cannot prosecute the soldiers of its foes for the soldiers' lawful acts of war." *Lindh*, 212 F. Supp. 2d at 553.

[8] *See* Articles 118 and 119, GPW III.

as indispensable by civilized peoples' for purposes of [C]ommon Article 3 of the Geneva Conventions." Under the M.C.A., unlawful enemy combatants who engage in hostilities against the United States or its co-belligerents, or materially support such, are subject to trial by military commission for violations of the law of war and other offenses made triable by that statute. *See* §§ 948a(1)(A)(ii) and 948b(a).

*   *   *   *

(ii) Salim Hamdan

Charges against Hamdan before a separate military commission were also dismissed on June 4, 2007. Following the CMCR decision in *Khadr*, supra, the commission granted a motion for reconsideration and a hearing was held on December 5 and 6, 2007. On December 19, 2007, the Hamdan military commission denied Hamdan's motion to dismiss for lack of jurisdiction, concluding:

> The Government has carried its burden of showing, by a preponderance of the evidence, that the accused is an alien unlawful enemy combatant, subject to the jurisdiction of a military commission. The Commission has separately conducted a status determination under Article 5 of the Third Geneva Convention, and determined by a preponderance of the evidence that he is not a lawful combatant or entitled to Prisoner of War Status. There being no Constitutional impediment to the Commission's exercise of jurisdiction over him, the Defense Motion to Dismiss for Lack of Jurisdiction is DENIED. The accused may be tried by military commission.

5. Geneva Protocol III: Additional Distinctive Emblem

On January 12, 2007, President Bush signed the instrument of ratification for the Third Additional Protocol to the Geneva

Conventions of 1949 and implementing legislation to protect the red crystal and red crescent emblems, Geneva Distinctive Emblem Protection Act of 2006, Pub. L. No. 109-481, 120 Stat. 3673 (2007). The Third Additional Protocol entered into force on January 14, 2007. A White House press release, excerpted below, is available at *www.whitehouse.gov/news/r eleases/2007/01/20070112-5.html. See also Digest 2006* at 1100–1104 and *Digest 2005* at 1042–43.

* * * *

. . . The Protocol created the Red Crystal as a new emblem for the International Red Cross and Red Crescent Movement that can be used by governments and national societies that face challenges adopting the cross or crescent symbols. By creating the Red Crystal, the Protocol also paved the way for Israel's Magen David Adom to join the International Red Cross and Red Crescent Movement, now more than 50 years after it became Israel's national society. U.S. leadership and significant international cooperation overcame longstanding obstacles to achieve this humanitarian success.

Ratification and implementation of this Protocol promotes the humanitarian objectives of the United States and advances the longstanding and historic leadership of the United States in the law of armed conflict. It reflects the commitment of the United States to international law, including the Geneva Conventions.

At the 30th International Conference of the Red Cross and Red Crescent, U.S. Department of State Legal Adviser John B. Bellinger, III, noted in his opening statement that the United States "understand[s] the importance the international community places on full implementation of the [Magen David Adom-Palestine Red Crescent Society Memorandum of Understanding], and we will continue to encourage all sides to implement fully the commitments made at the 29th International Conference." *See www.us-mission.ch/Press2007/ 1127BellingerRCRCStatement.html.* A November 30, 2007, press release by the U.S. Mission to the United Nations in Geneva at the conclusion of the conference summarized the progress made on that issue as excerpted below. The full text of the press release is available at *www.us-mission.ch/ Press2007/1130RCRCFinal.html.*

* * * * *

The 30th International Conference marked the first time that the Palestine Red Crescent Society (PRCS) and the Magen David Adom (MDA), the national societies of Palestine and Israel, participated in an international Red Cross and Red Crescent conference as full members. The United States was pleased to have facilitated their admission into the Movement at the 29th International Conference held in June 2006. Since their entry into the movement in 2006, these two societies have worked together to strengthen humanitarian assistance for those in need and to build bridges between their peoples.

The 30th International Conference adopted by consensus a resolution urging the two societies to enhance their cooperation, calling on the authorities concerned to facilitate this cooperation, and calling for the appointment of an Independent Monitor to monitor the implementation of the 2005 Memorandum of Understanding between the two societies. Mr. Bellinger said, "the U.S. Government is extremely pleased that the resolution was adopted by consensus, without acrimony or politics. The U.S. Government is committed to full implementation of the MOU between the two Societies."

The United States was also pleased that the delegations from Israel and the PRCS were able to work out the final operational details that enabled for the first time five PRCS ambulances to enter into service today in East Jerusalem. The United States Government and the American Red Cross served as official witnesses to the signing as part of their facilitation of cooperation among the Government of Israel, the PRCS, and the MDA.

* * * * *

6. 2005 Protocols to the UN Convention for the Suppression of Unlawful Acts Against the Safety of Maritime Navigation and to Its Protocol on Fixed Platforms

On October 1, 2007, President Bush transmitted to the Senate for advice and consent to ratification the Protocol of 2005 to the Convention for the Suppression of Unlawful Acts Against the Safety of Maritime Navigation ("2005 SUA Protocol") and the Protocol of 2005 to the Protocol for the Suppression of Unlawful Acts Against the Safety of Fixed Platforms Located on the Continental Shelf ("2005 Fixed Platforms Protocol"). S. Treaty Doc. No. 110-8 (2007).

Excerpts follow from the report of the Department of State, included in the transmittal, discussing proposed understandings to Articles 3 and 4(5) of the 2005 SUA protocol concerning the meaning of the terms "armed conflict" and "international humanitarian law," and the effect of the exception for activities undertaken by military forces. The same understandings were proposed for Article 2 of the 2005 Fixed Platforms Protocol, which incorporates the substantive provisions of the 2005 SUA Convention relevant to fixed platforms. *See also* C.6. below and Chapter 3.B.1.f.

* * * *

Article 3 of the 2005 SUA Protocol adds Article 2*bis* to the Convention to address the interaction of the Convention with other rights, obligations, and responsibilities of States and individuals. Paragraph 1 provides that nothing in the Convention shall affect other rights, obligations and responsibilities of States and individuals under international law, in particular the purposes and principles of the Charter of the United Nations and international human rights, refugee, and humanitarian law. Paragraph 1 is based on the similar provisions contained in Article 19(1) of the Terrorist Bombings Convention and Article 21 of the Terrorism Financing Convention, but adds specific reference to international human rights and refugee law to take into account the interests of seafarers.

Paragraph 2 of Article 2*bis* contains two important exceptions to the applicability of the Convention with respect to activities of armed forces and other military forces of a State. It states that the Convention does not apply to: (i) "the activities of armed forces during an armed conflict, as those terms are understood under international humanitarian law, which are governed by that law"; and (ii) "the activities undertaken by military forces of a State in the exercise of their official duties, inasmuch as they are governed by other rules of international law." This exception restates similar language in Article 19(2) of the Terrorist Bombings Convention.

The first exception is meant to exclude from the Convention's scope the activities of national and sub-national armed forces, so long as those activities are in the course of an "armed conflict." To ensure that suspected offenders cannot claim the benefit of the "armed conflict" exception in Article 2*bis*(2) to avoid extradition or prosecution under the Convention, it would be useful for the United States to articulate an understanding clarifying the scope of this exception, consistent with the understandings it included in its instrument of ratification for the Terrorist Bombings Convention with respect to the similar provision in Article 19(2) of that Convention and in its instrument of ratification for the Terrorism Financing Convention with respect to the reference to the undefined term "armed conflict" in Article 2(1)(b) of that Convention. Both of those understandings were based upon the widely accepted provision in paragraph 2 of Article 1 of Protocol II Additional to the Geneva Conventions of August 12, 1949, and Relating to the Protections of Victims of Non-International Armed Conflicts ("Additional Protocol II"), S. Treaty Doc. 100-2, which states that "armed conflict" does not include "internal disturbances and tensions, such as riots, isolated and sporadic acts of violence and other acts of a similar nature." Including an understanding that specifies the scope of "armed conflict" in a manner consistent with Additional Protocol II would help to counter attempts by terrorists to claim protection from this exception in circumstances for which it is not intended. As in Article 19 of the Terrorist Bombings Convention, Article 2*bis*(1) and (2) use the term "international humanitarian law," which is not used by the United States and could be subject to varied interpretations. Accordingly, it would be appropriate for the United States to include an understanding that, for the purposes of this Convention, this phrase has the same substantive meaning as the phrase "law of war." I therefore recommend that the following understandings to Article 3 of the 2005 SUA Protocol be included in the United States instrument of ratification:

> The United States of America understands that the term "armed conflict" in Article 3 of the Protocol of 2005 to the Convention for the Suppression of Unlawful Acts against the Safety of Maritime Navigation (which adds, *inter alia*, paragraph 2 of Article 2*bis* to the Convention for the Suppression of Unlawful Acts against the Safety of Maritime Navigation) does not include internal disturbances and tensions, such as riots, isolated and sporadic acts of violence and other acts of a similar nature.
>
> The United States further understands that the term "international humanitarian law" in Article 3 of the Protocol of 2005 to the Convention for the Suppression of Unlawful Acts against the Safety of Maritime Navigation (which adds, *inter alia*, paragraphs 1 and 2 of Article 2*bis* to the Convention for the Suppression of Unlawful Acts against the Safety of Maritime Navigation) has the same substantive meaning as the "law of war."

The United States included substantially identical understandings in its instrument of ratification for the Terrorist Bombings Convention and, with respect to the meaning of "armed conflict," in its instrument of ratification for the Terrorism Financing Convention.

Given the importance of protecting the flexibility of the United States to conduct legitimate activities against all lawful targets, the second exception in paragraph 2 of Article 2*bis* was also an important objective of the United States when negotiating the Protocols. This provision exempts from the Convention's application "the activities undertaken by military forces of a State in the exercise of their official duties, inasmuch as they are governed by other rules of international law." This language is consistent with Article 19(2) of the Terrorist Bombings Convention. Although this exclusion might be thought to be implicit in the context of the Protocols, the negotiators thought it best to articulate the exclusion explicitly. It is intended to exclude all official acts undertaken by U.S. and other State military forces from the scope of criminal offenses. Because the Convention does not impose criminal liability for the official activities of State military forces, it similarly does not impose criminal liability for persons, including non-military, policy-making officials of States, who direct, organize, or otherwise act in support of the activities of State military forces. Recognizing the importance of this provision, I recommend that the following understanding to Article 3 of the 2005 SUA Protocol be included in the United States instrument of ratification:

> The United States of America understands that, pursuant to Article 3 of the Protocol of 2005 to the Convention for the Suppression of Unlawful Acts against the Safety of Maritime Navigation (which adds, *inter alia*, paragraph 2 of Article 2*bis* to the Convention for the Suppression of Unlawful Acts against the Safety of Maritime Navigation), the Convention for the Suppression of Unlawful Acts against the Safety of Maritime Navigation, 2005, does not apply to:
>
>> (a) the military forces of a State, which are the armed forces of a State organized, trained, and equipped under its internal law for the primary purpose of national defense or security, in the exercise of their official duties;
>> (b) civilians who direct or organize the official activities of military forces of a State; or
>> (c) civilians acting in support of the official activities of the military forces of a State, if the civilians are under the formal command, control, and responsibility of those forces.

*   *   *   *

7. Iraq

a. *Executive Order*

On July 17, 2007, President Bush issued Executive Order 13438, "Blocking Property of Certain Persons Who Threaten Stabilization Efforts in Iraq." 72 Fed. Reg. 39,719 (July 19, 2007). *See* Chapter 16.A.4.

b. *U.S. operations within Iraq*

On January 31, 2007, the Department of State responded to questions raised by Senate Foreign Relations Committee Chairman Joseph R. Biden and Senator Jim Webb in a hearing held on January 11. Excerpts follow from the letter from Jeffrey T. Bergner, Assistant Secretary of State for Legislative Affairs, to the two Senators.

*   *   *   *

In the President's January 10 speech to the American people on the Administration's New Way Forward in Iraq, he made clear that Iran was providing material support for attacks on American forces. He emphasized the importance of disrupting these attacks and interrupting the flow of support from Iran and Syria. The President also noted our intention to seek out and destroy the networks that are providing the advanced weaponry and training that threaten our forces in Iraq. . . .

The Administration believes that there is clear authority for U.S. operations within the territory of Iraq to prevent further Iranian- or Syrian-supported attacks against U. S. forces operating as part of the Multinational Force—Iraq (MNF-I) or against civilian targets. Such attacks directly threaten both the security and stability of Iraq and the safety of our personnel; they also continue to threaten the region's security and stability. U.S. military operations in Iraq are conducted under the President's constitutional authority and the Authorization for Use of Military Force Against

Iraq Resolution of 2002 (P. L. 107-243), which authorized the use of armed force to defend the national security of the United States against the continuing threat posed by Iraq and to enforce all relevant United Nations Security Council resolutions regarding Iraq. The United Nations Security Council has authorized all necessary measures to contribute to the maintenance of Iraq's security and stability, which encompasses MNF-I conducting military operations against any farces that carry out attacks against MNF-I or Iraqi civilian and military targets.

*   *   *   *

c.   U.S.–Iraq security relationship

On November 26, 2007, President Bush and Iraqi Prime Minister Nouri Kamel Al-Maliki signed the Declaration of Principles for a Long-term Relationship of Cooperation and Friendship Between the Republic of Iraq and the United States of America. A fact sheet released by the White House on the same date explained the significance of the declaration, as excerpted below. The full text of the fact sheet is available at *www.whitehouse.gov/news/releases/2007/11/20071126-1. html.*

President Bush's statement congratulating Iraqi political leaders on their August 26 communiqué, noted below, is available at 43 WEEKLY COMP. PRES. DOC. 1118 (Sept. 3, 2007).

---

*   *   *   *

. . . [T]his Declaration is the first step in a three-step process that will normalize U.S.-Iraqi relations in a way which is consistent with Iraq's sovereignty and will help Iraq regain its rightful status in the international community—something both we and the Iraqis seek. The second step is the renewal of the Multinational Force-Iraq's Chapter VII United Nations mandate for a final year, followed by the third step, the negotiation of the detailed arrangements that will codify our bilateral relationship after the Chapter VII mandate expires.

- The UN Chapter VII resolution that is binding under international law gives the MNFI legal authorization to "take all necessary measures to preserve peace and security". Both the U.S. and Iraq are committed to Iraq moving beyond an international presence based on a UN Security Council Chapter VII mandate.
- Iraqis have expressed a desire to move past a Chapter VII MNFI mandate and we are committed to helping them achieve this objective.
- After the Chapter VII mandate is renewed for one year, we will begin negotiation of a framework that will govern the future of our bilateral relationship.

The Declaration Is A Continuation Of A Commitment That Began This August

The governments of Iraq and the United States are committed to developing a long-term relationship as two fully sovereign and independent states with common interests.

The August 26 Communiqué signed by the five political leaders— Prime Minister Nouri al Maliki, the three members of the Presidency Council, and Kurdish leader Ma'sud Barzani—on August 26, 2007, and endorsed by President Bush states: "The leaders considered it important to link the renewal of UN Resolution 1723 for another year with a reference to the ending of Iraq's Chapter VII status under the UN Charter and the concomitant resumption of Iraq's normal status as a state with full sovereignty and authorities and the restoration of Iraq's legal international status, namely the status that it had before UN Resolution 661 of 1990. In this context, the leaders affirmed the necessity of reaching a long term relationship with the American side . . . that is built on common interests and covers the various areas between the Republic of Iraq and the United States of America. This goal should be realized in the near future."

*   *   *   *

The Declaration Sets The U.S. And Iraq On A Path Toward Negotiating Agreements That Are Common Throughout The World

The U.S. has security relationships with over 100 countries around the world, including recent agreements with nations such as Afghanistan and former Soviet bloc countries.

The relationship envisioned will include U.S.-Iraqi cooperation in the political, diplomatic, economic and security arenas. The United States and Iraq intend to negotiate arrangements based upon a range of principles.

*   *   *   *

The Declaration of Principles is set forth below and is available at *www.whitehouse.gov/news/releases/2007/11/20071126-11.html.*

As Iraqi leaders confirmed in their Communiqué signed on August 26, 2007, and endorsed by President Bush, the Governments of Iraq and the United States are committed to developing a long-term relationship of cooperation and friendship as two fully sovereign and independent states with common interests. This relationship will serve the interest of coming generations based on the heroic sacrifices made by the Iraqi people and the American people for the sake of a free, democratic, pluralistic, federal, and unified Iraq.

The relationship of cooperation envisioned by the Republic of Iraq and the United States includes a range of issues, foremost of which is cooperation in the political, economic, cultural, and security fields, taking account of the following principles:

First: The Political, Diplomatic, and Cultural Spheres

1. Supporting the Republic of Iraq in defending its democratic system against internal and external threats.
2. Respecting and upholding the Constitution as the expression of the will of the Iraqi people and standing against any attempt to impede, suspend, or violate it.
3. Supporting the efforts of the Republic of Iraq to achieve national reconciliation including as envisioned in the Communiqué of August 26.
4. Supporting the Republic of Iraq's efforts to enhance its position in regional and international organizations and institutions so that it may play a positive and constructive role in the region and the world.

5. Cooperating jointly with the states of the region on the basis of mutual respect, non-intervention in internal affairs, rejection of the use of violence in resolving disputes, and adoption of constructive dialogue in resolving outstanding problems among the various states of the region.
6. Promoting political efforts to establish positive relationships between the states of the region and the world, which serve the common goals of all relevant parties in a manner that enhances the security and stability of the region, and the prosperity of its peoples.
7. Encouraging cultural, educational, and scientific exchanges between the two countries.

Second: The Economic Sphere

1. Supporting Iraq's development in various economic fields, including its productive capabilities, and aiding its transition to a market economy.
2. Encouraging all parties to abide by their commitments as stipulated in the International Compact with Iraq.
3. Supporting the building of Iraq's economic institutions and infrastructure with the provision of financial and technical assistance to train and develop competencies and capacities of vital Iraqi institutions.
4. Supporting Iraq's further integration into regional and international financial and economic organizations.
5. Facilitating and encouraging the flow of foreign investments to Iraq, especially American investments, to contribute to the reconstruction and rebuilding of Iraq.
6. Assisting Iraq in recovering illegally exported funds and properties, especially those smuggled by the family of Saddam Hussein and his regime's associates, as well as antiquities and items of cultural heritage, smuggled before and after April 9, 2003.
7. Helping the Republic of Iraq to obtain forgiveness of its debts and compensation for the wars waged by the former regime.
8. Supporting the Republic of Iraq to obtain positive and preferential trading conditions for Iraq within the global marketplace

including accession to the World Trade Organization and most favored nation status with the United States.

Third: The Security Sphere

1. Providing security assurances and commitments to the Republic of Iraq to deter foreign aggression against Iraq that violates its sovereignty and integrity of its territories, waters, or airspace.

2. Supporting the Republic of Iraq in its efforts to combat all terrorist groups, at the forefront of which is Al-Qaeda, Saddamists, and all other outlaw groups regardless of affiliation, and destroy their logistical networks and their sources of finance, and defeat and uproot them from Iraq. This support will be provided consistent with mechanisms and arrangements to be established in the bilateral cooperation agreements mentioned herein.

3. Supporting the Republic of Iraq in training, equipping, and arming the Iraqi Security Forces to enable them to protect Iraq and all its peoples, and completing the building of its administrative systems, in accordance with the request of the Iraqi government.

   The Iraqi Government in confirmation of its resolute rights under existing Security Council resolutions will request to extend the mandate of the Multi-National Force-Iraq (MNF-I) under Chapter VII of the United Nations Charter for a final time. As a condition for this request, following the expiration of the above mentioned extension, Iraq's status under Chapter VII and its designation as a threat to international peace and security will end, and Iraq will return to the legal and international standing it enjoyed prior to the issuance of U.N. Security Council Resolution No. 661 (August, 1990), thus enhancing the recognition and confirming the full sovereignty of Iraq over its territories, waters, and airspace, and its control over its forces and the administration of its affairs.

   Taking into account the principles discussed above, bilateral negotiations between the Republic of Iraq and the

United States shall begin as soon as possible, with the aim to achieve, before July 31, 2008, agreements between the two governments with respect to the political, cultural, economic, and security spheres.

8. Iran

On June 8, 2007, U.S. Permanent Representative to the United Nations Ambassador Zalmay Khalilzad responded to a question from reporters concerning the U.S. position in a Security Council discussion of statements made by Iran concerning Israel, stating:

> . . . [T]oday there was a discussion with regard to the statement made by the President of Iran with regard to the destruction of the state of Israel. And there was a good discussion that a statement by a head of state calling for or implying the destruction of a member state of the United Nations is as a matter of principle unacceptable. And this is an issue of threat to international peace and security. Now with regard to criticizing, that statement does not mean that one should not be critical of policies, or activities, or actions of Israel. But it is different than calling for the destruction of Israel by a head of state. That's a different category. And therefore we felt as did a number of other member states that this was worthy of a statement by the Security Council and of course as you saw a similar judgment was made by the Secretary-General. You can't be indifferent to the threats made or calls made for the destruction of a country, of a state, a sovereign state, a member of . . . the United Nations.

The full text of Ambassador Khalilzad's press release is available at *www.usunnewyork.usmission.gov/press_releases/ 20070608_145.html.*

B. ARMS CONTROL

1. Treaties with the United Kingdom and Australia Concerning Defense Trade Cooperation

On September 20, 2007, President Bush transmitted to the Senate for advice and consent to ratification the Treaty Between the Government of the United States of America and the Government of the United Kingdom of Great Britain and Northern Ireland Concerning Defense Trade Cooperation, done at Washington and London on June 21 and 26, 2007. S. Treaty Doc. No. 110-7 (2007). In a letter of September 4, 2007, submitting the treaty to the President, Secretary of State Condoleezza Rice stated: "This self-executing Treaty is intended to create an exemption to provisions of the Arms Export Control Act regarding authorizations and notifications associated with certain exports and transfers, as defined in the Treaty. The Treaty envisages the conclusion of implementing arrangements, which may be entered into as Executive Agreements." On December 3, 2007, President Bush transmitted the similar Treaty with Australia Concerning Defense Trade Cooperation to the Senate. S. Treaty Doc. No.110-10 (2007).

An Overview of the U.K. treaty prepared by the Department of State, enclosed with the Secretary's letter and also included in S. Treaty Doc. No. 110-7, is excerpted below. *See also* Chapter 4.B.2.

* * * *

For several years, the United States and the United Kingdom have sought to negotiate a legally binding agreement that would provide a mutually agreeable exemption for exports to the United Kingdom of defense articles controlled pursuant to the Arms Export Control Act (22 U.S.C. 2751 et seq.) (AECA) from some requirements, such as the licensing requirements, of Section 38 of the AECA and its implementing regulations, the International Traffic in Arms Regulations ["ITAR"] (22 C.F.R. 120–130) (ITAR).

Section 1 of the AECA recognizes that "[t]he need for international defense cooperation among the United States and those friendly countries to which it is allied by mutual defense treaties is especially important . . ." and asserts that "it remains the policy of the United States to facilitate the common defense by entering into international arrangements with friendly countries which further the objective of applying agreed resources of each country to programs and projects of cooperative exchange of data, research, development, production, procurement, and logistics support to achieve specific national defense requirements and objectives of mutual concern" (22 U.S.C. 2751). Section 38(a)(1) of the AECA authorizes the President "to control the import and the export of defense articles and defense services," to "designate those items which shall be considered as defense articles and defense services," and to "promulgate regulations for the import and export of such articles and services" (22 U.S.C. 2778(a)(1)). The AECA further provides that the President may regulate the import and export of defense articles and services pursuant to licenses (22 U.S.C. 2778(b)).

In the proposed Treaty between the Government of the United States of America and the Government of the United Kingdom of Great Britain and Northern Ireland Concerning Defense Trade Cooperation, done at Washington and London June 21 and 26, 2007 (the Treaty), the Government of the United Kingdom would be bound to a regime that would provide appropriate protections for U.S. defense articles and defense services exported under the Treaty through the application of the United Kingdom Official Secrets Act rather than through revisions to its export control regime. For this reason, the Treaty will not be entered into pursuant to the authority contained in section 38(j) of the AECA (22 U.S.C. 27780).

The Treaty establishes a comprehensive framework for the export of certain defense articles and defense services from the United States to certain facilities and entities of the United Kingdom. Where the Treaty applies, such export may occur without a license or other written authorization from the Department of State's Directorate of Defense Trade Controls, which is the office responsible for developing and implementing the ITAR. Once exported, these Defense Articles may be transferred within what is referred to as an

"Approved Community" without case-by-case review and approval by the Directorate of Defense Trade Controls. Transfers out of such Approved Community would, however, be subject to Directorate of Defense Trade Controls authorization requirements, and any unauthorized transfers would constitute violations of the AECA.

As noted in the Treaty's Preamble, this Treaty is self-executing in the United States. The purposes for which exports may occur pursuant to this Treaty and the defense articles that may not be exported pursuant to the Treaty will be identified in separate Implementing Arrangements, as well as in regulations intended to clarify this matter. The list of facilities and entities in the United Kingdom that may receive defense articles and defense services through exports pursuant to this Treaty will be identified through processes established in separate Implementing Arrangements.

This Treaty establishes an exemption from the operation of the licensing and notification requirements contained in the AECA and the ITAR. As stated below, compliance with the procedures established in accordance with this Treaty shall constitute an exception to these requirements. Conduct outside of the procedures established in accordance with this Treaty must comply with the normal requirements. Although the Treaty is self-executing, it will be necessary to promulgate a number of regulatory changes to the ITAR to effectuate the licensing exemption. Once the Implementing Arrangements have entered into force, they will be made available to the public, and changes to the ITAR will be published in the Federal Register.

*　　*　　*　　*

Scope of the treaty

Article 3 identifies the activities in support of which Defense Articles may be Exported or Transferred without a license or other written authorization. The Treaty applies to the movement of Defense Articles that are required for agreed combined military or counter-terrorism operations; cooperative security and defense research, development, production, and support programs; security and defense projects where the Government of the United Kingdom is the end-user; and for United States Government end-use. Either Government may exclude certain Defense Articles from the application of the Treaty.

The Treaty does not apply to the provision of Defense Articles pursuant to the Foreign Military Sales program. The process for providing Defense Articles pursuant to that program will remain unchanged. Once such Defense Articles are provided, however, they may be transferred within the Approved Community pursuant to the Treaty.

An exporter may request a license or other authorization from the Directorate of Defense Trade Controls in which case the terms of such license or authorization will apply instead of the procedures that will be established to implement the Treaty.

Approved community

Articles 4 and 5 identify the persons and entities that may Export or Transfer Defense Articles without a license or other written authorization. Specifically, Article 4 identifies the persons, entities, and facilities of the United Kingdom that may send or receive such Defense Articles; and Article 5 identifies the persons, entities, and facilities of the United States that may send or receive such Defense Articles.

                                *   *   *   *

United States Government personnel with appropriate security clearance and a need-to-know may be provided access to Defense Articles exported or transferred pursuant to this Treaty. Employees of the nongovernmental United States entities referred to above who have appropriate security clearance and a need-to-know may be provided access to Defense Articles Exported or Transferred pursuant to this Treaty.

The facilities, entities, and personnel described in Article 4 comprise the United Kingdom Community. The facilities, entities, and personnel described in Article 5 comprise the United States Community. The United Kingdom and United States Communities comprise the Approved Community.

                                *   *   *   *

Enforcement

Article 13 provides that if persons or entities Exporting or Transferring Defense Articles pursuant to the Treaty comply with the procedures established pursuant to this Treaty, including its Implementing Arrangements, and any regulations promulgated to implement the Treaty's effect on existing law, they shall be exempt from the generally applicable licensing requirements established pursuant to the Arms Export Control Act with respect to exports and transfers of Defense Articles. If, however, persons or entities Exporting or Transferring Defense Articles engage in conduct that is outside the scope of the Treaty, including certain of its Implementing Arrangements, and any regulations promulgated to implement the Treaty's effect on existing law, that conduct remains subject to the applicable licensing requirements and implementing regulations of the AECA.

Because the Treaty is self-executing, this exemption will be created through ratification of the Treaty; no additional legislation will be required to implement the exemption in United States law. Those Implementing Arrangements constituting terms of the exemption are authorized by this self-executing Treaty. They will not be submitted for Senate advice and consent to ratification and also require no further legislative action to become a fully effective part of the exemption.

*   *   *   *

Implementing arrangements

Article 14(1) of the Treaty provides that the Parties shall conclude, on an expedited basis, Implementing Arrangements for this Treaty, which may be amended or supplemented by the Parties from time to time. For example, the Implementing Arrangements will establish eligibility requirements for persons to be considered part of the United Kingdom Community.

Article 14(2) further provides that the Parties will include in such Implementing Arrangements a process by which entities in the Approved Community may transition from the requirements of U.S. government defense export licenses or other authorizations issued under the ITAR to the regime established under the Treaty.

The Administration does not intend to submit any of the Implementing Arrangements to the Senate for advice and consent, but is prepared to provide these Implementing Arrangements to the Senate for its information.

*   *   *   *

2. Russian Suspension of Conventional Armed Forces in Europe Treaty

On November 29, 2007, Russian President Vladimir Putin signed a law suspending, as of 0000 hours on December 12, 2008, Moscow time, Russia's observance of its obligations under the Treaty on Conventional Armed Forces in Europe, done at Paris November 19, 1990, S. Treaty Doc. No. 102-8 (1991); 30 I.L.M. 1 (1991). As explained in a Department of State fact sheet of June 18, 2002:

> The Treaty on Conventional Armed Forces in Europe (or CFE Treaty), signed in Paris on November 19, 1990, by the 22 members of NATO and the former Warsaw Pact, is a landmark arms control agreement that established parity in major conventional forces/armaments between East and West from the Atlantic to the Urals. It provides an unprecedented basis for lasting European security and stability. The original CFE Treaty (which is of unlimited duration) entered into force in 1992. Following the demise of the Warsaw Pact and the enlargement of NATO in the 1990s, the then 30 CFE States Parties signed the Adaptation Agreement at the Istanbul OSCE Summit on 19 November 1999, to amend the CFE Treaty to take account of the evolving European geo-strategic environment.

The United States ratified the original treaty in January 1992, and it entered into force on November 9, 1992. *See Cumulative Digest 1991–1999* at 2222–30 and *Digest 1989–1990* at 578–79. President William J. Clinton signed the Adaptation Agreement on November 19, 1999, but conditioned transmittal of the instrument to the Senate for advice and consent to ratification on fulfillment by Russia of certain commitments. *See Cumulative Digest 1991–1999* at 2234–38. The Adaptation Agreement has never been submitted to the Senate.

In a statement issued December 12, 2007, Department of State Spokesman Sean McCormack noted that suspension is not provided for under the CFE treaty, and expressed U.S.

disappointment in the Russian action. The statement is provided in full below and is available at *www.state.gov/r/pa/prs/ps/2007/dec/97151.htm.*

The United States of America deeply regrets the Russian Federation's decision to "suspend" implementation of its obligations under the Treaty on Conventional Armed Forces in Europe (CFE) on December 12, 2007. Russia's conventional forces are the largest on the European continent, and its unilateral action damages this successful arms control regime. This "suspension," which is not provided for under the terms of the CFE Treaty, is the wrong decision.

The CFE Treaty has demonstrated its importance through unprecedented reductions in levels of military hardware in Europe and a transformation of the political context of our security dialogue from suspicion to mutual confidence.

Russia's action is particularly disappointing because the United States and NATO Allies have been engaged for the last several months in an intensive dialogue with Russia to address the issues Moscow has raised, while taking account of the concerns of all 30 States Parties. We have offered constructive, generous proposals for parallel actions on ratification of the Adapted CFE Treaty and fulfillment of remaining commitments that were made at the OSCE's Istanbul Summit in 1999, with the objective of achieving our common goal of entry into force of the Agreement on Adaptation to the CFE Treaty.

Together with our NATO Allies and Treaty partners, we will carefully monitor Russia's actions with regard to its CFE Treaty obligations. We encourage Russia to reverse its decision and to work with us to resolve all outstanding concerns of all States Parties.

> Representatives of the Russian Federation continue to participate in the Joint Consultative Group, the CFE Treaty deliberative body that is composed of representatives of the states parties to the Treaty.

3.   International Traffic in Arms Regulations

Department of State responsibility for the control of the permanent and temporary export and temporary import of defense articles and services is governed primarily by the Arms Export Control Act ("AECA"), 22 U.S.C. § 2778, and Executive Order 11958 as amended, 42 Fed. Reg. 4311 (Jan. 24, 1977). The AECA, among other requirements and authorities, provides for the promulgation of implementing regulations, the International Traffic in Arms Regulations ("ITAR"), 22 CFR §§ 120–130. See *www.pmddtc.state.gov/ itar_index.htm*.

During 2007 several amendments were made to the ITAR, discussed below.

a. *Prohibited exports and sales to certain countries*

(1) *Countries affected*

At the end of 2007, 22 C.F.R. § 126.1, "Prohibited exports and sales to certain countries," provided as follows in its general subsection (a):

> It is the policy of the United States to deny licenses and other approvals for exports and imports of defense articles and defense services, destined for or originating in certain countries. This policy applies to Belarus, Cuba, Iran, North Korea, Syria, and Venezuela. This policy also applies to countries with respect to which the United States maintains an arms embargo (e.g., Burma, China, Liberia, and Sudan) or whenever an export would not otherwise be in furtherance of world peace and the security and foreign policy of the United States. Information regarding certain other embargoes appears elsewhere in this section. Comprehensive arms embargoes are normally the subject of a State Department notice published in the Federal Register. The exemptions provided in the regulations in this subchapter, except Sec.123.17 of this subchapter, do not apply with respect to articles originating in or for export to any proscribed countries, areas, or persons in this Sec.126.1.

(i) Somalia

Effective May 22, 2007, the Department of State amended § 126.1, deleting a specific reference to Somalia previously appearing in paragraph (a) *supra*, and adding a new paragraph (m) to that section. 72 Fed. Reg. 28,602 (May 22, 2007). As explained in the summary section of the Federal Register notice, the amendment would "make it United States policy to consider on a case-by-case basis licenses, or other approvals, for exports of defense articles and defense services destined for Somalia that conform to the provisions of United Nations Security Council resolution 1744 which amends United Nations Security Council resolution 733." The notice explained the change in policy as follows.

* * * *

On February 20, 2007, the United Nations Security Council (UNSC) adopted resolution 1744 which, inter alia, amends the complete embargo on weapons and military equipment imposed by UNSC resolution (UNSCR) 733 (1992). In resolution 1744, the UNSC decided that the embargo shall no longer apply to the export to Somalia of weapons and military equipment, technical training, and assistance when intended solely for either of two purposes: (1) Support for the African Union Mission to Somalia (AMISOM), an effort to establish an initial stabilization phase in Somalia, and (2) support for the purpose of helping develop security sector institutions in Somalia that further the objectives of peace, stability and reconciliation in Somalia. Proposed exports for the latter purpose will require advance notification by the United States Government to the UN Somalia Sanctions Committee and the absence of a negative decision by that Committee. In addition, exemptions from licensing requirements may not be used with respect to exports to Somalia without prior written authorization by the Directorate of Defense Trade Controls.

* * * *

(ii) Venezuela

Effective February 7, 2007, the Department of State amended the ITAR by adding Venezuela to the list of countries in the second sentence of § 126.1(a) "as a result of its designation as a country not cooperating fully with anti-terrorism efforts, and in conjunction with the August 17, 2006 [71 FR 47,554] announcement of a policy of denial of the export or transfer of defense articles to an[d] revocation of existing authorizations for Venezuela." 72 Fed. Reg. 5614 (Feb. 7, 2007).

(iii) Libya

The February 7 notice also amended the ITAR regarding Libya "to make it United States policy to deny licenses, other approvals, exports or imports of defense articles and defense services destined for or originating in Libya except, on a case-by-case basis for non-lethal defense articles and defense services, and non-lethal safety-of-use defense articles . . . as spare parts for lethal end-items." The new policy appears in a new subparagraph (k) to § 126.1, and Libya was deleted from subparagraph (d) listing countries designated as state sponsors of terrorism, reflecting the rescission of Libya's designation on June 30, 2006.

(iv) Vietnam

On April 3, 2007, the Department of State amended 22 C.F.R. § 126.1 regarding Vietnam by deleting it from the list of countries in the second sentence of subparagraph (a) and by adding a new subsection 126.1(l). 72 Fed. Reg. 15,830 (April 3, 2007) As explained in the Federal Register notice:

On November 2, 2006, the Secretary of State modified the U.S. arms transfer policy toward Vietnam allowing the sale, lease, export, or other transfer of non-lethal defense articles and defense services to the country. Subsequently, the President issued a determination December 29, 2006 that the furnishing of defense articles and services to Vietnam would strengthen the security of the United States and promote world peace.

The new policy will not permit the export or other transfer to Vietnam of: (a) Lethal end items, (b) components of lethal end items, unless those components are non-lethal, safety-of-use spare parts for lethal end items, (c) non-lethal crowd control defense articles and defense services, and (d) night vision devices to end-users with a role in ground security.

(2) List of countries embargoed under UN sanctions

Effective December 18, 2007, the Department of State amended 22 C.F.R. § 126.1(c), "Exports and Sales Prohibited by United Nations Security Council Embargoes," to add a list of countries subject to such UN embargoes. 72 Fed. Reg. 71,575 (Dec. 18, 2007). Section 126.1(c), as amended, follows.

(c) Exports and sales prohibited by United Nations Security Council embargoes. Whenever the United Nations Security Council mandates an arms embargo, all transactions that are prohibited by the embargo and that involve U.S. persons anywhere, or any person in the United States, and defense articles or services of a type enumerated on the United States Munitions List (22 CFR part 121), irrespective of origin, are prohibited under the ITAR for the duration of the embargo, unless the Department of State publishes a notice in the Federal Register specifying different measures. This would include, but is not limited to, transactions involving trade by U.S. persons who are located inside or outside of the United States in defense articles or services of U.S. or foreign origin that are located inside or outside of the United States. United Nations Arms Embargoes include, but are not necessarily limited to, the following countries:

(1) Cote d'Ivoire

(2) Democratic Republic of Congo . . .

 (3) Iraq
 (4) Iran
 (5) Lebanon
 (6) Liberia
 (7) North Korea
 (8) Rwanda . . .
 (9) Sierra Leone
(10) Somalia
(11) Sudan

4. Strategic Arms Reduction Treaty

In 2007 the thirtieth and thirty-first sessions of the Strategic Arms Reduction Treaty ("START" or "Treaty") Joint Compliance and Inspection Commission ("JCIC") were held in Geneva ("JCIC XXX" and "JCIC XXXI"). At each of these sessions, the START parties issued coordinated statements of policy and agreed to changes in site diagrams of certain START facilities.

The START provides in Article XV that the parties may "agree upon such additional measures as may be necessary to improve the viability and effectiveness of [the] Treaty." This allows the parties to agree on administrative or technical changes (often called "V & E changes") to improve the implementation of the Treaty that would not affect the substantive rights and obligations of the parties. Such documents have taken two forms: JCIC Agreements, in which a provision of one of the Treaty's Protocols (or another of the Treaty documents such as the Treaty's Memorandum of Understanding) is amended; and JCIC Joint Statements, in which the parties come to a legally-binding "understanding" as to how a specific provision of the Treaty or of a Protocol should be interpreted. One type of Joint Statement is known as an S-Series Joint Statement, which codifies the parties' agreement on changes in site diagrams.

At JCIC XXX, the coordinated statement addressed concerns of the United States regarding reentry vehicle inspections of SS-25 ICBMs. All parties' statements were substantially identical; excerpts follow from an unclassified annex to the plenary statement of the United States, May 23, 2007. The full text is available at *www.state.gov/s/l/c8183.htm.*

The United States of America notes that in order to confirm that the SS-25 ICBM is not deployed with more reentry vehicles than the number of warheads attributed to it under the START Treaty, the Russian Federation, as the inspected Party, conducted a demonstration in connection with reentry vehicle inspections of the SS-25 ICBM (hereinafter, the demonstration) for the United States of America, as the inspecting Party, at Vypolzovo ICBM base for road-mobile launchers of ICBMs on February 14–16, 2006. The results of the demonstration are recorded in the demonstration report signed by the representatives of the inspecting and inspected Parties on February 16, 2006. The report contains the results of the official measurements of additional cover parameters made during the demonstration. . . .

In this connection, the United States of America understands that the Russian Federation will supplement the existing procedures for conducting reentry vehicle inspections of SS-25 ICBMs with procedures for additional measurements of the covers used during such inspections, as well as additional procedures for visual examination and the use of seals. These procedures are intended to confirm that the cover used during a reentry vehicle inspection of an SS-25 ICBM (hereinafter, the cover) has been installed on the front section of the inspected missile in the same configuration as was observed during the demonstration. . . .

* * * *

. . . [T]he United States of America understands that the Russian Federation will be prepared to use the aforementioned additional procedures during each reentry vehicle inspection of SS-25 ICBMs, beginning 45 days after all the Parties exchange statements on this matter.

The United States of America notes that this statement, and the statements made by the other Parties on this matter, will enter into force 30 days after completion of the first reentry vehicle inspection of SS-25 ICBMs conducted after all Parties exchange such statements, provided that during those 30 days, the United States of America does not raise questions through diplomatic channels that: 1) were recorded in the report for that inspection; 2) addressed the inability of inspectors to confirm indirectly that the inspected SS-25 ICBM contained no more reentry vehicles than the number of warheads attributed to it; and, 3) were not resolved on-site during the inspection.

One important accomplishment at JCIC XXXI was reaching agreement among the parties on issues arising out of the Russian Federation's development of a prototype missile ("RS-24") that has not attained the status of a "new type" of missile, accountable under the Treaty. The U.S. versions of two coordinated plenary statements on this topic are excerpted below; the coordinated plenary statements of the other parties are substantially identical. The full texts of the statements, contained in an unclassified annex to the U.S. closing plenary statement of December 5, 2007, are available at *www.state.gov/s/l/c8183.htm*.

JCIC Coordinated Plenary Statement on Conversion Procedures and the Manner of Accountability for the One Road-Mobile Test Launcher of the RS-24 ICBM Prototype

The United States of America takes note of the Russian Federation Statement on Conversion Procedures and the Manner of Accountability for the One Road-Mobile Test Launcher of the RS-24 ICBM Prototype.

The Russian Federation declares that:

— procedures for converting the one road-mobile test launcher of the SS-27 ICBM to a road-mobile test launcher of the RS-24 ICBM prototype consist of the replacement of cabling and boxes of equipment for preparing and conducting launches;

— until such time as the RS-24 ICBM is accountable under the Treaty Between the Union of Soviet Socialist Republics and the United States of America on the Reduction and Limitation of Strategic Offensive Arms (hereinafter the Treaty), this converted launcher will be included by the Russian Federation in the Memorandum of Understanding Relating to the Treaty as a "road-mobile test launcher of the RS-24 ICBM prototype" for the facility where it is located;

— this launcher will be subject to the relevant notifications and provisions of paragraph 2(d) of Article IV of the Treaty;

— during data update inspections at the Plesetsk test range, in-country escorts during the pre-inspection procedures will declare the presence at the inspection site of a road-mobile test launcher of the RS-24 ICBM prototype, and it will be subject to inspection;

— the converted road-mobile test launcher of the RS-24 ICBM prototype will be distinctively marked with paint or in a similar manner to guarantee identification of this launcher during upcoming inspections;

— a photograph of the aforesaid distinctive marking will be provided to the United States of America.

The United States of America agrees that:

— the one road-mobile test launcher for the SS-27 ICBM which was converted for launching the RS-24 ICBM prototype is considered to be a test launcher of the RS-24 ICBM prototype as of the time when, after completion of all conversion operations, it first left the structure where its conversion took place;

— what has been set forth in this statement is sufficient to reach agreement on the procedures for converting this road-mobile test launcher of the SS-27 ICBM to a road-mobile test launcher of the RS-24 ICBM prototype and for the manner of its accountability under the Treaty.

Coordinated Plenary Statement On Verification Procedures for the RS-24 ICBM Prototype at the Portal of the Votkinsk Machine Building Plant

The United States of America takes note of the Russian Federation Statement on Verification Procedures for the RS-24 ICBM Prototype at the Portal of the Votkinsk Machine Building Plant.

*   *   *   *

In connection with the foregoing, the United States of America believes that the verification procedures currently in use at the portal of the Votkinsk Machine Building Plant are sufficient to confirm type of launch canister for the RS-24 ICBM prototype, and that there is no need to agree on additional verification procedures as provided for in paragraph 4 of Section XVI of the Protocol on Inspections and Continuous Monitoring Activities Relating to the Treaty.

> Finally, the Russians sought to change the site diagram for two of their inspectable facilities. Pursuant to Annex J to the Memorandum of Understanding on the Establishment of the Data Base Relating to [START], the parties must agree to certain of those changes; they do so by means of an "S-Series" JCIC Joint Statement. JCIC Joint Statement S-27 (May 23, 2007) addressed changes to the boundary of the Plesetsk Test Range; JCIC Joint Statement S-28 (December 5, 2007) addressed changes to the boundary of the Kostroma ICBM base for rail-mobile launchers of ICBMS. In Annex A to each of the statements Russia provided compliance information. Annex A to JCIC Joint Statement S-27 is set forth below; Annex A to S-28 contains similar information about the Kostroma site. The full texts of the two joint statements, with attached Annex A in each instance, are available at *www.state.gov/s/l/c8183.htm* (each of the annexes referred to in these texts as "Annex B," is classified and not included).

The Russian Federation:

(1) pursuant to subparagraph 19(a) of Annex J to the Memorandum of Understanding on the Establishment of the Data Base Relating to the Treaty, hereinafter referred to as the Memorandum of Understanding, declares that the requirements set forth in the first sentence of paragraph 2 of Section IX of the Protocol on Procedures Governing the Conversion or Elimination of the Items Subject to the Treaty have been met with respect to the portions of the Plesetsk Test Range to be excluded from within the boundary shown on the site diagram of the facility dated September 30, 2002;

(2) pursuant to subparagraph 19(b) of Annex J to the Memorandum of Understanding, states that all structures that were ever shown within the boundaries shown on the site diagrams of Test Sites No. 7 dated October 1, 1999, No. 9 dated October 1, 1999, No. 12 dated October 1, 1999, and No. 16 dated September 30, 2002, of the Plesetsk Test Range pursuant to subparagraph 9(b)(iii) or 9(b)(iv) of Annex J to the Memorandum of Understanding and that will be excluded from within the boundary of this facility pursuant to this Joint Statement, are unchanged but will no longer be used for items of inspection as of April 12, 2007.

5. Trafficking in Small Arms and Light Weapons

In a press release dated December 3, 2007, the Department of State Spokesman announced that the United States and the Caribbean Community ("CARICOM") countries had "pledged to enhance regional cooperation to prevent, combat, and eradicate the illicit trafficking in small arms and light weapons in the region. Illicit trafficking in small arms and light weapons poses a serious threat to the security of the Western Hemisphere because this thriving black market provides weapons to terrorist groups, drug traffickers, gangs, and other criminal organizations." The full text of the fact sheet, which includes the text of the initiative, is available at *www.state.gov/r/pa/prs/ps/2007/dec/96146.htm.*

C. NONPROLIFERATION

1. U.S.–Russia Joint Statement

On July 3, 2007, President Bush and President Putin issued a joint statement:

We are determined to play an active role in making the advantages of the peaceful use of nuclear energy available to a wide range of interested States, in particular developing countries, provided the common goal of prevention of proliferation of nuclear weapons is achieved. To this end, we intend, together with others, to initiate a new format for enhanced cooperation.

*   *   *   *

We are prepared to enter into discussions jointly and bilaterally to develop mutually beneficial approaches with states considering nuclear energy or considering expansion of existing nuclear energy programs in conformity with their rights and obligations under the NPT. The development of economical and reliable access to nuclear energy is designed to permit states to gain the benefits of nuclear energy and to create a viable alternative to the acquisition of sensitive fuel cycle technologies.

Further excerpts from the statement follow; the full text is available at 42 Weekly Comp. Pres. Doc. 895 (July 6, 2007). The U.S.–Russia agreement initialed in 2007 and noted below would establish the legal framework required by U.S. law for peaceful nuclear cooperation between the United States and Russia related to, e.g., transfers of nuclear material, reactors, and major reactor components. *See also* joint statement of July 17, 2006, available at 42 Weekly Comp. Pres. Doc. 1356 (July 24, 2006).

*   *   *   *

. . . [W]e acknowledge with satisfaction the initialing of the bilateral Agreement between the Government of the Russian Federation and the Government of the United States of America for cooperation in the field of peaceful use of nuclear energy. We share the view that this Agreement will provide an essential basis for the expansion of Russian-U.S. cooperation in the field of peaceful use of nuclear energy and expect this document to be signed and brought into force in accordance with existing legal requirements.

We share a common vision of growth in the use of nuclear energy, including in developing countries, to increase the supply of electricity, promote economic growth and development, and reduce reliance on fossil fuels, resulting in decreased pollution and greenhouse gasses.

This expansion of nuclear energy should be conducted in a way that strengthens the nuclear nonproliferation regime. We strongly support the Treaty on the Non-Proliferation of Nuclear Weapons, and are committed to its further strengthening. We support universal adherence to the IAEA Additional Protocol, and call on those who have not yet done so to sign and ratify it. We support the activities of the IAEA with respect to both safeguards and promotion of peaceful nuclear energy, and fully understand the need for growth of its capabilities, including its financial resources, commensurate with the expanded use of nuclear energy worldwide.

We are prepared to support expansion of nuclear energy in the following ways, consistent with national law and international legal frameworks. These efforts build on, reinforce, and complement a range of existing activities, including the work at the IAEA for reliable access to nuclear fuel, the initiative of the Russian Federation on developing Global Nuclear Infrastructure, including the nuclear fuel center in the Russian Federation, the initiative of the United States to establish the Global Nuclear Energy Partnership, the IAEA International Project on Innovative Nuclear Rectors and Fuel Cycles, and the Generation IV International Forum.

*   *   *   *

The energy and nonproliferation challenges we face today are greater than ever before. We are convinced that this approach will permit substantial expansion of nuclear energy and at the same time strengthen nonproliferation. We welcome the cooperation of states that share this common vision and are committed to jointly taking steps to make this vision a reality.

2. U.S.–India Agreement

On July 27, 2007, the United States and India completed negotiation of a bilateral agreement, the U.S.–India Agreement for Cooperation Concerning Peaceful Uses of Nuclear Energy, also known as the 123 Agreement, as part of the U.S.–India Civil Nuclear Cooperation Initiative. The text of the agreement is available at *www.state.gov/r/pa/prs/ps/2007/aug/90050.htm.*

A State Department Fact Sheet, available at *www.state. gov/r/pa/prs/ps/2007/89552.htm,* describes the agreement as well as the remaining steps that must be taken for the agreement to enter into force. A joint statement issued by Secretary of State Condoleezza Rice and Indian Minister of External Affairs Pranab Mukherjee is available at *www.state. gov/secretary/rm/2007/89522.htm.* In an on-the-record briefing of July 27, R. Nicholas Burns, Under Secretary of State for Political Affairs, described the agreement and its significance, as excerpted below. The full text of Mr. Burns's statement is available at *www.state.gov/p/us/rm/2007/89559.htm.*

*　　*　　*　　*

In this agreement, the United States commits to full civil nuclear cooperation with India. And that includes research and development, nuclear safety, commercial trade in nuclear reactors, in technology and in fuel. And the agreement essentially provides a legal basis for the two countries to cooperate in this fashion.

We have also reaffirmed in this agreement the fuel supply assurances that President Bush and Prime Minister Singh agree[d] to in March of last year. And we do so by supporting the creation of an Indian strategic fuel reserve and for committing to help India gain access to the international fuel market. Both of us—the United States and India—have granted each other consent to reprocess spent fuel. To bring this reprocessing into effect requires that India would first establish a new national facility under IAEA safeguards dedicated to reprocessing safeguarded nuclear material.

Our two countries will also subsequently agree on a set of arrangements and procedures under which reprocessing will take place. And for those of you who are steeped in this, you know that that's called for by Section 131 of the Atomic Energy Act of 1954.

In this agreement, India has committed to safeguard in perpetuity all civil nuclear material and equipment and also committed that all items under this agreement will only be used for peaceful purposes.

Those are the major features of what we have agreed upon, and it represents a tremendous and historic step forward for both of us. If we look back at the past decades of our relations with India, we know that our differences over nuclear issues have constituted the most significant divisive element in this relationship. The agreement that we announced today removes that fundamental roadblock and will bring us much closer together as two countries as a result.

And that is something that we Americans see as vital to our national interest, not only today but for the decades to come. And that is the first and most important strategic benefit of this agreement.

There are four other related benefits to this agreement as well. The first concerns nonproliferation. Some critics have said that this arrangement undermines the international nonproliferation regime and the NPT. We think that is absolutely incorrect. We think that the U.S.-India agreement strengthens the international nonproliferation regime. For 30 years, India has been on the outside of that system. It has been sanctioned and prevented from taking part in civil energy trade. With this agreement, India will open up its system to international inspection and it puts the majority of its civilian reactors under IAEA safeguards. This deal now brings India, soon to be the world's largest country, back into the nonproliferation mainstream in a way it was not before. And that is a tangible gain for India, as well as the United States and the rest of the world.

The agreement also sends an important message to nuclear outlaw regimes such as Iran. It sends a message that if you behave responsibly in regards to nonproliferation and you play by the rules, you will not be penalized, but will be invited to participate more fully in international nuclear trade. India has not proliferated, unlike North Korea in the past. India is willing to subject itself to full IAEA safeguards, unlike Iran today. And India has not violated its nuclear obligations, as Iran has and continues to do. Iran, of course, has reneged on its most important international commitments.

An additional related benefit is something we're all growing more concerned about everyday, and that is clean energy. We need to find alternatives to the polluting fossil fuel sources that the world has become so dependent upon. And India looks poised to continue its very substantial economic growth. It will require energy to sustain that growth. And with this deal, India will be in a greater position to increase the percentage of its energy sources and energy mix coming from clean nuclear power. That will help in the fight against global climate change.

The agreement also gives India greater control and security over its energy supplies, making it less reliant on imports from countries in the future, like Iran. That's currently a major problem for India; the fact that it needs these external supplies. And so India wants to find a way to resolve this problem, and so do we. And we believe this agreement can contribute to that cause.

The final benefit will be that American firms will be, for the first time in three decades, able to invest in India's nuclear industry. American companies have the finest nuclear technology in the world, and we are looking forward to American firms having the opportunity to bring their latest technology to the Indian market. We are confident that American companies will have equal access to this huge market and that they will succeed there.

So in all respects, we believe this agreement is in the unquestioned national interest of the United States. To put it into effect, there are three remaining steps that need to be taken: first, India will now have to negotiate an IAEA safeguards agreement, and we hope that can happen as soon as possible; second, we will work together, along with many other countries in the Nuclear Suppliers Group, to help India gain access to civil nuclear trade with all the countries of the world; and third, when we have finished those two steps, President Bush will send this agreement to Congress, as he has promised to do, for a final vote by the United States Congress.

* * * *

In October 2007 Mr. Burns commented further on criticism from some sources on the new agreement, as excerpted below. *See* "America's Strategic Opportunity With India," 86 Foreign Affairs 131 (Nov./Dec. 2007); also available at *www. state.gov/p/us/rm/2007/93728.htm.*

* * * *

The benefits of these historic agreements are very real for the United States. For the first time in three decades, India will submit its entire civil nuclear program to international inspection by permanently placing 14 of its 22 nuclear power plants and all of its future civil reactors under the safeguards of the International Atomic Energy Agency (IAEA). Within a generation, nearly 90 percent of India's reactors will likely be covered by the agreement. Without the arrangement, India's nuclear power program would have remained a black box. With it, India will be brought into the international nuclear nonproliferation mainstream.

Some have criticized this dramatic break from past orthodoxy, especially the decision to grant India consent rights to reprocess spent fuel. But in fact, the United States has granted reprocessing consent before, to Japan and the European Atomic Energy Community. Moreover, these rights will come into effect only once India builds a state-of-the-art reprocessing facility fully monitored by the IAEA and we agree on the specific arrangements and procedures for it. The agreement with India will not assist the country's nuclear weapons program in any way. And should India decide to conduct a nuclear test in the future, then the United States would have the right under U.S. law to seek the return of all nuclear fuel and technology shipped by U.S. firms.

. . . This agreement will deepen the strategic partnership, create new opportunities for U.S. businesses. . . .

*   *   *   *

3.   North Korea

a.   Six-Party Talks

(1)   Initial implementation

On February 13, 2007, at the conclusion of discussions held in Beijing among the Democratic People's Republic of Korea, the People's Republic of China, Japan, the Republic of Korea, the Russian Federation, and the United States ("Six-Party

Talks"), the parties released a joint statement entitled "Initial Actions for the Implementation of the Joint Statement." The Joint Statement referred to in the title of the 2007 action plan was issued on September 19, 2005, available at *www.state. gov/r/pa/prs/ps/2005/53490.htm.*

The substantive paragraphs of the 2007 action plan follow; the full text is available at *www.state.gov/r/pa/prs/ps/ 2007/february/80479.htm.*

---

*   *   *   *

I. The Parties held serious and productive discussions on the actions each party will take in the initial phase for the implementation of the Joint Statement of 19 September 2005. The Parties reaffirmed their common goal and will to achieve early denuclearization of the Korean Peninsula in a peaceful manner and reiterated that they would earnestly fulfill their commitments in the Joint Statement. The Parties agreed to take coordinated steps to implement the Joint Statement in a phased manner in line with the principle of "action for action"

II. The Parties agreed to take the following actions in parallel in the initial phase:

1. The DPRK will shut down and seal for the purpose of eventual abandonment the Yongbyon nuclear facility, including the reprocessing facility and invite back IAEA personnel to conduct all necessary monitoring and verifications as agreed between IAEA and the DPRK.

2. The DPRK will discuss with other parties a list of all its nuclear programs as described in the Joint Statement, including plutonium extracted from used fuel rods, that would be abandoned pursuant to the Joint Statement.

3. The DPRK and the US will start bilateral talks aimed at resolving pending bilateral issues and moving toward fill diplomatic relations. The US will begin the process of removing the designation of the DPRK as a state-sponsor of terrorism and advance the process of terminating the application of the Trading with the Enemy Act with respect to the DPRK.

4. The DPRK and Japan will start bilateral talks aimed at taking steps to normalize their relations in accordance with the Pyongyang Declaration, on the basis of the settlement of unfortunate past and the outstanding issues of concern.

5. Recalling Section 1 and 3 of the Joint Statement of 19 September 2005, the Parties agreed to cooperate in economic, energy and humanitarian assistance to the DPRK. In this regard, the Parties agreed to the provision of emergency energy assistance to the DPRK in the initial phase. The initial shipment of emergency energy assistance equivalent to 50,000 tons of heavy fuel oil (HFO) will commence within next 60 days. The Parties agreed that the above-mentioned initial actions will be implemented within next 60 days and that they will take coordinated steps toward this goal.

III. The Parties agreed on the establishment of the following Working Groups (WG) in order to carry out the initial actions and for the purpose of full implementation of the Joint Statement:
   1. Denuclearization of the Korean Peninsula
   2. Normalization of DPRK-US relations
   3. Normalization of DPRK-Japan relations
   4. Economy and Energy Cooperation
   5. Northeast Asia Peace and Security Mechanism

The WGs will discuss and formulate specific plans for the implementation of the Joint Statement in their respective areas. The WGs shall report to the Six-Party Heads of Delegation Meeting on the progress of their work. In principle, progress in one WG shall not affect progress in other WGs. Plans made by the five WGs will be implemented as a whole in a coordinated manner. The Parties agreed that all WGs will meet within next 30 days.

IV. During the period of the Initial Actions phase and the next phase—which includes provision by the DPRK of a complete declaration of all nuclear programs and disablement of all existing nuclear facilities, including graphite-moderated reactors and reprocessing plant—economic, energy and humanitarian assistance up to the equivalent of 1 million tons of heavy fuel oil (HFO), including the initial shipment equivalent to 50,000 tons of HFO, will be provided to the DPRK.

The detailed modalities of the said assistance will be determined through consultations and appropriate assessments in the Working Group on Economic and Energy Cooperation.

V. Once the initial actions are implemented, the Six Parties will promptly hold a ministerial meeting to confirm implementation of the Joint Statement and explore ways and means for promoting security cooperation in Northeast Asia.

VI. The Parties reaffirmed that they will take positive steps to increase mutual trust, and will make joint efforts for lasting peace and stability in Northeast Asia. The directly related parties will negotiate a permanent peace regime on the Korean Peninsula at an appropriate separate forum.

VII. The Parties agreed to hold the Sixth Round of the Six-Party Talks on 19 March 2007 to hear reports of WGs and discuss on actions for the next phase.

(2) Second-phase implementation

> Following further Six-Party Talks in Beijing, on October 3, 2007, the PRC Foreign Ministry released a joint statement by the parties on second-phase implementation. Second-Phase Actions for the Implementation of the September 2005 Joint Statement, available at *www.state.gov/r/pa/prs/ps/2007/oct/ 93217.htm*. This document, excerpted below, established December 31, 2007 as the deadline for disablement of facilities and provision of a complete and correct DPRK declaration.

---

*   *   *   *

The Parties listened to and endorsed the reports of the five Working Groups, confirmed the implementation of the initial actions provided for in the February 13 agreement, agreed to push forward the Six-Party Talks process in accordance with the consensus reached at the meetings of the Working Groups and reached agreement on second-phase actions for the implementation of the Joint Statement of 19 September 2005, the goal of which is the verifiable denuclearization of the Korean Peninsula in a peaceful manner.

I. On Denuclearization of the Korean Peninsula

1. The DPRK agreed to disable all existing nuclear facilities subject to abandonment under the September 2005 Joint Statement and the February 13 agreement.

The disablement of the 5 megawatt Experimental Reactor at Yongbyon, the Reprocessing Plant (Radiochemical Laboratory) at Yongbyon and the Nuclear Fuel Rod Fabrication Facility at Yongbyon will be completed by 31 December 2007. Specific measures recommended by the expert group will be adopted by heads of delegation in line with the principles of being acceptable to all Parties, scientific, safe, verifiable, and consistent with international standards. At the request of the other Parties, the United States will lead disablement activities and provide the initial funding for those activities. As a first step, the US side will lead the expert group to the DPRK within the next two weeks to prepare for disablement.

2. The DPRK agreed to provide a complete and correct declaration of all its nuclear programs in accordance with the February 13 agreement by 31 December 2007.

3. The DPRK reaffirmed its commitment not to transfer nuclear materials, technology, or know-how.

II. On Normalization of Relations between Relevant Countries

1. The DPRK and the United States remain committed to improving their bilateral relations and moving towards a full diplomatic relationship. The two sides will increase bilateral exchanges and enhance mutual trust. Recalling the commitments to begin the process of removing the designation of the DPRK as a state sponsor of terrorism and advance the process of terminating the application of the Trading with the Enemy Act with respect to the DPRK, the United States will fulfill its commitments to the DPRK in parallel with the DPRK's actions based on consensus reached at the meetings of the Working Group on Normalization of DPRK-U.S. Relations.

2. The DPRK and Japan will make sincere efforts to normalize their relations expeditiously in accordance with the Pyongyang Declaration, on the basis of the settlement of the unfortunate past and the outstanding issues of concern. The DPRK and Japan committed themselves to taking specific actions toward this end through intensive consultations between them.

III. On Economic and Energy Assistance to the DPRK

In accordance with the February 13 agreement, economic, energy and humanitarian assistance up to the equivalent of one million tons of [Heavy Fuel Oil ("HFO")] (inclusive of the 100,000 tons of HFO already delivered) will be provided to the DPRK. Specific modalities will be finalized through discussion by the Working Group on Economy and Energy Cooperation.

*   *   *   *

On November 3, 2007, Ambassador Christopher R. Hill, Assistant Secretary of State for East Asian and Pacific Affairs and head of the U.S. delegation to the Six-Party Talks, announced that an American team had gone into the DPRK two days earlier. The team was to "begin the process of disabling the DPRK plutonium production facilities in Yongbyon" in anticipation of the December 31 disablement deadline. Excerpts follow from a press conference held by Ambassador Hill in Japan on November 3; the full text is available at *www.state.gov/p/eap/rls/rm/2007/94608.htm.*

---

*   *   *   *

This will be the first time those facilities have ever been disabled. And, of course, the idea of disablement is to create a situation where it is very difficult to bring those facilities back online and certainly a very expensive, difficult prospect of ever bringing them back online. . .

We anticipate; indeed, we welcome the other Six-Party members taking part in these disabling actions. . . .

In addition, we look forward—probably in the next week or two—to begin to discuss with the DPRK a list of all of their nuclear programs that must be disabled and dismantled pursuant to the requirements set forth in the September '05 agreement, where the DPRK undertook the obligation to abandon all of its nuclear programs and nuclear weapons. . . .

. . . Clearly, we have to make sure that—as we get to the end of this process—not only is there no plutonium being produced, but we also need to make sure that there's no uranium being enriched. So that is also an ongoing process.

*   *   *   *

. . . [A]s we begin '08, we need to focus very much on the fact that North Korea has already produced some 30, 40, 50—we will know precisely from the declaration—kilos of weaponized plutonium. So that is something that the DPRK needs to abandon pursuant to the September '05 agreement. In addition, we would look, as I mentioned earlier, to move from disabling to dismantling of the nuclear facilities.

*   *   *   *

. . . [A] number of us have agreed to move ahead on our bilateral relationships. Japan and the DPRK have an ongoing bilateral working group, as does the United States. From the U.S. perspective, we made very clear to the DPRK that we are prepared to achieve normalization of our relations, but we will not normalize relations with the DPRK until the DPRK is fully denuclearized. That is, there will be no normalization of relations with a nuclear DPRK. But we are prepared to move along this road. It doesn't mean that all our disagreements with the DPRK will be over, but it does mean that if they denuclearize, we can have a normal relationship, where we will continue our dialogue as we deal with disagreements as we do with many other states in the world.

In addition, the United States has agreed to participate in an effort to end the Korean War by replacing the Armistice with some sort of peace process. We are prepared to begin our participation on substantial disablement by the end of this year, but we are not prepared to conclude a peace process, a peace mechanism on the Korean Peninsula. We are not prepared to conclude that until there is denuclearization. That is, again, we cannot get to the end until the DPRK gets to the end of denuclearization.

Finally, the United States is also prepared to participate in the overall creation of a Northeast Asian peace and security dialogue or forum. The purpose of this is to begin the process of building a neighborhood in Northeast Asia. In no way is it designed to replace the very key bilateral relationships, the bilateral alliances that the

United States has and is very proud to have with a number of countries in Asia, including with Japan and with the Republic of Korea. But it is an effort to begin, I think, a long-term project building a sense of neighborhood in Northeast Asia. And I do like to believe that the Six-Party process, as difficult and as frustrating as it has been over the months and years, has gotten a start on getting countries in the region to work together toward a common goal. And so we would look to see that—once this denuclearization is achieved—we can continue to build on the foundation of the Six-Party process, so that we can have a more permanent forum on the landscape of Northeast Asia. So with those sorts of introductory comments, let me maybe go to questions.

QUESTION: . . . DPRK transfer of nuclear technology to Syria or proliferation to Syria is emerging as an issue. In your negotiations with DPRK, have they guaranteed that they are not proliferating nuclear technology to Syria? . . .

ASSISTANT SECRETARY HILL: Well, first of all, our interest in being engaged in a Six-Party process stems from our concern about the DPRK's possession of nuclear weapons and what it means in the region—to the stability of Northeast Asia—but also [what it] means in terms of proliferation. Proliferation has been a primary concern of ours all along. We have approached the DPRK on the subject many times. We have received assurances that they will not transfer and have not been transferring or engaging in proliferation. . . . [Y]ou saw in the October 3 agreement that they did make a declaration of no transfer—I think that's not enough for us. I think we have to be very vigilant and continue to watch for this problem. I believe the Six-Party process is the appropriate process for dealing with proliferation.

*   *   *   *

QUESTION: . . . First of all, very shortly the (delisting) process will begin. Specifically, what will this process involve? . . . It seems that what you're explaining to Japan and what you're explaining to DPRK may or may not be different. . . .

ASSISTANT SECRETARY HILL: Well, they are consistent. The DPRK wants very much to be delisted, and we are prepared to work with them. Indeed, we are obligated according to the February agreement to have begun this process, which we have begun. And whether or not we get to the end of this process, of course, depends on future developments. It's not just dependent on denuclearization; it's also dependent on the statutory requirements of this U.S. law with respect to the terrorism list. . . . So what we are doing in the U.S. is to work with the DPRK to ensure that, if they want to be delisted, that they have to qualify to be delisted.

. . . They have to address the terrorism concerns that put them on the list in the first place. So we will be working with them on that. . . .

. . . We are in very close contact with Japan on our mutual efforts to achieve . . . meaningful progress on the matter of the Japanese citizens so brutally abducted some years ago by the DPRK. So we will continue to work very closely with Japan on this issue of delisting and the relationship of this issue to the abduction issue.

* * * *

. . . On disablement, we have agreed on a number of measures . . . which in their totality, we believe, will make sure that even if on a certain day the North Koreans wanted to restart the pluto-nium—which, by the way, would be a very bad day for all of us—that it would take them well over a year to do that. So we have a concept that disabling should be something that, in order to reverse the disabling, you would need more than a year.

* * * *

(3) End-of-year status

In a daily White House press briefing on December 7, 2007, White House Press Secretary Dana Perino responded to a question from a reporter concerning a letter sent by President Bush to North Korean leader Kim Jong-il. Ms. Perino stated:

. . . [T]he President sent a letter to every member of the six-party talks. And we are at a critical juncture, as the President would say, that this is a time when we're nearing the end of the 2005 agreement, that it has to be done by December 31st. And what that means is that North Korea has to make a complete and accurate declaration. And the President was reminding Kim Jong-il and the other members of the six-party talks that at the highest levels of this government we support the effort, and we are working to make sure that everyone is on the same page, and reminding North Korea that they have an obligation and a responsibility to send in a complete and accurate declaration. . . .

The full text of the press briefing is available at *www.white-house.gov/news/releases/2007/12/20071207-2.html.*

North Korea did not complete its disablement and declaration by the December 31, 2007, deadline. In a press statement on December 30, 2007, Department of State Deputy Spokesman Tom Casey stated:

It is unfortunate that North Korea has not yet met its commitments by providing a complete and correct declaration of its nuclear programs and slowing down the process of disablement. We will continue to work with our close allies Japan and South Korea, and partners China and Russia, as we urge North Korea to deliver a complete and correct declaration of all its nuclear weapons programs and nuclear weapons and proliferation activities and complete the agreed disablement. The United States is committed to fulfilling our obligations under the Six Party agreements as North Korea fulfills all its obligations.

The press statement is available at *www.state.gov/r/pa/prs/ps/2007/dec/98147.htm.*

b. U.S. sanctions

During 2006 North Korea launched ballistic missiles in July and conducted a nuclear test in October. In response to the nuclear test, the Security Council adopted Resolution 1718 under Chapter VII of the UN Charter imposing sanctions on North Korea. On December 7, 2006, President Bush issued Presidential Determination No. 2007-7, directing U.S. agencies "to impose on North Korea the sanctions described in section 102(b)(2) of the Arms Export Control Act, as amended (22 U.S.C. § 2799aa-1) and section 129 of the Atomic Energy Act of 1954, as amended (42 U.S.C. § 2158)," based on his determination in accordance with applicable law "that North Korea, a non-nuclear-weapon state, detonated a nuclear explosive device on October 9, 2006." 72 Fed. Reg. 1899 (Jan. 16, 2007). *See Digest 2006* at 1265–71.

Effective January 26, 2007, the Department of Commerce, Bureau of Industry and Security ("BIS"), issued a final rule "imposing restrictions on exports and reexports of luxury goods" to North Korea, and "continuing to restrict exports and reexports of nuclear or missile-related items and other items included on the Commerce Control List (CCL)." Excerpts below explain the operation of the amended Export Administration Regulations. 72 Fed. Reg. 3722 (Jan. 26, 2007).

* * * *

Under this final rule, in accordance with UNSCR 1718 and the foreign policy interests of the United States, the Bureau of Industry and Security (BIS) will require a license for the export and reexport to North Korea of all items subject to the Export Administration Regulations (EAR), except food and medicines that are not on the Commerce Control List (CCL). Although a license is already required to export and reexport to North Korea all items controlled on the CCL for Nuclear Nonproliferation (NP) and Missile Technology (MT) reasons, BIS also will require a license for these items (except for items classified under Export Commodity Classification Number (ECCN) 7A103) in accordance with the President's December 7, 2006 directive regarding implementation of Section 102(b) of the Arms Export Control Act.

Pursuant to new Section 746.4(c) of the EAR, BIS will review license applications for the export or reexport of luxury goods to

North Korea under a general policy of denial. This policy of denial applies to, but is not limited to applications to export and reexport luxury goods including, for example: Luxury automobiles; yachts; gems; jewelry; other fashion accessories; cosmetics; perfumes; furs; designer clothing; luxury watches; rugs and tapestries; electronic entertainment software and equipment; recreational sports equipment; tobacco; wine and other alcoholic beverages; musical instruments; art; and antiques and collectible items, including but not limited to rare coins and stamps. These and similar items have been imported by North Korea for the use and benefit of government officials and their families, rather than for the good of the North Korean people. In new Supplement No. 1 to part 746 of the EAR, BIS will provide further detail regarding the illustrative list of luxury goods set forth in Section 746.4(c). The determination of whether an item is a luxury good will be made on a case-by-case basis. In some cases, the end-use or end-user will be relevant to this determination. For example, an item being exported to a humanitarian organization for purposes of providing humanitarian assistance to the people of North Korea may not be considered a luxury good, but the same item going to a different end-user might be considered a luxury good and might not be approved. Computer laptops and luxury automobiles will be exempted from the general policy of denial if they are being exported or reexported to organizations legitimately involved in humanitarian relief efforts, other internationally sanctioned efforts, or in the interest of the U.S. Government.

BIS will review under a general policy of approval license applications for the export or reexport of humanitarian items other than food or medicine (e.g., blankets, medical supplies, heating oil, and other items meeting subsistence needs) intended for the benefit of the North Korean people. This policy applies to license applications to export or reexport items in support of UN humanitarian efforts and programs. The general policy of approval also extends to agricultural commodities (as defined in Section 102 of the Agricultural Trade Act of 1978) and medical devices (as defined in Section 201 of the Federal Food, Drug, and Cosmetic Act) that are determined by BIS, in consultation with the interagency license review community, not to be luxury goods. Applications for all other exports and reexports of EAR99* items will be reviewed on a case-by-case basis.

Consistent with UNSCR 1718 and existing U.S. export control policy, BIS will review license applications for arms and related materiel controlled on the CCL and items controlled on the multi-lateral export control regime control lists (the Missile Technology Control Regime, the Nuclear Suppliers Group, the Australia Group, and the Wassenaar Arrangement) under a general policy of denial. This includes items specified in UN documents S/2006/814, S/2006/815 and S/2006/853. BIS will also generally deny applications to export and reexports other items that the UN Security Council or the Sanctions Committee has determined could contribute to North Korea's nuclear-related, ballistic missile-related or other weapons of mass destruction-related programs. In addition, applications to export or reexport items controlled on the CCL for NP and MT reasons (except ECCN 7A103 items) will be reviewed under a general policy of denial. Applications to export or reexport other items on the CCL will be reviewed in accordance with the licensing policy set forth in Section 742.19 of the EAR (Antiterrorism: North Korea). Section 742.19 is being amended to make technical corrections and also to provide that applications to export or reexport parts and components for safety-of-flight will be reviewed on a case-by-case basis.

License Exceptions

This final rule makes inapplicable for North Korea most license exceptions set forth in part 740 of the EAR. The only license exceptions that remain available for North Korea, as provided in new Section 746.4(b) are: TMP (15 CFR 740.9(a)(2)(viii) only) for items for use by the news media; GOV (15 CFR 740.11(a), (b)(2)(i), and (b)(2)(ii) only) for items for personal or official use by personnel

---

* Editor's note: "EAR99 is a designation for dual-use goods that are covered by the EAR but are not specifically listed on the Commerce Control List. EAR99 items can be shipped without a license to most destinations under most circumstances. In fact, the majority of commercial exports from the United States fall into this category. Exporters of most consumer goods, for instance, may find their product listed under EAR 99." *See www.export. gov/regulation/exp_001498.asp.*

and agencies of the U.S. Government, the IAEA, or the European Atomic Energy Community (Euratom); GFT (15 CFR 740.12) for the export or reexport of gift parcels not containing luxury goods by an individual to an individual or a religious, charitable or educational organization, and for the export or reexport by groups or organizations of certain donations to meet basic human needs; TSU (15 CFR 740.13(a) and (b) only) for operation technology and software for lawfully exported items and sales technology; BAG (15 CFR 740.14 (a) through (d) only) for exports of items by individuals leaving the United States as personal baggage; and AVS (15 CFR 740.15(a)(4) only) for civil passenger aircraft on temporary sojourn.

* * * *

4. Iran

a. *Security Council Resolution 1747*

On March 24, 2007, the UN Security Council, acting under Article 41, Chapter VII, of the UN Charter, adopted Resolution 1747. In addition to reaffirming its earlier directives (*see* UNSCR 1737 (2006) and 1696 (2006)) that Iran must cooperate with the International Atomic Energy Agency and suspend certain proliferation sensitive nuclear activities, the Security Council in paragraph 4 "decide[d] that the [asset freeze] measures specified in paragraphs 12, 13, 14 and 15 of resolution 1737 (2006) shall apply also to the persons and entities listed in Annex I."

The list set forth in Annex I includes "entities involved in nuclear or ballistic missile activities" (including Bank Sepah and Bank Sepah International, already sanctioned by the United States, *see* 4.c. below), "Iranian Revolutionary Guard Corps entities," "Persons involved in nuclear or ballistic missile activities," and "Iranian Revolutionary Guard Corps key persons."

Paragraph 5 of Resolution 1747 imposed a ban on exports of arms from Iran, the Security Council deciding:

Iran shall not supply, sell or transfer directly or indirectly from its territory or by its nationals or using its flag vessels or aircraft any arms or related materiel, and that all States shall prohibit the procurement of such items from Iran by their nationals, or using their flag vessels or aircraft, and whether or not originating in the territory of Iran . . .

In paragraph 6 the Security Council also called upon all states "to exercise vigilance and restraint in the supply, sale or transfer directly or indirectly from their territories or by their nationals or using their flag vessels or aircraft o[r] any battle tanks, armoured combat vehicles, large caliber artillery systems, combat aircraft, attack helicopters, warships, missiles or missile systems as defined for the purpose of the United Nations Register on Conventional Arms to Iran," and to do the same with respect to any related technical assistance.

In paragraph 2 the Security Council called on states to exercise "vigilance and restraint regarding the entry into or transit through their territories of individuals who are engaged in, directly associated with or providing support for Iran's proliferation sensitive nuclear activities or for the development of nuclear weapon delivery systems." It also decided that states are to notify the 1737 Committee "of the entry into or transit through their territories of the persons designated in the Annex to resolution 1737 (2006) or Annex I to this resolution" and others so designated, "except where such travel is for activities directly related to [certain equipment when such equipment is for light water reactors or certain low-enriched uranium when it is incorporated in assembled nuclear fuel elements for such reactors]."

Annex II attaches the proposals for a negotiated resolution put forth in June 2006 by China, France, Germany, the Russian Federation, the United Kingdom and the United States, with the support of the European Union's High Representative. *See* U.N. Doc. S/2006/521. Paragraph 10 of Resolution 1747 "welcome[d] the continuous affirmation of the commitment" of the countries to that negotiated solution and "encourage[d] Iran to engage with their June 2006 proposals."

Ambassador Alejandro Wolff, Acting U.S. Permanent Representative to the United Nations, provided the views of the United States in a statement to the Security Council, also on March 24. Mr. Wolff's remarks, excerpted below, are available in full at *www.un.int/usa/press_releases/20070324_ 064.html*. Also on March 24, the foreign ministers of China, France, Germany, Russia, the United Kingdom, and the United States, with the support of the high representative of the European Union, issued a statement reconfirming its proposals for a negotiated solution. The text of that statement is available at *www.un.int/usa/press_releases/20070324_065.html*.

For discussion of events in 2006, including the February 2006 IAEA report to the Security Council of Iran's noncompliance with its nuclear-related obligations and subsequent Security Council action, *see Digest 2006* at 1272–84.

The United States is pleased that the Security Council has once again unanimously taken action against what is clearly a grave threat to international peace and security. The Iranian leadership's continued defiance of this Council in failing to comply with Security Council Resolutions 1696 and 1737 requires that we uphold our responsibilities defined in the Charter of this esteemed body and take necessary action. And while we hope Iran responds to this resolution by complying with its international legal obligations, the United States is fully prepared to support additional measures in 60 days should Iran choose another course.

We are here today because of the decisions of Iran's leadership. Their actions include more than 20 years of deception of the IAEA; a nuclear program hidden from the international community, in violation of the Nuclear Non-Proliferation Treaty (NPT); a program that is emerging from the shadows slowly, and incompletely, only due to the efforts of international inspectors and outside groups.

Let me quote from the IAEA Director General's latest report summing up the basic problem: "given the existence in Iran of activities undeclared to the Agency for 20 years, it is necessary for Iran to enable the Agency, through maximum cooperation and transparency, to fully reconstruct the history of Iran's nuclear program. Without such cooperation and transparency, the Agency will not be able to provide assurances about the absence of undeclared nuclear material and activities in Iran or about the exclusively peaceful nature of that program."

The unanimous passage of Resolution 1747 sends a clear and unambiguous message to Iran: the regime's continued pursuit of a nuclear weapons capability, in violation of its treaty obligations as well as its obligations as a Member State of the United Nations, will only further isolate Iran and make it less, not more secure.

In light of this history, it is not only appropriate, but the responsibility of the Security Council to act. And we have done so in a careful and deliberate manner. In July of last year, we adopted Resolution 1696, which demanded that Iran verifiably suspend all of its uranium enrichment-related and reprocessing activities and cooperate fully with the steps required by International Atomic Energy Agency. That resolution was ignored by Iran. Resolution 1737, adopted unanimously last December, took appropriate action against the regime in light of the failure by Iran's leadership to comply with the decisions of this Council. It, too, was ignored by Iran. Instead, Iran has expanded its enrichment activities and continued construction of the heavy water research reactor at Arak, while scaling back even further its cooperation with the IAEA. Iran called the Council's decisions "invalid" and "an extra-legal act" and vowed that the "new resolution won't be an obstacle in the way of Iran's nuclear progress."

Sadly, Iran continues to defy the will of the international community, the decisions of this Council, and its obligations under international law. For this reason it is entirely appropriate and necessary that we have adopted stronger measures to persuade the regime to make its country more secure by abandoning its pursuit of nuclear weapons. Should Iran choose a different path, this resolution makes clear that we are prepared and willing to adopt additional measures. Indeed, in the face of Iran's continued defiance, the United States expects that the Council will continue to incrementally increase pressure on the Iranian regime.

Let me be clear, though, to the Iranian people: these measures we are adopting today are in no way meant to punish the civilian population of Iran. Resolution 1747 is properly tailored to target Iranian institutions and officials that support Iran's nuclear and missile programs. It forbids Iran from providing any arms to anyone, anywhere and calls on all nations not to export to Iran any major arms. The world has benefited greatly from the rich, vibrant culture that the people of Iran have to offer. My own country is proud to be the home to hundreds of thousands citizens and residents of Iranian origin—and we are fortunate to benefit from their many contributions to our society. We hope for a different dynamic with Iran. As President Bush has stated,

> "Iran now has an opportunity to make its choice. I would hope they would make the choice that most of the free world wants them to make, which is there is no need to have a weapons program; there is no need to isolate your people, it's not in your interest to do so. And should they agree to verifiably suspend their enrichment, the United States will be at the table with our partners."

The decisions of the Iranian leadership, however, required the Council to act. It is our solemn responsibility to take measures which will not only halt the development of Iran's nuclear weapons programs, but to encourage the leadership of Iran to choose a different path, which will benefit the entire Iranian nation—including its government-professed aspiration for nuclear energy.

With respect to the measures adopted today, we would also like to note our understanding that the new resolution does not introduce any changes to the provisions in paragraph 15 of Resolution 1737. The asset freeze, therefore, does not prevent a person or entity designated in the annexes to UN Security Council Resolution 1737 and to this resolution from making payments due under a contract entered into force before that person or entity was listed in cases covered by paragraph 15.

The Iranian leadership has claimed that this Council seeks to deprive Iran of its right to peaceful nuclear energy—and we may hear this again today. This is simply not true. The six governments, including my own, that have been trying in vain to get to negotiations with the Iranians over the past year recognize Iran's right to peaceful, civil nuclear energy in conformity with all articles and obligations of the NPT. In fact, the generous proposal put on the table by the six parties last June—an offer that remains on the table today—includes assistance in the construction of civilian light water nuclear power plants. These plants would generate electricity for the people of Iran, but be of no use to Iran's nuclear weapons program. Many other governments around the world, including some represented on this Council, enjoy national civilian nuclear energy programs without any difficulties, demonstrating that there is no incompatibility between a country's right to a peaceful nuclear energy program and its non-proliferation obligations. Iran's rejection of this offer sends a deeply troubling signal to the entire international community. Nonetheless, my government associates itself with the statement read by the United Kingdom reaffirming our offer and willingness to resolve this issue through negotiations.

Mr. President, the current path chosen by Iran's leadership poses a direct challenge to the very principles on which the United Nations was founded. Iran's leadership openly proclaims that this Council is "illegal" and its resolutions are "torn pieces of paper." And Iran's Supreme Leader has pledged that Iran will undertake "illegal acts" if the Council proceeded with adoption of this resolution. Article 2 of the Charter makes clear that all Members shall refrain in their international relations from the threat or use of force against the territorial integrity or political independence of any state. Calls by Iran's leaders to have Israel, a Member State of the United Nations, "wiped off the map" stand in stark contrast to everything for which this body stands. This contrast is amplified by Iran's continued well-known role as one of the world's leading state-sponsors of terrorism.

*   *   *   *

Mr. President, in closing let me reiterate that the United States remains firmly committed to finding a peaceful and diplomatic solution to resolve what we all feel is a grave threat to international peace and security. And, while we regret the need for this resolution, our vote here today shows that the Council can and will act accordingly when countries violate their international obligations.

b.   Further statement by P5 + 2

On September 28, 2007, the Department of State Office of the Spokesman issued a "statement by the Foreign Ministers of the United States, China, France, Germany, Russia and the United Kingdom with the support of the High Representative of the European Union issued today in New York." The group, consisting of representatives of the five permanent members of the Security Council plus Germany and the European Union, is referred to as the "P5 + 2."

The statement is set forth below and available at *www. state.gov/r/pa/prs/ps/2007/sep/92944.htm.*

1. The proliferation risks of the Iranian nuclear program remain a source of serious concern to the International Community, as expressed very clearly in UNSC Resolutions 1696, 1737 and 1747.

2. We are committed to the Treaty on the Non-Proliferation of Nuclear Weapons and underline the need for all States Party to that Treaty to comply fully with all their obligations. We seek a negotiated solution that would address the international community's concerns over Iran's nuclear program. We reiterate our commitment to see the proliferation implication of Iran's nuclear program resolved, and have therefore met today to reaffirm our commitment to our dual track approach.

3. We remain ready to engage with Iran in negotiations on a comprehensive long-term agreement to resolve the Iranian nuclear issue. Creating the conditions for such negotiations requires that Iran fully and verifiably suspend its enrichment-related and reprocessing activities, as required by UNSC Resolutions 1737 and 1747. The Security Council has offered Iran the possibility of "suspension for suspension"—suspension of the implementation of measures if and for so long as Iran suspends all of its enrichment-related and reprocessing activities, as verified by the IAEA. We call upon Iran to accept that offer and allow for negotiations in good faith.

4. We urge Iran to engage in a dialogue to create the conditions for negotiations based on our June 2006 proposals for a long-term comprehensive agreement, based on mutual respect, that would reestablish international confidence in the exclusively peaceful nature of Iran's nuclear program and open the way to wider co-operation between Iran and all our countries. We have asked

Dr. Javier Solana, the European Union's High Representative for Common Foreign and Security Policy, to meet with Dr. Ali Larijani, Secretary of Iran's Supreme National Security Council, to lay the foundation for future negotiations.

5. We welcome the agreement between Iran and the IAEA to resolve all questions concerning Iran's past nuclear activities. We call upon Iran, however, to produce tangible results rapidly and effectively by clarifying all outstanding issues and concerns on Iran's nuclear program, including topics which could have a military nuclear dimension, as set out by the relevant IAEA Resolutions and UNSC Resolutions 1737 and 1747 and by providing all access required by its Safeguards Agreement and Subsidiary Arrangement and by implementing the Additional Protocol.

6. Full transparency and cooperation by Iran with the IAEA is essential in order to address outstanding concerns. We reiterate our full support for the IAEA and its staff in the execution of its verification role and for the role of the UN Security Council. We look forward to DG El Baradei's November report to the IAEA Board of Governors on the level, scope, and extent of Iran's cooperation and transparency.

7. In view of the fact that Iran has not fulfilled the requirements of UN Security Council Resolutions 1737 and 1747, including the suspension of its enrichment and reprocessing activities, we agree to finalize a text for a third UN Security Council Sanctions Resolution under Article 41 of Chapter VII of the Charter of the United Nations with the intention of bringing it to a vote in the UN Security Council unless the November reports of Dr. Solana and Dr. El Baradei show a positive outcome of their efforts.

> In an on-the-record press briefing of the same date, Under Secretary of State for Political Affairs R. Nicholas Burns explained that in the statement,
>
>> the P-5 and German ministers have agreed to reaffirm our strategy on Iran's nuclear ambitions. They specifically reaffirmed the dual track, meaning that we are offering negotiations to Iran; but should Iran not be able to meet the terms of those negotiations, we are prepared to sanction them further. . . .

. . . That offer stands on the table. But the statement is very clear and the discussion was very clear that we are also prepared to continue the sanctions process. And in that regard, the ministers agreed to finish writing the text of a third Security Council resolution in the weeks ahead. . . .

In response to a question concerning the U.S. view on the IAEA process with Iran, Under Secretary Burns stated as excerpted below. The full text of Mr. Burns's briefing is available at *www.state.gov/p/us/rm/2007/92953.htm.*

* * * *

. . . We have always welcomed the involvement of the IAEA and find it positive. But what we've said very clearly—and Secretary Rice has said this to a number of you—is it's not sufficient. It's part of the international effort, but it's not the totality.

And let me explain it this way. The IAEA is looking into the past activities of the Iranian Government. Now, that's important. It's important to know that when President Ahmadi-Nejad said publicly last year we're engaged in P2 centrifuge research, it's important to know whether, in fact, they are and why they are because countries have concerns about that.

What the IAEA process does not do is look at what the Iranians are doing today. And the focal point of the international concern is their enrichment and reprocessing activities at Natanz, their plant at Natanz. The Security Council over the last 18 months has focused on that. The sanctions are based on that and the suspension is required on that.

And so our view is that the IAEA and the Security Council are two halves of a whole; both are important. And so we do welcome the IAEA process, but on its own it's not going to stop the Iranians. The Security Council has a chance to do that through effective sanctions.

* * * *

On December 18, 2007, Ambassador Zalmay Khalilzad, U.S. Permanent Representative to the United Nations, addressed the Security Council on the situation with Iran. The full text of Ambassador Khalilzad's statement, excerpted below, is available at *www.un.int/usa/press_releases/20071218_375.html.*

---

*   *   *   *

The 90-day report makes clear that Iran is not complying with its Security Council obligations.

This is an issue of fundamental importance to this Council and we must remain seized of the matter until all concerns with Iran's nuclear program have been addressed.

As Dr. ElBaradei, the IAEA Director General, has stated on three occasions since 1747 was adopted in March—Iran has failed to comply with its obligations to suspend all proliferation sensitive nuclear activities. Although very limited progress has been made on the Iran-IAEA Work Plan, Iran is still failing to cooperate fully and transparently with the IAEA in its investigations.

Mr. President, Iran must:

1) Suspend its proliferation sensitive nuclear activities without delay, which would then allow negotiations within the framework of the P5+1; and

2) Give the IAEA its full cooperation in implementing the Work Plan.

The United States remains deeply troubled by Iran's noncompliance. The P5+1 continue their consultations in capitals, and we hope to have a text of a new sanctions resolution before the full Council as soon as possible.

In closing, Mr. President, let me say a few words about the recent announcement by the Russian Federation to send Iran enriched uranium for use in the nuclear power plant being constructed at Bushehr.

Resolution 1737, while prohibiting states from assisting Iran with sensitive elements of the nuclear fuel cycle, makes an exception for providing Iran with assistance and fuel for light water reactors such as Bushehr. As President Bush has noted, while he supports Russia's decision, Russia's arrangement to supply nuclear fuel for the entire period of Bushehr's operation demonstrates one thing: Iran does not need to pursue uranium enrichment and other sensitive aspects of the nuclear fuel cycle to have access to nuclear power.

We have joined Russia and other members of the P5+1 in offering Iran, if it complies with the requirements of the Council, cooperation in the development of a civil nuclear power program. This includes active international support in building state-of-the art light water power reactors and reliable access to fuel cycle, to nuclear fuel. If Iran is, in fact, serious about using nuclear power to meet its energy needs, the best way for it to proceed is to suspend its proliferation sensitive nuclear activities and accept the P5+1 offer. We await Iran's answer.

c. U.S. sanctions on Iranian individuals and entities

During 2007 the United States imposed sanctions on Iranian individuals and entities pursuant to both Executive Order 13382, "Blocking Property of Weapons of Mass Destruction Proliferators and their Supporters," 70 Fed. Reg. 38,567 (July 1, 2005) (*see Digest 2005* at 1125–31, most recently continued by notice of November 8, 2007, 72 Fed. Reg. 63,961 (Nov. 13, 2007)) and Executive Order 13224, "Blocking Property and Prohibiting Transactions With Persons Who Commit, Threaten to Commit, or Support Terrorism," 66 Fed. Reg. 49,079 (September 25, 2001); *see Digest 2001* at 881–93. These actions are discussed here; *see also* C.11. below for additional sanctions.

On February 9, 2007, the Department of the Treasury, Office of Foreign Assets Control, issued a notice of the designation of Bank Sepah, Bank Sepah International PLC, and Amad Derakhshandeh under Executive Order 13382. 72 Fed. Reg. 7919 (Feb. 21, 2007).

The Department of the Treasury made additional designations of three entities on February 16, 2007: Kalaye Electric

Company, Kavoshyar Company, and Pioneer Energy Industries Company (72 Fed. Reg. 25,835 (May 7, 2007)); four additional entities on June 8, 2007: Fajr Industries Group, Farayand Technique, Pars Trash Company, and Mizan Machine Manufacturing Group (72 Fed. Reg. 33,280 (June 15, 2007)); and two individuals on June 15, 2007: Mohammad Qannadi and Ali Hajinia Leilabadi (72 Fed. Reg. 36,103 (July 2, 2007)).

On March 28, 2007, the Secretary of State, in consultation with the Secretary of the Treasury, the Attorney General, and other relevant agencies, designated an additional Iranian entity, "Defense Industries Organization (a.k.a. Defence Industries Organisation; a.k.a. DIO; a.k.a. Saseman Sanaje Defa; a.k.a. Sazemane Sanaye Defa; a.k.a. 'Sasadja')." 72 Fed. Reg. 15,930 (Apr. 3, 2007).

On October 25, 2007, the Department of the Treasury and Department of State announced extensive sanctions against a number of Iranian entities and individuals under both Executive Order 13328 and 13224. A fact sheet released by the U.S. Department of State spokesman on that date summarized the actions taken under both the weapons of mass destruction and terrorism executive orders, with indications where designations were also reflected in Security Council Resolution 1737 or 1747, as excerpted below. The full text of the fact sheet, including a list of all entities and individuals designated, is available at *www.state.gov/r/pa/prs/ps/2007/oct/94193.htm. See also,* for actions discussed below, 72 Fed. Reg. 62,520 (Nov. 5, 2007) (designations including Bank Melli and Bank Mellat under E.O. 13382); 72 Fed. Reg. 65,837 (Nov. 23, 2007) (designation of Bank Saderat and the Qods Force under Executive Order 13224); and 72 Fed. Reg. 71,991 (Dec. 19, 2007) (designation of MODAFL and IRGC under Executive Order 13382).

The U.S. Government is taking several major actions today to counter Iran's bid for nuclear capabilities and support for terrorism by exposing Iranian banks, companies and individuals that have been involved in these dangerous activities and by cutting them off from the U.S. financial system.

Today, the Department of State designated under Executive Order 13382 two key Iranian entities of proliferation concern: the Islamic Revolutionary Guard Corps (IRGC; aka Iranian Revolutionary Guard Corps) and the Ministry of Defense and Armed Forces Logistics (MODAFL). Additionally, the Department of the Treasury designated for proliferation activities under E.O. 13382 nine IRGC-affiliated entities and five IRGC-affiliated individuals as derivatives of the IRGC, Iran's state-owned Banks Melli and Mellat, and three individuals affiliated with Iran's Aerospace Industries Organization (AIO).

The Treasury Department also designated the IRGC-Qods Force (IRGC-QF) under E.O. 13224 for providing material support to the Taliban and other terrorist organizations, and Iran's state-owned Bank Saderat as a terrorist financier.

Elements of the IRGC and MODAFL were listed in the Annexes to UN Security Council Resolutions 1737 and 1747. All UN Member States are required to freeze the assets of entities and individuals listed in the Annexes of those resolutions, as well as assets of entities owned or controlled by them, and to prevent funds or economic resources from being made available to them.

The Financial Action Task Force, the world's premier standard-setting body for countering terrorist financing and money laundering, recently highlighted the threat posed by Iran to the international financial system. FATF called on its members to advise institutions dealing with Iran to seriously weigh the risks resulting from Iran's failure to comply with international standards. Last week, the Treasury Department issued a warning to U.S. banks setting forth the risks posed by Iran. (For the text of the Treasury Department statement see: http://www.fincen.gov/guidance_fi_increasing_mlt_iranian.pdf.) Today's actions are consistent with this warning, and provide additional information to help financial institutions protect themselves from deceptive financial practices by Iranian entities and individuals engaged in or supporting proliferation and terrorism.

Effect of Today's Actions

As a result of our actions today, all transactions involving any of the designees and any U.S. person will be prohibited and any assets the designees may have under U.S. jurisdiction will be frozen.

Noting the UN Security Council's grave concern over Iran's nuclear and ballistic missile program activities, the United States also encourages all jurisdictions to take similar actions to ensure full and effective implementation of UN Security Council Resolutions 1737 and 1747.

Today's designations also notify the international private sector of the dangers of doing business with three of Iran's largest banks, as well as the many IRGC-affiliated companies that pervade several basic Iranian industries.

Proliferation Finance—Executive Order 13382 Designations

E.O. 13382, signed by the President on June 29, 2005, is an authority aimed at freezing the assets of proliferators of weapons of mass destruction and their supporters, and at isolating them from the U.S. financial and commercial systems. Designations under the Order prohibit all transactions between the designees and any U.S. person, and freeze any assets the designees may have under U.S. jurisdiction.

The Islamic Revolutionary Guard Corps (IRGC): Considered the military vanguard of Iran, the Islamic Revolutionary Guard Corps (IRGC; aka Iranian Revolutionary Guard Corps) is composed of five branches (Ground Forces, Air Force, Navy, Basij militia, and Qods Force special operations) in addition to a counterintelligence directorate and representatives of the Supreme Leader. It runs prisons, and has numerous economic interests involving defense production, construction, and the oil industry. Several of the IRGC's leaders have been sanctioned under UN Security Council Resolution 1747.

The IRGC has been outspoken about its willingness to proliferate ballistic missiles capable of carrying WMD. . . .

Ministry of Defense and Armed Forces Logistics (MODAFL): The Ministry of Defense and Armed Forces Logistics (MODAFL) controls the Defense Industries Organization, an Iranian entity identified in the Annex to UN Security Council Resolution 1737 and designated by the United States under E.O. 13382 on March 30, 2007. MODAFL also was sanctioned, pursuant to the Arms Export Control Act and the Export Administration Act, in November 2000 for its involvement in missile technology proliferation activities.

MODAFL has ultimate authority over Iran's Aerospace Industries Organization (AIO), which was designated under E.O. 13382 on June 28, 2005. . . . The head of MODAFL has publicly indicated Iran's willingness to continue to work on ballistic missiles. . . .

Bank Melli, its branches, and subsidiaries: Bank Melli is Iran's largest bank. Bank Melli provides banking services to entities involved in Iran's nuclear and ballistic missile programs, including entities listed by the U.N. for their involvement in those programs. . . . Through its role as a financial conduit, Bank Melli has facilitated numerous purchases of sensitive materials for Iran's nuclear and missile programs. . . .

Bank Melli also provides banking services to the IRGC and the Qods Force. . . .

Bank Mellat, its branches, and subsidiaries: Bank Mellat provides banking services in support of Iran's nuclear entities, namely the Atomic Energy Organization of Iran (AEOI) and Novin Energy Company. Both AEOI and Novin Energy have been designated by the United States under E.O. 13382 and by the UN Security Council under UNSCRs 1737 and 1747. . . .

IRGC-owned or -controlled companies: Treasury is designating [nine] companies listed below under E.O. 13382 on the basis of their relationship to the IRGC. These entities are owned or controlled by the IRGC and its leaders. . . .

IRGC Individuals: Treasury is designating the individuals below under E.O 13382 on the basis of their relationship to the IRGC. One of the five is listed on the Annex of UNSCR 1737 and the other four are listed on the Annex of UNSCR 1747 as key IRGC individuals.

Other Individuals involved in Iran's ballistic missile programs: E.O. 13382 derivative proliferation designation by Treasury of each of the [three] individuals listed below for their relationship to the Aerospace Industries Organization, an entity previously designated under E.O. 13382. Each individual is listed on the Annex of UNSCR 1737 for being involved in Iran's ballistic missile program. . . .

Support for Terrorism—Executive Order 13224 Designations

E.O. 13224 is an authority aimed at freezing the assets of terrorists and their supporters, and at isolating them from the U.S. financial and commercial systems. Designations under the E.O. prohibit all transactions between the designees and any U.S. person, and freeze any assets the designees may have under U.S. jurisdiction.

IRGC-Qods Force (IRGC-QF): The Qods Force, a branch of the Islamic Revolutionary Guard Corps (IRGC; aka Iranian Revolutionary Guard Corps), provides material support to the Taliban, Lebanese Hizballah, Hamas, Palestinian Islamic Jihad, and the Popular Front for the Liberation of Palestine-General Command (PFLP-GC).

The Qods Force is the Iranian regime's primary instrument for providing lethal support to the Taliban. . . .

The Qods Force has had a long history of supporting Hizballah's military, paramilitary, and terrorist activities, providing it with guidance, funding, weapons, intelligence, and logistical support. . . .

In addition, the Qods Force provides lethal support in the form of weapons, training, funding, and guidance to select groups of Iraqi Shi'a militants who target and kill Coalition and Iraqi forces and innocent Iraqi civilians.

Bank Saderat, its branches, and subsidiaries: Bank Saderat, which has approximately 3200 branch offices, has been used by the Government of Iran to channel funds to terrorist organizations, including Hizballah and EU-designated terrorist groups Hamas, PFLP-GC, and Palestinian Islamic Jihad. . . .

Secretary of State Condoleezza Rice and Secretary of the Treasury Henry Paulson announced the new sanctions against Iran and discussed their context and purpose in a press conference held on October 25. Secretary Paulson's remarks are excerpted below; the full text of the remarks is available at *www.state.gov/secretary/rm/2007/10/94133.htm.*

*   *   *   *

The Iranian regime's ability to pursue nuclear and ballistic missile programs in defiance of UN Security Council resolutions depends on its access to international commercial and financial systems. Iran also funnels hundreds of millions of dollars each year through the international financial system to terrorists. Iran's banks aid this conduct using a range of deceptive financial practices intended to evade even the most stringent risk management controls.

In dealing with Iran, it is nearly impossible to know one's customer and be assured that one is not unwittingly facilitating the regime's reckless behavior and conduct. The recent warning by the Financial Action Task Force, the world's premier standard setting body for countering terrorism finance and money laundering, confirms the extraordinary risks that accompany those who do business with Iran.

* * * *

The IRGC is so deeply entrenched in Iran's economy and commercial enterprises, it is increasingly likely that if you are doing business with Iran, you are doing business with the IRGC. We call on responsible banks and companies around the world to terminate any business with Bank Melli, Bank Mellat, Bank Saderat, and all companies and entities of the IRGC.

As awareness of Iran's deceptive behavior has grown, many banks around the world have decided as a matter of prudence and integrity that Iran's business is simply not worth the risk. It is plain and simple: reputable institutions do not want to be bankers to this dangerous regime. We will continue to work with our international partners to prevent Iran from abusing the international financial system and to advance its illicit conduct.

> On the same day, Under Secretary of State for Political Affairs R. Nicholas Burns and Under Secretary of the Treasury for Terrorism and Financial Intelligence Stuart A. Levey held a press briefing concerning the new sanctions. The full text of the briefing, excerpted below, is available at *www.state.gov/p/us/rm/2007/94178.htm.*

---

* * * *

UNDER SECRETARY BURNS:

*   *   *   *

This is in our view a powerful statement that the United States is making today and it has been in the works, of course, for quite some time, because we believe increased pressure needs to be put on the Iranian Government for its activities in two areas. First, Iran continues its nuclear research at its plant in Natanz into enrichment and reprocessing, as Mohamed ElBaradei's reports have shown over the last few months. . . .

*   *   *   *

On the terrorism issue, we are designating the Qods Force for terrorism purposes. If you remember back to UN Security Council Resolution 1747, and one of the strongest . . . measures in that resolution—Iran is prohibited by . . . the resolution, from transferring arms to anyone, any group, or any country outside of Iran. And since the passage of that resolution in late March, Iran has transferred arms to Hamas and to Hezbollah in Lebanon and to the Shia militant groups in Iraq and to the Taliban in Afghanistan. And so Iran has willfully violated the UN Security Council resolution. . . .

*   *   *   *

UNDER SECRETARY LEVEY:

*   *   *   *

The reasons that we've designated [Iran's banks] and the reasons that Bank Sepah was designated at the United Nations should concern financial institutions and other legitimate businesses all over the world when they think about whether they want to do business with Iranian entities. There was a significant development two weeks ago in the Financial Action Task Force; . . . [E]ssentially, 34 of the largest economies are members of the Financial Action Task Force. It is an organization set up by the G-7 to set standards for anti-money laundering and terrorist financing activities for countries all over the world.

In addition to those 34 countries that are members, over a hundred countries around the world have signed on to those standards set by the FATF through subsidiary bodies. On October 11th, the FATF put out a statement which recognized Iran as providing a significant vulnerability to the integrity of the entire international financial system because it does not have a comprehensive anti-money laundering or counterterrorist financing regime.

So if you put that statement together, which again is put out by a multilateral technical body, which includes Russia and China and others as members, about the significant vulnerability posed by Iran, you put that together with them using their state-owned banks in a consistent way as we've laid out in the fact sheet—Bank Sepah, Bank Melli, Bank Mellat, Bank Saderat—Iran's conduct is quickly turning it into a financial pariah and that is an aspect that I think of today's actions that I'd like to highlight.

*   *   *   *

QUESTION: . . . [W]hat's the difference between putting someone on the list as a terrorist organization and putting someone on the list as supporting terrorist organizations, as appears to be the case here with the Qods Force? In practical terms, what does that mean?

UNDER SECRETARY LEVEY:

*   *   *   *

In terms of the difference between the two sorts of actions, one being what we've done today, which is designating the Qods Force for providing material support to the Taliban and other terrorist organizations, as opposed to naming it as a terrorist organization, which we have not done—we have previously identified Iran as a state sponsor of terrorism and this is essentially identifying the portion of Iran's Government that it uses to export terrorism, in a sense. And it is the conduct that we are focusing on, which is not engaging in terrorist activity directly but providing material support to the Taliban, to Hamas, to Hezbollah and others. Incidentally, providing support to the Taliban is not just something that we have a domestic interest in stopping, but that is a violation of another UN Security Council Resolution 1267 which forbids . . . any entity from providing material support to the Taliban.

*   *   *   *

. . . [U]nder the Executive Order . . . 13224 designation, all U.S. persons wherever located have to block and freeze all property under their jurisdiction, or that comes into their jurisdiction, that the Qods Force has an interest in. . . . If an entity is identified as a foreign terrorist organization, the requirement only applies to financial institutions and . . . the requirement that they block funds . . . applies [only] to funds not all property. Whereas, for example, . . . if there were other types of property besides funds that came into the hands of a U.S. person and not a financial institution that would have to be blocked pursuant to the kind of designation that we've done today.

. . . There are legal differences. All U.S. persons, not just banks. All property, not just funds.

*   *   *   *

UNDER SECRETARY LEVEY: We're not threatening secondary sanctions on institutions. . . . [F]inancial institutions are making these decisions on their own and that's, we think, a positive development.

*   *   *   *

d. 2007 National Intelligence Estimate

On December 3, 2007, the Office of the Director of National Intelligence released a new U.S. National Intelligence Estimate ("NIE"). In a public summary entitled Key Judgments, the NIE stated in part:

A. We judge with high confidence that in fall 2003, Tehran halted its nuclear weapons program[1]; we also assess with moderate-to-high confidence that Tehran at a minimum is keeping open the option to develop nuclear weapons. We judge with high confidence that the halt, and Tehran's announcement of its decision

---

[1]   For the purposes of this Estimate, by "nuclear weapons program" we mean Iran's nuclear weapon design and weaponization work and covert uranium conversion-related and uranium enrichment-related work; we do not mean Iran's declared civil work related to uranium conversion and enrichment.

to suspend its declared uranium enrichment program and sign an Additional Protocol to its Nuclear
Non-Proliferation Treaty Safeguards Agreement, was
directed primarily in response to increasing international scrutiny and pressure resulting from exposure
of Iran's previously undeclared nuclear work.

*   *   *   *

G. We judge with high confidence that Iran will not be
technically capable of producing and reprocessing
enough plutonium for a weapon before about 2015.
H. We assess with high confidence that Iran has the scientific, technical and industrial capacity eventually to
produce nuclear weapons if it decides to do so.

The full text of the public summary is available at *www.dni.
gov/press_releases/20071203_release.pdf*.

In a press conference on December 4, 2007, President Bush
responded to a question on the NIE as excerpted below. The
full text of the press conference is available at 43 WEEKLY COMP.
PRES. DOC. 1555 (Dec. 10, 2007). *See also* December 3 statement
by National Security Advisor Stephen Hadley, available at *www.
whitehouse.gov/news/releases/2007/12/20071203-5.html*.

\-\-\-\-\-\-\-

*   *   *   *

Q: Mr. President, a new intelligence report says that Iran halted its
nuclear weapons program four years ago, and that it remains frozen. Are you still convinced that Iran is trying to build a nuclear
bomb? And do the new findings take the military option that
you've talked about off the table?

THE PRESIDENT: Here's what we know. We know that
they're still trying to learn how to enrich uranium. We know that
enriching uranium is an important step in a country who wants to
develop a weapon. We know they had a program. We know the
program is halted.

I think it is very important for the international community to
recognize the fact that if Iran were to develop the knowledge that

they could transfer to a clandestine program it would create a danger for the world. And so I view this report as a warning signal that they had the program, they halted the program. And the reason why it's a warning signal is that they could restart it. And the thing that would make a restarted program effective and dangerous is the ability to enrich uranium, the knowledge of which could be passed on to a hidden program.

. . . [T]he NIE provides an opportunity for us to rally the international community—continue to rally the community to pressure the Iranian regime to suspend its program.

You know, the NIE also said that such pressure was effective, and that's what our government has been explaining to other partners in keeping the international pressure on Iran. The best diplomacy, effective diplomacy, is one of which all options are on the table.

*   *   *   *

5. Nuclear Nonproliferation Treaty

a. Deterring and responding to withdrawal by treaty violators

In a release dated February 2, 2007, the Department of State Bureau of International Security and Nonproliferation provided U.S. views on deterring and responding to withdrawal from the Nuclear Nonproliferation Treaty ("NPT") by treaty violators. As noted in the release, the analysis was occasioned primarily by North Korean actions, starting with its announcement in January 2003 that it intended to withdraw from the Treaty:

> Its statements and actions before and since that date—not least in conducting a nuclear detonation in October 2006—demonstrate that North Korea's withdrawal is precisely the sort of conduct that the international community cannot permit if the NPT is to continue to serve its purposes.

The full text of the release, excerpted below, is available at *www.state.gov/t/isn/rls/other/80518.htm. See also* Department of State fact sheet dated April 18, 2007, "Challenges of Noncompliance," summarizing compliance obligations under the NPT and discussing challenges from Iran and North Korea, available at *www.state.gov/t/isn/rls/other/83398.htm.*

---

*   *   *   *

. . . NPT States Party should consider Article X [providing for withdrawal in limited circumstances] with great care. The question of how best to deter and, if necessary, to respond to NPT withdrawal by Treaty violators is both important and urgent. Prompt and effective international action is imperative. States Party should place this issue high up on their agenda for the current NPT review cycle, build upon the excellent preparatory work done on Article X issues for the 2005 NPT Review Conference (RevCon), and work closely together in order to implement appropriate measures as quickly as possible.

Treaty Benefits and Treaty Good Faith

All States Party to the NPT enjoy enormous security benefits from the Treaty, most of all in the assurances it helps provide that a non-nuclear weapon state (NNWS) neighbor or rival will not develop nuclear weapons—and in the consequent assurances the NPT also helps provide to all humanity against the emergence of dangerous new nuclear arms races. This is the basic purpose of the Treaty. This purpose, however, is undermined if States Party do not comply with the NPT, and if such states feel free to withdraw from it without consequence.

Parties to the NPT enjoy certain benefits not available to those states that have chosen not to adhere to the Treaty. Among those benefits is participation in deliberations at Review Conferences and Preparatory Committee meetings, which discuss important aspects of the operation of the Treaty. The Treaty's benefits also include an assurance of access to nuclear cooperation and a broad range of technical support in the use of nuclear technology for peaceful purposes. A state Party that enjoys these benefits while clandestinely violating its NPT obligations, however, demonstrates its contempt for the Treaty and perpetrates a sort of fraud against all other States Party. A State Party that withdraws from the NPT after violating the Treaty should not be permitted to avoid corrective action by the international community to deprive it of the benefits derived while in violation of the Treaty.

Withdrawal does not absolve a state of any violation of the Treaty that was committed while still a party to the Treaty. Should a party withdraw from the Treaty before it remedies its violations, it should remain accountable for those violations. Pursuant to Article X, countries have a right to withdraw from the Treaty, but they do not have a right to profit from their violations, and other States Party should ensure that they do not.

* * * *

The Existing Framework

Should a party announce its intention to withdraw, the NPT and the nuclear nonproliferation regime already provide an opportunity (three-months' advance notice) for the international community to address the situation. It is clear, moreover, that the Treaty envisions that Parties will consider withdrawal only in the most serious of circumstances: those which jeopardize its supreme interests. Pursuant to the text of Article X.1,

> *Each Party shall in exercising its national sovereignty have the right to withdraw from the Treaty if it decides that extraordinary events, related to the subject matter of this Treaty, have jeopardized the supreme interests of its country. It shall give notice of such withdrawal to all other Parties to the Treaty and to the United Nations Security Council three months in advance. Such notice shall include a statement of the extraordinary events it regards as having jeopardized its supreme interests.*

By requiring three months notice before withdrawal is complete, Article X allows parties and the United Nations Security Council (UNSC)—and thereby implicitly nearly any interested party with influence it might bring to bear—time to seek to influence the withdrawing party or to prepare to deal with the consequences of a completed withdrawal. The requirement that the withdrawing party include a statement in its notice of withdrawal explaining the circumstances it believes jeopardize its supreme interests affords the international community an opportunity to review and evaluate the motivations and reasons of the withdrawing party. Although a decision to withdraw is solely a matter of national sovereignty, the international community should seek to exercise any avenues of redress that may be available to it if it is clear that such reasons are offered in bad faith, especially with the intent of continuing pre-existing NPT violations.

The NPT conveys no power to *stop* withdrawal from taking effect if the reasons given are in the judgment of the international community frivolous or improper, but neither would the Treaty prevent the international community from taking appropriate steps against a withdrawing party, especially a party that had demonstrated that its actions posed a threat to international peace and security. Given the destructive capabilities presented by nuclear weapons, the possession of which is regulated by the Treaty, NPT withdrawal would ordinarily raise issues within the competence of the Security Council. Withdrawal by a country that had already violated its NPT obligations should be of very great concern indeed.

Responding to Withdrawal

NPT Parties should undertake a wide range of actions to seek to dissuade a state from withdrawing while in violation of the Treaty, and to express opposition to such a step—before, during, and after the Article X notice period. Such measures, depending on the circumstances, could include:

1. UN Security Council: Because an NPT violator's intention to withdraw from the NPT will likely be coupled with the intention to acquire nuclear weapons, the Security Council must carefully consider the potential consequences of the intended withdrawal for international peace and security. Upon its receipt of a notification of withdrawal, the Security Council, therefore, should meet promptly to consider the "extraordinary events" cited by the party as jeopardizing its supreme interests and thereby giving rise to its intention to withdraw, as well as the likely consequences for peace and security of the withdrawal and the possibility that alternative measures short of withdrawal might address and resolve the circumstances cited by the party.

The Security Council has made clear that proliferation of nuclear weapons constitutes a threat to international peace and security. Accordingly, in a case of withdrawal from the NPT by a violator, the Council should consider the full range of options provided by the Charter, including under Chapter VII, as may be warranted by the circumstances of the case. Withdrawal by a party in breach of NPT commitments raises particular concerns because other Parties may have based their security calculations and decisions regarding nuclear cooperation on the withdrawing party's compliance with those commitments.

The Security Council could ask the International Atomic Energy Agency (IAEA) for all relevant information it may have about the country in question, including the status of safeguards compliance by the withdrawing state. The IAEA may be able to provide other information such as the state's capabilities in reprocessing and enrichment and any holdings of enriched uranium and plutonium, as well as its inspectors' assessments of activities known to be underway there.

The Security Council also may wish to undertake consultations with the withdrawing party and make clear the possible future steps the Council might take. Should the requirements of Article X.1 of the NPT be fulfilled and withdrawal completed, the Council should carefully consider whether the situation resulting from the withdrawal constitutes a threat to international peace and security. Upon making such a determination, the Council should consider all appropriate measures, including invoking its authority under Chapter VII of the United Nations Charter to impose specific conditions of transparency and accountability upon nuclear-related activity in the country in question, and/or regulate the scope of permissible nuclear-related dealings with that country.

2. IAEA Board of Governors: The International Atomic Energy Agency has no specific role in matters of Treaty withdrawal *per se*. It has specific statutory authorities and responsibilities in the event of a Party's noncompliance with nuclear safeguards, however, which might become important in instances in which a Party violates safeguards obligations prior to attempting Treaty withdrawal.

The Agency also has some ability to shape safeguards obligations in such a way as to lessen the danger that withdrawal would immediately result in nuclear materials and technology being subject to no safeguards at all. Accordingly, the IAEA and its Board of Governors could consider the following:

1. Measures for continued safeguarding of nuclear equipment and material in a withdrawing state, should that Party complete the requirements of Article X;
2. Prompt reporting to the UN Security Council of any safeguards or other compliance concerns;
3. Suspension of supply agreements between the IAEA and a state in noncompliance with its safeguards obligations;
4. Suspension of IAEA technical assistance to such a Party, whether on grounds provided in the IAEA Statute, as a matter of policy, or as directed by the UN Security Council; and
5. Withdrawal of material or equipment provided under IAEA auspices to a state in noncompliance with its safeguards obligations, pursuant to Articles XII.A.7 and/or XII.C of the IAEA Statute.

3. Nuclear Supply: There should be no further nuclear supply to a country in violation of the NPT that has withdrawn or made a notification of withdrawal. Nor should such a withdrawing party be allowed to benefit from the use of nuclear materials and equipment that it imported while it was party to the Treaty. NPT Parties engage in nuclear cooperation based on a good-faith assumption of Treaty compliance and, in the case of a NNWS recipient, on its acceptance of comprehensive IAEA safeguards required in connection with the NPT. A withdrawing state that has violated the NPT should not continue to enjoy the benefits acquired while it was a party to the Treaty.

To this end, NPT nuclear supplier states should seek through appropriate means to halt the use of nuclear material and equipment previously supplied to the withdrawing state, and to secure the elimination of such items or their return to the original supplier. Nuclear suppliers should reserve these rights in their bilateral nuclear supply arrangements, and exercise them wherever appropriate.

Return of such items could also be directed by the Security Council in a Chapter VII resolution, if such an action were deemed necessary to respond to a threat to international peace and security. Finally, even in cases where there has been no supply, nuclear supply arrangements might be terminated, where possible, as an expression of disapproval.

(We note in this connection that, as indicated above, Article XII.A.7 of the IAEA Statute gives the IAEA the right to "withdraw any material or equipment made available by the Agency or a member" in furtherance of an Agency project if a recipient state does not comply with the relevant safeguards requirements and fails to take corrective action in a reasonable time. Article XII.C has a similar provision. The concept of removing materials and equipment from a State based on its failure to meet nonproliferation norms is not a new or novel concept, and thus it is reasonable to adapt the concept in cases of NPT withdrawal by a country that has failed to meet nonproliferation norms by violating the NPT.)

Finally, states may have their own resources to bring to bear against the efforts of withdrawing Parties to develop further nuclear capabilities, including with regard to information-gathering and various means of interdiction. In the event of a withdrawal by an NPT violator, States with such resources could focus their assets on the withdrawing state as a country of proliferation concern in an attempt to stop any clandestine transfers directed at the acquisition of a nuclear weapons capability or of the proliferation of such technology to others.

Conclusion

The right to withdraw from the NPT remains a sovereign right enshrined in the Treaty itself. But nothing in the NPT gives countries the right to benefit from their violation of the Treaty's provisions, or to shield themselves from the consequences of such acts. And Parties to the NPT, indeed all countries, have a sovereign right to consider the ramifications of such a withdrawal for their individual and collective security. States Party should make clear that they will ensure that all appropriate consequences will flow in the event of withdrawal from the Treaty by a violator. By doing this, they will also help deter such actions and further the goal of universal adherence.

It is of critical importance to the nuclear nonproliferation regime that NPT States Party work together to develop and implement prompt and effective measures to deter withdrawal by Treaty violators and to respond vigorously should it occur. Prompted by North Korea's announcement of withdrawal in 2003, much valuable work was done on this subject in connection with the 2005 Review Conference. This issue should be a top priority for the current NPT review cycle as well, and States Party should work diligently to ensure agreement upon effective steps. The review cycle has a valuable role to play in helping develop and encourage such measures, and in reaffirming the norms of the NPT and the broader nonproliferation regime they reinforce.

b. Disarmament obligations

On March 17, 2007, Dr. Christopher A. Ford, U.S. Special Representative for Nuclear Nonproliferation, addressed an annual workshop hosted by the Center for Nonproliferation Studies in Annecy, France to exchange views on the Nuclear Nonproliferation Treaty review process. Excerpts below from Dr. Ford's remarks discuss the U.S. position on disarmament. The full texts of Dr. Ford's paper and related working papers are available at *www.us-mission.ch/Press2007/0317Annecy.html*.

See also statement of April 10, 2007, by U.S. Representative John A. Bravaco exercising the U.S. right of reply in the UN Disarmament Commission to respond to Iranian statements regarding U.S. compliance with its Nuclear Nonproliferation Treaty disarmament obligations, available at *www.un.int/usa/press_releases/20070410_081.html* and June 12, 2007, statement by Ambassador Christina Rocca to the UN Conference on Disarmament in Geneva, describing U.S. nuclear disarmament efforts, available at *www.us-mission.ch/Press2007/0612ConferenceonDisarmament.htm*.

*   *   *   *

A. *The U.S. Record*

[One U.S. position] paper sets forth the United States' outstanding record of accomplishments related to nuclear disarmament. . . . These accomplishments continue today.

We have eliminated more than 13,000 nuclear weapons since 1988 and gotten rid of more than 1,000 ballistic missiles and 450 missile silos. But this process is not over. The Bush Administration dismantled the last W-56 warhead for the Minuteman II missile in June 2006, and it has requested significant *increases* in the current budget for nuclear warhead dismantlement. We are currently in the process of drawing down our strategic warhead numbers in order to meet Moscow Treaty targets. When we have completed this task, our nuclear arsenal will be at about a quarter of its size at the end of the Cold War, and will have reached its lowest level since the Eisenhower Administration. The Bush Administration has also continued longstanding reductions in delivery systems, and we recently announced that we will eliminate about 400 Advanced Cruise Missiles currently deployed with the B-52 bomber fleet.

We have not produced any uranium for use in nuclear weapons since 1964, nor any plutonium for such purposes since 1988, and we have scrupulously observed the nuclear testing moratorium we announced in 1992. We have also been actively *removing* fissile material from our nuclear weapons programs, placing some of it under International Atomic Energy Agency (IAEA) safeguards, and down-blending some 90 tons of highly-enriched uranium (HEU) from defense nuclear programs for use in civilian power reactors. The most recent step in this process occurred as recently as November 2005, when the Bush Administration announced that it would remove another 200 metric tons of HEU from any further use as fissile material in U.S. nuclear warheads. This is enough material, according to IAEA figures, to make 8,000 nuclear weapons. Meanwhile, the United States in May 2006 became the first (and so far only) country to introduce a draft Fissile Material Cutoff Treaty (FMCT) at the U.N. Conference on Disarmament.

The United States is also beginning development of the Reliable Replacement Warhead (RRW), which will help us to continue to meet our deterrence needs until the total elimination of nuclear weapons can be achieved, but to do so with safer warheads, fewer warheads, and less potential need to resume nuclear testing. The RRW, which adds no new nuclear weapons capabilities, thus supports and will help advance the disarmament objectives of the NPT.

For those of you who now acknowledge the reductions we have made since the end of the Cold War but think the United States may nonetheless be *increasing* its *reliance* upon nuclear weapons, rest assured that this is false. Indeed, pursuant to our Nuclear Posture Review (NPR) of 2001, the United States is reducing its formerly exclusive reliance upon nuclear weapons for strategic deterrence. In place of the exclusively nuclear strategic "Triad" of the Cold War, the United States relies increasingly on a combination of non-nuclear offensive strike capabilities, active and passive defenses (including ballistic missile defenses), and a robust and responsive defense industrial infrastructure to satisfy the requirements of strategic deterrence with a lessened emphasis on nuclear weapons.

The Strategic Arms Reduction Treaty (START I) will expire in 2009, and the Moscow Treaty in 2012. We have already begun high-level discussions with the Russians about what our future strategic security relationship should look like. It is too early to say much about those talks, but I should emphasize that U.S. officials have made it clear that they hope to ensure that transparency and confidence-building measures remain an enduring part of the U.S.-Russia relationship as it continues to mature in a post-Cold War environment. The reductions that followed the end of the Cold War highlight the role that easing tension and strengthening trust among nations must play in achieving the goals of Article VI and the Preamble to the NPT.

Finally, I wish to stress the link between nonproliferation compliance and disarmament progress, a link that Article VI itself makes by stressing the need to end nuclear arms race behavior. Strict compliance with nonproliferation obligations is an essential step toward disarmament, and the world cannot expect to achieve and sustain the elimination of existing nuclear weapons programs if it cannot prevent the development of new ones.

As the non-aligned members of the [UN's Eighteen Nation Disarmament Committee ("ENDC")] noted in a 1965 draft resolution during NPT negotiations, a guiding principle was for the draft treaty to be "*a step towards* the achievement of general and complete disarmament and, more particularly, nuclear disarmament." Nonproliferation alone, in other words, is not sufficient as the goal for the international community, but it is absolutely *necessary* if the world is to have any hope of finally achieving disarmament.

*   *   *   *

6.   2005 Protocols to the UN Convention for the Suppression of Unlawful Acts Against the Safety of Maritime Navigation and to Its Protocol on Fixed Platforms

As discussed in A.6. *supra,* on October 1, 2007, President Bush transmitted to the Senate for advice and consent to ratification the Protocol of 2005 to the Convention for the Suppression of Unlawful Acts Against the Safety of Maritime Navigation ("2005 SUA Protocol") and the Protocol of 2005 to the Protocol for the Suppression of Unlawful Acts Against the Safety of Fixed Platforms Located on the Continental Shelf ("2005 Fixed Platforms Protocol"). S. Treaty Doc. No. 110-8 (2007). Among other things, the protocols contain new nonproliferation provisions, including what the President's transmittal letter described as a "a shipboarding regime based on flag state consent that will provide an international legal basis for interdiction at sea of weapons of mass destruction, their delivery systems and related materials, and terrorist fugitives." The President's letter noted that the protocols "promote the aims of the Proliferation Security Initiative," discussed in C.7. below. Excerpts below from the report of the Department of State transmitted with the President's letter describe the nonproliferation initiatives and a proposed understanding. *See also* understanding concerning certain definitions, A.6. *supra,* and discussion of law enforcement provisions in Chapter 3. B.1.f.

---

*   *   *   *

Non-proliferation provisions
Article 3bis(1)(b) makes it an offense to transport on board a ship:

(i) any explosive or radioactive material, knowing that it is intended to be used to cause, or in a threat to cause, death or serious injury or damage for the purpose of intimidating a population, or compelling a government or an international organization to do or abstain from doing any act; or

(ii) any [biological, chemical and nuclear weapons and other nuclear explosive devices ("BCN weapon")], knowing it to be a BCN weapon as defined in Article 1; or

(iii) any source material, special fissionable material, or equipment or material especially designed or prepared for the processing, use or production of special fissionable material, knowing that it is intended to be used in a nuclear explosive activity or in any other nuclear activity not under safeguards pursuant to an IAEA comprehensive safeguards agreement; or

(iv) any equipment, materials or software or related technology that significantly contributes to the design, manufacture or delivery of a BCN weapon, with the intention that it be used for such purpose.

These nonproliferation offenses make significant advances to counterterrorism efforts by filling a gap in the existing international treaty framework. The Convention requires criminalization of certain transports of nuclear-related items associated with nuclear weapons or nuclear explosive devices and thus provides a complementary law enforcement element to the nuclear nonproliferation regime. Article 3*bis*(1)(b)(iv) of the Convention goes beyond the NPT in requiring criminalization of the transport of equipment, materials or software or related technology that significantly contributes to the design or manufacture of delivery systems for nuclear weapons (other than those of NPT nuclear-weapon States Parties). The nonproliferation offenses further the objectives of, and are complementary with, the nonproliferation obligations set forth in United Nations Security Council Resolutions 1540 (2004) and 1673 (2006).

Article 3*bis*(2) constitutes an important nonproliferation "savings clause" by specifying that nuclear transport activities remain permissible under the Convention in certain circumstances, notwithstanding the wording of the offenses in Article 3*bis*(1)(b). Article 3*bis*(2) states that it shall not be an offense within the meaning of the Convention to transport an item or material covered by Article 3*bis*(1)(b)(iii) or, insofar as it relates to a nuclear weapon or other nuclear explosive device, Article 3*bis*(1)(b)(iv), if such item or material is transported to or from the territory of, or is otherwise transported under the control of a State Party to the NPT where: "(a) the resulting transfer or receipt, including internal to a State, of the item or material is not contrary to such State Party's obligations" under the NPT, and "(b) if the item or material is intended for the delivery system of a nuclear weapon or other nuclear explosive device of a State Party" to the NPT, "the holding of such weapon or device is not contrary to that State Party's obligations under that Treaty."

This nonproliferation savings clause in Article 3*bis*(2), coupled with the general provision in Article 2*bis*(3) declaring that the Convention shall not affect the rights and obligations of States Parties under the NPT, ensures that the Convention is consistent with the rights and obligations of the States Parties to the NPT (except to the extent that the Convention goes beyond the NPT with respect to nuclear weapon delivery systems). As provided in Article 3*bis*(2), the Convention would not require criminalization of the transport to or from the territory of, or under the control of, an NPT State Party of source or special fissionable material, or of equipment or material especially designed or prepared for the processing, use or production of special fissionable material, as long as the resulting transfer or receipt of such items or materials is not contrary to the NPT obligations of the NPT State Party. This is the case even when a non-NPT party is on the "other end" of the transport to or from (or under the control of) the NPT State Party.

I recommend that the following understanding to Article 3 and Article 4(5) of the 2005 SUA Protocol be included in the United States instrument of ratification to clarify the applicability of new

Article 2*bis*(3) and Article 3*bis*(2) of the Convention to the offense in new Article 3*bis*(1)(b)(iii) of the Convention:

The United States of America understands that:

(a) Article 3 and Article 4(5) of the Protocol of 2005 to the Convention for the Suppression of Unlawful Acts against the Safety of Maritime Navigation ("the 2005 SUA Protocol") (which add, *inter alia*, Article 2*bis*(3) and Article 3*bis*(2), respectively, to the Convention for the Suppression of Unlawful Acts against the Safety of Maritime Navigation (together referred to as "the NPT savings clauses")) protect from criminality under the Convention for the Suppression of Unlawful Acts against the Safety of Maritime Navigation, 2005, the transport of source or special fissionable material, or equipment or material especially designed or prepared for the processing, use, or production of special fissionable material

(i)   from the territory of, or otherwise under the control of, a State Party to the Treaty on the Non-Proliferation of Nuclear Weapons ("NPT") to the territory of, or otherwise under the control of, another NPT State Party or a state that is not an NPT party, and

(ii) from the territory of, or otherwise under the control of, a state that is not an NPT party to the territory of, or otherwise under the control of, an NPT State Party,

where the resulting transfer or receipt of such items or materials is not contrary to the NPT obligations of the NPT State Party.

(b) The following are illustrative examples of transport of source or special fissionable materials (hereinafter referred to collectively as "nuclear material") and especially designed or prepared equipment or material that would not constitute offenses under the Convention for the Suppression of Unlawful Acts against the Safety of Maritime Navigation, 2005, by virtue of the savings clauses:

- Transport of nuclear material (from either an NPT State Party or a non-NPT party) to an NPT nuclear-weapon State Party, regardless of whether the nuclear material will be under safeguards in the NPT nuclear-weapon State Party, because the resulting receipt of the item or material is not contrary to the NPT obligations of the nuclear-weapon State Party;

• Transport of nuclear material to a non-nuclear weapon State Party to the NPT for non-nuclear use without safeguards, in accordance with the provisions of the recipient country's IAEA comprehensive safeguards agreement (INFCIRC 153) allowing for exemption of the nuclear material from safeguards or the non-application or termination of safeguards (e.g., for specified *de minimis* amounts, or use in a non-proscribed military activity which does not require the application of IAEA safeguards or in a non-nuclear use such as the production of alloys or ceramics);

• Transport of nuclear material or especially designed or prepared equipment, as described in Article 4(5) of the 2005 SUA Protocol (which adds Article 3*bis*(1)(b)(iii) to the Convention for the Suppression of Unlawful Acts against the Safety of Maritime Navigation), from an NPT State Party to a non-NPT party, so long as the relevant material is for peaceful purposes and placed under IAEA safeguards, consistent with the NPT State Party's obligations under Article III.2 of the NPT. If the nuclear material transferred for peaceful purposes is subject to an INFCIRC/66 safeguards agreement or other IAEA safeguards arrangement but is not required by that agreement actually to be under safeguards (e.g., under an exemption for *de minimis* amounts or provision permitting safeguards termination for non-nuclear use), the transport would not constitute an offense under Article 3*bis*(1)(b)(iii) of the Convention for the Suppression of Unlawful Acts against the Safety of Maritime Navigation, 2005.

*   *   *   *

Shipboarding

Article 8(2) of the 2005 SUA Protocol adds Article 8*bis* to the Convention. Article 8*bis* creates a shipboarding regime by establishing a comprehensive set of procedures and protections designed to facilitate the boarding of a vessel suspected of being involved in an offense under the Convention. The boarding procedures do not change existing international maritime law or infringe upon the traditional principle of freedom of navigation. Instead, the procedures eliminate the need to negotiate time-consuming ad hoc boarding arrangements when facing the immediacy of ongoing criminal activity. Additionally, the boarding regime builds upon existing regimes under bilateral and multilateral agreements to which the United States is a party, including agreements with respect to fisheries, narcotics, illegal migrants, and WMD interdiction.

The first three paragraphs of Article 8*bis* set forth general parameters for the shipboarding regime. States Parties must cooperate to the fullest extent possible to prevent and suppress offenses under the Convention, in conformity with international law, and to respond to requests under the boarding regime as expeditiously as possible (paragraph 1). This provision is derived from Article 17(1) of the 1988 UN Convention against Illicit Traffic in Narcotic Drugs and Psychotropic Substances (1988 Vienna Narcotic Drug Convention), S. Treaty Doc. 101-4, and Article 7 of the Protocol against the Smuggling of Migrants by Land, Sea and Air, supplementing the United Nations Convention against Transnational Organized Crime (Migrant Smuggling Protocol), S. Treaty Doc. 108-16. The United States is a party to both Conventions.

Each request should, if possible, contain the name of the suspect ship, the IMO identification number, the port of registry, the ports of origin and destination, and any other relevant information (paragraph 2). In addition, each State Party must take into account the dangers and difficulties involved in boarding a ship at sea and searching its cargo, and give consideration to whether other appropriate measures agreed between the States concerned could be more safely taken in the next port of call or elsewhere (paragraph 3).

The United States will implement its obligations to "cooperate to the fullest extent possible" under Article 8*bis*(1) by designating a competent authority at the national level for making, receiving, processing, and responding to boarding requests under the Convention, as we have done for counternarcotics, migrant, fisheries, WMD interdictions, and other similar law enforcement agreements. The competent authority, who will most likely be the Commandant of the U.S. Coast Guard, will execute its obligations through a national level command or operations center, which will have immediate access to all national vessel registry data, as well as procedures established for realtime U.S. Government coordination, including the Maritime Operational Threat Response Plan. See further the discussion of Article 8*bis*(15) below.

Pursuant to paragraph 4 of Article 8*bis*, if a State Party has reasonable grounds to suspect that an offense under Articles 3, 3*bis*, 3*ter*, or 3*quater* of the Convention has been, is being, or is about to be committed involving a ship flying its flag, it may request the assistance of other States Parties in preventing or suppressing that offense. The States Parties so requested shall use their best endeavors to render such assistance within the means available to them. This provision is derived from Article 17(2) of the 1988 Vienna Narcotic Drug Convention and Article 8(1) of the Migrant Smuggling Protocol. This provision does not obligate the United States to board or take law enforcement actions on foreign flagged ships, except to the extent it is required to use best endeavors to render assistance within the means available to it upon request of a flag State to assist in prevention or suppression of an offense specified under the Convention. The absence of a reference in paragraph 4 to "marks of registry" (both "flying its flag" and "displaying marks of registry" are used in paragraph 5) is of no consequence because each refers to indicia of the nationality of the vessel permissible, as reflected in Articles 5 and 6 of the 1958 Convention on the High Seas ("High Seas Convention"), TIAS 5200, and Articles 91 and 92 of the United Nations Convention on the Law of the Sea, ("Law of the Sea Convention"), S. Treaty Doc. 103-39. See Article 8*bis*(5)(a), (b) and (d).

*　　*　　*　　*

A State Party may provide advance consent to board ships flying its flag or displaying its mark of registry pursuant to subparagraphs

(d) or (e) of Article 8*bis*(5) by notification to the IMO Secretary-General. A notification pursuant to Article 8*bis*(5)(d) would grant the requesting Party authorization to board and search a ship, its cargo and persons on board, and to question the persons on board in order to locate and examine documentation of its nationality and determine if an offense under Articles 3, 3*bis*, 3*ter*, or 3*quater* of the Convention has been, is being, or is about to be committed, if there is no response from that State Party, within four hours of acknowledgement of its receipt of a request to confirm nationality. Notification pursuant to Article 8*bis*(5)(e) would provide general advance consent for other States Parties to board and search such ships, their cargo and persons on board, and to question the persons on board in order to determine if an offense under Articles 3, 3*bis*, 3*ter*, or 3*quater* of the Convention has been, is being, or is about to be committed. These optional notifications may be withdrawn at any time. Advance consent pursuant to either subparagraph (d) or (e) is not authorization for detention of the vessel, cargo, or persons on board or any other enforcement action. The United States will not file a notification with the IMO Secretary-General granting either such form of advance consent.

*   *   *   *

Paragraph 9 of Article 8*bis* sets forth overarching principles for the use of force by officials acting under the shipboarding regime. It directs States Parties to avoid the use of force "except when necessary to ensure the safety of its officials and persons on board, or where the officials are obstructed in the execution of the authorized actions." It also specifies that any such use of force "shall not exceed the minimum degree of force which is necessary and reasonable in the circumstances." The language of Article 8*bis*(9) is drawn from Article 22(1)(f) of the Agreement for the Implementation of the Provisions of the United Nations Convention on the Law of the Sea of 10 December 1982 Relating to the Conservation and Management of Straddling Fish Stocks and Highly Migratory Fish Stocks, S. Treaty Doc. 104-24, to which the United States is a party. Article 8*bis*(9) is also similar to use of force provisions in other maritime law enforcement agreements to which the United States is a party. As such, this use of force provision reflects and is consistent with current practice on the use of force in international law and U.S. maritime law enforcement.

*   *   *   *

Subparagraph (b) of Article 8*bis*(10) establishes a framework for liability and recourse arising from any damage, harm, or loss attributable to States Parties taking measures under Article 8*bis*. It clarifies that authorization to board by a flag State shall not per se give rise to its liability. Liability for damage, harm, or loss as a result of shipboarding activities arises under two circumstances: first, when the grounds for shipboarding measures prove to be unfounded, provided that the ship has not committed any act justifying the measures taken; and second, when such measures are unlawful or unreasonable in light of the available information to implement the provisions of Article 8*bis*. States Parties are obligated to "provide effective recourse in respect of any such damage, harm or loss." This provision does not require a State Party to provide a specific remedy, forum, or venue, and it does not require any form of binding dispute resolution. Accordingly, the manner of "effective recourse" remains at the discretion of each State Party. Article 8*bis*(10)(b) of the Convention is consistent with the claims provisions of existing relevant international treaties, including Article 22(3) of the High Seas Convention, and Article 9(2) of the Migrant Smuggling Protocol. As a matter of policy the United States compensates innocent people whose property is damaged by Federal officers during maritime law enforcement operations. Congress has established mechanisms that permit the United States Navy (10 U.S. Code 2734, 7622; 32 CFR Part 752) and the United States Coast Guard (10 U.S. Code §§ 2733, 2734; 14 U.S. Code 646; 33 CFR Part 25) to consider and pay meritorious claims for damaged property arising from maritime law enforcement operations. These mechanisms are administrative procedures, rather than judicial remedies, which permit the consideration and payment of meritorious claims by Executive Branch agencies. Accordingly, no new legislation is needed to comply with Article 8*bis*(10)(b).

*   *   *   *

The shipboarding provisions under the Convention do not apply to or limit boarding of ships conducted by any State Party in accordance with international law, seaward of any State's territorial sea. Paragraph 11 of Article 8*bis* confirms this understanding of the Convention's applicability. Other lawful shipboarding measures include, but are not limited to, the right of approach and visit, belligerent rights under the law of war, self-defense, the enforcement of United Nations Security Council Resolutions, actions taken pursuant to specific bilateral or multilateral instruments such as counter-narcotics agreements, the rendering of assistance to persons, ships, and property in peril, authorization from the flag State to take action, or the historic role of the armed forces in law enforcement activities on the high seas. In addition, the United States has often employed its military forces abroad to protect U.S. citizens and to enforce provisions of U.S. law. Article 8*bis* would not affect these rights.

* * * *

7. Proliferation Security Initiative

The Proliferation Security Initiative ("PSI") was first announced by President Bush in May 2003, stating:

> The United States and a number of our close allies have begun working on new agreements to search planes and ships carrying suspect cargo and to seize illegal weapons or missile technologies.

See Digest 2003 at 1095–99. During 2007 the United States signed PSI shipboarding agreements with Malta on March 15, 2007, and Mongolia on October 23, 2007, for a total of seven bilateral agreements. The agreements are available at *www.state.gov/t/isn//c10390.htm*, as are the Statement of Interdiction Principles adopted in 2003 and further information.

In an address to the Center for Oceans Law and Policy in Heidelberg, Germany, on May 25, 2007, Capt. J. Ashley Roach, JAGC, USN (ret.), Office of the Legal Adviser, U.S. Department of State, addressed among other things, certain concerns and misconceptions related to the Proliferation Security Initiative.

The full text of Mr. Roach's address, excerpted below (most footnotes deleted), is available at *www.state.gov/s/l/c8183. htm.*

* * * *

. . . [Bilateral shipboarding agreements negotiated by the United States] and the PSI Statement of Interdiction Principles are based entirely on compliance with national and international law and frameworks, including full respect for flag State jurisdiction and coastal State sovereignty. This truth is not understood by those who suggest that its implementation is not, or may not be, consistent with international law. Uncertainty has been expressed about the meaning of what would constitute WMD material, the geographic area of application, identification of "States and non-state actors of proliferation concern", possible negative impact on regional politics and stability, and lack of scientific technical knowledge with regard to WMD materials and how to deal with them. Let me address each of these concerns in turn.

Definitions

Some claim to be uncertain about the meaning of "WMD materials". I would refer them to UN Security Council Resolution 1540 (2004), binding under Chapter VII, which contains definitions of the relevant terms: WMD, related materials and delivery systems.[26] The US PSI bilateral shipboarding agreements contain substantially identical definitions.

Geographic scope of application

Some countries have expressed concern that application of the PSI principles in the various maritime zones and in national airspace would not be in conformity with the Law of the Sea Convention and the Chicago Convention, notwithstanding the commitment of all PSI participants to act in accordance with them. Legal experts from the 20 participant countries in the PSI Operational Experts Group continue to examine these very issues

---

[26] See http://www.state.gov/t/isn/c18943.htm

to ensure that any PSI activity in the territorial sea, contiguous zone, straits used for international navigation, archipelagic waters including archipelagic sea lanes, the EEZ, the high seas, and national and international airspace are consistent with the governing international law. All participants in PSI are committed to act in that manner and respect the international legal regimes for the maritime zones. It is simply wrong to assert that the PSI Participants, particularly those with major interests in freedoms of navigation and overflight, seek to limit those freedoms through PSI. Rather, PSI Participants fully recognize that responding to the extreme danger to international peace and security posed by the proliferation of weapons of mass destruction must be done in ways that fully respect those freedoms, especially when proliferators seek to take advantage of them.

Consequently, PSI participants are agreed that it is best to act in those locations and as to those ships and aircraft over which a particular participant has clear legal authority: in its ports and internal waters, on its land territory, in its national airspace, and over ships having its nationality wherever located. The participants have come to appreciate that rigorous application of national customs, import and export control, and money laundering laws and regulations, coupled with the willingness of ship owners, port states and shippers to cooperate, are particularly effective tools.

It is also instructive that UNSCRs 1718 (2006) and 1737 (2006) require States to take such actions regarding proscribed material to or from North Korea or Iran respectively, and that paragraph 8(f) of UNSCR 1718 calls upon all States to take cooperative action in that regard, consistent with international law, including the inspection of cargo to and from the DPRK, as necessary.

Identification of "States and non-state actors of proliferation concern"

Since the Statement of Interdiction Principles was adopted in 2003, the UN Security Council, acting under Chapter VII, has brought greater clarity. UNSCR 1540, reaffirmed in UNSCR 1673 (2006), calls upon all States to prevent the proliferation of WMD. UNSCRs 1695 (2006) and 1718 (2006) have identified North

Korea, and UNSCRs 1696 (2006), 1737 (2006) and 1747 (2007) have identified Iran, as States of proliferation concern. Identification of the A.Q. Khan network and enhanced enforcement of customs and financing controls has identified many of the non-State actors of proliferation concern. Indeed, UNSCRs 1737 and 1747 identify many of them involved in the Iranian programs.

Possible negative impact on regional politics and stability

Some countries have neighbors who are States of proliferation concern or within whose borders non-state actors of proliferation concern operate. Those countries should have an even greater interest in curbing proliferation and thereby promoting regional stability, rather than view PSI as having a negative impact on stability.

Lack of scientific and technical knowledge with regard to WMD materials and how to deal with them

The PSI OEG recognizes that the so-called "dual use" goods, those that could have legitimate or illegitimate uses, are the most difficult to recognize and that it requires specialized knowledge, training and equipment to deal with these WMD materials. They are working to remedy that situation. In addition, the US Department of Energy also provides Commodity Identification Training to customs and border control officials around the world.

Voluntariness

Some States have sought to justify their unwillingness to endorse the PSI Statement of Interdiction Principles because of their country's lack of human and material resources to carry out the actions contemplated. Many, indeed most, PSI participant countries have limited capabilities to carry out all of their political commitments. But that is understood by all. Participants acknowledge that participation in PSI itself and in any PSI activity is entirely voluntary.

Shipboarding

Finally, some authorities continue to argue that flag States have no authority to permit other States to board ships having their nationality, arguing that such action would be a surrender of its jurisdiction to third countries, violate its territorial sovereignty or be an affront to their sovereignty. These assertions conflate a flag State's undeniable international legal authority to permit a third state to board one of its ships on the high seas with national legal limitations on boarding of its ships by third States, and on what may be done if illicit activity is found as a result of that boarding,[29] as well as perpetuate the myth that a merchant ship, yacht or warship is a piece of its national territory. Only the last enjoys sovereign immunity.[30]

*　　*　　*　　*

8.　U.S. Missile Defense

During 2007 the United States commenced negotiations with Poland and the Czech Republic with a view to concluding agreements that would allow elements of the U.S. ballistic missile defense system to be based in those countries. A fact sheet released by the Department of State on April 16, 2007, explained that such negotiations, if favorably concluded, "would allow the fielding of ten U.S. long-range ground-based defensive interceptors in Poland and a tracking radar in the Czech Republic." The fact sheet continued:

- The proposed U.S. missile defense assets in Europe would defend the U.S. and much of Europe against long-range ballistic missile threats launched from the Middle East. The U.S. would benefit from greatly enhanced protection from attacks originating in the Middle East, while Europe would gain defenses where none previously existed.
- Some southern European countries do not face long-range threats from Iran given their proximity to the

---

[29] See Appendix 1, Article 8*bis*, paragraphs (5)(c), (6), (8) and (14) of the 2005 SUA Protocol.

[30] See articles 32, 42(5), 95, 96, 110(1) and 236 of the Law of the Sea Convention.

Middle East. NATO has focused its missile defense development efforts on countering shorter range threats. The United States and NATO efforts are complementary and could work together to form a more effective defense for Europe.

The full text of the fact sheet is available at *www.state. gov/p/eur/rls/fs/83119.htm*. Additional information on U.S. missile defense is available at *www.state.gov/t/isn/c21764. htm*.

9. Amendment to the Convention on the Physical Protection of Nuclear Material

On September 4, 2007, President Bush transmitted the Amendment to the Convention on the Physical Protection of Nuclear Material ("Amendment") to the Senate for advice and consent to ratification. S. Treaty Doc. No. 110-6 (2007). The Amendment was adopted at the International Atomic Energy Agency in Vienna on July 8, 2005, by a conference of States Parties to the Convention on the Physical Protection of Nuclear Material, adopted on October 26, 1979.

Excerpts from the report of the Department of State, transmitted with the President's letter, follow. In addition, the Amendment also includes important exceptions to the applicability of the Convention with respect to "armed conflict" and "activities undertaken by the military forces of a State in the exercise of their official duties, inasmuch as they are governed by other rules of international law," and uses the term "international humanitarian law." The State Department report recommended understandings related to these terms consistent with the understandings proposed for the 2005 SUA and Fixed Platform Protocols; *see* A.6. *supra*.

The Amendment to the Convention on the Physical Protection of Nuclear Material ("the Amendment") was adopted on July 8, 2005 by a diplomatic conference of States Parties to the Convention on the Physical Protection of Nuclear Material, adopted October 26, 1979 ("the Convention") at the International Atomic Energy Agency (the "IAEA") in Vienna, Austria. The IAEA serves as the depositary for the Convention. This Overview provides background on the need to amend the Convention and a paragraph-by-paragraph analysis of the Amendment.

Background

The United States led the initiative among the States Parties to pursue adoption of the Amendment. The Convention, which was negotiated in the 1970s and adopted in 1979, entered into force on February 8, 1987. Since that time, the physical protection provisions of the Convention have proven to be too limited in scope, particularly in the face of mounting evidence of increased illicit trafficking in nuclear and other radiological materials in the early 1990s and greater terrorist interest in acquiring weapons-usable nuclear material following the September 11, 2001 terrorist attacks on the United States. The physical protection provisions of the original Convention apply only to nuclear material used for peaceful purposes that is in or is to be placed in international nuclear transport. Although other provisions apply to nuclear material used for peaceful purposes while in domestic use, storage, and transport, no provisions in the original Convention explicitly apply to nuclear facilities.

*   *   *   *

. . . As of April 4, 2007, 124 States and EURATOM are Parties to the Convention. Pursuant to Article 20 of the Convention, the Amendment will enter into force for each State Party that deposits its instrument of ratification, acceptance, or approval of the Amendment on the thirtieth day after the date on which two-thirds of the States Parties have deposited their instruments of ratification, acceptance, or approval with the depositary. Thereafter, the Amendment will enter into force for any other State Party on the day on which that State Party deposits its instrument of ratification, acceptance, or approval of the Amendment. As of May 4, 2007, nine States have deposited such instruments of ratification, acceptance, or approval.

The Amendment, once it enters into force, will significantly strengthen the worldwide physical protection of nuclear material used for peaceful purposes and nuclear facilities used for peaceful purposes. The Convention, as amended, will have three purposes: (1) to achieve and maintain worldwide effective physical protection of nuclear material used for peaceful purposes and nuclear facilities used for peaceful purposes; (2) to prevent and combat offenses relating to such material and facilities worldwide; and (3) to facilitate cooperation to those ends among States Parties.

To accomplish these purposes, the Convention, as amended, will cover the physical protection of nuclear material used for peaceful purposes in domestic use, storage, and transport, as well as in international nuclear transport, and of nuclear facilities used for peaceful purposes. Among other things, the Amendment will establish: (1) new international norms for the physical protection of nuclear material and facilities, including protection from sabotage; (2) strengthened obligations for cooperation among States Parties to the Amendment on matters of physical protection, for protection of the confidentiality of physical protection information, and for the prosecution or extradition of those committing offenses involving nuclear material and nuclear facilities used for peaceful purposes; and (3) new criminal offenses that must be made punishable by each State Party to the Amendment under the national law of that State Party.

The Convention, as amended, will not apply to nuclear material used or retained for military purposes or to a nuclear facility containing such material. It will also not apply to a nuclear facility used for non-peaceful purposes, whether or not it actually contains military nuclear material. Also, the Amendment provides that nothing in the Convention will affect other rights, obligations, and responsibilities of States Parties under international law, in particular the purposes and principles of the Charter of the United Nations and international humanitarian law. The Amendment also includes a "military exclusion provision," similar to the one in the 1997 International Convention for the Suppression of Terrorist Bombings ("Terrorist Bombings Convention"), which was critical to the ability of the United States to support and join in adoption of the Amendment at the diplomatic conference.

* * * *

10. Fissile Material Cutoff Treaty

On February 8, 2007, U.S. Permanent Representative Ambassador Christina Rocca addressed the Conference on Disarmament ("CD") stressing the urgency of negotiating a treaty on fissile material cutoff. Ambassador Rocca's statement is set forth below and available at *www.us-mission.ch/Press2007/ 0208CDstatement.htm. See also* working paper, "The United States and the Fissile Material Cutoff Treaty," provided to the Center for Nonproliferation Studies workshop in Annecy, France, available at *www.us-mission.ch/Press2007/Annecy FMCT.pdf.*

The United States believes strongly that negotiating a legally binding ban on the production of fissile material for use in nuclear weapons and other nuclear explosive devices cannot be delayed any longer. The international community has expressed a desire for such a treaty in one form or another for decades. Here in the Conference on Disarmament, the history of this issue is somewhat shorter, but equally unsuccessful, despite the overwhelming support that negotiation of such a treaty enjoys. The United States believes that last year's CD session set the stage for negotiations to finally begin, and that this year's organizational plan for the CD might prove to be a successful vehicle for this beginning. This opportunity must not be lost. As a matter of record, there is a draft text from which we may begin. It is at once disarmingly simple and understandably complex. To establish the legal norm in a treaty is, in itself, simple. The discussions necessary to codify this ban will be complex. Nevertheless, the goal of ending the production of fissile material is achievable. The world community expects it of us. Now, we must demand it of ourselves.

I note with interest the statement made earlier by the German Ambassador on behalf of the EU. According to that statement, the EU supports the immediate commencement of negotiations on FMCT "bearing in mind the Report of the Special Coordinator." This comment deserves further scrutiny. In that regard, it is instructive to review what the Special Coordinator had to say about the most contentious issues surrounding FMCT, so I will quote from the report at some length:

> "During the course of my consultation, many delegations expressed concerns about a variety of issues relating to fissile material, including the appropriate scope of the convention. Some delegations expressed the view that this mandate would permit consideration in the Committee only of the future production of fissile material. Other delegations were of the view that the mandate would permit consideration not only of future but also of past production. Still others were of the view that consideration should not only relate to production of fissile materials (past or future) but also to other issues, such as the management of such material.
>
> "It has been agreed by delegations that the mandate for the establishment of the ad hoc Committee does not preclude any delegation from raising for consideration in the ad Hoc Committee any of the above noted issues.
>
> "Delegations with strong views were able to join consensus so we could all move forward on this issue. This means that an Ad Hoc Committee on Cut-Off can be established and negotiations can begin on this important topic."

So, what does it mean to "bear in mind" this report? If it means that there are many contentious issues that can only be resolved in the course of negotiations, then the United States is in full agreement. To that end, the mandate we proposed for such negotiations last year fully captures what is agreed and what is not. Our proposed mandate focuses on the one element on which we all agree, that is, that there should be a negotiation in the CD to ban the production of fissile material for use in nuclear weapons or other nuclear explosive devices. Beyond that essential point, our proposed mandate does not rule anything in during a negotiation, nor does it rule anything out; and it perfectly reflects the Shannon Report's conclusion that any delegation may raise any issue it deems important in the course of negotiations.

As to the Treaty itself, the United States has given considerable thought to what an FMCT should look like. The draft treaty that we have put forward sets forth the essentials needed for an FMCT that would meet the objective of ending expeditiously the production of fissile material for use in nuclear weapons. Our presentations last year made clear our position on some of the difficult issues we will encounter during the course of negotiations. To summarize our draft, the basic obligation under the treaty, effective at entry into force, would be a ban on the production of fissile material for use in nuclear weapons or other nuclear explosive devices. The definitions set forth in the U.S. draft treaty on "fissile material" and "production" represent the outgrowth of the decade-long international discussion regarding what an FMCT should encompass. In our draft, stocks of already existing fissile material would be unaffected by the FMCT. Finally, also in keeping with past discussions of this issue, the production of fissile material for non-explosive purposes, such as fuel for naval propulsion, would be unaffected by the treaty.

Our draft Treaty contains all the elements necessary to support a negotiation and we urge our colleagues, as we begin our discussion of Agenda Item II, to focus attention on this document as the most efficient means to finally begin this process. We have just spent three informal sessions on nuclear disarmament. As we said during those discussions, a necessary step in the achievement of a world free of nuclear weapons must of necessity be a ban on the production of nuclear material for those nuclear weapons. We also reiterate our view that, pending the conclusion of a Cutoff Treaty and the Treaty's entry into force, all states should declare publicly and observe a moratorium on the production of fissile material for use in nuclear weapons, such as the United States has maintained since 1988.

> On March 23, 2007, the CD considered a proposal by the P6 (a group composed of the six ambassadors serving on a rotational basis as CD president during the year), which included calling for the appointment of Ambassador Carlo Trezza of Italy as Coordinator "to preside over negotiations, without any pre-conditions, on a non-discriminatory multilateral treaty banning the production of fissile material for nuclear weapons or other nuclear explosive devices." *See* press release at *www.unog.ch/un og/website/news_media.nsf/(httpNewsByYear_en)/6EBFD 0E966CBEA55C12572A70066C70D?OpenDocument.*

Ambassador Rocca stated that the United States would join consensus on adoption of the P6 proposal, despite certain concerns, stating that the proposal

> . . . represents what, in the considered judgment of the six presidents, could garner consensus and allow this body to return to its primary task: negotiating international instruments. The U.S. well realizes that the Presidential document has been carefully crafted with each word and idea weighed and balanced. It is no secret that the United States would have preferred a clear cut decision to start negotiations on FMCT based on the mandate we tabled (CD/1776) without reference to any other issue. We have spoken against linkages for years and we are not convinced that all linkages have yet been broken as result of this plan—it bears a very close resemblance to the A-5 proposal, something we oppose.

The full text of Ambassador Rocca's statement is available at *www.us-mission.ch/Press2007/0323CD.htm.*

11. Other Sanctions

a. *Executive Order 12938*

Effective September 26, 2007, the Department of State Bureau of International Security and Nonproliferation issued a notice imposing nonproliferation measures on two Iranian entities (Aerospace Industries Organization, or AIO, and Shahid Hemmat Industrial Group, or SHIG) and a North Korean entity (Korea Mining and Development Corporation, or KOMID), including a ban on U.S. government procurement, as excerpted below. 72 Fed. Reg. 54,708 (Sept. 26, 2007). The sanctions were imposed under Executive Order 12938 of November 14, 1994, as amended, "Proliferation of Weapons of Mass Destruction."

*   *   *   *

1. All departments and agencies of the United States Government shall not procure or enter into any contract for the procurement of any goods, technology, or services from these entities including the termination of existing contracts;

2. All departments and agencies of the United States government shall not provide any assistance to these entities, and shall not obligate further funds for such purposes;

3. The Secretary of the Treasury shall prohibit the importation into the United States of any goods, technology, or services produced or provided by these entities, other than information or informational materials within the meaning of section 203(b)(3) of the International Emergency Economic Powers Act (50 U.S.C. 1702(b)(3)).

These measures shall be implemented by the responsible departments and agencies as provided in Executive Order 12938.

In addition, pursuant to section 126.7(a)(1) of the International Traffic in Arms Regulations, it is deemed that suspending the above-named entities from participating in any activities subject to Section 38 of the Arms Export Control Act would be in furtherance of the national security and foreign policy of the United States. Therefore, for two years, the Department of State is hereby suspending all licenses and other approvals for: (a) Exports and other transfers of defense articles and defense services from the United States; (b) transfers of U.S.-origin defense articles and defense services from foreign destinations; and (c) temporary import of defense articles to or from the above-named entities.
Moreover, it is the policy of the United States to deny licenses and other approvals for exports and temporary imports of defense articles and defense services destined for these entities.

b. Executive Order 13382

Effective January 4, 2007, the Department of the Treasury, Office of Foreign Assets Control ("OFAC"), designated three Syrian entities whose property and interests in property were blocked pursuant to Executive Order 13382 of June 28, 2005, "Blocking Property of Weapons of Mass Destruction Proliferators and Their Supporters." 72 Fed. Reg. 7919 (Feb. 21, 2007).

The entities so designated were the Higher Institute of Applied Science and Technology (HIAST), Electronics Institute, and National Standards and Calibration Laboratory (NSCL).

On January 31, 2007, OFAC published the name of one previously-designated entity it was removing from the list of Specially Designated Nationals and Blocked Persons under Executive Order 13382: Great Wall Airlines Company, Limited (a.k.a. Great Wall Airlines; a.k.a. Changcheng Hangkong). 72 Fed. Reg. 4561 (Jan. 31, 2007). As explained in the Federal Register notice, OFAC had "determined that this person no longer continues to meet the criteria for designation under the Order and is appropriate for removal from the list. . . ."

c. Export Administration Regulations: End-user entity list

Effective July 12, 2007, the Department of Commerce Bureau of Industry and Security amended the Export Administration Regulations ("EAR") to add five entities located in Iran to the Entity List. 72 Fed. Reg. 38,008 (July 12, 2007). As explained in the Federal Register, "[t]he Entity List is a compilation of end-users that present an unacceptable risk of using or diverting certain items to activities related to weapons of mass destruction. BIS requires a license for most exports or reexports to these entities and maintains the Entity List to inform the public of these license requirements."

d. Foreign Assets Control Regulations

On January 9, 2007, the Department of the Treasury, Office of Foreign Assets Control, amended the Foreign Assets Control Regulations, 31 C.F.R. pt. 500, to prohibit U.S. persons from registering vessels in the Democratic People's Republic of Korea, or from otherwise obtaining authorization for a vessel to fly the North Korean flag. 72 Fed. Reg. 4960 (Feb. 2, 2007).

Cross References

Applicability of Geneva Conventions in extradition of Manuel Noriega, **Chapter 3.A.1.b.**
Nuclear terrorism convention, **Chapter 3.B.1.e.**
Effect of armed conflict on treaties, **Chapter 4.B.4.**
Claims under Alien Tort Statute based on Israeli military actions in West Bank, **Chapters and 5.A.2.a.(2)** and **10.B.2.a.;** *based on sale through Foreign Military Sales Program*, **Chapter 5.A.2.a.(1).**
Law of war and human rights law, **Chapter 6.A.2.a. and b.**
Weapons and Outer Space, **Chapter 12.B.4.**

Table of Cases

Index